The Gower HANDBOOK of MANAGEMENT

SECOND EDITION

The Gower HANDBOOK of MANAGEMENT

SECOND EDITION

Edited by
Dennis Lock and Nigel Farrow

First published 1983

Second edition published 1988 by

Gower Publishing Company Limited,
Gower House,
Croft Road,
Aldershot,
Hants GU11 3HR,
England

Gower Publishing Company,
Old Post Road,
Brookfield,
Vermont 05036,
U.S.A.

Reprinted 1989

British Library Cataloguing in Publication Data

The Gower handbook of management—2nd ed.
  1. Management
  I. Lock, Dennis   II. Farrow, Nigel
  658   HD31

Library of Congress Cataloging in Publication Data

The Gower handbook of management.
Includes index.
1. Management   I. Lock, Dennis.   II. Farrow, Nigel.
III. Gower Publishing Company.
HD31.G684   1987   658   87-144

ISBN   0–566–02662–7

Printed and bound in Great Britain by
Anchor Press Ltd, Tiptree, Essex

Contents

PART 1 PRINCIPLES, POLICY AND ORGANIZATION

PART 6 PRODUCTION AND PROJECT MANAGEMENT

Illustrations

Notes on contributors

Bryan Atkin BSc (Econ) (Pricing) has been engaged in industrial market research and business consultancy for more than 20 years. In 1984, he became a founder director of Research Solutions Limited and currently specializes in research and consultancy for the information technology industry. He has extensive experience of the analysis, through research, of the purchasing process and the role of price in decision taking. He has also devised and implemented specific research procedures for testing price sensitivity and/or acceptability in relation to a wide range of products and services. Bryan Atkin directed the *How British Industry Buys, 1974* report sponsored and published by the *Financial Times* and co-authored a study into industrial pricing practices, *How British Industry Prices*, published by IMR Limited in 1975. In 1978 he spent six months on secondment to the Price Commission.

Stephen Badger (Sources of Finance) is a Director in the Corporate Finance Department of Morgan Grenfell & Co. Limited. He was educated at Sherborne School in Dorset and Pembroke College, Oxford, where he read Greats. He joined Morgan Grenfell on leaving Oxford and became a director in 1977. He is an Associate of the Institute of Bankers and of the Institute of Chartered Secretaries and Administrators.

Peter Baily (Procurement Policy *and* Purchasing Procedures) is a Senior Lecturer in Business Studies at the Polytechnic of Wales. He started off as a telecommunications mechanic and later worked in machine tool manufacturing and textile industries as buyer, materials controller, chief buyer and assistant to company secretary. Mr Baily has worked with the Business Education Council for several years as Board member, moderator and member of the Validating Committee and of several working parties and has been a member of the Education and Training Committee of the Institute of Purchasing and Supply. Author of several books and numerous articles, he has addressed conferences and contributed to courses in the USA, Ireland, Holland, Italy, Switzerland, Singapore and the UK. He is co-author of *Materials Management Handbook* (Gower, 1982).

Gordon Bell (Effective communication), a lapsed scientist, is the Senior Partner in Gordon Bell and Partners, a London-based firm of consultants specializing in teaching communications skills in industry and commerce. Gordon Bell and Partners have been conducting successful courses since 1956, not only in the UK but in many countries overseas. Gordon Bell is a broadcaster, and a contributor to *Handbook of Engineering Management* (Heinemann). He is the author of *Successful Speaking and Presentations*, also published by Heinemann.

Ted Bennett (Managing the Electronic Office) is an independent consultant/ business analyst who entered data processing in 1967, following a degree in Chemical Engineering and a period as an engineer. He has worked in a wide variety of organizations as a systems analyst, project manager, information systems manager and consultant. He specializes in construction/project management; financial applications; office automation; and problem analysis.

Denis Boyle (The Strategic Planning Process) is Managing Director of Service Management International Ltd., a firm which specializes in the process of strategy creation and implementation for accelerated profit growth. Formerly, he was Director of the Scandinavian Institutes for Administrative Research in London and Milan, and adviser to the Institute for Industrial Reconstruction in Rome where he helped to create new approaches to state planning in such sectors as special steel, telecommunications and banking. Currently, he acts as a consultant to several leading multinationals, working particularly with developing service quality as a strategic competitive weapon. Mr. Boyle lectures widely in Europe and the United States and is a visiting professor at the University of Bocconi, Milan. His publications include numerous articles on strategic planning and implementation and he is co-author of *The Challenge of Change* (Gower, 1981).

Ron H Bradnam (Corporate Strategies for the Future) works in private practice as a consultant in technology management with special interests in working with scientists, engineers and technologists in various management fields. After his military service he worked for EMI, Mullard and Plessey where he was responsible for the engineering design and management of research and development projects for commercial and military applications. While with EASAMS he planned and managed several important innovation projects before moving to Urwick Technology Management where his assignments were concerned with improvements to the management of technical and business functions. Mr Bradnam has had a varied academic career, acting as a visiting lecturer and course leader at various academic institutions. His present appointments include visiting lectureships at the University of Southampton and Cranfield School of Management.

A Brearley (Design Management) first worked as a design engineer after an engineering degree and military service. He became Production Manager of the Talbot Stead Tube Company and then a Works Engineer with ICI. He then worked for five years as a management consultant with PA Ltd before becoming Managing Director of the heavy engineering company Adamson and Hatchett. His next appointment was as Managing Director of Don International, a major manufacture of automotive friction materials and components. Dr Brearley is currently Professorial Fellow in Management Development at Bradford University. He also works as chairman and a director of a number of public companies. He advises a range of major multinational companies on management development, and is a consultant to Arthur Young. He holds an MSc in Management Sciences and a Doctorate in Management and Administration. His publications include *Management of Drawing and Design* (Gower, 1975) and *The Control of Staff Related Overheads* (Macmillan, 1976).

Keith G Cameron (Salary Management *and* Wage Management) is Personnel Director of Currys. A graduate in Social Science, he was formerly Personnel Director of Levi Strauss for Northern Europe and has worked for three other international companies.

E S M Chadwick (Manpower Planning) started his working life in local government administration but after war service joined the then Anglo-Iranian Oil Company (now British Petroleum). He has had long and varied experience in industrial and commercial management both at home and abroad and later as a consultant. As Manager, Manpower Research and Planning for the British Petroleum Group he was one of the pioneers in the development of corporate manpower planning. He was a regular contributor to management conferences and seminars and is the author of a range of articles in journals published here and abroad and of chapters on manpower planning in a number of books on management techniques.

J L Cookson (Employee Relations) is Principal Lecturer in Labour Law in the Department of Management at Manchester Polytechnic. After graduating in Law from Cambridge University, he spent four years in private legal practice followed by three years in corporate planning overseas. His particular academic interest is in labour law and its impact on industrial relations at organizational level, on which subject he has lectured extensively in both the public and private sectors of industry. He has acted as Independent Chairman of the Lancashire Health Authority's Conciliation Panel for Dispute Settlement and as an external arbitrator on collective disputes in the private sector. His publications include *Handbook of Industrial Relations* (Gower, 1972).

J C Craig (Taxation) is a taxation partner of KMG Thomson McLintock, chartered accountants, in Glasgow, where he deals with both personal and company taxation. He is a Member of the Institute of Chartered Accountants of Scotland and a former convener of its taxation committee.

Michael Day (Management Development) is Manager of the Employee Relations Division of BP Oil Ltd. Most of his career has been within the BP Group where he has held a number of posts including those of training officer, personnel manager and internal organization consultant. While with BP Oil he has previously managed the personnel resources and personnel policies division. Mr Day is a visiting lecturer at the University of Manchester Institute of Science and Technology. He is co-author of several papers and contributed two chapters to *Administration of Personnel Policies* edited by Naylor and Torrington (Gower, 1974).

R Dick-Larkam (Energy Management) started his career as a chartered engineer at the National Physical Laboratory and during the war served as an Engineer Officer in the RAFVR. He worked on engineering development in various companies before joining BOC Ltd in 1954 where he held various engineering appointments. Before his retirement he became an internal consultant and energy manager for the UK companies. He has lectured on productivity and energy management both within BOC and to many other companies as well as at the Management Centre Europe. His publications include *Profit Improvement Techniques* (Gower, 1973), *Cutting Energy Costs* (Gower, 1978) and a 'Practical Approach to Energy Conservation' (*Accountants' Digest* 45). Mr Dick-Larkam is a Liveryman and Freeman of the City of London.

Ken Firth (Warehouse Operation and Management) has an international reputation in storage handling and distribution in which he has been involved throughout his career. His industrial experience culminated in the position of Senior Project Manager for a large manufacturer of storage and handling equipment. He joined the NMHC in February 1971 as Advisory Service Manager and combined consultancy work with the setting up of short courses for in-career students. He became appointed as Assistant Director, National Materials Handling Centre, in 1974 and recently has been appointed as Operations Director of NMHC Consulting Group Ltd. His is a contributor to many publications and contributed the section on warehousing techniques to the *Handbook of Physical Distribution Management* (Gower, 3rd edition, 1983).

John Gentles (The Total Cost Approach to Distribution) was, for a number of years, a management consultant in the London office of Booz Allen & Hamilton. In this capacity he completed a large number of manufacturing and distribution assignments for such industries as domestic consumer products, automotive supply, aerospace and medical supplies. He is now Materials Management Director of Allegheny International.

Patricia George (Working Conditions) was Senior Adviser of the Industrial Society's Information and Personnel Advisory Services Department. Miss George is an Associate Member of the Institute of Personnel Management, and is now a Principal Personnel Officer working for Surrey County Council.

Norman Hart (Corporate Relations) is Managing Director of Interact Seminars Ltd, having been Managing Director of Interact Communications Ltd and Director of the CAM Foundation. His previous career with Unilever, Morgan Grampian and Roles and Parker, has been mainly in marketing, advertising and public relations. He is a regular international speaker on these subjects and has written or contributed to many books including *Marketing Handbook* (Gower, 1981). Mr Hart is a Fellow of the Institute of Public Relations and the Institute of Marketing, and holds an MSc from the University of Bradford.

R S Henderson (Office Services) is Chairman and Managing Director of the specialist office planning and design consultancy, Space Planning Services plc. He took an engineering degree at Jesus College, Cambridge, and is a member of the Institution of Civil Engineers. He is past Chairman of the National Council of the 10000-member Institute of Administrative Management and has been particularly active in the IAM's Facilities Management Group. He has written many articles for professional journals on office planning, design, property markets and corporate strategy. Mr Henderson joined Space Planning Services in 1969, has been Managing Director since 1971 and became Chairman in 1986.

John Hobson, CBE (Advertising) Honorary President of the Advertising agency Ted Bates Limited, is a former President of the Institute of Practitioners in Advertising, a former Chairman of the Advertising Association and a former President of the European Association of Advertising Agencies. He formed his own agency, John Hobson & Partners, in 1955 and merged it in 1959 with Ted Bates New York to form Hobson, Bates & Partners.

R C Horsley (International Trade) is a manager at the centre for Physical Distribution Management in London. He has previously worked for ICI Ltd, the Rank Organization and Fisher Price in posts associated with distribution. Mr Horsley is a Fellow of the British Institute of Management, the Chartered Institute of Transport and the Institute of Physical Distribution Management.

P T Humphrey (Recruitment and Selection) is a Managing Consultant with Price Waterhouse Management Consultants. Previously he was Managing Director, Ashton Containers (Southern) and Personnel Director with The Mettoy Company Ltd. He is a Companion of The Institute of Personnel Management, a Fellow of the British Institute of Management, and Member of the Institute of Management Consultants. He is a contributor to *Administration of Personnel Policies*, edited by Torrington and Naylor (Gower, 1974) and author of *How to be Your Own Personnel Manager* (Institute of Personnel Management, 1981).

Peter Jackson (Production Control) is a Principal Tutor/Consultant at CMTC Management Training Centre. He specializes in management techniques and computer training. He was previously with P.A. Management Consultants and started his career in GEC Telecommunications where he worked in production management and control.

Colin Jones (Patents, Trade Marks and Designs) is a partner in a provincial firm of chartered patent agents. After graduating from Cambridge in Mechanical Sciences, he joined Metropolitan Vickers (later AEI and now part of GEC) as a graduate apprentice. After working on steam turbine engineering he entered the patent profession in private practice where he qualified and became a Fellow of the Chartered Institute of Patent Agents. He is a contributor to the *European Patent Handbook* (Longman Professional, 1986) and *CIPA Guide to the Patents Act 1977* (Sweet & Maxwell, 1984) both of which are published by arrangement with the Chartered Institute of Patent Agents.

Arthur Lawrence (Distribution channels) is a freelance writer and consultant. His experience includes thirty years' involvement in manufacturing, general trading and retailing in the UK and many countries overseas. For ten years he was an internal consultant with the Unilever group, specializing in organizational effectiveness, productivity and the introduction of systems to sales and marketing operations. He is author of *The Management of Trade Marketing* (Gower, 1983).

Alan R Leaper (Budgetary Control) was Financial Controller of Hoover Worldwide Eastern Region Headquarters for ten years in which capacity he was responsible for review and control of the budgets of thirteen overseas subsidiaries. His previous experience include three years in Canada on cost and general accounting assignments and eleven years with the Frigidaire Division of General Motors Ltd in various factory accounting positions. Mr Leaper is now managing his own retail and wholesale business. He is a member of the Advisory Committee to the Managing Division of Management Centre Europe where he frequently chairs various seminars and Round Table meetings.

Dennis Lock (Editor of this Handbook, author of Project Management and co-author of Solution Engineering and Stock Control) qualified in applied physics and began his career with the General Electric Company, where he was an electronics engineer. His subsequent management experience has been long, successful and exceptionally wide, in industries ranging from sub-miniature electronics to mining engineering and heavy machine tool engineering. He is a Fellow of the Institute of Management Services, a Member of the British Institute of Management and of the Institution of Industrial Managers. Mr Lock has carried out lecturing and consultancy assignments in the UK and overseas, and has written or edited many management books, mostly for Gower. He is now a full time freelance management writer, specializing in management subjects.

Colin McDonald (Market Research) has twenty-five years' experience of market research on a wide scale in both commercial and social contexts. During this time he has written numerous articles on various aspects of the subject. He is an Oxford graduate and has worked for Reckitt & Sons Ltd, Distillers Co. Ltd and the British Market Research Bureau Ltd. Mr McDonald is now Chairman of Communication Research Limited.

J Mapes (Planning for Production) is Senior Lecturer in Operations Management at Cranfield School of Management. Earlier in his career he worked for

ICI in Productivity Services before taking up a lectureship in the Department of Management at Middlesex Polytechnic. Prior to his present appointment he worked as an internal consultant for Clayton Dewandre Ltd. Mr Mapes holds degrees from Cambridge and Brunel and is joint author of *Model Building Techniques for Management* (Gower, 1976).

Dr Andrew Melhuish (Executive Health) is a general practitioner in Henley-on-Thames. He has also been medical adviser to the staff and members at Henley, The Management College, for the last sixteen years during which time he has developed a particular interest in managerial health. With Professor Cary Cooper of UMIST, Manchester, he is involved in a large long-term prospective study of managers' health involving members of Henley and big groups from ICI Paints and Mars. He lectures widely to managers and is the author of *Executive Health* and *Work and Health*. He is at present contributing a monthly article on health to *The Director*.

John Muir (Employee Benefits) is Associate Consultant with Cockman, Copeman & Partners Limited, Remuneration and Benefits Consultants. He was for some years a full-time official with a white collar trade union before assuming senior industrial relations posts with London Transport and the P & O Shipping Group. He has a Bachelor of Commerce degree from the London School of Economics. He is a Fellow of the Institute of Personnel Management, a Fellow of the Chartered Institute of Architects and an Industrial Fellow of the International Management Centre from Buckingham. He lectures on employment law, undertakes representation at industrial tribunals and teaches negotiating skills. Mr Muir is the author of *Industrial Relations Procedures and Agreements* (Gower, 1981).

Peter Mumford (Redundancy) was a personnel manager in industry and now lectures in management at Brighton Polytechnic. He has been a management consultant for a number of years, specializing in management and organizational development and has worked with a variety of industrial organizations, as well as local government departments. Following his book *Redundancy and Security of Employment* (Gower, 1978) he has written a number of video scripts for training programmes, including 'Styles of Leadership' and is now devising and writing a series of CBT training programs 'Office Skills' for VPS Interactive.

C C New (Planning for Production) is Professor of Operations Management at Cranfield School of Management where he was also Director of the MBA Programme 1983-1986. Professor New took his first degree in Engineering at Cambridge before working with Rolls Royce Ltd in the Aero Engine Division. He joined London Business School in 1971 as a faculty member after taking his Masters Degree in Business Studies there. He completed his PhD shortly after joining Cranfield in 1978. Professor New is the author of numerous books and articles and is an acknowledged expert on manufacturing planning and control systems.

Dr John S Oakland (Quality Assurance) is Senior Lecturer in Production Management at the Management Centre, University of Bradford, England, one of the largest business schools in Europe. Over the last six years he has taught quality management to members of over 500 organizations. He has directed several large research projects on quality control in UK industry, funded by the British Government. This has brought him into contact with a diverse range of companies and his work has been widely acknowledged and published in international journals. John started his career with the British Iron and Steel Research Association. He has worked for Sandoz, the multinational Swiss-owned company on the development of manufacturing processes and in 1976 he became Production Manager in an agro-chemical company, controlling a wide range of plant and processes. He joined the Bradford Management Centre in 1979 since when his interests have centred on Production Management and Quality Control education. He has written *Statistical Process Control* (Heinemann, 1986). He is a Fellow of the Institute of Quality Assurance (and a member of its Council), a Chartered Chemist, Member of the Royal Society of Chemistry, and Fellow of the Royal Statistical Society.

Sydney Paulden (Overseas Marketing) is Publisher and General Manager of *Export Times*, editor of *Export Times Trade Finance Handbook* and Dun & Bradstreet's *Creditnews* and a Consultant to UNCTAD/GATT International Trade Centre, Geneva. He is a Cambridge graduate and was Churchill Fellow in Marketing in 1969. He undertook a research project in Mexico, Venezuela and Brazil and has been a correspondent in Mexico for *Financial Times* and *Sunday Times*. He has written several books including *Export Agents* (Gower) and *How to Deliver on Time* (Gower, 1983).

A W Pearson (Managing Research and Development) is Senior Lecturer in Decision Analysis, Director of the R&D Research Unit and the MBA Programme at the Manchester Business School. He gained industrial experience with Pilkington Brothers Ltd and Henry Simon Ltd before becoming Lecturer in Economic and Social Studies, University of Manchester. Subsequently he was appointed Lecturer in Operational Research at MBS and has been Director of the R&D Research Unit since 1967. He is Editor of *R&D Management* and co-editor of *Transfer Processes in Technical Change* and of *Managing Interdisciplinary Research*; member of the International Advisory Board of Interstudy – International Association for the Study of Interdisciplinary Research – and a member of the Board of COLRAD – the College of R&D of the Institute of Management Science.

Christian Petersen (Sales Promotion) was the youngest-ever member of the Institute of Practitioners in Advertising and of the Advertising Association, and is a Fellow and Life Member of the Institute of Sales Promotion. He was Chief Editor of *The Handbook of Consumer Sales Promotion* (1976-77) and is the author of *Sales Promotion in Action* (Associated Business Press, 1979). He was a founder and Managing Director of KLP Group plc, Britain's first publicly quoted sales promotion group, retiring in 1986 to read history at Oxford.

W P Ridley (The Annual Accounts) is a partner in Wood Mackenzie and Company, a firm of stockbrokers he joined in 1973 after five years as a financial consultant with Merrett Cyriax Associates. He read law at Oxford and became an Associate of the Institute of Chartered Accountants in 1961. He taught in Uganda and at Hendon Technical College before joining the Economic and Investment Research Department of the Bank of London and South America. Between 1965 and 1968, Mr Ridley worked for the Commonwealth Development Corporation.

F W Rose (Company Law *and* Contracts between Companies) is principal lecturer in the Law Department of Birmingham Polytechnic. He graduated from King's College London with a Master's Degree in Law and was called to the Bar at Gray's Inn. After working as a company secretary he began teaching full time and has acted as Course Director successively for a law degree course, the Solicitor's Final Examination Course and the Common Professional Examination Course. For several years he has also taught professional courses for a number of commercial undertakings and acted as an external examiner for various professional bodies. His publications include *Employment Law* (Ravenswood Press, 1984).

Don Rushton (Solution Engineering) is a Director at the UK office of Ingersoll Engineers Inc. He is currently a Member of Council of the Institution of Production Engineers, and Chairman of its Working Party on Manufacturing Strategy. He is a Councillor of the West Midlands Region of the CBI. After graduating in Mechanical Sciences at Cambridge, followed by practical training with De Havillands and English Electric, he was automatic machinery engineer for Procter & Gamble, Works Manager of a shoe machinery factory, and held a marketing position in the machine tool industry. He has been with Ingersoll since 1968, and has published papers on advanced manufacturing technology and related subjects.

Tessa V Ryder Runton (Capital Project Planning) who has a Cambridge Science and Law degree, started her career as a patent examiner. She studied further at the London School of Economics and worked as a financial analyst for the Rio-Tinto Zinc Corporation. She has lectured on financial analysis at several business schools in England and Scotland. After retraining in science she has been teaching at a comprehensive school. She contributed to *Financial Management Handbook* (Gower, 3rd edition, 1988).

Philip Sadler (Principles of Management) is Principal of Ashridge Management College, a position he has held since 1969. After graduating from the London School of Economics with first class honours in 1953 he was employed in various research posts in the private and public sectors before being appointed Ashridge's first Director of Research in 1964. He is the author of several texts and numerous articles on management. He is a Companion of the British Institute of Management and holds the Institute's Burnham Medal, awarded in 1972. He is also a Fellow of the Institute of Personnel Management, a Fellow of the International Academy of Management and a Fellow of the Royal Society of Arts. He was awarded the CBE in 1986.

George S Sanders (Corporate Strategies for the Future) is a Freelance Consultant in Management Development. He is a Chartered Engineer and started his career with ICI in plant construction and maintenance. He also had several years' experience in the electronics industry as Production Director with the Solartron Electronic Group. Most of his career, however, has been spent with management consultants Urwick Orr and Partners Ltd starting as a Production Consultant and finishing as Director of the Urwick Management Centre as well as a main board Director. He has written many articles on management themes and was joint author of *Urwick Orr on Management* (Heinemann, 1980). Mr Sanders is a Fellow of the Institution of Mechanical Engineers, of the Institute of Management Consultants and of the British Institute of Management.

Bill Scott (Negotiating), having held senior appointments in both the industrial and the academic world, is now an independent consultant specializing in communication, negotiation and management development. His clients are in industry, commerce, engineering, and international organizations. He works regularly in Europe, Asia and Australasia. Mr Scott is author of the best-selling Gower books *The Skills of Negotiating* and *The Skills of Communicating* and co-author (with Dr Sven Söderberg) of *The Art of Managing*.

Leon Simons (Working Capital and Management Ratios) is a graduate of Glasgow University and a member of the Institute of Chartered Accountants of Scotland. He has wide experience of finance and accountancy acquired in industry, the City and the profession. He is now an independent management consultant specializing in finance and pricing in which subjects he lectures extensively in the UK and has also lectured in Europe and America. He is a non-executive director of a public company and has contributed to many books and journals.

John Stapleton (Marketing Planning) completed his full-time education at the University of Aston in Birmingham, is a recipient of the Lord Mayor of London's Marketing Award, a Queen's Award to Industry and has appeared in the British High Court as a marketing authority. Mr Stapleton has had a varied in-depth career in marketing management and practice, having been a salesman, sales manager, market research manager, marketing manager, and a senior lecturer in advertising, media and statistics. He has worked in the printing, pharmaceuticals, telecommunications, detergents, construction, publishing, and computer industries for British, American, and European companies, large and small. He has written a number of books on marketing, including *How to Prepare a Marketing Plan* (Gower, 4th edition, 1988), *Teach Yourself Marketing*, *Elements of Export Marketing* and *Glossary of Marketing Terms*. Since 1969 he has been an independent consultant, and provides diagnostic and monitoring services into company marketing plans, advertising campaigns, and new product promotions.

Derek Torrington (Industrial Training) is Senior Lecturer in Personnel Management at the University of Manchester Institute of Science and Technology. Previously he spent fifteen years in the engineering industry and five years at Manchester Polytechnic. Publications include *Successful Personnel Management* (Staples Press, 1969), *Face to Face* (Gower, 1972), *Handbook of Industrial Relations* (Gower, 1972), *Handbook of Management Development*, with D F Sutton (Gower, 1973), *Administration of Personnel Policies*, with R Naylor (Gower, 1974), *Encyclopaedia of Personnel Management* (Gower, 1974), and *Comparative Industrial Relations in Europe* (Associated Business Press, 1978). His major text book *Personnel Management* was published in 1979 by Prentice-Hall International. He is a Companion of the Institute of Personnel Management.

Brian Walley (Plant Layout) is a director of Ferodo Ltd. His career has included appointments as production controller, operational planning manager and internal consultant with Metal Box Company, J. Bibby and Sons, and Turner and Newall Ltd. He is the author of over sixty articles and eight successful books including *Management Services Handbook, Efficiency Auditing, Profit Planning Handbook* and the best-selling *Production Management Handbook* (2nd edition, Gower, 1986). Currently he is the Chairman of a group of engineers, systems personnel and Production planners and managers introducing MRP II.

A N Welsh (Personal Organization) is a Senior Adviser with the Hong Kong Management Development Centre. He obtained a History Degree at Oxford University, and started his industrial career with ICI; he then moved via management services work to general management in FMCG, then to consultancy, latterly as Director of Training for W. D. Scott & Co. He moved to Pembrokeshire as managing director of various small companies, interspersed with property development and farming on his own account (enterprises which are now managed by one of his sons), and for four years he was Management Adviser for West Wales with the Welsh Development Agency. Mr Welsh wrote *The Skills of Management* (Gower, 1980) and has contributed many articles on business and historical topics. In 1986 he published a novel *Halog* (The Book Guild) set in an eighteenth century farming background.

Philip Westwood (The Administration of Commercial Property) is a Senior Lecturer in the Department of Building Economics at South Bank Polytechnic. A chartered surveyor and chartered builder, he holds a MPh degree in Building Legislation. Before becoming a full-time lecturer he worked for many years for Walter Llewellyn & Sons Ltd as a surveyor and estimator. He has lectured for a number of years in building economics, building technology and management to surveyors and building technologists. He is currently embarking on a research programme into cost modelling related to building legislation and its effect on building design and construction.

E N White (Maintenance) has held a number of management posts in quality control, product support, customer service and engineering maintenance, and was for ten years managing director of a technical services company. He has published many papers, is a frequent speaker in the UK and overseas, and manages a number of training programmes. His book *Maintenance Planning, Control and Documentation* (Gower, 2nd edition, 1979), has become a standard reference work for engineering training.

Dennis Whitmore (Industrial Engineering) is Director of the Short Courses and Consultancy Unit associated with Harrow College of Higher Education and also works as a management consultant. Previously he was Senior Production Manager with Mullards and a Senior Consultant with Philips. Dr Whitmore was educated at London, Brunel and Surrey Universities and is a Fellow of the British Institute of Management. He has written numerous books including *Work Study and Related Management Services* (Heinemann, 1976), *Work Measurement* (Institute of Management Services, 1976) and *Management Sciences* (Teach Yourself Books, 1979). He has also written the standard text on work measurement for the People's Republic of China.

John Williams (Sales Promotion) is the Chairman of Innovation Ltd, a business development and sales promotion consultancy. Previously John was the New Product Development Manager at Watneys, responsible for the launch of Fosters Draught. He has also been an Associate Director of Dorland Advertising and Consumer Promotions Manager, and Persil Automatic Brand Manager at Lever Brothers. John Williams is the author of *The Manual of Sales Promotion*, the definitive guide to sales promotion in the UK.

Michael Williams (Management self-development) is an independent management consultant who operates both in the UK and Western Europe. His clients include universities, business schools, professional bodies and a wide range of companies, in both the private and public sectors. He is the author or co-author of several books in the fields of industrial psychology and management practice. His areas of specialization include senior executive development, the assessment of managerial potential, leadership development and team building. He has had extensive experience of the business world, in personnel, marketing, sales and production. He gained his MSc from the University of Aston and he served full time and as a volunteer reservist with the Royal Navy (Intelligence) and the Royal Marines (Commando and SBS).

John Wilson (Security) is a security adviser and writer, recently retired from his position of Company Security Officer for the IMI Yorkshire Imperial Group where he held an omnibus remit for advising on all aspects of security policy. A former Detective Chief Inspector and Deputy Head of CID in the Leeds City Police, he is a Fellow and past governor of the Institute of Industrial Security, former National Chairman of the International Professional Security Association and its representative on the Home Office Standing Committee for Crime Prevention from 1975 to 1981. He has been visiting lecturer on security in industry to the Home Office Crime Prevention School at Stafford for the last decade and to management seminars in the UK and abroad. He is co-author of the textbooks for the Institute examinations and a security chapter contributor to other textbooks dealing with management, distribution, administration and computers. With Eric Oliver, Mr Wilson wrote *Practical Security in Commerce and Industry* (Gower, 5th edition, 1988).

M T Wilson (Managing a Sales Force) is Managing Director of Marketing Improvements Ltd, the leading international marketing consultancy and training group. Operating from offices in London and Singapore and through associates in Europe, MI covers all major markets and languages on behalf of its numerous clients in the consumer, industrial and service sectors. Marketing Improvements was formed in 1964 by Mr Wilson following experience in the Institute of Marketing and Ford Motor Company, which he joined on graduating from Manchester University. He is widely known for the seminars and courses on all aspects of marketing which he has run in all five continents, and for the highly creative consultancy advice given to companies throughout Europe, including multinationals. His *Managing a Sales Force* (Gower, 2nd edition, 1983) and *The Management of Marketing* (Gower, 1980) have both achieved worldwide success.

R M S Wilson (Cost Analysis) is the Pannell Kerr Forster Professor of Accounting at Trent Business School in Nottingham. His commercial experience was gained via appointments with a number of organizations covering consumer goods, industrial goods, and services. He is actively involved as a consultant with various organizations, and has also held non-executive directorships. His other publications include *Financial Analysis: A Managerial Introduction* (Cassell); *Managerial Accounting: Method & Meaning* (Van Nostrand); *Financial Dimensions of Marketing* (Macmillan); *Cost Control Handbook* (Gower); and *Management Controls & Marketing Planning* (Heinemann).

Frank Woodward (Managing Transport Services) is a Fellow of the Chartered Secretaries and Administrators, a Fellow of the Royal Society of Arts and a Member of the Chartered Institute of Transport with over thirty years' practical experience in all types of fleet operation. Before retiring in 1983, he was Managing Director of a large industrial fleet of over 3500 vehicles. An author, journalist and well-known speaker at conferences and seminars, he has written many books on fleet management and finance and on road transport distribution. He is co-author of *Controlling Company Car Costs* (Gower, 1985).

John Woolhouse (Organization Development) is Director of Education Programmes at the Manpower Services Commission where his responsibilities include the £900 million Technical and Vocational Education Initiative (TVEI) designed to promote a wider curriculum for 14–18-year-olds in secondary schools and colleges throughout the country; the Commission works with the Further Education system and with universities and polytechnics to increase the supply of qualified scientists and technologists in the UK. Before his secondment to the MSC in 1983 he was an international management consultant with the W S Atkins Group specializing in education, training and organization in both the public and private sectors. From 1972 to 1978 he was an Assistant Director of Kingston Polytechnic and founder Director of the Kingston Regional Management Centre; he worked with Rolls-Royce Limited for 18 years and held appointments as Personnel Director of Rolls-Royce and Associates and as Company Education and Training Officer of a 'high tech' business with over 80 000 employees.

Avison Wormald (International Trade) is Executive Vice-President of Lansberg, Wormald Humble y Asociados C.A., Management Consultants, Caracas, Venezuela, Professor of International Trade at the Universidad Metropolitana, Caracas and author of *International Business*, published by PanBooks. He was Director and Managing Director of Fisons Limited, London from 1950 to 1962, Chairman Grace Bros. Limited (W.R. Grace and Co.) and a director of many companies in six countries. He graduated from London University with first class honours and is a Fellow of the British Institute of Management.

David Wragg (Promotional Public Relations) is the Head of Press and Public Relations for the Bristol & West Building Society. He entered public relations in 1974, joining the P&O Group, where he eventually became Manager, Public Relations Services, before leaving in 1979. He subsequently handled a number of short-term PR projects as an independent consultant, including one for the Chartered Institute of Transport, before joining Twinlock in 1981. He took up his present appointment in 1986. A member of the Institute of Public Relations, Mr Wragg is the author of *Publicity and Customer Relations in Transport Management* (Gower, 1982) and has written eleven books on aeronautical history. He is a contributor to the Inter Company Comparisons and Keynotes series of industry reports.

The once and future manager

Nigel Farrow

Merlin, wizard and medieval management consultant, is sitting in his study. He is wrestling with one of his most difficult assignments: the tuition of the future King Arthur in the arts of management.

The course is full of practical work. Using his magical powers and the experience of already having lived in the future, Merlin often projects himself and King Arthur into the twentieth century in order to work on real business problems. Together they have designed a small car for Rover, which has taken 60 per cent of the domestic market. They have negotiated free entry into the Japanese market for British products and services and modernized French agriculture. They have found an uncontested site for the third London airport and re-financed Poland. In 1933 they bought IBM and in 1965 they sold Rolls Royce. Merlin believes in the case study method.

But Arthur notices that whenever a particularly difficult issue arises, Merlin consults a big book which lies on his desk, along with his portable crucible, philosopher's stone, and bottled bat's blood.

Arthur   *Merlin, please tell me what's in that great volume you keep referring to? Is it a book of spells?*

Merlin   No, it's *The Gower Handbook of Management*, which I acquired on a quick trip to 1988. . . . There's no wizardry in it, just sound advice on almost every aspect of management.

Arthur   *But was it written by a wizard?*

Merlin   Not by a wizard, but by many experts. Over 60 of them.

Arthur   *(after some thought) – Merlin, there's something that's been troubling me. If there are going to be so many management experts in those days-yet-to-come and so much written and published on management and so many people tutored in the arts of management, why will they have so much trouble with their business?*

Merlin   Because they will attempt so much. It will be an heroic age. Ordinary managers, without the weapons of social privilege or personal wealth, will be required to ride out as champions of the whole kingdom to defeat poverty, ignorance and sloth.

Arthur   *You make these managers sound like a new order of chivalry. I thought that they would be arriving as bag-men and the servants of bag-men. People who will be out to line their own pockets.*

Merlin   It may well start like that, but it will have become something very different by the time *The Gower Handbook of Management* is written. I see that a little yet-to-be-history lesson is required.

First, I will let you into a secret about the system of free business enterprise, which by some will be called 'capitalism'. Contrary to reports, mostly put about by its own practitioners, it will be a tremendous success. By the twentieth century, it will provide the material means of feeding, housing and clothing huge populations. It will sustain individuals and groups of individuals regardless of their origins and promote their fortunes largely on the basis of their usefulness to society. It will transmit wealth and knowledge around the world. It will finance science and encourage the arts. In fact, it will be far too successful for its own good.

Arthur   *What do you mean?*

Merlin   Because of its success, governments and individuals will link their hopes and programmes for social development to its economic performance. By the middle of the twentieth century, business will be the main source of income in work and in retirement for most men and many women. Through taxation, business will contribute massively to the welfare services of the community, as well as developing many health, educational and housing schemes of its own. Through legislation, business will be obliged to advance racial and sexual equality, protect the natural world and train the young. Not content with the controls of taxation and legislation, governments will force themselves into partnership with business so as to be able to direct its resources to the achievement of their social goals.

Arthur   *But will this be a bad thing? If, as you tell me, the Age of Chivalry cannot last forever, then the Age of Business Enterprise sounds as though it will provide a better life for most people than many of the ages that will come between now and then.*

Merlin   Indeed it will. And that's the point. Having had their expectations raised, people and their popularly elected governments will seek to extract from business enterprise ever better conditions of living. You only have to look at the contents of this Handbook to see that by the late twentieth century the manager will have taken over many of the functions performed in previous ages by the feudal lord, the priest, the teacher, the money-lender, the physician, the lawyer, the watchman and even (*he glances with suspicion at the section on market research*) the astrologer.

Arthur *Are you saying that the decline of some businesses in the late twentieth century is therefore not the responsibility of the managers but the fault of society?*

Merlin Of course not. Management incompetence, fraud and idleness will contribute their share of failures, as in all other occupations. But the feeling of weakness that you have observed in some areas of business and government during our visits to the mid-to-late twentieth century is in large part a reflection of managers' frustration with their social roles and people's disappointment at the failure to fulfil their expectations. Indeed, some businesses will fail just because the original purposes and skills of business management – buying, making, selling – will be lost in a mass of unproductive administration. For a while, this trend will be encouraged by the very people who should stand out against it – the Business Schoolmen. They will be teaching high finance to those who need low cunning; planning to those who should be doing; organizational theory to those who need personal skills. It will take a great recession in business in the 1970s to bring some of them back to teaching the basic arts.

Arthur *Merlin, you said that the system of free business enterprise will be a success. And that to cope with this success and the expectations that it will create, the arts of business management will be developed. However, in spite of this development, the managers will not always be able to deliver all the benefits that the people expect. Does that mean that in the end management and managers will be rejected as the means of controlling business? On our study tours, we have never been beyond 1988. What happens after that?*

Merlin Ah . . . I'm not going to tell you the answers before you have done the practical research. You will have to wait and see. But you should have already observed that towards the end of the 1970s there will be significant changes in the context of management.

Small businesses, whether owned by their managers or by large corporations, will come back into favour. Governments will notice that small businesses employ the majority of people. Large corporations will realize that smaller operating units have smaller costs of administration. The costs of basic resources – manpower, energy, materials – will all rise dramatically as the owners of these resources realize that they can fix a market price for them – and that society is no longer prepared to risk wars or revolutions in order to hold down the cost of such resources. More people and nations will acquire the means of production and the skills of management, so that competition will increase faster than custom. As a function, management will be invaded by machines, which will take over the task of assembling and analysing information, and by working people, who will seek to participate in the process of decision making.

Arthur   *So, what will this mean for the manager?*

Merlin   That he needs to go back to the basics of business – and with the consent and encouragement of a society which has a better appreciation of the true role of business. Increased competition will mean getting closer to the customer and involving the whole workforce in the satisfaction of his needs. The scarcity and expense of resources will mean developing better ways of making things and generating less waste. With more machine-produced information and analysis, there will be a greater need for human judgement. Smaller business units employing better educated people will require more effective styles of leadership.

These are all reasons why *The Gower Handbook of Management* will be such a good guide for businesses in the latter part of the twentieth century. It is concerned with the basic practicalities of managing a business and it also contains a section on personal skills, such as negotiation, communication, and self-development.

Arthur   *If it is so full of wisdom and management is so important to the future, I think I should have the copy of this Handbook. After all, I am the 'once and future king'.*

Merlin contemplates this suggestion. For Arthur to study the book himself would save a lot of time in tutorials. Time in which he could be earning fees from other consultancy assignments, like the plan to start a quality circle for knights called the Round Table. But Merlin considers that to let *The Gower Handbook of Management* out of his possession could be dangerous for his own business. It is the Middle Ages: wizards are two a penny, but good management consultants are few and far between. It is better not to risk spoiling the market.

Merlin   No, thank you, Arthur. I think it would be most appropriate if I kept the book – just for the next few hundred years.

With apologies to T. H. White, author of *The Sword in the Stone*.

Part One
PRINCIPLES, POLICY AND ORGANIZATION

1 Principles of management

Philip Sadler

When practising managers are faced with difficult and complex problems – for example, designing and organization structure for a new manufacturing plant, or attempting to motivate a workforce characterized by apathy and low productivity – they quite naturally feel the need for a set of principles to turn to, in order to help them reach the right decisions.

This is sensible when it involves a willingness to learn from the experience of others as opposed to a stubborn determination to learn only from one's own mistakes. There is also the risk that so-called 'principles' which carry all the authority of tablets of stone, but which are frequently based on limited experience, may be accepted uncritically as if they were eternal truths and used by managers as substitutes for their own thought processes.

The principles of management are, of course, quite unlike the principles of mathematics or the laws of the natural sciences. In the management field there is no universal agreement as to what the principles are, nor can it be said that the principles of management are valid for all situations. (There is little point in adding the qualification 'other things being equal' since in the human context in which management is set the 'other things' are rarely if ever 'equal'.)

It would, perhaps, be better not to use the term 'principles' at all, but to refer instead to 'guidelines'. They are, quite simply, sets of potentially useful generalizations about the factors which make for success in management. People have been making such general statements for thousands of years, usually as a result of thinking deeply about their own experiences in organizations. In modern times the wide-ranging types of experience gained by successful management consultants has been a particularly fertile source of such ideas.

In this chapter the historical development of management principles will be traced briefly in order to set the scene for a more detailed examination of some of the more recent and contemporary writings on the subject. The chapter will conclude with a statement of some management principles which have emerged from experience and research in recent years.

THE BEGINNINGS OF MANAGEMENT THOUGHT

The search for 'principles of management' – rules or 'laws' which, if observed, will result in effective managerial performance in all situations – has been going on for thousands of years (George, 1968). Early Egyptian writings show that the builders of the pyramids recognized certain basic principles such as authority, responsibility and specialization. The Babylonian Code of Hammurabi set out principles of control and responsibility and Moses developed principles of organization when leading the tribes of Israel on the flight from Egypt. Mencius, writing in China in 500 BC emphasized the importance of the systematic application of principles of management: 'Whoever pursues a business in this world must have a system. A business which has attained success without a system does not exist.' Plato, in the *Republic*, argued the merits of the principle of specialization, and Socrates stressed the universal nature of management: 'I say that over whatever a man may preside he will, if he knows what he needs, and is able to provide it, be a good president, whether he have the direction of a chorus, a family, a city or an army.'

Many instances of early management thought come from the writings of great military strategists, for example, the staff principle, probably first used during the reign of Alexander the Great (336-323 BC). Machiavelli, in the sixteenth century, developed four principles – reliance on mass consent; cohesiveness; leadership; and the will to survive. Although he was writing about government in his time, the same principles might be applied to the management of companies today.

Modern industrial management theory dates from the introduction of the factory system. Techniques for financial control, incentive payment schemes, planning systems and investment appraisal methods were rapidly developed and applied. A rational approach to management was developed in the nineteenth century, and became known as 'scientific management'. Typical of pioneering work of this kind was the development of techniques such as product forecasting, production planning and work study at the Boulton, Watt Co. Engineering Works in England in the early years of the century. At the same time, in the United States, Eli Whitney was developing cost accounting, quality control and the concept of interchangeable parts. In Scotland, Robert Owen laid the foundations of modern personnel management at the New Lanark Mill, demonstrating that concern for employee welfare and the provision of good working conditions were compatible with a profitable and thriving business.

In 1881 the first business school (the Wharton School at the University of Pennsylvania) was established – some eighty or more years before the decision to establish business schools in London and Manchester.

Thirty years later Frederick Winslow Taylor published the work which has possibly had more influence on management practice than anything published since, his famous *Principles of Scientific Management* (Taylor, 1911). He advocated that managers should gather together all the traditional knowledge possessed by workmen and then classify it and reduce it to laws, rules and formulae. They should then develop a 'science' for each element of a man's work to replace old rule-of-thumb methods and 'scientifically' select and train workmen in the new methods. Finally, managers should take over certain tasks, such as planning and scheduling of work, which were previously left to the workmen to cope with as well as they could.

THE PRE-WAR MANAGEMENT WRITERS

Taylor's work had a profound and far-reaching influence on works management and much workshop practice today still reflects this. In the field of general management, however, a number of writers, in the years up to the Second World War, exercised a similarly powerful influence – most notably Henri Fayol, a French mining engineer; Elton Mayo, a Harvard professor; Mary Parker Follett, an American educationalist trained in philosophy, law and political science; Chester Barnard, president of the New Jersey Bell Telephone Company; and Lyndall F. Urwick, a British army officer who became a management consultant.

Fayol's work was first published in France in 1916 under the title *Administration Industrielle et Générale* and failed to be noticed in Britain and North America until translated and published by Pitman in 1949 as *General and Industrial Management* (Fayol, 1949). He analysed management activity into five elements – planning, organizing, commanding (or directing), co-ordinating and controlling – an analytical framework which has been borrowed and built upon by countless writers since. He also argued that, to be effective, management should be founded upon fourteen principles as follows:

1 Division of work and specialization
2 Authority must match responsibility
3 Discipline
4 Unity of command (one man, one boss)
5 Unity of direction
6 Subordination of individual interest to the general interest
7 Remuneration must be fair in relation to effort
8 Centralization
9 The scalar or hierarchical principle of line authority
10 The principle of order (a place for everyone and everyone in his place)
11 Equity
12 Stability of tenure of personnel
13 Importance of initiative
14 Importance of *esprit de corps*.

This represented the first attempt at a complete theory of management. The fact that it received widespread recognition and acclaim when published in the English language more than thirty years after it was originally written is an indication of the extent to which Fayol was regarded as an authority on management matters.

Elton Mayo's distinction lies in the fact that his contribution was based on research rather than on direct personal experience, and in the way he shifted attention away from the more mechanistic issues of structure and control on to the human factors affecting industrial performance. The now famous studies he conducted at the Hawthorne Works of the Western Electric Company (Mayo, 1933) led to the conclusion that questions of human motivation and the emotional response elicited by the work situation were more important than logical and rational arrangements in determining output. Mayo also held that social relationships in working groups were the most important factor influencing the satisfaction the workers derived from their work.

Mary Parker Follett (Follett, 1949), reached similar conclusions, but on philosophical grounds rather than as a result of applied research. She emphasized the importance of group processes in decision making and had much to say that is relevant today on the question of resolving conflict.

Chester Barnard was a practising manager, but his analysis of the managerial role and the nature of organizations in *The Functions of the Executive* (Barnard, 1937), constitutes an important part of our sociological literature. His analysis linked together hitherto unrelated ideas about the factors affecting individual performance, the nature of organizations and the role of the manager.

The final figure in this group of people writing in the 1930s and '40s is Lyndall F. Urwick, whose most influential work was *The Elements of Administration* (Urwick, 1949). He produced a new synthesis based on the work of such people as Taylor, Fayol and Follett.

The principles which Urwick gathered together in this way have come to be known as the 'classical' principles of management. They are based on a combination of experience and philosophy rather than rigorous research and have been widely criticized for this. They have attracted criticism on other grounds also. First, the underlying assumption of their work – that there exists a common set of principles applicable to management in all types of situation – has been frequently challenged. Second, their work is criticized (perhaps unfairly) on the grounds that the world in which they had their experience no longer exists and that the principles they derived from that experience have little or no validity for the contemporary organization operating in the modern business environment. (An example of the way ideas have changed in recent years is the widespread loss of confidence in the so-called economies of scale; another is the extent to which the principle of specialization has been challenged as a result both of new ideas and much research and experimentation in the field of job design.)

Thus, changes in our ideas about management have conspired with the march of events to destroy the credibility of the classical management principles. The main changes which have affected the managerial role and altered it beyond recognition in the last quarter of a century include:

1 The impact of the computer, and more recently the microprocessor, on information processing tasks in production and administration

2 The increase in the pace of technological change generally, with consequences for the speed with which manufacturing processes and products themselves become obsolete

3 The growth of international trade and the associated intensification of competition, together with the growth of the multinational corporation and the impact on business of unstable exchange rates

4 The much greater impact of legislation on business activity – in such fields as employment protection consumer protection, environmental care, health and safety, etc

5 Changes in social climate leading to demands for employee participation in decision making

6 High rates of inflation.

These and other factors have brought about a geometric increase in the complexity of the management task such that decisions can not easily be taken in the light of a few clearly formulated principles or guidelines of the classical kind.

MANAGEMENT THEORY IN THE POST-WAR ERA

The post-war era has seen great expansion in the volume of literature on management. The range and variety of approaches is so great as to defy any simple grouping or system of classification into schools of thought, but some commonalities can be detected.

First, the tradition of the consultant or practitioner theorizing on the basis of his experience has continued, primarily because this approach genuinely meets the needs of many practising managers seeking to bring a greater degree of system and order into their own thinking. Often the most successful writers in this category have been those who can most clearly communicate, and elaborate into a system of thought, what practising managers already believe to be the case on the basis of their own experience. The best-known writers in this category in the English language have been such eminently successful consultants as Brech, Louis Allen and, above all, Peter Drucker.

Drucker in particular has taken account of changes in the nature of business environment and the managerial task, and has been successful precisely because he speaks to the contemporary manager and deals with the issues that currently concern him (Drucker,1971).

Second, and closely related to the first group, is a smaller number of highly influential writers who have illuminated management thought with shafts of humour or satire. The most outstanding in this respect are C.Northcote Parkinson's *Parkinson's Law* (Parkinson, 1957); Robert Townsend's *Up the Organisation* (Townsend, 1970) and Antony Jay's *Management and Machiavelli* (Jay, 1967).

The ideas of these writers are well known outside management circles and indeed Parkinson's work has a place of its own in the literature of post-war society.

Third, there are the propounders of functional principles or of principles concerned with part rather than the whole of the management task. We have already seen that the classical principles of management were developed by people such as Fayol and Urwick on the basis of earlier work in production management by Taylor and others. In the post-war period we have seen considerable elaboration of theory in such areas as principles of marketing (Levitt, 1969, and Kotler, 1976), principles of personnel management (Pigors and Myers, 1969) and corporate strategy and planning (Ansoff, 1965).

This third group differs from the previous two in that it is dominated by academics as distinct from practitioners or consultants, reflecting the growth of management studies as an academic subject in the universities and the growing influence of the business school – initially in the US but more recently in Britain and other European countries. This group, in consequence, overlaps to some extent with the fourth and perhaps most important group – the management researchers. Primarily industrial psychologists and sociologists, their work builds on the tradition pioneered by Elton Mayo of detached, empirical and comparative studies of behaviour in industrial organizations. In turn they can be subdivided according to the main focus of their research. Looked at in this way the field breaks down quite logically into studies of the individual industrial worker and his motivation; studies of the behaviour of industrial work groups; studies of the factors influencing organization effectiveness and researches into managerial and leadership behaviour.

Under the first heading three American psychologists, Herzberg, McClelland and Maslow, have had a strong and enduring influence on management theory and practice.

Herzberg is best known for his distinction between 'motivators' such as the work itself, achievement, responsibility and recognition, and what he describes as 'hygiene' factors, which do not provide motivation but merely act so as to prevent workers from being dissatisfied. These factors include pay, working conditions and relations with supervisors. Herzberg's work has led to important experiments in job enrichment as well as casting doubt on the effectiveness of many financial incentive schemes (Herzberg, 1959).

McClelland's researches emphasized the importance of the motivation to achieve in relation to the performance of work (McClelland, 1969), while Maslow's most important contribution was to draw attention to the way in which human needs are ordered into a hierarchical system, with basic needs such as survival and security as the foundation of motivation but with higher-order needs such as belonging, esteem, achievement and self-actualization acting as the more important day-to-day motivators in advanced societies where survival and security can reasonably be taken for granted (Maslow, 1954).

Insight into the behaviour of industrial work groups has been provided by researchers on both sides of the Atlantic. Outstanding examples include Gouldner's study of gypsum mineworkers (Gouldner, 1954), and Walker and Guest's work on assembly line workers in the US (Walker and Guest, 1952), while in Britain there have been equally illuminating studies such as Lupton's participant observation of shop floor behaviour (Lupton, 1963).

The functioning of whole organizations and relationships between different forms of organization structure and effectiveness have been the focus of a great deal of research on both sides of the Atlantic. This work in particular has had a powerful influence both in demolishing the credibility of the simple classical principles and in establishing new but more complex guidelines for management decisions.

In Britain, the work of members of the Tavistock Institute of Relations has demonstrated the importance of taking account both of the constraints imposed by technology and the needs of human beings for satisfying social relationships when designing organization structures. From their work emerged the principles of 'joint optimisation of the social and technical systems', which stresses the need to search for forms of organization in which technical requirements and human aspirations are simultaneously fulfilled (Rice, 1963, and Trist et al, 1963).

Joan Woodward (in her studies of organization structures and levels of technology) conclusively showed that there is no one best way to organize a business and that the form of organization advocated in the classical principles, with its emphasis on unity of command, hierarchy and clarity of structure, was far from universally adopted by successful firms (Woodward, 1965).

In a similar vein Burns and Stalker were able to demonstrate that the classical principles worked well in firms with highly stable technologies and markets but failed to be associated with successful performance in firms faced with the need for rapid adjustment to changing conditions (Burns and Stalker, 1961).

Organization studies in the US that have contributed to the theory and practice of management include the work of Rensis Likert and in particular his concept of the organization as a series of interlocking groups (Likert, 1961). These US studies also include the analysis by Lawrence and Lorsch of the problems faced by firms which need on the one hand to differentiate their activities to be able to relate to different markets, but which must simultaneously integrate these activities into a coherent and cohesive organization for purposes of control and co-ordination (Lawrence and Lorsch, 1967).

Among the many studies of managerial behaviour, those of Mintzberg in the US (Mintzberg, 1973), and Rosemary Stewart in Britain (Stewart, 1967) have thrown much needed light on what managers actually do, and how the job content of managers with different roles in the organization varies. The relationship between leadership style and management effectiveness has also proved to be a fruitful area of research, with outstanding contributions to our knowledge of leadership processes emerging from the work of Bass (Bass, 1960), and Fiedler (Fiedler, 1971) in the US.

The fourth and final group of contributors to modern management theory can be traced in its origins to two main sources: first, the application of scientific methods and mathematical problem-solving techniques to the solution of operational problems in wartime and second, to the subsequent development of computers and related mathematical approaches to solving complex problems. This fourth group is variously known as operational research or management scientists. It has included a number of eminent thinkers who have moved beyond the development and application of techniques to develop whole theories of management and organization based on concepts derived from systems theory or information theory. In the US the outstanding personalities are March and Simon of the Massachusetts Institute of Technology (March and Simon, 1958); Diebold, the 'father of automation' (Diebold, 1965) and Norbert Weiner (Weiner, 1948), the man who first developed ideas in the field of cybernetics and related them to management.

In Britain, Stafford Beer clearly falls into this category. Beer exemplifies the approach of this group of writers in several ways. He is enthusiastic about prospects of management becoming more 'scientific'. He regards the computer as a potential tool for revolutionary changes in the practice of management. He conceptualizes management as an information-processing activity and management's task as primarily one of *control*. Given that cybernetics is the science of control systems, it follows that the principles of cybernetics are also the key principles of management (Beer, 1972).

The management world described by Beer and others writing in the same vein is one with a strange language of its own – familiar perhaps to specialists in control engineering or to consultant neurologists, but foreign to generalists, and marketing and personnel specialists to whom terms such as 'heuristic', 'negentropy' and 'reticulum' convey little or nothing. At the same time it is a world in which problems of labour relations, emotions, attitudes, irrational conflicts and organizational politics have no place.

The main influence of this school of writers has been in the design, development and application of mathematically based operational research techniques to the solution of certain types of business problem.

MODERN MANAGEMENT PRINCIPLES

To what extent is it possible to draw from these various approaches a body of knowledge which, when summarized and distilled down to its essentials, could be said to represent the principles of modern management as distinct from the 'classical' ones? The task is a daunting one, not only because of the sheer volume of literature that now exists, but also because the principal trends have been towards divergence of theory, specialization of topic and fragmentation of knowledge rather than reflecting convergence, integration and synthesis.

It is possible, however, to identify a number of recurring ideas or themes which, albeit given different treatment by different authorities and accorded differing degrees of importance in different conceptual schemes, would, nevertheless, command widespread acceptance. What follows is an attempt to state these.

The main propositions, 'principles' or guidelines about management which command widespread agreement today are:

The organization as a complex system

The achievement of the purposes of a human organization will involve a wide range of activities which are interconnected so as to form a system, such that changes to the pattern of activities in one part of the system will trigger related changes in other parts of it.

The technical and social sub-systems

The organization as a system is made up of two principal sub-systems – the technical and the social. The former is made up of such elements as the plant and machinery in use, the work flow between the different production stations and the system of production adopted (batch, mass production, continuous flow, etc.). The social system consists of the pattern of relations between the people who work in the organization. In designing organizations regard must be given both to the need to adapt the structure to the technical system and to provide a structure which makes for a satisfying pattern of human relationships.

The organization as an open system

The existence of any organization depends on some process of exchange of goods or services with other organizations, social units or individuals in its environment. From this it follows that in the long run, organizations cannot survive if they are managed exclusively in ways which meet the needs of their members. Management is, therefore, partly the process of achieving a delicate balance between the expectations and needs of such internal 'stakeholders' as shareholders, managers, employees and pensioners on the one hand, and the demands and constraints imposed upon the organization by its markets, its customers, its suppliers, trades unions, government departments, pressure groups of various kinds and, not least, by the strategies and tactics of competitors. To create and preserve such a balance calls for the continuous monitoring of the organization's environment and the will to bring about appropriate responses on the part of the organization.

The key resource of the modern business organization in advanced industrial societies is knowledge

The key workers are the 'knowledge workers'; management, therefore, is more to do with the profitable exploitation of knowledge than with the productivity of labour or the utilization of physical capacity. 'Knowledge' in this context may mean product knowledge, process 'know-how' or knowledge of the market. It is the task of management to ensure that the organization's level of investment in the acquisition of new knowledge is

11

sufficient to give it the competitive strength it requires to achieve profitable growth.

Management's key task is to secure the future survival of the organization by means of appropriate and timely innovation

The classical principles of management tend to conjure up a vision of some mythical factory for producing 'widgets' which has always produced widgets and always will, using the same technology for the purpose and selling them in a stable market to loyal customers and without any Japanese competition! In the modern organization, by contrast, successful innovation in both products and processes is indispensable to survival. Effective management, therefore, involves the ability to develop an innovative, creative climate, to establish an efficient system of market intelligence so as to discover needs for new products and to generate the funds needed for R & D and investment in new plant and equipment.

Management is the process of getting things done by other people

From this proposition it follows that the achievements of an organization will reflect the degree of motivation and commitment of employees. Motivation is an extremely complex aspect of human behaviour about which we still have much to learn. We have, however, advanced beyond the naïve belief that it is a simple response to reward (in the form of financial incentives, for example) or punishment (fear of 'the sack'). Other factors such as job satisfaction, leadership and recognition clearly play an important part.

Management as an activity is universal but does not take the same form in all situations

Managers in all organizations and at all levels have to get things done by others, have to ensure that decisions are taken and cannot escape the need to exercise leadership. At the same time the qualities and skills required in the chief executive of a large organization are very different from those required in a first-line manager, while the qualities needed to be effective as manager of a building site differ from those required in the successful manager of an R & D group in the electronics industry.

There is no one best way to organize a business

The most successful systems of organization differ markedly from one kind of business to another. Any one business must continuously adapt its organization to meet the demands of changing circumstances.

Small is beautiful

Entrepreneurial drive, creativity, adaptability and innovation alike are stifled by the bureaucratic systems of administration and control which characterize large, monolithic organizations. Effective management structures therefore involve autonomous profit centres, served rather than directed by small head-office teams.

Management is a process involving a mix of rational, logical decision-making and problem solving activities and intuitive, judgemental activities

In this sense it is both science and art. An important skill is to be able to recognize which problems and decisions fall into which category and to treat them accordingly.

None of the foregoing statements, whether they are described as generalizations, precepts, principles, or guidelines, has necessarily any enduring validity. There is no point in smashing one set of tablets of stone in order to create another. Given the high level of uncertainty and, indeed, turbulence in today's business environment, coupled with the value system of our modern society, and the stage of development of our economic institutions, these statements provide some indication of the likely paths to success. Should further radical changes take place in the nature of the environment, new guiding principles will inevitably be needed.

FURTHER READING

Ansoff, H.I., *Corporate Strategy*, McGraw-Hill, New York, 1965

Barnard, C., *The Functions of the Executive*, Harvard University Press, Cambridge, Mass, 1938

Bass, B., *Leadership, Psychology and Organisational Behaviour*, Harper, New York, 1960

Beer, S., *Brain of the Firm*, Allen Lane, The Penguin Press, London, 1972

Burns, T. and Stalker, G. M., *The Management of Innovation*, Tavistock, London, 1961

Diebold, J., *Focus on Automation*, British Institute of Management, London, 1965

Drucker, P., *Drucker on Management*, Management Publications Ltd, for the British Institute of Management, London 1971

Fayol, H. *General and Industrial Administration*, Pitman, London, 1949

Fiedler, F., *Leadership*, General Learning Press, New York, 1971

Follett, Mary P., *Freedom and Coordination*, Management Publications Trust, London, 1949

George, C.S., *The History of Management Thought*, Prentice-Hall, Englewood Cliffs, NJ, 1968

Gouldner, A.W., *Patterns of Industrial Bureaucracy*, The Free Press, Glencoe, Ill, 1954

Herzberg, F.J.,*The Motivation to Work*, Wiley, New York, 1959

Jay, A., *Management and Machiavelli*, Hodder & Stoughton, London 1967

Kotler, P., *Marketing Management*, Prentice-Hall, Englewood Cliffs, NJ, 1976

Lawrence, P.R. and Lorsch, J.W., *Organisation and Environment*, Harvard Business School, Cambridge, Mass, 1967

Levitt, T., *The Marketing Mode*, McGraw-Hill, New York, 1969

Likert, R., *New Patterns of Management*, McGraw-Hill, New York, 1961

Lupton, T., *On the Shop Floor*, Pergamon Press, Oxford, 1963

McClelland, D.C. and Winter, D.G., *Motivating Economic Achievement*, Free Press, New York, 1969

March, J.G. and Simon, H.A., *Organisations*, Wiley, New York, 1958

Maslow, A., *Motivation and Personality*, Harper & Row, New York, 1954

Mayo, G.E., *The Human Problems of an Industrial Civilization*, Harvard Business School, Boston, Mass, 1933

Mintzberg, H., *The Nature of Managerial Work*, Harper & Row, New York, 1973

Parkinson, C.Northcote, *Parkinson's Law*, John Murray, London, 1957

Pigors, P. and Myers, C.A., *Personnel Administration*, McGraw-Hill, New York, 1969

Rice, A.K., *The Enterprise and its Environment*, Tavistock, London, 1963

Stewart, R., *Managers and their Jobs*, Macmillan, London, 1967

Taylor, F.W., *Principles of Scientific Management*, Harper and Brothers, New York, 1911

Townsend, R., *Up The Organisation*, Michael Joseph, London, 1970

Trist, E.L., Higgin, G.W., Murray, H. and Pollock, A.B., *Organisational Choice*, Tavistock, London, 1963

Urwick, L., *The Elements of Administration*, Harper and Brothers, New York, 1944

Walker, C.R. and Guest, R.H., *The Man on The Assembly Line*, Harvard University Press, Cambridge, Mass, 1952

Weiner, N., *Cybernetics*, Wiley, New York, 1948

Woodward, J., *Industrial Organisation: Theory and Practice*, Oxford University Press, Oxford, 1965

2 Corporate strategies for the future

George S Sunders and Ron H Bradnam

Corporate strategy cannot exist in isolation from the world in which the customer lives, in which the business must exhibit acceptable behaviour and from which the business draws its resources. Hence this chapter contains some speculation concerning possible developments for the future in the hope that it may help businesses to adopt strategies that are compatible with the opportunities and threats they may face. No attempt has been made to forecast quantitatively – partly because of the inherent uncertainty in the process but more importantly because each business must research its own input data in accordance with its unique markets, technologies and resources.

Strategy must take into account:

– future social attitudes
– future legal structures

and must be considered in relation to:

– future markets
– future resources
– future technologies
– future organization and management style.

Each of these factors will now be examined in broad outline, with particular emphasis on those that are liable to affect the enterprise at strategic level.

FUTURE SOCIAL ATTITUDES

There is a growing feeling among leaders in industrialized nations that the assertion 'everyone has the right to work' (Universal Declaration of Human Rights) may have to change to 'everyone has the right to an income'. Europe and the US appear to be entering an age where:

1 If work is defined as toil in exchange for money, then providing work for all is becoming increasingly difficult

2 If work is so defined, an ever-increasing amount of creative work is enjoyed and undertaken for no monetary return – including 'do it yourself', home food growing and preparation, charitable work and arts and crafts. In some advanced countries this has been estimated as accounting for a large proportion of the gross national product (GNP)

3 More people are finding satisfaction from working on their own or in small groups earning money (or engaging in barter) from efforts that may well have started as hobbies.

Work has traditionally provided people with their means of livelihood, status in the community and an outlet for contributing. Unless an alternative can be found of providing these three, work remains the essential vehicle. It is the responsibility therefore of management to find ways of creating suitable work opportunities for all people for reasonable periods of their lives. The greatest problems (or, more correctly, opportunities to influence this situation) currently lie in the lower age range. There are particular problems with school leavers whose lack of experience means that they have less to offer an employer. However a strength of their situation is to be found (with the right motivations) in their willingness to learn and adapt to circumstances. This motivation can be developed by the creation of closer bonds with the establishments that provide the workforce (i.e. schools, colleges and universities) in order to foster a better understanding of industry, commerce and government. All companies, if they have not already started, should be encouraging the concept of continuing education throughout the careers of their staff. Training and public relations consume time and resources but the consequence of ignoring the needs of the present and future employee cannot be underestimated. In addition, once the work has been provided, there is an increasing demand for the work to be more satisfying and 'owned' by the worker, while at the same time the employer is endeavouring to improve the competitiveness of the operation.

One outcome of this trend may well be that employment, as it has been known, will no longer be for life but may last for less than half life. New opportunities must therefore be sought to provide for continuing employment, which may include the acceptance of other forms of work. The implications reach beyond the usual scope of most corporate plans, but if we accept that the organization must respond to the environment in which it operates, there is an urgent need for management to get out into that environment and learn from it. Businesses will have to meet the expectations of the community by creating opportunities to discuss the activities of the business and perhaps also to participate (if only by visits, etc.) in operations being undertaken. Improvements in the relationship with the community include the need to create closer links with, and awareness by, policy makers in government and the financial institutions. Planners can sometimes get quite skilled at 'sorting out the wood from the trees' but often they have no idea of what view they wish to see when emerging from the forest at the far side! These changes will become unacceptable in companies practising a more open management style. Ronald Ellis, one time managing director of the Truck and Bus Division of British Leyland, has observed that there are six stages to 'managing to survive':

1 entrepreneurial stage
2 survival stage
3 stabilization
4 reputation and pride
5 uniqueness and adaptability
6 contribution – to society, industry, profession.

He suggested that companies tend to grow through these stages but can, all too easily, slip back to an earlier stage if anything goes wrong. He considered that far too few companies reached the last stage – that of social responsibility – and found it relatively difficult to remain at that stage for long periods. Yet that is increasingly what is expected of the organization.

These changes in social attitudes could affect the strategy of the medium-sized and the large companies in the following ways:

1 Companies may be forced to employ more people on shorter working weeks (shift work) and part timers, despite the difficulties in training, change overs, continuity and planning, etc. and the adverse effect on costs
2 Since the result of work which appears as GNP is only part of the picture, market forecasting will have to be reassessed to take into account this changing social practice
3 A move towards work sharing, once dismissed by all European governments as 'an impractical method of reducing unemployment', has been officially promoted in the Netherlands with the aim of reaching a target of 25 per cent of the working population by the end of the decade.

Each of these issues arouses different responses. In the Netherlands experiment, the Government subsidized both the company and the employee to buffer the effects of lower wages and increased indirect costs. However, a prominent industrialist has suggested, quite independently, in a private communication, a way in which the costs of work sharing may not be so prohibitive as at first thought, and the administrative burden kept small by implementing adjustment at the company level before the company pays its dues to the Government.

Another factor that will undoubtedly affect corporate strategy in the years ahead is the growing public concern over the potential dangers in high technology. Harmful side effects of drugs, factory explosions with or without noxious emissions, fear of nuclear energy – all these and others have illustrated the need for extreme caution in launching new products and commissioning new processes. And yet the paradox is that, given a choice, the buying public do not seem willing to pay the premium for more safety, more testing and more precautions (lead-free petrol marketed in the US at a few cents per gallon above normal pump prices just didn't sell).

There is also public concern at the more obvious results in heavy industry and the throw-away society. Pollution by noise, fumes, throw-away packaging or ugly buildings, tips and pylons will be increasingly resisted; and the possibility exists of stronger legislation in this area.

A study published in 1979 for the UK Department of Energy set out six prerequisites for full employment in an environment of technological change:

1 An adaptable and better educated workforce
2 More trained manpower in electronics and software skills and traditional skills
3 An expanded retraining effort
4 Less hierarchical industrial structures
5 Greater willingness by management to consult
6 Positive attitude to opportunities in new technology.

These prerequisites assume that, with the increase of technological choice, effective planning and policy making is essential. Important steps have already been taken to aid effective planning, but with industry moving towards basic technologies and modules requiring systems of management based on project rather than on functional structures. The development of appropriate strategies, methodologies and auditing techniques must proceed.

These and other issues are now explored, with the aim of ensuring that human and material resources are responsibly used.

FUTURE LEGAL STRUCTURES

Ever since the earliest Companies Acts (notably incorporation in 1844 and limited liability in 1855), company law reform has continued on the basis of a commission every 20 years or so. Succeeding Acts made small changes based upon problems that cropped up as business activities developed. In recent years, however, and largely in response to EEC directives, changes have been coming faster. To the harassed small business man these changes seem too fast, whereas to others they seem pitifully inadequate. One commentator has remarked, 'If we have a mess in 1981, we ought to expect chaos by 1984. What kind of company law will we have in 2001? If neither the politicians nor the administrators ask this question, then those who will be most affected must do so for themselves. The initiative must be taken by commerce, industry and the professions, on the American pattern. There is little enough time.' (Sealey)

As well as company law reforms and EEC harmonization, there are various voluntary codes and guidelines that should also be acknowledged as having an impact on corporate strategy. For OECD member countries, there are guidelines on international investment and multinational enterprises amongst other matters; from various pressure groups there is a bewildering array of codes concerning product liability and environmental impact. In 1976, a certain chemical plant under construction in the US required 26 permits from 13 separate government agencies.

The corporate strategist must be aware of current and impending legislation that could affect his company's plans. Admittedly a large amount of legislation will have only minor effects on tactical plans but some laws can have major impact: some companies have already been forced to abandon products that cannot be brought into line; in some processes excessive investment is needed to meet new safety requirements; other companies have had to invest huge sums in R & D to meet future standards (car exhaust emissions for example). These problems due to legislation are all in addition to fiscal changes in respect of which Sir David Steel said '. . . I must repeat my frequently expressed concern at the growing tendency of governments, not least in the UK, to alter the terms on which business is conducted' (BP Annual Report, 1980).

Consider just four areas where changes in legislation will probably have increasing influence on corporate strategy:

1 directors' responsibility
2 employee rights
3 product liability
4 environmental impact.

For each of these areas, points that may need consideration in relation to planning are briefly discussed.

Directors' responsibilities have long been catalogued but in response to public disquiet and to EEC directives, changes are imminent. Already the UK Companies Act of 1980 requires directors to have regard to the interests of their employees. Many will assert that they always have had such regard, which anyway is in the long-term interests of shareholders, so only time and case law will give clear interpretation.

Attempts to force more responsible attitudes take broadly two forms; firstly a demand for more disclosure and secondly for more nonexecutive directors (including employee representatives) on company boards.

Disclosure is already dramatically different from what was considered acceptable 25 or 30 years ago when most businessmen saw no need to disclose anything more than was required by law and often no more than a couple of sheets of typescript was issued to shareholders. Now glossy multicoloured annual reports are commonplace, perhaps reflecting the company's need to woo the shareholder but also containing much social reporting (community activities, waste recycling, pollution control, employment practices, etc.). If all the other current codes were followed (for example intragroup trading practices, third world technology investment, etc.) the present day 40 page annual report would double or treble in size.

The pressure for more nonexecutive directors has already led to two-tier boards in West Germany and a wide range of consultative devices in other countries. In the UK there will probably be a continuing desire requiring management and trade unions to agree arrangements for participation. The problems of ensuring joint regulation of strategic planning will no doubt be fiercely debated. It would be a disaster, however, if fear on either side of industry were allowed to stop progress towards consultation. Still far too few companies hold regular meetings between the board and employee representatives.

In parallel to these statutory approaches, City of London institutions, alarmed at the effect of more dramatic revelations of director behaviour, have appointed a bureau to promote the appointment of nonexecutive directors. The theory, presumably, is that directors who do not depend on the company for their livelihood will probably be willing to challenge proposals that are morally dubious. Of course, in theory, the shareholders are supposed to watch over the behaviour of those they have elected as directors; but many directors have grown up in the period when shareholder power was minimal, when private investors (often referred to as absentee landlords) were interested only in short term capital gain. Growth in the power of the institutional investor is fairly recent and there have been a number of cases of pension fund trustees and the like becoming openly critical over company revelations (take overs, gratuitous payments, etc.).

Enormous changes in the laws governing employee rights in the UK took place in the 1970s. Equal pay, discrimination, health and safety, redundancy compensation were all the subject of legislation. Trade Union immunity was strengthened and the closed shop protected, though this was later modified. Minority groups are also being increasingly safeguarded. Since 1980, every directors' report must include a statement on company policy over employment of the disabled (companies with over 250 employees only). There is no doubt that pressure from other minority groups for similar consideration will follow.

As far as product liability is concerned, the current laws tend to be based upon proven negligence. It seems probable that strict liability will become the determining factor. The need for harmonization in product liability laws is important. Without it, the country with lenient legislation risks becoming a dumping ground for products of foreign manufacturers who cannot meet the high standards elsewhere. Similarly their own manufacturers would have difficulty in exporting products that meet only domestic lower level requirements. It is also of interest to note that in the USA, in the event of a take over, the principal corporation must accept liability for product damages caused previously by the taken-over company. In addition, putting a guilty subsidiary into liquidation, whilst not affecting the rest of the group, is a procedure which will probably not be accepted much longer. Future corporate strategy may require closer control of product quality by headquarters than has hitherto been customary.

Environmental impact is an immensely wide subject. Opencast mining, the laying of underground pipes, the effect of throw-away packaging, non-degradable plastic rubbish as well as noise and air pollution – all these affect almost every company directly or indirectly. Corporate sensitivity is already manifest in many advertising campaigns claiming responsible behaviour. Those companies who intend to introduce some new product or process in the future will have to think deeply about its environmental impact and take steps to alleviate any adverse effects or spend time and money to change public attitude.

FUTURE MARKETS

During the 1960s and 1970s financial management skills dominated strategic thinking. This was a period when thriving businesses based their success on growth. In the 1980s, slow growth and intense competition have meant that strategic thinking must be dominated by marketing skills. Indeed marketing is proving the critical management function in strategic terms. However, marketing has not been able to slide easily into the driving seat; rather it has had to earn its position through greatly improved productivity. With sales and distribution costs rising rapidly and advertising getting keener, innovative thinking is necessary. The new thinking must include more effective promotional methods (the information revolution is supposed to be imminent and promotion is, after all a form of communication) and must:

- cover novel distribution methods (many congested city centres will not now tolerate heavy goods traffic)
- experiment with breaking bulk and assembling locally, and
- computerize all the routine operations of stock control; regularize reordering, delivery and invoice documentation (which could extend to computer-to-computer links).

Let us consider three separate types of business and their market future:

1 Bespoke goods, major capital equipment and all such specials which, in general, are not made until a customer is found and has ordered. In this situation, marketing is followed by selling and then by manufacture
2 Standard goods, consumer durables and consumables where marketing is followed by manufacture and then by selling
3 Service industries selling financial skills, technology, consultancy licences, software franchises, etc. where marketing and operating are so closely linked as to be inseparable.

In the first case, marketing and selling are closely linked and will probably continue so. The larger the unit sale, the more the marketing/selling process becomes prolonged and often political. Under such circumstances the problem of keeping a manufacturing or operating unit occupied becomes of secondary importance. Peaks and troughs of activity are difficult to avoid and with world politics in a turbulent state continuous production is not going to get easier to achieve. Strategically it would seem wise to maintain a lean operating unit capable of handling the work load in the troughs and to subcontract the peaks.

In the second case, manufacture of consumer and industrial goods, the skills of forecasting and careful control of unsold stock will be paramount. In this type of business, the marketing man has traditionally thought in terms of volume and market share and has used these measures as his main objectives and controls. In future broader thinking will become necessary and the marketing man must start thinking of contribution and return on investment. His goals must be set in these terms which will take account of stocks and productive capacity left idle through unequal loading. For many marketing men, the idea that it will be his duty to load the factory to capacity will come as a shock.

There will also be a greater need for marketing to give better guidance to produce R & D with clearer indication of customer needs and attractive product features.

In the third category, service and sales of know-how, opportunities in the export field will dominate. For more than a century, countries rich in raw materials have sold them to developed countries who have had the skills of conversion. Now many of the developing countries are rapidly acquiring their own skills of conversion, so developed countries have moved towards the provision of capital goods for the factories, power stations and general infrastructures of the developing world. Following this will be a thriving market in the provision of technical, management and training skills. Countries which have moved in one generation from a nomadic or agrarian culture require an immense amount of help in adopting a manufacturing and commercial culture. This must however be provided with sensitivity and due regard for underlying cultural mores. The company that can so provide should reap a rich harvest.

Important to those who trade in know-how, is the protection of their wares. The patent system of the world although complex is reasonably effective. The same cannot always be said for trade marks and copyright. Whether tapes contain music or computer programs, they are easily and widely copied. The development of security systems protecting intellectual property is long overdue.

In summary marketing competence is at a critical stage and must be greatly improved to face the slow-growth highly competitive markets of the next decade. It is not surprising that some will adopt the strategy of diversification into the sale of their know-how via service contracts or franchise operations to overseas markets keen to become self-sufficient and hungry for help to achieve this.

FUTURE RESOURCES

Corporate manpower, apart from the obvious impact of technology, will probably change in method of employment. For the shorter working week to become practical, for instance, much greater versatility will be necessary. Since the first industrial revolution, specialization has been the goal as mechanical tools were developed and special skills were needed to operate them. Now the trend could well reverse, leading to general machine minding and maintenance skills in both manufacturing industry and information-dominated commercial and administrative offices. The implications for training, trade union organization and social attitudes are considerable and such changes are expected to be slow.

As has already been mentioned, an increase in numbers of small specialist companies and even sole practitioners and self-employed craftsmen is to be expected. Some businessmen have already taken advantage of this trend by establishing business format franchise operations. Carl-Henry Wingwist, a former Secretary General of the International Chamber of Commerce said 'the need to rekindle the entrepreneurial spirit is urgent in all our countries. A restoration of confidence and a rise in the world's standard of living depends on this vital point' ('Tomorrow the World', *Vision*, November 1981).

As far as the larger business is concerned, corporate strategy will probably include the greater use of subcontractors, consultants, software houses, and so on, leaving the principal leaner, more flexible and with clearer corporate goals associated with the kernel of the business.

As a result the problems to be solved will become more complex, also the art of managing people will require further development if the workforce is to help freely in the problem-solving process. Indeed a 'no threat' environment is going to be required in most enterprises, if the decision takers are to be expected to perform in an effective way. The advent of the cheap microcomputer, and its associated software make the possibility of 'what if?' modelling a practical option for even the smallest company. Given a degree of competence in the specialized requirements of the business and a certain general business experience and understanding of the economy, the possible consequences of decisions will be easily computed before major investments are made.

A major change experienced in the last decade has been the increase in worldwide trade and co-operation. The procurement of resources is no exception. As examples:

1 manpower, the ready international exchange of staff
2 materials, procured in a world market
3 machines and facilities, bought, hired, leased
4 finance, available in all the money markets
5 time, intercontinental sharing of computer systems
6 management, exchange of know-how, experience and information.

A further complication for the strategist is to be found in the potential 'problem resources', that is those whose availability is limited and may become scarce by the year 2000; these include: aluminium, copper, gold, lead, mercury, natural gas, petroleum, tin, silver and tungsten. Any user of these materials needs to model the implications of future supply, as the necessary data becomes available.

In the 1980s the main change has been the ease with which information on such resources can be obtained, processed and reviewed by the judicious and careful use of the technologies developed in the 1970s. With more reliable inputs, decisions will be quicker and themselves more reliable. Additionally, it will become easier to test the sensitivities of decisions before they are taken, and so enable a greater degree of realism to be built into the modelling. A demand will arise for more flexibility than currently exists in many organizations, if advantage is to be taken of this new capability. The workforce will have to be prepared and protected in the transition period.

With increased flexibility will come a need for improved specification of what is to be achieved and the resource procurement function will become a more professional activity; by the end of the decade, the existing make/buy and inventory management decision, is expected to be replaced by decisions in the field of employment strategies and business policy (for example, should company X purchase finished sub-assemblies or design, develop and manufacture the item itself). To be able to contribute effectively to such decisions will require a keen awareness of what the practicalities of any particular situation may be, and how external changes in the environment may influence the performance of the enterprise. The contributor will therefore have to extend his vision from the relatively narrow functional approach to a more system oriented approach. The real aim is to map out the possibilities and to make the optimum selection, a very much more attractive prospect.

FUTURE TECHNOLOGIES

All too often, new technology is seen as a threat. Corporate strategy in the future must be founded on technology as an opportunity.

The ability to forecast future growth technologies has been the dream of strategists for at least 20 years. In the late 1960s technological forecasting was popular. Now with the benefit of hindsight, many of the forecasts of those days can be seen to be unimpressive.

It has been said that anything is possible in a technical field given enough money. Although an exaggerated statement, there is more than a grain of truth in it. The technological advances coming from the conquest of space happened only because two great powers decided to fund space exploration, mainly for political reasons. Novel techniques and equipment that have been developed enabling oil majors to explore deep sea concessions and drill at ever increasing depths would never have been developed if oil were still traded at $2 per barrel. The need and the finance must precede the research and development; on the other hand, the Swiss watch industry was transformed almost overnight by the advent of quartz as a time piece. The mistake in the 'technological forecasting' era was to forecast from a starting point of scientific feasibility rather than the starting point of need; science push instead of needs pull. Jantsch (1967) made a valiant effort to redress the balance with his review of frameworks, techniques and organization of the technological forecasting function. Of course both viewpoints – science push and market pull – are necessary but each must be given its proper weight.

As far as strategy in the future is concerned, we are looking at relatively short term developments in the pure science timescale and so new ideas for exploitation within ten years are already born. The question is more which will die in infancy and which will reach maturity.

There are some obvious candidates that are already mature and, to continue the analogy, are themselves ready for selective breeding. Such is the general area known variously as the information explosion, informatics, telematics, etc., mostly dependent upon microcomputer technology. Predictions on how this will affect our lives are legion, ranging from programmable domestic hardware to the total disappearance of paper as the medium for information storage and transmission. Forecast spin off effects include the absence of commuter traffic assuming everyone will work at home (somewhat neglecting the social aspects of work) and the evanescence of transport and stocks and spares and component parts; local manufacture will be possible using computer controlled machines receiving instructions, by satellite if necessary, from a remote head office.

We are concerned in this chapter with shorter term technologies of the type that have already been born and are now adolescent.

In the food industry it has been estimated that much of the world's food is wasted before reaching the point of consumption, and this may become the spearhead to action. With large areas of the world still at starvation level, any developments which could satisfy this need are likely candidates for investment in the short term. Among these are marine farming, enzyme technology and hydroponics. In the packaging and distribution of food, retort packaging will go a long way to replacing cans and frozen foods.

In the medical field, improved methods of diagnosis are expected to have a marked effect on health and life expectancy.

Mechanical equipment of all kinds will probably become more durable. Increased durability will be achieved by greater use of adhesives to replace rivets and welds, by the introduction of ceramic unlubricated bearings and by the adoption of design lives of 20 to 30 years instead of the present 3 or 4 years. A motor car, for example, consumes more energy in its construction than in its propulsion in a 10-year life. Doubling its life will save more energy than making marginal improvements to its fuel consumption. This appreciation must inevitably lead to the adoption of 'whole life cost' concepts (already used in the defence and space technologies) in everyday industry, commerce and consumer affairs.

In the field of metal manufacture, means of conserving and recycling are likely to see rapid development. In assembly, robotics should of course make further progress.

Rising crime rates and terrorist activity could lead to the development of security systems capable of recognizing individuals, with probable spin offs into the management of money and financial transactions.

Lasers have been with us for almost 25 years but many hold the view that their development is only just starting. The fields of information processing, telecommunications, metal forming and medical work are still open to considerable development.

Free thinking speculation can be a valuable technique for the strategist but positive and negative feedback must be taken into account. The authors of *The Limits to Growth* used system dynamics as developed by Professor Jay Forrester at the Massachusetts Institute of Technology to explore the effects of such feedback. The questions posed when considering any new development were:

1 What will be the side effects, both physical and social, if this development is introduced on a large scale?

2   What social changes will be necessary before this development can be implemented properly, and how long will it take to achieve them?
3   If the development is fully successful and removes some natural limit to growth, what limit will the growing system meet next? Will society prefer its pressures to be the ones this development is designed to remove?

The third industrial revolution is about to begin! The question that arises is 'where do we join in?' Ansoff and Stewart (1967) suggested four categories of participation:

– first to market
– follow the leader
– application
– me too!

What management has to decide is where their particular organization should be, and the probable answer for most is a blend of all four, so that risks may be balanced and opportunities adequately exploited.

When a new product or process is developed the company has to decide if it should patent, publish or keep the idea secret until exploitation. Sometimes secrecy is the best policy because the rate of innovation is so great that the product is out of date by the time it is available in the market place; but in other cases, awareness of the risk must be based upon knowledge of competitors' capability. One multinational has reported that a particular competitor needs only about six months to produce a competing product from scratch – and that with no evidence of commercial espionage. Patents provide some safety in such situations, but it is worth considering whether the cost of international production is worthwhile; using the same funds to reduce the selling price and so making it more difficult for competition to take the market, might be an alternative worth considering.

It is worth considering also, that there is ample scope for useful exploitation of intermediate technologies – particularly in the developing countries.

FUTURE ORGANIZATION

The organization of most present day businesses and public institutions is based upon the principle of delegation and orderly specialization. This pattern has changed little from the day when a few knowledgeable managers administered a largely manual labour force. Indeed it is still a relevant pattern where such a situation still exists, as in agriculture, high volume manufacture or assembly of a single product (or product family) as well as in routine clerical industry. Such a pattern is becoming less and less relevant in the growing knowledge-based businesses where multifunctional decisions must be made by those who have the knowledge and local perspective.

Traditional organization based mainly on functional specialization has dominated management thinking for almost a century. This thinking has penetrated deeply and has spawned job descriptions, definitions of authority and responsibility, functional procedures, training programmes and the whole structure of rewards and promotions. Under such a system, there is a risk that functional and parochial objectives will dominate and obscure overall business objectives. The popularity of long range planning and management by objectives was due in part to this dichotomy. In addition the demand for in-house management development courses to focus on interfunctional interdependence indicates a recognition of the deficiencies of traditional organization.

In response to the needs of the more knowledge-based and innovative business, two trends have evolved in recent years and are expected to accelerate in the future.

The first trend is towards small self-sufficient units. It has been argued that '. . .there is every reason why a business unit should grow to an optimum size and no good reason for growing beyond it. This, of course, looks like a self-justifying statement that makes sense when 'optimum' is defined – which will never be easy.. . . A whole business might still grow but on the biological principle of the dividing cell.' (Latham and Sanders, 1980). Professor A. Piatier (1981) argues similarly pointing out that up to a certain size the economies of scale enhance the results but thereafter the diseconomies of scale take over. These economic arguments are supported by many writers from the behavioural viewpoint. Dr Sheane forecasts the era of self management within power distributed federations. That remarkable prophet Dr. Schumacher said '. . . we must learn to think in terms of an articulated structure that can cope with a multiplicity of small scale units'.

The second trend is towards the superimposition of project teams, task forces, new venture teams – call them what you will – operating within the hierarchical structure. The leaders of more enterprising businesses have discovered that if they want entrepreneurial or innovative management then they must delegate those responsibilities with a broadly defined strategy to small multidisciplinary teams of knowledge workers. Project management has grown in popularity, in practice, in publications, and in management training by leaps and bounds. Teams which can be given one single clear objective are usually highly motivated and are an ultimate manifestation of management by objectives. In the construction and civil engineering industries, project teams assigned to the dam, the hospital, the motorway or the factory building are the only logical way of organizing. Aerospace and many other high technology businesses do likewise. It is in the more traditional industries where functional organization has thrived that project teams have found that cohabiting is uncomfortable; yet it is in these industries more than any that change and innovation are long overdue.

As for top management and its responsibilities for overall strategy, it is vital that these three organizational systems – hierarchy, small units and transient project teams – are not seen as alternatives or as mutually exclusive. As Peter Drucker has pointed out (1973) '. . .just as statesmen learned long ago that both good laws and good rulers are needed, so organisation builders (and even organisation theorists) will have to learn that sound organisation structure needs both a hierarchical structure of authority and decision making, and the capacity to organise task forces, teams and individuals for work both on a permanent and temporary basis'.

The role of top management must increasingly move towards the identification of overall strategy within which small teams can turn social and market needs into possible opportunities. Thereafter, top management must provide support coupled with reward systems that identify contribution to overall goals rather than functional and parochial objectives. The top manager of the future will be a spokesman and representative of the business to the outside world in general and to the external stakeholders in particular. The top managers and indeed all managers will see their role as a service to the wealth generating units – a service of helping, facilitating, supporting and training. The top manager will talk and think less about 'subordinates' and more about 'colleagues', 'teams' and 'juniors'. He will set high standards but will never underestimate the contribution of others.

Perhaps the most important strategic role of the future manager in an organizational context is the provision of strategic continuity. The average middle manager or project team leader is unlikely to be in his post more than three years (if he is any good) and yet major strategic decisions can take ten years to implement. It follows that middle managers, team leaders and small unit executives are unlikely to be motivated to give care and consideration to ten-year decisions; the top management team must provide that input. To do so effectively will need a new skill and much time spent in listening, travelling, reading and debating and will (to quote Drucker again) '. . .require thinking and understanding in at least three areas – the functional or operating; the moral; and the political' (1968).

FURTHER READING

Ansoff and Stewart, 'Strategies for technology-based businesses', *Harvard Business Review*, November/December, 1967

Drucker, P.F., *The Age of Discontinuity*, Heinemann, London, 1968

Drucker, P.F., *Management: Tasks, Responsibilities, Practices*, Heinemann, London, 1973.

Halley, J.C.G., *Management Issues of the '80s – Topic Papers*, BIM, London, 1980

Jantsch, E., *Technological forecasting in Perspective*, OECD, 1967

Latham, F.W. and Sanders, G.S., *Urwick Orr on Management*, Heinemann, London, 1980

Meadows, Meadows, Randers and Behrens, *The Limits to Growth*, Earth Island, London 1972

Piater, A., 'Innovation, information and long-term growth', *Futures*, October, 1981

Schumacher, E.F., *Small is Beautiful*, Blond and Briggs, London, 1973

Sealey, L. 'A company law for tomorrow's world', *The Company Lawyer*, vol.2, no.5

Sheane, D., 'Beyond Bureaucracy', *Management Research*, 1976

3 The strategic planning process

Denis Boyle

The failure of traditional corporate planning systems to resolve fundamental business problems of the 1980s has led to the development of a new approach to the strategic planning process, which is the subject of this chapter. The 'hockey stick effect' (Figure 3.1) where plans and performance are consistently not achieved, depicts graphically the reason for these new concepts. Today, in its new form, strategic planning provides corporations with a powerful tool for creating and sustaining profit growth.

TWO STRATEGIC PLANNING PHILOSOPHIES

Traditional corporate planning was to a large extent an extension of the annual budgeting process. In a highly rational process goals were set, broken down into sub goals, and the process of implementation initiated. Diagrammatically this is shown in Figure 3.2. In a stable environment where, for example, competitors are well known, industry pricing is stable, cost structures are well understood, and customers behave in a predictable fashion, such 'traditional corporate planning' worked well.

In the world of the 1980s companies were faced by a radically different environment. Step changes and irreversible trends made detailed plans drawn up one year scarcely relevant the next. Industry invaders, new technology, deregulation and shock cost changes demanded a different kind of strategic planning process. This was concerned with formulating a view of the business and its competitive environment in the future, and also of the immediate short run steps which must be achieved. Thus the focus shifted from planning to implementation of action programmes which in the short run would produce visible results against which the long run strategic vision could be further refined. This new approach is shown diagrammatically in Figure 3.3. The fundamental difference between the two philosophies is that traditional planning assumes that all relevant knowledge is available at the beginning of the process whereas the 'new strategic planning' approach is designed to exploit information as it is acquired. The annual budgeting and financial forecasting cycle still provides a framework for systematic new strategic planning. However, the elements of strategic thinking and action are given equal weight.

New strategic planning in action

The process is cyclical, its main elements being interlinked as shown in Figure 3.4. It begins with a review of the strategic situation of both the company and the industry in which it operates. The results of this are translated into 'high leverage' action plans designed to have maximum impact on the company's competitive position and profit growth.

These plans are implemented in a highly effective manner with results monitored and fed back 'real time' with the beginning of the next planning cycle providing a systematic mechanism for an overall review before the process continues.

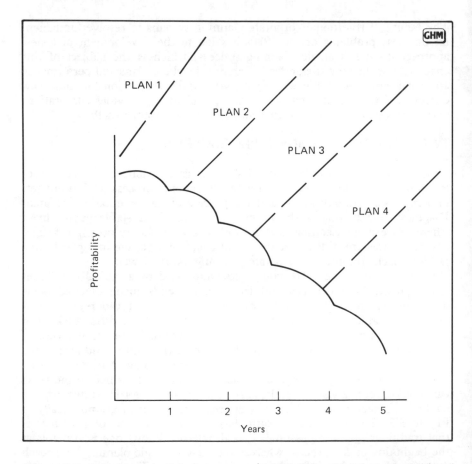

Figure 3.1 **The hockey stick phenomenon, highlighting the crises of traditional planning**

Organizing the strategic review

Since the process is designed to strengthen a 'whole business' it must be organized around different business areas within the company. For example a chemical manufacturer may have four business areas such as:

- industrial paints
- pharmaceuticals
- agricultural chemicals
- special coatings

Each has its own unique success factors and needs to be treated as a distinct planning unit. To collect the necessary data for the strategic review the top management typically appoint 'fact finding groups' of relevant managers from different functions. The strategic planning staff provide methods

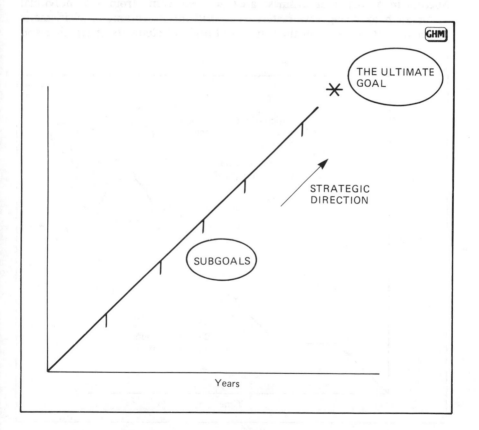

Figure 3.2   The traditional planning process with goals, subgoals and action plans

for analysis as well as co-ordination of the overall process. In a complex multi-business it will be essential to examine interdependencies between different business areas so that these can be optimized for the benefit of the whole company. Individual business area plans will be harmonized to maximize benefit to the total corporation while minimizing risks.

In initiating the work of the fact finding and analysis groups the board should set challenging but realistic objectives in both financial and business performance terms. These need to be discussed and, if necessary, renegotiated.

To operationalize the conclusions of the strategic review actions are defined as specific projects, and these become the responsibility of functional departments or specially set up cross-functional teams.

The importance of analysing the total business concept for each business area

Success in a particular business area does *not* come from any individual factor such as cheap raw materials, a brilliant invention, or charismatic leadership. It depends on the way a multitude of elements fit together and

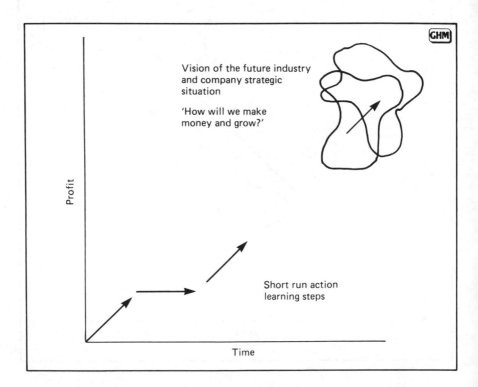

Figure 3.3   The new strategic planning approach

mutually reinforce each other. This 'total business concept' is the basis of market segment dominance and long term profitability. During the strategic review everyone should refine their understanding of the main elements (Figure 3.5):

- the target customers 'who are our good customers?'
- the product service price offering 'what are they really selling?'
- the company's production and delivery systems 'how do we produce better quality at lower cost than our competitors?'
- the company's organization structure and culture 'how do we make our organization and systems support our way of making money and growing?'
- the corporate image 'what image do we want and how do we project it?'

The 'fit' or harmony between these different elements is learned through success in the market place. Equally when structural changes arise they result in 'misfits', the real cause of business problems, and a weakening

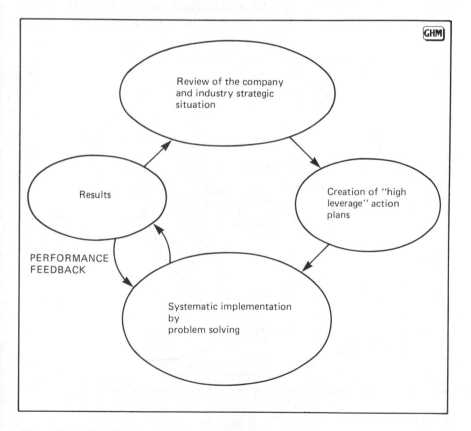

Figure 3.4   The four elements of the planning cycle

33

of competitive strength. The strategic review should identify these misfits and propose actions to resolve them.

Consider an example from today's insurance industry. Most institutions are organized on product lines such as fire insurance, car insurance, house insurance and so on. This is shown diagrammatically in Figure 3.6.

Following a dramatic change in the industry environment success now depends on customer orientated marketing. Strategic action is therefore needed to transform organization structures and control systems to once again create fit or harmonize with the needs of the new industry.

The creation of high leverage action plans

The objective of the strategic review is to understand the company's total business concept for each business area and how this can be effectively developed. This requires the creation of high leverage action plans. Based upon the strategic review 'diagnosis', top management focus on those actions critical to their winning strategy. For example, suppose that following its strategic review an airline decided that it must target full fare, high frequency business travellers. To get more of their business it identified several

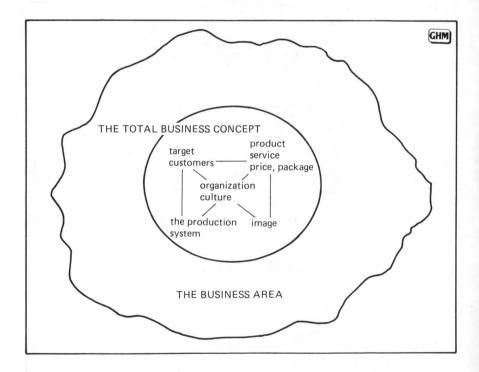

Figure 3.5   Fit and the total business concept in each business area

misfits which had to be tackled. Its timekeeping performance was poor, its air hostesses were not friendly and its hub airport did not function very efficiently. Action programmes were focused on these in the high leverage pay-off areas.

In selecting an appropriate strategy the strategic review process will have quantified the likely outcome in approximate financial terms. As individual action programmes are developed the overall financial impact can be more closely assessed and, if necessary, appropriate adjustments made.

There are, in addition to the high leverage plans, five important preconditions for successful strategy implementation which must also be effectively planned.

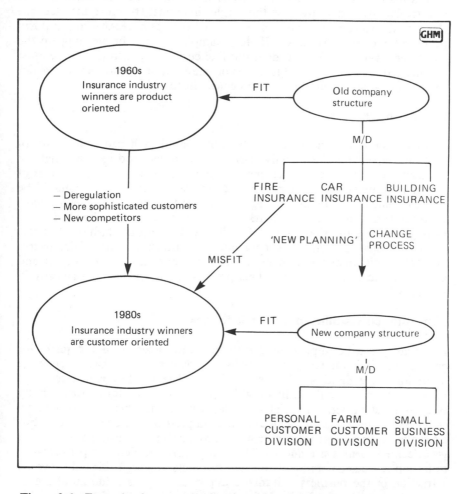

Figure 3.6   Example of an organizational problem or 'misfit' caused by a structural industry change

Visible commitment

Top management must visibly demonstrate commitment to its strategy. Since people believe actions rather than words it is essential always to act in line with the strategy. This means for example that if resources are necessary for a critical programme then they are made available.

Removing organizational blockages

The organization structure, and the people in key positions, must support the strategy. Consider, for example, a manufacturer of jeans. Suppose that this firm's strategy is to refocus activities on its core products. To tackle this effectively, divisionalization of the single functional structure into teenage jeans wear, women's wear and men's wear becomes necessary to pin down problems and responsibilities. If, for example, the person heading up the customer service department does not like customers, then clearly he must be changed. Organizational blockages of one form or another are the major reason for failure to implement strategies effectively.

Internal marketing

Many organizations underestimate the potential of their people for contributing to implementation if only they were to understand exactly what the strategy was. Planning internal marketing is therefore a crucial element of the 'new strategic planning process'. Everyone in the company should be told the conclusions of the strategic review and be given their own opportunity to contribute. Internal marketing to be effective must be carried out through the organizational lines of authority in a cascade fashion, but also by the top management team parachuting to the front line. This ensures not only rapid dissemination of the message but also less distortion and a high degree of involvement. This process is shown diagrammatically in Figure 3.7.

Performance visibility and fast feedback

No strategy can be implemented if there are not adequate mechanisms for getting feedback on progress. Usually companies do not have a shortage of performance monitors. The secret is to select the few which are most relevant and give feedback in a highly credible way. Performance visibility systems must provide financial and qualitative data. There is a very interesting knock-on effect of using even the simplest of strategy monitors. For example, an engine manufacturer wished to develop his customer service. It was decided to measure and feed back regularly the delivery performance to its top ten customers for its top ten products. Though this only covered a fraction of the business a dramatic improvement was made in all areas.

Performance standards should be set to be bold, challenging and capable of attainment within a relatively short time.

Systematic implementation by problem solving

The heart of successful implementation is decentralized problem solving. The main strategic programmes are broken down into hundreds of action programmes each with a clearly defined responsibility and time scale. Problems which come within one functional area are relatively easy to handle. Cross functional problems require the establishment of special teams and careful follow-up to ensure that they do not simply fall between chairs.

As with any complex system improving total business performance is more a question of 'one hundred changes of one per cent than one change of a hundred per cent'. This means the responsibility for problem solving implementation must be pushed all the way down the organization. Front line supervisors are particularly important people in this process.

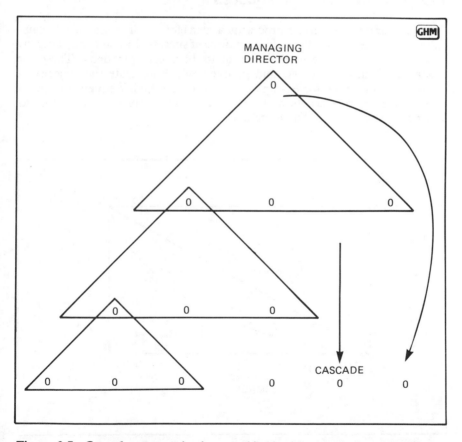

Figure 3.7 Cascade communication combined with parachuting for effective internal marketing

Systematic reinforcement of success

Motivation and the power of the problem solving process is greatly enhanced by feeding back every possible success. People enjoy being winners and strategy implementation can be made an exhilarating 'game'.

In situations where the company has faced severe problems it may well be necessary to overcome the problem of image lag. This phenomenon is shown diagrammatically in Figure 3.8. People tend to remember performance as it was, not as it is. The classic example is that of an automobile manu-facturer who once had a reputation for rusty cars. Though today they have probably one of the best records in the world people still talk about the problem they experienced more than ten years ago. If employees see that their efforts are not being appreciated they can easily be demoralized.

USING THE PLANNING PROCESS TO CREATE THE SELF-REINFORCING SPIRAL OF SUCCESS

The new strategic planning process is a management instrument for main-taining a business in a self-reinforcing circle of success. In year one a company will focus on the 'core of the core' of its business operations. These are made up of those customers and products which generate the majority of its profits. An airline for example may choose the high frequency business travellers in Europe as its first step. Or an automobile manufacturer its top three models in its home market.

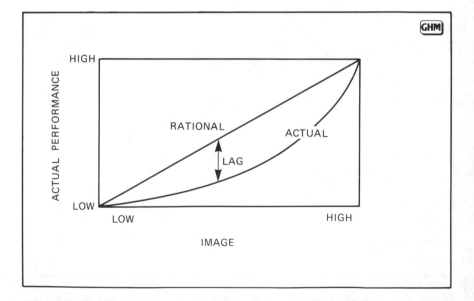

Figure 3.8 Planning to overcome image lag

Success during the first year provides experience and confidence to expand the core of the core so that for example the airline might begin to tackle its transatlantic routes and the automobile company its top-selling cars across Europe.

With every cycle the depth of understanding of the company's strategic situation is enhanced. The internal strategic language becomes more refined. Crude though adequate organizational measures taken during the first cycle can be greatly refined during the second. Information systems on an *ad hoc* basis provide the foundation for longer term development. So it is that with each cycle misfits are eliminated and the competitive strength of the business is improved. Thus strategic thinking and action become one in a mutually reinforcing circle of success (Figure 3.9).

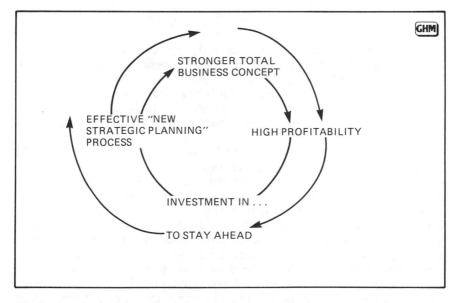

Figure 3.9 Using the new strategic planning to create a self reinforcing spiral of success

4 Organization development

John Woolhouse

Managing an organization in a constantly changing environment, often against formidable national or international competition, is a task that calls for exceptional skill, judgement and resourcefulness. The purpose of this chapter is to explore some aspects of this task and to describe some of the ways in which a manager can plan and implement those changes that are essential to the proper functioning of the organization for which he or she is responsible.

The term 'organization development' is used in this chapter to describe a planned programme of organizational change designed to help an organization to achieve the strategic purposes and objectives for which it was created. The concepts discussed do not apply only to the problems of changing existing organizations; they apply equally to the creation of new institutions or enterprises. In many parts of the world the creation and rapid growth of new industry, commerce, government departments and public services present serious organizational problems. There is a need, as yet too rarely understood, to apply to the design, formation and development of new organizations, the disciplines of systematic planning that are common practice in the design, construction and commissioning of buildings, plant and other physical facilities.

In discussing the relationship between strategy and organization, Professor K. R. Andrews of the Harvard Business School sums up the theme to be developed in this chapter, as follows: 'It is at once apparent that the accomplishment of strategic purpose requires organisation. If a consciously formulated strategy is to be effective, organisational development should be planned rather than left to evolve by itself.'

Organization development concerns not only structure, procedures or systems, but also such intangible factors as the styles of leadership, teamwork, collaboration between functions or departments, the motivation of staff, and the problems of power and influence, of co-ordination and conflict that arise in the working life of an organization.

THE NEED FOR PLANNED ORGANIZATION DEVELOPMENT

The need for a planned programme of organizational development will arise in many situations. Perhaps the most common are:

1 The creation of new institutions or enterprises in industry, commerce, government or the public services
2 Enabling existing organizations to adapt more readily to changes in their external environment (for example in markets, in products or services, or in the range, scale or location of their operations)
3 Where the organization is failing to accomplish its objectives in terms of output, quality or profitability, and where the nature of the organization is itself limiting the performance of those who work in it
4 Where the adoption of new technology, systems or methods requires corresponding changes in the organization for their proper implementation.

Organizations vary in purpose, in constitution, in the methods and technologies which they use to achieve their purpose, and in the scope, size and location of their operations and markets. Furthermore, they exist in different economic, political and social environments, and in different cultures and subcultures.

Organizations are not merely a product of a particular technology; they are designed and directed by individuals with different values, experience and perceptions, and are to some extent a reflection of the personality of those who direct and shape them. Each organization is, in a sense, a social experiment which is constantly evolving and adapting in response to changes in the environment.

The structure and style of any particular organization, at any given time in its history, are the products of a complex mixture of technology, culture, environment and personal styles, so that there is no single solution to the problem of what constitutes the best organization in a given situation.

The management of organizational change is complex because it involves an understanding, first of organizational purpose, secondly of organizational structure, procedures and systems and thirdly of what may be described as the 'dynamics' of organization; that is, the relationships between people and between groups, the role of leadership and teamwork, and the significance of learning and motivation in creating an understanding of the need for change, and in generating commitment to action.

The unique character of each organization indicates that the objectives and content of any programme of organizational change will vary with the situation for which it is designed, but the theme common to all programmes is that the development of an organization can be systematically planned and managed.

STRUCTURE, PROCESS AND STYLE

What exactly is an organization, and how does it work?

In the space of this chapter, it is not possible to examine this extremely complex subject in depth, but it is appropriate to identify some of the elements involved.

Industrial organizations are socio-technical systems which incorporate three main subsystems:

1 The 'executive system' by which the organization is directed and controlled
2 The 'operating system' by which it carries out work
3 A 'representative system' through which consultation and negotiation with members of the organization is conducted.

What an organization *is* can be described in terms of structure, procedures and systems. What it *does* can be defined as 'processes'. The *manner* in which it conducts those processes is usually called the 'style' of the organization.

The structure of any organization is a product of many inter-related factors including the culture of the society in which it was created, and the idiosyncracies of those who direct it. Among the factors on which the design of a new organization should be based, or an existing organization assessed, are:

1 The strategy or purpose which the organization is designed to achieve
2 Legal status, accountability and sources of financing
3 The methods of technology by which the strategy is to be implemented
4 The information process and procedures for making decisions, for planning and control and for operating and resourcing
5 The geographical distribution of resources and of markets or clients
6 The scale and range of the activities and resources to be controlled.

The variety of structures that have developed, particularly in large industrial, government and military organizations is so great that it has become a subject in its own right. Simple line, staff, and functional structures have been superseded by the creation of profit centres and cost centres within organizations; by project, programme and product management groups; by various forms of matrix organization for managing multi-skill or multi-discipline resources; by the extensive use of 'temporary' structures such as project teams, task forces and working parties.

What forms of both 'permanent' and 'temporary' structures are appropriate to any particular organization at any particular stage in its evolution is a question requiring detailed and thorough examination of each unique situation.

The chief executive is the architect of the organization. It is his vision of what the organization should and could become that will generate the need for change; it is his judgement as to when change is needed and what form that change should take. He must, above all, be aware that old structures are rarely an effective way of implementing new strategies.

Organizational 'processes' are the interactions, communications, and 'transactions' between people. This 'dynamic' aspect of organization is of special significance for all those involved in organizational change. Every organization is in essence an interlocking set of contracts between people. These contracts determine what people will do, and how they conduct the thousands of 'transactions' such as giving and receiving information, or authorizing the acquisition, deployment or disposal of resources. In effect all the members of an organization enter into a complex set of contracts by which they relate to other members. The majority of these contracts are not legal contracts; they are informal 'psychological contracts'. They are not written down; they are frequently changed; they are determined partly by logical factors, and partly by subjective and emotional factors.

By looking at the day-to-day activities of an organization in terms of 'contracts' regulating action and behaviour, and of 'transactions' between individuals and groups who are collaborating and communicating with each other, it is possible to gain a much clearer idea of what happens when changes are made in structure, technology, procedures or systems; the result of all such changes is that informal 'contracts' between people have to be renegotiated, not necessarily in a legal sense, but certainly in a psychological sense. Any change such as the introduction of a new piece of equipment, or of a new management information system, requires the renegotiation of the contracts which regulate what a member of the organization does and how he or she does it.

The *manner* in which relationships and transactions between people, and between groups, between managers and subordinates, between departments, divisions and functions are conducted, is usually referred to as the 'style' of the organization. A considerable amount of research has been conducted into organization and leadership 'styles', and into the psychological factors which determine or influence behaviour. Some of this research is summarized in Chapter 1 under the heading 'Management theory in the post-war era', and the subject of leadership is discussed briefly later in this chapter.

THE ROLE OF THE CHIEF EXECUTIVE

With this perspective, it is possible to examine more closely the responsibility of the chief executive or general manager for organization development, and to do so in the knowledge that it is the will to achieve, the will to survive, the will to manage and the will to work that are the sources of the energy which drive an organization.

The chief executive and those of his colleagues who share his responsibility for the direction of an enterprise perform four basic functions. They must:

1 Define strategy
2 Specify the methods, technology and resources by which that strategy is to be achieved
3 Prepare plans and programmes
4 Create and manage an organization through which those plans and programmes will be implemented.

Andrews describes the role of the general manager in the following terms: 'The successful implementation of strategy requires that the general manager shape to the peculiar needs of his strategy the formal structure of his organization, its informal relationships, and the processes of motivation and control which provide incentives and measure results. He must bring about the commitment to organisational aims and policies of properly qualified individuals and groups to whom portions of the total task have been assigned. He must ensure not only that goals are clear and purposes are understood, but also that individuals are developing in terms of capacity and achievement and are reaping proper rewards in terms of compensation and personal satisfactions. Above all, he must do what he can to ensure that departmental interests, inter-departmental rivalries, and the machinery of measurement and evaluation do not deflect from organizational purpose into harmful and irrelevant activity'.

Translating these issues into specific activities is the task of the chief executive who must ensure that:

1 Key tasks and decisions are identified and defined
2 The responsibility for carrying out tasks and making decisions is assigned to individuals or groups; the authority for acquiring and allocating resources is defined
3 Procedures are established for planning, co-ordinating and controlling the activities or work programmes to be undertaken by each work group
4 Information systems for obtaining, storing, analysing and retrieving the data needed both for management and operational purposes are designed and installed
5 Activities are arranged in a programme to be completed within defined time and resource limits
6 Individuals or groups are made accountable for the achievement of objectives and their performance is evaluated against time, quality and resource standards
7 Actual performance is monitored quantitatively against programmes, estimates or budgets, and qualitatively by the judgement of managers and supervisors, or by feedback from users, customers or clients
8 Procedures for internal consultation and communications are established so that information can be transmitted and feedback obtained on any given activity and on problems encountered in carrying it out
9 Individual staff are selected, recruited, trained and assigned to particular roles, and roles are adapted to make optimum use of the skills which are available or which can be acquired
10 A system of rewards and constraints is established, and procedures are developed for negotiating change with members of the organization or with their representatives
11 Arrangements are made to facilitate and encourage the acquisition and development of individual technical, professional and managerial skills, and for the improvement and adaptation of methods, systems and procedures.

These tasks and procedures are part of the agenda that will be considered in planning the content of any programme.

PLANNING A PROGRAMME OF ORGANIZATION DEVELOPMENT

The purpose of an organization development programme may be to create a new organization, or to adapt an existing organization in ways that will enable it to achieve the purposes for which it was established. In most cases the institution will seek to achieve those purposes with the minimum consumption of time, energy and resources.

Because each institution or enterprise is unique it must define *for itself* the criteria that will guide the development of its organization. Because all institutions are subject to change these criteria will need to be redefined at intervals in response to changes in strategy, environment or technology.

Figure 4.1 illustrates some criteria that can be used in analysing the extent to which existing or proposed organizational arrangements help or hinder the achievement of purpose, and in identifying priorities for change. In practice

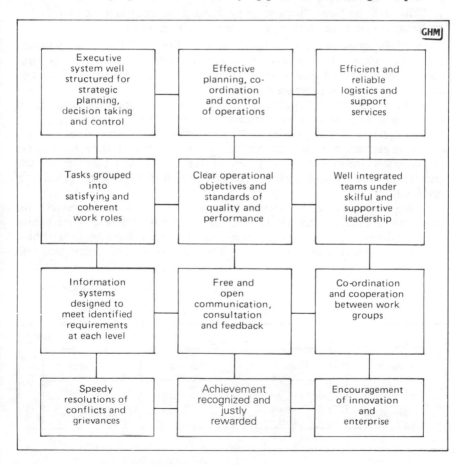

Figure 4.1   Criteria for organization development

attention and effort must be focused on a limited selection of factors which are critical to successful performance, and which the institution itself has the capacity to change. If the programme is too narrowly based it will be ineffective; if it is too ambitious it will be impossible to implement. The structure and content of each programme will vary according to the needs of the organization concerned, but most programmes will include four main stages (see Figure 4.2).

The first stage is concerned primarily with defining, diagnosing and understanding the task to be performed or the problems to be resolved. A useful starting point for Stage 1 is a discussion in which senior managers define the present state of the organization by seeking answers to the following questions:

1   Where are we now?
2   Where do we want to get to?
3   What are the forces helping or preventing us from getting there?
4   What do we have to change to enable us to get there?

While these questions are an apparent over-simplification, it is common experience among those engaged in organization development that the process of analysing and questioning the 'status quo' is an essential first step in the planning of a programme.

Feedback on what is happening within the organization may be obtained by informal discussion or by a systematic survey depending on the nature and complexity of the problem. What is important is that those aspects of the organization which are under review – whether they be matters of procedure, relationships, attitudes to work, or to new plans or to new technology – are tested against reactions and responses of those directly involved.

Issues arising from this examination will often become a subject for much more detailed analysis of specific problems of roles, relationships or procedures, and for action planning in the second phase. This phase is usually conducted by one or more internal management teams who will

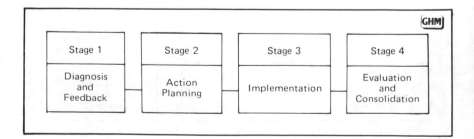

Figure 4.2   Stages in an organization development programme

often be given training in the use of appropriate analytical and planning techniques.

In the implementation phase, which may last for many months in cases of major changes in the organization or its procedures, it is very important to obtain feedback on problems experienced in practice, and to include arrangements for making any modifications necessary to the success of the programme. Every programme is an experiment in managing change, and the implications of that statement must be understood and acted upon by everyone involved.

Evaluation should be made against realistic criteria agreed at the outset of the programme. There are several difficulties in evaluation which must be acknowledged: organizational changes may take a long time to become effective and a proper evaluation can be made only after a reasonable period of operation of new structures or procedures. Some of the most important benefits of a programme, particularly those concerned with management styles, with cooperation between teams, or with job satisfaction cannot be quantified and can only be assessed by collecting and analysing responses from managers and staff who have taken part.

At the end of the programme it is vital to consolidate and reinforce those changes that prove effective in practice. It is only too easy to lose the advantages of a programme by failing to ensure that successful procedures and processes become a permanent part of the organization's ways of working.

Diagnostic methods

Because organizations exist to accomplish strategy, any organizational design or analysis must begin with a definition of strategy, and an examination of the extent to which existing structure, systems and procedures constitute logical and effective means of implementing that strategy. It is relatively easy to conceive new ideas and new strategies. Because the time and effort needed to implement change is considerable, particularly in large organizations, there is a tendency for organization structure and systems to 'lag' so that the enterprise is trying to tackle today's or even tomorrow's problem with yesterday's organization. The time-lag problem can also be serious when major structural or procedural changes have been introduced because, in the absence of any action to accelerate the 'natural' rate of change, members of the organization can (if not helped to make the adjustment) take a long time to absorb the implications of change and to modify their actions accordingly.

In a comprehensive programme a variety of analytical or diagnostic methods will need to be employed. These methods may, for example, include:

1 Examination of work roles and of co-ordination between individuals, or between departments and functions
2 Evaluation of procedures for planning, co-ordinating, allocating re-

    sources, setting performance standards, monitoring performance, output quality or cost

3　Analysis of information systems and information flows

4　Collecting and analysing feedback on operational problems, on attitudes, morale or job satisfaction

5　Assessment of leadership styles, or of the relationships within or between work groups

6　Review of rewards and incentives and of opportunities for personal development or career progression

7　Investigating internal procedures for negotiating terms and conditions of employment, or for resolving conflicts and disputes.

In programmes involving a study of work organization it may also be necessary to use such techniques as process analysis, task analysis, activity analysis, method study or operational research to analyse work flows or procedures for planning and controlling operations in the allocation of resources. Studies of this type are best carried out by small multi-discipline teams which include members with expertise in appropriate technology, in operational research and in organization development. In specialist industries and services, teams of this type can make a powerful contribution to the development of structures, systems and procedures which are properly matched to the technological requirements of the enterprise.

    Underlying all structural and procedural issues there is, in every organization, a 'culture', and 'atmosphere', a set of values which is partly a reflection of the style of leadership within the institution itself, and partly of the society within which the institution operates. Technology is a major factor in determining structure and systems, but social and cultural factors are the main determinant of organizational style.

    The most important and intangible of these factors are concerned with leadership, with motivation and with team work. All organization development programmes centre on the role of leadership, on the use of teams as the agents of change, and on the use of learning and feedback.

STYLES OF LEADERSHIP

There is no single 'best' style of leadership, just as there is no 'best' type of organization structure. Different situations call for different styles of leadership. One of the problems in developing an effective organization is to develop a style that is appropriate to that organization.

    The effect of leadership style on individual performance, team work and morale can be studied by analysing feedback from people in the organization. Feedback can be collected and analysed in many different ways ranging from informal interviews with individuals or groups to highly structured diagnostic procedures. Two of the best known diagnostic methods are the 'Managerial Grid' developed by Blake and Mouton and Rensis Likert's 'System 4'. In his work at the Michigan Institute for Social Research, Likert found evidence to suggest that the prevailing management style of an organization could be depicted on a continuum from 'System 1' (a very authoritarian style) to 'System 4' (a style based on team work, trust and confidence). In most of the companies studied, those closest to 'System 4' were more likely to have a continuous record of high productivity. The extent to which such instruments are useful in any particular situation is a matter for judgement, but the following summary by Hersey and Blanchard of Likert's four systems illustrates some of the issues which need to be explored in a study of the leadership style.

System 1

Management is seen as having no confidence or trust in subordinates, since they are seldom involved in any aspect of the decision-making process. The bulk of the decisions and the goal setting of the organization are made at the top and issued down the chain of command. Subordinates are forced to work with fear, threats, punishment and occasional rewards and need satisfaction at the physiological and safety levels. The little superior-subordinate interaction that does take place is usually with fear and mistrust. Although the control process is highly concentrated in top management, an informal organization generally develops, which opposes the goals of the formal organization.

System 2

Management is seen as having condescending confidence and trust in subordinates, such as master has toward servant. The bulk of the decisions and goal setting of the organization are made at the top, but many decisions are made within a predescribed framework at lower levels. Rewards and some actual or potential punishment are used to motivate workers. Any superior-subordinate interaction takes place with some condescension by superiors and fear and caution by subordinates. Although the control process is still concentrated in top management, some is delegated to middle and lower levels. An informal organization usually develops, but it does not always resist formal organizational goals.

System 3

Management is seen as having substantial but not complete confidence and trust in subordinates. Broad policy and general decisions are kept at the top, but subordinates are permitted to make more specific decisions at lower levels. Communications flow both up and down the hierarchy. Rewards, occasional punishment, and some involvement are used to motivate workers. There is a moderate amount of superior-subordinate interaction, often with a fair amount of confidence and trust. Significant aspects of the control process are delegated downward with a feeling of responsibility at both higher and lower levels. An informal organization may develop, but it may either support or partially resist goals of the organization.

System 4

Management is seen as having complete confidence and trust in subordinates. Decision-making is widely dispersed throughout the organization, although well integrated. Communications flow not only up and down the hierarchy but among peers. Workers are motivated by participation and involvement in developing economic rewards, setting goals, improving methods, and appraising progress towards goals. There is extensive, friendly, superior-subordinate interaction with a high degree of confidence and trust. There is widespread responsibility for the control process, with the lower units fully involved. The informal and formal organizations are often one and the same. Thus, all social forces support efforts to achieve stated organizational goals.

TEAMS AND TEAM BUILDING

Teams are the building blocks from which organizations are constructed, the cells from which the various organs of the corporate body are assembled. An organization development programme is a planned programme of learning and action, carried out over a considerable period of time, in which *teams*, rather than individuals, are the agents of change. In recent years valuable research has been carried out into the dynamics of group behaviour, for example at the National Training Institute in the US and at the Tavistock Institute in the UK.

Work has been carried out by these Institutes both on individual relationships within a group, described as *intra-group* relations, and on the relationships between groups, known as *inter-group* relations. The results of this research, and of experience in large industrial and military organizations, are of great practical value to managers because they provide the foundation for team building programmes which form a central part of all organization development programmes. Advice and assistance in team building is now available from many sources and the skills needed are within the capability of most competent managers.

Team building sessions (in which diagnosis and feedback of problems at several levels in an organization are linked together as part of an integrated programme of problem identification, feedback, analysis, planning and implementation) are a major component of all programmes designed to accelerate the development of new organizations, to facilitate the transfer of an introduction of new technology, and to improve the performance of existing organization. They also provide one of the main instruments for coping with conflict between levels or functions within an organization or between the organization and external groups such as suppliers and distributors.

The methods used in any particular circumstances will differ with the objectives of the programme but all processes depend on providing the group as a whole, and its individual members, with feedback or situations with which they have to cope. The intelligent and sensitive use of feedback is fundamental to any process of organization development. It is the experience of most researchers into organizational problems, first, that a significant proportion of problems whose causes are either not known, or are attributed to individual deficiences, are the result of organizational defects; and secondly that many of these defects can be identified by feedback from individuals and by methodical examination of the logic underlying the definition of responsibilities, procedures and information flows. The key to all change in behaviour is learning. Not theoretical learning, but learning about the facts, the myths and the conditions which are present in every human and social situation.

This type of learning process is one in which the 'agenda' is not a syllabus but a real problem: it draws on the combined knowledge and experience of members of a group, incorporates any 'external' advice that may be appropriate; and its purpose is to take action and not solely to acquire knowledge or skill. The result is that the approach makes a real contribution to the difficult task of changing perceptions, attitudes and behaviour in organizations. Difference enterprises use different terms to define this process: action-learning, group-learning, achievement learning, joint development programmes, and quality circles, which have attracted so much attention in recent years, are all attempts to tap the latent energy of groups and individuals by creating opportunities for learning related to the need for action and the need for change. The management of change is a complex process; but collaborative or 'synergistic' learning is a powerful catalyst of change.

A full-scale organization development programme is appropriate only where major organizational change needs to be managed. Team building programmes can be started, with proper preparation and instruction, by any departmental manager or project manager who wants to improve the performance of his team. A day or two spent in the early stages of team formation, given wise selection of team members, can yield rich returns in collaboration, cooperation and personal development features essential to successful project work.

CHARACTERISTICS OF A SUCCESSFUL PROGRAMME

Richard Beckhard of the Massachusetts Institute of Technology in his essay on organization development lists eight characteristics of a successful programme:

1 It is a planned programme which involves the whole of an organization, or of a relatively autonomous unit within an organization
2 It is not a programme to improve managerial effectiveness in the abstract. It is designed to create organizational conditions that will directly help the institution to accomplish a specific strategy
3 The senior management of the organization are personally committed to the goals of the programme
4 It is a long term effort, because two or three years are usually required

51

for any significant organizational change to be planned, implemented, and its benefits realized and rewarded

5 The programme is action-oriented. In this respect an organizational development programme differs from a training programme in which the individual is left to transfer any knowledge or skill acquired, because the programme is designed from the outside to generate action by those involved

6 Particular emphasis is placed on changing perceptions, attitudes and behaviour, and not solely on structural or procedural change

7 It relies on some form of experience-based learning through which participants can examine the present situation, define new goals, and explore new ways of achieving them

8 The basis of all programmes are the groups or teams from which the organization is constructed.

CONCLUSIONS

No discussion of an organization or of organization development can be concluded without reference to the character and quality of the people who work in it. The selection, training and development of individual managers and staff is discussed elsewhere in this book. It is sufficient here to observe that while the relationship between individual competence and organizational success is widely understood, the extent to which organization structure and style encourages or inhibits individual growth and development is not always so clearly perceived. People create organizations; successful organizations develop capable people: capable people to keep organizations flexible and responsive to changing needs and goals.

FURTHER READING

Beckhard, R., *Organisational Development: Strategies and Models*, Addison-Wesley, Reading, Mass, 1969

Bennis, E.G., *Organisation Development: Its Nature, Origins and Prospects*, Addison-Wesley, Reading, Mass, 1969

Blake, R.R. and Mouton, J.S., *Building a Dynamic Corporation through Grid Organisation Development*, Addison-Wesley, Reading, Mass, 1969

Bower, M., *The Will to Manage*, McGraw-Hill, New York, 1966

Burns, J. and Stalker, G.M., *The Management of Innovation*, Tavistock Publications, London, 1961

Hersey, P. and Blanchard, K.H., *Management of Organisational Behaviour*, 3rd edition, Prentice-Hall, Englewood Cliffs, NJ, 1977

Jaques, E., *Work, Creativity and Social Justice*, Heinemann, London, 1970

Katz, D. and Kahn, R.I., *The Social Psychology of Organisations*, Wiley, New York, 1965

Lawrence, P.R. and Lorsch, J.W., *Developing Organisations: Diagnosis and Action*, Addison-Wesley, Reading, Mass, 1969

Learned, E.P., Christensen, C.R., Andrews, K.R. and Guth, W.D., *Business Policy*, Irwin, Homewood, 1969

Mant, A., *The Experienced Manager: A Major Resource*, British Institute of Management, London, 1969

Parker, H., Bower, M., Smith E.E. and Morrison, J.R., *Effective Boardroom Management*, London, 1971

Schein, E.H., *Process Consultation: Its Role in Organisation Development*, Addison-Wesley, Reading, Mass, 1969

Sofer, C., *The Organisation from Within*, Tavistock Publication, London, 1961

Sutermeister, R.A., *People and Productivity*, McGraw-Hill, New York, 1969

Tannehill, R.E., 'The Management of Technological Change', *Manufacturing Engineering and Management*, 1971

Tannehill, R.E., *Motivation and Management Development*, Butterworth, London, 1970

Walton, R.E., *Interpersonal Peacemaking: Confrontations and Third-party Consultation*, Addison-Wesley, Reading, Mass, 1969

5 Corporate relations

Norman Hart

The need for a planned programme of corporate relations stems not from some new management concept but from the fact that organizations are realizing sometimes to their dismay, the need for a formalized corporate strategy. This has been dealt with earlier in the book but, simply stated, it is no longer good enough to take random actions for long term effects: rather it is necessary to give mature consideration to future objectives and the means of achieving them. Such objectives will incorporate financial investment, labour force and staffing, marketing aspects, production, research and development and of course profit. This is no more than a move from past practices, in which future events were just allowed to take their natural course, to a position in which a company sets out deliberately to move to a predetermined position. The weakness of any attempt at corporate planning is that unforeseeable events are bound to cause the objectives to be changed, but this is no reason for not taking action to influence the course of events so as to hit the desired target as closely as possible. Corporate relations is but one of the management functions which can be used to help achieve this goal.

The need for corporate goals and for a strategy to achieve them stems from a growing number of influences, external and internal, which if ignored may well undermine the profitable development of a company and indeed threaten its very existence. The increasing tendency by governments to impose controls is a major factor as are international regulations at one extreme and a vigorous consumerist movement at the other. Thus trade barriers and constraints, scarcity of raw materials, inflation and high taxation are factors which now play a larger part in the development of business. Equally the growing interest by employees and trade unions with their sometimes massive influence must be taken into consideration in any future planning.

This chapter will examine corporate relations from the point of view of *what* they are, *why* they are necessary, to *whom* they should be addressed, *when*, and *how*. Finally, it will consider the all important question of the results that might reasonably be expected of such an activity.

First, *what*. Corporate relations is a term used to signify the deliberate attempt by an organization to maintain the best possible relations with each and every identifiable group of people whose interests and activities might be supposed to have an effect, for good or ill, on the prosperity and progress of the business. Such an operation is linked with communications in both directions since without communications of some kind it is difficult to see how any change or impact can be achieved. It is important at the outset to realize two things. First, that no matter how efficient any corporate communications system may be, it will be of no avail unless the object of the communication is sound. In just the same way no amount of advertising will ever sell an unsatisfactory product. The second point to be made is that every single source of communications must be considered for possible use, not just the classical PR media such as press releases, factory visits, booklets and special events.

What then are corporate communications? A good example was given in a report by *The Financial Times,* as summarized in Figure 5.1. The list is not, and was not intended to be, comprehensive. It misses for instance the communications element of the product, its packaging and branding, as well as the place from which it is distributed. It does not touch on the vital role of employees, from people answering the phone and writing letters, to salesmen meeting customers. Then there is the appearance of the factory, the livery, the letterheading: the list is endless. Corporate relations then is the building-up of a good *reputation* with a company's many and varied publics. An old-fashioned term sums it up very well – *goodwill.*

Public	Example of communication GHM
Consumer	media advertising
	press release
Supplier	trade exhibitions
Employees	house journal
Trades unions	statement of company policy
Competitors	public lectures
Local residents	local radio information
Trade association	journal article
Technical groups	technical journal articles
Shareholders	annual reports
Financial community	financial press release
Government	co-operation with CSO
Distributors	promotion literature
Universities	scientific information
Other pressure groups	local community action

Figure 5.1 The company public and an example of a typical outward communication for each component of that public (The Financial Times)

Clearly the kind of activity being described is going to cost money. Hence the need to ask *why?* The fact is that all companies have an image whether they like it or not, or even if they are totally unaware of it. A company is perceived by people in a variety of ways, depending upon the messages, conscious or unconscious, they have received about it. And the perception varies from one public to another. Customers may view a supplier as a thoroughly reliable and trustworthy organization with which to do business, whereas its employees may take the very opposite view. The reason *why* corporate relations is important, then, is that it is only when relationships are positive and sound that the most effective and efficient business can be conducted. For example, is it reasonable to expect the best possible applicants for a job with a company which has a very poor reputation as an employer? It may be argued that in such a case the solution is to change the conditions of employment so that they are really attractive, but this is overlooking the essential ingredient of corporate communications for if people are unaware of a situation they cannot react to it. And if, as often happens, they are misinformed about it the opposite result to what was intended may be the outcome. The reason *why* corporate relations is important, then, is that on the one hand the company is receiving messages about itself from all the interested publics and on the other hand it is sending out messages to those same people to ensure that they are fully informed, that they understand and that they are convinced. The reason why, then, is in order to establish and maintain a series of relationships in which business can be conducted most efficiently.

To *whom* is corporate relations meant to apply? Once again a simplified diagram taken from *The Financial Times* shows the answer (Figure 5.2). In addition, of course, each individual company will have a number of specialist groups whose goodwill it is vital to maintain. These might be termed 'special interest groups' such as Women's Institutes, teachers, consumerists, youth movements and even, say, cycling clubs, bird-watchers and farmers.

The *when* of corporate relations can be dealt with simply. A reputation is with a company all its life. It is no use having a corporate relations function and a corporate communication programme for a couple of years and then closing it down. People's memories and attitudes are dynamic and will change over time. A company must decide whether or not it is really serious in the matter of building its reputation. If it is, and it wishes to maintain it, this can be achieved in one way only, and that is by a continuous programme of activities. It is as well also to bear in mind that achieving any major change may take years rather than months, so advance planning is required as well as continuity.

Turning now to *how* corporate relations is to be implemented. First, it is necessary to draw up plans, both strategic and tactical, to set objectives, to measure results, to co-ordinate all related and parallel activities, and to ensure that an adequate administration and professional facility exists to ensure proper execution.

STRATEGIC PLANNING

The key to successful strategic planning for good corporate relations is in the setting of comprehensive objectives. Two examples have been chosen

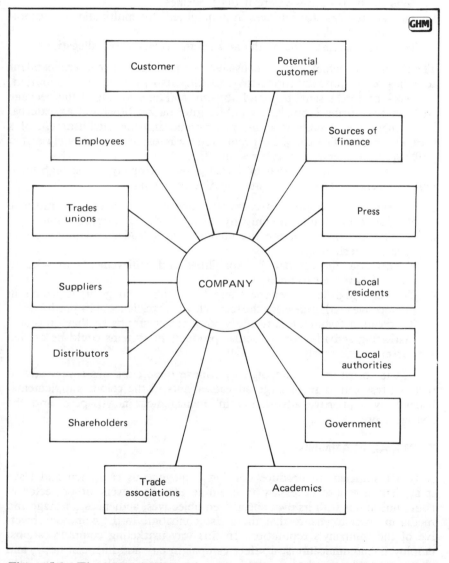

Figure 5.2   The company as a corporate citizen and its communication links
    (The Financial Times)

to illustrate this point. First, a major multinational corporation which listed five aims:

1 To increase the share of people's minds available to the company
2 To engender favourable attention and acceptability from its diverse publics
3 To explain the realities of the company's social and economic contributions to the countries where it does business
4 To state the case for business in general and for multinational corporations in particular
5 To correct some of the myths and refute irresponsible allegations.

The programme which evolved consisted of a package of five interdependent activities, each mutually supporting, making its own unique contribution, but working to the same plan and objectives. The elements of the package were an advertising campaign, a public information brochure, an external house magazine, a press relations programme and the establishment of a speaker's panel. The complete programme was based on a publicly stated philosophy of openness, frankness and fact.

The second example is that of a well-known company in the high technology business. The programme had five objectives:

1 To extend the company's corporate identity and to enhance/improve attitudes held towards the company among the defined target audiences
2 To establish and promote the company as a leader and innovator in advanced technology
3 To promote the company's capabilities and achievements in selected areas of advanced technology
4 To create high level awareness and knowledge among target groups in prospective market areas for the technological excellence of its products
5 To create a favourable attitude among target groups so that divisional marketing activities for particular products or systems could be carried out more effectively.

The main thrust of the campaign to achieve these aims was a very adventurous press campaign of large advertisements in the colour supplements, backed by supportive advertising in 'management newspapers' and the specialist press.

TACTICAL PLANNING

It is not sufficient to produce one big homogeneous campaign and leave it at that; it is also necessary to examine each and every other sector of communications with its own specialized objectives, audiences, message and media in order to ensure that these also contribute to the common objective of the company's reputation. In this way marketing communications, employee communications, a safety campaign, city and financial news, and all the rest add together to make up a synergistic whole. It can be seen that organizationally there is a need for the provision of top management direction to ensure the proper orchestration of all the many parts which are being conducted on a day-to-day basis.

The second part of tactical operations relates to what might be termed 'reactive activities'. This is the response to events which, if not handled properly, can work against the corporate objectives, or alternatively fail to give the potential support which might otherwise be achieved. Examples might be an industrial dispute where bad handling can undo much of the goodwill which may have been built up over a period of years. Equally, but in the opposite direction, failure to exploit fully the securing of a major overseas contract is a loss in terms of the very favourable light in which such an achievement can be shown to the target groups which together make up the corporate public.

Such contingencies cannot by their very nature be incorporated in any plan, but the organization must be sufficiently flexible to be able to react quickly to each of them and to have in mind not just the event itself and how to deal with or exploit it, but also the overall objectives.

CORPORATE RESEARCH

Early in the growth of the marketing concept and of corporate planning, communications activities were characterized by 'prestige advertising' and by a narrow form of public relations which relied mainly on what was loosely termed 'press relations'. It was unusual to have specific goals, and large sums of money were spent in putting out almost self-congratulatory messages about the company without much regard to the interest of the audiences or indeed what the effect on them might be. Companies indulging in these activities became sceptical of their value and as economic conditions became tougher interest in buying prestige declined.

The growth of corporate affairs as a function, and corporate relations as an activity has been accompanied by the precise setting of objectives in quantified form, and by a programme of research to ensure that any investment was achieving results. Businessmen have begun to demand that expenditure in this area should be accountable and the effects measurable.

The starting point of any properly constructed programme of corporate communications is to make benchmark measurements against which progress can be compared as the campaign proceeds. It is no use making such measurements at the end of a campaign as by that time it is too late to take any corrective action. A company might decide that it wishes to increase the level of awareness amongst certain discrete publics and at the same time gain an improved attitude towards itself and its products. Sample groups from each segment must be chosen and an assessment made of their current level of awareness and the nature of their attitudes. Only with this information can an effective plan be drawn up. From this a budget is set with the task of moving from a perceived level A to a targeted level B in a given period of time. Using the same audience segments, methods of sampling and questioning techniques, research must be planned at intermediate stages to find out whether the results are on schedule, in advance of it or behind it. Variations can be made at this stage to bring the campaign back on course; changes may be in the direction of the campaign, or it may be necessary to increase expenditure, or for that matter cut it back. So the operation breaks down into four stages – set objectives, quantify, research, verify.

ORGANIZING FOR CORPORATE RELATIONS

If corporate relations is not recognized as a top management function it stands little chance of success. If there is not to be a corporate affairs director, at least the executive responsible must have direct access to the chief executive and the top-level strategic thinking which is going on at that level. The person concerned needs professional communications expertise across all channels of persuasion and information, but more than that he must have the perspective of an all-round businessman equally at home with financial matters as with technical, personnel and marketing.

Depending on the size of the company he may require a small staff, but increasingly there is a reluctance to add what almost amounts to a fixed overhead, and the alternative of outside services is looked upon with greater favour. It is said that outside consultants find it difficult to relate closely to the company and its inside and outside complexities. This may be so and is one of the reasons for having at least one really good staff man. On the other hand, the body of knowledge and expertise in corporate activities, particularly in effective communications, is limited and in all probability will not be found among more than a handful of consultants. The position is further complicated by the fact that many corporate campaigns have been devised and executed by advertising agencies, and so the acquired cumulative experience is shared between two professional groups of practitioners. There are signs that a new breed of total communications agencies will emerge which will set out to provide counselling at a corporate level and then follow on with a full range of services on an *à la carte* basis so that a client company can select which executive activities he will take upon himself, and which he will leave in the hands of the outside service. This combination, all under one strategic plan, facilitates the use of the respective strengths of both the consultant and the client, is highly flexible, professionally more effective, and arguably cheaper.

BENEFITS

A well constructed and properly funded corporate relations programme can lead to many benefits of which the following are but a few of the more obvious examples.

1 Increased market reputation and market share
2 Happier and more satisfied employees
3 Rise in share price
4 Greater productivity

5 Favourable government support
6 Better quality applicants for jobs
7 Improved treatment from suppliers
8 Better understanding by, and less criticism from, outside pressure groups.

While benefits will accrue to any company as a result of a planned corporate relations effort the chances are that the larger the organization, the greater the need for a formalized corporate policy. This applies to an even greater extent where the products concerned fall into the category known as 'undifferentiated'. With little to choose between one brand and another (for example with petrol, oil, banks, cigarettes, detergents) what are the real determinants of a purchasing decision? There is a good deal of evidence to suggest that the customer will prefer the brand or name he knows best and for which he has the greatest regard. Where products are intrinsically the same, the most important factor must become that undefinable property which lies behind the product – its reputation.

THE FUTURE

There can be little doubt that corporate relations as a new management function is here to stay. Increasingly corporations are having to accept a social responsibility and, what is more important, to be seen to accept it. Customers, employees, shareholders and all the other interested public groups wish to be better informed and to feel comfortable in the knowledge that they are not being unfairly exploited by faceless, impersonal organizations whose sole purpose is to make as much profit as they can, regardless of the feelings or sensitivities of others.

One portent of future growth is to be found by looking at the United States where there are many indicators of the firm foundation and significant benefits of corporate relations. Other industrialized countries have a long way to go in comparison, but it would be surprising if corporate relations did not become a way of business in most of them during the next decade.

FURTHER READING

Bernstein, D., *Company Image and Reality*, Holt, Rinehart and Winston, London, 1985
Hart, N.A., *Effective Corporate Relations*, McGraw-Hill, Maidenhead, 1987
Hayes, R., and Watts, R., *Corporate Revolution*, Heinemann, London, 1986

Part Two
FINANCIAL MANAGEMENT

6 Sources of finance

Stephen Badger

In theory three sources of wealth are available to a company – land, labour and capital. These are not wholly interchangeable, but to some extent the balance in any given company can be changed by the entrepreneur; land can be turned into capital by sale and leaseback (see Long-term facilities, below) or a given process can be made more capital-intensive and so generally require less labour (or vice versa). These decisions are within the scope of management, one of whose functions is to optimize the balance between the different factors of production. The first step before raising capital is therefore to ensure that it is really financial capital that is required.

WHY CAPITAL MAY BE REQUIRED

Capital is required to finance the conduct of the business. When a manufacturing business is first established, for instance, factory and office premises will be needed and plant and machinery and transport vehicles. These can either be bought outright or hired; in the first case the expenditure represents capital permanently invested in the business (for the second, see Medium-term facilities, below). In addition funds will be required to finance production from the initial purchase of raw materials until the sale of the finished product to an external purchaser, to pay wages and to meet overheads: these funds are known as working or revolving capital. As the business expands, fresh injections of both permanent and working capital will be required. If on the contrary it contracts (or is merely run more efficiently) capital will be freed for alternative uses. When the original fixed assets need replacing, more expenditure will be needed. This should have been adequately provided out of profits by depreciation provisions over the life of the assets, but in times of inflation there may well be a shortfall which will need an injection of new capital.

Capital may also be required for acquisitions.

TYPE OF CAPITAL REQUIRED

Capital is conventionally described as short-term, medium-term or long-term. The distinctions are not rigid, but short-term capital may be regarded as any liability repayable within one year; medium-term as being replayable between one and ten years in the future; and everything else as being long-term capital (this covers both the proprietor's ordinary risk capital, or equity, and long-term borrowings, or debt capital). In general, working capital requirements should be financed by short-term capital and capital permanently invested in the business should be long-term. Medium-term capital is useful to give added flexibility and balance to the overall financial structure: if a project is expected to generate sufficient cash flow to repay the initial investment within, say, seven years, medium-term financing may be appropriate.

This chapter deals primarily with sources of long-term finance (both debt and equity) but sources of short and medium-term finance are considered in outline.

SOURCES OF LONG-TERM FINANCE FOR UNLISTED COMPANIES

The types of finance available to a company that is not listed on a stock exchange are much the same as those for one that is. The difference in the two situations is that the unlisted company is restricted to a much narrower range of sources, since many potential lenders or shareholders will be unwilling to put up funds if their investment is unlisted and so not marketable. In addition, if the company is private in the legal sense it is not permitted to make any invitation to the public to subscribe for shares or debentures.

In the first place an unlisted company may rely on the permanent capital put up by its promoter and his friends and relations, supplemented by bank borrowings. But in due course, if the company expands faster than retained earnings by themselves allow, there will come a time when these individuals are unable to find all the funds required; or they may wish to realize part of their investment. If the company has not yet reached a stage where a public flotation is appropriate, it should be possible to find one or more institutions to put up more capital (consisting either of ordinary shares or a mixture of ordinary and loan capital) on the basis that a flotation will take place within a few years so that the institutions will then be able to realize their investment if they wish. There are a number of specialist institutions providing this kind of finance, such as Industrial and Commercial Finance Corporation, a subsidiary of Investors in Industry, which is owned by the Bank of England and the clearing banks. The merchant banks are also active in this field, and insurance companies, pension funds and investment trusts may participate in a placing if the company is large enough.

In addition the wish of the UK government in recent years to encourage the entrepreneur has combined with an increasing appreciation of the profitability of investment made early in a company's life to produce a flourishing venture capital market. There has been a wide proliferation of institutions willing to provide both venture capital in start-up situations and what is sometimes referred to as mezzanine capital at a rather later stage. An example is Equity Capital for Industry, a body originally set up to channel institutional funds into industry, which now concentrates almost exclusively on venture capital situations. Most banks now have a venture capital subsidiary and a considerable number of other funds are active in this area, some specializing in high technology and others operating more generally. Private capital is also tapped for this purpose by Business Expansion Scheme funds, which take advantage of the legislation allowing the cost of such investments to be charged for tax purposes, and so appeal to investors with high tax rates.

Substantial funds are also available for what are referred to as management buy-outs (MBOs). These are situations where, for instance, a company is willing to dispose of one or more subsidiaries and the existing subsidiary management is willing or even eager to take it over. The managers will put up a relatively small amount of capital with the bulk of it coming from institutions, usually in a mix of ordinary shares, preference shares and loan capital (see Types of security, below). But the institutions are prepared to give the management a financial incentive and thus the finance is structured so as to maximize their equity investment so long as they succeed in increasing profits. A number of MBOs have shown very good rates of return and therefore the range of institutions prepared to invest in them has increased. Syndicates have also been set up commanding large amounts of funds so that decisions can be made quickly by the syndicate leaders: there have been examples in the UK of MBOs running into hundreds of millions of pounds, and in the USA the amounts are very much larger. Some of the privatizations carried through by the government have also involved a sort of MBO with a high percentage of all employees being encouraged to put up at least a small amount of capital – The National Freight Corporation is one of the best examples of this.

Investments in unlisted companies (whether tiny start-ups or large MBOs) all tend to be unmarketable. There will come a time when some or all of the investors in any circumstances will need to realize their capital. At this stage the company may be taken over by another one or it may go public on the Stock Exchange.

GOING PUBLIC

Obtaining a listing on the Stock Exchange is a most important step in any company's development. But at the end of 1985 there was a total of more than 868 000 companies registered in Great Britain of which about 862 000 were private companies (in the legal sense) and only 2616 were listed on the Stock Exchange, including nearly 500 overseas companies. Many companies will therefore never reach a stage at which a listing is appropriate, or their proprietors may for various reasons not wish to seek a listing; taking in new shareholders provides an additional source of capital, but at the same time involves added responsibilities towards those shareholders typified by the Stock Exchange's requirements on disclosure. The interests of 'outside' shareholders may at times differ from those of 'family' shareholders and the future management of the company must reflect the new spread of interests represented.

The reasons for going public are usually among the following:

1 To make the shares marketable and hence more valuable
2 To diversify the family investment holdings and so to reduce the degree of risk
3 To provide funds to meet capital transfer tax liabilities when necessary
4 To make acquisitions of other companies for shares practicable
5 To raise new funds once the resources of the existing shareholders cease to be adequate.

This chapter is concerned with the last of these, but it is important to realize that going public does not necessarily involve raising new money for the company – the shares sold to the public are often existing shares being sold on behalf of existing shareholders.

There is a small over-the-counter market sponsored by Granville & Co. but to go public on the Stock Exchange a company must either join the Unlisted Securities Market (the USM) or else obtain a full listing. The USM caters for smaller companies – entrants do not need to wait until they can show a five-year record, advertising requirements are less and only 10 per cent of the capital need be made available to the public, often in a placing. It therefore appeals particularly to newer high technology campanies which may well command a high rating. Even so, a high proportion of the money raised is often consumed by the expenses of issue. More substantial companies will tend to apply for a full listing straightaway and the mechanism used for this is an offer for sale. To give an idea of scale, gross issues on the USM in 1985 amounted to £181 million whereas it can be seen from Figure 6.2 that total corporate issues of ordinary shares exceeded £3.4 billion.

The offer for sale will be made by a merchant bank or a firm of issuing brokers. The offer will be underwritten so that the money is available even if sufficient public subscriptions are not forthcoming. But it is most important for the company's future capital-raising ability that the issue should be successful, which means that it should be fully subscribed, that the shares should open at a premium and that a free after-market should be maintained. To achieve this it is essential that the company should have continuity of good management and attractive prospects and that large shareholders should not continue selling frequent blocks of shares once the offer for sale is complete. The amount of money that can be raised initially will depend primarily on the present and future profit levels of the company and hence on its ability to pay reasonable dividends on the increased capital: the figures can range from a million pounds to hundreds of millions depending on the size of the company.

SOURCES OF LONG-TERM FINANCE FOR LISTED COMPANIES

Once a company has taken the important step of going public it can seek to raise funds from the whole range of investors, both private and institutional, without restriction.

In recent years private investors have tended to an increasing extent to channel their savings through life assurance policies, pension schemes and unit trust purchases rather than making direct investments in securities themselves. Figure 6.1 illustrates this by showing, for recent years, selected uses of funds by the personal sector and by financial institutions (other than the banking sector). This shows that there has been a steady net divestment of corporate securities by individuals with a brief pause in 1985, whereas financial institutions have been substantial net purchasers. They have also increased their rate of investment in property significantly. Any company wishing to raise funds therefore has to try to issue the sort of security that will appeal to this type of investor – primarily insurance companies, pension funds and unit and investment trusts.

Figure 6.2 shows some of the ways in which companies have in fact raised finance over the same period. It can be seen from this that bank lending plays a very important role, since banks are the first (and often the cheapest) source of finance to which all companies turn. Even more important in the overall picture are internally generated funds: the figures in Figure 6.2 must be viewed in the perspective of a total figure for undistributed income adjusted for unremitted profits of £31 576 million in 1985.

YEAR	PERSONAL USES OF FUNDS		USES OF FUNDS BY FINANCIAL INSTITUTIONS		GHM
	Investment in company securities £m	Life assurance and pension funds £m	Ordinary shares £m	Other corporate securities £m	Land, property and ground rents £m
1976	−1511	5568	1135	7	1111
1977	−1817	6138	1815	−117	1084
1978	−1152	7333	1924	− 37	1368
1979	−2105	9302	1990	− 61	1365
1980	−2026	10688	2501	− 1	2013
1981	−1648	13270	2540	276	2328
1982	−2525	13996	2707	502	2136
1983	−1086	15244	2089	625	1618
1984	−3048	17059	3488	487	1726
1985	471	17739	6104	1149	1582

Figure 6.1   Uses of funds by individuals and institutions (CSO Financial Statistics)

Types of security

The types of security usually issued are the following:
1 Ordinary shares
2 Preference shares
3 Debentures, secured either by a floating charge or a specific mortgage
4 Unsecured loan stocks
5 Unsecured loan stocks with conversion rights or warrants attached
6 Foreign-currency bonds

Ordinary shares

These represent the equity or risk capital in a business. They entitle their holders to a share of the profits by way of dividend only to the extent that the directors think fit. Thus if the business prospers its ordinary shares may become very valuable, but if it declines they may become valueless. Ordinary shareholders are also usually entitled to control the company's activities by voting at general meetings.

Preference shares

Preference shares carry the right to receive a fixed dividend in every year that the company makes a sufficient profit, but to no further participation unless they are specifically participating preference shares. They may in some cases be redeemable at a fixed future time or at the company's option and they can also be issued on the basis that they are convertible in a specified ratio into ordinary shares of the company, but they will normally only

YEAR	BANK BORROWING £m	OTHER LOANS AND MORTGAGES £m	UK CORPORATE ISSUES £m		ISSUES OVERSEAS £m
			Ordinary shares	Fixed interest (net)	
1976	2398	439	785	42	6
1977	2966	38	730	−67	102
1978	2939	386	829	−73	−43
1979	4772	616	906	−22	−59
1980	6795	667	902	419	−15
1981	5847	618	1660	738	−34
1982	6563	768	1033	245	−43
1983	1559	725	1872	608	−46
1984	7165	412	1127	249	298
1985	6562	591	3406	860	770

Figure 6.2 Selected sources of capital funds of industrial and commercial companies *(CSO Financial Statistics)*

carry full voting rights in special circumstances. Preference shares became relatively unpopular after the tax changes introduced by the Finance Act 1965, but more recently they have been more used as a way of increasing the capital base without diluting the interests of ordinary shareholders.

Debentures and loan stocks

The other types of capital are generically referred to as loan capital, which may be either secured or unsecured. It can be seen from Figure 6.2 that the use of these instruments has picked up in recent years but still represents a small proportion overall.

A debenture, according to s455 of the Companies Act 1948, includes debenture stock, bonds and any other securities of a company whether constituting a charge on the assets of the company or not; but in stock exchange parlance the expression debenture normally means a secured stock, while unsecured loan stock is used to refer to a stock which is not secured. This is the terminology used here.

Unlike shareholders, holders of a debenture or unsecured loan stock are not members of a company, simply its creditors. They are therefore entitled merely to receive the agreed rate of interest (which is normally paid semi-annually) and to receive repayment of capital on final maturity. Their rights will be incorporated in the trust deed constituting the stock which will be made between the company and (usually) a trustee on behalf of the stockholders. It is a requirement of the Stock Exchange that there must be such a trustee if the stock is to be listed; the trustee will normally be one of the insurance companies or investment trusts which specialize in this type of work.

Investors in fixed-interest stocks have historically required a long life to final maturity. In fact most stocks issued in the London market have a term of twenty to twenty-five years, although some medium-term issues have been seen. There is usually a period of five years before final maturity when the company can repay the stock without penalty and the average life of the stock may be reduced by the operation of a sinking fund. Since the creditworthiness of a company, and even the nature of its business, can change materially over an interval of this length the trust deed constituting the stock will impose certain restrictions on the company. These will vary from case to case, but they may include limitations on such things as disposing of more than a certain proportion of the business, changing the nature of the business and giving security. An unsecured loan stock deed issued domestically will also probably contain a permanent limit on the overall borrowings of the company and its subsidiaries and a separate limit on secured borrowings and the borrowings of UK subsidiaries. A debenture deed will not impose a continuing limit but will require the presence of a certain level of cover in terms both of income and of assets before any further issue of another tranche of the stock can be made. In general, debenture stock holders, since their claims are supported by security, will require rather less in terms of restrictions than the holders of an unsecured loan stock who merely rank alongside trade and other unsecured creditors.

71

But in either case the trustee will have the power to declare the stock immediately repayable if interest is not paid or if the company defaults on certain other obligations.

Convertible and warrant stocks

These are a compromise between borrowing and equity. A convertible is an unsecured loan stock which initially merely carries a fixed rate of interest but which, on specified dates or within a specified period, may be converted, at the option of the holder, into ordinary shares of the company at a fixed ratio. Warrant stocks are stocks which are not convertible but which are issued together with warrants which entitle the holder to subscribe for ordinary shares of the company at specified times and at a specified price. Convertible stocks have been popular for a long time, but warrant stocks have never really become familiar in the UK domestic market.

The advantage to a company of issuing convertible stock is that for the initial period it can service the stock at a lower rate of interest than would be necessary for a stock that was not convertible, that when it is finally converted the effective price of issuing the resultant shares will be higher than it could have been initially, and that in the interval the interest payments (unlike ordinary dividends) will have been an allowable expense for tax purposes. A warrant stock gives the company a long-term borrowing (at a lower rate of interest than a simple borrowing), and when the warrants are exercised there is a further inflow of cash into the company. Both kinds of stock will impose the same sort of restrictions on the company as an ordinary unsecured loan stock with additional provisions to protect the holders' rights to convert or exercise their warrant rights.

Foreign-currency bonds

Only the very largest companies will want long-term loans in foreign currencies. In the great majority of cases, the UK market will be amply sufficient as a source of capital and in general it is unwise to incur a foreign-currency liability unless one has corresponding assets in that currency. Moreover only the largest companies would be well enough known to attract the interest of foreign lenders. However, in the 1960s a substantial international capital market developed in eurodollars (US dollars deposited outside the USA, but not necessarily in Europe, and so not subject to any national restrictions on capital flows). A large number of US, and a smaller number of European, companies have taken advantage of this to raise quoted eurodollar loans (both fixed interest and convertible) and there have also been issues in Deutschemarks, French and Swiss francs, eurosterling and artificial units such as the European unit of account. Unlike domestic issues, eurobond issues usually have a life to final maturity of not more than fifteen – and in some cases as little as five – years. With the abolition of exchange control in the UK the dividing line between domestic and Euro issues in sterling has become blurred and indeed current trends suggest that large companies may find it most convenient to raise long-term funds on an unsecured basis in the eurosterling market.

METHODS OF ISSUE WITH A LISTING

The four chief methods of making an issue for cash on the Stock Exchange are:

1. Offer for sale
2. Rights issue
3. Open offer
4. Placing

Offer for sale

In this case all members of the public are invited to subscribe for the issue by advertisements inserted in the press. The offer is usually made at a fixed price. Sometimes an offer for sale by tender is used where only a minimum price is fixed and applicants decide themselves how much they are willing to pay; a striking price is then fixed at a level at which the issue will be fully subscribed and the shares issued at that price to all applicants who applied at that price or above. In either case, only a fixed number of shares are available for issue and, if a greater number of applications is received, each application is scaled down proportionately. Priority is sometimes given to existing shareholders or employees who are sent special application forms.

An offer for sale is normally used when a company goes public for the first time, as described earlier. It may also be used in an issue of loan capital where the amount of capital required is very large or where it is necessary to appeal to a particularly wide circle of investors for some other reason. In most cases, however, a placing is preferred because of its speed and simplicity (see below). By comparison an offer for sale involves significantly larger advertising and administrative costs.

Rights issue

In a rights issue new ordinary shares or other securities are offered to existing shareholders of the company *pro rata* to their holdings. Shareholders can then choose between taking up their entitlement (their rights) by subscribing the set amount per share, or they can sell some or all of their rights in the market if these are quoted at a premium. If they choose to sell they of course receive money rather than paying it out, but their percentage holding in the company is reduced so that in theory the effect is the same as if they had sold some of their existing shares. From the company's point of view the subscription money will still be received from the purchaser of the rights.

It is a requirement of a listing on the Stock Exchange that new equity shares (or other securities involving an element of equity) should only be issued for cash to existing shareholders of the company in proportion to their holdings (unless they consent otherwise in general meeting), and this has now been given wider application by the Companies Act 1980. As a result, issues of ordinary shares or convertible stocks are normally made

73

by way of rights so that shareholders have the opportunity of maintaining their proportionate stake in the company.

Open offer

An open offer is an offer of loan capital restricted to shareholders (and possibly the holders of loan capital) of the company making the issue. However, the offer is not made *pro rata* to their holdings. Each shareholder can apply for as much stock as he wishes or for none; if more applications are received than stock is being issued, each application will be scaled down proportionately. This method of issue is relatively infrequent, but it may be used if it is thought that the stock being issued may attract a large premium and the benefit of this should accrue to shareholders. It is appropriate only where the company has a large number of shareholders, but in that case the effect is very similar to an offer for sale but without the attendant advertising costs.

Placing

In a placing, stock is offered direct to a relatively small number of large institutional investors who are the principal holders of fixed interest stock; it is therefore a quick and effective method of issue which allows the most precise pricing. Placing for an unlisted company was considered under Sources of Long-term Finance. Stock exchange permission must be obtained for a placing with a listing and it is a condition of such permission that a proportion of the stock should be available publicly in the market. As already noted, a placing of new equity issued for cash is only possible with shareholders' consent but, because of its simplicity, placing has become the most usual method of raising loan capital for UK companies.

Underwriting and expenses of an issue

Once a company has decided that it needs money, it will clearly wish to be assured of that money as soon as possible, come what may. Rather than making an issue itself it will therefore go to a merchant bank or issuing broker who, in addition to advising on the documentation and terms of the issue, will arrange for it to be underwritten; that is, the issuing house will undertake to subscribe or find subscribers for the issue on the terms fixed in so far as it is not fully subscribed by the public or shareholders as the case may be. In return for accepting the risk and for its overall co-ordinating work on the issue, the issuing house normally charges a total commission of 2 per cent, $1\frac{1}{4}$ per cent of which is passed on to the sub-underwriters, that is the institutions who agree to take up different amounts of the issue *pro rata* to the extent that it is not fully subscribed. In the case of a placing, however, the stock is placed directly with a number of the same institutions. Accordingly, no sub-underwriting commission is required and only a placing commission of perhaps $3/4$ per cent (varying with the size of the issue) is payable; however, the issue terms will be slightly worse so that the net proceeds receivable by the company will be much the same. The other major expense of an issue of share capital is capital duty levied at a rate of 1 per cent on the value of the shares being issued. Duty is no longer payable on the issue of loan capital but, in the case of a convertible stock, capital duty arises on conversion. By comparison the administrative costs of an issue, especially in a placing, are small.

OTHER METHODS OF SUPPLEMENTING CASH FLOW

The main methods of raising long-term capital with a listing have now been outlined. It remains to consider briefly the various other possible methods of supplementing cash flow, which are of course open to quoted and unquoted companies alike. Some of these can provide relatively long-term finance, but the majority are short-term.

Long-term facilities

These include mortgages, sale and leaseback transactions, and public authority and specialist institution lending. The main sources of mortgage and sale and leaseback finance are the insurance companies and pension funds. In the case of a mortgage loan, a single lender will advance up to two-thirds of the value of a building for a specified term on the specific security of that building – the borrower retains the ownership of the building but his rights are subject to a mortgage charge for the term of the loan. In a sale and leaseback transaction he will actually sell the building (and so forfeit any appreciation in value) in return for a capital sum and at the same time lease the building back for his own use from the purchasing institution for a long period at a specified rent. Other sources of relatively long-term facilities include the Department of Industry (for specified purposes in development areas and in accordance with such schemes as may be in effect from time to time), local authorities where employment is being created in their areas, and various specialist semi-official organizations such as Investors in Industry, Agricultural Mortgage Corporation and National Research Development Corporation, all of which exist to lend for certain purposes.

Medium-term facilities

These include leasing, hire-purchase, project finance and term loans.

Leasing and hire-purchase are most appropriate for items such as vehicles, plant, machinery and office equipment. In leasing, the ownership of the item remains with the lessor, but the lessee is entitled to the use of it for a specified term in return for regular payments under the lease. A tax-based lease may be particularly attractive to a company with no immediate liability to taxation. In a hire-purchase transaction the purchase price of the item and interest thereon is paid in instalments over a set period, at the end of which ownership of the item does pass to the hirer. There are a large number of finance houses which specialize in these activities.

Similarly, merchant and other banks may undertake to arrange finance for a specific project. This will involve tapping a number of different sources of finance in accordance with the cash flow requirements of the individual project and is a particularly flexible form of financing.

Finally, banks sometimes engage in term lending for periods up to five or even ten years. A term loan could come from a single bank or it might be syndicated among a number of different banks. It might be at a fixed rate of interest, but it will more usually be on a roll-over basis; that is, with interest fixed periodically at the prevailing rate. In the latter case it is also possible to arrange for drawings to be made in different currencies at different times.

Export finance

The UK Government (in common with governments of other major industrial countries) assists UK exporters to finance their contracts with overseas buyers by running an export credit programme which has two purposes: first, to provide insurance against political and commercial risks which may affect performance and payment under export contracts; and second, to ensure that the terms of any credit offered to overseas buyers of UK goods and services can be made as attractive as possible. The banking system plays a crucial role as provider of funds and of specialist export finance advisory services. The official UK export credit authority providing insurance guarantees and a level of financial subsidy is the Export Credits Guarantee Department (ECGD) which operates as an autonomous government department with a direct reporting line to the Secretary of State for Trade.

Typical export funding structures

With ECGD support, finance can be made available in several different forms. For short-term transactions a supplier can insure 90 – 95 per cent of his receivables with ECGD and assign the proceeds of his insurance policy to a bank, thereby enabling him to obtain finance from his bank on attractive terms. For transactions attracting medium-term credit (usually the supplier of capital goods), the structure is more complex so as to reduce the impact of deferred payments on the exporter's balance sheet. Under a medium-term supplier credit structure, the supplier would insure deferred contract receivables, evidenced by Bills or Notes accepted/issued by the buyer, with ECGD. Under a bank facility, the supplier would then be able to sell the Bills or Notes to his bank, who, in turn, is entitled to a 100 per cent unconditional guarantee from ECGD. ECGD has the right of recourse to the exporter in the event that the bank guarantee is called but the exporter may offset the recourse liability against his ability to claim up to 90 – 95 per cent under his insurance policy. Under this structure, therefore, the supplier carries a continuing residual 5 – 10 per cent financial risk on the buyer throughout the credit period. For larger-sized contracts and major investment projects, the more usual structure is a 'buyer's credit', under which the supplier enters into what is essentially a cash contract. Instead of taking out insurance cover for deferred payments, the supplier is paid by means of disbursements from a loan made available by a bank to the foreign buyer. ECGD provides a 100 per cent unconditional guarantee for the principal and interest due under this loan. ECGD is entitled to take recourse on the supplier in the event of a claim by the bank under the guarantee only in circumstances where the UK supplier is in default under his contract. Although opinions differ on the real extent of this recourse burden (much of the onus of proof of the contractual default lies with ECGD), suppliers would generally agree that they would have no continuing financial risk throughout the credit period as would be the case under a medium-term supplier credit.

The terms available for support of UK export finance transactions vary from straightforward commercial funding for short-term transactions to officially supported interest rates. For transactions involving a credit period of more than two years, the UK authorities acting through ECGD make it possible for exporters to offer the minimum fixed rates permitted by the international consensus on export credit terms subscribed to by OECD member countries. The minimum fixed interest rates currently vary between 8.8 per cent for the poorest category of borrowing country to 11.2 per cent for the richest category. For particular projects in selected markets, it may be possible to obtain even finer 'soft' terms under the 'Aid and Trade' programme administered by the Overseas Development Administration and the Department for Trade and Industry. In cases where an officially supported fixed rate is to be offered to a borrower in connection with a medium-term credit, ECGD agrees with the banks providing the funds that they will receive 'interest make-up' to provide them with:

(a) the difference (if any) between the fixed rate and the cost of funds, and
(b) a margin over the cost of funds.

The cost of interest rate support provided by the UK authorities has continued to give rise to concern in recent years, despite a reduction in the overall cost of the scheme due to an increasing alignment between OECD minimum rates and market interest rates. Increasing attention is thus being given to funding medium-term credits from purely commercial financial sources.

If it is thought that finance will be required in connection with an export order, it is advisable to contact a merchant/clearing bank as well as ECGD sooner rather than later in view of the wide range of financing options which may need to be considered and the difficulties which can be encountered in obtaining ECGD support after a firm contract has been struck.

Short-term facilities

These include bank overdrafts and loans, bank acceptance credits, bills of exchange, trade credit, invoice discounting and factoring. Of these, bank overdrafts and loans are the most common and are used universally by companies as Figure 6.2 shows. They may be supplemented by acceptance credits, where a bank undertakes to accept approved bills of exchange up to a certain limit so that the bills can be discounted at the finest rates. Alternatively, bills of exchange can be used as a form of trade credit, whether or not discounted with a bank or discount house, or various arrangements may be made between buyers and suppliers as to the length of credit given in payment for goods. Finally, invoice discounting and factoring are undertaken by various specialist institutions. Invoice discounting means financing the collection of specific invoices (at the risk of the selling company). Factoring involves making immediate payment against invoiced debts which are then normally collected at the factor's own risk for an appropriate charge. All these methods have in common that they finance relatively small revolving trade transactions, but in aggregate they provide the finance for a vast amount of business on a continuing basis.

Current trends

The willingness of lenders to lend for long periods will depend on their being able to foresee a reasonable rate of return in real terms. In times of high inflation there is therefore a reluctance to tie up funds in this way except at rates so high as to be unacceptable to many borrowers. Equally, companies may prefer to borrow for relatively short periods in the hope of being able to refinance their obligations later at a lower rate. For these reasons, there has been a considerable shift over the years away from long-term issues to more flexible short-term borrowing. This has been encouraged by the greater availability of bank credit following the new monetary policy adopted by the Bank of England from 1971 onwards in its new approach to competition and credit control.

The banking market has been very competitive and in many cases lending margins have shrunk drastically. The banks have also been active in devising new products to appeal to their customers who are now offered note issuance facilities (nifs) and revolving underwriting facilities (rufs) to supplement the staid overdraft. There is also an active market in swaps both for currencies and interest rates which allow a company to optimize its own position by benefiting from the countervailing position of another party. More recently still, the UK commercial paper has been inaugurated, thus allowing companies to obtain funds outside the banking system. It must be said however that many of these instruments are suitable only for the larger listed company and have little relevance for many finance directors.

LOOKING AT THE OVERALL CAPITAL STRUCTURE

We have now outlined the chief avenues open to a company wishing to raise new capital. Before raising any new capital a company should consider what the capital is needed for, whether it is permanent or likely to be repaid out of cash flow within a period and what rate of return it is likely to earn. One can then go on to decide how it can best be supplied. For instance in the case of an investment with a high degree of risk the best source of finance is likely to be equity (or risk) capital; but, if it is a relatively risk-free long-term investment, loan capital may be more appropriate. If it is a specific project of medium-term duration, project finance should be considered, while if it is a working capital requirement, bank overdraft facilities are likely to be the answer. In all cases the various methods of supplementing cash flow in other ways must be borne in mind so as to minimize the amount of new capital actually required. Finally, the rate of return must be set against the cost of the capital to ensure that an adequate margin exists to justify the investment.

One of the most important considerations is to preserve a proper balance between debt and equity in the company's financial structure. This relationship is described as the company's financial gearing; if the company's source of income is reasonably stable and assured (such as the rental income of a property company) it is safe for it to be highly geared, but if it is operating in a cyclical industry (such as machine tools) it is prudent to keep the gearing (that is, the element of borrowing) at a low level, for interest on borrowings has to be paid in adverse as well as favourable times and if a temporary setback combined with high interest charges results in the company making a loss, its overall status will suffer. The degree of gearing will depend both on the absolute amount of borrowing and the extent to which any of this borrowing is at fluctuating interest rates which may rise faster than the company's income. In inflationary times, borrowing at a fixed cost can be most advantageous to a company. But the closer the company gets to what is thought to be an unduly high level of borrowings, the more reluctant lenders will be to provide new funds and the more the equity interest of existing shareholders will be endangered.

The object of company financial management should be to see that the company has adequate funds at the lowest cost consonant with all these factors and so to seek to maximize its earnings for ordinary shareholders.

FURTHER READING

Admission of Securities to Listing, Stock Exchange, London, revised 1984

Brearley, R.A., and Pyle, C., *Bibliography of Finance and Investment*, Elek Books, London, 1973

'Competition and Credit Control', Bank of England, reprinted in *Bank of England Quarterly Bulletin*, June 1971

Leach, J.H.C., 'The Role of the Institutions in the UK Ordinary Share Market', *Investment Analyst*, December, 1971

Leach, J.H.C., 'The Weight of New Money – Once again', *Investment Analyst*, September, 1975

Merrett, A.J., Howe and Newbould, *Equity Issues and the London Capital Market*, Longmans, London, 1967

'New Capital Issues Statistics', *Midland Bank Review*, commentary published annually in Spring edition

Report of the Committee of Enquiry on Small Firms (Cmnd 4811), HMSO, London 1971

Report of the Committee on the Working of the Monetary System (Radcliffe Report) (Cmnd 827), HMSO, London, 1959

Royal Commission on the Distribution of Income and Wealth (Diamond Report), Report No.2 (Cmnd 6172), HMSO, London, July, 1975

'The UK Corporate Bond Market', *Bank of England Quarterly Bulletin*, March, 1981

The various volumes of evidence given to the Committee to Review the Functioning of Financial Institutions (the Wilson Committee) and published by HMSO may also be of interest.

7 Capital project planning

Tessa V Ryder Runton

Capital project planning is the process by which companies allocate funds to various investment projects designed to ensure profitability and growth. Evaluation of such projects involves estimating their future benefits to the company and comparing these with their costs. Such analysis is appropriate not only to the purchase of long-lived physical assets, but to any decision which has impacts extending into the future. Thus capital project planning can encompass, for example, long-term contracts for goods and services, marketing expenditures, disinvestment by sale, mergers and plant closures. While capital project planning is a process that takes place in an organizational context over extended periods of time, certain elements of this process are essential to good project planning. These are:

1 Access to the appropriate information
2 Knowledge of the company's required financial return
3 Realistic evaluation of the prospective cash flow and profit impacts of projects
4 Analysis of the costs and benefits of projects with attention to the timing of their occurrence
5 Evaluation by senior management of the strategic implications of large projects
6 A well-defined approval process
7 Consistency with strategic planning and budgeting procedures
8 A review procedure.

THE GOALS OF CAPITAL PROJECT PLANNING

Businesses have responsibilities to various interested groups including employees, customers, suppliers, banks and shareholders. Most companies claim that their financial goal is to satisfy their shareholders. This goal is met by maximizing the total market value of the company's shares. The capital market values shares at the present value of current and future cash flows attributable to shareholders. If the company maximizes the net present value of all the operations that make up its business, the sum will be the maximization of the value of the company. This value, net of debt, belongs to shareholders. Companies pursuing other objectives whether social or technological must primarily be profitable. Should shareholders, corporate members or financiers become dissatisfied with the company's operations, they may withdraw their support, causing such awkward problems as loss of morale and personnel, shortage of funds, a fall in the company's share price if it is publicly quoted, or stormy annual general meetings. Any of these can lead to undesirable vulnerability and result in a takeover, close-down or governmental interference.

REQUIRED RATE OF RETURN: STANDARDS AND THE COST OF CAPITAL

Cost of capital is a major standard of comparison used in financial analysis and is a vital company statistic needing careful calculation. The return on capital resources must equal or exceed the cost of that capital. Although zero or negative returns are acceptable in special cases, the necessary subsidies may lead to costs in another form.

The realities of commercial life have caused the cost of capital to be a very complex subject. Any comparisons must be made between like numbers. A percentage profit before tax made on a hotel in Bermuda bears no relationship to the same figure made after tax on a farm in Scotland. A profit expressed as a percentage of capital employed should not be compared with a discounted cash flow internal rate of return. Many measures of company performance can be devised but these are valuable only to those who are completely familiar with the definitions involved. The appraisal of projected cash flow discounted at a rate equal to a carefully estimated required rate of return leads to fewer pitfalls. In particular, the time-value of money is taken into account, all the financial effects are assessed, and tax and inflation are taken into account in the calculation of the cash flow and the estimation of the cost of capital.

Capital investment analysis aims to discover the financial truth about the plan under investigation. If it does not meet the survival standard of the organization, that fact should be stated clearly before the discussion as to its desirability begins. In practice many apparently unprofitable processes go on in any business because they enhance the profitable activities which, of course, should outnumber them. Obvious examples are the provision of catering and other services for the workforce, advertising, research and so on. It used to be thought that discounted cash flow analysis led to categorical 'yes' or 'no' judgements on any plan; in fact, all it does is marshal the financial facts for the guidance of the decision-takers. In addition, it can point to the least unprofitable way of tackling a loss-making but necessary job.

The cost of capital to the firm

Most companies raise funds from many sources – retained earnings, new equity, grants and many forms of loans. The overall cost of capital to the firm is the return it must earn on its assets to meet the requirement of all those providing it with financing. Lenders require interest payments and shareholders expect to receive dividends and see capital growth.

In the past, UK shareholders have expected to earn a real net return of about 8 per cent after tax on average risk shares. To obtain this required net return in money terms, the expected inflation rate must be added. If this expected inflation rate is 10 per cent, the required return on the company's present equity and retained earnings is 18 per cent. The cost of new equity raised by means of 'rights' is a little more than this to allow for the costs of the issue. Other forms of new equity issues incur further costs of about 2 per cent.

Although the average real expected return on shares is about 8 per cent, companies in risky industries or with high gearing (borrowing relative to equity funds) will have more vulnerable shares than average. The real return required by their shareholders will be commensurately higher. This means that borrowing is not necessarily a cheap way of raising funds. Although the interest rate on borrowing may be lower than the return expected by shareholders, increased gearing will raise the risk of shares and not change the overall cost of funds to the company. (For a more detailed discussion see Franks and Broyles, 1979).

If a company maintains a proportion of debt capital agreed with its lenders, it can compute a *weighted average cost of capital*. For example, if the interest rate on debt is 10 per cent, and the company has 25 per cent debt and 75 per cent equity, the weighted average cost of capital in money terms including 10 per cent average inflation is (0.25 x 10 per cent) + (0.75 x 18 per cent) = 16 per cent. This cost does not allow for the tax savings from interest payments. This benefit is added separately.

In deciding the appropriate standards for an organization, the marginal cost of capital is a vital guide. In a growing company, new capital will be needed and, therefore, the return on a project of normal risk should be judged against a standard of the weighted average cost of new capital. Companies making investment decisions continuously should use this marginal cost of capital as the standard for all projects with risks normal to the company's business. If a project cannot pass this test, it will diminish the company's value.

Required rates of return on projects

Obviously projects involve differing risks. Some, such as cost-saving investments and lease or buy decisions, are of low risk; others, such as research projects, involve greater than average levels of risk. A company should classify its risk categories for projects and set required returns for each. A large project of risk significantly different from normal can alter the overall character of a company, its cost of capital, its accepted gearing and the returns expected by financiers.

The required rate of return for a project can be significantly different from the weighted average cost of capital for the company. High-risk projects are characterized by high fixed operating expenditure and high revenue variability. These should be expected to earn high rates of return. The exact return required will depend upon a judgement about the level of risk in the project compared with the average risk of the company. In the case shown above, where the weighted average cost of capital in real terms is 6 per cent, the real required return on a project twice as risky as the market should be 12 per cent. With 10 per cent expected inflation the required return should be 22 per cent on a cash flow projected in money terms.

The use of a separate required rate of return for each individual project is most important when the projects are large relative to the company and/or when the projects being considered have long lives. A typical classification scheme, in increasing order of risk is: cost reduction, replacement, scale expansion, new products. The risks of these different types of investment differ, and so should their required returns.

By evaluating different projects using discount rates equal to different required rates of return, the company is seeking to protect its shareholders. Shareholders require high rates of return for higher levels of risk, and receive compensation for high risk in the capital markets. Companies undertaking high-risk investment decisions must seek to achieve higher returns than their shareholders can earn for that level of risk in the capital markets.

Effect of debt finance on required returns

Unless there are non-financial incentives, a project is acceptable only if it stands on its own feet – that is, its cash flow should at least meet the company's return criterion for whatever risks are involved. With the possibility of debt financing is the position changed? A typical case arises where new assets simply increase the total assets on a proportion of which debt is available. Some people argue that, even apart from tax advantages, debt is cheap since the interest rate is lower than the cost of equity funds. This argument ignores the hidden cost of debt: the increased vulnerability of the equity as more borrowing is undertaken. The total operating risk of the company remains constant as more debt financing is used, so it is unrealistic to believe that the overall cost of funds can be reduced in this way.

One advantage that borrowing does confer is the reduction in taxes caused by the deductibility of interest payments. The impact on cash flows of this tax saving is simply the future stream of tax payments that are saved by the interest payments on the debt. The value of these tax savings can be added to the value of the operating cash flows from the project to get an overall value including the benefits of debt financing. This is preferable to using a weighted average cost of capital including the cost of debt at an after-tax rate. Use of the latter assumes that the debt available for a project will be very long term and will be the same proportion of the project financing as it is for the company. Both these assumptions can be very erroneous when projects have short-maturity debt or very high or low gearing.

Care needs to be taken when a project merits special loans. Usually these are projects of significant size for which government incentives are available, or for which special working capital loans can be raised, or involving mortgageable property. If the result is a new company finance structure, then cost of capital and risk classifications must be reassessed. Some large capital investments, such as in mining, involve parent companies in special financial guarantees and these need special attention. Other capital investments, such as in research, do not result in increased total assets which can be partly debt financed.

TRADITIONAL TECHNIQUES FOR TESTING VIABILITY

The natural question: 'When do I get my money back?' has often been answered by the traditional technique of adding up the forecast net cash inflow (sometimes the sum of the profit before depreciation from the forecast profit and loss account) year by year until the amount of the original capital investment is reached, thereby giving the years to payback. Such a calculation is inconclusive because standards vary, definitions of the original capital vary, tax is not always deducted and most of the benefits of tax allowances are obscured. The method ignores the *time-value of money*, cannot cope with inflation and takes no account of the later profits, if any. Whether, in fact, any profit is made on the investment is not measured at all. Payback calculations give some guidance in matters of liquidity in which case the cash inflow should be carefully defined and be free of any 'accounting numbers' such as 'tax provision' instead of 'tax payable'. A better payback calculation is the discounted payback, which is computed using the present values of the future cash inflows.

Another traditional technique involves the use of balance sheet ratios for current and proposed operations. These include the ratios of profit to capital employed, of profit to sales, and many others concerning the stock, current assets and liabilities, and working capital. These ratios are useful for regulating smooth operations but are unhelpful for judging profitability owing to definition problems and the choice of standards, but mostly because the time-value of money is not included.

One ratio used is the return on capital known as 'the accountant's return' or the 'book rate of return'. An average profit, before or after tax is calculated for a number of years of the proposed project and this is expressed as a percentage of the capital employed. The latter is often defined as the initial investment or the average capital employed over the years, thereby allowing for further investment and depreciation. This procedure suffers from the same snags as the techniques mentioned above and, in addition, smooths out the effect of irregular annual profits. Clearly, quick profits are preferable to a slow build-up, but advantages or disadvantages arc obscured.

MODERN TECHNIQUES FOR TESTING VIABILITY

The traditional techniques take no account of the time-value of money. But money received today is much more valuable than the same money received later. Present inflationary conditions magnify the difference. This is the principal fact which modern analysis techniques have incorporated to improve on past procedures. Analysis concentrates on the incremental cash flow of a project. The cash flow is discounted at the project's discount rate to the present time, giving a present value. The work involved has increased, but once an analysis discipline has been set up, decision-takers can expect that the realities of the given data for some plan will be clearly identified. They can then concentrate on the non-financial problems involved, judge whether the data are sufficient to work with and act accordingly.

The concept of moving money in time using the relevant discount rate is not new. Today's quoted price for benefits to be received in the future can be judged by netting the price, or capital cost, from the present value of the future cash flow. A positive resultant net present value (NPV), if properly calculated, shows that the transaction is financially worthwhile. The value of the transaction can also be assessed by judging its internal rate of return (IRR).

CASH FLOW DISCIPLINE IN CAPITAL PROJECT ANALYSIS

The discounted cash flow techniques use as their raw material the incremental cash flow resulting from some plan. Profit flow study is necessary for proper annual accounting as required by shareholders, but it is the cash flow that should be studied to identify the return forecast and the finance that is required. Provisions for depreciation are excluded, but expenditures on working capital and capital expenditures are included. The cash flow of a project is a forecast of the total monetary effects computed periodically (usually annually or monthly) over the whole life of the project, including scrap values. Such items as tax savings achieved on other profits of the organization because of allowances due to the new project or any other cash effects which would not occur without the new project – for example, the cost of head office extensions or replacing an executive who would be transferred – should be included. Interest payments are often wrongly deducted from the cash flow, but they are not operating flows, being part of the cost of funds included in the cost of capital. A project can be defined as any procedure which alters the organization's cash flow. Projects, therefore, include opportunities for cost savings and productivity improvements, where capital cost is not necessarily involved. What, therefore, is analysed is the total cash flow effect of an opportunity, that is, the net incremental cash flow which is the difference between the cash flow in the company if the project is undertaken and the cash flow if it is not.

This analysis must be in real terms or in money terms with respect to inflation and, if necessary, alterations must be made so that real terms cash flows are judged by a real terms required return standard and money cash flows are judged by a money terms required return standard. Tax allowances and loan-servicing schedules are always in money terms but sales and cost figures are usually forecast in real terms. It is usual for the marketing and production departments to project schedules showing changes in sales percentages or production costs without allowing for external price changes. However, the estimation of taxable profits and taxes requires that these data be converted to money terms. In cases of high inflation forecasts, or different effects on prices and costs, and for lengthy projects, some estimate must be made of the inflation pattern over the life of the project. This estimate could differ for use on prices, on costs and on the overall situation including the cost of capital. All figures must be converted to money terms so that expected tax payments can then be estimated.

It should go without saying that cash flows are forecast after the effects of company taxes when paid. Because tax allowances are normally in money terms, consistent cash flows almost certainly have to be forecast in money terms, unless real terms tax allowances can be calculated. Sometimes it is necessary to consider any likely future changes in tax structure. In this, as in treating inflation and in all problems of data uncertainties, it is important not to be over-meticulous, particularly at the outset. Analysis of the most roughly prepared cash flow will show whether it is worth spending any further time attending to the details. The first question to answer is: 'What is the profitability of the given set of data (warts included)?' If the answer looks promising it is then sensible to take the time to examine the given data, prepare a detailed net incremental cash flow in money terms and look at possible outcomes of the project as opposed to one set of data. The analysis should then examine sensitivities, risks and probabilities and the effect of the project on the organization as a whole. Decision-takers prefer consistent analysis disciplines so that they can use consistent standards of judgement and comparison.

NET PRESENT VALUE (NPV) AND INTERNAL RATE OF RETURN (IRR) IN MORE DETAIL

The use of the concept of net present value (NPV)

The net present value (NPV) of a project is the net present value of the net incremental cash flow discounted at the project's required rate of return. A zero NPV shows that the project repays the capital invested plus the minimum acceptable return on the invested capital throughout the project's life. The minimum acceptable return is equal to the opportunity cost of that capital including a return required for the risk taken by investing in that operation for that period. NPVs show that the minimum return is achieved plus extra value.

Given a discount rate of 11 per cent for a project, the NPV is found as shown in Figure 7.1. Other things being equal, this project looks financially acceptable. One could pay up to £199 more for the opportunity and still not lose. NPV represents the analyst's estimate of the net increase in the value of the company which would accrue from the project. If the discount rate used is the capital market's capitalization rate for the risk

GHM

Time in years from today	Cash flow (£)	11% Discount factor	Present value (£)
0	(1500)	1.00	(1500)
1	100	0.901	90
2	1000	0.812	812
3	1000	0.731	731
4	100	0.659	66

The NPV, the sum of the present values of the cash flow = +£199

Figure 7.1   Calculation of net present value (NPV)

of the project, the NPV represents an estimate of the incremental market value of the firm due to the project. The NPV technique thus gives a simple assessment tool, but is inaccurate if there is doubt or dispute as to the correct discount rate.

The use of the concept of internal rate of return (IRR)

The internal rate of return (IRR) is also known as the discounted cash flow yield (DCF), the DCF return or the actuarial return. IRR is defined as the break-even financing rate for the project. This is not to say that the capital released by the project earns such a return. Reinvestments, whether wise or not, should be kept separate from the analysis of a project on its own merits. The IRR of a project is judged against the cost of capital standard or the minimum required return.

The mathematical definition of the IRR is that it is the discount rate which, when used to discount the net incremental cash flow, gives a zero net present value for the project. The NPV (which is calculated at the project's required rate of return discount rate) should not be confused with the many net present values which can be calculated using other rates.

The calculation of the NPV consists in setting out the cash flow, discounting it to the present time and adding up the net total. DCF or IRR calculations necessitate trial and error. If, however, the graph shown in Figure 7.2 is borne in mind, the process need not be lengthy.

Most practitioners find it convenient to calculate the NPV first. If this shows, for example by being positive, that it is worth doing more sums, a guess must be made of the next trial rate. A positive NPV indicates that the DCF/IRR will be greater than the cost of capital rate, how much greater can sometimes be guessed by the size of the NPV. Trial rate A per cent

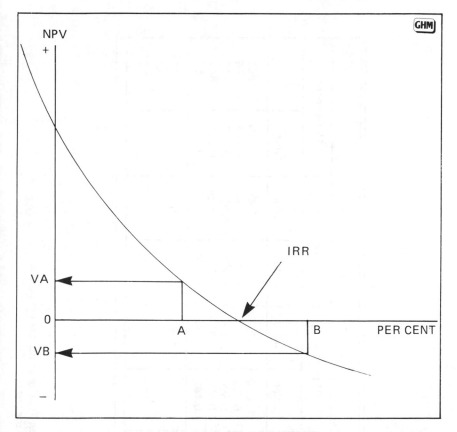

Figure 7.2   The use of trial rates to calculate the internal rate of return (IRR)

is used and will give a net present value VA. Consideration of this result might lead to trial rate B per cent and VB. Having thus both over- and under-estimated the answer, the true IRR can be found by mathematical interpolation, or by drawing a similar graph (always provided that the trial rates are not more than one or two percentage points apart – if they are, the curve that represents the relationship will give too inaccurate a result, which should be checked by another trial and interpolation or extrapolation).

An example will show how this procedure applies. Suppose that the cost of capital is 11 per cent, and an investment is being considered which costs £1500, lasts four years, and has no terminal value. All calculations are tabulated in Figure 7.3. By interpolation between the net present value calculated at 16 per cent and 17 per cent the IRR is found to be:

89

Time in years from today	Cash flow (£)	Cash flow discounted at:									
		11 per cent		20 per cent		17 per cent		16 per cent			
		Discount factor	value	factor	value	factor	value	factor	value		
0	(1500)	1.000	(1500)	1.000	(1500)	1.000	(1500)	1.000	(1500)		
1	100	0.901	90	0.833	83	0.855	86	0.862	86		
2	1000	0.812	812	0.694	694	0.731	731	0.743	743		
3	1000	0.731	731	0.579	579	0.624	624	0.641	641		
4	100	0.659	66	0.482	48	0.534	53	0.522	55		
Net present values			199 this is the NPV		(96)		(6)		25		

GHM

Figure 7.3 Tabulation using actual and trial rates, leading to calculation of IRR (The calculation process is described in the text)

$$16 + \frac{25}{31} = 16.8 \text{ per cent}$$

The same result is obtained extrapolating from the 17 per cent and 20 per cent:

$$IRR = 17 - \frac{3 \times 6}{90} = 16.8 \text{ per cent}$$

Interpolation between the 11 per cent and 20 per cent figures, however, gives the answer:

$$11 + \frac{9 \times 199}{295} = 17.1 \text{ per cent}$$

which may be too inaccurate, although in this case the return would probably be quoted at 17 per cent. These figures could also be found graphically.

The use of present value: mid-year discounting

Discount tables are available for all periods – weeks, quarters, years – and to various numbers of places of decimals. It is not normally helpful to calculate the cash flow in too small periods or to discount it using more than four-figure tables. It is more important to notice that the tables usually refer to points of time and the cash flows represent a total for a period. A fitting assumption is needed. It is easy if the majority of receipts and payments occur at the beginning or at the end of the periods. For flows which are continuous and irregular over the periods, the total cash flow is often assumed to arise mid-year. The calculation should therefore be refined. If only annual discount tables are available, the half-year discount factor at r per cent can be calculated from the equation:

$$\text{Discount factor} = \frac{1}{\text{Square root of } (1+r \text{ expressed as a decimal})}$$

Example A

Suppose the investment is bought today and the operation is immediate and continuous. The NPV calculation becomes:

Time from today	Cash flow (£)	Present value at 11 per cent	
		Discount factor	Present value
0	(1500)	1.000	(1500)
½	100	0.949	95
1½	1000	0.901 x 0.949	855
2½	1000	0.812 x 0.949	770
3½	100	0.731 x 0.949	69
			NPV = 289

The IRR now needs to be recalculated to take account of the refined timing.

The IRR is now $21^1/_2$ per cent because of the earlier cash flow.

Example B

Suppose again that the operation were to be built up and paid for over one construction year. In this case the £1500 cash flow is similarly assumed to be mid-year and the other cash flows occur six months later than before. The NPV can then be obtained from the first calculation, which has so far given a present value six months from today, by discounting the result by six months. NPV today equals

$$199 \text{ x } 0.949 = £189$$

The IRR is 17 per cent in this case, as at first, because it is mathematically true that the same yield is given wherever period zero is assumed to occur if the succeeding time periods bear the same relationship to period zero.

In some cases, such as natural resource projects, which involve large negative cash flows at the end of the project, a special problem arises in using IRR. Projects of this sort can have more than one IRR, some of which may be above the required return and some below. Complex techniques have been developed to salvage the IRR method in these circumstances. These adjustments usually involve procedures similar to the present value approach, and fewer problems will be encountered by the use of the NPV rule in these circumstances.

The use of present value – optimization of mutually exclusive alternatives

Financial analysts are constantly being asked to advise as to which of two viable alternatives is financially preferable. Such choices include large long-life machinery versus cheaper short-life machinery, labour versus automation, the choice of site, speed of construction, shaft versus open-pit mining, air versus sea transport, and so on; in each case choice of one excludes the possibility of choosing the other alternative. Use of the net present value calculation is the easiest approach. Suppose that in a company with a cost of capital of 11 per cent the choice is between:

Method A (which is capital-intensive) showing a NPV of +£1500 and
Method B (with a lower capital cost) showing a NPV of +£1300

If the analyst calculates NPVs using the minimum acceptable return discount rate for the risk of the project, different discount rates might be appropriate to A and B. For example, one method might involve installing a possibly risky unproven technological improvement, whereas the other method would re-equip as before.

The actual question to be answered, since both methods are financially desirable, is whether the expenditure of the extra capital involved on Method A is worthwhile. The incremental investment, which is represented by the difference between the cash flows of the two alternatives (cash flow A and cash flow B, for each period), shows a NPV of +£200 (NPV A – NPV B). It is therefore worth spending the extra money. Where the patterns of the alternative cash flows are very different, the incremental approach avoids problems in comparing projects with different levels of capital expenditure. Indeed, different cash flows can arise from the same total capital invested but the incremental cash flow analysis still gives the financially preferable operational plan.

Use of the DCF/IRR approach is also straightforward but contains a snare for the unwary. The question of whether the incremental investment would be desirable is answered by finding the DCF/IRR on the incremental cash flow (cash flow A minus cash flow B, for each period). If the incremental IRR is greater than the company's minimum acceptable return, then alternative A is financially preferable. When setting out the results, however, an apparent problem frequently arises. For example:

Method		11 per cent NPV	IRR
A	Expensive	+£1500	14 per cent
B	Cheaper	+£1300	16 per cent
A-B	Incremental investment	+ £200	13 per cent

It looks as though one should choose method B because the IRR is better than that in A. This is an illusion because the capital on which the yield is earned is different in each case. The analysis of the incremental investment points to the same answer whichever method is used. It is often argued that, perhaps, the incremental capital should be spent on some other investment which might show a better return than the 13 per cent here. This could be the case in conditions of severe capital rationing when investments yielding 13 per cent cannot be financed. In other conditions there is no conflict and both investments are desirable. Of course, more than two projects might be available, in which case, several incremental investment choices would be necessary. It is easier simply to compare the NPVs – the most preferable choice has the highest NPV.

Some practitioners approve the calculation of the NPV but find the answer, which is of necessity expressed in currency, difficult to use. The *profitability index* is therefore sometimes used, particularly when projects need to be ranked because budgets are limited. The index is calculated by dividing the present value of the net cash returns by the present value of the net cash investments. In the example shown in Figure 7.3 the profitability index is 1699/1500 = 1.13 which means that every unit of investment earns 1.13 units of present value in the project. Care must be taken not to confuse this with the IRR which is 17 per cent. In practice many analysts report the profitability of a project both in terms of NPV in currency and of IRR as a percentage to assist understanding.

When mutually exclusive opportunities are being analysed, equal project lives should be compared. This is often difficult, but a three-year life machine can be compared with a five-year machine by assuming that the longer-life machine will be sold at the end of the third year. Alternatively a fifteen-year period can be taken with five three-year machines compared with three five-year machines. The most sensible assumption will be obvious.

Present value and expected value – decision trees

Much of capital investment planning involves arranging a continuous series of actions which may be altered in the light of future events or future actual patterns of marketing. It is possible to set out likely outcomes in a map known as a decision tree – it grows as it is extended further into the future. NPVs of each likely chain of events can be prepared and this could help the decision that must be taken later. Very often decision-tree calculations are of the expected value of the outcome. To calculate expected values the probabilities of likely intermediate events of outcomes are incorporated. Decision trees have been described extensively. A decision tree is shown in Figure 7.4.

Faced with the need to decide whether or not to install a computer, the possibilities or likely events might appear as shown in the figure. The decision taken would depend, financially, on the relative NPVs or expected values of the three good possibilities. Expected values are weighted by the relevant probability; for example, if there is a 60 per cent chance of an NPV of £100 and a 40 per cent chance of an NPV of zero, the expected value is £60.

COMPUTATIONAL RESOURCES

Although computers, big and small, are invaluable as calculating aids for complex problems they should not be used indiscriminately because the cost, and the time taken to eliminate errors, can become disproportionate to the problem being analysed. Time-sharing on computer terminals using borrowed working programs can be invaluable. Modern analytical methods can generally be employed for problems, using everyday hand calculators.

Calculation short-cuts and standard procedures for all problems are often sought in this field. If, however, they are used without understanding or without necessary adaption to the different circumstances of each case, much more time can easily be wasted than if the problem were initially approached from first principles.

DATA

The collection and sifting of project data normally leads to far more problems than the analysis. This is no reason for allowing less than rigorous analytical techniques. If a quick look at the first set of data indicates a promising idea, it is sensible to re-examine the data before extending the analysis. Data

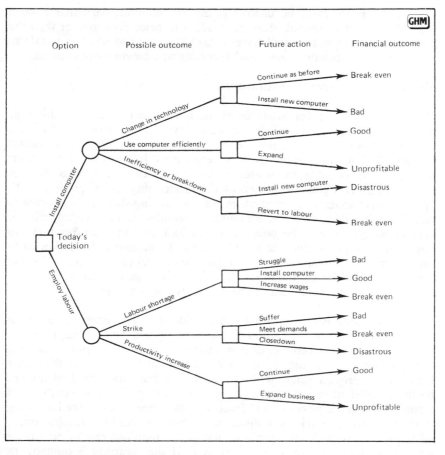

Figure 7.4 Example of a decision tree

are given, begged, borrowed or stolen, but in spite of (or because of) the uncertainties involved the best way to obtain good understanding leading to better decisions is to establish good communications with the project initiators as a top priority.

Discussions should be held 'on site' as early as possible so that there is no suggestion of ivory tower thinking. Diplomatic approaches to the hard-worked estimators who have to grapple with difficult forecasting problems can lead to a good understanding, not only of the best realistic guess at some figure, but also of the possible range in which it may lie and of the probabilities involved. Conversation with outsiders often helps clarification. Much the best hunches are those agreed by two or more experts. Special and outside experts can be called in to advise on variables found by sensitivity analysis to be critical enough to merit the cost of the advice.

A special problem to be tackled is that of inflation, particularly when costs are subject to special pressures leading to price rises greater than the general rate. The analyst will have to take a view as to when it is safe to assume that, on balance, costs and revenues will be similarly inflated.

Missing data – reverse economics

Very often, data are not available for such vital factors as the achievable price for a new product, the size of the reserves in a new oilfield, the time required to obtain safety clearance or planning permission, or the market or technological life period. Reverse economics is the formal technique whereby it is possible to define the achievable or viable range for the missing data. If a graph is drawn of the profitability (NPV or IRR/DCF) of the project against invented values of the missing data, it is possible to find the value that gives the minimum acceptable result. If that value is very unrealistic, it may be possible to conclude that the new product will not be profitable, or that the oilfield cannot be economically exploited in present circumstances. A decision might then be taken to stop any further expenditure on the promotion of the idea. If a project must be killed off or frozen it is far better halted early before reputations become involved.

This technique is also useful when considering the merger, takeover or sale of a company, or its flotation on the public market. An attempt is made to forecast the foreseeable cash flow of the company – possibly including benefits caused by savings in the new managerial context. The difference between the present value of the forecast cash flow and the debt divided by the number of issued shares will give a measure of the acceptability of a quoted or offered price, or will indicate what price to set at the beginning of negotiations. In a takeover situation the buyer should use the incremental required return for the project, that is the required rate of return for the risk of the company being taken over. If the company is quoted, the value of its equity share capital is given in the market-place, unless there are undisclosed facts such as technological advance, or unless the market has anticipated a possible merger. The premium paid should be less than the NPV of the merger benefits.

Uncertain and erroneous data

A good approach to uncertain data is to attempt to identify the range in which the answer may lie. This is sometimes done by adding to the best guess two more guesses, one of which is the most pessimistic and the other the most optimistic. In this way it may be possible to exclude too much subjectivity on the part of the estimator, who might previously have thought that his future depended on the success of his estimates and who therefore, understandably, introduced too much conservatism. In large organizations a chain of conservatism may be introduced. In such cases the analyst must try to assess the realities, and it is helpful if the motivations of the personnel are adjusted so as not to interfere. Over-estimating can be as wrong as under-estimating and can easily lead to raising too much finance or premature expansion.

Often data are manipulated, either innocently or deliberately, to achieve the desired result – perhaps acceptance of a scheme by head office or of a contract in a tendering competition. The results can lead to public embarrassment, if not disaster. A good review discipline can help to avoid or to sort out such problems.

Once the range in which critical data lie is found, sensitivity analysis can be carried out. Alternatively, a calculation of the likely profit or loss, should everything turn out for the worst, can help in a discussion. If the organization simply cannot survive such a loss and the chances of it are significant, then the project may well have to be forgone.

Sensitivity analysis

This technique can highlight the facts and problems caused by the risks and uncertainties of the plan under discussion. It has limitations but can be carried out with a minimum of calculating aids if necessary. The aim of this analysis is to discover the value of an uncertain variable at which the project is just profitable. Two or three calculations will give the necessary sensitivity curve.

Example of sensitivity analysis

A project is showing a negative net present value at the company's cost of capital rate. What would need to be done to make it profitable? The sensitivity graph is drawn (Figure 7.5) and shows that the operating profit would need to be raised by 10 per cent to give a zero NPV of the net incremental cash flow for the project. All other things are assumed at first to remain constant (capital cost, speed of coming into operation, life of the project, tax, inflation etc.).

Data which give the desired result:

	Original estimate	Acceptable estimates					
Price per unit (£)	20	21	20	20	20	20	20.3
Volume/number sold	10	10	10.5	10	10	10	10.15
Labour cost (£)	40	40	40	30	40	40	38
Materials cost (£)	50	50	50	50	40	50	47.5
Overhead cost (£)	10	10	10	10	10	0	9.5
Operating profit	100	110	110	110	110	110	111.045

It is thus possible to say that the project would be acceptable if either the price could be raised by 5 per cent, or the volume sold increased by

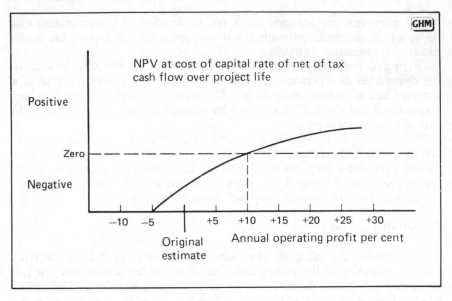

Figure 7.5   Graph of project viability's sensitivity to profit variation

5 per cent, or if the labour cost could be lowered by 25 per cent, or the materials cost by 20 per cent or the overhead cost by 100 per cent. Another possibility to explore would be if (as shown in the final column) both the price and volume sold could be raised by $1^1/_2$ per cent at the same time as all costs are reduced by 5 per cent. However, one should try to ensure that joint changes in variables are not contradictory and fit a plausible and consistent scenario. The graph could have been plotted using IRR and the company's required rate of return as the cut-off line but this involves more sums.

One more uncertainty can be explored to extend the analysis. Suppose, for example, that the market for the product is thought to last ten years but could be hit by competition in eight to twelve years' time; further calculations give the graph shown in Figure 7.6. Annual operating profit is thought likely to lie between 95 and 120. Assuming the variables examined to be the most critical, the profitability 'envelope' is shown by the two outer curves and the dotted connecting lines. This envelope is divided into two parts by the cut-off line of zero net present value. By inspection of the two areas it is possible to conclude that the project has roughly only a 40 per cent chance of being viable. The worst likely outcome is also shown. The decision may then be taken more easily.

Should the whole envelope be above the cut-off line it would be possible to conclude that the project is profitable in spite of the uncertainty in the variables considered, which are then defined as uncritical. Further effort could then be concentrated on other variables. This technique is limited

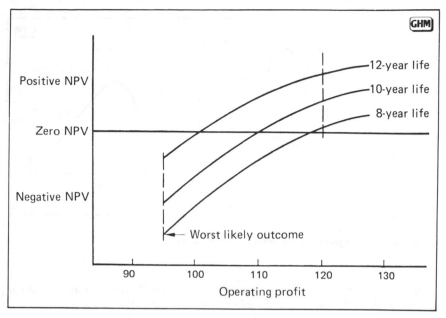

Figure 7.6   Two variable sensitivity analysis graph

to two dimensions. It is, however, of great value, even without calculating aids, because of its simplicity in demonstrating the effect of apparently daunting uncertainties.

PROBABILITY ANALYSIS

This is the ideal towards which sensitivity analysis is the first step, but the calculation usually requires the help of a computer. Great efforts are being made by large organizations and consultants to prepare flexible computer programs to conduct probability analyses on a wide variety of projects.

The data required are further examined to discover a range of probabilities for every variable which may lie in each part of the likely range. Subjectivity is not avoided by this, but the further discussion can sometimes help clarify the situation. The results could be shown for each variable in a histogram, which is a practical approach to the underlying mathematical curve. An example is shown in Figure 7.7. Mathematical sampling using such data for each significant variable results in the type of profitability/probability graph shown in Figure 7.8. The peak of the curve in Figure 7.8 shows the most likely outcome, but there is a significant chance that the yield might be negative or that the original investment would not be recovered. The area under the curve being taken as unity, the area to the left of the cost of capital or required rate of return cut-off line, if measured, gives the probability of unprofitability. The use of sensitivity and probability

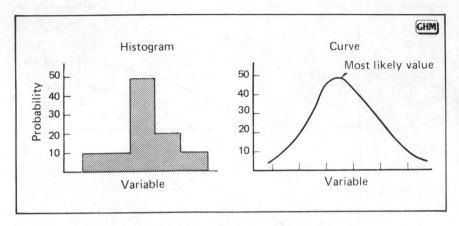

Figure 7.7   Examples of probability distributions

analyses does not remove uncertainty and subjectivity of data; it helps decision-takers to judge the likelihood of profit or loss in projects.

RISK

Uncertainty of data is not the only unknown bedevilling projects. There are also many possible events which could have a significant effect. Such events include acts of God (earthquake, flood), of governments (tariffs, nationalization), of competitors, of technological improvement. Some risks can be insured against. In every case it is helpful to define the risk and

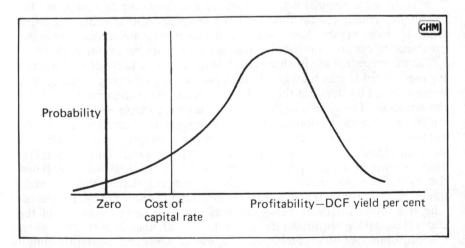

Figure 7.8   Example of a profitability/probability graph

assess its possible effect ('what happens if. . . ?') and in particular when such an effect might occur. If the likely loss caused by risky circumstances were to be disastrous to the company, then perhaps the venture is too risky. There are several ways in which organizations of different kinds can proceed to minimize the effect of risk. Obvious examples are diversification, both geographically and in the nature of the business, the tying of customers or suppliers to long-term contracts, and the cautious introduction of new or different scale business. Other risks can be eliminated through markets in which risk is traded. A surprising variety of risks can be insured against and others, such as commodity price variation and exchange rate variations, can be hedged in future markets.

THE DISCUSSION FORUM FOR CAPITAL INVESTMENT PROBLEMS

Good decision-taking depends more than anything else on good communication. The decision-takers (at a level appropriate to the size of the proposal) do well to arrange a free debate between the project sponsors, the experts, the analysts and themselves. Documentation of the proposal, the analysis, the decision and any argument or discussion are of great value to all concerned in future planning, as well as to interrelated projects in the context of the organization's future as a whole. The techniques described in this chapter contribute only by assembling such facts as can be established and highlighting the likely probabilities. This, however, is of great value in releasing management effort for the interpretation of the problems.

Most private organizations are to some extent limited as to the amount of capital available, particularly for unspectacular investments. It would be convenient if all projects turned up simultaneously and could be ranked in order of profitability and then accepted in turn until available funds were used up. (Such a procedure is to a certain extent available to the public sector at budget time). In most companies, however, capital investment or operational optimization opportunities turn up irregularly. It is therefore highly desirable to establish and monitor a clearly understood set of criteria and discount rates, reflecting the company's required rates of return for different risks, against which each scheme can be measured as it arises and progresses. With the aid of the right criteria there is some chance that a good source of investments will have been chosen so that, at the minimum, returns can exceed costs; and the company's value can be increased, leading to a healthy financial context for future development.

Tactics

When analysis precedes or accompanies negotiations with governments, financiers, associates or opponents, it is usually helpful to make calculations in order that one can understand the opposite point of view, which might be based on different methods or criteria.

Few organizations can avoid differences of opinion which lead to apparent or very real conflicts. The experienced decision-taker and his advisers can normally recognize the behavioural signs. Avoidance of discussion is not always for good reasons, such as a real emergency. Emergencies can be contrived by skilful delays and, perhaps, decisions can be precipitated by prompted outside pressures. Decisions taken in real emergencies should be appraised and documented as soon as possible. If a decision-taker is known to be susceptible to private discussions, then project sponsors will be quick to arrange suitable lobbying. Such a situation has obvious dangers.

A very real problem can arise in planning investments which can or should be phased. The purchase of options or expenditure on pilot plants, which lead either to subsequent large investment or to embarrassment if the second stage is deemed unacceptable, should not be appraised in isolation. Appraisal of the first stage should be accompanied by a best guess of the likely subsequent history, and the project should be discussed at the level relevant to the whole operation, in which case the decision will be taken after consideration of the future commitments. The decision-tree technique examined earlier can help.

When a superficially attractive proposal is financially marginal, special care must be taken. At this time criticism may be made of the company's criteria which were otherwise accepted when the proposals were better than marginal. Such criticism at this time may not always be valid. In this situation excessive subjectivity may be introduced into uncertain data; in fact, some estimators claim to be able to produce estimates which pass company tests. Wide discussions of parameters, perhaps calling in outside advice, as well as the discipline contained in carrying out sensitivity and probability analysis, go some way to reduce this risk. Afterwards a well-established routine of project monitoring reappraisal, review or *ex post* evaluation, or whatever the subsequent comparison of forecast with actual results is called, may be especially appropriate.

REAPPRAISAL: EX POST EVALUATION AND CAPITAL EXPENDITURE REVIEWS

It has been said that, without subsequent re-examination, formal planning appraisal techniques are largely counter-productive. *Exante* evaluation – the prior preparation of forecast results – is very necessary when raising finance for a project, either internally or externally, and obtaining the desired go-ahead. There is, however, no certainty that the combined estimates and skills which resulted in the forecasts have been optimized unless a subsequent view is taken.

There are well-established commercial routines whereby periodic (weekly, monthly, quarterly, annual) accounts are compiled of both financial and physical resources used and benefits achieved, and reports are made to relevant technical and financial monitors. Usually the results are compared with annual and three- or five-year plans for the project and for the organization as a whole. Variations are studied and adjustments are made.

Projects which were initially appraised using cash flow disciplines should be reviewed using the same disciplines. If the conclusions drawn differ, speedy action may be desirable or, if it is not, it would be nice to know that it is not.

It is unfortunately necessary to take a cynical look at projects built for less than the forecast cost, sales that noticeably exceed budget, and other such successes. If the planners' faults were not in their stars but in themselves they should remain as underlings. People have gone as far as saying that it is useless to plan at all unless one also reviews the results. But, as always, too much is as bad as too little.

It is not always clear who should conduct reappraisal reviews. Conflicts may be avoided if the project operators undertake the review in the normal course of their duties. It is highly desirable also to include some sort of outside view to ensure a balanced opinion as to why the resulting return differs from that first forecast. The review should, of course, cover all the unquantifiable as well as the measurable aspects. If the organization sets up a separate reviewing team, its members may need great powers of diplomacy as well as of detection and endurance.

Reviews are discussed preferably at the same forum as are capital expenditure proposals, or, at least, the decision-takers should check that re-evaluation has taken place. Very often the lessons do not need to be driven home but have been learnt in the course of the operation.

The introduction of this routine is often problematical. As usual, opposition may be a cover. Other avoidance tactics can include radical changes of scope of a project leading, among other things, to a delay in the review date. Significant changes of scope should be appraised as rigorously as new projects.

FURTHER READING

Franks, J.R., and Broyles, J.E., *Modern Managerial Finance*, Wiley, New York, 1979

Merrett, A.J. and Sykes, A., *The Finance and Analysis of Capital Projects*, 2nd edition, Longman, London, 1973

Merrett, A.J., and Sykes, A., *Capital Budgeting and Company Finance*, 2nd edition, Longman, London 1973

Thomas, Howard, *Decision Theory and the Manager*, Pitman, London, 1972

8 The annual accounts

W P Ridley

Anyone interested in the management of a company, whether taking an active part or merely investing capital, needs to have financial information of two kinds concerning the company:

1 Where the capital is invested (shown in the balance sheet)
2 The return earned from the investment (shown in the profit and loss account).

Those in active management can call for financial reports and accounts to be designed according to their own requirements. But, for investors and others, forms of balance sheet and profit and loss account have been laid down by Acts of Parliament. This chapter starts by describing the formal requirements, and then proceeds to discuss other aspects of the accounts, including the interpretation of accounts in order to judge a company's financial performance.

ACCOUNTING REQUIREMENTS OF THE COMPANIES ACTS

The form of the published accounts and the directors' report is set by the Companies Act 1985, which consolidates the Companies Acts 1948 – 1983. They set out what must be included in the profit and loss account, the balance sheet and the directors' report (including notes). The accounts of a company, when based on this selected information, are termed the statutory accounts.

Growth of information required

The information required for the statutory accounts has grown enormously during the past sixty years, owing to pressure from investors and the general public. The pressure from investors for more information has grown with their increasing separation from management in industry and commerce. This separation has led to a need for investors to learn as much as possible of the state of the companies, in order to assess the security of their investment. The general public, which in this connection includes creditors and potential investors, are concerned to know how companies are being managed, and whether they are financially sound. (This demand for information becomes especially apparent when public confidence in company administration has been shaken by a well-publicised fraud. Successive governments have responded to these two pressures in their legislation.)

The government itself may wish to have more information made public if it feels that this will have a beneficial effect upon industry or commerce as a whole. Thus the publication of export figures by each company, for example, can have the effect of increasing emphasis on overseas sales and thereby stimulating trade. As a result, the successive Companies Acts tend to set increasingly stringent requirements for company disclosure while accounting standards are continually being tightened to achieve uniformity in reporting.

STANDARD PRESENTATION

While there are some variations allowed in presentation, Figure 8.1 shows the information required in a profit and loss account. Specifically, the object is to show:

1 Operating income
2 Investment income – splitting income from associated companies from other income
3 Income from ordinary activities separately from extraordinary income, charges or tax.

In addition, other information has to be given either in the accounts or in a statement attached to the accounts:

1 The directors' remuneration must be given, either in the accounts or in a statement attached to the accounts. All directors' remuneration and past directors' pensions, paid by the company or by any other person, either for their services as directors or for services in other capacities, must be shown. Likewise the statements or accounts must show any compensation paid by the company or any other person to past or present directors for loss of office. In addition the statement must show the number of directors who have waived their rights to emoluments and the aggregate amount that has been waived. The chairman's emoluments must be shown separately, and also those of the highest paid director if these are in excess of the chairman's emoluments.

The number of directors must be shown, broken down into income groups; that is, the number of directors whose emoluments do not exceed £5000, the number whose emoluments exceed £5000 but do not exceed £10 000, and so on for each successive integral multiple of £5000. For each of these items, the term 'emoluments' does not include contributions paid by the company for the benefit of directors under any pension scheme.

2   Auditors' remuneration
3   Amount set aside for redemption of share capital and loans
4   Turnover with analysis by geographical market
5   The average number of staff (by category) to be given with the aggregate amount of wages, social security costs and pension costs incurred.

GHM

 1 Turnover
 2 Cost of sales (*a*)
 3 Gross profit or loss
 4 Distribution costs (*a*)
 5 Administrative expenses (*a*)
 6 Other operating income
 7 Income from shares in group companies
 8 Income from shares in related companies
 9 Income from other fixed asset investments (*b*)
10 Other interest receivable and similar income (*b*)
11 Amounts written off investments
12 Interest payable and similar charges (*c*)
13 Tax on profit or loss on ordinary activities
14 Profit or loss on ordinary activities after taxation
15 Extraordinary income
16 Extraordinary charges
17 Extraordinary profit or loss
18 Tax on extraordinary profit or loss
19 Other taxes not shown under the above items
20 Profit or loss for the financial year

Notes

(a) Cost of sales: distribution costs: administrative expenses

These items shall be stated after taking into account
any necessary provisions for depreciation or diminution
in value of assets

*(b) Income from other fixed asset investments: other interest
receivable and similar income*

Income and interest derived from group companies shall
be shown separately from income and interest derived
from other sources

(c) Interest payable and similar charges

The amount payable to group companies shall be shown
separately

(*d*) The amount of any provisions for depreciation and
diminution in value of tangible and intangible fixed
assets shall be disclosed in a note to the accounts

Figure 8.1   Profit and loss account format

Taxation items. The more detailed requirements about disclosure of taxation items are covered by the layout shown in Figure 8.2.

The balance sheet

Figure 8.3 provides a format for a company's balance sheet, together with the notes which relate to the corresponding figures shown in the table. The principles of valuation are also set out.

1 Fixed assets: the amount to be included in respect of a firm's fixed assets is the amount of its purchase price or production cost less provisions for depreciation. Similar principles shall be applied where goodwill or development costs (only rarely to be treated as an asset) are given balance sheet values.

For fixed assets shown at valuations, the year in which the valuations were made must be disclosed. For fixed assets valued during the last financial year, the names or qualifications of the valuers and the bases of valuation they used must be given.

Freehold land must be shown separately from leasehold land, and land held on a long lease (one having not less than fifty years to run) must be distinguished from that held on a short lease (having less than fifty years to run).

There must also be shown (i) the aggregate amount of fixed assets acquired during the year: and (ii) the book value at the date of the last balance sheet of fixed assets disposed of during the year.

GHM

Taxation based on profits for the year:

Corporation tax at 35%(including £ [previous year £] transferred to deferred taxation) on profits excluding those of associates	x	x
Less relief for overseas taxation	x	x
	x	x
Overseas taxation	x	x
Prior-year adjustments	x	x
Tax on share of profits of associates	x	x
Total tax charge	—	—

Note : No provision has been made for tax, deferment of which is reasonably certain for the foreseeable future.

Figure 8.2   Presentation of taxation details

GHM

ASSETS

A Called up share capital not paid (a)

B Fixed assets

I Intangible assets
   1 Development costs
   2 Concessions, patents, licences, trade marks and
      similar rights and assets (b)
   3 Goodwill (c)
   4 Payments on account

II Tangible assets

   1 Land and buildings
   2 Plant and machinery
   3 Fixtures, fittings, tools and equipment
   4 Payments on account and assets in course of construction

III Investments
   1 Share in group companies
   2 Loans to group companies
   3 Shares in related companies
   4 Loans to related companies
   5 Other investments other than loans
   5 Other loans
   7 Own shares (d)

C Current assets

I Stocks
   1 Raw materials and consumables
   2 Work in progress
   3 Finished goods and goods for resale
   4 Payments on account

II Debtors (e)
   1 Trade debtors
   2 Amounts owed by group companies
   3 Amounts owed by related companies
   4 Other debtors
   5 Called up share capital not paid (a)
   6 Prepayments and accrued income (f)

III Investments
   1 Shares in group companies
   2 Own shares (d)
   3 Other investments

IV Cash at bank and in hand

D Prepayments and accrued income (f)

LIABILITIES

A Capital and reserves

I Called up share capital (k)

II Share premium account

III Revaluation reserve

Figure 8.3 Balance sheet format

GHM

IV Other reserves
   1 Capital redemption reserve
   2 Reserve for own shares
   3 Reserves provided for by the articles of association
   4 Other reserves

V Profit and loss account

B Provisions for liabilities and charges
   1 Pensions and similar obligations
   2 Taxation including deferred taxation
   3 Other provisions

C Creditors (*l*)
   1 Debenture loans (*g*)
   2 Bank loans and overdraft
   3 Payments received on account (*h*)
   4 Trade creditors
   5 Bills of exchange payable
   6 Amounts owed to group companies
   7 Amounts owed to related companies
   8 Other creditors including taxation and social security (*i*)
   9 Accruals and deferred income (*j*)

D Accruals and deferred income (*j*)

Notes

(*a*) This item may be shown under the heading of Assets

(*b*) Amounts in respect of assets shall only be included in a company's
     balance sheet under this item if either
        (i) the assets were acquired for valuable consideration and
             are not required to be shown under goodwill; or
        (ii) the assets in question were created by the company itself

(*c*) Amounts representing goodwill shall only be included to the
     extent that the goodwill was acquired for valuable consideration

(*d*) The nominal value of the shares held shall be shown separately

(*e*) The amount falling due after more than one year shall be shown
     separately for each item included under debtors

(*f*) This item may be shown in an alternative position

(*g*) The amount of any convertible loans shall be shown separately

(*h*) Payments received on account of orders shall be shown for each
     of these items in so far as they are not shown as deductions from
     stocks

(*i*) Other creditors including taxation and social security. The amount
     for creditors in respect of taxation and social security shall be shown
     separately from the amount for other creditors.

(*j*) Accruals and deferred income. The two positions given for this
     item are alternatives.

(*k*) Called up share capital. The amount of allotted share capital and
     the amount of called up share capital which has been paid up shall
     be shown separately.

(*l*) Creditors. Amounts falling due within one year and after one
     year shall be shown separately for each of these items and their
     aggregate shall be shown separately for all of these items.

Figure 8.3   Balance sheet format (concluded)

If the detail to be disclosed is considerable it might best be given on a statement attached to the accounts, reference thereto being made in the balance sheet.

2   Current assets shall normally be valued at production costs or purchase price (which may be calculated on a last in first out or first in first out price or average weighted price). However, where the net realisable value is estimated to be lower than this cost, this lower value will be substituted.

Items requiring disclosure

Other matters to be disclosed in the published accounts (by notes if not otherwise shown) include:
(a) The corresponding figures for the preceding year
(b) The nature and amount or estimated amount, of any contingent liabilities not provided for; financial commitments (including pensions); charges for other companies;
(c) The amount or estimated amount of any contracts for capital expenditure, so far as not provided for, and of any capital expenditure authorized by the directors but not yet contracted for;
(d) The bases on which foreign currencies have been converted into sterling;
(e) Any special circumstances affecting the company's taxation liability for the current or succeeding financial years;
(f) The number of employees (other than directors of the company) whose emoluments for the year (from the company, its subsidiaries or any other person in respect of services to the company or its subsidiaries):
exceeded £20 000 but did not exceed £25 000
exceeded £25 000 but did not exceed £30 000
exceeded £30 000 but did not exceed £35 000
and so on in successive integral multiples of £5000;
(g) The information concerning each of the company's subsidiaries;
(h) Similar information – normally capital reserves or profit or loss for the year:
   (i) where the company holds equity shares in another company (other than a subsidiary) exceeding one-tenth of the nominal value of the issued equity capital of that other company, or
   (ii) where the company holds shares in another company (other than a subsidiary) which, in the investing company's balance sheet, are shown at an amount exceeding one-tenth of the investing company's assets (as stated in its balance sheet);
(i) Under s 5, a subsidiary has to give the name and country of incorporation of its ultimate holding company.
(j) Allotments of shares during the year; outstanding options; amount of redeemable shares; debentures issued redeemed and the amount that can be re-issued. In addition, any financial assistance given by a company for purchase of the company's shares shall be noted;

(k) Dividends recommended; any fixed cumulative dividend in arrear;

(l) Reserves and provisions at the beginning and end of the year, together with any material movements. Any revaluation reserve should be shown separately;

(m) The amount of any provision for taxation other than deferred taxation shall be stated.

THE DIRECTORS' REPORT

The directors' report must accompany the balance sheet and profit and loss account filed with the Registrar of Companies, and must be sent to all members of the company, debenture holders and other interested parties.

The report, which is presented by the board of directors, contains much relevant information concerning a company's activities, and its minimum contents summarized below, have been considerably extended. It should be especially noted that these minimum contents are required by legislation and are not subject to directors' choice any more than the information contained in the statutory accounts.

Minimum contents of directors' report

Review

A review of the company's affairs during the period covered by the accounts: particulars of important events that have occurred since the year end; likely future developments; an indication of research and development activities.

Dividends

The amount(s) recommended to be paid by way of dividend.

Reserves

The amount(s) proposed to be transferred to reserves.

Activities

The principal activities of the company and significant changes in these activities.

Directors

The names of all directors who acted in such a capacity at any time during the period under review.

Changes in fixed assets

Significant changes in the company's fixed assets. If the market value of land is substantially different from the value shown in the balance sheet, an indication of the difference in value.

Contracts

Contracts with the company (except service contracts) in which a director of the company has an interest; the parties to the contract, the director involved, the nature of the contract, and the nature of the director's interest must be specified.

Arrangements between company and directors

Any arrangement whereby the directors are able to obtain benefits by the acquisition of shares or debentures in the company or any other body corporate.

Directors' interests

Directors' interests (at the beginning and end of each year) in shares or debentures of the company. This requirement is extended to include the directors' spouses and infant children (the directors' 'family interests')

Matters showing the state of the company's affairs

Particulars of any matter required for an appreciation by its members of the state of the company's affairs, so long as in the opinion of the directors the publication of such information would not be harmful to the company.

Relative profitability of different activities

Turnover and profit or loss of each class of business carried on by the company, if such classes differ substantially.

Persons employed

The average number of persons employed in the UK by the company (on a weekly basis) during the year, and the aggregate remuneration paid or payable to such persons in respect of that year. This information is not required where a company has fewer than one hundred employees.

Political and charitable contributions

The amount of contributions, if exceeding £50 given for political or charitable purposes, and the identity of the political party concerned.

Exports

The turnover from exports when the value exceeds £50000, and a note where no goods are exported.

Previous year

The corresponding amounts in each section for the immediately preceding year.

Employment policy

The arrangements for health, safety and welfare at work and for involvement in the business. Provisions for employment of disabled persons.

JUDGING A COMPANY FROM ITS ACCOUNTS

Reports by a company to its shareholders are regulated in detail by law. As a result, outside assessments of the financial standing of a company are almost inevitably based on the information given in these reports (normally issued annually) rather than on other publications of the company or on its trade reputation. Increasingly it is being realized that this outside assessment is important to the company – in raising finance, whether by loan or equity, in merger discussions with other companies, or in trading negotiations. It is therefore advisable for senior company executives to consider in detail the standards against which their company's financial performance – as set out in the fully audited report to shareholders – will be judged.

PROFIT AND LOSS ACCOUNT FOR PANGLOSS PLC

This chapter takes the abridged accounts of a company called Pangloss PLC to highlight information on which a financial examination is based (see Figure 8.4).

In the year to 31 March 1985 Pangloss earned £1.4m before a charge of £0.4m for depreciation; depreciation is singled out because it does not represent a direct cash outflow but an accounting adjustment to the value of fixed assets – some of which are likely to have been bought many years before. Therefore when considering the cash resources available to the company both the level of depreciation and retained profits will be taken into account. The trading surplus net of depreciation gives pre-interest profits – an important indicator of company trading performance – of £1.0m (see Figure 8.6).

Interest charge

The interest charge depends on the amount of loans and overdrafts outstanding, which is an integral part of the financing of the company's assets, rather than of current trading. It is therefore of prime significance to those providing finance whether as lenders or investors. From the point of view of a potential lender, the relation of the interest charge to the level of pre-interest profits gives some indication of the security for loans; in

		GHM
YEAR TO 31 MARCH 1985		
		£m
	Trading surplus (before depreciation)	1.4
Less:	Depreciation	0.4
	Pre-interest profits	1.0
Less:	Interest	0.3
	Pre-tax profits	0.7
Less:	Tax	0.3
	Available to shareholders	0.4

Figure 8.4   Abbreviated profit and loss account of Pangloss PLC

this case with interest at £0.3m he is likely to be deterred by the relatively high ratio of 30 per cent of pre-interest profits (of £1m) already absorbed by interest. From the point of view of the equity investor, this ratio represents the gearing given to the amounts available to ordinary shareholders. Thus if pre-interest profits increase by 70 per cent to £1.7m with interest remaining at £0.3m pre-tax profits will double to £1.4m, while if they fall by 70 per cent, pre-tax profits will be reduced to nil. So the element of gearing offers both opportunity for increasing the return to shareholders where the company is successful and additional risk if trading returns fall. The degree of gearing that investors are prepared to accept varies according to the industrial risk and this must be borne in mind by the company executive when negotiating loans, overdraft facilities or equity finance.

Tax charge

The tax charge depends not only on the rates of tax ruling in the countries where profits are earned, but also any special allowances or grants offered. Where the charge appears abnormal it will be analysed to ascertain whether this is due to temporary or permanent factors. The tax charge shown for Pangloss, however, of £0.3m on £0.7m represents a tax rate only slightly higher than normal. This leaves £0.4m available for distribution to shareholders, which will be evaluated by investors with reference to the number of shares issued.

RETURN TO SHAREHOLDERS

Earnings of £0.4m on 2 million shares (see Figure 8.5) are equivalent to 20p per share in Pangloss. The value of the share is normally directly related to this figure; thus, if the share price is £2 an investor will consider whether it is reasonable to buy or sell the share given that £2 is equivalent to ten times the earnings attributable to that share (that is a p/e ratio of 10). The dividend must also be considered – for long-term investors, this represents the direct return. At a price of £2 the dividend of 10p per share represents a 5 per cent net return on the investment; because tax is already deducted, the dividend is free of tax up to the standard rate in the hands of the recipient. The 5 per cent return is therefore worth 7.0 per cent in gross terms to the standard taxpayer at current rates of tax. Better returns are offered by an investment in gilts. The investor has therefore to judge whether the trading prospects of Pangloss offer scope for this dividend to be steadily increased.

TRADING PROSPECTS

The record of Pangloss will first be examined to assess the management's abilities to secure satisfactory returns. Figure 8.6 shows the ratios normally applied to the results published in the accounts to judge the management's ability in running the trading of the business.

Performance

Figure 8.6 shows Pangloss's performance measured against sales and capital

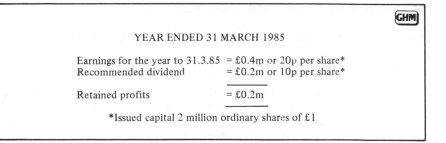

GHM

YEAR ENDED 31 MARCH 1985

Earnings for the year to 31.3.85 = £0.4m or 20p per share*
Recommended dividend = £0.2m or 10p per share*

Retained profits = £0.2m

*Issued capital 2 million ordinary shares of £1

Figure 8.5   Earnings, dividends and retentions of Pangloss PLC

employed. These criteria are used as a guide to management efficiency, as they allow comparison with other companies in the same industry, as well as to the underlying viability of the company. In this table, pre-interest profit (taken because it excludes interest which depends on the method of funding of the capital employed) has advanced by a quarter from £0.8m in 1983 to £1.0m in 1985; with turnover (up from £8m to £9m) and capital employed (up from £10m to £11m) both rising less fast, margins on sales and return on capital have increased over the period. Margins at 11 per cent in 1985 are the same as for the industry as a whole, which therefore indicates normal trading returns and one without volatile fluctuations; return on capital however at 9 per cent is well below the industry level of 11 per cent, indicating that the amount of capital employed is high com-pared with other companies in the industry. Moreover, since the return of 9 per cent falls below the general level of interest rates, it is insufficient to justify the use of new capital in the business; indeed disposal of the existing assets or a change of management – whether through merger or staff recruitment – could be justified in these conditions. For the business cannot justify to its shareholders the employment of funds which could be better invested elsewhere. Thus return on capital forms a key element in the financial assessment of a company; capital in this context however has to be carefully defined and this is considered in detail with reference to the Pangloss balance sheet.

INDUSTRIAL AVERAGE			YEAR ENDED 31 MARCH		
			1983	1984	1985
	a	Pre-interest profit (£m)	0.8	0.9	1.0
	b	Turnover (£m)	8.0	8.0	9.0
11%		Margin on sales a/b	10%	11%	11%
	c	Capital employed (£m)	10.0	11.0	11.0
11%		Return on capital a/c	8%	8%	9%

Figure 8.6   Performance ratios for Pangloss PLC

BALANCE SHEET FOR PANGLOSS PLC

Pangloss's balance sheet is given in abbreviated form in Figure 8.7.

Value of shares

The first point of interest raised by the balance sheet is the book value of the shares. Of the £11m capital employed in Pangloss at the end of the 1985-6 year, £6m is shown to be financed by shareholders' funds giving a book value of £3 each for the 2m shares. (This allows for the assets of the company fetching the £11m shown and thus providing £6m surplus after paying off the debt finance of £5m).

Scope for raising funds

Secondly the balance sheet gives an indication of the scope for raising further finance. In this case with borrowing at £5m against £11m capital employed, it is unlikely that lenders would be interested in advancing further funds to Pangloss. In addition to checking the company's ability to service the interest charge out of current profits, lenders are concerned with the asset backing for loans. It is rare for a company to obtain half its funds from borrowing. Within the £5m debt the £3m 4 per cent debenture explains the relatively low interest charge given in the profit and loss account. However, since it falls to be redeemed in 1986, it can be

		£M	**GHM**
Sources of Finance			
Share capital 2 million ordinary shares of £1		2	
Retained profits		4	
		—	
Shareholders' funds		6	
Debt finance			
4% Debenture 1986	3		
Bank overdraft	2	5	
	—	—	
Total funds		11	
Assets Employed			
Fixed assets			
Property	5		
Machinery	1		
Vehicles	1	7	
Net current assets	—	4	
Total assets		11	

Figure 8.7   Abbreviated 1986 balance sheet for Pangloss PLC

considered, with the bank overdraft, as short-term finance; the refinancing of the debenture could well be at a rate of interest of 10 per cent instead of 4 per cent, increasing the interest charge by £180 000 from £120 000 to £300 000. Thus the funding problems of the Pangloss Company are clearly likely to discourage investors; for shareholders will expect to be asked to contribute further equity finance.

Assets employed

However, close attention must also be paid to the assets shown in the balance sheet, for the value attributed to these assets is critical to measuring the efficiency of the company through the rate of return on capital and the potential debt finance that they can secure. In particular the value given to the property must be considered; for if the book figure represents cost or an out-of-date valuation, the current value may be considerably higher provided the property is freehold or on a long lease. The annual report must therefore be examined for details of the basis of valuation of the property; if the up-to-date value of the Pangloss property was for instance £8m against £5m shown, the total assets employed come to £14m; and with pre-interest profits of £1m, return on capital is little over 7 per cent, indicating that higher rewards could be gained by investing the money in gilt-edged stocks. (This assumes the machinery, vehicles and current assets, which include stocks and debtors net of creditors, raise their book value of £6m.) On the other hand the prospect of raising debt finance is clearly less forbidding; not only does property tend to appreciate but legal rights to it can be granted to lenders. As a result up to two-thirds of the value of the property can commonly be raised by debt finance and, provided it is invested at a rate of return that exceeds the interest charge, this offers opportunities for expansion. Property may make Pangloss attractive as a takeover prospect whether on a break-up basis or on the possibility of improving the present returns.

Assets other than land have to be treated more cautiously; the value of the plant may be minimal on a break-up basis, while current assets, such as debtors and stock, may not fully realize their book values – particularly if the company does not impose sufficient financial control. The trend of these assets to turnover will therefore be examined closely to see whether normal business standards are being achieved. On a forced realization, these assets may recover much less than their book value if standards have not been maintained.

Other information

There is much other information that can be taken from the report, for instance on the extent of capital commitments, or the subsidiaries and associated companies of the group. These do not however affect the key standards applied to the balance sheet and profit and loss account that have been examined here. These standards are used for assessing the company from several standpoints. For the shareholder the attraction of the company may be measured by the trend in earnings per share. Potential lenders will look at the cover for the interest charge, the proportion of capital funded by loans and the type of security offered. Management will be assessed by the margin on sales and return on capital that it has secured. The significance of the information given in the annual report is therefore of fundamental importance to a company in any assessment of its financial standing and the efficiency of its management.

INFLATION ACCOUNTING

As inflation is becoming more and more an accepted part of the economic environment, considerable attention has been paid to adjusting company results to take this factor into account. A simple approach is to charge to the profit and loss account the amount that is required to maintain the real value of the equity base.

However, a more complex approach is to apply adjustments to the profit and loss account that reflect the rate of change of prices experienced by each company in its existing business, rather than the general rate of inflation – as represented, for instance, in the changes in the retail price index. The purpose of this approach is to identify the success of the company in maintaining its business activities rather than providing for the equity base to be maintained.

FURTHER READING

Firth, M., *The Valuation of Shares and the Efficient Markets Theory*, Macmillan, London, 1977

Hay D., and Morris, D., *Industrial Economics: Theory and Evidence*, Oxford University Press, 1979

How to Read a Balance Sheet, ILO, Geneva, 1975

Merrett, A.J., and Sykes, A., *The Finance and Analysis of Capital Projects*, Longman, London, 1973

Reid, W., and Myddelton, D.R., *The Meaning of Company Accounts*, 3rd edition, Gower, Aldershot, 1982

Rockley, L.E., *The Meaning of Balance Sheets and Company Reports*, Business Books, London, 1975

9 Budgetary control

Alan R Leaper

All businesses have some form of budgetary control in existence whether or not they recognize it or call it by that name. Someone in the organization co-ordinates the resources of the business in some degree to achieve some sort of plan, but whether they examine alternative plans, ideal criterion and harmony of objectives is possibly another question.

There are many benefits to be derived from the introduction of a formalized budgetary control system among which are:

1 It defines the objectives of an organization as a whole and in financial terms
2 It provides yardsticks by which to measure efficiency for various parts of the organization
3 It reveals the extent by which actual results have varied from the defined objective
4 It provides a guide for corrective action
5 It facilitates centralized control with delegated responsibility.

The disadvantages of a formalized procedure are by no means so readily identifiable; in general terms they usually concern the following:

1 The additional costs/personnel necessary to perform the function
2 The suspicions aroused by its introduction that it is merely another vehicle to implement cost reduction programmes
3 The complacency of paper work becoming routine with the eventual possibility that little notice or action is taken.

Immediate benefits should not be expected from the introduction of a budget procedure. It may take a year or two to educate those concerned in the proper compilation of the data required and in the proper application of the data subsequently made available.

WHAT IS A BUDGET?

A budget, in business planning, is the expression in financial (and rather summarized) terms of a comprehensive short-term operational plan for a business entity. The financial numbers relate to specific action programmes, which give rise to asset acquisitions and disposals, the earning of revenues and the incurring of expenditure. A budget in which these financial numbers have been 'pulled out of the air' is worse than useless.

Many alternative plans may be considered before the final one showing the most practical profit is chosen. Executives and other responsible officials from all functions of the company must contribute towards the plan. Data in the unit terms of each of the functions concerned must be collected and translated into monetary terms. For example, the sales manager is primarily concerned with units of the finished article or service and he would therefore contribute the volume and models to be included in the plan. The production manager talks in standard hours and efficiencies. The personnel manager will be responsible for the levels of wage rates, absenteeism factors, welfare schemes, etc. The chief executive must be fully convinced of the benefits to be derived from the plan and really believe in it.

Budgetary control is the process of managing these facets – planning and co-ordinating all functions so that they work in harmony and control performances and costs. It establishes the responsibility, throughout the corporate structure, of all managers for achieving the company's budgeted objectives. It entails measuring at suitable intervals how the plan is actually progressing and, if divergencies are occurring, taking the necessary corrective action to ensure that the company gets back on course again.

By having a budget built up in this manner it is possible to fix responsibility at every level of the organization – and this is important.

Most managements have found that it is not sufficient to face the problems of a business on a day-to-day basis or even on a year-to-year basis; medium-term operational (or programme) planning is therefore carried out over a time-horizon of three to five years ahead. Generally, such planning involves a projection of the total market for the company's products and an assessment of what the company's share of that market should be, based on historical performance and management objectives. Obviously the degree of accuracy of the projections and plans varies with the period covered. As a matter of fact, in view of the many uncertainties involved in projecting activities over, say, a three-year period, the usual procedure is to prepare plans for the first year in considerable detail, i.e., the Budget, and then to resort to summary projections for the remaining two years. As each year's plan is done, refinements are made on the basis of recent experience and a new third year is added.

BUDGET CENTRES

Efficient control requires acceptance that costs are best controlled at the point where they are incurred. The transport manager should therefore control the transport department's cost. But the control span of any one person should not be unduly large. The area controlled by an individual is known as a *budget centre*, defined by the Institute of Cost and Management Accountants as 'A section of the organization of the undertaking defined for the purposes of budgetary control.'

Budgets prepared at a given level of budget centre are then consolidated at the next level up (profit centre, division or company, as the case may be). A substantial business organization will generally comprise a number of operating units, each with primary responsibility for its own profits and cash flow (profit centres) as well, perhaps, as its own capital investment (investment centres). Thus a business may include several profit centres which, in larger organizations, may be grouped into investment centres or divisions. Every division will normally have its own financial controller, responsible for preparing the divisional master budget (see the following section of this chapter). Larger profit centres may also employ their own management accountants, who prepare draft profit and loss and cash budgets. Within each budget centre there may be other smaller areas to which costs are attributable: for example, it may be desirable to identify and control groups of trucks in a transport department. Such a smaller area of control is defined as a *cost centre*, which the Institute of Cost and Management Accountants describes as 'A location, person or item of equipment, or a group of these, in or connected with an undertaking in relation to which costs may be ascertained and used for purposes of cost control.'

Within each budget centre, only one person should be responsible for incurring costs. Ultimate responsibility for budgetary control lies with the chief executive.

COMPILING A BUDGET

There is really no established order in which budgets should be prepared provided all parts are geared into a common factor. This is generally the principal limiting or bottleneck factor which varies for each individual company.

Most companies tend to establish a sales target determined on market potential and their share of the market as the basis of their budgets. Many others prefer to establish their production capacity and plan a budget to ensure the full utilization of available equipment. The ideal, of course, is to achieve a harmony of both of these important items. However, there are many other factors which may determine the level of activity to be budgeted, amongst which are insufficient cash to finance expansion, a scarce raw material, and, possibly, the non-availability of skilled labour.

Having established the basis for compiling the budget all known external factors which could have a bearing on its fulfilment must be examined – national wage awards, sales taxes, credit squeezes, the movement of purchase prices, etc.

In larger organizations a budget committee is usually formed to review these items and determine, as best it can, the likely effect they will have on business during the period to be used in the budget. Having determined these external factors, the budget accountant/committee would advise functional and departmental managers of their effects and provide guidelines for the compilation of the subsidiary departmental budgets, the main examples of which are considered below.

Sales budget

The sales budget should show total sales, expressed both by value and quantity. It may be further analysed by product, by area, by customer and, of course, by seasonal pattern of expected sales. The main problems arise in determining quantities and in the calculation of standard prices. Constraints such as competitive activity have to be borne in mind (new products and aggressive pricing policies).

The budget should be compiled by the sales manager. He will seek the opinions of his salesmen and use any statistical forecasting techniques arising from market research. Other considerations include general business and economic conditions, company advertising policy, new products, supplies, product demand and plant capacity. A special pricing study is usually helpful at this stage, and this should show the complete product range, the relevant market sector, competitive models or products (taking into account both the pricing and the features available), introduction dates, discount structures and advertising strategy. In some cases, when jobbing production is involved, budgets must be made in terms of the expected sales value only.

Production budget

The production budget is a statement of the output by product, and is generally expressed in standard hours. It should take into consideration the sales budget, plant capacity, whether stocks are to be increased or decreased and outside purchases. The form the production budget would take depends on circumstances. Usually, the quantities are shown for each department (budget centre) and information is taken from machine loading charts, material specifications, time schedules and other production or time-study records.

When computing labour cost, the average labour rate used depends on the wage plan in effect. For hourly rated employees not on incentive bonuses, an overall plant rate may be sufficient. In other cases, departmental or labour grade rates may be used. When a straight piece rate plan is in force, the labour cost is the amount paid per unit produced. When other incentive plans are used, labour rates have to be computed to include estimated amounts for bonus payments. In companies using standard costs, cost accounting records can be very useful in determining budget requirements for non-productive direct labour. Many cost accounting systems are sophisticated enough to indicate the breakdown of non-productive direct labour into down time, waiting time, changeover or set-up time, etc.

The plant manager will prepare the production budget in close collaboration with accountants, production engineers, work study engineers and other key personnel. Adequate lead times for the delivery of new equipment and the development of new processes must be considered.

At this stage, the sales and production budgets should be compared to ensure maximum utilization of capacity aligned to satisfactory sales growth. If the sales budget exceeds production capacity, then decisions on capital expenditure and new plant may be required before proceeding further. If, on the other hand, significant under-utilization of capacity is denoted, decisions on how best to use this spare capacity must be taken (to determine, for example, if sub-contract work would be profitable, if a revised pricing structure could increase the volume of sales, or if plant should be declared surplus and sold off or scrapped, etc.).

Production costs budget

This supplementary budget should determine the 'cost of sales' allied to the required production.

Generally, by far the largest element in cost terms is direct material. This part should be compiled by the chief buyer in conjunction with the production manager. Using the sales and production budgets, it will determine the requirements of raw material and piece-parts, period by period, to meet the output, and will be evaluated in cash cost terms. Considerations should take into account bulk buying, delivery periods, stock holding, suppliers' credit terms and trade discounts, as well as recognizing any changes in material specifications, new model introductions, etc. In timing the purchase of raw materials, piece-parts etc., consideration must be given to the necessity to keep inventory levels to the very minimum and thereby not tie up valuable capital. Special competitive pricing exercises should be undertaken from potential suppliers to ensure that costs are strictly controlled and keen.

Direct labour is another most important element of production costs. The work study department should be called upon to establish standard times for individual units. These may then be evaluated by the required volumes and converted into direct labour requirements. The degree of labour efficiency must be determined, as must the type of employee necessary, that is, male/female; skilled/semi-skilled/unskilled.

Direct expense budgets covering warehousing, transportation, warranty and special tools should be determined by the appropriate managers responsible for incurring or approving the respective expenses.

Factory overhead costs (burden) should be established by departmental foremen and consolidated by the production manager. Expenses of all types should be considered and some assistance may be necessary from the finance department in determining depreciation, insurance and other expenses possibly beyond the control of the local foremen.

Personnel budget

This is a headcount schedule of the total labour requirements necessary to carry out the sales and production budgets and, in fact, run the whole business from managing director to office boy and production worker to office cleaner. It should be prepared by the personnel department in conjunction with all other functional departmental heads.

The schedule will show the number of personnel required, the hours to be worked, wage rates, salaries etc., and should be built up by departments. The respective costs should, of course, be incorporated in the applicable departmental budgets. The recruitment and training policies of the company will be incorporated in the budget and cognizance should be taken of all labour-related costs – for example, national insurance, and pension schemes.

Operating and service department budgets

The type of department falling into this category may be administration, finance, selling, advertising and service, and might also include warehousing and shipping. The departmental head of each of these functions will be responsible for compiling his individual budget. The data included will cover personnel requirements by number and grade and be cost-determined in conjunction with the personnel manager; and departmental running costs detailed by account, namely utilities, operating expenses, depreciation, insurance, rates, etc.

Special note should be taken of competitors' activity in determining the size and use of the advertising budget.

If raw material or bulk purchases are necessary, the usage and cost of these will be planned with the purchasing agent or chief buyer.

The basis of determining costs included in these budgets invariably depends on the actual trend in previous years adjusted, of course, for known changes. It should also be remembered that historical costs will include inefficiencies and these must be identified and determined if likely to continue. The considered effects of volume and activity should also be borne in mind.

Capital expenditure budget

This supplementary budget is usually compiled by senior management in conjunction with engineering and technical services.

The budget will show details of the capital expenditure proposals in the period of the master budget and will probably be prepared for a number of years because of its longer-term implications. Items included will be distinguished by the various types of asset – land, buildings, equipment, furniture, etc., and should also state the reasons for proposals – replacement, new methods, capacity, etc.

Back-up data should also accompany the proposals to justify the expenditures, and will take the usual forms of capital evaluations, such as return on investment and discounted cash flow analysis. The strain on cash resources should also be considered when compiling this budget.

Profit and loss account

The first component of the master budget is the budgeted profit and loss account. This budget will summarize the effects of all the relevant data contained in the supplementary operating and service budgets, sales, purchasing, personnel and capital expenditure (depreciation, salvage receipts) budgets. It will be prepared in months or other chosen periods and be compiled by the financial controller. A sample profit and loss statement incorporating provisions for budget and standards is shown in Figure 9.1.

Cash budget

The second component of the master budget is the cash budget, which is critical in view of the possible constraints that an unsatisfactory cash availability position may have on the required expansion of a business and hence on the acceptability of the master budget as a whole.

The financial controller, with the assistance of all other management, should determine the timing by period, usually monthly, of production, sales, fixed asset purchases etc., and then prepare the effects on the cash balance. The reason for this budget is to determine by period where additional cash may be required or where surplus cash may be available for short-term investments.

The income side is built up from the sales and debtors budget plus any other miscellaneous receipts, such as loans, new capital, sale of assets, grants, interest, etc. On the expenditure side will be the incurred expenses of the production and service department budgets, purchasing and capital expenditure budgets plus other payments relating to the distribution of profits, such as dividends and income taxes.

Balance sheet

The third component of the master budget is the projected balance sheet which will show the net effect of the budgets on the financial position of the company. Again, being compiled by the financial controller, it will consider information contained in the budgeted profit and loss account, capital expenditures and cash and the related movement of the working capital and financing.

Management must examine these results of the profit and loss, cash and balance sheet master budgets that result from the consolidation of the subsidiary budgets and determine if they are acceptable. Do they show the most practical overall profit to be accepted as a plan for the ensuing year or period to be budgeted? If the answer is negative then the problem areas should be determined and the departments concerned advised specifically of their short-comings. As all the budgets are mainly interrelated, such

	Budget	%	Standard	%	Actual	%	Variance
Current Month							
Gross Sales							
Less: Deductions from sales							
Total Net Sales							
Manufacturing Standard Costs							
Material							
Labour							
Burden							
Direct expense							
Total Standard Costs							
Standard Manufacturing Gross Profit							
Budget and Volume Variances							
Actual Manufacturing Gross Profit							
Expenses							
Selling							
Advertising							
Administrative							
Engineering							
Total Expenses							
Operating Profit							
Net Profit Before Taxes							
Income Tax Provision							
Net Profit							

GHM

Figure 9.1   Example of a profit and loss statement with provision for budgets and standards

a change generally means the re-submission of all the subsidiary budgets. Whilst this exercise may appear to be rather long-winded and even time-wasting, it is one of the real values of preparing budgets in this manner in that the consideration, discussion and communication of the short-term profit objective of the company involves all levels of management in its achievement, and by this process is most likely to reveal the maximum practical profit objective for the company.

In practice, a lot of companies tend to take either sales or production in isolation and agree independently what the level of activity should be in these fields; once decided on, they proceed to build all the other budgets around them. If the resultant profit is in excess of the outlook for the current year, they are happy to leave it as such. However, assuming that the job is to be tackled properly, it is at this stage of review that any attempts at over-budgeting or, worse still, conservative budgeting, should be weeded out. The level of responsibility for performance of the plan from each manager should be agreed upon, so that he fully commits himself to its attainment.

When the master budgets have been finally agreed upon and accepted, they should be adopted formally by management as its policy and plan for the forthcoming year or period and thereby provide a budget against which performance or achievement will be measured.

CONTROLLING THE PLAN

As indicated, budgets are built up by responsibility. It follows, therefore, that operating statements will be prepared to each budget centre involved. These operating statements should form part of the management information system used to control actual performance against the budget plan.

Good budgetary control follows the theory of 'management by exception'. Whilst management is provided with full details of expenditure, sales, production, etc., under its functional control, reports and information should be focused on matters that are adverse, or that show an unusual favourable variance, so that its energy is concentrated in the right direction and its effort is not being diluted with a lot of information which merely indicates that things are going as planned.

There are differing schools of thought on the amount of detail that should be provided to management. Some management accountants prefer to provide only data over which managers have some degree of control. For instance, if depreciation policy is decided by the board, there is no point in giving an operational manager a depreciation charge for, say, the machine shop. He has no control over what that charge will be; according to this theory, this information is unnecessary and does not help him to perform his part of the plan under normal conditions. This theory does not give management the full picture and lacks the important benefit of enabling management to see the overall effect and contribution of its department to the business as a whole. The statement may be broken down into two sections labelled 'controllable' and 'uncontrollable'. Just what is controllable or uncontrollable can be surprising. For example, a shop foreman shown a list of fixed assets in his area on which there is a depreciation charge may well indicate items of equipment which are surplus to his requirements but for which he has not bothered to raise a disposal request. These items can then be removed from the department, sold with good salvage values being obtained, valuable floor space being released, routine maintenance checks ceasing and administration time and effort being saved in searching for and identifying equipment at physical inventory time.

Timing of feedback

Timing is of great importance. When should the measurement of control be effected, and over what period? Having decided what period the budget is to cover (usually annual) the budget itself will be divided into sub-periods: possibly months and quarters, or perhaps into thirteen four-weekly intervals, depending on the type of business. In addition to the detailed annual budget, most companies have some form of long-range planning for a number of years ahead covering, for instance, the profit and loss account, balance sheet, cash flow and capital expenditure.

This longer-term planning concerns itself primarily with determining whether or not the internal fund flow of the business will cover its commitments and capital expenditure programme, etc., but of course the longer-term plans will not be prepared in anything like the same detail as the yearly short-term operating budget. It is a matter of individual company requirements to determine which data is best controlled on a quarterly, monthly, weekly or even daily basis.

An organization must generally have a fairly sophisticated accounting system to generate and disseminate information on a daily basis and this type of data is generally confined to production data. Standard hours produced, finished units, efficiencies, absenteeism, etc., all lend themselves to daily control. Billings in terms of unit sales and value would best be reviewed on a weekly basis, although for local consumption this, again, may be preferred on a rough daily basis.

All other profit and loss and cash flow data would be embodied in monthly financial statements. A balance sheet could be prepared on a quarterly basis.

Whatever is right for a business must be determined by the constraints within which it works and what is needed to control the situation. Normally, data of a daily and weekly nature are restricted to middle management to facilitate operational control and are not fed through the pyramid of top management unless a special situation demands such close control. As a general rule, the lower down the management line one goes, the sooner information should be in management's hands. The foreman should have his output in standard hours measured against budget and his material usage for his batch of machines during the following morning so that he can take the necessary action to correct any deviation from his target.

Thus it has been said that this first-line information is the life blood of the business, and the accounting results which follow at the end of the month confirm and quantify an already known situation.

FLEXIBLE BUDGETS

One criticism sometimes levelled at budgetary control is its rigidity. In practice, actual results may be the outcome of circumstances which have changed from those existing when the budget was first prepared. Budgets, when set and agreed upon, can only be based on one set of circumstances. As actual conditions seldom equate with budgeted conditions, the difference between actual costs and budgeted costs must be demonstrated. Information should therefore be available to suggest the appropriate level of expenses, generally known as budget standards, which fluctuate at varying levels of production activity or sales volume.

Flexible budgetary control (as opposed to fixed budgeting) was introduced to control this situation. Flexible budgeting is applied in businesses where it is impossible to make a firm forecast of future conditions. Although fixed budgeting should be satisfactory for the more stable industries, these are very few and far between. Flexible budgeting is more widely applicable.

Flexible budgeting is designed to provide a more realistic picture of the variance between actual expenses and budgeted expenses. One expects to be able to distinguish that part of the variance which is due to volume and for which a manager will not have control, and that part of the variance over which the manager should have control. To achieve this, one must be in a position to calculate budget standards at varying levels of activity.

The application of this calculation is demonstrated below by considering first a report on the basis of fixed budgeting and then showing a similar report calculated on a flexible budgeting basis. Before looking at these reports, it must be clear that costs are classified for flexible budgeting purposes. This in itself is a most difficult task and one that may be tackled in many ways which cannot be amplified in this chapter. However, for the purpose of this exercise, the following broad categories are used:

Expense type	Budget (£)	Actual (£)	Variance (£)
Material	10 000	12 500	+ 2500
Labour	5 000	5 900	+ 900
Rent	3 000	3 000	—
Salaries	1 000	1 100	+ 100
GHM	19 000	22 500	+3500

Figure 9.2 Example of fixed budgeting

1 Fixed costs – costs which do not vary in the short term with volume
2 Variable costs – costs which do so vary
3 Semi-variable costs – costs which will vary with volume but not in direct relationship.

The later chapter on cost accounting gives more details of these types of costs: of course, if standard costing is already applied in the company, the setting of a flexible budget is rendered considerably easier. If standard costs are not available, the technique of marginal costing will need to be applied in dealing with individual costs to determine the degree of variability. Scatter graphs or the regression theory may be used. Figure 9.2 is based on fixed budgeting and demonstrates how much the actual is off target. This type of measurement is an improvement on, say, measuring against last year's performance when circumstances may have been different. The report provides some conception of the amount by which actual experience varies from budgeted plans.

However, if one is to adhere to one of the basic principles of budgetary control, that people should only be responsible for cost over which they have control, this report may not provide the solution.

Figure 9.3 applies similar information but is calculated on the basis of flexible budgeting. Thus, clearly, the advantages of flexible budgeting are demonstrated by the second report. It shows in reality that instead of the manager being responsible for an adverse variance of £3500 as he was in the first report, he is, in fact, only responsible for the adverse variance of £500, the remaining £3000 being due to increased volume in production which may be the result of conservative sales forecasting, or some other factor which must be taken up with some other department in the organization.

GHM		Budget			Actual	Variance Analysis	
	Standard per unit	Fixed budget	Flexed budget			Control-able	Volume
Output in units		10 000	12 000	12 000		—	+ 2 000
% of original budget		100%	120%	120%		—	+ 20%
		£	£	£	£	£	£
Variable Costs							
Material	£1.00	10 000	12 000	12 500		+ 500	+ 2 000
Labour	£0.50	5 000	6 000	5 900		– 100	+ 1 000
Fixed Costs							
Rent		3 000	3 000	3 000		—	—
Salaries		1 000	1 000	1 100		+ 100	—
TOTAL		19 000	22 000	22 500		+ 500	+ 3 000

Figure 9.3 **Example of flexible budgeting**

Flexible budgeting is thus extremely useful for getting behind the causes of variances, particularly if quantities, as well as costs, have been budgeted. With sales variances, for example, one can determine whether the variance is due to prices, volume, outlet mixture, product mixture, or a combination of these.

USE OF COMPUTERS

Generally, manual methods of making the planning computations are time-consuming, with the result that only a few alternative plans of operation can be fully evaluated when setting a budget and analysis of variances may be limited by time constraints. Computerized financial models have been developed to assist in simulating what the results would be under many different assumptions as to volume, products and plans of operation. Most steps in budgeting usually involve some alternative assumptions or decisions, and the final outcome of the budget process can vary greatly in terms of the profits and resources which will result from each assumption or decision. As a practical matter, the burden of making the planning and budgeting computations, under even one set of assumptions, is generally considered to be all that a company can expect its people to carry in addition to their current operating responsibilities. Very often the work is such that deadlines are missed and budgets for the new year are not available on time. The computerized financial model takes the drudgery out of the computations, once the computer programs are prepared, by applying the given relationships to different sets of assumptions and conditions. This process of simulating different methods of operations is a big help in exploring the alternatives available in the planning process.

ZERO-BASE BUDGETING

Zero-base budgeting is a technique for short-term operational planning, whereby existing levels of expenditure on ongoing activities are systematically questioned. This is in contrast to the more common 'incremental' approach. In incremental budgeting, the benchmark tends to be the level of activity and expenditure in the immediate past, budget proposals being related to this in terms of 'more' or 'less'. In zero-base budgeting, the benchmark is the 'minimum survival' level of activity and expenditure as seen by the manager of the activity in question. If the budget proposal is only to maintain the existing level of activity, assuming this to be above the 'minimum survival' level, the proposal must explain why the additional expenditure involved over and above the 'minimum survival' level is justified. A manager in charge of several activities will be required to state which level of expenditure on each of these activities he would choose if he could only spend, say, 80 per cent of his budget. The point of this approach is to squeeze out 'budget slack' at the lower levels of decision-making and to allow the senior levels to decide how, if at all, the balance of the budget will be spent.

INSTALLING THE SYSTEM

The organizational chart should be examined with a view to determining where the responsibility for sales, costs and profits really lies. Revisions, where appropriate, may be considered at this time. The organization structure should be so developed as to fix responsibility right down the line. There must be an organization chart which clearly defines the levels of responsibility and the chain of command, setting out who is responsible for what and to whom. It is desirable to support each functional position with a job description defining the function, duty and responsibility. Tradition must be ignored, responsibility and control being given to those who are responsible for taking the decisions, but care must be taken to preserve the 'business flair' of an organization, and those given the responsibility should be placed where their individual resources can be best used.

The key factors should then be determined before designing the system most suitable to the company's needs. The system design should cover flow diagrams of the information generated, collection data necessary for budget preparation and control reports to be subsequently prepared. During this period consideration should be given to the level of sophistication of the existing information system, whether the proposed system will provide an improvement and also the level of human resources with which one has to work the new system.

Having obtained a positive reaction to these considerations, the next step is to test the initial design with various personnel at all levels in order to determine its suitability to meet their requirements for management information.

Once initial design is finalized, the next step is to prepare a series of seminars and teach-ins to explain the thinking behind the purpose and operation of the system. Questions, constructive criticisms and improvements should be invited so that all are involved and communicate at all levels.

A timetable for installation of the programme should be established. A critical path analysis is the ideal basis for identifying the order in which the budget data should be collected and which information is to be cross-referred to two or more departments.

Now is the time for the collection of information for the 'first budget'. Considerable time, assistance and guidance should be made available to staff at this stage, and perseverance on behalf of those taking responsibility for the installation of the system will be required. It is vital that all levels of management go through the discipline of thinking through and preparing their portion of the budgets. Miracles should not be expected from the first results. It is not unusual for a company to take two or three years to get a control system of this nature fully operational. However, at each stage one should expect to produce some results which are usable even in the first year. What these results will be may differ from company to company but initially they usually provide a good insight to sales and cash flow data. An important by-product is management education and awareness of what the business is all about.

Budget period

There is no general rule governing the selection of a period of time for a budget. This will be decided by the particular circumstances of the business. For instance the fashion industry must, of necessity, have a very short budget period, sometimes of three or four months' duration, whereas in the shipbuilding industry a budget may range over three or four years. For most businesses, however, the calendar year is normally the accepted period: it is broken down into twelve monthly periods and the information is complementary to the published accounts.

However, if there is a strong seasonal influence affecting sales, it is sometimes prudent to have a 'model year' upon which to base the budget and this usually starts just ahead of the main selling period. Businesses which rely mainly on the summer or Christmas trade may well justify a model year. Model years, as the name implies, usually commence with the introduction of new models. A car manufacturer, for example, may run its model year from September to the following August in order to have a good start to the year following the autumn motor shows and new year car registrations. The motive behind this is that if business has not gone as well as expected there is still sufficient time before the end of the model year to curtail activity, restrict costs and reconsider expansion programmes or introduce special promotions in order to keep profits in line with, or better than, budget.

Budget manual

It is helpful to have such a document available within the company so that there is no ambiguity about what is required of each individual in relation to budgets. The type of information one might expect the budget manual to contain is a brief explanation of the purposes of budgetary control as practised within the company and organization charts and job descriptions showing quite specifically the budget responsibilities for each function; routing of budgetary control forms for collection and control documentation; timetables or programmes for completion of budgets and control data feedback; budget periods; samples of reports and statements to be employed and accounts classification and coding data.

Budget committees

The question of who should control the preparation of budgets and who should review these controls is one that each organization arrives at during some stage of the budget preparation.

It is desirable that top and middle management contribute to and agree levels of activity to be budgeted, although it must be recognized that the human factor involved makes this difficult to achieve. A keen manager, anxious to please at a budget review meeting, will possibly incorporate a stretch element to his plan. Another manager setting his own targets against which his performance is to be measured may be inclined to be over-cautious (particularly if an achievement bonus is paid). Investigations have been made in this area and the results carry important lessons for the business man interested in making the most of his budget system. One conclusion is that the budgets studied were used as pressure devices for constantly increasing efficiency, but because of the effects on people, the budgets tended to generate a long-run result of decreased efficiency. Naturally enough, this is attributed to the lack of participation in the budget preparation phase by those being budgeted and to the lack of sales ability on the part of the accounting personnel. Another study concludes that successful budgeting is more concerned with human relationships than with accounting techniques and that if good principles of human relationships are applied, successful budget practices become inevitable. Yet another appraisal of current business budgeting indicates that important weaknesses in practice are the result of superficial appreciation of budget concepts by management, inadequate techniques, and the absence of a disciplined environment in many organizations. Upon reflection, it becomes apparent that the requirements for a successful budget operation are not restricted to accounting or finance planning techniques but that successful managers are those who keep such considerations in mind while executing the more mechanical aspects of the budget process.

There are various views held on this point. If operating managements are made responsible for profits, then one of the objectives of budgetary control, that is, the proper co-ordination of the organization, is achieved.

The same processes should be involved as with the control aspect. What an organization should attempt to achieve is the total commitment of all levels of management to the plan. Each level of management should review its plans and performances through the usual management committees, be they formal or informal groupings, right up to the chief executive, and the overall objective should be clear and unambiguous at each stage.

However, one person will be responsible for pulling together the various parts of the master budget. This job usually falls on the chief accountant or financial controller or his department. Larger companies employ a budget manager and, of course, this co-ordinating exercise naturally falls into his lap. He may be called upon to undertake a number of exercises to determine what the various results thrown up mean within the overall company objectives, but it must be emphasized that his role is one of support. The responsibility is fixed upon the persons committing and accepting stewardship over resources.

The budget organization can be regarded as analogous to a telephone company operating an important communications system; it is responsible for the speed, accuracy and clarity with which the messages flow through the system, but not for the content of the messages themselves.

Information codes

Budgetary control has extended control information beyond the more traditional accounting information to broader aspects of control, setting out data in terms of hours worked, output of production in standard hours, information on market share, quality of product, etc. This is all necessary for the achievement of the plan. However, looking at the pure accounting contribution to budgetary control, a suitable system of accounts coding should be designed so that the information is collected and analysed within the budget and cost centres.

The accounting code should be what is commonly called a subjective/objective system. The subjective part of the code should qualify information into its primary or traditional classification, that is, the nature of the expenses, for example, wages, fuel, rent, etc. The objective part of the code will be used to analyse the expenditure to the cost and burden centres, that is machine X in the machine shop.

It is important to give considerable thought to the design of the coding system, as it should not only be able to cope with existing needs for information, but also have the flexibility to be expanded to meet future demands. A system of this sort should enable a company, using the subjective code, to produce information necessary for the preparation of the traditional statutory accounts. And by going through the objective section of the code, the information required for budgetary control and management accounting can be produced which should be made available to those drawing up the budgets as appropriate.

CONCLUSIONS

Budgetary control often strikes apprehension or fear into non-financial people. People tend to be sceptical or untrusting of having their performances measured against a standard. This is a human and understandable response. Most people, at some time during their careers, have had budgetary control used against them as a cost reduction tool.

It is up to finance managers to clarify and emphasize that budget flexing and control is an essential and deliberate need of modern-day management. It is a management tool designed as a *fair* basis upon which to measure performance against a predetermined plan, and conduct business in the most efficient manner possible, thereby improving profitability.

FURTHER READING

Batty, J., *Corporate Planning and Budgetary Control*, Macdonald & Evans, London
Cave, S.R., *Budgetary Control and Standard Costing*, 3rd edition, Gee, London, 1973
Willsmore, A.W., *Business Budgets in Practice*, 5th edition, Pitman, London, 1973

10 Working capital and management ratios

Leon Simons

LIQUIDITY

The working capital of a company is its net current assets, which are its current assets less the current liabilities. In modern balance sheets current liabilities are termed 'Creditors – amounts falling due within one year'. In the balance sheet of Standard plc (Figure 10.1) the working capital is seen to be £1 406 000 (at line 11), being £5 675 000 − £4 269 000 (line 9 − line 10).

The amount of working capital indicates the liquidity of a company. Two management ratios are commonly used to express the degree of liquidity. One of these is the current ratio, which is simply the current assets divided by the current liabilities. The current ratio for Standard plc (Figure 10.1) is therefore $\frac{5675}{4269}$ = approximately 1.3.

Some accountants consider that it is more useful to ignore the value of inventories when looking at liquidity, since these could take considerably longer to convert to cash than debtors or creditors. These accountants feel that it is more pertinent to compare the quick assets (current assets minus inventories) with the current liabilities. This is known either as the quick ratio, or the acid test ratio. Again taking the balance sheet of Standard plc as an example, the calculation of the quick ratio is as follows:

$$\frac{\text{quick assets (lines } 6 + 7 + 8)}{\text{current liabilities (line 10)}} = \frac{3389}{4269} = 0.79$$

There is no generally ideal current ratio, since companies differ so greatly from each other. A current ratio of 1.3 may be appropriate for a light manufacturing group with a short production cycle (like Standard plc). The same ratio, however, may be too low for a company with a longer cycle and a proportionately bigger stock investment. On the other hand, a

GHM

STANDARD plc

CONSOLIDATED BALANCE SHEET
at 31st March 1985

			1985 £'000	1984 £'000
	Fixed assets			
1	Tangible assets	10	6697	5014
2	Investments	11	1406	365
3			8103	5379
4	**Advance corporation tax**		175	151
	Current assets			
5	Stocks	12	2286	1852
6	Debtors	13	3269	2693
7	Short-term deposits		—	250
8	Cash at bank		120	206
9			5675	5001
	Creditors			
10	Amounts falling due within one year	14	4269	4616
11	**Net current assets**		1406	385
12	**Total assets less current liabilities**		9684	5915
	Creditors			
13	Amounts falling due after more than one year	15	89	1214
14	**Provisions for deferred taxation**	16	380	300
15			9215	4401
	Capital and reserves			
16	Called-up share capital	17	1944	1392
17	Share premium	18	3277	151
18	Capital reserve	18	697	697
19	Retained profit	18	3297	2161
20	**Shareholder's funds**		9215	4401

Figure 10.1 Annual accounts of Standard plc – balance sheet

137

supermarket with no work in progress (because it does not manufacture) and no debtors (because its business is purely cash) would very likely have a current ratio of less than one. In other words, it would have current liabilities which exceeded its current assets.

One should try neither to maximize nor to minimize the liquidity ratios. One should try to optimize them in relation to the objective, which in the case of a commercial public company is the maximization of profit on capital employed. The lower the liquidity ratios are, the more vulnerable the company is to pressure from creditors which it is unable to meet. The

---

STANDARD plc GHM

CONSOLIDATED PROFIT AND LOSS ACCOUNT
for the year ended 31st March 1985

Line		Notes	1985 £'000	1984 £'000
1	**Turnover**	1	15220	13124
2	Cost of sales		10083	8544
3			5137	4580
4	Distribution and administration expenses	2	2958	2799
5	**Operating profit**		2179	1781
6	Associate companies		56	
7	Investment income	3	46	50
8	Interest payable	4	(81)	(233)
9	**Profit on ordinary activities before taxation**		2200	1598
10	Taxation	6	533	428
11	**Profit on ordinary activities after taxation**		1667	1170
12	Extraordinary income less taxation	7	70	111
13	Profit for the year		1737	1281
14	Dividends	8	583	350
15	Retained profit for the year		1154	931
	Profit for year retained by:			
	Holding company		576	411
	Subsidiaries		522	520
	Associates		56	–
			1154	931
16	Earnings per ordinary share	9	9.05p	7.52p

Figure 10.2   Annual accounts of Standard plc – profit and loss

higher the liquidity ratios, the more the capital is not being fully exploited in terms of the return earned on it. One should seek, therefore, to have as little working capital as is consistent with not being unduly vulnerable to pressure from creditors. This ideal level of liquidity would vary not only from company to company, but through time within one company, as conditions changed.

STOCK

Excess stockholding has an adverse effect on liquidity. The ratio used for assessing stock level is the stock/turnover ratio. The stock/turnover ratio for Standard plc is found as follows:

$$\frac{\text{stock (line 5, Figure 10.1)}}{\text{turnover (line 1, Figure 10.2)}} = \frac{2\ 286}{15\ 220} = 0.15$$

On its own, this ratio has little significance but, as with most other management ratios, it can be used to monitor changes through time. Standard's stock/turnover ratio of 0.15 could be expressed instead as a proportion of a year which, in their case, is 8 weeks. We do not know if 8 weeks' average stock is too high or too low, or how great a deviation there is around the average. Like liquidity, stockholding has to be balanced: it should neither be maximized nor minimized, but optimized in terms of profit. Too much stock means that the money tied up in it is costing more than it is contributing. Too little stock means that the cost of lost sales (owing to stocks not being available to meet orders) exceeds the savings made by not holding the additional stock.

There are other factors to be considered in deciding the optimum stock level. For example, are there additional costs attributable to holding increased stock rather than just the interest on the capital? If the stock level were to be reduced by a given amount, would the company then be able to vacate a warehouse, with consequent savings in rates, rent, insurance, heating, etc? How many storemen could be dismissed or redeployed?

Stock appreciation should also be brought into account. If the company uses volatile commodities it might save a great deal of money by holding more than its immediate requirements of a material whose market price is expected to rise during the period covered by the holding. This saving could far outweigh the extra stocking costs and throw in, as a bonus, freedom from the danger of being caught out of stock.

The stock ratio is not ideal in a number of respects. First, the turnover is at selling prices, while the stock is at cost. Second, the turnover covers a period, while the stock is quoted at a point in time which may not be typical of that period. Third, the cost of the stock is not factual but is a function of the company's costing system which includes arbitrary assumptions.

DEBTORS

Apart from inventories, a major element of working capital is in the credit taken by customers. This does not of course apply to those retailers and others who do not conduct a credit trade. The debtors/sales ratio is

---

GHM

	Line		Group	
13 Debtors falling due within one year			1985	1984
			£'000	£'000
	1	Trade debtors	3173	2659
	2	Prepayments and accrued income	96	36
	3	Amounts due from subsidiaries	–	–
	4		3269	3693

			Group	
14 Creditors falling due within one year			1985	1985
			£'000	£'000
	5	Trade creditors	1347	1477
	6	Other creditors	634	816
	7	PAYE and Social Security	172	157
	8	Accrued charges	237	182
	9	Bank overdraft	654	–
	10	Proposed dividend	408	238
	11	Corporation tax	596	641
	12	Amounts owed to subsidiaries	–	–
	13	Medium term loan	20	20
	14	Non-convertible unsecured loan stock 1984/45	201	1085
	15		4269	4616

The bank overdraft is secured on the group's freehold land and buildings.

Interest on the loan stock is payable at the rate of 1% below the rate at which three months' deposits are offered in the London Inter-Bank Market for sterling subject to a maximum of 11% per annum. The loan stock is redeemable at par on not less than 3 months notice from stockholders and in any event no later than 31 December 1985

Figure 10.3   Extract from notes to the annual accounts of Standard plc

the measure, and this again is usually expressed in weeks. In the case of Standard plc, the debtors/sales ratio is derived from information contained in Figures 10.2 and 10.3 as follows:

$$\frac{\text{Debtors (line 1, Figure 10.3)}}{\text{Sales (line 1, Figure 10.2)}} \quad = \quad \frac{3\ 173}{15\ 220} \quad = \quad 0.208$$

(20.8 per cent, or about 11 weeks).

The debtors/sales ratio has the same disadvantage as that mentioned concerning the stock ratio, namely that the point of time at which the debtors are taken may not be typical of the period to which the turnover relates. Alternatively, there may be a strong seasonal bias within the year's total sales figure. For example, if two-thirds of the year's turnover was sold in the second six months, then the ratio is

$$\frac{3\ 173 \times 26\ \text{(weeks)}}{10\ 147} \quad \text{which is just over 8 weeks.}$$

However, this is a problem only for external readers of the report, since managers with access to the management accounts could take the seasonal bias into consideration when calculating the ratio.

CREDITORS

Creditors are the opposite side of the coin to debtors. They are a source of funds to the company, and the more capital the company can borrow from this source, the less it requires from others (or, alternatively, the more funds it has available to deploy in various assets for building up the activity – and possibly the return – on the same net capital).

The creditors, being money owing in respect of purchases made by the company, will be compared with the purchases in the recent period and expressed in weeks. Although the cost of sales figure appears in the profit and loss account it includes manufacturing wages as well as purchases, and purchases are not shown separately. However, the figure for purchases will be available to the managers; they should use it in the same way as the debtors ratio by allowing for any seasonal bias.

Readers of the published accounts can make the assumption that purchases are roughly the same proportion of sales in the recent year as they were in the previous year. They can then compare the movement of creditors with that of debtors. Standard's debtors increased from £2 657 000 to £3 173 000 (line 1 in Figure 10.3) or by 19.4 per cent. The creditors, however, fell from £1 477 000 to £1 347 000 (line 5 in Figure 10.3) which is 9 per cent. Since the rise in debtors is similar to the rise in sales, it is the movement of creditors which is surprising. This inference is reinforced by the increase of stock from the previous year. It would appear that either the company is voluntarily paying more quickly (which would be strange in view of the poorer cash position) or that suppliers are applying more pressure, or perhaps offering better cash discount incentives to attract prompt payment.

Whatever the reason, the decrease in trade creditors of £130 000 and the increase in trade debtors of £516 000 combine to result in a total reduction of cash flow of £646 000, which accounts for virtually the entire bank overdraft.

However, the average length of credit time taken by the company from its suppliers is still not known. Suppose, for the sake of argument, that the £1 347 000 (line 5 in Figure 10.3) represents two months' credit – meaning that average monthly purchases have been running at half that level. Then an increase by one month to three months' credit will, other things being equal, raise borrowing from this source by about £673 000, at the same time eliminating the bank overdraft. The total current liabilities will remain the same, but the company will have substituted additional borrowing from its suppliers for what it previously borrowed from the bank. The effect of this change on profit, assuming overdraft interest at the rate of (say) 14 per cent, would be a gain of about £94 000. Moreover, this is not just a once and for all gain; it will continue at that rate for as long as the additional credit is taken. This assumes that:

1 purchases continue at the current level
2 interest rates continue at 14 per cent and
3 relations with suppliers remain unaltered.

If there are changes in either (1) or (2), the effects can easily be ascertained, but assumption (3) requires careful consideration. If we take more credit from a supplier, will that supplier react and, if so, how will his reaction affect us?

There are a number of things the supplier can do, from writing a letter (which costs the customer nothing) to withholding supplies (which may cost the customer a great deal). Between these extremes, he may reduce quality, increase prices, cut down deliveries and so on. However, there is doubt about the validity of these intermediate reactions.

He may reduce the quality of the product or the frequency of delivery or after-sales service, but this may not be acceptable to the customer who may then withdraw his custom. Before taking any of these steps, the supplier would have to be prepared for this eventuality, the effect of which would be the same as if he himself withheld supplies.

Similarly, if the supplier increases his prices, the higher prices may or may not be acceptable to the customer. If they are, why did the supplier not increase them previously? If they are not, he once again risks losing the business. Therefore, the question facing the supplier is whether or not he can risk losing the business.

From the customer's point of view, he must decide whether he can tolerate loss of supplies from this source because, even though it may not be in the supplier's best interest to stop supplies, he may act irrationally and the customer must be prepared for this. The summary of this discussion is that the customer's ability to take longer credit from a particular supplier depends on the balance of power between them.

Since this varies with different suppliers it follows that an individual credit policy with at least the major suppliers is necessary if optimum credit is to be taken. If a blanket credit policy is adopted to cover all suppliers, this assumes that they are all equally powerful, which is most unlikely to be the case. The consequence of this would be to take from some less credit than one could take with impunity, and to take from others more than is wise.

These arguments apply with equal force to debtor control, and since sales exceed purchases tight debtor control is even more important.

It is often suggested that if a company takes longer credit from its suppliers, its own customers will in turn extend their credit and the move will be self-defeating. This is woolly thinking.

Customers cannot know how a company behaves to its suppliers, save in the exceptional case where customer and supplier are the same and a two-way trade is conducted. In the normal case, the customer will take whatever credit he thinks he can get away with. This consideration is based on the same assessment of relative power as already discussed concerning creditors.

However, many companies recognize the importance of intelligent debtor control and designate it as a specific management function, whilst attention is paid to prompt invoicing and follow-up procedures. It is the treatment of credit obtainable from suppliers that is relatively neglected.

Cash discount

So far we have not considered the effect on one's credit policy if one is offered a discount for prompt payment. For example, a supplier may offer a discount of $2^1/_2$ per cent on invoice for payment within 30 days.

If one pays two months from date of invoice and forgoes the discount, one has in fact borrowed for one extra month (since the first 30 days would be taken in any event) at a cost of $2^1/_2$ per cent which is equivalent to a straight annual cost of $12 \times 2^1/_2$ per cent = 30 per cent. The discounted annual rate would be even higher than this. If one is borrowing at say 15 per cent from the bank, 30 per cent is far too dear to contemplate. Break-even point would occur with 3 months' credit; i.e. 2 extra months at a cost of 2½ per cent = $12 \div 2 \times 2½$ per cent or 15 per cent p.a. Therefore, it is only worthwhile losing the discount if one can take at least 3 months' credit. However, if bank facilities are scarce it will pay to borrow at more than 15 per cent from suppliers if the benefit derived from the utilization of the extra credit exceeds the cost.

So far in this chapter the various factors concerning liquidity have been discussed. We have seen that suboptimal utilization of working capital is expensive. At the least, it costs the interest on the unnecessary money used, but it also prevents that money from being properly employed in the company and could inhibit the company's growth through lack of cash.

Cash flow

Liquidity is the life-blood of the company and lack of cash is the only thing which could force the company out of business. Cash flows into the company by direct cash sales and the collection of debts from customers, and also, though less regularly, from the sale of assets. Cash flows out in direct purchases and payments to creditors, in payment of wages and other costs, and in the purchase of capital equipment. It also flows out in payment of taxes and interest on borrowed money and dividends to shareholders.

These flows have to be predicted and controlled. This is done by forecasting and budgeting (see Chapter 9). Cash has always to be available to meet committed expenditure. If not, the company can be forced into liquidation by its creditors even though it has an overall excess of assets over liabilities. The company can also obtain additional transfusions of cash from time to time by means of additional bank facilities, which are likely to be relatively short-term, by raising fresh loans which are likely to be long-term and by rights issues of further ordinary shares which are permanent funds.

PROFITABILITY

We shall assume, since there is not the space here to argue it, that the objective of a public commercial company is the maximization of profit on capital employed. The objective covers the total future and, of course, does not apply to any single year. Almost every company could make a bigger profit this year if in so doing it was prepared to jeopardize the future. The cessation of advertising and research, for example, would often increase this year's profit but might cripple the business in the following year.

Profit on capital employed, on its own, does not mean very much. Are we talking about profit before tax or profit after tax, shareholders' capital or total capital, for example? In fact, different definitions of profit are appropriate at different levels in a company because of varying degrees of authority to control resources and make decisions.

At parent company board level, the directors are directly accountable to ordinary shareholders, and therefore the capital for which the directors are accountable is the ordinary shareholders' funds (OSF) which consists of the ordinary share capital plus reserves. Similarly, the profit which the directors are seeking to maximize is the profit attributable to the ordinary shareholders. This profit is often referred to as the company's earnings, and the earnings divided by the number of ordinary shares in issue is the earnings per share (EPS). The earnings are the trading profit less all interest charges, taxation, minority shareholders' interest and preference dividend, since these are all the deductions which must be made before the ordinary shareholders are entitled to the remainder.

Thus the profitability ratio relevant to the assessment of directors' performance is earnings divided by OSF which, in the case of Standard plc, is:

$$\frac{£1\ 667\ 000\ (\text{Figure } 10.2,\ \text{line } 11)}{£9\ 215\ 000\ (\text{Figure } 10.1,\ \text{line } 20)}$$

which is approximately 18 per cent. Notice that the earnings figure is struck before deducting ordinary dividends. The earnings can be used by the directors, either in paying a dividend to the ordinary shareholders or by retention in the company as an addition to the OSF. How the directors dispose of the earnings is entirely within their discretion. The earnings figure is also struck before extraordinary items (line 12 in Figure 10.2) because these are of a non-trading and non-recurring nature.

Let us now look at the position of the chief executive. He is directly accountable to the board of directors and is sometimes called the managing director (if he also sits on the board) or the general manager (if he does not). The chief executive is accountable for profit since he controls both sides of the profit equation – income and expenditure. However, he does not control dividends, since he does not raise capital, and for the same reason he does not control loan interest. On the other hand, he does control the level of bank borrowing by his credit policies, etc., and so he is accountable for bank interest.

Taxation is affected within the company by board decisions, particularly those regarding capital expenditure and the raising of capital. Capital expenditure gives rise to government capital allowances. New capital may be raised by a rights issue of shares (on which dividends are paid) or by the issue of loan stock (on which interest is paid). However, interest (being a cost) is allowable for corporation tax. Dividends, which are distributions of profit, are paid after corporation tax has been charged, but are paid net of income tax. With corporation tax at 35 per cent and the basic rate of income tax at 29 per cent, every £1 of gross interest actually costs the company 65p and a £1 of gross equivalent dividend costs 71p.

Minority interests are no concern of the chief executive since the decision of whether to own subsidiaries partly or wholly is a board decision. The chief executive is therefore accountable for trading profit ÷ total investment. Trading profit is defined as a profit after bank overdraft interest but before deducting loan interest, taxation, minority interests and dividends. Total investment is the total long-term capital made available by the board to the chief executive. It consists of the ordinary shareholders' funds, plus preference capital, plus loan capital, plus minority interests.

Standard plc's $\frac{\text{trade profit}}{\text{total investment}}$ is $\frac{£2\ 163\ 000^{1}}{£9\ 255\ 000^{2}}$ or about 23 per cent.

The chief executive's ratio is different from the board's, but contributes towards it: the better the trading profit, the better the earnings (other things being equal). The chief executive's profitability is almost always higher than the board's because his is before tax and theirs is after.

---

[1] The £2 163 000 comprises the operating profit of £2 179 000 (see Figure 10.2, line 5) less the £16 000 bank overdraft interest. (This overdraft interest appears in notes to the accounts which are not reproduced here.)

[2] The £9 255 000 in the OSF of £9 215 000 plus a medium term loan of £40 000 (noted in a part of the accounts which is also not reproduced here).

These profitability ratios have little absolute significance, since both profit and capital employed are worked out in an arbitrary manner, and within a given factual context there is a wide range of possibilities for both.

The elements which make annual profit arbitrary are depreciation, stock valuation and the capitalizing or writing off of expenditure. Capital employed is arbitrary because assets are often included at cost, or at cost less depreciation, or at valuation. It is not uncommon to find a balance sheet with some assets at cost less depreciation, some assets at 1965 valuation, and other assets at 1982 valuation all added together as if they were the same currency.

The only logical value of capital employed is the deprival value (the current market value) of the assets less the liabilities. (This argument is explained in Simons, 1986, Chapter 8, pp 103–106).

The main use of ratios is in monitoring trends. It might be thought that a given ratio at one time can be compared with the equivalent ratio at another time if, although they have certain arbitrary elements, they are calculated consistently.

This would only be partly true. Suppose, for example, that assets are entered in the balance sheet at cost, or at cost less depreciation, and not at value. At a time of inflation, profit will reflect the effects as prices and costs rise, except for depreciation which is usually based on historical cost instead of replacement cost. However, capital employed, in being consistently 'valued' at cost, will depart more and more from reality and so, therefore, will the return on capital employed. The ratio will tend to rise, simply because the conventions used are holding back the denominator to a far greater extent than the numerator.

Whereas the shareholders have to accept the accounts as they are published, and make the best of what is too often a bad job, fortunately more can be done by management, in this case the board of directors. They can ensure that the accounts (at least the management accounts if not the published ones) are prepared with maximum reality in order that they can provide a basis for management decision-making.

In the calculation of profit, stocks should be based on net realizable value instead of cost which is irrelevant. Depreciation should be the reduction in the market value of the assets between the beginning and end of the year plus the increase in the replacement cost of these assets during the year.

The reduction in the market value of the assets should be deducted from the asset value in the balance sheet at the end of the previous year to arrive at the balance sheet value at the end of the current year. In this way the assets will always be included at market value, which is the only treatment of relevance to the readers of the balance sheet.

The increase in the replacement cost of the asset will not be deducted from the balance sheet value as this could eventually cause a negative value of the asset which is of course impossible. Instead, it is taken to an asset replacement provision on the balance sheet. Thus when an asset is sold, a figure similar to the balance sheet value should be obtained, in addition to which depreciation has been provided between the historical cost and realizable value of the asset, and between the replacement cost and the historical cost, so that the company will have provided sufficient funds for the replacement of the asset. Conventional historical cost depreciation does not achieve this, as a result of which profit is overstated, non-existent profit may be distributed as a dividend, and the company may leave itself short of the capital necessary to continue the business at the same level as before.

Gearing

The principle of gearing is a very important one in any decision to raise new capital and it is also one of the differences between the board's profitability ratio of $\frac{\text{earnings}}{\text{OSF}}$ and the chief executive's ratio of $\frac{\text{trading profit}}{\text{total investment}}$. The measure of gearing is the gearing ratio, which is $\frac{\text{total investment}}{\text{OSF}}$. Most financial commentators quote a gearing percentage rather than the ratio, which is the percentage that net borrowing is of shareholders' funds.

Total investment has already been described as the total long-term capital, including OSF, preference and loan capital. OSF (ordinary shareholders' funds) is the ordinary share capital and reserves. Except for the loan of £40 000 mentioned above, Standard's long-term capital is the OSF, and it is thus virtually ungeared. The ratio of an ungeared company is 1.

Now suppose that an ungeared company has OSF (and thus total investment) of £10m, and that it makes a trading profit of £2m. The profitability ratios can be set out thus:

Trading profit	£2 000 000
Loan interest	nil
Profit before tax	2 000 000
Corporation tax (35 per cent)	700 000
Earnings	£1 300 000

The chief executive's profitability is $\frac{\text{trading profit}}{\text{total investment}} = \frac{£2m}{£10m}$ which is 20 per cent.

The board's profitability is $\frac{\text{earnings}}{\text{OSF}} = \frac{£1.3m}{£10m}$ which is 13 per cent.

The chief executive now makes an application to the board for £4m additional capital, the new funds being required for a long-term project on which the chief executive is confident of making his present 20 per cent return. The board, after examining his proposals, and comparing them with alternatives, decide to go ahead with the project and raise the necessary capital. Basically, the choice facing them is a rights issue to increase the equity (owners' capital or OSF) or an issue of 10 per cent loan stock. We shall look at both possibilities on the assumption that the chief executive (CE) meets his forecast of 20 per cent return. Here are the figures:

147

	Case 1 (rights issue)	Case 2 (loan stock issue)
OSF	£14m	£10m
10% loan capital	nil	4m
Total investment	14m	14m
Trading profit	2.8m (CE's ratio = 20%)	2.8m (CE's ratio = 20%)
Loan interest	nil	0.4m
Profit before tax	2.8m	2.4m
Corporation tax at 35%	0.98m	0.84m
Earnings	1.82m (board's ratio = 13%)	1.56m (board's ratio = 15.6%)

In case 1, the board's ratio is $\dfrac{1.82m}{14m\ (OSF)}$ and in case 2 it is $\dfrac{1.56m}{10m\ (OSF)}$

Case 2 is preferable because money has been borrowed at 10 per cent pre-tax, and invested at 20 per cent pre-tax, the difference going to the benefit of the ordinary shareholders with no further investment on their part. The gearing ratio in case 1 is 1 and in case 2 is 1.4.

Gearing, however, is a two-edged weapon. It will magnify the effect of a change in trading profit on the earnings. Suppose that in the following year (year 2) trading profit doubles and in year 3 it falls to half of the year 1 level. Then, assuming the capital structure in case 2, the positions would be as follows:

	Year 2	Year 3
Trading profit	£5.6m (CE's ratio = 40%)	£1.4m (CE's ratio = 10%)
Loan interest	0.4m	0.4m
Pre-tax profit	5.2m	1.0m
Corporation tax at 35%	1.82m	0.35m
Earnings	3.38m (board's ratio = 33.8%)	0.65m (board's ratio = 6.5%)

Notice that in the year 2 the $\dfrac{\text{earnings}}{\text{OSF}}$ has more than doubled from 15.6 per cent to 33.8 per cent and from year 1 to year 3 it has more than halved from 15.6 per cent to 6.5 per cent.

A simple and dramatic example of the effect of gearing is to be seen in the case of the private house. A man buys a house for £50 000 and finances it by a deposit of £10 000 and a 25-year endowment-linked building society mortgage of £40 000. He sells the house for £150 000 and repays the mortgage. The gearing ratio is $\dfrac{\text{total investment}}{\text{OSF}}$ which is $\dfrac{50\ 000}{10\ 000} = 5$.

		Time of purchase	Time of sale	
Deposit	(equity)	£10 000	+1 000%	£110 000
Mortgage	(loan capital)	40 000		40 000
House	(total investment)	50 000	+200%	150 000

Although the house has appreciated by only 200 per cent, the owner's equity has increased by five times that proportion (since the gearing ratio is 5), namely, 1000 per cent. Equally, of course, if the house had fallen in value by £10 000, which is 20 per cent, the fall in the equity would have been 5 × 20 per cent = 100 per cent. In other words, the owner would have lost his entire capital since the remaining £40 000 in the value of the house would have been just sufficient to repay the mortgage.

There is no generally ideal gearing ratio. It can be seen that gearing adds a speculative element to a company in the method of financing it, but the degree of speculation tolerated in the financial structure of the company depends on how basically speculative the company is. A nice steady company which is relatively unaffected by seasonal and cyclical variations in profit can stand a considerable degree of gearing whereas a company whose profit fluctuates a great deal is perhaps better left ungeared or low geared.

SOLVENCY

Finally, we come to the concept of solvency. Just as liquidity is concerned with a company's ability to meet its current liabilities out of its current assets, solvency is concerned with the ability of the company to meet its total liabilities out of its total assets. The solvency ratio is

$$\frac{OSF}{\text{total assets}} \times 100 \text{ per cent which in Standard's case is}$$

$$\frac{9215 \text{ (Figure 10.1, line 20)}}{13953 \text{ (Figure 10.1, lines 3+4+9}}, \text{ which is approximately 66 per cent.}$$

This means that 66 per cent of all Standard's assets are financed by the owners and, therefore, borrowed money is the source of the remaining 34 per cent of the assets. In other words, even if 66 per cent of the assets are lost, the company is still solvent since there is enough value remaining just to repay all the borrowing and no more.

Once again, optimum solvency is a question of balance. A company financing too high a proportion of its total assets by equity is not maximizing its profitability (since the denominator of the profitability ratio is unnecessarily high) even though it is extremely safe. The art is in judging how much external financing an individual company can stand.

The true degree of solvency, like the true degree of liquidity and gearing, can only be ascertained if the values of the assets in the balance sheet are realistic. Book values based on cost are of no help in making these assessments.

FURTHER READING

Simons, L., *The Basic Arts of Financial Management*, 3rd edition, Business Books, London, 1986 (Business Books is an imprint of Century Hutchinson)

11 Cost analysis*

Richard M S Wilson

Everything that a manager does, as well as many things he fails to do, has an associated cost. Although not all such costs are identifiable or measurable, this does beg the question of what is meant by cost. Cost is characterized by the word *sacrifice*. As such, it is very much in management's interest to control, and where possible reduce, the sacrifices involved in achieving desired results.

SOME CONCEPTS OF COSTS

Non-financial costs

Non-financial costs are those which are not directly traceable through cash flow. Such costs certainly involve sacrifices and can lead (in complex ways) to a future cash flow reduction but they are not immediate cash outlays. Psychic costs are a good example: these are the costs of mental dissatisfaction such as would be found, for example, in reduced morale following a 5 rather than a 10 per cent pay rise for the workforce, or when a manager is passed over for promotion. Another non-financial cost is that associated with diminution of a company's reputation, (reflected in a fall in the value of its goodwill – if only we had a satisfactory way of measuring this).

Non-cash costs

Non-cash costs are financial sacrifices that do not involve cash outlays at the time when the cost is recognized. Two important examples are depreciation charges and opportunity cost.

---

* Some of the material in this chapter has been drawn from the author's other published work with the approval of Cassell (relating to '*Financial Analysis: A Managerial Introduction*'), and Gower Publishing (relating to '*Cost Control Handbook*', 2nd. edition, and chapter 13 in '*Handbook of Management Accounting*', 2nd edition). The author is grateful to those publishers for their permission to draw on the material in question.

Depreciation charges

When a long-lived asset (such as a major item of plant) is bought there is clearly a cash outlay but, since the price paid is almost certainly deemed to be at least equal to the value of the asset to the business at the time of purchase, there is no diminution of value and hence no sacrifice (other than in terms of financial flexibility). However, as the asset is used it will physically deteriorate or otherwise lose value (for example through obsolescence). This is seen as the depreciation cost to be charged periodically against revenue of the business. Thus depreciation charges are costs, but they are not a cash outflow at the time they are recognized.

Opportunity cost

Every manager and consumer is accustomed to being unable to do everything that he or she would like to do owing to the problem of limited resources. If scarce resources are allocated for one purpose, they cannot be used simultaneously for another. The potential benefits of strategy X are foregone if all the resources are applied to strategy Y. The foregone benefits of strategy X constitute the opportunity cost of strategy Y. It is seen that there is no cash outlay corresponding to the opportunity cost.

Cash costs

Cash costs are the sacrifices reflected in actual cash outflows. The cost is incurred at the same time as the cash expenditure (as, for example, when a fare is paid on public transport). In a corporate setting it is a reasonable approximation to equate operating expenses (excluding depreciation) with cash outlays, provided that stock levels are not fluctuating significantly.

Cost, revenue and profit

Business transactions usually involve reward (revenue) and sacrifice (cost), with the difference being gain (profit). Thus:

$$\text{Reward} - \text{sacrifice} = \text{gain}$$
$$\text{Revenue} - \text{cost} = \text{profit}$$

It is important to recognize that the term *cost* only has meaning in a given context and must always be qualified by an adjective. There are different cost concepts appropriate to different circumstances, and no simple cost concept is relevant to all situations.

THE ROLE OF COST ACCOUNTING

Product costing

Cost accounting has conventionally been associated with *product costing*. This is concerned with determining the amount of cost to be assigned to each unit of manufactured output as a basis for:

1 Valuation of stocks (as shown in a balance sheet)
2 Computing the cost of goods sold (deducted from sales revenue to show profit).

Apart from these uses, product costing is employed in the cost-plus approach to pricing (for example in some construction contracts).

The approach to product costing is generally to assign a 'fair share' of the total cost of operations to each unit of output. This is straightforward for a single product (or single service) company, but complexity increases in proportion to the number of product lines. In a single product company *all* costs are attributable to that product (for example, an output of 1 000 000 units at a cost of £5 000 000 gives a unit cost of £5). If there are two product lines (or 2000 lines) the problem is much more difficult and it is impossible to measure accurately the cost of any single item.

Segments

In addition to product costing, cost accounting is also used to derive costs for other units of activity. Products are not the only cost units; it might be necessary to know the cost of operating particular departments, of operating in different territories, of serving different customer groups, of servicing orders below a particular value, of hiring a new salesman, and so forth.

The analysis of *segments* is usually concerned with measuring the profit from each defined segment of the market, with the segments chosen according to such criteria as the age, occupation, number of children, and income (in the case of individual customers) and SIC code in the case of organizational customers. In order to ascertain the profitability of supplying specified products to identifiable market segments it is necessary to match the revenues from the sales made to each segment with the costs of supplying these segments. The revenue aspect is not difficult, but the cost analysis is fraught with problems. For example, it is too simplistic to allocate a proportion of total marketing and distribution costs to each segment in relation to the percentage of revenue obtained. Any attempt to apportion fully each elemental category of cost is likely to be misleading because variable costs are a function of activity level, whereas fixed costs are a function of time. If, for example, it was decided to withdraw from segment X, it would not follow that the fixed cost element of servicing X would be avoided, even though the variable costs are likely to be. It is important, therefore, to consider the purpose for which costs are being computed and the implications of using the various concepts of cost and alternative analysis techniques.

Services

In comparison with the costing of physical products, relatively little attention has been given to the costing of services (such as those supplied by accounting firms, advertising agencies, architects, solicitors and engineering consultants). This is partly due to the difficulty of defining and measuring that which has to be costed. For example, is it the audit certificate in the case of the accounting firm, or the television commercial in the case of the advertising agency?

Payroll items are by far the largest category of expenditure in service firms. But individuals have different rates of pay and work different numbers of hours, the quantity and quality of their output vary, so that to cost a service on the basis of (say) staff hours is not a very realistic approach. The increasing size of the service sector in the British economy makes this a problem of growing significance. There are, of course, internal departments within manufacturing and service organizations which provide services as inputs to the final market offer, and the costing of some of these is considered later.

The main purposes of cost accounting

In broad terms, the main purposes of cost accounting are:

1 To show the cost structure of each activity carried out by the enterprise in order to facilitate planning
2 To facilitate product costing for inventory valuation
3 To show whether or not a profit has been made on the business as a whole
4 To show whether or not a profit has been made in each division, or on each job or product, or in any other segment, thus assisting in planning the mix of jobs or products to optimize overall profitability
5 To aid the pricing decision by distinguishing between fixed and variable costs, with the latter forming the lowest price level that should be set
6 To prevent wastage by the use of an efficient system of stores and wages control
7 To provide data on which to base tenders for government and other contracts
8 To secure more efficient operations and more effective use of resources, by comparing actual results with predetermined standards (variance analysis)
9 To permit the establishment of uniform cost accounting systems for interfirm comparison purposes
10 To achieve control by assigning costs to responsibility centres
11 To help in decision-making by giving a basis for evaluating alternative courses of action, such as:
    (a) What would be the effect on a company's net profit of discontinuing product A and re-allocating the resources to product B?
    (b) If an order or contract is accepted at a given price, will that price be sufficient for the company to earn a profit on the job?
    (c) What would be the effect of a given wage increase on product costs and, hence, on profits?
    (d) What effect would replacing specified equipment have on costs?

These purposes relate essentially to the managerial tasks of planning, decision-making and control, so it is appropriate to consider the relevant cost categories applicable to these tasks.

COST ANALYSIS FOR PLANNING

Whilst plans are concerned with the future, the process of planning usually starts from the present (or recent past) by examining the pattern of resource allocation and its effectiveness. This can be illustrated by thinking of available resources as *effort*, and then seeking to know how that effort was applied in the recent past, and with what results.

For example, an enterprise might operate in five sales territories, prompting the questions:

1 How much effort was applied to each sales territory last year?
2 How much revenue and profit did each territory generate?

Two issues are especially important in this context:

1 The focus of attention can be on any activity (or 'cost object') of managerial interest. The origins of cost accounting (and the subsequent preoccupation of most costing systems) are in product costing, and this explains the traditionally introspective focus of costing on manufacturing processes. But manufacturing does not produce profits or generate sales; it is transactions in the market place that bring in revenue. This highlights the relevance of sales territories, product lines, customer groups, distribution channels and size of order as legitimate alternatives to the unit of manufacture for cost consideration.
2 In seeking to establish the pattern of resource allocation it is necessary to use simplifying assumptions and techniques that inevitably involve approximations of an unknown (and unknowable) 'full' cost for selected activities. As a result, full cost data can only be used as a basis for asking questions. For example, 'which product lines are earning their keep in overseas markets?' or 'how well are salesmen performing relative to one another?' It is inappropriate to use full cost data as a basis for making decisions (such as adding or dropping product lines, eliminating particular channels of distribution, and so on).

Distinction between direct and indirect costs

Whatever cost object (or activity) is selected as the focus of attention, some costs will be *direct* in the sense of being traceable to the activity (such as direct labour and direct material inputs into a unit of manufactured output) whilst others will be *indirect*. By definition, indirect costs cannot be traced directly to cost units, so any procedure whereby these costs are assigned to cost units will mean that the resulting full (or 'absorbed') cost is inaccurate to an unknown extent. The assigning of a 'fair share' of indirect costs, along with direct costs, to cost units is at the heart of *absorption costing*.

A particular cost item can only be termed direct or indirect once the cost object has been specified. Thus a salesman's salary will be indirect in relation to the individual product lines he sells (assuming he carries a range of products), but it will be a direct cost of the territory in which he is operating. In the same way the costs of distributing various products to wholesalers may be indirect with regard to the goods themselves but direct if one is interested in costing the channel of distribution of which the wholesalers are part.

By considering the way in which the full cost of units of production might be determined, it is possible to show how this procedure can be adapted for use in other settings. Data will be derived from the following sources.

Labour

The initial point to observe in relation to payroll data is that the cost of employing a man is not just his gross wage or salary. In addition to gross earnings the company must pay its contribution for national insurance, superannuation, and so on.

In a manufacturing or distribution environment, time sheets can be used to record, in summary form, time spent by each operative on different jobs. The onus will often be on an operative to record the time that he spends on each job during a week. This highlights a major danger. Unless there is some incentive towards the accurate booking of time, the validity of labour costings will be highly suspect. An operative may attach little importance to recording the time worked on different tasks if he fails to understand the importance of this function. Further, he may be reluctant to record times accurately because lost time, idle time and waiting time can reflect partly on himself, partly on his supervisor and partly on his colleagues. These indirect bookings might, therefore, be left unrecorded by the operative, the 'missing' time being made up by spurious inflation of the direct bookings to jobs.

An analysis of indirect labour hours (especially where reasons can be given clearly) is of great value in pinpointing areas of weakness. Account codes can be drawn up to facilitate such an analysis, so that each source of indirect labour expense can be recorded against its particular code as it is incurred. Idle time, for example, might be given the following breakdown of codes:

X123 Waiting for orders
X124 Waiting for stock
X125 Waiting for materials from previous operation
X126 Waiting for fitter
X127 Waiting for power
X128 Waiting for supervisor
X129 Waiting for drawings
X130 Waiting for maintenance
X131 Waiting for jigs
X132 Waiting for instructions

If the cost of idle time booked to X126 amounted to (say) £7500 during a year, a good argument could be made for employing another fitter. A weekly report can be compiled to show how lost time is made up, and the proportion which it bears to direct labour time.

Methods for pricing materials issues and valuing stocks

Every issue of materials should be authorized by a requisition which states:

1 Stock or part number and description of the materials
2 Quantity required for issue
3 Job number (or other number) for cost allocation
4 Originator's name
5 Authorizing signature

Note that the quantity requested may not be available. In such cases the requisition must either be held until the full quantity does become available, or a reduced quantity can be issued and the requisition amended accordingly to record the amount actually issued.

A difficulty arises in deciding the cost to associate with each issue of materials. It might appear simple to charge *actual* material cost (the price paid) against production. However, the stock will probably comprise materials purchased on several occasions at different prices. 'Actual cost' then has several meanings, and some systematic method for pricing must be chosen. Once a method has been decided, it is customary to use it for the valuation of material stocks, perhaps with adjustment according to the 'lower cost or market value' convention.

Suppose that the information available for a particular stock item (material *A*) is as shown in the following list (given in chronological order) and that a unit price is required for each issue, and a valuation of closing stock:

(a) Opening stock	100 units	Cost £1.00 per unit	£100.00
(1) Issue	75 units		
(b) Purchase	400 units	Cost £1.10 per unit	£440.00
(2) Issue	100 units		
(3) Issue	50 units		
(c) Purchase	80 units	Cost £1.20 per unit	£96.00
(4) Issue	150 units		
(5) Closing stock	205 units (ie assuming no wastage)		£636.00

First in, first out (FIFO) method

This method assumes that the various units of material are used in the order in which they are received. Closing stock will consist of the last items purchased. Whenever stores are issued the issue price will be calculated by working forwards from the oldest batch in stock; see Figure 11.1.

This method is easy to operate unless many small purchases at different prices occur. Stock balances represent nearly current costs, and costs are recognized in a manner which should correspond to the physical use of the

	Stock (a)	Purchase (b)	Purchase (c)		GHM
Issue (1)	75 x £1.00			= £75.00	
Issue (2)	25 x £1.00 +	75 x £1.10		= £107.50	
Issue (3)		50 x £1.10		= £55.00	
Issue (4)		150 x £1.10		= £165.00	
Stock (5)		125 x £1.10 +	80 x £1.20	= £233.50	
	100 units	400 units	80 units	£636.00	

Figure 11.1   FIFO method

stock. However, the system is inequitable if a sudden change in price results in similar jobs being charged with different material costs, and where stock turnover is slow and there are substantial price changes, current material costs will not be apparent in the account.

Weighted-average cost method

This method assumes that all material of a given kind is so intermingled that an issue cannot be made from a particular lot and the cost should therefore represent an average of the entire supply. A new issue price is calculated every time a purchase is made by dividing: (the cost of material received plus the cost of material on hand) by (number of units received plus the number of units on hand).

Issue (1) 75 x £1.000   = £75
Issue (2) 100 x £1.094 = £109 $\left.\right\}$ $\dfrac{(25 \times £1) + (400 \times £1.10)}{25 + 400} = 1.094$
Issue (3) 50 x £1.094   = £55
Issue (4) 150 x £1.118 = £168 $\left.\right\}$ $\dfrac{(275 \times £1.094) + (80 \times £1.20)}{275 + 80} = 1.118$
Stock (5) 205 x £1.118 = £229
$\underline{\underline{£636}}$

Note that the calculation may be done on a periodic basis instead of on the occasion of every purchase. Issue and stock pricing would then be recalculated as follows and no entries would be made until the end of the period:

$$\frac{£100 + £440 + £96}{100 + 400 + 80} = £1.093 \text{ per unit}$$

This method is easy to operate, smooths out the sudden jumps likely to occur in pricing under other methods, and gives stock balances that represent relatively current costs. However, the influence of a large purchase on favourable terms may influence stock pricing for many periods if usage is slow.

Last in first out (LIFO) method

This method assumes artificially that the last items purchased are the first used. Closing stock will be valued at the price of the first goods purchased. Whenever stores are issued the issue price will be calculated by working back from the most recent batch received (see Figure 11.2).

The only advantage of this method is that it matches recent material cost with current revenue – hence cost of goods manufactured will fluctuate with the market price of material used (unless stock levels are sharply reduced). However, stocks are valued at prices paid for the earliest purchases (including previous periods) which may deviate considerably from current market values.

	Stock (a)	Purchase (b)	Purchase (c)	
				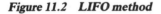 GHM
Issue (1)	75 x £1.00			= £75.00
Issue (2)		100 x £1.10		= £110.00
Issue (3)		50 x £1.10		= £55.00
Issue (4)		70 x £1.10 +	80 x £1.20	= £173.00
Stock (5)	25 x £1.00 +	180 x £1.10		= £223.00
	100 units	400 units	80 units	£636.00

Figure 11.2   LIFO method

Materials costing – application of methods

If prices are reasonably stable it matters little which of the above methods is employed. Average cost would probably be best, but any of the three methods should be satisfactory, if applied consistently.

If prices are not stable, the fact that all the above methods (and other methods) are considered 'generally acceptable' for internal management use and for external reporting is alarming. Some means of isolating the effect of price changes is essential both from a control point of view and an income reporting point of view. One suggestion is to use LIFO for pricing issues and FIFO for pricing stocks and transfer the ensuing 'difference' to a 'price gains' or 'price losses' account. A far better solution is to employ standard costing whereby all material pricing is based on attainable standards as calculated at the beginning of the period. The effect of unforeseen price changes is then automatically segregated and can be both examined for control purposes and reported separately in income statements.

Once purchased, some materials are difficult to control as a result of their physical nature. For example, temperature changes may affect the apparent volume of an issue of a liquid chemical; wastage may arise due to inevitable evaporation or because issues do not correspond with purchases (e.g. galvanized wire may be purchased by the tonne but be issued in coils or lengths). These are all examples of *unavoidable* causes and allowances can (and should) be made for such losses and gains. If experience shows that only 19 issues of 10 kilos can be made from a purchase of 200 kilos of material X at a cost of £20, it will be necessary to use the following formula to compute the cost per *usable* kilo of material X: $\frac{20}{190}$ (i.e. £0.105 per kilo) as opposed to $\frac{20}{200}$ (or £0.100 per kilo).

Avoidable losses are, however, quite a different matter. Such losses may result from:

1 Pilferage
2 Careless handling
3 Careless measurement of issues
4 Incorrect allowances for variations due to evaporation, absorption of moisture, changes in temperature, etc.
5 Unsuitable storage

Care should be taken in deciding which issues to value on an individual basis and which to value on a collective basis. Items of small value (e.g. nails, nuts, etc.) are of the latter type, and although they are strictly in the nature of direct materials (i.e. their cost can be specifically identified with particular products) it will usually be unnecessarily expensive in terms of clerical labour to do this. The usual procedure, therefore, is to issue such items in bulk and classify them in the overheads as consumable stores rather than issue them at a specially computed price to specific jobs.

Indirect cost items (overheads)

Indirect (or overhead) labour costs will be obtained from work sheets and labour summaries, and indirect material costs (such as the nails referred to above) will be obtained from requisitions. Further indirect cost details covering electricity and other utilities, bought-out services, supervisory and managerial salaries, depreciation, and so on will be obtained from expense summaries compiled from either invoices or internal work sheets. The next step is to develop overhead rates by which the indirect costs may be absorbed into the manufactured output. A basic procedure for doing this involves the following steps:

1 Analyse and classify all costs into their direct and indirect categories. (This can be done as a retrospective exercise using actual costs, or as a predictive exercise using estimated costs.)

159

2 Relate direct costs to the particular jobs, processes, etc., for which they were/are to be specifically incurred.

3 Of the indirect costs, some will relate to particular production departments through which products pass in the course of the manufacturing cycle, and others will relate (on a responsibility basis) to service or ancillary departments (i.e. non-production departments such as maintenance, production control, stores, costing, etc.). The cost of these service departments is then apportioned to the production departments on some 'fair' basis relating to the benefits enjoyed by different production departments.

The most important criterion in selecting a base is to relate the overhead cost to its most causal factor: machines require maintenance, space involves paying rates, outputs require inputs. Nevertheless, the whole methodology of apportioning service department costs is plagued by the necessity of having to rely on some arbitrary rules (i.e. relating to 'benefit or 'fair share') that have been developed in order that service department costs might be rationally spread over production departments. Such apportionments are carried out solely for product costing purposes: the control of individual overhead costs will not be achieved by cost apportionments, and nor will the method of cost apportionment influence cost control.

4 An overhead rate can be established for each production department or cost centre, determined by the formula

$$\frac{\text{departmental overheads + apportioned service overheads}}{\text{level of activity}}$$

and applied to each job, process, or whatever. This is termed the *recovery of overheads*. (A simpler alternative of obvious use in a single product company, but also applicable in other circumstances, is to have a single, company-wide overhead rate. However, even in the single product company it will often be desirable to know the cost of each operation and the cumulative cost of the product as it passes through the various stages of manufacture).

Overhead rates in practice are generally determined once a year (preferably in advance rather than retrospectively) but, in changing circumstances, it will be advisable to revise them. The level of activity at which a department is expected to operate during a given period is of crucial importance and whenever overhead rates are determined in advance very careful attention must be paid to estimating this dimension.

There should be some cause-and-effect link between an overhead cost and the basis of absorption (e.g. if supervisory labour is apportioned to productive cost centres on the basis of direct labour cost, then it should be absorbed into product costs in accordance with direct labour costs).

It is not always necessary to distribute each overhead cost separately: some fixed costs (such as depreciation, rates, insurance premiums, and rent) can be spread collectively on the basis of, say, machine hours (since this factor represents the time during which a product 'rents' the machinery and premises).

Other costs, such as maintenance, certain utilities, operating supplies, and so forth, may be distributed on the basis of units of output. However, those costs that are proportional to direct labour (such as indirect labour, supervision, holiday accruals, overtime premiums, welfare services, personnel department, etc.) can be distributed on the basis of labour cost, man–hours, or the number of people employed – whichever seems most appropriate.

The apportionment/absorption routine is summarized in Figure 11.3. The first step is to separate service centre costs from production department overheads. The service department overheads are then apportioned over the production departments. Finally, the departmentalized overheads are absorbed into units of production.

It should again be emphasized that when a company produces a hetero-geneous range of jobs/products, with each receiving an unequal amount of attention as it moves from one cost centre to another, it is essential to develop and apply departmental overhead rates (rather than one total company-wide overhead rate) to each job if the resulting product cost is to bear any relation to the true (but unknown) full product cost.

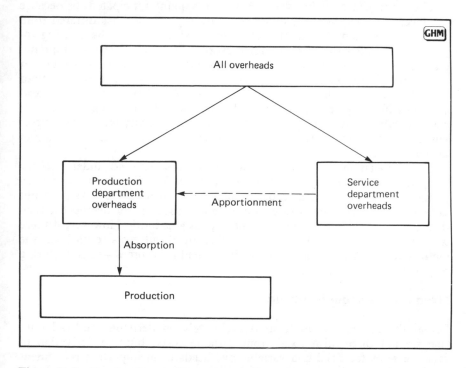

Figure 11.3 Overhead apportionment and absorption

The actual overhead costs of a particular period will only be equal to the applied overheads of that period (i.e. predetermined overhead rate × number of units produced) by chance (unless, of course, the period's costs and activities were all rigidly determined in advance, or the forecaster was in the improbable position of having a perfect view of the future).

Over- and under-absorption of overheads

If more overheads are applied to units of output than are actually incurred, then overheads are said to be *over-absorbed* (or over-applied or over-recovered). Conversely, if too little overhead is applied to units of output, then overheads are said to be *under-absorbed* (under-applied, under-recovered). The degree to which overhead costs are over- or under-absorbed is a useful piece of management information. A record should be kept of the extent to which the overheads of each cost centre are over- or under-absorbed, and this can be a guide that indicates when overhead recovery rates require adjustment. (Because over- and under-absorbed overhead costs are charged directly to the profit and loss account, they are not reflected at all in any product cost. Clearly this is unsatisfactory in an absorption costing system that exists purely for product costing reasons).

An over- or under-absorption of overheads may arise because the actual level of overhead costs has varied from the amount anticipated, or because the level of activity actually experienced during a period has differed from the level predicted. Either of these causes (or the two of them acting together) can render the predetermined overhead recovery rate inappropriate. (It is also possible for these two causes to act together in such a way that the overhead rate remains appropriate: thus an expected level of activity of 10 000 direct labour hours in conjunction with a predicted level of overhead costs of £20 000 gives an overhead rate per direct labour hour of £2.00. If costs actually amount to £25 000 and the level of activity was 12 500 direct labour hours, the effective overhead recovery rate remains £2.00 per direct labour hour).

The explanations behind the major causes of over- and under-recovery are price rises, an expanding level of general economic activity, poor marketing, and so on. If plant capacity along with materials are available but sales volume is so low as to create an under-recovery of overheads, then this may be considered to be a marketing responsibility. However, if there is a backlog of orders and under-absorbed overhead costs result from the ineffective use of manufacturing facilities, then it becomes a manufacturing responsibility.

Fixed and variable overheads

So far the discussion has focused exclusively on deriving overhead rates that do not distinguish fixed from variable costs, but the derivation of separate rates for fixed and variable overheads is an important refinement of absorption costing.

Consider, for instance, a labour-intensive cost centre having estimated fixed overheads of £40 000 for a period, and estimated variable overheads of £30 000 for the same period, with an expectation of working 20 000 direct labour hours. A fixed overhead recovery rate of $\frac{£40\ 000}{20\ 000} = £2.00$ per direct labour hour, and a variable overhead recovery rate of $\frac{£30\ 000}{20\ 000} =$ £1.50 per direct labour hour can be readily derived. If the actual figures for the period in question are:

Fixed overheads	£41 500
Variable overheads	£31 500
Direct labour hours	£19 500

then the fixed overhead will be under-applied by £1000 [i.e. £40 000 − (19 500 x £2.00)] whilst fixed overhead prices have risen by £2500 [i.e. £41 500 − (19 500 x £2.00)]. Variable overheads to the extent of £29 250 (i.e. 19 500 x £1.50) will have been absorbed, but the actual variable overheads incurred (£31 500) are made up of price changes and inefficiencies of £2 250 (i.e. £31 500 − £29 250).

Job or process costing

Having described the various direct and indirect cost elements, we can put all the pieces together to show how the full cost of a job, batch, process or other activity can be ascertained. Figure 11.4 shows a job cost sheet for a job which passes through two departments. Direct material costs are obtained from the cost codes given on the relevant stores requisitions. Direct labour costs come from labour analyses. The overhead costs are applied according to the costing method employed.

In the job costing example shown in Figure 11.4 no attempt is made to compute the cost of running a department, but process costing is based on knowing the cost of operating each processing department. Figure 11.5 gives an example of a cost sheet for a process costing exercise in a company having two processes – X and Y. The cost per unit (tonne) can be built up as production progresses from raw materials to the finished product through, initially, process X and then through process Y.

Process costing is associated with flow production in industries such as chemicals, oil, textiles, plastics, paints, glass, and so on. All costs of each process (i.e. direct material costs, direct labour costs, any direct expenses and overheads) are accumulated and related to the units produced. During any period for which costs are accumulated it is probable that there will be some incomplete units of product on hand at the beginning of the period and, similarly, some partly processed units will be present at the close of the period. In order to work out a unit cost for the process it is necessary to convert all partly processed units into the equivalent of fully processed units. Thus 100 units that were complete in terms of material inputs but

| JOB COST SHEET | | | | | | | GHM |

Product _____   Date started _____   Order number _____

Stock _____   Date completed _____   Quantity _____

Customer _____

DEPARTMENT A

Direct material			Direct labour			Overhead	
Date	Code	Cost	Date	Code	Cost	Date	Cost

DEPARTMENT B

Direct material			Direct labour			Overhead	
Date	Code	Cost	Date	Code	Cost	Date	Cost

SUMMARY

Selling price

      Dept A   Dept B   TOTAL

Costs: Direct material
        Direct labour
        Overhead
Gross profit

Figure 11.4   Example of a job cost sheet

PROCESS COST SHEET   Month_____

Details	This month actual		This month budget		Year to date		Budget to date		Remarks
	£	per tonne	£	per tonne	£	per tonne	£	per tonne	
Process X									
Materials									
Wages									
Expenses (detail)									
Overhead allocation									
Process Y									
Material									
Wages									
Expenses (detail)									
Overhead allocation									
Office and establishment overheads									
Selling overheads									
Cost of sales (A)									
Sales									
Deduct : outward freight									
containers									
Net sales (B)									
Profit (B-A)									
Quantity of sales		tonnes		tonnes		tonnes		tonnes	

Figure 11.5 A process cost sheet

only half finished in terms of the labour and overhead input would be converted into *equivalent units* in the following way:

	£
Material input (total)	600
Labour input (50 per cent)	200
Overhead allocation (50 per cent)	100
	900

The completed units would cost:

	£
Material input	600
Labour input	400
Overhead allocation	200
	1200

Equivalent units are thus $\frac{900}{1200}$ x 100 = 75 units.

Segmental analysis

It is usually found that enterprises – especially smaller ones – do not know what proportion of their resources is devoted to their various activities or segments, or the profitability of these allocations. Producing useful computations of segmental costs and profit contributions can readily be achieved using analytical methods which, whilst not difficult in principle, are not widely adopted (due largely to a preoccupation with manufacturing cost accounting).

The fact that most companies do not know what proportion of their total marketing outlay is spent on each product, area, or customer group may be due to the absence of a sufficiently refined system of cost analysis, or it may be due to vagueness over the nature of certain costs. For instance, is the cost of packaging a promotional, a production, or a distribution expense? Some important marketing costs are hidden in manufacturing costs or in general and administrative costs (including finished goods inventory costs in the former and order-processing costs in the latter).

Since few companies are aware of costs and profits by segment in relation to sales levels, and since even fewer are able to predict changes in sales volume and profit contribution as a result of changes in marketing effort, the following errors arise:

1 Marketing budgets for individual products are too large, with the result that diminishing returns become evident and benefits would accrue from a reduction in expenditure.
2 Marketing budgets for individual products are too small and increasing returns would result from an increase in expenditure.
3 The marketing mix is inefficient, with an incorrect balance and incorrect amounts being spent on the constituent elements – such as too much on advertising and insufficient on direct selling activities.

4 Marketing efforts are misallocated amongst products and changes in these cost allocations (even with a constant level of overall expenditure) could bring improvements.

Similar arguments apply in relation to sales territories or customer groups as well as to products. The need exists, therefore, for control techniques to indicate the level of performance required and achieved as well as the outcome of shifting marketing efforts from one segment to another. As is to be expected, there exists great diversity in the methods by which manufacturers attempt to obtain costs (and profits) for segments of their business, but much of the cost data is inaccurate for such reasons as:

1 Marketing costs may be allocated to individual products, sales areas, customer groups, etc., on the basis of sales value or sales volume, but this involves circular reasoning. Costs should be allocated in relation to causal factors, and *it is marketing expenditures that cause sales to be made* rather than the other way round: managerial decisions determine marketing costs. Furthermore, despite the fact that success is so often measured in terms of sales value achievements by product line, this basis fails to evaluate the efficiency of the effort needed to produce the realized sales value (or turnover). Even a seemingly high level of turnover for a specific product may really be a case of mis-allocated sales effort. (An example should make this clear: if a salesman concentrates on selling product A which contributes £20 per hour of effort instead of selling product B which would contribute £50 per hour of effort, then it 'costs' the company £30 per hour he spends on selling product A. This is the *opportunity cost* of doing one rather than another and is a measure of the sacrifice involved in selecting only one of several alternative courses of action).

2 General overheads and administrative costs are arbitrarily (and erroneously) allocated to segments on the basis of sales volume.

3 Many marketing costs are not allocated at all as marketing costs since they are not identified as such but are classified as manufacturing, general, or administrative costs instead.

Distribution cost accounting (or analysis) has been developed to help overcome these problems and aims to:

(a) Analyse the costs incurred in distributing and promoting products so that when they are combined with production cost data overall profitability can be determined.

(b) Analyse the costs of marketing individual products to determine their profitability.

(c) Analyse the costs involved in serving different classes of customers and different areas to determine their profitability.

(d) Compute such figures as cost per sales call, cost per order, cost to put a new customer on the books, cost to hold £1 worth of inventory for a year, etc.

(e) Evaluate managers according to their actual controllable cost responsibilities.

(f) Evaluate alternative strategies or plans with full costs.

These analyses and evaluations provide senior management with the necessary information to enable them to decide which classes of customer to cultivate, which products to delete, which products to encourage, and so forth. Such analyses also provide a basis from which estimates can be made of the likely increases in product profitability that a specified increase in marketing effort should create. In the normal course of events it is far more difficult to predict the outcome of decisions that involve changes in marketing outlays in comparison with changes in production expenditure. It is easier, for instance, to estimate the effect of a new machine in the factory than it is to predict the impact of higher advertising outlays. Similarly, the effect on productive output of dropping a production worker is easier to estimate than is the effect on the level of sales caused by a reduction in the sales force.

The methodology of distribution cost analysis is similar to the methodology of product costing. Two stages are involved:

1 Marketing costs are initially reclassified from their *natural* expense headings (e.g. salaries) into *functional* cost groups (e.g. sales expenses) in such a way that each cost group brings together all the costs associated with a particular element of the marketing mix.

2 These functional cost groups are then apportioned to control units (i.e. products, customer groups, channels of distribution, etc.) on the basis of measurable criteria that bear a causal relationship to the total amounts of the functional cost groups.

Whilst costs can be broken down in a microscopic manner, there are dangers and limitations which should not be overlooked since they can hinder the control of marketing costs. If the outcome of functionalizing all marketing costs is to compute a unit cost for every activity, then this can be misleading. At the least a distinction should be made between fixed and variable costs, and the focus should be on the *purpose* for which a particular cost is to be derived and not simply on the *means* by which a figure is computed. Thus costs and units can be looked at separately, thereby avoiding myopic confusion.

An important distinction to make in distribution costs analysis – beyond the basic fixed–variable split – is that between *separable* fixed costs and *non-separable* fixed costs. A sales manager's salary is a fixed cost in conventional accounting, but in so far as his time can be linked to different products, sales territories, customers, etc., his salary (or at least portions of his salary) can be treated as being a separable fixed cost attributable to the segments in question in accordance with time devoted to each. In contrast, corporate advertising expenditure that is concerned with the company's image is not specific to any segment, hence it is non-separable and should not be allocated. Any non-specific, non-separable cost allocations would inevitably be very arbitrary, and such costs should therefore be excluded from all detailed cost and profit computations.

An illustration of segmental analysis

In Figure 11.6 a number of segments are illustrated for a hypothetical engineering company, ABC Ltd. It is possible to measure the costs and revenues at each level in order to highlight the profit performance of each segment. Thus, for example, the profit performance for the calculator market may be measured along the lines shown in Figure 11.7. The approach adopted in Figure 11.7 is a *contribution approach*, with costs and revenues being assigned to segments on bases that are essentially direct. Common costs have not been assigned to segments at all.

Whilst the contribution approach avoids the controversies surrounding the apportionment of indirect costs to segments there can be benefits in carrying out apportionments – provided the bases are clearly thought out and have a causal connexion with cost levels. This approach gives the foundation of *marketing productivity analysis*.

The steps to be followed in carrying out productivity analyses were hinted at above. They are:

1 Determine the analysis to be made
2 Classify costs into appropriate categories (as discussed above)
3 Select bases for apportioning indirect costs to functional activities
4 Allocate revenue and direct costs to the chosen segment
5 Apply indirect costs to the segment
6 Summarize 4 and 5 into a statement showing the net profit of the segment.

It is vital to recognize that this net profit approach to segmental analysis can only raise questions; it cannot provide any answers. (The reason for this, of course, is that the apportionment of indirect costs clouds the distinction between avoidable and unavoidable costs, and even direct costs may not be avoidable in the short run). The application of the above steps to a company's product range may produce the picture portrayed in Figure 11.8.

The segment could equally be sales territory, customer group, etc., and after the basic profit computation has been carried out it can be supplemented (as in Figure 11.9) by linking it to an analysis of the effort required to produce the profit result. (Clearly this is a multivariate situation in which profit depends upon a variety of input factors, but developing valid and reliable multivariate models is both complex and expensive. As a step in the direction of more rigorous analysis one can derive benefits from linking profit outcomes to individual inputs – such as selling time in the case of Figure 11.9).

From Figure 11.9 one can see that product A generated 43.7 per cent of total profits, requiring only 16.9 per cent of available selling time. This is highly productive. By contrast, product E produced only 6.8 per cent of total profits but required 10.2 per cent of selling effort. Even worse, however, is the 24.8 per cent of selling effort devoted to products G and H which are unprofitable.

A number of obvious questions arise from this type of analysis. Can the productivity of marketing activities be increased by:

1 Increasing net profits proportionately more than the corresponding increase in marketing outlays?
2 Increasing net profits with no change in marketing outlays?
3 Increasing net profits with a decrease in marketing costs?
4 Maintaining net profits at a given level but decreasing marketing costs?
5 Decreasing net profits but with a proportionately greater decrease in marketing costs?

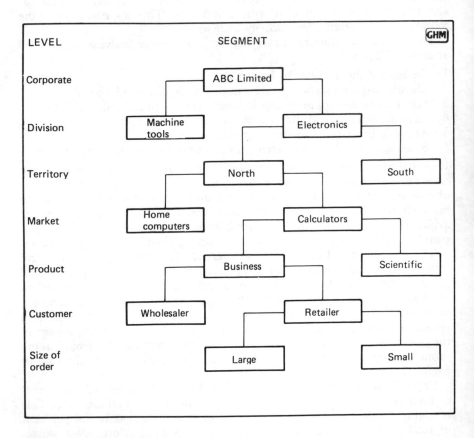

Figure 11.6   Segmental levels

COST ANALYSIS FOR DECISION MAKING

In making decisions, managers must pay a great deal of attention to the profit opportunities of alternative courses of action. This obviously requires that the cost implications of those alternatives are assessed. An important aspect of such cost analysis (but, as explained later, not the most important one) is that made between fixed and variable costs. A cost can be classified as being either fixed or variable in relation to changes in the level of activity within a given period. (In the long run, of course, all costs are variable.)

PRODUCT : CALCULATORS	NORTH TERRITORY	SOUTH TERRITORY	TOTAL
	(£)	(£)	(£)
Net sales	xxx	xxx	xxxx
Variable manufacturing costs	xx	xx	xxx
Manufacturing contribution	xx	xx	xxx
Marketing costs			
Variable:			
Sales commissions	x	x	x
Selling expenses	x	x	x
Variable contribution	xx	xx	xxx
Assignable:			
Salesmen's salaries	x	x	x
Manager's salary	x	x	x
Product advertising	x	x	x
Product contribution	xx	xx	xx
Non-assignable:			
Corporate advertising			x
Marketing contribution			xx
Fixed common costs:			
Manufacturing			x
Administration			x
Net profit			xx

Figure 11.7   Segmental contribution statement

Fixed costs

A cost is fixed if, within a specified time period, it does not change in response to changes in the level of activity. For example, a managing director's salary will not vary with the volume of goods produced during any year; interest payable at 10 per cent per annum on a loan of £500 000 will not vary within changes in a business's level of activity; and the road tax payable for a motor vehicle will not vary with the vehicle's annual mileage.

Figure 11.10 illustrates a typical fixed cost curve. (If one looks beyond the current time period, however, the managing director's salary may change – but not purely in response to changes in output.)

If we relate fixed costs to the level of activity (e.g. road tax to miles travelled) we will find that the fixed cost *per unit* of activity is variable: as activity increases, so the fixed cost per unit decreases, and vice versa.

	GHM
PRODUCT	% CONTRIBUTION TO TOTAL PROFITS
Total for all products	100.0
Profitable products:	
A	43.7
B	35.5
C	16.4
D	9.6
E	6.8
F	4.2
Sub-total	116.2
Unprofitable products;	
G	−7.5
H	−8.7
Sub-total	−16.2

Figure 11.8 Segmental profit statement

An enterprise's fixed costs can be categorized in the following way:

1 *Committed costs*. Costs that are primarily associated with maintaining the company's legal and physical existence, and over which management has little (if any) discretion. Insurance premiums, rates, and rent charges are typical examples.
2 *Managed costs*. Such costs are management and staff salaries that are related to current operations but which must continue to be paid to ensure the continued operating existence of the company.
3 *Programmed costs*. Costs that are subject both to management discretion and management control, but which are unrelated to current activities. R & D is a good example, and it will be apparent that these costs result from special policy decisions.

PRODUCT	% CONTRIBUTION TO TOTAL PROFITS	% TOTAL SELLING TIME
Total for all products	100.0	100.0
Profitable products:		
A	43.7	16.9
B	35.5	18.3
C	16.4	17.4
D	9.6	5.3
E	6.8	10.2
F	4.2	7.1
Sub-total	116.2	75.2
Unprofitable products:		
G	−7.5	9.5
H	−8.7	15.3
Sub-total	−16.2	24.8

GHM

Figure 11.9 Segmental productivity statement

Variable costs

A variable cost is one that changes in response to changes in the level of activity. Sales commissions in relation to sales levels, petrol costs in relation to miles travelled; and labour costs in relation to hours worked are obvious examples. Figure 11.11 shows a variable cost curve for direct materials. It will be apparent that, with certain exceptions, variable costs tend to be fixed per unit of output but are variable in total in relation to the level of output.

The exceptions result from costs that do not vary in direct proportion to changes in the level of activity. One underlying reason for this as far as labour costs are concerned is the *learning curve*. Learning curve theory was initially developed in the US aircraft industry, when it was observed that man–hours spent in building planes declined at a regular rate over a wide range of production. This effect arose from the capacity of human beings to learn, enabling them to avoid earlier errors and become more generally efficient in the execution of their jobs. In general, the greater the frequency of repetition, the greater will become the efficiency in performing the task. A learning curve pattern is shown in Figure 11.12. Evidence suggests that the improvement is predictable, and that there is greater scope for improvement in connexion with the more complex tasks.

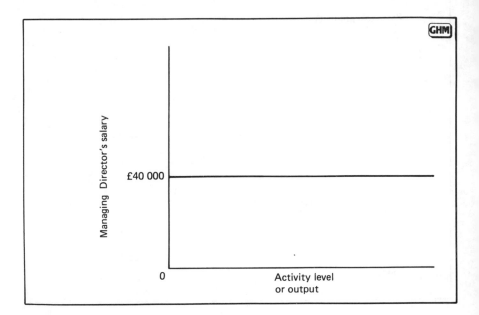

Figure 11.10   Fixed cost curve

On the other hand, when a factory is operating at or near full capacity it may be necessary for overtime to be worked, and this will increase the labour cost per unit of output.

When fixed and variable costs are combined, the results are as shown in Figure 11.13.

Mixed costs

Certain costs are of a hybrid nature, being partly fixed and partly variable. An example is found in telephone charges – the rental element is a fixed cost, whereas charges for calls made are a variable cost. Figure 11.14 (a) illustrates this behaviour pattern, and Figure 11.14 (b) shows the semi-variable cost behaviour that would be found if new telephones are installed as the level of business changes.

Some mixed costs are characteristically semi-fixed. Up to a given level of output it may only be necessary for a factory to work one shift and it may only need one foreman – a simple instance of a fixed supervisory cost. However, beyond that level of output it may be necessary to start a second shift and recruit a further supervisor, and this gives rise to the stepped cost pattern of Figure 11.14 (c). Maintenance costs payable on a contract basis

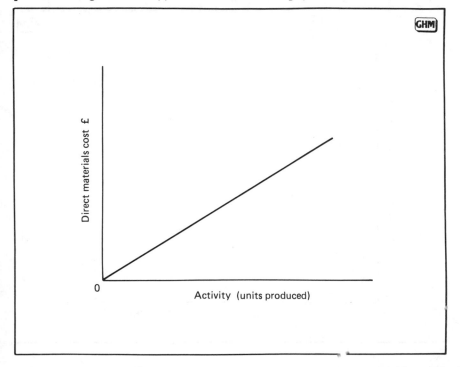

Figure 11.11   Variable cost curve

would tend to follow the pattern of Figure 11.14 (*d*) if more machines are bought as output increases.

With mixed costs the question arises of whether to treat the cost as partly fixed and partly variable, or as wholly fixed or wholly variable. The answer must depend on the degree of variability of the cost itself and the level of activity.

Separating fixed and variable costs

The total cost at any level of operations is the sum of a fixed cost component and a variable cost component. If the variable cost per unit of a particular item is £1.25, fixed costs for the period are £10 000, and the output of the period is 12 000 units, then the total cost will be:

Total cost   =   Fixed cost   +   Variable cost
£25 000   =   £10 000   +   £(12 000 x 1.25)

When the values of the fixed and variable components are unknown it is

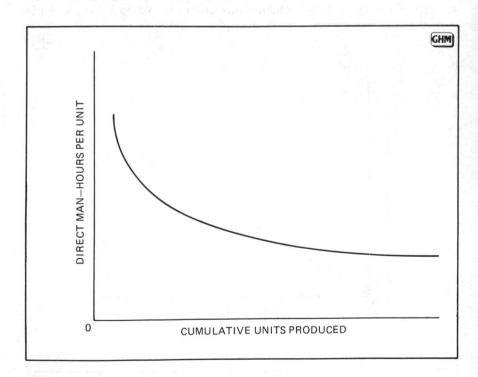

Figure 11.12   Learning curve

possible to estimate them so long as the total costs are known for any two levels of activity. The procedure is as follows:

1 Deduct total cost at the lower of the two levels from total cost at the higher level. Since fixed costs do not vary with volume, the difference must be entirely composed of variable costs
2 Divide the difference in cost by the difference in volume (i.e. units produced) to give the unit variable cost
3 Multiply one observed level of activity by the unit variable cost and deduct this from the total cost of that level to give the fixed cost component.

The following example will clarify the method fully:

Total cost at output of 15 000 units per period: £25 000
Total cost at output of 10 000 units per period: £20 000
Difference   5 000 units £5 000

The unit variable cost is therefore £5000/5000 = £1. At the higher level of activity the variable cost must be 15 000 x £1 = £15 000. Since total cost is £25 000 it follows that fixed costs must be £10 000. (This answer can be checked by applying the same reasoning to the lower level of activity).

This method is simple and rather crude. More refined statistical techniques can be applied to obtain more precise results.

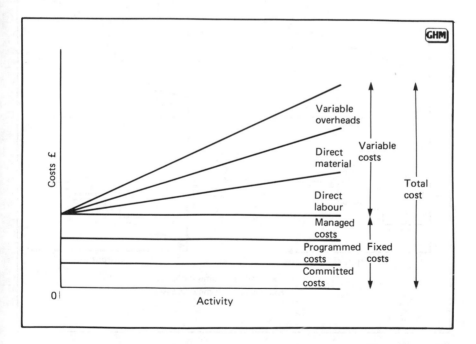

Figure 11.13 Classified cost pattern

Usefulness of the fixed–variable split

The importance of separating variable from fixed costs stems from the different behaviour patterns of each, which have a significant bearing on their control: variable costs must be controlled in relation to the level of activity, whilst fixed costs must be controlled in relation to time. From a decision-making point of view, it is also important to know whether or not a particular cost will vary as a result of a given decision.

By plotting a company's (or division's) total fixed cost curve and then adding the variable cost curve for the expected possible levels of activity in a forthcoming period, the total cost curve shown in Figure 11.15 (*a*)) is obtained. Alternatively, if the variable costs are plotted and the fixed costs added (Figure 11.15, (*b*)), the same total cost curve is obtained but by another means.

Because fixed costs must be incurred even when there is no activity, the fixed cost curve (and hence the total cost curve) cuts the vertical axis above the origin, and this results in the total cost curve being proportional – but not strictly proportional – to the level of activity.

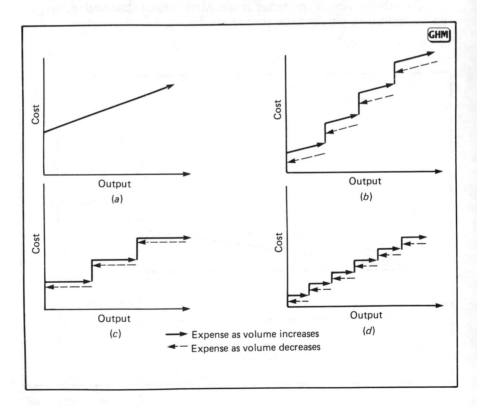

Figure 11.14   Cost behaviour patterns

If a revenue curve is superimposed on the same graph as the cost curves, the result is the break-even chart (see Figure 11.16) which depicts the profit/loss picture for several possible cost-revenue situations at different levels of activity. Various assumptions underlying break-even analysis – such as constant prices, a constant sales mix, and a greater degree of independence amongst costs, revenue, and profits than can be found in most real-life situations – make the break-even chart a basic tool. Nevertheless, provided its user appreciates the static nature of this technique he should be able to employ it effectively.

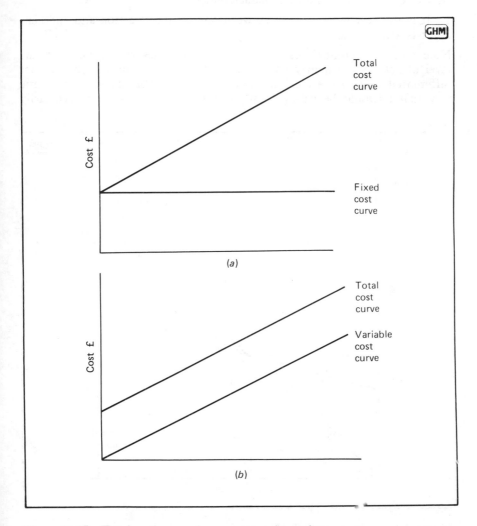

Figure 11.15   Total cost curves from same total cost data

In particular, break-even analysis is useful as a background information device for reviewing overall cost and profit levels, but it can also be used in connexion with special decisions such as selecting a channel of distribution or make-or-buy decisions.

Differential cost

It was stated earlier in this chapter (page 171) that the fixed-variable split was not the most important one for decision-making purposes. That distinction goes to the notion of *differential cost* which, in a situation of choice, exhibits the following characteristics:

1 It is the cost which differs between one course of action and another
2 It is a future cost.

Note that a differential cost may be one that varies with changes in the level of activity, or it may not. Thus it would be wrong to suppose that differential costs are exclusively composed of variable costs in the same way that it would be wrong to suppose that direct costs are necessarily

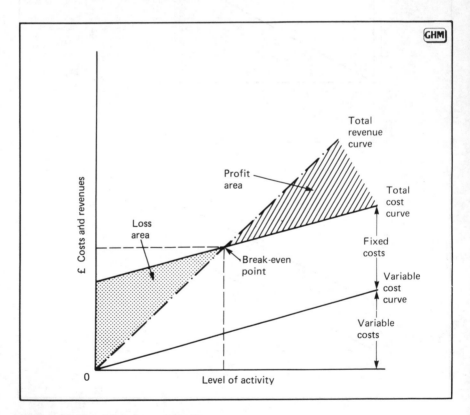

Figure 11.16   A break-even chart

variable: it all depends on the particular situation and the question at issue.

Avoidable and unavoidable costs

When the choice lies between an existing way of doing something and a new alternative it is helpful to think in terms of *avoidable* versus *unavoidable* costs: thus the costs of adopting an alternative are avoidable if one persists with the present way of doing things, but not all of the present costs will necessarily be avoidable if one changes to an alternative.

If, for example, a company is manufacturing gas appliances, and plans are being made to bring out a new product range and cease an existing range, then (according to British Gas Corporation rules) it will continue to be necessary to maintain an inventory of spares for the outgoing range for 15 years after its discontinuance. There are unavoidable costs in this case, in the maintenance of these spares stocks.

Sunk costs

Once funds have been committed to a particular purpose – especially in the case of capital expenditure – the chances of recovering them depend upon how much can be obtained from either disposing of the asset, or selling the output from the asset. The funds so committed are termed *sunk costs*, and are irrelevant in deciding whether to abandon or continue operations, or to replace an old asset with a new one. This is so because no present or future action can undo the decision to spend the money. The money has been spent regardless of what happens next.

Marginal costs

Finally in this section we might note the problem over terminology concerning costs for decision-making. Differential costs are also known as relevant costs, incremental costs, and marginal costs. Strictly, *marginal* cost refers to the change in total cost resulting from the production of one more (or one less) unit of output. Almost certainly, therefore, marginal cost is a variable cost concept, whereas the other versions may be treated as synonyms and are not restricted to variable costs.

COST ANALYSIS FOR CONTROL

Controllable and uncontrollable costs

The most important categories of cost for control purposes are *controllable* and *uncontrollable* costs. Costs can only be controlled if they are related to the organizational framework: in other words, costs should be controlled in accordance with the concept of responsibility – a cost should be controlled at whatever level it is originated and initially approved by the individual who did the initiating and approving. In this way it will be clear that certain costs are the responsibility of, and can only be controlled by, the chief executive of a company (such as corporate public relations expenditure) whereas others are controllable by responsible individuals at lower levels of the organizational hierarchy (e.g. a departmental manager will be responsible for the salary expense of those who work within his department, and a foreman will be responsible for the cost of consumable materials used in his productive department. Strictly, a foreman should only be held responsible for usage rather than prices due to his lack of control over the latter.) Cost control can only be effective if individuals are held responsible for the costs over which they have authority. This is the essence of responsibility accounting.

At this stage, however, it is important to distinguish between costs that are controllable at a given level of managerial authority within a given period of time, and those that are not. This distinction is not the same as the one between variable costs and fixed costs. For example, rates are a fixed cost that are uncontrollable – for a given time period – by any managerial level, whereas the annual road licence fee for a particular vehicle is a fixed cost that is controllable by the fleet manager who has the power to dispense with the vehicle. In the same way the insurance premium payable on inventories is a variable cost (fluctuating with the value of the inventory from month to month) that is not controllable at the storekeeper level, but it is controllable at the level of the executive who determines inventory policy (subject, of course, to the environmental vagaries of such factors as consumer demand which can never be removed).

Controllability is affected by both managerial authority and the element of time. (A short-run fixed cost can become a long-run variable cost. Thus a managing director's salary is fixed for 12 months, but is variable thereafter.) All costs are controllable to some extent over the longer term, even if this involves a change in the scale of operations or a relocation of the company.

The problem of distinguishing between controllable and uncontrollable costs is more difficult in relation to overheads as opposed to direct costs. It is vital that costs be regulated at source, and this means that for many overhead items the beneficiary of cost incurrence is very often not the person to be charged with the cost. Obvious examples are overhead services – maintenance, the personnel department, post room/switchboard facilities – from which all members of the company derive benefits, but for which cost responsibility is accorded to the respective supervisors and managers of these service functions.

In a control sense, overhead absorption rates and full product costs (made up of direct labour cost, direct material cost, and applied overhead) are not helpful. These rates and product costs must be broken down into their constituent parts and these parts must be controlled at source. It is impossible for one manager to control an overhead *rate*, but it is possible for him to control those specific costs over which he has authority.

To sum up so far, the approach to cost control that is based on the concept of responsibility accounting involves designing the cost control system to match the organizational structure so that it reflects realistically the responsibilities of departmental managers, supervisors, etc.

In devising an accounting system for securing cost control that accords with the organizational structure it will usually be found necessary to define more closely the duties of responsible individuals, and various responsibilities will have to be re-assigned in order to give a logical structure to an organization that may have grown in a haphazard manner. All subsequent organizational changes that lead to changes in individual responsibilities should be accompanied by suitable modifications to the cost control system.

Standard costing

Once the organizational structure, and associated responsibilities, have been established it may prove helpful to the control exercise to employ a standard costing system.

Standard costs are costs that should be obtained under efficient operations. They are predetermined costs and represent targets that are an essential feature of cost control. An important measure of performance is derived from a comparison of actual performance and standard performance. For example, if the standard material input for a unit of production is 50p and the actual cost is 48p, then the variance of -2p is the appropriate measure of performance and (assuming a satisfactory quality level) the actual performance is an improvement on the standard. It is better to compare actual costs with a cost standard than with, say, comparative figures from the company's previous financial results. The main reason for this is that a comparison between current results and previous results presupposes that the previous results were at a level of efficiency that was sufficiently suitable to be emulated: this will rarely be the case. The future is a much better perspective, and future circumstances will almost certainly differ from past circumstances. If this year's profit is £3m and last year's was £2m, this may be seen as a remarkable improvement and a highly desirable state of affairs – but maybe this year's profit should have been £5m.

The establishing of standards as a basis for setting standard costs is an important part of the work of the industrial engineer. Without standards, a company's management has no way of knowing if the company's overall performance, or the performance of one of its divisions, for example, was average, below average, or exceptional.

Whilst standards are closely related to budgets, the two are not identical. A budget is a prediction of probable future results that has been formalized into a plan whereas a standard is a cost level that should be achieved by efficient working under prevailing conditions. (Budgets are also authorities to spend, or to limit spending, and are prepared for all departments and operations of a company, but standards are simply benchmarks that tend to be used mainly for manufacturing activities).

The general nature of a standard costing system is shown in Figure 11.17, which is self-explanatory. The major difficulty lies in setting realistic standards, accompanied in many instances by the educational problem of introducing such a system into a company for the first time.

Among the benefits of standard costing are the following:

1 It results in simpler systems
2 It produces the same costs for physically identical products, whereas a batch or process costing system would probably not

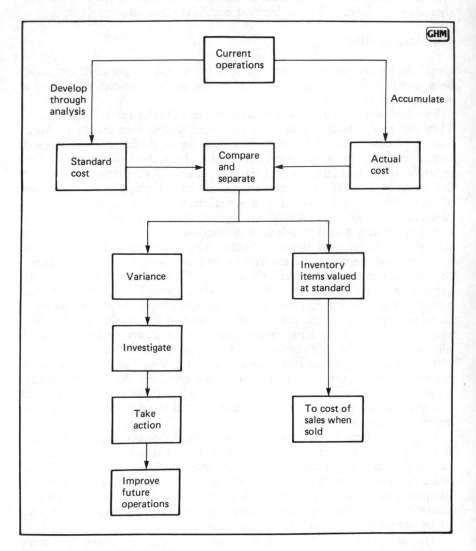

Figure 11.17 A standard costing system

3   The whole costing system need not be based on standards, but selected parts only (e.g. material costing) may be 'standardized' and the remainder based on actual costs

4   Control information is specific, and produced for each appropriate level of management, thereby permitting delegation to be effective

5   Management by exception is permitted by setting both standards and tolerance limits

6   A forward-looking attitude is encouraged throughout the firm

7   It segregates the effect on costs of temporary variations in the level of output and sales.

ALTERNATIVE COSTING SYSTEMS

Contract costing

Contract costing is adopted for large jobs undertaken by civil engineering or building concerns, often lasting through several accounting periods. Essentially it is a large-scale application of the job costing system described earlier in the chapter.

When, as is usually the case, most of the work is done on site, it is simple to collect the direct costs for the contract. The only overheads to assign are head office and central stores, perhaps with the addition of central fabrication expenses.

Direct costing

The absorption costing system attracts criticism through the treatment given to overheads which, at best, can be little more than arbitrary and, at worst, can be positively misleading. An alternative approach is to use variable, marginal or direct costing (these terms are interchangeable). This differs from absorption costing in that no attempt is made to absorb fixed overheads, with the result that only costs of a variable nature are applied to the chosen cost object.

The assumption behind direct costing is that fixed manufacturing costs (i.e. overheads) are of the same nature as administrative expenses – they are incurred to support the productive activities of the firm. As a result, they are not considered to be product costs to be assigned to the units produced, but treated instead as 'period costs' and charged wholly against profits in the period in which they arise.

The question to be answered is *not* whether direct costing is better than absorption costing, but whether direct costing is better *in a particular situation*. The disadvantages and advantages of direct costing in each specific case must be considered and, if the former do not outweigh the latter, then direct costing should be adopted. (These advantages and disadvantages should relate to the information that management will receive, and not to the theory of cost accounting).

Direct costing has the following advantages:

1   It is simple to operate, since there are no problems of fixed cost allo-

cations, and the direct costs are easy to identify and accumulate.

2 The effects of inventory fluctuations on profits are eliminated because no varying element of fixed costs is included in the inventory valuation.

3 The difficulties of explaining fixed overhead absorption are avoided, and fluctuations in income are easier to explain as they result from changes in sales volume and not from changes in inventory.

4 The relationship among cost, volume, and profits is highlighted, thus helping to decide between alternatives.

Inevitably, there are also general disadvantages, including:

1 The omission of fixed cost allocation presupposes that allocating these overhead costs serves no useful purpose, but this is not necessarily true, especially when a variety of different products are made.

2 The substitution of a 'contribution' (i.e. revenue less direct cost) for 'gross profit' (i.e. revenue less absorption cost) can lead to confusion.

3 The exclusion of fixed overheads from product costs can give a feeling of false security over performance, with the possible result that fixed overheads are ignored for control as well as product costing purposes.

4 The absence of an approximation to 'full' cost may discourage cost reduction efforts.

The choice between using absorption or direct costing will be determined by such factors as:

1 The system of financial control in use (e.g. responsibility accounting is inconsistent with absorption costing).

2 The production methods in use (e.g. marginal costing is favoured in simple processing situations in which all products receive similar attention, but when different products receive widely differing amounts of attention absorption costing may be more realistic).

3 The significance of the prevailing level of fixed overhead costs.

Uniform costing

This is not a separate system of accounting, but indicates the adoption of common definitions and practices within an industry, or among the member firms of a trade association. The major benefit of uniform costing is in inter-firm comparisons, where it is necessary to compare like with like. It also enables new or small firms to use an adequate accounting system, developed by experts for their type of business, which otherwise might have been beyond their means to design. (It does not necessarily require a high-salaried expert to operate a uniform costing system, but it takes a specialist to develop one.)

CHECKLIST ON COST ACCOUNTING

1 Is the company's costing system tailored to the company's needs?

2 Have cost centres been clearly defined?

3 Are the benefits of the system commensurate with its costs?

4 Are all costs classified into their direct and indirect, fixed and variable, controllable and uncontrollable, and separable and joint categories?

5 Is the behaviour of different costs understood in relation to changes in the level of activity?

6 Are cost reports made available promptly? How often? How quickly?

7 Could statements be presented earlier if more estimates were used? (Are estimating procedures reliable?)

8 Are figures rounded so that results are more easily understood?

9 Can any figures of small value (as shown on the chart of accounts) be grouped?

10 Are the descriptions of reported items clear?

11 Are unusual items adequately explained?

12 Will further (or less) mechanization affect the overhead of cost accounting?

13 Can the effectiveness of cost accounting procedures be improved?

14 Has sufficient thought been given to the type of costing system to use? (That is, standard costing, absorption costing, or marginal costing.)

15 Has the purpose for which costing is being performed been fully considered? (For example, pricing, product costing, cost control.)

16 Is the costing system adequate in determining the relative efficiencies and profitability of divisions, processes, product lines, jobs, etc?

17 Is the costing system adequate for the needs of EDP and operations research analysts?

18 Are ratios, graphs, etc., used to supplement the figures produced by the costing system?

19 Is a satisfactory procedure being operated to price material issues from stores?

20 Are all withdrawals of stock and ordering of goods from outside suppliers duly authorized by requisitions?

21 Are job allocation numbers recorded against labour time, material usage, etc., in all cases?

22 Do employees understand the importance of recording the allocation of time to jobs? How are they encouraged to do this accurately?

23 What is the basis for the apportionment of each service department's costs? Is the most suitable basis selected in every case?

24 How are overheads absorbed into productive output? Is the most suitable basis used?

25 What action is taken on the basis of over- or under-recovery of overheads?

26 Are normalized overhead recovery rates used? If not, why not? For example, is the level of activity stable from month to month?

27 Have separate overhead rates been developed for fixed overhead costs and variable overhead costs?

28 Why are overheads absorbed (if they are absorbed)?

29 Is the contribution margin concept understood within the company?

30 Is cost-volume-profit analysis undertaken?

31 Is marginal costing undertaken?

32 Has the company's margin of safety ever been worked out?
33 Are the comparative advantages and disadvantages of marginal costing versus absorption costing fully appreciated?
34 Is the costing system closely geared to the type of production processes operated?
35 What role does cost accounting play in relation to special decision-making?

FURTHER READING

Belkaoui, A., *Cost Accounting: A Multidimensional Emphasis*, Dryden Press, Chicago, 1983. A technically comprehensive text that draws on a range of disciplines to show how to analyse costs.

Cowe, R., (ed.) *Handbook of Management Accounting*, 2nd edition, Gower, Aldershot, 1988. A comprehensive array of commissioned contributions from experts across the domain of management accounting (covering planning, control, and much more).

Horngren, C.T. and Foster, G., *Cost Accounting: A Managerial Emphasis*, 6th edition, Prentice-Hall, Englewood Cliffs, NJ, 1987. The leading international text in the field, offering lucid and comprehensive coverage.

Solomons, D. (ed), *Studies in Cost Analysis*, 2nd edition, Sweet & Maxwell, London, 1968. An excellent collection of articles looking in an authoritative way at a range of relevant issues concerning the aims and methods of cost analysis.

Wilson, R.M.S., *Cost Control Handbook*, 2nd edition, Gower, Aldershot, 1983. This text deals in considerable detail with cost analysis for planning and control, and illustrates the application of costing methods in all major functional areas.

Wilson, R.M.S. and McHugh, G., *Financial Analysis: A Managerial Introduction*, Cassell, London, 1987. Within this broad-based book, especially written for those with little formal financial background, cost analysis is explained in a way that aims to help the non-specialist.

12 Taxation

J C Craig

Tax law is mainly based on the Income and Corporation Taxes Act 1970, the Taxes Management Act 1970, the Capital Allowances Act 1968, the Capital Gains Tax Act 1979 and annual Finance Acts. The first of these Acts brought together the combined effects of the Income Tax 1952 and subsequent Finance Acts to 1969 with the principal exception of personal capital gains tax; this is now governed by the Capital Gains Tax Act 1979 which consolidated the law on capital gains tax up to 5 April 1979.

Each year (sometimes more frequently) following the budget speech, a Finance Act is introduced, so it is always necessary to look at the accumulated effect of amendments when examining a tax problem.

Interpretation of the law follows the standard pattern of court decisions, and there are now more than two thousand references to decided cases, each of which is normally binding on everyone in similar circumstances, unless reversed by a subsequent enactment or by a decision in a superior court. (Very occasionally the House of Lords will overturn a previous decision of the same Court.)

RETURNS AND ASSESSMENTS

Every person who receives income of any kind is under statutory obligation to complete a return of income each year; the senior partner deals with the form for a partnership, and the officers for a limited company. Personal responsibility for making correct returns cannot be avoided even if an agent is employed to complete the return form.

Tax assessment

Assessments for tax are made by local Inspectors of Taxes in accordance with the return of income and supplementary figures supplied by the taxpayers, including a copy of the annual accounts of a business. Where necessary, an assessment may be altered within six years of the end of the accounting period to which it relates, for example if a mistake is discovered by either the Revenue or the taxpayer. However, there is no time-limit to the correction of assessments which were wrong because of the fraud, wilful default or neglect of the taxpayer. A case heard in 1970 (Rose v. Humbles) referred to assessments stretching back to 1942.

Appeals against assessment

Where the taxpayer does not agree with the Inspector's assessment, he may appeal in writing within thirty days. Usually the appeal is settled by correspondence or at a meeting with the Inspector, with or without professional advice. If agreement cannot be reached the taxpayer may have the appeal heard by either:

1 General Commissioners, who are leading local citizens, unpaid, not civil servants and not specialists in tax, but hear each case on its merits and aim to give a fair decision according to the facts; or
2 Special Commissioners, who are civil servants concentrating wholly on the complexities of tax and therefore better able to unravel an argument of a complex nature.

It tends to be more costly to ask for the appeal to be heard by the Special Commissioners because, though no charge is made, it may be necessary to travel some distance with professional advisers for the appeal to be heard, and it is usually advisable to brief Counsel to put the case.

A decision of the Commissioners is binding on both Revenue and taxpayer unless it can be shown that the query is based on an interpretation of the law, when permission may be asked to appeal to the High Court in England or the Court of Session in Scotland.

Further appeals may go beyond the High Court to the Court of Appeal and then to the House of Lords, or in Scotland from the Court of Session to the House of Lords, if it can be shown there is still doubt as to whether the law has been interpreted correctly. Occasionally in England an appeal may be taken direct from the High Court to the House of Lords.

Appeals are an expensive, troublesome activity. A good working relationship between the company's management, its auditors who commonly handle the tax returns, and the local Inspector of Taxes, with the management taking a close personal interest in the tax computations, is recommended as the most practical approach to tax.

Interest on tax assessments

If tax is not paid on its due date, or if unpaid tax is held over for too long pending an appeal, interest will be payable at 11 per cent – not allowable for tax purposes. In practice it is preferable to avoid this charge by paying tax not in dispute and buying a certificate of tax deposit for the balance. If after negotiations the amount of tax in dispute is payable the certificate can be surrendered in satisfaction of the tax and there will be no interest charges. If the tax is not payable the certificate can be encashed or used to pay other tax and interest will be received.

ADJUSTMENT OF PROFIT AND COMPUTATION OF AMOUNT LIABLE TO TAX

The normal pattern for an industrial or commercial business is to measure and adjust the income from all sources, to arrive at the total on which corporation tax is payable as shown in Figure 12.1.

	£	GHM
(a)		
Income		
Gross trading profit	700 000	
Rent from industrial premises let to tenants	20 000	
Interest from bank deposit account	6 000	
Dividends from shares held	10 000	
Interest from debentures held (gross)	4 000	
	740 000	
Expenditure		
Depreciation	26 000	
Salaries, wages, employer's contributions to national insurance and graduated pensions	60 000	
Directors' salaries and fees	10 000	
Bad debts	300	
Specific provision for the bad debt of a named customer	100	
General provision for bad debts	800	
Legal expenses	200	
Rent, rates and insurance	3 000	
Superannuation (company's contribution to an approved scheme)	2 000	
Heating and lighting	1 000	
Travelling expenses	2 000	
Entertainment expenses	600	
Distribution costs	20 000	
Sundry expenses	3 000	
Loss on sale of machinery	1 000	
	130 000	
Net profit	610 000	

Figure 12.1 *Example of a corporation tax computation*
Shows the profit and loss account (a) adjustment for corporation tax purposes (b) and the calculation of corporation tax (c)

191

(GHM)

	£
(b)	
Net profit shown in the accounts	610 000

Add back items not allowable

Depreciation	26 000
General provision for bad debts	800
Entertainment expenses	600
Loss on sale of machinery	1 000

	28 400
	638 400

Deduct items, either not taxable or taxable
under different headings

Rent	20 000
Interest income	6 000
Dividends	10 000
Interest	4 000

	40 000
	598 400

Less
Capital allowances (in lieu of depreciation) — 28 400

Case I Income — 570 000

(c)

Case I income – business profits adjusted	570 000
Case III income – untaxed income from bank deposit interest	6 000
Schedule A income – rent	20 000
Income received subject to deduction of income tax at source – debenture interest but not dividends	4 000

	600 000
Corporation tax at 35% on £600 000	210 000
	390 000

Dividend income, not liable to corporation tax, is not part of the computation	10 000
Remainder, which may be retained or paid out as dividend	400 000

Figure 12.1 (concluded)

In making the adjustment of profit to arrive at the amount liable to tax, the starting point is the profit shown in the ordinary profit and loss account. Expenses not allowable must be added back; income which is either not taxable or taxable under a different Case or Schedule must be deducted, to arrive at the adjusted trading profit assessable under Schedule D Case I (or Case II).

Apart from advance corporation tax paid to the Collector of Taxes following the payment of dividends (dealt with later), the balance of the liability to corporation tax (the 'mainstream' liability) is due for payment nine months after the end of the accounting period except in the case of companies which carry on the same trade as they did prior to 1965. Such companies may have a longer interval; normally they pay their mainstream liability on 1 January in the fiscal year following that in which the accounting period ends, unless there has been a change of accounting date.

Rate of tax

The rate of corporation tax is announced for each financial year, which runs from 1 April to the following 31 March, in the Chancellor's end-of-year budget. For the financial year 1985, which ended on 31 March 1986, a rate of 40 per cent applies and for financial year 1986 the rate is 35 per cent. For 'small' companies the rate of corporation tax on income is 30 per cent for financial year 1985 and 29 per cent for financial year 1986. For this purpose a company is small if profits do not exceed £100 000 (unless the company has associated companies, in which case a lower level applies); a sliding scale applies to profits between £100 000 and £500 000.

Accounting year

If the company's accounting year spans two financial years in which the percentage differs, the profits are apportioned on a time basis. In, for example, the accounting year ended 31 December 1986, three-twelfths of the profit (for January, February, March 1986) will be taxed at the rate applicable to financial year 1985 and the remaining nine-twelfths at the rate for financial year 1986.

ALLOWABLE EXPENSES

For any expense to be allowable, it must have been incurred 'wholly and exclusively' for purposes of the business. Certain forms of expenditure are disallowed, either by definite statements in the Acts, or as a result of cases decided by the Courts. It would be impossible to give an exhaustive list here, particularly as many of them concern only a restricted range of industries, but a selection of the more common ones is given below.

General advice is: when in doubt, check with the detailed tax textbooks; if these do not settle the doubt, claim the expense is allowable and see the

Inspector's reaction. There is no penalty for this approach provided the true nature of the expense is stated openly and honestly.

Salaries and wages

Salaries and wages of employees and directors are normally allowable in full. However the deduction allowed for excessive payments to part-time directors is liable to be restricted if the Inspector is not satisfied that the amount is reasonable considering the services rendered.

Entertaining

Entertainment expenses are not allowable, except for entertaining overseas customers, and even in this case the amount must be reasonable considering the potential business arising. A UK resident agent of a foreign customer is not an overseas customer for this purpose.

'Entertainment' includes gifts of food, drink and tobacco – for example, as Christmas presents.

When a senior employee is reimbursed for the cost of entertaining UK customers, the amount is not treated as part of his personal income, but if he is given an allowance to cover entertaining, among other expenses, it becomes part of his earned income from which he cannot deduct any part of the cost of the entertaining.

Bad debts

A general reserve for bad debts is not allowable, but actual bad debts and a specific provision for the bad debts of a named customer are allowable.

Depreciation

Depreciation is not allowable, but capital allowances are given in appropriate cases instead.

Capital expenditure

No kind of capital expenditure is allowable other than by way of capital allowances. Capital profit or loss on the sale of an asset is excluded from the computation of business profit, but may be subject to a separate calculation for capital gains tax.

Legal expenses

Some legal expenses are and some are not allowable, the distinction being broadly that they are allowable if they relate to a transaction of a revenue nature but not if they are of a capital nature. For example, legal expenses for the preparation of a service agreement for a manager, or the collection of debts, or the renewal of an existing short lease are revenue and allowable, but legal expenses in connection with the purchase of freehold premises or a long lease are capital and are not allowable.

Retirement benefits

Retirement benefits for employees are allowable whether they are direct pensions or contributions to a superannuation scheme approved by the Inland Revenue. A moderate lump sum to an employee on his retirement would be allowable, but an exceptional lump to a superannuation fund would be spread forward over future years.

RELIEF FOR INCREASE IN STOCK VALUES

Stock relief was introduced by Finance Act 1975 and survived in various forms until withdrawn with effect from 12 March 1984.

History

In times of inflation, an increasing amount of cash became tied up in trading stock, causing cash-flow problems. To alleviate these difficulties, stock relief was introduced. Relief was first granted as a deferment of tax by the Finance Act 1975, and was extended by Finance (No.2) Act 1975. A more permanent relief was provided for in the Finance Act 1976: broadly the taxable profit for an accounting period was reduced by the increase in the value of stock held less a percentage of the Case I or II profit which would otherwise be liable to tax. In any period in which there was a decrease in the value of stock held, taxable profit was increased by the amount of the fall or the amount of unrecovered past stock relief, whichever is smaller.

Because a large potential charge to tax existed in many companies should their stock levels fall, the Finance (No.2) Act 1979 provided that certain stock relief granted be excluded from the amount of unrecovered past stock relief and thus effectively be written off.

In November 1980 a new system was introduced (by the Finance Act 1981) under which relief was given by reference to an 'all stocks' index published monthly by the Department of Industry. The movement in the 'all stocks' index over the period of account was applied to the closing stock of the previous period less a *de minimis* amount of £2000. If there was a reduction or no movement in the index no relief was granted and no addition made to taxable profits. There was no clawback of relief unless trade ceased or the scale of activities in the company became small in relation to past levels.

Unused stock relief

Unused relief under the Finance Act 1981 may only be carried forward for six years. If it is unused by that time the relief is lost. There are rules for determining the order of set-off of reliefs available in each year. Unused relief under the old systems may be carried forward without time limit.

THE NECESSARY BOOK-KEEPING

Adjustment of profit and computation of tax payable are made outside the double-entry book-keeping system, but settlement of the tax requires three ledger accounts:

1 Corporation tax account (including advance corporation tax and tax credits)
2 Income tax account for unfranked investment income
3 Income tax account for PAYE deducted from employees' income.

The foundation for accounts 1 and 2 is that a company suffers corporation tax but not income tax on its own income. Income tax which has been deducted at source from investment income received by the company may be offset against income tax deducted from payments made out by the company, and if a net balance is due by the company it is payable to the Collector of Taxes. If a balance is due to the company it will be treated as a payment to account of any corporation tax due for the period. It is important to keep franked items separated from unfranked, and PAYE separate from both.

The necessary entries are summarized in Figure 12.2

CAPITAL ALLOWANCES

Capital allowances exist on seven main types of fixed assets used wholly and exclusively for purposes of the business:

1 Industrial buildings
2 Plant and machinery
3 Agricultural land and buildings
4 Mines and oil-wells
5 Capital expenditure on scientific research
6 Patents
7 Know-how.

Only the first two types will be considered in detail here.

When any asset which qualifies for allowances is purchased, the year's allowances are given in full for the company's accounting period no matter how late in the period the asset was obtained. This rule may need to be modified where the accounting period is shorter than twelve months.

It is important to consider the overall position before deciding whether or not, or to what extent capital allowances should be claimed.

Corporation tax account   with double entry in: **GHM**

Debit:
(a) adjustment for overprovision of last   Profit and loss
    year's liability   (appropriation) a/c

(b) Excess tax suffered on unfranked   Unfranked investment
    investment income tax   income a/c

Credit:
(a) Estimated rax on the profits for the   Profit and loss
    year now ending   (appropriation) a/c

(b) Adjustment for under provision for   Profit and loss
    last year's liability   (appropriation) a/c

Tax on unfranked investment income account

Debit:
Income tax suffered at source on   Unfranked investment
unfranked investment income received   income a/c

Credit:
Tax retained when paying out debenture   Accounts for debenture,
interest and other annual interest   etc interest paid
payments

Where credit is greater than debit, the
difference is settled by paying tax to the
Collector   Bank a/c

Where debit is greater than credit, the
difference is settled by transfer to
corporation tax a/c   Corporation tax a/c

Advance corporation tax

Debit:
Tax credit accompanying franked   Memorandum only – not
investment income received   passed through books of
                                                account

Credit:
ACT paid when paying out dividends

Figure 12.2 Entries to make in the tax accounts

Industrial buildings

The nature of the business must be industrial as distinct from commercial, retailing or wholesaling, or professional. Even for an industrial company the allowance is not given for offices and showrooms, except where these form an integral part of a factory and account for less than 25 per cent (10 per cent prior to 16 March 1983) of its whole cost. The allowances to the first owner are as follows:

1 Initial allowance: this was abolished for expenditure after 31 March 1986 (other than for expenditure in enterprise zones). Previously the rates were as follows:

	%
After 10 March 1981	75
After 13 March 1984	50
After 31 March 1985	25

2 Writing-down allowance of 4 per cent of the cost price (or 2 per cent if the building was erected before November 1962).

In the year of disposal, instead of the writing-down allowance there is a balancing allowance or balancing charge to bring total allowances into line with net cost.

Where the building is sold for more than it cost, the balancing charge cannot exceed the total of allowances already received. (There may, however, be a taxable capital gain in addition to the balancing charge).

On sale of a factory built before November 1962 there is no balancing adjustment if it is sold after it is fifty years old, and for factories built since November 1962 none after they are twenty-five years old.

Cost price includes: the building, plus the architect's fees, plus cost of tunnelling, levelling and preparing the land; installing main services, fences, perimeter walls and roadways on the site.

It does not include: the cost of land, legal and estate agency fees; preparation of a lease; purchase price of a lease; demolition of a former building.

When a building is demolished, the cost of demolition is added to the original cost before working out the balancing adjustment.

For the second and subsequent owners, the allowances are equal to the residue of cost spread over the remainder of twenty-five or fifty years. An example is given in Figure 12.3. The importance of distinguishing between land and buildings is vital, with seller and buyer having opposing interests.

From 12 April 1978 industrial buildings' allowances were extended to apply also to certain qualifying hotels, the rate of initial allowance being 20 per cent, with a writing-down allowance of 4 per cent. With effect from 1 April 1986 the initial allowance was abolished.

Expenditure incurred between 26 March 1980 and 27 March 1983 on small workshops of up to 2500 square feet and expenditure incurred between 26 March 1983 and 27 March 1985 on very small workshops of up to 1250 square feet qualified for an initial allowance of 100 per cent and a writing-down allowance of 25 per cent on any part disclaimed.

Any industrial or commercial structure or qualifying hotel in an Enterprise Zone (an area designated as such by the Government) also qualifies for 100 per cent initial allowance; if a reduced allowance is claimed, 25 per cent writing-down allowance is available on the amount of the reduction.

Plant and machinery

Allowances may be claimed by any type of business assessed as trading income under Case I or Case II of Schedule D, or against Schedule A assessments on income from real property, or in respect of assets owned by an employee and used by the employee for his employer's business, or against profits of a trade assessed under Schedule D Case V.

The definition of 'plant and machinery' spreads remarkably widely to include office and canteen equipment, furniture, dry docks and virtually every type of fixed tangible asset which is not 'building'.

The allowances available for plant are as follows:

(a) First year allowance: these are abolished for expenditure incurred after 31 March 1986 unless incurred before 1 April 1987 on a pre-14 March 1984 contract, but were previously given in the year of purchase at the following rates:

	%
After 26 October 1970	60
After 19 July 1971	80
After 21 March 1972	100
After 13 March 1984	75
After 31 March 1985	50

GHM

Original cost to first owner, 1977		£10 000
Initial allowance in first year 50%	£5 000	
Written-down allowance 4% a year for 10 years	4 000	9 000
Written-down value in 1986 (end of year)		1 000
Sell on 1 January 1987 for		7 350
Balancing charge of first owner		£ 6 350

Second owner: residue of cost is £7350
  balance of 25 years is 15 years
  so annual allowance is £490 a year

Check: £490 x 15 = £7350

Figure 12.3 Example of allowances for expenditure on industrial buildings

(b) Writing-down allowance: any expenditure not qualifying for the first year allowance and the balance of the previous year's qualifying expenditure after deducting any first year allowance given is added to the pool of expenditure and a writing-down allowance of 25 per cent is taken on the pool value.

(c) When an asset is sold or scrapped, its disposal price is deducted from the pool figure on which writing-down allowances are being calculated, unless sale proceeds exceed cost in which case the deduction is restricted to cost.

It is possible for the company to take any smaller amount of allowances and so defer allowances to subsequent years. First year allowance applies equally to new or secondhand assets unless a secondhand machine is bought from a connected company or transactions are entered into mainly with a view to obtaining a larger allowance, in which case the first-year allowance is restricted.

Private cars do not qualify for first year allowance unless hired on a short-term basis in the course of a trade, and no capital allowances are given on assets bought for purposes of business entertainment. Details of cars should be shown in a separate 'pool'.

Private cars costing over £8000 (£5000 prior to 12 June 1979) are kept separate from other assets and qualify only for a writing-down allowance at 25 per cent of the written-down value but restricted to a maximum of £2000 per year, starting in the year of purchase and with a balancing adjustment for the year of sale.

From 1 April 1986 it is possible to elect for separate items of plant to be treated as short-life assets. Each asset forms its own pool of expenditure outside of the general pool. If the assets are still held after four years the residue of expenditure is transferred into the general pool.

For assets acquired on hire purchase, allowances are given on the equivalent of the cash price, and the hire charge is treated as an allowable revenue expense in the years in which it is paid. For assets on straight hire, contract hire or lease, there are no capital allowances but the rental is allowed as a revenue expense in the years in which it is paid.

The lessor will be eligible for capital allowances like any other trader but subject to certain conditions. These are that the asset is used for short-term hire in the UK or the asset is used for the 'requisite' period, of four years (or shorter if the asset is sold within four years) by a trader who would have been granted first-year allowance had he purchased the asset himself. If the lessee does not fall into one of these categories the lessor will be entitled to 25 per cent of writing-down allowance on the cost of the asset.

Where private cars costing £8000 are hired a proportion of the rental charge payable by the lessee is disallowable.

Expenditure incurred on the provision of a new ship has a degree of flexibility not available on other assets. The taxpayer is able to postpone allowances and take them in the period in which it is most advantageous.

LOSSES

Setting losses against profits

A trading loss in one accounting period may be set against:

1 Other sources of profit in the same accounting period in which the loss is suffered
2 The trading profit of the immediately preceding accounting period provided that the company was then carrying on the trade
3 Other sources of profit in that preceding accounting period.

To the extent that a trading loss has been created by first-year allowances it may be set against profits in the three years preceding the year of the loss (again provided that the trade was then being carried on).

Claims for relief in this way are optional. If they are not made, or if they leave a balance of loss still unrelieved, the remaining loss may be set against the first available future profits from the same trade, but not against future profits from other sources.

The right to carry forward any losses is ended when a majority of the shares changes hands and there is a major change in the nature or conduct of the trade being carried on. The effect of this restriction has been virtually to end the sale of tax-loss companies.

An example of a normal loss claim is given in Figure 12.4.

Terminal loss relief

A loss suffered during the final twelve months up to the time a trade is discontinued may be carried backwards and set against the trading profits of the three preceding years. An example is given in Figure 12.5.

Note particularly that to make a terminal loss claim it is sufficient that the trade has been permanently discontinued. This is not necessarily the same as winding up the company, as a company may have more than one activity and its existence may continue without the discontinued trade, or a fresh trade of a different nature may be started after the loss-making enterprise has been discontinued.

Directors' remuneration as it affects loss

It will be seen that skill is needed in arranging a company's affairs in the way to take the best advantage of the many variations of the loss relief rules. For example, even in a small private company it may be sound policy to pay the directors at least a portion of their customary remuneration, even though this makes the loss larger. Otherwise the directors might be without income from which to offset their personal tax reliefs.

Example

Williams is sole director and principal shareholder of WL Ltd. He customarily draws £5000 a year from the company as director's remuneration and leaves the company with no profit to suffer corporation tax. In 1985/86 trade is poor and before paying himself any remuneration there is trading loss of £1000. If Williams forgoes remuneration his personal reliefs will be wasted, so he declares himself £3600 and leaves the company showing £4600 loss (the liability to employer national insurance contributions has been ignored).

His personal income then is		£3600
from which he deducts:		
Personal allowance	£3455	
Dependent relative relief	£ 100	
		3555
		£ 45

Income tax payable by Williams will be only:
£45 at 30 per cent = £13.50

The company's trading loss will go forward to set against future trading profits if Williams is confident he can restore the profit-making basis of the trade. His personal reliefs would have been wasted had he not taken any remuneration, as they cannot be carried forward.

GHM

PQ Ltd — Accounting period to 31 December annually:

Trading results	— 1983 profit	£20 000
	1984 loss	60 000
	1985 profit	8 000
Unfranked investment income	— 1983	5 000
	— 1984	7 000
	— 1985	6 000

Set off of loss		
1	Other income in 1984	7 000
2	Profits in 1983 (£20 000 + £5 000)	25 000
3	Trading profit in 1985	8 000
4	Carry forward against future trading profits	20 000
		£60 000

Losses carried forward may only be set against future profits from the same trades and not other income hence unfranked investment income in 1985 is taxable. Corporation tax payable for the year to 31 December 1983 would be cancelled, or if already paid it will be refunded.

Note the cash flow advantage of submitting promptly the figures for 1984 and the claim for loss relief.

Figure 12.4 Example of normal loss relief

ADVANCE CORPORATION TAX

On the occasion when a company pays a dividend (or other distribution to members), it is required to make a payment of advance corporation tax (ACT) to the Inland Revenue. The rate of ACT is fixed annually and applied to the actual or net dividend but is equivalent to income tax at the basic rate on the gross of the dividend plus the ACT. Payment of ACT is due quarterly and must be made fourteen days after the end of the quarter in which the dividend is paid. When the dividend is paid, the member is given a tax credit for the ACT in respect of the dividend.

Treatment by shareholders

Every individual in the UK who receives a dividend and tax credit can treat the tax credit as if it were a voucher for income tax paid. If he is liable at the basic rate of income tax, no further liability will arise; if he is liable at more than the basic rate, he will be required to pay only at the excess of his higher rate over the basic rate. If his income is so small that he pays no income tax, he will recover the tax credit.

Where a company receives a dividend with a tax credit the sum of the two will be treated as 'franked investment income', i.e., income which has already borne corporation tax and therefore income upon which no further tax is payable. The company may set the amount of the tax credit against an obligation to pay ACT in respect of its own dividends, and pay only the balance to the Inland Revenue.

		RS Ltd	TU Ltd
Profit for the year to			
31 December 1981		£40 000	£40 000
31 December 1982		15 000	15 000
31 December 1983		10 000	10 000
31 December 1984 (Loss)		(80 000)	(80 000)
RS closed trade at 31 December 1984			
31 December 1985			5 000
TU closed trade at 31 December 1985			

GHM

RS Ltd will have a terminal loss claim of £80 000 which will successfully be off-set to the extent of £65 000 against the profits of 1981, 1982 and 1983. TU Ltd has no terminal loss because the loss was not made in the final twelve months and so will only be able to use normal claims against 1983 (£10 000) and 1985 (£5000).

Figure 12.5   Example of terminal loss relief

Treatment of ACT by company paying dividends

In respect of dividends paid during an accounting period, ACT is treated as a payment to account of the corporation tax liability for that accounting period and only the balance (or mainstream liability) is payable nine months after the balance date (or later in respect of certain companies – see Adjustment of profit, above). The ACT must, however, be set against corporation tax on income – it must not be set against tax on capital gains – and the maximum which may be set off is the ACT on a distribution such that the sum of the two is equal to the income charged on corporation tax.

Any ACT not relieved in this way may be carried back for two years and any balance still not relieved may be carried forward. An example is given in Figure 12.6. During the year to 31 March 1986, when the rate of corporation tax was 40 per cent and of ACT three-sevenths, Z Ltd had the taxable profits shown in Figure 12.6.

		GHM
Trading profit, Schedule D Case I, year to 31 March 1986		£520 000
Unfranked investment income		20 000
Capital gains £40 000 less excluded £10 000 (see section on capital gains tax, below)		30 000
In May 1985 Z Ltd paid a dividend of £413 000 on which ACT amounted to £177 000		
The mainstream liability is computed:		
Taxable profits — Income £520 000 + £20 000		£540 000
— Capital		30 000
		£570 000
Corporation tax at 40 per cent		£228 000
ACT for set-off — £177 000		
Restricted to tax on 'gross' dividend of £540 000, i.e., to (Since £378 000 + ACT thereon of £162 000 = £540 000)		162 000
Mainstream liability		£ 66 000

Figure 12.6   Example of set-off of Advance Corporation Tax (ACT)

GROUPS OF COMPANIES

There are special concessions in the taxation of groups of companies, their main effect being to reduce or cut out the tax on inter-company transactions within the group. It requires considerable skill to arrange group affairs to take the best advantage of these arrangements, and the administrator should either make a specialized study or else form a regular practice of consulting the group's professional advisers before making transfers of assets or dividends within the group.

For example, for some purposes a 'subsidiary' is one in which the parent company owns more than half the ordinary shares, for others the minimum is 75 per cent of the ordinary shares, and for yet others 75 per cent of the whole equity capital including certain non-commercial loans. The main advantages of group taxation are:

1 *Subsidiaries*
A subsidiary may pay dividends to its parent company with or without paying ACT thereon. It may be valuable to pay the dividend without ACT when the parent company is not making distributions to its own shareholders, or when it has other sources of franked investment income receivable net and no trading income of its own
2 *Loss on one company against profit in others*
When one company has suffered a trading loss, this may be set off against the profits of any one or more members of the group. It should be noted that this concession does not extend to capital losses and careful planning is essential prior to a disposal where there are capital losses within the group
3 *Transfers of capital assets*
No chargeable gain arises when capital assets are transferred between members of a group. Care is required however when a company which has received an asset leaves the group within six years of the transfer.

CAPITAL GAINS TAX

Companies pay corporation tax on chargeable gains as well as on income but a proportion of the capital gain is excluded from the assessment at the full rate of corporation tax to bring the effective rate of corporation tax on capital gains down to 30 per cent – the normal rate for individuals. All forms of property are included as assets for capital gains tax purposes but certain of them are exempt from charge. These include:

1 Wasting assets with a predictable life of less than fifty years, if they are chattels (tangible moveable objects) but excluding assets which have qualified for capital allowances
2 Gains on certain government securities and qualifying corporate bands
3 Winnings from betting or lotteries
4 Gains on discharge of liabilities (e.g. the repayment of debentures at less than their issue price).

If assets were acquired before April 1965 any part of the gain arising before that date is not taxable.

The list is not exhaustive and does not include assets such as dwelling houses for which the gain may be exempt if made by an individual. When a capital gain made by a company has suffered tax and the balance is paid out to shareholders, a further round of tax is deducted. For example, if it sells its premises and goes into liquidation the position is as shown in Figure 12.7. This example has been simplified to illustrate the principle, which in an actual company would be clouded but not overthrown by the existence of other assets.

Underlying capital gains

A company with an underlying capital gain in its assets is always better sold

---

GHM

Purchase price of asset, £400 000 – absorbed into the business as a fixed asset, or alternatively the shares are purchased.

The position of the seller is as follows:

Sell the asset and then go into liquidation:		Alternatively sell the company's shares	
Selling price 1986	£400 000	for	£400 000
Cost price 1965	300 000	Cost price 1965	300 000
Capital gain	£100 000		£100 000
Tax at effective rate of 30%	30 000		
Balance distributed to shareholders	£ 70 000		£100 000
Less: Personal capital gains tax 30%	21 000		30 000
Net gain in the hands of shareholders	£ 49 000		£ 70 000

NB: Indexation allowance has been ignored for the purposes of this example.

If the shares are purchased, the asset will be owned by a subsidiary of the buying company. It may subsequently be sold to the parent company which may declare a dividend to dispose of its capital gain without suffering any tax; alternatively, the proceeds may simply be lent to the parent company.

Figure 12.7 Simplified example to show that sale as a going concern is better than liquidation where assets have appreciated

as a going concern than put into liquidation, and to the purchaser it may be a matter of indifference whether he obtains ownership of the valuable assets in the one way or the other. He is not obliged to run the company as a trading concern when he has acquired its shares. The directors of a private company should give thought to the chances of 'retirement exemption' before disposing of their shares. For disposals after 5 April 1985, the first £100 000 (previously £50 000) of gain will be exempt if they are aged over sixty and have been full-time directors for not less than ten years and hold either:

1 Not less than 25 per cent of the voting share capital in own right, or
2 Not less than 5 per cent in own right, and members of immediate family own more than 50 per cent.

A proportionate amount of relief is available if the shares have been owned for less than ten years (but more than one year). The exemption is restricted to the underlying chargeable business assets; it is not available in respect of portfolio investments held by the company.

Replacement of assets

Deferment of tax on capital gains may be claimed where the asset has been used only for trading purposes and is replaced by fresh assets (not necessarily of a similar nature, or even serving the same function) if they are of one of the following classes:

1 Land, building, fixed plant and machinery
2 Ships
3 Aircraft
4 Goodwill
5 Hovercraft.

It is important that the replacement is bought within twelve months before or three years after the sale of the previous asset. These time limits may be extended at the discretion of the Inland Revenue. Deferment continues indefinitely if the replacement asset is permanent, but if a 'depreciating asset' is bought it will continue only for ten years. If the depreciating asset is sold within ten years and replaced by a fresh permanent asset, the permanence of the deferment is established, but if it is replaced by a fresh depreciating asset the deferment ends immediately.

Depreciating assets for this purpose are assets with an expected life of less than sixty years, i.e., they are wasting assets, or items which will become wasting assets within ten years. The most common example is fixed plant. Full deferment is given only where it is requested and where the whole proceeds from sale of the previous asset are used for the purchase of the replacement. Where only a portion of the sale proceeds are used, the amount on which deferment can be claimed is restricted.

THE COMPANY AS A TAX COLLECTOR

Although the company does not itself pay any income tax, it is obliged to serve as an unpaid collector by withholding income tax when making payment of:

1 Wages and salaries, for the PAYE system
2 Annual interest, the most common example being debenture interest

The amount of PAYE deducted in a month has to be passed to the Collector of Taxes on the nineteenth of the month next following. For example, month from 6 April to 5 May; tax to be paid on 19 May. Income tax on annual interest is payable quarterly, fourteen days after the end of the quarter.

Extension for close companies: When a close company does not pay a sufficient dividend, part of its income may be treated as if it had been distributed by the company and income tax thereon at the higher rates applicable to its members may be recovered from the company.

CLOSE COMPANY DISABILITIES

1 If money is lent to a 'participator' an amount equal to tax at the basic rate on the grossed up amount of the loan is payable by the company. This is repaid to the company as and when the participator repays the loan.
2 Where a close company fails to make an adequate distribution out of income, tax may be payable as if such a distribution had in fact been made. The amount of the shortfall in distributions is apportioned to members and the appropriate income tax is computed; this income tax may be paid by the members or by the company.

For a trading company the maximum which may be apportioned is its distributable investment income, plus 50 per cent of its estate income abated by the appropriate fraction, namely:

$$\frac{\text{Estate income}}{\text{Estate plus trading income}}$$

Estate income of less than the appropriate fraction of £25 000 is disregarded and if less than the appropriate fraction of £75 000, it is reduced by 50 per cent of the difference. In addition distributable investment income is arrived at after deduction of the smaller of 10 per cent of the estate or trading income or £3000.

It is always open to a trading company to justify a smaller distribution, on the grounds that the company needs to retain more of the profit to meet the requirements of its business – to finance improvements, modernization or expansion and to repay short-term loans; cash required to finance a wholly new trade will be treated as a business expense for this purpose.

Negotiations with a view to ensuring there will be no apportionment of income should be opened by an approach to the Inspector backed by a clear statement of intentions such as the forecast of sources and application of funds which forms part of the management accounting routine of most companies.

CONTRAST BETWEEN LIMITED COMPANY AND PARTNERSHIP

Partners pay income tax at graduating rates on the whole of their profit, which is regarded as earned income in their hands, except in the case of a limited (or 'sleeping') partner whose share is normally treated as investment income for tax purposes.

In a limited company, corporation tax is payable on the profit after deducting remuneration of its directors, who are classed as employees. Profit remaining in the company after paying corporation tax is not subject to further tax, but if it is withdrawn as dividend this may be liable to income tax at the higher rates as personal investment income of the shareholder.

From purely a tax viewpoint, there is a distinct advantage in the tax rates applicable to a company compared with personal tax rates. From 1 April 1986 the full rate of corporation tax is 35 per cent whereas income tax rates for 1986/87 rise from the basic rate of 29 per cent on income of up to £17 200 to a top rate of 60 per cent on income over £41 200.

There are many powerful legal advantages in running a limited company and these often far outweigh the importance of tax differences. The larger the business and the more involved its ownership, the more important it becomes to operate it as a limited company. Also a company pension scheme for the directors can provide better benefits than a self-employed retirement annuity scheme. On the other hand certain undertakings, such as most of the professions, are not allowed to operate through limited companies.

CHANGES IN PERSONAL AND CORPORATION TAX

From 1973/74, income tax and surtax were replaced by a single unified tax, but the change was one of administration. It did not alter the total tax liability, the only real difference to the taxpayer being that the new high rates of tax on large incomes are payable more promptly than the surtax they replaced (but now only marginally so: surtax was due nine months after the year end, higher rates of the new unified tax were originally due three months after the year end but this was extended to eight months in 1980).

Changes in the corporation tax system were effected from 1 April 1973 when the system was changed from a 'classical' one (corporation tax on profits, with income tax deducted from dividends) to an 'imputation' one (corporation tax on profits, part of the tax being passed on as credit to the recipients of dividends). The object of the change was to make the corporation tax on retained profits as heavy as the combined tax on distributed profits. This reduces the incentive to retain profits for reinvestment in expansion of the company's business, the plan being strangely at odds with the then government's supposed encouragement to increased industrial investment.

DEFINITIONS OF SOME PHRASES USED IN THE CORPORATION TAX RULES

Accounting date
The date to which a company makes up its accounts.

Accounting period
The period for which corporation tax is charged: this will normally be a period for which a company makes up its accounts but it may be a shorter period and must not exceed a year.

Close company
A UK resident company under the control of five or fewer participators, or any number of participators who are directors, or if more than half of the company's income could be apportioned for tax purposes among five or fewer participators or among any number of participators who are directors. However, any company in which shares carrying at least 35 per cent of the voting power are held by the public is excluded from the definition provided such shares have been dealt in and officially listed on a recognized stock exchange within the preceding twelve months.

Participator in a close company
Primarily a person who is a shareholder or has an interest in the capital or income of the company.

Distribution
Any dividend paid by a company, including a capital dividend. It also includes any other distribution out of the assets of a company, whether in cash or otherwise, except for a repayment of capital on liquidation or any amount for which new consideration has been given. Also excluded is a company purchasing its own shares, satisfying certain conditions.

Franked investment income
Income from a source which has already suffered corporation tax and is consequently not liable to further corporation tax in the hands of the receiving company. Dividends from UK companies are the most common example.

Unfranked investment income
Income from a source which has not suffered corporation tax and is therefore to be included in this company's total income for corporation tax purposes. Debenture interest from other companies is a common example.

VALUE ADDED TAX

The scope of the tax

The tax is chargeable on the supply of goods and services in the UK and on the importation of goods and certain services into the UK. The tax will be charged only where the supply is a taxable supply and where the goods are supplied by a taxable person in the course of a business which he is carrying on. The tax is normally payable by the person supplying the goods or services. Tax is chargeable on the importation of goods whether for business purposes or not and the tax is payable whether or not the importer is carrying on a business. In cases where imported goods may be used for private purposes the tax cannot be the subject of a VAT input deduction but a separate claim to the Commissioners for repayment. Where goods are imported by a registered taxable person who imports goods in the course of his trade, payment of the tax can be deferred. New rules applied from 1 January 1978 where certain overseas services are imported. In such instances the taxable person in the UK has to account for the tax as if he had supplied the services to himself. Also with effect from 1 January 1978 the supply of services includes the letting of goods on hire and the making of certain gifts or loans of goods.

The arithmetic of the tax

Strictly speaking, value added tax is not a tax on value added in the true economic sense. Rather it is a tax on consumption, collected at each stage in the economy, on the difference (broadly) between the purchase price of goods and services acquired to make the product and the sale price of that product. Purchases are called inputs, and the tax which a business pays on buying those inputs is called input tax; sales are called outputs, and the tax which a business charges on its customers is called output tax. The excess of output tax over input tax is payable by the business to Customs and Excise, who are responsible for administering the tax, but if the input tax exceeds the output tax the difference is repayable by Customs and Excise to the business. Assuming then that a business is wholly within the VAT system, the business bears no VAT itself but recovers all the tax it pays on its inputs either by way of deduction from its output tax or by way of repayment from Customs and Excise.

Rates of tax

There are three classifications of goods and services. Exempt, zero-rated and standard-rate goods. Standard rate of VAT has been 15 per cent since 18 June 1979.

Zero rating

References should be made to the Finance Act 1972, Schedule 4 (as amended) for a list of zero-rated items. These are principally food, books, newspapers, periodicals, news services and advertisements, fuel and power, transport and certain drugs and medicines. In addition, the export of all goods and most services is zero rated. This ensures that no VAT enters into the price of any export.

Exemption

Exemption is of two kinds:

1 Finance Act 1972, Schedule 5 (as amended) gives exemption to a list of items of which the most important are land, insurance, postal services, certain financial services (mainly banking), education and health
2 Small traders whose turnover of taxable supplies does not exceed £20 500 per annum are exempt but they may elect to come within the system if it is to their advantage to do so.

The difference between zero rating and exemption is that a business dealing in zero-rated supplies charges VAT at the rate of zero per cent but is nevertheless fully within the system; thus it can recover from Customs and Excise any input tax which it has paid on its purchases. Exemption on the other hand is generally a less favourable status in that, whereas the business cannot charge VAT on its supplies, it cannot recover the VAT on its purchases; thus the exempt business must either bear any input tax itself, or if it can, pass it on in the form of higher prices.

Many businesses are taxable on some part of their sales (whether at the standard rate or zero rate) and exempt on another part. In these cases an apportionment of the input tax is made, and only that part considered to be referable to taxable sales is deductible.

Time of supply

In order to determine which VAT accounting period a transaction falls into, the time of supply has to be ascertained. Broadly the time of supply is as follows:

Goods

1 If the goods are to be removed the basic tax point is the time when they are removed
2 If the goods are not to be removed the basic tax point is the time when they are made available to the person to whom they are being supplied
3 There are special rules for sale or return and for certain other transactions. A hire purchase transaction is deemed to be a sale. The construction industry is subject to special rules
4 Where a tax invoice is issued within fourteen days after the basic tax

point, the invoice date becomes the tax point unless the taxpayer elects to use the basic tax point instead. The fourteen-day period may be extended by agreement with Customs and Excise

5 If a tax invoice is rendered before the date of the basic tax point or if payment is received in respect of a supply before the basic tax point, the earlier of the invoice date and the payment date becomes the tax point. The taxpayer in this case has no option to elect for the tax point in 1 or 2 above.

Services

1 The basic tax point in the case of the supply of services is when those services are performed.
2 If a tax invoice is issued within fourteen days after the basic tax point (extendable by negotiation with Customs and Excise), the invoice date is the tax point unless the taxpayer elects to the contrary.
3 In other cases, the tax point is the earlier of the tax invoice and the date on which payment is made for the services.

Businesses should ensure that where an option is open they choose the best tax point for their accounting and administrative systems.

Place of supply

Broadly, if goods are supplied within the UK for use in the UK, the supply is a taxable supply. If goods are supplied in the UK and exported, the goods are still a taxable supply but at the time of export are zero rated. Goods supplied outside the UK but imported into the UK are liable to VAT at the time of importation. There are special accounting rules for VAT purposes which are designed to ease the cash flow problems of importers. A supply of goods made outside the UK but not imported into the UK is outside the VAT net altogether; this applies whether or not the goods are ordered from the UK.

The rules regarding the place of supply of services initially only applied to a supply rendered and enjoyed within the UK and services rendered in the UK for the benefit of someone outside the UK. The implementation of the EEC Sixth Directive on VAT has extended the scope of the tax in the UK to include the importation of certain services. Where a taxable person receives, from a person who does not belong in the UK, any of the services listed in Schedule 2A to the Finance Act 1972 (except services which would be exempt if supplied in the UK) he is required to account for tax as if he had supplied the services himself.

The tax invoice

No special form of tax invoice is laid down but certain minimum requirements have to be met. In particular every tax invoice must show an identifying number, the date of supply, the name and address and VAT registration number of the supplier, the name and address of the person to whom the supply is made, the type of supply (i.e., sale, lease, etc.) a description of the supply, the price for each supply before the addition of VAT, any discount offered and the rate and amount of tax chargeable. An abbreviated form of tax invoice may be used in some cases; these are generally small transactions at retail level.

It is not necessary, unless requested, for a retailer to issue a tax invoice. Tax invoices need not be rendered where the transaction is zero rated. In the case of exempt transactions it is not legally possible to issue a tax invoice.

Discounts

Where a discount is offered for prompt or immediate payment, VAT should be shown on the tax invoice as though the discount had been earned by the person to whom the goods or services are being supplied. If in the event the discount is not earned no recalculation of the VAT should be made. Where a trade discount is offered, VAT should similarly be calculated on the discounted price. Where on the other hand a contingent discount is offered which will be available, for example, when a certain level of purchases have been achieved by the customer, the VAT should be calculated on the assumption that the volume target will not be reached.

Retrospective adjustments

Where a downwards adjustment to the price charged for a supply is made, the VAT on the original invoice will be overstated. This may be corrected by showing VAT on a credit note issued to the customer; the VAT must be at the same rate as that originally charged by the supplier. Retrospective adjustments of any kind can be made by the use of the credit note mechanism.

Bad debts

In line with the EEC Sixth Directive the Finance Act 1978 introduced relief for VAT on bad debts. However, relief is restricted in that a taxable person is not entitled to relief unless he has proved the insolvency and the amount for which he has proved is the outstanding amount of the consideration less the amount of his claim. The relief applies where the person liable to pay the outstanding amount of the consideration becomes insolvent after 1 October 1978.

Secondhand goods

In principle, secondhand goods are treated in the same way as new goods. There are, however, special schemes for secondhand works of art, antiques, precious stones, postage stamps, scientific collections, cars, motor cycles and caravans. The effect of these schemes is to make liable to VAT only the dealer's margin rather than the full sale price.

Capital goods

In principle, capital goods are treated in the same way as any other items and there is no question of spreading the input tax over the life of the asset or indeed in any other way. Thus, heavy purchases of plant within a short period may put a business into a temporary repayment position. The effect on cash flow ought to be studied before engaging in large-scale plant acquisitions.

Disallowances of VAT

Powers are given to Customs and Excise to disallow certain amounts of input tax even though the expenditure is for the purposes of a taxable business. The two main disallowances at the present time are for business entertaining (other than of overseas customers) and business cars.

Apportionments

Reference has been made above to the part-exempt business. A business whose outputs are part taxable and part exempt may have a disallowance of some part of its input tax.

Special apportionment schemes are prescribed for retailers. These are somewhat complicated and Public Note No. 727 (as amended) should be consulted.

Groups

Provision is made so that groups of commonly controlled companies can be treated as one single VAT paying entity. Transactions within companies in such a group are then ignored for VAT purposes and a single return is made by the 'representative member' of the group to Customs and Excise. Not all members of a Companies Act group need be grouped for VAT purposes, and the cash flow of a Companies Act group can be improved if the correct selection of companies is made.

Divisions

A company organized in divisions may request to have each division treated separately for VAT.

Accounting period

The basic VAT accounting period is three months but a company which is in a habitual repayment position may elect for a one-month period. This minimizes the delay between the payment of input tax by a business and its recovery from Customs and Excise.

Accounting records

The quarterly VAT return (form VAT 100), which has to be submitted to Customs and Excise, requires information to be extracted from the accounting records of the registered person in such a way that the trader can make his own assessment.

For VAT recording purposes, the accounts will have to provide the following figures:

1 VAT – output tax
2 VAT – tax on imports
3 VAT – deductible input tax
4 Total outputs (sales etc.)
5 Total inputs (purchases, etc., excluding wages and salaries).

It is very important therefore to ensure that the accounting records are maintained in such a form that the tax return can be completed with the minimum of additional work.

Although accounting for VAT is a burden on most businesses the quarterly return imposes a discipline on the accounting function and should be used as a method of providing up-to-date information for the trader, and thus result in increased efficiency.

Retention of records

Invoices both in and out should be retained for a minimum period of three years to enable Customs and Excise to perform their periodical audit of the business's VAT position. By agreement with Customs and Excise, invoices may be kept in microfilm or any other form. Invoices should be stored and recorded in such a way that the periodical VAT return can be completed without difficulty. The amount of record keeping which has to be done is likely to be far greater than many businesses are used to.

Cash flows

The combination of the rules on the tax point and the date on which tax is payable to Customs and Excise gives rise to cash flow advantages or disadvantages. Thus a business which secures a long period of credit on its purchases will very likely not have to pay the VAT on the purchase price until after it has received credit for the tax on the purchase. On the other hand a business which allows long periods of credit on its sales may find that it has to pay the appropriate output tax to Customs before receiving payment of that tax from the customer. The rule must therefore be that the maximum credit should be obtained from one's supplies but the minimum credit should be given to one's customers. This is not at variance with normal financial strategy.

Appeal procedures

Large numbers of disputes have arisen between businesses and Customs and Excise. If agreement cannot be reached with the local VAT office, it is usually prudent to seek a ruling from Customs and Excise head office in London. If agreement is still not possible, an appeal may be lodged to a VAT tribunal. These are presided over by lawyers, and meet in various parts of the country. Their proceedings are sometimes publicized and sometimes not; in so far as they are not, Customs clearly have an advantage over the taxpayer. A determination by a tribunal on a question of fact is final but on a question of law there is a right to appeal first to the High Court (in England), then to the Court of Appeal and (with permission) to the House of Lords, or Court of Session (in Scotland) and (with permission) to the House of Lords.

Professional advice

It is evident, in an area of taxation which is a mixture of law and administrative practice, that the taxpayer is at a disadvantage in dealing with Customs and Excise. It is important, therefore, to take professional advice not merely in negotiations with Customs and Excise but also in the handling of appeals.

FURTHER READING

The aim in this chapter has been to highlight those aspects of company taxation which appear to be of most consequence to administrators. All the rules are hedged around with ifs and buts which make it imperative to check details before making major decisions.

Useful explanatory booklets may be obtained free from the Revenue; (these include Corporation Tax; Capital Gains Tax; Directors' Benefits and Expenses; Capital Allowances on Plant and Machinery); and from Customs and Excise.

The taxation of banks, insurance companies, building societies and other financial organizations, and of agricultural concerns, is outside the scope of this work.

The following books may prove useful:

Cretton, Colin, *Practical CGT*, Butterworth, London, 1982

Gammie, Malcolm, *Tax Strategy for Companies*, Oyez, London, 1981

Ritchie, K.J.M., *Official Tax Forms Manual*, Oyez, London, 1981

Wheatcroft, G.S.A. and Avery Jones, J.F., *Encyclopaedia of Value Added Tax*, Sweet & Maxwell, London, 1973 (updated annually)

Whiteman and Wheatcroft, G.S.A., *Income Tax*, 2nd edition, Sweet & Maxwell, London, 1976 (with supplements)

Also, the following are published by Tolley Publishing Company, Croydon, annually:

Tolley's Capital Gains Tax
Tolley's Corporation Tax
Tolley's Income Tax

Part Three
MARKETING

13 Marketing planning

John Stapleton

Every marketing activity is an investment in time, energy and money. Few companies would spend thousands of pounds on, say, a purchase of capital equipment without a full investigation into its justification, the alternatives available, and the expected return on expenditure. Yet every year the vast majority of companies allocate a substantial part of their revenue to marketing actions without fully assessing the value or likely return on that investment. By introducing the disciplines arising from marketing planning a company should be able to ensure that the costs of marketing show an equitable return and are subject to measurement in the same way as all other business investments.

Many executives believe that the costs of marketing form an additional expense that has to be borne in order to sell their goods. Whilst it is true that many companies use certain tools of marketing for this purpose, it is true also that the most successful companies accept marketing as an essential and integral part of the company's total commercial operation, for it is an essential cost in just the same way as production or finance.

Companies often avoid marketing planning procedures because of the effort needed to express their forward policy in a written form. Executives commonly consider that their time is too valuable to spend on anything other than pressing operational problems; those that face them from day to day. In fact, the manager who devotes his time to dealing with current administrative detail is almost certain to have ignored proper planning in the past. For if properly prepared the marketing plan will contain sufficient details of the company's policy and operational strategy for the implementation to be undertaken by an assistant. As the many alternative courses of action are programmed it is merely necessary for the assistant to activate the appropriate remedy or decision. Only unusual situations need be dealt with by the manager.

The first step in preparing a marketing plan is that of producing the information necessary for decision making. Usually, a company will have within its own administration and control system the raw material necessary for the plan's foundations. In addition, there is an abundance of published information which is made available by government departments, para-governmental bodies, institutions, associations, and the national, trade, and technical press.

Marketing research is an activity which has yet to be fully exploited by the majority of companies. It has so far only been used by companies that have recognized that their existing information sources are inadequate. Because of the scale of operations that now confronts the typical businessman it is essential that investment decisions are based upon relevant information, so reducing the number of variables and, hence, business risk.

STANDARDS FOR MEASURING PERFORMANCE

For a marketing-oriented activity to produce lasting results the entire operation has to be systematically planned. By producing basic information in written form and establishing goals and aims for the future the company is creating standards against which actual performance can be measured. Documentation of detailed policy actions then provides the basis for monitoring and controlling the company's operation. Future trends may be predicted through the investigation of all factors that are likely to influence company results.

It is, however, unusual for future opportunities to be easily isolated or even defined. The possibilities are infinite, but it is essential that the most promising are fully investigated and the potential assessed. It is particularly important that the person responsible for planning be a senior executive, for the full appraisal of market opportunities will enable that executive to gain far more intimate knowledge of the workings and the environment of the business operation than could be achieved from a lifetime of working within the close confines of the limited philosophy and procedure of one company. The executive will be able to learn about the interactive forces that affect the company, the industry and, more important, its markets.

In studying the company's future market the businessman will try to discover basic needs for which there is no satisfaction or possibly where there is an inadequate match. It is by discovering the peculiar needs of each existing and potential customer that the enlightened company starts its marketing-orientation. It is upon such special needs that the foundations are laid. Looking at the market and listing the operational needs of each industry, then measuring the extent of each need and then the value that the market places on overcoming the problem gives an indication of the potential – in volume and in profit opportunity.

The main approach adopted by firms is to segment the market either demographically or psychographically. Having isolated part of the market, a brand differential is created sufficient to provide the company with a competitive advantage. This is the step towards a unique selling proposition.

THE NEW PRODUCT DEVELOPMENT PROGRAMME

From this stage the company will embark on a new product development programme in an effort to resolve the problems that face the market. Once a satisfactory product has been produced the basis for a promotional campaign is already apparent, as the original market assessment will have shown the prospects either by size, industry or location, and the product feasibility studies will have indicated the most appealing stimulus to demand for advertising and field selling purposes.

It must be apparent from these observations that success in marketing cannot be achieved overnight except by coincidence or good fortune. Often a minimum of three years will be required before the first hopeful signs become apparent. Successful use of certain marketing activities alone does not automatically mean a company is marketing-oriented. This situation frequently presents management with an almost insoluble problem. As the whole company has to become involved with marketing principles for success to be possible, it is unlikely that a new recruit hired for his expertise will be able to win sufficient confidence from colleagues by results in the time span that is normally allowed a new manager.

There is usually only one person in a company who can inspire the confidence and support that is necessary and who will automatically have the authority to implement the total changes that may be justified, and that is the chief executive. Introducing satisfactory marketing-orientation is more likely to be successful if the present chief executive delegates most of his daily activities to an assistant or to senior line managers and devotes his entire energies to planning, than if a manager is appointed with such responsibilities.

DETERMINING COMPANY OBJECTIVES

Few company executives have ever formally determined their company's business activity. If they have it is often specified in terms of the means by which the business activity is achieved, e.g. printing rather than communications; or the end-product, e.g. aero-engines rather than propulsion; or by convention, e.g. insurance rather than security. The only sure means of defining the business activity is by thinking in terms of applications for a product, for whilst products, no matter how successful they are now, are heading for eventual decline, the need will usually remain – to be satisfied by the latest innovation. Companies may overcome this problem by cultivating a brand image and encouraging the development of a brand personality based on the unique selling proposition. People do not buy products; they buy brands and brands can achieve buyer loyalty. Brands can have a reputation monopoly.

Determining the appropriate business activity is the first essential step in the marketing plan. In this first step the executive will establish the parameters within which his efforts should be confined initially, but will also rely upon the know-how, expertise, market reputation, and resources the company has accumulated during its history.

At the preliminary planning stage the company will need to decide upon the course that it wishes to take and the stages that have to be reached during each step in the journey. These objectives have to be achievable and yet sufficiently challenging to enable executives and staff to take pride in their fulfilment. The aims and goals of each company have to be expressed in the marketing plan in a way that is beyond dispute while being capable of measurement and comparison. The only medium that achieves these standards is money – the means by which company prosperity is valued. The prime requirement for the survival and development of any business is profit. Too many managers still regard profit as the amount of money that is left over after all the operating expenses have been met. This view almost has connotations with a death wish, for profit is the prerequisite of all business activity and as such must be the first cost to the business.

PROFIT IS THE FIRST OPERATING EXPENSE

By writing in the profit required as its first operating expense the company recognizes its major priority and then gears all its other objectives to ensure the acquisition of that profit. The sales volume needed, the orders to be won, the tenders or quotations to be sent out, the inquiries to be solicited, and all the means by which they are obtained are secondary objectives to be achieved before the prime objective becomes possible – in practice. Properly organized the marketing effort can be used to manage demand itself. It can be used to control the levels of demand and its timing.

Any objectives of this sort must be based upon certain assumptions. It may have to be assumed that raw materials will continue to be available or that the government will not cause a market to dry up following an Act of Parliament. Whatever the objectives they will depend for their satisfaction on certain events happening or not happening. These assumptions are incorporated in the plan with a cross-reference to the strategies that will have to be implemented or the tactics employed should the assumptions become invalid. The strategies a company adopts are the means by which the company approaches its market opportunities and by which it adjusts its resources to exploit those opportunities. Its tactics are the methods it uses to meet short-term situations or more frequently the steps it takes when in immediate contact with customers.

In documenting the preliminary marketing plan it is also necessary to list all the major problems that have faced the company during its immediate history, as well as those that are expected to confront the company in the future. At the same time it is prudent to list all opportunities that have been under consideration with the expected profit return, when they are to be achieved and under what circumstances. Both problems and opportunities are then subjected to the same appraisal as the objectives and assumptions when the company strategies are built into the plan.

Every company struggles to improve its profit performance and any attempts planned for the period of the marketing plan, in detail for one year and in outline for five years, should be included. It is possible that improved productivity at the plant will make it possible for the company to improve its profitability through increased sales volume. Sales may be improved either by additional expenditure on marketing actions or by reducing price in an effort to expand the total market. It is by marketing planning that a company can be sure that whatever action it chooses will be based upon facts and information obtained from the marketplace.

Every action and every decision taken by the company executives will have an effect somewhere in the business. It may be favourable, it might be unfavourable. In formulating a marketing plan the company will be formalizing its actions, weighing its alternatives, and deciding the most appropriate route open to it. Unless each marketing decision is made with the full and detailed consideration of the known, likely and possible effects upon the business, the investment that marketing actions require will be unmonitored and the management will have lost effective control of a major asset and the benefits that should accrue from that asset.

DEVELOPING THE MARKET PLAN

Preparing a sales forecast, the basis of the total marketing plan, is not just a matter of looking at past sales and trying to establish trends, but a conscious effort to look into the future and assess potential sales opportunity.

A company has started to be objective about its future when it attempts to evaluate the future and forecast what the market will require in the way of new or improved products. Most companies, in making long-range, sales forecasts, choose a period varying between five and twenty years, while more detailed sales targets are usually prepared for the financial year immediately ahead. Many products which will be available in five years' time are already on the market and firmly established in the product range. It is often possible to use such historical sales performance as the basis for projections into the future, but only as the basis, for such projections are dependent upon future events being similar to events which have happened in the past. Allowance must be made for changes due to economic circumstances and changes in competitive forces within the industry under investigation.

Demand forecasts are not based on purely functional needs. People in the affluent societies buy to satisfy psychological drives. So many successful brand personalities are based on abstract promises often appealing to the subconscious, a segmentation and brand differential all in one.

Comparison of movements, either short-term fluctuations or medium- to long-term trends, can often be achieved using the published economic data. Sometimes, acceptable degrees of correlation can be traced and these tied indicators will be useful parameters in forecasting.

The sales forecast can be as sophisticated or as simple as is justified by the business. The small- to medium-sized business is usually better placed than its larger competitors for maintaining close contact with its markets and can use elementary methods of forecasting which often produce better results than the methods employed by larger firms, where customer contact has become more remote because of larger lines of communication.

While the larger company will normally handle the research necessary to prepare a sales forecast by using its own personnel, the smaller concern cannot justify the expense of recruiting and retaining specialist staff. Where such forecasts are prepared, outside agencies are usually brought in for the task and, in recent years, multi-client projects have been evolved to cater for this demand. As the cost of research is spread over several sponsors, the research organization can afford to employ highly skilled staff and carry out projects in some depth across a wide front. In addition, the research organization is often able to prepare a report confidential to each client concerned.

BIAS TOWARDS ONE'S OWN COMPANY

Any sales forecast is subject to numerous influential factors, each of which must be isolated and measured. Some factors will have more effect than others and the forecaster must attempt to isolate and grade those factors according to their significance in such a way that weightings can be applied and an acceptable forecast determined within tolerable limits. In forecasting there is inevitably some bias towards the forecaster's own company and this must be avoided otherwise operating budgets, based on the forecasts, will be over-estimated, adversely affecting profitability.

It is also necessary to predict trends in related industries which provide indirect competition to the company's own products and which could have a bearing on the growth rate of the industry concerned. It is here that the forecaster can discover opportunities for product innovation or new product development. Since new products are the lifeblood of a company their discovery, development and subsequent production programming are necessary parts of the sales forecasting procedure.

To maintain a constant growth rate it is essential that every company estimates the life cycle of each of its products and introduces new products at the apex, or earlier, of an established product's life cycle in order to continue company growth. New products should not be introduced in a haphazard manner, but properly planned to fit the firm's expansion programme.

Price cutting, the most often observed tactical device in the struggles against competition, is a negative approach unless done from a position of strength with the company anticipating growth in the market and increased consumption achieved as a result of the price stimulus. Skilled marketing based on market segmentation, brand differentiation, and reputation monopoly provide a haven against price competition. People believe they are buying something unique that is superior to others. For them it seems better value even if dearer.

New markets are occasionally created following new legislation by government. Such changes can also be the cause of a substantial growth or decline in established markets and are often put forward as attempts to improve the social and/or economic life of the nation. Sudden changes in taste or fashion can cause sudden shifts in demand. Climatic changes can seriously affect sales of products which rely on extremes of temperature for their sales volume. Economic recessions, strikes or industrial disputes often bring in their train changes in purchasing habits.

CONTINGENCY PLANNING

Fortunately, many of these factors are predictable. There will certainly be any amount of published comment indicating possibilities. Research into future events is sometimes sponsored by trade and professional bodies; many thousands of words are produced by numerous authoritative writers in scores of newspapers, magazines, and trade and professional publications. These reports can be very valuable to businessmen seeking an insight into the future.

While one cannot forecast accurately what is going to happen, plans can be laid to cover any eventuality in advance of the event, at different levels of effectiveness. If the consequences of events are quantified in purely monetary terms, the businessman will be able to equate consequences with sales volume and, thus, profitability. Where necessary, contingency plans can be brought into operation.

It is true to say that many manufacturers take their products for granted and rarely investigate the uses to which they are put by customers, or how relevant they are to the customer's applications. Research can establish whether new features introduced by the manufacturer in good faith in the belief that they provide a plus for the buyer are not really required and not used, although paid for by the customer in the original selling price. It is possible, of course, that customers may not have realized the significance or relevance at the time of purchase.

In assessing product performance the businessman needs to relate application to product characteristics. Several companies have developed their share of the market as a direct result of providing a superior finish or excellent design. Buyers are often impressed by tales of long life for some mechanical item and sometimes make buying decisions in favour of such devices because the cost can be amortized over several years' operational life.

Where a brand personality has been established, whether it be a consumer product or service or an industrial product or service, the need for that personality survives in the buyer's mind. The marketing-orientated company has bought that position in the consumer's mind, and has therefore bought the customers it wants. The future has been virtually secured.

In arriving at the final assessment based on established standards relating each factor to every other factor, the researcher can compare the total significance of these in terms of market share and will be able to relate the performance of individual companies according to factors on which they concentrate. Comparison of results is the only certain way of monitoring company performance in a competitive commercial environment.

The standards established in the appraisal of competitor profiles provide the foundations for a full analysis of market shares. Companies desiring to break into a completely new market will need to examine the extent to which policies adopted by those already serving this market have been successful.

Having obtained full information on total market size it is necessary to assess the extent to which the market can be penetrated either by winning a share of the existing market or by concentrating on growth and winning the business which would otherwise have gone to present suppliers. Once this work has been done the company can make a full and realistic evaluation of the marketing budget necessary to achieve its objectives – objectives based on the right product (differentiated) the right target audience (segmentation) and the right message (unique selling proposition).

It may be easier in some industries to take business from established suppliers than to expand the total market. In other projects it may be more feasible to opt for developing the growth market potential than to get involved in a battle with those already active in the market. Only when the business activity of the company has been decided should any attempt be made to measure the total market and to prepare a reasoned definition of the market.

DEFINITION OF THE TOTAL MARKET

Many people are confused about the total market for a particular product. It is the total amount of money spent in satisfying a need, irrespective of the products which satisfy that need. This means that all types of food are in competition with one another, the various forms of transport are competitors, and all aids to business efficiency are locked in combat for the purchaser's money. This is direct competition, but because buyers have a wide range of choices across different product groups, the real competition is for the consumers' or buyers' money; to change their scale of preferences.

The market situation for any given company or industry is continually changing and violent fluctuations can occur in market shares from day to day. Over a period, shifts in the pattern of demand will become evident and it is imperative that a check be kept on such trends. Steadily rising sales turnover is not, in itself, a true indicator that a company is making the best use of its potential. It is quite possible for a company to achieve reasonable increases in sales year by year yet find that it has a rapidly diminishing share of the market. It will be losing sales opportunities unless sales volume is rising at least as rapidly as that of the industry as a whole.

A company also needs to keep track of its competitors' market shares and be able to explain any change that becomes apparent. There must be a reason why a competitor is expanding his market share faster than anyone else. If, on the other hand, a competitor with a strong marketing team is seen to be losing out on a market share, it could be that he has decided to diversify because of a forecast over-capacity or a decreasing growth rate. It is for these reasons that it is vital to carry out constant analyses of market share at frequent intervals, even if in a simple form, rather than rely on occasional extensive research projects, no matter how sophisticated.

Confusion sometimes arises when referring to marketing research and market research. The former is the activity which examines all the elements which make up marketing practice, including markets, products, channels of distribution, pricing behaviour and opinions. Market research is only one element of marketing research, albeit the most widely known and practised.

When it comes to getting the goods to the customer, different companies use different channels of distribution. While some use stockists or distributors, others deliver direct to the retailer or even direct to the ultimate consumer. Different channels of distribution achieve different levels of success in selling their suppliers' products, and their effectiveness can be critical to the sales volume achieved by any one company. Channels of distribution in the consumer field have undergone considerable change in recent years. The development of supermarkets and self-service stores has progressed very rapidly in some areas of retailing, more slowly in others. Some companies have achieved considerable growth through the provision of mail order facilities, while others have built their share of the market through new selling methods such as party plan or vending machines or through selling direct to the household.

In the industrial field there have not yet been such fundamental changes in the pattern of distribution, although some changes have become apparent, for example leasing of factories and capital equipment, and the use of time sharing for data processing equipment.

CONTROL OF DISTRIBUTION

It is not generally realised that the cost to industry of distributing a product may range between 5 and 60 per cent of the final selling price, depending upon the nature of the product and the method of distribution selected. Active control of distribution can reduce these expenses and allow a substantial increase in profitability. Many related activities could be improved following an improvement in actual distribution.

The marketing executive must endeavour to reconcile the needs of the customer for a full service with his company's requirements for the provision of an economic level of service. If he decides that the most appropriate way to win sales from a competitor is by providing a superior distribution service, then that is a deliberate expense incurred in the marketing budget as an alternative to other marketing activities and expenditure.

Because of the forces of competition, demand for any one product from one source can vary considerably. It is the distributive function to provide a contingency against wide fluctuations in demand, and the businessman's responsibility to develop a distributive pattern to cater for those deviations from the norm. Some are more predictable than others and the product mix from the factory must be adjusted to cope with the demand.

Properly controlled, the distributive system can protect a company against giving customer dissatisfaction and will enable it to achieve a high

229

level of productivity by ensuring economical production runs according to pre-determined planning.

MONITORING THE MARKET PLAN

No matter how carefully a management may plan, some objectives will always be more difficult to achieve than others. Marketing planning is not a panacea for all commercial and industrial problems.

Ideally the marketing plan will include any action which may have to be taken to avoid diminution of profits. Even if actual performance exceeds all expectations there should be built-in provisions for the favourable conditions which have become apparent. If proper care has been taken to structure the marketing plan the contingency section should be straightforward, being no more than the detailed consideration of alternative courses of action. The contingency plan should include action which may need to be taken in the short term to minimize or maximize the possible consequences of deviation from the schedule as well as the medium- to long-term action necessary to exploit a changed environment.

To ensure that the right action is taken at the right time – to ensure best results – it is essential that a barometer of company and industry performance be developed. Steps must be taken to monitor actual results against forecast company sales and forecast market shares.

There are several specialist organizations which provide, at reasonable cost, performance comparisons within an industry. If one of these organizations is used, the company needs to develop only an internal early warning system. This can be done by plotting orders received by major product groups against the purchasing industry by standard industrial classification.

In the shorter term, signals can be provided by relating actual inquiries, quotations, orders received, and sales by major product groups against the forecast. Then if the average timelag between inquiry and order is, say, six weeks, and between order and delivery is four to six weeks, the company will have, automatically, nearly three months' notice of an imminent fall-off in sales. Care must be taken to ensure that conversion ratios between each stage do not vary, or that if they do adjustment be made accordingly.

Whilst it would not be wise to institute remedial action as a result of one deviation from plan – for occasional fluctuations *do* happen – once a trend becomes apparent, the cause should be established and appropriate action taken. In addition to showing industrial performance as a whole, some specialist comparison organizations quote the detailed performance of unspecified companies against which the performance of one's own firm can be measured.

Here, the company should be able to judge the extent to which it will be able to exert influence on the market. If the entire industry is suffering the same deteriorating position, it is probably wise to curtail any plans for expansion unless there is a clear indication that the present circumstances can be favourably exploited. The timing and extent of any cutback in this area should be provided for in the contingency plan, which should show detailed profit and loss statements for 70, 80, 90, 110 and 120 per cent actual performance against forecast. Each of the detailed accounts should include the appropriate departmental budgets and head counts. The major driving principles must be to preserve net profit and indemnify future profits. These considerations often prove incompatible in practice and a working compromise may be necessary. Sometimes, profit comes from the last 15 to 20 per cent of sales, after overheads have been covered, and when costs become marginal. Under such circumstances a reduction of 20 per cent in sales volume will warrant, perhaps, a cut of 30 per cent in expenditure in order to maintain net profit at par value.

A company can sometimes avoid the disaster of a temporarily poor market position by acquiring another company. A study of competitive profiles in the marketing plan, followed by detailed investigation of suitable partners, may disclose a competitor which could supplement, or ideally complement, the company's own operations.

Although the possibility of making a takeover bid will almost always be considered first, realistic management must not discount the advantages of soliciting a bid for one's own company, as this may be more prudent.

Detailed consideration of both rationalization and diversification policies should form a logical part of any contingency plan. There is nearly always conflict between the sales department, anxious to meet individual customer requirements, and the production department needing long production runs and the elimination of time-consuming 'specials'.

INVESTMENT IN COMPANY RESOURCES

Although the need for improved efficiency and productivity has long been accepted by manufacturing processes in industry, and a similar need recognized for some time in the marketing function, it has never been satisfactorily resolved in the latter because of the difficulties of reconciling accounting principles with a business function which is considered part art and part science. While many marketing activities operate under disciplines not widely appreciated – let alone understood – by management, the practice of marketing is still an investment in company resources. If control is to be maintained marketing will be subject to the same accounting appraisal as any other form of investment.

The cost of handling orders of varying sizes must be ascertained if stock levels are to be controlled with great accuracy. It may be found more profitable to refuse orders selling below a price level considered to be uneconomic. Such selective selling often increases profitability. Location of warehouses, planning of sales territories and routes of salesmen can be organized, using accurate cost statistics rather than intuition. Improving direction and supervision of salesmen through the setting of performance and activity targets can result in increased selling and operating efficiency.

Management in many companies is not always able to recognize that its products or services are mediocre or even inferior to others on the market. Where such blindness exists the company is unlikely to introduce new methods or procedures to assist in rectifying or overcoming the problem. In the same way the firm is unlikely to experiment with new ideas or make a fresh approach in an attempt to improve its future prospects. In these circumstances the only avenue left for that firm is to continue in its own fashion no matter how much the position may deteriorate.

Because of the pace of technological change, a greater demand is manifesting itself for information to be employed in decision making. Investment decisions become more and more complex as businesses grow. The businessman must endeavour to forecast growth potential, and the factors likely to influence his company's penetration of that potential, in an attempt to reduce the risks facing every business enterprise.

Companies should be able to identify the influences on their major activities and show how they are being controlled to the benefit of the entire organization. The extent to which the information provided is relevant to the company's needs should be assessed. Executives need to eliminate unused material being prepared and to discover additional information previously unknown. Such research into the marketing effort will help to ensure that an economic level of expenditure is being maintained. Appropriate marketing policies should ensure that all products are developed according to the needs of the market and resources are not wasted on products which the market shows as unsatisfactory.

COMMUNICATING PROFIT RESPONSIBILITY

One of the important developments in marketing consumer goods is the change in emphasis to impersonal selling techniques such as advertising and point-of-sale display. Personal selling still has the most important role in industrial marketing. Improvement in the function and performance of industrial sales forces justifies more attention than is now perhaps necessary in consumer goods selling efforts. These salesmen cannot be expected to sell the ideal product mix without guidance and direction nor differentiate between the profitability of various products.

In any organization the level of profit responsibility must not only be decided but also widely communicated to ensure the satisfactory implementation of the most critical of business activities.

The marketing plan and all its ancillary documents must be used by executives as a day to day control and development manual. The planning process must not be treated as an annual political exercise suffered by busy executives concerned with other tasks. Planning, organization, direction and control are basic management jobs and, in a successful marketing-oriented company, will fill the management's working days. Each manager needs to understand the interactive nature of the individual tasks which have to be completed during each period of the marketing plan.

The timing of each step, at all levels, and in each function, is critical if the total plan is to be satisfactorily co-ordinated and the anticipated results achieved. A flexible attitude to planning principles needs to be adopted so that management recognizes the need for contingencies and their control within corporate strategy.

Unforeseen events create a different scale of priorities, and flexibility in policy interpretation as allowed for in the plan must be recognized if the company's interests are to be best served. The results of monitoring actual performance against forecasts have a definite value in personnel development and in operating efficiency, as does the preparation of forecasts itself.

The chief executive of any marketing-oriented company retains the final responsibility for marketing policies. The marketing manager gives advice in the field of marketing and may well carry a line responsibility. If the marketing concept is to be adopted the entire company and, in particular, the management team must be oriented towards customer satisfaction. And this is the essence of planning in marketing. For the end result – the marketing plan – is not so important as the benefits gained from the input. The effort, study, appraisal, and evaluation of the business environment provides the major bonuses from the preparation of the plan and it all starts from considering customer needs.

In the foreseeable future most companies will become increasingly involved in computerization. Even if not directly concerned as users, companies will become involved by the extent to which suppliers, competitors and customers become geared to electronic data processing. Every businessman must appreciate how the computer can be applied to marketing problems. He needs some appreciation of the effects of computers on present-day and future marketing decisions. Future growth potential of computer-linked terminals making computerization possible and economic for many smaller firms will certainly assist in the scientific application of marketing. The day is not far off when a company's entire planning process will be subject to computer storage and processing.

FURTHER READING

Allen, Peter, *Marketing Techniques for Analysis and Control*, Macdonald & Evans, Plymouth, 1977

Kitler, Philip, *Marketing Management: analysis, planning, and control*, 4th edition, Prentice-Hall International, London, 1981

McDonald, Malcolm H.B., *Marketing plans, How to prepare them: How to use them*, Heinemann, London, 1984

Stapleton, John, *How to Prepare a Marketing Plan*, 4th edition, Gower, Aldershot, 1988

Wilson, Richard M.S., *Management Controls and Marketing Planning*, Heinemann on behalf of the Institute of Marketing and the CAM Foundation, London, 1979

Winkler, John, *Winkler on Marketing Planning*, Cassels/ABP, London

14 Market research

Colin McDonald

It is a favourite military adage that 'time spent in reconnaissance is seldom wasted'. Market research is the way in which industry does reconnaissance. It seeks to provide knowledge of customers, how they behave and to what they respond and, the current and expected state of the market. Without this knowledge it would be very much more difficult and less safe to plan marketing, to decide between options and to evaluate the effect of decisions.

Market research is by no means all the information a marketer needs, but it is a quite specific sector of it. The military analogy is useful here. 'Reconnaissance' is a survey of the ground before a battle, knowledge of the enemy and how his troops are disposed. It cannot itself determine military objectives; other information (for example, about the resources available on one's own side and their state of readiness) is necessary for this. Nor can it decide the political objectives of the war. But it can modify the general's appreciation of his objectives and suggest the best ways of achieving them (provided of course that it is good reconnaissance; misleading information is worse than none, as Napoleon doubtless felt after Moscow). In the same way, well-conducted market research provides systematic and accurate knowledge of the market 'out there', the people we are trying to sell to; it can correct false impressions and aid understanding of their needs and responses. It cannot *by itself* determine marketing objectives but, allied to a proper appreciation of the product it helps the resources of a business to be deployed effectively.

Market research does not guarantee success. Even the best-conducted intelligence service may be misinterpreted or misused; Napoleon did not fail at Moscow through lack of information, but because he refused to pay attention to the information he had available. Market research costs money, and there are often strong pressures to skimp on it or to think of it too late, instead of integrating it into the marketing plan. Market research provides an important part of the basis for better, more cost-effective marketing, but only if it is well designed and well thought out in accordance with marketing objectives, and if the results are taken seriously and understood.

THE GROWTH OF MARKET RESEARCH

Although the beginnings of market research can be said to date back to the turn of the century, when advertising agencies such as the J. Walter Thompson Company in America began to build successful businesses on the basis that they understood the market, its growth into a substantial industry is entirely post-war. In Britain a few advertising agencies had established market research subsidiaries before the war, and one or two successful entrepreneurs (A.C. Nielsen, Gallup, Mass Observation, for example) had set up their own specialized services. Government work for the Ministry of Food and other departments kept these bodies in operation during the war, but when the Market Research Society was formed in 1947 there were only a dozen market research agencies in the country, six of which still operate today: British Market Research Bureau (the oldest *ad hoc* agency in Britain), Bureau of Commercial Research, Mass Observation, Nielsen, Research Services and Gallup.

Today the market for research in Britain is estimated to be worth over £150 million. During the 1970s the increase in real terms (adjusted for inflation) was more than two-thirds. The turnover of companies belonging to the Association of Market Survey Organizations (AMSO), whose members account for 80–90 per cent of all interviewing, increased by 87 per cent between 1980 and 1984. Over 4000 people are thought to be employed in market research, three-quarters of whom are members of the Market Research Society, and there are over 250 supplying agencies.

It is still the case that the industry depends heavily on consumer goods clients, especially in food and drink. Advertising agencies, the original founders of most market research suppliers, now directly commission less than 10 per cent; the post-war years have seen the development of in-house research departments, staffed by professionals, with an established place in the marketing organization of their companies, and the decline of the full-service agency. In 1986 the following distribution of research revenue was estimated (based on the returns of members of AMSO, the Association of Market Survey Organizations, adjusted for non-members):

Food, drink and tobacco	28
Media and advertising	17
Pharmaceuticals and cosmetics	14
Household products	10
Government and public services	7
Motoring	6
Retailers	4
Financial services	4
Travel services	3
Industrial products	3
Other	4
	100 per cent

Whilst it would not be surprising if growth did not continue at the same rates as in the past, the revolution now taking place in financial services is likely to accelerate the spread of research into new areas; as companies appreciate the benefits of marketing, research will follow.

THE OCCASIONS FOR MARKET RESEARCH

The variety of problems presented for treatment by market research methods, and of sources from which they come, is so great these days that no classification can give its full flavour. However, some sort of intelligible grouping is needed to break up the subject. Let us consider first the occasions when, and the purposes for which, market research is used. Since this book is intended for managers, we shall concentrate on market research for industrial and commercial clients making consumer goods; but much of what follows will apply in the different context of work for government departments, local authorities, nationalized and non-consumer industries or university research projects. All of these use the same tools of the trade in differing degrees.

As a first step, one might distinguish three aspects of business where market research is naturally involved:

1 *Description* of the market
2 *Monitoring* how the market changes
3 *Action* taken by the company, both at the state of *initiation* (choosing which action to take) and *evaluation* of the results of action taken.

Each of these three can be applied at two levels of distribution: the level of the *retailer*, and the level of the eventual *consumer*. Thus we can think of the field divided into a sixfold framework:

	Retailer level	Consumer level
Description		
Monitoring		
Action (initiation and evaluation)		

The way in which research methods fit into the cells of this framework will be discussed later, but first these three aspects of business will be described.

Description

The primary purpose for which research is required. The need is obvious for a company coming new to a market. To work out the overall strategy, to formulate the product correctly and to decide how to market and promote it, it is clearly necessary to learn whatever relevant information is not already known about the brands (if any) already in the market, how they are distributed, their share of market, who the users are, how frequently and how they use the brands, whether they are single- or multiple-brand users, and the reasons why they make their choices. A new entrant would *have* to learn these things but it is equally important, if less obvious, for an established brand that those who market it should keep up to date with the context in which their product is bought.

Yankelovitch, in a paper in 1966, tells the story of the runaway success of Timex watches in the United States, and attributes it to their correct appreciation of the actual demand in their market. The Swiss manufacturers, against whom Timex were competing, discovered (from a survey which they misunderstood) that low-cost Timex watches were being purchased not merely by low-income groups but by high-income groups also. They failed to appreciate that as many as two-thirds of the watch-buying population either wanted a low-cost watch which they could replace if it wore out, or a reliable watch (paying extra for the quality); in both cases a *practical* purchase. They continued to address all their promotion to the remaining third of the market, which saw a watch solely as a gift for a special occasion with an emotional content. The quality watch companies stressed the symbolic aspect in their advertising and concentrated it all around Christmas and graduation day, leaving the rest of the year uncovered. Timex exploited the gap with brilliant effect. It is unusual to find so clear a case history, but there have been other examples quoted publicly, by managers responsible for brands of acknowledged success and prestige, which have stressed the importance they attach to keeping up to date their knowledge of the 'health' of the brand, and the place this takes in their marketing strategy.

Monitoring

By this is meant period checking for *changes*, in the brand's share or distribution, usage or image. There are obvious dangers in formulating plans on out-of-date information when significant changes have occurred since the original picture was taken.

A typical research strategy might involve periodic studies of a market in some depth, taking a cross-section at a certain point in time, linking these together by continuous measurement of a limited number of key variables which are expected to be liable to change.

Action

Whereas 'description' and 'monitoring' refer to obtaining information about the market 'out there', the 'action' heading would include all the ways in which market research can help a company to operate within that situation, both in initiating and deciding between options, and in evaluating action taken. It can include the following areas of activity:

1 New product launches and development
2 Alteration to existing products (i.e., testing for acceptability)
3 Developing and evaluating advertising campaigns, in matching creative treatment and media to target markets
4 Developing and evaluating promotions, sampling drops, mailing shots etc.
5 Promoting the company's image.

Another area of research which really deserves a separate heading, although it is not included in the 'management' scheme above, is *media*. Information on the audiences for different media is needed on a continuous basis to provide the currency in which agency buyers can deal with media sellers. Television viewing, radio listening and newspaper and magazine readership are all regularly measured in surveys paid for by media owners and controlled by joint industry committees representing media, agencies and advertisers. Apart from these, a number of specific surveys are carried out to establish the coverage or effectiveness of particular media.

WHY RESEARCH AT ALL?

As already stated, market research is not the whole of the information needed for marketing, but a special kind of information, obtained by survey methods from the population of potential consumers or from the distribution system. Before moving on to consider how the different purposes outlined above are satisfied by different research methods, it is pertinent to ask why we need market research at all. After all, it costs money to collect and process research data, and it is not so long ago that there was no market research at all. Didn't people manage then, and are there not firms who seem successful enough today without it?

It is tempting, especially in times of financial stringency, to believe that a company's own knowledge of its product and contacts with the trade should be adequate. Nor would it be right to decry the know-how of (for example) a good sales force. But there are several problems in relying solely on reports from salesman or other departments. One is lack of the coverage we need: salesmen's contacts with the trade are not likely to tell us enough about *customers'* attitudes. Second, what salesmen are able to discover is limited by the contacts they make among retailers and will not represent them all. Third, information gathering is not their principal job, and their selection and interpretation of what seems important will inevitably be affected by their primary interest in selling. Although information from salesmen or other sources may have considerable qualitative value, we need to be sure that the information on which decisions are based is as far as possible complete and representative in coverage, and objective.

To ensure representativeness and objectivity, market research makes extensive use of *sampling*.

Sampling in market research

Sampling is not, of course, exclusive to market research; it is a familiar concept in quality control. It is the only practical way of measuring the composition (taking a sounding) of a very large population which it would be impossible, or prohibitively expensive, to measure in a complete census (a 'population', by the way, in statistics means any defined group of people or things which is to be sampled).

If a sample is selected by correct methods, every member of the population will have an equal probability of being selected (or, if not equal, a known and deliberately weighted probability). There is thus no bias in the selection, so that the results remain unknown and uncalculated.

Central to the theory of sampling is the concept of standard error. From a very large population, there is a very large number of ways, almost an infinity of ways, of selecting samples. Suppose a very large number of different samples of a given size were selected. What would we expect the variation to be in any estimate derived from samples? To make it concrete, let us suppose we want to find out the proportion of all adults who are men. We happen to know it should be about half, but the same principle applies to any other unknown proportion we want to estimate. The different samples will not give exactly the same estimate, but we would expect *most* of them to give *roughly* the right estimate; otherwise sampling would be of little value. In fact, we know from sampling theory that the estimates given by a very large number of samples fit into a standard pattern, called the *normal distribution*, a bell-shaped curve in which most of the sample estimates bunch together around the centre while some tail off in either direction, above and below the central estimate. It is possible to calculate how sample estimates form themselves into a normal distribution, by calculating the standard error, two-thirds of all the estimates would be within plus or minus one standard error of the average (central) estimate, 95 per cent within two and 99 per cent within three standard errors. Thus we know, by calculation based on sampling theory, the probability that the true proportion for the population (or the average estimate from a number of samples, which approaches closer to the true proportion as the number of samples approach infinity) lies within a certain range of the estimate given by our *one* sample.

A very important point here, and one often not understood by laymen, is that the error probability we can calculate for a sample depends only on the size of the sample itself and *not at all* on the proportion of the population sampled. People are often surprised at the idea that one can estimate a quantity for a population of many millions from 'only' 500 or 1000 people. But if it is a properly selected sample, the error calculation depends only on the sample size and the fact that the sample is only a tiny proportion of the population is irrelevant. If from a sample of 1000 people we estimate that 45 per cent of the population of the country is male we know that there is a 95 per cent chance that the true figure will lie between plus or minus 3 per cent (in other words, there is only one chance in twenty that any similar sample would have produced an estimate lower than 42 per cent or higher than 48 per cent). If the sample size were increased to 4000, the range of error would be reduced to plus or minus 1.5, i.e., between 43.5 per cent and 46.5 per cent. The general rule is that to *halve* the standard error you have to increase the sample size by four times.

The above explains why sampling theory provides a safe and economical procedure for accurate estimation of large populations. In practice, in market research, the pure theory just described nearly always has to be modified. This is because we sample people, and people living all over a country are expensive to contact and interview; a simple equal probability sample of the population of Britain would involve a great deal of expensive travelling by interviewers to contact isolated individuals.

Basic sampling theory has been developed in many ways so as to combine statistical validity with practical cost-effective interviewing. The two most important modifications are *clustering* and *stratification*. By clustering is meant that, instead of sampling across the board, we sample in *stages*, selecting first a sample of geographical areas (e.g. wards, polling districts or census enumeration districts) and taking the sample of people within those districts. Clustering slightly increases the standard error of a sample, but this is calculable and is normally a small price to pay for the benefit of cost-effective interviewing, since interviewers can be given assignments with contacts all living reasonably close together and can then achieve a higher rate per day's work. Stratification means that before selecting the geographical areas (normally called sampling points) within which we are to sample, they are arranged in an order which makes sure that we include in correct proportions all relevant local characteristics: north and south, urban and rural areas and so on. There are now in existence very sophisticated methods for classifying geographical areas, based on information from the census, and computer programs for picking stratified sampling points.

There are many possible ways of sampling individuals but they group essentially into two: random and non-random. In random, or probability, sampling, the interviewer has no choice: he has to try to contact a specific individual pointed out to him. Most samples in the UK are picked from the electoral register, and there are systems for picking either households or individuals from the register and for sampling adults with the correct probability from selected households even if they are themselves not registered. With a probability sample one knows what proportion of the selected sample could not be contacted and therefore has a chance to estimate any bias in the results; the statistical calculations of standard error, etc., all apply. Probability samples are usually demanded for government surveys and for others which are required to be publicly accountable. There is however a cost penalty, since it is more expensive to require interviewers to contact specific individuals, calling a number of times if necessary, than to allow them some latitude in their selection of persons to interview. For this reason, many market research projects use a form of non-random, or quota sampling, in which interviewers are required to deliver certain numbers of interviews with specified types of people whom they must find themselves. Quotas can be set in line with what is known of the population. Strictly, quota sampling does not have the statistical theoretical base of random sampling, although empirical tests of the consistency (stability) of non-random samples are possible. In much sampling practice quota samples are selected multi-stage, with the primary sample of areas (wards etc.) being chosen by strict probability methods after stratification. The interviewers are issued with lists of street numbers and given strict instructions to obtain their interviews within those streets. The only quota controls which then remain necessary are those relating to the probability of someone being at home: typically, interviewers have to find a certain proportion of working women or women with children, and must interview men in the evening so as not to find only unemployed or shift workers. Most of the major research agencies operate a system of this general kind.

The above account of sampling applies (obviously) to consumer research. But the variety of problems which can arise often calls for ingenuity in devising new ways of sampling, often in cases where there does not exist a 'universe' from which the sample can be drawn: industrial firms, people in professions, people with certain minority characteristics, users of certain products etc.

RESEARCH METHODS

We can now consider in broad terms the research approaches which are appropriate for the different levels of information required, classified above as description, monitoring and action. It should not be thought that these are hard-and-fast distinctions. Good research is always designed to fit a specific problem and there are cases, for example, where retailers or manufacturers are properly researched by sample survey (certainly where we are involved in measuring their opinions). Much detail is omitted from the table in Figure 14.1. Nevertheless, it is a convenient way of breaking up the subject so that we can *start* thinking about it.

Retail audits

The retail audit is one of the earliest known types of research, pioneered by Nielsen in the United States. It stemmed from the realization that relying

GHM	For retailers	For consumers
Description of market	Retail audit	Sample surveys
Monitoring changes and trends	Retail audit	Panels or sequential surveys
Action: Initiation	Test market	Experimental tests
Evaluation	Area evaluation	Product tests etc.
The media	Not applicable	Sample surveys or panels

Figure 14.1   Market research appropriate to different purposes

on measurements of sales ex-factory was not fast enough or accurate enough to identify areas of weakness in distribution or adverse trends that would need correction. A falling demand could be concealed by stock build-up at the wholesalers; conversely, retailers might be content to tolerate shortages of stock in areas where a little activity could stimulate a healthy demand, etc. It was necessary to go to the front line, so to speak, and observe directly what consumers were taking off the shelves.

Retail audits work in the following way. A panel of stores is recruited to represent the universe (grocery outlets, chemists, off-licences or whatever the definition is) being stratified so that different turnover levels and types of organization (multiple, independent, voluntary group, cash and carry etc.) are represented. The audits are carried out at regular intervals, usually bi-monthly. At each audit, an interviewer counts the stock of the audited items on display on the shelves and in the storeroom, and all goods invoiced since the previous check. Movement off the shelf between two checks is then calculated by the simple formula:

(Stock at check 1) + (Goods invoice since check 1) – (Stock at check 2)

The key data normally reported for audited product fields are sales brand shares and volume trends, purchase brand shares and volume trends, and distribution. These are broken down by relevant classifications such as area of the country, type of shop or turnover level, and all shown both in unit volume and sterling value terms: where relevant, pack sizes within brands are also broken out separately. Advertising expenditure is usually monitored and fluctuations in this can be set alongside sales and purchase movements, although it may be dangerous to draw simple conclusions about relationships between them. Most retail audit companies will, for a lower charge, supply a distribution check which merely tells one what proportion of stores have the brand in stock and on display. Merchandizing material and display advertising can also be monitored.

Setting up a retail audit panel and the facilities to process the data is an expensive investment, and it is crucial to this kind of operation that it should be *syndicable* (that is; sold to a number of clients). Syndication is economically possible because, once the initial investment of recruiting and visiting the panel is made, it is relatively inexpensive to collect the data for a large number of product fields. Following the pattern pioneered and still operated by Nielsen, clients pay agreed subscriptions for packages of selected brands within a defined product field, reported and presented so that the information is tailored to their needs.

Although most retail audit work is thought of in connexion with grocery and chemist products, audits are run in hardware stores, tobacconists, garages, off-licences, travel agents, record shops and other specialist outlets. Prescription auditing, in which either chemists' invoices or doctors' prescriptions (from duplicate pads) are counted, is also an established service.

In buying an audit, of course, one always has to be aware of the proportion of trade that passes through outlets *other* than the particular group being measured by the audit.

It is widely expected that the spread of new technology, especially electronic data capture at the checkout, will eventually change the face of auditing. Through scanners, retailers can acquire instant, accurate and continuous knowledge and therefore control to assist them in their day-to-day management. They may not wish to make this information available to competitors; alternatively, they may agree amongst themselves upon the extent to which information for the whole trade (or the few companies responsible for 80 per cent of it) is to be disseminated and shared. The detail available from scanners will make traditional auditing seem very slow and old fashioned; on the other hand part of the market (the smaller outlets) will be relatively slow to adopt scanners. In America (where some 4000 stores now have scanners) there are already a number of research firms who have set up consumer panels in association with scanner stores, so that these people's purchases can be logged automatically over time (without trouble to the respondent) and related to their opportunities for seeing advertising, etc. It will be a few years yet before new-look audit facilities are in being but eventually (we may be confident) scanner-based data will win on cheapness as well as quality and new types of service will compete for the business.

Consumer sample surveys

These are what most people automatically think of as 'market research': the interviewer with a clipboard, the structured questionnaire, the so-called opinion poll. Indeed, these methods are still the backbone of market research, and are likely to remain so. To stop short at the level of the retailer's counter is not enough; marketers must know what consumers do with their products, how they buy them, what they like or dislike, what needs are unsatisfied. New products could not otherwise be optimally designed and launched; existing ones could not be promoted to best effect.

The personal interview, with the interviewer knocking at the door or stopping people in the street, is the popular picture of consumer surveying but not the whole story. Occasionally the necessary data are collected by *observation*. Often *self-completion* questionnaires are used, either in the course of a personal interview, or left with informants to return by post or to be collected later. Self-completion is used for the Target Group Index (a syndicated survey of 25 000 people covering usage of over 2000 brands and services and media). It is also a good procedure for certain kinds of scaled attitude data. Finally, there are the alternatives of *postal* and *telephone* interviewing.

Personal interviewing is the most costly alternative, and this trend is likely to continue. The reason is obvious: it is a highly labour-intensive method. Interviewers are paid about £20 for a roughly six-hour day, depending on their quality and experience. Pay is increased for unsocial hours (evenings or weekends) which are necessary in most surveys these days even when only housewives are being interviewed, since so many of them are out at work during the day. In addition, interviewers have to be paid for their time in travelling to the place where the work has to be carried out, which may be some distance from their home, and their mileage expenses, which must increase in line with petrol prices. The days of interviewing as a relatively low-cost part-time job are over. More importantly, a large section of the time paid for is 'dead' time, travelling to and between contacts, and this lowers the effective daily interviewing rate, which is the principal variable determining the cost of a survey.

Nevertheless, for many survey purposes personal face-to-face interviewing is considered necessary. A good interviewer forms a rapport with respondents which can lead them to focus their minds in a relaxed and concentrated way on the subject under discussion. The interaction between two people plays a part in improving the quality of the response. Stimuli can be shown, ranging from words on a card through photographs to actual products. Also, a questionnaire can be taken in a designed order, with respondents not being alerted to questions due to come later and which could affect the earlier response.

A device commonly used to offset the high cost of face-to-face surveys where the method is judged necessary is *syndication*, in which the data collection costs of the survey are shared between a number of subscribers. The commonest form of such syndication is what has come to be known as the 'omnibus' survey. In this a regular sample is interviewed weekly (so many housewives or adults) and subscribers buy questions on the survey at a standardized fee per question and sample size. Many regularly repeated surveys, advertising tracking studies and so on, have been successfully and economically run on omnibus survey vehicles. The only serious limitation is the length of the interview. No individual can tolerate being interviewed for too long, however fascinating the subject matter, and if a number of topic areas for different subscribers have to be fitted into an interview the amount of time which can be allowed for any one of them is clearly much less than would be the case if the whole interview could be given over to that topic. For this reason, if a subject has to be explored in some depth by a large number of questions, an omnibus is unlikely to be suitable and a tailor-made survey will probably be required. The same is true if there is some special requirement in the sample which cannot be fulfilled by the general purpose sample used for the omnibus. But if only one or two things are required to be known and if a representative sample of the total population will do, an omnibus can offer significant savings. A special advantage of an omnibus is that because relatively large samples are interviewed weekly it can be an excellent way of finding minority samples quickly; for example where questions are to be asked of users of a product which is known to be used by only 2 per cent (say) of the population. With a tailor-made survey the cost of contacting the other 98 per cent to find out that they are not eligible for our survey is considerable, but on the omnibus that cost is almost entirely shared between the other subscribers.

Postal and *telephone surveys* are ways of interviewing which do not incur the cost penalties of sending interviewers out to people's homes to make their contacts.

The postal survey is perhaps neglected a little unfairly in the UK except where a special sample assumed to be highly interested in the subject matter is involved (for example, the members of an organization being asked their opinions about that organization). There is an obvious incentive to use postal surveys where we have a population to sample for whom it is easy to obtain names and addresses and where the sample is so scattered as to make the cost of face-to-face interviewing prohibitive (the same applies, of course, to telephone interviewing). There are two main potential disadvantages with postal interviewing. The first is that a respondent can scan the whole questionnaire before he answers it (there is no possibility of leading the respondent through one stage a time) and he can take as long over answering it as he likes; postal surveys are therefore suitable for 'considered opinions' but not for 'instant reactions'. The second and more serious disadvantage is that it is so easy for people not to reply at all. The normal procedure is to send out the questionnaires with reply-paid return envelopes, to send a reminder (with a spare questionnaire) after (say) ten days, and a second reminder some ten days after the first.

Even so, it is common to get not more than 40-50 per cent of the sample responding, and it has been known to be as low as 20 per cent. There is no simple answer to this difficulty, the important question being whether the non-respondents are *biased* in some way which would affect our interpretation of the survey results. However, this is certainly not a reason for avoiding postal surveys altogether. Postal surveys are suitable for an *interested* population, and much can be done to encourage people to respond by good design, good layout and (occasionally) incentive payment; non-response bias can be checked by telephone calls on a sub-sample.

Telephone interviewing is, in Britain and other industrialized countries, the most likely main development for the future. In the United States, where 95 per cent of the population have telephones, it is now a major data collection method. In the UK the proportion with a telephone at home has passed the 70 per cent mark, which is about the point at which telephone interviewing began to take off in the US several years ago. At these levels the question of what bias there may be among non-telephone households assumes less and less importance for most marketing interests.

Telephone interviewing preserves the interviewer-respondent interaction but in a rather different form: the interviewer's *voice* becomes crucial, other aspects of the interviewer's personality much less so. It is acknowledged that telephone interviewing is a different type of operation with its own requirements of questionnaire design and the kind of person suitable to be an interviewer. It can achieve much greater productivity than face-to-face interviewing because it can be centrally organized. No costs are incurred in travel to locate respondents and many more calls (both contact calls and successful interview calls) can be made in a day. Moreover, there is a facility for instant supervision and correction of interviewer error which is lacking in a face-to-face survey. As technology improves, telephone interviewing will make possible the automated questionnaires and immediate data capture and processing by computer which are already in operation to a limited extent in the United States.

There are some obvious limitations. One cannot show stimulus material over the telephone (although it is possible to mail stimulus material to people already recruited to a sample with instructions not to look at it until the interview). There are worries also about the psychological reaction of respondents to the telephone: will they be nervous of a disembodied voice or resentful at the intrusion into their privacy that the telephone may seem to represent? American experience does not suggest that these are serious problems, but only time will tell whether in other countries there is an anti-telephone feeling.

An experimental study carried out in 1985 by the Market Research Fund showed that, for most purposes, telephone gives results comparable with face-to-face interviewing, but there are some points of difference which may need to be considered when planning a survey.

Although telephones are not yet used widely in general consumer surveys in Britain, they are extensively used for surveys among respondents at the executive level who can, of course, most easily be contacted by telephone. Frequently such respondents are recruited by telephone for face-to-face interviews in greater depth.

Panels

If you wish to measure *change* in attitudes or behaviour, an obvious approach is to interview the same set of people twice. Any change observed is subject to the standard error of the one sample only, whereas, if two separate samples are used, there are two standard errors to take into account. One can get a more direct, more accurate picture of change within people, and perhaps that can be related to a stimulus such as a new advertising campaign. The drawback, of course, is that one must be careful not to alert people by questions which in themselves could lead them to notice things or to modify their behaviour and thus distort their answers the second time round.

Any repeat interviewing of the same people could be called a panel. Normally, in research parlance, a panel has a more restricted meaning than that. *Either* it is a sample which agrees, on recruitment, to be available for contact on all sorts of subjects (some firms run telephone panels on this basis) *or* (more commonly in the UK) a panel is recruited to provide *continuous* information over a period, typically information which needs to be recorded day by day otherwise it would not be remembered. Such panels may be run either as continuous syndicated services (requiring an investment too great for a single company to underwrite) or for specific *ad hoc* projects. Examples of operations suitable for panel treatment include:

1　*Retail audits*, where the data are provided from panels of shops
2　*Consumer audits*, where panel members keep records of purchases and interviewers periodically call and check stocks (one method is the so-called 'dustbin check', where special containers are provided for used cans or cartons of the product being measured)

3 *Media*; the television audience measurement required for the industry is provided by a panel of homes with meters showing when the set is switched on and to which channel; diaries record who was watching. The radio audience measurement is based on diary panels
4 *New product launches*; there are well-established techniques for covering the launch period of a new brand with a panel record of purchases and, forecasting from that, the eventual development of penetration and repeat purchasing.

Panels on any scale are expensive to operate. If the panel is continuous, new members have to be continuously recruited to replace those who drop out or have to be dropped because they grow stale or too 'professional'. With diaries or similar records the task is heavier than with a single interview, and panel members may need much more in the way of 'nursing' by frequent calls from interviewers (if not more practical incentives) to make certain they keep at it. And panels generate very large amounts of data, which are seldom analysed in enough detail to get full advantage from the panel's unique capacity to trace changes over time within individuals; better analysis of panel data may be expected to be one of the major benefits of new technology in the next few years.

Experimental design

Hitherto we have been thinking mainly of strategic research, with population descriptions and monitoring of change. But much market research is concerned directly with marketing action, not only planning but evaluating it. Which option to take? What happens if we do that? What has happened as a result of action already taken, and how should it be modified in future?

The key to such questions is *comparison*, and the problem is to control for other possible sources of variation than the one we are trying to measure. Suppose we want to try out, or learn the effect of, a new advertisement. A typical approach would be (assuming the advertisement had not yet appeared on the air) to show the advertisement to a group of people and then ask questions about the brand, their attitudes to it and what the advertisement conveyed to them. The trouble is that from just this one sample it would be difficult to be sure just how far their answers were being determined, not by the new advertisement at all, but by previous experience of the brand, other advertising seen, and other influences triggered off by our questioning. To deal with this difficulty we could take another sample, like the first in all relevant respects (such as social grade, age groups, usage of the brand) and ask them the same questions but *without* showing the advertisement. Comparing the two sets of answers gives one a much better basis for believing that the *differences* between them are due to the advertisement, since that is the only relevant factor we have allowed to vary.

Many research users do not distinguish clearly enough between *survey* and *experiment* in market research, or appreciate the important part that well-designed experiments could play in their decisions.

A survey has description as its main purpose and may range widely in its coverage, but it must be based on a sample which represents the population properly. Experiments may be (and usually are) based on representative samples, but the point is less crucial for them; much more important is the matching of samples to control for extraneous sources of variation. An experiment is set up with a specific objective, usually to establish the relation between two specific variables (for example, seeing advertising and changing one's state of awareness or attitudes) and it achieves that objective by ensuring as far as possible that other sources of the effect are accounted for. The objective of an experiment determines how it is designed and how the results are to be looked at, and as a rule it is not possible to follow more than one such objective at a time.

One of the commonest types of experimental research is *product testing*. When a new version is developed (for example, a new flavour) it needs to be tested out on consumers in natural conditions to establish whether it is a good investment. Alternatively, opportunity of economy may arise by a change in the ingredients, but this must be tested on the consumers to assess whether they notice or object to any difference. There are many approaches to product testing. Members of the sample can compare two or more versions directly, test them one at a time, or the comparison can be made between samples testing one product each. The versions can be tested blind, or in their full dress concept; it may be the package or the label which is to be tested, etc. The correct design should be chosen to obtain, as economically as possible, what is needed for decision: for example, a blind paired comparison would often be appropriate if one was trying to check that a minor alteration in ingredients would remain unnoticed whereas, if two clearly different versions were being tested for overall preference, a good approach would be to take two matched samples and test each version blind on one of the samples against a 'control': since the control is common to both samples, the two sets of differences between test product and control can be compared. Sample sizes should be chosen on the basis of the degree of difference required for decision; for instance, if it is decided that a new ingredient should be adopted *unless* the old one is preferred by a difference of 10 per cent or more, the sample would be set so that a 10 per cent difference would be unlikely to occur in the sample by chance.

When testing reactions to advertisements, packs or displays, *hall testing* is often used. Instead of respondents being interviewed in the street or in their homes, they are invited to come to a central location. The advantage is that equipment can be set up to show advertising or display packaging, etc. Sometimes the equipment used may be very sophisticated (for example, tachistoscopes, which artificially vary the times of exposure so that the speed with which a design can be identified is measured). Displays can be set up which simulate real-life viewing situations.

In real life, in the market-place, it is usually impossible to set up perfect laboratory-style experiments. Human beings and their environments are so complex that the influences which *could* affect relevant attitudes or behaviour cannot all be controlled. This does not invalidate the experimental approach; it merely means one has to keep one's head. *Advertising evaluation*, for example, is often done by a 'before and after' approach: a survey is done before the new campaign and another done after it has finished (with perhaps others at stages during it) and the differences between them measured. There can often be a problem with timing: the precise point at which the second measurement is taken could affect the result according to how long it is after the end of the campaign. It may therefore be advisable, even if a little more expensive, to run a continuous tracking measurement or, alternatively, to obtain some measure of probable exposure to the advertisement so that one can compare *within* the sample those likely and unlikely to have seen it. There are no general rules; the right tactics have to be worked out according to the case. But common sense and intelligent thought about the research design and the required outcome *before* embarking upon it pay dividends.

Test marketing for new brands, and *area tests* of advertising weights and treatments, are normal management practice for most major consumer goods companies. The reason is that however careful one may be to test the effect of product or promotional variations on a small scale, there are so many influences on consumer behaviour in the market-place which cannot be controlled that the only secure way of predicting what will happen after a major launch decision is to try it out in real life. The basis of all such work is implied experimental comparison, involving an estimate of what sales *would have been* in the test area without the action taken (taking account of all other known special features of the test area which make it different from other areas) and a comparison of that prediction with sales actually achieved.

There are many difficulties with test marketing. Suitable areas for test are difficult to select and isolate in a small country like Britain. Some operators believe that the domination of the retail trade by a few large multiples has now made test marketing in a restricted area much less practical, since they are often unwilling to negotiate the special deals required. Nevertheless, provided the maximum care is taken to understand all the factors which could affect a test, it is usually thought better to subject a plan to the discipline of an area evaluation, depending on the marketing circumstances. Time can be a problem; practitioners of test marketing usually stress the importance of allowing the test market to continue for long enough to allow the product to settle down in a normal sales pattern. With an advertising test, since advertising interacts with many other variables to induce sales, one should beware of generalizing too readily that a relationship found in a test would always be reproduced.

Qualitative research

It would be wrong to conclude their brief review of market research methodology without a mention of qualitative research. Qualitative research is a form of research in which small groups of people, not sufficient for *sta-*

tistical analysis or for quoting as numbers representing the population, are interviewed in much greater depth and a more free-ranging manner than is possible with a quantitative survey. Typically this is done through group discussions, or by single taped, in-depth interviews; the interviewers or group leaders follow through points raised from a discussion brief, instead of asking fixed-format questions from a questionnaire precoded for instant analysis.

The distribution between qualitative and quantitative is often presented as a rather sterile conflict between opposing research schools. It should not be so. Each method has its benefits, its limitations and its place. Qualitative methods may provide deeper insight into a situation, and are often a necessary preliminary for the selection and correct wording of questions in a quantitative survey which, in turn, is needed to provide sound numerical estimates. The two approaches are thus complementary. Danger can come from ignoring either aspect. Questionnaire design is the most difficult part of research, and a base of qualitative understanding may enable one to avoid stupid mistakes through, for example, not realizing the way in which people talk about a subject naturally. On the other hand, reliance on qualitative work only, because it is cheaper, can lead to unwarranted assumptions about what the population believes. This does not mean that qualitative work ignores the need to be representative. Frequently, great care is taken to set quotas, and in major projects as many as thirty or forty groups may be recruited from different strata of society and areas of the country. But the inference that the results represent the population remains an inference, not based on statistical theory.

ANALYSIS, INTERPRETATION AND USE

Even a modest research project may produce very large amounts of data, in the form of cross-tabulations and combinations of variables. The management of this information can pose problems. The development of data handling by computer has made it very easy to produce pages of tabulation; it has not made it easier to draw relevant and useful information from the data in a form which management can appreciate and use. The expensive research report gathering dust on the library shelf is, unfortunately, very often a reality.

The key to the problem is integration. Research will be effective if it is planned as part of a marketing process into which the information produced fits in its proper place. It follows that before going to the expense of collecting information one must have a clear picture of where that information is to fit in the scheme of things, how it is to be used and the actions or consequences which are to follow from different anticipated results. Indiscriminate, undirected information is an expensive luxury. It follows that thought must be given in advance not merely to the content of the information but also to its dissemination: the right people must have it presented to them in a form which they can use.

These considerations should be effective not merely at the analysis and reporting stage of a research project but at the beginning, when it is being planned and designed. This is not to say that there will be no scope for creative ideas once the survey has gone out into the field. It usually happens that the process of analysis itself suggests new ways of looking at the subject which are worth following through. But this does not absolve a researcher from recognizing in advance the limitations of any research proposed and designing the project to take advantage of those limitations. If the marketers who commission work are to get full value from their investment, they need themselves to be aware that the research will only answer the questions it is designed to do, and to realize the importance of being clear about their objectives so as to ensure that the design will meet them.

Normally a research project begins with a written brief from a client to one or more agencies. It is sadly true that most briefs from commercial sources are very badly written indeed. It is often impossible for the reader to draw from the brief a clear idea what the research is intended to do or how it will be used: if it is to be descriptive, what measures are relevant; if experimental, what are the criteria for action.

The best results nearly always require that the research designer be taken into his client's confidence. His speciality is to map out the route from A to B, but to do that effectively he must know where B is. Interaction between a researcher and his marketing client can be very fruitful. Research designers do not seek to have everything cut and dried in a brief, but they must obtain somehow a clear, agreed view of the objectives; from this, the design, the choice of methods and the analysis often fall naturally into place. It is relatively easy to choose the best route and means of travel, once one knows where one has to go and how quickly. Research can never be an alternative to clear thinking on the part of the management which commissions it.

The objectives determine the design and the main thrust of the analysis in one go. Analysis in quantitative survey or experimental work is rarely exploratory: it confirms or tests ideas rather than searches for them. Computers have made possible an increasing sophistication in analysis, but it is a mistake on the part of the researcher or his client if this is allowed to get out of control and confuse the reader. It is very tempting to think that, since it is easy to obtain certain tabular breakdowns in the same computer run, we 'might as well have it' because 'it may show something', even if there is no purpose in mind. This temptation has to be resisted firmly. Unnecessary tables adding to thick volumes increase the probability that none of the tables, including the most useful ones, will be read at all.

It is important to pay attention to the way in which results are presented. It is common practice to prepare research reports at least at two levels:

1 A detailed commentary with technical appendices. This gives the specialists a clear account of the basis from which conclusions are drawn.
2 A summary of the main findings, with their conclusions and implications. This part of the report is for the benefit of senior management, who need such information as a basis for decisions, but who do not have

the time or inclination to absorb all the detail. This summary can be reinforced by visual presentation in person, which gives the opportunity for questions and discussion. The executors of the research should not be too shy to make recommendations where the results justify them.

New technology is making it increasingly possible to access data banks in a flexible way. Random access storage of information on disks and the use of on-line terminals enable a client to buy not merely a set of tabulations on paper but also the right to run off tabulations of his own, piecemeal, at relatively little expense. As these facilities spread, especially with continuous research services, the habits of users will change and they will become accustomed to *interacting* with a data source, asking questions of it to order, and linking data banks together. With the development of on-line data sources, the dusty books on the shelf should become an anachronism.

FURTHER READING

Davies, Anthony H., *The Practice of Marketing Research*, Heinemann, London, 1973

Green, Paul E., and Tull, Donald S., *Research for Marketing Decisions*, Prentice-Hall, Englewood Cliffs, NJ, 1975

Harris, E. Edward, *Marketing Research*, 2nd edition, McGraw-Hill, New York, 1978

Rawnsley, Alan (ed.), *Manual of Industrial Marketing Research*, Wiley, Chichester, 1978

Stacey, N.A.H., and Wilson, A., *Industrial Marketing Research*, Hutchinson, London, 1963

Stapleton, John, *How to Prepare a Marketing Plan*, 4th edition, Gower, Aldershot, 1988

Wentz, Walter B., *Marketing Research: management and methods*, Harper & Row, New York, 1972

15 Advertising

John Hobson

In a modern industrialized society virtually the whole population has some discretionary spending power, with money to spend on goods that, unlike basic food, shelter and clothing, are not essential. People have the capacity to buy improved utilities, extra amenities and modest luxuries. Industry responds by providing goods and services to suit a wide variety of tastes. But no one could want or afford all of these. People have to choose.

In order to make a choice, the consumer needs suggestions and information about what is available, what might suit personal preferences and what could be new or interesting experiences. Before buying, the consumer will want to hear about the performance or satisfaction to be expected from the goods or services offered. Goods may be seen displayed in shops or supermarkets, and their potential satisfactions made known through advertising. Taking the total range of modern advertising, as it appears in all the media, it is not unreasonable to view it as a kind of supermarket of satisfactions.

Although advertising owes its existence in this way to the service it gives the consumer, it becomes a vital service also to the producer. To him advertising offers the lowest-cost channel of communication for his messages offering the goods or services he has for sale. As a result of low-cost communication to millions of people with considerable frequency, he can achieve economies of scale which enable him to reduce prices. He can influence demand in such a way as to maintain a steady flow, which in turn enables him to maintain a flow of production. He can modify seasonal influences on demand with the same advantage, and can assure himself of the rapid pay-off of investment in new production lines and machinery and in research and development. Although advertising is only one element – the communication element – in the marketing mix, it very often can be the critical factor in a marketing decision because it can control the speed at which vital costs can be reimbursed, and new products or improvements to existing products launched.

As a result, advertising has a vital role to play in the economy of the consumer societies of the West. It is one of the most vital tools of competition and innovation which maintain the dynamics and the initiative of industry. It provides the outlet for the results of sound research and development, without which an industrial nation must go into a decline. Advertising helps to maintain employment and the uses of all resources, at a steady pace, without undue swings in supply or demand. It increases the aspirations of the public so that the desires to work harder and earn more money are increased. It improves the quality of material life for the mass of the public. It may be objected that it puts too much emphasis on material aspiration and well-being, but advertising is only responding to social trends, encouraged by the redistribution of wealth over the last century. Advertising does not govern the shape of society; it only reflects the shape that exists.

Advertising is basically communication. There are many kinds of advertising other than in the marketing context: government propaganda, advertising for churches and charities, financial news, advertising to fill jobs and get jobs, and so on. In the rest of this chapter, the word 'advertising' is used in the context of the commercial functions of advertising.

ADVERTISING AS A MARKETING ACTIVITY

The impression the public has of advertising might be that a vast amount of money and effort is being spent on a lot of bright ideas or momentary inspirations. It is a misunderstanding for which even the less well-informed social observers could be pardoned, but it is curiously prevalent also among many people concerned with industry even in the consumer goods fields.

In fact, good advertising is the result of careful planning and research, which lead in almost every case to each advertisement being given its particular content or form, and its direction to a selected audience of potentially interested consumers. The serious sponsors of advertising have no money to waste; for them it is not an art form, or a display of ego or personal interests. When industry spends over £2000 million a year on consumer goods advertising it not only expects to get, but actually does get, what it regards as a proper return for its outlay.

The basic purpose of advertising, then, is to offer goods and services for sale. Each particular advertising campaign for a particular product at a particular time is part of what one may term a deliberate marketing intention on the part of the sponsors, who base their carefully considered strategy and tactics in the first instance on the properties and utilities, shape, packaging and colour of the product, and calculate the latest trends of public behaviour, recreation or outlook, new factors in retail distribution and effect of competition. The marketing intention takes in the method of transport, trade margins, price merchandising, wholesaling and retailing decisions, the role of the sales force, the after-sales service facilities, and a number of similar considerations. It will comprise a careful identification of the best potential market in terms of people, geography, seasons and spending power; and will duly arrive at the advertising message, and the deployment of budget best calculated to carry it. The choice of advertising is virtually the last element to be decided in the marketing complex, and, although it may represent a very large part of the financial outlay and may in the result determine the success or failure of the whole marketing plan, it is in itself very largely governed by the other elements in the plan. Because the advertisements are the main, and certainly most obvious, outward and visible signs of the plan, many people get the impression that the advertising is the only really important element, that it *is* the plan in its own right.

Next, it is worth remarking that virtually no two marketing plans, or their consequent advertising programmes, have identical intentions. There are, of course, certain broad groups of similar circumstances which call for fairly similar treatments; but with each tactical situation, on which each plan is based, there are differing weights of contributory factors which make every case different from any other. It is not feasible to lay down a kind of blueprint that will fit the needs of a number of marketing or advertising intentions.

ADVERTISING OBJECTIVES AND TECHNIQUES

The two most important stages in developing an advertising campaign are (*a*) the strategic decision on objectives and (*b*) the choice of creative treatment. The former is bound up in the total marketing intention; the latter is a matter of advertising techniques.

The considerations leading to decisions of strategy are as wide and various as the field of commerce itself. Nevertheless, it is possible to list five main types of consideration which normally affect the advertising objectives:

1   The range, type and intensity of consumer wants comprising the market for our product, together with estimates of the trends of public outlook or trade development, which may affect those wants in the future
2   The efficacy of the product itself
3   The strength of the sponsor's resources for promoting it
4   The existing disposition of competitor's strength
5   The type of purchasing occasion arising from the character of distribution for this type of product.

One talks of 'the market' for a type of product, but this apparently straight-forward concept of the market conceals a wide variety of types and degrees of want varying by age, geography, outlook, habit, price, occasion of usage, availability and so on. By means of a painstaking assembly of facts through market research, retail contacts, and all other methods of fact finding, the size of the potential sale for our product, associated with each degree of necessity can be calculated, thus setting up a choice of differing objectives for the advertising. It is axiomatic that no product is ever equally perfect for all sectors of the market.

The first consideration in choosing an objective will probably be the special qualities or performance of a product. The addition or adjustment of qualities would be considered in order to create a better advertising proposition. The decision will also be affected by the areas of strength or weakness of the competition. It is no good tackling an objective head-on where strong competition is entrenched.

A vital factor is the resources which our sponsor can put behind his campaign. Only too often, ambitious sponsors with slender resources attempt an objective too big for them.

The strategic advertising decision will also be greatly influenced by the type of purchasing occasion, e.g. an impulse market, a carefully considered purchase, a product limited by distributive conditions to tied outlets, a cut-price supermarket situation etc.

Finally, one must look forward from the market, the competition and the distribution, as they now exist, to possible developments foreseen as a result of trends in public spending, outlook and living patterns, and position of the product in its market accordingly.

An illustration of the strategic advertising decision might be given in the case of the breakfast cereal market. Here are five products which have been deliberately aimed at five sectors of the market. The market leader uses his dominant resources to promote a broad sense of pleasure and wholesomeness, which can apply to everyone. Another brand with a more rugged product and a lower budget concentrates on youngsters through their sporting interests. A third attacks a limited but specific health area. A fourth goes for the children's market with the appeal of a sense of fantasy and fun, while a fifth tackles the same market with the appeal of premium gifts.

It is probable that this strategic decision overrides even the creative decision of importance. The most sparkling and competent creative execution will be wasted if the policy objectives are not correctly chosen. It happens only too often. At the same time, within the right strategic decision there is a wide scope for success or failure, brilliance or dullness, competence or incompetence, in the creative execution.

There are three main considerations likely to influence the approach to the creative decision: (a) the tactical objective of the particular phase of advertising (b) the choice of main and secondary selling arguments, and (c) the manner or atmosphere of the presentation of those selling arguments.

TACTICS

There is an infinite variety of tactical situations. To name a few – we may be launching a new product with new utilities which need proclaiming and explaining. A dramatic piece of news like a price reduction or a new model may be announced, or the memory of an established brand name may be merely sustained with a fresh rendering of its well-known claim. The virtues and the responsibility of a serious industrial concern may be expounded to an audience of managers, or the objective may be to give a company in the popular consumer goods field a favourable image against which its goods will sell automatically. A race for our brand against a very similar brand of some other firm to gain a larger share of the market may occupy much of our time, or it may be that greater concern is felt for widening the total market for a class of goods because, if the market widens, our brand must automatically gain the lion's share.

There are probably three main elements in the tactical case of advertising – to penetrate, remind and create favourable associations. The relative importance of each element in the plan of the particular campaign will tend to determine which type of media or campaign approach will be used. For example, television and large spaces in the press and magazines are ideal outlets for telling a story in depth, while posters and smaller spaces in the press and short television flashes (little more than moving posters) are good for repetition which, as Dr Kelvin points out in *Advertising and the Human Memory*, not only prevents us forgetting but serves as the means of progressive assimilation of the advertising message.

Then the question of the selling arguments arises. It might seem as if the choice were obvious, determined simply by the properties of the product. This, however, is unlikely to be so in the majority of cases. It will be true at the moment when a product has clear and simply expressed product advantages over its competitors; but this situation will not hold good for long because it will only be a matter of time before the competition is forced to include those same advantages. Look around the whole field of consumer goods and you will find very few markets in which there is not a handful of equally good competitive brands. If one has edged ahead in product quality, the others have caught up. Indeed, this continuous competitive improvement is one of the great merits of the system of which advertising is a part. In this situation advertising has to find some aspect of a brand on which to focus, an aspect on which the competition has not focused. Nor is this limitation of the scope of the product claim to a single aspect a disadvantage; indeed quite the reverse. The consumer finds it far easier to identify, and therefore to remember at time of purchase, a product which has one single claim associated with it. So, however many good points a product may have, it is wise for the purposes of advertising to focus on one only, and allow the other values to emerge in course of use. Naturally, that one point must be an important one capable of influencing a sizeable part of the market.

ADVERTISING AND MARKET RESEARCH

What are the techniques for assessing the best choice of product claim? First, there is the obvious selection of an objective built-in utility superior to that of competition, but this is usually a short-lived advantage. Next, there is the historic flair and inspiration of the salesman for judging what the public wants most in the area of this product, and for concentrating on this aspect of the brand's properties. This competence, whether rational or intuitive, is one of the chief qualities of a great industrialist or a great salesman.

But in the intensive competition of today, and where the stakes are high and the penalties great, the hit-or-miss risks of intuition are not always acceptable. Market research, and especially depth research, are employed more and more to help in defining those areas to which the product's copy claims can best be directed. Market research covers all types of consumer investigation, but is generally associated with research designed to establish a pattern of behaviour. From the patterns of behaviour by people of various descriptions the motives of that behaviour are deduced. Depth research, or motivation study as it is called, consists of interviews directly designed to establish attitudes, motives and feelings about products and their usage, without the risks of deducing them from behaviour patterns.

A lot has been written and spoken about 'hidden persuaders' since Vance Packard's book of that title was written. Certainly, the book overdramatized what is a very natural and sensible process. Let us be clear that in buying, as in many aspects of life, the number of decisions that can be taken on strictly rational grounds is very few; not only because it is seldom possible to assemble all the facts, but also because rational decisions involve a painful and complicated mental process which only a few people are either capable of or willing to undertake. Therefore, the majority of decisions are made out of feelings, habits, instincts and impulses. It is commonsense, therefore, to try to chart those feelings, habits and impulses which surround the purchase of goods being sold.

The purpose of any such research, as indeed of the alternative – flair and intuition – is to establish that aspect of the product's claims which interests a large enough market, which has been neglected by competitors, and with which therefore this particular brand can become associated with major selling effect. Sometimes, of course, the need for being different leads to an exaggerated or partly untenable vision of a claim, even among well-intentioned salesmen. The public's safeguard in this case is that, since the success of any product depends on repeat purchases, not merely on a single purchase, and since nothing makes the public react against a product more than disappointment in an advertised claim, it is bad commercial policy as well as undesirable ethically to call into the trap of exaggerated or dishonest claims.

DEVELOPING IMAGE AND SUBJECTIVE VALUES

The third main area of consideration in the approach to the creative decision is the associations with which the advertising can endow the product. This is something quite apart from the substance of the claims one makes for the product, yet it is of very real significance in the selling situation. It is the same subjective element which, when applied to corporations, is sometimes called the 'image'. It arises from the fact that when people make a purchase, they do not only buy something having objective values, but they buy satisfaction which includes subjective values also. The most obvious case is a woman buying a hat. She does not only buy a head-covering or a piece of coloured felt; she buys a satisfaction that includes such subjective values as fashionableness, a feeling of style, a sense of daring or renewed youth or whatever. But while this is an obvious case, the same principle applies just as readily to purchases of everyday things. With petrol you buy a sense of power or the feeling of a wise bargain. With beer you may buy a sense of manliness, or a sense of fun or a sense of healthfulness. With chocolate biscuits you may buy a feeling of gaiety, and with a car you certainly do not only buy a means of transport, but also a feel of dashingness, of luxury, of importance, or smartness, or whatever attribute has been added to the machinery by the advertising, the line of the bonnet, or the number of marginal gadgets.

There is plenty of evidence to show that these subjective values represent a very real increase of satisfaction in the purchase and use of the product; and the improved product commands a definite preference, and often a higher price, from the buyer than the same product not so improved. In the advertising aspect of their creation (and it is one of the most potent effects of advertising) the method is usually that of building up certain deliberate associations by the type of verbal or visual treatment, the use of colour and the associated pictures or personalities. It is as if a pattern of subjective associations is integrated with the substance of the product and becomes a real part of it. In an economy where the public could afford to pay for nothing except objective values this situation could hardly arise, but in an affluent society where almost everyone has a spending power in excess of physical needs, scope is widening for following one's whims into the area of subjective satisfactions.

Techniques of advertising presentation are a subject of endless fascination. They embrace all the most intricate aspects of perception, communication and persuasiveness. They cover everything in verbal and visual techniques from journalism to poetry, from realism to impressionism, from the *News of the World* to *Vogue*. One can only hope to touch on a few of the main points.

The first is to recognize the different audiences to whom the advertising must be addressed: top management or the housewife in the Durham back streets; children or the fashion-conscious women of society; bank managers or miners. The tone, the contents and the treatment will vary according to the audience. But certain factors will remain reasonably constant.

The first need for any advertisement is to gain attention. By and large, people do not aim to read advertisements – though in fact the advertisement section of a woman's magazine has a high readership in its own right. However, even here one is wise to start with the assumption that people will not want to read a particular advertisement. In the newspapers advertisements have to capture attention. On television there is much talk of a captive audience, but this can be misleading. The audience may be captive, but its attention is not necessarily so; it may be talking or knitting or reading.

TECHNIQUES OF ADVERTISING

Here is a first axiom for getting attention: that it is the interest of the message that attracts attention – not the size, visual impact or its violence. The eye and mind work so fast that they shrug off instinctively a first impact of size or surprise or violence in an advertisement, before they have even assimilated what it is about, unless subconsciously there is an awakening of genuine interest. Clearly, interest in a product message is not universal; it will always limit itself to some section of the total public. For example, even a little advertisement headed 'Indigestion' will be noticed by the 3 or 4 per cent of people who at that moment are conscious of having a problem of indigestion. One of the reasons why advertising gets a bad name for being excessive or boring is that far more people every year are being exposed to far more messages than can be of interest to them personally. Men particularly become irritated with all the household advertisements which have no interest for them. In newspapers one can select those advertisements on which, because they say something of personal interest, one wants to focus, and ignore the rest. On television it is not so easy to ignore those of no personal interest, and this is why television tends to get a worse name in the context of intrusion that the press does.

Since the attention of an advertisement is gained by the first awakening of interest, it is vital that the attention-getting element should signal the sector of interest the advertisement aims to attract. Otherwise, one may only attract interest that cannot lead to sales. Humour, so beloved of many superficial observers of advertising, is a dangerous weapon for this reason, because (although it can add a certain cheerfulness to the image of the product) it too often attracts the attention of masses of people who are not potential buyers, and it may obscure or even damage the serious appeal to those who are.

The second key factor is the essential need to offer a benefit to those forming the potential market. People neither buy, nor want to think about buying, something that does not promise them a benefit for their money. It may sound a self-evident truth, but it is surprising how often it gets overlooked in the intricate and elaborate process of advertisement creation. Ideally, the benefit should be clearly conveyed in the attention-getting element in the advertisement. Sometimes the sponsors of advertisements, or their creators, are so shy about their whole function of selling they will go to great lengths to avoid seeming to intrude anything so blatant as a selling-point in the advertisement. But really the function of advertising is not to amuse, not to educate; not to decorate the hoardings or enliven the newspapers, but to sell; and only when an assured commitment emerges can it afford to do the other things as well.

The third element worthy of focus as important is that of giving a 'reason why', i.e. the reason why the product can offer such and such a benefit. More is often achieved through an appeal to the emotions than to the mind (because people are lazy about using their minds); but people are both mind and emotion, and their emotions react more easily if they are offered some concession to their logical process as well. It is wiser therefore to say 'X is better because . . .' than just 'X is better'.

The final element in a good advertisement is a bold display of the brand name. Once again this may seem obvious. After all, the function of an advertisement is to get the public to ask for a product or at least to recall its name in the shops. But there are some people who believe that a prominent display of a brand name will make people pass on from your advertisement because they believe they know what you are going to say about that product. This is a risk which must be taken, and be counteracted by the other elements in your advertisement. There are advertisers who believe that their advertisements are so well-liked and recognized that it is a good idea to leave the name out altogether. This is treating advertising as some kind of parlour game, not the expensive, productive and important process it really is.

THE UNIQUE SELLING PROPOSITION

Ideally the benefit should be one which the product alone can offer: it may be desirable to go back to the product formula and build-in some unique added benefit that its competitors do not possess. It may only be possible to seek a unique way to express the benefit, or a unique aspect of the benefit to stress. Most products can offer a whole spectrum of benefits ranging from solid factors such as the price and performance, to elaborate subjective benefits derived from the manner of presenting either the product or the advertising. Somewhere at some point of this spectrum the advertising can be coloured with a unique shade, giving it a separate identity from its competitors. It is vital to end up by leaving in the public's mind a clear identity for your product – a uniqueness in an important selling area; what has been termed by one great American expert, Rosser Reeves, a Unique Selling Proposition.

This positive proposition of a benefit can then be enhanced by any one of a wide range of subjective associations which, providing they are relevant to the purchase of the product, can add to its total attraction. Such associations may be gay or fanciful or fashionable; they may offer a sense of a bargain, youthfulness, or keeping up with the Joneses. These are well-tried examples; there are many others. From these elements the total advertising presentation is built up to do its job of making a potential market interested in trying this product through the promise of a satisfaction which is part objective and part subjective.

THE ADVERTISING CAMPAIGN

A campaign concerns the total effect and sequence of the advertisements for a product. This technique was crystallised by Sir William Crawford, one of the great advertising technicians of the early days, in the three-word precept, 'concentration, domination, repetition'. It is still, and must always be, the clearest reflection of the processes which go to make up mass selling.

Concentration

This is the selection of one shade in the spectrum of possible appeals for the product and the avoidance of diversity of appeal and dispersal of resources. It implies, of course, the careful selection of the appeal best calculated to gain a response from a sector of the market, which in turn is calculated to offer the best sales potential, having regard to the particular attributes of the product, the state of competitive activity and the resources available for promotion. It would be useless to select an area of product appeal which brought head-on collision with a competitor of much greater resources or to comprise a sector of wants to which the available budget was insufficient to do justice. It implies also the virtues of simplicity and single-mindedness in execution.

Domination

Domination is the gathering of the available forces of money and presentation techniques in such a way as to create a dominant impact on the minds of the chosen public. It will comprise an element of size at the initial stages of the campaign so as to gain attention and outweigh competitive claims. It will ensure that in the selected area of consumer needs, the name of the product will come out top of the alternatives in the memory of the potential customers. Given a budget insufficient to cover all areas, classes or segments of the public, domination will necessitate a concentration of effort in terms of geography or choice of media or some other means so that in that area of concentration the product can outweigh all rivals.

Repetition

Repetition is an essential part of the techniques of all advertising. With most consumer goods it is the repeated purchase that makes the selling investment pay off. The product drops only too easily out of mind and memory, and is supplanted by some lively newcomer unless the satisfied customers are reminded. Then it must be remembered that virtually no first impact of advertising reaches everybody; what appears to be repetition is very often merely a continuation of first impact on groups of customers not previously reached with the message. Every week of every year a new group of potential customers grows into the market. The advertising campaign therefore needs to be continued over a period of time, and a disposition of available resources must be made accordingly.

THE STRATEGIC FRAMEWORK OF ADVERTISING

The above are the salient factors which go to the strategic framework of an advertising campaign. There are executive processes which have then to be considered.

First and foremost comes the creative execution. To some people the creative element appears to be the most important, and certainly it is usually the most noticeable. A campaign tends to be judged superficially on its creative impact; in fact, unless the marketing conception is right, the creative impact can increase and intensify the misdirection of the expenditure and effort. Creative execution can only be considered after the strategic conception. It is usually a wise plan to present the strategy as a document for agreement by all concerned before going to the next stage of writing or visualizing the actual advertisements.

Clearly, there must be vitality, craftsmanship, humanity and hopefully, a touch of creative inspiration, to turn a campaign plan into warm, sparkling communication. The agreed campaign message can be given vividness and brilliance, but it is wise to remember that vividness and brilliance have their own glamour and can divert the critical instinct from the fact that the basic message may be the wrong one. Both in the creative process and in the initial selection of the creative executive, those concerned must keep their eyes firmly on the ball.

It is of little value to try to define the right ingredients for creative quality. Too many experts would give different answers. Tastes change from year to year. Different media require different treatment. If an advertisement is to be as helpful as possible to the consumer in making a choice, it needs to portray a realistic situation with which that consumer, usually a woman, can identify. In that situation her need is defined, and the usefulness of the product or service in satisfying that need realistically presented. The creative quality will emerge in the vividness, the impression, the humanity, in which the need and its satisfaction are pictured. Television is of course an ideal medium for this kind of treatment, because realism and demonstration are a natural part of it. The essence of creative ability then becomes the capacity to stand in the very shoes of the people you are appealing to, understand their needs, sensitivities and feelings, so that the process of identification comes most cogently to them.

A good deal of advertising creativity concerns itself wrongly with over-emphasis on technique, and the intrusion of the creator's own ego and feelings. A typical case is the use of sex interest or symbols into irrelevant contexts, simply because the creator is interested in these symbols. Many advertisements appealing to women portray sex interests which are clearly male because the creator is a man. A certain amount of advertising also betrays the creator's desire for applause for his own cleverness among his own confrères, rather like the centre forward who has just scored a goal, lifting up his arms and waiting to be embraced by his colleagues. And other advertising betrays a misuse of techniques admired and copied from more relevant contexts, which in a wrong context become just plain silly.

The right creative execution is a vital part of the marketing concept of the campaign because clearly the more effectively and cogently the advertisement can communicate with the maximum number of potential buyers, the quicker the budget cost of the advertising will pay off, to the profit and success of the advertiser.

MEDIA PLANNING

The next step in the executive process will be the choice of media. Indeed, it may need to be considered at an early stage because it may govern both the economics and the creative execution of the whole campaign. The choice of media is a whole subject in its own right. Suffice it to say here that the essence of the choice is to reach the maximum number of the clearly defined target audience, in the right atmosphere for the particular message, at the lowest cost. Since target audiences for a particular product seldom identify themselves, in the consumer goods area, exactly with media readership, the problem very often comes down to choosing the media with the minimum wastage. Again, however, television which may involve maximum wastage may nevertheless be the best choice simply because it offers the best medium for the message. The available media statistics, whether sifted by computer or other techniques, can offer extensive guidance to relate coverage of a particular audience to cost, but there still remains an imponderable element of choosing the best media to suit the character of the product or the particular type of message.

THE AGENCY RELATIONSHIP

The other aspect of running an advertising campaign that this chapter will cover is the function of the advertising agency in this context. The basic contribution of the agency must be its expertise in particular services – top creative ability, experienced media men for selecting and buying media, good technicians in the printing and blockmaking and other mechanical processes, and competent co-ordination, at executive level, of all the many details of a campaign. It is possible for an advertiser to buy many of these services from specialists outside the service agency, but, in the UK at least, there is no real sign that advertisers prefer to take on the job of co-ordinating such outside services themselves. The agency package is still the most convenient method.

There is, however, one other great value in the agency arrangement. The manufacturer tends to look at his marketing proposition from the boardroom downwards. He relates it to his manufacturing, profits, raw materials, distribution and the like. It is, to many manufacturers, an enormous advantage to have the compensating service of people who look at the same proposition from the market upwards. This is the special competence of the good agency. The manufacturer's personnel, even if they have the ability and training to take a consumer's view may, in certain circumstances, not have the independence to prevail on the board to make essential changes. The agency is an independent body and will be listened to more readily by the board. Finally the manufacturer, being concerned with his own type of business and immersed in it, may not have had the useful experience of outside industries, of successes and failures in other related or unrelated fields, which an agency with many clients can gather together. The manufacturer values someone competent to trade ideas with as a means of measuring his own interests against outside criticism.

ETHICS

Much has been written about the ethics of advertising. Essentially, since advertising is a communication process, the ethics of advertising are the ethics of those who utter the communication. The advertising of bad products or services is bad ethics. Sometimes, also, the urgent search for additional sales may lead an advertiser into promoting his product for purposes outside its normal range, for which it is of dubious value. But good marketing, which is offering products which clearly have a true and well calculated market, does not need 'sell at all costs' advertising.

Within the limits of advertising itself there are two aspects of ethics which may be considered. The first is the honesty and truthfulness of the satisfactions offered and the information given. In the UK this requirement is controlled by the combination of the Advertising Standards Authority (operating through the Code of Advertising Practice Committee) in relation to print and other non-broadcast media, and the control committee of the Independent Broadcasting Authority, in relation to television and radio. And the International Chamber of Commerce operates a Code of Advertising Practice that applies throughout the world.

The second is a much more subjective area of advertising, what may be called the helpfulness of the advertisement to the consumer in making his or her choice. Questions of relevance, good taste, sufficient information, and other factors which cannot be controlled by a rule-of-thumb system as easily as truth and honesty can be, are inevitably left to the good sense and sensitivity of those, whether advertisers or agencies, who are practising advertising. At the same time, self-interest works to encourage the advertiser to make his advertisements helpful, because they will improve the long-term goodwill of his business, and the confidence of the public in his advertising. Social sense and business expediency combine, and in the long run the factor of consumer acceptance will be paramount.

FURTHER READING

Jefkins, F., *Advertising Made Simple*, W.H. Allen, London, 1973

Nicholl, D., *Advertising: its purpose, principles and practice*, Macdonald & Evans, London, 1973

White, R., *Advertising: what it is and how to do it*, McGraw-Hill, Maidenhead, 1980

16 Sales promotion

Christian Petersen and John Williams

Sales promotion is an integral part of today's marketing dialogue with the consumer. Every day it reaches out to the consumer, salesman, and retailer. Promotion techniques are used to market a vast variety of goods and services. In many markets, expenditure on sales promotion equals or exceeds expenditure on advertising. In the UK, where it is of similar size to advertising expenditure, the amount spent on sales promotion is estimated to be in excess of £5 billion.

This importance is recent. Although the techniques involved have been in use for decades, and often for centuries, the spectacular growth of promotion dates only from the mid-1960s. In many markets sales promotion expenditure (discounting inflation) has grown *five times or more* in the last twenty years.

Such dynamism reflects a change in western economies. There has been a change from 'pull' purchasing to 'push' selling. In the 1950s and the 1960s, the growth of consumer spending power, accelerated by easily available credit, meant that people were keen to purchase whatever could be manufactured and retailed.

With the slowing and then flattening of the demand trend, the primary effort has switched to 'push' selling, in order to maintain, as far as possible, the momentum of manufacturing and retailing.

The dramatic changes in how brands, products or services are retailed to the consumer have been responsible for fuelling this trend. The advent of supermarkets, hypermarkets, self-service outlets (petrol stations, banks and the like) have dramatically shifted the balance of power between manufacturer and retailer. Never before have so many brands been competing for the consumer's attention.

As more inducement is now necessary to get people to purchase, sales promotion techniques have come into full play. Sales promotion is the technique which makes brands shout 'buy me' at the point of purchase.

WHAT IS SALES PROMOTION?

Sales promotion covers just about everything you can do to give people a *tangible* incentive to purchase. Everything, that is, on top of the basic sales message.

The variety of promotional techniques is as extensive as our ingenuity can devise, and as disciplined as the laws of different countries allow. New developments and refinements of technique happen every year. And because sales promotion is part of the total marketing mix, and usually co-exists with other forms of marketing, it is often difficult to decide what sales promotion is, and what it is not.

No one has yet produced a wholly satisfactory definition of sales promotion. A definition that attempts to be thorough and precise is usually too limiting for so dynamic a function. Such definitions, if accepted, cut out creative opportunism. Loose definitions hardly help either, since they give no firm idea of promotion, and often could be defining marketing as a whole. Also, the practical dimensions of sales promotion vary from country to country, so definitions adopted from other markets can be misleading and even legally dangerous.

The reader may like to experiment with his own definition of sales promotion. Any valid definition is likely to include the following elements:

1 There must be *a featured offer* (something done as a normal part of trade and not featured in any special way does not count as sales promotion)
2 The offer must be of *tangible advantage*. A message alone is intangible
3 The offer must be designed *to achieve marketing objectives* – during a defined time period – which will usually, but not necessarily, mean sales.

These are, of course, rather abstract terms. An easier, though less objective, way of recognizing sales promotion is to look for any of these *four key propositions:*

SAVE!
FREE!
WIN!
GIVE!

Just about every known form of sales promotion will include one or more of those propositions.

WHAT CAN SALES PROMOTIONS DO?

Sales promotions can encourage the consumer or retailer to behave more in line with the economic interest of the manufacturer or supplier. Sales promotions can assist in:

1 Smoothing out costly buying troughs
2 Stimulating stock movement
3 Encouraging repeat purchase

4 Securing marginal buyers
5 Increasing penetration of new or existing products
6 Increasing volume
7 Avoiding uneconomic production runs
8 Avoiding uneconomic delivery drops
9 Bringing forward buying peaks, e.g. seasonal sales
10 Attracting customers to premises
11 Correcting poor distribution levels
12 Increasing consumer awareness
13 Increasing consumer loyalty
14 Increasing purchase frequency
15 Securing display in-store
16 Obtaining retailer support
17 Disposing of models before a new introduction
18 Drawing attention to a company's product range
19 Boosting sales in particular geographical areas
20 Stimulating a new use for the brand
21 Increasing the appeal of the brand to specific target audiences.

WHAT CANNOT SALES PROMOTIONS DO?

Sales promotions cannot change long-term trends in the life of a brand or take the place of advertising or personal selling. Promotions are one element of the marketing mix and it is important to consider whether or not investment in other areas (e.g. on improving the product, or changing the packaging) might meet the marketing objectives in a more cost-effective manner. In general, brand strength determines promotional effectiveness. Brands can be broadly classified into one of three types – growing, holding and declining. The effects of promotions on these are as follows:

Growing brands
Promotions enable the brands to make gains and hold them.

Holding brands
Promotions enable the brands to make short-term gains which are not held.

Declining brands
Promotions may slow down the rate of decline but cannot reverse it without a significant and lasting change in the value (product- and image-based) that the brand offers the customer.

SALES PROMOTIONS ACT DIFFERENTLY

Sales promotions differ widely in their effectiveness at addressing particular marketing problems. Sampling, free offers, and reduced price offers (coupons or offers) are particularly effective at increasing penetration of new or existing brands. Free draws, sweepstakes, contests and phone-ins are ideal tools to increase consumer awareness. Techniques, however, overlap considerably and consequently there will generally be more than one technique available to solve the problem. Selection of a particular technique is generally governed by four criteria:

1 The nature of the problem the promotion is to solve (penetration, repeat purchase, distribution and so forth)
2 Budget available
3 Nature of the brand (product or service)
4 Target group the promotion is seeking to influence.

THE KEY SALES PROMOTION PROPOSITIONS

Save!

People have always loved a bargain. And keen pricing is central to 'push' selling.

The promotional use of bargains, where featured offers of a price saving are made, can be classified under the following headings:

1 A retailer's price cut
2 A manufacturer's price cut
3 Coupons
4 Rebate schemes
5 Self-liquidating offers

1 A retailer's price cut
The format is usually simple: the retailer cuts the price of a product or service and features the promotional price on store material and perhaps in his advertising.

Many retailers now consistently cut the price of the goods they stock, so that the prices they offer are no longer specially featured bargains of a promotional nature, but an integral, and often *the main*, aspect of their business.

2 A manufacturer's price cut
Again, usually a simple format. The manufacturer cuts the price of his product and features the promotional price on his pack, or on display material, or in advertising.

Most promotions of this kind are straightforward and regular aspects of a brand's existence. Sometimes, however, a price cut can be exploited in spectacular fashion.

For example, the British motorist has become aware that a car costs more to buy in the UK than the identical car bought in most parts of Europe. In March 1982 the Ford Motor Company announced substantial cuts in the UK prices of many of its more expensive models, presenting this as the company's single-handed effort to bring UK prices into line with Europe.

Ford's competitors rushed into print to say that the savings were not all that exceptional, but Ford had scored a major victory in putting its proposition into the front of the consumer's mind, in a believable way.

3 Coupons

A coupon is a promissory note entitling the consumer to a saving on a product or service.

Some coupons are printed on or inserted in a pack, entitling the consumer to money off his or her next purchase. Manufacturers and retailers print millions of coupons each year to stimulate consumer demand.

Coupons are a popular method of offering savings, and can be more precisely targeted than price cuts. An audience can be selected by placing a coupon in a newspaper with a particular kind of readership, or an area can be selected by delivering coupons door-to-door there. Increasingly, promoters select a retailer and make a coupon redeemable only in his stores. A development of the technique in the United States is that the manufacturer issues a coupon for, say 3 cents off his product, and an individual retailer offers to double the value of the coupon if it is redeemed in his stores.

4 Rebate schemes

The rebate scheme offers either cash or a coupon by return if the consumer *mails in* a stated number of proofs of purchase.

An advantage of the rebate technique over coupons is that the promoter receives proof of purchase, whereas ordinary coupons can be wrongly used for other purchases (the two categories of wrong redemption are *malredemption*, where the wrong use is deliberate and *misredemption*, where the wrong use is accidental. Because coupons are, effectively, currency, malredemption and misredemption are serious dangers).

Rebate schemes are frequently used to retain the loyalty of customers. Effectively, the loyal customer is receiving a volume discount. The proofs of purchase required can be carefully calculated against the regular user's repeat purchase pattern, and the rate can be speeded up (e.g. five packs purchased over the time usually taken to purchase four packs).

A variant of the technique is the *step-sum rebate* where each proof of purchase qualifies for a rebate amount, say 20p per proof of purchase. This variant can be used to attract the occasional purchaser or the non-purchaser sampling for the first time. And, of course, once a customer starts on the scheme, there is an incentive to go on collecting proofs of purchase in order to qualify for more and more money.

Shareouts or giveaways give a rebate scheme excitement as the rebate received depends upon the number of entries received. Here a sum of money or other divisible prize is shared equally amongst entrants according to the total number of 'shares' (proofs of purchase) received. The number of proofs of purchase that constitute a share are predetermined. So if the shareout fund consists of £10 000 and 10 000 entries are received, each entry is worth £1, with 2000 entries the sum awarded is £5 and so forth. Usually a minimum sum, irrespective of the number of entries received, is guaranteed.

Another variant of the technique is the accelerator rebate scheme. Here the proofs of purchase are worth different amounts, say 50p, 30p and 20p according to when they are sent in. This adaptation is designed to bring forward sales.

5 Self-liquidating offers

The first four 'save' techniques relate to savings on the price of the promoted product. The self-liquidating technique involves the offer of a bargain price on another item, which the consumer usually applies for by mail.

The price the consumer pays for the offer item covers all the costs of making the offer – hence the term 'self-liquidating'. Essentially, the promoter is acting as a direct marketer, buying the item in bulk and cutting out profit margins.

In a class of merchandise where regular retail prices and margins are high, significant success can be achieved with a dramatic bargain offer. But consumers can be suspicious, expecting the offer item to be of inferior quality. Therefore it is usual to seek items which carry well-known brand names and are of that manufacturer's regular quality, or to offer the item on approval.

Of course, as mass retailing spreads to cover most classes of merchandise, and prices and margins fall, it becomes difficult to find known, branded items, which can be liquidated at a price below retail, especially when the increasing costs of postage have to be offset.

There are two ways round that problem. One is to regard the self-liquidating offer as a nil-cost opportunity to develop the character of a brand. A coffee manufacturer, for example, might offer a coffee mug imprinted with the brand name – an item unique to the product. This is a simple and frequent use of the self-liquidating technique.

A more ambitious way of communicating brand values is shown by the case of the Ovaltineys LP. Ovaltine (Ovomaltine in Europe) is a food beverage; its TV campaign recalls the brand's advertising of the 1930s, when it was known to everyone via a Radio Luxembourg show featuring the 'Ovaltineys of the Air': children who sang songs and made jokes. So, in 1980 an LP record was made of the Ovaltineys singing many of their famous songs. This was offered to Ovaltine's customers at a self-liquidating price. But the LP was also put on sale in leading record stores throughout the country (at a price £1 higher than the bargain price available to Ovaltine purchasers), and copies of the record were given to radio disc jockeys for airplay. Also a short television film of the singing Ovaltineys was made and offered to producers of suitable TV shows for inclusion in their programmes.

The overall effect was to create increased awareness of the brand, not only through on-pack promotion but also via free radio and television exposure (the value of this exposure, if it had been purchased at ratecard cost, was around £750 000).

Another creative use of the self-liquidating technique was developed for Marlboro cigarettes: the mail-in element was eliminated. Marlboro retailers were offered cigarette lighters carrying the Marlboro name for resale to their customers at a price of 89p if the customer did not also purchase Marlboro cigarettes, or 69p if he or she did. This simple mechanism produced very big business – Marlboro became the biggest selling brand of cigarette lighter, and the effect on Marlboro cigarette sales was very beneficial too.

Free!

'Free' is a very powerful word. Most people are irresistibly drawn to the prospect of something for nothing.

Of course, for a free offer to be of commercial value, the something will usually be for something. And the power of the promotion will depend on whether the value offered is as good as it appears to be at first sight. It is possible to lose customers by misleading them with the word 'free', and it is also possible to attract the attention of the regulatory authorities.

There are two main types of free offer – the free product and the free item.

1 Free product

Here the promoter gives away some of his product. For example, a *free sample*, distributed door-to-door, or included in a magazine, or handed out in-store, or banded to another product. Or *extra product free*, where, for example, a product usually sold in a 100g size will be sold in, say, a 120g size at the same price. Free product promotions are often an excellent way to get occasional purchasers or trialists to buy your brand. Where the offer is being made on-pack, a devastatingly effective 'sales appearance' is achieved.

2 Free item

Here the promoter gives away an item with his product. It can be fixed on or packed inside the product; or the product can be packed in it – for example, a free storage jar containing coffee.

The free item can be handed out to the customer, and sometimes purchase is not required; the item serves as an advertising device. Such giveaways were legion in the nineteenth century. For example, that great promoter, H J Heinz, drew massive crowds to his stand at the World's Columbian Exposition in Chicago in 1893 by advertising a free badge to all asking for it. The badge showed a pickle with the name Heinz enamelled on it. The crowd was so dense that the floor sagged under their weight. And the pickle badge became the trademark of the Company.

Or the free item can be available by mail. An attractive free item allows the promoter (where permitted by law) to 'charge' a large number of proofs of purchase.

A remarkable free offer was mounted for Chivers Jelly in the UK in the early 1970s. The marketing objective was to persuade consumers to buy the Chivers brand loyally (and to take the opportunity to try out the various flavours). In return for *eighteen* proofs of purchase mailed in, the consumer was offered a free family of goldfish! Five live goldfish were delivered to the consumer's house (in an aerated water-filled container); there was also a self-liquidating offer of a fish tank if the consumer didn't already have one. Considerable planning and management went into the organization of that promotion, which was a huge success.

The free item offer gave rise to two forms which are almost techniques in their own right. The *free picture card*, inserted in or printed on a pack, was originally developed in the cigarette industry. When cigarettes were sold in paper packets, a piece of card was put in to stiffen the pack. In Canada, in 1879, someone had the idea of printing something on the card and this developed into the 'cigarette card'. Cigarette cards were issued in series, and each series had a theme – famous actors, flowers, warships – to encourage collection (and therefore loyal brand purchasing). Though cards disappeared from cigarettes a long time ago, the picture card is still a widely used free in-pack offer.

The other major development of the free item offer is the *trading stamp promotion*. A retailer issues trading stamps in proportion to the amount you spend in his store; you save the stamps and then redeem them against a wide range of gifts published in a catalogue. The same mechanism applies if you substitute a 'voucher' for a stamp: vouchers related to free gifts in a catalogue have been widely used to motivate retailers and salesmen.

Win!

Promoters did not invent the idea of winning a prize. Gambling and prize contests and games of skill have been part of life in most civilizations. In the UK in 1978, for example, gamblers laid out £7 000 000 000 on stakes (though £6 000 000 000 was returned in the form of prize money). Apart from horse-race betting, we trade fortunes in casinos and bingo halls, on dogs and in amusement machines, doing the football pools, and a host of other activities. Games of skill – crosswords, Monopoly, and now video games – provide hours, even weeks, of amusement.

All this would continue if there were no sales promotion. But sales promotion can harness the appeal of winning to marketing, and can do so very effectively.

The most important quality of a prize promotion is, or should be, *excitement*. This is often ignored. One attraction of a prize promotion is that the value of the prizes, and therefore the main cost of the promotion, is usually fixed. This appeals to promoters who want to mount activity which won't overrun budget. With such pedestrian ambition, these promoters run contests as routine and often poorly executed activities. They attract few entrants, and those few contain a proportion of *professional* contest entrants.

Lose excitement and you have lost the basic value of a prize promotion. The main types of prize promotion are:

1   A *contest*, in which success depends to a substantial degree upon the exercise of mental or physical skill
2   A *free draw*, in which success depends on your name being drawn at random
3   A *sweepstake*, in which success depends on the chance receipt of a winning leaflet, or other device. Recognition or detection of success must be easy
4   A *game*, where you compete but your success does not depend primarily upon skill

5 *A lottery*, where you purchase (or make a contribution of some kind to get) a ticket which entitles you to entry into a prize draw of some kind.

It must be stressed that the laws relating to prize promotions are individual to different countries and are usually vigorously policed. Expert advice is needed when planning a prize promotion.

Some examples of prize promotions

One of the most effective prize promotions ever run in the UK is *free bingo*, tied to the sale of daily newspapers. The promotion format was pioneered by *The Daily Star*, immediately taken up by *The Sun*, and soon copied or adapted by every popular national daily and Sunday newspaper. Taking advantage of highly sophisticated random printing techniques, the promoters deliver cards with assortments of numbers to every home in the UK; you check your numbers against those published in the newspapers and, when you have matched all the numbers on your card, you can claim a large cash prize.

The mechanics of the game are the same as in the traditional game of bingo played in halls and social clubs for generations: the excitement comes from the scale of the exercise and the size of the prizes.

The drawback to the promoters is that since *every* popular newspaper is running its own variant of the scheme, the high expense is not being matched by additional circulation. Only a truce, or fresh creative thinking, can free the promoters from a costly battle.

A quite different kind of excitement was achieved by a British Airways contest. Everyone buying a British Airways ticket to any destination became eligible to enter; the prize was a place on a British Airways' Concorde aircraft making a special flight to the 1982 World Cup venue, Madrid. The beauty of this scheme is that it associates the excitement of the World Cup with British Airways' most exciting product – and the prize is unique. The idea justified British Airways in heavily advertising the scheme.

What is sales promotion and what is not? A remarkable kind of prize contest, demanding extraordinary skill, was the core idea of a book, *Masquerade*; the book contained a series of highly cryptic clues, woven into the storyline; if a reader correctly solved the clues he or she would find a jewel, buried somewhere in England. Finally, after phenomenal world sales of the book, someone did find the jewel. It is very rare indeed for a book to have this kind of built-in *real* dimension.

The use of prize promotions is heavily regulated in many European countries; for example, in France entry to a contest must be open to purchaser and non-purchaser alike. This discipline should make the promoter aim for fresh ideas which create news and interest around his product. One example: a vermouth manufacturer staged an angling contest – an enjoyable day's fishing of the normal kind – but with the added bonus that some of the fish in the river had been specially marked with indelible ink. If you hooked one of the marked fish you won an angling holiday for two in Norway!

Give!

Sales promotion's 'big three' – Save! Free! Win! – have recently been joined by a fourth – Give!

Promotions linked to charitable causes appeared only rarely until the early 1970s. Now charity promotions form a very large and visible part of promotional activity in the United States and in the UK – less so, as yet, in the rest of Europe.

The basic charity promotion asks the consumer to collect the promoting brand's proofs of purchase, and then hand them in or mail them to the promoter, who will donate to the chosen charity a specified amount per proof of purchase.

Frequently the charitable aspect is coupled with a free offer, especially where children may be involved. Badges and wallcharts relating to the charity's sphere of action can be very popular.

Charity promotions offer tremendous PR opportunities at both local and national level and they are difficult for stores to reject. Often they can provide a national link with the brand's advertising theme such as Captain Morgan Rum and the RNLI, the Andrex Guide Dogs. On the downside potential, overtones such as with the Moscow Olympics can cause problems and some charities are over-exploited.

The Olympic Games gave the first serious impetus to charitable collections – to raise funds to train a country's athletes. Rothman's cigarettes were linked to a major appeal for 1972, and many promoters have since followed the Olympic theme. Association with sporting endeavour, and the achievements of the national team, can be a very effective form of publicity.

The H J Heinz Co. has chosen a charitable theme for several of its annual, block-busting, multi-brand promotions. Heinz twice ran an appeal to raise funds to build a new children's home. In 1980 they pursued the charitable theme into a wholly new area – the public were asked to collect labels, against which Heinz would make a donation, to provide the things needed by schools that had registered with the scheme – sports equipment, for example. Since such material had traditionally been financed out of public funds, the promotion raised some eyebrows. And you did have to collect a lot of labels to get anything worthwhile!

The *Sunday Express* commented: 'Three thousand five hundred cans of baked beans for a football? Isn't it a mercy for hundreds of little tummies, not to mention the Clean Air Society, that they hadn't set their sights on a swimming pool?'

In 1980/81, Golden Wonder, makers of crisps, snacks and nuts, linked with the World Wildlife Fund to celebrate that fund's twentieth anniversary. Against the proofs of purchase received, Golden Wonder financed the cost of six specially equipped Landrovers for use by the WWF in protecting the game parks of East Africa; the scheme was coupled with the offer of a free set of badges showing the various endangered animals helped by the WWF. Thirty million proofs of purchase were sent in to Golden Wonder.

SALES PROMOTION MEDIA

Sales promotion is a combination of content – the various techniques – and *media* – the channels via which the promoter reaches the market. All forms of advertising can be used, and frequently are used, as sales promotion media.

In addition, there are certain media specially associated with sales promotion:

1 The pack
2 Point-of-sale material
3 Field personnel
4 Direct mail
5 The telephone
6 Presentation material
7 Scratch-cards

1 The pack

The pack in which a product travels is a fine communication medium. Admittedly, it does not have moving pictures, nor does it talk, but it is umbilically bound to the product; it is there at the point of sale at the time of sale; it goes into the home; often a pack offers space, the advantages of colour printing, and the facility of a proof of purchase. And since the pack is required in any case, the extra cost of having it carry a sales promotion message is minimal.

2 Point-of-sale material

A promotion should not exist in limbo: it should be an integral part of the marketing mix, and in many cases the most significant integration will be between the promotion and the *total effect* created at the point of sale.

The pack is an item of point-of-sale material. So too are window bills, showcards, shelf-strips and many other vehicles for point-of-sale advertising. The trend to mass retailing through supermarkets and superstores has created many disciplines for, and often against, point-of-sale material of the conventional kind. Such material can be messy, and, in fairness, it has to be admitted that much material was produced with no idea of the real situation in-store. So many retailers have banned display material. The resulting drabness has been fashionable for some time, but is likely to give way to revived point-of-sale advertising if that material is designed with awareness and flair.

3 Field personnel

Field personnel – salespeople, demonstrators, and merchandisers – augment the regular sales teams of their clients. They can be used in many ways – to offer samples, or coupons, to show how a product works, to give information and answer questions, or just to ask people if they'd like to buy the product. And specially hired personnel are often used to sell goods into the trade, reinforcing the regular sales people.

4 Direct mail

Though direct mail can succeed simply through the use of words, most direct mail solicitations include a promotional offer of some kind.

Heavy direct mail promoters, such as magazine publishers, usually offer a price cut to a new subscriber, or a free gift such as an atlas or set of cutlery.

The key to effective direct mail is the quality of the mailing list. Thorough up-dating of the names on a list is vital, especially if the message is to be personally addressed. Changes of status must be meticulously monitored. Don't send a message 'Dear Mr. Smith, You as a captain of industry . . .' to a man who has just been made redundant.

A great amount of thought has gone into the writing and designing of direct mail messages, and into the development and use of successful incentives. Because most direct mail asks the recipient to respond in some way, the responses can be counted and carefully analysed: every ingredient can be thoroughly tested. So direct mail can be an exceptionally accurate promotional medium.

5 The telephone

Few people today write letters as a matter of personal choice. Most people use the telephone. And since many promotional techniques require the public to respond in some way, it is natural to choose the means of response that they normally prefer.

Consumers can be asked to telephone to claim a voucher; or to enter a prize promotion; or to hear further details of an offer. Complications are that the cost of a telephone call varies by distance, and a customer may be loath to call long-distance; a list of local telephone numbers can be presented, but some administration is needed to set that up. And it is difficult to obtain proof of purchase via the telephone.

But the telephone offers considerable scope for immediacy, and creativity in promotion.

6 Presentation material

A manufacturer mounting a promotion will want to tell his salesforce and retailers about it. So printed and audio-visual media are used to communicate the message. Generally speaking, these presentations are accorded low priority by marketing departments and are often poorly executed. This is thoroughly bad business practice: improved presentation must be a chief objective for promoters in the 1980s, particularly with the advent of interactive video techniques.

7 Scratch-cards

Over the past decade, scratch-cards have evolved into an important sales promotion medium. They can be used with most sales promotion techniques from instant win and competitions through to chance/skill games and collection schemes. They can generate considerable excitement and participation. Scratch-card promotions, however, have to be carefully thought out and executed. Security is of paramount importance in the staging of scratch-card games particularly in terms of printing as well as field distribution.

SPECIAL TARGETS

Most of this chapter is about consumer promotion. But all the techniques can be used for *industrial promotion*, both to reach new customers (frequently via personal selling, exhibitions, and direct mail), and to maintain business with existing customers. There are many factors specially relevant to industrial promotion which cannot be covered in this chapter. A useful guide to these will be found in *Sales Promotion – Its Place in Marketing Strategy* by Peter Spillard.

Promoting to retailers is an important aspect of manufacturer's marketing, with techniques ranging from special discounts to free gifts to competitions. Such activity is governed by law in many countries, and there can be a fine dividing line between legitimate promotion and bribery.

And, of course, most companies will seek to motivate their own sales teams with incentives ranging from cash bonuses to holiday prizes to free items. If it is true that a salesman loves being sold to, then sales motivation must be particularly effective.

INTERNATIONAL SALES PROMOTION

The opportunity to mount international marketing campaigns will be substantially increased by the development of satellite television. It is therefore possible to conceive of a sales promotion campaign operating simultaneously in many countries.

But different countries have different laws. Even the individual states of the USA have different laws affecting certain kinds of sales promotion.

There has been much talk of a 'harmonization' of the laws of EEC countries which affect sales promotion. This task, which would make Europe-wide promotion an attractive possibility, has proved to be difficult, if not impossible, to progress. Harmonization, if it comes at all, is likely to be a long way off in the future.

RESEARCHING AND EVALUATING SALES PROMOTION

Most kinds of sales promotion activity can be easily evaluated; sales performance can be measured, and redemptions and applications can be counted, and compared with track record.

Promotions are rarely researched in advance, largely because the activity is likely to be of short duration, with few strategic implications. There is an important trend, however, towards *strategic sales promotion*, where one technique, or one 'strategy platform' is intended to apply for many years. In this case, researching the technique or platform is as valuable and essential as researching a long-term advertising strategy.

SUMMING UP

A short chapter in a wide-ranging book can touch on only the most important aspects of sales promotion. More comprehensive information is available in the books listed below. And the reader must look carefully at the nature and practice of sales promotion in his or her own market, because the differences are not only interesting, but of crucial practical importance – differences of law, for example.

Moreover, sales promotion is dynamic, and what applies today can have changed dramatically in many respects within a few years.

This very dynamism makes sales promotion a key marketing tool. It is especially relevant to 'push' selling market conditions, but in tough or prosperous economies modern sales promotion has a major role to play.

FURTHER READING

Petersen, C., *Sales Promotion in Action*, Associated Business Press, London, 1979

Piper, J., (ed.), *Managing Sales Promotion*, Gower, Aldershot, 1980

Spillard, P., *Sales Promotion – Its Place in Marketing Strategy*, 2nd edition, Business Books, London, 1975

Toop, A., *Choosing the Right Sales Promotion*, The Sales Machine, London, revised (paperback) 1978

Toop, A., *'Only £3.95?!' – The Creative Element in Sales Promotion*, The Sales Machine, London, 1978

Williams, J., *The Manual of Sales Promotion*, Innovation Limited, London, 1983

17 Pricing

Bryan Atkin

Setting and maintaining the right prices for its products is perhaps the most delicate and important of all the problems facing a company. Whatever other things impinge on sales volume and on profitability, the pricing executive can be sure that the consequence of *his* decisions will be reflected in his firm's financial performance. However successful a firm may appear, poor pricing will inevitably result in sacrificed profit either through loss of sales or loss of margin or both. The importance of the pricing decision is, moreover, not diminished by limitations faced by the individual firm in its degree of flexibility in setting prices – even relatively small differences or changes in price can have a dramatic effect on the profitability of a product or service.

It is, however, a reality of business life that there is probably no area of business activity in which practice differs so widely from theory as the area of pricing. The simple – and well attested – truth is that in a great many firms, prices are set in a way which is disorganized, inconsistent and often illogical. The reasons for this are not hard to find. Pricing decisions, even under the best of conditions, are difficult to make and frequently have to be taken against what can often seem overwhelming odds – inadequate information; time pressures; corporate demands; changing and sometimes unpredictable competitive situations; higher than budgeted R and D and other overhead costs; inflationary pressures on labour, material and other production costs. Added to this, those responsible for pricing in the firm are often managing directors, sales or marketing managers or financial managers who face a great many other demands on their time.

The purpose of this chapter is to provide a framework within which the reader can evaluate the opportunities for greater profitability available to his own firm through the development of a more rational pricing policy and implement practical procedures leading to the shaping, introduction and control of this policy.

ECONOMIC THEORY AND THE PRACTICAL BUSINESSMAN

There is a substantial body of economic theory dealing with price and pricing. The practical businessman can, however, expect little direct help from the academic in applying economic theory to the solution of everyday pricing problems. Certainly, theories of price are effective in describing *in general* the way markets behave: demand and to some extent supply volumes do respond to price approximately as predicted by theory and markets do vary in the degree of responsiveness to price changes as provided for by the concept of price elasticity. Technically, price elasticity is measured by dividing the percentage increase or decrease in the volume of demand (or sales) resulting from a change in price by the percentage change in price. 'Elastic' markets are those where the change in demand is more than a proportionate price change. Conversely, 'inelastic' markets are those in which a change in price is greater, proportionately, than the effective change in demand.

The problem is that the theory breaks down when applied in particular cases largely because the assumptions on which theoretical calculations are based turn out to be inappropriate in real life. For one thing firms rarely possess the empirical data required to construct actual demand or revenue curves for their products and are often unable to distinguish costs sufficiently clearly to construct cost curves. Second, the goals which businessmen set themselves and the constraints which surround their achievement are usually far different – and less rational – than the idealized principles and responses of the theoretical firm. Third, markets do not in practice display the assumed characteristics of perfect competition and rational purchasing behaviour on which theory is based.

Nevertheless, since it has long enjoyed a certain popularity, an adaptation of economic theory worth mentioning at this point is the concept of 'breakeven'. The concept, in its simplest form, purports to show the minimum quantity of its product(s) a firm has to sell simply to cover its costs. Figure 17.1 shows the classic breakeven chart in its most widely reproduced form.

In the chart, the line AB represents gross revenue from unit sales at a specified price, and the line FK denotes the total costs of making those units. These total costs are made up of fixed costs (incurred whether or not the product is made and sold at all) and variable costs (which vary according to the number of units produced). The intersection of lines AB and FK represents breakeven – the point at which gross sales income is exactly equal to the costs involved in producing those units (Y) for sales. At the price set, the firm makes increasing losses with every unit as sales fall short of Y and an increasing profit with every unit in excess of Y. The chart can be developed to show alternative breakeven points at assumed different selling prices (represented by lines AB_1 and AB_2 in Figure 17.1).

The attractiveness of the 'breakeven' idea – which in principle can be applied both to individual products and to the firm as a whole – is obvious in the context of a chart on the managing director's wall dramatizing what the firm has to do to stay in business *once selling price has been determined*, by indicating the volume of sales to be achieved to reach breakeven. However, the concept is of little help in actually setting prices because of the crude and unrealistic assumptions which the theory assumes about the level of, and relationship between, price, demand and costs. Thus:

1   The sales income line (AB) takes no account of the price elasticity of demand. The breakeven quantity (Y) is a 'formula' calculation – not a forecast of the actual sales, which would still need to be made to determine the profits likely to be generated at a particular price (or indeed whether break-even were achievable at all at that price)
2   The assumptions that variable costs increase proportionately with unit output (as represented in line FK) and that fixed costs remain the same irrespective of the level of output are poor representations of business reality.

In Gabor (1977), a more sophisticated variant of the concept is described. This takes account of the relationship between price and quantity in drawing the curve of gross sales returns, but goes on to observe that its practical value is similarly diminished by the lack of information on costs and demand elasticity available to the average firm.

One of the problems in applying the concept of elasticity is that the theory assumes a constant relationship between demand volume and price, when in fact research has shown that consumers (and industrial buyers) respond differently to the *size* of price changes – particularly when these are measured in a competitive (one brand versus another) rather than a global (total market change) context. Depending on the circumstances therefore a market can be both elastic and inelastic in terms of response to the pricing

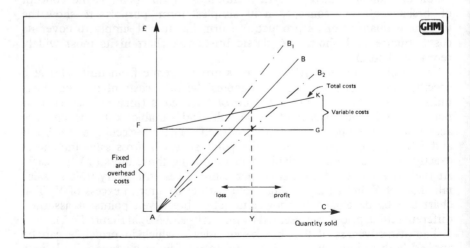

Figure 17.1   Simple breakeven chart

activities of the individual firm – a paradoxical situation requiring sound judgement and market knowledge.

At best the 'breakeven' concept – which is closely associated with cost-based pricing formulae described later – is mostly of value as a simple 'rule of thumb' method for evaluating pricing options in the context of other market-oriented information on (potential) demand and competition.

PRICING POLICY, STRATEGY AND TACTICS

Before looking in more detail at pricing decisions and the way they are arrived at, it is useful to draw a distinction between three terms often used rather inter-changeably by businessmen – in so far as they are used at all! These terms are *pricing policy, pricing strategy* and *pricing tactics.*

Pricing policy refers to the framework of rules and constraints within which pricing decisions are taken. The nature and scope of this framework can vary widely from one firm to another, even within the same industry or between firms with apparently similar pricing problems. At one extreme pricing policy can be little more than a rationalization of rule of thumb judgements or historical practice. At the other end of the scale can be policies devised and spelled out in considerable detail. An example is the policy operated by the Metal Box Company (1978) described by the Price Commission as comprising the following elements:

1 An immediate objective of raising return on capital to 17 per cent
2 Through the discount structure to pass on to large customers the cost savings commensurate with the scale, continuity and stability of their demand
3 For non-standard containers to price these at a level related to the operating costs of the lines while producing these containers
4 To ensure that customers share with the company the benefits arising from productivity improvements and reductions in specification
5 In the case of new business, selling prices are to be set on the basis of (achieving) 70 per cent capacity usage of (production) equipment. (If demand fails to reach target volume, a decision has to be taken whether to increase selling price or to eliminate the product)
6 To obtain high export prices wherever possible but retain flexibility to use marginal cost techniques for opportunistic business
7 Regular review of standard margins to ensure equity across the range.

Simply having a pricing policy, however formal, does not imply that it is either logical or sensible in the broader arena of the market place. Nor does the existence of a policy guarantee that it will be observed in practice – policies are often more honoured in the breach than the observance. Indeed it is entirely feasible for a firm to trade without a pricing policy at all or for decisions to be justified by reference to a policy which is to all intents and purposes a *post hoc* rationalization. This is often the case with small companies where price, like many other decisions, is in the hands of one forceful personality – a situation in which whim, prejudice and ignorance can easily play a powerful role.

Whereas *pricing policy* is the outcome of largely internalized objective of a financial or other corporate nature, or statements of pricing principles, *pricing strategy* reflects the (longer-term) market-oriented (or externalized) objectives of a firm. In effect *pricing strategy* involves the systematic manipulation or planning of pricing decisions and policies over a period of time in the context of achieving the broader objectives contained in corporate and marketing plans. It implies recognition of the role of price as an active, and important, component of the overall marketing 'mix' rather than a largely intractable obstacle which marketing has to overcome in order to compete successfully. In so far as pricing policies and strategies are the expression of needs and objectives over different time periods and on different planes it is not unusual for firms to have a pricing *policy* but no pricing *strategy*.

Whereas pricing strategy is concerned with the projection over the long term, without regard to short-term fluctuations in market conditions, pricing tactics are concerned with the manipulation of prices themselves, and the way in which prices are presented to achieve optimum response from a targeted customer group against competition. Pricing tactics take as much from interpreting the psychology of the buyer as from more rational 'economic' judgements. Tactics are, by their nature, often short-term. They may be changed several times during the life of the strategy of which they form a part. Such changes are the practical means of responding on a more day-to-day basis to changing market conditions. There are a great many variations of pricing tactics, some of which are described later in this chapter, and in practice they are often mistakenly elevated to the level of pricing strategy.

Oxenfeldt (1960) sees the pricing process involving a series of decisions taken over a period of time, rather than a single all-embracing solution. The six steps he proposes are:

1 Identification of target markets
2 Choosing an appropriate image
3 Constructing the marketing mix
4 Selecting a pricing policy
5 Determining price strategy (and tactics)
6 Definition of a specific price.

This multi-stage approach has a particular relevance to new product development but can be recycled wholly or in part as a means of reappraising existing products. The approach is particularly interesting in the emphasis it gives to broader issues of market segmentation and planning the marketing mix as the essential framework for pricing decisions.

PRICING POLICIES AND TECHNIQUES

In Wilson (1972), pricing is described as 'an exercise which must be undertaken on two dimensions. First it is necessary to think in terms of establishing the right price and second of using the correct methodology for arriving at it.' In a way this observation neatly encapsulates the practical dilemma facing most firms. At one level the pricing process takes place within a framework which is the product of many influences, inside and outside the firm. These factors, which provide the basis for defining pricing policy, strategy and tactics, include:

Internal	External
Corporate objectives and business goals – both generalized and specific	The nature, strength and pricing behaviour of competition (direct and indirect; existing and potential)
Cost structures – direct and indirect	The role and importance of distri-butors and their attitudes and needs
Existing prices (e.g. of other products in the same or other product lines)	relating to price (including need to create/maintain acceptable margins)
Historical practice and precedent in price setting within the firm	(Pressure from) suppliers of raw materials, components etc. used in the product
Degree of market knowledge (or ignorance) of key executives	The size, structure and perceived price sensitivity of demand
Pressures from feedback of other individuals within the firm, e.g. salesmen	The purchasing procedures and motivations of (potential) customers
Levels of R and D and pace of new product development	Existing and anticipated government policies
	General conditions prevailing in different markets (especially where export markets are concerned).

At the second level, pricing should involve a sensible and coherent procedure for determining the final selling price. That this procedure or methodology needs to be conceived and operated within a broader framework of attitudes and subjective judgements which may not always be logical (and may even be in conflict) is simply a fact of commercial life.

However, pricing policies and strategies do not necessarily define, or even imply, a particular methodology for arriving at the selling price itself. In many cases this is set as much by guesswork, trial and error, historical analogy and simple entrepreneurial judgement as it is by some more formal procedure.

There is no single 'correct' methodology or golden rule for arriving at the right price. For example, the pricing decision process and the degree of flexibility available are heavily conditioned by whether prices are *declared* or *negotiated* (the pricing system). At one extreme the executive responsible for setting catalogue or list prices is in theory at least creating a structure of 'ruling' prices for his products which will remain in force for all or a substantial proportion of sales until a change is notified; at the other extreme the executive involved in contract or tender pricing is faced with a new pricing decision with each new order or customer. The apparent coherence and stability of published prices have to be seen, however, in the context of the discounts, concessions, rebates, differentials and other devices employed by firms to manipulate the prices actually paid by customers. For many firms, list prices can be said to exist mainly as a basis for discounting with the bulk of turnover being generated from sales at discounted and negotiated prices (see Atkin, 1975). An apparently logical framework of declared prices can, therefore, be rendered meaningless and misleading by the reality of a haphazard system of informal discounts and/or individual negotiations with strong customers. See Discounts and discounting later in this chapter).

The 'right' price is not necessarily what theorists would call the 'best selling price' in the sense that it maximizes profit for a given product considered by itself. In any meaningful sense what is 'right' can only be assessed in the context of what the firm identifies as its general strategic or operational goals. Because these differ according to the size, product range, historical development, future ambitions, geographical trading pattern, financial resources and management philosophy of individual companies, so the concept of 'right' price will vary.

The precise combination and weighting of factors will depend on the product, the market and other circumstances. The following paragraphs look in more detail at five categories of factor which both shape pricing policy and contribute to the process of actual price setting. To the extent that one of these categories may carry the greatest weight it is possible to talk about pricing which is profit, cost, competition, demand- (customer) or distribution system-oriented.

Profit targets and other corporate objectives

Perhaps the most widely quoted of all business aphorisms is that it is the objective of every firm to maximize its profits. The most cursory examination of this proposition in practice, however, shows it to be one which should not be taken too literally. Firms rarely set out even with the *theoretical* objective of maximizing profits (or return on capital employed) and often introduce criteria into pricing strategies and policies the deliberate effect of which is to contain profits at a level below that which otherwise might be achievable.

Few would deny that, in a free market economy, a firm exists to make a profit and, indeed, needs to make a profit to exist. More fundamentally, perhaps, the profits generated by the firm have to be sufficient to satisfy the providers of the capital – shareholders, bankers, etc. – on whom the firm's existence and future ultimately depend. Simply making a profit does not itself guarantee the continued flow of funds required to renew current plant and invest in facilities for producing new products. Equally, given the scarcity and cost of capital, it is nonsense to suggest that a firm would be able, even if it wished, to continue to pour capital into the production of a product until the last drop of profit has been extracted from the market.

Profit is therefore a less meaningful criterion for judging performance in the longer term than return on capital employed or 'return on investment'. Thus the Price Commission commented, with respect to UG Glass Containers Ltd (1978), that 'for [the company's] profit to be adequate it must be sufficient after paying for the cost of capital to fund all expenditure on fixed and working capital necessary to maintain the fabric of the business and to make a contribution towards capital required for expansion'. The Commission went on to state that the company's corporate strategy provided specific targets relating to pre-tax profit and return on investment to be 'achieved and maintained'.

The question of time dimension also needs to be considered. A quick glance at the city pages of any national newspaper shows that profits achieved by even the largest firms fluctuate from year to year for reasons, often connected with the general economic, environmental and trading conditions, over which the firm has no control. Financial objectives can therefore be expressed both as long-term and immediate.

Longer-term financial objectives tend to be set in the context of achieving a targeted average level of return on investment or profit for the whole of the company which is considered to be 'reasonable' taken over a period of years (and across all products). Judgement of what is reasonable is in this context largely a pragmatic affair, owing more to general perceptions within society of what might be considered as 'fair trading profit' or to historical experience or analogy, than to the projection of a mechanistic formula. In the short term, different targets may be set either for return on capital for profit or for margins or contributions (difference between selling price and *direct* costs usually expressed as a percentage) which reflect prevailing economic and market conditions in individual years or even short planning periods.

As indicated earlier, however, financial objectives are not the only determinants of corporate policy and are therefore by no means the only factor underlying pricing decisions. Other considerations include:

1 (*Market*) *growth aspirations*. Targets relating to achievement of an annual percentage rate of growth in revenue and/or volume terms or of an overall target for a period of time (for example, a five-year plan)

2 *Market share*. Targets relating to achievement either of some specific share of total industry sales (or consumer uptake) of some or all of the company's products or of some more vaguely defined objective such as 'market leadership'

3 *Corporate stability/expansion*. Development of products and businesses to achieve more broadly conceived goals concerning the longer-term stability and growth of the firm as a whole with implications for balancing investment decisions, R and D expenditure and other aspects.

Decisions which appear unattractive from a purely financial standpoint in the short term may have important longer-term implications for the firm's financial health either individually or as part of a framework of such decisions

4 *Corporate image*. Pursuit or rejection of a course of action in the light of judgements – objective and subjective – about the way the company wishes to be seen in the market place. This may be related to protection of an existing image, for example where a manufacturer of a range of products with a reputation for quality rejects the chance of selling a range of popularly priced goods (however profitable potentially) because of the risk of tarnishing a carefully fostered image. Or it may be related to development of a targeted image (e.g. for product reliability, speed of after-sales response, innovative design) which has attendant implications for costs and prices

5 *R and D*. This can be both the lifeblood to and a leech on corporate profitability depending on the extent to which it is controlled and goal-oriented. Where R and D, especially in fast-moving high-technology industries, becomes tied up with the image and reputation of a company it is possible to generate sunk costs which for reasons of competition or strength of demand are difficult to recover through the prices the company is able to command in the market place

6 *Costs and efficiency*. Corporate plans often contain cost reduction and efficiency objectives linked to opportunities that provide for keen competitive pricing and/or greater margins

7 *Customer/public opinion*. Winning and retaining the regard of customers and perhaps of a broader public through performance or specific design, e.g. safety aspects of equipment for which profit may be a secondary consideration, or by being seen to be trading 'responsibly'

8 *Competitive arena*. Implementation of strategies for pre-empting, containing or meeting competition

9 *Capacity*. Gearing of pricing and marketing strategies to achieve acceptable level of use of production capacity.

An example of the way in which various strands of corporate policy combine to affect prices was demonstrated in the Price Commission report on BOC Ltd (1979) which stated:

The company's central thinking is based on the need to manage a portfolio of businesses. Essentially, this is to invest for market growth and to increase market share on the assumption that scale benefits on costs will be obtained. This gives the investor market dominance based on competitively low cost which in turn provides the power further to secure market position by keen pricing. When the growth slackens off the rate of investment can be reduced to yield a positive cash flow which may be reinvested in another growth market. . .

The role of costs in pricing

It has often been claimed that the pricing of industrial products is based on costs and very little else – a process which Wilson has derided as 'faith, hope and fifty per cent'. The argument runs that the cost accountant and the engineer have dominated the pricing process and that neat formulae based on cost are most easily comprehended by these types of executive whose knowledge of, and exposure to, the market place itself is limited. Research into pricing behaviour has tended to support this view of the pricing process: when asked directly about the pricing of their products firms will indeed claim that they arrive at their prices largely by the application of some formula related to costs.

How rigidly companies stand by such formulae or, indeed, whether they actually have a formula at all, is very much open to doubt. Gabor claims that 'pricing is not in fact carried out by the alleged mechanistic application of cost-based formulae' and goes on to quote Edwards: 'the manufacturer has "hunch" as to the price at which his article can be sold and makes use of "costing" or "estimating" to justify that price'. In other words a price 'derived from cost' can often be in effect the reverse procedure, with margins and contributions justified *post hoc* by reference to costs when in fact they are subsumed from price. Nevertheless if prices are rarely based exclusively on cost, it is equally rare for costs not in some way to form the starting point either for calculating prices or for evaluating the profit consequences of various prices indicated or set by reference to other factors.

In order to use costs at all in pricing it is obviously necessary for the firm to have a clear idea of what its costs are and how these should be allocated to individual products. This is all very well for the firm producing only one product since all costs are, by definition, attributable to that product. Where more than one product is concerned, as it is for most firms, cost allocation can be exceedingly complex and the solutions at best arbitrary. The costs of producing and selling a range of products can be classified broadly into three main components:

1 *Variable (including direct) costs* – costs which vary in relation to output, e.g. materials and components, labour, advertising
2 *Fixed costs* – costs which do not vary in relation to output except in the longer term, e.g. buildings, machines, vehicles
3 *Overhead costs* – costs attributable to management.

The problem of allocating management overheads will be obvious but what of variable and fixed costs? *Shared costs* are a common feature with respect, say, to vehicles and buildings but can also occur with respect to materials and labour. Consider, for example, the furniture factory which uses the same labour force, the same machinery and to some extent the same materials to make beds, wardrobes and dining room tables. Add to this a constantly changing balance of production volume between these different product lines – and within each product line between different model ranges – and the problems of allocation assume daunting proportions. The cost accountant might be able to devise an acceptable formula for allocation if each product was always produced in the same proportions but the formula becomes increasingly unworkable and arbitrary where these are constantly changing. Basing a formula on historical experience is equally undesirable as it makes pricing for the future dependent on past and possibly greatly outdated sales levels. The scale of difficulty increases still further where several products are produced by the same process (as in oil refining or dairy processes) and therefore incur, not so much shared costs as *joint costs*, or where a marketable product is a by-product of the production process for another good.

The problems outlined above become highly relevant when costs are used as a means of calculating price. There are two main concepts or procedures for cost-based pricing – *absorption or full cost pricing* and *variable cost or incremental cost pricing*.

Absorption cost pricing, to put it simply, involves the principle of adding a pre-determined mark-up to total unit costs derived from the formula

$$\frac{\text{total of fixed and variable costs attributable to the product}}{\text{total units produced}}$$

By this procedure, sometimes known as 'cost-plus', each product produced by the firm is made, in theory, to cover all of its costs and make a known profit on each unit of sale or order.

Variable cost pricing is based on the principle of relating prices not to total costs but to variable costs only with the mark-up on costs (or the price less variable costs if the price is set by a procedure independent of costs) making a *contribution* to fixed costs and to profit, the scale of which depends on sales objectives being achieved. Gabor distinguishes two variants of variable cost pricing: one is based on average variable costs (for a predicted level of output) and the other, which he calls incremental cost pricing, is based on the incremental or additional cost of producing a particular batch of the product which may be different from the variable costs of total production when considered in unit terms. Incremental cost pricing is a concept particularly appropriate to pricing individual orders, in cases where demand is made up of discrete orders or batches, or in evaluating the relative contribution of alternative possible orders where the price available is fixed by some other means perhaps beyond the firm's direct control.

Absorption cost pricing is a method which has had particular appeal to the firm with a substantial proportion of its total costs in the form of fixed costs and overheads, since it places all products, in theory, on a sound profit footing and eliminates cross-subsidization and below-cost trading. It is particularly useful in tender or contract pricing as a reference basis for pricing where there are no other useful indicators and in setting some practical limits to prices of new products with no relevant competitors. However, absorption costing has a number of major drawbacks as the basis for pricing. The arguments can be summarized as follows:

1   It is not always easy to isolate the total costs attributable to a particular product where there are several product lines and ranges. Depending on the conventions and assumptions used to apportion costs, the outcome of absorption cost pricing could be substantially varying price levels for individual products

2   There is, anyway, no compelling reason why any particular segment of the business, individual product, or specific order *should* be made to bear its proportionate or 'fair' share of overheads even where these can be calculated. Looked at in an overall corporate sense, the ability to offer a full product range, stability of production, attraction or retention of a major customer, response to a change in the competitive environment and many other factors may in individual cases and pricing decisions be considered to carry greater weight

3   Absorption costing takes no account of demand. The fact that a price can be computed by this method does not guarantee that consumers will buy the item at that price or at the predicted volumes. Nor are firms willing in reality to implement one of the apparent implications of the method which is to *raise* prices when demand falls short of expectations or declines from a previous level (since total costs will be spread over a smaller volume of output). The inclination of most firms in this situation would be to *reduce* prices

4   Absorption costing takes no account of competition. No firm can guarantee that its competitors will play by the same rules either by adopting the same method of costing or by allocating its overhead and fixed costs to particular products on the same basis. The firm rigidly applying absorption cost pricing would find its products highly vulnerable to a competitor using direct or incremental cost methods or simply pricing irrationally.

The proponents of incremental cost pricing tend to use arguments which are the obverse of their criticisms of absorption cost pricing emphasizing the flexibility of the method as a means of responding to changing demand and competitive conditions. Thus, it is pointed out, for example, that since market conditions vary between different industry segments of a given national market and even more, perhaps, between different national markets it is logical to seek (or accept) prices which reflect those conditions. Using a direct or an incremental cost approach enables the firm to operate at different prices in different markets while maintaining overall control over the aggregated contribution derived from sales. This provides a means of assigning supply priorities in the event of demand outstripping capacity. Similarly the method enables the firm to consider and respond to individual orders in a way appropriate to specific circumstances. Thus, at times of high demand a means is provided of selecting orders or pieces of business which yield the greatest contribution and at times of low demand of indicating how far the firm might reduce its prices before an order ceases to make any contribution at all.

Despite its apparent pragmatism, variable or incremental costing is not without its dangers. In the first place, it has been said with some truth that all costs become variable if the firm is to survive – that is, in the end, the firm depends on making sufficient revenue from its sales to cover all costs incurred whether variable, fixed or overhead. Incremental cost pricing cannot therefore be pursued unchecked. It must be conducted within some framework of required contribution based on profit targets for return on capital invested.

Second, firms using incremental cost pricing to justify accepting an order at reduced contribution may find they have made a rod for their own backs in subsequent dealings with the same customer. However logical the concept of variable pricing might be to the seller, the buyer is given a weapon to use in subsequent negotiations, when general demand conditions have improved and the firm has been able to command higher prices. If the seller gets to the point of refusing an order offered at too low a price there is a danger that the buyer may simply eliminate him from future consideration or allow a competitor to gain entry.

Third, there is always a risk of provoking price retaliation from competitors, resulting in reduced margins all round and a steep hill to climb back to acceptable profitability in a market environment which can become accustomed with remarkable rapidity to low prices.

Finally, it must be appreciated that it is not always easy to determine clearly either the variable costs attributable to a particular product or the incremental costs associated with a particular batch or order. Some so-called variable costs are not, in fact, more than marginally variable, at least in the shorter term. Few firms are able or willing, for example, to manipulate the size of their labour forces constantly to reflect changes in the level of orders. Unionization and a natural desire on the part of firms to keep a trained and effective work force together play an important role here. It is easy for firms to delude themselves therefore as to what the incremental or marginal unit cost of a product actually is. Similarly, taking on an additional order in certain circumstances may have its own 'hidden' incremental costs in the form of overtime working, loss of efficiency in output in machines pushed closer to maximum capacity, extra 'blocks' of production space requiring heating, lighting and maintenance and many other items.

Pricing is not only difficult in practice to base entirely on costs but it renders the firm vulnerable in other respects. In a strictly competitive sense it hardly matters a jot how reasonable a profit mark-up or contribution target a firm sets in relation to its own costs if these costs are higher than those of competitors. Indeed the costs which ultimately matter are those of the lowest-cost producer. Of course, most markets support producers who vary in efficiency, but the greater the disparity in efficiency, the greater is the pressure exerted on the least efficient.

More broadly, cost-based pricing formulae often provide little encouragement to company management to consider improving margins by reducing costs as distinct from raising prices. Firms rarely explore as rigorously as they might the various ways in which costs might be cut, from better materials purchasing to tighter control of office costs. This is not, however, the only way costs can be cut and here we return again to the need to be alive to *market* needs and conditions. Research has consistently shown over the years that products and services can quite simply be 'over-engineered' – that is contain features to which the user attaches little economic significance or which are designed to a quality standard which exceeds customer needs. By eliminating these features from the product the firm may well be able to make considerable savings in costs without reducing prices to anything like the same extent.

Competition and pricing

There are few products or services indeed for which there is no effective competition. Even when a firm has no direct competitors – as in the case of an innovative product – it usually has to take into account products capable of acting as alternatives or substitutes in some way, or the prospect of competition developing.

Long-term monopolies are therefore rare outside the realms of state enterprises but it is possible for short-term monopolies to develop on the basis of new products, particularly where high technology is involved. Firms may be able to protect themselves for a time from direct competition by taking out patents, as Xerox Corporation did with plain paper copiers and Polaroid Corporation with instant photography. But in the end competition will come, either through expiry of patents or through a competitor finding a means of entry which does not infringe the patents. The short-term monopolist needs to consider pricing in the context of the breathing space he has to establish himself in the market place before competition develops, rather than in terms of the apparent freedom of action of the true monopolist.

At the most fundamental level, the product competes on the basis of its usefulness or value to the buyer compared with the many other items on which income or resources can be expended.

Price acts as an element in competition therefore at up to three levels: it can help determine whether or not a product is bought at all (or whether the decision to purchase is taken now or at a later date); it can help determine in which of a number of alternative ways a particular need is satisfied; and it can help determine which supplier's product is selected.

It is not surprising then that in most cases prices are set and maintained with some reference to the general level and range of competitive prices. In a more specific sense, however, pricing against competition can become in itself a technique of pricing. This can work in one of two main ways:

1   By establishing the prices being charged by all (or a selected cross-section) of the competitive suppliers active in the market and positioning one's own price to occupy a certain position in the range. This may reflect either 'safety' pricing (pricing in the middle of the range) or 'aggressive' pricing (pricing at either extreme). In the latter case particularly, given that price variations reflect product differentiation, the adoption of competition pricing also tends to imply judgements about demand response and price segmentation in the market (see below)

2 By gearing prices to those charged by a specific competitor on the basis
   of achieving parity with them or of achieving a designated discount or
   premium. This approach is often used where one company has achieved
   a position of such pre-eminence in the market place that both sellers
   and customers accept its prices as a reference level. An example is the
   market for open-top containers in relation to which the Price Commission
   commented that 'where prices are negotiated by individual contract they
   are set by reference to Metal Box levels'.

In so far as competitors' prices are declared or easily established,
competition-orientated pricing is relatively straightforward and has the advantage of placing prices within the known parameters of the market place.
The price structure of markets is not, however, always easy to establish.
Published price lists often give a highly misleading guide to actual price
levels which may be arrived at largely by discounting or special negotiation.
Further, buyers are frequently reluctant to indicate even to independent
researchers, let alone company salesmen, the terms of a bargain struck with
a competitor. There is always a danger therefore that prices may be set on
the basis of a competitive price structure which is different in reality from
that assumed.

The extent to which firms are willing and able to take a competitively
independent line in setting and maintaining prices is partly a reflection
of factors such as market share, established reputation, financial strength,
distinctiveness of product and relative costs of production, and partly a
reflection of competitive psychology. Many writers on pricing have drawn
attention to the fact that price competition often tends to be of a muted
and controlled nature in which a few (perhaps only one or two) dominant
suppliers (price leaders) both set the price levels and pricing systems around
which competition is fought, and determine the timing and scale of price
changes. Other firms (price followers) are essentially content to respond –
raising and lowering prices in line with the price leaders. Markets operating on this basis can become highly conservative and regulated structures
in which price competition is to all intents and purposes eliminated.
In certain industries, typified by large commodity-type businesses such
as cement, animal feeds and tyres, the institutionalization of competition
among a small number of large companies has resulted in prices fixed and
maintained at very similar levels with price rises taking place in rounds
under the 'leadership' of one company – a situation to all intents analogous
to the outlawed 'price ring'.

In theory, price leaders 'undertake' to behave in a responsible manner with
respect to price setting and act as 'policemen' for any firm threatening to
take a more aggressive and independent pricing line. However, in practice
the *status quo* is protected more by mutual compliance than any genuinely
effective sanction which the price leaders can bring to bear. As Japanese
companies have demonstrated repeatedly in European markets, complacent
and conservative competitive environments – which in turn lead to reduced
interest in increasing efficiency and cost savings – are highly vulnerable to
a bold and determined aggressor.

The attitudes and motivations of the buyer

Price is rarely, if ever, the only factor entering into the purchasing decision and is sometimes only secondary. The success of pricing decisions is therefore highly dependent on the ability of the firm to comprehend and respond to the purchasing environment into which its products are sold. Many ineffective, even disastrous, pricing policies can be traced back to misconceptions about the attitude of buyers to price and the role of price in the purchase decision. These misconceptions are often rooted in a popular industry folklore the credibility of which has been reinforced by constant repetition to a point at which the desire or willingness of firms to go against this conventional wisdom has been almost totally sapped. The philosophy of price cutting as the only effective means of competition which pervades some industries is often due more to uncritical acceptance of this folklore than to a sober analysis of marketing options.

Distinguishing fact from fiction in the market place is therefore the first task of the would-be rational pricing executive. Consider some of the marketing-related factors bearing on the role of price in the purchase decision. The most important of these is the concept of 'product differentiation'. This relates to the differences in functions, performance, design and other product-related or physical attributes which a manufacturer can introduce to distinguish his products from those of his competitors. The greater the differentiation, it is argued, the more invidious direct price comparisons by the buyer become, thus giving the firm greater flexibility in turn to gear its prices to the value it believes, or can persuade buyers to believe, attaches to the features or benefits it is offering. In many industrial markets this is characterized by the weighting attached by buyers to factors such as 'technical specification' and 'quality'. The range of price competition in such markets reflects the fact that buyers vary in the value they attach to different product features. The principle of segmentation – designing and pricing products to cater to a particular target group of customers within the market as a whole – derives from the concept of differentiation.

Economists usually assume, in theorizing on purchasing behaviour, that the buyer, being rational and efficient, will tend to purchase at the lowest price prevailing in the market place, for the product which best fits his needs and requirements. Where there is little or no product differentiation, such as in the case of electrical cable or industrial fasteners, he might be expected to look for the lowest price *per se*. Where there is substantial differentiation, such as in an industrial engine or a conveying system, then the buyer will weigh up all the economic aspects of the alternatives to arrive at the product which offers him the highest cost benefit. As consumer goods companies and advertising agencies have long appreciated, the domestic consumer is neither rational nor efficient but there is a widely held belief that the industrial buyer, being a 'professional', cannot be deceived as easily and will go unerringly to the 'bottom line'. Research into the buying decision has consistently shown this simply not to be true when considered in any detail.

In the first place, economic factors are not the only criteria employed in the purchase decision. Even in the case of non-differentiated products, many other factors can intrude to justify purchases at other than the lowest price available. These include:

1 Delivery (firms are often prepared to pay more for fast delivery or guaranteed delivery or for a delivery particularly convenient to the purchaser)
2 After-sales service/availability of spare parts
3 Previous good experience of the product or other things produced by the same manufacturer
4 Proximity of supplier to the purchaser
5 Security of supply/risk spreading (e.g. by dividing requirements between two or more suppliers)
6 General reputation of supplier/advice and recommendation of own staff and other firms in buyer's industry
7 The volume of other goods purchased from the same supplier
8 Good personal relationship with salesman, technical staff and other aspects of the supplier's organization.

Second, economic considerations can go far beyond the 'price' of the product. In the case of a capital product such as a commercial vehicle, a forklift truck or a machine tool, the purchase price of the product is only one of several cost-related considerations such as running costs (in terms of fuel and power, cost of spare parts); 'whole life' cost (the estimated total cost of the machine or vehicle over the whole of its expected operational life, reliability in service, running costs and disposal value); facilities for financing the purchase (are credit or deferred payment terms available? Is a leasing or rental facility available as an alternative to purchase?).

Third, industrial buyers are perfectly capable of being irrationally influenced by factors such as a persuasive salesman; clever advertising; cosmetic product features such as colour; fashion trends within the industry and simple prejudice. A manufacturer of circular knitting machines for whom the author once carried out a research project found it hard to accept that many customers rejected his technically well-engineered but old-fashioned looking product in favour of a streamlined, push-button import with, by objective standards, an inferior price/performance relationship. Various writers have drawn attention to cases where new products have been unsuccessful initially because they were priced too cheaply, thus creating buyer suspicion, and became successful when the price was brought more into line with what the buyers expected to pay! Differentiation is therefore feasible at a level well short of genuine product differences.

Finally buyers rarely have perfect knowledge of the markets for all the products they have to buy. Thus the buyer for a fabrications firm may have an extensive and systematically compiled knowledge of the suppliers and prices for the steel products which make up a substantial proportion of his firm's costs but has neither time nor the inclination to develop the same knowledge for less significant items he may also be responsible for such as paper clips and toilet rolls.

It has rightly been said that the price the final buyer is prepared to pay for a product is, in the end, the best guide to optimum pricing. Because it is the best guide, however, it is inevitably the most difficult concept to employ as a practical technique in pricing. The attraction of cost-based pricing formulae and using competitors' prices as a yardstick for price setting can be attributed at least in part to the fact that they are simple to understand and employ information which, in theory at least, is readily to hand or easily generated. By contrast it is often exceedingly difficult to establish in a direct way how much customers for a product are prepared to pay for it, or put another way, how many customers would be won at different alternative prices, given the variety of factors which affect the purchase decision of individual buyers. Nevertheless it is within the capacity and resources of most firms to develop sufficient information from their own knowledge and experience of trading in particular market places or by talking to some potential customers, or by some experimentation or by extrapolating the results of market research surveys. Then they can make broad assumptions about the size and structure of demand for a product and responsiveness to price in a competitive context which can be used to narrow the limits within which price should be set and define the strategy and tactics which best fit market conditions.

Distribution structure

Where a product is sold direct from manufacturer to end user, as many industrial products are, the pricing executive has only to consider pricing at a single level. The situation becomes more complex when distributive intermediaries – agents, wholesalers and retailers – are involved, as he then has to consider not just the price at which the product is sold to his immediate customer, say a wholesaler, but also the price at which it ultimately sells to the final consumer after it has passed through one, two or even three sets of hands, each of which have added their own mark-up. Wholesalers and retailers tend to price by adding a designated percentage mark-up to the price they buy-in the product in order to cover overhead and sales costs and yield a profit. It is, however, relatively unusual for a single fixed percentage to be applied to all products. Rather the percentage mark-up is manipulated between products according to circumstances or design around some overall average (which may itself reflect long-standing practice or folklore in a particular industry rather than any independent judgement on the part of the distributor).

Since the ending of resale price maintenance the manufacturer is unable to dictate the ultimate selling price of his products (and therefore in effect distributors' margins). Distributors may therefore manipulate margins in a way which favours or disfavours the products of the individual manufacturer and thereby impacts on ultimate sales. Pricing to the *distributor* but with an eye to reselling prices is therefore a special component of the art of pricing.

It should also be recognized that the effect of passing on, say, a reduction (or an increase) in the cost of materials or components is heavily affected by the length of the distribution chain. Not only might the change be much smaller proportionately in respect of the final selling price than it is to the ex-factory price but distributors can choose to pass on the change across a spectrum of options ranging from no price adjustment at all to one in excess of that made by the manufacturer.

AIDS TO PRICING

Models and computer simulations

In the main, however practical or logical the basic technique adopted, pricing decisions tend to involve a great deal of individual judgement by the pricing executive. Because the individual has to apply precise weightings to the many influences bearing in practice or in theory on this decision, the final outcome is at best an approximation of the best selling price and is as good, or as bad, as the quality of judgement applied to it. Various attempts have been made to construct 'models' of a more formal nature designed to help the firm fix the optimum price of its products under actual competitive conditions. These models differ widely in their nature, purpose and origin, but most frequently relate to the pricing of goods for retail sale (particularly fast-moving goods such as baked beans and washing powder) and pricing in a competitive bid or tender situation.

All models work by simulating, in terms of mathematical relationships, the interaction of the variables – company-, competition- and demand-related – which govern the pricing decision. They share therefore inevitable problems in defining and assigning a value to each variable. Their success depends on the quality of research or of the market knowledge or insight the firm is able to feed into the model, and on the manipulation of the variables which normally requires access to a computer. In the past the cost and complexity of model building tended to make it the preserve of the largest firms only. However, with the development of modestly priced personal computing systems and off-the-shelf software the ability to perform at least some price modelling is now within the compass of even the smallest firm.

Market research

Whether or not a pricing model is being developed, firms still require information on customers and competitors to help them reach sensible pricing decisions. This information is rarely readily available 'off the shelf' and some level of active information gathering is therefore predicated. The most widely employed source of intelligence is the salesman. The reasons for collecting information via the salesman are, naturally, seductive; the salesman is already employed by the firm 'on the road' and he is in constant contact with customers. In theory he ought to be particularly alive both to competitors' prices and to the price sensitivity and purchasing considerations of the buyer. In practice, however, salesmen are a highly unreliable source of pricing intelligence and tactical judgement. Research into the pricing of industrial products has suggested that it is not unusual for salesmen to convince themselves that they have lost orders on the basis of price when in fact other factors were of greater or equal importance in the purchase decision and it seems likely that many buyers use price as an excuse for not placing an order with a particular firm rather than give the real, possibly more contentious, reason.

While it is not suggested that firms should give up monitoring price through feedback from salesmen, it would seem prudent that where key pricing decisions are concerned, such as pricing a new product or a change in pricing strategy, information should be generated where required by means of more systematic market research conducted by a reputable and competent consultancy with experience in asking and interpreting questions about price and setting these in the context of other data on market structure and the purchasing process. Market research can make a valuable contribution to the analysis of pricing situations and the selection of appropriate strategies and tactics. For example, by providing detailed feedback on actual price levels and discounting procedures operating in the market, by monitoring terms and conditions associated with pricing, and by planning price in a meaningful perspective in relation to other influences on the purchase decision. Market research by individual specialist agencies is not usually a tool for setting actual selling prices, mainly due to the difficulty of measuring likely response to hypothetical price levels. Nevertheless, research based techniques have been developed for constructing pricing models.

DEVISING PRICING STRATEGY AND TACTICS

Entry strategies

The concept of pricing strategy as an element in the achievement of specific marketing goals was mentioned earlier. This involves the co-ordination of pricing decisions in the context of their longer-term impact and implications rather than their short-term or tactical benefits and requires the firm to take an extended view of such factors as probable product life; volume and price sensitivity of potential demand; opportunities for segmentation of demand by price; pace of likely consumer acceptance taking into account competitive, alternative and substitute products; build-up of production capacity and the opportunity for scale economies in unit costs; timescale for recovery of R and D costs.

The most sensitive, and probably the most important, time for strategy formulation is before the launch of a new product – whether or not the product concerned is an innovative or unique one with no direct competitors or is a new brand entrant on an established market place. It is frequently stated that at the stage of market entry the firm has a choice between two basic strategy options known as *skimming* and *penetration*.

Skimming strategies involve the deliberate setting of an initial price which is high in relation to anticipated long-term price levels towards which the price will be progressively lowered as competition and demand conditions change. The benefits of this strategy derive from the high gross margins achieved at the outset against which R and D and other 'sunk' costs and often heavy initial promotional costs can be set and from the flexibility afforded for using subsequent price changes as a means of controlling market expansion (since, setting aside inflation, the direction of price changes will be downward) and meeting merging competition by aggressive pricing. Skimming enables the firm to cream off that component of demand prepared to buy the product at its highest price before attacking the broader potential market which may exist for the product at a lower price. In so far as the progressive effective price reductions can be implemented on a 'step-wise' basis, the market may be, in effect, creamed off at different (and progressively larger) levels. The firm employing a skimming entry strategy also gives itself the option of approaching the anticipated longer-term downward adjustment in price by introducing variations of its original product or even a different brand rather than by simple price reduction, thus enabling it to maintain a premium price on its original product. This strategy might be termed progressive segmentation. A further advantage of skimming which should not be overlooked is that it conforms to the well attested dictum that it is easier to correct a pricing mistake in a downward direction than in an upward one.

Penetration strategies are intended to generate the highest possible volume of sales from the outset by keen (low margin) pricing. In practice they can be divided into two categories – demand-oriented and competition-oriented strategies (see Figure 17.2). Demand-oriented penetration strategies are based in the main on a combination of an expected high level of price sensitivity among potential buyers and a need for high volume of demand to justify plant investment or achieve projected economies of scale in production (i.e. some products have to be produced in volume or not at all). Competitively they have the advantage of potentially creating a strong market position or an image as market leaders before competition emerges (although this will depend on the speed and strength of the competitive response).

One specific variant of demand-oriented penetration strategies is worth mentioning – this might be called the 'razor and razor blades' strategy. Basically it involves pricing a unit of hardware (e.g. razor, labelling gun, copier, abrading machine) at a level which achieves the maximum market penetration or placement so that profits can be achieved on repeated sales of related consumables. If the consumable can be made unique in some way to the hardware, at least initially, a curious combination strategy of penetration for the hardware and what amount to skimming on the consumable presents itself.

Demand-oriented penetration strategies usually assume a slight underlying downward trend in prices under the impetus of further economies of scale and competitive pressure. This assumption is not necessarily true of competition-oriented penetration strategies. Penetration pricing in the broadest sense can be regarded as a means of deterring potential competitors by pressuring the margins which can be achieved to offset the costs of entry implicit in product development, investment in production facilities

GHM		
Skimming	Penetration: demand-oriented	Penetration: competition-oriented
Anticipated short product life (technological changes, fashion)	Anticipated long product life	Anticipated need to tempt users to try new product rather than continue with existing functional alternatives (gain foothold especially where differentiation not immediately clear to, or valued by, consumers)
Slow initial consumer acceptance (new applications, new technology)	Belief in rapid consumer acceptance/high price elasticity	
Uncertainty over ultimate scale and elasticity of demand	Economies of scale in output – threshold sales level before economies can be achieved	
Market segmentation – 'cream' those prepared to pay high price before moving to mass market (perhaps with lower priced variants)	Expectation of rapid competitive response – establish sound market position/market leadership before competition can develop	Pre-emption of competition – exclude prospective competitors by raising entry costs/establishing entrenched position
Inelastic production costs/capacity constraints	Exploitation of established reputation/sales, marketing, distribution strengths	Displacement of entrenched competition by aggressive pricing in directly competitive market (market launch of similar or identical product)
Recovery of high R and D costs		
Generation of funds for mass marketing	Create platform for continued sale of related products e.g. labelling machines and labels	
Competition slow to develop due to patent protection, research lead time, high production entry costs		
Exploitation of established reputation/differentiation aspects of product		

Figure 17.2   Evaluation of entry price strategy

and marketing/promotional efforts. To this extent bold penetration pricing might be employed to pre-empt the (immediate) risk of competition. Even so the strategy may still call for prices to be kept, in relative terms, around the launch level or even drifting lower to keep up the deterrent.

Two situations exist, however, where the strategy may be one of low entry price and an underlying plan for either a sharp or gradual increase in price. First, where a new product is being launched in a market where the competition comprises substitute or alternative products, price has been used as a means of persuading potential users to try the product (about which they may have, for example, technical doubts) on the assumption that when it has proved itself they would be prepared to pay a price equal to, or higher than, the existing alternatives. The second example concerns the use of a low entry price as a means of displacing or forcing out entrenched competition from an established market place or of gaining a substantial market share on the basis of which prices can subsequently be increased to a more profitable level. This highly aggressive strategy is one which has been successfully employed by Japanese companies in European markets for a wide variety of products. An example is marine engines. 'The prime target for the Japanese . . . was the European market and the view in the trade was that their strategy would follow the familiar pattern of gaining a large initial market share at cut prices, forcing the opposition out and then raising prices'(*Marketing*, 1979, Oct., p.32).

The temptation to use price as an entry wedge becomes increasingly great the more difficult it is for the firm entering a well established existing market to differentiate its product sufficiently clearly from those already available to ensure achievement of a satisfactory foothold on other competitive grounds. It can, however, be a high-risk strategy: if competitors have the resources to fight a rear-guard battle or even to step up the price war or if customers do not respond to the entry price as expected, the firm employing this strategy might find itself blocked, forced even to lower prices with consequent loss of profit margins all round or even faced with a situation in which serious resistance is encountered to the subsequent price rises implied by the strategy.

In general terms the more innovative the product the more the firm is likely to incline towards a skimming rather than a penetration strategy, particularly if R and D costs have been high and production capacity is limited, at least in the short term. However, the right strategy will depend on the firm, the product and the market.

Reviewing strategy after entry

Although pricing strategies are conceived as operating over a period of time, ignoring short-term fluctuations or pressures which may demand a tactical response, this does not mean that the strategy does not need to be kept under regular review. Nor that it is not necessary for strategies to be changed if conditions in the market place become sufficiently different from those that prompted the original plan.

The firm which has adopted a skimming strategy is faced with the need to decide when to implement the price cuts envisaged by the strategy and how large these should be on each occasion. There can be no hard and fast rules to guide these decisions. Depending on the pace at which competition develops – and this may be slowed down by patent protection, high entry costs and other factors – a high initial price might be retained for some considerable time before it needs to be reduced. On the other hand it can be advantageous to make the first cut well ahead of competition as a pre-emptive measure. Equally the timing and size of the cut may be best related to taking advantage of the demand interest opened up by initial entry to boost sales by a substantial cut in price justified by reference to cost savings from increased scale of production and greater efficiency. Similar considerations apply to subsequent cuts.

The firm which has implemented a penetration strategy has less room to manoeuvre in terms of price adjustments in the face of developing competition. The major problem facing pricing executives is maintaining a long-term view of price developments when competitive pressures appear to be forcing the firm into a growing number of reactive or short-term tactical decisions most probably associated with price cuts. In order to maintain its strategic grip the firm must be able to retain a broader view of the development of demand, its sensitivity to price changes and its susceptibility to non-price differentials.

It is probable that for many products, pricing decisions shade from the strategic to the tactical in the longer term whichever entry strategy is adopted as competition develops, as product differentiation becomes increasingly difficult to sustain and as sales approach saturation. Even so it would pay the firm to be alive to the opportunities which exist for using a deliberate change in strategy to revitalize its position in the market place or improve profits. The strategic options are legion, but they include:

1 Switching from a skimming strategy to a penetration strategy to exploit mass market potential of a product initially pioneered at a high price – perhaps by introducing a simplified and cheaper version rather than by cutting the price of the original product
2 Introduction of replacement or second generation products which can be differentiated sufficiently to command a premium price (return to skimming strategy)
3 'Re-packaging' of products in a way which takes them out of the competitive arena. A good example is the development of 'electronic office' concepts linking more conventional pieces of equipment in a unique total way (return to skimming strategy)
4 Concentration of attention on more profitable market segments even at the cost of volume – diversion of released production resources into other products
5 Improve margins by concentration on cost savings through more efficient production rather than by increasing prices (although the ability of the firm to use this strategy is limited by the long-term tendency of all production methods to ape the most efficient).

Tactical considerations

In theory, strategy precedes tactics in the pricing process, the latter providing the short-term dimension which governs the actual prices charged and the way these are expressed to the customer. In practice it is not always easy to separate the two. Tactics can be considered at two levels. First there are tactical decisions which relate to gearing actual price levels, and the form they take, to what might be termed the 'psychology' of the customer and the nature of the purchasing process. Such tactical considerations, in so far as they hold true over a period of time, in effect form part of strategy.

The semantics of such pricing tactics tend to be those of the consumer market and retail pricing. However, many have a more universal relevance whatever the product or service being sold. Probably the most widespread tactical device is discounting and this is considered in more detail below. However, mention might also be made of such tactics (based on Wilson, 1972) as:

1   Offset – low basic price, 'lost' margin recouped on extras, replacement parts or consumables
2   Diversionary – low basic price on some products (in range or line) developing overall image of low cost
3   Discrete – tailoring of price to bring product within the purchasing competence of a given seniority of buyer (relevant where the location of purchase decision is determined by corporate price ceilings)
4   Price lining – price kept constant but quality of product or extent of service adjusted to reflect changes in costs
5   Financing – alternative options to purchase such as leasing and rental (can be used as a specific means of extracting greater profit by changing the bases on which 'price' is assessed by the customer); might be coupled with special credit terms, trade-in allowances and special offers.

The above tactics are basically concerned with price. However, these need to be considered alongside what might be termed non-price differentials – ways of competing with command customer loyalty outside the framework of direct price competition, such as delivery services, after-sales support, technical back-up and advice and advertising and promotion effort.

In addition to these 'tactics of strategy' there are tactical questions of a more practical day-to-day level: what is the best way to pass on a price increase forced by rises in costs? Should ways be sought of keeping prices stable by modifying the product? Is it better to make price changes at regular and infrequent intervals (as until recently was mainly the case) or often in line with cost changes (as inflation is increasingly forcing on firms)? Should prices be changed to take into account positions of short-term strengths or weaknesses in the market place? How should the firm react to changes in competitors' pricing – is is necessary to react at all? By how much?

The combination and application of tactics require, if they are to have the desired effect, a detailed knowledge of the customer groups to which they are applied and the way these take purchasing decisions as well as a good appreciation of the likely response from competitors and the tactics which they are using themselves.

DISCOUNTS AND DISCOUNTING

The principle of discounting, whether formal or discretionary, is entrenched in most sectors of manufacturing industry where list prices of some kind or other are employed. The variations in discounting practice in everyday use are numerous. Four main types of discount: quantity discounts, trade discounts, cash discounts and seasonal/load shedding discounts are summarized in Figure 17.3. Other types of discount include those based on geographical factors (e.g. zonal pricing based on delivery distance); delivery method (e.g. discounts for customer collection); trade-in allowances on old equipment; 'free' supply of related consumables (e.g. labels used in price marking equipment). There are various ways also in which discounts are actually effected: they can be based on physical volume or money sales; be a percentage discount or a cash difference from a 'list' price; be shown as a flat sum rebate or a net price; be made 'on invoice' or 'off invoice'. Finally discount structures can be formal (with details published for customer use) or discretionary (in the form of guidelines within which sales managers can negotiate) or a combination of the two.

Special contract or 'net price' arrangements with key customers are, in effect, an extension of the discounting principle but with the essential difference that the terms of the sales agreement are usually the result of direct negotiation between buyer and seller rather than a development of the existing discount formula. Prices are inevitably keen but how much so will depend in individual cases on the bargaining strength of buyer and seller at the time and can be obscured by the introduction of product modifications, non-standard delivery arrangements and other special conditions. Special terms can come to dominate sales, for example, approximately 80 per cent of the sales of the Metal Box Company (open-top group) in 1977 were covered by special arrangements.

Of course in theory and in practice there are excellent reasons for operating a discount policy, some of which are indicated in Figure 17.3. Carefully operated and controlled, discounting provides firms with a flexible facility for fine-tuning response to (changing) demand and competitive conditions while retaining the overall integrity of catalogue and list price structures. The danger of discounting as general practice is that it can lead to inconsistency and lack of control. Special terms to important customers can individually be defended on the basis of pragmatism and expediency but add up in total to a jungle of prices which inevitably becomes perpetuated in successive deals with the same customers.

Discounts and special details in effect represent the reality of pricing while formal price lists and formulas represent the theory. The greater the flexibility or informality of the discounting procedure, and the more discretion which is granted to individual sales executives in negotiating

	Method of operation	Reasons for use
Quantity discounts or rebates	1 Single order – discount based on physical volume purchased at one particular time	1 Respond to individual purchasing power of customer in a competitive environment
	2 Cumulative – discount based on physical volume purchased over a fixed period of time (usually one year)	2 Pass on cost savings involved in servicing larger orders (economies in packaging, transportation, sales, administration)
	3 Guaranteed offtake – version of cumulative discount involving commitment by the buyer to take up either a fixed minimum quantity over the period as a whole or in specified amounts at fixed intervals (e.g. monthly) or both. Sometimes penalties in the form of sur-charges are made for exceeding a contract offtake as well as for falling short. In other cases bonuses can be paid for exceeding contract minimum	3 Encourage customers to purchase in larger quantities than they might otherwise do
		4 Discourage small orders which are expensive to process or unprofitable
		5 Promote repeat purchasing
		6 Create stability in demand and foster greater regularity and consistency in supply (benefits in stock-holding, organization of transportation, operation of product lines, etc.)

Figure 17.3 Types of discount

306

Trade discounts	Usually percentage discount from a specified 'list' price, designed to represent the distributors' operating expenses and profit. Alternatively may be represented as net trade prices available only to recognized 'trade' customers.	1 Aid in controlling or guiding final selling price (subject to legislation)
	Where more than one level exists in the distribution chain, discounts may discriminate between levels (e.g. between wholesalers and retailers)	2 Means of discriminating between different types of distributor, e.g. wholesaler and retailer; general distributor and special distributor who may offer additional or enhanced service
	Trade discounts may be characterized as a flat rate trade concession (e.g. 25 per cent to trade, list to other buyers) or combined with a quantity discount	3 Simplicity – easily understood by distributors
		4 Economy – reduce need to keep changing catalogues (since discounts, not 'list' prices can be manipulated
		5 Protection of distributor against direct buyers
Cash discounts	Deductions offered by the seller if payment of an invoice is made within a specified time period	Encourage immediate or early payment thus saving costs involved in the extension of credit and management of overdue accounts
Seasonal discounts/ load shedding	Differential prices according to season, day of week or time of day, where demand has a cyclical pattern and supply is fixed or intractable – most appropriate in consumer markets	Encourage spreading of demand, diversion of peak loading, boosting of demand at low periods Examples – electricity, coal, hotels, cross channel ferries, public transport, cinemas

Figure 17.3 Types of discount (concluded)

actual prices, then the more the difficulty the company faces in maintaining a firm grip over the effects of its pricing activities. Anticipating revenues and profit is a basic component of financial budgeting and control. However, the ability to make realistic forecasts and impose meaningful controls is directly related to an appreciation of the way prices are actually arrived at, the extent and 'mix' of sales at discounted prices and the relationship these prices have with formal price structures.

The firm operating discounts should keep asking itself:

1 *Do we need to discount at all?* Tradition and convention often play a major role in the operation of formal discount policies and structures. Yet firms have successfully fought the weight of conventional practice. For example, one major US-owned manufacturer of office furnishing systems has successfully operated a list price only policy for sales of whatever size in a market where discounting is notoriously widespread

2 *What types of discount should we offer?* The types and scales of discount appropriate in individual cases cannot be embodied within a general set of rules. These will depend on the markets concerned, on the cost structures faced by the firm, perceived customer sensitivity to price changes, on the competitive situation and many other factors. What is important is that discounting procedures are subjected to rational evaluation of all the factors involved and kept consistent with changes in cost, sales structure and the market environment. Discount structures have a habit of becoming entrenched so that they remain in force long after they have ceased to be relevant to the firm's business. A manufacturer who has switched from selling through distributors to mainly direct sales does not, for example, need to offer trade discounts pitched at a level which encourages heavy stocking

3 *What proportion of sales will be made at discounted prices?* Company management should be aware of the sensitivity of revenue and profit to the extent and level of discounting. This should include a particular appreciation of the role of special terms negotiated with large customers and the impact of a wide flexibility or discretion in fixing discount prices.

REPRESENTING PRICE TO THE CUSTOMER

Preceding paragraphs have shown how pricing can depend, legitimately, on a balance of demand and competition-related issues. It is also the case that firms can set prices in ways designed deliberately to frustrate the ability of the buyer to make direct comparisons, and even to foster price perceptions which are at variance with objective reality. Techniques which are frequently used by firms include:

1 *The 'optional extra' routine.* This involves pricing a product in a basic version with a variety of enhancements priced separately as 'optional extras'. To the extent that the value of the product to the buyer is likely to require at least some 'optional extras', this approach implies an expectation that the buyer will be drawn into a greater expenditure

commitment than he might otherwise have been prepared to agree to, particularly if other suppliers have included these 'extras' in their original basic price. The pricing of cars is a good example of this practice – some European manufacturers, especially, still charge extra for many items which Japanese manufacturers fit as standard, thus obscuring the true difference in price.

2   *Bundling.* This is, in practice, the obverse of the 'optional extra' approach and involves making up a package unique to a specific supplier and offered at a special price which makes invidious a comparison with a competing product without the special elements. The process can be represented as offering the buyer an attractive overall discount. A good example is the way some computer companies have packaged their personal computers with a number of software packages and/or peripherals such as a printer or a monitor. However, bundling also enables the supplier to dispose of outdated or uncompetitive products in a commercially attractive way. For example, the software bundled with a personal computer may be an earlier release than that marketed as a separate product.

3   *Artificial recommended selling prices.* Although resale price maintenance (the practice of enforcing specific resale prices) is outlawed in many countries, it is often perfectly legal for a manufacturer to declare a *recommended* selling price. Retailers can use this price if they wish or, more often, to demonstrate how keen his prices are (ie. lower than the Manufacturer's Recommended Price, MRP). However, MRPs can be used to provide what in reality is a spurious reference level, since no retailer from the smallest to the largest would actually sell at that price. The pricing of many items of furniture and domestic appliances has long reflected this practice.

PRICING AND NEW PRODUCT PLANNING

It can be said that the only time a firm genuinely has complete discretion in pricing is before it has committed itself to developing and marketing a new product at all! Once resources start to be committed to R and D, and even more, once production facilities have been invested in, the pricing options available to the firm become progressively narrowed by practical consideration: the costs 'sunk' in bringing the product to market; the fixed costs represented by the scale of plant laid down to produce it; the direct costs of production consequent on choice of production process and scale of production; the constraints imposed by demand and competitive conditions and by the pricing of existing product lines with which the new product might be expected to interact.

New product development has always been a high-risk activity – various studies in the USA have shown failure rates among those actually launched running as high as 60 per cent. Many others are abandoned before they reach the production stage after large sums have been spent on R and D. The risks are moreover tending to become greater as the pace of technological change and competitive pressures force up development costs. The more greedy on resources new product development is, the more careful the firm needs to be that the products selected for development are those standing the best chance of achieving a good rate of return on investment when the product finally goes into production. Many writers on new product planning have emphasized the need for establishing clear frameworks of controls, systems and guidelines for appraising the relative merits of new product ideas so that management time and resources are channelled to those products offering the most attractive investment opportunity.

The process of new product appraisal is one which involves a large number of corporate and marketing considerations. However, anticipation of the price ranges at which the product is likely to sell and the market conditions or assumptions underlying those ranges is something which should normally take place at the earliest stages of product planning and be held under review throughout the development process. In effect it is argued that firms should think far more concretely about gearing new product development to a broad target selling price derived in turn from a realistic valuation of potential demand and the nature of competition than they do at present. This would have several major benefits:

1 It would contain the tendency in R and D to 'over-engineer' products (since the price target will also imply production cost targets which would have to be met if satisfactory profits are to be made)
2 It would prevent the development of products based on unrealistic assumptions about likely sales volumes (which often result from the use of cost plus formulas to project price, at the planning stage)
3 It would provide a framework for 'fine-tuning' the product during the later stages of development to maximize competitive success within the selected price range.

Admittedly this approach is not easy to apply to the product which is itself a dramatic technological breakthrough or creative innovation for which existing price indications in the market place are inadequate and hypothetical testing of consumer responses at best unreliable. However, the great majority of new products do not fall into this category but relate in some reasonably direct way to established applications and existing products against which price targets can reasonably be set.

PRICING AND PRODUCT LINES

A great many pricing decisions take place in the context of product lines or ranges rather than as entirely independent exercises. Product lines or ranges comprise individual products linked together in some identifiable way – by a common function, by a common design or structure, by a common production process, by a common user group or application area. An office equipment manufacturer may, for example, offer a range of copiers of different print speeds or output capacities; within each model type a choice of features, e.g. automatic or manual operation, ranges of other office products, e.g. typewriters, word processors and facsimile transceivers.

The basis for product-line policies and the justification for offering different models, lines and ranges is a subject in itself. It is sufficient to note here that the existence of product lines raises particularly complex issues of pricing because of the way demand for each individual product interacts. Product lines as a whole may be mutually supportive but individual products within the line can easily be competitive with each other, particularly if encouraged by lack of care in pricing. Simply applying a common mark-up to each individual product is clearly unsatisfactory since it is probable that each product will vary in its production and marketing cost profile and in the opportunities and constraints implied by demand and the competitor environment it is selling into. This argues for a pricing policy which provides for each product in a line to be individually priced according to costs and market conditions subject to certain broad principles of consistency to minimize the risk of anomalies leading to the firm competing with itself.

Even so the firm faces sensitive issues each time a product line is extended, supplemented or modified by introduction of revised models or when a new product line is introduced. An example of the dangers faced, in the author's own experience, is provided by a building board company which tried to launch a new and superior grade of board at a premium price in a market which turned out to place much less value on the higher quality offered by the new product than the company expected. The result was that as the price of the new product was forced down to a level close to that of the firm's existing range of building board, buyers of the original range simply switched allegiance to the new product forcing the price of the original range still lower in order to maintain sales. What started off as an exercise in market segmentation turned out to cause disastrous loss of profit all round.

SUMMARY

This chapter has sought to demonstrate why pricing is perhaps the most complex and demanding – and least clearly understood – of all tasks facing company management. Some conclusions are now drawn which might help the financial executive, in particular, contribute more effectively to pricing policy formulation and price setting.

1 *Pricing is much more of an art than a science.* There is no universal formula or golden rule for arriving at the right price. Those responsible for price setting have to balance and allow for a variety of factors and influences both internal to and external to the firm itself which, far from the ordered and rational world of the theoretical economist, may not always be logical and may even be in conflict. Nevertheless, profitability can significantly be enhanced by injecting greater coherence into the rules and principles, whatever these may be, which govern the way prices are fixed and maintained. The financial executive has an important part to play in the preparation and implementation of pricing policy

2 *Successful pricing decisions cannot be based on costs alone.* Prices are far less often arrived at by the mechanistic application of cost-based formulae than is widely believed. Even so, costs and cost-related profit targets remain a major obsession of many firms in pricing, particularly in the case of industrial products. Financial executives have tended on the whole to encourage and reinforce this essentially inward-looking approach. The success of pricing decisions is, however, highly dependent on the ability of the firm to comprehend and respond to *market* needs and conditions. The contribution of the financial executive to pricing decisions would be substantially enhanced by greater recognition of the role of such factors as competition, buyer attitudes and motivations and the impact of distributive systems in optimum pricing

3 *Price is a much neglected and potentially powerful element in the marketing mix.* Price is widely treated more as a handicap which has to be borne rather than as a positive tool for achieving designated marketing goals. This chapter has looked at the ways pricing can contribute to overall marketing plans both in the longer term (pricing strategy) and in the short term (pricing tactics). The financial executive should be prepared to be 'sufficiently flexible in his own advice and policies not to inhibit sales and marketing personnel from manipulation of price as a marketing weapon

4 *Pricing considerations are a key element in product planning.* Anticipation of price ranges and market conditions are an essential precondition to effective investment and product planning. The financial executive should seek to ensure that pricing factors are introduced at the beginning and not at the end of the planning cycle for new products.

REFERENCES AND FURTHER READING

Atkin, B. and Skinner, R., *How British Industry Prices*, IMR, 1975

Price Commission, *Compressed Permanent Gases and Dissolved Acetylene Sold in Cylinders, Cylinder Rentals and Fixed Charges* (BOC Ltd), HC 223, 1979

Gabor, A., *Pricing, Concepts and Methods for Effective Marketing*, 2nd edition, Gower, Aldershot, 1988

Price Commission, *Open Top Food and Beverage Cans and Aerosol Cans* (Metal Box Ltd), HC 135, 1978

Oxenfeldt, A.R., 'Multi-stage Approach to Pricing', *Harvard Business Review*, July/August 1960

Price Commission, *Report for the period 1st February to 30th April 1980*

Price Commission, *Prices of Glass Containers* (UG Glass Containers Ltd) HC 170, 1978

Wilson, A., *The Marketing of Professional Services*, McGraw-Hill, Maidenhead, 1972

18 Distribution channels

Arthur Lawrence

'Getting distribution' for a marketed product (or even for a marketed service) is the term we give to the process of moving it through from the producer and making it conveniently available to its universe of final users. The aim is to do this through whatever channels will provide the greatest sales and the lowest costs and so generate the maximum profit.

In using distribution channels we are not concerned only with the processes of merely physical distribution; that is, the actual storage, handling, transportation and delivery of goods. It is unfortunate that only the one word 'distribution' is available to describe both the physical operations and the wider marketing concept. Perhaps a clearer distinction could be made by describing the physical operations as 'logistics', and this term is sometimes used. A whole later section of this book is devoted to physical distribution; what is being discussed here are the methods of getting a product 'into' distribution, and so made available to its potential users.

MARKETS

Distribution, or trade, channels are simply the institutions which exist – or which could be created – to bring about the consummation of buying and selling between potential consumers and producers, in a given market. A market has to be defined both geographically and by the type of product in question. Geographically, the considerations are whether the product is to be marketed only in its own home town or district; or regionally; or with full national coverage; or even further afield. Distributing beyond the national boundaries of course means 'export', which still in many minds implies a barrier beyond which everything is strange and different, although membership of the EEC (supposed to be a common market) was designed to do away with such restrictions. Nevertheless, the larger the distribution area is geographically, the more possibility there is that different distribution channels will be required for different parts of it.

As to market differentiation by product, every individual product can

313

be said to have its own market, in so far as it appeals to a unique set of users. But for purposes of considering distribution channels, there is one great divide in product classes; that is, whether the product is designed for consumption by the general public as individuals; or whether it is intended as an input product for use in other sectors of industry and business. This distinction is fundamental. The public buys its needs in the main in retail shops and stores. Equally generally, commerce and industry does not.

General public or industry?

Products aimed at the individual customer can of course be subdivided again and again from the point of view of the distribution channels they require. A main subdivision would probably be into products which are recurrent necessities for everyone (food, clothing, household supplies) and those of a rarer, more specialist appeal. The former are likely to have to jostle for a place in the main retailing market place, while for the latter more exclusive outlets may be available. Each main group can again be broken down as to the 'class' of consumer aimed at, typically as regards spending power, sophistication of interest and so on.

Supplies to industry and commerce will have their own specialized channels or routes to the user. Even when the identical product is in use by both the general public and various sectors of industry it will usually be found necessary to supply it through different channels of distribution in each case. Industry expects to deal more directly with the producer and get lower prices than are charged in the public shops; while the public does not normally have access to the channels provided for industry.

Reviewing alternative channels

The first fact of distribution is that whatever institutions and channels may exist in a particular market, their cooperation in actually providing distribution to users cannot by any means be taken for granted, either for the launch of a new product or for the continued throughput of an existing product. A new product has to be suitable for and of interest to its prospective distribution channel, just as much as it must appeal to its ultimate user. Distribution channels are constantly evolving; completely new ones become available, and the old ones by degrees change their methods and their interests or even disappear altogether. New and competitive products come on the scene to oust older traditional lines, not just in their appeal to the user, but in the esteem of their distributors as well. The current arrangements for securing the distribution of a product may therefore not always be adequate for its development and expansion, and may at times be vulnerable to changing circumstances. The proper study and assessment of all available and alternative distribution channels is therefore a vital part of marketing planning for both new and existing items.

In considering the kind of distribution channels that could be used between the producer and the ultimate user in any marketing situation, the following main alternatives present themselves immediately. There is the choice of:

1 Using no third party intermediary or middleman between producer and end user
2 Using only one level of intermediary trader between producer and end user
3 Using more than one level of intermediary trader between producer and end user

These alternatives apply in practically every distribution situation, whether for individual consumer goods or for supplies to industry, and in very many cases more than one of these alternatives may have to be used. Each of these categories can be considered in turn.

SELLING DIRECT TO THE USER

Where no intermediary trader is used between producer and consumer, the producer becomes a direct seller to the end user, that is, the producer himself provides or controls or buys in all the necessary services for contacting potential users in his own name, concluding sales with them, and delivering the goods to them. It is immaterial that some of the services involved may be provided by third parties. The producer may well use a transport contractor for deliveries rather than run his own delivery fleet; or use a mailing house to send out circulars; or even use commission agents to bring in orders. The essential point is that deals are concluded directly between the producer and the user, and property in the goods passes directly from the one to the other.

Direct to industry

For products intended as inputs to industry or to commerce rather than for the general public, this method of selling would probably be the first to be considered. The more specialized the product, and the fewer (and therefore the more individually important) the potential users of it, the more inclination there will be to deal with them direct. If the product is more or less tailor-made for each user, or needs complicated installation and user instruction, there may be little alternative but for the producer to see to things for himself. However widespread the market in geographical terms, the producer must contemplate undertaking all the costs of providing salesmen and other services for customer contact. On the other hand he need not allow for any third party to make a profit out of his transactions.

Direct to the public

At the other extreme, for products aimed at the public's daily needs, it would be out of the question for the producer to contact all potential users direct – or almost so. On a purely local basis there can certainly be exceptions. The small town baker can still sell all his output through his own shop. In developing countries the peasant farmer (or his wife) takes their own produce to the market and sells it there. But where daily needs are concerned in sophisticated markets, the public tends to buy little and often and seeks as many different items as possible in the one establishment. This rules out buying from the producer direct. On the other hand, for more specialized products aimed at the general public, the possibilities for the producer to deal directly with the user begin to multiply considerably.

Mail order

To make any impact at all, products being sold by mail order must be intensively advertised, probably in the national media or by the equally expensive distribution of catalogues and mail shots. Potential sales must therefore be sufficient to carry this cost. The question is whether the allure of advertising will be enough to make up for the product not being available in the shops where the public can see it and touch it. Will the attractiveness of presentation be a substitute for active selling by the shops – if shops ever do perform active selling? As against the impulse buy, the would-be customer has the added chore of writing off for what he wants. (But perhaps local agents can be employed to do this for him).

Despite these drawbacks, mail order selling for personal possessions and household goods can be tremendously successful. Clothes, furniture, items for specialized interests, all kinds of leisure equipment, books, records – the list is so extensive that mail order cannot be ruled out as being of possible application in almost any field. Possibilities are also liable to increase if the use of 'electronic shopping' ever becomes widespread. The technology for this is already in existence – cable TV or similar arrangements can allow the customer to call up pictures and details of the items in which he is interested, and to key in his order quoting his credit card number, all in his own home.

Direct contact

For items of very high unit value, the employment of salesmen calling door to door can be cost-effective. Domestic house improvements such as double glazing and central heating are the prime examples, but personal services can be included – notably life insurance. Fifty years ago in the UK the list would have included vacuum cleaners and domestic brushware, which nicely illustrates how wage costs have increased in relation to merchandise unit value.

In a specialized field it is not wholly out of the question for a producer to operate his own retail outlets as a channel of distribution direct to the individual user. Examples exist in the clothing industry. However with vertical integration on the one hand and the sub-contracting of production on the other, it becomes quite hard to distinguish between organizations which are really producers having some interests in shops, and those which are really retailers having some control over production.

In summary, direct selling to the user can be viable both for industrial and for general public merchandise, in specific circumstances; and can be implemented either by salesmen's visits, by use of the media, or even by the establishment of local sales centres.

SINGLE LEVEL DISTRIBUTORS

In the supply of consumer goods to the public, probably the most common situation is the use of a single level of distributor between the producer and the individual user. The consumer finds his or her needs in the retail shop or store, and the producer sells directly to these outlets. In the more highly developed markets, several complementary trends can be observed in this system of retail distribution. Producers (through mergers and growth) become larger and fewer in number, each operating as far as possible nationally; and retail establishments similarly develop into widespread chains and multiples, each covering very large areas, if not all, of the national market. Thus a smaller number of centrally organized producers supplies an ever larger share of total needs to a smaller number of centrally organized retailers, and it is not surprising that each should deal directly with the other. At the same time, an ever wider range of merchandise is being put through the mass retailing system. The public is doing more for itself rather than employing small tradesmen for the purpose, so that materials and equipment which previously would have been distributed as trade supplies are now suitably packaged and retailed to the home user. Manufacturers have had to adapt themselves to selling a larger part of their output at retail and changing their distribution channels accordingly.

Retailing establishments can be categorized in all sorts of ways, but from the point of view of the distribution mechanism the principal distinctions are as follows:

National or regional multiples

Irrespective of differences in the range of merchandise or the house style or any such qualitative aspects, retail multiples are essentially organizations which implement a uniform merchandising and selling policy throughout all their many branches. Into this category come hypermarkets, food supermarkets, clothing chains, furniture warehouses, do-it-yourself chains, multiple chemists, electrical and photographic multiples – in fact any large scale retailer exercising central control over branches. To exercise this control, multiples operate in two principal ways:

Central buying and warehousing

Very large single deals are negotiated with suppliers, for delivery in bulk to the central warehouse, which in turn supplies to branches according to their needs. Branches place no orders directly with suppliers. From the suppliers' point of view, bulk deliveries to a single point mean a great saving in transport and order processing costs, and there is no need for an expensive sales force to visit the individual stores to get orders. Since the multiple is bearing the cost of warehousing and delivery to branches, the price concession demanded from suppliers will be correspondingly steep. Suppliers may also find that in practice they still have to send salesmen to call on branches, if only to ensure that the latter remember to order stocks from their central warehouse, and to give them proper display.

Listing and local ordering

The multiple negotiates prices and terms centrally with suppliers, for estimated total requirements over a period. In return, the suppliers' products are then 'listed' to branches as items which they are authorized to order directly from the suppliers, at their own discretion. Suppliers in practice have to send salesmen to call to get these orders, and still have to bear the expense of making smaller individual deliveries to each branch. To obtain a 'listing' at all, the supplier will also have to make some price concession.

Any given multiple may operate either or both systems, and may even give a supplier the option of which system he prefers to use. It is essential in either case for suppliers to calculate all their selling and delivery costs correctly, so as to know exactly what price concessions they can afford to make.

Department stores

Originally, the classic department store was a collection under one roof of a great variety of merchandise departments, each individually managed as to its selection of merchandise and its buying policy. There would be overall guidelines and financial controls, but the department buyer had the last word on ordering. Thus department stores were in a way the exact opposite of retail multiples; one location in place of many, but many buyers in place of one. For the specialist supplier, dealing with only one department out of a huge establishment, there would be little difference from dealing with any other single retail shop. Department stores in the classic mould, apart from one or two famous exceptions, appear to be dying out, and through mergers are evolving more into retail multiples. While outward appearances may remain the same, the individual departments are becoming parts of a centrally managed chain which now makes the principal buying decisions. The supplier must therefore check carefully exactly how each establishment operates, in assessing what his costs of selling and supplying to it are going to be.

Independents

Other retail outlets fall by default into the category of independents – independent in the sense of buying decision. An independent may of course have more than one selling location, as long as there are not so many branches as to raise the status to that of a small multiple. (It is an interesting point that cooperatives can be in either category: in some areas, buying is centralized in multiple fashion; in others, quite small groups act independently.) The characteristic of dealing with the independent retailer as a channel of distribution is that each has to be sold to individually, usually through visiting by salesmen. Costs of selling are high, coupled with the higher costs of small order quantities and widespread deliveries. Against this, the supplier hopes that terms will be easier than with multiples.

Groups

Independents also are evolving, chiefly by becoming members of voluntary buying groups. In this way the group of independents begins to operate very much like a multiple, in that bulk buying decisions are now made centrally by the group headquarters, which may also operate its own warehouse. Discipline among the independent members is of course not nearly so tight as in a wholly owned multiple, and the supplier has less assurance that the single central negotiation will be effective in getting his merchandise into every store. To be sure of this, the supplier may have to retain as much direct contact with individual members as when they were truly independent.

Franchising

The ultimate in grouping is franchising, where the merchandising and selling policy for the particular goods or service are centrally controlled and enforced as rigidly as by any multiple. The fact that individual outlets are independently financed makes no difference to buying policy, which will usually leave the franchisee free to purchase at his own discretion only the most minor local supplies.

In all the foregoing retail categories, size of establishment and method of organization make no difference to function as a channel of distribution. Retail outlets are available to the producer as single level trading intermediaries between himself and the ultimate users, should he wish to avail himself of them. It is up to the producer to make his product of sufficient interest to those categories of retailer which offer the best channel of approach to potential users.

Industrial distributors

The producer of goods for industry and commerce will generally have more incentive to deal direct with his users than the producer of goods for the public. Nevertheless, where these users are both individually small and numerous in total, the industrial producer also has to seek intermediaries to provide an alternative channel of distribution. This will be especially the case where the product is neither so technical nor so purpose-made as to make direct contact essential between manufacturer and user. Thus as direct counterparts to retail outlets for the general public, there exist distributors to industry and commerce in every field of product. Builders' merchants act as stockists of bricks, tiles, cement and every kind of material and accessory for construction work. Agricultural merchants stock animal feeds, seeds, fertilizer and every farm need, down to wheelbarrows and rubber boots. Steel stockholders supply engineering works. Office equipment suppliers stock everything from paper upwards. Even the hotel, restaurant and catering industry is covered by specialist wholesaling stockists, usually of the cash and carry type.

Similar categorizations exist among industrial distributors as among retail distributors. While the trend towards mergers and nationwide organizations is perhaps not so marked as in retail, it still occurs, and the equivalents of national multiples exist, in practically every field of industrial distribution. The individual producer thus has similar alternatives of central negotiation for bulk contracts with multi-branch organizations, or individual deals with a multiplicity of smaller independent traders.

A particular case of industrial distributor is the agent or stockist in a foreign market. While producers can and do still deal direct with large and important export customers, they are likely to feel more need than in their home market for an intermediary distributor to act between them and the majority of potential users abroad.

MORE THAN ONE LEVEL OF DISTRIBUTOR

When potential users of a product are too numerous for the producer to be able to contact all of them direct, he makes use of an intermediary distributor. When, in turn, the first level of intermediary distributors becomes too numerous to contact direct, the producer has to seek a higher level of distributor to deal with all the others.

This situation arises mainly in the market for the general public. Despite the trend for the displacement of small independent retailers by large centrally controlled multiples, there remain enough of the former in some sectors to constitute a problem. In the UK, for example, there are over 50 000 retail shops selling newspapers, magazines, confectionery and tobacco. There are also nearly as many grocers or general food shops. For any one producer to attempt to deal with all of these directly, obtaining their orders and making individual deliveries, is unlikely to be economic. Therefore in each class of trade, both in the UK and in other markets, there is an important stratum of 'wholesalers' or higher level distributors between producer and retailer.

Wholesale and cash and carry

Many of these wholesalers operate on the basis of cash and carry, which is self-selection by their retail customers and payment on the spot, with the buyer providing his own transport. Others for a higher price provide delivery and credit. All of them most jealously guard against the general public being able to gain access and buy for themselves at wholesale prices, thereby short-circuiting the retailer. In dealing with wholesalers, the producer saves the cost of selling and delivering direct to thousands of retailers, but must now allow in his pricing for both wholesaler and retailer to make a profit – and probably must take steps to ensure that the position of each is protected.

Main distributors

In industrial situations the use of more than one level of distributor is perhaps rarer if only because of the smaller number of primary outlets likely to be involved. It will be unusual for there to be more first level distributors than the producer can readily deal with directly. Nevertheless there will be instances of specialized items – agricultural machinery for example – where an advantage is found in having an upper level of main distributors who will undertake supply of occasional 'one-offs' to less specialized sub-dealers. The sub-dealer knows the customer who may prefer to deal with him rather than with a distant specialist. Again, in the export field there may be grounds for having a single main distributor in a foreign territory to handle sales to all other stockists.

CHOOSING DISTRIBUTION CHANNELS

For any producer seeking distribution for a newly launched item or reviewing the current arrangements for existing lines, the first area of decision is likely to be whether any one distribution channel will satisfy all requirements, or whether there may be grounds for using more than one channel at the same time.

Parallel channels

Many producers will find that no single channel of distribution is ideal for all the product range in all sets of circumstances. In the sector of products aimed at the general public, the manufacturer may feel that the best prospect for sales is through having the product stocked and promoted by the retail shops specializing in that class of trade. But what if retailers fail to carry stocks and large sectors of the public are left without opportunity to buy? It may be necessary to encourage direct mail ordering from the public, at the same time as stepping up pressure on retailers to stock. The advertising message will have to be: 'Available from all good retailers, or by mail direct from . . .'. Some book publishers practise this as a matter of course; as do manufacturers of specialized items where retail distribution is not widespread.

The commonest situation in the consumer goods market is where the manufacturer can and must deal directly with the largest retailers, but cannot economically sell and deliver directly to all the smaller ones. A typical case is where the larger outlets, accounting for around 20 per cent of all shops, may handle 80 per cent of all sales; while the remaining 80 per cent of smaller shops account for only 20 per cent of total sales. The manufacturer cannot afford to forego this last 20 per cent of sales altogether, but equally cannot afford to contact all of the smaller shops direct. If possible, a way must be found to interest wholesalers in handling supplies to the smaller outlets, while the main stores are dealt with direct.

In developing markets overseas, producers commonly sell their output through only a few large traders, who supply smaller outlets and market traders through possibly several levels of re-selling. But in order to stimulate sales in particular areas, the producer may have to bypass them all and from time to time sell direct to the public from mobile vans in the market place.

Goods for the industrial and commercial market face the same kind of choice. While the majority of sales can be handled through specialized merchants and stockists, very large users must be dealt with by direct negotiation, for two main reasons:

1 Large users insist on buying only from manufacturers on grounds of price
2 The size of their requirements would probably exceed the financial and physical capacity of intermediary dealers.

Very large users nowadays include governments and state organizations, for whom special terms are always necessary.

Conflicts

Where more than one distribution channel has to be used simultaneously there is thus a fundamental conflict; the producer is trying to make sales to the customers of his own customers. The reasons for trying to do so have to be compelling, and the distributors being bypassed have to be protected and their cooperation retained. Some or all of the following means can be employed:

1 Make clear in advance to intermediary distributors the circumstances in which it may be necessary to bypass them
2 Explain that the purpose is not to deprive them of business but to make the sales which they cannot get themselves and which otherwise would be missed altogether
3 Point out that gaining extra market share for the product in this way will be to their advantage in stimulating total demand for it
4 Try not to undercut distributors' prices when bypassing them to sell direct; then there is no reason why distributors should not do this class of business themselves in future
5 If a lower price is necessary to get some special direct business, point out to distributors that they would not have been able to match this price themselves.

Whatever the arrangements for operating more than one distribution channel it is essential to make clear to all the parties involved just what these arrangements are, and also to make provision for changes should these ever become necessary. Distributors should never be allowed to think that they have a monopoly right to sales being made only through them; the manufacturer must reserve the right to intervene in special cases, giving whatever protection he can to the distributors' position.

Regulated distribution

A secondary dilemma in choosing distribution channels is whether to sell through as many distributors as are willing to handle the product, or to restrict it to selected distributors only.

Having the product available in as many outlets as possible fulfils one of the prime functions of achieving distribution. User demand is stimulated through the widespread presence of the product and no potential sale is lost through non-availability. This however is achieved at the risk of excessive competition between outlets, leading to price cutting and eventual loss of interest by the trade in handling the product at all.

Restricting the product to selected distributors permits a regulated market, where each distributor has a more or less exclusive position in his own area. Demand is concentrated on fewer distributors so that they can in turn concentrate on the product to the exclusion of other competitive lines. At the extreme, distribution becomes a network of exclusive dealerships.

Exclusive territories

Regulated distribution is more the norm for industrial and commercial supplies than for general public merchandise. With markets much smaller in terms of numbers of users it is the more essential not to overcrowd them. For many industrial products, technical service, support, spares and special equipment are required and distribution must be limited to those dealers who can provide them. Their investment in the product must be given some guarantee of protection thereafter. These arrangements would normally be the subject of a distribution agreement with the rights and duties of both sides clearly set out. The distributor may be given exclusivity in one particular territory, and in such cases it is essential to make provision for changes if the arrangement does not work out. It may often be better to have more than one dealer in a territory so that none has a complete monopoly.

In the public sphere, regulated distribution also occurs. The sale of motor cars is an obvious example; dealers are appointed for each make on a territorial basis again on the grounds that each has to provide specialized spares and service. Less obviously, many other lines of merchandise are restricted in their outlets. Expensive cosmetics and perfumery are on sale only in boutiques and drug stores with the requisite level of sophistication and would never be allowed to reach the shelves of a common supermarket. Technical items for specialist leisure activities will only be supplied through stores offering know-how and service.

Free consumer market

For the great majority of consumer goods, the maximum exposure in the largest number of retail outlets usually far outweighs any considerations of market regulation. Since competition is regarded as of ultimate benefit to the consumer there may be legal issues involved in trying to regulate it. In the UK for example it is illegal to try to impose a minimum retail selling price. In practice, suppliers stipulate minimum order quantities, offer discounts for large deliveries, and require a minimum level of display. This ensures that the product is stocked only in those outlets considered suitable. The difficulty for manufacturers is usually in the other direction, in trying to keep the product on sale in all sizes of retail outlet when the larger organizations use their buying power to squeeze price concessions. With these concessions in hand, retail prices can be cut to levels with which the smaller outlets cannot compete. Given the higher costs of selling and delivering to them, manufacturers cannot reduce prices comparably to the smaller outlets.

From the manufacturers' point of view there can be considerable temptation to supply only to the large retail multiples through single negotiations, with bulk deliveries to a central warehouse; and to ignore the smaller independent retailers altogether. In this way the bulk of the public can be reached adequately, and the costs of selling and delivery are minimal. On the other hand, terms will be onerous and, if a single sales negotiation falls through, the manufacturer may be left with no distribution at all.

THE CRITERIA FOR CHOICE

The basis for choosing a distribution channel or combination of channels is very clear in principle; it will be the one which promises to yield the highest ultimate net profit, calculated as sales volume times margin, less the associated selling and supply expenses. Estimates are therefore required of sales volume, margins attainable, and costs of selling, through different channels.

Sales volume

Sales forecasts have to based largely on experience, but it should still be possible to estimate whether sales would be greater or less when using different distribution channels. For example, sales could be made:

1 Through mail order direct to users
2 Through retail shops
3 Through wholesalers to retail shops
4 By a combination of some or all of these methods.

Presumably sales through a channel which is shared with another would be less than if that channel were used exclusively. The question is whether total sales through shared channels would be greater than by using either one alone. Estimates should be made for all possible methods and combinations of methods.

Margins

Assessing margins entails knowing what levels of profit the different classes of distributor would require to motivate them to stock and promote the product properly. It is essential to start with the price the end user can be expected to pay, then deduct the distributors' margins. The manufacturer gets what is left, and must make his profit out of it. To start with a manufacturer's selling price, leave distributors to add what they like, and hope that end users will pay what they are asked, is not marketing – it is simply throwing a product on to the market. The complete pricing structure through all alternative levels of distribution should be worked out, allowing for distributors' costs in stocking, handling and re-selling the product, plus whatever profit will be required. The less distributors are used, the higher the remaining margin to the manufacturer; but out of this the manufacturer will have to incur higher costs of his own in selling more directly.

Selling costs

The calculation of selling costs per channel must include the costs of handling orders and making deliveries as well as salesmen's wages, travel costs, telephones and so on – in fact every cost which is incurred as a direct result of using any particular distribution channel. Costs which are incurred whatever the channel can be left out of the comparison. The distributive trade is essentially passive towards suppliers, supporting its own interests rather than theirs. Customers are left to make their own choice between competitive products, rather than any one product in particular being promoted. Therefore in addition to the cost of selling 'in' to distributors there may be further support costs in helping and persuading distributors to sell 'out'. Selling-in costs will themselves vary widely as between making single large scale negotiations with central multiples, and making sales calls on thousands of small shops throughout the country.

When all estimates have been made, it is a straightforward matter to work out sales times margins less costs by each alternative method and see which promises the best net result.

Intangibles

At the same time, the intangibles must not be overlooked. Alternative distribution channels may appear to produce similar financial results, but the more direct method might offer an additional advantage in closer control over the market place, and a sounder base from which to launch new products in future. Or a channel which offers a lower return in the short term might be one which provides a higher market share, greater exposure to the public, and thus better prospects for expansion. All intangibles will in the end reveal themselves in terms of financial reward, but it is as well to cross check that they have not been left out of the financial calculations.

PLANNING FOR DISTRIBUTION

Obtaining distribution channels for a product or range of products should not be looked on as a secondary matter which can be attended to once all arrangements for the presentation of the product to its users have been perfected. Except in the specific case where the manufacturer proposes to contact all users directly – as by mail order, or through own sales force – the product will only ever reach its users if the appropriate trade distributors choose to take it on. Many of the features of the product designed to appeal to users will do so only through the active participation of the trade. The appearance, performance and quality of the product will impress potential users only if the trade stocks it and allows them to see it. Its attractive price to the user depends on the trade accepting the margin proposed. Sales promotion schemes will work only if the trade cooperates. Only media advertising allows a manufacturer to appeal to his potential users directly; all other aspects of consumer marketing depend on trade participation.

Dual marketing strategies

Launching a product successfully through distribution channels therefore demands a dual marketing strategy aimed both at the intended user and at the trade sector chosen for distribution. Financial calculations will have shown which method of distribution should be the most advantageous; it remains to select the individual distributor organizations or groups or sectors most suitable for giving the product the exposure it requires. As trade outlets become concentrated into a smaller number of large organizations, it is vital to succeed in appealing to the ones whose cooperation is counted on. The absence of even one large organization from the distribution plan may mean the loss of a substantial part of the user market.

The trade's interest in a product line depends essentially on two things: the trade margin offered, and the extent to which the trade thinks the product will appeal to users. Thus an advertising campaign addressed to potential users should not overlook the secondary aim of impressing the trade as well as with the effect it will have on their customers.

A customer marketing plan culminates in an estimate of the volume which will be sold to users. It is essential to cross check this with the corresponding volumes which will have to be handled through each distribution channel and to consider whether these volumes are in turn feasible. What do these volumes imply in terms of:

1 The numbers of outlets that would have to handle the product
2 The stock availability required
3 Display, storage and servicing facilities
4 The level of finance needed from the trade?

Distribution implications may therefore bring realism to consumer marketing plans, or at least provide throughput targets per channel for regular monitoring.

Working out a strategy for achieving distribution through the channels chosen should be thought of as marketing to the trade, and given as much priority as the strategy for consumer marketing which it is designed to complement. Only through joint marketing plans for both trade and consumer can a product attain maximum success in reaching its targets.

FURTHER READING

Foster, D., *Mastering Marketing*, Macmillan, London, 1982

Lawrence, A., *The Management of Trade Marketing*, Gower, Aldershot, 1983

Stapleton, J., *Marketing*, Hodder and Stoughton, Sevenoaks, 1985

Wilmshurst, J., *The Fundamentals and Practice of Marketing*, Institute of Marketing, Heinemann, London 1978

19 Overseas marketing

Sydney Paulden

There are many companies that derive the major part of their business from overseas markets. There are others that export a smaller part of their production but generate a higher rate of profit on exported goods than on goods sold in the domestic market. However, the factor that is common to all companies that export successfully is the commitment that they make to their overseas markets. Failures, and they can be costly, occur when export markets are only turned to in times of emergency, when overseas buyers suddenly appear to be lifesavers during severe recessions on the home market. Export marketing requires a long-term commitment. It requires the support of senior management. It must be allocated the resources, in management, manpower and investment, commensurate with the volume of business that a company regards as feasible. This means, therefore, that the overseas markets have to be approached on similar lines to those described in earlier chapters for the domestic scene. Business from foreign buyers should be part of the corporate strategy, targets must be defined as the result of research, and resources must be allocated in order to achieve the targets. There must also be the same lead time as for the opening of any type of domestic market, or possibly a longer lead time. Disappointments often occur in overseas markets simply because senior management despatches a salesman on an overseas sales trip and judges the potential or the performance by the orders brought back in the salesman's briefcase. Yet this approach would hardly be regarded as adequate for the testing of a brand new market at home, unless it was the launch of a miracle product.

Overseas marketing, therefore, is usually best left to a time when a company has established itself on the home market when there is less likelihood of a shortage of management time or of capital. The export 'pipeline' is longer than that for domestic transactions. It can take longer to become established, longer to deliver goods and to receive payments. Communications are more stretched, after-sales service more critical, so that it is all the more vital for possible teething troubles with a new company or a new product to have been overcome before launching into overseas territories.

MARKET SELECTION

Once a company knows that it has a product suitable for export and once it has checked that it has sufficient capacity for growth into export markets on a long-term basis, then the moment has come for selection of priority markets overseas. It is rare for a launch to be successfully carried out into many foreign markets simultaneously. Resources have to be focused on those areas that are likely to yield the most immediate returns.

It is stressed again and again in export marketing literature that it is essential for exporters to travel in person to their overseas markets. That is undeniably true, but it is also true that an enormous amount of effort and money can be wasted by hurrying to foreign territories without sufficient advance preparation. The first essential is to carry out so-called 'desk research' at home in order to identify the initial target markets, picking, from the 150 or more potential new territories, those that stand the best chance of being profitable.

Desk research

This encompasses any relevant published material that can help to create a picture of market conditions and opportunities; and also includes visits within the home market to any organizations that can provide an insight into trading overseas. There are usually scores of possible sources of data and assistance. They include government export service bodies, clearing banks, merchant banks, branches of banks from the overseas markets, specialist libraries, trade associations, general chambers of commerce, as well as those chambers relating to particular foreign territories.

The data can take the form of market surveys, bulletins, reports from trade missions that have visited the territories, statistics on exports to the overseas territories, statistics on the overseas territories' imports from the world at large. (Some suppliers from second and third markets might be supplying your type of goods, even if there is little export from your own country.) It is also frequently possible to obtain catalogues of competitive product lines that are available on the foreign markets through the services of the trade commissioners at overseas embassies, enabling the would-be exporter to compare quality, design and even price.

Newspaper articles and surveys should not be forgotten. The national press and trade papers frequently review prospects in different overseas markets, giving a broad or a specialist analysis of a country's economy, imports and future plans.

There is a growing array of computerized bibliographic databases that give access to an astonishing range of information of immediate interest to the export market researcher. Several organizations, for example, offer the facility to use one's own desk-top terminal to read the world's newspapers – *Financial Times, The Guardian, The Washington Post*, and so on – selecting articles from the previous three months, one year or even three years, and searching by any combination of keywords one pleases. An example might be to tap in the words: *Australia, schools, re-equip, construction.* The screen then gives a list of newspaper articles that have included any or all of these words. It is then possible to tap in a number in order to call up the article in question to be read on the screen. In this way, up-to-date leads can be gleaned for the sale of schoolbooks or educational laboratory apparatus to new establishments planned for Australia. Databases can thus enable a researcher to do in minutes from his desk what would otherwise take days and days of work in a number of different libraries, or might otherwise necessitate an expensive field trip abroad.

A fascinating exercise is to pinpoint some easily obtainable statistic that can give a valuable guide to the potential market for your product range. A company selling graphite, for example, was able to relate the use of sulphuric acid to the need for its products. Although there were virtually no statistics available on the purchase of graphite products, figures could fairly easily be obtained for consumption of sulphuric acid by industry worldwide, broken down by country, and this led directly to the largest potential markets. A leather shoe manufacturer was also able to obtain details of the sale of shoe polish in a country and this gave an immediate guide to the volume of shoe sales and the shoe colours that were popular.

In desk research the trick is not only to identify markets that have been using your products in volume, but also, and even better, to spot those that are about to embark on a much greater use of them. It might then be possible to move into a new market before competitors have become too strongly established there. In today's world, markets can change very rapidly and even the veteran exporters might be missing an opportunity that the newcomer can spot.

In this decade, oil has been a significant influence on the buying power of countries. Oil producers have had more money to spend as the revenue per barrel has increased, and oil consumers have had proportionately less to spend on other imports. Then, as the oil price has dropped, so money has become tight in the previously oil-rich countries, but opportunities have grown for business in the non-oil markets.

Even in the most debt-ridden nations, there can be opportunities for sound business. The knack is to identify products that just have to be imported. These can include military supplies (and remember that Kruschev once pointed out that the buttons that hold up soldiers' trousers are military supplies), spares and raw materials for basic industries, plant for major new development projects and essential foodstuffs. One 'military order' was a batch of violin strings for the band of the Thai army.

It is even possible to get credit insurance cover for exports to otherwise non-creditworthy countries if the export is considered 'in the national interest' of the exporting country; i.e. it is considered essential to keep out competitors for the future or maintain friendly relations with a strategically placed ally.

Aid funds

Desk research can easily identify countries in which the supranational aid agencies have continued faith and to whom they are making substantial loans. A multi-million dollar project, funded by aid, can encompass a wide range of supplies. It can generate a need for temporary housing for the thousands of workers on site for several years. It can demand catering equipment, earthmoving machinery, communications apparatus, training materials, water treatment facilities, and so on, in addition to the turbines or textile machinery or whatever special plant is needed for the project itself.

Cost saving

The point about desk research is that it is less costly to dig for data at the home market end than in the overseas territory; especially when the exporter might be making a bee-line for the wrong territory, anyway. First select the target markets, then check every possible aspect before travelling there; and make sure that every trip is well prepared, with introductions to useful contacts prior to flying from home. Hotel bills, food, local travel and entertainment expenses can be very high, even in the apparently poorer areas of the world. In fact, often the poorer countries cost more *per diem*, because the traveller simply cannot risk living cheaply. It is essential to stay at the best hotels and eat in the best restaurants, whereas a seasoned traveller might well know his way to using more modest facilities in a market such as the US, say, or Germany, where the range of suitable accommodation is much wider.

It should also be remembered that a wasted trip not only costs money and time; it might also cause such disappointment that the whole approach to export marketing can wind down as a result, losing a company all the potential that could exist in the right markets.

PREPARATION OF A SALES/RESEARCH TOUR

It is usually cost-effective to plan a sales-cum-research trip to a group of markets rather than to a single market. However, it is also wise to guard against taking in too many new territories on one tour. A businessman can tire after a given time away from home and from then on there is less and less value to be gained from each successive market visited. A rough survey of a number of different exporters suggests that five weeks is probably the limit to a foreign tour, that three weeks is probably optimum for distant markets (over 8 hours' flight, say), whilst one working week of five or six days is not a bad idea for markets closer to hand (3 to 8 hours' flight). One or two days are frequently allocated to a visit to a market no more than 2 hours away. It is a trade-off between making use of the money spent on the longer flights and keeping alert and enthusiastic whilst away. Also, it has to be remembered that a trip is not ended when the businessman arrives home. The real finish only comes when all the leads have been followed up; when the information requested by people met on the trip has been collected and despatched; when letters and telexes have been sent to confirm arrangements; when people back at head office or at the factory have been briefed on what they have to do to meet orders, prepare prototypes or set up a marketing channel for the new markets.

One common failing in preparing a foreign sales tour is to neglect to allocate sufficient time for tying up all these ends at the finish of the actual travelling. There is always a huge pile of accumulated work on the desk awaiting the returning traveller and then the true value of the trip can be lost due to neglect of the follow-up.

Once the main target markets have been defined for a visit, an agenda for the trip should be drawn up. A possible checklist of such an agenda might be:

1 Identify current and future size of market for product range
2 Identify methods of distribution to major buyers
3 Shortlist suitable agents or distributors
4 Appoint or interview potential agent
5 Check competitive prices, trade credit terms and product quality
6 Check best method of carriage of goods (air, sea, road)
7 Double check any technical or import tariff complications
8 Meet major buyers in person

To achieve these objectives, within a reasonable time to be spent in the field, a lot of groundwork must be done before departure. The businessman should have arranged appointments with, say, the trade officials at his embassy, with officers of the relevant chamber of commerce, with local banks, trade associations and so on. It is often a good idea to fill the first two or three days with pre-arranged appointments, leaving plenty of spare time in a market to follow up the leads that arise on the spot. Markets and opportunities always look very different once one is there, compared with the view that might be created from afar. This is the whole point of making the trip in person.

OVERSEAS SALES AGENTS

Much more than half the world's international trade is conducted through agents of one kind or another. The selection and management of agents in overseas markets is the key to success. A common failing is for a would-be exporter to appoint the first agent who approaches him and then to leave the market in the hands of the agent, complaining later if the market does not live up to its potential.

The prime objective of most first visits to overseas markets is to find and appoint the best possible form of representation. To do this, the exporter must first have a detailed picture of the market, so that he can devise the best strategy and then home in on an agent that fits it. The following factors will greatly influence the choice of a representative in a market.

Geography

It is seldom wise to give an agent in one country the rights to business in another country, even though this might appear to be a very convenient arrangement. It is rare, for example, for Finns to welcome US or British goods sold to them through an agency in Sweden, or for Thais to feel easy about buying through Malaysia.

Nor can it be assumed that a single agent is capable of representing an exporter's interests in the whole of the agent's own country. There can frequently be problems relating to local geography or traditional distribution channels, or even ethnic and language barriers. The USA and West Germany, for example, are very fragmented markets, being federal countries with a lot of trade focused on the different commercial centres in each separate state or *Land*. Very few agents would have the necessary contacts in each part of the country where the exporter might have a big potential market. New York salesmen can rarely cover the rich markets of California. A Hamburg firm is not likely to spend a lot of time selling in Munich or Nuremberg. Similarly, there could be problems in even a tiny country such as Belgium, where there are linguistic and commercial differences arising from the divide between Flemish and French-speaking buyers.

On the other hand, there are often areas that are regarded regionally as centres of trade, where representatives can cover a wider field. Hong Kong and Singapore, for example, are seen in the East as professional trading centres and, being very small territories, have developed traders who are often capable of tackling other neighbouring markets on behalf of principals. Singapore-based agencies often take on the rights for Malaysia and Indonesia. However, it is vital for an exporter to check how acceptable this arrangement might be – not with the agent, but with the potential customers. How do they view it? And has the agency the resources to cover more than one territory?

Customer contacts

Is the market for the product range segmented? If so, can a single agent tap each segment effectively? Some products or services might have applications in industry and at the same time find outlets through retail trade stores (hand tools for example); or a product might have two very distinct market segments, such as the construction industry and the vehicle repair industry, or the original equipment industry and the spares and replacement trade. The distribution channels feeding these industries and trade might differ from one market to another. Can one importer cope or should there be two?

Size of representation

Exporters very often face the agony of decision between a potential agent who is well established but who handles scores of different product lines, and the new firm that is hungry for business. One has the age-old contacts and reputation, but may not give a new line very much attention. The other will have to spend time building up contacts and might also have problems in financing his expansion. There is no rule-of-thumb guide to this problem. It is the exporter's decision, but it is well to be aware that the problem exists and give it thought. Often, the newcomer to an overseas market does not have the choice, as the older agencies already have competitive lines on their books. More and more, however, in the rapidly developing territories, young capable staff are leaving the older agencies and setting up their own, and these go-getters welcome the chance to prove themselves with a new principal. Again, these people can rarely be identified from afar in the home market. It takes a personal visit to the territory to track them down.

Service facilities

Service is often a function of size of representation. If a product requires substantial technical back-up or personal attention, the exporter has to be satisfied that the representation appointed in a market has the capability to provide the service *in all the corners of the market that are allocated as his territory*. Does the agent cover these remoter areas effectively? Can the potential customers be expected to communicate with the agent's headquarters?

FINANCIAL CONSIDERATIONS

Export finance is covered in Chapter 6 of this handbook but it is very necessary to look at finance as part of the export marketing strategy. There are two important aspects to be considered. First, there is the question of financing export business, seen from the exporter's own point of view. Second, there is the financing of exports seen from the point of view of the buyer. How attractive are the financial terms to him, compared with offers from other exporters or from domestic suppliers within his own territory?

Financing exports

The problem is that exporting has a lengthy pipeline and there can be a long period between production of the goods and receipt of final payment. The situation can be aggravated by one of the rosier aspects of exporting – the average size of order from overseas is frequently much bigger than that from the home market. Importers often place orders for a whole territory, whereas home orders are for tiny pieces of a market. It is usually economic for foreign buyers to purchase in larger units, because of transport costs. Long credit terms are also the fashion in exporting, due to the fierce competition between the exporting nations of the world. A foreign importer might expect 120 days, whereas a home market transaction might assume 30 or 60 days.

Export finance facilities exist that can transform the credit sale into a cash sale. Naturally, they imply a discount and so the exporter must investigate these facilities prior to quoting a final price to the foreign buyer, as the cost of finance may have to be built into the price to be paid by the overseas importer. It is a common complaint in financial circles that exporters too often land an order and only then run to the financial experts for help in handling the credit – to find that they cannot afford services that would otherwise have been ideal.

There is a whole host of export finance services and this is obviously a critical topic that must be studied carefully in relation to the type of business on hand. Exporters should call on the services of financial specialists. However, it is possible to provide a very brief review of some of the possibilities, so that the exporter can appreciate how important it is to study the topic further and also how the financial side can affect the pricing of export orders and even the approach to a market.

Credit insurance

Export credit can be insured through an exporter's official bodies, such as the Export Credits Guarantee Department (ECGD) in the UK. This form of insurance in the UK not only provides cover against possible default by the foreign buyer after he has received the goods and against political risks (the foreign government stopping all foreign payments, for example) but can often be used to raise money at favourable rates of interest. Invoices for exported goods covered by credit insurance can often be used as collateral to support an overdraft at the bank.

In the UK the private sector is beginning to offer services in credit insurance either in competition with ECGD or in conjunction with ECGD. Trade Indemnity, the company known for insurance against bad debt on the domestic market, has launched policies that cover customer default in foreign markets and also political risk. It is also possible, through a broker, to have political risk for specific shipments insured by a Lloyds underwriter. A company called Unicol offers exporters the opportunity to become insured through its umbrella policy with ECGD. Each insurer will look at a proposal and accept it, amend it or reject it depending on its own circumstances and its own view of the risk, so it does not mean that if an exporter is refused cover by one that he will be refused by them all. The proliferation of services makes it possible to shop around for the best deal.

Factoring

There is a growing range of export factoring services. These mainly apply to companies that have a large number of export deliveries to a wide range of overseas buyers on open account, with up to, say, a maximum of 90 or

120 days credit. The factoring company, often the subsidiary of a major bank, can provide two distinct services. One is the management of the export sales ledger, sending reminders to the foreign buyers and taking responsibility for insurance of the debt and for collection of the payments, permitting the exporter to concentrate on sales and production. The second service is the provision of working capital, by remitting a given monthly sum to the exporter that is an average of what can be expected back from foreign payments. This enables the exporter to plan his cash flow programme, ironing out the unpredictable nature of foreign receipts.

Forfaiting

This is a service whereby a finance house buys the debt from an exporter at a discount immediately on shipment of the goods. The exporter has his money in the bank just as with a cash transaction. Payment is in the home currency, no matter which hard currency has been used for the invoice. The exporter then has no exposure to currency exchange risks during the period of credit. This technique is valuable for one-off transactions for capital goods of some substantial value.

Confirming

A confirming house can greatly assist an exporter in setting up a financial package for a foreign buyer that provides the buyer with good credit terms and the exporter with immediate cash for his consignments. The confirming house can *contract with the buyer* to provide a loan to purchase the goods in the buyer's own currency with a favourable term of credit. This loan is then used to pay the exporter on shipment in his own currency. The exporter is relieved of the exchange risk, of the risk of default and of the problem of financing the term of credit.

Marketing tool

These services can be used by the exporter as a marketing tool, because nowadays the financial package that accompanies the offer of goods can rank in importance with quality, delivery and price. In the developing countries, particularly, buyers aim to finance the purchase of foreign goods or equipment from the profits made with the goods during the period of credit. The financial services available to the exporter can enable him to tailor a package to suit the needs of the buyer and his own need for funds.

One warning should be sounded, however. Export finance almost always relates exclusively to the financing of post-shipment credit and does not make life easier for the exporter who needs funds to expand his production in order to produce the goods for export. This kind of pre-shipment finance is only available in connection with huge capital plant contracts, where foreign buyers might be expected to agree to stage payments during manufacture.

Instruments of payment

Documentation for shipment and for payment is an area of exporting that requires careful attention. Again, it needs study with the assistance of financial experts from a bank or consultancy to ascertain the best means of payment and of raising the documents. Strangely enough, the most common form of transaction is open account exporting, just as in domestic marketing. The supplier sends an invoice and expects payment within an agreed time limit of 30, 60 or so days. The exporter must, however, be sure that the buyer is creditworthy and reliable and should carry out checks through specialist agencies and banks.

However, there are still very large numbers of export transactions that require special payment documentation, particularly on sales to the non-industrialized countries. Documentation has to cover insurance (of carriage and of credit), customs regulations, transportation requirements, and methods of payment.

It is an appalling truth that over 50 per cent of claims on insurance and over 25 per cent of documents lodged for payment with banks have errors or omissions that seriously delay handling of the transactions. These delays add to the cost of exporting and can erode profit margins, so it is essential for exporters to set up systems that ensure accuracy and expertise in producing documentation. Help is available through the banks and also through the government services that provide advice for exporters. There are specially devised 'aligned documentation systems' that ensure that once a basic document has been prepared with all the relevant data, then there are no errors in transcribing that information to the various different forms that have to be produced from it.

Nowadays, it is necessary to think in terms of a computer for the production of complex documentation. It might take a while (usually longer than you expect) to get the computer working effectively, but it is worth the effort, because once the first set of data on a contract has been fed into the machine, then it will be possible to use it again and again for every subsequent set of documents required without the possibility of introducing errors. The computer can also be programmed to ensure that no documentation is omitted or overlooked.

The avoidance of delays in payment, the certainty of getting paid resulting from accurate and complete documentation can make computerization a rewarding investment. Literally millions of pounds of payments are lost and even more millions of pounds of unnecessary interest is paid on late receipts every year in the UK alone. The semi-Government organization, SITPRO (Simplification of Transport Procedures), has developed a software package for the handling of export documentation expressly to avoid these problems.

Letters of credit

Letters of credit (l/c's) are a common form of payment arrangement in exporting that are often misunderstood or misused. A letter of credit is a document that is signed by the importer or buyer, giving a bank instructions to pay the exporter when the exporter has performed to the terms of the sales contract. The exporter proves his performance with the presentation of documents that are enumerated in the letter of credit. They are likely to be bills of lading, certificates of origin, and so on, to show that the right kind of product has been dispatched by the agreed form of transport by the due date.

A letter of credit is given by the importer to his local bank. The bank then guarantees that the funds are available to pay on performance. This then makes the l/c an *irrevocable* letter of credit, as the bank has the importer's funds available to pay the exporter as soon as the right documents have been presented. The buyer cannot revoke payment provided that the exporter carries out the correct procedure.

The local bank can pass the l/c to a bank in the country of the exporter. This bank can then *confirm* that it will pay the exporter on sight of the correct documents, or within an agreed period of credit after receipt of the completed documents. This then makes the l/c a *confirmed* irrevocable letter of credit – in other words, the exporter's bank will pay even if the buyer's bank goes bust. It is a very safe way of ensuring payment according to contract, but only if the exporter's documents are in good shape. If even one tiny discrepancy arises, the banks in the middle will not be authorized to pay on behalf of the buyer and the exporter is then vulnerable – the goods may have been despatched and there is no certainty of payment.

CONCLUSION

Export marketing brings in its wake an obvious spread of complications in relation to transport, communications, pricing, credit, financing and cash collection. That is precisely why it is advisable to enter the field in a planned and gradual way, so that the international scene is opened up steadily, market by market. This gives the chance to a company's management to digest the market, exploit it effectively and iron out problems on the way. The best way to learn is to get the maximum amount of advice to avoid obvious pitfalls and then gain personal experience. Expertise can readily be accumulated.

A steady, regulated approach to export marketing does not mean an inordinately slow entry. The words 'steady and regulated' are relative. They can suggest a new market every two years to a company whose marketing cycle is lengthy, or a new territory every three months to one that has an easily shipped product with no service or back-up complications. It is still vital, however, to get pricing right, to get the right representation locally and to ensure reliable receipt of payments. No export contract is complete until payment is in the bank, providing a profit on the transaction.

The steady entry into overseas markets demands an allied development of management facilities. There are those companies that have a brisk early success but whose export performance falls off as they fail to relieve the salesman of the administration that builds up as a consequence of his very success. In-house administration and documentation facilities have to be provided, or outside services hired, to ensure that the successful export salesman is kept free of encumbrance. It is a surprising and illogical fact that the average export salesman is expected to produce a turnover about ten times greater than his home market equivalent and that he normally has less than half the back-up of the domestic salesman. Cinderella treatment eventually leads to declining success.

A salesman might be allocated the task of identifying and opening a string of new markets. Then it might be necessary to appoint area or regional salesmen to specialize in groups of markets, supporting and monitoring agents in several territories; for example, in the five markets of ASEAN, or the four agents located in the USA and Mexico, or the three or four markets of Scandinavia or possibly there might be one man supervising sales for the whole of West Europe.

The product quality, price and the reliable performance of the exporting company are vital ingredients in export success, but there is no denying the enormous impact of the personality of the export salesman, the relationships he creates with agents and buyers and his dedication to his territories. Personal relationships seem more vital to success in overseas marketing because a market is linked to the company very much more through the single contact of the regular salesman. On the home market, a buyer is exposed to a large number of contacts with a supplier. He is likely to see more salesmen, to see management more often, to read of a company in the local press, see its advertising and so on. Links between supplier and overseas market are much more restricted as a general rule, putting all the more responsibility for success on the performance of the salesman. And his performance will be influenced by the kind of support he receives from the company at home.

FURTHER READING

Branch, A.E., *The Elements of Export Practice*, Chapman and Hall, London, 1979

Horten, H.E., *Export-import Correspondence in Four Languages: English, French, German and Spanish*, Gower, Aldershot, 1970

Katz, B., *Managing Export Marketing*, Gower, Aldershot, 1987

Livingstone, J.M., *International Marketing Management*, Macmillan, London, 1976

Noonan, C., *Practical Export Management*, Allen & Unwin, London, 1985

Paulden, S., *How to Deliver on Time*, Gower, Aldershot, 1977

In addition, *Export Times* is a monthly newspaper, published in the UK, which deals with problems and opportunities for export marketing.

20 Managing a sales force

M T Wilson

The strategy of marketing is concerned with arranging the resources of the company so that the needs of customers can be satisfied by presenting to them a product/price offering which when purchased provides a profit to the firm. This strategy is implemented through a number of tactical tools, some concerned with finding out what the needs are (marketing research), some with ensuring the product/price offering is correct (product development and testing), and some with presenting the offering to the customer. The sales function is a major tactic in this last area, while having a role to play in the first two.

The importance of the sales function cannot be over-emphasized in those companies where the bulk of the presentational effort is carried by the sales force. This covers most industrial and speciality markets and many consumer goods industries. In fact, it is not exaggerating far to say that in some markets – for example, office equipment and life insurance – the main difference between competing companies lies in the quality of their sales forces.

Moreover, the sales force can make valuable contributions in the definition of market segments and customer needs, and product development and rationalization. This is particularly true in industrial markets, where formal market research is less used. Obviously, since salesmen are not usually trained researchers, the information they collect has to be treated with care.

As sales management is a function (often the most important) within the marketing strategy, it is essential for the sales manager at least to be aware of the other tactics of marketing so that he can contribute to and benefit from them. These include:

1 New product development
2 Distribution
3 Sales forecasting
4 Pricing

5 Advertising and sales promotion
6 Public relations
7 Marketing planning and control (particularly the financial aspects).

In some companies the sales manager will directly control some of these; in others, they will be looked after by marketing staff. In every firm, the sales manager must integrate his activities with the rest of the marketing effort if the maximum value is to be gained from marketing expenditure.

The sales manager is the key man in developing a successful sales operation. He must do this by managing his team – not by doing their jobs for them. As a manager he is responsible for working through others to achieve economic objectives, but this process is hindered by the difficulties of dealing with geographically spread subordinates who spend most of their time with people other than their colleagues.

To do his job successfully, the sales manager must possess knowledge and skill in four major areas: selling, management, sales management and marketing. Only then can he claim to be a fully productive member of the executive team.

Sales management comprises five key elements – planning, organization, training, motivation and control. It is on these that this chapter concentrates.

HOW TO PLAN THE SALES OPERATION

The planning process is only one part of the basic and repetitive management activity necessary in any company seeking to grow. The firm must continuously answer three questions:

1 Where are we going? This is the objective-setting process
2 How shall we get there? This is the planning process
3 How shall we know if we are getting there? This is the control process.

These questions first appear at top management level and the answers constitute the corporate objectives, corporate plans and policies, and corporate control mechanisms. Typically they will result in a statement of the profit objectives of the company (usually expressed in terms of return on capital employed), a description of the business the company is in and its desired position in that industry, its plans and policies for each function of the company, and specific goals and targets to be met within set time-periods.

The whole process will then be repeated for each function of the company. Thus marketing, production, R and D, finance and so on, will each formulate its objectives, plans and controls. Within the marketing framework, the sales manager must specify his answers to the three questions in order to produce a format for his staff to work to. Each salesman may well be required to repeat the process with individual customers.

The sales manager's role in the continuum is obviously critical. If he fails to set clear objectives that are compatible within the hierarchy and does not initiate the appropriate action, the whole firm must suffer.

Setting sales objectives

The sales manager will commence by considering the marketing objectives, policies and strategies and control criteria. He will probably have a forecast of sales by revenue and volume, a forecast of gross profit required, perhaps an expense budget, a description of the product range available with additions and deletions, price structure, promotional support, etc.

Forecasting sales

In many firms the sales manager will be involved as a member of the marketing team in the definition of these items. The process will normally start with forecasting sales for the next period. This is the most critical prediction in the company as it will determine the production schedule, raw materials and finished stocks, promotional expenditure, etc. It is best to approach the forecast in two stages. First, what will sales be, assuming all variables in the situation are the same in the future as they have been in the past? Second, which variables will change and what will the impact be? Some of the variables will be internal factors which management decides to change; others will be external factors which are uncontrollable by the company but whose effect must be predicted.

Developing the sales plan

Having set the sales forecast and targets, the manager must now consider how they can be achieved. Obviously some thought will already have been given to the plan in formulating the objectives. After the plan is written it might well be necessary to reconsider the goals that were previously identified.

The sales manager has to consider five basic questions:

1 What is to be sold?
2 To whom?
3 At what price?
4 By what methods?
5 At what costs?

In some of these areas, notably the product range and pricing structure, he may well have limited influence; they are often controlled by the marketing planning department, through a brand or product management structure. In respect of all five he will certainly have to consider the inputs of other parts of the business. What stocks will be available from production, what money is available from finance, what advertising and sales promotion support is planned, etc.?

Deciding what is to be sold

In determining what the product range should be the sales manager can at least advise his marketing planning colleagues on the saleability of the various items in the range as well as new product requirements.

From a sales management viewpoint he will have to decide whether the full range should be sold to everybody. In some capital equipment markets, for example, where the distributor has to make a heavy investment in stock, it may not be in the interests of the company to supply dealers whose resources may not be adequate to finance the more costly products. Likewise, companies who have to make after-sales service arrangements may well decide not to sell products to customers who are geographically isolated.

To whom are the products to be sold

Next, the sales manager must consider the customers and prospects for his products. First, he will study the existing markets and decide whether business with them is likely to increase, decrease or remain static. This judgement will be based on a study of previous buying records.

By analysing customers in terms of their potential and actual purchasing of the various products he has to offer, he can identify the areas to be attacked. Prospective customers can be analysed in the same way.

Choosing the methods

Having identified from the product/market analysis the segments to be attacked, the sales manager can now consider the methods most likely to achieve the objectives set.

The first question to be answered is – what sort of service should the sales force provide in order to influence the buyer? For example, a crop-protection firm pondering how to increase sales to agricultural merchants will have to consider how the merchant will market the product to farmers. Perhaps the job of the sales force in this case will be to help the merchant develop his skills.

Such an analysis of the kind of sales effort needed will lead to identification of the appropriate sales methods. The complexity of seller/buyer relationships becomes rapidly obvious. It is only by such definition that the sales manager can develop the presentational approach that will enable him to succeed in the face of product/price parity.

Having identified the nature of the sales method he can then consider the scale of effort required. He must calculate how many customers and prospects should be called on how often.

The customers are relatively easy to specify because obviously they are known by name to the company. The level of prospecting is more difficult to calculate; as in many companies potential customers cannot be identified by name. At least, however, the sales manager can indicate the characteristics of likely prospects. Such a profile can then be used by the sales force to select prospects to be called upon. Alternatively, the sales manager can plan simply to allow a certain percentage of time or calls for seeking new business, giving the salesmen the responsibility of using the time or calls wisely.

How often calls should be made is always difficult to assess. Obviously different categories of accounts will require different call frequencies. In some trades where there is an established buying pattern, usually little is gained by calling at a different frequency.

The support of the field force will also be covered by the sales manager's study of the methods required to achieve his objectives. Parts of the supplier/buyer relationship can often be more economically handled by techniques other than personal visiting by representatives. Telephone selling is one method that is successfully used to handle routine ordering, thus freeing the salemen's costly time for more creative work.

Evaluating the costs of selling

The best approach is to look at the cost-effectiveness of the methods used and particularly to try to analyse the values gained for the costs incurred. For example, if the manager were concerned with the cost of generating prospects he could compare the cost per prospect from advertising, direct mail and cold canvassing. If he were analysing sales force activity, he might question what value was gained from 'courtesy calling' (i.e. routine visiting to check that the customer is satisfied with the products and service supplied). In such a case the manager might experiment by eliminating such calls in a test area and evaluating what, if anything, happened to the sales.

HOW TO ORGANIZE THE SALES FORCE

Many sales organizations have developed without objective analysis of their purpose or structure. Today they are out of date and unable to fulfil the purposes for which they were originally designed. This is because the traditional hierarchical structure is based upon conditions which no longer hold true in a great number of firms. Such organizations assume that there is a large number of relatively small, geographically separate and independent buying-points all with similar requirements, and that these can be serviced by a large number of geographically separated salesmen who can perform similar tasks and who represent the major promotional activity of the company.

Changes in buyer/seller relationships

The foregoing suppositions have been made obsolete by two fundamental changes in the buyer/seller relationship.

First, the buying power in many industries is no longer evenly distributed. In a large number of markets, a few big firms control the majority of the purchasing decisions. These oligopolies, developed largely through the processes of merger and acquisition, have resulted in a dramatic reduction in the numbers of independent outlets in the trades concerned. Thus, whilst sales organizations' structures have in many cases changed little, the number and type of customers with whom they deal have altered dramatically.

Second, the development of new marketing techniques has meant that some tasks traditionally performed by the sales force can be more economically or efficiently handled by other methods. The development of advertising and sales promotion in general, as well as the growing use of specific techniques such as telephone selling and contract ordering, have all had an impact on the nature and scale of the sales effort required. Furthermore, the reduction in sales force sizes and improvements in communications have in some cases obviated the need for regionally based management.

The prime objective of all salesmen is to gain business. From an organizational point of view, however, how they are to achieve their goals must be defined in order to identify what kind and quality of skills are required.

Matching the sales effort to customer requirements

Organizing the sales effort so that it matches the reality of the market place can alleviate such problems. First, the level and quantity of customer service must be defined and the personnel concerned identified.

Such an analysis will also begin to identify the work-loads of each level and suggest ways of grouping the various elements so that they can be better managed.

The sales force structure should also be scrutinized. A geographical split may be the most economical in that travel time is minimized. It may not, however, be the most effective. In one glass-container company it was seen that the prime service to be provided to the buyer was a technical knowledge of bottling as applied to the customer's particular industry. Thus the sales force was regrouped on an industry basis, changing the organization structure. Obviously there was some increase in travel costs because each industry group worked nationally but this was more than offset by the increase in sales.

At sales force level common groupings other than geographical are by industry, by customer size category, by buyer type (for example, purchasers and specificers), or by service to be provided (for example, order taking and merchandising).

By conducting a customer service requirements analysis the sales manager can identify which organizational approach is appropriate.

The number of salesmen needed

The aim of building an organization is to give the appropriate level of service to each customer and the appropriate amount of work to each man. The only factor common to all salesmen is the number of working hours and this should be the starting point for a work-load analysis, which is the only really logical way of constructing a sales force. The amount of work per salesman can then be calculated by assessing the elements and the time taken on each. Typically, they include: prospecting, travelling, waiting, selling and report writing. If the number of actual and potential accounts to be visited and the frequency of visiting can be assessed, it is possible to calculate the number of salesmen needed as follows:

$$\frac{\text{Number of actual and potential customers} \times \text{Call frequency}}{\text{Average daily call rate} \times \text{Number of working days per year}}$$

TRAINING THE SALES TEAM

The art of selling is the presentation of product benefits in such a way that the buyer is persuaded that his needs will be satisfied. If the salesman is to be successful he must not only be knowledgeable about his product and his customer but also skilful in the presentation of this knowledge.

Induction training

When a new salesman joins a company he should be given some form of training. Too often, even when training is given, the whole time is devoted to company and product knowledge in the hope (usually unfulfilled) that the salesman will somehow pick up sales techniques in the field.

This initial training can be critical to the ultimate success of the new man as it will affect both his ability and morale. It must therefore be very carefully planned and skilfully executed.

The programme material will obviously vary from firm to firm, particularly in terms of the company and product knowledge to be taught.

There are, however, some basic areas of the sales job that should be included in most initial training courses, although with specific biases being given by different companies. Ten major elements should be covered.

1 *The marketing concept and the role of the sales force.* The salesman must understand fully the part he plays in the total effort of the company. Otherwise he will find it difficult to integrate his work with that of other departments
2 *The nature of salesmanship.* It is essential that the salesman has a clear definition of what selling is, its role in society and the basic requirements of the sales job
3 *Communications.* As selling depends on persuasive communication, the salesman must understand the inherent difficulties of interpersonal relationships and be given techniques for overcoming these problems. He must be skilled in other forms of communication, such as reporting and talking on the telephone
4 *Preparation for selling.* This is normally a very weak area of sales skill and yet if a coherent, logical approach to the customer is to be adopted, it has to be structured in advance, and the technique for doing this has to be taught
5 *Prospecting.* Every business depends to some extent on gaining new customers. This is probably the most difficult part of selling and the salesman should be taught a systematic approach to the finding of

potential buyers. Having learnt how to look for new business, he will also be better motivated and less likely to avoid prospecting, as so often happens

6 *Opening the sales.* Obtaining interviews with buyers and making the right impression in the early stages of the presentation are areas where skill is required. A casual approach will lead to failure to pass the receptionist or even when that is achieved, to curtailed, unsuccessful interviews

7 *Making sales presentations.* To be effective as a persuader, the salesman must be skilled in oral presentation, visual aid handling and product demonstration. There is a body of techniques that can be learnt which will help the salesman to communicate convincingly

8 *Handling objections.* Every sales interview is likely to produce customer objections on such topics as price, delivery, etc. Some of these can be prevented, others overcome. Certainly most objections can be predicted and the salesman trained in the answers to be given and the methods of expressing them

9 *Closing the sale.* Again, this is normally a very weak area because the salesman fears rejection. He therefore tends to avoid it by never asking for the order. If he never asks the buyer to buy, the buyer never has to refuse. Obviously the whole point of selling is to gain sales and the salesman can be encouraged to request orders more often and more persuasively by thorough training in proven closing techniques

10 *Work organization.* The main emphasis of initial training is on improving the quality of the salesman's skill. Due regard should also be paid to the quantity of selling so that the man knows how to utilize his very limited time to the maximum. He should be taught techniques of journey planning and day planning.

Concept of customer orientation

Throughout the initial training programme certain themes will have to be constantly emphasized as some of the basic concepts are hard to instil. One of the most fundamental of these is the philosophy of customer orientation. Without this approach, the salesman will find it hard to succeed and yet it is difficult to ensure that it will be practised.

Every salesman must recognize that buyers buy to satisfy needs, both rational and emotional. These needs are fulfilled by benefits of the product and these benefits are derived from product features.

Because of the difficulty of reversing the viewpoint in this way, successful training in this concept can be hard to achieve. It is helped if a product analysis is demonstrated and this technique is inculcated so that the salesmen analyse the needs, benefits and features of a situation before they commence selling.

Field training

The objective of field training is to ensure a continuous improvement in the salesman's performance. To achieve this goal there are five tasks that must be carried out by the manager:

1 Field performance must be assessed systematically against known standards
2 Deficiencies must be identified and agreed and coaching given in the knowledge and skills necessary to correct the identified faults
3 Guidance must be given on the self-training that is expected from the salesman
4 Information should be collected about common faults that can be more economically or effectively corrected on a collective basis
5 The effectiveness of the initial training should be assessed so that it can be improved in the future.

Sales meetings

The regular gatherings of the sales team create the other major opportunity for developing sales force performance. In all but the smallest sales forces, these are held at local level, where the regional, area or district manager meets with his salesmen. Where there are no intermediate supervisory levels between the national sales manager and the sales force these gatherings have to be held on a national basis. The objectives of such meetings should be:

1 To administer corporate training and development
2 To inform and get feedback from the sales force
3 To stimulate and if necessary rekindle the salesmen's enthusiasm and motivation
4 To provide a meeting place and forum for all the salesmen.

HOW TO MOTIVATE THE SALES FORCE

The motivation of salesmen is probably the most common topic of conversation whenever sales managers meet. Every manager has his own pet theories on how to get the best out of his team. The reason why it is such a popular discussion point is because salesmen can be directly supervised only intermittently. It is therefore vital to success that they are deeply motivated to work on their own. Moreover, the sales job inevitably involves loneliness and certain customer contacts which can depress the morale of any but the most enthusiastic salesmen.

The nature of motivation

Because of the geographical separation and the wearing aspects of the job, it is vital for success that the sales manager possesses or develops the ability to motivate his men. In order to do so he needs a clear understanding of why people work and what they wish to gain from their work. Only then can he create an environment which will cause his men to apply their full abilities to their jobs.

Incentives and disincentives

The basis of motivation is the provision of incentives which encourage salesmen to give of their best and the removal of disincentives which prevent them from devoting their whole energies to their work. Unfortunately, far too often, motivation is equated with incentives only, although it is common to find that the elimination of disincentives – for example, unfair treatment – is the more powerful influence.

It must also be recognised that virtually every incentive brings with it a disincentive, either for the same person or for his colleagues. For example, a competition may be a strong motivation for the winners; but it can be demoralizing for the losers, particularly if they believe that because of the poor construction of the contest they never had a real chance of winning.

The task of the manager is therefore to consider the needs of his team, both individually and as a group, and to arrange a balance of motivational influences that will encourage them to achieve the company's objectives. In essence, this is best done by ensuring that the individual's own goals in life are consistent with the aims of the firm. For example, there is little point recruiting people who are highly money-motivated into a company which offers security as its major satisfaction.

Although recognizing that everyone has his own individual need pattern, there are five motivational influences that the sales manager must fully understand. These are:

1 Remuneration
2 Direct incentives
3 Job satisfaction
4 Security
5 Status.

Remuneration

First, management should define the salary grades appropriate to the job level. This grade will represent the market value of the position as well as the worth of the job to the company. The bottom of the category will represent the remuneration of a man entering the position exhibiting minimum standards of performance, the upper limit being paid to a man who can achieve completely all the criteria of the job.

Second, the position of any individual within his grade should be determined by his performance against the job standards. An average performer would therefore be paid at the mid-point of the grade. Thus, the salary philosophy will reflect the two main elements of a logical payment structure: the degree of responsibility carried by the position, and the effectiveness with which the man discharges it.

Payment by results system

Such an approach to job grading and appraisal presupposes that the salesman will be remunerated at least in part by salary. Many sales forces are of course paid in addition, to some degree or another, according to results. In a relatively small number of companies the salesmen are paid entirely on commission. The choice of remuneration system – salary only, salary plus some form of commission, or commission only – will depend upon the desired mix of security and incentive.

Direct incentives

This term is used to cover the many systems of payment in cash or in kind other than basic remuneration. It includes fringe benefits, merchandise awards, point schemes and competitions. Apart from fringe benefits, such schemes do not usually make a significant difference to total earnings and their basic intention is motivational. Merchandise awards and competitive schemes are best used to focus short-term attention on particular aspects of the business. They are a tactical rather than a strategic motivational weapon. When employed in this way, they can be very effective to concentrate sales force attention on, for example, gaining new accounts, increasing sales of lower volume products, or even submitting call reports on time!

Job satisfaction

Direct incentives in either cash or kind are important elements in any motivational scheme. The so-called 'psychic wages' of the job however must be given at least equivalent priority. Salesmen spend more than half their waking life working. It is not surprising therefore that they seek fulfilment in the job as well as rewards for the job. It is an essential function of any manager to ensure that such satisfaction can be gained by the sales force from their work.

Security

The need for security is a very common, although seldom admitted, motive. The nature of the remuneration system and the relative importance of salary and commission will obviously affect job security and must be considered from this aspect.

However, the less obvious facets of security should not escape the sales manager's attention. In companies where insecurity is a constant feature of the environment morale tends to be low and, although there is often an appearance of frenetic action, achievement is usually very limited.

Status

The sales manager can help to improve the status of selling within the company and the market by ensuring that the job titles given carry as much prestige as possible. He should ensure, too, that the rest of the company realizes the importance of the function so that when a customer telephones and asks for one of the field force by name, the switchboard operator does not reply that as Mr. Smith is 'only one of our salesmen (or worse still, "travellers"), he is not in the office'. Likewise when the caller is eventually put through to the sales department, he should be greeted by a girl who says she is Mr. Smith's secretary. She can, of course, be 'secretary' to a number of other salesmen as well.

The salesman should be provided with the best possible equipment for his job. Well-printed visiting cards with his name in the middle, a well-made brief-case or sample case and good literature all contribute to his status in the eyes of his customers. His car is perhaps the most significant symbol of all, not only to his buyers but also to his family and friends.

HOW TO CONTROL THE SALES OPERATION

In order to control any activity, there must first be an objective and a plan. Unless it is known what is to be achieved and how, whether it is being achieved cannot be assessed. Conversely, there is little point in setting goals and defining actions unless there is an evaluation procedure.

For example, in one business equipment firm, the sales manager developed a system whereby he could analyse the monthly performance of every salesman under eighteen different categories of activity. Thus he could identify how many hours each man had spent on each facet of his job. He could ascertain for instance that salesman X spent seven and half hours on prospecting, salesman Y eight hours on report-writing. He obviously believed that control was constituted by the collection of detailed information. Such attitudes are common among sales management and part of the impact of computerization is that data suddenly becomes available in vast quantities, thus apparently giving even more minute control.

The concept of control

It must be realized that the collection of information, however accurate, up to date and detailed, in itself in no way constitutes control. This is for the very basic reason that there is little point in knowing what *has* happened unless there is a clear conception of what *should* have happened. Control can then be exercised by comparing actual performance with planned performance and deriving variances. It is on these variances that corrective action should be based. Control can be summarized therefore as:

$$A - S = \pm V$$

where A is the actual performance, S is the pre-set standard and V is the variance between the two.

To know that salesman X spent seven and half hours prospecting is meaningless by itself. However, if the standard for this activity is ten hours then there is a minus variance of two and half hours and it is this figure which should cause the manager to take corrective action. If, however, the standard were seven and half hours, as the actual performance is equivalent to the desired standard no managerial action is required. Only by adopting such a concept can management time be economically utilized.

Setting standards of field sales performance

To identify appropriate standards for control, the manager should ask two questions:

1 What constitutes success?
2 What affects the achievement of success?

Descriptive standards

In a sales operation success can usually be defined as the achievement of the sales targets. These serve as the prime standards of control. By themselves, however, they are insufficient. The achievement or otherwise of the annual sales target constitutes a descriptive standard. It measures what has happened but it is then usually far too late to redress the balance. Moreover, it does not indicate *why* the performance has been poor.

Diagnostic standards

Diagnostic standards, which help to identify why performance is varying from target, are defined by asking the second question: 'What affects the achievement of success?'

The manager must consider in the case of a particular salesman failing to achieve target what actions by the salesman himself should lead to the goals being met. Surprisingly, there are only four and these can be identified by the following questions:

1 What kind of people does he call upon?
2 How many does he call upon?
3 How often does he call?
4 What does he do while he is there?

How to set standards

One of the aims of setting standards is to control the sales activity at an early stage to prevent failure to achieve orders. This aspect of control can be further refined by evaluating planned performance against standard before the activity takes place. In fact it is only by assessing the intended action of the sales force that the sales manager can directly prevent failure. Obviously he must check his own plans to ensure that, if achieved, they reach the desired objectives. He can go further by assessing each salesman's activity plans before they are put into action. This is normally done by the submission of weekly calling plans on which each man identifies whom he is intending to visit, for what reason and when he last saw this customer (if applicable).

Variance production and analysis

Variances are produced by comparing actual results against the pre-set standards. However, this simple method may need refining as high variances can result which reflect the forecast error of the standards. For example, if the average daily call rate is set at eight, there is probably no cause for alarm if this varies between six and ten. Because so many of the standards are produced by averaging past performance it may well be necessary to process the actual results before comparing them against standard.

When the actual results are compared with the standards, variances will become apparent. These discrepancies may need more careful analysis before corrective action is taken. For example, in one firm it was known from past experience that most of the selling depended upon seeing the senior management of the customers, which could only be done by appointment. The results of some salesmen, however, were disappointing despite the fact that the percentage of calls by appointment was well up to the pre-set standard. But when performance against other standards was examined it was noted that their call rate was below par. Thus although the appointment to total call ratio was high, this was due to a smaller number of other calls rather than to an over-achievement of appointments. Furthermore, it was discovered that as they increased their number of appointments, their overall call rates decreased markedly.

What in fact was happening was that these men, in their enthusiasm to gain appointments, had not controlled the timing of such meetings. They had placed them in the middle of the mornings and afternoons, thereby limiting their ability to make other calls. The more experienced men systematically made appointments early in the morning, immediately before lunch, immediately after lunch or late afternoon, leaving mid-morning and mid-afternoon free to make cold calls which, although not as important, resulted in enough business to make their results superior. It would have been very easy to jump to the conclusion that the disappointing results of the less experienced men where due to a lack of sales skill. It was only by careful variance analysis that the real problem of appointment timing was identified.

Taking corrective action

Having identified the true nature of the variance, the sales manager has to decide whether it results from faulty standard setting or inadequate salesman performance. If the former, the standards will have to be modified. If the latter, the performance of the man will have to be improved, usually by some form of training or instruction. If the man is to improve he must be given specific targets to achieve within specific time periods, otherwise little or no change will result.

FURTHER READING

Lidstone, J.L., *Motivating Your Sales Force*, Gower, Aldershot, 1978

Lidstone, J.L., *Training Salesmen on the Job*, 2nd edition, Gower, Aldershot, 1986

Wilson, M.T., *Managing a Sales Force*, 2nd edition, Gower, Aldershot, 1983

21 Promotional public relations

David Wragg

If one ignores the jargon, public relations is concerned simply with the relationship between an organization and the community as a whole. Occasionally, there is some confusion between public relations and press or media relations, which are important parts of PR, and this is because these different means of mass communications are important to the whole of public relations. A PR man can never forget the media: he has to think like a journalist when advising his employers or clients, and he has to think like a manager when dealing with the media, whether they be press, television or radio. The media are one of the main avenues for communication and it is important to realize their value in influencing attitudes or bringing a message to the notice of the greatest number of people in the shortest time.

PUBLIC RELATIONS WITHIN THE ORGANIZATION

Most large organizations have their own public relations staff, and sometimes they will break the activity of the PR department down into those handling PR and those handling press relations, as the simpler and more junior task. This is seldom a wise move, not only because it tends to devalue press relations, but also because it can lead to duplication of effort, and press relations must be seen as a part of a wider picture.

Many organizations use consultants. PR consultants, unlike advertising agencies, seldom have any major item of expenditure on which their fees can be based. This is why the term 'consultant' is used, implying that payment is for their advice, while advertising agencies are agents who place advertising, although they also do other things. This is a simplification in both cases, for in the case of the public relations consultant, it implies that they do little more, when in fact most draft and distribute press material, arrange interviews and facilities for journalists, organize photography and even, sometimes, prepare brochures and mailing shots, help in the preparations for an exhibition or a conference, or produce a house newspaper

355

for the client. Consultants are sometimes paid an agreed fee for a specific project, but normally they are appointed for a year at a time and the fee is based on the amount of executive time required, usually paid quarterly (but sometimes monthly) in advance plus the costs incurred, sometimes with special inclusive charges for such items as press releases to account for the cost of paper and postage, and for the clerical or secretarial time involved in despatch.

Hybrid consultant and in-house arrangements are quite common. Sometimes the consultancy will do the donkey work, despatching releases and so on, but it is not unknown for the in-house PR person to be relatively junior and working under the wing of an experienced consultant. More usually, the consultancy will handle a specific project or a certain area of activity. Some managements keep a consultant on a retainer, which grants them the right simply to telephone and consult; anything further is charged for as an extra. Others will use a consultant for corporate or financial relations, or to ease the pressure of work in the in-house public relations department, especially when a certain promotional task creates a short-term workload.

It is sometimes worth while employing a locally based consultant when a company moves away from its normal home base, and where local knowledge and language can be useful.

A number of companies believe that their managers ought to act as communicators, usually with guidance and co-ordination from a central PR staff. This can be an excellent approach, but only if the guidelines are understood by all concerned, and for that there must be a sound management communications programme which keeps all members of management fully in the picture. The advantages are that this system enhances the status of the local manager, giving him a broader view of his company and his industry, and also pleases the local media who would far rather deal with him than with a distant press office.

MEDIA RELATIONS

The prime rule to remember when using the media to gain attention for a company's products or services, is that the media are not working for the company, but for their own readers, viewers, listeners or subscribers. Even though a manager in a company which is a substantial advertiser may feel that he is entitled to preferential treatment, it is important to remember the ethical requirement for impartiality on the part of the journalists, and the fact that without the provision of an adequate service to readers, listeners or viewers, there could be no medium in which to advertise.

A frequent plea from many managers is that they have not received coverage in the media for a considerable period. Sometimes, this is allied to a complaint that their competitors are receiving more attention. However, the media do not allocate space on the basis of fair shares, although they would not like any one company to appear to monopolize their output.

To them the main question is whether or not the story would interest the reader, listener or viewer; does the company have something worth saying? Of course, good media contact will ensure a flow of potentially useful material for the media, to the benefit of the company or organization.

The media need news, pictures and features. Some complain that only bad news is ever printed, but this is not really true and the object of a successful promotional public relations campaign is to ensure that the good news, the new products or services, or improvements to existing products and services, appears in print or is broadcast. New products and services do receive attention, but the object of the exercise in the view of the media is not to help the producer to sell, but to advise their readers, listeners or viewers. This means that a substantial proportion of the readership has to be interested, in the view of the editorial staff, before space can be provided, and the significance of a new product, for example, has to be considerable before national or regional coverage can be provided. There are limits on both time and space, and strong competition from major national and international developments. These pressures vary, so that a story which one day might be given some prominence can, just a few days later, be given low rating and little space on an inside page. Time is most at a premium on broadcast news bulletins.

One picture remains worth a thousand words, if not more, in terms of publicity. A good picture provided by an organization seeking to draw attention to itself or its products will be used if the subject is newsworthy enough, or if it appeals to a certain slot, such as a gardening or travel page, or is an appealing gimmick (although really good gimmicks are extremely rare). The national press has a strong preference for using the work of its own photographers or those of the major press agencies, and some object to anything which displays a company name too strongly. As a rule, the local press and specialized media are far less demanding.

Of course, one buys a newspaper, listens to the radio or even watches television for far more than just the news. All types of media seek to entertain as well as to inform, and this means that there is usually a demand for good features material as well. Features vary, from those giving the background to the news to those which entertain, including travel, motoring, gardening, hobbies, new products and women's columns. Even when a company has nothing interesting to say, there are occasions when its products or services may find a slot on the features pages. Trade or specialized publications are sometimes anxious to find companies on whose products and management they can write a background article.

Into the news

Obtaining news coverage is a highly disciplined procedure, rather than luck or influence. A number of steps must be taken before news coverage can be expected, and ideally one should start by asking the following questions:

1   Is it newsworthy? If so, to whom?

2 Which media will be most interested? National, regional, local, special interest or trade? Are there any contacts who might be interested?

3 When should the news be released? Avoid weekends, but will it be worth while offering it to the periodicals early, so that they do not miss it because of their longer production and distribution periods?

4 Does any statement give the salient points simply, without raising fresh questions or misunderstandings? Remember:

   (a) Never say 'announces'; the fact that it is a press statement is sufficient.

   (b) The essence of the news must be in the headline.

   (c) The first paragraph should contain the most important points, so that it can be used on its own if necessary, if the journalist should be too lazy or busy to go any further.

5 Would a photograph help, and if so which of the media would use it?

6 Is any follow-up action necessary? Are there arrangements for handling press enquiries?

One important outlet for any British company is the Central Office of Information, which will translate and release British news stories of sufficient importance to the media abroad. This can be invaluable for companies with an interest in reaching export markets, or hoping to find agents or to license overseas manufacturers to produce the goods.

Sometimes, it can help to release news stores early, protected by an *embargo* to prevent early publication. This gives journalists the time to research the story accurately and fully, and the embargo will usually be observed for fear of being denied future news. However, it might not necessarily keep the news from your competitors, who may be telephoned for comment by the media.

On to the feature pages

Many organizations rely heavily on the features pages for public attention, whether it be gaining the interest of holidaymakers, or perhaps those interested in different types of sporting or cultural events, including the theatre, or those who might attend a country show or agricultural fair, as well as those who might look at the new products pages, the beauty and fashion pages, the books, gardening, hobbies, motoring or home interest pages of the daily and weekly press. Also of considerable importance are the specialized and technical press, helping to reach either particular segments of the market, or wholesalers and distributors and their staff, or even retailers. Good press coverage even in specialized publications can be a cost-effective alternative to additional visits from members of the sales team.

Some aspects of features work require the product or service being publicized to be relatively newsworthy. Take, for example, a new play or film that will need to be publicized while it is still new, and not after it has been running for several months. The same can be said about sporting events, which often justify news coverage pure and simple. Motoring correspondents have been known to react bitterly, and in print, to manufacturers who have offered foreign journalists an earlier opportunity of testing a new car than they themselves have enjoyed; and boating journalists have been known to take a similar attitude. Fashions must be promoted while they are still fashionable. Others tend to be relatively timeless, such as a handy gadget or compound for use in the garden, or for servicing the car, and others are seasonal, insulating material for example, which can sometimes hope for press coverage every autumn!

Holidays and holiday travel facilities can sometimes prove to be unusual in that they have to be promoted indirectly. A ferry company might only obtain the features coverage in the travel pages that is necessary if it indulges in promotion of the destination, for example, and joins with a tourist authority to do this. This is because few people travel for the sake of it. A manufacturer of home improvements products may, on the other hand, find that his best chance of features publicity arises when a journalist is writing on the subject generally, mentioning many of the products available, and so the manufacturer finds his goods mentioned along with those of competitors and those which are suitable for other jobs around the home. However, on the assumption that the reader is interested in getting on with the job, this type of publicity, even if it is merely a passing reference, can be extremely valuable.

The means of attracting the attention of features writers vary. Publishers, record manufacturers, and many others, send samples of their wares, sometimes with a covering press release, a handout article of their own, or a brochure. In many cases, photographs will be offered. A motor vehicle manufacturer will invite specialized motoring writers to sample the new cars, following this up later with the opportunity of an extended trial. This concept of testing the product tends to be essential, whether journalists do so *en masse*, so that a new product can be launched, or as individuals, so that an existing product, a holiday, a boat or a car, can be written about at some length, providing valuable follow-up publicity. Clearly, it is pointless to waste time and effort, not to mention money, on journalists who will not be interested; neither is it worth while considering those who are more interested in a free gift or a free ride, and this is where good knowledge of the requirements of the media can prove so useful.

In many cases, parties of journalists can be organized. If the product or service on show is not new, the best way to ensure coverage of a holiday destination, for example, is to keep journalists from rival publications away from the same party, allowing them some scope for exclusivity, with perhaps a typical mix including a national daily, a regional newspaper, an up-market magazine and a general woman's interest magazine, with perhaps a trade journalist. Freelance journalists can be very valuable, often writing for several outlets.

Facing the media

For many managers, facing the media is not a question of 'if' but of 'when'. Media contact should not always be regarded as a good thing. After all, what does the journalist want to know? Is a particular manager ideal, or should someone else be found? It is as well to know a little beforehand, to avoid wasting everyone's time.

Contact with the press, radio or television, apart from that over the telephone, can take the form of an interview or a press conference, with a press reception being a further possibility. One should usually leave it to the journalist to request an interview, although it can sometimes be offered. Press conferences should be reserved for important developments, such as heavy capital investment programmes, significant acquisitions, or clarifying a matter of urgent general interest (perhaps if a subsidiary company has collapsed, or there has been criticism of a product). Press receptions can be useful for minor announcements and also for a more generalized 'getting to know' contact with specialized journalists, maintaining or establishing a relationship.

Many press conferences and receptions will require a speech, possibly drafted by the public relations adviser. Leaving aside the obvious recommendation that these should be 'short and sweet', it is important to provide copies of the speech for journalists, and to ask them, and a member of the PR staff, to check the speech against delivery, so that changes are noted.

In facing the media the following points should be borne in mind:

1 Interviews and telephone conversations are always liable to be quoted and attributed to the interviewee unless understood to be
   (a) *off the record* and for background briefing only, or
   (b) *non-attributable*, in which case they can be quoted, but without reference to the source
2 Journalists will seldom allow their copy to be vetted, but if they do, alterations must be restricted to points of accuracy
3 No confidences, no hints! Never try to be too clever
4 Avoid using jargon
5 Never forget to provide additional information or photographs when requested
6 Always accept the journalist's deadline
7 Keep the PR adviser at the interview, partly to brief him and partly so that he can deal with any follow-up work, and of course he will be a witness if anything is subsequently misquoted
8 Particularly at conferences, it is a good idea to ask the PR adviser to draw up a list of possible questions beforehand, getting the management to prepare answers, which can be circulated within the organization as a management briefing exercise.

Obviously, every media contact must be put to good use. While long questions are in order, long answers can be misunderstood, and even catch the interviewee himself off-guard. Too short an answer is rather rude, and misses the opportunity to expand a little.

It is easy to ensure that good black-and-white photographs are available and can be offered to the press, showing equipment, new products, even premises and staff, and all pictures have to be captioned. Background articles and illustrations, especially useful for the trade press, must be up-dated at intervals.

Always remember that if a customer or a distributor is involved in any PR effort, he must be consulted and the story cleared with his management first.

EXHIBITIONS

Exhibitions are a form of promotional public relations which offers direct contact with customers, distributors, wholesalers and retailers, as well as the benefit of media coverage in publications, and even broadcast programmes, covering the event and those taking part. The media coverage varies widely, and it is obviously best for those exhibitions with a wide appeal, such as the London Boat Show, the Ideal Home Exhibition and the National Motor Show, although even very specialized exhibitions can attract national media coverage if the subject is newsworthy and there is felt to be some novelty about the exhibits.

Whether or not an exhibition is viewed as an avenue for sales will depend on the nature of the business. Cars and boats are sold at exhibitions; aircraft seldom are. In many cases, even though orders may be timed to be announced during an exhibition, exhibitions are also offering a chance of informal contact with customers and prospective customers, developing a relationship which may ultimately lead to business, or perhaps discussing a problem with an existing customer. Ideas can be floated, and the sales staff do not have to feel that they are wasting a customer's time since the customer for his part has ventured into this particular market place, and is obviously interested in what may be on offer.

Unfortunately, exhibitions are relatively costly, and the space occupied by the stand is but a small part of the total expense. One must add staff time, the cost of travel, subsistence and accommodation, the preparation of the stand and special sales literature. It is worth while ensuring a good position for the stand; the cost of the stand space, even if it is in a prime spot, is such a small proportion of the total cost that any saving by moving to a cheaper and less prominent position can never match the loss of opportunity. Do it properly, or not at all!

When considering participation in an exhibition, the following questions should be asked:

1 What is the aim of the exhibition? Will it reach the right customers?
2 Are the timing and the location suitable?
3 Is the layout suitable, allowing space where the organization will want it, with an adequate flow of visitors past the stand?

4 Can sufficient staff be made available? Remember that staffing must be adequate and must allow for staff to be absent from the stand on occasion.
5 Does the company have anything worth showing? There can be times when this question might not seem so silly!

It is a fortunate man who can put a house, or lorry or a boat on his stand to fill the space and provide a focal point. However, even such a stand needs some thought as to its presentation. Good exhibition stands need not be difficult, and if planned wisely, they can be used again and again, with any illustrations suitably up-dated. It is usually a mistake to insist on a purpose-built stand; instead it is wiser to use standardized components from one of the several ranges available, and which can be adapted to different stand sizes and layouts, since these will vary from exhibition to exhibition. Ideally, the standardized components will break down easily and be reasonably light, so that they can be carried in an estate car or even a good hatchback. It should be possible to assemble or dismantle such a stand in two or three hours.

Naturally, a good stand will not be too crowded, and will have room for visitors to circulate. It should not be too bare. It should convey a message and leave visitors in no doubt as to its purpose. Some literature should be available for visitors, but it can make sense to display only a cheap general-purpose leaflet leaving the more elaborate and expensive brochures out of reach of casual visitors. If any serious discussion is to take place, there should be a secluded area with seating in which customers can relax and talk with the sales team.

DEALER COMMUNICATIONS

Sales literature and point-of-sale material will usually be provided as an extension of the work of the advertising agency and the marketing department. However, public relations techniques are frequently of assistance in maintaining and developing contact with dealers and even customers.

There is frequently a need for a newsletter, possibly monthly or bi-monthly, or even quarterly, providing up-to-the-minute information on new products, changes to existing products, management changes, alterations to distribution patterns, and so on. A flow of regular information in this way enhances the contact which dealers or customers may have with the company. Some companies elevate the enterprise above this fairly simple and direct level, and provide a newspaper or magazine for their dealers, and large industrial customers, basing this on a house newspaper format, with rather more than just the basic company and product news. One pharmaceutical manufacturer has provided a tabloid (i.e. *Daily Mirror* format) newspaper for general practitioners, including articles on hobbies, such as angling, and the problems of general practice, as well as information on new products. The newspaper format was enhanced by including advertisements, in fact the manufacturer's current advertising. This type of approach is ambitious and needs to be done well. That said, it can be at least as acceptable as many trade publications (notably those controlled circulation 'free sheets' which rely entirely on advertising for their revenue, and to a great extent on editorial copy supplied by company PR departments whose style is dreary and where the sales pitch is barely concealed). Obviously, if the major customer, dealer or retailer accepts such a publication, and even becomes accustomed to looking out for it at a certain time each month, it is doing much to improve contact and to create additional goodwill.

Before starting publication of a newsletter, or any of the more sophisticated variations on this theme, it is important to take two important factors into account:

1 The amount of news and features material which can be published
2 The frequency of publication.

Nothing can be more harmful than starting with a publication and then finding, as time passes, that there is insufficient material of interest to fill the space available. Start cautiously, after careful consideration of an editorial programme running several issues ahead. If necessary, the publication can be enlarged or expanded later, when the change will be a sign of success, which is better than having to reduce the size, suggesting failure or loss of enthusiasm. It is unlikely that any such publication will be more frequent than monthly but, if it is too infrequent, the audience, the dealer or customer, will not become used to looking out for it. Publication should never be less than quarterly, and then only for major reviews (usually in glossy magazine format) while monthly or bi-monthly is better. It may be wise to avoid publication in December and August, the festive and holiday months, when attention will be elsewhere (unless early December publication of a suitably festive issue can be arranged).

There can also be a strong case for bringing together dealers or agents, and in some instances large customers, for events. There can be occasions when a conference for dealers will be supported, especially if this is arranged around a preview of new products and suitable hospitality. In some cases, an evening reception or a buffet luncheon, both of which allow people to circulate, might be better. If dealers have to travel from a wide area and are reluctant to leave their businesses, a solution sometimes lies in hosting an event at their annual trade association conference. Remember, make the event, whatever it is, worthwhile for the dealer, it must be profitable or fun, and ideally it should be both!

One other form of dealer communication shouldn't be forgotten – training, especially for the dealer's employees, since these will normally be the people selling or servicing your product. Training programmes for dealer employees, sometimes on their premises if numbers warrant this, will reinforce the relationship between the dealer, his staff, and your company. Visits to factories, research and development establishments, or to other premises operated by the company if it is a service rather than a manufacturing business, will also help.

At all of these opportunities for face-to-face contact with dealers and their employees, one of the most important benefits is to give them an opportunity to communicate with your company, since good communications should be a two-way process, and in this instance it can also provide manufacturers with useful additional market intelligence.

COMMUNICATING WITH THE SALES FORCE

Most companies today have some form of employee publication. The members of the sales force are different from other employees in that they are usually working on their own, sometimes from a regional sales office, but in many instances salesmen and women are based on their homes. While companies vary in this, the business lives of these people are often lonely compared to those of other employees who work alongside each other throughout normal office hours. Of course, those based in their own homes will see the regional manager from time to time, and they will probably make regular visits to a regional sales office, with yearly or half-yearly national sales conferences as well, but there is a need for a regular form of communication, aimed purely at the sales force.

In a sense, communications with the sales force have more in common with management communications than with normal employee communications. The object is to ensure rapid and frequent up-dating of information which will enable the sales team to work more efficiently and effectively. Usually, written communications are used, but these tend to be simpler in production than the glossier general employee communications, and this is another point in common with management communications. The function is not one which can be delegated to regional sales managers because the basis of these communications is that a uniform message should be received by everyone at the same time.

The information which the sales force will require can be summarized quite simply:

1 Advance notice of product changes
2 News of large orders, since nothing succeeds (or sells) like success, and this will impress their customers
3 News of product changes by competitors, or special promotional offers by competitors, with explanation and comment (what are you going to do?)
4 Information on developments with large customers, such as take-overs, difficulties or opportunities, so that sales people are aware of the situation in the industries to which they are trying to sell
5 Information on sales progress, perhaps with a league table so that successful sales people stand out
6 Personal news, such as 'John Smith has just joined' or 'congratulations to Fred Green and his wife Jane, who has just given birth to a baby boy' – remember, this is a lonely existence!

Many marketing and sales managers will send such communications in the form of a long letter or memorandum. There is no harm in this, just so long as everything is covered and it does not become too stiff and starchy. Professional PR advice in drafting may also be welcome, since it must be clearly written, without ambiguity.

This is only part of the communication, however, since forms will have to be devised so that sales people can provide comments, effectively acting as correspondents for the newsletter, and sharing their market intelligence with their colleagues, with the newsletter acting as the communication exchange. What other employees may say to each other over a cup of tea, sales people will say through the newsletter.

While written communication remains the basis of such a programme, companies and other organizations, such as building societies, are increasingly using video for sales training and communication. Dealing with individual salesmen by means of videos can be expensive, since everyone will have to have a video cassette recorder, and a large number of copies will have to be produced. Videos can be used for briefing sessions during visits to regional offices by the sales people. In addition, in stores, bank and building society branches, a video machine can be justified so that everyone working at the branch can watch the tape being played. Details which would otherwise be included in the newsletter to the sales force can be presented on video tape, with far greater impact than the written word. The drawbacks are the cost of producing a good tape, of making copies, and of providing machines for every branch. Good video production is a skill of its own, and may require the use of a specialist producer. It will be wise to back up every tape with background notes so that after watching the video, employees have something to which they can refer.

SPONSORSHIP

Sponsorship is one of the oldest activities of followers of the arts and of sport, and today it is one of the fastest-growing areas of publicity. The privilege of sponsorship has passed from the monarchy and the nobility, and from wealthy individuals, to the company. This is partly because of the effect of inflation and taxation but also because, for certain types of business, sponsorship is a way of furthering their publicity plans, and for some the only way. The prime example is the sponsorship of sporting events by the tobacco industry, as a way around the ban on television advertising of their products.

Sponsorship takes many forms, but can generally be considered as the funding by business of otherwise uneconomic activity. It can be sport or the arts, or it may be an entertainment or even some feat of endurance. Not only does the activity to be sponsored vary enormously, but the way in which sponsorship can be applied also varies. The only common element should be that it earns its keep for the sponsor, and is not a waste of money or time, remembering always that ill-used management time is a waste which no organization can ever recover.

The main ways in which sponsorship works are that it either publicizes an organization and its product directly, or it benefits the customers. One company might sponsor an orchestra, and in doing so will meet a proportion of its costs which it is agreed between the orchestra and the sponsor are unlikely to be covered by box office receipts. If the orchestra does better than expected, its funds benefit, but if it fails, the sponsor has safeguarded himself by limiting his support. In such a scheme with an agreed level of sponsorship, the sponsor will be able to obtain a considerable initial publicity benefit from having committed a certain sum, and will of course still expect to have either the company or one of its products credited with the sponsorship in programme and publicity material.

An alternative method would be to agree to cover the shortfall between receipts and costs, provided that seats are sold at normal rates. However, this can take on the form of an open-ended commitment, and worse, there is some reduction in the publicity benefit simply because the media love to be able to put a firm price tag on any sponsorship. On the other hand, if all goes well, costs could be much lower than anticipated. This type of sponsorship is really for the gambler, rather than for the professional manager.

A sponsor should expect the organizers of any event which is benefiting from the sponsorship to have some idea of the demand for tickets. This is important, not only because of the cost of sponsorship, but also because those tickets which are unlikely to be sold can be used by the sponsor as part of the agreement as gifts to customers or agents, or even as an incentive to members of the sales staff. There is no reason why the sponsor should not ask for a certain number of tickets for every performance or match, but if attendance or audience is likely to vary, it is sound financial sense to confine this to the poorly attended events.

To some extent, sporting sponsorship is more limited. Not all sports, for example, permit the sponsor's name on players' clothing. There can also be difficulty over changing the name of a horse to one acceptable to a sponsor, but this apart, it is possible to sponsor a horse, a yacht or even a motor racing team. Alternatively, a particular event can be sponsored, for example a race, a race meeting, or perhaps a series of competitions leading eventually to a trophy and prizes offered by the sponsor. Not every sport requires the sponsor to cover all costs, but some do! Any company contemplating sponsoring sporting or artistic events would do well to seek the professional advice which is available from certain specialists.

Of course, it is also open to a company to sponsor its own brass band (which can also do much for staff morale), provide a scholarship for gifted children to continue their studies, or even award a prize for students of a relevant professional body (which is reasonably inexpensive but can associate the organization with the aims of a profession). The smallest firm can afford to take a page or two in the programme for a charity event or sponsor local people on a charity walk, gaining purely local publicity and goodwill, but which can still be of value if the business is confined to a certain area.

Which is the ideal form of sponsorship? Some cynics say that firms sponsor their chairman's favourite activity and there is some truth in this, partly because the support of the chairman is sometimes essential to overcome management opposition. Many managers are still very cynical about sponsorship, and sometimes with justification, since there have been instances of companies being misled by those whom they have sponsored. In any case, companies must be clear whether or not they are seeking publicity as a result of sponsorship, or indulging in philanthropy (although this can sometimes also show publicity benefits).

On the positive side, the chairman's involvement is sometimes beneficial because he often knows his customers, and he and they have something in common. On this basis, one insurance broker has sponsored a particular rugby football match every year because many of his clients support one or other of the two teams. An insurance company sponsored a series of cricket matches and found that, with its name displayed liberally around the pitch, market awareness of the company had risen sevenfold (the snag was that the increased awareness was among male television viewers and cricket fans!).

To be truly effective, sponsorship must be directed at an audience interested in both the event being sponsored and in the product or service provided by the sponsor. It would be silly for a fishing-rod manufacturer to sponsor motor racing, but it could make good sense for ferry operators, motor manufacturers, or oil companies, amongst others. Point-to-point racing or gymkhanas are ideal if the market lies amongst country people, possibly making sense for a tractor manufacturer. A firm sponsoring classical music performances would have a fairly up-market clientele, suitable for an insurance company or a bank for example.

Novelty in sponsorship can be a good thing, and it can be cheaper than other established forms of sponsorship, but of course the risk of failure is that much higher.

It is seldom a good idea to sponsor a beauty contest. All too often the winner receives a number of prizes but few of the sponsors receive a worthwhile mention; terms such as 'car' or 'holiday' are used, bringing little benefit to the sponsor. Prizes in charity draws can be more effective, although often the potential market which hears of these is rather limited.

The management of a potential sponsor should consider the following:

1 Do our competitors sponsor?
2 If not, then why not?
3 What interests the customer?
4 Where are the customers located?
5 Would they hear of the event, or is it likely to be broadcast?
6 What are the snags in this form of sponsorship?
7 What will the costs be – at the outside?
8 Have the budgets been properly prepared?
9 What will the organizers provide in turn? For example:
   (a) mention in their publicity
   (b) first refusal of advertising opportunities

(c) change of name of the event, if practicable
(d) cooperation in the sponsor's publicity, if necessary
(e) good planning and costing
(f) public appearances on behalf of the sponsor
(g) a reasonable chance of a favourable press reception to the play, etc.
(h) reliability.

The list may be daunting, and constructive scepticism is called for. However, if done well, sponsorship can produce a highly cost-effective success for the firm or its products. Since much of the funding for sponsorship comes from publicity or advertising budgets, and quite rightly, bear in mind too that the advertising agency is likely to be hostile to the idea.

The constituent parts of a public relations programme can only be effective if managed well, and if occasional opportunities for publicity are not ignored. It is this flexibility, and the ability to react quickly, which is amongst the strengths of public relations. The scope of PR activity is wide. Promotional work is but a part of the whole, with sound corporate work often doing much to enhance the image of a company and its products, with far-reaching benefits.

FURTHER READING

Bland, M., *Be Your Own PR Man*, Kogan Page, London, 1981
Jefkins, F., *Public Relations*, Macdonald & Evans, Plymouth, 1980
Lloyd, H., *Teach Yourself Public Relations*, 3rd edition, Hodder & Stoughton, Sevenoaks, 1980
Wragg, D.W., *Publicity and Customer Relations in Transport Management*, Gower, Aldershot, 1981
You're On Next, Kogan Page, London, 1979

Part Four
RESEARCH AND DEVELOPMENT

22 Solution engineering

Dennis Lock and Don Rushton

Consider a company which has a need to establish a new, complex machining plant. Starting from a knowledge of product design and the volume of output required, it would be usual for the company to approach at least two potential suppliers to obtain competitive proposals for providing the machinery. Except in the very simplest case, it can be taken for granted that the number of machining arrangements proposed will be at least as great as the number of bidders. At one extreme a supplier may be able to suggest a range of equipment taken from his standard catalogue, offering a solution which requires no development costs but which may have to be a compromise, not exactly tailored to manufacturing needs. At the other end of the scale is the bidder who offers to design purpose-built, fully automated equipment – very expensive in terms of initial investment but capable (theoretically) of superb performance and low manufacturing costs.

In arriving at a final solution with any potential supplier a dialogue takes place between the customer and the supplier's sales engineers. During this process the supplier has to learn the customer's problems and work with him to develop a mutually acceptable working solution. In the course of these discussions, manufacturing methods, work practices and even the design of the product itself could be changed to facilitate the establishment of an efficient manufacturing system. The supplier has to arrive at a solution which will satisfy the customer's needs for volume of output, product quality, plant life and reliability and total manufacturing cost; however, the equipment must not be *too* superior, driving its cost up beyond economic limits (there is no point in designing plant with an expected life of twenty years for a product that will become obsolete in five). The bidder who gets this balance right deserves to win the order. The whole process, from first contact to the signing of a sales contract, is known as 'solution engineering'.

Capital investment in manufacturing plant is only one example of a sales negotiation involving solution engineering. Any contract for the construction of a building, supply of a computer system or any other complex project with no obvious single solution is bound to involve lengthy discussion and development before a final solution is reached. A contractor's solution engineering capability is bound to be a major factor in his chance of winning orders against competition. Solution engineering is in any case an essential procedure for ensuring that:

1   A customer's order accurately specifies his requirements
2   The contractor's internal sales specification and manufacturing or construction plans generate the equipment or buildings which the customer *thinks* he ordered
3   The final costs to the customer and to the contractor are in line with the estimates, so that the customer is satisfied and the contractor makes an equitable profit.

THE NATURE AND SCOPE OF SOLUTION ENGINEERING

Generally speaking, the provision of a solution to any industrial problem which can be solved through investment in new plant or buildings can be regarded as solution engineering. For simplicity, the discussion in this chapter will centre upon an organization which supplies and installs manufacturing plant. Although the arguments are based on a solution embodied in a sales proposal, it should also be recognized that a similar logical approach is involved when an engineering consultant is engaged. The difference here is that the consultant is less likely to have any vested interest in recommending a particular machine type or make.

Objectives

From the contractor's point of view the objectives of solution engineering must be to produce a scheme which satisfies the customer's requirements, results in a profitable deal and enhances the contractor's own reputation in the market place. This is a summary definition of a complex process. It is obvious that there will be many cases where these objectives simply cannot be met, and where the contractor should decline to commit his solution engineering team to a quest for a non-existent solution to an impossible problem.

In order to win the contract for the company, the solution offered must not only meet the requirements specified by the potential purchaser. Given several choices by different vendors or contractors, he will select the solution which solves his own business problem most effectively. Thus in the preliminary discussions, a broad experience is helpful in drawing out from the purchaser an adequate understanding of the real business problems he is anxious to solve. This understanding will often help to ensure the preparation of a more precisely designed user requirements specification.

Organization and people involved

Since solution engineering takes place before a contract is signed, it is usually regarded as part of the marketing process. It therefore falls within the scope of the marketing director. It is desirable that the potential customer should only have to deal with one point of contact in the contractor's organization from the start, in order to keep communications simple and to avoid later expensive contractual contradictions. The wise contractor will ensure that only one of his most competent, professional engineers is allowed to spearhead such an operation. Although many others may become involved, the identification of one co-ordinating individual throughout the formative stages ensures continuity. his individual, although under the control of the marketing department during solution engineering, need not be a marketing man himself. He could be one of the engineering staff. An excellent practice, when planning and workload allow, is to arrange for the person who heads the solution engineering phase to become the project manager (or project engineer) in the event of a contract being signed.

Solution engineering for any but the very smallest company will involve several departments outside the sales and marketing organization. In order to prove a possible solution it is often necessary to set up a small team comprising engineers and designers, draughtsmen, planners, cost estimators, buyers and production management representatives. This is necessary to ensure that the eventual solution is practicable, and properly assessed for its costs and effects on company workload. At this stage the managers of all contributing departments are really committing themselves to the solution. These managers must afterwards be held responsible if work actually goes ahead. But, although many individuals may come together from a number of departments during solution engineering, the process remains a marketing function and control should be vested in the marketing manager or his senior delegate.

Just as it is sensible for the contractor to nominate one individual to act as a contact for the customer, it also makes sense for the customer to reciprocate (if he can) by appointing his own representative.

Functions necessary

Quite obviously, engineering at the highest possible professional level is necessary to arrive at the best solution, and to assure a potential customer of the expertise and credibility of the contractor. While solution engineering centres on this engineering design function, it is useful here to list some of the other functions needed to achieve a total solution.

It may be that the engineer appointed to the task is brilliant at his job, but is not a skilled communicator and has little sales ability. Such shortcomings must be recognized by the controlling marketing person, and the necessary guidance and support given to assist in face to face meetings with the customer. In other words, business awareness (of a high order) is one of the contributing functions.

Where manufacturing forms part of the work plan, production management and production engineers may need to be consulted. In any case the production management will need to consider the effect on workload. Early discussions between production engineers and the solution engineers can often lead to discovery of cost saving methods, thus allowing a relatively low price to be given in the final quotation.

In the last few years techniques of simulation have evolved rapidly, which enable the engineer or designer to consider more alternatives, and evaluate them, than hitherto possible. In the field of product design, computer graphics now enable the engineer to consider a large number of variations, or combinations, and offer only the most promising alternatives. In the field of plant or equipment design, graphical simulation packages permit the flow of production to be portrayed and analysed through different combinations of equipment. When linked with financial models, the capital investment, space characteristics and production rates can be related to financial benefits, providing impressive factual arguments to support the sales effort.

Although setting the selling price is not part of the solution engineer's job, the data which he assembles are obviously essential to the price setting process. Here, the company's estimating engineers have a vital role to play, and their estimates usually require augmenting with quotations from all subcontractors and outside suppliers of large components likely to be involved. Such requests for quotations may have to be channelled through the purchasing department.

In addition to price, the customer is also going to ask when he can expect completion of his order – the date when he can take up occupation of a new building, the date when he can first cut metal on his new machining installation, or a date when he can change over from clerical control to a proven new computerized system. Such predictions have to be made realistically. Too much optimism at the order stage may be good for winning one order, but broken delivery promises are a very good way of achieving a terrible market reputation. Delivery dates must, therefore, be estimated with care, and those responsible for day-to-day planning and workload should be consulted during the process.

Reliability of delivery performance has been improved beyond recognition in recent years by companies who have integrated the flow of data through their businesses in one corporate data base. Direct linking of common data is possible without errors of transmission (inevitable where human intervention is necessary in data transfer) from design through manufacturing engineering to the CNC machines used to make parts which are right first time, every time. One leading machine tool builder has achieved 100 per cent deliveries on the promised date, and at the same time removed several months from the combined design and manufacturing lead time. This is only one example of computer integrated manufacturing. It will be the way of the future.

Solution engineering is, then, a team effort. With the number of people needed, performing all the functions just mentioned, it is clear that solution engineering is also expensive. If an order is not obtained, substantial costs may have to be written off.

STAGES OF SOLUTION ENGINEERING

Initial screening

The first stage of solution engineering is deciding whether or not to commit expensive company resources to a customer's enquiry. Further attention to an enquiry must depend upon the likely success of any proposal. The enquiry will be rejected (politely) if such success seems remote, if the contractor does not want the business, or if it is suspected that the customer is not in earnest or is not a desirable partner for a contract. An alternative to outright rejection is to allow a limited amount of preliminary study in order to evaluate the enquiry and its possibilities, but such limited work must have clearly defined upper expenditure cut-off for obvious reasons. Screening decisions have to be made at top level and are not part of the solution engineer's responsibility. They are particularly relevant here, however, since they authorize the solution engineering process and (usually) set a limit to the amount of expenditure that can take place before a further review.

It is prudent to set up regular, formalized screening committee meetings. Such assemblies would include the marketing director, senior sales engineers involved in customer contracts, the engineering director (or his delegate) and senior representation from the manufacturing organization. Each customer enquiry would be presented by the sales engineer responsible, and considered on its merits. If the committee decided that the enquiry showed promise, the committee would decide upon a course of action directed towards the preparation of a sales proposal. In order that the committee's decisions receive due attention, without ambiguity, it is important that an *action plan* is drawn up at this stage. Action plans list every significant stage of the solution engineering process authorized, with required completion dates alongside each item, the names of those responsible for carrying out the actions and the budget allowed. A very promising enquiry may be given a full go-ahead, while more doubtful projects would typically be given partial clearance, to be reviewed more critically as each intermediate stage is reached.

Problem definition

The first step is to learn the customer's requirements and define his problem. He may not even know himself where the problem lies. Solution engineering has to start, therefore, from the customer's declaration of his own long-term objectives. The contractor's job then is to ensure that the objectives are sufficiently clear, and supported by quantities where necessary.

For example, if the problem is to design a new building to house a commercial organization, the fundamental details needed are the numbers of people to be housed, standards for office accommodation according to grades of people employed, common service requirements such as conference rooms, catering, air conditioning, ventilation, lighting standards, and so on and so on. Coupled with a knowledge of communications between different departments of the customer's organization, the solution engineers (architects and their supporters in this case) can proceed to plan the building layout and suggest construction methods.

Even in cases where the client specifies building layout and office sizes, a potential contractor's design staff must still establish many details of the customer's needs before producing a fully costed solution.

Similar complexities arise in defining solutions for manufacturing organizations. The introduction of robotics has added a new dimension to automated production systems, and this increases the possible number of solutions to some production problems. Here is a case where the solution seeker must try to establish with the customer the expected life of the production requirement. If the product is expected to continue in high volume production for a number of years, flexibility may not be necessary in the plant. If, on the other hand, the customer is uncertain about the life of his product, the use of standard machines, or of re-programmable robots, may provide the more flexible approach appropriate to this situation.

An example of the task definition sequence for a manufacturing system is show in Figure 22.1. Such a logic diagram, prepared at the start of a project:

1 Helps the engineers to thread their way systematically through a mass of information
2 Can be discussed with the client to give him confidence that a realistic approach is to be followed
3 Highlights all essential input data about the client's existing production practices – a necessary starting point and essential as a basis for comparing potential advantages offered by new solution proposals
4 Can be used to monitor progress
5 Shows that the heart of good problem definition is the work of gathering realistic workload data
6 Maximizes the opportunity of building shop experience into the problem definition and gives people in the customer's workshops the feeling that they have made a contribution.

From the morass of data collected and sifted during this phase the problem summary will be prepared. This identifies those things which a good solution must eliminate or overcome.

Problem definition review

For complex problems it is essential that the contractor reviews his problem definition with the customer. This would certainly be necessary in the manufacturing system example quoted above, when a working session would have to be organized at which key client personnel would be given a formal presentation of the facts as understood by the contractor. Review meetings of this nature carry sufficient importance to ask that priority is given to attendance, and the use of visual aids in the presentation is fully justified and recommended.

The review meeting with client's staff is, of course, far more important than a one-way presentation. Those attending will be asked to contribute

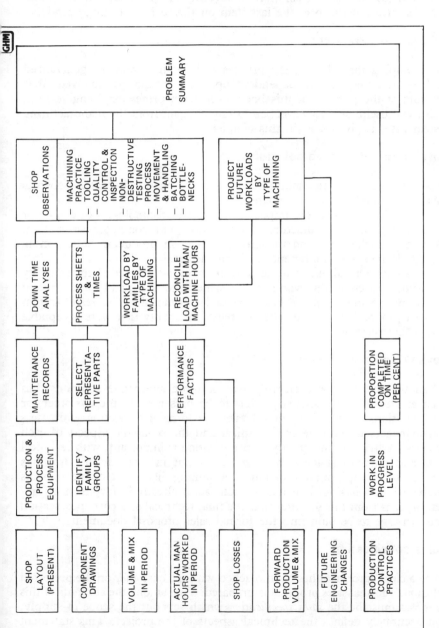

Figure 22.1 *An example of problem definition sequence (for a component manufacturing system) (Ingersoll Engineers Inc.)*

any additional data or experience considered relevant, to confirm the data presented, and to point out any anomalies or areas which may have been missed. In effect, the review meeting completes and ratifies the problem definition. From this base solution engineering can proceed, and the guidelines for future work form the last item on the review meeting agenda.

Solution development

In developing the solution, the process and details cannot be generalized here because they are too dependent upon the technology involved. It is not part of the purpose of this book to instruct professional engineers in their own disciplines. However, an example (again from the manufacturing system case) is given later in this chapter.

Developing alternative solutions

As a continuation of the solution development phase, alternative schemes have to be developed and evaluated.

It is in this area that the impact of the newer technologies of computer aided design and manufacture (CAD/CAM) and computer simulation, referred to earlier, has had the greatest effect in producing better, more reliable designs and equipment in shorter times.

The ability to recall earlier designs has immeasurably speeded up the ability to respond to enquiries, while at the same time the quality and content of the information available has increased enormously. The result is that modern proposals far exceed the standards of quality that were acceptable only a few years ago.

Review and recommendation

When the solution (or preferably two or more alternative solutions) has been arrived at and evaluated, it has to be presented to the customer for consideration. This review should take the form of a meeting with users and managers to examine the technical and the economic aspects of each proposal. Obviously the quality of presentation is important, with technical facts and financial statements properly set out in clear charts, drawings and any other appropriate visual aids. Assuming that the customer remains interested, and has not rejected the contractor already in favour of a competitor, it is from this meeting that the final technical and cost specification must emerge to be built into the formal sales proposal document.

Sales specification

Once a clear agreement has been reached with the customer on the preferred solution, a formal sales proposal is prepared. Vital among the contents of this proposal must be the *sales specification* which sets out the scope of supply, and accurately defines the technical aspects of the project. This statement crystallizes all the work done during the solution engineering phases, and provides the unambiguous basis from which detailed design and production follow on. Obviously, the sales proposal contains much more information, notably the commercial and contractual terms of the proposed deal, but it is the sales specification element which is particularly concerned with the solution description.

The sales specification must define the equipment or other items to be supplied in clear terms, by reference to statements of performance and dimensions, and with adequate back-up drawings and schedules. It is usual for such specifications to undergo several revisions during discussions with the customer, and such revisions *must* be properly accounted for and documented. When any significant change is made, the specification has to be updated and reissued accordingly. Changes in the text should be highlighted by writing the revision number alongside the affected paragraph (an alternative method is to draw a set of parallel vertical lines in the margin, with the number of lines corresponding to the revision number). The correct revision numbers of all associated drawings and schedules must also be given – it is safer to avoid stating any revision numbers for such complementary documents in the text (where they could easily be missed during revisions) but to list them instead in a schedule of 'documents which are to be read with and form part of this specification'.

Subsequent stages

Remaining stages follow only if a contract is concluded. They are outside the role of solution engineering, although the original solution engineering team will have a continuing involvement in the progress. The follow-on stages are: setting up planning, work scheduling and cost control, preparation of detailed drawings and manufacturing instructions, procurement of bought-out items and materials, actual production, work on the customer's site, commissioning and final hand-over.

Summary of solution engineering stages

Although the sequence given is not rigid, with overlaps and reruns to be expected, the established logic outlined above has been found to be the most rewarding in handling solution searching. The summary is:

1 *Screening* – decide whether or not to bid against a customer's enquiry and, if appropriate, produce an action plan with dates and expenditure limits
2 *Task definition* – find out, in depth, exactly what the customer's requirements are
3 *Task definition review* – go back to the customer and review the interpretation of his problems with the users and managers to ensure that the task has been correctly defined
4 *Solution development* – which involves the development of a solution, plus

alternatives if possible, all of which have to be analysed and evaluated for their technical and economic merit

5 *Solution review and recommendation* – present the alternative solutions to the customer and work with his users and managers to arrive at a preferred solution

6 *Specification* – write up the solution in a detailed sales specification to ensure that the project proceeds into production and fulfilment exactly as the customer intended.

EXAMPLE OF SOLUTION ENGINEERING – 1

In this example a system for machining large automotive engine crankcases was studied. Six variations of the crankcase were to be produced, and a detailed analysis and comparison of all six designs was made to determine which features were common and which needed special treatment.

Where a greater number of variants is to be machined, the logical approach is to classify them into 'families' based on manufacturing criteria and the commonality of design features, with a representative part being chosen for each family. Detailed study of representative parts has proved to be satisfactory for planning purposes in many projects, provided that a capability check for all parts is not omitted, covering size envelope ranges and all specific features.

Design of the manufacturing system in this example commenced with consideration of the amount of cast iron stock to be removed. Foundry and pattern making practices and problems were questioned to establish the minimum stock removal that could be anticipated repeatedly. Next the method of location and qualifying was decided, and some changes were introduced to permit automatic location to optimize metal removal before clamping for the first operation: to mill location pads used as datum for all subsequent operations.

The machining process

The major job of deciding the optimum machining sequence and selection of appropriate machine tools was a complex task. It was subdivided into three sections, by type of machining:

– flat surface
– boring
– drilling and tapping

Each of these areas was considered in turn, commencing with an understanding of the present practices adopted in the factory and the reasons for them. Special attention was paid to the causes of quality problems in each machining area. Alternative approaches and machine combinations were identified and compared, and the best available selected for each area. The logical sequence in which this project was approached is illustrated diagrammatically in Figure 22.2.

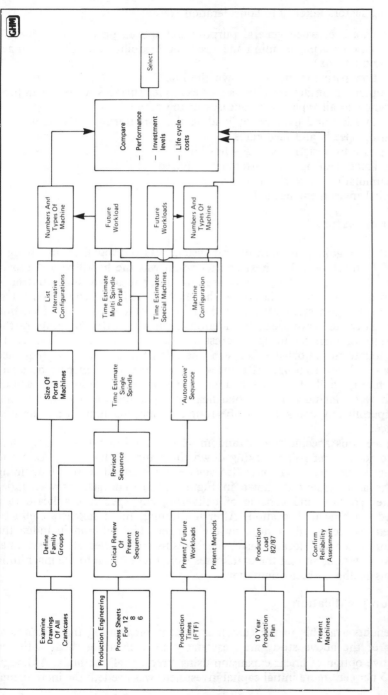

Figure 22.2 *Example of a solution engineering sequence in the selection of short-term investment for the manufacture of crankcases (Ingersoll Engineers Inc.)*

Among factors taken into consideration were:

1 The choice between general purpose and special purpose machines in each case (bearing in mind the need for flexibility for future changes in product mix)
2 The flow path for the part down the line
3 Grouping of similar operations (for example, surfaces to be flat milled, common to all types of crankcases in the range)
4 Part location and fixtures for holding the part during machining
5 Cutting speeds and feed rates
6 Response to design changes – flexibility
7 The amount of operator attention required
8 Accumulation of work in progress
9 Capital investment needed.

The total system

From the foregoing, the best overall system was put together, involving a total of 15 machines. The next consideration was the handling and movement of this family of large crankcases. In order to obtain total control of the movement of the crankcases in the shop, a computer controlled inter-operation storage system was required with discreet identification of location of each individual crankcase, and identification within the computer of the exact state of manufacturing progress which it had reached. Further, to accommodate the imbalance between operation times within the sequence for one crankcase routing, differences between the different part numbers in the family, and at the same time to maximize utilization of machine tools, it was concluded that a total flexible capability was required which would permit any crank case to be routed to any machine in any desired sequence.

To meet this specification a random access inter-operation storage area was provided using pallet racking down the centre of the shop. Access to pallets was obtained by a controlled stacker for each side of the machining line (the arrangement is shown in Figure 22.3). The stacker was under computer control, and capable of delivering any specific crankcase to a required machine tool location. After machining, the crankcases could be collected and returned to store by the stacker. The solution included the provision of separate local transfer mechanisms and reorientation devices at some workstations so that the crankcases were presented into the machining positions in the correct orientation.

Solution justification

The benefits available to the customer from implementing the recommendations of the above study are best stated by comparing them with the alternative option of linear expansion using 'traditional' methods. Although some 15 per cent more initial capital investment was needed, the incremental

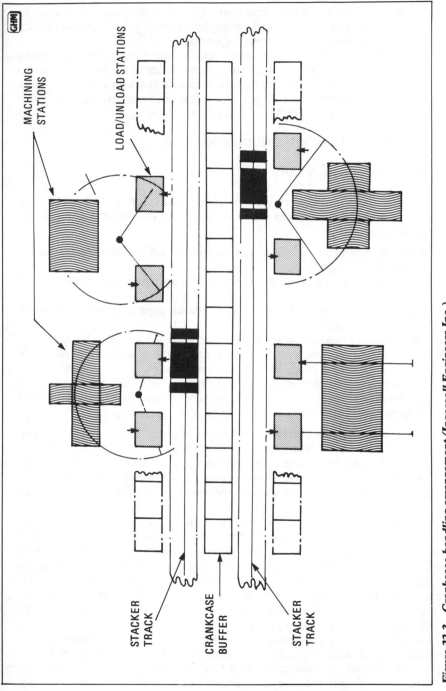

Figure 22.3 Crankcase handling arrangement (Ingersoll Engineers Inc.)

investment was recoverable in three years. On a cash flow analysis at current costs, the break-even point would be reached in four years, compared with the seven years needed for a linear expansion.

The performance figures were substantially improved using the results of the study. Manufacturing lead times were reduced from ten weeks to only two, coupled with a 57 per cent reduction in work-in-progress. These results were obtainable for a 60 per cent increase in output, and the whole plant occupied considerably less factory floor space.

EXAMPLE OF SOLUTION ENGINEERING – 2

Planning an engine factory

In a comparative evaluation of alternative sites for a new generation engine factory, advantage was taken to maximize the benefits from recent developments:

1 It was to produce a new family of engines which had been 'rationalized' during the design phase
2 Maximum advantage had been taken of improving the 'producibility' of the components
3 Subassemblies were to be tested and 'quality approved' before reaching the assembly line
4 Only 'quality assured' parts were to be supplied to assembly
5 'Cold testing' devices were to be included in the assembly line to ensure correctness before proceeding to the next station
6 Finally, computerized engine testing in fully automated test cells, but on relatively short cycles, would ensure correct performance before despatch, and provide a birth certificate for each engine.

These requirements together with the other relevant data about production volumes, mix, and manning policy statements, were collected into a descriptive document (the task definition). This document was reissued several times during the course of the project, additional facts being added as they became available so that all members of the team could be kept up to date.

The level of integration was the first major factor to be established. Parts requiring dedicated high-volume transfer machinery were identified for in-house manufacture (cylinder blocks, cylinder heads and connecting rods). So were other parts specific to the engine design but which could be manufactured on dedicated lines of standalone machines (gear housings, manifolds, flywheels, flywheel housings, being some of the principal items). Forgings and some other items requiring heavy capital investment were selected for purchase from appropriate vendors.

For all those parts considered as possible for in-house manufacture, machining lines were planned and detailed estimates made for the manning, space and capital requirements. 'Make or buy' decisions were made later on the basis of unit cost for each item. The best assembly sequence for the family of engines was determined from assembly logic diagrams, and maximum use of subassemblies was made. The engine test cycle and procedures stipulated by the designers were met in concepts using the latest available computer control of test cycles.

Resulting from this work, a plant layout was developed (the best being selected from several alternatives) and the area of the building determined. Specifications for building services together with the factory layout enabled preliminary capital estimates for the factory building to be made. As a forward looking plan, low energy concepts were used for the building construction.

A radical approach to manning levels was adopted. Equipment was selected to minimize the number of direct operators required to perform an operation on each engine or component before it could proceed. Indirect tasks were screened for elimination, but necessary supporting tasks were carefully defined, and manpower allocations developed so as to complete the assessment of true product unit cost.

Significant reductions were achieved against the numbers employed in traditional plants by vigorously adhering to strict planning guidelines. For example all parts were contracted to be delivered packed in a manner to be determined by the user. Strict limits were determined for the number of days of stock to be held ahead of the line, depending on whether the item was sourced from UK, Europe, or transocean. Automatic counting and recording were used wherever possible to eliminate clerical work and direct links were specified between the production control computer and each operating line, thus eliminating many traditional 'office' personnel.

The planned productivity levels which this study revealed could be achieved on a practical basis represented a very significant gain over the performances currently achieved in existing plants. Also the true cost difference of operating at each of the different sites was identified, so that in the final decision-making process management was able to assess these differences against the significant commercial or political considerations favouring one or other site locations: for example, the existence of a workforce with relevant skills, the availability of grants to assist in capital investment or the need to redevelop an existing site and utilize its assets more effectively.

CONCLUSION

The two foregoing examples illustrate the benefits available to the end user after successful solution engineering carried out by a contractor or consultant. There was obviously a large element of high-level production engineering involved in achieving the benefits quoted, but this only describes a part of the total function of solution engineering. Complementing the benefits experienced by the plant user are those enjoyed by the project contractor who, as a result of the clear specification and cost estimates provided by the solution engineering team, has been able to carry out the work with clear objectives and within a well-defined and documented design and cost budget framework – vital as a basis for profitable project fulfilment.

Although manufacturing examples have been used in this chapter, proficient solution engineering is the essential forerunner of any industrial project. As technology advances and international competition grows still keener, the company with the best solution engineering capability has a head start over its competitors in the winning and profitable execution of engineering contracts.

FURTHER READING

Leech, D.J., *Management of Engineering Design*, Wiley, London, 1972

Lock, D., *Project Management*, 4th edition, Gower, Aldershot, 1988

Topalian, A., *The Management of Design Projects*, Associated Business Press, London, 1979

23 Managing research and development

A W Pearson

Investment in research and development must be looked at in the same way as any other investment in the business – the benefits it produces must exceed the costs. However, it is by no means easy to ensure that the practice lines up with the theory. The available evidence from a wide range of companies suggests that the costs incurred in the R and D phase of well-managed projects can be reasonably controlled, but that the time to completion is often significantly underestimated. Problems are also frequently encountered in the implementation phase and this causes further delays. Lengthening of the timescale to completion can have adverse effects upon the benefits stream which may not only be delayed but may be significantly altered due to external influences: for example, competitive activity and changes in economic, social, political and environmental factors. It is also clear that assessing benefits is a very difficult task, which must take into account a wide range of effects and compare the anticipated futures with the likely situation if the R and D had not been undertaken.

Financial planning must recognize these uncertainties, particularly with respect to longer-term work. Appropriate monitoring or control procedures must be instituted which are capable of recognizing significant changes and indicated corrective action as early as possible.

In practice it has been found to be useful to approach the problem from two directions: first, to consider the overall allocation of funds to R and D based on identified organizational needs, and second, to consider the planning and monitoring of individual projects. The evidence is that attention to the former has a significant influence upon the success of the latter, allowing individual initiatives to be encouraged and managed within an agreed overall framework. The two approaches are complementary and in most organizations both will be used as starting points, with links becoming apparent at a very early stage, as the next two sections aim to show.

TOP-DOWN PLANNING

In the late 1960s the word 'relevance' was frequently heard in discussions about the allocation of funds to R and D. Very simply this was meant to direct attention to the need to support R and D work which if successful would be put to effective use by the organization. In the late 1970s the phrase 'top-down planning' was used very frequently. This refers to an approach which systematically questions where the organization is going, and examines the structure of the organization in terms of its size, the nature of the component parts, their growth and profitability and their strengths and weaknesses in relation to competitive and other environmental forces. The purpose of this exercise is to identify where the organization is likely to end up if it continues in the way it has done in the past, and where it may need to change in order to improve its viability in the future.

Such an analysis will usually be undertaken by individuals or groups of people who are responsible for, and knowledgeable about, a specific area of activity and will often follow organizational lines, for example, focused on products or areas of like characteristics. Within the analysis a 'technological audit' should be undertaken and this will reveal both the level and type of R and D activity which can be directly related to the support of specific areas of the organization. Such information then forms the necessary background to detailed discussion about the relationship (or 'relevance') of the R and D expenditures to the needs of the organization, with emphasis being placed on the longer- as well as the short-term needs.

The time orientation of the people involved in such discussions may be different, with R and D tending to look further ahead than, say, production or marketing people. This must be accepted. The purpose of top-down planning is to focus attention on the organization needs and each function should have an opportunity to make its view clear about these needs, bearing in mind the specialist knowledge it can contribute to the discussion. Differences of opinion are best brought out into the open at this stage, and it must be accepted that there is no certainty about the future. All opinions must be listened to. Where wide differences arise more information may need to be collected, and more views canvassed. However, it may well be that such differences still persist, and in this case it may be necessary to consider the variation of views as being a good representation of the actual situation, i.e. to accept that a high level of uncertainty exists about the future. In this case a decision may have to be taken to authorize a programme of work which will cover the different views and hence allow flexibility. This will almost certainly require the allocation of more resources to the area, with a consequent reduction in the risk. If this is the accepted strategy efforts must be focused on identifying those features of the situation which can be monitored to indicate at the earliest possible time which areas should be given priority.

Top-down planning is therefore a way of focusing senior management attention on the needs of the organization. It forces people to ask questions about the relationship between the expenditures on the different functional areas and the alternative futures which the organization may encounter. In this process the R and D people should have every opportunity to put their own views forward and to make a significant contribution in respect of, for example, potential new technologies which may be seen as threats or opportunities. A thorough discussion of all these issues will reveal areas for attention and will generate commitment to a project, by the organization and by the project leader and the team. Such a commitment is a necessary condition for success.

It is not, however, also a sufficient condition, as many champions of 'non-successful' projects know to their disappointment. Many other factors need to be taken into account and as some of these change over time, for example legislation, it is important to have a planning and monitoring procedure which will provide useful information to all parties. Such a procedure can form an important part of the 'bottom-up' form of planning.

BOTTOM-UP PLANNING

This approach implies that individual activities or projects are the starting point for analysis. In many areas this is indeed the case. Ideas arise in a variety of ways: from discussions, casual meetings, problems, etc., and they often form the basis for a request for funds to develop the idea into a proposal backing a request for a larger allocation of resources. Requests for small amounts of funds for developing ideas should always be encouraged and seriously considered. In general such ideas will lie within areas which will be of potential relevance, simply because they will utilize the skills of people who have been recruited in line with the organization's needs. The major cost of encouraging such requests is in fact the 'opportunity' one of not applying the same resources to other ongoing or preselected projects. However, the positive side of this is the increased motivation which can be generated by allowing some freedom for individuals to pursue their own ideas, and to convert them into projects which they can 'champion'. In most organizations the decision as to how much of this type of activity to encourage, and in which direction, is left to the R and D director, whose responsibility it is to develop and maintain an exciting and creative environment which will be a positive asset to the organization. Many R and D directors report a lack of initiative on the part of their scientists and technologists in bringing forward new ideas, rather than any excessive demand. In some organizations this is partly due to pressure from projects of a more immediate concern to the organization's needs, which itself can be due to lack of an adequate planning and monitoring system.

The important point about the bottom-up planning approach is that it focuses attention on the level of resources which will be required to service all the projects which have been accepted into the R and D portfolio. If these projects are to be progressed well they cannot command in total more resources than are available, at any one time. This may sound an obvious statement, but the evidence is that many organizations consistently fail to complete projects on time due to the pressure on resources. If this is the case, corrective action must be taken either to reduce the number of projects which are being progressed simultaneously, or to bring in assistance from outside agencies, for example contract research organizations. Both of these are essentially short-term measures. In the long term serious consideration needs to be given either to reducing the number of projects which are accepted into the portfolio or to increasing the level of in-house resources in areas which are causing delays. If the first of these alternatives is chosen it will be necessary to examine carefully all the projects and to assess their relative importance to the organization, so that any trimming down can be done in areas which are likely to have less significant effects. This can only be done after due consideration of the plans produced by the approach discussed in the previous section, and hence the top-down and bottom-up approach will come together when questions of direction and priority are raised. An important point to note is that unless this trimming down is well managed there will be a continuing scramble for resources which will lead to the not uncommon situation in which progress meetings end up as being primarily concerned with establishing priorities. The inevitable consequence is a lowering of motivation of the people involved in low-priority projects and a reduction in financial return when compared with that planned.

Project evaluation and selection

This is an area fraught with difficulty. The literature is full of methods which have been designed to be helpful. These range from simple cash flow models, the use of net present value and internal rate of return accounting procedures, checklists, various forms of decision analysis incorporating probabilities of technical and commercial success and the more analytical approaches which are based on mathematical programming techniques. In practice the evidence suggests that the simpler approaches are the ones most commonly used, this often being justified because adequate data for the more mathematically based models are lacking. The simple cash flow models and weighted checklists are therefore much in evidence.

More recently, emphasis has been placed on the behavioural aspects of decision making, and a number of multi-criteria approaches (some using microcomputer facilities) have been described. These look very promising, and it is expected that they will become increasingly accepted as valuable aids to decision making.

PLANNING AND MONITORING

The success of the approaches outlined in the previous two sections will depend upon the degree to which the performance on individual projects matches up to the expectations. The purpose of a good planning and monitoring procedure is to ensure that any differences can be quickly identified and appropriate action taken. A number of methods are available for doing this, and the choice should be made in the light of the organization's needs, with one point being emphasized – the simplest and most flexible approach should be adopted. Many people still consider that the introduction of formal planning and control procedures into R and D will stifle creativity and initiative. Most attempts to impose standardized systems seem to have met with little success. It is comparatively easy for an individual or group to get around a system they do not see as useful and which takes up time they feel could be better allocated to their scientific and technical activities.

Planning and monitoring must be seen as a positive aid to the individual, the project group and the organization. Any techniques used should be seen as valuable aids to the team-building and leadership needs of a project. They should help focus attention on both the task and the people aspects of management. They should take into account the variables which are specific to the situation (for example, the development level of the team members) as well as the technical and organizational complexity of the project. This leads to a variety of methods being used for individual projects, the choice depending on the type of work and the project leader's management style.

There is a need for a reporting and monitoring procedure which will provide common information across the whole of an R and D establishment, and which places emphasis on obtaining and presenting information in a form which is useful for management purposes. Some approaches which have proved useful in practice are discussed in the following sections of this chapter.

Project planning

Several methods have been described in the literature, and further information can be obtained from the sources listed in the bibliography. Briefly, they fall into the following categories.

The bar chart

This is probably the oldest and yet still the most commonly used method in many R and D establishments. The chart is really a calendar planner on which individual activities are identified, with the time over which they are expected to be progressed indicated by a bar. The degree to which a particular activity has been completed is often indicated by a dotted line under the main bar. The advantages of this approach are its simplicity and its visual impact. It is not, however, always easy to update, and not so easy to show dependencies between activities. Although both these disadvantages can be overcome, more complicated projects are often planned using a form of network diagram.

The network diagram

This can take a variety of forms. Until recently the most commonly met was the simple form of PERT or activity on arrow diagram. Standard computer programs are available which allow easy presentation and analysis of such networks and also easy updating. In most cases the same programs allow for the printing out of a standard bar chart for any section or all of the network. They also include facilities for multi-project scheduling and for resource levelling, which can be very useful. Networks of this type are most commonly encountered in larger projects of a more development type and particularly where external inputs are required, and external deadlines have to be met. They are used also where standard practices must be followed to satisfy, for example, government and legislative requirements.

Alternative forms of network diagrams are available, notably the activity on node, or activity in box method sometimes referred to as the metra potential method (MPM). As the name implies, the activities are written inside the boxes or nodes and these are linked by arrows which show the dependencies. This variation is claimed to provide more flexibility at the initial project design stage and is more closely related to the engineering flow diagrams with which many scientists and technologists are already familiar.

Arguments against the use of networks have, however, been put forward by many people who believe they are too structured and inflexible and not capable of handling the uncertainties associated with R and D projects. Some of these arguments have been countered by the further development of the methods, for example, to allow alternative outcomes to be considered at any node or activity completion point. A such points allowance can also be made for recycling by incorporating feedback loops into the diagram.

Research planning diagrams (RPDs)

A further development of the network diagram, essentially following on from the activity in box approach, specifically calls for the incorporation of decision nodes. This is a very valuable addition in an area like R and D and the approach has been found most useful. Another point in its favour is the similarity to the commonly accepted logic or flow diagram which is used in other areas of business activity. A very simple example, showing the basic format, is given in Figure 23.1.

The milestone chart

This is perhaps the simplest of all approaches and is generally used to provide a summary of the information which has been spelled out in more detail using one or more of the previously outlined methods. As will be seen later, it can form the basis of a very effective reporting and monitoring system. The basic characteristic of the approach is the identification of milestones, or key events, which can be readily identified in advance and recognized when they occur in time. In the case of R and D projects these may be defined in terms of, for example, technical specifications which have to be met, tests which must be completed, pilot plants built, production facilities designed, or specific market research information gathered, etc. The dates by which these activities should be completed then become the milestones. These will often be associated with specific review meetings.

The milestone chart is used in many organizations and expanded versions often include a breakdown of the activities by function or by individual, so that the responsibility for actions can be clearly identified. For this reason the name 'activity matrix' has been used to describe this form of presentation.

Monitoring

The purpose of outlining some of the approaches to planning individual projects was to illustrate the variety. As stated earlier, the preference for a particular method will depend upon the type of project, and the management style of the team leader. Any method must be seen as an aid to, and not as a substitute for, management. The project leader is responsible for planning, or agreeing the plans, and for progressing the project. However, it must be accepted that many things can change during the course of the work, and corrective action may need to be taken during the life of a project. The first person to recognize this is likely to be the project leader,

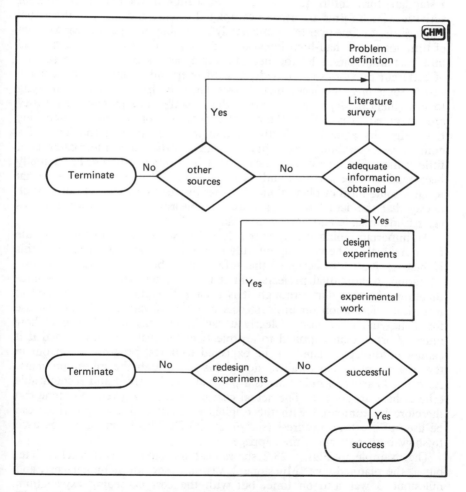

Figure 23.1   The research planning diagram (RPD) format

who is responsible for taking the necessary initiatives. The purpose of a good monitoring procedure is to record progress and to report actions which have been taken which were not originally planned and which might have consequences for the organization. In addition it should highlight, if necessary, where actions are not being taken at the correct time.

The monitoring procedure should be essentially a communication system which adds to, but does not replace, the direct contact which is always necessary between the various parties interested in a particular project. It will almost certainly provide some historical information, but its value will be significantly increased if it also focuses attention on future expectations.

Historical analysis

Most organizations require all people involved in project work to record on a standard form information about the allocation of their time on different activities. Such forms are usually completed weekly and relate to the actual expenditure of time over the immediately preceding time period. Breakdown of time may be in half-hour intervals, half or whole days. This is converted into cost information by the use of simple factors based on the salaries of different categories of individuals with overheads being added in many cases. Sometimes the accumulated costs form the basis for direct charging to customers or departments within the organization. In most cases they are presented so as to show the actual expenditure on the project alongside that originally agreed. Such information may be given in the form of a cumulative expenditure chart, but it is obvious that such information is of little value unless one can be clear about how much progress has actually been made on the scientific and technical work. That is why it is essential to have some form of plan, along the lines discussed earlier, set out in such a way that the actual work progress can be assessed at regular intervals against identifiable and agreed criteria.

An important point to note is that it is the exception rather than the rule for individuals to be working on only one project at any given time. If this is the case, it must be accepted that information about time, and hence cost, allocation to individual projects cannot be accurately assessed. Experience therefore suggests that although it is usually thought necessary to collect historical information on project costs it is not of very great practical use for management purposes. Clearly it can be used as an indicator of how much effort is being applied to a project, but its value is diminished if it cannot be directly related to the expected technical progress as set out in the original plan. One way of doing this is through the milestone chart. As defined earlier, a milestone is a point at which agreed and recognizable criteria have to be met. The actual cost of reaching a given milestone can therefore be compared with the original estimate and a simple chart can be used to illustrate progress (see Figure 23.2). This diagram can be used to show both cost and time slippage.

The example in Figure 23.2 shows that milestone 1 was reached late, but at the planned cost. Milestone 2 was on time, but at higher cost, and milestone 3 was also on time, but with the cost exceeding expectation.

However, such a chart only indicates actual achievement against milestones and information about progress between these key points cannot be easily gained without a more detailed breakdown of the project into smaller activities. It is possible to do this and at the extreme every activity can be individually monitored and progress of cost and time against expectation assessed almost continuously. This is often referred to as the work breakdown approach. In this case computer analysis is useful, but in general the amount of information required and generated becomes too much to handle effectively, and it often leads to an anti-reaction from scientists and technologists who think too much of their time is taken up in what they

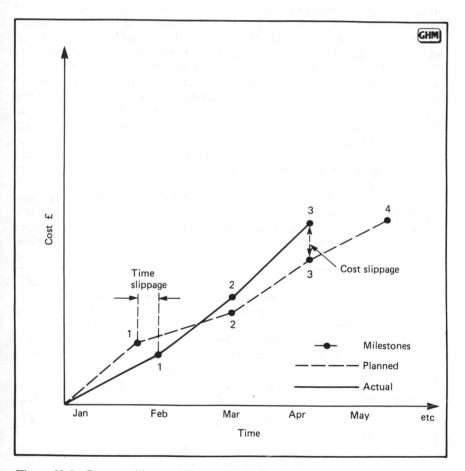

Figure 23.2   Progress illustrated by a milestone chart

see as unnecessary administration. This is particularly so in projects with a relatively high degree of uncertainty, where they feel they may require to take initiatives which were not specifically planned but which will ultimately be of advantage in steering the project to a successful conclusion. Such initiatives should be encouraged in R and D and it has been found possible to allow a reasonable degree of flexibility by staying with the broad milestone approach but calling for information about future expectations as well as accounting for past expenditures as outlined in the following section.

Progress charts

When a project is selected, and a project leader identified, a plan is drawn up and agreed. This plan may be based on only one of the approaches outlined earlier (bar chart, network, RPD, etc) but the key point is that it should highlight important decision criteria or milestones. The number of these will depend on the type and size of project, and on the anticipated ability of the team to manage the work, including anticipated variations within the plan. The milestones need not be very close together, but they should not be so far apart that the opportunity for taking corrective action is delayed too long. They may coincide with review points, and estimates of both time and cost to reach them should be made however uncertain these may appear to be at the outset. Such estimates can be updated as more information becomes available and as such the learning of the project is more clearly indicated.

This information could be added to the simple historical analysis chart described earlier, but this would very quickly become confusing if many changes occurred in the estimates of the time and cost required to reach future milestones. An alternative is to consider the time and cost variables separately and it has proved to be most useful to emphasize the time variable in the first instance partly because this can be more accurately monitored but also because time delays usually indicate the need for corrective action

					Calendar time			
		Jan	Feb	Mar	Apr	May	June	etc.
	Jan	1	2	3	4	5		6
	Feb	1	2	3	4	5		
Review	Mar	1	2		3	4		5
time	Apr	1	2		3	4		
	May	1	2		3			4
	Jun							
	etc.							

GHM

Figure 23.3   Example of a slip chart

which if not taken is likely to reduce considerably the financial return on a project.

The simplest of the time-based charts in use has been referred to as a 'slip' chart, because it very clearly shows when progress is slipping (see Figure 23.3).

The numbers refer to key stages or milestones in the project, and the chart acts as a historical record of how the estimates of the time required to reach a particular stage have changed as the project is progressed. In this respect it provides future-oriented information which is extremely valuable for planning purposes. Anticipated slippage is clearly shown as a movement to the right in the number associated with the milestone, and commands the attention of all interested parties. The chart therefore acts as an extremely powerful communication device. The information contained in the graphical presentation can quite easily be put on to a computer. Print-outs can then be obtained as required of the progress of any individual project or of groups of projects associated, for example, with one area of activity or under a single management, or relevant to and perhaps supported by a particular client.

Other forms of presentation can also be of value. For example, progress against expectations for an individual project can be portrayed graphically (see Figure 23.4).

A plot of the progress of a project on these two dimensions will show up deviations from plans as overruns above the line and ahead of schedule

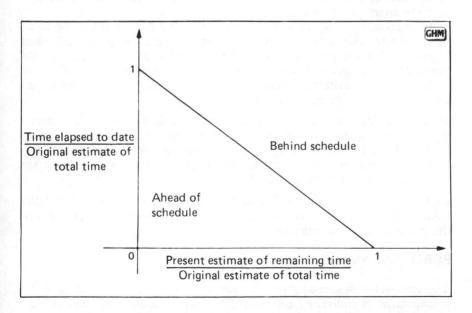

Figure 23.4   Progress against expectations for an individual project using time dimensions

below the line. Both these methods are simple to use and are visually very easy to understand. They clearly indicate deviations from plan, not only those that have occurred, but also any that are expected in future periods. This is most important if corrective action is to be taken.

The reason for choosing time as the major variable on which to focus was discussed earlier. Overruns on time are more frequent, often much larger, and the effects of such overruns on the financial return can be very large.

This does not mean, however, that cost can be ignored. Historical methods of accounting were discussed earlier, and these can be extended to include future projections in a number of ways.

Many organizations now require a cost to completion forecast at major review times. This information should be provided by the project leader, based on the best possible estimates of work outstanding (including any originally unforeseen requirements). Estimates can be derived from extrapolation from the information to date of actual against planned expenditures. In some cases this is not an unrealistic approach, as past problems frequently indicate future difficulties. The work breakdown method lends itself neatly to this approach through the identification of 'efficiency' factors. Care must be taken, however, to ensure that such an approach is not applied mechanistically. The aim of a good monitoring and reporting procedure should be to highlight problem areas as quickly as possible, allowing corrective action to be taken that will improve future performance.

Future cost estimates can be incorporated directly into the simple type of monitoring chart shown in Figure 23.2, or they can be presented as a cost slip chart (see Figure 23.5).

An organization may choose to emphasize time or cost reporting as its needs dictate. However, it is obvious that both can be useful and taken together will often provide additional information. For example, keeping time and cost progress charts side by side will enable slippage in either or both of these parameters to be considered at the same time. Some conclusions which might then be drawn are as follows:

1 Time overruns but not cost overruns suggest a lack of effort on the project
2 Cost overruns but not time overruns suggest problems are being encountered but extra effort is being allocated which looks like overcoming them
3 Cost overruns and time overruns suggest there are problems which are proving more difficult to handle.

Each of these will require different types of management action and the value of the reporting system is the simple indication which it provides of the possible areas for attention.

PORTFOLIO ANALYSIS

The approaches described above are essentially designed for assisting in the management of individual projects. The project leader and team are the people who supply the information and as such are the first people to identify deviations from the plan. They are therefore able to take corrective action if this is within their terms of reference, or to suggest alternative courses of action if they require additional resources and/or support from other key people in the organization. The value of the approaches must therefore be that they do not take away the responsibility for managing a project from those most closely concerned with its progress. Essentially what they do is recognize the uncertainty associated with research and development and encourage project leaders to provide regular position reports in the light of the progress made.

The individual planning methods focus attention on key decision points, milestones or review points. At these times the project leader will be expected to make a more detailed report on the project. Such review points will normally be agreed in advance. The progress chart, by its very nature, provides much more up-to-date information about the state of a project but without requiring this information in a detailed form. If milestones are not going to be met then the sooner this is recognized the better. In some cases this can lead to more rapid corrective action being taken; in others it may lead to an earlier decision to terminate a project which would otherwise become a cash drain with little prospect of providing an adequate financial return.

An important point about the progress chart approach is that it is clearly first and foremost an information system, with the project leader at the centre of the information network and primarily responsible for any necessary

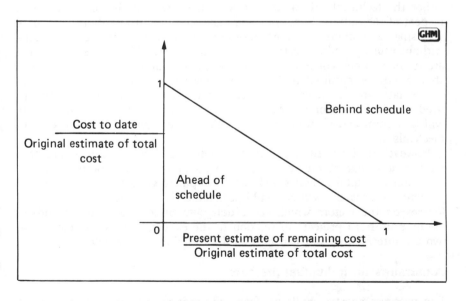

Figure 23.5 Progress against expectations for an individual project using cost dimensions

actions. It is possible to go further than this and provide some information to management on a more general basis by presenting information in alternative forms. For example, the basic information already provided for the progress charts can be converted into ratio form, as follows:

$$\frac{\text{Cost to date}}{\text{Original estimate of total cost}}$$

$$\frac{\text{Present estimate of remaining cost}}{\text{Original estimate of total cost}}$$

which becomes

$$\frac{\text{Original estimate of total cost} - \text{cost to date}}{\text{Present estimate of remaining cost}}$$

In this case, a ratio of one would indicate that a project was on schedule for cost (but not necessarily for time). A ratio of less than one indicates the likelihood of overspending on the project.

Ratios can be used in conjunction with other information (for example, with expenditure to date) but they must be treated with caution. They can clearly form part of a management by exception system but here there is a danger that they will take away the main feature of the progress chart which is its value as a communication device. Management by exception systems can too easily become the tools of people who know little about either the technical side of the work or the needs of the organization in respect of the output. Some projects may need urgent attention when only very small exceptions are reported; others can tolerate much larger variations without causing undue alarm. The people who should be most concerned are those closely concerned with the project and outside interference should only be required if they are not taking the necessary actions. The use of ratios must therefore be seen essentially as a back-up mechanism, used mostly for senior management to monitor key projects. Their value will be diminished if an attempt is made to use them as the main control mechanism.

However, it is useful to consider whether additional information of a more general nature might be obtained about the overall performance of an R and D establishment which could be put to good use. There are two particular approaches which should be given serious consideration. The first focuses on the factors which cause delays to projects and the second on the outputs from projects in relation to the expectations. Obviously these two are interrelated, but can be usefully examined separately.

Constraints on individual projects

The progress chart is built up from information supplied by the project leader. Deviations from the original plan will be due to a variety of causes. A simple request for information about the nature of factors causing delays can be very illuminating. In practice these usually fall into a few categories, for example lack of resources, external factors, technical problems.

An analysis of all the projects in the R and D establishment may also reveal a significant number of delays due to the same factor. If so, corrective action should be taken, which will reinforce the value of the planning and monitoring system, as people will see that the information they are providing is being used to their advantage. For example, if lack of resources is a common constraint then action to increase the level of resources or to reduce the number of projects will be much appreciated. It will also be of considerable motivational value to project leaders who will have to spend less of their time fighting for priority and working with inadequate support facilities. The advantage of the progress chart is that it focuses attention on any likely changes in future resource requirements on individual projects due to changes in expectations about the achievement of particular milestones. Taken over the R and D establishment as a whole this information is of great value from the resource allocation point of view.

Output assessment

At the beginning of the chapter the potential value of top-down planning was discussed. The actual value of this approach will be partly determined by the ability of the R and D establishment to complete the projects which are agreed to be relevant to the different needs of the organization. A coding system can be developed which shows the relationship of an individual project to a particular need, e.g. business area, short or long term, product or process development, etc. Projects can then be identified readily and at appropriate intervals, say quarterly or annually; all projects related to a given need can be examined and their progress noted. This analysis may well reveal areas for concern, for example, that short-term projects are being progressed more effectively than long-term ones, etc. From the financial planning point of view, it will provide a simple breakdown of the expenditures and the progress which has been made against the expectation in each area. Deviations between these two can then be examined to see whether corrective action needs to be taken.

It must also be remembered that an R and D establishment will have activities which cover a wide range of uncertainties. The proportion of low to high probability of success projects will depend upon the needs of the organization at a particular point in time as well as the attitudes to risk of the key decision makers. This balance must be reviewed at regular intervals and the monitoring procedure should highlight those projects in which the uncertainty is not decreasing over time at the expected rate. Again, the project leader will be the first to recognize the lack of uncertainty reduction, but this will also be highlighted through the lack of progress towards meeting defined milestones within the agreed timescales and cost. Decisions on whether to continue with such projects are not easy to make, as many major innovations have come about after sustained effort over many years with success always looking possible but always appearing to be just out of reach. In such cases the size of the potential benefits will usually be the deciding factor in obtaining further backing, but this must be balanced against the potential losses of not being successful, or of being beaten by competitive activity. There are many examples of organizations falling into difficulties through backing innovations requiring excessively large cash outflows with benefits appearing very far in the future.

CONCLUSIONS

A financial planning and control system is just as necessary in research and development as in any other area. However, it must take into account the uncertainty surrounding the activity. It must be flexible and it does not need to be complicated. It must be motivational rather than penalizing and the responsibility for management has to remain at the level at which the work is being done.

There is considerable evidence that the internal evaluation of projects is very compatible with external evaluations where the goals are agreed and accepted. The aim therefore is to provide the right environment in which the project leader and team are motivated to be honest with themselves and with the organization in the reporting of progress. The monitoring system can then be oriented towards signalling deviations about which other people might express different concerns than those most closely connected with the work. Such signals will encourage communication and agreement on actions which will be of benefit to all interested parties. The emphasis is on the positive aspects of monitoring which are too often hidden by disagreements about the reasons for deviations and the implied blame which often leads to the adoption of defensive positions by the different parties. The value of good feedback which can be provided through a simple planning and monitoring system cannot be over-emphasized.

Planning methods can be allowed to vary within the organization, although there may be some advantage in agreeing the type of approach which is likely to be most suitable for different types of projects. Monitoring is more useful if there is a high degree of standardization, so that comparative analysis can be done and attention paid to those factors which will improve the overall management of the R and D establishment.

In looking at possible approaches more emphasis is placed on forward than on historical analysis, with time being considered of prime importance. It must be remembered that the largest part of the cost of an R and D establishment is in the people, and unless significant amounts of outside work can be rapidly commissioned it is not easy to overspend significantly on the overall budget. The evidence is that many organizations fail to live up to their expectations in respect of completed projects in any given time period. It must therefore be more sensible to develop a monitoring system which focuses on outputs and the approaches outlined in the previous sections are of assistance in this respect.

The basic characteristics of the suggested approaches should be carefully examined before any new system is considered, as experience suggests that the imposition of formal planning and control systems on R and D has not met with a great deal of success. Any system which is likely to be accepted and effectively used will be one which can be seen to be helpful to all parties. In this respect a monitoring of the system itself is also necessary, so that adaptations can be made in the light of experience, to ensure that the maximum use continues to be made of the information generated.

REFERENCES AND FURTHER READING

Beastall, H., 'The relevance tree in Post Office R & D', *R & D Management*, vol. 1, no. 2, February 1971

Brooke, D.G., 'The use of slip charts to review research projects', *R & D Management*, vol.4, no.1, October 1973

Costello, D., 'A practical approach to R and D project selection', *Technological Forecasting and Social Change*, vol.23, 1983

Davies, G.B. and Pearson, A.W., 'The application of some group problem solving approaches to project selection in research and development', *IEEE Transactions on Engineering Management*, vol. EM-27, August 1980

Davies, D.G.S., 'Research planning diagrams', *R&D Management*, vol. 1, no. 1, October 1970

Dunne, E.J., 'How six management techniques are used', *Research Management*, March–April, 1983

Fishlock, D., *The Business of Science*, Associated Business Programmes, London, 1975

Hardingham, R. P., 'A simple model approach to multi-project monitoring' *R&D Management*, vol.1, no.1, October 1970

Lanford, H.W. and McCann, T.M., 'Effective planning and control of large projects – using work breakdown structures', *Long Range Planning*, vol.16, no.2, 1983

Liberatore, M.J. and Titus, G.J., 'The practice of management science in R and D project management', *Management Science*, vol. 29, no. 8, August 1983

Mansfield, E., 'How economists see R and D', *Harvard Business Review*, November–December 1981

Parker, R.C. and Sabberwal, A.J.P., 'Controlling R and D projects by networks', *R&D Management*, vol. 1, no.3, June 1971

Pearson, A.W., 'Planning and monitoring in research and development – a 12-year review of papers in R and D management', *R&D Management*, vol.13, no.2, 1983

Pearson, A.W. and Davies, G.B., 'Leadership styles and planning and monitoring in R and D', *R&D Management*, vol 11, no.3, 1981

Souder, W.E., 'A system for using R and D project selection methods', *Research Management*, vol. 21 no.5, 1978

24 Design management

A Brearley

This chapter considers issues relevant to the design and drawing activity. It examines arrangements for investigating and analysing design and drawing office work, for improving output quality, for improving productivity and for reducing cost. The technical aspects of design are not discussed.

A very concise definition of design describes it as a creative process by which product innovations and ideas are reduced to an economically viable arrangement, this arrangement being set down on paper as a proper scheme. The concept of economic viability can be expanded to include:

1 The economic objective
2 A product to meet that objective
3 How effectively the product meets the economic objective
4 How well the product works
5 How the product can be made
6 Hence, how much the product will cost to make
7 What the product will cost to maintain.

To these can be added consideration of how the product will look, quite apart from effects on appearance resulting from the above criteria alone, without concern for attractiveness. This is the area of design commonly known as styling. Apart from the general desirability of elegance, styling is of fundamental importance in many products such as fabrics or motor cars. It is of less significance, even unimportant, in such products as aero engines.

It follows that design management involves the initiation, organization and control of all those matters to enable effective results to be obtained. This involves design staff, a design organization and a design process, the whole interaction taking place within design and drawing offices of various kinds.

It might seem self-evident that design does actually require to be managed. However, wide-ranging experience of investigating design matters does lead to the conclusion that in what is a creative activity there is very often a failure to appreciate the need for the process to be managed carefully and skilfully. Also common is a tendency to give inadequate attention to design costs, which in themselves then form a part of product cost. These issues are considered later in this chapter.

COMMON ISSUES

Some key issues relevant to the management of design and drawing can be summarized, as in the following sections.

Management control

Senior management often takes the view that it has inadequate information and skills to enable it to control design and drawing office work and to bring it within a reasonable framework of sound management. This attitude does not seem to depend particularly on whether senior management is itself technically qualified and experienced or not. As a result, productivity and cost figures and controls for the drawing office are often inadequate. It is also often found even in an integrated design-to-manufacture business that the design and drawing office organization is not readily recognized as part of the production or construction facilities of the business.

Staff attitudes

Technical staff traditionally have little interest in administration and organization. Its members consider themselves as creative (which is obviously true to some extent) and tend to take the view that since they are creative they are not suitable for normal managerial control. There is often little appreciation of the importance of improved productivity and of reduced unit costs.

These issues are important for designers and draughtsmen; they are considerably more important when the same attitudes are found among design and drawing office managers, supervisors and higher management. There is not infrequently a reluctance to accept the managerial disciplines which would be regarded as normal in other parts of a business enterprise.

Ineffective use of staff

Because of inadequate attention to management organization and control, highly qualified design staff often spend too much of their time in work that does not involve the exercise of their particular skills. The resulting inefficiency is obvious, and will be discussed later. At the same time resentment is felt by qualified design staff at the high proportion of their time spent on tasks which they quite reasonably regard as beneath them, but which nevertheless have to be carried out.

Inadequate standardization

It is not unusual to find insufficient attention being given to the standardization of materials, components and finished products. The general attitude to productivity and cost within the drawing office as mentioned above encourages this and may well show itself in the design and detailing of the product. The lack of management and accounting expertise means there is often an insufficient attempt (if any) to evaluate the total cost of meeting the design requirements.

Unreliable completion and priority information

Inadequate information for calculating design completion dates means that design completion estimates may be unreliable, and the consequent extended through-put times cause expensive and damaging pressures on the purchasing and manufacturing or construction processes. At the same time drawing office priorities become subject to changes as a result of inadequate planning and (since the effects of those changes are difficult to evaluate in advance) the time given to developing ideas is frequently inadequate. Again, time pressures often result in inadequate consideration being given to alternative materials, processes and designs, and design modifications or errors result in expensive production or construction interruptions.

Inadequate definition of responsibilities

Insufficient attention to managerial control often leads to overlapping and confusion in the various departments of the business responsible for design and specification; sales departments, product development engineers, sales engineers and others who have an influence on design do not work to clear understanding of how their influence is to be applied and how broad it is to be. When coupled with inadequate attention to the definition and limitation of the authority to create modifications to existing or to new products, the scope for expensive confusion is considerable.

TYPES OF DESIGN AND DRAWING OFFICE

There is a very wide range of design and drawing office types. Attempts to separate them into exclusive categories are of little real value. The best approach in classification is to consider where any particular design or drawing office lies between a number of possible extremes:

1 The office designing and drawing custom-built products at one extreme.
   The office designing and drawing standard products at the other extreme
2 The production detailing office with negligible design work at one extreme.
   Offices where the design content is higher, usually meaning that output in terms of finished drawings is not closely related to the number of hours worked, at the other extreme
3 Offices with a very high level of creativity, usually found where the design content is high, at one extreme.

Offices with a very low level of creativity, which is still possible when the design content is high, at the other extreme.

The production of designs and drawings is obviously not an end in itself. The objective is to give clear instructions to the user (in other words to the production or the construction department) on the configuration and methods of manufacture or construction of the final product. The medium for doing this will usually be some combination of drawings and written instructions but, as will be discussed later, many variations are possible.

The unit of output from a design and drawing office, however defined, will have a relationship to the amount of work carried out which will vary considerably in different types of office. In general, offices with a high design content or high creativity levels will have instruction outputs bearing a less direct relationship to the input of design and drawing effort. Offices with a lower creativity level and a greater element of detailed drawing rather than design will have much closer correlation.

As would be expected, the more creative the work the more difficult it is to supervise it, control it and measure it. Figure 24.1 shows the variability involved. In cases of higher creative levels, however, the scope for improving the value of the product and for reducing its manufacturing or construction costs through better design is greater. If the aim is to improve effectiveness, the greatest scope will lie in improving the product rather than in reducing the unit cost of creating the instructions.

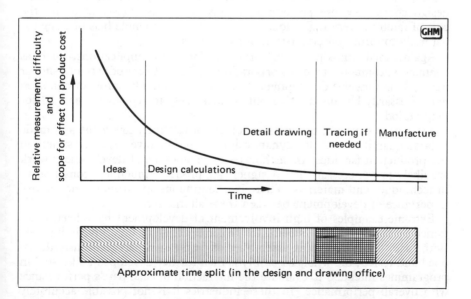

Figure 24.1   Work measurement in the design and drawing process

Some attempts have been made to classify design offices in relation to the annual production or construction costs controlled by the work carried out in that office. The costs of operating a design office are often a small proportion of the costs controlled or influenced by that design office. In those circumstances when considering any programme of reorganization or improvement we again need to give priority to improving the product rather than to improving the efficiency of the office as measured by the output of instructions related to the expenditure of design and drawing effort.

DESIGN AND DEVELOPMENT

In some industries design is an easily identifiable function, moving from a broad specification to the production of detailed drawings, whilst throughout the process striking agreements and compromises with relevant interests so that finally a product can be made or constructed. Various frameworks for the design process are considered later in this chapter.

In many fields, particularly in engineering, the additional function of development may have to be incorporated in some way into the scheme. The whole design process is an iterative one as is emphasized below. In many cases development (involving the manufacture and testing of prototypes so that the design assumptions can be tested and the results fed back into the design process) becomes a major part of that design process.

Obviously the significance of development varies greatly with the end product and the investment structure of the particular industry. A business making heavy capital equipment must give priority to getting the initial design correct because prototypes usually cannot be constructed and the cost of failure is very high indeed. In such cases the whole bias of design is naturally towards conservatism in most aspects.

Again, small mass-produced products for static applications, such as containers, components for incorporation into domestic products and similar items, do not involve development to a major extent. The initial design need not necessarily be conservative but is then likely to remain unchanged for long periods.

At another extreme, products which are of relatively low value and made in large quantities often for dynamic applications involve large investment in the production facilities. In such cases large amounts of development work are likely to be necessary and designers are probably much less conservative in techniques and materials. There is a continuous spectrum of the relative importance of development between these alternatives.

Extreme examples of high involvement of development have been mentioned by Perkins (1974) as being in the aerospace and automotive industries. Both cases involve complex assemblies of parts, each part rigorously developed and tested; the whole assembly is then further developed and tested in programmes intended to evaluate the interaction of each part's performance with overall performance. In these industries it is not possible accurately to quantify the parameters affecting performance of either the individual components or the completed assembly. Emphasizing the importance of development as an integral part of the design process is the only feasible solution.

The actual organization of the design function will obviously vary to take these differences into account and this question is considered later.

CREATIVITY IN DESIGN

Clearly design is a creative process although the depth and sophistication of the creative element varies greatly in different industries and with different products. The actual periods of creative activity are often comparatively short and are overshadowed by longer periods of calculation, technical administration and drawing.

Figure 24.2 shows a broad view of the scope for creative inputs as the design process proceeds. This shows a factor which is of considerable importance, namely, that the greatest scope for creative inputs is in the earlier stages of the design. It can also be seen that, since the cost of making important

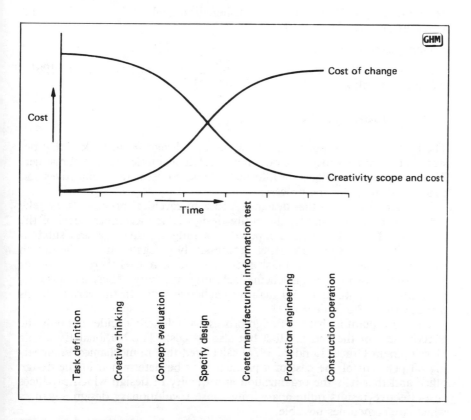

Figure 24.2   Curves of creativity and cost

changes in design increases as the process proceeds, it is highly desirable to ensure that as far as possible a major creative effort is encouraged in the earlier stages (though obviously not excluded from any stage).

There are a number of conceptual frameworks which encourage creative thinking. Most of these are well summarized in Twiss (1974). This chapter is not the place to set them out in detail; all stem from the distinction between analytical or convergent methods (in which we move towards an answer by logical deduction from known facts) and creative or divergent methods (in which we stimulate imagination in situations where the facts do not encourage or permit logical deduction and a range of possible answers can be created). There appear to be many barriers to creative thinking imposed by conformity, by lack of willingness to challenge obvious conclusions, by self-imposed idea limitations, by a belief in one 'best' answer or by a reluctance to be thought a fool for introducing ideas which look improbable.

Among techniques for assisting creativity the following should be considered:

Analytical techniques

Attribute analysis (Twiss, 1980); morphological analysis (Twiss, 1980); and needs research (Haines, 1968).

Non-analytical techniques

Brainstorming (Rickards, 1973; De Bono, 1969); synectics (Gordon, 1961); and lateral thinking (De Bono, 1969 and 1971).

DESIGN FRAMEWORKS

The first and crucial point to make about any design framework is that design is an iterative process; it does not occur in a simple sequential manner. There is constant feedback of information and adjustment of objectives and concepts throughout the process.

The second point is that design is also a hierarchical process. If we take a motor car as an example, the entire design is at the highest level of the hierarchy. The task is then composed of a range of divisions and subdivisions, with the design task being progressively delegated down the design structure as the scale of each task decreases. At each level there is scope for all the functions in a design scheme including creativity. There is, however, in addition a continuous and iterative exchange between the various levels if success is to be achieved.

The third point is that the design process very largely decides not only the effectiveness of the end product but also its cost. The National Economic Development Office (London, 1974) calculated that in mechanical engineering 80 per cent of the cost of a product may be determined in the design office and that it is the organization and quality of design which produces cost-effective results quite apart from those revolutionary design advances which are sometimes possible.

There are considerable organizational problems involved. Also there is a real risk that a product is designed as a set of components with much less interaction than is desirable. These points are mentioned again later.

Many writers have discussed the processes involved in design, an interesting early example being Marples (1960), a later one Allen (1965). It is useful to set out a simple conceptual framework for the design process. This enables us to clarify our minds about that process whilst reminding ourselves of the risk to oversimplification and of the obvious need to avoid any simple framework becoming dogmatic. One suitable framework is set out below.

Definition of the task

It is first necessary to set out the task in specific and qualitative terms. A specification is needed in a form which will describe both the functions to be carried out and the performance tolerances. A suitable specification provides a guide to continued design activity and enables us to judge both the final design and the various ideas raised as the design progresses.

Application of creative thinking

It now becomes necessary to formulate a concept which may meet the defined task, and it is now that we draw on the designer's experience and knowledge. The creative process can also be helped by group discussion and a conscious use of various aids to creativity mentioned later in this chapter. A range of possible concepts will probably emerge, all of them ill-defined in the early stages. As the process advances and the definition improves it should be possible to arrive at one or more primary concepts to meet the specification.

Evaluation of the concept

In formulating the concept clearly it is neither possible nor desirable to eliminate an informal evaluation of it as the idea develops nor would we wish to. It can, however, be inhibiting if that evaluation is carried too far at the earlier stage. It is now that the concept or range of concepts should be considered, evaluating them by later quantitative analysis and by qualitative judgement. It should then be possible to arrive at an evaluated concept which seems likely best to satisfy requirements. The specification of the solution is then largely complete.

Specification of the solution

The solution can now be more formally specified, although possibly still retaining one or more alternatives. Clearly, if a single choice is not made, the cost in time and resources of the next stages will be greatly increased.

Creation of the manufacturing information

Detailed manufacturing information is now created following detailed design work. This information can be in a range of forms, written instructions, detailed drawings, sketches, photographs, physical models and others. By this stage the investment in time and resources is very considerable.

Building of prototypes and testing

This stage may not always exist, particularly in the case of large capital projects. More typically it does exist and the implications of it for the relationship between design and development have already been mentioned. It is at this stage that the iterative nature of the process becomes particularly clear.

Development of production methods

Detailed production or construction methods can be defined; the implications and problems are outlined later in this chapter.

Production, building and operation

The obvious last stage in the process but still very much part of the iterative scheme. Aircraft and motor cars are clear cases where this part of the scheme frequently results in considerable feedback. This is also true in many large capital projects such as process plant.

Figure 24.2 showed an approximate picture of the curve of cost of design changes as the work proceeds. This is also referred to later in considering the role and timing of creative inputs.

SYSTEMIZED DESIGN

A number of design methods have been developed in an attempt to ensure that design is approached in a systematic and logical way so as to make certain that vital issues are not missed. Most of these involve systematically asking a series of questions. Obviously there is a risk that designers will give the stock answer to schemes of this kind in many areas of management, namely, that they already do all that but without the paperwork. It is also obvious that asking questions of itself creates nothing unless answers of depth, breadth and originality are forthcoming.

No system should ever be allowed to become a rigid, dogmatic structure. Systemized approaches must, therefore, be approached with caution. The particular approaches mentioned are themselves subject to change and the three examples are given so that the use of systems of this kind, suitably amended for specific circumstances, can be considered.

Fundamental design method

Fundamental design method (FDM) was developed by Matchett. The method is devised to increase the designer's awareness of his thought process. It is really an application of method study thinking to design, intended to ensure that the designer analyses problems in a controlled and disciplined way.

Problem analysis by logical approach (PABLA)

Problem analysis by logical approach (PABLA) was developed by the United Kingdom Atomic Energy Authority (UKAEA), Aldermaston, for design work involving new processes and unfamiliar environmental conditions. The approach can be regarded as an extension of FDM. A set of charts covering four main areas of design are shown below.

Chart 1: operational and environmental aspects

This chart (Figure 24.3) is used as a first step. It provides a storage space for the factors affecting a job; the limitations, the resources, operational requirements, experience, etc., are all recorded.

The titles on each box are in effect labels on pigeon holes in which information can be filed; however, the titles are also intended as questions to ensure that all factors are considered. These titles are interpreted in their widest possible meaning. For example, 'Test and install' means how do we

Operational and environmental aspects		GHM
Usage	Influences	Existing resources
Occasion 1	Environment 2	Previous designs 3
Duration 4	Safety 5	Existing equipment 6
Frequency 7	Policies 8	Services available 9
Sequence 10	Test and install 11	Experience 12
Operators 13	Time scale 14	15
Maintenance 16	Finance 17	18
Personnel acceptability 19	Manufacture 20	

Figure 24.3 PABLA chart 1: operational and environmental aspects

move the job from A to B, who does it, will it go through the doors, will we need specialized labour, is the lift big enough, who will test it, to what specification, before or after installation, do we need test equipment, test points on the job and can we test it? And so on. The titles are used as a prompt for systematic scanning over a broad area rather than as a question requiring a single answer.

This chart then is a word picture of the whole environment of the job; any conceivable factor that can influence a decision is shown. It is axiomatic that, unless all the parameters have been determined, it is unlikely that a correct decision will be made.

Chart 2: engineering design specification

On this chart (Figure 24.4) the true objective of the problem is defined, together with the performance expected of the solution. The assumptions made in determining the objective are also listed.

Chart 3: principles of systems

The primary thinking about possible solutions is recorded on this chart, which is shown in Figure 24.5 and is used as follows:

All possible means of meeting the objective are listed in the first column; no attention must be paid to whether they are practical or not – this can come later. It is essential at this stage to cast off inhibition and just to put

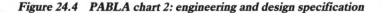

Engineering design specification			**GHM**
Objective	Performance	Assumptions	This specification to be read in conjunction with chart nos.
			Effect on environment
			Limitations

Figure 24.4   PABLA chart 2: engineering and design specification

down anything that could do the job. The aim should be to get a long list of ideas, no matter how practical or otherwise. These ideas should only be rough ones. If 'layout' type ideas come to mind one is thinking in too much detail.

Expand the ideas to cover the ground needed before they can become usable. First, is the theory of this idea known? If not, why not? What are the practical problems in using this idea? Is it an unusual size, etc.?

It is a quicker process to expand the ideas into theory and practice as a first step. Then check with charts 1 and 2 to see what it is that stops them being used. This can be noted in the 'Conflicts with' column. Having eliminated some of the ideas the remainder can be expanded further and eventually either only one will be left or the different problems associated with a number of solutions will be exposed. The choice of the best line of attack can then be made.

Chart 4: requirements of system features

Chart 4 is shown as Figure 24.6. Having selected our proposed design we break down the complex system into discrete units and note the performance required for each one, the feature we know, the questions needed to be answered and, more important still, who has to answer them. This is an essential part of the process for only by considering the constituent units side by side can one see their effect on each other. Each feature is listed at the top of the column whilst beneath it is a short description of its function and method of functioning. Beneath that again is shown what is known it has to do, whilst further down is shown the unknown areas concerning this item. This enables anyone reading the chart to see what is needed before the design can be completed.

GHM												
Principles of systems												
		Considerations										
Methods of fulfilling requirement	conflicts with	Theoretical	conflicts with	Practical	conflicts with	Size and material	conflicts with	Production aspects incl. manufacture test, install, transportation	conflicts with	Probable cost, research needed	conflicts with	

Figure 24.5   PABLA chart 3: principles of systems

Information flow

The information flow system for the PABLA method is summarized in Figure 24.7.

Integrated component approach

Middleton and Martin (1974 and 1975) describe an approach intended to ensure that the interaction of various components in a design assembly is carefully considered using a suitable mathematical model.

The approach starts from the assumption that, in many design situations, after consideration of the design effort required the work is then frequently divided among several people or groups, each with separate design responsibility. As a result, it is suggested, many products are designed as sets of independent components with each designer or group tending to proceed with little reference to the design effects of that work in other areas of the design. In the result, although the design of each component may be optimized, the final product may be less than adequate.

This approach to design is sometimes assumed to be the only practicable way to proceed if the design is to be completed in a reasonable time. Arguably, however, it leads to the rapid production of information and manufacturing

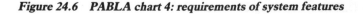

	Requirements of system features								GHM
Feature									
Function and method of functioning									
Characteristics {	Decided								
	Undecided								
Decision by {	Customer								
	Project engineer								
	Design engineer								
Source of supply {	Stores								
	Purchase								
	Design								
	Existing								

Figure 24.6   PABLA chart 4: requirements of system features

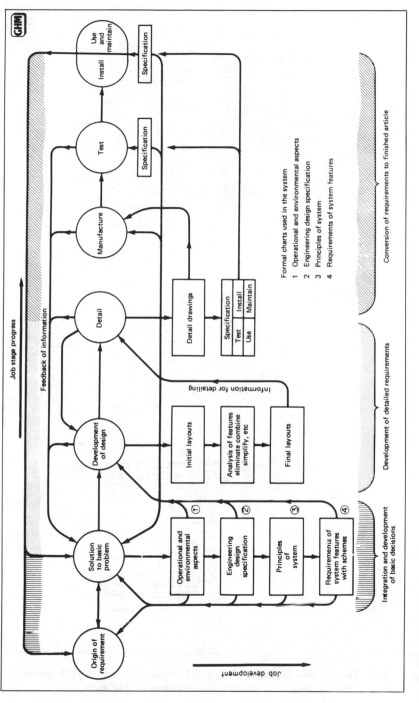

Figure 24.7 PABLA information flow chart

417

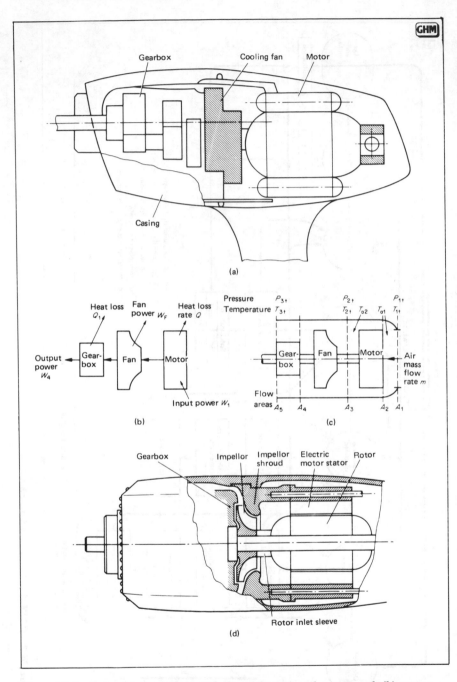

Figure 24.8 *Integrated component design: (a) proposed power tool; (b) power balance model; (c) cooling air conditions; (d) section*

instructions without necessarily resulting in the design of the most suitable product.

A procedure developed by Middleton and Martin includes the systematic examination of component interactions. Design begins with an examination of the requirements and constraints of the whole system and development of qualitative information on the static and dynamic interaction between components. A model of the system – mathematical, analogue or scale model – is then developed with concentration on a mathematical model as being quickest and cheapest. The construction of this theoretical model involves identification of all the basic physical phenomena controlling the behaviour of the product. Analysis of the model is devised to relate to the real thing, and wherever possible the behaviour of the model is checked against the known behaviour of an existing system before design starts.

The accuracy of the correlations may well depend on the assumptions made to simplify analysis, and in applying the results to a particular problem it is often necessary to change both the model and the assumptions as the design proceeds. The model is first examined with its operating parameters set for nominal values, thus providing an indication of behaviour under normal running conditions. It is then advisable to move away from the design values so that a complete range of conditions is examined. The calculations frequently justify the use of a computer although in simpler cases a tabular method is used. Middleton and Martin give an example of the successful design of a mass produced hand-drill using this system; outline drawings of the tool and two of the design models are given as Figure 24.8.

DESIGN FOR PRODUCTION

As shown in Figure 24.2 the cost penalty of design changes rapidly increases as the stages in the design process evolve. At the stage of detailed drawing preparation and transmission to the production or construction department the cost of changes is very high. It is essential that by this stage the problems of production or construction and the limitations of the production and construction processes have been fed back into the design chain.

This is often done in a haphazard way, relying on the informal production or construction knowledge of designers or on a hurried examination of the drawings by a production or construction planning department before issue. It is preferable to ensure that an organized approach to the feedback of this information is devised either by suitable administrative procedures or by organizational arrangements – possibly including consideration by joint teams of designers with production and construction people. This is crucial in applications where product economies may justify expensive rearrangements to overcome the present limitations of the production or construction techniques and facilities.

There seems little doubt that the interaction of the techniques of value engineering (VE) and value analysis (VA) with all their associated disciplines can be of great value in such matters. These techniques are briefly described in Gage (1967 and 1970) and Miles (1961).

THE COMPUTER IN DESIGN

This chapter is not the place to examine in any great detail the use of the computer in design. It is necessary only to set the scene and to comment on the effects of the computer on the design function. Cooley gave a good concise guide to the computer in design as matters stood in 1972 and particularly emphasized the effects on staff.

Until recently the computer was used only for very complex calculations, mainly in the larger companies. Now it is common to find computer terminals and mini- or micro-computers in design and drawing offices. This results from the development of time sharing and multi-programming systems in recent years and from the later development of mini- and micro-computers.

The extent of computer use varies enormously with the sophistication of the particular design process, and there are many design areas in which the computer is never likely to play a major part. The computer's main advantages are the reliable performance of functions which need large data storage, rapid retrieval and an ability to make computations and logical decisions at very high speed. Clearly the computer can only do this if the sequence can be predetermined in great detail.

On the other hand, the design engineer brings to his problems a large, ill-defined store of knowledge about his environment, about the world in general, about his own design situation and about his personal experience of products, events and relationships. He can form qualitative judgements, and only he can introduce the innovative and creative elements into the design situation. He is also capable of making intuitive judgements at various stages of the design at which inadequate information is available, then of checking and possibly of changing those judgements at later stages.

The problem throughout is to use the design engineer for the work which only he can do but also to give him the appropriate computer-based facilities to enable there to be a continuous interaction between the designer and the computer throughout all the iterations of the design process. There are thus at present two broad areas where computers are used in design.

Computing and analysis

Hand calculators are now available in increasingly sophisticated versions at comparatively modest prices and are of course widely used. Design calculations, however, range from simple arithmetic up to highly sophisticated multi-factor problems, and it is at the more sophisticated level that computers have increased their use in recent years.

The manipulation of large quantities of data and the solution of equations are tasks frequently given to the computer. Also the more difficult tasks of analysis, when the design concept is sufficiently developed to enable a conceptual model to be constructed, can often be performed and the limited example given by Middleton and Martin (1974) points to the sort of work involved although a very wide range of more complicated examples exists. Many programmes have been developed in the high-technology industries, such as the aerospace and automotive industries, and also in structural applications.

Recent years have witnessed an enormous increase in the complexity of engineering design codes and standards. Although these are still theoretically within the capabilities of manual preparation methods, they effectively preclude economic designing without recourse to computer facilities (especially important to consider in relation to the increasing pressures of cost competition between companies).

Software is readily available to handle not only complex stress analyses and analytical design, but also the progression of design in accordance with codified requirements until the final solution is achieved. This is particularly the trend in the fields of civil, structural and fluids engineering.

Computer graphics

The application of computer graphics began with the off-line transmission of graphic information to the computer, and a wide range of equipment is available for this purpose. The arrangements have particular value in the preparation of drawings in a range of scales and projections and sometimes for the direct preparation of manufacturing templates. In some systems the computer can interact with the designer to prepare three-dimensional mock-ups while the designer relates other factors. In the container industry designs have been used to prepare and optimize material and structural requirements, for example.

Later developments sometimes described as 'active' computer graphics allow the design to input directly to the video display unit or to a 'graphics pad'. These facilities allow rapid design changes and have reduced the complexity of the machine interface considerably. One application of such a system using a microcomputer allows civil engineers to calculate areas or volumes of various alternative designs on an immediate and interactive basis.

A stage has now been reached where active graphics systems can finally provide the design engineer with the capability he needs. There is communication in the designer's natural medium; there is the facility for continuous interaction between the designer and the machine; and the designer can work at his own pace with the machine carrying out the time-consuming analyses, whilst maintaining a continuous record of the current stage of the design. The machine can also be used to integrate various sections of a design, to display the result and to convert internally stored designs to copies when needed.

Computerized graphics also enable the efficient transfer of drawings between distant centres. For example, a construction site equipped with a graphics terminal can receive instantaneous drawing revisions from the design office. The digitized data can be sent in the form of a magnetic tape, or transmitted via telephone or radio links (including the use of radio satellites).

The greatest benefits from computer graphics are seen when the technique is used in direct conjunction with computer aided manufacturing. The abbreviations CAE (computer aided engineering), CAD (computer aided design) and CAM (computer aided manufacture) are now in common use. There are hundreds of CAD/CAM equipment and software suppliers, many operating in the UK.

ORGANIZATION OF DESIGN AND DRAWING

Organization patterns

There is a very wide range of alternatives in the organization of companies and hence of the position of the drawing office within the company. There is also a wide range of variation in the internal organization of drawing offices. In those circumstances any attempt to specify the 'best' type of organization in particular circumstances will inevitably fail. What is important is to familiarize oneself with the objectives and plans of the business and with the organizational patterns used in various businesses, so that the appropriate pattern for the particular circumstances can be kept under constant review.

Wearne (1973) gives an excellent survey of the principles of engineering organization which should be read when considering the present pattern in any business and the possibility of changes to that pattern. In any one business at any one time it is necessary to take a clear view of the most appropriate patterns of organization for the time being and the various possibilities are briefly examined below.

Company structure

Company structure and the relative importance of the design and drawing office functions vary greatly between industries and between organizations of differing capital and cost structures. Wearne (1970-71) gives a number of specific examples from manufacturing, consulting engineering and contracting and capital project promotion; there are many others.

Also to be considered are the various broad categories for the grouping of people in business. The general structure of design decisions was discussed earlier and the structure adopted has significant implications for the grouping of people in the business as a whole. There are a number of broad alternatives and the choice will depend on the decision structure adopted. Among the possible choices are the following:

Grouping by phase

In this system people are grouped according to the phases of the project, one group carrying out feasibility studies, the next group doing overall design of each project and so on.

Grouping by experience levels

In this grouping the authority to make decisions is formulated in a hierarchy based on the experience and technological ability of the people concerned. This method has clear affinities with grouping by phase.

Grouping by functional subject

In this system people are grouped by technological specialism such as electrical, fluid flow, etc., or by component type specialism.

Grouping by project

In this system the teams needed for one particular project are grouped together. This is obviously used in 'one time' organizations, but can be used in organizations carrying out projects of various sizes and complexity at different times.

Matrix organization

A final interesting variant is the matrix organization in which the various responsibilities and alternatives, both project and specialist, are combined in a matrix permitting wide variability. In the formal sense this type of organization is very rare. In the informal sense, however, almost any organization, however structured, takes on some limited aspects of the matrix system. This should particularly be borne in mind when considering changes in the organization. The apparent formal organization may in fact operate rather differently than appears and it is possible that the matrix element of the organization, even though it is not obvious, is making a major contribution to its actual operation.

IMPORTANT ORGANIZATIONAL FACTORS

A number of general points can be made.

Geography

The organization pattern decided will be used to settle the geographical dispersion of the people concerned. That is inevitable but immediately raises problems of communication and problems of rigidity.

Definition

Even though an organization may frequently change, it is of importance that the position of the drawing office in the organization is defined in writing if reasonable managerial control is to be effective. The relationship with other functions, with customers and in particular with the manufacturing or construction function requires clear definition. The responsibility and authority for giving executive instructions, such as firm commitments to purchase materials and components and to manufacture, needs clear definition.

Drawing office management

Equally important is a clear definition of the responsibility and authority of drawing office management. It is frequently necessary to clarify the drawing office manager's responsibility for managing the drawing office in its full sense as opposed to the technical supervision of the office. Surprisingly, it is still often found that drawing office management is reluctant to accept full responsibility for matters other than technical areas; in particular the responsibility for employee relations and for meeting completion and cost targets will need definition. If the executive in charge of the drawing office is not already called the drawing office manager a change to that title may well be effective in emphasizing the role.

Integral organization

The remarks made above about the organization also apply to the internal organization of the drawing office. The range of possible groupings by phase, by experience level, by function or by project are all relevant and possible methods of organization. Again almost any system will in practice have some of the characteristics of a matrix.

In the small drawing office the drawing office manager will himself deal with the pre-drawing problems and will issue work to the individual draughtsmen; he will supervise the details and will note the progress of the work. This organization is necessarily modified when the drawing office is larger and more complex. When the drawing office is larger a number of changes are possible, among these are the following.

Section heads

Section heads may be appointed. These are responsible for a specific part of the work of the office divided on functional, experience level or component lines and they act as subordinate managers directly responsible to the drawing office manager. They should preferably supervise administration and discipline in their sections as well as technical matters. This not only relieves the drawing office manager of a sizeable load but also ensures that section heads do not stand aside when administration and disciplinary problems are at issue. Their duties should be defined in writing.

Separate drawing offices

In the larger company separate drawing offices may be set up for different aspects of the work. Each drawing office then has its own manager and subordinate section heads. The basis for separation may be any of the variants mentioned above for a geographically integrated drawing office. This approach is sound but, as the work load on different offices may be difficult to balance, a procedure for easy transfer of staff is vital.

Contract engineers

Contract engineers may also be appointed. Their main job is usually to deal with customer liaison on technical matters and to relieve the drawing office manager and section heads of this work. They will be of senior status, usually senior to section heads. Contract engineering is a functional responsibility and does not normally affect the line management relationship between the drawing office manager and section heads. The presence of a number of contract engineers, each calling on the same resources, emphasizes the need for a proper loading, planning and progressing procedure within the drawing office.

Project engineers or leaders

Project engineers or leaders may be appointed for the duration of projects. This type of arrangement may be formalized as a matrix organization as already discussed. Project teams can encourage efficient use of manpower by good communications within the groups and by breaking down the sometimes artificial boundaries. It should be remembered that externally imposed delays may leave a project team under-employed unless it has a reservoir of other work or can readily transfer men to other teams.

Production methods engineers

In the NEDO Report (1974) the view was expressed that 80 per cent of product costs in engineering can be determined in the design and drawing office. If this is accepted then clearly the infusion of detailed knowledge of production engineering methods into the drawing office is vital. It is not necessary to repeat the points already made about the VA and VE techniques. The point here is that production methods engineers are often appointed as members of the drawing office staff to provide the necessary knowledge.

Work control

The question of production control within the drawing office is discussed later. The type of work control methods clearly affects organization and vice versa. Figure 24.9 shows a conventional drawing office organization with the section heads holding responsibility for parts of the organization split in one of the ways mentioned earlier. The various subsections or individual staff members may be combined in one of the various ways mentioned above. Any section head may have subordinates of one functional specialism or in a combination suitable to the organization actually in being.

There is an obvious problem with this organization as it stands. The only managerial link between the various section heads is the drawing office manager himself. In practice this problem can be overcome in a variety of informal ways. It may, however, be very desirable particularly in the more complex drawing office to introduce some form of central planning unit reporting to the drawing office manager with responsibility for planning, scheduling, controlling and progressing the work throughout the office. This arrangement can be used to introduce a greater flexibility in the arrangement of capacity or it can simply be used for the routine functions

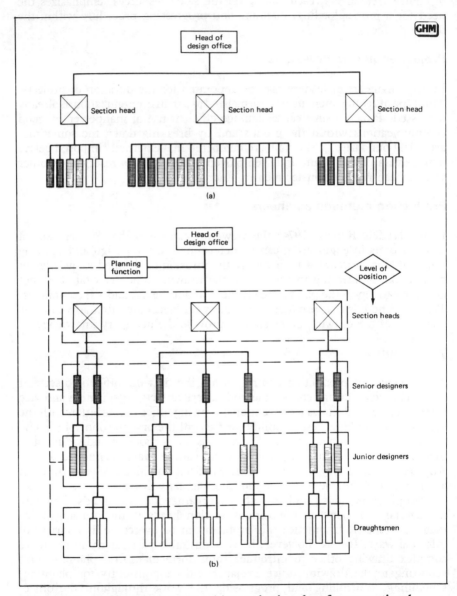

Figure 24.9 **Organization patterns: (a) organization chart for conventional design office; (b) organization with planning function**

with an additional responsibility for drawing attention to areas and periods when work loads are, or will be, out of balance.

Feiner (1969) gives an example of two methods of organization used to introduce maximum flexibility and these are illustrated in Figure 24.9. Figure 24.10 shows the change in work distribution seen as a result of introducing this method of operation into a sample group of drawing office situations, although the sample is not necessarily a fully representative one.

Checking work for errors

It is often still the custom for all drawings and calculations to be checked by a draughtsman other than the one originating the work. This procedure can be wasteful and inefficient; the extra work involved can amount to between 20 and 30 per cent. Even if the checker spends as long on the job as the originating draughtsman he can miss unfamiliar details. Checking by another draughtsman can induce a slacker attitude in the originating draughtsman, and the final effect is a reduced sense of responsibility for his own work. The section head and the drawing office manager should both feel a responsibility for work quality and style; although they cannot check all details, they should make an overall inspection; checking by another draughtsman tends to reduce their sense of responsibility also. A random check can sometimes be used if necessary but even this is open to doubt.

Any errors or omissions on drawings will usually be quickly discovered in the manufacturing or construction function. Reporting them immediately should be encouraged and immediate action should be taken to correct them. Obvious exceptions to this philosophy on checking are design areas where safety is of crucial importance and where errors are unlikely to be discovered until it is too late or too expensive; for example, the stress calculations in civil engineering structures.

Other functions

Drawing office productivity is a crucial issue. In industry generally since the industrial revolution, massive productivity increases have been achieved with a considerable contribution made by the concept of division of labour. There is, however, an obvious dilemma which has been discussed since that industrial revolution began. If the division of labour is increased, efficiency increases but very often job satisfaction and motivation decrease. If the decrease in job satisfaction and motivation goes far enough, there may be a drop in efficiency offsetting the increases hoped for from the division. The question of motivation is thus fundamental.

In drawing offices, where the staff are intelligent professional people although at widely differing levels of education and skills, the problem of division of labour is particularly important. No simple rules are possible. It should be borne in mind when considering the division of drawing office work that job satisfaction and motivation are very easily impaired, especially where the work has a significant creative element. It is very often desirable

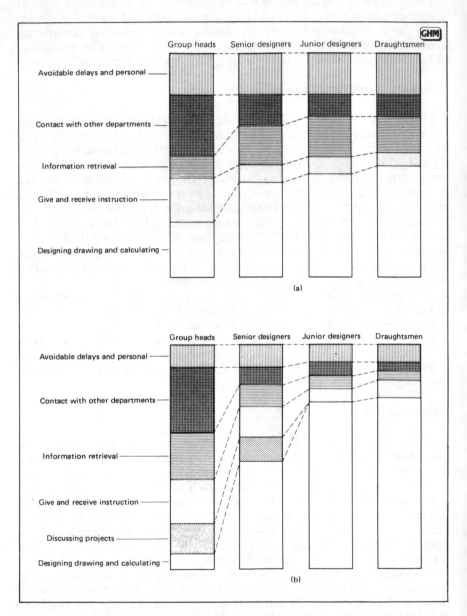

Figure 24.10 **Design drawing office work distribution: (a) work distribution in a conventional engineering design office; (b) work distribution in an engineering design office with planning function**

to avoid the elimination of some of the activities which may apparently reduce productivity but which may be vital to job satisfaction. The following
groups of work often carried out in drawing offices should be considered
with these issues in mind.

Development

In the larger companies (as already discussed) development may be a separate
function but in smaller companies it will often be mixed with design and
drawing. If the design and drawing office organization includes project teams
or has a matrix structure, it will be possible to treat a development project
in much the same way as any other project.

Sales estimating

Sales estimating is not generally regarded as drawing office work but
in many companies will be found there. The attitudes required by a sales
estimator are different from those required by a draughtsman. The estimator
should be more ready to approximate, and commercial acumen is required
in addition to technical knowledge. If this work is done in the drawing
office it is desirable to have specialist staff doing it. In many cases there
is also scope for improving the mechanics of estimating; better synthetics,
multiple regression using commonly recurring parameters in the types of
work undertaken, improved data retrieval and other methods are all often
appropriate.

Specifications

Specifications other than initial design specifications may be written for sales
purposes or for use in other departments. It is possible in large companies
for this work to be done by specially trained staff. Writing specifications is
difficult; they require economical language but will often be read by people
with less technical knowledge than the writer, and technical staff frequently
do not have an adequate command of the appropriate skills.

Parts lists

Parts lists vary from simple lists of parts referred to on drawings up to lengthy
descriptions of parts listed. They are frequently contained on drawings but
are best prepared as separate documents. It is often desirable to have a
parts list prepared by a different member of staff from the one originating
the relevant drawing, as this ensures adequate checks, and results in better
detailed lists. Parts explosions are sometimes produced by computer.

Parts lists should be recorded and filed in a similar way to drawings and
they require cross-reference to the drawings involved.

Materials lists

In some offices materials lists may be more important than parts lists, and the same considerations apply.

External relations

The following are among the important external relations of the drawing office.

Relations with manufacturing or construction

It is necessary to clarify in writing the channels of communication with production or construction departments on such matters as drawing errors and proposed shop-floor modifications. The relationship between the drawing office work control function and the overall production control function of the business must be defined – usually involving close co-ordination. Already mentioned are the effects of VA and VE techniques on relations with manufacturing or construction departments and the possible appointment of production methods engineers which also affects the relationship.

Relations with customers

There should be clear definition of the aspects of customer relations to be dealt with by the drawing office manager, contract engineers, project engineers, section heads and draughtsmen, respectively. If contract engineers are employed it is often preferable for most of these contacts to be made by them and, if so, possible overlap with sales functions must be carefully controlled.

Relations with other business functions

The important issue again is a clear definition of the channels and of where authority and responsibility lie in the matters dealt with by those channels.

Technical information service

Any drawing office, however small, should maintain a library of essential publications and technical information, and in large companies a fully comprehensive library service may be desirable. A sound working relationship may also be established with the local lending and reference library; the free assistance thus available is considerable. Contact is best maintained by one person, who can acquire familiarity with sources and avoid individual draughtsmen wasting time. Collecting technical information is a specialist job.

In recent years access to published information has been widened by the establishment of online bibliographic data bases, centred in the UK or overseas, and accessed from a small terminal or micro-computer over ordinary telephone lines. Several agencies exist, and the facilities offered allow searching of massive files using titles, authors or subject 'keywords'.

Standard practice

The main code of practice for drawing offices in the UK is BS 308 (British Standards Institution). This will be found useful in standardizing actual drawing methods. Even where offices have already standardized on this specification, however, the fact will sometimes not have been stated in writing, and individual draughtsmen may be deviating from it. This can result in difficulty in reading drawings, in customers being given a bad impression and in wide variations in work content for similar drawings made by different draughtsmen. The question of functional draughting is discussed later and, as will be seen, company standards for drawings may permit a far greater degree of simplification than indicated in BS 308. For general standards reference there should be an up-to-date copy of the *BSI Yearbook*.

Since standard practices are of crucial importance to the usefulness of drawings and to the efficiency with which they are produced it is necessary for the responsibility for issuing and maintaining the standard practices approved for use in the company to be very clearly defined. A comprehensive schedule of the standards to be used is essential and a system for disseminating the information thoroughly is needed.

WORK SCHEDULING AND OFFICE CONTROL

The design and drawing office as a production department

In an organization of any size and complexity the design and drawing office is itself a major production department. In some cases the drawing office can be of such size and complexity that the work scheduling and control problems are as difficult and important as the production control problems of many factories.

It seems clear that four basic steps are involved in achieving effective control in any managerial situation:

1 Plan what should be achieved
2 Record at regular intervals what is being achieved
3 Compare actual achievement with planned achievement
4 Take action to correct any deviation from the plan.

It is also possible to see each of these steps in four distinct but interdependent aspects of control, namely, work scheduling, managerial control, manpower budgeting and supervision or work control. These are considered below.

Time estimates

Without some form of time estimates satisfactory control is not possible. Even in the least sophisticated systems some estimates are made, even though they may be informal and not set down in writing at all. For methods of work measurement and time estimating in offices see Brearley (1975 and 1976). In this chapter it is assumed that some form of time estimates are created for use in the control system.

If the design and creative content of the work is low, the problem is fairly simple and output figures for satisfactory control can readily be defined. If the design content is high, a varying number of solutions to each design problem may have to be tried and evaluated before an acceptable solution is found and then suitable control measures are more difficult to define. Possible control parameters are numbers and values of products for which design solutions are found; alternatively the estimated value increase or cost reduction between the various alternative solutions and the one finally adopted. Always a key control is the conformance with scheduled delivery dates for drawings and designs.

Even so it is essential to have time estimates prepared in advance for the work content of designs and drawings to be used for planning forward loads, for setting clear control targets and for advanced pricing for tenders where necessary.

When making time estimates the following points should be borne in mind:

1 *Validity* – care must be taken to avoid unknowingly including time spent on extraneous activities when accepting staff time recording as a basis for analysis. This requires a good knowledge of the work
2 *Improvement* – the target times for planning will not remain static, but will reduce as methods, skill and experience are improved (often referred to as the 'learning curve' effect)
3 *Adjustment* – time targets set for planning will be continually adjusted as made necessary by changes in organization and methods.

Unless these points are acted upon the time estimates will become fixed, so that over a period a distorting (and possibly slackening) effect on efficiency will result.

Work scheduling

A scheduling system is necessary in the drawing office for a wide range of reasons:

1 Providing accurate completion dates for projects
2 Providing accurate completion dates for drawings for parts of projects as work proceeds, so as to give targets for staff motivation
3 Providing sound sequencing of parts or projects so that external requirements such as materials orders can be dealt with
4 Providing a means of checking in advance the need to change the capacity of the drawing office or of a part of the project
5 Providing a means of balancing load against capacity in order to achieve acceptable delivery times at economic target levels.

The broad needs of such a scheduling system are as follows:

1 *Information provision.* A system for collating the results of all preliminary

information such as initial investigations, feasibility studies and overall design parameters

2   *Forward load.* A medium- to long-term forward load picture which shows the forward load and indicates the smoothing necessary to maintain adequate control, and the extension of load shedding to other sources of help if that is appropriate

3   *Work planning.* A system of planning the work in the shorter term, allowing for the work already in progress and waiting to start, and then balanced to the total capacity available or planned. If the drawing office is closely linked to production or construction facilities where major unpredicted changes of plan may be created, then this system will need to be very flexible. This short-term plan is also a major factor in productivity and cost control and these aspects are dealt with later in the chapter

4   *Work issue.* A system intended to ensure that the requirements of the work schedule are communicated in adequate detail to the management and staff responsible for doing the work and to ensure that acceptance of that work is clear

5   *Progress.* A system to check the progress of all work in the drawing office, revealing delays and potential delays so that information can readily be obtained to ensure corrections to the arrangements. This also enables information on any really unavoidable delays to be fed back into the forward load and work planning systems.

Work scheduling techniques

A wide range of techniques at various levels of sophistication is available for carrying out this work. The most likely techniques are as follows, the likely usage depending on the complexity and character of the work:

1   Project critical path networks, possibly scheduled by computer
2   Load simulation using mathematical techniques
3   Aggregation of loads within control periods for a range of projects, possibly by computer
4   Job sequencing to groups or to individuals, probably by the use of visual bar charts in one form or another.

This subject is discussed in greater detail in Chapter 34.

Managerial control

Managerial control is necessary to fulfil two objectives.

First, it provides a system of access by senior management in the drawing office and outside it to the scheduling systems mentioned earlier so that decisions on changes in priorities, acceptance of urgent demands and the possible build-up of drawing office delivery problems can be made with adequate information to hand. It also provides rapid access to accurate progress information on particular projects and gives summary information on such matters as achievement of the programme and of delivery promises.

Second, it provides senior management in the drawing office and outside it with information enabling them to take a broader, long-term view and to set budgets for the main features of the drawing office activity, such as staffing levels, productivity and cost. It also provides management with a means of comparing actual results with budgeted results so that action can be taken to maintain high levels of productivity and the lowest possible levels of drawing office cost.

The object of any management control system is to provide each manager with key information on the activities under his control in a clear quantified way, thus promoting action by management. It needs to be prompt, frequent, directly relevant, sufficiently accurate, and stimulating in that it contrasts actual results with standard results in a clear manner. All this information can only be available if some form of measurement has been applied as discussed earlier. The information necessary for management control is discussed in Brearley (1975).

Manpower budgeting

The importance of medium-term manpower budgets, in other words determining the staff requirements to deal with the required workload – has already been mentioned. This process can sometimes be carried out for a twelve-month period, although sometimes a shorter period is necessary. In considering the calculation of staff levels on the basis of the future twelve months (whilst remembering the possibility of other periods being more suitable) appropriate stages in the procedure are as follows:

1 Determine the workload for the next twelve months
2 Calculate the effective staff requirement
3 Modify the staff figures to make provision for holidays and other absences
4 Review the figures to see whether fluctuations in staff requirements can be levelled
5 Consider the effect of short-term work cycles.

Determination of workload

Clearly in a reasonably stable situation the workload can be based on figures for the previous twelve months amended for any expected changes over the next twelve months. There will be some stability in the drawing office, overlaid with information from forward visualization. The required workload in units of output is reached by multiplying the work unit value by the number of output units. Work unit values would be in the time units of any of the various work measurement systems. Where the mix of work changes very little, this calculation may be speeded by choosing the predominant unit and by calculating an equivalent time for the remaining units. The workload is calculated for each month or accounting period and the workloads then tabulated by months or by accounting periods.

Determination of effective staff requirements

Effective staff requirements can be defined as the equivalent number of full-time staff working a complete week. The requirement for the forecast volume is determined by two factors: the length of the working week allowing for meal breaks, and the expected performance of staff taking into account their motivation and the type of work they perform.

In the absence of direct monetary incentives, but with good control procedures, it is reasonable to expect performances around 70 per cent effective use of time, though a judgement is necessary for each office. In this way the effective staff requirement can readily be calculated and again tabulated by month or by accounting period.

Holidays and other absence

The effective staff figure makes no allowance for time lost through holidays and absence and therefore needs to be adjusted. A suitable procedure is to determine the percentage incidence of holidays and sickness from an analysis of past records; these figures should then be adjusted to allow for management policy, such as any changes in holiday entitlement or the retirement or dismissal of those frequently absent through illness. This adjusted percentage must then be converted to the equivalent number of staff lost. Finally, the total staff required is calculated by the addition of the effective staff required and the effective staff lost through holidays and sickness.

Levelling staff requirements

Staff requirements often show variations from month to month. To achieve optimum manpower usage some means of dealing with these variations is necessary. Possible solutions are as follows:

1 *Change the work flow pattern* by changing requirements which can be shown to be the cause of peak workloads. Examine the possibility of adjusting the seasonal characteristics of the work if such characteristics exist
2 *Employ temporary staff.* If peak requirements are essentially seasonal this is often a solution. It is, however, one which is over-used and uncontrolled in many businesses and is not welcomed by drawing office staff
3 *Transfer staff internally* or combine departments. A system of easy temporary transfers can be set up. In some cases compatible departments can be combined, making the interchange of staff easier and enabling peaks and troughs to be balanced.

Short-term levelling

A procedure of the kind already mentioned allows for monthly fluctuations throughout the year. It is also necessary to consider fluctuations in workload over much shorter periods and to answer the fundamental question of what work delay is acceptable; in many cases a preplanned reasonable work delay can be tolerated and, if so, work patterns should take this into account.

Where requirements exist for dealing with peaks as they occur, possible solutions are borrowing staff from other sections, employing part-time staff and using controlled overtime. Clearly a considerable degree of extra-staff flexibility will be essential and this can present a training problem for staff and also for managers in setting up adequate control systems.

WORK SUPERVISION OR CONTROL

By work supervision or control is meant close day-to-day control of the work of a group or section by the supervisor. The manager immediately supervising design and drawing office staff is the key figure in improving and maintaining the performance of the section. Depending on adequate time estimates or work measurement standards for control, work supervision is essentially day-to-day and hour-to-hour control; the objectives are to increase productivity by eliminating non-productive time, and to improve service by reducing work backlogs and delays. The fundamental aspects of work control needed to meet these objectives are clear:

1 Determine the time required to complete each job
2 Schedule the work to staff in manageable units, so as to maintain an even work flow
3 Maintain records from which the supervisor can see the work in progress and take action to reduce delays
4 Report results, especially exceptions, to management at suitable regular intervals.

These fundamentals can only be fully achieved if realistic work standards are available to the supervisor. The standards can then be presented to supervisors so that they are both easy to understand and quick and effective to use. The precise manner in which results are presented to supervisors will vary considerably but would normally be either tables or work values or variable manning tables. Detailed methods are summarized in Brearley (1975).

IMPROVING DRAWING OFFICE PERFORMANCE

There is clear evidence of considerable scope for improvement in design and drawing office performance. Such improvements can be classified broadly into three areas:

1 *Improved output quality* – improving the end result of the instructions; in other words improving the design of the product functionally or in its cheapness of production.
2 *Changing the output* – changing the balance of instructions to more effective means by reconsidering the proportion of drawings, sketches, written instructions, photographs or models.
3 *Improving productivity* – increasing the output of instructions from the drawing office for every unit of design and drawing input effort.

As in productivity investigations in most other areas of management the balance between these three aspects needs to be very carefully considered. It would clearly be pointless to concentrate on internal productivity improvements in a drawing office if those improvements were to be gained at the expense of a deterioration in the effectiveness of the output instructions produced.

A recommended comprehensive scheme for investigating and improving the operation of design and drawing offices is set out in Brearley (1975). This chapter is not the place for a detailed treatment of the subject, but some aspects are dealt with below.

Change of output

The output can be changed in the following way:

1　Reduce unnecessarily high grade drawing. (The concept of functional draughting is outlined below in this context.)
2　Increase the use of sketches and written instructions using the simple cost information which is often made available as a result of measurement and control to decide which methods are in fact the most effective.

Functional draughting

A particularly important potential area of change is that of functional or simplified draughting. The objective of producing a drawing is to communicate information; this information is intended to depict the shape and to give details of dimensions and tolerances. The first approach to functional draughting is to consider whether the information is being communicated in the best way. In many cases it is found that much of the information can be communicated by technical notes or sketches, and detailed drawings either are unnecessary or can be produced for only part of the communication need.

It is not necessary to summarize the detailed procedures examining drawing specification; these are summarized in Brearley (1975). Reference to Figure 24.11 shows the type of simplification possible even in an unsophisticated example. It is immediately clear from this figure that enormous scope can be found in most drawing and design offices for the simplification of drawings. The important point to be made in this chapter is that early realization of the possibilities before the investigation gets under way will greatly simplify the evaluation of those possibilities at this stage.

Improving drawing office productivity

Drawing office costs can be reduced, and the effectiveness of the output instructions increased by:

1　Increasing the output from each draughtsman by drawing simplification
2　Possibly, increasing the output effort made by draughtsmen
3　Eliminating delays and the inefficient use of time

4   Using effective work scheduling with realistic dates; but avoiding being over-ambitious in raising productivity so that schedule dates become too optimistic

5   Saving office space and creating functional layouts for optimum super-vision and communications

6   Increasing productivity through improved general office and working conditions (e.g. lighting)

7   Reducing the incidence of drawing mistakes, therefore reducing time needed to make corrections – and reducing the risk of production scrap later

8   Encouraging the application of VA and VE techniques

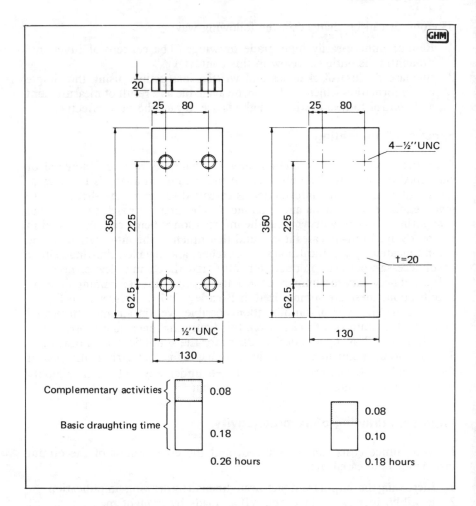

Figure 24.11   Functional draughting results

9 Providing for better liaison between drawing office and production departments, and to customers where appropriate, so as to provide a good service on technical queries and attendance to complaints
10 Improving supervision and management control
11 Updating draughting equipment to take advantage of modern digital techniques, ranging from draughting machines with co-ordinate readouts to full-scale CAD facilities.

Improvement of management control

The following measures contribute to more effective management of the drawing office:

1 Clarifying the position of the drawing office within the company management structure and reducing any confusion of objectives
2 Improving administrative procedures within the drawing office and ensuring that these are compatible with procedures in the remainder of the organization
3 Providing internal productivity information which can form a basis for establishing drawing office performance standards
4 Providing overall control information on drawing office performance for use by management
5 If necessary, reducing the difficulties of recruitment and staff training.

Improvement of morale and employee relations

This improvement can be achieved in the following manner:

1 General working conditions and equipment must be adequate, and should be improved if necessary
2 Costing and control information can be used as a foundation for the payment of adequate and sensibly graded salaries
3 A more equitable work distribution can be created
4 Improved control information can provide management with additional opportunity for assessing drawing office managers, supervisors and other staff. This information can frequently be used for formal management and staff appraisal, and it can sometimes be used as part of an improved salary review procedure
5 The availability of better information for setting detailed objectives and for providing better means for controlling and motivating staff can, if properly used, contribute to the development of managers, supervisors and other staff
6 Obviously no internal improvement can counteract external effects on workload, a decrease in which could lead to redundancies. It should, however, be possible to reduce the risk of redundancies by the use of sound manpower planning and workload balancing techniques.

Use of time: increasing productivity

Many consultants and executives carrying out productivity investigations emphasize that their programmes do not involve staff in 'working harder'. This contention is rather difficult to sustain and the thinking behind the comment requires further investigation. In most cases it is found that the major proportion of any productivity increase in the drawing office does not come from increased effort in the work study sense – i.e. it does not come from individuals achieving higher ratings whilst actually working. The improvement comes in the main from a significant reduction in delay time of all kinds. The survey of possible productivity gains given later shows this. A particularly important issue is to ensure that studies are capable of isolating delay time of all kinds so that the amount can possibly later be reduced by sensible control and motivation.

Of even greater significance is that in discussions with staff during all the consultation and participation processes of any reorganization work it is specious and undesirable to talk about staff not being asked to 'work harder'. It is vastly better to put all the relevant issues to the staff concerned and, if the end result desired is a reduction in delay time and ineffective time, then this should be openly discussed to see if active cooperation is possible, which it frequently will be.

The scale of possible performance improvements

It is possible to evaluate improvements under any of the foregoing headings in financial terms, although it is obvious that this must sometimes be extremely difficult. There is a considerable body of evidence that the general effectiveness of white collar workers in offices without adequate control is around 50 per cent. This figure is well substantiated by reference to a wide range of design and drawing office reorganization studies; substantial improvements in productivity are clearly obtainable theoretically.

Improvements in direct productivity vary considerably, as might be expected. The sort of average figures found to be available are set out below, with the average figure for overall increase in output for a draughtsman being 35 per cent.

Reductions in actual drawing work after the application of functional draughting techniques average 30 per cent, ranging from 10 to 80 per cent. Allowing that, before any improvement, the average effectiveness was 50 per cent, then this 30 per cent reduction of effort is equivalent to an improvement of 15 per cent in productivity. Productivity improvements from the elimination of unnecessary tasks could add another 5 per cent, with better planning yielding 15 per cent. Obviously these figures are given only as averages, and they are taken from a wide range of actual figures.

If part of the increase in productivity is applied to the value engineering aspects, the indirect benefits can be considerably larger than the direct benefits quoted above. Better products, more sales and higher prices through improved quality are probable. Reduction in manufacturing costs are also probable, with multi-component products being most likely to benefit.

Dramatic possibilities for productivity improvement are opened up when suitable computer systems are introduced into the design (CAE) and draughting (CAD) functions, especially when these can be integrated with a manufacturing (CAM) system. However, the investment involved in equipment, software, maintenance contracts, staff training and even in time spent evaluating possible systems is likely to be heavy, so that the company must be satisfied that work throughput will be sufficient to justify the capital outlay.

THE DESIGN AUDIT

However much care and attention is given to the management issues relevant to design, problems may still arise in manufacture or use. It has therefore become widely accepted that some further assurance is required that new designs do not have features which lead to manufacturing or service failures. An overview technique is therefore desirable. A particularly useful one is *design audit*, an outline of which is given in Jeffries and Westgarth (1981) which describes the work developed by the Design Audit Group of British Steel. The technique has been developed for use on high-cost capital plant, but it has obvious possibilities of development for other applications.

The design audit is a multi-disciplinary activity conducted by a team of managers and investment analysts to examine the design of new plant to ensure that it is built to the optimum specification with a minimum of design deficiencies. The technique is a development of review procedures used by NASA in the space programme. The audit can typically be operated at two distinct levels: total systems level or component level.

Total system audit

The total system audit studies the overall process and engineering route. It identifies the capital, operational and maintenance costs associated with each functional unit within that system. It then optimizes these costs to attain minimum life-cycle cost comparable with reliability and easy maintenance. Basic design features of the plant are studied using systems engineering and reliability modelling techniques to appraise and modify the plant layout.

Component audit

This is design auditing of individual components as an integrity assessment. At this level it is directed at the individual plant items to ensure their fitness for purpose under working conditions within the total plant design. The analysis is carried out in detail and takes account of such requirements as:

Component capacity
Reliability
Maintainability
Stress tolerances
Environmental compatibility, etc.

441

Components may, when required, be subject to detailed examination and testing to ascertain their performance under specific plant operating conditions. Consideration is given to basic design, the effect of environmental conditions, accessibility for maintenance, component wear rate, compatibility of parts, and the ways in which these interact to influence component reliability. The timing of the audit function is obviously critical to derive the best value from design trade-offs, and should preferably occur prior to the finalization of plant or equipment design.

The audit programme

While the course of any individual design audit depends upon customer plant and equipment requirements, as does composition of the audit team, there is a common logical format for most circumstances:

Stage 1: familiarization

Following initial customer discussions, a specific design audit team is formed. This team then acquaints itself with plant operation, examines relevant documentation and establishes with the customer the availability of the necessary customer, plant and contractor's data, drawings and design parameters. It is essential at this stage that clear and regular lines of communication between customer, contractor and audit team are set up and maintained throughout the audit study.

Stage 2: criticality study

Further to the preparatory work of stage 1, a detailed examination and evaluation of the plant and equipment design is conducted in the light of the proposed layout, process considerations and the in-service environment. Critical items of plant, particularly interfaces with other plant and equipment, are identified and examined in detail, through reliability studies. In conjunction with this engineering and design evaluation, an economic assessment is conducted to establish and quantify the proposed trade-offs between plant design, reliability requirements and the total.

Stage 3: finalization and recommendation

This is the most necessary element and, as common practice, the independent audit team has detailed discussions with customer and contractor to ensure complete understanding of the design analysis and reliability assessments to reach tripartite agreement.

The final report encompasses all the design analyses conducted on the plant and is presented in a simple, readable layout.

There seems no doubt that design auditing is a valuable technique to facilitate the efficient operation of high-cost capital plant by minimizing construction, maintenance and replacement costs. The technique has proved itself to be cost-effective in those circumstances and it will inevitably be extended to other applications.

USEFUL ORGANIZATIONS

ASLIB, 26 Boswell Street, London WC1M 3JZ
Tel. 01-430 2671
(For information and guidance on specialist libraries and bibliographic databases)

The British Standards Institution, Linford Wood,
Milton Keynes MK14 6LE
Tel. 0908 320066

The Design Council, 28 Haymarket, London SW1Y 4SU
Tel. 01-839 8000

FURTHER READING

Allen, T.J., *Problem Solving Strategies in Parallel Research and Development*, Working paper 125-65, Sloan School of Management, MIT, Mass., 1965

Brearley, A., *The Management of Drawing and Design*, Gower, Aldershot, 1975

Brearley, A., *The Control of Staff Related Overheads*, Macmillan, London, 1976

British Standards Institution, *Engineering Drawing Practice*, BS 308, British Standards Institution, London, published in three parts, 1,2 and 3, 1984, 1985 and 1972 respectively

Conway, H., 'Design and Produce – The 1977 George Bray Memorial Lecture', *The Production Engineer*, London, May 1977

Davies, R.S., and Clarke, A., 'A Surface Modeller for the Turbine Blade Industry', *Chartered Mechanical Engineer*, London, December 1979

De Bono, E., *Mechanism of the Mind*, Cape, London 1969

De Bono, E., *Practical Thinking*, Cape, London, 1971

Gage, W.L., *Value Analysis*, McGraw-Hill, Maidenhead, 1967

Gage, W.L., *Outline of Value Analysis*, DATA, Richmond, Surrey, 1970

Gibbs, P.J., 'Computer Aided Integrated Systems', *Chartered Mechanical Engineer*, London, February 1980

Jeffries, B., and Westgarth, D., 'The Design Audit – A Management Tool for the 1980s, *Chartered Mechanical Engineer*, London, March 1981

Marples, D.L., *The Decisions of Engineering Design*, Institution of Engineering Designers, London, 1960

Middleton, J., and Martin, P., 'Design Rationalisation, the Key to Cost Reduction', *Chartered Mechanical Engineer*, London, January 1975

Middleton, J., and Martin P., 'A Design is more than the sum of its parts', *Chartered Mechanical Engineer*, London, July 1974

Miles, L.D., *Techniques of Value Analysis and Engineering*, McGraw-Hill, New York, 1961

Perkins, C.A., 'Development, its Influence on Design', *Chartered Mechanical Engineer*, London, November 1974

Rickards, T., 'Brainstorming in an R&D environment', *R and D Management*, No.3, June 1973

Simkins, P., *The Computer as a Production Tool*, CAD Centre, Cambridge, 1980

Twiss, B.C., *Managing Technological Innovation*, 2nd edition, Longman, London, 1980

Wearne, S.H., 'Systems of Engineering Organisation' *Proceedings of the Institution of Mechanical Engineers*, 185, No.3, 1970-71

Wearne, S.H., *Principles of Engineering Organisation*, Arnold, London, 1973

25 Patents, trade marks and designs – intellectual property rights

Colin Jones

Historically, patents, trade marks and designs were referred to collectively as industrial property. In recent years it has become usual to refer to 'intellectual property' so as to include more clearly copyright, 'know-how' and trade secrets. All forms of intellectual property can be bought, sold and licensed.

PATENTS

Patents for inventions (until recently 'Letters Patent') have a long lineage in England. They were being granted by the Crown, along with other monopoly rights, in pre-Tudor times, but the first legislative enactment was the State of Monopolies of 1623, which made all monopolies void except (under s6) those granted for fourteen years (now twenty) in respect of 'any manner of new manufacture'.

The latest of a long series of enactments is the Patents Act 1977 (referred to in this chapter as the 1977 Act) which came into force on 1 June 1978. There are still in force some patents ('existing patents') which were granted under the Patents Act 1949 (referred to here as ('the old Act'). Another major change was the coming into force (also on 1 June 1978) of the European Patent Office (EPO) in Munich. A further development is the Community Patent Convention (CPC), which will not come into force for a considerable time because ratification of the EPC and the CPC by Denmark and the Irish Republic will entail amendments to the constitutions of these two countries.

The EPC provides a system whereby a single application at the EPO designating a number of member countries (which will include all the Western European countries when all the signatories have ratified the Convention) selected by the applicant will be examined by the EPO and, if accepted, will result in the grant of a bundle of identical patents in the designated countries.

The CPC will go further, in that an application at the EPO designating the EEC will (if successful) result in the granting of a single 'Community patent'. Thus, there will be three kinds of patent in the UK:

1 National Patents, granted by the UK Patent Office (UKPO) and effective only in the UK
2 European Patents (UK), granted by the EPO and effective only in the UK (although identical patents in the bundle will be effective in the other designated countries)
3 Community Patents, granted by the EPO and effective as a single entity throughout the EEC

All three kinds of patents are enforceable by the UK courts, but validity of Community Patents will be under the jurisdiction of the EPO with an appeal to a Community Patent Court (COPAC), yet to be established.

INVENTION

An adequate guide to the meaning of 'invention' for present purposes is that an invention is a new article or substance, or a new machine, or a new method or process of carrying out an industrial operation – the word 'industrial' including agriculture and horticulture. Computer programming is not included, but new computer programs now enjoy copyright protection.

Further types of activity may, with the advance of technology, become suitable for patenting in the future, and the 1977 Act provides that such new developments can be included within its scope by Statutory Instrument, without the need for legislation.

Not all inventions can be *validly* patented; certain attributes are necessary to make an invention 'patentable'. Before considering these, we need to know more about the nature of patents.

PATENT SPECIFICATION

The grant of a patent can be regarded in a sense as a contract between the State and the patentee under which the State grants the patentee a twenty-year monopoly in making or using the invention in return for a disclosure to the public of the invention and how to put it into practice. The vehicle for this disclosure is the patent specification, a document printed and published by the Patent office as a prerequisite to every granted patent.

The claim

Besides disclosing the invention, the specification has another essential function: the definition of the area of monopoly to which the patentee claims to be entitled, this being contained in the *claims* of the specification.

It has long been recognized that to confine the patentee's monopoly exactly to his invention would stultify the whole system, since a competitor could evade the monopoly simply by making an inconsequential variation.

The patentee is therefore allowed to include in this monopoly a range of constructions or processes centred on the original invention but in return he must by means of the claims define precisely the scope of the monopoly for which he wishes to have protection and to which he believes himself to be legally entitled.

A simple example will help to clarify this rather difficult concept. Suppose the invention is a ball-cock for a cistern. It is a piece of mechanism which includes a float in the form of a hollow sphere. If the patent monopoly were confined to the exact mechanism as conceived by the inventor, a competitor might be able to evade it quite easily by replacing the sphere by an egg-shaped float or even perhaps a rectangular one. So the patentee does not refer in his claim to a 'hollow spherical float' but to a 'hollow body serving as a float' or perhaps just to a 'float'.

The extent to which the inventor can extrapolate from his original invention is dealt with in the 1977 Act by the provision that the claim must be supported by the matter disclosed in the specification (s14(5)(c)), but this can in the last analysis only be a subjective judgement by the tribunal considering the matter.

Explaining the nature and function of patent claims is not made easier by the fact that the word 'invention' is used not only as above to mean the concrete article or process devised by the inventor but also in the quite different sense of 'the invention claimed' – that is the area of the monopoly. Although these two meanings are hallowed in the legal phraseology of patents and by time-honoured usage generally, the word will in this chapter be used only in the first of the above senses, thus removing at least one semantic obstacle from the reader's path.

WHAT IS A PATENT?

We can now consider what sort of thing a patent is. A simple analogy may be helpful. A patent can be likened to a fence erected round an area of technology and bearing the sign 'trespassers will be prosecuted'. The area of technology will be recognizable as the claims discussed above, while somewhere near the middle of the area is the 'invention'.

By way of illustration, let us vary the theme from a ball-cock to a chemical process – say a process for making sulphuric acid by passing sulphur dioxide over a catalyst at a temperature of $x°C$. The patentee will probably have been allowed to include in his claim a range of catalysts and a range of temperatures on either side of x. The fence delimits these ranges.

It will be observed that the fence in itself does not prevent anyone from trespassing on the forbidden area, or *infringing* the patent as it is called. But once the fence is crossed the patentee has a cause of action in the High Court claiming damages and (usually much more significant) an injunction to stop the infringer from doing it again.

VALIDITY OF PATENTS

The validity of a granted patent can be the subject of proceedings in the Patent Office acting in a judicial capacity, or the Patents Court, which is a branch of the High Court. If the patent is held to be invalid, it is revoked.

The grounds of revocation under the 1977 Act are of three types:

1 That the invention is not patentable
2 That the patent was granted to somebody who was not the inventor(s) or a person deriving title from him or them
3 That the specification does not adequately tell the expert (in the 1977 Act a 'person skilled in the art') how to put the invention into effect.

The state of the art

The fundamental requirements of patentability are concerned with the relationship of the invention to the 'state of the art'. This phrase means the sum total of the knowledge available to the public in the relevant 'art' (i.e. technology) at the 'priority date' of the patent. The knowledge can be documentary, e.g. in the technical journals or above all in prior patent specifications (usually referred to for short, but inaccurately, as 'prior patents'), or it can be by virtue of what has been done before (so-called 'prior use'), provided the nature of the use was known to the public, e.g. as a product available on the market.

Under the old Act the knowledge had to exist in the UK to be effective, but under the 1977 Act it can be anywhere in the world. This will not make as much difference as might be thought, because most technical publications, including patent specifications, become available here shortly after publication.

Novelty

The first requirement for patentability is that the invention shall be new. This means that if a comparison is made between the alleged invention and the state of the art, there must be some genuine difference between them. In making the comparison, account must be taken not only of the express wording of the relevant documents, but also any clear implications. The approach is to ask the person skilled in the art what, on a fair reading, the document actually means to him.

Obviousness

The commonest ground of invalidity is probably that the invention is 'obvious and does not involve any inventive step' having regard to the state of the art. This means that while there is some difference between the invention and the prior art, so that it can properly be described as new, the difference is such as would have been obvious to the person skilled in the art such as, for instance, a 'mere workshop variant'. To justify a monopoly the inventor must have taken an 'inventive step'. This need not be of breakthrough proportions; quite the contrary. In one case it was held that a 'mere scintilla of invention' will suffice. What is certain is that there is no definition of what it consists of. As in the case of the phrase 'supported by' the description in the specification as referred to above, it is a matter of the subjective judgement of the tribunal considering the case. It is possible by a study of the decided cases to arrive at various generalizations to assist in judging particular cases but such a study would not be appropriate here.

There is, however, one criterion which is worth discussing as it enters in one form or other into most arguments on obviousness. Let us take as an example, the mixing of two well-known fungicides. One's first reaction is likely to be that this cannot be inventive, especially as it is generally well known that biocidal agents can be mixed in order to enlarge their 'spectrum' of activity. If, however, the inventor shows that the fungicides have a marked synergistic effect on each other, so that the mixture is more effective than the sum of the components, it is very difficult to say that it was obvious to make the mixture. The incentive was there, but nobody before the inventor thought of doing it. That the invention produces an unexpected advantage is thus often decisive in justifying a finding of inventiveness, although it must be emphasized that it is not an indispensable condition.

What it amounts to is that, if there had been an incentive for some time to come up with the new development but no-one had thought of it before the inventor, it is hardly possible to regard it as having been an obvious thing to do.

Secret prior use

Prior use which was 'secret' (i.e. the nature of which was not known to the public) is not part of the state of the art, and is not available under the 1977 Act as a ground of invalidity.

The word 'secret' is a little unfortunate, as it covers a normal works operation, provided the public are not admitted. If members of the public had access and could find out what was going on, the relevant activity is part of the state of the art and is available as such under both Acts.

It is fundamental that a patent should not be granted which could stop a person from continuing to do what he was doing before, even if he was doing it 'secretly'.

The 1977 Act, recognizing that the secret use is not part of the state of the art, provides that if a person other than the inventor was using the technology before the priority date of the patent, he shall have a free licence to continue doing so. Thus the patent remains valid and enforceable except against the individual or company who operated the invention before the priority date.

Is the technology an invention?

Patents can only be validly granted for patentable inventions. Before patentability is considered, the question must be asked: 'Is the item of technology in question an invention at all'? To enable this question to be answered, the 1977 Act includes a definition of the sort of technology that can be patented in that section, i.e. s1 of the Act which defines the requirements of a patentable invention. We have given a simplified version of this definition above.

Ground of invalidity concerned with the specification

The specification must disclose the invention in a fair and intelligible manner. It must reflect the breadth of the scope of the claims and it must not withhold significant information on its optimization, because this information is the consideration for the grant of the patent. Failure to comply with this requirement is a ground of revocation.

The whole of the above discussion on validity needs qualifying in view of our determination not to use the word 'invention' in a double sense. To understand the point it may be helpful to return to the analogy of a fence round an area of technology – defined with precision by the words of the patent claim – and think of the area as covering a whole range of articles or processes roughly centred on the invention. Then everything which has to be satisfied by the invention to make the patent valid must also be satisfied by the whole range of variants included in the fenced-off area. It is this which is the main factor in restraining the inventor from claiming too great an area, for the bigger the area, the more chance there is that some variant near the periphery will contravene one of the requirements for validity. In that event the whole claim is invalid – patent claims cannot be like the curate's egg, good in parts.

EMPLOYEES' INVENTIONS

In the absence of any rule of law to the contrary, an invention, including any patent rights in it at home or abroad, belongs to the inventor or joint inventors. However, an invention made by an employee is the property of the employer if:

1 The duties of the employee might reasonably be expected to lead to the making of an invention, and
2 The invention was made in the course of those duties.

The first is a legal question to be decided by the Patent Office or Courts considering a particular case. They could, however, be assisted if a job description agreed between the employer and employee included a specific statement that the job was expected to result in inventions.

Compensation to employee inventors

The 1977 Act (s40) introduced the concept of awarding compensation to employee-inventors in appropriate circumstances.

Entitlement to an award can arise in either of two cases as follows:

1 If the invention belongs to the employer and a patent granted in respect of the invention is of outstanding benefit to the employee
2 If the invention belongs to the employee and a patent granted in respect of the invention has been assigned or exclusively licensed to the employer.

The first case can only arise where the invention was made after 1 June 1978 and the second case can only arise where the assignment or licence was effected after 1 June 1978.

An application for an award can be made by the employee (even if his employment has ceased) to the UKPO or to the Patents Court at any time up to one year after the patent has ceased to have effect and any number of applications may be made. The 1977 Act (s41) sets out the considerations which the tribunal must have in mind (such as relative contributions to the success of the invention by the inventor and by others and remuneration or payment already received by the inventor from his employer) in deciding how much compensation (if any) should be awarded.

An employee is debarred from making a claim to the UKPO or the Patents Court for an award of compensation if he is a member of the trade union which has entered into a 'collective agreement' with his employer relating to payment of compensation.

Since time is required before it can be seen that a patent has been an outstanding benefit to the employer, very few applications for compensation awards have yet been made.

Contracts on employee inventions

The 1977 Act overrides the ordinary law of contract in certain cases. Thus, s42 renders unenforceable any contract between an employer and employee inventor which reduces the statutory rights of the employee, if the contract was made *before* the invention. A contract relating to an invention belonging to an employee which was entered into after the invention was made is clearly enforceable, and presumably the same applies to inventions belonging to the employer.

A collective agreement with a trade union relating to employee inventions is enforceable in respect of members of the union only. It appears that non-members retain their full statutory rights under the Act, even if they benefit from the collective agreement, but the tribunal could probably take this into account in awarding compensation.

INFRINGEMENT OF PATENTS

A patent is infringed by anyone who makes, imports, uses or sells an article or machine protected by the patent, or uses a process protected by the patent, or sells the direct product of such a process (whether the process is conducted in the UK or abroad). To decide whether a given article is protected by the patent it is necessary to construe the definition constituted by the patent claim and determine whether the article falls within or without the definition.

British patent law is strict in holding the patentee to the words of his claim but there are two qualifications. The first is that the *de minimis* rule (that the law takes no account of trifles) applies as always. The second is the doctrine of *equivalents* or 'pith and marrow', according to which a man infringes a claim if he substitutes an element of it by an equivalent (as for instance a non-spherical float in a ball-cock claim confined to a spherical float) so as to take the pith and marrow of the claim even if it is not within its exact wording. This doctrine grew up in the days before the patentee was required to delineate the boundary of his monopoly by an accurately drafted patent claim. Further reference to this question is made in the section on European Patents.

Court action

If the patentee wishes to go to the limit in enforcing his patent against a supposed infringer, he must issue a writ for infringement in the Patents Court. If he cannot tell from any product sold by the alleged infringer whether what the latter is doing infringes the patent (as in the case of a chemical process, for example) he can ask the Court for an order for discovery and inspection on the basis of a reasonable suspicion.

It is routine in an infringement action for the defendant to counter-claim for revocation of the patent on the basis that it is invalid on one or more specified grounds. The question at issue at the trial is therefore whether any valid claim of the patent has been infringed.

What also constitutes infringement?

1 *Contributory infringement*. (This is only a very brief summary of a section of the Act which will prove difficult to interpret). This applies to patents where the invention essentially involves the use of some unpatented material, substance or article. $S60(2)$ of the 1977 Act provides that anyone selling such unpatented material etc. knowing that the customer intends to use it for infringing the patent is guilty of infringement. $S60(3)$ makes the additional qualification that if the material etc. is a 'staple article of commerce', the supplier must actually induce the customer to infringe before he (the supplier) can be held to infringe. A typical example would be the issue of a data sheet to customers recommending the infringing use

2 *Pharmaceutical use*. A method or process of treating the human body is not a patentable invention ($s2(6)$). However, the 1977 Act provides that a patent can be obtained for a new pharmaceutical use of a substance and such patent will be infringed by a person supplying the substance for the patented use, even though the use itself, being a treatment of the human body, is not deemed to be an infringement. In other words the pharmaceutical manufacturer can be sued, but not the doctor.

Threats

An important practical point in the relationship between a patentee and a person he suspects of infringing his patent is the matter of threats. Under *s*70 of the 1977 Act, anyone who makes unjustified threats to bring proceedings for infringement against somebody, such as a retailer, who is re-selling an article or product, renders himself liable to an action to restrain these threats. The threat need not be spelt out in so many words, provided what is said or written would be regarded as a threat by a reasonable business man. A patentee is free to threaten the manufacturer or importer to his heart's content.

EUROPEAN PATENT LAW

The function of the EPO has been touched on above, and the procedural aspects will be dealt with later in this chapter. At the moment we will deal with the substantive law embodied in the EPC.

The question can be considered quite briefly because the law is mainly confined to matters relating to the criteria for granting and validity of a patent; in other words, what is a patentable invention? It is, moreover, the express intention (*s*130(7)) of the 1977 Act to bring UK law into line with the EPC so far as it is practicable to equate an Act of Parliament with an international treaty. It follows that the EPC law on patentability is essentially as set out above in relation to UK law.

The need to harmonize UK and EPC law is increased by the CPC. Although, as mentioned above, this convention cannot yet be ratified, the 1977 Act had to make provision for eventual ratification. Since community patents, which will be granted by the EPO under the EPC, will be effective as such in the UK after granting, it is essential that UK patent law should be assimilated to the law of the EPC.

PATENTING PROCEDURE IN THE UNITED KINGDOM

Each country has its own system of patent law and administrative procedure. In broad outline the principles set out in the preceding sections, although directed primarily to the UK and EPC law, are valid for overseas countries, with a few important exceptions which will be referred to later. Administrative procedures, however, differ substantially from country to country. Those obtaining in Great Britain will be considered first.

Priority dates

The first step in obtaining a patent is to file an application at the UKPO. It has always been a special feature of the British system that the application need be accompanied only by a 'provisional' specification, which does not require the inclusion of the monopoly-defining 'claims' and that the application need not be completed until twelve months after the filing date.

For the sake of harmony with the EPC, the 1977 Act has formally abolished provisional specifications, but the substance of the system has been retained by an ingenious device.

Under the 1977 Act, the applicant need only file a description which can be informal; in particular, he does not need to include claims. In fact, the description can be just the same as a provisional specification under the old Act. Such a document serves to establish the applicant's priority date for his invention. But in order to proceed to the granting of a patent, the claims must be filed within twelve months. Alternatively, a new application containing a specification with claims may be filed and this is particularly useful if the applicant wishes to add new matter to his description. If such new application is filed within twelve months of the first application, the priority date established by the latter remains effective. The system is thus essentially the same as the old provisional and complete specifications.

Publication

The specification with claims is published, usually just as it is filed, at 18 months from the priority date. The specification is printed and indexed in a comprehensive classification system, and copies can be bought at the Sales Branch of the UKPO. It should be noted that this document only fulfils one part of the function of a patent specification – the provision of technical information about the invention. The other function – defining the scope of the claimed monopoly – cannot be fulfilled until the patent has been granted.

On publication of the specification, the Patent Office file of the case becomes open to public inspection, and remains so for the life of the patent and thereafter.

Search and examination

When the claims have been filed and the prescribed search fee (£80) has been paid, the application is remitted to an examiner who makes a search among prior documents (in practice, existing patent specifications) and reports those which are relevant to the invention as claimed. The applicant then has the opportunity of deciding whether, in the light of the search report, it is worth proceeding to the next step. The sort of considerations which usually arise can be illustrated with reference to our ball-cock invention.

Let us imagine that the applicant thinks he is entitled to claim a ball-cock with any kind of float, but that (surprisingly) an elliptical float is especially advantageous in some way. The examiner cites a specification describing a ball-cock with a spherical float. This clearly destroys the patentability of the broad claim to any kind of float but not of a claim limited to the case in which the float is elliptical. To cater for this (very common) type of situation the law provides that the applicant can make a whole series of claims directed to successively smaller fenced-off areas, each within the confines of the previous one, and that in litigation the validity and infringement of each claim is to be considered separately. In our case claim 1 would include any kind of float and claim 2 would be restricted to an elliptical float; so that on being notified of the examiner's citation, the applicant would simply strike out claim 2 and accept the grant of a patent based on claim 2.

The applicant must make up his mind whether there is enough chance of securing allowance of a claim or claims which are of worthwhile scope, to justify spending the further fee of £100 for *examination* of the application.

If he decides in the affirmative, the case is sent back to the examiner, who determines on behalf of the Patent Officer whether, in his view, the prior documents totally destroy the patentability of the invention, in which case he will refuse the application; or whether (as is more likely) there is something left which could be patented, in which case he reports to the applicant, who can amend his claims accordingly. If the examiner is satisfied, usually after some argument to and fro, a patent is granted.

It should be emphasized that acceptance by the examiner is in no way a guarantee of the validity of the claims. In our illustration he could have missed the ball-cock specification in his search, so that a patent was granted containing claim 1 as well as claim 2, and this could be challenged in litigation by a defendant who managed to discover the prior specification the examiner had missed. The court would then hold claim 1 invalid but might hold claim 2 valid. If the defendant had made a ball-cock with an elliptical float, the court would order an injunction and (subject to a defined discretion) damages for infringement of claim 2, at the same time ordering the cancellation of claim 1.

The patent in its granted form is reprinted, using the same number as the previously published specification but with the letter B added. The letter A is used for the first published version.

Conflict between co-pending applications

It can happen that an applicant *B* files a patent application after an application by *A* for closely similar subject-matter, but during the 18 months between *A*'s priority date and publication of his (*A*'s)final specification. This is particularly so in intensively research-based industries. We then have the paradox that *A*'s specification was still secret at *B*'s priority date and therefore ought not to count against *B*, yet patents ought not to be granted to both *A* and *B* for the same invention. To overcome this difficulty, both in the UK and in the British 1977 Act, *A*'s specification in our illustration is deemed (during the period before its publication) to be part of the 'state of the art'. However, the prior unpublished specification is only half way to being in the state of the art: it counts against the *novelty* of the later application but cannot be used as a basis for proving *obviousness*.

Adjudication of patents

Under the 1977 Act, the UKPO has jurisdiction over the validity of patents granted by the UKPO and by the EPO although, in the latter case, the jurisdiction is confined to the UK part of the bundle. Opposition before grant of a patent has been abolished. Anyone interested in securing the revocation of a patent at any time in its life can apply to the UKPO for revocation under *s*72 of the 1977 Act. There is a right of appeal to a new branch of the High Court called the Patents Court, but appeal from this to the Court of Appeal only lies in respect of particular grounds listed in the 1977 Act (*s*97(3)).

The Patents Court can also adjudicate on validity at first instance, for example if a defendant in a patent infringement action puts in (as he invariably does) a counter-claim for revocation of the patent.

PATENTING PROCEDURE IN EUROPE

Since procedure under the 1977 Act has been devised to correspond closely with that under the EPC, only a few further points need be added under this heading.

Language

The EPO is an autonomous international organization set up by a treaty (the EPC). It has no connexion with the EEC. It is staffed by officials from all member countries.

Patent applications must be filed in one of the official languages: English, French or German. Since the system is accessible to nationals of any country, a large number of applications originate in the USA or Japan. More applications are filed in the English language, therefore, than in either of the other two official languages. When a patent is granted, the *claims* will have to be translated into the other two official languages. Most countries (but not the UK) require that the specification be translated into their official language when this differs from the language of publication of the grant.

Application for a European patent

There are two main differences between procedures in the EPO and the UKPO. The first is that there is no counterpart in the EPO to the British specification without claims. Priority can be claimed in the EPO from a British preliminary specification, but this is part of the International Convention system (see below) rather than a specifically EPC procedure.

Secondly, as mentioned above, the applicant has to 'designate' the countries in which he wishes the European patent, if granted, to be effective, a designation fee of £84 approx being payable for each country, including of course the UK.

Opposition

Although the EPO is basically concerned only with the *granting* of patents, which then revert to the national jurisdictions of the respective designated countries, there is one exception. Within nine months after grant, a European patent can be 'opposed' at the EPO. This is similar to British revocation proceedings at the UKPO. If an opposition is successful, the European patent as a whole (i.e. in respect of each designated country) is revoked.

Which route: European or national?

If a prospective applicant wants to cover his invention in more than one member country of the EPC, he has the option of applying at the EPO (the 'European route') or of filing separate national applications in each of the countries concerned (the 'national route'). The considerations which arise are as follows:

1 Financial: obviously the greater the number of countries involved, the greater the financial advantage of the European route. The calculation is complicated because it involves professional as well as official Patent Office fees, and both of these vary from country to country in the case of national applications. It also involves the cost of translating the granted European patent for those countries where such translation is required. As a rough guide it can be said that there is a break-even point of 3 or 4 countries at which the European route becomes less expensive than the national route
2 National patents can be obtained very easily in a number of member countries (e.g. France, Belgium, Italy, Spain). If the European route is chosen, fairly strict criteria for allowing an application will be applied by the EPO, and in any case one would be putting all one's eggs in one basket
3 In the case of a European patent, a single opposition can destroy the patent in all the designated countries
4 The amount of time and effort which has to be spent by the applicant and his patent agent in securing protection in more than one country should be less by the European than the national route
5 British patent agents who are also European patent attorneys can act directly at the EPO, whereas if the national route is used local agents have to be employed for each country.

COMMUNITY PATENT CONVENTION

We have indicated briefly the nature of the CPC, which will provide for the granting of a *single* patent for the whole Common Market. This will raise interesting questions of jurisprudence which have not yet been resolved. Procedure under the CPC should fit comfortably into that of the EPO and the UKPO. The main problem will be the cost, since the annual renewal fees to keep the patent in force will be very high.

Further discussion of the CPC in this book would be premature until ratification by all the member countries takes place, and this may be years ahead.

FOREIGN PATENTS

Nearly all the countries of the world have their own patent offices and fully autonomous patent systems. This includes the members of the EPC, whose national systems will continue to operate in parallel with the EPO. There are two treaties which operate worldwide:

1 The International Convention for the Protection of Industrial Property
2 The Patent Cooperation Treaty (PCT).

The PCT is concerned with providing a single filing and searching facility for all the countries which a patent applicant may wish to cover. This sounds like a simple matter, but in fact the technical and procedural complications are immense and so the PCT is not popular among patent agents.

THE INTERNATIONAL CONVENTION

This dates from 1883 and now includes all the industrial countries of the world and many more. We shall call it simply 'the Convention'.

The EPC counts as a 'Convention country', on the same footing as each individual European or other member country.

The main provisions of the Convention are:

1 That the laws of a Convention country will be applied equally to citizens of all Convention countries
2 That if a patent application for an invention is filed in one Convention country and within twelve months an application for the same invention is filed in one or more other Convention countries, then such other applications will have the priority date of the first one. Hence it is very desirable for a UK applicant to file foreign applications within twelve months of his British application. Thus if the latter was filed with a preliminary specification, the filing of the claims in the UK normally coincides with the filing of foreign 'Convention applications'
3 If a ship or an aircraft, which has on board equipment used for the operation of that craft, temporarily enters a country where such equipment has been patented by a third party, no proceedings for infringement may be taken.

If an applicant (usually from abroad) files a Convention application in the UK, he files a certified copy of the original foreign application and this serves to establish his priority in much the same way as a British preliminary specification does for a British applicant in the UK.

Diversity of laws

It is not possible here to touch on the different procedures in different countries and only salient differences in substantive laws can be mentioned.

In the USA and Canada, the inventor's priority does not stem from the date of filing a patent application, but from the date he 'conceived' the invention.

No country except the UK and some of the old commonwealth countries has the preliminary specification system.

The examination to which a patent application is submitted before grant varies as follows:

1 Full examination of all possible grounds of invalidity – for example, the

USA, Japan, Germany and other northern European countries including the UK
2 Little or no examination at all – for example, Italy, Belgium, Spain and Latin countries generally. France has provision for an official search, although it is left to the applicant whether to take action on the search report or not
3 Germany, Holland, Australia and Japan have adopted the system of 'deferred examination' whereby the application is not examined unless the patentee or an interested party requests it and pays the appropriate fee within the specified period, failing which the application lapses.

There used to be a fundamental difference in the way the UK, on the one hand, and the civil law countries and most of the rest of the world on the other (with the USA somewhere in between but nearer the UK) approached the questions of definition of the monopoly area and validity. To take Germany as a typical example, there is no definition of the monopoly area in the claims or the rest of the specification or in any other document. Whether any particular manufacture is within or without the patent can only be a matter of subjective judgement after considering the description and claims in the light of the prior art and any statements made by the patentee to the Patent Office to persuade them to grant the patent. On the other hand, the validity of a patent once issued tends to be taken for granted unless a challenger brings up fresh facts, such as items of prior art which were not before the examiner. This is somewhat the reverse of the British position where the monopoly is tightly defined by the claims and the question of validity is more open. For inventions, steps are being taken to bring laws on validity and infringement into line.

Renewal fees

In all countries except the USA and Canada, renewal fees have to be paid to keep a patent in force. These vary greatly in amount, but they are generally payable annually, and they usually increase with the life of the patent. Renewal fees are onerous in West, and especially East Germany.

LICENSING

Instead of using his 'fence' to keep out the competition, the patentee may decide to exploit it by allowing one or more parties in for a consideration. A licence in its simplest form is a promise not to sue the licensee for infringement if he enters the forbidden territory. If at the same time the patentee agrees not to let anyone else in, and to stay out himself, the licence is 'exclusive' within the meaning of the 1977 Act. Such an exclusive licensee has most of the rights and privileges of the patentee, including the right to sue for infringement.

If the patentee undertakes to grant no further licences, but does not exclude himself from working the invention, the licence is known as a 'sole' licence. This carries none of the statutory rights of the exclusive licence.

Territory

The effect of a licence is to give the licensee permission to do something which would otherwise be an infringement of the patent. This may be limited to a part only of the technology covered by the patent and to a part only of the UK, though the latter is probably rare in these days. If there are corresponding patents in other countries, the agreement may include a licence in one or more of these countries. A not uncommon arrangement would be to grant a British company an exclusive licence to make, use and sell in the UK and a non-exclusive licence to sell in other countries where there are patents, thus leaving it open for manufacturing licences to be granted to other companies abroad. The licensee does not need a licence to sell in countries where there are no patents, but he may (subject to legal restrictions which obtain in various countries - see below) agree collaterally *not* to sell in specified countries.

Financial arrangements

The consideration for the grant of a licence is normally monetary, and may take the form of a royalty based on use of the invention, an annual minimum payment and/or a down payment. The royalty can conveniently be expressed as a percentage of the sales value of an article, or the product of a process, covered by the patent. If, however, the article is a machine, for example for making shoes, it is difficult to get a fair return by charging a percentage of the value of the machine unless the percentage is an intimidatingly high figure. It is more realistic to charge a small percentage on the value of the shoes made by the machine. Similar considerations arise if the invention is for example a mixture of petrol and an additive present in very small quantities, in which case a royalty based on the value of the petrol has a more realistic appearance than one based on the value of the additive.

If the licence is exclusive, the patentee has a prime interest in ensuring adequate performance by the licensee. This is usually provided for by requiring the licensee to make up the royalty payment to a stated annual minimum payment. The licensee for his part is willing to do this since he is effectively buying a monopoly as well as a right of entry. The licensee may either covenant outright to pay the annual minimum or he may reserve the right not to pay it in which case he submits to a penalty such as termination of the licence or conversion to a non-exclusive one.

A down payment is appropriate if the deal includes the initial transmission of technical information ('know-how') such as drawings, to enable the licensee to commence manufacture.

Miscellaneous terms

If the parties so agree, the licence may permit the licensee to grant sub-licences to third parties.

The question of infringement usually arises during negotiations. There are two quite distinct issues: what is to happen if a third party infringes the licensed patent, and infringement of a third-party patent by the licensee. On the first issue, the licensee is justified in objecting to pay royalty if an infringer is operating for nothing. The agreement can therefore provide that the payment of royalty shall be suspended until either the infringement is stopped by the patentee or the infringer is granted a licence (assuming the original licence was non-exclusive). What is not reasonable in view of the high cost and uncertainty of patent actions is to expect the patentee to covenant to sue an infringer.

The question of infringement of a third party's patent by the licensee is not directly connected with the licence, and the licensor is justified in refusing to take any responsibility. The fact that a licensee's operation is covered by two patents, one of them being the subject of the licence and the other belonging to a third party, is in no way derogatory of the former. A patent gives no right to anyone, even the patentee, to manufacture the subject of the patent, as can be seen if we remember the fence analogy. To revert to the ball-cock example, if A gets a patent with a claim worded widely enough to cover any kind of float, but in which the specification describes only a spherical float, and later B discovers that an elliptical float has a special unexpected advantage, B may be able to get a valid patent for that particular variant and this would in no way reflect on the validity of A's patent. If B grants a licence to C there is no reason why B should be responsible for the fact that in operating under the licence C will infringe A's patent. It is up to C to make terms with A (with the sanction of a compulsory licence in the background if A's terms are so unreasonable as to frustrate exploitation of B's invention).

The duration of a licence is normally for the life of the relevant patent and it is provided in the 1977 Act ($s45$) that it shall be terminable by either party when the patent expires.

Know-how

It often happens, especially if an exclusive licence is contemplated, that the parties agree to transmit know-how and improvements to each other. The point to note here is that an essential part of such an agreement is an exact definition of the technological field. If this is to be coterminous with the fenced-off area of the patent, the agreement should say so; it is not, as is often believed, an accepted meaning of the word 'improvement'. The agreement should also be clear about what rights will accrue in respect of *patentable* improvements. Possibly each party will be able to exploit these in his own territory.

Another important point is the right to use the know-how after termination of the agreement. In the absence of an explicit provision there is no such right, and this can have very serious consequences for the recipient of the know-how.

461

Know-how licence

Of course, technology does not need to be patented to enable it to be licensed. It is not unreasonable for secret unpatented know-how to be licensed in return for a royalty payment so long as the know-how remains secret. In the case of know-how which is not secret, a single payment or stage payments are more appropriate as all the licensee is doing is saving himself the trouble of seeking out know-how for himself.

Forbidden terms

In English law, parties can negotiate a patent licence (or for that matter any other intellectual property licence) on any terms they please provided it is not in restraint of trade – a common law doctrine of fairly narrow compass – and (when a patent is included in the licence) does not contravene s44 of the 1977 Act. This provides that the patentee shall not extend his monopoly right by making it a condition of a licence that the licensee shall buy from the patentee unpatented raw material, for example, unpatented phosphoric acid for use in a patented metal-finishing process. This is in fact frequently done, especially by implication, but the patentee is risking the enforceability of his patent if the practice ever comes to light.

In the USA and the EEC this matter comes in the province of the anti-trust or competition laws, which are being applied with even more stringent effect to restrict what a licensor and licensee can lawfully agree. It is impossible here to go into any detail on this subject, but readers will be aware of the importance of not falling foul of these laws.

The practice of applying restrictions to licence agreements has been spreading in recent years, especially in developing countries, where the main motives are to foster local development and reduce the payment of royalties to other countries.

EXISTING PATENTS

Existing patents are patents granted under the old Act, i.e. on applications filed before 1 June 1978. Existing patents can be recognized in that their numbers are in the 1 000 000 range whereas patents granted under the 1977 Act are numbered from 2 000 000 onwards. Since the term of a patent is 20 years, the last existing patent is not due to expire until 1998. The law on validity of existing patents differs from that applicable to patents granted under the 1977 Act but it is rare for these differences to be of great significance.

The law on infringement of existing patents, on the other hand, is that prescribed under the 1977 Act as described above, unless the infringement commenced before 1 June 1978. Since, at the time of application for an existing patent, the term of the patent was sixteen years, an existing patent is deemed endorsed 'licenses of right' for the seventeenth to twentieth years of its life. This means that anyone wishing to take a licence under the patent must be given one. If the prospective licensee cannot agree terms with the patentee, these will be settled by the UKPO.

TRADE MARKS AND SERVICE MARKS

It has long been part of the common law that if A has a reputation in a trade name or trade mark and B sells his goods in association with the trade mark in such a way as to lead the public to believe that his goods emanate from A, then A has a cause of action against B for 'passing off' his goods as A's. In such an action, A has the onus of proving both the reputation of his mark and the confusion caused by B's use of it.

By the Trade Marks Act of 1875, the owner of a trademark was given a new right: to enter his mark on a Register of Trade Marks, thereby gaining an entitlement to stop anyone else from using the mark – always assuming that the registration was valid. The current registration is provided by the Trade Marks Act 1938, as amended by the Trade Marks (Amendment) Act 1984 and the Patents, Designs and Marks Act 1986.

Under pressure from trade mark agents and persons providing services rather than selling goods and in anticipation of a future Community Trade Mark Regulation, the Trade Marks (Amendment) Act 1984 was passed to enable registration of service marks.

An essential part of the system is that the registration must be in respect of a specified range of goods on which the owner uses or intends to use the mark or services which he offers or intends to offer, and that the registration is infringed only by use of the mark in connexion with goods or services within this 'specification of goods' or 'specification of services'.

The Register of Trade Marks

The Register of Trade Marks is kept by the Registrar, who is in fact the same person as the Comptroller of Patents. As in the case of patents, an application to register a mark is examined to see if it complies with the requirements of the Trade Marks Act. The examination extends to almost all the grounds on which a registration could be held invalid. The guiding principle is that the mark must be distinctive (in the sense that it distinguishes the owner's goods or services from those originating or provided elsewhere) either inherently or because past use has in fact made it distinctive. The former is in effect a subjective judgement by the examiner or tribunal considering the matter while the latter is determined by evidence furnished by persons in the relevant trade. There are, however, two categories which are difficult to register no matter how much distinctiveness is proved, namely words of which the ordinary significance is either a geographical name or a surname ($s9$ of the Trade Marks Act). The opposite of a distinctive mark is one which is descriptive of the goods in question. This fact, coupled with the overriding requirement ($s11$) that the mark must not be deceptive, shows the narrow path which has to be trodden in many cases. For example, 'Silico' for polishes might be held descriptive if they contained silicones but deceptive if they did not.

All goods are divided into thirty-four classes and separate applications must be made for goods in different classes. Services are divided into eight further classes.

Conflicting marks

A further requirement of registration (s12) is that the mark must not resemble too closely a mark already on the Register for the same or similar goods or services, unless the applicant for registration can prove 'honest concurrent use' of the two marks for a period of some years. In borderline cases the Registrar will accept the consent of the owner of the mark already on the Register as justification for allowing the marks to coexist. Whether the consent is given and if so, subject to what conditions, is a private matter between the two parties, but in practice consent is often given gratis on the assumption that the consenting party may want the same favour from the other on some future occasion.

Opposition and rectification

There is provision for opposition to the registration (s18)and for an action to 'rectify the Register' by removing an existing registration (s26). One ground of removal which will not have been considered at the registration stage is that the owner had no bona fide intention to use the mark and has not in fact used it; or that he has not used the mark for a continuous period of five years.

Trade mark and service mark use

It is most important that a mark (whether registered or not) should be used correctly if the proprietor is to retain his exclusive rights in the mark.

Specifically in the case of a word mark, the proprietor should aim to prevent his mark from becoming a generic name for the goods or services in question. To this end, it is recommended to use the mark always in conjunction with the conventional noun for the goods or services, and to write the mark in some special way (such as between quotation marks, in capital letters, or in bold letters). The proprietor should monitor the trade press to ensure that any reference to his trade mark which may appear also includes a reference to the ownership of the mark.

Licensing

The right to use a trade mark or service mark (whether registered or not) can be licensed by the owner but he must be careful to require the licensee to adopt his standards of quality for the goods in question, since otherwise the public may be deceived, with the result that the owner will lose his rights in the mark. It is advisable in the case of a registered mark to get the official seal of approval on the terms of the licence by making the licensee a 'registered user' under *s*28 of the Trade Marks Act. This has the further advantage that use of the mark by the registered user counts as use for the purpose of *s*26.

International

Trade marks (but not service marks) are included in the International Convention for the Protection of Industrial Property, but the priority period is six months as distinct from twelve months in the case of patents. The trade mark laws and practice of other countries differ from each other about as much as they do for patents, the main point to watch being that in some countries, notably France, there is no concept of ownership of a trade mark until and unless the mark is registered, prior use being of no consequence. Hence a company that has failed to register a valuable mark in France can see it lost to a third party simply by registration.

Discussions have been in progress for some years under the aegis of the EEC for the setting up of a Community trade mark system. It will be at least a couple of years, probably more, before this is finalized and put into operation. As in the case of the EPC, national systems will continue to exist in parallel with that of the EEC.

DESIGNS AND COPYRIGHT

Literary and artistic copyright has a long history and protection for industrial designs has followed in the wake of copyright legislation. The current Designs Act is the Designs Act 1949 with some minor amendments. A design registered under the Designs Act must be in respect of a named article and gives the proprietor the exclusive right to make, import and sell such articles to which that design is applied. The design may be in respect of the 'shape or configuration' of the article (which is usual in the case of three-dimensional articles, such as furniture), or in respect of the 'pattern or ornamentation' (which is more usual in the case of two-dimensional articles, such as wallpaper and textiles). Features of the design which are dictated solely by the function of the article are not protectable under the Designs Act.

The current Copyright Act is the Copyright Act 1956, with amendments. It covers artistic copyright, literary copyright and musical copyright and performing and broadcasting rights. Artistic copyright includes not only copyright in artistic drawings, paintings, sculpture and photographs but also copyright in original engineering drawings and this is where copyright is particularly important to the industrialist. Such copyright is conveniently called 'industrial copyright'. By virtue of a recent amendment to the Copyright Act, it has been confirmed that computer programs are protectable as literary works. Copyright other than industrial copyright and copyright in computer programs is outside the scope of this handbook.

A design registration is infringed by anyone who, without permission, makes, imports, sells or hires articles to which the same or a similar design has been applied. There need not be any actual copying for infringement to be found. The reliefs available are an injunction to restrain further infringement and damages.

Artistic and literary copyright is infringed by anyone who, without permission, *copies* the author's work or a material part of it and sells the copies. In the case of artistic copyright, it is also an infringement to copy a three-dimensional reproduction of a two-dimensional drawing. This means that a product which has been made or reproduced from original drawings or sketches effectively enjoys copyright under the Copyright Act. 'Original' means that the drawing is not merely a copy of an earlier drawing or of a model. The remedies available are an injunction to restrain further infringement, an account of profits or 'conversion damages'. Conversion damages are equivalent to the value of the infringing articles to the infringer and not just the damage suffered by the copyright owner. For this reason, a mere threat to bring a copyright infringement action will often bring an infringer to heel.

However, care is needed when threatening to bring a design registration infringement action since the person threatened has the possibility of bringing an action for restraint of threats which are unjustified. Unlike threats of patent infringement proceedings, there can be danger in threatening a manufacturer or importer with design infringement.

The Designs Register and filing design applications

The Designs Register is kept by the Registrar who is again the same person as the Comptroller of Patents. An application to register a design is filed at the Designs Registry and must be accompanied by 'representations' illustrating the article to which the design is applied. The representations can be drawings or mounted photographs but, in either case, there must be sufficient views to illustrate the whole of the exterior of the article. Only features which are judged solely by the eye are protectable, so views of the interior of the article must not be included.

The design must be new at the date of filing of the application. Novelty is judged in relation to what was available to the public in the UK before the filing date. Thus, the proprietor of a design must file his application *before* making his design available by publication or by sale of articles to which the design is applied. The application is examined by the Registry and a search confined to previous design registrations is carried out. An opportunity is given to correct formal defects and to reply to any objections.

The registration is dated as of the filing date and lasts for five years, renewable for two further periods of five years each on payment of the prescribed fees.

There is no procedure for registration of copyright. Copyright is an inherent right which arises when the original work is made. The copyright term in respect of most artistic and literary works is for the life of the author and for 50 years after his death.

Licensing

Registered designs and copyright can be licensed in much the same way as patents. An exclusive licence of copyright carries with it a right of the licensee to sue infringers. Whilst an exclusive licensee under a registered design does not have any statutory right to institute infringement proceedings, a true exclusive licence will probably include the right of the licensee to sue. A restrictive condition concerning articles not the subject of a design registration or copyright should be avoided, for fears of running foul of EEC anti-trust laws.

International

Designs are covered by the International Convention but, as with trade marks, the priority period is six months. A design filed under convention is dated as of the priority date, not the filing date.

There are two copyright conventions, namely the Universal Copyright Convention and the Berne Copyright Union. Each of these conventions in principle extends the copyright under domestic legislation of each member country to nationals of all other member countries. The Berne Union imposes more conditions on member countries as to the content of their copyright laws. The UK is a member of the Universal Copyright Convention but not of the Berne Union. The UK recognizes countries party to either or both of these conventions for the purpose of providing copyright protection under the Act.

Only those countries whose copyright laws follow closely those of the UK provide for 'industrial copyright' protection of the kind described above. On the other hand, many countries have an unfair competition law which can provide remedies similar to those under the UK passing-off law and UK industrial copyright law (except that they do not provide for conversion damages).

MARKING

Since patents, registered designs, trade marks and copyright are exclusive to the proprietor, it is to the benefit of the proprietor that his competitors should know of the existence of those rights. Therefore the proprietor is well advised to advertise that he has such rights by marking the patented product, or article protected by a registered design with the patent or design number or by indicating the number of any trade mark which is registered. Indeed such marking is compulsory in some countries and where marking is not compulsory, failure to mark may result in failure to obtain damages for infringement.

A false claim to protection is, in general, an offence punishable by a fine or imprisonment or both. Accordingly, when an application for a patent, a design registration or a trade mark registration has not been granted, it is necessary to use wording such as 'Patent applied for, No.86 54321'.

In the case of unregistered trade marks, it is useful to include the marking such as 'ACME is a Trade Mark of PQR Ltd'. This makes it clear that PQR Ltd has staked its claim to the trade mark.

Copyright is somewhat different in that it does not have an identification number and in that it automatically extends to all countries recognizing the relevant convention. The marking in accordance with the copyright conventions consists of the letter C in a circle followed by the year of publication followed by the name of the copyright owner, thus '© 1986 XYZ Ltd'. Failure to use this prescribed marking can mean that, in some countries, no damages can be recovered for infringement.

FUNCTIONS OF PATENT AGENTS AND TRADE MARK AGENTS

Patent agents have a function in relation to patent law and practice which is analogous to that of solicitors in relation to other branches of the law. Owing to the technological subject-matter involved, a patent agent has to have achieved at least GCE 'A' level standard in a science or engineering subject, and usually has a university degree, before sitting for the qualifying examinations which the Chartered Institute of Patent Agents administers on behalf of the Department of Trade and Industry.

There is a contradiction between the difficulty of the concepts underlying the patent system and the familiarity of its main visible product – the patent specification. In many industries, patent specifications are an important if not the main source of information on recent developments and they are constantly handled by technical personnel of all grades. This means that laymen who are familiar with 'patents' (as they incorrectly term patent specifications) as items of technical information are unlikely to learn the underlying concepts of the system but substitute a rough-and-ready version which usually has little relation to reality. There are, in fact, very few matters connected with patent law or practice in which it is safe to proceed without consulting a patent agent.

It is usual for patent agents to include trade marks in their practice, some training in trade marks being necessary in order to pass the patent agent's qualifying examinations. Although this is elementary compared with the training in patents, a patent agent will either have acquired a full understanding by assisting an expert or will employ a fully qualified trade mark agent in his practice.

Unlike the profession of patent agency, that of trade marks is not closed, but there is an Institute of Trade Mark Agents which administers a rigorous examination as a condition of membership. Many patent agents are members of both institutes.

The bread-and-butter work of the patent agent is the preparation of patent applications, the main part of which is the patent specification, for filing in the UK and abroad in accordance with the various local procedures; dealing with objections raised by the various examiners and with any oppositions; securing the grant of a patent; and ensuring the renewal fees are paid on it as long as the patentee requires. To do the job properly the patent agent ought to be in direct touch with the inventor in any particular case.

Analogous work arises in relation to trade marks and here the agent should be in *direct* touch with the relevant marketing executive. Trade mark matters sometimes seem simple, but in fact this is deceptive and the agent needs to have direct access to the principal actually involved just as much as he does in patent matters.

Representation before the UKPO in connexion with design registration application is also an open profession. Nevertheless, it is usually conducted by patent agents and sometimes by trade mark agents.

The role of the patent agent in copyright questions is purely advisory. Many patent agents develop substantial experience in industrial copyright because of the overlap of interests with other intellectual property matters.

European patent attorneys

Professional representatives (practitioners) of any EPC member country can act directly at the EPO, in contradistinction from the national patent offices which require the representation to be held by a local patent practitioner. Qualification to act before the EPO is by an examination of similar scope to that in the UK, run by the EPO. Qualification leads to membership of the European Patent Institute (EPI).

Most foreign practitioners, when speaking English, call themselves 'patent attorneys'. Recognizing that this could put British agents at a disadvantage when competing for EPO business (for example in the USA or Japan) Parliament approved the name 'European patent attorney' for use by British practitioners qualified to act before the EPO (in $s85(1)$ of the 1977 Act).

The same expression was subsequently approved by the EPI for use by all professional representatives, irrespective of nationality. Equivalent expressions in French and German have also been approved.

COSTS

The costs of obtaining and maintaining patents contain two components: government fees and professional charges. The Patent Office in each country has to carry out a number of clerical and technical operations on each patent application, the latter requiring skilled manpower, and the objective is to charge applicants and patentees enough to make the Patent Office self-supporting. The fee in the UK for an application is a nominal £10, the search fee is £80, and the examination fee is £100. The patent agent's charges depend on the nature of the job but are not likely to be less than £250 for a preliminary specification and £350 for an application with claims. Much higher charges may be made for lengthy or complex work.

The costs for foreign applications vary a good deal from country to country. A large fraction of the costs in foreign language countries goes for translation. An idea of the order of magnitude and range of costs can be given by quoting estimates of £700 for an average case in India, and of £1500 in West Germany.

It is impossible to estimate the cost of prosecuting an application since it depends on the subject matter, the procedure of the country concerned and the objections the examiner happens to turn up. The cost can vary from a few pounds in some countries to hundreds of pounds for a difficult US case.

The annual renewal fees necessary to maintain a patent in force also vary enormously from country to country, and over the life of the patent (generally increasing with age). The UK range is from about £76 to £292, exclusive of agent's charges.

Charges for trade mark work follow a similar pattern, but on a lower scale, perhaps a quarter to one half of the charge for analogous patent work. Renewal fees are required only at relatively long periods: for example in the UK every fourteen years after an initial period of seven years.

Charges for design registration applications are generally of the same order as those for trade marks.

★ ★ ★

The Copyright, Designs and Patents Bill was introduced into parliament as this book went to press. The Bill attempts to reform the system radically and, if enacted, will effectively repeal all the existing copyright and patents legislation introduced in the last 30 years.

FURTHER READING

Blanco White, T.A. and Jacob, Robin, *Patents, Trade Marks, Copyright and Industrial Designs*, 3rd edition, Sweet & Maxwell, Concise College Texts, London, 1986

Flint, Michael F., *A User's Guide to Copyright*, Butterworth, London, 1985

Hearn, Patrick, *The Business of Industrial Licensing*, 2nd edition, Gower, Aldershot, 1986

Meinhardt, Peter and Havelock, Keith R., *Concise Trade Mark Law and Practice*, Gower, Aldershot, 1983

Phillips, Jeremy, *Introduction to Intellectual Property Law*, Butterworth, London, 1986

Reid, Brian C., *A Practical Guide to Patent Law*, ESC Publishing, 1984

Part Five
PURCHASING AND INVENTORY MANAGEMENT

26 Procurement policy

Peter Baily

Manufacturing organizations typically spend over half of their total sales revenue on the purchase of materials, components and services from outside organizations. Retailing organizations of course spend an even higher proportion, since what they sell is what they buy. In the case of manufacturing organizations, what they sell is what they make, and most of their purchases constitute the materials and components required for the manufacture of their products.

Although this chapter is mainly about procurement policy for manufacturers, a brief comparison between the situation for manufacturers and that for retailers will be useful to establish the policy variables. Any trading organization needs to determine, and continually to reconsider, its *market offering:* what products it offers, what prices it charges, how its products are publicized or promoted and how they are distributed to the customer or to places convenient to the customer.

A small independent retailer selects the products offered from those available at the wholesalers, cash and carry outlets, etc. A large chain store on the other hand may develop its own products and seek suitable producers for them. It may also purchase 'own brand' goods which are sometimes nationally available products, bought at a cheaper price without the national brand label. The main trading advantage of the chain store is in fact its ability to buy in bulk and thus both to rationalize its purchases and to get cheaper prices.

A small manufacturing firm will also make much use of wholesalers, and other organizations which specialize in supplying goods and services to manufacturers; but such organizations sell standard products, and even the smaller manufacturer needs to buy special products made to its own design. A large manufacturer may devote the major part of its purchasing effort to finding and trading with suppliers of components and materials which are not nationally available but are specifically called for by the design of the products which it is offering.

Very large manufacturers, and those occupying a *de facto* monopoly position as buyers, are in a position to exert so much leverage on their supply markets that they need to consider, whenever they take a major purchasing decision, the future state of the supply market which will result from it.

Such organizations as the National Coal Board, British Telecom, IBM and General Motors constantly need to bear in mind such considerations, and much research and thought may be needed to decide whether a two-supplier market would be better than a three-supplier market, for instance.

The normal purchasing situation for the larger customer is what economists call *bilateral oligopoly:* that is, a small number of powerful suppliers dominate the supply market and a small number of powerful customers dominate the sales market. No formula will determine whether supplier or customer has the whip hand. Negotiation is used to decide the arrangements for supply: the specification, the contract quantity and the delivery quantities, the price and terms of payment, the inspection or quality assurance agreement, etc.

PROCUREMENT STRATEGIES

Corey (1978) classified procurement strategies into three groups:

1 Cost-based negotiation
2 Market-price-based negotiation
3 Competitive bidding.

While these were distinguished from each other basically by pricing mode, they also differed according to Corey in the product scope of the procurement (which could be narrow or broad), in the number and kind of suppliers contacted (ranging from one or very few in the case of cost-based negotiation to many in the second group), in price-quantity determination (including risk-sharing arrangements and the form in which quotations were requested) and in negotiating strategy (which varies considerably between the three groups).

Supplier selection was not just a matter of selecting the type and number of source; it involved the construction of a sourcing system in which different suppliers had different roles, for instance, technical development, price leadership, etc. Long-term supply availability, domestic versus foreign sources, distributors versus manufacturers and the strategy of numbers were some of the factors to be considered. Single sourcing and the stability of vendor relationships were topics of considerable importance while, in certain circumstances, it could be quite difficult to persuade a supplier to accept an order. If a manufacturer needed to demarket his product, then the customer needed to market his demand – a reversal of the traditional supplier–customer relationship which may become increasingly prominent if material shortages loom larger.

Negotiation has become the subject of an enormous literature and many training courses are available for buyers, sellers, labour union representatives, management representatives, and many others with special interests. Most of this training material stresses the importance of the groundwork which precedes negotiating sessions, in which objectives are set, the relevant facts are assembled and conclusions drawn, and tentative agenda established for the negotiations.

Corey's work is based on research carried out at six very large American corporations during the 1970s. Purchasing could be carried out, and in fact in all six cases was carried out, at plant level, divisional level, and corporate level; but a strong trend was noticed to centralize procurement decision-making to corporate level, mainly perhaps because of the increasing importance of the function as perceived by corporate management. Supply shortages and long-term planning of material availability, effective response to a changing business environment, profit improvement by means of purchase cost reduction, and better selection, use and development of purchasing talent were listed as reasons for this trend.

During the 1980s the main trend was towards single sourcing of major parts and materials. This resulted from the widespread adoption of just-in-time (JIT) methods in production planning and control and in stock planning and control. Goods delivered had to meet conformance standards without goods inwards inspection by the customer, so that the supplier had to comply with severe requirements for supplier quality assurance. Goods had to be delivered on time, which in terms of JIT requirements could be very specific (say at 14.20hrs on 3 March, rather than 'during the first week in March').

Suppliers had to plan ahead very thoroughly to comply with these requirements, which meant that they had to have a detailed, accurate and thorough grasp of the customer's forward planning. Inevitably many suppliers could not or would not comply, and they had to be dropped. Other suppliers would also have to be dropped because, for one reason or another, they too failed to meet JIT requirements. More and more, suppliers of major purchases were seen as extensions to the customer's own organization. They were taken into confidence about future plans. Problems with prices, quality or deliveries were seen as common problems, to be resolved jointly for mutual benefit.

All this left less room for two or more suppliers in competition with each other, and resulted in the widespread adoption of single sourcing for major parts and materials.

INPUT MANAGEMENT

Similar trends have been reported by Farmer (1981), in his discussion of the management of input to the firm from its supply market. Input in the sense in which it is used here refers to the components and materials used in producing the firm's end products. It is argued that too many firms have confined their strategic planning to output management and the marketing of their end products, regarding the input area as operational rather than strategic. This thinking may indeed have been appropriate to the supply market conditions of the recent past, but it is doubtful if it continues to be appropriate in the present and likely that it will become quite inappropriate to future supply market conditions.

Farmer argues that while input management is one of the variables in a business system, and its importance varies from company to company and from time to time, it is nevertheless hardly ever to be regarded as insignificant. And while the operational aspects of input management are certainly important to the functioning of the business, it has strategic aspects which have often been overlooked in the quest for operational efficiency. The effectiveness of the whole business is not the same thing as the efficiency of the various functions which are elements within it. Co-ordination and balance should be sought between the various functions, and between input and output management, at the strategic as well as at the operational levels. To focus solely on cost reduction in the input and conversion stages of a manufacturing system, and to look for profit opportunities solely at the output end, may well, according to Farmer, have been a major contributing factor in the decline and even demise of many manufacturing businesses.

Purchasing policy should thus be seen as part of business policy, purchasing strategy as part of business strategy. Long-term as well as short-term aspects need to be considered, as indeed they have been by successful Japanese manufacturers of motor cars, motor bikes, and TV sets, and by successful retailers such as Marks & Spencer.

Professor Farmer in this paper was looking particularly at the long-term and strategic aspects of supply planning; but the short-term and operational aspects are also important in the determination of procurement policy. Materials requirement planning, greatly facilitated by the more powerful computers and better systems which became available in the early 1980s, brought great improvements to supply and production operations in those companies which implemented it successfully. The insistence that management should devise and authorize a rational, feasible and appropriate master schedule, coupled with the ability to explode this into detailed schedules of what parts, components and materials to make or buy, week by week, over the whole planning horizon, came like a revelation to companies which had previously operated on a chaotic mixture of stock-controlled production and customer priorities.

Materials management was a different but related approach, also intended to improve operational efficiency, but this time by a change in departmental structures.

MATERIALS MANAGEMENT

The term 'materials management' presumably referred originally to the management of the activities within an organization which had to do with the planning, purchasing, transport, storage and handling of the materials required by the organization, using materials in the general sense to refer to the whole range of goods and services obtained from outside the organization in order to provide finished products for sale. However, increasingly materials management has come to refer to the grouping together of these materials-related activities into one department under a materials manager. A typical theoretical approach is shown in Figure 26.1.

In practice, surveys have shown that adoption of some kind of materials

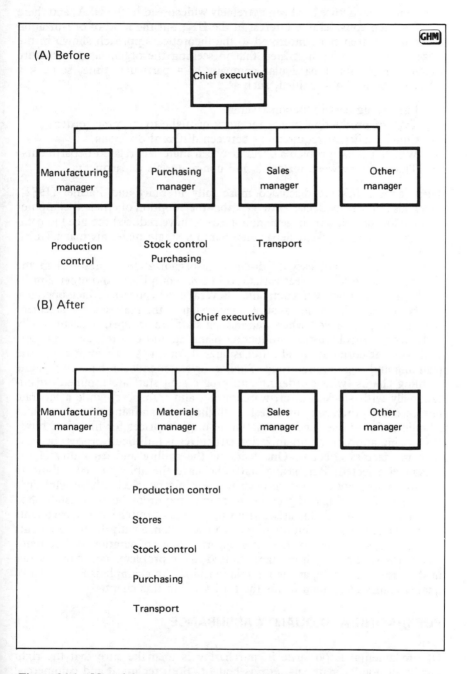

Figure 26.1   Materials management reorganization

management structure has been extremely widespread in the USA, and there has also been considerable interest in the UK; but the kind of organization adopted has often not conformed to the theoretical approach shown in the diagram. It has been suggested that in seeking the organization structure which is right for a particular company at a particular time, some key variables should be identified, such as:

1 Purchasing cost reduction leverage
2 Type of production: make for stock or make to customer order
3 Commonality of requirement between different divisions
4 Whether most problems occur between materials-related departments
5 Trade-offs between materials and non-materials departments

These approaches are discussed more fully in Baily and Farmer (1982), which also quotes evidence to suggest that the adoption of efficient computer systems for materials management appears to have reduced the need to combine the materials-related departments into a single materials management department.

It is obviously not easy to discuss the organizational questions in the abstract because of the great variations in size, complexity and other dimensions which exist between companies. Several large concerns which operate a number of establishments favour some version of the materials management structure at plant level, where purchasing staff are grouped departmentally with stock control, stores, production planning and control, and transport staff while at corporate level purchasing and contracts staff form a separate planning and negotiating group. Similar developments can be seen in some retailing chains, where ordering and progressing staff are grouped organizationally with stock control, warehousing and transport, while a separate headquarters purchasing unit deals with the merchandising aspects, such as adoption of new lines and negotiation of original prices for first-time buys.

Devising appropriate organization structures is a difficult process because so many factors affect it. One factor is the calibre and capability of the personnel affected. Purchasing staff who have the ability to contribute to long-term strategy are not necessarily the same people as those who do a sound job of ordering and progressing regular requirements from established suppliers. Another factor arises from the fact that purchasing departments exist to arrange for the supply of goods in accordance with the requirements of other departments, so that inter-departmental cooperation and communication is particularly important. Indeed many problems occur in practice in this area of inter-departmental relationships. An example is the matter of quality assurance, which forms the final topic in this chapter.

PURCHASING AND QUALITY ASSURANCE

Of fundamental importance in purchasing is to make sure that the right quality of goods, materials, etc. is bought. Both technical and commercial considerations are involved. The purchasing department operates jointly with other departments which also have important roles to play in this crucial aspect of arranging for the supply by outside organizations of what is required.

Although a number of different activities or stages occur in the process of purchasing quality assurance, it is convenient to group them under two headings:

1 Specification quality
2 Conformance quality.

The first part of the process is concerned with specifying the quality required. This may consist of a comparison of available merchandise and the selection of suitable brands or standards, or it may involve the preparation of engineering drawings and other forms of internally prepared specifications. Such a specification is a detailed statement of the features or characteristics required in a material, part or product. These features or characteristics may include chemical composition, such physical characteristics as ductility, viscosity, conductivity, weight, colour, surface finish, and physical size or dimensions – to name a few. The tolerance should also be stated: that is, the range of values within which a characteristic may vary without making the product unacceptable.

The second part of the process is concerned with arrangements to ensure that goods received conform with the specification, and that their important features or characteristics are within the allowed tolerances.

Normally in manufacturing industries a specialist department such as design, engineering, standards, etc. is entrusted with the responsibility for specifications. Such a department needs to take account of inputs from marketing (what can be sold) and from purchasing (what can be bought), as well as the production implications. It is difficult to generalize about the role of the purchasing department in this connexion beyond saying that it must play some part, and that its concern will naturally be with the commercial rather than with the technical aspects of the product. Commercial aspects include the relative cost and availability of alternative materials or products, and also the feasibility of obtaining the quantity required for bulk production at an acceptable price.

A single instance may illustrate the last point. A certain company manufactures agricultural chemical products, for use mainly by farmers but also by home gardeners. New products are continually being developed by the research and development laboratories. If approved by the new products committee, which is heavily marketing-oriented, they are put into a two-year field trial process intended to uncover any unwanted side-effects as well as to provide evidence that the products will in fact produce the effect claimed. During this two-year period, a purchasing research section within the purchasing department investigates the availability on world markets of all the ingredients required by the formulation of each new product under trial. Naturally at the end of the two-year trial it is not possible to change the formulation before going into bulk production. But it would be a mistake for management to authorize bulk production if some of the ingredients could not be supplied in sufficient quantities.

The second part of the process is concerned with the selection of suppliers, the approval of their quality control systems and the inspection of goods received. Inspection is an expensive process, and should not need to be carried out at all if suppliers could be relied on to supply acceptable goods. Increasingly, purchasing organizations are taking steps to ensure that this is so.

Many organizations carry out their own investigations of suppliers, but third-party investigations are also used quite widely: the British Standards Institution and other organizations operate in this connexion. Most systems for investigating the quality capability of suppliers classify the work into three levels, depending on the extent to which the customer relies on the supplier.

At the simplest level, all that the customer needs to know is whether the supplier has satisfactory instruments, test equipment and inspection procedures for final inspection of his products.

Many intermediate-level products require inspection at a number of successive stages of manufacture, with a reliable system for corrective action if faults occur, so that a more comprehensive system of quality control would need to be certified.

When a supplier is responsible for design as well as for manufacture, the investigation of his quality capability needs to be still more extensive and thorough.

Industries such as aerospace, motor car manufacture, atomic energy and other parts of electrical manufacturing, are already subject to strict official regulation of certain aspects of quality (mainly those which have to do with safety) and this has been one of the factors leading to the development of British Standards such as BS 5179.

At the same time as official regulation of safety and other quality standards has increased, and official guidance as to procedures for ensuring that suppliers are capable of supplying and do in fact supply goods to the standard specified has become more widespread, a parallel development has been occurring within companies. Quality is everybody's business; job security and progression for the individual depends on the organization's ability to survive and prosper, which in turn to a large extent depends on the quality of its products.

Quality circles are a recent example of many approaches which organizations have adopted to encourage individual and small group initiative in maintaining and improving the quality of the product.

Technical inspection of incoming goods is a costly business which in principle could be dispensed with if suppliers could be relied on to supply acceptable goods. The investigation and selection process described above is intended to ensure that suppliers are in fact to be relied on, and is often used in practice to classify suppliers into three groups:

1 Accept goods on supplier's certificate

2 Accept goods after sample inspection
3 Inspect all goods received; do not order from this supplier if an alternative supplier is available.

If goods received require technical inspection before acceptance, it is often possible to obtain satisfactory results by inspecting a sample rather than every piece submitted. A large body of theory exists which can be applied in this connexion to select the size of the sample and to draw conclusions from the results.

REFERENCES AND FURTHER READING

Baily, P.J.H., and Farmer, D.H., *Purchasing Principles & Management*, Pitman Publishing, London 1986

Baily, P.J.H., and Farmer, D.H., *Materials Management Handbook*, Gower, Aldershot, 1982

Corey, E. Raymond, *Procurement Strategy, Organisation and Decision-Making*, CBI Publishing Company, Boston, Mass., 1978

Farmer, D.H., 'Input Management', *Purchasing & Supply Management*, Institute of Purchasing & Supply, Ascot, Berks, August 1981

Farmer, D.H., *Purchasing Management Handbook*, Gower, Aldershot, 1985

27 Purchasing procedures

Peter Baily

Management will naturally wish to adopt or devise purchasing procedures which suit the individual requirements of their own organizations. Retailers do not in general use quite the same systems and procedures as manufacturers, while civil engineering contractors have their own variations: procedures need to be appropriate to the type of operation.

Some small organizations employ local purchasing staff, while others operate on a national or worldwide scale. Purchasing procedures can be affected by the scale of operation.

Procedures are also affected by the type of office technology employed. Communications between buyer and seller can be face to face, by word of mouth, handwritten or typed and sent through the post, or some form of electronic mail can be used. Telex and facsimile have been in use for many years. Communicating word processors, teletext and direct links between customer's computer and supplier's computer are in the early stages of adoption.

The standard operating procedure for purchasing will be affected by the type and scale of operation and by the type of communications and records employed, but in addition to the standard procedure, a number of special procedures may be used. For instance many organizations adopt special procedures for routine low-value purchases, and also for non-routine high-value capital expenditure transactions. Procedures need to be appropriate to the type of purchase. A single standard procedure for all purchases, although having the merit of simplicity, is not always the best way to do things.

This chapter outlines a standard purchasing procedure in four successive stages:

1 Initiation
2 Supplier selection
3 Contract stage
4 Completion.

Reference is made in each stage to the special or non-standard variations most commonly encountered, with examples of forms. The process is illustrated in Figure 27.1.

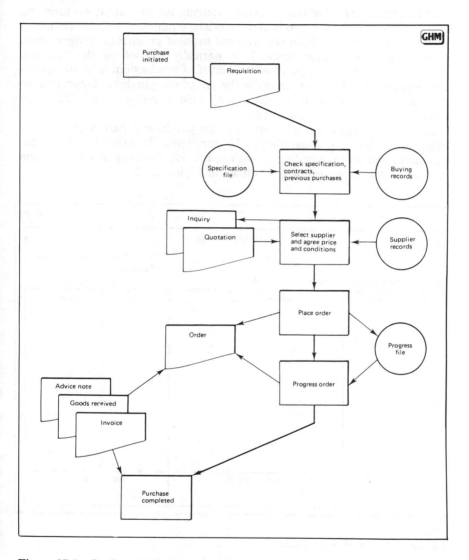

Figure 27.1   Outline of standard purchase procedure

INITIATION

Purchasing for organizations involves arranging for the supply on time and at a suitable price of the goods and materials, equipment and merchandise, services and supplies which are required to meet production programmes, sales plans or operating needs. It is normally the job of the purchase department to make the purchase on behalf of production, sales or operating departments. It is not normally the job of the purchase department to determine what needs to be purchased: most purchases are initiated by *requisitions* from other departments.

A purchase requisition is a request to the purchase department from any other department for something to be purchased. It serves to initiate the purchase, and also for audit purposes to provide evidence of authorization and action taken. An example is shown in Figure 27.2.

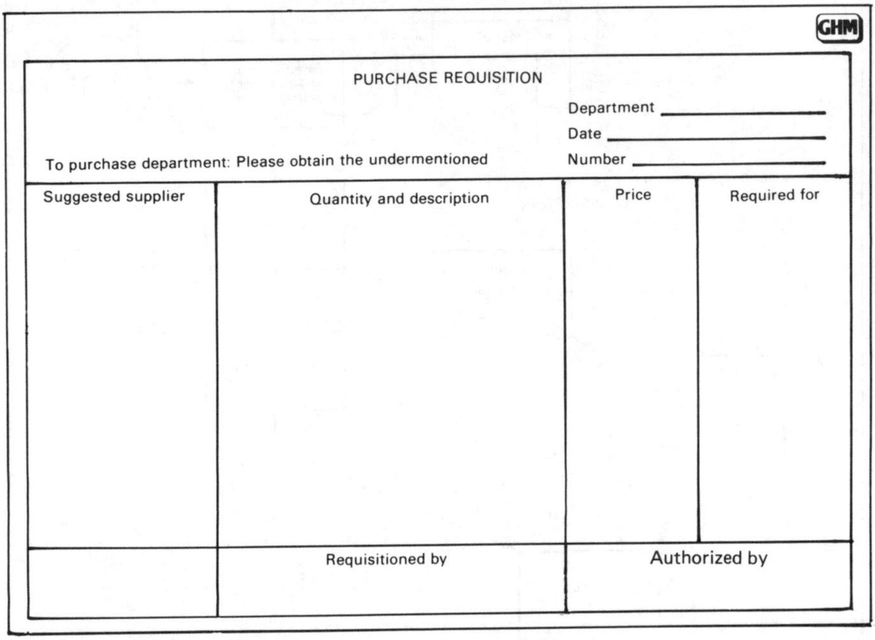
GHM

PURCHASE REQUISITION

Department ______

Date ______

Number ______

To purchase department: Please obtain the undermentioned

Suggested supplier	Quantity and description	Price	Required for
	Requisitioned by	Authorized by	

Figure 27.2 Purchase requisition

Such requisitions are date-stamped on receipt by the purchasing section and allocated to an appropriate member of department for action. The buyer may need to check the requisition against specification files, buying records and contract files. Some editing may be required, since requisitioners do not always express their requirements in terms suitable for communications with suppliers. If the item requisitioned is covered by a contract, an order will be placed immediately. Otherwise, a supplier may need to be selected.

After the order has been placed, the requisition is filed for a limited period in case of query: two years should be quite adequate.

Many stock items and MRO (maintenance, repair and operating) requirements are ordered several times a year, and for these a *travelling requisition* will save time. This is a card kept in the initiating department on which is entered permanent data (such as description) and variable data (such as quantity required and date). It is sent to the purchasing section to initiate a purchase. After ordering the goods, details are entered on the card which is returned to the initiating department. An example is illustrated in Figure 27.3.

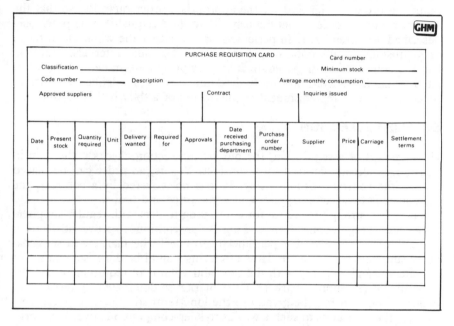

Figure 27.3 Travelling requisition

Systems for production planning and control used by manufacturers, or for stock planning and control used both by manufacturers and service industries such as retailing, normally generate a large group of purchase requirements periodically. Rather than prepare separate individual requisitions for each item affected, a *blanket requisition* or schedule of requirements is produced.

Materials Requirement Planning (MRP) systems are particularly suitable for jobbing and batch production. With suitable adaptations they have been used in mass production ever since Henry Ford devised the first assembly line for motor cars. The process starts with the regular production or revision of a master production schedule which states, period by period, what quantities of each end product need to be completed to meet sales commitment or management plans.

For each end product the quantities due in each period are exploded by means of a parts list or bill of materials to determine what parts or materials are required for its completion, and this is offset by lead times to yield a time-phased schedule of gross requirements for parts and materials. Adjustments are then made for uncommitted stock on hand and orders due to produce a time-phased schedule of net purchase requirements, or blanket requisition.

Stock control systems fall into two main groupings: continuous, and periodic. In continuous systems, each stock item is assigned an order point and an order quantity. Whenever a stock item quantity falls to the order point, an order is triggered for the appropriate order quantity, so that the system produces orders continuously. Travelling requisitions as previously described are often used. In periodic systems, either the whole stock range or a substantial subsection of it is reviewed at regular intervals. Stock on hand is compared with target stock as previously determined, or as calculated dynamically from previously determined rules. A blanket requisition, schedule of stock replenishment requirements or a 'buy list' is produced.

SUPPLIER SELECTION

Upon receipt of a requisition, the purchasing section checks if the item in question is already covered by a contract. If it is, an order can be placed against the contract without delay. If it is not covered by a contract, the next stage is to select a supplier and agree price and terms.

There is a strong preference for continuing to deal with regular suppliers in the case of regular purchases, so long as they continue to prove satisfactory. Nevertheless it is advisable periodically to check the market, to see what other suppliers have to offer. How often this should be done is a matter for judgement, and will vary with the type and volume of requirement and the structure of the supply market. If the market is dominated by one or two major suppliers it may be greatly to the long-term advantage of purchasers to place their business in such a way as to keep competition alive. Very large purchasers which dominate a market on the customer side often devote a good deal of time and thought to the optimum supply market structure, and sometimes take direct action to support minority suppliers or to develop new suppliers.

It is good practice for purchasing staff to know their regular supplier well, to be personally acquainted with the people who process and make decisions about their orders, to keep in touch with business plans, product developments and so forth. Suppliers are a major resource without which neither manufacturers nor traders could operate, and the management of supply markets can be a very important matter which calls for advance planning, forethought, and some difficult decisions.

When making a new purchase for which there is no regular supplier, or when checking the market for regular purchases, the usual procedure is to send a *request for quotation* to a short list of possible sources. Names of potential suppliers are obtained from trade associations, commercial directories and buyers' guides, the trade knowledge of the buyers and their colleagues, advertisements and editorial material in the trade press, salesmen and technical representatives who call on the purchaser, and catalogues and other

GHM

Dear Sirs,

PURCHASE ENQUIRY

Your quotation is invited not later than ....
for the supply and delivery of the goods specified below, carriage
paid, to ....

Your tender must clearly state (a) the price which will
remain firm, (b) the terms of payment, (c) details of appropriate
discounts, and (d) the period required for delivery. It must also
incorporate all the conditions (general and special) set out overleaf.

Dear Sirs,

CONTRACT ENQUIRY

Your tender is invited for the supply and delivery of the
goods specified below to any of the Board's depots listed overleaf.

Your tender must clearly state (a) the price which will remain
firm throughout the period of the contract, (b) the terms of payment,
(c) details of appropriate discounts, and (d) the period required for
delivery. It must also incorporate all the conditions (general and special)
set out overleaf.

If your tender is accepted you will then supply and deliver
the goods in accordance with draw-off orders issued by the Board's
supplies officers and invoices should be submitted for payment in
respect of such draw-off orders.

I shall be pleased, therefore, to receive your tender not
later than .... in a plain sealed envelope marked
"contract enquiry number ...."

Period of contract:
Description of goods:

Yours faithfully,

(Purchasing and Stores Controller)

Figure 27.4   Request for quotations (enquiry)

direct mail material which is received. A number of computerized buyers' guides are also available, which can be consulted on-line or by a telephone call; their main advantage is that they can be kept up to date continually, whereas printed directories can only be updated periodically when they are reprinted. As industrialization spreads to new parts of the world, the search area for potential suppliers continues to widen; particular care should be taken before committing sourcing arrangements for important requirements to an untried overseas source, but major competitive advantage may result.

The request for quotation form (or enquiry as it is sometimes called) is shown in Figure 27.4. The form itself is simply the usual letterhead with, to save typing, a standard preprinted text asking the addressee to quote price, terms and delivery date for supply of the undermentioned goods on the terms and conditions stated overleaf.

There is, however, sometimes considerable scope to structure the request for quotation in such a way as to facilitate subsequent negotiation in order to arrive at a mutually satisfactory agreement which gives better value: alternatives may be put forward as to total contract quantity, sub-quantities to be ordered against contract or delivered in particular places at particular times, terms of payment and other aspects of the deal. In some cases suppliers are asked to support their price quotation by a cost breakdown, which will be compared with a price/cost analysis prepared internally by estimating staff attached to purchasing. This latter technique is particularly favoured by mass-production manufacturers, the very scale of whose requirements limits possible suppliers to one or two in a given national economy.

In most cases the information a supplier gives on his tender or quotation needs to be supplemented by information in financial stability, quality capability, performance record, etc., which has to be obtained independently by purchasing staff. Reference was made in the previous chapter to supplier inspection visits in connexion with quality assurance. All these matters are of particular importance in sourcing new requirements or considering new suppliers. When considering regular purchases or established suppliers, the track record is of particular importance – although it should not be forgotten that past history is not a sure guide to future behaviour. Management does change, new developments occur, new products are launched, new customers found; nevertheless it would not be prudent to ignore the record of how a particular supplier has behaved in the past. *Vendor rating* is an attempt to systematize this information.

Vendor rating

Vendor rating, or supplier evaluation as it is sometimes called, is the process of systematically accumulating information about a supplier's actual performance and presenting it in numerical form. The usual aspects of performance to be measured are:

1 Quality
2 On-time delivery

3 Service (although this is usually estimated rather than measured)
4 Price.

Quality is delivered or conformance quality: essentially, the proportion of goods delivered by a supplier which are accepted. In practice several rules are used to calculate a figure appropriate to the needs of a particular purchaser: one for instance is:

$$\frac{60 \,(\text{number of batches accepted})}{\text{number of batches delivered}} + \frac{40 \,(\text{number of parts accepted})}{\text{number of parts delivered}}$$

The delivery measure is again based on goods-received records and is essentially the proportion of goods delivered on time. Since the meaning of 'on time' may not be the same in a large-scale mass producer (within ten minutes of the due hour and date?) and a small-scale batch producer (within two weeks of due date?), rules are specified to suit purchasing needs.

The price rating may be based on a comparison of the price quoted by the supplier in question with that quoted by competitors: the lowest price would score 100, and a price twice as high as the lowest would score 50 in one scheme. Often such a comparison is not feasible, and the price rating is based on a comparison of latest price with standard budget price, or last year's price, or latest target price.

It is not particularly difficult to calculate these ratings manually, since the system will be applied only to a minority of purchases from a relatively small number of supliers, but computer salesmen have made much of the system as a further argument for extending the application of computers.

In most systems, after calculating individual numerical scores for the supplier characteristics being measured, a further calculation is made by weighting and combining the individual scores to arrive at an overall figure which is regarded as an index of the supplier's total performance – in fact a vendor rating or supplier evaluation figure which can be used in deciding how to allocate business between potential suppliers and also in persuading delinquent suppliers to improve their performance!

Such systems are considered in more detail in purchasing textbooks, and in books about industrial marketing, but it must be admitted that recent accounts in books which have a practical rather than a strictly academic bias are somewhat less than enthusiastic about their use in practice and tend to stress their limitations.

THE CONTRACT STAGE

A contract is a business agreement for the supply of goods or the performance of work in return for a price, and subject usually to a number of terms and conditions. An order on the other hand is an instruction to a trader or manufacturer to supply something.

In most cases both order and contract are incorporated in a single document, the purchase order form. Normal practice is to make it a rule that all purchases, subject to certain clearly defined exceptions, must be made by means of the official purchase order form. This is for practical rather than for legal reasons. The purpose of the rule is to prevent sharp practice, whether by some unscrupulous employee or by some shady dealer outside the organization, and also to establish clearly what the organization is committed to accept and pay for. Regular suppliers are made aware of the rule by printing it on the order form, or by stipulating that the order number must be quoted on advice notes and invoices. Goods-receiving personnel can then be given instructions not to accept goods which are delivered without an official order number.

Exceptions to this procedure take several forms. The contract, or agreement with the supplier, may cover the supply of aggregated requirements over a considerable period of time, or over a large geographical area as when corporate contracts are signed by headquarters staff for common requirements at a number of divisions or branches. If such a contract is placed on the standard purchase order form it might cause some confusion if the same form is also used for instructions to supply specific quantities of goods against the contract to specific locations.

Three solutions have been observed in practice. First, a special form is used for the contract document, and normal purchase orders are used to order goods against it. Second, the normal purchase order form is used for the contract, and special forms are used for the orders; these may be known as delivery schedules, delivery instructions, contract releases, or call-offs. Third, the same form is used both for order and contract, and care is taken to state on one: 'This is an order against contract', and on the other: 'This is a contract against which goods should not be delivered until orders are placed.'

Most organizations use a preprinted multipart set of forms for purchase orders. Four or five copies are usually provided, and these are distributed to supplier, goods receiving, possibly accounts, possibly originator (department which produced the requisition), to purchase order open file, and possibly to order progress file.

Some organizations have adopted computer-output order forms and such developments as communicating word processors and computer-to-computer links (via telex, telephone or other form of communication channel). These developments are making the traditional method of typewritten order forms sent by letter post less economic than the newer methods of electronic communication. A review of the current position, rapidly changing as it is, can be found in the second edition of Baily, P., *Purchasing Systems and Records*. Blanket orders or systems contracting methods are often used with considerable commercial advantage where it is possible to group together either numbers of different item requirements from one source, or else a sequence of requirements of one item over a substantial period of time, say, six months or a year. Instead of treating each order, or requisition, as an independent closed transaction, the idea is to look at the flow of requirements over a time and buy the flow. Instead of taking a bucket to the well every day, a waterpipe is laid on.

For example, a small or intermediate value purchase is carbon paper. Instead of placing a series of orders every month or so for the various sizes and grades required, with this technique once a year there is a review of requirements, alternative specifications and sources. Twelve months' requirements are then covered with just one or two orders which specify so many reams of A4 standard weight, so many reams of lightweight, etc., to be delivered each month. If stocks start to build up or fall short during the year, one or two adjustments may be required. Apart from that, supplies come through automatically; and the price, based on a twelve-month contract, is low.

A group one or two production purchase may not seem at first glance amenable to this approach if production programmes are not fixed twelve months in advance. There will usually be a sales forecast going at least a year ahead, and a firm production programme going only one or two months ahead.

The solution then may be to approach management to authorize purchasing to make firm commitments for 50 per cent of the sales estimate for the year, thus getting the benefit of a lower price and also the benefit of a bank stock of finished parts to handle cyclical fluctuations. In one actual case, component X was being bought in lots of 1000 approximately at a price of 26p a piece. It was built into a product with a current sales estimate of 12 000 a year. Contracting for 50 per cent of this, that is 6000 pieces, with delivery called off at 1000 a month, enabled the buyers to bring the price down to 20p, a 23 per cent reduction in invoice cost, with further reductions in administrative costs and paperwork. Both cost and availability are improved, and if sales fall short of forecast, it may well take nine or twelve months instead of six months to clear the components but they would still be used up within the year. This is a useful technique for plastic mouldings, castings, electrical and mechanical parts.

SMALL ORDER PROCEDURES

Wherever possible the small orders should be put through a special procedure. If they are repeating or regular requirements they should be bought once a year in one lot, or perhaps twice a year: it is obviously uneconomic to expend £15 worth of man-hours, cheques, stamps and paperwork in procuring an item with a usage value of only £15 a year, but it happens. Non-repeating small orders are often such things as maintenance requirements, design and development prototypes, laboratory requirements. The requisitioner knows exactly what he wants and where to get it and the price is often a listed price. One solution to this problem is the order/requisition/cheque form devised by Kaiser Aluminium in the USA, and adopted by other organizations, including one in the public service. Through clever forms design, the same document which the requisitioner prepares as a requisition serves as an order, and a blank cheque accompanying it (marked 'not valid above £X') cuts out the invoicing/purchase-ledger/payments procedure.

Other approaches to the small order problem include: local cash purchase

– a man with a bag of cash goes round in a van picking up requirements and paying for them as he goes; and laundry list – the local stockholder calls one a week and delivers a wide range of sundry materials against a laundry list type of order: invoices come through one a month and prices are negotiated annually.

THE COMPLETION STAGE

Contracts (or orders) are completed when goods are delivered or work is done in accordance with the agreement and payment is made as provided.

Obtaining delivery on time can be difficult: the sub-contract and component supply section of the engineering industries have got themselves a bad name for late delivery, although large numbers of purchasers throughout industry and commerce have few problems in this connexion and would rightly regard late delivery as an exceptional event, to be dealt with by crisis measures when it occurs.

The fundamental step in obtaining delivery on time is to decide accurately and firmly exactly what is wanted at what time, to communicate this decision to those concerned, and to insist that delivery is made at the time specified. All too often firms which complain of late deliveries by suppliers are themselves to blame for inaccurate delivery schedules, continually amended. When both customer and supplier are struggling to operate with production planning and control systems which are defective in practice and misconceived in principle it is astonishing that anything is ever delivered on time, yet this has been the situation in certain sections of the engineering industry. Materials-requirement planning systems, if properly designed and operated, have brought great improvements in this connexion to manufacturers of complex products.

The next step is to ensure that suppliers know that on-time delivery is a very important element in their marketing mix: in the combination of characteristics which results in their customers doing business with them. If valid due dates are stipulated it becomes easy to measure supplier performance in meeting due dates, and delivery performance tends to improve significantly once it is measured and reported. Customers with accurate, stable and reliable schedules of delivery requirements, who insist on delivery at the time scheduled, and measure and report supplier delivery performance, are on the whole quite satisfied with the results they get. In many cases it has been shown that 99 per cent on-time delivery is normal when suppliers know and are fully aware that the schedule is accurate and that every time they fail to meet the schedule they are going to have to explain it to their customers. Nevertheless, progressing (chasing, expediting or follow-up) of orders remains necessary in many cases. This may be done:

1 At the date when tool or jig designs are to be ready
2 When the items from these designs should be available
3 When materials or components should be marshalled for production
4 When the various stages of production can be achieved

5   When final assembly and testing will be completed.

Often critical items can be identified which deserve special attention. For example, casting with long delivery times might be delivered to suppliers, only to be rejected. In consequence, some companies extend their progressing activities to include secondary suppliers (to the foundry in this example).

Methods which help to ensure that orders are controlled (chased when they ought to be) include:

1   Copy orders filed in date-due order, being actioned, say, one week before that due date in general, or as necessary in the particular case
2   Five divisions made at the top of the copy order numbered one to five (representing weeks in any month). A signal of a different colour is then allocated to each month and one is attached to the relevant square in the particular case. (Thus if January were red and the item were due in week three of that month, a red signal would be placed on square three.) The order copies are then filed in alphabetical order by supplier
3   A diary system with the serial numbers of orders which are due being entered on the appropriate page of the diary.

It is often useful to provide space on the order form to record the date of progress action, reply, etc., as shown in Figure 27.5.

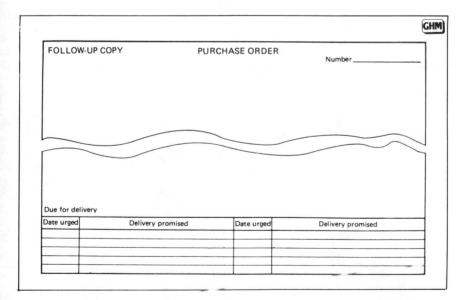

Figure 27.5   Follow-up copy of purchase order

Finally, the supplier dispatches the goods to the customer, usually including a packing note and copy advice note with the goods and also forwarding an advice note by post. The postal copy is passed to the purchasing section to note that goods are in transit and the same morning is passed on to the goods-receiving section. Each day the goods-receiving section check through their file of advice notes and if any goods appear to have been lost or delayed in transit they initiate appropriate action. When goods are actually delivered, a goods-received note is prepared, usually on a multipart form to notify purchasing, accounting, and originating sections of the delivery.

REFERENCES AND FURTHER READING

Baily, P., *Purchasing & Supply Management*, 4th edition, Chapman & Hall, London, 1978

Baily, P., and Farmer, D.H., *Purchasing Principles & Management*, Pitman, London, 1986

Baily, P., *Purchasing Systems and Records*, 2nd edition, Gower, Aldershot, 1983

28 Stock control

Peter Jackson and Dennis Lock

Investment in stocks can represent a high proportion of the capital employed in any typical manufacturing company. Total inventory comprises purchased materials and components held in stores, stocks of finished goods awaiting sales, and all the work in progress. The value of work in progress includes not only the relevant materials costs, but also the value added in terms of labour costs incurred in machining, assembly and all the other process operations throughout the factory. Stocks and work in progress away on subcontractors' premises also contribute to this total investment. Since so much capital is attributable to inventory holding, it follows that sensible and efficient control of stock levels is an essential ingredient of profitable management.

For a given level of factory output, the value of work in progress must depend largely on the average throughput time taken by work through the plant. Put very crudely, a factory with an average throughput time of three months would probably carry about twice the amount of work in progress as another factory making the same product, at the same rate, but with a throughput of six weeks. Thus efficient production control and materials movement between work-stations is obviously another very important factor. Since production control and plant layout are important elements in the control of work in progress, the chapters in Part 6 are particularly relevant.

Distribution managers rightly take a wider view of total inventory costs because their responsibility extends to goods in warehouses and other premises off site, and in vehicles and vessels plying between those places. These distribution aspects are complex, and solving the problem of providing good customer service while avoiding excessive stock levels and transport costs becomes a challenging exercise in logistics. This subject is covered in Chapter 37.

This chapter is concerned with the control of stocks in the factory stores. Although there may be a person in the organization with the title 'stock controller', in reality the management of local stock levels is a team function involving the purchasing, stores, stock control and production control personnel.

Stock control is a balance between having too little (and so running out of items when they are needed) and having too much (thus incurring high costs). The point of balance depends on circumstances, but if an organization never runs out of stock it is probably holding too much.

If only a few items are stocked, control can be kept by common sense and experience. Where hundreds of thousands of items are dealt with, routine clerical systems are required. The clerical effort of stock control itself costs money, so this is a further item to be balanced.

STOCK RECORDS

Later in this chapter, various aspects of stock level control will be discussed. First, however, it is fairly obvious that no control over stock levels can be exercised at all unless a firm knows, with reasonable accuracy, the actual levels of stocks held at all times. All records systems cost money to operate, whether they are carried out manually or by computer. It is useful to consider the classes of stock items according to the financial value that each represents, in order that systems and management attention can be concentrated on the most significant items.

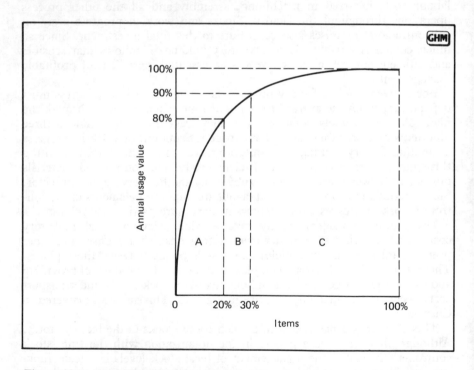

*Figure 28.1   **ABC Classification of stocks.*** *By concentrating stringent control on the few most expensive* **A** *items effective inventory reduction can be achieved for least effort*

ABC stock classification

Clerical costs can be minimized by concentrating the available effort on items which cost most to stock, and keeping their stock levels as low as possible. Conversely, larger stocks of those items which are cheap to stock can be held, reducing the need for tight control.

An item is expensive to stock either because it has a high usage, or because its unit cost is high. If, for each item, the annual usage value is found (annual usage × value = annual usage value) we find that a small proportion of items accounts for a large proportion of the total annual usage value. By arranging items in descending order of annual usage value and working out cumulative totals, a 'Pareto' curve can be plotted (Figure 28.1). From this Pareto analysis, stock can be divided conveniently into three categories:

1 *A items*, the 20 per cent of items which account between them for, perhaps, 80 per cent of the total annual usage value
2 *B items*, which lie in the intermediate classification, and require less stringent control than the *A* items
3 *C items*, which form the large majority of items in stock, but which make up only a small fraction of the total annual usage value because they are cheap, or because they are slow moving, or both. Holding a relatively high stock of these, in weeks usage, will cost little and allow the adoption of simple and inexpensive control procedures.

Basic stock record information

Many stock record systems depend on index cards, the information on which is entered and updated as stores inputs and issues occur. In the past such systems were duplicated in the stores and in the stock control (or purchasing) departments and where such duplicated or triplicated sets of records existed it was always a fairly safe bet that (owing to errors) no two sets of records would ever agree exactly. This is one area where a centralized computer can prove really useful, with terminals located in the stores and purchasing departments that allow information to be updated immediately stock movements take place. Whatever system is used, and whether it is clerical or computer based, the following data are usually required for each stock item:

A code number

This must be unique to the particular stock item, which allows the item to be identified without ambiguity for all purposes. This code may well be allocated to fit in with the firm's own drawing numbering system, or the costing system, or (preferably) both.

Description

This is used in conjunction with the code number for identification. This may include a summary of technical data for purchased components. Descriptions are necessary as back-up identification, to avoid expensive mistakes when clerks make copying errors when writing down long code numbers. Descriptions are also obviously vital when the code number has been forgotten or is not known.

Quantity held in stock

A function of movements into and out of stock. It is usual to record these movements in addition to the actual residual stock quantity. Where issues are made, details of relevant job numbers are entered; when new stock arrives the particular batch quantity is entered together with the purchase order number.

Stores location or bin number

A coded address that positively indicates the rack, shelf, bin or other location where the item is normally stored.

Stock control information

This includes (according to the system for control in use) planned maximum and minimum stock quantities, the stock level at which reordering should take place, and so on.

Cost data

This shows the cost per unit of issue (for example, in pounds sterling per litre). Typically, such costs are computed and entered afresh for each new intake batch. However, in standard costing systems, such entries are used to assist the accounts department in calculating historical variances and in setting up periodically new standard cost levels.

Selling price

This is occasionally needed, especially where stock lists are generated for issue to sales staff, or where the stores is actually responsible for handling and invoicing customers' orders.

Issue restrictions

These may include the reservation of certain stocks for particular jobs. Recording such information in the stores stock record system can prevent the inadvertent issue of stocks that are required against some other vital need (such restrictions are known as pre-allocations).

There is probably no such thing as a typical stock record card, because systems vary greatly from one company to another. Figure 28.2 shows an example produced by Kalamazoo which caters for a fair proportion of the requirements listed above.

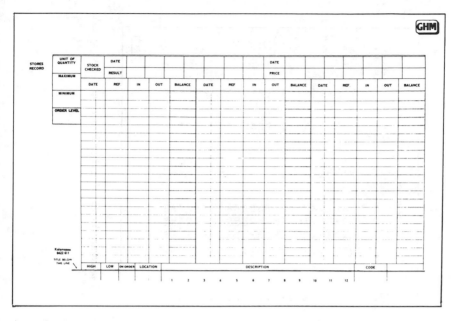

Figure 28.2 **Stock record card.** *This stock record card carries most of the data needed in a typical stock control system (Kalamazoo Limited)*

Computerized stock records

Stock record systems and computers are a logical combination. Using the stock code number as the principal identifier for each item, it is a straightforward job to set up a database. Once this has been done, computer terminals in the stores and in related departments can be used to interrogate the database at any time, and fresh information on stock movements or the issue of purchase (or manufacturing) orders for replacement stocks can be fed into the system without delay.

Later in this chapter, some systems for calculating economic stock control decisions will be described: the application of such systems can become fairly automatic when a computer is used with suitable software.

Once a stock database has been set up, the computer can be made to produce reports which are edited or sequenced to suit a number of different departments in the factory. These could include a listing of all stocks, sorted according to stock numbers or by an alphabetical sorting of the first character in the description. Where, for example, retail prices are printed out alongside all items, stocklists become valuable to salesmen and others who deal directly with taking customer orders. A large 'mainframe' computer is not always required, and minicomputers can often cope. A reasonably straightforward program produced the illustration in Figure 28.3 using a minicomputer.

PGH23 V00   STOCK USAGE   DATE: 10.08.81   RUN: 0001   PERIOD: 01   PAGE: 0001

PRODUCT CODE	DESCRIPTION	PHYS. LEVEL	ALLOC STOCK	BACK ORDER	ON ORDER	USAGE PERIOD	USAGE TO DATE	LAST INV DATE	REORDER LEVEL	MIN. LEVEL	NO.MIN REPORT	REMARK RO MIN
A123	CLOCKS	149	2	0	140-	1	1	10.08.81	150	50	0	**
B100	BRACELET GATE 5 BAR	92	5	2	100-	8	8	10.08.81	15	5	0	
B101	BRACELET GATE 4 BAR	50	0	0	50-	0	0	00.00.00	15	10	0	
B102	BRACELET GATE 3 BAR	50	0	0	50-	0	0	00.00.00	15	10	0	
B103	BRACELET GATE 7 BAR	48	0	0	50-	2	2	10.08.81	10	5	0	
B123	EARRINGS STUDS	159	0	0	160-	1	1	10.08.81	150	100	0	
C100	CHARMS CHURCH 9C	60	0	0	60-	0	0	00.00.00	5	2	0	
C101	CHARMS CROSS 9C	48	0	4	50-	8	8	10.08.81	5	2	0	
C102	CHARM RABBIT 9C	47	0	0	50-	3	3	10.08.81	5	2	0	
C123	BRACELETS	53	0	0	3-	0	0	00.00.00	100	50	0	**
D123	GOLD BANDS	161	5	0	5-	4	4	10.08.81	50	40	0	
E123	TIARAS	15	0	0	6-	3	3	10.08.81	2	1	0	
R100	PLAIN GOLD BAND 9C	24	0	0	25-	1	1	10.08.81	20	9	0	
R101	PLAIN GOLD BAND 18C	34	0	0	35-	1	1	10.08.81	20	10	0	**
R102	PLAIN GOLD BAND 22C	29	3	0	30-	1	1	10.08.81	10	4	0	
R103	RUBY RING GOLD	27	2-	5	35-	8	8	10.08.81	10	5	0	
R104	DIAMOND SOLITAIRE GOLD	33	0	0	23-	2	2	10.08.81	6	2	0	
R105	DIAMOND SOLITAIRE 18C	32	0	0	32-	2	2	00.00.00	15	4	0	
R106	DIAMOND SOLITAIRE 22C	8	0	0	9-	2	2	10.08.81	10	3	0	
R107	SILVER WEDDING RINGS BAND	20	0	0	17-	1	1	00.00.00	15	5	0	
R108	WHITE GOLD BANDS	24	0	0	25-	7	7	10.08.81	10	4	0	
S100	STUDS FLOWERS 9C	18	0	0	25-	0	0	00.00.00	15	5	0	
S101	STUDS CROSS 9C	40	0	3	50-	13	13	10.08.81	15	5	0	
S102	STUDS DIAMONDS 9C	24	2	1	20-	6	6	10.08.81	10	3	0	
S103	STUDS KEYS 9C	23	0	0	25-	2	2	10.08.81	10	5	0	
S104	STUDS LOOPS 9C	27	1-	0	25-	1	1	10.08.81	5	2	0	

RANGE: A123 TO T123

GHM

Figure 28.3 Stocklisting by minicomputer. This report was specially prepared to demonstrate the type of stocklist layout and content possible from a very small computer system located in the stores area (Triumph Adler)

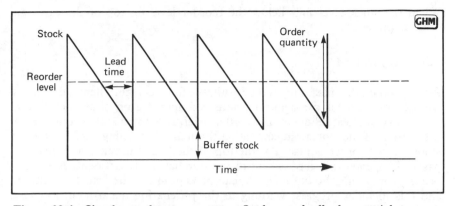

Figure 28.4 Simple stock usage pattern. *Stock control tells the materials manager when to reorder, how much to order, and what level of buffer stocks should be kept*

METHODS FOR CONTROLLING STOCK LEVELS

There are many methods of stock control. Those shown here are typical, and would be suitable for the stock classification indicated in each case.

In general, stock will fall over a period of time, and then be replenished suddenly as an order is delivered. The cycle will then repeat itself, as shown in Figure 28.4.

ordering on past usage (Max–min)

The max–min system is suitable for *B* items. When the stock level falls to a certain level a new order is raised. This reorder level is found from:

Reorder level = weekly usage × lead time (weeks) + buffer stock.

For example, if 50 units of a particular stock item are being used per week, and the delivery lead time is 6 weeks, then fresh stock must be ordered when or before the stock level falls to 300.

Accurate data on past usage and lead times is not always available, and in any case such figures are liable to random variation and long-term change. This explains why it is necessary to carry a buffer stock (or safety stock). The size of buffer stock needed will vary with the availability and accuracy of the data. It can be determined statistically or, more commonly, by trial and error (for example, by holding (say) 3 weeks' usage as a trial buffer stock and seeing what overall level of stockouts this gives).

This system is usually controlled by a stock card for each item. Each card (see the example in Figure 28.2) would show:

Receipts
Issues
Current stock.

When the stock level falls below the reorder level on top of the card, an order is placed.

Two-bin method

A variation on the max–min method, suitable for C category items, dispenses with the use of stock cards and relies instead upon the physical stock levels. A quantity of stock, equal to the reorder level, is put in a sealed container at the bottom of the stores bin containing the item. A warning card telling the storeman to reorder is placed at the top of the sealed minimum. When the packet is opened this card is sent to the purchasing department. A smaller packet, containing the buffer stock, can be kept inside the sealed minimum, and this includes progress warning to the purchasing department to chase the order. When the order is delivered the two packets are made up again, and the cycle repeats.

The main advantage of this system is that stock issues do not have to be recorded. Items are given on demand. As this system of sealed minimum is commonly used for the C items, which can comprise 70 per cent of all stock, substantial clerical savings are possible. The only record is kept by the purchasing department, who record the frequency of orders and (therefore) overall usage.

Ordering on predicted usage (free balance)

The assumption of max–min systems is that past usage patterns will continue. Protection against change is obtained by holding safety stock. For high usage/high value items (such as the A category stock) it might be worth the clerical effort of predicting future requirements from the forward sales plan, and ordering to cover them.

For a given period ahead (at least as long as the lead time) is calculated:

Free balance = stock in hand + existing orders due – requirements

The free balance is thus the amount which would be in stock at the end of the period if all went to plan. If it is negative, or below a predetermined minimum, an order is placed. A special stock card can be used, as shown in Figure 28.5.

In the simplified case illustrated, it is seen that on 4 May, 70 items will be needed in 6 weeks' time. Posting this allocation causes the free balance to become negative. This prompts an order for the order quantity of 100, leaving the free balance at 30.

When the order is delivered the stock rises by 100. When the 70 are issued the total stock level falls to 30. Thus it can be seen that the left hand side of the card anticipates the physical movements of the left hand side. This system can only be used if allocations can be posted further ahead than the lead time.

| DESCRIPTION : **Base Plate** | | | | | Part No : **P-123** | | **GHM** |
ORDER QUANTITY : **100**							
Date	Allocations	Orders	Free balance	Receipts	Issues	Stock
4 MAY	**70**		**-70**			**0**
4 MAY		**100**	**30**			
3 JUNE				**100**		**100**
12 JUNE					**70**	**30**

Figure 28.5   Stock card used for reordering by predicted usage

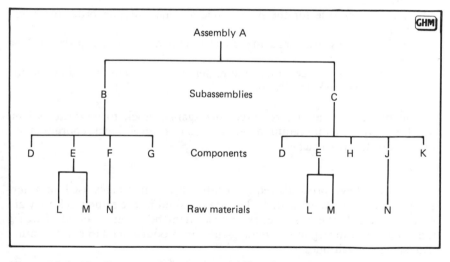

Figure 28.6   Family tree arrangement of bills of material, essential to material requirement planning

Material requirement planning (MRP)

Material requirement planning is a computerized version of free balance stock control. The basis of the system is a series of parts lists (bills of material) for all assemblies, showing the relationships between the items in a family tree arrangement (see Figure 28.6). The family tree stages are referred to as levels.

Usually, level O is used for assemblies, level 1 for subassemblies, and so on.

The bills of material each show the quantities required to build the particular assembly or subassembly. Stock control information held about each item will include:

Part number
Description
Unit of quantity (for example, each or metres)
Delivery lead time
Supplier (or supplier's code)
Order rule or quantity (for example, one-for-one or batch size)
Stock level

Netting

Orders for end products are fed into the computer. These are usually for final assemblies, but could include items from lower levels ordered for spares. At each level the computer compares the requirements with actual stock, and calculates the difference. For example:

1 If there is an order for 10 models type A, and there are 3 in stock, the difference is 7
2 If the order rule for the item is one-for-one, then an order for 7 will be generated
3 If the models are made in batches, then a batch size order will be generated
4 These orders will generate requirements for the next level down in the bills of materials family tree

So the process of netting requirements against stock to generate orders, which in turn generate requirements for the next level down, continue until the bottom level is reached.

Batching

As the breakdown proceeds requirements for common parts used on different assemblies are generated. If they are required in the same week they are simply added. If there is a series of small demands over a period of weeks it is possible to incorporate batching rules to produce one large order rather than several small ones.

Offsetting

Given the delivery dates required for the end product orders and the lead times for each item the computer works out when each item is required and thus when each generated order should commence.

There are two snags to this

1 Lead times are information that is often hard to come by. They are at best variable and often inaccurate. If, working from the top assembly

level, a series of lead times are added together to find out when raw material orders should be placed, the overall result may be considerably out.

2 The assumption is that quoted delivery dates are achievable. The MRP breakdown may show that action should have commenced several weeks previously. In some systems there is provision for doing 'dummy runs'. End orders are fed in with provisional dates. Whilst the computer does not change the information on its files or print out order paperwork, it checks to see if the provisional dates are achievable.

Although MRP is a computer based technique, many companies go through a similar process manually. The computer based procedure indeed has its roots in earlier manual systems, used before computers became available. Using the computer not only saves considerable calculation time and clerical effort, but it brings the great benefit of being able to respond quickly to changes in the production requirements.

Economic order quantity

Stocks for continuous or batch production are liable to be over-ordered because of the lure of quantity discounts. Against any advantage in lower prices obtained through bulk ordering must be set the increased costs of storage, risk of obsolescence and the cost of capital employed. By comparing all the costs involved in carrying inventory with purchase prices in relation

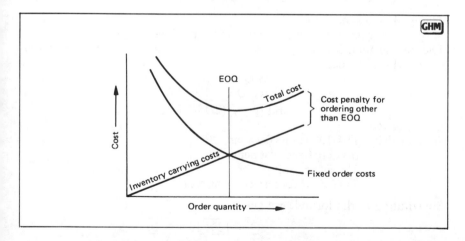

Figure 28.7 Economic order quantity. This diagram shows that the economic order quantity for each batch of purchased items will correspond to the lowest point on the curve of total costs. This curve is also of use in determining batch quantities for manufacture, in which case the set-up costs have to be considered, either instead of or in addition to the inventory-carrying costs

to quantities, it is theoretically possible to produce a set of curves similar to those shown in Figure 28.7. These curves show that there is one particular order quantity where the advantages of quantity discounts are just balanced by the increased costs of inventory carrying, this quantity being regarded as the economic order quantity (EOQ) for the particular commodity under consideration.

In practice many other factors determine the actual quantity to be ordered. It may be, for example, that delivery times from suppliers are so long that high stocks must be held in order to avoid lost production time through stockouts. Also, it is generally recognized that considerable flexibility can be exercised in varying the amount ordered above or below the precise economic level. The curve representing total cost is usually shallow around its lowest point and, provided one does not stray too far from the optimum quantity, differences in the amounts ordered will not have a great effect on the total unit cost.

The formula for the economic order quantity is usually derived thus:

The annual fixed costs of acquisition are equal to the number of orders per year multiplied by the fixed cost per order

$$= DS/Q$$

where D = annual sales volume for the demand (units)
S = fixed cost per order (or setup costs for a manufactured batch)
Q = order quantity (units)

The annual variable costs of possession are equal to the average stock held (monetary value) multiplied by an inventory-carrying-cost factor. This is

$$\tfrac{1}{2} QVI$$

where V = cost per unit
I = (cost of carrying inventory)/(value of inventory)

The annual total inventory service cost is at its lowest when the two are equal, which is when

$$DS/Q = \tfrac{1}{2}QVI$$
$$\text{whence } Q^2 = 2DS/VI$$
$$\text{and } Q = \sqrt{(2DS/VI)}$$

EOQ example

Suppose that: D = 1000 units per year
S = £10 fixed cost per order
V = £4 per unit
I = 25% inventory carrying cost

Substituting in the formula we get:

$$Q = \sqrt{\frac{2 \times 1000 \times 10}{4 \times 0.25}}$$
$$Q = \sqrt{20000/11}$$
$$= 141 \text{ units}$$

This would suggest seven orders per year.

In practice there is no need for many tedious calculations. There are many EOQ tables and nomographs available. EOQ theory will certainly not cope with every type of inventory problem. Its success depends, to a large extent, on a reasonably stable usage figure. Nevertheless, its application has given many firms considerable financial benefits.

Order levels and safety stocks

Consider the artificial situation in which production is started using an initial stock of a particular item, with reordering taking place at prearranged intervals so that the stock is replenished at precisely the correct economic time. Each order is placed for the economic quantity (EOQ) and orders are spaced so that the stockholding just falls to zero as the next supply arrives. By this approach the perfect condition is presented where the average amount of inventory held is kept to a minimum. The situation is represented in Figure 28.8(a).

In practice, of course, the perfect situation can never occur. Many variables will wreck any attempt to achieve the perfect stock condition. These variables include:

1 Uneven stock usage for production
2 Unexpected wastage or losses
3 Failure by suppliers to maintain consistent delivery times
4 Goods received short or damaged from suppliers.

Some of these variations can be accommodated in planning. For example, seasonal fluctuations can often be predicted and allowed for. However, some safety factor must always be provided and this takes the form of safety stocks, sometimes called buffer stocks. A more realistic stock-level pattern is seen in Figure 28.8(b) and this illustrates the way in which buffer stocks safeguard against possible contingencies. The skill of the stock controller must be exercised in determining reorder levels and reorder quantities in order to achieve the planned maximum and minimum actual stockholdings.

The situation depicted in Figure 28.8(b) starts from the point at which production stocks have been assembled at the start of a product range. The curve shows that, for the stock item being considered, 6000 units have been provided against a predicted usage rate of 1000 units per month. In other words, sufficient stocks have been laid in to cover the first six months of production. In order to safeguard against unforeseen contingencies (a phrase familiar to most production managers) a 'safety stock' of 2000 units has been planned. With the economic order quantity having been calculated at around 6000 units, the reorder point occurs when stocks fall to 4000 units (for a supplier's lead time of two months).

In the diagram, it is apparent that all went as planned during the first 'stock cycle'. Usage took place at the predicted 1000 units per month, and an order was placed for 6000 fresh units when stocks fell to the planned reorder point of 4000. The supplier performed as promised, and stocks were replenished to the planned maximum level of 8000 units after the expected lead time of two months. The first 'unforeseen contingency' took place during the end of the second stock cycle, after the second replacement

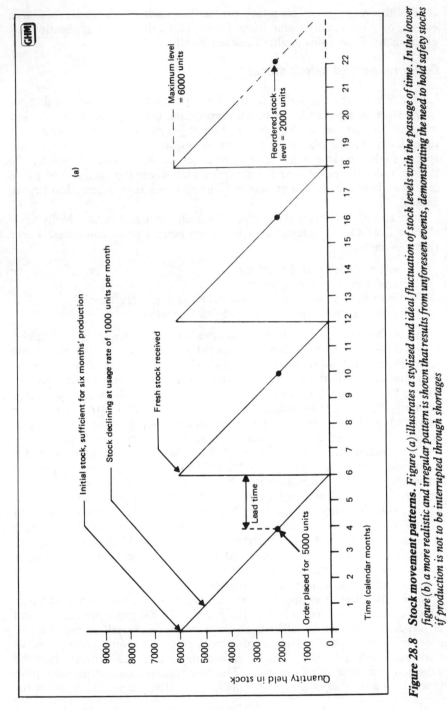

Figure 28.8   Stock movement patterns. *Figure (a) illustrates a stylized and ideal fluctuation of stock levels with the passage of time. In the lower figure (b) a more realistic and irregular pattern is shown that results from unforeseen events, demonstrating the need to hold safety stocks if production is not to be interrupted through shortages*

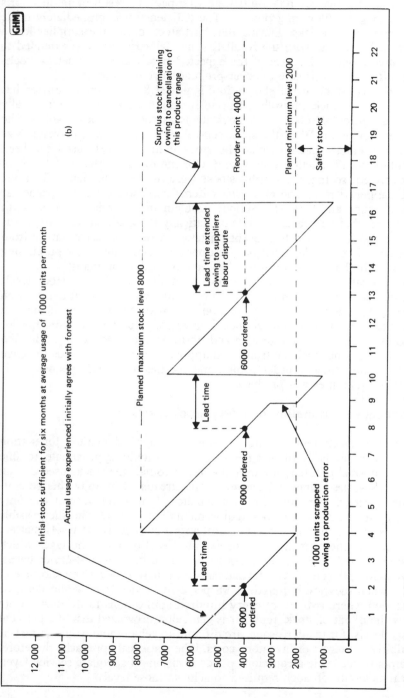

Figure 28.8 *(concluded)*

509

order had been placed: 1000 units were scrapped as a result of an operator's error during a guillotining process. The deficiency was immediately made good from safety stocks. During the third stock cycle, the supplier had a strike on his hands, with the result that his delivery time was extended to over three months, in place of the expected two. Again, the safety stocks were sufficient in this case to cover production requirements.

In the last stock cycle shown in Figure 28.8(b) a small disaster has occurred. The stock controller, true to his instructions, has automatically placed an order for 6000 fresh stock items as soon as stocks sank to the 4000 reorder point. What the stock controller did not know, however, was that the product range on which this stock item was solely used had been discontinued. Production ceased only one month after the new batch of stock arrived, so that the surplus stocks were in fact redundant. The same thing happened to all the other stock items used solely on this particular product range and created a serious problem of redundant stocks. With any system that generates orders automatically for fresh stocks, safeguards must be rigidly applied to prevent mistakes of this expensive nature from happening. Every order must be questioned by a production or purchasing manager who has access to forward sales and production plans.

Determination of planned maximum, minimum and reorder stock levels must obviously start from the production plans (which in turn derive from the sales forecasts). What may not be so obvious is that any change in these plans must be communicated immediately to those responsible for ordering stocks. Given a thorough and up-to-date knowledge of production requirements, the stock controller can apply a number of methods to arrive at reorder quantities, reorder points, and the theoretical safety stock levels that these quantities will produce.

Statistical determination of safety stock levels

For routine stock replacements, a commonly applied method for setting safety stock levels is to arrange that these should approximate to one month's normal production requirements, or to half the stocks used during the purchase lead time, whichever is the greater. Naturally this rule-of-thumb approach can give rise to anomalies. It is arguable that the only true way to decide safety stock requirements is to consider all the possible variables, and then to adopt a statistical approach to arrive at levels that are reasonable in the context of the probability level of stock shortages which can be tolerated. This problem can be described in terms of 'service levels' where a 100 per cent service level means that there is never any shortage of stocks when they are required. A 98 per cent service level would describe a situation where two out of every hundred applications to the stores were met with an 'out of stock' reply. It is generally recognized that 100 per cent service levels, for many reasons, are difficult to achieve and would in fact be prohibitive in terms of inventory costs. The statistical approach, therefore, attempts to reconcile a conscious policy decision on adequate service levels with the amount of stock required to achieve those levels.

Once the realms of statistics are entered, mathematical solutions beyond the understanding of most stock control clerks are encountered. The subject is complex, and the results will only be as good as the estimates of demand and the accuracy of production plans.

Figure 28.9 is a normal-distribution curve, of the type familiar to statisticians. An average (or 'mean') event has the highest probability (at the peak of the curve), while the probability falls away on both sides as the individual events differ more and more from the average. The extent to which the curve spreads out is measured by a quantity called the 'standard deviation' (sd) of the distribution: 68 per cent of cases fall in the region between mean minus 1 sd and mean plus 1 sd while 96 per cent of cases fall in the region between mean minus 2 sd and mean plus 2 sd.

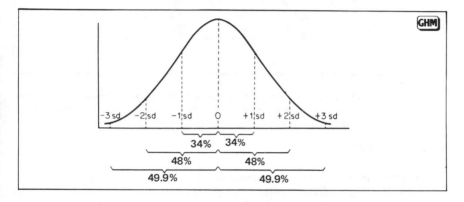

Figure 28.9 *Normal distribution curve. The figure shows a normal distribution curve and illustrates the dispersion about the average, in terms of standard deviations related to percentage probabilities*

In the field of stock control, the mean can be taken as the average monthly usage of a stock item. As the curve falls away on both sides, it can represent the probability that (production plans remaining unchanged) demand will differ from the average.

Records of stock usage can be used to find the mean and standard deviation of monthly usage for a particular item. Then, to guarantee a particular level of protection against stockout on that item it is necessary to have a safety stock of K times the standard deviation of monthly usage, where K is given by the table in Figure 28.10. It can be seen that achieving better protection against stockout requires an increasingly large investment in safety stocks.

Calculations of standard deviations demand access to detailed records of past stock usage. These records must not only be accurate, but they must also relate to present-day production requirements. If the current situation is significantly changed from that which existed when the records were taken, there is no reason to suppose that the standard deviations calculated will have any justification in future computations.

K value	Protection (%)
0	50
0.84	80
1.04	85
1.28	90
1.41	92
1.56	94
1.75	96
2.05	98
2.33	99
2.57	99.5
2.88	99.8

GHM

Figure 28.10   Table of K values against stockout protection. Amount by which the standard deviation of monthly usage must be multiplied in order to achieve particular levels of protection against stockout

STOCKTAKING

Stocktaking is a tedious and laborious chore that has to be performed annually to the satisfaction of the company's auditors in order to evaluate the quantities of stocks of materials and work in progress. The results are used in preparing the company's financial accounts and are also important for management control. Stocktaking verifies the accuracy of stock records and discloses possible frauds or other losses. The Inland Revenue and the auditors (representing the shareholders) will need to be satisfied that suitable standards of accuracy are achieved. Some large organizations find it profitable to engage their own internal audit staff to undertake continuous stocktaking, but whether or not this is the case, every company should practise stock checks periodically in between the main annual events.

Stocktaking needs careful planning to ensure that the whole exercise can be completed during the prescribed period. This is commonly arranged during a weekend or at some other time when production will not be interrupted. This is a necessary arrangement because stores receipts and issues have to be suspended while stocktaking is in progress. Because of the large amount of work involved all available staff have to be deployed. These will include people outside the normal stores function or people who have no connexion with materials or even production during their normal working time. The role of storekeepers during stocktaking should be confined to that of guides so that the actual counting is always carried out by people who are independent of the usual stock records and stores functions. This is a safeguard against the perpetuation of errors or the concealment of possible fraud. The whole exercise can be supervised by the accountants.

Books of serially numbered tickets or, alternatively, pre-numbered list sheets have to be provided. Serial numbering means that every ticket or sheet issued can be accounted for when the accountants come to tot up all the values. The first step is for every item of stock, whether in the stores or on the factory floor, to be counted, either as a physical quantity or by weighing or measuring volume. The stores code or description is entered on a ticket together with the counted quantity. Tickets are left in prominent positions on the actual stocks. Supervisory staff or other checkers make random checks of items already counted to verify the accuracy of the 'first-line' stocktaking staff. Finally the auditors themselves may wish to carry out their own counts on selected items. Naturally, more attention will be paid to the most expensive goods.

Stocktaking provides an opportunity, which should not be missed, of identifying obsolete and redundant stocks, the disposal of which can release both cash and space.

It is important to understand that the objective of stocktaking is not simply to verify the accuracy of stock records, but to assess the total value of stocks and work in progress. This means that all stocks have to be counted and valued, including materials, components and assemblies throughout the factory and its stores and stockyards. The value of these items is not represented solely by the material stocks contained in them; the investment of wages and salaries used in all work in progress has to be included.

FURTHER READING

Baily, P., *Successful Stock Control by Manual Systems*, Gower, Aldershot, 1971

Baily, P., and Farmer, D., *Materials Management Handbook*, Gower, Aldershot, 1982

Goldratt, E., *The Goal*, Gower, Aldershot, 1986

Storey, R., *Stock Control Systems and Records*, 2nd edition, Gower, Aldershot, 1984

Thomas, A.B., *Stock Control in Manufacturing Industries*, 2nd edition, Gower, Aldershot, 1980

Part Six
PRODUCTION AND PROJECT MANAGEMENT

29 Planning for production

J Mapes and C C New

Production management is concerned with managing the physical resources necessary to create products in sufficient quantities to meet market requirements. In manufacturing organizations the majority of the workforce and a very high proportion of the total capital investment expenditure will be devoted to the production function. Efficient production management is therefore absolutely critical to the success of such organizations.

Although production management is most closely associated with the manufacturing sector, the techniques of production management are increasingly being applied in service and non-manufacturing organizations. Because of this the modern definition of a production system has been broadened to cover systems for the creation of both manufactured items and services. The problems are very similar for both manufacturing organizations and service organizations. One of the main differences is that the 'product' of service organizations is highly perishable and must be consumed immediately.

While the primary emphasis in this chapter will be on manufacturing organizations, most of the techniques discussed are equally applicable to service organizations like banks, hospitals and public utilities.

THE PRODUCTION MANAGEMENT TASK

The production management task can be divided into two main areas. First, there is the design of the production system. This will involve decisions regarding the performance requirements and desired output levels of the production system. Then decisions will need to be made about the number of production facilities which will be required and their location, the methods of production to be used and the management control procedures to be introduced.

Second, there is the task of operating the production system in order to meet the specified performance requirements. This will include production scheduling and control, inventory management and quality control.

THE PLANNING OF PRODUCTION

The planning of production in an organization can therefore be considered at two levels, strategic and tactical. Strategic planning is concerned with the design of the production system. Tactical planning is concerned with the running of the operating system. Figure 29.1 shows the kind of planning decisions which have to be taken in production and their relative time horizons.

				GHM
Strategic	Long-term	2 years +	Introduction of new products Number and location of facilities Type of technology to be used	
	Medium-term	1–2 years	Relative mix of products Changes in capacity	
Tactical	Medium term	1 year	Size of workforce Subcontracting Overtime working Stockholding policy	
	Short-term	3 months	Production schedule Output targets	

Figure 29.1   Time-scale for planning decisions

Strategic level decisions

At the strategic level decisions will be required regarding:

The product range

While this is primarily a marketing decision the production capabilities of the organization together with any limitations on production capacity must also be taken into account.

Product design

By taking into account production implications at the design stage substantial reductions in manufacturing costs and processing time can be achieved.

Selection of processing methods, plant and equipment

Usually there are several alternative methods of manufacturing the product, each being the most appropriate for a particular output range. The choice will depend on the trade-off between capital cost, operating costs and performance requirements.

Plant location

The number of plants, the capacity of each plant and the location of each plant must be decided. This will be influenced by the transport costs for raw materials and finished goods, availability of labour, delivery performance requirements and economics of scale.

Plant layout

Within each plant the number of departments and their relative location must be decided. Within each department the location of machines, storage areas and support facilities must be decided in order to simplify movement and handling of materials between operations.

Planning and control systems

An important part of the design of a production system is the development of procedures for planning and controlling the production process.

Decisions at the tactical level

At the tactical level decisions will need to be taken regarding:

Production control

This covers the detailed scheduling of operations, allocation of jobs to machines and monitoring of actual against planned production. The aim should be to produce a schedule which is practicable and also meets performance objectives in terms of operating costs and delivery.

Stock control

In order to ensure acceptable delivery times nearly all organizations have to carry some stocks of raw materials, subassemblies or finished products. For each item held in stock decisions must be made about when to replenish stocks and what the replenishment quantity should be.

Quality control

The quality specification will be set at the design stage. The operational task is to ensure that, as far as possible, all items which leave the factory meet this specification. Decisions must be taken on methods of inspection, on when a batch of items should be rejected or re-worked and on when machines should be reset.

Maintenance

The servicing, repair and replacement of equipment is an essential part of ensuring optimum operating effectiveness. Decisions must be taken regarding the frequency of equipment overhaul, the scheduling of maintenance work and the frequency of equipment replacement.

Labour control

Labour costs are an important part of total production costs. In many industries labour costs are the main component of production costs. In order to exercise effective control the work content of each task must be determined. This enables realistic work scheduling and monitoring of actual against planned performance to be carried out.

While the relative importance of these decision areas will vary for different industries and different companies every organization will need to give some attention to each of the areas mentioned.

STRATEGIC PLANNING

Clearly strategic planning of production can only take place within the context of the overall corporate planning process. Traditionally the strategic task for the production function has been seen as the design of a production system capable of meeting the requirements of the marketing strategic plan. This is likely to lead to insufficient account being taken of the production implications of alternative strategies at the corporate planning stage. This frequently results in conflicting demands being placed on production which are impossible to resolve. Naturally the marketing department wish to provide as good a service as possible to the customer. As a consequence they

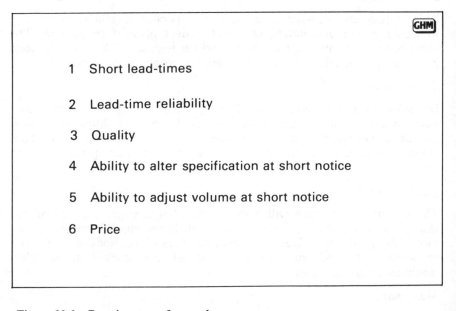

Figure 29.2   Requirements for market success

may require production to manufacture special products to customer specifications using the same production facilities as standard products with no increase in production lead-times. Alternatively they may ask for immediate availability of all products while insisting that the increased stockholding costs incurred cannot be passed on to the customer.

In developing a strategic plan which adequately reflects both market requirements and production capabilities, the production function must play an integral part in the process of strategy formation.

An essential first step must be to gain a clear understanding of the performance measures leading to success in the market-place. Figure 29.2 lists the most common criteria for success. While most organizations would ideally like to meet all of these criteria this is not possible as many of the criteria are in conflict. In achieving short lead-times, increased costs will be incurred leading to increased prices. If quality is an important criterion then it is unlikely that very short lead-times can be achieved.

Of course the key criteria may be different for different product groups provided separate production facilities are used. Problems only arise when the same production facility is required to satisfy different criteria for two product groups at the same time. Setting priorities can be almost impossible if, for example, one group of orders must be completed at minimum cost (implying high levels of machine utilization) while another group of orders must be completed as rapidly as possible (implying low levels of machine utilization).

Once the tasks which are vital to corporate success have been identified, a production capability analysis should be carried out. The main purpose of the analysis is to assess whether the organization is likely to be able to meet the performance requirements of the market with currently available resources.

If there is a mismatch between the capabilities of the existing production system and market requirements then either the production system must be modified or the strategy must be altered. Otherwise the consequences can be extremely serious. When the Babcock and Wilcox Corporation in the United States tried to enter the nuclear pressure vessel business they encountered very severe problems. They had considerable expertise in the manufacture of steam pressure vessels where the requirement was for a standard product with a short, reliable lead-time, sold at a competitive price. The nuclear power industry required absolute product reliability and reliable delivery but the length of the lead-time and the price were relatively unimportant. Also the large size of nuclear pressure vessels, coupled with the fact that each vessel was a special item fabricated to a very precise customer specification meant that manufacturing methods suited to steam pressure vessels were quite unsuitable for nuclear pressure vessels. Consequently, during the first three years of operation only three pressure vessels were completed instead of the twenty which were scheduled. Eventually the two main contractors transferred fourteen part-completed pressure vessels from Babcock and Wilcox to competing organizations. Between 1967 and 1969 company profits fell from $33m to $5m.

Once the production capability analysis has been completed then decisions will need to be made on the following main components of the manufacturing structure:

Plant and equipment technology

This covers the processing methods to be used, the choice of equipment and the level of automation.

Production systems

These define the procedures for detailed planning and control of production and the performance standards to be met.

Personnel policies

These specify policies on the degree of job specialization, payment systems to be employed and the type of work group organization to be adopted.

Product design

This is concerned with those aspects of product design which simplify manufacture and reduce production costs.

Organization and management

This specifies the organizational structure adopted within the production function and the allocation of responsibilities between staff.

FORECASTING DEMAND

An essential requirement for the planning of production is a forecast of demand for each product. For each forecast an indication of the likely forecasting error should be provided. For forecasts with a high expected error contingency plans can then be made to cope with the occasions when actual demand is much higher or lower than the forecasts.

Forecasting techniques tend to be classified into short-term, medium-term and long-term depending on the underlying assumptions which have been made. In short-term forecasting it is assumed that the underlying trend is linear and stable with changes in external factors having little effect on demand. This enables very simple extrapolative techniques to be used. However, the assumptions are only likely to be valid when forecasting just a few months ahead. The simplest method of short-term forecasting is to use moving averages to identify the underlying trend line and then to project the trend line forward. Figure 29.3 shows the results obtained using a five-period moving average.

Increasingly, however, simple moving averages of this kind are being replaced by weighted moving averages in which the greatest weighting is given to the most recent data. The most popular technique of this kind is

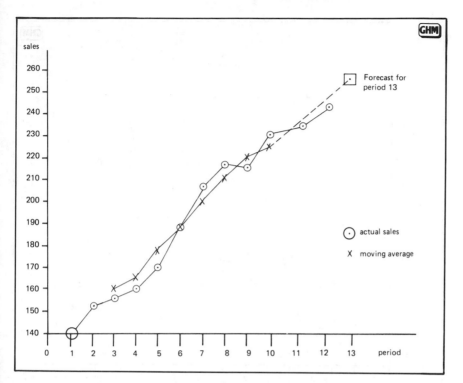

Figure 29.3 Forecast based on a 5-period moving average

called exponential smoothing. This involves updating the moving average each period using the following calculation.

new moving average $= a \times$ sales for this period $+ (1-a)$
$\times$ moving average for previous period

where a is called the smoothing constant and is normally given a value between 0.1 and 0.3.

Forecasts based on exponential smoothing tend to be more accurate than forecasts based on a simple moving average, particularly when there are frequent fluctuations in the trend. Figure 29.4 shows the results of using exponential smoothing for short-term forecasting when there are marked short-term fluctuations in sales.

Medium-term forecasting techniques are based on the assumption that the underlying trend follows a regular curve. The most commonly used approach is to fit a curve of the appropriate type to the data and then to project the curve forward to obtain the forecast.

In long-term forecasting it is recognized that external factors will have a considerable effect on the forecast. The emphasis is therefore placed on establishing the quantitative relationship between demand and those factors

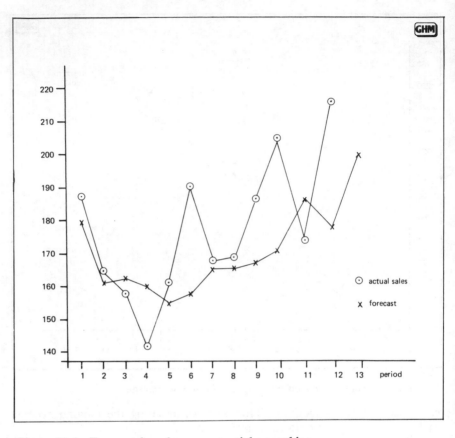

Figure 29.4   Forecast based on exponential smoothing

which influence demand, using the techniques of regression analysis. This enables an equation to be developed which can then be used to forecast demand.

THE MAKE OR BUY DECISION

One very important part of the strategic planning process is the decision regarding which items are to be manufactured and which items are to be bought in. This decision will be taken primarily on financial grounds but there are other factors which should also be taken into account. Purchase of items gives greater flexibility if large fluctuations in demand occur. It also allows access to specialist skills and economies of scale which may not be available internally. On the other hand manufacture gives greater control over quality and delivery dates.

For most items a change from manufacturing to purchase or vice versa would involve such a major change to the nature of the company that it would not be acceptable on policy grounds. However, there will be a number of items which could either be manufactured or purchased depending on which involves the lowest cost.

When making cost comparisons it is important that only incremental costs are taken into account. Any costs which will be unaltered by a switch between manufacturing and purchasing should be ignored.

In practice the decision is very dependent on current utilization of internal resources. Manufacturing will nearly always be more attractive if labour and equipment would otherwise be under-utilized. On the other hand buying-in is likely to be preferable if the decision to manufacture the item will involve substantial capital investment and the recruitment of labour. Purchasing will be particularly attractive if there is a possibility of a fall-off in the future level of requirements for the item in the long term.

PREPARING AN OPERATING PLAN

Once demand for each product has been forecast, and it has been decided which items will be manufactured and which will be purchased, then an operating plan must be devised aimed at ensuring that the company's marketing objectives are met.

In order to predict delivery periods and decide on stockholding policy a production stage chart should be constructed. This is a diagrammatic representation of all the stages in the production process including supplier delivery periods, product design and final dispatch to the customer. Estimates of the time to complete each stage are included so that the delivery time can be assessed. An outline of a production stage chart for a pigment is shown in Figure 29.5.

If the delivery time is likely to be acceptable to customers, the organization can operate as a make-to-order company, only carrying out work on firm customer orders. Usually, however, the delivery time will be unacceptable and it will be necessary to carry out some stages in the chart in advance of customer orders. In some cases it will only be necessary to pre-order raw materials and hold stocks based on forecasts of future usage. In other cases, where customers require very short lead-times, stocks of the finished product will need to be held so that new orders can be met immediately from stock.

The next step should be to decide whether the forecast demand can be satisfied and the desired lead-times met with currently available capacity. To estimate capacity requirements, current capacity and forecast demand need to be expressed in the same units, for example, litres of paint or numbers of electric motors. However, with a varied range of products there will be no common physical unit of capacity and so forecast demand will need to be converted into standard hours of manufacturing time.

If average weekly demand exceeds average weekly capacity, a decision must be taken on whether capacity should be increased. This decision is likely to be influenced by the following factors:

1   Long-term forecasts of changes in market size and market share

Activity	**GHM**
	Weeks
Purchase raw materials	1
	2
Manufacture intermediates	3
	4
Manufacture base pigments	5
Standardize	6
Blend final product and test	7
Dispatch	8

Figure 29.5   Production stage chart for pigment manufacture

2   The expected return on the capital investment required
3   Possible future innovations in the product or the production process.

If it is decided that an increase in capacity cannot be justified then one or more of the following alternatives can be considered:

1   Increase the number of purchased or subcontracted items
2   Use overtime or shift working to increase effective capacity
3   Eliminate items with low profit margins from the product range releasing capacity for more profitable product lines.

Aggregate planning

The analysis described above should ensure a reasonable match between capacity and demand on an annual basis. In addition there will be the need to cope with variations in demand over the year. These may be due to seasonal variations, changing economic conditions or random fluctuations in orders from week to week. A company which has sufficient capacity to meet average demand will find that there are periods during the year when demand is appreciably above average. As a consequence either sales will be lost or delivery periods will become unacceptably long. On the other hand, if capacity is based on peak demand then the utilization of labour and equipment will be low during periods of below average demand.

Aggregate planning is an attempt to schedule production over a six- to twelve-month period taking into account forecast variations in demand. The following methods of handling fluctuations in demand can be considered:

1 Vary the number of hours worked each week by the use of overtime or additional shifts during periods of peak demand
2 Vary the size of the workforce by recruiting casual workers during peak periods
3 Use spare capacity during periods of low demand to build up stocks of finished goods for use during periods of above average demand
4 Increase the amount of sub-contracted work during periods of high demand.

Each alternative will incur substantial additional costs. The use of overtime or sub-contracting involves premium charges relative to the cost of manufacturing internally during normal working hours. Changes in the size of the workforce involve recruitment and lay-off costs. Stock building involves high stockholding and obsolescence costs. The optimum solution will be the combination of these alternatives which minimizes total costs. A number of techniques for aggregate planning have been developed. The main approaches are outlined below.

The linear decision rule

This technique for obtaining a minimum-cost solution to the above problem was developed by Holt, Modigliani, Muth and Simon. The approach takes account of normal time and overtime labour rates, recruitment and lay-off costs, inventory holding, back ordering and machine set-up costs. These are used to derive two linear decision rules for computing the workforce levels and production rate for each period taking into account forecasts of sales for each period over a specified planning horizon.

This approach provides an optimum solution and is easy to apply once the two decision rules have been derived. However, the assumptions on cost structure may provide a poor approximation to reality. Also there are no restrictions on the size of the workforce, the hours of overtime worked or the number of units held in inventory so that the solution generated by this technique may be impractical.

Linear programming

The Simplex method of linear programming takes the same cost data as the linear decision rule approach and also generates a minimum cost solution giving workforce size and production rate period by period. An advantage over the linear decision rule method is that capacity constraints can be incorporated into the model. A major limitation of linear programming is that all constraints and cost functions must be linear. This will be unrealistic whenever economies of scale exist. A further limitation is that only a single objective can be optimized at a time whereas aggregate planning is usually concerned with satisfying a number of conflicting objectives simultaneously.

Goal programming is an extension of linear programming which to some extent overcomes the problem of being limited to a single objective. A set of management goals is specified and a solution is generated which is as close to this set of goals as possible.

Search decision rule

This is an iterative procedure which starts with an initial solution and determines the overall cost of this solution. The procedure then searches for an alternative solution with lower costs. This continues until a solution is reached for which further alteration would not yield significant cost reductions. Unlike the first two procedures this does not yield a mathematical optimum solution. In other words it yields a good but not necessarily minimum-cost solution. However it has the advantages of being less complicated and requiring less computation.

Management coefficients method

This is a method developed by Bowman in which management's past planning decisions are analysed statistically to determine the decision criteria which were used. A set of decision equations are then derived in which the numerical coefficients are based on this statistical analysis. These decision equations can then be used to prepare future schedules using the same criteria. This should result in an improvement in performance due to the criteria being applied more consistently.

Parametric production planning

This is a technique suggested by Jones which uses a search procedure to quantify four parameters associated with minimum cost in aggregate planning. The four parameters are then inserted into equations which are used to determine workforce size and production rate for each period. The method involves no constraints imposed by the mathematical structure of the model and the parameters and equations are specific to the company. While the method is non-optimizing it is claimed to produce very good results.

A performance comparison of the alternative aggregate planning procedures

Lee and Khumawala carried out a comparative study of alternative aggregate planning procedures in a company manufacturing capital goods. The aggregate planning procedures evaluated were the linear decision rule, the search decision rule, the management coefficients method and parametric production planning. The application of these procedures was simulated and the profit performance achieved compared with the actual performance of the company. All the planning methods yielded better profits than the company's own planning procedures. The greatest improvement (14 per cent) was achieved using the search decision rule.

Tactical planning

Once the aggregate plan has been prepared all the key policy decisions will have been made. The next step is to prepare a detailed operating plan. This will involve a series of tactical decisions regarding:

1 The operations necessary for the manufacture of each product or order and their sequence
2 Allocation of jobs to facilities
3 Scheduling the start and finish times of each operation.

These tasks are more appropriately dealt with as part of production control.

FURTHER READING

Bowman, E.H., 'Consistency and Optimality in Managerial Decision Making', *Management Science* 9 January 1963. This article provides a detailed description of the management coefficients method of aggregate planning

Buffa, E.S., *Modern Production Management*, 5th edition, Wiley, New York, 1977. An excellent and comprehensive coverage of the techniques of production management

Constable, C.J., and New, C.C., *Operations Management*, Wiley, New York, 1976. A good general introduction to production management with particular emphasis on the strategic aspects

Holt, C.C., Modigliani, F., and Muth, J.F., *Planning Production, Inventories and Workforce*, Prentice-Hall, Englewood Cliffs, 1960. Covers all aspects of aggregate planning with particular emphasis on the linear decision rule method

Jones, C.H., 'Parametric Production Planning', *Management Science* 13, July 1967. This article describes the parametric production planning technique for aggregate planning

Lee, W.B., and Khumawala, B.M., 'Simulation Testing of Aggregate production Planning models in an Implementation Methodology', *Management Science* 20, February 1974. This article describes the comparison of alternative aggregate planning techniques referred to in the text

Skinner, W., 'Manufacturing–Missing Link in Corporate Strategy', *Harvard Business Review*, May–June 1974. This article discusses how top management can take a more active role in the formation of manufacturing strategy

Taubert, W.H., 'Search Decision Rule for the Aggregate Scheduling Problem', *Management Science* 14, February 1968. This article describes the search decision rule for aggregate planning

Twiss, B.C., 'Developing and Implementing Strategy for Production', *Long Range Planning*, April 1974. This article provides a framework for the strategic planning of production

Wheelwright, S.C. and Makridakis, S., *Forecasting Methods for Management*, Wiley, New York, 1973. A useful handbook for all managers involved in preparing or using forecasts

30 Productivity improvement

The British Council of Productivity Associations

Productivity improvement, in the sense of making better use of the resources employed in meeting the needs of the consumer, is a continuing preoccupation of the managers of all manufacturing or service operations. Whether by investment in more efficient plant, development of more effective systems, energy conservation, the reduction of scrap or stimulation of employee performance, the pursuit of improvements in productivity is an everyday concern. But the focus of this chapter is on improvements in these – and other – areas which are brought about in a systematic way.

A PLANNED APPROACH TO PRODUCTIVITY IMPROVEMENT

The kind of measures referred to above represent, by definition almost, a piecemeal approach to productivity improvement. Typically they are reactive, stimulated by an increase in some element of cost – labour or materials or energy or capital, or perhaps where some malfunction has focused attention on a part of the system. Even where this kind of action is co-ordinated into a more comprehensive attack on one of these elements through an organization-wide programme, the approach is still essentially a tactical one. Recent years, however, have seen a growing realization that substantial benefits can follow from a strategic approach to productivity improvement.

There are a number of reasons for this. First is the realization that there is more to the productivity equation than the measurable inputs to, and outputs from, some part of the system: man hours per unit of production or ton miles per vehicle per day. Such measures are essentially indices of the efficiency of some component of the conversion process but take no account, for example, of effectiveness (of the output's contribution to the organization's wider objectives) or of the social impact of change. Thus, investment in expensive plant in the narrow interest of reduced conversion costs can lead to a lack of flexibility in the face of rapidly changing markets. And there is nothing more demoralizing than to engage energies in bringing about operational improvements to a part of the business which subsequently falls victim to a change in business policy.

Then again, the growth of the service sector, where outputs are less tangible, has raised problems of measurement which can only be met by introducing some element of quality of service into the equation.

To recognize these additional dimensions to the output side of the productivity equation – effectiveness, quality and social impact – is to realize that to bring about an improvement is likely to involve diverse inputs also.

Conventional approaches to productivity improvement tend to be rooted in a particular discipline rather than focused on some aspect of business performance. There are many fables which describe how some problem was addressed by industrial engineering, personnel, accounting, operations research and so on, each seeing the problem and the solution in terms of their own specialization. This is not to belittle the contribution of such specialists, which is totally indispensable, but to make the point that where the effort is directed at a broader outcome, the advantages of a multi-disciplinary approach become more obvious.

In discussing the subject of productivity we are, by definition, talking about manipulation of operational resources. In a commercial undertaking there are a variety of ways in which its prosperity can be enhanced by actions which, whilst having important impacts on the operating system, have origins which lie outside it. Thus, more astute financial management which makes more funds available for investment; mergers and acquisitions which provide the opportunity to take advantage of economies of scale; new product developments which provide wider market opportunities and so on, all originate outside the present operating system. Such actions will present those responsible for managing day-to-day operations with both problems and opportunities and their responses may well bring about beneficial change in the overall productivity of the systems in their charge. But the effect will not invariably be benign; there is a whole range of profitable change through improved service to the customer which may well have adverse effects on the utilization of resources. Where there is improvement it will be a mere by-product of the pursuit of policies which have other, wider objectives.

The argument is that the narrow pursuit of productivity of resources is not necessarily beneficial to the business as a whole. Nor, conversely, do wider policy decisions necessarily have a beneficial effect on resource productivity as such. What is required is a recognition that there is an important interaction between policy decisions and the productivity of the operating system. Initiatives taken to raise the level of utilization of input resources can have the effect of opening up opportunities for the business: business policy decisions can have important implications for the utilization of such resources.

Formal programmes of productivity improvement need to take notice of the nature of these interactions for the particular business. For example, business strategies which depend on the relationship between cumulative product experience and lowered costs will only succeed where positive steps are taken to manage the operating system down the experience curve.

A PRODUCTIVITY IMPROVEMENT PROGRAMME

To be successful, a productivity improvement programme must be based first of all on a global review of the main resources used in the business – finance, technology, plant, people. This should identify not only their potential contribution to the achievement of policy objectives but make an assessment of the organization's readiness for change. This assessment needs to consider what resources (in terms of management skills and financial strength, for example) will be required and whether they are in place or can be made available to ensure the success of the programme. If existing resources are fully stretched in coping with the day-to-day business in a tough competitive environment, then it will be unwise to proceed until some space has been created to take on the additional load.

In addition to assessing the obstacles which a shortage of resources might represent, there is a need also to consider those positive factors which contribute to organizational readiness. These would include a climate within the organization which is conducive to change, a record of innovation, of challenges successfully taken up.

If the assessment of readiness is favourable, detailed planning can begin. One of the problems with productivity improvement plans is that they have come to be associated mainly with manpower productivity and, in the prevailing economic climate, with a reduction in employment opportunity. The issue has to be faced squarely and, where the primary objective is cost reduction, it must be recognized that employees will be legitimately interested in how the savings are to be divided.

Many companies recently have found themselves in a situation where drastic action has been necessary for survival and it has been possible to convince employees of the seriousness of the situation and secure their active cooperation in bringing about necessary change. But it has been an uncomfortable process. For others, it has seemed impossible to embark on any kind of programme which involved a collaborative approach.

In the introduction of a formal productivity improvement programme, five separate steps can be identified.

Step 1 Awareness

First is the need to establish an awareness throughout the organization of the objectives of the programme and the way in which it is to be implemented. The methods used to establish this awareness will depend on the established patterns of communications within the company. Plans have been launched which involve a considerable amount of direct training of managers, supervisors, union officers and employee representatives. Such training will often embrace some introduction to problem solving or other relevant techniques or may be confined to an understanding of the processes of change in organizations, presented in the context of the proposed plan. In other cases, information will be imparted through internal newsheets, through briefing groups, through presentations on videotape and so on.

There is much to be said for making the keynote of the campaign a very positive one: successful programmes have been run which do not look for mere improvement but challenge every item of cost to be justified in terms of contribution to profit. Other programmes have been based on the need to match the annual rate of increase in controllable costs with comparable overall savings. But it is very important to make sure these kinds of programmes are consistent with the objectives of the business. Whilst reduction in costs is always desirable there is generally a trade-off between use of resources and service to the customer which should be recognized in the main thrust of the programme.

Step 2   Motivation

One of the objectives of measures taken to raise levels of awareness is to create a climate favourable to change. The next step is to turn that to a positive motivation. Action here will depend critically on the earlier assessments of readiness, particularly those aspects which are concerned with enthusiasm and morale. Where the management team is already innovative in style, the focus may be on convincing them that a productivity improvement programme is an appropriate weapon to use in the current situation.

Where there is a degree of inertia to be overcome, the facts revealed in the awareness campaign – of competitive pressures for example – may of themselves create the necessary motivation. But however this phase of the exercise is directed, an essential component will be some very explicit commitment to the programme on the part of senior management. Without such a demonstration the exercise is unlikely to succeed.

The best recipe for a strongly motivated workforce is a combination of leadership and involvement. To provide leadership, senior management need to maintain a high profile where the programme is concerned, taking part in presentations where appropriate and making sure that progress reports are on the agenda at operating meetings. They can also make clear by example that attendance at team meetings enjoys a high priority. They can insist that the reward system takes account of individual contribution to the programme.

In considering the other component, there is abundant evidence that participation in teams is a powerful motivator. To spread the opportunity for participation as widely as possible consistent with sensible control is to take maximum advantage of the benefits which such involvement brings. And that participation should extend not only to the search for opportunities for improvement but to setting targets for improvement as well.

Finally under the heading of motivation is the question of reward. Programmes have been run successfully in which achievement of targets is one of the factors taken into account in assessing bonuses for managers. But it has to be stressed that other, more direct indicators of job performance dominate the system. Generally it is held that direct financial reward is not appropriate but that some form of recognition is desirable. The method chosen should take account of any established system in the company for achievement of targets for quality, safety, lost time or other subjects of interdepartmental competition.

Step 3 Tactical planning

The next step is concerned with tactical planning – where to begin? Some form of force field analysis may be appropriate to establish a comprehensive view of the factors, both favourable and hostile, which will influence success in any proposed area of change. Early success is a great morale booster in change programmes, but avoid the fate of boxers whose reputations are built on a series of inadequate opponents only to be floored by the first serious opposition! Rather than picking the easy options there is much to be said for starting in areas where changes can be made – and be seen to be made – quickly. For it is the achievement of actual change which will build up the momentum of the programme rather than an accumulation of proposals whose implementation is necessarily delayed – by the need to purchase and install equipment for example or to develop computer software. Once agreement has been reached on some form of employee participation in the programme, nothing is more discouraging for its supporters than a period when nothing appears to be happening.

Step 4 Implementation

In considering the implementation of the programme there are two main areas for decision. First is the choice of an appropriate organizational frame-work. Most programmes involve the establishment of some structure which is divorced from the day-to-day running of the business. There are many alternatives and we explore three different examples later in this chapter. Each of these involves the establishment of one or more teams, task forces – call them what you will – which will carry out the detailed analysis of the present situation and development of alternative solutions. These teams will typically be multi-disciplinary and must have access to further specialist resources, both inside and outside the organization.

In addition to such teams there will be a need for some co-ordinating activity to ensure that individual team efforts constitute a coherent whole, and that this is consistent with the overall objectives, whose importance has been stressed at some length above. It will also be desirable to establish some means of direct communication between teams, to provide for the exchange of ideas and experiences and for mutual support.

A second important decision concerns the resources which are to be made available to the programme. Focusing initially on the problems of raising levels of awareness and motivation, it is a common experience that managements greatly underestimate the amount of effort required to satisfy the levels of expectation that have been aroused. Of course there are limits to the amount of change which any individual part of the organization can absorb in a given time without some aspects of performance being affected.

But, nevertheless, for any given amount of resource which can be made available to the programme, it will probably be wiser to concentrate it rather than spread it so thinly that early enthusiasms cannot be adequately followed up.

Step 5   Monitoring

Finally a mechanism for monitoring the progress of the exercise will be desirable. It is not uncommon for programmes to be designed around some quantifiable target of improvement – say 5 per cent – in utilization of plant or personnel or in delivery performance or in the reduction of scrap or energy consumption, the choice being made in the light of potential contribution to the objectives of the business. Team members will want to see the cumulative effect of their efforts on progress towards such targets and management will want to monitor the outcome of the programme in relation to the resources they have made available.

Since commitment to change is the essential ingredient of success, there is much to be said for a monitoring system which requires proposals to be set out with some formality and which clearly identifies actions, responsibilities and timing.

ORGANIZATIONAL STRUCTURE

The paragraphs above have sketched in a framework for the establishment of a productivity improvement programme. Throughout there has been an implication that the programme will be based on teams. There has also been an implicit assumption that a team approach is likely to be more successful than any of the alternatives. This assumption is based on experience of the power which a small, well managed team can bring to bear on the problems and opportunities which a productivity improvement programme can bring to light. The actual composition of such teams and the relationship between them has been only lightly touched on. Some of the alternative arrangements are illustrated in the following examples.

Company A

Company A is a subsidiary of a large engineering group and manufactures industrial products at a single site employing some 400 people. The factory has its own industrial engineering capability and is able to call on a limited range of other specialist help from the headquarters of the group. They set up their productivity improvement plan with teams consisting of departmental managers and supervisors. There are eight teams in all, one in each of the production departments, one each representing maintenance and plant services and one from production planning. The teams have four or five members and may co-opt members as they think fit. There is also a team co-ordinator and an action group. The general structure of the plan is as follows:

1 Teams meet once a week for about two hours
2 Each team has a leader whose responsibilities are:
   (a) To maintain records of meetings, actions agreed, responsibilities and timing
   (b) To maintain links with other teams and with specialist departments
   (c) To prepare project proposals for the team co-ordinator
3 The team co-ordinator is a senior member of the factory industrial engineering department whose responsibilities are:
   (a) To assist the teams to develop and progress their proposals
   (b) To prepare proposals for submission to the action group
4 The action group consists of the factory manager, chief engineer, chief accountant, personnel manager and the team co-ordinator. The group meets monthly, and its responsibilites are:
   (a) To examine project proposals
   (b) To decide priorities and timing for implementation
   (c) To progress implementation of proposals in line with agreed dates.

Before proposals are put before the action group a detailed examination of costs and benefits is carried out. Three months after changes are brought about, an investigation is carried out to establish that the benefits are being secured and that the costs are in line with estimates. The results of this investigation are reported to the action group for attention.

Company B

Company *B* is in the service sector and has more than twenty branches. These branches, whilst differing considerably in size, share a common technology and employ substantially similar procedures in the service of their customers.

Because of the similarity between branches, and in their way of working, it seemed that the opportunities for exchange of experiences were particularly strong. It was accordingly decided to set up a productivity improvement programme which would have a strong element of direction from the centre. A small team was set up at the head office under the leadership of a senior manager from one of the branches. The team was to visit each location and, with the active participation of the local manager, to review each aspect of the unit's activity. The purpose of the review was to be the identification of opportunities for profitable change and to get commitment to action plans to turn such opportunities into results.

The choice of the team leader was seen as critical. He needed to be a manager whose own success had earned him the respect of his colleagues and whose personality would set a tone of encouragement and confidence. He was assisted by a member of the head office productivity services unit and an accountant with a good knowledge of branch procedures. The team leader worked to the following brief:

Work programme

The team will need to develop a programme. Its work at each site will have some aspects of an audit and must therefore be systematic and comprehensive in its review of site activities. The programme should provide for study in depth, the team spending from two to three weeks at each main site. The team's activities at each site will include:

1 Briefing sessions with the local manager to gain understanding and commitment to objectives, methods of working, confidentiality, reporting, follow-up
2 Briefing sessions with other officers, supervisors and graded staff as may be appropriate
3 Review of site activities: a useful starting point will be provided by an organization chart which accounts for every employee, and by the site budget and expenditure control reports
4 Detailed examination of selected areas with emphasis on the opportunities for profitable change
5 Establish priorities, action plans and assign responsibilities
6 Draft terms of reference for projects requiring further work. (An example of a suitable form is shown in Figure 30.1)
7 De-briefing, agree follow up procedure.

Control system

The essence of the programme is to gain the commitment of local management by working with them in finding opportunities for profitable change. At the same time there will be a need to keep the programme moving forward. It is proposed that all information, notes of discussions, reports and other data generated by the team at any location should be confidential to the local manager and not disclosed to anyone else without his express permission. The local branch manager will be required to report on the projects to which he has agreed as a part of his regular reporting procedure.

General

The emphasis of the whole programme must be upon action and results. In many directions where opportunities exist, the obstacles to change are clear to see. It will be a prime task of the central team to re-appraise these obstacles and seek ways in which they can be surmounted. In some areas there may be a need to re-establish the confidence of local managers. Much will depend on the ability of the central team to gain the confidence of local managers in discussing their problems; no sense of recrimination over past performance must be allowed to enter into these discussions.

Company C

Company *C* is a manufacturing company which has two main activities. Contracts division is concerned with meeting customer demands with products

		GHM
COMPANY B	**TERMS OF REFERENCE FOR PRODUCTIVITY IMPROVEMENT PROJECT**	

Location .... Project No. ....

Project title

Brief title for identification

Initiated by ....

Start date .... Date for completion ....

Project objective

What will the project achieve?

Present situation

What happens at present?

Reasons for project

What makes you think an improvement is possible?

Action requested and end product

What the project team is being asked to do and what the end product will be?

Constraints

What constraints are imposed on the solution in terms of costs, time, etc?

Team manager   Team members

Figure 30.1   Form used by company B to specify terms of reference for a productivity improvement team

which are designed and built to individual customer specification. Products division markets a highly specialized range of industrial products which are very competitive in their field.

In considering the appropriate structure for a productivity improvement programme, the company distinguished sharply between the two divisions. It set out proposals for them in the following terms:

Contracts division is an important growth area for the company. The chief preoccupation of management is the planning and execution of contracts, particular emphasis being placed on the achievement of shorter delivery times through improved procurement and sub-contracting procedures and on detailed planning and control of manufacturing processes.

However, if the expansion which is planned for the business is to be built on sound foundations, management information and control systems must be developed which will support such future growth. With this in mind, a team should be set up with the specific task of examining, on a regular and systematic basis, the procedures by which the operation of the business is controlled. This systems review team should comprise:

Manufacturing manager
Procurement manager
Chief accountant

The team, which will report to the general manager, will draw on such outside assistance as appears helpful including, in particular, computer services.

Products division has remained very static for some time. Control information and operating statements indicate that standards are being met and that most adverse variances arise from causes beyond the control of management.

If products division is to achieve the profitable expansion planned for it, a detailed review of the whole operation should be taken as a priority. What is needed is an approach which will challenge all the accepted constraints on the technology, and on the manufacturing and distribution operations. Resources from outside the division will be needed and structured so that creative problem analysis techniques can be brought to bear.

TEAM BUILDING

All the approaches that have been described involve the creation of teams whose composition will depend upon the circumstances and the objectives of the particular programme. Experience shows that there is benefit to be gained if a new team can take a short period of time soon after it has formed to examine how it is going to work, what its methods, procedures and work relationships will be and what the principal concerns of its members are. Training will take the form of discussions covering the following topics:

1 Statement, discussion and clarification of the team's mission – its objectives, timetable, work tasks
2 Discussion of the concerns and hopes of the team members – about their roles, relationship with the team, relationship with the departments from which they are seconded, how the group will follow or depart from tradition, what will happen when the project is complete
3 Presentation and explanation of the team leader's plan to organize the project; organization structure, relations with others, general ground rules
4 Discussion of each individual's special contribution, area of responsibility and authority
5 Development of methods of communication within the team and with people outside the team. Conduct of meetings, preparation of minutes, reports, memoranda
6 Development of the team's relationship with local managers; legitimacy, confidentiality, expectations
7 Arrangements for a follow-up meeting.

FURTHER READING

Gmelch, W. and Miskin, V., *Productivity Teams*, John Wiley, New York, 1984

Gregeman, I., *Productivity Improvement*, Van Nostrand Reinhold, New York, 1984

Lawlor, A., *Productivity Improvement Manual*, Gower, Aldershot, 1985

Saunders, G., *The Committed Organisation*, Gower, Aldershot, 1984

31 Plant layout

Brian Walley

The signs of a poor plant layout can seldom be hidden. There are delays to be seen in the manufacturing process, with products and materials following no direct or obvious path. Aisles become cluttered with materials and components. Manual handling of materials, including machine loading and unloading, is commonplace. Service areas and stores are sited so that operatives are forced to leave their machines frequently to walk long distances for the collection of cutting tools, work instructions and materials. Production plant is under-used, and machines are seen to be idle, waiting for previous processes to be finished.

In a perfect world the layout of plant would allow an uninterrupted flow of work through the factory. Machines and workers would always be gainfully occupied, and they would be arranged so as to take up the least amount of space consistent with safe and efficient operation. Unfortunately, this happy state of affairs is rare. A definition of the subject, and a look at the factors and people involved in plant layout decisions will suggest why this is so.

A plant layout study is the analysis of all the factors involved in siting machinery, work stations, ancillary equipment, storage, services, manufacturing flow pattern and the functional design of buildings. The objective is to produce an arrangement which will minimize production costs.

The study must involve a wide range of specialists, either directly or as consultants. These can include architects, draughtsmen, ergonomists, design, mechanical, civil, electrical, process control, and production engineers, work study and operations research people, production planners and controllers, safety officers, materials handling experts, factory inspectors, local shop stewards and other trades union officials and (of course) line management. Paradoxically, the abundance of expertise, with so many diverse aims, can make the process of designing a plant layout difficult to achieve logically and simply. In all respects, plant layout design is a complex task.

BENEFITS OF A GOOD PLANT LAYOUT

Potential benefits are many, but achievement depends largely on careful planning before production starts. It is obviously far more difficult to attempt re-laying out a plant arrangement after production has got under way. The following list of benefits is useful as a checklist against which any new layout proposals should be assessed. A perfect layout would ensure:

1 Best possible use of production warehousing and stores space
2 Most economic investment of capital in new plant, materials handling equipment, tooling, general facilities and the building itself
3 Efficient routing of services, so reducing installation and subsequent maintenance costs of electrical, steam, gas and air services, and of ventilation
4 Minimum movement of materials between processes, so reducing handling costs and the volume of work in progress
5 Through increased efficiency, a lower requirement for ancillary workers; fewer storekeepers, general labourers and internal transport drivers
6 Easier movement of staff around the factory
7 Reduced operator fatigue through the provision of mechanical handling aids where appropriate, and the sensible positioning of materials in relation to plant and machinery
8 Elimination of fatigue and low morale attributable to a bad working environment (poor lighting, excessive noise, vibration, dust, fumes, heat and humidity)
9 Reduced energy consumption
10 Production management made easier (production control and progressing, materials and stock control, work booking, costing, etc.)
11 More effective supervision and management
12 Better housekeeping – easier to keep everything clean and tidy
13 More easily predictable – and achievable – output and cost objectives
14 Sensitivity to changed requirements of production volume or to product mix and new designs
15 Promotion of good industrial relations.

Even if some of these benefits are mutually exclusive, this remains a powerful argument for taking the trouble to plan a good plant layout.

CONSTRAINTS

Anyone analysing a plant layout will quickly come up against a series of constraints having a serious effect on the search for the most efficient layout. Of necessity, a plant layout has to accommodate a number of compromises. Suppose, for example, that all potential risks to health and safety could be ignored (for instance, by operating all machinery without guards). Such an approach might allow very high levels of production. The fact that hazards do have to be considered could result in slower working, and in a more tortuous and less well-utilized production operation than would otherwise be the case.

Constraints, therefore, need to be built into the layout. These will probably raise production costs and reduce potential efficiency beyond the best theoretical limits. The most common and most important constraints are:

1   The site and the structure of the building (a single-storey building, for example), access to road and rail transport, and structural strength. It is still comparatively rare for a layout to be prepared and then a factory building put round it. A single-storey unit will make expansion easier and facilitate natural lighting, but will cost more per square metre of manufacturing or storage space. The multi-storey alternative will be cheaper per square metre but perhaps less flexible, with doubts about structural strength on upper floors

2   Second only in importance to the structure and the site are environmental constraints:

   (a) *Pollution:* the main causes of pollution are oil mists, dust and fumes and gases of various kinds. Elimination of oil mists from drillers, grinders or lathes would mean the full enclosure of a machine which may not be practical

   (b) *Dust:* there are various regulations covering such things as quarry dust and the use of asbestos. Wet manufacturing processes instead of dry ones will help to eradicate dust problems, though complete enclosure of dust-producing areas where operatives can wear masks is also a possibility

   (c) *Fumes and gases:* these are also potential pollutants. Sealing off fume-producing activities where extra ventilation is installed is perhaps the only practical way of reducing fume hazards

   (d) *Ventilation:* this is necessary even where dust hazards are minimal. Humidity control is important

   (e) *Lighting and heating:* lighting and heating installations need to conform to the Factories Act of 1961

   (f) *Noise:* noise is recognized as a prime health hazard and cause of fatigue and its supervision needs to be considered carefully

   (g) *Factory amenities:* seating, cloakrooms, rest rooms, lavatories, changing rooms, are requirements whose minimum standards are listed in the Factories Act

   (h) *Fire and safety precautions:* will determine fire escape needs, escape routes and state how the building should be used, the restrictions on its use, and the number of people to be employed in it

   (i) *The Health and Safety at Work Act:* provides the framework for good housekeeping and all this entails in plant layout.

3   Productivity requirements may sometimes impose a constraint on technical excellence. There may be occasions when a conscious decision has to be taken to sacrifice a degree of product quality or other technical objective in order to speed up a process, thus maximizing production at a lower (but still acceptable) level of quality.

4   Capital available for investment may be restricted. In any case one of the recognized project appraisal techniques should be used to test the

economic viability of any investment project. For short-duration projects, where results can be expected in (say) a year or so, the payback method is usually sufficient. For the more customary project durations in new plant installations, the investment appraisal will have to consider the cash flows and taxation position over several years, and in these circumstances all alternative proposals should be compared using the discounted cash flow technique, or other method acceptable to the company's accountant.

PRINCIPLES OF PLANT LAYOUT

The skills needed to ensure success in plant layout design are often complex and occasionally difficult to weld together to ensure a coherent result. While method study may, theoretically, be easy to apply, its relationship with production engineering is not always an easy one. It seems important, therefore, that the plant layout team is able to refer to a set of overall principles which can guide the team's efforts and eventually provide a means of measuring whether the outcome is as satisfactory as it might appear.

The checklist which follows can be used as a fixed reference for the layout team. The principles are obviously superior to any one technique, specialist skill, or even point of view. They provide the means for answering the basic question of 'How is the layout we have proposed?'

1 The least possible space should be taken up. Any plant layout should be judged, at least in part, on the number of cubic metres and square metres needed

2 Working conditions must be such that a safe working environment is produced, conducive to high work activity. The layout should promote good working practices which help to reduce manufacturing cost, increase flexibility and maintain or improve good industrial relations

3 Interdependent operations, processes, activities and departments should be placed in proximity to each other, with as little product travel as possible

4 The layout should facilitate flow process type manufacturing operations, as this tends to utilize machine and labour

5 All product handling and re-handling should be eliminated as far as possible

6 Material/product movement both in times and distance should be minimized

7 Movements of products/material should be continuous as far as possible. Lead-times for manufacturing should be as low as possible

8 Manual handling of all kinds should be eliminated and mechanized where appropriate

9 The installation and speed of machines should be such that few, if any, bottlenecks occur. The production process should set a uniform pace which will optimize the use of production machinery, handling equipment and associated personnel

10 While machines should be utilized as fully as possible, in some instances production personnel may be the resource to utilize fully. Comparative costs, the need for flexibility, the imbalance in the process, may determine which resource needs to be given priority for efficient utilization

11 The simplest possible materials handling equipment should be used. For example, gravity or roller conveyors are preferable to powered conveyor track. They are cheaper and often more flexible

12 If materials or products have to be moved any distance they should do so as a 'unit load', i.e., a quantity rather than a single item, perhaps on a pallet

13 Receiving and dispatch departments should be located near entrances and exits. Dispatch departments, obviously, should be at the end of the production line

14 There should be centralization of the most widely used services, such as maintenance or inspection

15 There should be logical positioning of all stores and service areas based on least travel between service and point of use

16 Obnoxious areas of dust, fume or noise pollution should be isolated. Dangerous sections need to be isolated, e.g. inflammable material stores and use

17 Delicate or mentally arduous work should also be isolated (e.g. production planning). This work can be carried out at any point provided that it is isolated, for example, by sound-proofed walls. (Isolation, however, does not imply banishment to an outer corner of the building).

18 Factory production facilities and associated clerical management activities should be interrelated. Production should be seen as a system with inputs and outputs, all of which need to be integrated within the plant layout. Management, supervision, production control, engineering and all other functions associated with the production activity should be embodied within the layout.

INFORMATION REQUIREMENTS

Information is a vital component in the analysis which the layout team will need to carry out. The team members themselves are unlikely to have all the information required and it will need to be obtained from market research people, the profit planning department, the accounting functions, engineering staff, who are not necessarily members of the team.

An opportunity to combine different objectives might occur as information is collected. For example, can finished goods stock be raised as a result of fast throughput time and reduced work in progress?

Information required is again set out in the form of a checklist in order to facilitate easy reference.

1 Range and volumes of production required based on marketing plans – types, quantities, raw materials, weights, volumes, product design, components, seasonality, delivery requrements

2 Budgeted revenue and costs of potential operations and, once an appropriate sequence has been determined, machines, machine speeds and potential utilization

3 Approximate costs of new plant, buildings and associated services

4 Site situations, building regulations, basic constraints of the site and any local environmental conditions which used to be taken into account – access to roads, railways or other means of transport

5 Volume of work in progress, raw materials and finished goods storage likely to be required

6 Labour and associated services required – canteens, rest rooms, lavatories etc.

7 General services required – maintenance, stores, boiler-house, toolroom, fitters' shop etc.

8 Office accommodation

9 Materials handling equipment required.

THE TECHNOLOGY OF PLANT LAYOUT

The technology of plant layout is a fundamental precept, often based on engineering principles which have become enshrined in plant layout activities. For example, the nature of the production process will normally fit a standard pattern and these patterns have become an accepted part of the technology.

1 Typical operation and process patterns are illustrated in Figure 31.1, in the following classifications:

(a) *Straight line* Figure 31.1(a). Raw materials are converted into one product by successive operations

(b) *Converging process* Figure 31.1(b). Several raw materials or components join a main line product. A motor car assembly plant is a good example

(c) *Diverging process* Figure 31.1(c). Materials converted into different products by separate processes or operations

(d) *Multiple process* Figure 31.1(d). A complex activity where cross-over between processes or operations is carried.

2 Site/floor plans – the production process will tend to prescribe the site configuration, but the site itself may be a major factor in the plant layout. Several site-production processes have become fairly common-place over the years and these are;

(a) *The 'I' plan* – a straight-line production process established in a simple rectagular building Figure 31.2(a)

(b) *The 'U' plan* – the production process is often a straight line one,

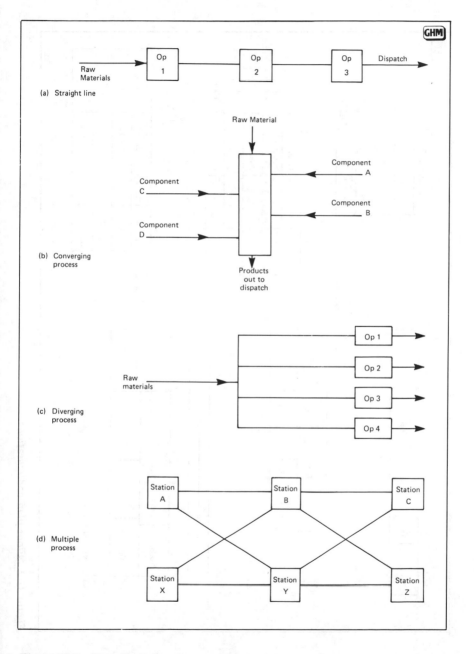

Figure 31.1 Four typical process patterns

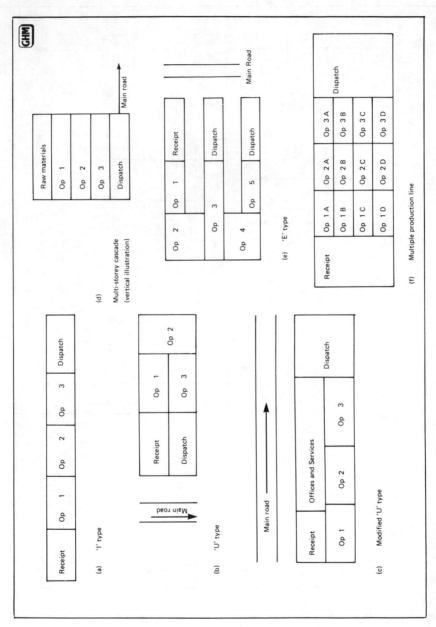

Figure 31.2 Floor plan configurations

548

but because of the need to have the receipt and despatch areas adjacent to each other, a 'U' plan is adopted as shown in Figure 31.2

(c) *Modified 'U' plan* – the position of a main road and the access provided to it often promote a modified 'U' plan as in Figure 31.2(c)

(d) *Multi-storey cascade* – multi-storey buildings provide the means to store raw materials on the top floor, and then allow manufacture to continue until completion on the ground floor as shown in Figure 31.2(d)

(e) *'E' plan, multiple production* – multiple product lines are normally more difficult to lay out effectively than single product manufacture. The 'E' plan Figure 31.2(e), and the multiple production line Figure 31.2(f) are two ways of tackling the problem.

3 Process versus product layouts: process and product layouts are often in contention in optimizing plant layout. A process layout is one where flexibility can be obtained in the manufacturing activity (Figure 31.3). Like activities are put together. One machine may make several different products. The process, therefore, is specialized and can be subjected to efficient supervision and maintenance.

Product layouts (as shown in Figure 31.4) are typified in car assembly plants. Such layouts should reduce handling costs and production time. Work in progress should be minimized.

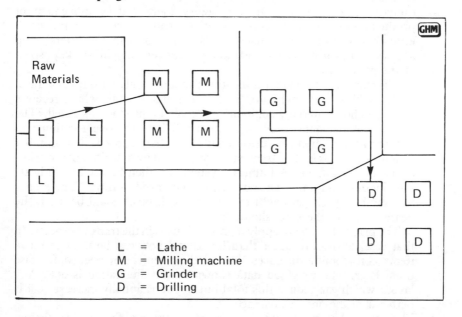

Figure 31.3 Process layout

549

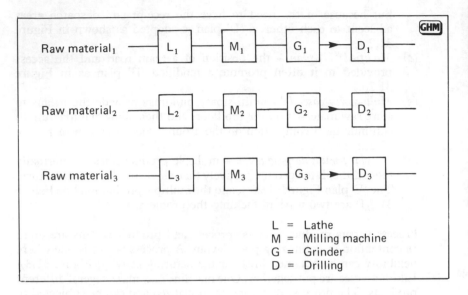

Figure 31.4   Product layout

   In many instances a combination of product and process layout is desirable.

4   Functional relationships: in any factory there will be movement of products, raw materials, tools, operatives, and services personnel of all kinds between processes, machines, stores, toolroom and fitters' shop and warehouse dispatch area. Minimizing movement will be a key aspect of the plant layout.

   The standard method for indicating functional relationships is a travel chart as illustrated in Figure 31.5. Each area or unit which receives or dispatches materials, components, tools or products is listed. The number of personnel who have to travel between one location and another as part of their duties should also be recorded. The number of journeys or weight of transfers should be shown against the units or areas receiving them. A numeric system can then be used to indicate the amounts and importance of items which need to travel. The higher the number (perhaps weight or quantity x distance could be used) the nearer together the parts should be.

   The principle may not apply if gravity is used in the transfer process. In that case downward rather than horizontal flow can be used to move items considerable distances, provided power is not needed to raise them later. The weighted data shown in the illustration is 568. Any layout which can reduce this total but not substantially increase cost is better than the one in existence.

5   The plant layout should be designed around five major factors (illustrated in Figure 31.6):

GHM

	A	B	C	D	E	F	G	H	TOTAL
A		31	12		11	12	10	—	76
B	11			40	12	13			76
C	21	—	61					17	99
D	13					70			83
E	41		20					16	77
F	11		20			24			55
G	21								11
H			60					21	81
TOTAL	118	31	173	40	23	119	10	54	568

Figure 31.5 Diagram of functional relationships

(a) *The product, its design and markets* – this will help to determine unit load possibilities, economic batch sizes, the need for plant flexibility, speed of delivery, degree of 'change-over' capacity

(b) *The process design:* the selection of equipment, dimensions of floor area to be occupied, manufacturing operatives, operation sequences

(c) *The operation designs:* methods study should help to set working patterns. Work measurement should help establish manning levels and equipment requirements

(d) *The design of facilities:* materials flow, storage areas, materials handling, power, steam, heating, environmental requirements

(e) *Site design:* using the site and building to best advantage

The design team should ensure that the interrelationships are well understood, the comparative importance of each process established

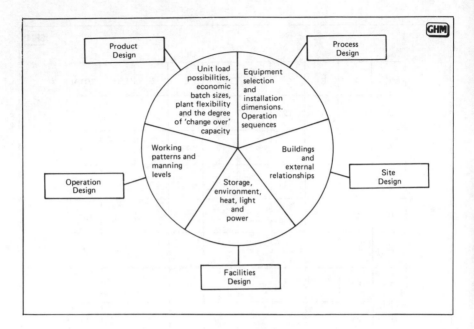

Figure 31.6 The design process

and suitable priorities made and the whole project set out as a PERT diagram or network.

6 Space considerations: the allocation of space between offices and factory, productive processes and service areas, in process and finished goods storage needs to be done according to predetermined rules and standards. For example, aisles are often allocated far too much space. If too much is allocated an aisle will degenerate into an inter-process storage area, holding up material flow and generally hindering the reason why aisles exist – rapid transport of materials and products, and personnel of all kinds.

Storage space too is often given an over-generous allocation of floor area. Maximum height stacking should be the rule rather than the exception, and materials handling equipment should be obtained to provide this facility.

Workplace design will often determine the space required for production machinery, rather than the machinery itself. Each workplace should be designed as a microcosm of the total plant so that it has its own receiving and dispatch areas, facilities and services and production equipment, established to maximize production efficiency. Workplace design should take account of potential scrap and finished production waiting to be moved, any inspection requirements, tools and tool storage, height of working surfaces, relationships between receipt and dispatch of materials, hazard elimination, degree of automation and mechanization anticipated, operator comfort and conditions, floor loading constraints and general environmental considerations.

7 Line balance considerations: a plant layout analysis should promote a balance between machine/labour utilization and use of in-progress storage space. This is often difficult where machines or operations have to be introduced which produce at a much higher or lower rate than perhaps the rest of the line.

The most common solution to this problem is to divide the work to be done into elements and thus combine them into activities which take up a similar amount of time. The related cost/performance calculations have been embodied into operations research techniques.

There are other ways of overcoming line balance problems, perhaps the easiest being the build-up of partly or semi-finished stocks so as to feed in production when required at the slower operations.

Another solution is to have a reasonably peripatetic workforce which has been trained to carry out work at several operations, wherever the line has become unbalanced.

Balancing the line grows increasingly difficult as the product range becomes more complex. Variety reduction will always help this problem.

8 Equipment selection: equipment can be bought to satisfy one or more of the following criteria. To:
(a) carry out a new activity
(b) replace a manual activity
(c) improve the environment and general working conditions
(d) make use of new technology
(e) improve line balance
(f) replace a worn-out machine
(g) reduce possibilities of accidents
(h) improve quality of products

9 Method study: using the simple method study symbols to describe a material flow process is often the simplest and best way of ensuring a record is made of actual or potential plant layout designs. String diagrams too can be of help.

10 The evaluation of alternative production methods and layout schemes is an essential part of any layout planning. This assumes, of course, that more than one potentially viable scheme does, in fact, exist. The merits of a proposal can be examined critically by asking how well the proposal would achieve any of the benefits listed at the beginning of this chapter, and checking that all constraint factors have been satisfied. By awarding a maximum possible number of 'score points' to each benefit factor (according to the degree of importance attached) a scale is made available against which the benefits of a scheme can be quantified. This helps to render any choice objective rather than subjective. It is obviously better still if the financial benefits of alternative schemes can be estimated and used in comparison.

MATERIALS HANDLING

The truism that 'handling adds nothing to value, only cost' suggests that materials handling should be an integral part of any consideration of a plant layout. Indeed it is difficult if not impossible to separate them. Materials handling is a term that embraces all aspects of material movement, other than when an actual production process is occurring. 'All aspects' are the physical transportation, equipment, methods, personnel and systems used in materials handling.

It must always be remembered that 'handling' is not an end in itself – the objective should be to contribute to a high performance of production, stores and despatch and to minimize the cost of production. Frequently this is synonymous with minimizing the cost of handling. Handling is a service function and should never be considered as a system independent of production of warehousing.

Many of the principles which materials handling specialists apply are similar to those used in plant layout. Handling and re-handling should be avoided where possible. Movement should be reduced in time and distance. Materials should be deposited as near as possible to the point of use and be prepositioned for use.

Continuous rather than intermittent movement should be a main aim. It is usually advantageous to establish definite routes for all material movement, vehicles and fork lift trucks.

Motion economy principles should apply wherever possible. Gravity should be used wherever it is feasible. Equipment and methods should be chosen to minimize in-process damage to products.

Equipment should be simple and cheap where possible. Mechanization or automation is often unnecessary. Equipment should be used which is flexible and requires no fixed floor space.

GROUP TECHNOLOGY

Group technology is an interesting and important development, concerned with the flow of inter-process materials. It is based on the assumption that grouping manufacturing resources such as machines and making them interdependent in a cellular fashion has many advantages over the functional layout which has normally been found in batch or job shops. Each cell has a mix of machines sufficient to carry out all processes on a part, or family of parts.

A functional layout where, say, groups of lathes or drilling machines are brought together, produces complicated product route patterns, resulting in high work in progress, bottlenecks and more orders delivered late than early.

An analysis of batch or job shop work usually reveals that products, far from being unique, can be seen to have family likenesses in dimensions, material types, functions and general appearance. This analysis is an important element in establishing group technology. So by batching small groups of work in accordance with family features, it is possible to create large batches of basically similar work. Large batch production tends to take the place of small batch production.

A precursor of introducing group technology, therefore, is the design of a product classification system which can be used to batch material. A definitive parts numbering (drawing numbering) code system is essential.

The design of group technology flow lines can roughly be defined as 'batch flow lines' which form an integral part of the manufacturing system. Individual operations can be formed into cells by linking roller conveyors. This ensures that batches of work do not 'queue jump' and are processed in the same sequence as they are fed into the cell.

The general applications of group technology suggest that operations can be optional, and so either machine or labour resources are consequently under-utilized to create a continuous flow of work. The cost of the disadvantage is usually more than outweighed by reductions in setting up or change-over time, work in progress and finished goods stock. The improvement in customer service is also important.

The size of each cell is determined by engineering considerations and span of control, and particularly the work relationships of the primary working group. Flexibility of labour within the cell is the norm; flexibility between cells an ideal. Incentive schemes are designed to take account of breaks in rhythm needed when operatives move from one machine to another.

AUTOMATION AND ROBOTICS

Mechanization and automation have often been confused when plant layouts are being determined. Mechanization is the replacement of human muscle by mechanical means. Automation is the substitution of the human brain. It is the latter factor that will become more and more important in plant layout.

Industrial robots came about when it was possible to harness digital electronic circuitry in this application with sufficient reliability to stand up to the rigours of a factory environment. A robot comprises a jointed arm, a 'wrist' and a gripper or hand. These limbs are attached to a body and control unit, which is programmable. The very simplest programs were set up by means of plugging leads into an electrically connected pegboard. Modern robots can be 'taught' to carry out all the necessary operations by taking them manually through the desired sequence, committing each action and limb position to the electronic memory, and then switching the device on to do the job repetitively, accurately and reliably.

Muscle power is such that work-pieces weighing 250 kilos can be positioned speedily with accuracy repeatable to a millimetre or so. Smaller robots have been developed which are capable of very fine assembly tasks.

Because robots are programmable, they are also *reprogrammable*. Unlike conventional automation, they do not have to be thrown away when a product is modified, redesigned or changed altogether. They are simply redeployed and 'taught' afresh.

The simplest robots are known as 'pick and place' devices, which means that they are capable of picking up a part from one given position, and placing it in another attitude and position. Such machines have a wide range of applications, but would not be suitable for work where every part of the path traced by the arm and gripper needed to be defined. In this case, a 'continuous path' robot would be required – useful for paint spraying and for seam welding for example.

One essential feature of plant layout and work planning with robots is that the part orientation must be accurately defined and controlled. A robot must be able to find the parts at the place where it has been 'taught' to find them, and in the correct attitude.

A robot can be set among a small group of machines, and sequenced to load, unload and operate them in an efficient, tireless fashion. Another application, such as in the welding of car bodies on a production line, uses stationary robots, with the work brought to them on a conveyor. A third arrangement is to mount the robots themselves on tracks or conveyors, with the workpiece stationary or on another conveyor.

Although robots contain their own controls and 'memory', they have to be sequenced and interlocked with all the surrounding plant. This needs the attention of control engineers during the planning stage, as with conventional automation.

The first successful use of robots on a useful scale was in diecasting, where one robot was able to operate two diecasting machines and a trim press, producing a product of consistent high quality, unaffected by the fatigue factor which overcomes human operators working in the hostile atmosphere of a diecasting shop.

There are now many applications for robots, which include:

> Diecasting
> Spot welding
> Arc welding
> Forging
> Investment casting
> Plastic moulding
> Machine loading
> Materials handling and palletizing
> Paint spraying
> and many, many more.

Research and development is very active, and the ambition of robot designers is to improve the intelligence of the machines, and to extend their use by giving a sense of feel or touch to the gripper, and by giving the robots some form of visual sense.

All responsible for plant layout and plant investment decisions must keep up to date with the possibilities offered by this technology if they are not to allow their companies to lose their competitive edge.

PLANT LAYOUT AND FLEXIBLE MANUFACTURING SYSTEMS

Application of flexible manufacturing systems does not invalidate any of the plant layout principles set out in this chapter. It does, however, demand a radical review of plant layout, without which many of the benefits possible from the use of a flexible manufacturing system could be lost. This is one instance where a gradual approach is inappropriate.

The basis of a flexible manufacturing system is the computer control of integrated manufacture. For example, on a production line making variants of one type of product the plant layout might comprise a main line incorporating the standard processing facilities. Branch lines, integrated with the main line, could then be used to carry out the non-standard operations needed to produce the product variants. All activities would be programmed by a computer-coded instruction to the main computer and all linked process computers. Such instructions would denote the product type, its dimensions, and the variations required.

FURTHER READING

Bolz, H. A. (ed.), *Materials Handling Handbook*, Ronald Press, 1963

Chrison, G.B. (ed.), *The Production Handbook*, Ronald Press, 1962

Clay, M.J. and Walley, B.N., *Performance and Profitability*, Longmans Green, London, 1965

Engleberger, J.F., *Robotics in Practice*, Kogan Page, London 1981

Gattorna, J., (ed.) *Handbook of Physical Distribution Management*, 3rd edition, Gower, Aldershot, 1983

Hollinggum, J., *Mass Production With Batch Work: Group Technology Explained*, Pergamon, Oxford, 1969

Mallick, R.W. and Gaudreau, A.T., *Plant Layout Planning and Practice*, Wiley, New York, 1963

Walley, B., *Production Management Handbook*, 2nd edition, Gower, Aldershot, 1986

32 Production control

Peter Jackson

Production control is concerned with producing goods in the right sequence in the least time at the lowest cost. As such it is a balancing act between contradictions. Good production control involves compromises and best fits rather than theoretical ideals. The main aspects are:

1 Loading and scheduling work
2 Provisioning material, parts and production aids
3 Monitoring and progressing work
4 Producing management information enabling the system to be controlled.

DIFFERENCES BETWEEN SYSTEMS

Every company will have a different system depending on its products and production facilities. Some relevant factors are:

Complexity of the product

Single-operation plastic mouldings are much easier to control then components going through any combination of up to twenty operations. This is especially true if assembly of components is included.

Length of cycle time

If a job stays on a machine for a fortnight it is much easier to replan than if each operation takes only a few hours.

Repeatability of the work

Regular jobs will have prdictable cycle times. The production facilities they require, such as tooling, will be known and available. One-off jobs are not so easy to control.

Forward notice available

Some companies know every job they will do for a year ahead and can plan accordingly. Others do not, or claim they do not, know a week ahead what orders will be required.

Dependence on outside suppliers and subcontractors

Where control is not completely within the company greater allowance must be made for slippage.

Seasonal nature of the workload

Where seasonal peak loads occur capacity utilization will obviously vary.

Availability and quality of information on capacity and workload

Companies which have detailed time standards, process layouts and up-to-date capacities can load to a fuller degree and schedule to a tighter time-scale than those which have to rely on rough estimates.

Despite all these differences companies with a wide range of products and production facilities have similar problems and have developed similar solutions.

LOADING AND SCHEDULING WORK

Loading is filling available capacity with sufficient jobs in a given time period. Scheduling is determining the desired sequence of jobs. The two are interrelated and in some procedures may be indistinguishable. When work is correctly loaded and scheduled optimum use can be made of capacity, completion times can be predicted and met and urgent jobs can be given priority without upsetting the rest of the work.

Stages

Loading and scheduling will probably be done in several stages from the overall factory planning when a new order is received to the detailed plan for each machine in the period immediately before production. The mechanics are similar at each stage. When the order is accepted little detail may be known of the work load involved or of the machine capacity available in the proposed production period, yet some estimates must be made to enable delivery dates to be quoted. Such forward loading is done on an overall basis using broad measures.

As the time for producing the order draws near the drawings, parts lists and process paperwork will have been extracted enabling loads on each machine to be calculated. Also, nearer the production time available capacity can be more realistically assessed. This enables detailed short-term loading to be done.

Data required

Units

The basic need is a common unit in which both capacity and load can be expressed. The most common unit is time. Load can be measured by work study or estimation or historical information can be kept. The accuracy required of these time standards depends on the degree of repetition of the work. Often good estimates are sufficient provided they are on average right. Where times for individual components are used they must be multiplied by the batch size and an allowance for setting time included.

Capacity in terms of time is easily expressed in man- or machine-hours with suitable allowances for breakdowns, re-work and other contingencies.

Where times are not available a physical count may provide a suitable unit. Foundry output is often expressed in tonnes. A shoe factory may make so many pairs a day. A warehouse may process so many orders. Here the load is already defined; capacity is found from historical data.

A third measure of capacity and load is money. Orders are often considered in terms of their financial value and this may be a convenient way of loading a factory. An output of £10 000 per week may be a good measure of a factory's production. Again capacity is measured historically. Because of the nature of material and labour costs it is unusual to use money as a unit for detailed machine loading.

Load centre capacities

A load centre is the production unit to which jobs are allocated. It could be a factory, a section, a machine group or an individual machine or operator. With several stages of loading it could be all of these in turn. When it involves more than one machine either all work loaded to it should be capable of being done on any of its sub-units or the mix of work should on average match the mix of the sub-units.

Before breaking the load down to individual machines it should be considered whether the production control department are the best people to do this. The foreman or supervisor will have detailed knowledge of the capabilities of particular men and machines and be able to react to break-downs and other immediate problems. It may, therefore, be realistic to load to machine groups leaving the final allocation to the man on the spot.

The capacity of the load centre is calculated in the appropriate units. Some capacity may be reserved for emergency work or special customers but this must be kept to a small proportion and revised regularly.

Processes

The sequence of operations, usually called the process layout, must be known if each operation is to be loaded separately.

Parts lists

Where assemblies are manufactured the parts list of each assembly and sub-assembly will be needed. The requirements for common parts need to be batched up. For some components it may be more economical to make for stock than make on a one-for-one basis for final assembly.

LOADING METHODS

There are two main methods: job sequence, in which each job is loaded in strict sequence against a time-scale, and control period where a list of jobs is planned for a defined time period but can be carried out in any sequence.

Job sequence loading

To load jobs in strict sequence against a time-scale requires some visual display such as a planning board. Such boards can be purchased ready made although a home-made version can often fit particular requirements better. The load centres are usually displayed along the left-hand edge with a time-scale along the bottom. Jobs are planned to load centres either by writing on the board with an erasable medium or inserting a card in a slot (see Figure 32.1).

Machine	Hour beginning							
	08 00	09 00	10 00	11 00	12 30	13 30	14 30	15 30
Capstan lathe	1053	1053	1053	1154	1154	1154	1154	1154
Herbert lathe	1186	1186	1186	1186	1186	1701	1701	1701
Holbrook lathe	1188	1188	1188	1188	1188	1188	1790	1790
Jig borer	REPAIR AND MAINTENANCE							
Universal miller	IDLE	IDLE	IDLE	IDLE	1185	1185	1185	1185
Horizontal miller	1081	1081	1081	1081	904	904	904	1225
Automatic — 1	1300	1300	1300	1300	1300	1300	IDLE	IDLE
Automatic — 2	IDLE	IDLE	IDLE	IDLE	IDLE	IDLE	IDLE	IDLE

Figure 32.1 A job sequence loading chart. This simple configuration is suitable for blackboard and chalk. The numbers in the squares are job numbers

This method is best used close to actual production for loading individual machines. It can only be used for forward planning where contracts cannot run simultaneously. An example of this would be forward planning ships on the slipways of a shipyard.

Advantages of job sequence loading

1 Clear visual display of information
2 Full utilization of capacity possible
3 Rapid throughput of jobs loaded on more than one load centre
4 Planning boards can be used for progressing.

Disadvantages of job sequence loading

1 Updating is difficult and time consuming
2 Only suitable for limited periods ahead because of the likelihood of the situation changing
3 Relies on precise measurement of load
4 Cannot cope with overall allowances for reduction of capacity, for example, 10 per cent allowance for breakdowns.

Control period loading

A list of jobs is produced for each load centre for a fixed period of time, the control period. The total load of these jobs equals the capacity of the centre. For example, a machine group of two lathes each worked 40 hours a week has a capacity of 80 hours if the chosen control period is a week. A list is produced of jobs for these machines up to a total of 80 hours. Any further work is loaded into the following week.

The list becomes the programme for that load centre for that period. Jobs can be done in any sequence on any machine in the centre, provided they are finished by the end of the control period.

Multi-operational jobs are programmed at one operation per control period resulting in all jobs going through at an equal pace. The completion time of each job can be predicted.

The choice of control period depends on the length of the jobs and the sophistication of the production control system. Setting a target of one operation per week may not be very ambitious but may compare favourably with what was achieved without a loading system. It is better to start with a long control period and shorten it when experience has been gained rather than start with an unrealistically short one.

Control period loading is used in long-term planning where the overall work load can be compared with the overall capacity; for example, accepting orders up to £50 000 value a month. It is also used for short-term planning on groups of machines. This allows supervision flexibility to allocate particular jobs to individual machines or operators.

Advantages of control period loading

1 Simple to operate
2 Not dependent on completion of every job. Late jobs can be caught up without upsetting the programme

3 Allows supervision discretion in allocating jobs to particular operators or machines
4 Enables forward load picture to be produced over a reasonable period.

Disadvantages of control period loading

1 Overall throughput time is slow compared to job sequence loading, although much quicker than if no planning is used at all
2 Work in progress is higher than for job sequence loading.

Forward and backward loading

Using either job sequence or control period loading it is usual to start at the present time and load jobs in the earliest available capacity, slowly building up a forward load picture. This is known as forward loading.

It is, however, possible to fix a completion date a number of weeks in advance and load backwards from this date thus arriving at a date when the job must start. This is called backward loading.

Assuming that delivery dates have been set realistically, backward loading ensures that jobs are not started needlessly early. If all jobs are loaded in this way capacity may well be exceeded as one of the main reasons for loading is to set achievable delivery dates. It may help to backward load a certain proportion of jobs, key ones whose delivery dates are important, and then fill in the remaining capacity by forward loading the less urgent jobs.

NEW APPROACHES TO LOADING AND SCHEDULING

Several new approaches to loading and scheduling have been developed. Typical of these are Kanban, just-in-time (JIT) and optimized production technology (OPT). The overall aim of such techniques is to reduce inventory to a minimum. The principles on which they are based include:

Close relationships with suppliers

Arrangements are made for materials to be delivered immediately before they are required for use.

Reduced set-up times

Machine setting times are reduced, so that batch sizes can be much smaller without incurring production cost penalties.

Improved plant layout

By analysing common sequences of operations and then reflecting the results in the positioning of machines, transfer batches can be made smaller and can be overlapped.

Manufacturing only to demand

Techniques vary, but the overall principle is that parts are not made just to keep men and machines busy, but are instead made according to the time when they are needed for the next manufacturing stage. Although this can lead to idle time at some work stations, it is better than increasing the amount of unwanted work in progress. Several computer programs are available to control work in this way but the basic Kanban system depends on the precept that work can only be performed at a work station when it receives a ticket requesting it from the following work station (the word Kanban is Japanese for a token or a ticket).

Concentrating on bottlenecks

OPT, in particular, places the control system emphasis on bottlenecks. It points out that an hour saved at a bottleneck in a plant means that an extra hour's output leaves the plant. Conversely, an hour lost at a bottleneck loses an hour's production for the whole plant. Thus the financial benefits of keeping a bottleneck working for an extra hour greatly exceed the immediate costs (such as overtime). On the other hand, an hour saved at a non-bottleneck is a mirage. By definition there should be some inactive time at non-bottlenecks. The traditional approach of keeping men and machines busy at all times to improve efficiency figures merely results in work being done that is not needed immediately, and this early production thus increases inventory.

Accepting that non-bottleneck work stations can be non-productive for some of the time affects batch quantities. Inactive time can be used for more set-ups, allowing smaller batches, less inventory and quicker throughput. Batch sizes at bottlenecks and at non-bottlenecks will be different.

Analysis of bottlenecks will affect investment policy in new plant. Automating a machine which is not a bottleneck may not result in any savings.

The OPT method requires that bottleneck operations are forward scheduled in detail. Buffers are provided before each bottleneck to ensure that work is always available for it. Non-bottleneck stages are scheduled more loosely, using backward loading.

PROVISIONING

Provisioning is ensuring that everything required is available when production is scheduled to start. This includes drawings, tools and gauges as well as parts and material. Such aids can hold up production just as much as material shortages and lack of them is often harder to put right.

Make or buy

Preliminary decisions must be taken on whether the part is to be made in-house or bought out or part sub-contracted.

Factors affecting the decision are:

Available capacity

This may fluctuate changing the decision.

Available skills and technology

Outside firms may specialize in certain processes.

Volume required

Normally a firm would not make its own nuts and bolts but if it used millions then it would.

Available lead-times

Much tighter control can be exercised over internal manufacture.

Where external suppliers or sub-contractors are used it is vital to obtain commitment to delivery dates. Progressing is best done by personal visits. In any case it is wise to build in latitude in the lead-times of externally sourced parts. Rating of suppliers on delivery is obviously worth while but cannot guard against every contingency.

Quantities

Certain items will be made on a one-for-one basis according to sales demand with perhaps a small allowance for scrap or spares. A few items may be made continuously throughout the year. The majority of items are made in batches. The size of the batch can be determined in two ways. Economic batch sizes can be calculated as shown in the chapter on stock control. Where a batch is manufactured internally the setting cost replaces the order cost in the formula.

An alternative is to make regular batches to return the stock to a desired level. These batches will vary in size but enable the factory to be programmed on a regular repetitive basis. For example, using the Pareto stock classification, *A* items might be made once a month, *B* items once a quarter and *C* items once a year.

In fact the mathematics of both methods are not dissimilar. If batches are made regularly the average stockholding is slightly higher than if economic batches are made when a reorder level is reached.

Kitting and pre-allocation

Before a job is issued to the shop floor it should be established that all things needed for its production are available. It should not be the job of a skilled operator to queue for drawings, tools and gauges before he starts work. Even less should he have to spend time searching on the section for missing items. All such production aids should be collected by stores staff before a job is issued. Where a job is repeated a card can be kept recording everything required for the job.

Where assemblies are produced kitting problems are more apparent. Often a set of parts will be collected for issue and shortages found. Either the job is issued incomplete or it is held in stores where it may tie up parts which could be used elsewhere. Such parts may be removed from the kit, further complicating the problem.

In such situations a paperwork exercise can be carried out where all the components are checked for availability though not physically collected. This dummy kitting or pre-allocation means that if it is not feasible to issue Job A because of shortages it may be possible to issue Job B using some of the components from Job A.

If parts lists and stock levels are kept on computer and are up to date such pre-allocation can be done automatically and rapidly with obvious advantages.

MONITORING AND PROGRESSING

The aims of monitoring and progressing are to:

1　Highlight jobs running late
2　Assist such jobs to catch up
3　Anticipate problems further down the production cycle that late jobs would cause
4　Enable customer enquiries to be answered.

The first principle is to progress by exception. Collecting a vast amount of information about jobs which are running to time may give people a feeling of achievement but does little real good.

The second principle is that information must be up to date. Elaborate computer runs analysing where jobs were three days ago may be ignored in favour of a physical search of the section.

Monitoring

The simplest way of monitoring the position of jobs is to utilize the work booking system. At the end of each operation the completed job card is used to update a master progress record which is held in the production control office. Problems may arise where booking is not done immediately at the completion of a job.

A similar system is to have a set of tear-off tickets attached to each job. As the job passed a control point the appropriate section of the ticket is detached and sent to update the master progress record.

Increasingly the completion of jobs is being recorded on data collection devices linked to computers. These can be on the shop floor beside the machines and can give an extremely rapid update of the production situation.

Progressing

When the current state has been monitored action has to be taken. As a job running late in its initial stages can cause problems all the way down the line progress meetings are often held for all those involved. Provided such meetings are kept short and involve more than marking up lists they can be valuable.

Progress men are often used firstly to monitor the state of jobs and secondly to urge priority jobs. Again if this is largely marking lists it could be done better by a good clerical booking system. Progress men oil the wheels by putting urgent jobs at the front of the queue and arranging special transport between operations. However, sometimes their work can be self-cancelling. In one engineering works there were fourteen progress men to one hundred machinists. Each of the five foremen could have up to fourteen people requesting that their job be done first.

Urgent jobs

It is common for urgent jobs to be given some distinguishing mark, a red label or a star for example. The trouble is that such labels multiply until 80 per cent of the jobs have red stars. Then someone gives the really urgent jobs two red stars and so the system escalates. Fifty urgent jobs are a contradiction in terms.

A strict upper limit, ten for example, should be placed on the number of urgent jobs. If another is required an existing one should be dropped from the list. To do this the person deciding the priorities should be senior enough to resist sectional pressures and see the overall picture. A shop floor supervisor can often be approached by many different people in the management structure each asking for different jobs to be given priority.

Long-term solutions

Although it is sensible to give a few urgent jobs an extra push, if late and rush jobs are a large and constant problem then the overall situation needs to be looked at. Are delivery dates being realistically set? Is there sufficient capacity? Could the effort spent chasing rush jobs be better spent improving the throughput time?

It may be possible to chase one job through the factory with it hardly touching the ground. What is not seen is the trail of delays and increased costs on other jobs that this action causes. Many customers will ask for jobs sooner than they need them because they know only priority jobs will be chased and the rest left to drift through.

One solution to the problem of conflicting priorities is to have each progress man responsible for all the throughput of one section. When operations are completed in this section the jobs become the responsibility of the progress man in the next section and so on. This is in contrast to the usual system where a progress man is responsible for all stages of a particular range of jobs. Sometimes there is a need for both types of progress but the balance must be held.

Where two or more divisions of a company share a common resource (for example, a machine shop), conflicts over capacity and priorities will often happen. Where possible such facilities should be split. If this cannot be done the capacity may need to be expanded over what might be theoretically required to allow for interference between the user departments.

MANAGEMENT CONTROL INFORMATION

A production control department processes vast amounts of information, levels of stock, states of orders, capacities available and so on. It should, therefore, be the source of the overview of production that higher management needs. Too often management will concentrate on solving particular problems using their authority to get things done. This may solve the particular issue but create a whole set of other problems and delays. It is management's job to look at the total picture, making decisions about capacity and load, leaving the day-to-day problems to those paid to cope with them.

The production control department can help by supplying regular information on relevant totals. The particular figures will vary but might include:

Order book

Forecast sales
Total orders received
Total orders dispatched
Total orders on hand

Customer service

Current average delivery times
Delivery promise achievements
Number of complaints

Factory performance

Total production
Programme achievement
Arrears
Forward load versus capacity

Stocks

Raw material
Work in progress
Finished goods

For most of these figures it would be difficult to set an ideal level though it is always good to aim for a target. The important thing is the direction in which the figures are going, improving, worsening or staying the same.

It may be necessary to break the total figures down into separate product lines. The temptation to produce lists of individual jobs for higher management should be avoided.

PAPERWORK

Production control departments produce a mass of paperwork, schedules, lists, tickets, progress records, computer printout. Over the years new systems may have been introduced partly duplicating existing ones. Records may be kept which are no longer required. Individuals produce and maintain their own systems.

It is possible to have a department called production control which produces a large amount of paper yet influences what happens on the shop floor hardly at all. It is said that when the weight of a ship being built exceeds the weight of paperwork required to build it then it is ready for launching.

Different production systems will require different paperwork but a typical outline is shown below.

Advanced warning

When an order is first received a document is raised to notify departments concerned. It will contain basic details of the order and the provisional delivery date quoted. An example is shown in Figure 32.2.

The receiving departments, typically industrial engineering, stock control and production, will confirm whether the provisional date can be accepted.

Job paperwork

Each job needs:

1 A loading/progress document which stays in the production control department and is used first to schedule the job and then to record its progress. It may well be a card which can be slotted into a planning board
2 An identification label which goes round with the job (job ticket)
3 Instructions for the people doing each stage of the job
4 Material or parts requisitions
5 Paperwork for booking each stage of the job. This may be in the form of cards which are returned to the production control office showing date, time, scrap and the operator's name.

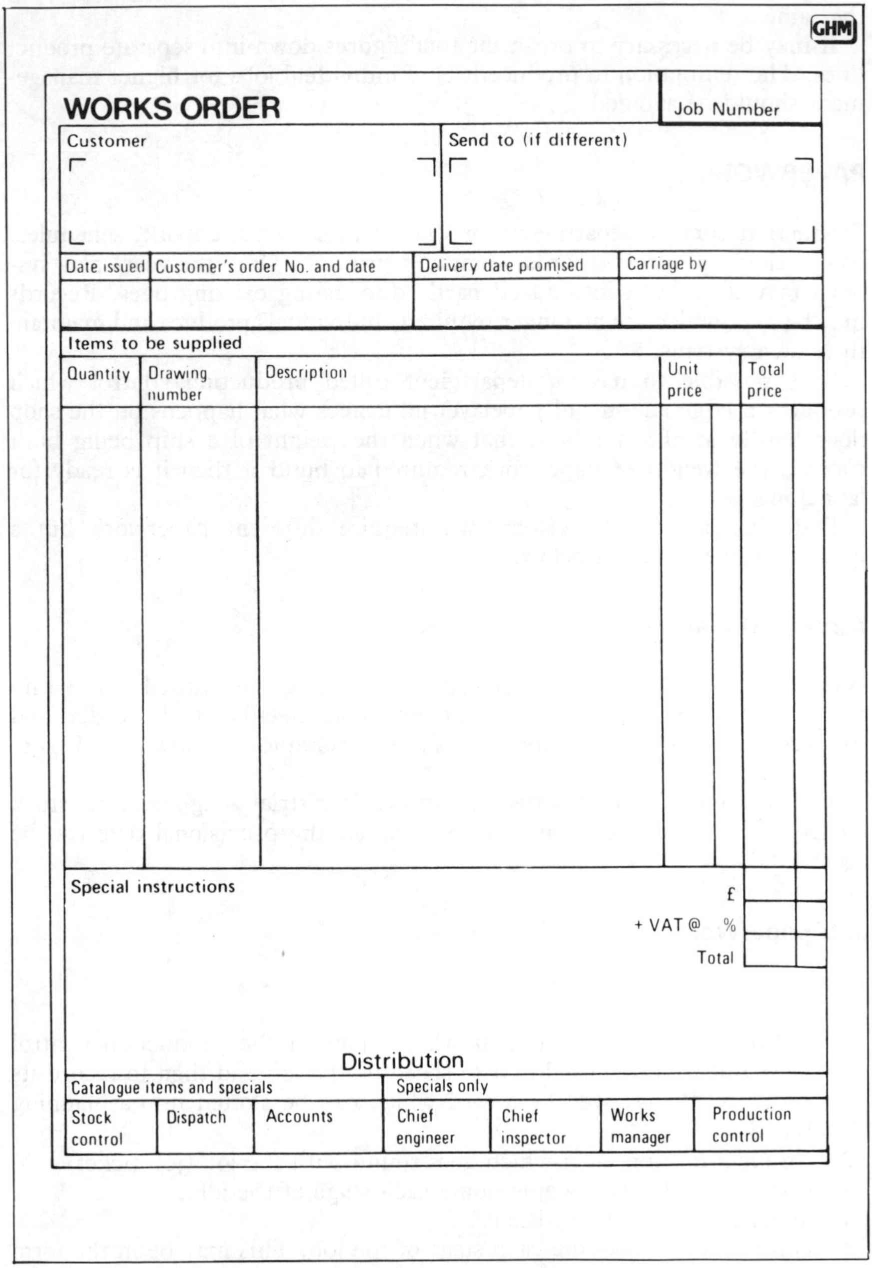

Figure 32.2 Works order

Examples of production control paperwork are given in Figures 32.3 and 32.4.

Schedules

Lists of jobs will be made of work to be done on a section in a given period. These may be in sequence or highlight jobs with a higher priority. These lists will also be used to progress the work.

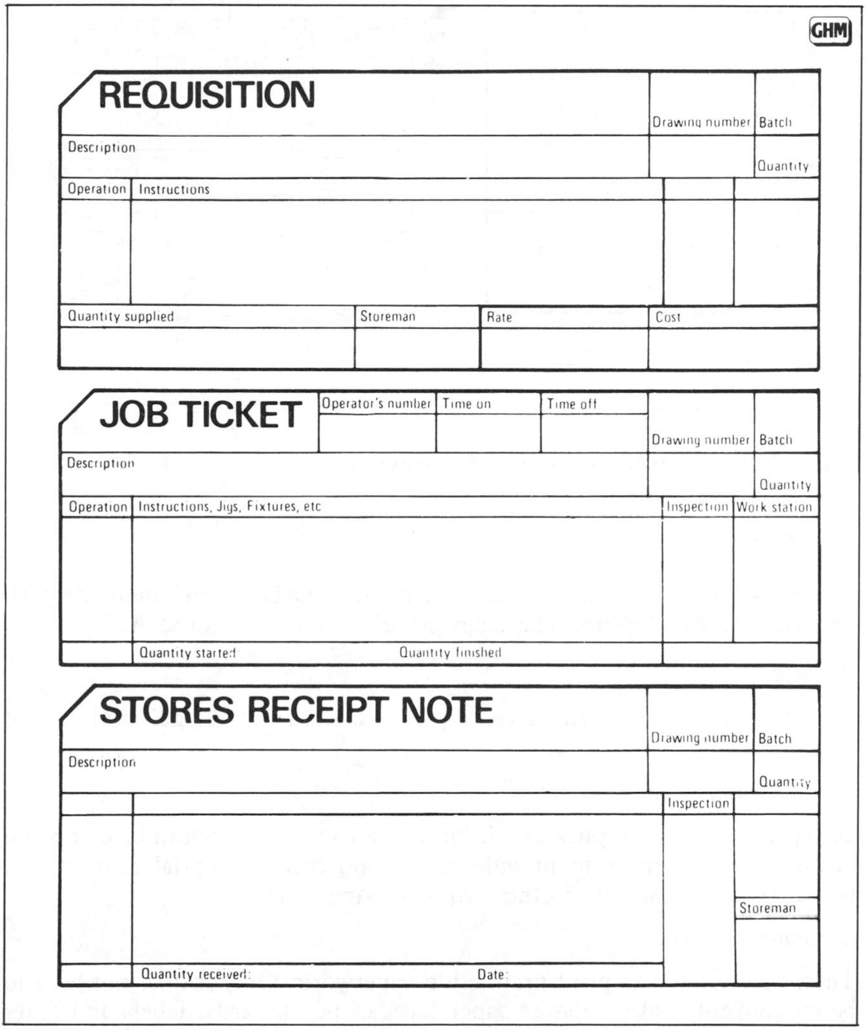

Figure 32.3   Requisition, job ticket and stores receipt note

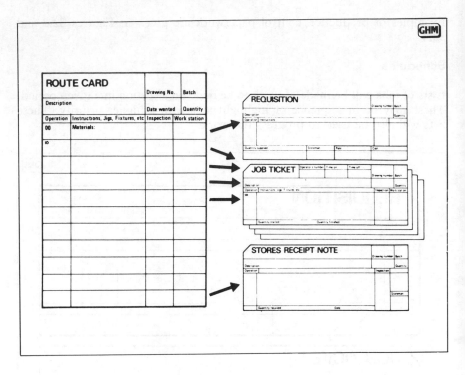

Figure 32.4 A production control document set

Methods

Various ready made paperwork systems are available but there may be limits on their flexibility. The main proprietary systems used are:

Stockcards

Visible edge filing can give rapid access to a large number of records.

Line selection systems

Using special spirit duplicators, information from a master can be combined in different sequences to provide sets of job cards, material requisitions, master progress cards and other required paperwork.

Computer systems

These can be used to print production paperwork. Output does not have to be on conventional computer paper but can be on cards, labels and other forms.

Whatever method is used it should be simple and functional. Periodically paperwork systems should be reviewed and improved or discarded where necessary.

COMPUTERS

Computers have been applied to production control since the 1950s with varying degress of success. With large mainframe computers at head office information was first punched on to cards and then fed into the machine when it was available from its other tasks and more importantly, when it was working. The result was that computers were good at showing what the production situation was a week last Friday.

With faster, smaller, more reliable and much cheaper computers it is possible to have one dedicated full time, at least in working hours, to production control. Remote terminals mean information can be input as it is generated on the shop floor or in the stores. Not only does this save time but it decreases copying errors. Output need no longer be thick piles of computer paper showing the current state of everything. Selective enquiries can be made via a terminal with the answer appearing at once.

Materials requirements planning

The principal use of computers in production control is for materials requirements planning (MRP). The forward order position is entered in terms of end products required per week. The computer checks these against finished stock and produces the net requirements. These are then broken down using the parts lists for each assembly. The requirements for each component for each week are totalled. These again are checked against existing stock and orders and the net requirements produced. These net requirements can be batched and turned into orders either manually or by computer. Lead-times can be included so that raw material is called for a number of weeks before the final assembly is due.

In complex situations assemblies may break down to subassemblies which break down to sub-subassemblies and so on. Up to as many as twelve such levels may be encountered before the basic parts of raw materials are reached. Using MRP the entire schedule of demand for each level can be produced in a few hours or less. Manually it would take weeks or months.

Conventionally the MRP file has been updated once or twice a week with all new orders, production achieved and stock delivered. It is becoming possible to feed in such changes as they happen giving a continuous updated materials requirement plan.

Using MRP, orders for components and materials are based on actual forward demand. Where this is not possible or feasible traditional stock control can be done on a computer. Predictions based on past usage and average lead-times are made. Reorder levels and batch sizes are calculated.

Loading and scheduling

Various computer packages (such as MRP II – manufacturing resource planning) are available for loading jobs on to machines. These are usually based on the critical path network approach.

The limitation of such packages is the sheer complexity of the task. To load even a few jobs on a limited number of machines can give several hundred possible combinations. With a realistic number of jobs and machines the possibility may be hundreds of thousands. Manually such loading can be done using a planning board. The human brain can produce a result that is adequate and takes most considerations into account. The computer can only try all possible combinations until it finds the one best solution. To shorten the process, jobs are assigned priorities and other simplifications are made. The result is still a lengthy computer run producing a result little better than a manual one. In a fast-changing production environment where machines break down, times overrun and priorities get altered the computer may not yet be the tool for sequential loading.

What the computer can do well is provide totals of loads on sections or machines so that advance warning is obtained of over- or underloads.

Future development

In the future production control will be almost entirely computerized, even in small companies. The chief requirement is for comprehensive, accurate, up-to-date information. Data recorders linked to each machine and to the computer will be a large step towards this. Increasingly, bar code readers are being used to update stock movements.

FURTHER READING

Burbridge, J.L., *Principles of Production Control*, 4th edition, Macdonald & Evans, London, 1978. A wide-ranging and practical book

Goldratt, E.M., *The Goal*, Gower, Aldershot, 1986. A very readable and unusual introduction to production control, especially OPT

Lockyer, K.G., *Production Control in Practice*, 2nd edition, Pitman, London, 1975. A good introduction, particularly to the numerical aspects of production control

New, C.C., *Managing Manufacturing Operations*, BIM Management Survey No.35, 1976. A survey of practice in 186 plants giving a good basis for comparisons

Walley, B.H., *Production Management Handbook*, 2nd edition, Gower, Aldershot, 1986

33 Industrial engineering

Dennis Whitmore

Industrial engineering is a generic term for techniques primarily aimed at increasing productivity. Many other disciplines and occupations help in the improvement of effectiveness, but this is often incidental to their main objectives. The accountant, for example, provides information for financial control, and the personnel manager must choose the most effective people for particular jobs. But the industrial engineer is *directly* charged with the task of improving productivity.

'Industrial engineering' has a transatlantic ring about it. Although the term is used in the UK, *management services* is often preferred, to avoid the connotation of machine shop-floor and tool-making which the word 'engineering' implies to many people. Some organizations still cling to the rather narrow term *work study* but investigations into productivity have advanced far beyond the original techniques of the first two decades of this century.

The disciplines and techniques of industrial engineering are outlined in Figure 33.1. They can be separated into four major groups, concerned with the improvement of:

1 The organization
2 Methods and equipment
3 Job conditions and environment
4 The product or service itself.

There are no watertight compartments. Techniques may overlap and be interchanged, but essentially the first two areas above can be investigated through *work study* for most manual work, *organization and methods* (O&M) is applicable to clerical and office work, and *operational research* (OR) is mainly concerned with corporate level operations. (Examples of such corporate level operations include distribution, product mix, planned maintenance, stock control and so on).

The safety, well-being, and comfort of the operator are the concern of *ergonomics*, which is often known as 'fitting the job to the worker'; exactly what it does. The subject demands a knowledge of the medical disciplines so that the ergonomists may be able to design jobs to suit people who must do them.

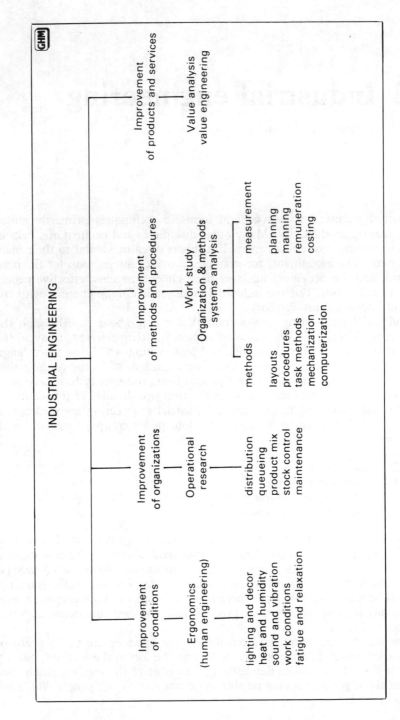

Figure 33.1 Industrial engineering techniques

Products and services may be designed to remove all unnecessary parts, or simplified to retain only those which are absolutely necessary for functional, aesthetic, or prestige purposes. When these cost-reducing devices are built in at the design stage the technique is known as *value engineering*, but its sibling, *value analysis*, may be used on existing products or services.

Over all these approaches there are the two fundamental disciplines which answer the two basic questions: how should the task be done? and how long should it take? The first of these must be tackled by a *problem-solving* technique and the second by *work measurement*.

THE IMPROVEMENT OF PRODUCTIVITY

The term 'productivity improvement' has been used for many years by companies and governments as a recipe for the salvation of industry. In essence, productivity is the producing of goods and services with the minimum of resources, consistent with adequate quantity, quality, utilization and other requirements. Thus it follows that productivity can be increased by raising production for the same or lower amounts of the input resources, or by maintaining the same levels with fewer resources. These resources are materials, labour, services and money.

Productivity measurement has posed problems because it is difficult to reduce all results to a common national or international basis. This obviously makes comparisons between different industries – or even companies – extremely difficult. It is a relative consideration: productivity may be measured both before and after improvement, and the two results compared to quantify the uplift in productivity.

As a simple example, suppose 6000 printed circuit boards are being assembled by fifteen people, and when a methods improvement is introduced only ten people are needed to produce the same number of boards in the same time. Productivity was 400 boards per person, while after the improvement it becomes 600 each, giving an increase of 200 boards per head. Usually the resources are more than labour so a common basis, such as money, may be used to measure the resource input (for example, the total cost of producing the boards).

A common form of productivity measurement is operator performance, assessed by the ratio of measured time to actual time taken. This index is discussed further in the section dealing with work measurement.

PROBLEM SOLVING

People are always solving problems and making decisions both in their domestic and working lives. Basically there are four types of situation:

1 An *improvement* problem, where there is a situation which needs improving in some way, such as an inefficient method
2 A *deviation* problem is one in which the situation differs from what it ought to be, or what one desires of it

3 A *creative* problem exists where one wishes to invent or design something, given the terms of reference, or objectives to be achieved

4 In *problem avoidance* one tries to anticipate troubles or problems before they actually occur, and thinks up remedies in case they do occur.

There may be an infinite variety of problems but all can be approached using a common strategy. The general procedure applies equally to method study, organization and methods, operational research or to any other technique.

1 *Problem definition.* Clearly, before a problem can be tackled the true problem, as opposed to the apparent problem, must be defined

2 *Data collection.* All the facts about the situation must be assembled before any solution can be attempted

3 *Examination.* The facts must be critically examined in either a logical way, or in some cases, using a completely illogical approach (*see* the following sub-section). From the results of this examination can follow:

4 *Development of a solution.* Examination will show up the deficiencies and point the way to a solution. This is now developed and tested during a 'dry run' period

5 *Installation.* When the proposed solution is as perfect as it can be, it is introduced to the situation

6 *Maintenance,* or continual monitoring and updating is necessary as the situation develops in the future.

Methods for problem solving

Problem-solving methods can be separated into logical and illogical. A chart showing how a particular technique may be selected is shown in Figure 33.2.

A logical, step-by-step method is traditional *critical examination* which asks *what* is done?, *when?*, by *whom?*, *where?*, *how?* are the goals achieved? and to all of this, *why?* Often tasks need not be changed or simplified, but can in fact be abandoned altogether as unnecessary.

An illogical approach is to use analogies to describe a situation, thereby making a complex one more easily understood by equating it to similar circumstances with which the observer may be more familiar, or by acting out the role of the situation.

The Kepner-Tregoe approach is to list all things about what the situation *is* and what it *is not*. From the lists, the *causes* of deviation from the desired condition are highlighted.

Another non-logical method of collecting ideas is *brainstorming*. This requires participants to throw in ideas as they occur to them in an uninhibited way, with no criticism. This method avoids stereotyped ideas, and often generates novel and 'way-out' ideas.

Trial-and-error, or heuristic methods are often used, each trial being improved upon until the optimum solution is achieved.

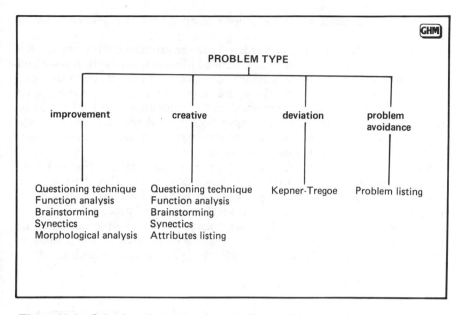

Figure 33.2   Selecting the appropriate problem-solving technique

IMPROVEMENT OF WORKING METHODS

Problem solving may be applicable to all situations, but method study capitalizes widely on the techniques. In the clerical field organization and methods is the principal tool for increasing effectiveness and productivity, and includes within its orbit the technique of method study.

The first stage is to define the true problem and terms of reference. For example, a goods-inwards procedure is labour-intensive and must be made more cost-effective. With such a brief must be included constraints such as costs, savings required and period of capital return.

The data collection period involves the employees through interviews about their jobs, and facts about the objectives and goals to be achieved. Information is displayed by means of flow charts, diagrams and models.

It may be necessary to investigate the document flow, goods handling and individual methods of doing the jobs (the two-handed chart). The investigator may wish to improve the layout, using a flow diagram as the basis, even using three-dimensional models, or templates which can be moved around in order to find the best configuration.

Having gathered the facts, the investigator is able to examine them and question the purpose and need for the various parts of the system. One of the problem-solving techniques outlined in the previous section of the chapter will be used. A method growing in popularity is function analysis, based on brain-storming. This technique is described later under 'value analysis', but in essence a team of specialists discusses the problem, tossing ideas for improvements into the general pool of knowledge.

These suggestions are then considered and the promising ones investigated further. From the final list of recommended ideas new methods, layouts and procedures are written up as a report to management for its consideration.

The parts of the report which are approved are then implemented gradually to replace the existing ones. Full consultation with staff would be maintained, of course, and their suggestions considered too. There would be many deficiencies in the new situation needing reconsideration, but eventually an integrated system would emerge.

Quite possibly the team may consider a computer configuration to be the best solution to the manual one being used at present. This is usually the province of *systems analysis*, responsible for the examination of existing or proposed computer installations and mechanization of procedures.

Over a period of time, situations change so it is important that the sixth phase of maintenance and updating is incorporated into any study of procedure, method or layout as a continuing process of monitoring.

THE MEASUREMENT OF WORK

Previous sections of this chapter have examined the processes of improving productivity through the medium of making work and organizations more effective. However, it is of small advantage if people do a well-designed job but do not perform the task at an effective pace. The whole object of redesigning a task by method study is to reduce the time in which it can be completed, and this reduction may be entirely negated if the operative takes twice as long to do it by working so slowly.

Moreover, unless an organization knows how long a job ought to take it cannot plan its completion and delivery dates, nor can it cost the labour content, nor even pay its employees if they are engaged on incentive payment schemes. But who is to say how long a job ought to take, and how can one determine this time?

Regardless of what some textbooks say, work can only be measured in three basic ways: by timing it with some form of chronometer, by using manuals of predetermined times, or by estimating it. Thus all work can be measured to a greater or lesser degree of precision (see Figure 33.3). One could even measure the time it would have taken Beethoven to write his Tenth Symphony by the last of the three methods! The estimate would be wild, but it *is* a time standard nevertheless.

The main objective of work measurement is to establish a time for a job which an experienced, trained, person could achieve while doing the job effectively and at a workmanlike pace. This may seem rather subjective but in practice it can be done. The techniques for setting such *basic times* are many, but they all fall under these three basic headings as shown in Figure 33.3. The most appropriate has to be selected from the toolbag of techniques. The two main guiding factors in this selection are (a) the precision desired, and (b) the speed of application or how long it takes the

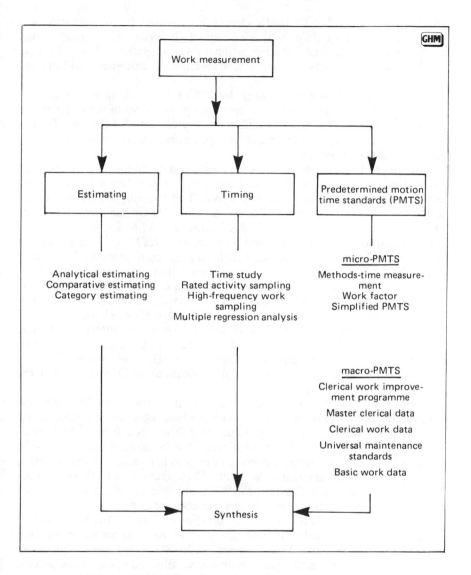

Figure 33.3 Techniques of work measurement

analyst to set the time standard compared with how long it takes to do the work.

The most precise standards are given by the generic group of predetermined motion time standards (PMTS). These exist in two main forms: micro-PMTS (with elements measured in thousandths of a minute) and macro-PMTS (with elements of the order of seconds). Many proprietary systems exist but international ones practised in USA, Europe, the Far East and Australasia are Methods-Time Measurement (MTM) and Work-Factor.

The principle of measuring work by PMTS is based upon the analysis of the work into suitable elements, looking up the tables of times for these, and then summing the times to obtain the overall time for the job. Typical elements of micro-PMTS are reach, grasp, release, move, walk, sit, stand, assemble, disassemble, etc.

The micro-PMT systems are very time consuming to use, so the originating concerns have simplified them to produce higher levels of data which are far quicker and easier to apply. The two major systems on the lowest level are Detailed Work-Factor and MTM-1. On the second level are the equivalent systems of Ready Work-Factor and MTM-2 respectively, and on the third level Abbreviated Work-Factor and MTM-3. Higher levels of data are developed in various ways including the combination of elements, the merging of moving distances, the elimination of some elements, and the simplifying of elements. For example, in Methods-Time Measurement the first-level elements of reach, grasp, and release were combined into one new element of get, while move and position become the new element of put.

Typical elements of a mythical system are shown in Figure 33.4. The analysis of a simple operation and the derivation of the subsequent basic time for this job are illustrated in Figure 33.5. This shows how elements are identified, and times extracted for subsequent addition to obtain the time for the complete job.

In PMT systems it is appreciated that certain factors will affect the time taken to do a basic element. A reach with the hand of 45 cm will take longer to accomplish than one of only 10 cm, so distance is a factor which must be considered (see Figure 33.5). Also care must be taken if the article to be grasped is delicate or dangerous to handle; another factor. If the article is heavy, this must be taken into account. These factors and others are considered when designing a system of PMT, and due allowance of extra time must be made when any of the factors are encountered.

The basic unit of measurement in Work-Factor is called the Work-Factor Time Unit, and is equal to 0.0001 min., while the time-measurement unit (tmu) of Methods-Time Measurement is 0.00001 hr. These tiny times originally were measured using high-speed film analyses, stroboscopic photography, stop-watches, and various electrical devices. As an example, a basic 30-cm reach with the hand with no manual control or weight would take 0.0046 min.

On the macro-PMTS level are Clerical Work Data, Clerical Work Improvement Programme, Universal Office Standards, and Office Modapts, together with Basic Work Data, MTM Maintenance Standards, Universal Maintenance Standards, and others.

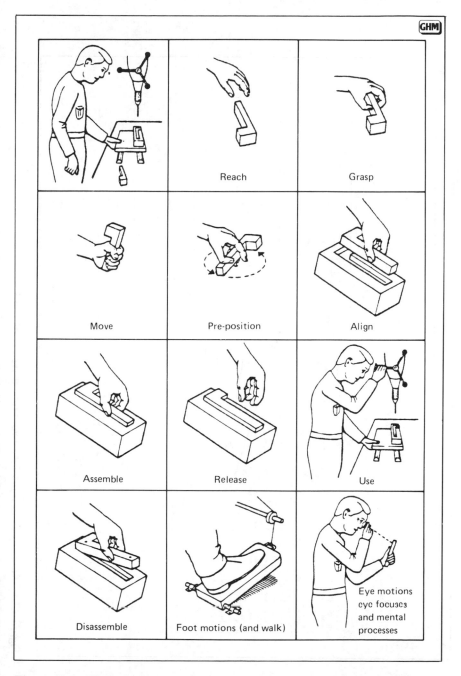

Figure 33.4 Typical elements for a system of predetermined motion times (PMTS)

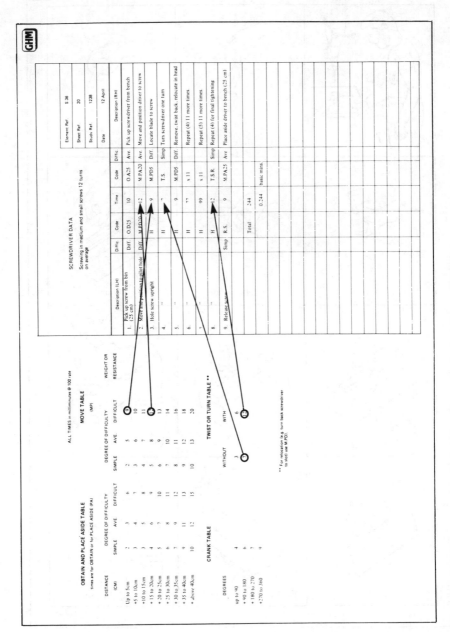

Figure 33.5 An analysis of a job by a hypothetical system of PMT

584

A typical PMTS analysis

The exact form of the analysis of jobs for PMTS varies according to the system being employed. An illustration of how a job may be analysed and the elemental times extracted from tables using a mythical system, is given in Figure 33.5. A more complete account of PMTS is found in Whitmore (1980).

Relaxation allowance

All techniques of work measurement produce basic times for each element of the job. However, it is recognized that people must have time to recover from their exertions periodically, and so a relaxation allowance (RA) is added to the basic time to allow for this. The resulting *standard time* is the one which is used by management for their various needs. The magnitude of the RA is derived from predetermined tables (see Figure 33.6) or is sometimes just estimated.

Timing techniques

The oldest method of formal work measurement is *timing* which goes back to the early part of the century to Frederick W.Taylor, Frank B.Gilbreth and Charles Bedaux. There are three basic forms of timing: time study, rated activity sampling, and timing using multiple regression analysis.

Time study is the setting of a basic time for a job (*not* for the person doing the job). This basic time is the time for one cycle to be performed with the operative working at a standardized pace, so that different jobs may be compared, and the time is absolutely unconnected with the person doing the work. Unfortunately people do not conveniently work at this standard pace but adopt their own natural speeds. Even this may vary throughout the day as people tire.

This problem is overcome by timing (using a stop-watch) workers doing the task to be studied and then adjusting this time to what it *would* have been had the operator been working at standard pace. The process of assessing the pace is known as *rating*. Thus if a worker took 0.6 min. to do a cycle of the job and the work study practitioner rated his pace as 50 (that is, half standard pace) he would have done the cycle in half the time were he working at standard (100) rating. This gives a basic time of 50 per cent of 0.6 min. or 0.3 basic min. All cycles are rated in the same way, to extend observed times to basic times using the same formula, which is (observed time) × (observed rating ÷ 100).

A typical study is shown in Figure 33.7. It will be seen that, after the addition of RAs, the standard time is 0.939 sm.

A variation of time study, suitable for measuring long-cycle jobs, is rated activity sampling. Unlike time study, jobs are not broken down into

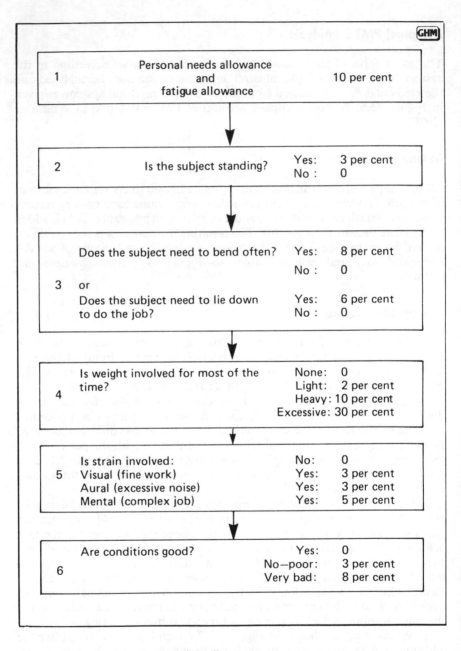

Figure 33.6 A table of relaxation allowances

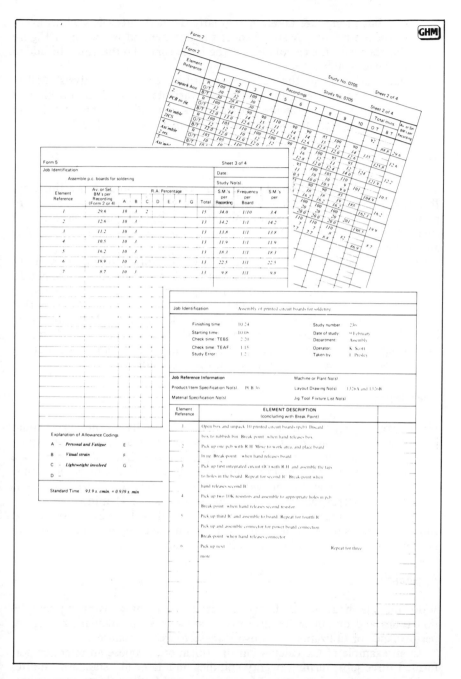

Figure 33.7   A typical time study, showing three of the most usual forms employed

elements, but ratings are taken at regularly defined intervals such as every minute, on the minute. A study sheet for this method is shown in Figure 33.8, together with the calculation of the basic time. To this must be added suitable RA of course.

A recent addition to the range is multiple regression analysis (MRA) which is extremely useful for measuring variable work. A description of this is beyond the scope of the present book but full accounts of this and all other techniques in this section are given in Whitmore (1975).

Estimating

The most rapidly applied set of work measurement techniques is estimating. It exists in three forms: analytical, comparative and category. The first of these required the analysis of the job into elements to which *synthetic times* (see below) are allocated. Those for which synthetic times are not available are estimated from experience.

Comparative estimating is a method based on work content comparison. Typical benchmark jobs are carefully measured and allocated to 'time bands' on spread sheets (Figure 33.9). Estimating is performed by the estimator comparing the job in hand with the benchmark jobs until he decides that those listed in a certain band compare in work content with the job being estimated. He then allocates the band basic time to that job. Category estimating is a variation of this but has no benchmarks, time band slotting being done purely on the experience of the estimator.

Synthetics

Much work is repetitive, so it is wasteful repeatedly to measure similar jobs over and over again. It makes more sense to create a library of study results which may be used to time future similar jobs. Such library times are *synthetic data*, which may be in the form of tables, formulae or nomographs. A typical formula may be for walking: time $= 0.006 \, S + 0.01$ where S is the number of steps taken. To walk 400 steps takes 2.41 min.

Synthetic data may be compiled from time studies, PMTS, or estimating. In complex cases formulae are derived from multiple regression analysis. An example of tabulated synthetics is given in Figure 33.10.

Applications

Work measurement standards may be used for planning, assessing completion times and durations for projects, costing of jobs, calculating operator performance or utilization, and using these to assess bonuses.

As an example of the calculation of utilization, suppose an operator performed three jobs; turning twenty spindles on a lathe (12 standard minutes each), drilling forty brackets (2.5 sm each), and fettling thirty components (3.0 sm), all in 450 min. Total earned minutes are $(20 \times 12) + (40 \times 2.5) + (30$

GHM

		DIGGING	RESTING	ABSENT

RATED ACTIVITY SAMPLING

JOB: DIGGING TRENCH ANALYST: A.J.B.

DURATION: 09.00 to 09.13 DATE: 10 JUNE

	DIGGING	RESTING	ABSENT
9.00.25		X	
50		X	
75		X	
1.00		X	
25		X	
50	95		
75	95		
2.00	90		
25	90		
50	90		
75	90		
3.00	100		
25	100		
50	100		
75	100		
4.00	105		
25	105		
50	95		
75	95		
5.00	95		
25	95		
50	100		
75	100		
6.00	95		
25	90		
50	90		
75	95		
7.00	85		
25	85		
50	85		
75			X
8.00			X
25			X
50			X
75			X
9.00			X
25			X
50	80		
75	80		
10.00	85		
25	85		
50	90		
75	90		
11.00	100		
25	110		
50	110		
75	110		
12.00	90		
25	110		
50	110		
75	95		
13.00			
25			

CALCULATION

$$\text{basic time} = \frac{\Sigma R \times \text{time interval}}{100 \times \text{vol. dug}}$$

time interval = 0.25 min

Vol. = 0.4 cu. metre

$$\text{basic time} = \frac{3710 \times 0.25}{100 \times 0.4}$$

$$= 23.19 \text{ b. min}$$
per cu. metre

| Total ratings R | 3710 | | |

Figure 33.8 **A rated activity sampling study with calculation of the basic time**

Department: Maintenance   Section: Plumbing

CATEGORY A Mean time = 9 minutes 0 to 20 minutes	CATEGORY B Mean time = 28 minutes 20 to 40 minutes	CATEGORY C Mean time = 55 minutes 40 to 80 minutes	CATEGORY D Mean time = 2 hours 80 minutes to $2\frac{3}{4}$ hours
Change tap washer Replace shower head Change short piece of burst copper pipe	Change immersion heater Replace stopcock Install bath tap and shower assembly Clean and replace waste trap on bath or wash basin	Install immersion heater Install stopcock in line Connect bath hot, cold and waste	Change cold tank in loft Install new outside tap Connect wash basin to existing supplies
etc.	etc.	etc.	etc.

Figure 33.9   A comparative estimating spread sheet

No. of items dusted	0	2	4	6	8	10	12
Area (sq.m)							
25	6.8	8.2	9.6	11.0	12.4	13.8	15.2
30	7.6	9.0	10.3	11.7	13.1	14.5	15.9
35	8.3	9.7	11.1	12.5	13.9	15.3	16.7
40	9.0	10.4	11.8	13.2	14.6	16.0	17.4
45	9.7	11.2	12.6	14.0	15.4	16.8	18.2
50	10.5	11.9	13.3	14.7	16.1	17.5	18.9
55	11.3	12.7	14.1	15.5	16.9	18.3	19.7
60	12.0	13.4	14.8	16.2	17.6	19.0	20.4
65	12.8	14.2	15.6	17.0	18.4	19.8	21.2
70	13.5	14.9	16.3	17.7	19.1	20.5	21.9
75	14.3	15.7	17.1	18.5	19.9	21.3	22.7
80	15.0	16.4	17.8	19.2	20.6	22.0	23.4
85	15.7	17.2	18.6	20.0	21.4	22.8	24.2
90	16.5	17.9	19.3	20.7	22.1	23.5	24.0

Data include vacuum cleaning carpets, and dusting items of furniture (times in standard minutes)

Figure 33.10   A table of synthetic data (for cleaning rooms)

× 3) which equals 430 sm. Actual time taken was 450 min. so utilization was (430 ÷ 450) × 100 = 95.6 (or 95.6 per cent efficiency). Furthermore, if each standard minute is costed at 20 pence, the labour cost of the spindles was 240 × 20p or £48, or £2.40 each. One thousand spindles would take 12 000 sm, or 27 days. If required within nine days, then three turners would be needed.

IMPROVEMENT OF PRODUCTS AND SERVICES

The subject of productivity would not be complete without consideration of the value of the product or service itself. The twin approaches of value analysis and value engineering are used to reduce the cost of an existing product, and a new design respectively. The philosophy of value analysis/engineering (VA) is to produce the same *function* in a cheaper way. Function, in this sense, has four facets. These are:

1 *Use function* – how the product or service performs
2 *Esteem function* – how it appears
3 *Exchange function* – how it will trade in
4 *Cost function* – value for money.

VA procedure follows the basic problem solving sequence:

591

1   Collection of data (orientation phase)
2   Examination of the situation (speculation)
3   Consideration phase
4   Recommendation phase (a report to management)
5   Implementation (when recommendations are put into operation).

VA is carried out by a team of specialists in different fields who meet at each of the phases outlined above. The orientation phase is used to collect data, costs, sales value, specifications and drawings, and specimens. The object of VA is to reduce the cost without reducing the necessary functions. This may involve removing unnecessary embellishments, combining functions, changing standards, sources of supply, designs, and simplification of the product.

Speculation uses brainstorming as its method of examination. The team suggests improvements using freethinking, with all judgements on ideas deferred until the consideration stage. Criticisms stem from prejudices against situations and methods, and generalizations which condemn certain proposals out of hand. Stereotyped thinking is another source of resistance to change. Brainstorming can sweep aside stereotype answers and come up with novel, original ideas.

After speculation, the team reconvenes to consider the ideas produced during that phase. Results of considering these ideas may be separated into 'rejected', 'recommended', or 'consider further'. Those eventually recommended are incorporated into a new design.

An example of a VA analysis sheet is given in Figure 33.11.

IMPROVEMENT OF CONDITIONS

The effectiveness of work can be improved, it can be measured and the product can be made less expensive. But the conditions under which the person is working must also be considered. The discipline which looks at this is *ergonomics*. The scope of ergonomics covers:

1   *The worker* – his own physical dimensions, the stresses imposed upon him and the way in which he reacts to events and conditions
2   *The workplace* – layout of work, design of equipment, furniture and seating
3   *The environment* – the effects of heat and humidity, lighting, noise, vibration and atmospheric conditions.

All of this requires some knowledge of physiology and anatomy, anthropometry and psychology.

Stresses on a worker arise from the environment, so working conditions must include suitable seating, work heights, arm rests, and footrests, correctly designed controls, good layout of controls, tools, materials, and equipment, and well-designed hours of working during shifts. Attention must also be paid to relaxation periods, both length and frequency.

VALUE ANALYSIS	GHM

SPECULATION SHEET

SPECULATION	ANALYSIS

CONSIDER WHETHER:

FUNCTION
the function can be eliminated,
the function can be achieved in a simpler way,
the function can be combined or integrated with any
    other function.

NON-CONTRIBUTORY ITEMS
any of the items contributing nothing to the prestige
    or use function can be eliminated.

TOLERANCES AND INSPECTION
the inspection can be eliminated,
quality control can replace 100% inspection,
tolerances are realistic,
gauging can replace measuring,
reduced quality of surface finish can be accepted,
alternative finish can be used,
alternative methods of applying finish can be used.

MATERIALS
standard items can be used to replace specially
    made items,
cheaper items can be bought from external suppliers,
cheaper alternative material can be used,
amount of material used per part can be reduced,
dimensions can be reduced,
design changes can reduce material used.

PROCESSING
a cheaper process can be used for the raw materials,
a cheaper process can be used to produce any components,
a cheaper process can be used for the finish on the
    article.

DESIGN
a new design will reduce the number of components
    used
a re-design will combine two or more functions,
a re-design will eliminate any item or function,
excess material, scrap, or number of rejects will
    be reduced by re-designing the item,
it would be cheaper to make the component in
    more parts,
the part or component could be re-designed to
    facilitate the use of power tools or plant.
the part or component could be re-designed to
    facilitate the assembly by improved method.

Figure 33.11   Example of a value analysis speculation sheet

593

The workplace must be designed so that tools and controls are within easy reach of the worker. Dials which must be read should be unambiguous, and easy to understand at a glance. Similarly controls must be simple to operate, and compatible; that is, apparatus must move in the direction which one would expect, so that a lever pushed upward should move the equipment (say fork-lift truck arms) upward. Some conventions are recognized, such as a clockwise turn of a knob for increase.

The environmental factors include noise, which may be disturbing, or can sometimes be dangerous. The most important considerations are the frequency or pitch, and the intensity of the sound. Instruments measure the intensity in decibels (dB). Recommended maximum levels are published, and these depend on whether the noise is intermittent, or sustained. Ultrasonic sound, used for detecting cracks in metal, or for cleaning oily or dirty components, is particularly dangerous because one cannot judge the intensity as it is inaudible.

If the source is not bright enough, lighting can be a problem. The ergonomist is concerned with other factors such as the type of lighting, colour, glare and reflection, and the décor of the place of work. Minimum criteria are laid down for corridors, general work, fine work and other conditions. Factors which affect the amount of light needed are size of object, contrast between object and its surroundings and reflectivity of the surface. Shadows can also be a problem unless they are needed for a three-dimensional effect. Colours are important in designing décor because they affect the psychological well-being of the worker. For example, grey, blue and green are cold colours, while red and orange make people feel warm. Purple is a shocking colour. Colours can also give a feeling of space, or claustrophobia.

Heat and humidity affect the effectiveness and comfort of people. Ergonomists advise on heat stress, and how it can be relieved. The ambient temperature is considered, but humidity can cause more discomfort than a relatively high temperature. Protection for the worker may be afforded in several ways, such as shielding the offending heat source. Special clothing may be worn, but often this restricts the movements of the worker.

From all this, it is evident that ergonomics is an essential part of any study into the raising of productivity.

OPERATIONAL RESEARCH (OR)

Operational research, originating between the two world wars, has been developed to assist in the solving of certain problems through mathematical and statistical theory. Extensive use is made of probability theory, of queuing and replacement theories, and of logical thought. Some applications of OR are:

1   Optimization of stock levels with fluctuating demands
2   Optimum use of labour, plant and machinery

3 Determination of policy for maintenance and repair of plant and machinery, and replacement of parts and components
4 Product-mix problems and determination of the levels of output for each product consistent with demand and cost
5 Minimization of transportation costs in a distribution system such as delivery of goods to wholesalers
6 Problems where queuing or congestion occur
7 Problems of sequencing, dealt with by critical path analysis.

Applying OR

In using OR it is necessary to formulate some logical approach, so again a five-step pattern of problem solving may be used.

1 *Define the problem.* It is essential to define the problem before a start is made otherwise a great deal of time may be spent on unnecessary data collection and problem solving
2 *Record the facts.* Once defined, the plan of action must be developed and the necessary data collected and assembled in suitable form. All variables and all constraints which may limit possible solutions must be determined and specified in order that the models, equations and inequalities may be constructed. Any information omitted may invalidate the solution. Historical data are used to assess the future. These can be gathered either by collecting data until sufficient information has been obtained, or by simulating the history with the use of 'hypothetical facts'
3 *Examine the facts.* The facts are next analysed and from the data equations (or models) are formed to represent the facts in mathematical form. In certain cases actual physical models can be made as in departmental layouts. A mathematical model is an equation or inequality which may be manipulated using mathematical processes. To form the equations, statements about the job are given mathematical symbols
4 *Derive and test the solutions.* The models are processed mathematically or physically and the solutions are derived. These solutions are then tested under actual operating conditions
5 *Application and maintenance.* The solution is translated into practical and concrete terms and these are put into practice. Modifications may be necessary in the light of new knowledge or changing conditions.

Some techniques and situations are now described.

LINEAR PROGRAMMING

Linear programming may be used to solve such problems as product-mix or distribution (allocation). As the name linear suggests there are no powers of the variables in the equations (that is, no x^2, x^3, etc.).

Product mix

These problems are of the type where there are several factors mixed into the problem which, if taken in the correct proportions, will produce an optimum solution for cost, time or other quantity.

For example, a tyre factory may be making its tyres from several types of rubber which are mixed together. The problem is to find the most economic mix consistent with safety, wear, durability and reliability. It would be an easy matter to mix up the cheapest materials without worrying about the *constraints* given above, but these restrictions make the problem more complicated.

In solving problems of this type it is necessary to construct mathematical models relating all the factors and constraints. For example, if a dog food contained three types of meat A, B and C, where A cost x pence per pound, B cost y pence, and C cost z pence, and the total cost must not exceed 160 pence per pound, then the model would be: $Ax+By+Cz < 160$, where A, B and C are the weights of the meats respectively. The solution to the problem would give the amount of each meat needed to make up the dog food at an economic cost, consistent with the constraints imposed.

Distribution

The use of OR in this case is to find the most economic way for distribution of goods from dispatching points to the receiving points. For example, in distributing goods to retailers it may be possible to send one van on the round to visit all the customers over the period of one week; or alternatively to send five vans out on the same day, each serving one-fifth of the customers. In the first case it is probably cheaper but in the second case it is more convenient to the customers. These and many other facts must be considered and processed before the solution can be determined.

QUEUING

A queue in the OR context is any line of items, people or products which are waiting for some sort of service or processing. Problems of queuing may include:

1 Queues at cash registers in a supermarket, ticket office or toll booth
2 Incoming calls at a telephone exchange
3 Aircraft stacking over a busy airport
4 Queues at a factory-stores hatch
5 Letters awaiting signature, or any documents or forms in an in-tray
6 Piece-parts awaiting processing in the flow line.

Characteristics of a queue are:

1 *The queue length.* This may be self-regulating as when people get tired of waiting, or fruit goes bad while awaiting shipment
2 *The service time.* This is the time taken by the server to deal with the situation and will vary according to circumstances, from constant to exponential time
3 *The arrivals* of items joining the queue may be: *regular* and cyclic, and thus may be predetermined, or *random* which are unpredictable, or *random but cyclic*, being in cycles (peak and slack periods) but the numbers are unknown.

Queuing problems may be simulated in the usual way using models.

PLANT REPLACEMENT

Under planned maintenance the scheme is often based on replacement theory. The problem is choosing between (a) running the system until something happens to disrupt the system (such as a breakdown due to component failure) or (b) replacing the components at regular intervals in order to prevent disruptions by anticipating them before they occur. The costs of these alternatives must be weighed up before a choice can be made. The costs of running until failure may include:

1 The cost of the breakdown
2 Damage to other components
3 Shutdown of whole line due to the breakdown of one process
4 Negligible cost if there are no breakdowns, making this policy the cheaper.

The policy of forestalling breakdowns may involve:

1 Cost of changing components which may still be perfectly good, and
2 A fixed cost, which will definitely be incurred, as against 4 above which may vary between zero and a very high value.

STOCK CONTROL

OR can be applied to problems of stock control. Again it is a choice between two different policies:

1 A large stock may be held to avoid running out of stock – expensive because of storage, insurance, depreciation, deterioration and handling cost, or
2 A minimum stock may be held with the risk of running out of stock, causing loss of production, time and customers.

The job of OR is to determine the optimum stock level to hold, and this is achieved by using statistical method, which includes probability theory.

FURTHER READING

Ackoff, R.L., *The Art of Problem Solving*, Wiley, London, 1978
De Bono, E., *P.O. Beyond Yes and No*, Penguin Books, Harmondsworth, 1977
Gordon, W.J.J., *Synectics*, Harper & Row, New York, 1968
Grandjean, E., *Fitting the Task to the Man*, Taylor & Francis, London, 1971
Karger, D.W., and Bayha, F.H., *Engineering Work Measurement*, Industrial Press, New York, 1977
Kepner, C.H., and Tregoe, B.B., *The Rational Manager*, McGraw-Hill, New York, 1964
McCormick, E.J., *Human Factors in Engineering Design*, McGraw-Hill, New York, 1976
Murrell, K.H.F., *Ergonomics*, Chapman & Hall, London, 1969
Osborne, A.F., *Applied Imagination*, Scribner's Sons, New York, 1965
Quick, J.H., Malcolm, J.H., and Duncan, J.H., *Work-Factor Time Standards*, McGraw-Hill, New York, 1962
Rivett, P., and Ackoff, R., *A Manager's Guide to Operational Research*, Wiley, London, 1963
Whitmore, D.A., *Measurement and Control of Indirect Work*, Heinemann, London 1970
Whitmore, D.A., *Work Study and Related Management Services*, Heinemann, London, 1976
Whitmore, D.A., *Management Sciences*, Teach Yourself Books, London, 1979
Whitmore, D.A., *Work Measurement*, Heinemann, London, 1980

34 Project management
Dennis Lock

If there is one single quality which sets a project apart from routine commercial or industrial operations, it is its novelty. No two projects are ever exactly alike, and the course of any project can never be predicted with accuracy or the final outcome completely guaranteed. A project is always a journey into the unknown, fraught with risk. Projects typically demand the use of resources that are scarce or expensive, but which have to be deployed over a most complex framework of tasks. The purpose of project management is to minimize, contain or counter the risks, and organize and direct the resources so that the project is finished on time, within budgeted costs and with the functional or other design objectives fulfilled.

PROJECTS AND THEIR OBJECTIVES

Projects obviously come in many shapes and sizes. It is possible to group them loosely under four headings:

1 *Manufacturing projects* – where the final result is a vehicle, ship, aircraft, piece of machinery, weapon system, or any other form of purpose-built hardware
2 *Construction projects* – resulting in the erection of roads, bridges, tunnels, railways or buildings. Mining and petro-chemical projects can be included in this group, all of which share the common characteristic that they start life in a design or architect's office, with the fulfilment phase taking place at some external site (which could be hundreds or even thousands of miles removed from the contractor's main offices)
3 *Management projects* – which include the organization or reorganization of work without necessarily producing a tangible result. Examples would be the design and testing of a new computer software package, relocation of a company's headquarters, or the production of a stage show
4 *Research projects*, in which the objectives may be difficult to establish, and where the results are unpredictable: such projects are unlikely to be amenable to the management techniques described in this chapter.

Objectives

A project usually has three objectives, which are:

Function or performance – the final result must satisfy the requirements of the end user. Considering a project to develop a motor car (for instance), the objectives must be to produce a vehicle that satisfies specified standards for performance, reliability and safety. Other design objectives also come into play in this example (styling is obviously an important feature if the car is to attract buyers, and the design must be such as to allow the vehicles to be produced at economic cost).

Containment of expenditure within budget is another criterion for project success. Continuing with the car development example, if the development costs were to exceed those planned, then their recovery from car sales could result in the selling price having to be increased too far above prices charged by competitors for their rival products. Projects must, therefore, be completed within their budgeted costs. In large capital projects it is usually necessary to ensure that expenditure is controlled not only against an overall budget, but also that the rate of expenditure is phased in accordance with the planned availability of project financing (cash flow management).

In project management terms it is correct, when generalizing, always to talk in terms of budgets rather than of achieved profits. By no means every project is conducted for profit (for example, projects originated and managed by local government bodies).

Timescale is the third factor. Some projects have very well defined delivery targets, whether these result from promises to customers or from some other predetermined date. In the motor car example it might be that the car has to be fully developed and proven in time for launch at the Motor Show.

PROJECT DEFINITION AND SPECIFICATION

If the purpose of project management is to meet the functional, cost and timescale objectives, then clearly these objectives must be properly defined from the outset. The technical or performance specification usually originates from a customer's stated requirements (allowing that the contractor may be his own customer for some in-house management projects). It is customary for the initial requirements to be discussed and modified during a dialogue between the customer and the contractor's sales engineers, with a design scheme or preferred solution emerging. It is essential that the agreed scheme is recorded without any possibility of ambiguity in a concise but comprehensive sales specification. This must describe in clear text the scope and technical performance of the project, supported by whatever drawings are necessary to define the agreed solution.

Since any eventual contract will be based on this specification, it is important that no significant element of the project is omitted, and that any special problems are foreseen. If the scope of work is to include the provision of training manuals, commissioning, and other related tasks, then this should be spelled out. Where projects require work to be carried out overseas, such as the installation of machinery or the construction of a building, then it is essential that any local standards are complied with (which might involve additional expenditure). Local climatic conditions could also be an important factor. The use of checklists is recommended under such circumstances: most contracting companies should be able to prepare such lists from their past experience of similar projects.

All drawings and other associated documents have to be catalogued in the specification, with identification numbers and any revision numbers listed. The procedure of solution engineering is discussed more fully in Chapter 22. If the contractor succeeds in his bid for the work, then the resulting contract document will refer to the sales specification by its number and revision number.

After contract award, the sales specification becomes the definitive project specification. Any subsequent change requested by the customer, or any deviation from the agreed solution proposed by the contractor, affects the basis on which the contract was signed and the contract must be amended accordingly, using a formal contract variation order procedure to ensure that the implications of every proposed change are properly considered and implemented (see Figure 34.1).

Project definition is a process which continues after contract award, right up to the final stages of commissioning. This comes about through the preparation of detailed design drawings (which amplify the original specification) and through the inevitable changes introduced as work proceeds (not least of which are modifications and corrections found to be necessary during final assembly or at the construction site). The total process of project definition, from initial customer enquiry to the archiving of 'as-built' drawings, is illustrated in Figure 34.2.

PROJECT ORGANIZATION

The project manager

Obviously the person at the head of the project should, ideally, be technically experienced and qualified in the type of work involved (although there have been exceptions). Provided that the individual concerned has appropriate management skills it is sometimes prudent to appoint as project manager the most senior member of the sales engineering team that won the order, since this must help to ensure adherence to the original intentions of scope and performance.

Otherwise, the project manager needs to be:

- perceptive (able to spot potential problems early)
- questioning (sadly, a project manager cannot always believe progress

PROJECT VARIATION

GHM

COST DATA   UNITS:

Total increase / decrease in cost =

PROGRAMME DATA

LIST OF RELEVANT DOCUMENTS AND DRAWINGS

DESCRIPTION OF CHANGE (Use continuation sheet if necessary)

APPROVALS

Originator	Project manager			Client
Date	Date			Date

Client   —

Project   —   Project No —

TITLE —   VARIATION No   revision   sheet

Figure 34.1 **A project variation summary form.** *Example of a form used to summarize details of a change requested by a project customer, together with the contractor's estimates of the effect on costs and timescale*

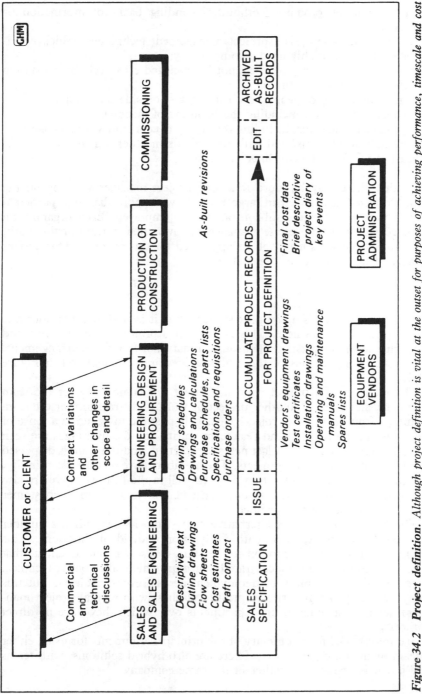

Figure 34.2 **Project definition.** *Although project definition is vital at the outset for purposes of achieving performance, timescale and cost objectives, the process of definition continues throughout the life of the project until as-built records are assembled and archived*

information or promises without demanding back-up information or proof)
- familiar with appropriate project management techniques (which nowadays almost invariably need a computer system)
- active and mobile (a project cannot be managed effectively by remaining behind a desk all the time)
- a good motivator of people, both inside and outside the company
- a capable organizer, including the handling of meetings
- a good communicator, including the ability to cooperate with management and staff at all levels, and with individuals in other organizations – not least of which is the customer or client.

Note that there may be more than one project manager working on the same project. This is seen in large projects with more than one participating contractor, or where subcontractors are employed. Each organization involved will need to exercise management over their portion of the work, and project managers may well be appointed for this purpose. This applies equally, if not more so, to the customer.

Team or matrix?

Project organization is a complex subject, but it is useful to consider one of the principal issues here. This is whether a project should be managed through a team organization or through a matrix or functional arrangement. The basic configurations of these alternatives are demonstrated in Figure 34.3.

The manager of a project team has direct line command over the team members, and there is no other project or work to distract him or the team members from their own project goals. It is possible to generate a sense of belonging to the project, and real team spirit. The disadvantages are seen when the project ends, or at last nears completion, and the team is dispersed and redeployed over other projects. The members have no career continuity, and may actually lose motivation to work well in the future. There are also problems when queries arise from a construction site or from the customer after the team has been disbanded.

The functional or matrix alternative comes into its own when a number of projects are in progress, with fairly short individual durations. This method avoids career disruption to the staff. It also has the advantage that specialist disciplines are concentrated in groups which allow better technical supervision and flexibility of deployment across several projects. But this same flexibility can give rise to priority clashes, with several project managers demanding action from departments over which they have no direct authority.

See Figure 34.4 for a summary of the principal arguments for using either a team or matrix organization. There are also hybrid solutions, with teams and a matrix operating together in the same company.

Communications

Organization also includes the important subject of communications, inside the company, with outside organizations, with the customer and (where relevant) with remote work sites. Many methods exist for transmitting information, ranging from ordinary mail to the use of datapost, couriers, airfreighted documents, telephone, telex, facsimile and other means.

An individual should be nominated at each location as the addressee for all written communications and technical documents. Each regular project channel should only carry serially numbered letters or consignments so that any missing envelope or parcel can be realised from the gap in received serial numbers (e.g. LS1, LS2, LS3, ... etc., for letters from London to site, and SL1, SL2, SL3 . . . ., and so on for documents travelling from site to London.

In the course of project work a great deal of management control information can be generated, especially where computers are concerned. Reports must be sorted and edited so that their scope and level of detail are appropriate to the management disciplines and levels at which they are directed. Regular distribution of documents must be on the basis of who 'needs to know' rather than who 'wants to know'. It is useful to define an agreed standard distribution of documents for each project using a chart such as that shown in Figure 34.5.

COST ESTIMATING AND BUDGETING

Once the scope of a project has been defined clearly in a sales specification it is necessary to estimate the likely costs of fulfilling all the work. Cost estimates form the basis of subsequent budgets for management control. They also provide a foundation for pricing (although the relationship between the estimated costs and the eventual contract price may not always be quite as direct as might be supposed). Pricing should be regarded by the project manager as a decision to be made (or certainly endorsed) by senior company management. However, any executive faced with the need to decide a selling price must be told how accurate and reliable the estimates are claimed to be.

There is no such thing as an accurate estimate. If eventual project costs turn out to equal the original estimates, then that is pure chance. By their very nature projects are not accurately predictable. But it is possible to classify estimates according to their probability of being correct. The degree of confidence in any estimate depends on several factors, which include principally:

1 The amount of information available concerning the scope of the project
2 The amount of detailed technical and design information available to the estimators
3 The degree of practical experience achieved with similar previous projects

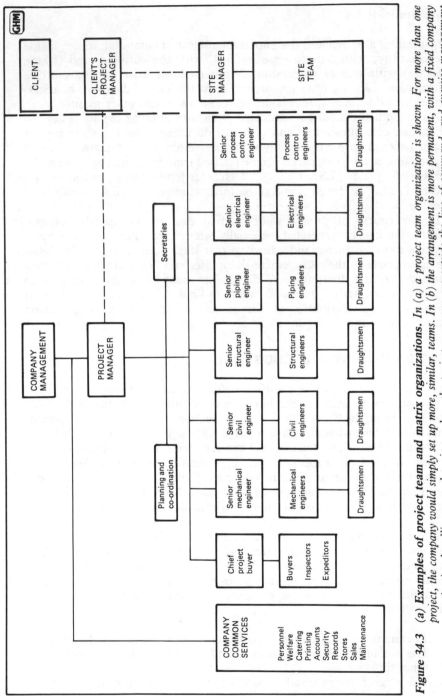

Figure 34.3 (a) **Examples of project team and matrix organizations.** In (a) a project team organization is shown. For more than one project, the company would simply set up more, similar, teams. In (b) the arrangement is more permanent, with a fixed company organization handling several projects where the project managers are outside the line of command, and exercise management through a functional link with each company specialist department

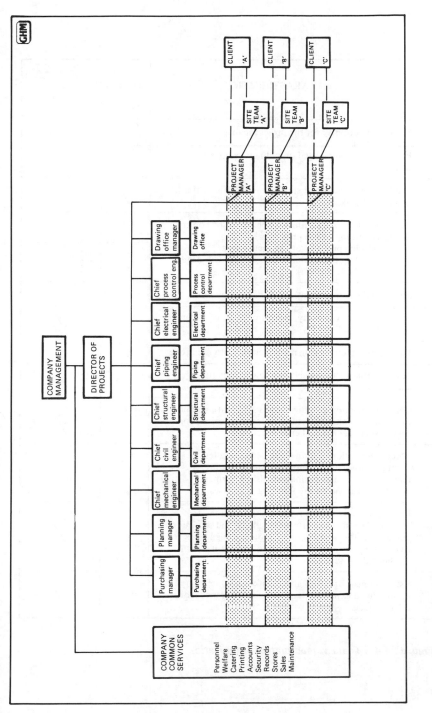

Figure 34.3 (b) Examples of project team and matrix organizations

CHARACTERISTIC	ORGANIZATION INDICATED GHM	
	TEAM	MATRIX
Maximum authority for the project manager	✓	
Freedom from duplicated or ambiguous lines of command	✓	
Maximum motivation of staff to meet difficult time and cost targets	✓	
High security — where information has to be confined to those working on the project — by enclosing project work in secure areas	✓	
— by restricting the total number of staff who need to know about the work	✓	
Most flexible deployment of total company resources		✓
Most effective availability, company-wide, of experts with rare specialist skills		✓
Large project, employing many people for a long time	✓	
Several projects, each needing a few people for a short time		✓
Career motivation of individuals — by creating senior job positions (and opportunities for promotion) for specialists (e.g. electrical engineers)		✓
Career motivation of individuals — by long term continuity of management structure, allowing managers time to assess individuals' performance, give guidance, and ensure fair long-term rewards		✓
Provision of advice or service to construction personnel on site, and after-sales advice and service to customers after completion of project design work (which may prove very difficult to arrange if a team has been disbanded)		✓
Establishment of information banks, in which accumulated experience can be kept for retrieval on later projects		✓

Figure 34.4 Team versus matrix organization

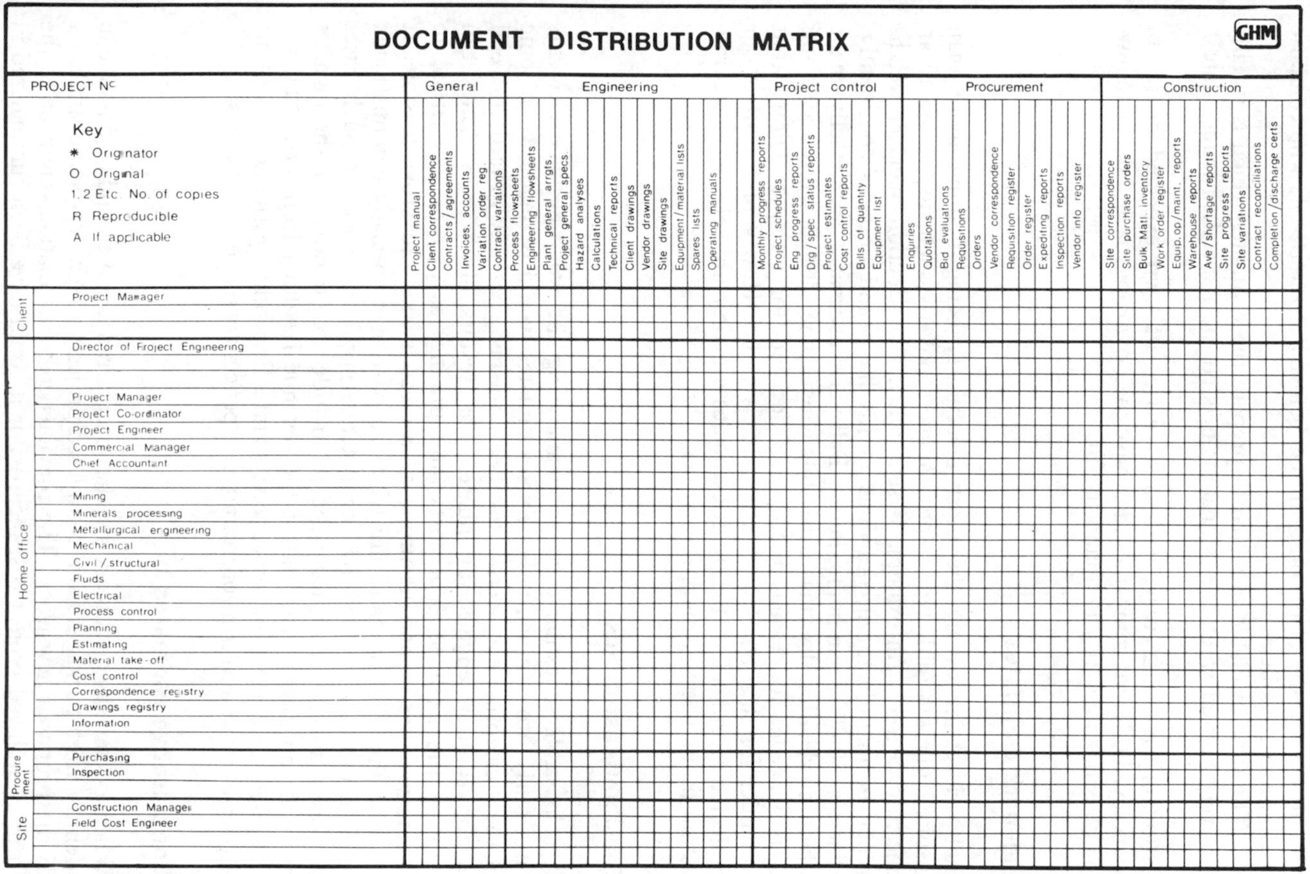

Figure 34.5 A document distribution matrix. Example of a chart used to show the standard, agreed distribution of project documents

609

4   The amount of complexity or uncertainty in the work (for example the possibility of strikes, lockouts, civil commotion, war, floods, earthquakes, or any of the other things beloved of the people who compose insurance policies)

5   The time available in which to prepare the estimate (which is usually very limited when the estimate is needed for a specified tender date).

Estimating methods vary, and each carries its own expected degree of accuracy. Different companies each have their own approach, but the following classifications may be found useful.

Ball-park estimates

Ball-park estimates are the most inaccurate, being nothing more than inspired guesses (although some managers possess such inspiration to an uncanny degree). An example is seen when a production manager weighs a pile of manufacturing drawings in his hand and declares confidently, 'There's 50 000 man-hours here'. Ball-park estimates are usually made where no detailed drawings exist, but when some idea of project scale and costs is needed for reasons of corporate decision (for example, 'Do we want to tender for this job? How big is it likely to be? How would it affect our projected workload?'). Ball-park estimates are very unlikely to be accurate within limits better than ± 25 per cent.

Feasibility estimates

It is possible to estimate costs by analysing the work package elements on a fairly broad brush basis. Such estimates would be made when some of the conceptual engineering has been finished, possibly towards the end of the solution engineering phase. The results of these estimates can indicate the likely level of costs (and pricing) as part of an exercise to decide whether or not the proposed project is likely to prove feasible. It may be that the estimates are made as part of a specially commissioned feasibility study, funded by the potential project owner. In such cases cost estimating is often extended to include consideration of the owner's probable operating costs and of the revenue resulting from operating the proposed machinery or processing plant. Feasibility estimates might be expected to contain errors of around ± 15 per cent of the real project cost.

Comparative estimates

When a detailed work breakdown has been arranged, it should be possible to identify work packages from completed projects which bear some similarity to the proposed new work. The previous cost information might be in the form of archived project cost records, or it could have been summarized in tables which employ mean values. It is important in these cases to allow for the passage of time and consequent inflation: when estimating work content it is always preferable to use time units (typically man-hours) and convert these to costs at the appropriate contemporary rates. Comparative estimates offer the most practical form of project cost estimating for the purpose of setting up budgets and establishing selling prices. A degree of error not greater than ± 10 per cent should be achievable.

Definitive estimates

As work on the project proceeds it is necessary to update the estimate continually by substituting known costs for estimated costs as soon as they are incurred or committed (e.g. when purchase orders and subcontracts are placed). Analysis of cost trends and regular reviews of the estimated cost-to-project-completion are essential for effective cost control. Allowances must be made for any change in project scope (whether or not sanctioned by an approved project variation order). The total project cost estimate obviously becomes more accurate as time proceeds and the known costs displace the initial estimates until, eventually, it must converge on the true cost. There comes a point in project progress, usually well into the production or construction phase, where the cost data have been established with sufficient certainty to justify declaration of the total cost prediction as a 'definitive estimate', with the residual error less than ± 5 per cent. At least, that is the theory but difficulties during erection and commissioning and late modifications can easily make nonsense of any estimate.

Allowances

Any estimate of project costs must recognize and allow for possible errors or risks. This is usually termed a contingency allowance, and forms part of a group of allowances and provisions which are known as the 'below-the-line costs'. One important element of these provisions is the allowance for cost inflation (termed 'cost escalation' by project managers) and it obviously requires a crystal ball of the very highest quality for projects that extend several years into the future. Variations in international currency exchange rates provide another interesting exercise in prediction. Customary practice is to translate all costs to one common 'control' currency, and to use this as the standard throughout the life of the project for all cost reporting.

Procedure

Cost estimating deserves careful attention and management, since errors of scale or omission could prove financially disastrous to the contractor. The value of checklists in ensuring a complete project specification is most important in this respect. The estimates themselves require a disciplined approach (with or without the aid of a computer) and standard tabulation formats are recommended. An example of an estimating form (in this case for total capital expenditure) is given in Figure 34.6.

CONTRACTS AND PRICING

There are many ways in which contract terms can be arranged between a purchaser and the contractor, and in some industries there are standard forms of contract. In the space available here it is necessary to consider some aspects of pricing, since these can have a pronounced effect on project management priorities and incentives.

'Cost-plus' contracts operate against agreed rates of payment for the materials and various professions and trades employed. They imply that the purchaser has access to the contractor's books to verify claims for payment, although such access is often achieved by means of an independent third party (a consulting engineer) to preserve the contractor's commercial confidentiality. Alternatively, payments can be made against independent certification of the value of work done, within the agreed schedule of working rates.

The rates paid for cost-plus work might include an element of profit. Alternatively, payment could be at cost, with a management fee added. There are many variations on this theme, but cost-plus working in general places more financial risk on the purchaser than on the contractor. The method is appropriate when project definition is difficult, and would be useful for contracted-out research and development work.

Fixed price contracts have become increasingly common in recent years, and in these most of the risk is borne squarely on the contractor's shoulders. If costs exceed estimates, the contractor's only recourse to additional payment from the purchaser lies in claiming for additional work caused by the purchaser (supported by approved project variation orders) or by claims for inflationary cost increases where these were specifically provided for in the original contract terms.

The route from estimating to fixed price tendering is, in theory, simply a matter of adding a target 'mark-up' sum to the total cost estimates, designed to achieve a target profit (usually expressed as a percentage of the costs incurred). In practice pricing is a matter for expert management decision, since the likely (guessed) level of competitors' prices, the desirability or not of obtaining the project contract, and the current in-house workload are all factors to be taken into account. A project intended for installation and commissioning in some war-torn area of the world would undoubtedly justify a higher price than a similar project in the home country. On the other hand, a project might be priced below its estimated cost in a period when the workload was very low, simply to retain the skilled project staff and to cover the costs of fixed overheads (a risky procedure if an underpriced project takes longer to develop than expected and lands bang in the middle of a peak workload when capacity is needed for other, profitable, projects).

Contract pricing typically includes incentives or penalties. Some contracts

Engineering Limited   London   England

ESTIMATE OF CAPITAL COST

Estimate No.

GHM

Company
Project   No
Plant
Plant Section

All values are in
• Curr = Currency in which value is to be paid
Exchange Rates
Estimate Base Date

Estimate Identifier
Sheet   of   sheets
Estimator (s)
Approved by

Rev 0 1 2 3 4 5

Discipline / Detail	Detail Extension	Classification	Quantity	Unit	Supply			Freight			I D S T			Sub-contract			Total cost
					Unit Rate	Cost Fob/For	• Curr	Gross / Ocean Tonnes	Rate	Cost	• Curr	Rate	Cost	• Curr	Rate	Cost	• Curr

Description

Sheet Totals

Figure 34.6 *Estimating form for project capital costs. This is an example of a form used by an engineering company to summarize capital cost estimates in orderly fashion for new mining projects*

613

have a target price, and any savings are shared between the parties (which could lead to skimping of quality standards by the contractor in the absence of good contract supervision). Similarly, there are cost incentive possibilities for early completion and penalty clauses for late delivery.

PLANNING AND SCHEDULING

Every project must be controlled from a plan of working, even if such a plan is difficult to produce. A bad plan is better than no plan at all, because it can be improved as the project proceeds and more information becomes available. Without effective planning, there can be no basis for subsequent control. This is true even for quite small projects (although these may not require application of the more sophisticated techniques available to the managers of major projects).

Ideally the promised project delivery or completion date will have resulted from careful planning. More typically, the completion timescale will have been determined in advance, based simply on past experience and without the benefit of detailed plans. This need not be disastrous, since contracting companies are expected to be expert in their own field of business. Under these circumstances the purpose of detailed planning is to provide the basis for work scheduling, issue, measurement and control, underpinning the committed delivery promise.

It is convenient to regard the formidable task of planning and controlling a large, complex project in the same way as a mathematician might approach a problem containing many unknown and variable factors. It is necessary to follow a pattern of thoughts and actions which ensure that the unknown quantities or variables are identified and dealt with one at a time, in a sensible sequence.

Work breakdown

Large projects must be considered in smaller packages for the purposes of planning and control. This procedure should result in the identification of sub-projects or groups of tasks that can be delegated to the responsibility of managers with the general or specialized experience best suited to the demands of each work package. The principle of a work breakdown structure is shown in Figure 34.7. This diagram shows the concept of a work breakdown, using the example of a project to build a railway connecting two main stations, with one halt in the middle. Obviously much of the detail cannot be included within the confines of a book page. Note, however, the way in which the different items fit together as a family tree, with the code numbers indicating the relationships between items at different levels. If A23 is the subproject for City Station, then it is easy to see that the footbridge job A235 relates to that station and, further, that the design activity A2351 is for that footbridge at that station. In an ideal system, such code numbers would be used for cost recording, for drawings and for numbering component parts.

The work breakdown structure should be designed to correspond with a numbering system that can be used to denote project areas, buildings, machines, tasks, cost elements, hardware components, assemblies, sub-assemblies, and indeed every part or activity of the project. Competent contracting companies develop standard numbering systems, which marry design information and the code of cost accounts, so that work breakdown numbering is predetermined within the standard framework. For a project involving a large new mine development, for example, the headframes might automatically include the generic code number 010, and all other headframes for all other mining projects handled by the company would carry the digits 010 in their drawing and cost codes. The addition of a project number enables costs and documents on each project to be separated from other projects, but the common 010 component in the number provides a basis for searching all files and collecting useful comparison data on headframes from the other projects (past and present).

The most significant benefits deriving from the use of a standard numbering system, coupled with logical project work breakdown structures, are:

1 Presentation of project work in packages of manageable size
2 Provision of a framework for estimating and planning
3 Establishment of a basis for costing work done, allowing detailed comparison against budgets
4 Provision of a common system for numbering drawings, material lists, specifications, and other documents needed for project fulfilment
5 The system extends automatically to provide identification numbers for the resulting hardware or construction elements
6 Standardization across all projects means that corresponding parts of different projects can be compared, in terms of costs (estimated and actual), duration, and design configuration
7 Design information can be identified and retrieved from past projects to reduce or remove entirely the need to produce completely fresh designs for a new project: it might be possible simply to modify drawings, thus avoiding the need to 're-invent the wheel' every time
8 The hierarchical nature of a code of accounts linked to a work breakdown structure should assist in selecting data for reporting to different levels and areas of management, especially where a computer is being used as a comprehensive planning, reporting and control tool.

Establishing a logical work sequence

The next stage in project planning is to assemble all the tasks in a practical working sequence. This is possible for small projects using a bar chart (Figure 34.8) or with a critical path network diagram (Figure 34.9). The critical path method provides an excellent notation for this purpose and is summarized later in this chapter.

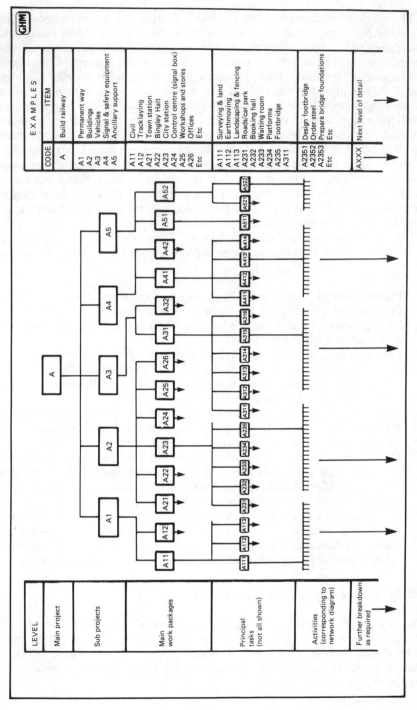

Figure 34.7 Principle of a work breakdown chart

Planning the project duration

The addition of estimates for the duration of each task enables the planner to add up all the expected durations in the work sequence to arrive at a planned project completion date. This exercise almost always predicts a completion date that is unacceptable, and the plan must then be reviewed and re-worked until the target dates are brought within reach. Such adjustments must always be made on the basis of sound judgement, such as running two jobs in parallel, overlapping others, or arranging for the early ordering of long-delivery bought-out items. It must not be done by substituting unrealistic, over-optimistic shortened job times that cannot possibly be achieved.

Scheduling resources

A plan of action is not complete until the use of resources has been taken into account. This is the process of resource scheduling. Critical path analysis is a most useful tool in this respect, because it allows a degree of criticality (float) to be assigned to each activity. This provides a sensible set of priorities when two or more tasks compete for one scarce resource (in which case the tasks with least float should be scheduled to start first). For small projects adjustable bar charts are useful for scheduling, since the bars can be shuffled around (but with the logical sequence constraints still observed) until the work load is as smooth as possible for each profession or trade. This process of resource allocation can be carried out by many of the commercially available computer critical path programs, but beware those systems which claim to be capable of resource scheduling but which can in practice only manage resource aggregation (which is simply showing the resources that would be needed to start all tasks at their earliest possible dates regardless of the impossible workload that would result).

If the schedules indicate that the project cannot be completed on time because the resources are insufficient, the planner has two options. He can go for a time-limited schedule, in which case the computer program will attempt to contain resource usage within the stated existing limits, but will ask for additional resources where these are essential (indicating the need for subcontracting, for shift operation of a bottleneck manufacturing centre, or for temporary recruitment). The other option is a resource-limited schedule, where the computer is instructed that the given resource limits must not be exceeded, acknowledging that the end date may have to be allowed to run out.

It is bad practice to attempt schedule shortening through the planned use of overtime to increase resource levels outside those available within the normal working days or shifts. Overtime should be regarded as a reserve capacity, to be called in only when crash action is needed (as it will be) to rescue jobs that are running late or to cope with unexpected additional work.

Some computer programs allow specification of two resource levels,

PROJECT DAY NUMBERS

ACTIVITY	Day numbers 1–54
Measure room	
Get computer sizes and weights	
Plan room layout	
Determine air conditioning needs	
Get power supply/dissipation data	
Design air conditioning system	
Order air conditioning	
Install air conditioning	
Commission air conditioning	
Design electrics and lighting	
Order electrics and lighting	
Install electrics and lighting	
Design Halon fire system	
Order Halon system	
Install Halon system	
Commission Halon and interlocks	
Specify data connections	
Order cable and connectors	
Install cable and connectors	
Inspect cable and connectors	
Specify decor	
Order decoration materials	
Specify false floor	
Order false floor	
Specify false floor cut-outs	
Install false floor	
Decorate room	
Final clean up	

GHM

PROJECT DAY NUMBERS

1 2 3 4 5 6 7 8 9 10 11 12 13 14 15 16 17 18 19 20 21 22 23 24 25 26 27 28 29 30 31 32 33 34 35 36 37 38 39 40 41 42 43 44 45 46 47 48 49 50 51 52 53 54

Figure 34.8 A project bar chart. This example shows the main tasks needed to convert an existing room into a computer suite. Compare this chart with the network diagram in Figure 34.9, which is another way of depicting the same plan for this project

employing a 'threshold' which can be exceeded at the expense of more costly working (which could correspond for example to the employment of temporary agency-supplied staff). Threshold resources are treated as another 'availability band' superimposed on top of the normally available resources. The computer will attempt to schedule without exceeding the threshold, but will do so if this is essential in order to preserve the planned achievement of target dates.

Resources such as money and materials can be scheduled using the same techniques. Space, especially if it is three-dimensional, is a little more difficult.

PLANNING WITH CRITICAL PATH NETWORKS

In Figure 34.8 a plan is shown in bar chart form for the conversion of an existing room into a small computer suite. Interpretation of such charts requires no special knowledge, and they are readily accepted by everyone, including workmen without specialist training in project management techniques. The chart is useful because it is drawn to scale and shows clearly the timing of every job. When a bar chart is assembled on an adjustable board it is a fairly simple matter to colour code the bars to denote the type of staff or workmen needed, add up the numbers of each type shown in each column (each day in this example) and shuffle the bars around until the workload looks reasonable, without peak overloads. Addition of a moveable vertical cursor, which can be set to 'today's date' as the project proceeds, highlights any job remaining to the left hand of the cursor as being late.

The snag with bar charts comes when the project is big, with hundreds or even thousands of activities to be planned, loaded and progressed. Although it is possible to set up a bar chart showing hundreds of different activities, it is difficult to show how the jobs relate to each other. It is also extremely difficult to cope with any change of plan, and any attempt at rescheduling can lead to mistakes. Experienced bar chartists never look one straight in the eye: they are unable to do so because their eyes are permanently crossed from the effort of trying to follow along the rows and up and down the columns of large charts without seeing the wrong activity or date (this problem is demonstrated even in the very simple chart of Figure 34.8).

The arrow diagram

Now please turn to Figure 34.9, which depicts the same computer room project as that shown in the bar chart of Figure 34.8, but this time planned as a critical path network. To those without specialist training there is nothing obvious about this version of the plan, and it may look difficult and a little intimidating at first sight. But in fact, the critical path technique is quite straightforward once explained. It is simply a specialist notation – a new language if you like – that has been designed for expressing the interrelationships between all the activities in a project. The method also allows for arithmetic calculations that can determine the relative priorities of all jobs for resource scheduling and progressing.

There are several variations of the critical path technique, but that shown here (sometimes known as an activity on arrow network) is widely used, practicable for most purposes, and certainly sufficient for the purposes of this chapter.

Ignore the small numbers written all over the network for the time being (these will be explained in due course). The first thing to note is that the network comprises a number of arrows which join up a series of circles. Every circle represents a definable and recognizable project event (such as the start or finish of a job. Thus the circle containing a figure 1 at the left hand end of the network is the start of all the work (i.e. the project start event) and the event numbered 26 at the right hand is the project completion event.

Each solid arrow represents the work or activity needed to progress from the left hand event (at the arrow tail) to the right hand event (at the arrow head). The arrows are called activities.

Critical path networks are drawn to flow from left to right, but they are not drawn to any scale, and the length of the arrows has no significance whatsoever.

By convention (and by commonsense logic) no activity can start until the event which precedes it has been completed. And for an event to be complete, all activities leading into it (from the left) must have been completed. For example, the activity called 'Order cable and connectors' (at the top of the diagram) cannot be started until event 8 has been achieved – which means in this case that the activity 'Specify data connections' must have been finished. These dependencies are called logical constraints. Similarly, event 20 must have been achieved before the false floor can be installed, which means that both activities leading into event 20 from the left must have been finished.

The dotted arrows are called dummies. They do not denote any work requirement, and they do not occupy any project time. They simply form logical links to show constraints between events. Thus event 7 cannot be declared achieved until both events 6 and 3 have been achieved.

Activities, dummies and events are the only important symbols to learn in network analysis. The trick is to put them together in the right order, so that they show a logical working plan (the network is often called a logic diagram). This requires some practice, but the knack is soon learned. Often the network is sketched out during a planning meeting at which the project manager and the supervisors or managers of key departments are present. A planning engineer (with network experience) asks the members of the meeting for information from which the network logic can be built up. A good planning engineer knows which questions to ask in order to elicit all the important facts and avoid logic errors.

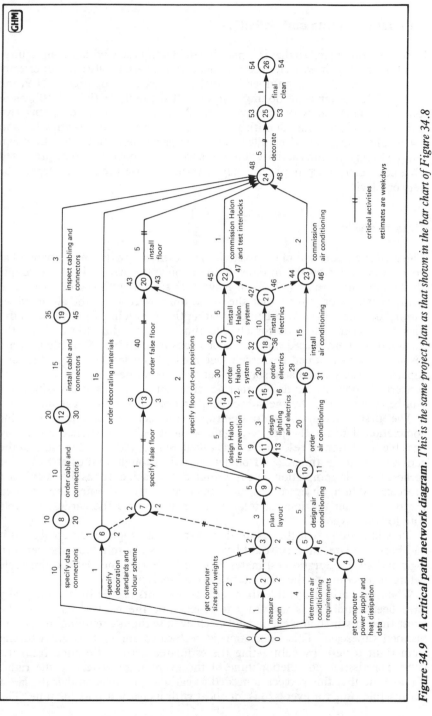

Figure 34.9 A critical path network diagram. This is the same project plan as that shown in the bar chart of Figure 34.8

Numbering events and activities

Events are numbered so that it is possible to identify them without ambiguity. In addition to their written descriptions, activities are identified numerically by their terminal event numbers. Thus, in the example of Figure 34.9, the activity 'Design air conditioning' can be called simply 'activity 5,10'. Note that the dummy activity 4,5 has been added simply to avoid having two activities with the same identification numbers (otherwise activities 1,5 and 1,4 would both have been called 1,5). It is particularly necessary to assign unique event (and thus activity) numbers when the network is to be processed by a computer, since network analysis programs use them to interpret the network logic.

Time analysis

The estimated duration of each activity is shown not by its length (which has no relevance) but by the number written above the arrow. In this example all the estimates are in weekdays. Any other suitable units could have been used, provided of course that the same units were used for all activities throughout the diagram. When estimating the durations of individual activities the concern must be for elapsed time (i.e. the duration and not the man-hour content) based on the use of a sensible number of people or other resources. This planned resource usage must obviously not exceed the total capacity of the particular resource, but there is no need at this stage to be concerned about demands of other activities on scarce resources (since this will be taken care of by the subsequent process of resource scheduling).

The first calculation is to determine the earliest estimated possible completion date for the project, again without being concerned about any possible limitation of resources. This calculation is performed by adding the activity duration estimates up from left to right throughout the network. The earliest possible completion date is written above each event as the calculation proceeds. Where an event has more than one activity leading into it, then the path having the longest total duration must give the earliest possible date for that event.

We will assume that the result (day 54 in this example) is acceptable. If it had been too late, then it would have been necessary to review the network logic and all the duration estimates in a bid to shorten the planned timescale before proceeding to the next stage in time analysis.

When the earliest possible times at which events can be finished logically have been found, it is necessary to re-examine the network and find the latest time at which any event can be achieved without extending the overall planned timescale. This calculation is performed for each event, working from right to left, by subtracting the estimated activity duration from the latest permissible completion time of the event immediately to the right. We assume that this project is needed as early as possible, so that the latest permissible time for event 26 is identical with its earliest possible time. The latest permissible times are written below the event circles. Where there is more than one activity following an event, the path yielding the earliest answer must be taken.

Now consider events 14 and 17, and the activity joining them. This activity could start, at its earliest, at day 10. However, its latest permissible start is day 12: in other words it could be delayed for two days without affecting the project end date. This activity is then said to have two days' float.

It can be seen that there is a series of events in the network of Figure 34.9 which have zero float (i.e. their earliest and latest times are equal). These events are called critical events. The activities joining them are critical activities, and they lie along the critical path. Network branching can sometimes result in two or more paths with equal durations, and this can lead to the existence of more than one critical path. Critical activities in the example are emphasized by two short parallel intersecting lines.

The more float an activity has, the less priority it claims for being started when there is competition from other activities for scarce resources. Activities with zero float must be given priority for scheduling, and for rigorous progressing. The process of resource scheduling was summarized earlier in this chapter.

Using a computer for critical path planning

Computer programs for time analysis and resource scheduling are available for running on hardware ranging from mainframe to microcomputers. The most sophisticated programs integrate the network analysis and resource scheduling results with information on drawings and engineering using a database approach.

Competent programs include error checking routines, which recognize and report any obvious error or omission in the input data. Among the types of recognizable errors are:

1 Duplicate activities (two or more activities input with the same start and finish event numbers)
2 A missing activity (identified when the computer finds a break in any path through the network)
3 A logical loop. This can be caused by transposing start and finish events for an activity, which reverses the flow direction of the arrow as seen by the computer. In certain circumstances, the reversed arrow joins other arrows in such a way that the work flow follows round and round a group of activity arrows which form a closed loop (getting nowhere).

CONTROLLING PROGRESS AND COSTS

At first glance it might seem strange to group the control of progress and expenditure under one heading, but in truth the two run hand in hand. Within the confines of this short chapter there is space to outline the most important factors.

Using the resource schedule

Assume that the project has been sensibly planned, using a computer loaded with a critical path program. The resulting schedules, provided they have taken resources into account, provide an invaluable tool for issuing work and for gauging subsequent progress. This issue of work starts with an authorizing document (such as a works order) which spells out the scope of work expected from each department, gives timescale and budget targets and provides a mandate for expenditure and work to start.

It is important to note that any computer planning or reporting technique is only a forecast and guide. A computer can control neither progress nor costs. Action can only come from management. If a job is running two weeks late, and the project manager knows from the schedule that the relevant activity has a float of only one week, then he does not have to ask the computer what to do. Action is obviously needed to speed up progress on that activity and its followers until the schedule is regained.

The original schedule must be updated to take account of progress achieved, of any job that has become too late to pull back into the plan, and of approved modifications that change the scope of work. Otherwise the schedule would cease to be valid for controlling the issue and gauging the progress of remaining work. All project critical path computer programs have updating routines which allow the input of such data, followed by recalculation of the critical path and resource scheduling.

Subcontracts and major purchases

Subcontracted services can often be regarded as an extension of the purchasing function, with the work being controlled and expedited by the company's purchasing inspectors. If the subcontracts are for large items, they really constitute projects in their own right and the subcontractors must be expected to have their own project management systems for ensuring compliance with their contract commitments. Some subcontract arrangements demand that the main contractor has the right not only to inspect the progress of work, but also to examine and approve the project management systems to be employed. Please refer to Chapters 26 and 27 for an account of purchasing in general.

It may be prudent to appoint a person with specific responsibility for progressing subcontractors. This function is sometimes combined with a degree of technical responsibility, so that the subcontract liaison engineer (as he/she is frequently called) can offer constructive advice on any technical problem that might arise or agree minor concessions. A different problem is seen with the subcontracting of design engineering, when in-depth understanding of the main contractor's engineering standards and design concepts must be conveyed to the outworkers. One answer in these circumstances is to take one or more senior engineers from the subcontractor in-house for several weeks to carry out the design layouts under direct supervision.

Those engineers are then capable of returning to their own design offices and controlling the detailing and checking of production or construction drawings.

Evaluating progress

From time to time it is necessary to gauge progress in terms of the value of work achieved. This is done for two reasons:

1 For the purposes of comparing the value of all work actually finished (as defined by the estimated costs for that same work) against the actual costs incurred. Such measurements provide a clue to the efficiency being achieved and allow predictions to be made of the probable final project costs
2 For the purposes of billing the client or customer for work done. Such work measurement usually requires certification by the customer's inspectors or by an independent professional person (such as a consulting engineer for a manufacturing project or a quantity surveyor or architect for construction work).

There are many ways in which progress can be evaluated, based either on absolute quantities (e.g. tonnes of earth moved) or stated as a percentage of work completed. Percentage completion estimates made by individuals usually err on the optimistic side: one important point to remember is that a job is only 100 per cent complete when it has been passed without let or hindrance to the next scheduled activity.

Progress meetings

Most managers reading this book will be familiar with the regular meetings that take place to review progress, whether these are for sales results, for factory production management, or for a number of other specialist reasons. In project management, too, it is the accepted norm to hold regular progress meetings at intervals of a month, a fortnight, or even weekly.

The purpose of a progress meeting is to short-circuit the usual communication routes in an organization and get key people together so that progress data can be reviewed, disputes debated, and agreements reached on the spot. The chairman must ensure that commitments made are properly defined, with specific dates (not simply 'as soon as possible') tabled and with those responsible for action clearly designated. Minutes containing this information must be brief but accurate, and they must be issued promptly while the news is still hot.

That is the conventional approach. But it is possible to control progress continuously against a detailed schedule in such a way that regular progress meetings become unnecessary. Dispensing with regular 'meetings for the sake of meetings' releases valuable senior staff time for more productive work. Meetings will still have to be called to resolve problems and in other emergencies, but these will no longer be run-of-the-mill affairs, and they will be seen as occasions demanding special attention and action.

Controlling costs

The first essential in cost control is to start with an approved budget, related item by item to each job or purchase, and with the timing of expenditure calculated to agree with the project work schedules. The same computer program which carried out resource scheduling can often be used to phase the budget over time in this way. It is possible, for instance, to divide the budget over all the activities (including those for the purchase of equipment), and the computer can treat costs as a resource and produce a timescaled accumulation. When plotted cumulatively against time, project costs typically produce an *S*-shaped curve (Figure 34.10). This *S*-shaped curve is characteristic of the way in which total project costs accumulate as the project proceeds. The initial build-up is at a slow rate, as the project is gradually mobilized. The intensive working and purchasing during the middle period is followed by the later, more drawn out activities of final commissioning, drawing modifications, customer training and similar work. The final stages of the curve should be asymptotic to the total project cost estimates, but (as shown) there is a danger that the late costs will continue to edge up while commissioning and other snags are ironed out.

If project staff are effectively managed, with industrial relations harmonious, in a company which is technically and commercially competent, then the battle for control of labour costs will depend largely on the control of project progress. When a project proceeds according to the schedule (which spreads the labour budget over the planned timescale) the costs will tend to take care of themselves. But if a project runs late, total costs will also overrun and there may also be expensive contractual penalties. Time is money!

The control of materials costs is somewhat different, and depends on an appreciation of the difference between actual expenditure and committed expenditure. Put simply, if an order is placed for an item of equipment at a cost in excess of its budget, or in such a loose contractual way that the costs must eventually exceed budget, then the costs have been committed and any consideration of the actual expenditure (when the invoices arrive) must be too late for any control action to be taken. Here is another case where the use of a computer for recording and reporting results (actual expenditure in this case) is fine for historical records but valueless for control purposes.

Progress reports

In large projects it is usual (it could be a contractual requirement) for the contractor to submit regular reports of progress to his client. These are typically produced at monthly intervals, and they may also be prepared for circulation to the project manager's superiors in his own company.

The reports could be large and glossy, supported perhaps by photographs of work in progress. Whatever the case, progress should always be quantified if possible. This could mean identifying key events or project milestones in the planning, and reporting progress with reference to these. Alternatively, progress could be reported in terms of quantities (e.g. the number of drawings issued as a proportion of the total required, or the number of metres sunk in a new mine shaft during the month). Quantified reporting might be a requirement for supporting monthly claims for progress payments.

If problems have been encountered which might endanger the programme, then the report should be truthful – the client may be displeased, but he would be really angry if the problems were covered up so that they were discovered later by default. For internal company reporting to higher management, or within the project organization itself, the value of exception reporting is stressed. This means highlighting problem areas needing corrective action, rather than simply dwelling on the successes already achieved.

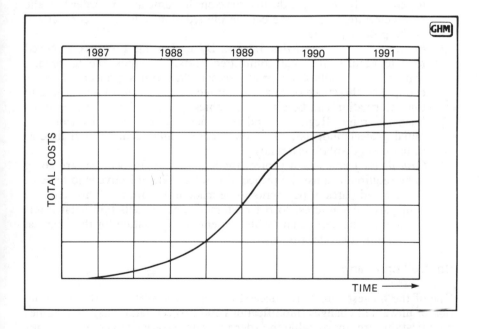

Figure 34.10 Time–cost relationship for a capital project

Reports of progress should never be divorced from consideration of the corresponding costs incurred, comparing these with the costs budgeted for the work actually achieved. Before cost reporting can take place effectively, there must be an adequate project cost accounting system which can record costs as they are incurred and allocate them to the appropriate cost codes. Thus actual costs are assembled in the records in such a way that they can be compared against budgets, either as a project total or against detailed breakdowns.

Another aspect of cost recording is the collection of committed costs, which would include the value of all purchase orders placed, subcontracts actually let, and so on. Committed costs have special value in reporting and control because they give the earliest warning of any possible over-expenditure, and it is only at or before the commitment stage that real cost control can be exercised.

There are three kinds of cost reporting in most common use:

1 *A report of total costs committed at the reporting date* (including all actual costs). This information is often plotted as a graph, building up an *S*-curve (see Figure 34.10). It is possible, and these days conventional, to plot a budgeted expenditure curve on the same axes in order that the total committed cost curve can be plotted alongside it for comparison as the project proceeds.

2 *Projected cost to completion reports.* By evaluating progress achieved to date against the total committed costs, it is possible to predict regularly the likely final project costs. Sometimes project managers extrapolate the curve of total committed costs so that those entitled to this information can be given a graphical presentation of the project's financial trend. Regularly updated, these predictions start from the initial project budgets and become increasingly accurate with time as actual costs displace estimates.

3 *Cash flow reports,* which project the amounts of finance that are going to be required against the project timescale. The objective is to forecast the size and dates of payments to be made in the future. This schedule is of particular interest to the customer, since it tells him what funds are going to be needed and when: essential information for the financial planning of a capital project.

Controlling changes

One of the biggest threats to successful project completion is the introduction of unwanted changes (modifications and project variations). Sometimes modifications are unavoidable in order to secure safety or to compensate for some unforeseen design problem. When faced with any request to make a change, it is useful to consider the nature of such change, and to classify it (if possible) under one of the following headings:

1 *Customer changes*. A change requested by the customer, although possibly disruptive, must obviously be carried out under most circumstances. A customer change has the advantage of constituting a change to the original contract, and should qualify for additional costs plus consideration for an extension to the agreed timescale. Do not under-rate the expense of such changes. Even a reduction in project scope can qualify for compensation as a result of abortive work. Under some circumstances contractors welcome customer changes, since the contractor is the sole seller, in a monopoly situation shorn of the competition that reigned when the original contract was won. If the project is running late or over budget, there might be a chance of making up some of the lost ground when the customer changes his mind over the specification. A project variation form, suitable for summarizing some kinds of customer changes, was shown earlier in this chapter at Figure 34.1.

2 *Unfunded modifications*. These are modifications which cannot be charged to the customer, where any additional costs must be set against project profit, and where any extension to the timescale has to be explained to the customer and could attract contract penalties. Unfunded modifications can be further classified as *desirable* (wouldn't it be better if . . . .?) or *essential* (unavoidable if the project is to be completed to meet the customer's original specification with safety and reliability).

The accepted method for authorizing and controlling all project changes is to appoint a change committee, comprising people with the technical ability to weigh all the consequences, and with the level of authority necessary to say yes or no to each proposal.

The control stages are as follows:

1 The proposed change is summarized on a change request form, which is given a serial number and registered by a clerk

2 The form is completed with details of all the estimated effects that the change would have on project costs and timescale, together with the reasons why the change was requested

3 The change is considered by the committee, who give their decision as soon as possible

4 The change form, authorized or not, is distributed to key project staff, including the change clerk, for action or cancellation according to the committee decision

5 The clerk follows each change request through the above stages to ensure that it is not unduly held up, and that authorized changes are added to the project programme. Typically the clerk would also follow authorized changes right through to see that new drawing issues emerge with updated revision numbers.

FURTHER READING

Lock, Dennis, *Project Management*, 4th edition, Gower, Aldershot, 1988
Lock, Dennis (ed.), *Project Management Handbook*, Gower, Aldershot, 1987

35 Quality assurance
John S Oakland

The reputation attached to a company for the quality of its products is accepted as a key to its success and the future of its employees. To prosper in today's economic climate, any manufacturing organization and its suppliers must be dedicated to never-ending improvement in quality and productivity. For industrial organizations, which are viable only if they provide satisfaction to the consumer, competitiveness in quality is not only central to profitability, but crucial to business survival. If manufacturing industry in the West is to continue, it must learn how to manage quality. A comprehensive quality policy is not merely desirable. It is essential.

THE MANAGEMENT OF QUALITY

Many day-to-day issues, often taken for granted, involve quality control in some form or another. For example, the safety and conformity of pharmaceuticals and food processing, the continuity of performance and safe operation of nuclear plants and offshore installations, the effectiveness of weapons, the relative merits and life-cycle costs of competing products, and the efficiency of services, all attest to the need for good control of quality.

The quality of products is important not only for users but also for suppliers. For manufacturers, quality deficiencies result in additional costs for inspection, testing, scrap, rework and the handling of complaints. Repeat sales and future market share will also be affected, with significant effects on profitability and survival. Quality must, therefore, be taken into account throughout all the areas of design, manufacture, marketing, and purchasing. It must be controlled in all these functions, and their activities co-ordinated to achieve a balanced corporate quality performance. Quality performance will not just happen; effective leadership and teamwork is the only sure recipe for success. Understanding commitment by senior management and explicit quality policies lead to an improvement throughout the entire organization, which in turn generates a momentum for quality improvement of products and performance.

Management must be dedicated to the continuous improvement of quality, not simply a one-step improvement to an acceptable plateau. There must be willingness to implement changes, even in the ways in which an organization does business, in order to achieve that improvement. In addition, innovation and resources are required to satisfy the long-term requirements of the customer and the company, which must be placed before short-term profitability.

A traditional approach to manufacturing is to depend on production to make the product and quality control to inspect it and screen out items which do not meet specifications. This is a strategy of *detection* and is wasteful, because it allows time and materials to be invested in products which are not always saleable. This post-production inspection is expensive, unreliable and uneconomical.

It is much more effective to avoid waste by not producing unsaleable output in the first place – to adopt a strategy of *prevention*. The prevention strategy sounds sensible and obvious to most people. It is often captured in slogans such as; 'Quality – right first time'. This type of campaigning is, however, not enough on its own. What is required is an understanding of the elements of a systematic control system which is designed to prevent defective manufacture.

DESIGN AND CONFORMANCE

In manufacturing, one of the most commonly misunderstood words is 'quality'. What is a high quality pair of shoes or a high quality washing machine? It is meaningless to make statements about the degree of quality of a product without reference to its intended use or purpose. Shoes which are to be used in the performance of a ballet would obviously have different requirements from those used in mountaineering, but both pairs of shoes may have the same level of quality, i.e. they are equally suitable for the purpose for which they were manufactured.

We define quality then as 'the degree of fitness for purpose or function', indicating that it is a measure of the satisfaction of customer needs. So the quality of a motor car, or washing machine, or a pair of shoes is the extent to which it meets the requirements of the customer. Before any discussion on quality can take place it is therefore necessary to be clear about the purpose of the product, in other words, what those customer requirements are. The customer may be within or without the organization and his or her satisfaction must be the first and most important ingredient in any plan for success.

A word of warning: the customer's perception of quality changes with time and the company's attitude to quality must, therefore, change with this perception. The skills and attitudes of the producer are also subject to change. Failure to monitor such changes will inevitably lead to dissatisfied customers. Quality, like all other corporate matters, must be continually reviewed in the light of current circumstances.

The quality of a product has two distinct but inter-related aspects:

1 Quality of design
2 Quality of conformance to design.

Quality of design

Quality of design is a measure of how well the product is designed to achieve its stated purpose. If it is low, the product will not work.

The most important feature of the design, with regard to the achievement of the required product quality, is the *specification*. This describes and defines the product and should be a comprehensive statement of all aspects of the product which must be present to meet customer requirements.

The stipulation of the correct specification is vital in the purchase of materials and components for use in manufacture. All too frequently the terms, 'as previously supplied', or 'as agreed with your representative', are to be found on purchasing orders for bought-out items. The importance of obtaining materials of the appropriate quality cannot be over-emphasized and this cannot be achieved without adequate specifications. Published standards should be incorporated into purchasing documents wherever possible.

A specification may be expressed in terms of: the maximum amount of tolerable variation on a measurement, the degree of finish on a surface, the smoothness of movement of a mechanical device, a particular chemical property, etc. There is a variety of ways in which the specification of a product may be stated and the ingenuity of man must be constrained in order to control the number of forms of specifications present in any organization.

A question frequently asked in manufacturing is, 'Why are the tolerances so tight?' This raises the question of the criteria for establishing the precision of the design, which should be predominantly the in-service performance requirements of the end product. Work on tolerance specification and relative process costs shows that movement towards tighter and tighter tolerances requires manufacturing processes which are more and more costly. This trend is represented by the manufacturing cost curve in Figure 35.1 which rises more and more steeply as attempts are made further to increase precision. Tolerances which are based only on 'idealistic design concepts' will result in extremely high manufacturing costs.

Given this relationship between precision and manufacturing costs, it follows that it is not sensible to aim for absolute perfection. The other side of the coin is the relationship between precision and market value or price. Higher precision will inevitably demand a higher market value but, owing to the reluctance on the part of the purchaser to pay more for effectively the same product, this value increases at a decreasing rate. This is represented by the market value curve of Figure 35.1 which rises less steeply as tighter and tighter tolerances are achieved. Hence the cost of trying to achieve perfection increases at an accelerating rate whilst the rate of increase in market value decelerates. The difference between the market value and the cost, the 'contribution', may be calculated and is shown as the dotted curve in Figure 35.1. The precision level at which the contribution per article is a maximum is the point at which the market dictates a manufacturer should operate.

There must be a corporate understanding of the company's quality position in the market-place. It is not sufficient that the marketing department

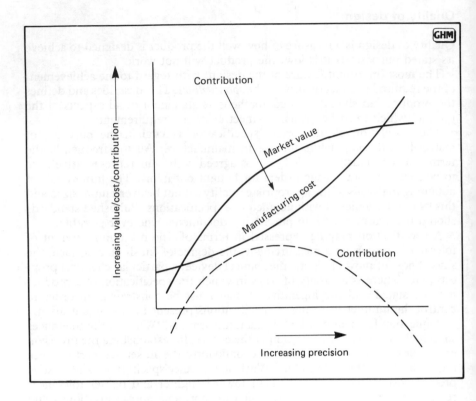

Figure 35.1 Contribution and precision of design

specifies a quality, 'because that is what the customer wants'. There must also be an agreement that the production departments can produce to that quality. Should production be incapable of achieving the desired quality, then one of two things must happen. Either the company finds a different position in the market-place or it substantially changes the production facilities.

Quality of conformance to design

This quality is the extent to which the product achieves the quality of design. What the customer actually receives should conform to the design, and manufacturing costs are tied firmly to the level of conformance achieved. Quality cannot be inspected into a product; the customer satisfaction must be designed into the production system. The conformance check then makes sure that things go according to plan.

A high level of final product inspection is often indicative of attempts to inspect in quality, an activity which will achieve nothing but spiralling costs increasing viability.

The area of conformance to design is concerned largely with the quality performance of the manufacturing function. The recording and analysis of data play a significant role in this aspect of quality, and it is here that the tools of 'statistical process control' must be applied effectively.

RESPONSIBILITY FOR QUALITY

'Quality is everyone's business' is an often quoted clichè but 'Everything is everyone's business', and so quality often becomes 'Nobody's business'. The responsibility for quality begins with determining the customer's quality requirements, and continues until the product is accepted by a satisfied customer. The management functions identifiable with this process, together with their duties (some of which are shared activities and appear under several functions) are as follows:

Senior management

1 Having a clear understanding of quality
2 Making a commitment to a defined quality level
3 Ensuring that the correct quality systems and attitudes pervade the organization
4 Supporting and encouraging the quality policy.

Marketing

1 Determining customer quality requirements
2 Knowing the competitors' quality levels
3 Setting of product specifications
4 Analysing customer complaints, sales staff reports, warranty claims and product liability cases
5 Downgrading of products for sale as seconds, etc.

Research, development and design

1 Setting of appropriate specifications (including raw materials, processes and products)
2 Setting up pre-production and prototype trials
3 Designing and specifying inspection equipment
4 Analysing some rework and rectification problems
5 Downgrading of products
6 Dealing with product complaints and warranty claims.

Production (including production engineering)

1 Agreeing specifications
2 Setting up pre-production and prototype trials
3 Training of manufacturing and associated personnel, including supervisors, foremen, etc.
4 Ensuring special handling and storage during production

5 Supervising and controlling quality at all stages
6 Arranging line or process control
7 Arranging finished product control
8 Analysing scrapped, reworked, rectified, replaced and downgraded products.

Purchasing

1 Establishing vendor rating and supplier approval
2 Procuring materials and components of the required quality.

After-sales and technical service

1 Dealing with product specification and performance evaluation
2 Evaluating pre-production and prototype product
3 Analysing customer complaints and material returned.

Stores, transport and distribution

1 Arranging special handling and storage
2 Receiving and checking of raw materials and bought-out items
3 Checking and despatching of finished products and replacement goods
4 Receiving, checking and sorting of returned products for replacement or repair.

Quality assurance

1 Dealing with quality planning
2 Providing quality advice and expertise
3 Training of personnel
4 Providing inward goods, process and finished products appraisal methodology
5 Analysing customers' complaints, warranty claims and product liability cases.

These quality tasks are represented on a 'responsibility matrix' in Figure 35.2. The shaded squares identify the main areas of responsibility for quality within the different functions of an organization.

A quality assurance system, based on the fact that all functions share responsibility for quality, provides an effective method of acquiring and maintaining desired quality standards. The quality assurance department should not assume direct responsibility for quality but should support, advise and audit the work of the other functions, in much the same way as a financial auditor performs his duty without assuming responsibility for the profitability of the company.

The actual control of quality during manufacture rests squarely on the shoulders of production management, who must ensure that all the appropriate concepts and techniques are applied to this task. Organizationally, this means that staff carrying out work to control quality must be within the production function.

A good quality management system must be documented. This usually

	MARKETING	RESEARCH & DEVELOPMENT	PRODUCTION	PURCHASING	SERVICE	STORES, TRANSPORT, DISTRIBUTION	QUALITY ASSURANCE
CUSTOMER REQUIREMENTS — determination of	X						
SPECIFICATIONS — setting and evaluation	X	X	X	X	X		
PRE-PRODUCTION and PROTOTYPE TRIALS		X	X		X		
QUALITY PLANNING							X
TRAINING — in quality and supervision			X				X
RAW MATERIALS and BOUGHT-OUT ITEMS — control of quality				X		X	
PROCESS CONTROL			X				
FINISHED PRODUCT CONTROL			X			X	
SUPERVISION OF QUALITY			X				
SPECIAL HANDLING and STORAGE			X			X	
INSPECTION —technology & methodology		X					X
DOWNGRADING	X	X					
SCRAP, REWORK, etc. — analysis		X	X				
COMPLAINTS and CLAIMS — analysis	X	X			X		X

Figure 35.2 Quality responsibility matrix

(but not necessarily) takes the form of a quality manual. The sections of a quality manual cover such matters as:

1 Who should be responsible for the functions affecting quality
2 Once installed, how the system should be reviewed to remain effective
3 The planning considerations involved in setting up the quality system
4 The documented work instructions required
5 The records that will be required
6 How defects may be found and corrected
7 Which design functions need to be controlled
8 The sort of system required for the control of documentation and changes
9 The control of inspection, measuring, and test equipment required
10 The control of purchased materials
11 The controls required during manufacturing operations
12 The requirements at final inspection
13 The sampling procedures which should be used
14 The control of non-conforming materials
15 The identification of inspection status of materials in the production process
16 The procedures required to protect and preserve product quality
17 The need for training.

The control of quality is a managerial function in which the quality of raw materials, processes and products is controlled for the purpose of preventing the release of defective goods. To meet this responsibility, organizations must use every device practicable to prevent, detect, and correct errors that occur in the steps of manufacture. This implies that, to achieve the control of quality, the variables which may affect quality and which can result from the actions of men, the nature of materials, and the performance of machines, must all be controlled.

Technologies and market conditions vary between different industries and markets, but the basic concept of quality management and the financial implications are of general validity. The objective should be to produce, at an acceptable cost, goods which conform to the requirements of the customer. The way to accomplish this is to use a systematic approach in the operating departments of design, manufacturing, quality assurance, purchasing, sales and others – nobody should be exempt. The systematic approach to quality control is not a separate science or a unique theory of quality control – rather a set of valuable tools which becomes an integral part of the 'total' quality approach.

THE COSTS OF QUALITY

Manufacturing a product which has 'fitness for purpose' is not enough. The cost of achieving quality must be carefully managed so that the long-term effect of quality costs on the business is a desirable one. These costs are a true measure of the quality effort. A competitive product based on a balance between quality and cost factors is the principal goal of responsible production management. This objective, which is highlighted in Figure 35.3, is best accomplished with the aid of competent analysis of the costs of quality. The balance works like this: as quality goes down, costs rise and (conversely) as quality goes up, costs fall.

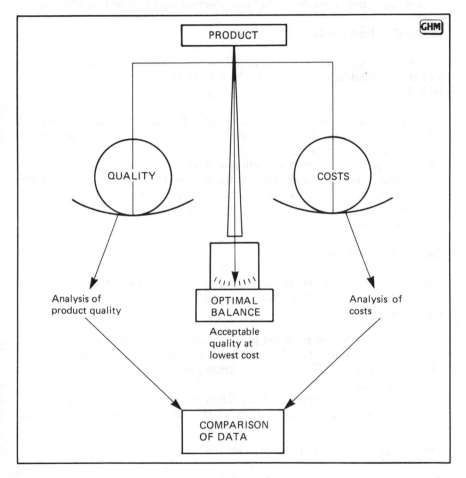

Figure 35.3   The balance between quality and cost

The analysis of quality costs is a significant management tool. It provides:

1   A method of assessing the overall effectiveness of the management of quality
2   A means of determining problem areas and action priorities.

The costs of quality are not different from any other costs, in that, like the costs of maintenance, design, sales, production, and other activities, they can be budgeted, measured and analysed.

Having specified the quality of design, the manufacturing plant has the task of making a product which matches this quality. This comprises activities which will incur costs that may be separated into the categories of failure costs, appraisal costs and prevention costs. Failure costs can be further split into those resulting from internal and external failure.

Internal failure costs

These costs occur when products fail to reach designed quality standards and are detected before transfer to the consumer takes place. Internal failure includes:

1 *Scrap* – defective product which cannot be repaired, used or sold
2 *Rework or rectification* – the correction of defective material to meet the required specifications
3 *Re-inspection* – the re-examination of products which have been rectified
4 *Downgrading* – product which is usable but does not meet specifications and may be sold as 'second quality' at a low price
5 *Failure analysis* – the activity required to establish the causes of internal product failure.

External failure costs

These costs occur when products fail to reach design quality standards and are not detected until after transfer to the consumer. External failure includes:

1 *Repair* – either of returned products or those in the field
2 *Warranty claims* – failed products which are replaced under guarantee
3 *Complaints* – all work associated with servicing of customers' complaints
4 *Returns* – the handling and investigation of rejected products
5 *Liability* – the result of product liability litigation and other claims.

External and internal failures produce the *'costs of getting it wrong'*.

Appraisal costs

These costs are associated with the evaluation of purchased materials, processes, intermediates and products to assure conformance with the specifications. Appraisal includes:

1 *Inspection and test* – of incoming material, process set-up, first-offs, running processes, intermediates and final products, and includes product performance appraisal against agreed specifications

2 *Quality audits* – to check that the quality system is functioning satisfactorily
3 *Inspection equipment* –the calibration and maintenance of equipment used in all inspection activities
4 *Vendor rating* – the assessment and approval of all suppliers.

Appraisal activities result in the *'costs of checking it is right'*.

Prevention costs

These are associated with the design, implementation and maintenance of the quality system. Prevention costs are planned and are incurred prior to production. Prevention includes:

1 *Product requirements* – the determination of quality requirements and the setting of corresponding specifications for incoming materials, processes, intermediates and finished products
2 *Quality planning* – the creation of quality, reliability, production, supervision, inspection and other special plans (e.g. pre-production trials) required to achieve the quality objective
3 *Quality assurance* – the creation and maintenance of the overall quality system
4 *Inspection equipment* – the design, development and/or purchase of equipment for use in inspection work
5 *Training* – the development, preparation and maintenance of quality training programmes for operators, supervisors and managers
6 *Miscellaneous* – clerical, travel, supply, shipping, communications and other general office management activities associated with quality.

Resources devoted to prevention give rise to the *'cost of making it right first time'*.

Direct costs of quality in relation to organization's ability

The failure, appraisal and prevention costs just described are termed the direct costs of quality. Their relationship with the ability of the organization to meet the customer requirements is shown in Figure 35.4. Where the ability is low, the total direct quality costs are high, with the failure costs predominating. As ability to meet the customers' requirements improves, by modest investment in prevention (and possibly appraisal) the failure costs drop, initially very steeply. There will be an optimum operating level at which the combined costs are at the minimum.

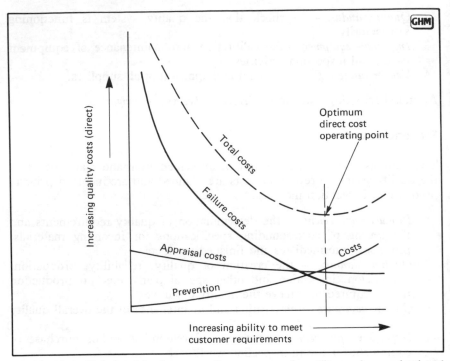

Figure 35.4 *Relationship between direct costs of quality and organizational capability*

Indirect costs of quality

So far little has been said about the often intractable indirect quality costs associated with customer dissatisfaction, and the loss of reputation or goodwill. These costs reflect customer attitude towards an organization, and they may be considerable. Figure 35.5 portrays the relationship between indirect quality costs and the organization's ability to provide customer satisfaction. It shows the effect of a developing poor reputation for quality – loss of market share.

Indirect quality costs, like direct costs, may be lowered by relatively small increases in prevention costs which subsequently reduce external failure (the cause of customer dissatisfaction and loss of reputation).

COLLECTION AND ANALYSIS OF QUALITY COSTS

Progressive managers, always anxious to reduce costs, should be looking closely at the costs involved in achieving and maintaining conformance to a predetermined design and standard of quality. Most of those who have attempted to do so have found ample scope for economies. Work in the USA and Japan by the doyen of quality management, Dr.J.Joseph Juran, shows that total direct quality costs in manufacturing lie between 4 and 15

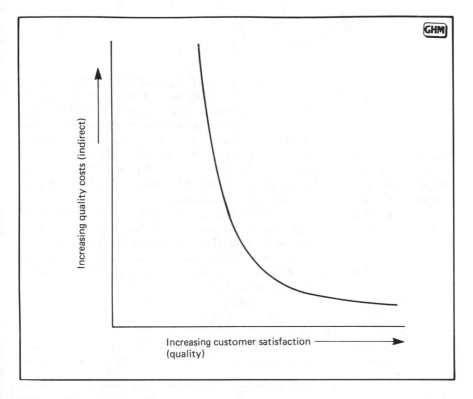

Figure 35.5 *Relationship between indirect costs of quality and customer satisfaction*

per cent of sales turnover, with an average of 10 per cent, and this makes them a subject worthy of attention. Indeed, it is necessary for effective management control that these expenditures be detailed and displayed. Yet efforts to discover the extent of quality costs prevailing in many companies have met with frustration for a variety of reasons. Quality costing tends to cut across normal accounting methods and cannot simply be secured by asking the accounting department for them. This will simply elicit the response, 'We don't keep the books that way'.

The information must be pieced together using the 'books' where possible and resorting to estimates and finding new data when necessary. The first rule of thumb is that successful quality costing involves working closely with the accountants and with the supervisors of the various departments to evaluate and estimate the costs associated with various activities.

Many useful reports may exist within a manufacturing company which aid the quality costing process. These reports might include, for example:

1 Production scrap and rework
2 Machine utilization

3   Material usage
4   Salesmen's visits
5   Analysis of credit notes
6   Analysis of repairs

A first estimate of the costs of quality in an organization can be made by combining data from such reports with estimates derived from discussions with appropriate managers and supervisors. Each assumption and estimate used in this first quality cost computation should be published in a document which is circulated to selected managers. This will produce heated arguments about whether certain costs are part of quality costs. It is unimportant whether these 'grey' items are included or not. Provided that there is consistency in including or excluding the debatable categories, the opportunities for reducing costs are not affected.

The next rule of thumb is to consider very carefully the presentation and scope for misinterpretation of the findings. A bar chart presentation is often the least troublesome. A typical one is shown in Figure 35.6. To be meaningful, quality costs must be expressed as both total costs and as some financial measure. The most generally used base is sales volume or turnover. Sales have the great advantage of being understood by all as a measure of a unit's activity. A change in the quality cost:sales ratio can be immediately converted into an effect on the organization's pre-tax profitability. For a given industry, the profit to sales ratio is one of the indices of financial success so its close relationship to the quality costs:sales ratio is another reason for favouring sales volume as the base for quality cost reporting.

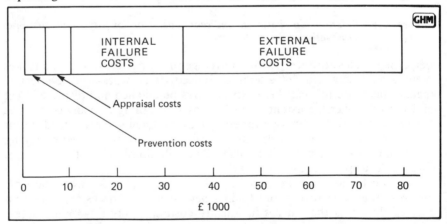

Figure 35.6   Bar chart presentation of quality costs

Ideally, quality costs should be recorded on a periodic basis on a running scoreboard. An annual once-off survey is a poor alternative. For regular reporting accountants should prepare the basic data and issue the report. This overcomes numerous problems of inconsistencies, duplication of effort, and the credibility gap created when financial data are produced from a non-financial source.

The quality–productivity link

Total direct quality costs, and their division between the categories of prevention, appraisal, internal failure and external failure, vary considerably from industry to industry and from plant to plant. Juran's work, showing that total quality costs in manufacturing average 10 per cent of sales turnover, means that in the average organization there exists a 'hidden plant', amounting to approximately one-tenth of productive capacity. This is devoted to producing scrap, rework, correcting errors, replacing defective goods and so on. Thus, a direct link exists between quality and productivity and there is no better way to improve productivity than to convert this hidden plant to truly productive use. A systematic approach to the control of quality is the best way to accomplish this.

QUALITY CIRCLES

One of the most publicized aspects of the Japanese approach to quality has been quality circles. The quality circle may be defined as a group of workers doing similar work who meet:

voluntarily
regularly
in normal working time
under the leadership of their supervisor
to identify, analyse, and solve work related problems
to recommend solutions to management.

Where possible quality circle members should implement the solutions themselves.

The quality circle concept first originated in Japan in the early 1960s, following a post-war reconstruction period during which the Japanese placed a great deal of emphasis on improving and perfecting their quality control techniques. As a direct result of work carried out to train foremen during that period, the first quality circles were conceived, and the first three circles registered with the Japanese Union of Scientists and Engineers (J.U.S.E.) in 1962. Since that time, the growth rate has been phenomenal, with an estimated one million circles, and ten million members alone in the early 1980s. During the mid-1970s, the concept spread to Taiwan, the USA and Europe, and circles in many countries became successful.

It is very easy to regard quality circles as the magic ointment to be rubbed on the affected spot and unfortunately many managers in the West see them as a panacea which will cure all ills. There are no panaceas and to place this concept into perspective, Juran, who has been an important influence in Japan's improvement in quality, has stated that quality circles represent only 5–10 per cent of the canvas of the Japanese success. The rest is concerned with understanding quality, its related costs, and the organization and techniques necessary for achieving customer satisfaction.

Given the right sort of commitment by top management, introduction, and environment in which to operate, quality circles can produce the shop floor motivation to achieve quality performance at that level. Circles should develop out of an understanding and knowledge of quality on the part of senior management. They must not be introduced as a desperate attempt to do something about poor quality.

Structure of a quality circle organization

The unique feature of quality circles is that people are asked to join and not told to do so. Consequently it is difficult to be specific about the structure of such a concept. It is, however, possible to identify four elements in a circle organization:

1 Members
2 Leaders
3 Facilitator or co-ordinator
4 Management.

Members – the prime element of the programme. They will have been taught certain problem solving and quality control techniques and, hence, possess the ability to identify and solve work-related problems.

Leaders – usually the immediate supervisors or foremen of the members. They will have been trained to lead a circle and bear the responsibility for its success. A good leader, who develops the abilities of the circle members, will benefit directly by receiving valuable assistance in tackling nagging problems.

Facilitator – the overall manager of the quality circle programme. This person, more than anyone else, will be responsible for the success of the concept, particularly within an organization. The facilitator must co-ordinate the meetings, the training and energies of the leaders and members, and form the link between the circles and the rest of the organization. Ideally, the facilitator will be an innovative industrial teacher, capable of communicating with all levels and with all departments within the organization.

Management – without whose open support and commitment quality circles, like any other concept, will not succeed. Management must retain its prerogatives, particularly regarding acceptance or non-acceptance of recommendations from circles, but the quickest way to kill a programme is to ignore a proposal arising from it. One of the most difficult facts for management to accept, and yet one which forms the cornerstone of the quality circle philosophy, is that the real 'experts' on performing a task are those that do it day after day.

Training quality circles

The training of circle leaders and members is the foundation of all successful programmes. The whole basis of the training operation is that the ideas must be easy to take in and be put across in a way which facilitates understanding. Simplicity must be the key word, with emphasis being given to the basic techniques. Essentially there are eight segments of training:

1 Introduction to quality circles
2 Brainstorming
3 Data gathering and histograms
4 Cause and effect analysis
5 Pareto (or ABC) analysis (the 80:20 rule)
6 Sampling
7 Control charts
8 Presentation techniques.

Most of these are not exclusive to quality circles or quality control and find applications in most fields of management. Data gathering, graphs, histograms, cause and effect analysis, Pareto analysis, scatter diagrams, sampling and control charts form the basis of good quality control.

Management should also be exposed to some training in the part they are required to play in the quality circle philosophy. A quality circle programme can only be effective if management believes in it and is supportive and, since changes in management style may be necessary, their training is essential.

Operation of quality circles

There are no formal rules governing the size of a quality circle. Membership usually varies from three to fifteen people with an average of seven to eight. It is worth remembering that as the circle becomes larger than this, it becomes increasingly difficult for all members to participate.

Meetings must be held away from the work area where members are free from interruptions, and are mentally and physically at ease. The room should be arranged in a manner conducive to open discussion and any situation which physically emphasizes the leader's position should be avoided.

Meeting length and frequency is variable but new circles meet for approximately one hour, once a week. Thereafter, when training is complete, many circles continue to meet weekly; others extend the interval to two or three weeks. To a large extent, the nature of the problem selected will determine the interval between meetings, but this should never extend to more than one month, otherwise members will lose interest and the circle will cease to function.

Great care is needed to ensure that every meeting is productive, no matter how long it lasts or how frequently it is held. Any of the following activities may take place during a circle meeting:

1 Training – initial or refresher
2 Problem identification
3 Problem analysis
4 Preparation and recommendation for problem solution
5 Management presentations
6 Quality circle administration

A quality circle usually selects a project to work on through discussion within the circle. The leader then advises management of this choice and assuming that no objections are raised, the circle proceeds with the work. Other suggestions for projects come from management, quality assurance staff, the maintenance department, various staff personnel and other circles.

It is sometimes necessary for quality circles to contact experts in a particular field, for example, engineers, quality experts, safety officers, maintenance personnel. This communication should be strongly encouraged and the normal company channels should be used to invite specialists to attend meetings and offer advice. The experts may be considered to be 'consultants', the quality circle retaining responsibility for solving the particular problem.

STATISTICAL PROCESS CONTROL (SPC)

Since the responsibility for manufacture lies with the production department, the responsibility for achieving the appropriate quality in manufacture must also lie with production. To fulfil this responsibility production staff must be provided with the tools necessary to:

1 know whether or not they are meeting the specifications,
2 make a correct adjustment to a process which is not meeting specifications.

Statistical process control methods, backed by management commitment and good organization, provide objective methods of process quality control.

A systematic study of a production process provides knowledge of the process capability and the sources of defective produce. This information can then be fed back quickly to the product design and production technology functions. Knowledge of the current state of a process enables a more balanced judgement of equipment, both with regard to the tasks within its capability and its rational utilization.

Statistical process control (SPC) procedures exist because there is variation in the characteristics of manufactured articles. The inherent variability of every manufactured process causes the articles produced to differ one from another. If this variability is considerable, it is impossible to predict the value of the characteristic of any single item. Using statistical methods, however, it is possible to take meagre knowledge of individual items and turn it into meaningful statements which may then be used to describe the process itself. Hence, statistically based process control procedures are designed to divert attention from individual items and focus it on the process as a whole.

SPC techniques can be used to measure the degree of conformance of raw materials, processes and products to previously agreed specifications. In essence SPC techniques select a representative, simple, random sample from the 'population', which may be a batch of finished products or the output from a process. From an analysis of the sample it is possible to make decisions regarding the quality of the whole batch or the current performance of the processor.

Types of quality data

Numerical information on quality will arise from one of the following:

1 Counting
2 Measurement.

Data which arise from counting can only occur at definite points or in 'discrete' jumps. There can only be 0, 1, 2, etc. defectives in a sample of 10 items. There cannot be 2.86 defectives. The number of imperfections on a polished surface, the number of defects in a length of cloth, the acceptability or unacceptability of the lining of a drum are discrete data and are called *attributes*. As there is only a two-way classification to consider, attributes give rise to discrete data, which necessarily vary in jumps.

Data which arise from measurement can occur anywhere at all on a continuous scale and are called *variable* data. The weight of a tablet, the length of a table, the tensile strength of a piece of rod, are all variables, the measurement of which produces continuous data.

Process variability

At the basis of the theory of process control is a differentiation of the causes of variation in quality during manufacture. Certain variations in the quality of product belong to the category of chance or random variations, about which little may be done, other than to revise the process. This type of variation is the sum of the effects of a complex interaction of 'random' or 'common' causes, each of which is slight. When random variation alone exists, no major part of it may be traced to a single cause. The set of random causes which produces variation in the quality of manufactured products may include: draughts, atmospheric temperature changes, passing traffic or machine vibrations, electrical fluctuations and changes in the operator's physical and emotional conditions. This is analogous to the set of forces which causes a coin to turn up heads or tails when tossed. When only random variations are present in a process, the process is considered to be 'in statistical control'. There is also variation in test equipment and test procedures, whether used to measure a physical dimension, an electronic or a chemical characteristic, or any other property. The inherent variation in testing contributes to the overall process variability and is always an important factor.

Causes of variation which are large in magnitude and readily identified are classified as 'assignable' or 'special' causes. For the most part, these consist of differences among: plant, processes, operators, materials and other miscellaneous factors. When an assignable cause of variation is present, process variability will be excessive and the process is classified as 'out of control' or beyond the expected random variation.

Control charts

A control chart is a form of traffic signal, the operation of which is based on evidence from the small samples taken at random during a process. A green light is given when the process should be allowed to run. All too often in manufacturing processes are adjusted on the basis of a single measurement, a practice which can make a process much more variable than it is already. The equivalent of an amber light appears when trouble is possibly imminent. The red light shows that there is practically no doubt that the process has wandered and that it must be stopped and corrected to prevent production of defective material.

Clearly, such a scheme can be introduced only when the process is 'in control'. Since the samples taken are usually small, typically less than ten, there are risks of errors, but these are small, calculated risks and not blind ones. The risk calculations are based on various frequency distributions.

There are different types of control charts for variables and attribute data. The most frequently used charts for variables are mean and range charts which are used together. Number defective or np charts and proportion defective or p charts are the most common ones in use for attributes. Other charts found in use are moving average and range charts, number of defects (c) charts, and cumulative sum (Cusum) charts. The latter offer very powerful management tools for the detection of trends or changes in attributes and variable data.

The control of variables

In the manufacture of products, having properties which are measured on a continuous scale, it is important to realize that no two items will ever be made exactly alike. The variation may be quite large and easily noticeable, such as in lengths of pieces of steel sawn by hand. When variations are very small, it may appear that the items are identical. This is in fact due to the limitations of measurement and instruments with greater precision will show differences.

Process capability

In sampling a continuous variable (for example, the diameter of a piston, the

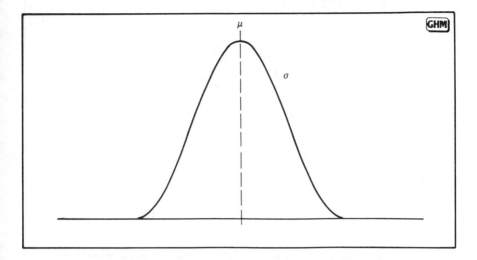

Figure 35.7   The normal distribution curve for a continuous variable

main assumption on which the statistical analysis is based is that the variable
– in this case the piston diameter) will be normally distributed - which is to
say that a graph plotted of its distribution will be bell shaped, as shown in
Figure 35.7.

The measure of accuracy or central tendency most frequently used in
industry is the *mean* or *average* (μ) of the bell-shaped process. The measure
of spread of values or precision of a process is obtained by calculating the
standard deviation, (σ).

Suppose the target of a sheet steel cutting process were 2150mm and
that the bell-shaped curve fell almost entirely within the limits 2135mm to
2165mm, then from a knowledge of the shape of the curve and the properties
of the normal distribution, the following facts would emerge:

68.3 per cent of the sheets are being produced within $\pm$ 5mm of the
average ($\mu\pm\sigma$)

95.4 per cent of the sheets are within average $\pm$ 10mm ($\mu\pm 2\sigma$)

99.7 per cent are within average $\pm$ 15mm ($\mu\pm 3\sigma$)

The usual aim in manufacturing is not to achieve every sheet with the same
length, but to obtain sheets or products within specified limits of tolerances.
No adjustment of the process is called for as long as there is no immediate
danger of falling outside the 'tolerance zone'. Ensuring that the tolerance zone
exceeds the spread of the distribution is thus an prerequisite to avoiding the
production of defectives. If tolerances have been set for the sheets of metal
at 2150 $\pm$ 20mm, then very few will fall outside the tolerances (Figure

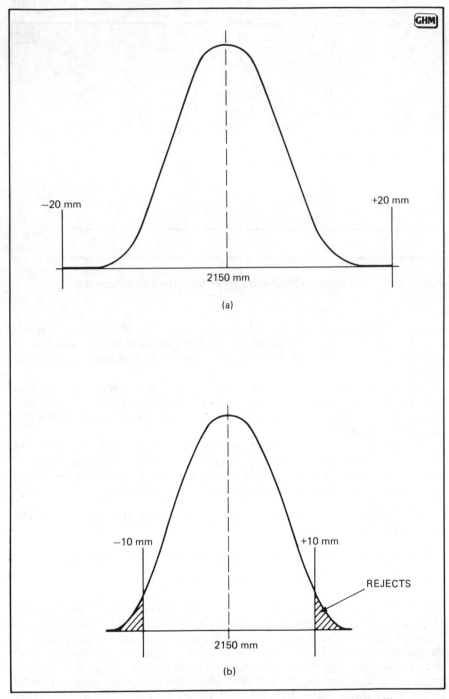

Figure 35.8 *The relationship between tolerances and process variability*

35.8a). Conversely, if the spread of the process exceeds the tolerance zone, e.g. 2150 ± 10mm, as in Figure 35.8b, then there will inevitably be reject material.

The standard deviation (σ) of a process distribution is one measure of variation. As the sample size in SPC is usually ten or fewer, a more convenient measure of spread is the sample range, which is the difference between the largest and smallest values in the sample. To control the plant or process it is necessary to check the current state of the mean and spread of the distribution. This can be achieved with the aid of mean and range charts.

Mean charts

Periodically samples of a given sample size are taken at reasonable intervals from the process when it is under control. The variable is measured for each item of the sample and the sample mean recorded on a chart. Figure 35.9 shows values of sheet rod lengths plotted on a mean chart. The sample size (n) = 5. The upper and lower action limits, and the corresponding warning limits, have been determined conventionally, as follows:

$$\text{Action limits at } \bar{x} \pm \frac{35}{\sqrt{n}}$$

$$\text{Warning limits at } \bar{x} \pm \frac{25}{\sqrt{n}}$$

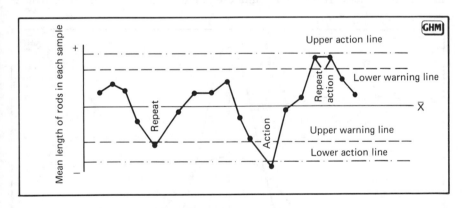

Figure 35.9 *A mean chart for controlling the length of rods*

If the process is running satisfactorily, almost all the averages of successive samples will lie between the lines marked upper action and lower action. The chance of a sample mean falling outside either of these lines is approximately 1 in 1000, unless the process has altered in some way. If a point does fall outside, the process should be stopped immediately for investigation. This does not normally suggest a serious fault (it might, for example indicate tool wear, and the need for resetting). The chances of being right in the decision to stop the process are approximately 999 in 1000.

Figure 35.9 also shows warning limits. The chance of a sample mean plotting outside these limits is about 1 in 40, or in other words it is expected to happen once in every 40 samples. When it does happen, there are grounds for suspicion and the usual procedure is to take another sample immediately, before making a definite decision about the state of the process.

Range charts

A process is only in control when both the accuracy (mean) and precision (spread) of the process are in control. A separate chart for control of the sample range as a measure of process variability is required. The range chart is very similar to the mean chart, the range of the sample (the difference between the highest and lowest values in the sample) being plotted and compared to predetermined limits. The development of a more serious fault than tool wear can lead to the situation illustrated in Figure 35.10, where the process collapses from form A to form B (e.g. due to failure of a tool). The ranges of the samples from B will have higher values than ranges in samples taken from A. If a range chart (Figure 35.11) is plotted in conjunction with the mean chart, similar action and warning lines can be drawn to indicate trouble.

This example covers the case of a process which is just capable of holding the tolerances. If one is fortunate enough to have conditions in which

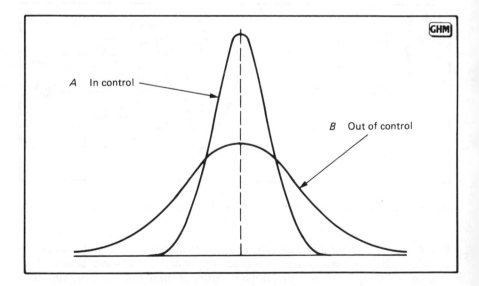

Figure 35.10   Increase of spread of a process

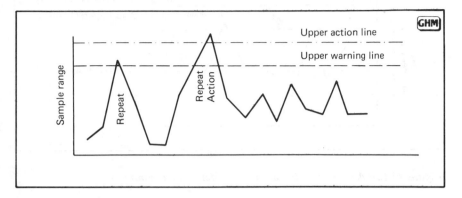

Figure 35.11   A range chart

the base of the process 'bell' is much narrower than the tolerance zone, the machine setting may be allowed to drift to a certain extent without giving trouble. Modified limits can be determined to accommodate such cases. The information for setting the control limits is obtainable in table form, making elaborate calculations entirely unnecessary. The whole process can, of course, be delegated to a micro-computer.

The control of attributes

In the case of attributes (e.g. colour, general appearance, surface finish, etc.) where each part is simply acceptable or a defective, it is clearly not possible to use the methods of measurement and control described in the previous section. Instead, a standard must be set with which all products may be compared. Control can then be exercised by means of a chart showing the number of defectives in samples of fixed size and the results plotted on a number defective or np chart as shown in Figure 35.12.

It is desirable to have a constant sample size, but this is not always possible and a chart showing fraction or proportion defective may be used. Before placing action and warning lines on a chart of this type, time should be allowed for the process to settle down. On many occasions the presentation of proportion defective in this form often gives production personnel valuable information, enabling them to reduce scrap and rework. The determination of control lines is clearly justified only when this initial effect has played its part and the process has settled down to a reasonably steady level. It is sometimes useful to insert lower warning and action limits on np and p charts. If points appear below the lower action limit, there would be only a slight chance of this happening unless there had been a significant change for the better in the process. In this case, it would be worthwhile investigating the cause of such a change, to discover how the improvement

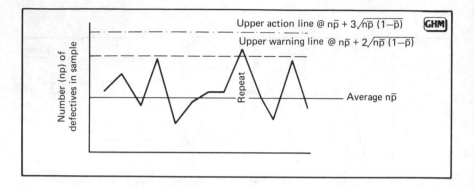

Figure 35.12   An np chart for number defective in a sample

could be made permanent. The only other reason for a point plotting below the action limit would be inaccurate inspection or defectives being passed as good.

Cusum charts

The cusum (cumulative sum) chart is a graph which takes a little longer to draw than the conventional control chart, but which gives a lot more information. It is particularly useful for plotting the evolution of processes because it presents data in a way that enables the eye to separate true trends and changes from a background of random variation. Cusum charts can detect small changes in quality very quickly and may be used for the control of variables and attributes. In essence a reference or 'target value' is subtracted from each successive sample observation and the result accumulated. Values of this cumulative sum are plotted and 'trend lines' may be drawn on the resulting graphs. If this is approximately horizontal, the value of the variable is about the same as the target value. An overall slope downwards shows a value less than the target and if the slope is upwards, it is greater.

Figure 35.13 shows a comparison of an np chart and a cusum chart which were both plotted using the same data (defectives in samples of 100 polyurethane form products). The trends, which are immediately obvious on the cusum chart, are difficult to detect on the conventional control chart.

Implementing process control

One of the first steps in any implementation programme must be the provision of education and training for:

Managers
Supervisors

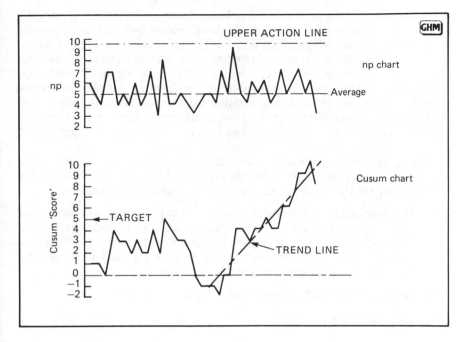

Figure 35.13   Comparison of cusum and np charts for the same data

Operators, and
Technical staff.

The courses, teaching methods, and materials used for this purpose must be very carefully selected, for much harm can be done by the insensitive teaching of 'statistics', which many people in industry find indigestible. It is possible to learn and apply excellent methods of process control without becoming immersed in heavy theoretical studies.

For the successful introduction of SPC, the training must have follow-up, which can take many forms. Ideally, an in-house expert can provide the lead through the design of implementation programmes. The most satisfactory strategy is to start small and learn through a bank of knowledge and experience. Each technique should be introduced alongside existing methods of quality control (if they do exist). This allows comparisons to be made between the new and old methods. When confidence has been built upon the results of the comparisons, the statistical techniques can take over the control of the process. Improvements in one or two areas of the company's operations, using this approach, will quickly establish SPC as a reliable tool for control of manufacturing processes.

Sometimes it is necessary to obtain help from outside sources – the prophet is rarely accepted in his own land – and many organizations can offer valuable assistance. Ideally, the people providing the initial training should also be involved in the follow-up activities, which should include 'workshop days' when specific process control and implementation problems are discussed.

The costs of introducing good methods of process control will be grossly outweighed by the savings which accrue. The inevitable reduction in scrap, rework and rectification costs, together with the increases in machine utilization and production capacity will directly repay the investment. The increased confidence and efficiency that derives from greater process knowledge will permeate the whole organization from design and purchasing staff through to sales and marketing. Moreover, the introduction of good process control methods will act as a 'spearhead' to draw through the organization many of the requirements of a good quality system.

Two of the most famous authors on the subject of quality management are Drs Walter Shewhart and W.Edwards Deming. From their book *Statistical Method from the Viewpoint of Quality Control* is taken this quotation:

> The long-range contribution of statistics depends not so much upon getting a lot of highly trained statisticians into industry as it does on creating a statistically minded generation of physicists, chemists, engineers and others who will in any way have a hand in developing and directing production processes of tomorrow.

This was written in 1939. It is as true today as it was then.

FURTHER READING

Oakland, J.S., *Statistical Process Control*, Heinemann, London, 1986
Price, F., *Right First Time*, Gower, Aldershot, 1984
Robson, M., *Quality Circles*, Gower, Aldershot, 2nd edition, 1988

36 Maintenance

E N White

The demands made upon the works department concerned with the maintenance of structures, buildings, services installations, plant and machinery, vehicles, equipment or instruments, grow with the increased dependence upon these assets in today's environment. Pressures on maintenance personnel increase as high-cost assets require efficient utilization with minimum out-of-use periods. At the same time, widening applications of new technology require added knowledge and improved techniques of servicing and repair. Clearly the role of the maintenance manager is expanded in this environment and improved systems and practices are often needed to ensure the correct degree of asset care. The manager of the maintenance function is seen as a major contributor to the 'assets management' programme of the organization and, as maintenance costs are recurring costs, he has an important part to play in controlling life cycle costs.

TEROTECHNOLOGY

The terotechnology concept grew out of a working party study on maintenance practices (see *Report by the Working Party on Maintenance Engineering*, HMSO). The scope of terotechnology is illustrated by the definition: 'A combination of management, financial, engineering and other practices applied to physical assets in pursuit of economic life cycle costs.'

This indicates the thinking behind the concept, namely, that attention to maintenance management alone would not provide the complete answer to the problems arising in the maintenance sector (or otherwise attributed to maintenance). It clearly was necessary to look at other management functions having an influence on the performance and costs of physical assets: in other words, those functions which contribute to assets management.

The broad application of the terotechnology concept is further illustrated by the note to the definition, which states:

> Its practice is concerned with the specification and design for reliability and maintainability of plant, machinery, equipment, buildings and structures; with their installation, commissioning, maintenance, modification and replacement, and with feedback of information on design, performance and costs.

659

Thus the terotechnology concept is applied both to buildings and plant, and to all stages of their life cycles from design to eventual replacement or disposal. Finally, terotechnology includes the feedback of data to produce management information.

The terotechnology system (Figure 36.1) is generally shown as a combination of management systems and communication channels which provide support for maintenance. Typical contributions include:

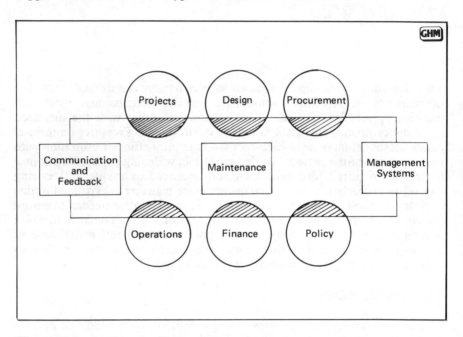

Figure 36.1   A terotechnology system

1   Design – assets designed for maintainability and reliability
2   Procurement – application of 'best buy' procurement techniques
3   Projects – provision of assets having operability and maintainability features
4   Operations – introduction of operating techniques which reduce downtime and improve care of assets
5   Finance – cost control, cost monitoring and feedback
6   Personnel – selection and training programmes for operating and maintenance personnel.

Strategies for terotechnology (new assets)

Assets management is a cradle-to-grave strategy which commences with techno-economic studies prior to an investment and proceeds through the implementation stages into the life cycle of use. During the period of use

Preparation phase
    Consideration of feedback (operations and maintenance)
    Planning (operating and maintenance policies)
    Technical forecasting
    Whole life planning
    Life cycle costing

Decision phase
    Direct participation by users (past and future)
    Preparation of procurement checklists
    Reviews of supplier profiles and quality ratings
    Specification of support systems
    Review of life plans and life cycle costs

Implementation phase
    Design (design records, design reviews, configuration control)
    Studies (maintainability, reliability, feedback from users)
    Project planning and control
    Support planning (information, training, spare parts)
    Information systems (disclosure of design data by manufacturers and suppliers)
    Preparation of documentation (manuals, specifications, training programmes)
    Maintenance planning (management systems and resources)
    Commissioning (testing, defect action, certification)
    Handover (operation, proving, final acceptance)

Utilization phase
    Operation, maintenance, condition monitoring
    Technical and costs records
    Analysis of records
    Feedback to operations, maintenance, design, procurement
    Improvements and updating (configuration control)
    Reviews of life plans and life cycle costing

Review phase
    Technical and financial reviews
    Disposal or replacement decisions
    Feedback to benefit future projects

Figure 36.2   Terotechnology considerations in a life cycle

there will be operation and maintenance strategies, designed to give best use at least cost, and eventually a replacement or disposal strategy will be formulated based on technical and economic reviews.

Asset provisioning can be considered in three phases: preparation, decision and implementation. In the preparation phase it is important to consider historical data and feedback from operations and maintenance, and to attempt whole life predictions with life cycle costs. These and other data are considered during evaluation and decision, and it is important here to consider the views of operations and maintenance management. Finally, in the implementation phase the programme includes design, installation, commissioning and proving stages until the assets are handed over to the operations and maintenance personnel. Some important considerations in these phases are listed in Figure 36.2.

The utilization phase requires the planned operation and planned mainten-ance of the asset with performance analyses and feedback of management information. Performance data should be recorded and used to benefit future designs and procurement decisions, and for frequent reviews of the whole life predictions. It is important also to apply controls to any modification programmes so that configuration control is maintained.

Finally there will be a review phase when all technical and economic factors are considered and the decision made to dispose of or replace the asset.

The terotechnology system demands that a number of 'trade-off' decisions be made. For example, the comparison between increased utilization of a new asset and the attendant costs of operation and maintenance, especially if new technologies are incorporated, can be considered in a 'trade-off' against statistics for the assets to be replaced.

Strategies for terotechnology (existing assets)

Actions to implement terotechnology in the management of existing assets may be considered in two groups – actions within the maintenance function, and actions by other departments. Each of these groups further divides into actions which follow accepted practice, and actions based on analyses of feedback.

As an example, within the maintenance function, the applications of planning and control to maintenance work is probably the first reaction of many managers to a terotechnology programme. The principles are well documented, case histories exist and planned maintenance is accepted prac-tice. However, at a later date, when the feedback inherent in a planned system is analysed, the control system may well be modified and condition-based maintenance introduced. It is the action based upon feedback which effects the most significant improvements. But it is often necessary to improve existing systems as a first step, so that meaningful analyses can be made as justification for further progress.

MAINTENANCE PLANNING AND CONTROL

Total maintenance planning embraces all activities necessary to plan, control and record all work done in keeping the assets to the acceptable standard. This includes preventive maintenance and corrective maintenance, planned overhaul, planned replacement, spares provisioning, workshop functions, repairs and renewals, plant history compilation, plant modification to facilitate maintenance, spare parts manufacture, preventive maintenance on spare parts, etc. In a fully controlled situation only the time spent on emergency work is 'unplanned' and this could well be less than 10 per cent of the available man-hours in the maintenance department. The three basic requirements of a planned maintenance system are:

1 A programme of maintenance activity for the buildings, plant and equipment
2 Means of ensuring that the programme is fulfilled
3 A method of recording and assessing results.

Figure 36.3 lists the basic elements of a planned maintenance system which is represented diagrammatically in Figure 36.4.

Assets register

A comprehensive register of all plant and buildings (or of that part of the plant and buildings which are the subject of the planning) is an essential base for the planning operation. Each asset must be positively identified in terms of:

1 Name and identity code
2 Description
3 Reference numbers – manufacturers, suppliers, etc.
4 Location – with provision for changes if item is interchangeable or mobile
5 Supplier's details.

The asset code can be numerical, or alpha-numerical and it usually replaces any existing plant numbering systems. Asset codes are given to buildings, plant, services installations and mobile plant, and are attached to the asset for identification. The codes can be preceded by other letters or numbers if required for corporate purposes (investment analyses, depreciation calculations, etc.).

Asset codes can identify asset type (PU = pump), accounts codes (primary and secondary) and physical locations. Additional numbers can be added to link the basic asset codes to spare parts, special tools, work specifications, or to drawings and manuals filed in the maintenance library. The asset code must be used on all work cards, defect reports, materials requisitions and other documentation as the key to effective communication, feedback and the compilation of history records.

Item	Description	GHM
1 Assets register	A complete inventory of the buildings and plant to be maintained	
2 Maintenance schedule	Schedules for inspection, lubrication and preventive maintenance of the items in the register. The schedules may also include planned overhaul	
3 Work specifications	Instruction cards or documents which identify exactly the tasks to be undertaken within the maintenance system	
4 Maintenance control system	A 'trigger' system which initiates the activities on the maintenance programme at predetermined intervals as listed on the maintenance schedule	
5 Resourcing schedule	A manpower allocation system to ensure that the resources are available to implement the maintenance requirements of the assets and that optimum use is made of labour	
6 Maintenance records	A record of maintenance carried out and a system for reporting to management	
7 Maintenance support organization	The organization of technical information, spare parts and tools, etc	
8 Liaison with production	An effective system of agreeing with the user management when maintenance work can be done	
9 Planned overhaul	Provisions for ensuring the planned overhaul of plant, either on a regular basis in accordance with the maintenance schedule or in response to condition monitoring	
10 Costing system	Costing procedures to ensure adequate cost control and apportionment of costs in the maintenance department	
11 Training	The necessary training of operatives and supervisors in the operation of the system	

Figure 36.3 Components of a planned maintenance system

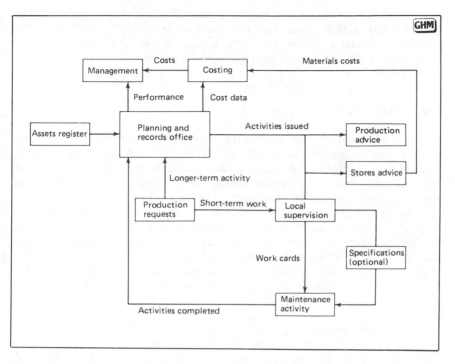

Figure 36.4   Typical maintenance control system

Maintenance schedules

Maintenance schedules list the requirements of each asset shown on the register in so far as routine maintenance is concerned. A typical schedule card indicates:

1 Grade of labour required
2 Frequency of the work to be done
3 Details of the work to be done
4 Estimated time for the execution of the work.

Where assets are identical or similar the schedules are repeated on additional cards so that a complete schedule exists for each asset. The preparation of the maintenance schedule is a skilled task. Not only must all necessary maintenance activities be identified and recorded, but the frequencies must be evaluated with availability for maintenance in mind as well as other more obvious factors including suppliers' suggestions.

Grouping work by slight adjustments of the frequencies can have a most beneficial effect on the operation of a maintenance programme.

Basic data can frequently be obtained from manufacturers' manuals but not all manuals have the necessary information, or have the information in the required form. The maintenance planning engineer must therefore use any available information as a basis but must interpret it in accordance with the local requirements and with his own knowledge and experience. (Obviously care must be taken within the guarantee period of new equipment to conform with any special instructions which form part of the supplier's guarantee.)

Maintenance controls

When the extent of the preventive maintenance activity is known, a suitable control system can be selected to 'trigger' activities at the required frequencies. Control systems range from a manually sorted card file, through automatic job-card sorter/printer devices to a system in which a computer printout represents the programme for the selected period.

If a computer-based system is used a study will be necessary, as with the introduction of any data-processing system, to determine the availability and the cost of programs, the cost of installation and the availability of computer time on any existing installation. When installing a computer-controlled system based on time from an existing computer it is necessary to safeguard the availability of that time before abandoning existing methods and accepting full computer dependence.

The functioning of a typical control system is illustrated by Figure 36.5. The 'trigger' system gives rise to the issue of the work card and materials; the detailed instructions (work specification) can be issued at the same time. At the completion of the scheduled work the documents are returned to the control office for recording and for any corrective work to be initiated.

Manpower resourcing schedule

Once the routine maintenance requirements have been determined for all items on the assets register, it will be necessary to table estimates of the man-hours needed from each grade of labour. Using these estimates, a phased schedule can be compiled by allocating the appropriate hours to the relevant dates for each planned activity. Such a chart will be made to show detailed requirements for a medium-term control period, with summaries added to extend the plan to two, three or even five years as a resource planning tool.

Manpower resourcing in the maintenance department only makes sense when full control and full support for the maintenance activity is provided. The routing of maintenance staff during work is important. Studies have shown that 15 per cent of the available working time can be devoted to obtaining instructions and making journeys to the work point in an industrial installation of average size. Full support in terms of test equipment, spare parts and technical manuals can reduce the number of journeys made to workshops or the stores.

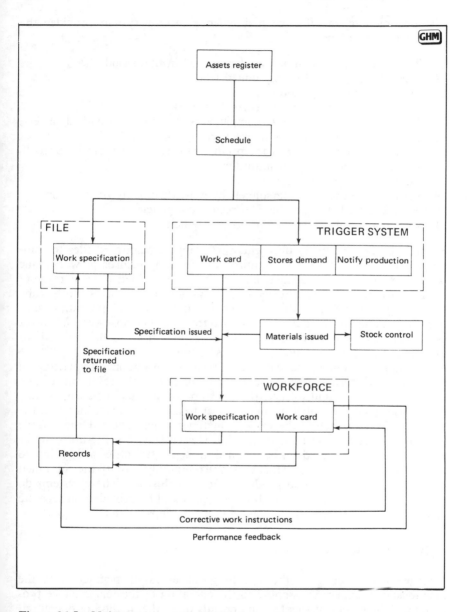

Figure 36.5 Maintenance control with trigger system

Maintenance records

The operation of an effective maintenance records system provides the following information:

1 The percentage of planned work achieved in the period
2 The ratio of planned to unplanned work
3 Downtime for the period
4 Ratio of preventive work to corrective work
5 Maintenance requirement comparisons between individual assets, between types of asset, or between groups of assets
6 Indicators for reliability of the products of particular manufacturers
7 Trends in spare parts consumption
8 Equipment failure patterns
9 Performance detail for personnel, by individual or by trade group
10 Materials used, for guidance on restocking policies
11 Indicators on possible standardization policies.

Records are kept in many different ways, ranging from card files to computer data stores. The labour required for updating records or work done is a deterrent to many managers and can only be justified if use is made of the information. If a computer is used, lengthy printout sheets can be time consuming also. However the computer is a useful tool for providing summary information on a regular basis so that trends can be observed. Whatever system of records is used, detailed investigations have to be reserved for individual situations in which the cost is justified.

In a simple system a practical level of recording is obtained by writing on the actual work card as issued. Successive workers on the asset can refer to the working history and to their predecessors' comments. This can be useful in passing on the defect history or wear trends but can precondition the worker in his approach to the work, sometimes to bad effect. Other simple systems provide for the issue of new cards each time but for up to six or ten of the completed cards to be retained in the control office at any time to give a short history record. Thus with a two-monthly activity the continued retention of six cards would produce a one-year history. These systems do not provide detailed financial records, which would be provided on separate cards or as a function of the company accounts department.

Liaison with the user

Effective liaison between the operating managers or planners and the maintenance planners is essential to the operation of the maintenance programme. The extent of this liaison depends upon the method of operation, the worst situation occurring when continuous use is required. However, in continuous process plants the awareness of the requirement for liaison is generally such as to encourage efficient planning. The most difficult situations occur where the degree of use or the volume of production fluctuates and a peak period can coincide with an intended maintenance activity.

In an ideal working environment both long-term (annual) and short-term (monthly) plans are regularly reviewed. Short-term release of assets for maintenance purposes can substantially reduce the need for weekend working by maintenance staff. Among the disadvantages of weekend working are the supervision problems, non-availability of materials, spares, and other services at weekends, and possible personnel problems as the maintenance staff tend to become socially separated.

Another important aspect of liaison is the request for service originated by operatives. When standby maintenance staff are available, requests for assistance are frequently made verbally. Formal requests include details of the fault and of the particular item requiring attention together with a priority indication, advice as to whether operations have been halted and an indication of the maintenance trade needed. Cost code information is required for any work undertaken by the maintenance staff in response to requests by operatives. Depending upon the arrangements for cost codes this allows expenditure to be allocated to particular machines, to individual buildings or to operators' stations.

Manpower allocation

In the operation of a planned maintenance system, staff of appropriate skills have to be allocated to various tasks in accordance with the requirements originated by the control office. The actual method of allocation may be a simple manual system or a computer program but this is one aspect of planning in which good local supervision often produces the best results.

A basic work programme must originate from the control system with a batch of work cards issued for the particular period. However, the issue of these cards to particular personnel is still, even in quite sophisticated systems, a matter for personnel control by the foreman/supervisor. There are many local factors which may affect the decision on sending Mr Smith or Mr Anderson on particular routes on a particular day. The system is satisfied if two men in a given labour grade are matched to a two man-day load, but with the foreman left to assign the two individuals between the jobs on the schedule.

Downtime analysis

The maintenance records must provide for an acceptable level of downtime analysis, either from the records themselves or in direct summary form from the maintenance requests (see Figure 36.6). Useful information produced in this way includes:

1 An indication of downtime per building, per machine, or if necessary per operator
2 The time taken for fault diagnosis and repair on various types of fault, or on specific machines, or by various personnel
3 Indications of the causes of breakdown.

Date	Item	Fault	Downtime (hours)
1	Main panel	Fuse blown	0.1
2	Spreaders	Latches snapped, main arm	1.3
6	Mixers	Gearbox shaft broken (spare gearbox fitted)	0.25
10	Main press	Burst pipe (guard to be fitted)	0.3
11	Water sprays	Valve burnt out (revert to manual – no spare)	0.1
15	Water sprays	New valve fitted	0.4
16	Dryer burner	Faulty electrode (spare fitted, jets cleared)	1.20
19	Compressor	Bearing collapsed (spare fitted – re-order)	3.00
22	Product lift	No upward drive (contacts cleaned)	0.4
24	Main press	Burst pipe (repaired – guard fitted)	0.5

Figure 36.6   Record of downtime

Among the useful points made clear by analysis 1 might be:

(*a*)   The true ratio of downtime to use time (to answer rumours or inaccuracies being quoted against the maintenance department)

(*b*)   The need for further investigation, by the operations or maintenance managements, of high downtime

(*c*)   The relationships between operator performance and the downtime on individual assets.

Analysis 2 may help to define:

(*a*)   High downtime areas where permanent standby repair staff or zone workshops might be beneficial

(*b*)   Suppliers to be avoided on future procurements

(*c*)   A requirement for specific training (e.g., electronic fault-finding) for maintenance workers

(*d*)   The most efficient members of the maintenance staff for the various types of work (fault-diagnosis, repairs, renewals, etc.).

Analysis 3 will define:

(*a*)   The spare parts and materials requirements for the various assets

(*b*)   Any requirement for increased operator training

(*c*)   Problems caused by variations in the product materials used in manufacturing processes.

It will be seen that downtime analysis is complementary to any cost-analysis work. However, downtime recording in detail is relatively expensive and, if economies are sought, may be applied only in certain areas rather than generally. The areas chosen may be high-risk areas containing plant which is vital to a high production figure, or may be areas of rising maintenance cost as defined by the normal cost summary, or areas in which large consequential losses could occur.

Costing

The maintenance control system must provide for accurate costing of work and materials for all maintenance activities. Work cards, materials requisitions, work instructions, maintenance requests, defect reports and time sheets must all carry significant codes to indicate cost allocations. The level of accounting practice adopted will determine the structure of the code system which may define costs in terms of:

1 Individual factories
2 Process lines
3 Individual machines
4 Separate buildings
5 Office units
6 Administration departments
7 Canteens and other special areas.

There is a wide variety of functional and physical hierarchies which may be adopted. The cost codes can conveniently be incorporated in the asset codes, so that costs to a particular asset are cross-referenced at once to the correct accounts.

COMPUTER-CONTROLLED SYSTEMS

A variety of computer systems has been developed for the assets registers, work control, manpower resourcing, stock control, maintenance accounts and, in some systems, analyses of feedback and costs. Often these are based on mainframe computers which, in industrial and commercial applications, are also employed for a variety of other purposes. This can give rise to delays, with the works department low in priority for computer time, especially when major financial programs are being run. The ideal computer system is interactive, dynamic and dedicated. 'Dedicated' means that it is always available to the maintenance department for logging vital information or for instant retrieval of data. These requirements can be met using a minicomputer or microcomputer system within the maintenance department.

Computer applications in maintenance planning and control include:

1 Recording or updating asset records or asset movements

2　Managing lubrication activities and modifying the schedules if required by feedback

3　Acting upon inspection reports from lubrication operatives

4　Managing preventive and corrective maintenance activities and incorporating emergency maintenance when necessary

5　Acting upon feedback from maintenance activities

6　Resourcing for capital works programmes

7　Acting upon feedback from emergency maintenance

8　Managing spare parts stocks.

Other uses for the computer in the maintenance department can include:

1　Management of the maintenance department stores

2　Planning and control of capital works programmes

3　Management of production tools, dies, moulds, etc.

4　Energy conservation through monitoring and control

5　Security and fire monitoring through remote sensors

6　Monitoring of automated processes or boiler plant

7　Co-ordination of condition monitoring inputs

8　Register of technical manuals and drawings

9　Register of defects and defect actions

10　Register of tests and quality documentation.

A fuller account of computer applications in maintenance management is given in White, 1979.

CONDITION-BASED MAINTENANCE

Condition-based maintenance work ordered as a result of the condition of an item as discovered during routine or continuous checking. Corrective maintenance ordered after the discovery of cracks in a wall or overheating noticed in a machine during a preventive maintenance check constitutes condition-based maintenance. Condition reports arise from human observations, checks and tests, or from fixed instrumentation or alarm systems grouped under the name 'condition monitoring'.

Benefits expected from a condition monitoring programme include:

1　Reduced expenditure on preventive maintenance

2　No unnecessary dismantling of plant items

3　Less (or less serious) breakdowns

4　Avoidance of consequential damage.

Levels of monitoring

Condition monitoring can be considered at four levels:

Level 1 Inspection monitoring based on the human sense, as in preventive maintenance schedules

Level 2 Assisted monitoring, using portable equipment

Level 3 Lubricant analysis and wear debris collection

Level 4 Fixed monitoring systems connected to alarm systems or data logging equipment.

The inspections at level 1 of the monitoring programme form part of the normal preventive maintenance schedules and are generally included in the daily and weekly activities. The inspectors are expected to use sight, hearing, touch and smell and to obtain a sensory impression of the condition of the asset. The senses may be assisted by magnifiers, viewing devices, temperature sensing strips or paints, stroboscopes, fixed instruments or indicators.

At level 2 the inspector is assisted by a range of portable test equipment to make a variety of measurements. Examples of the tests to be made and the types of equipment used are:

Measurements	*Equipment*
Speed and running time	Tachometers, counters
Electrical quantities	Test meters
Fits and tolerances	Proximity testers
Temperature	Thermography
Vibration wear	Vibration analyser or shock pulse tester
Movement	Frequency analysis
Deterioration of materials	Radiography; ultrasonics; dye penetration

This type of monitoring is applied to selected assets from the asset register for which a condition history file is built up. Quantities and characteristics are recorded and variations observed and interpreted.

Level 3 monitoring is confined to lubricated items and consists of checks on component wear together with checks on contamination of the lubricant. Wear of components is usually indicated by metal particles and debris in the lubricant. Contamination of the lubricant is detected by sampling and subsequent spectrometric analysis.

Fixed monitoring systems for level 4 monitoring range from simple remote alarm systems to comprehensive data gathering systems based on minicomputers or microprocessors. A wide variety of contact points, transducers, accelerometers, counters and other sensors are employed. Data can be transmitted directly to the display or can be electronically processed on a time-shared signal transmission system.

CAPITAL PROJECT MANAGEMENT

The stages in the life cycle of a new capital project are:

1 Conception – formulation of project idea

2   Approval – preliminary discussion and agreement on study
3   Formulation – study of various implementation methods
4   Procurement – selection of suppliers
6   Design – development of concept
7   Construction – manufacture of hardware
8   Installation – construction and installation (often run concurrently)
9   Commissioning – often referred to as 'start-up'
10 Hand-over – buyer accepts responsibility
11 Proving – testing under normal conditions.

The hand-over is sometimes partial and proving is then necessary before final acceptance by the buyer.

If time and money are to be spent in a study of a project idea, approval is sought and budgetary provisions made. This study might entail consideration of:

1   Life-cycle costs, and return on investment for the existing installation (if applicable)
2   Predictions for these after the project has been implemented
3   Predictions after implementation by the various methods available
4   The development costs, operating costs, maintenance costs and possible problems arising if new technologies are introduced
5   The possibilities for achieving similar results (technical or financial) without introducing new techniques and non-standard plant.

The operating and maintenance aspects must be fully considered and the maintenance manager consulted. The effect on maintenance investments for a separate plant or an extension of an existing plant may include increases from the sources listed in Figure 36.7.

Typical operating costs for the maintenance department will include:

1   Salaries for the additional personnel
2   Other payments for the additional personnel
3   Spares and materials costs
4   Depreciation of buildings occupied by the maintenance staff
5   Overhead charges, insurances, etc.
6   Depreciation of workshop plant, tools, spares and equipment
7   Sub-contract costs.

In the first year of a new installation additional costs may include:

1   Excessive overtime working during familiarization period
2   Increased use of vendor service engineers
3   High spares consumption caused by start-up problems and also some wastage
4   Further training requirements for maintenance staff.

In addition, low utilization rates and increased downtime are sometimes features of first-year working.

Item	Separate plant	Extension
Maintenance accommodation	New maintenance building or floor space allocation in new buildings	Possibly a zone workshop. Additional floor space if existing accommodation inadequate
Workshop plant, tools and access equipment	An appropriate proportion of the project costs based on existing knowledge	Equipment for zone workshop with an evaluation of use to be made of existing main workshop. Transport between zones
Staff requirements. Installation and commissioning	Manager or assistant manager and staff. Allocation of maintenance management and staff during installation phase to achieve familiarity with new plant	Supervisors and additional staff
Product support	The capital cost and charges arising from the documentation and training aspects	
Spares provisioning	A complete range of plant spares plus standard stocks of parts and materials	The recommended range of spares, less any adjustments for rationalization
Staff training	Requirements for special staff training, above the machine training provided by the vendor, if new techniques are introduced	
Maintenance Consultancy	Development of maintenance policy, organization of effective product support and introduction of maintenance planning	

Figure 36.7 **Effect on maintenance investments**

The maintenance budget may be 7 to 10 per cent of the total investment in an industrial installation (although actual budgets vary enormously). The approximate allocations within the maintenance budget may be:

Cost item	Allowance
Materials and subcontract	25 per cent
Personnel – total costs	40 per cent
Depreciation and overheads	25 per cent
Other items	10 per cent

The maintenance manager may request a number of studies by the project engineers. Typical studies are:

1 Study of supplier's proposals for assistance.

  (a) Should the proposals for training, etc., be accepted?
  (b) Should training and product support be subcontracted to specialist firms?
  (c) Are independent commissioning engineers to be used?
  (d) Is a servicing contract desirable?

2 Study of operating and maintenance requirements.

  (a) Will required utilization be achieved?
  (b) What numbers and grades of manpower are necessary?
  (c) Have all services requirements been clarified?
  (d) Are all aspects of maintenance support provided for?

3 Study of maintenance planning and control systems.

  (a) Is planned maintenance provided for?
  (b) Which control method will be used?
  (c) Can this plant and others be combined to justify more sophisticated planning systems?
  (d) Will a maintenance consultant be appointed?

4 Study of spare parts requirements.

  (a) Are supplier's recommendations acceptable?
  (b) Will drawings be supplied for local spares manufacturer?
  (c) Is the spares investment at acceptable level?
  (d) Are original sources of spares known?
  (e) Are spares compatible with existing stocks?

5 Study of monitoring techniques.

  (a) Is vibration analysis or other condition monitoring included?
  (b) Is remote control or centralized surveillance desirable?
  (c) Are adequate alarms provided?
  (d) Are fault diagnosis methods provided for?

GHM

	Factor	Remedy
1	Insufficient attention to reliability and life maintenance predictions during research and development phase	Improved R and D management disciplines and design analysis
2	Procurement on lowest tender without regard to possible life maintenance costs	Increased technical vetting by maintenance manager during procurement
3	Procurement without specification of and enforcement of product support requirements to be met at time of installation	Include spares, maintenance manuals, tools, training assistance, commissioning, etc.
4	Insufficient appreciation of role of maintenance by works managers, production managers, etc.	Maintenance appreciation courses for managers of associated departments
5	Failure to plan the maintenance operation and to budget accordingly	Information and training for project planners, and chief engineers
6	Ineffective communication in the maintenance hierarchy	See items 3 and 8
7	Inadequate training for maintenance staff beyond basic skills level	Maintenance training courses of wider scope (fault-finding and repair training, for example)
8	Insufficient management training for engineers required to manage maintenance departments	Training in communication, management by objectives, budgeting, control and planning, terotechnology and maintenance improvement techniques

Figure 36.8   Factors adversely affecting maintenance efficiency

677

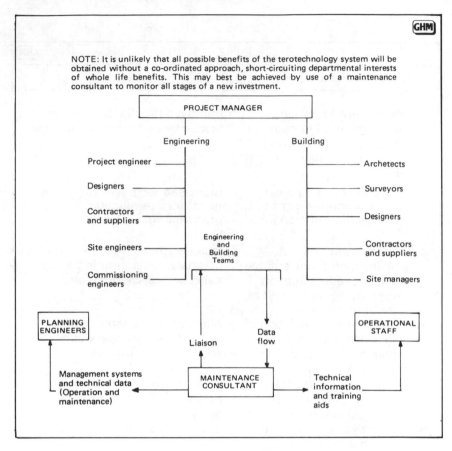

NOTE: It is unlikely that all possible benefits of the terotechnology system will be obtained without a co-ordinated approach, short-circuiting departmental interests of whole life benefits. This may best be achieved by use of a maintenance consultant to monitor all stages of a new investment.

Figure 36.9   A maintenance consultant in a project team

These and other studies set the pattern for subsequent maintenance of the plant at an acceptable utilization factor.

The total involvement of the maintenance manager in new project work is essential if effective maintenance is to be a feature of future years. If effective maintenance planning and control methods are used in an existing maintenance department, the maintenance manager should be available for participation in new work programmes.

Figure 36.8 lists a number of factors contributing to efficiency which merit attention when a capital project is planned. Possibly the most important is item 3 – the inclusion of the support items within the penalty clauses.

It is the responsibility of the project planner, with assistance from the maintenance manager or chief engineer, to set the pattern for a controlled situation in the maintenance department. The introduction of planning methods, control systems and effective supporting organizations depends upon the disciplines imposed at procurement, first, upon the planner to know what is required and to provide for it, and second, upon the plant suppliers to meet their obligations. It is the responsibility of the project planner to discipline all concerned into a successful project. This may entail the appointment of a terotechnology consultant (see Figure 36.9). His duties would include:

1   Formulation stage – evaluation of maintenance aspects of various methods and development of monitoring and maintenance policies
2   Procurement stage – vetting of contracts for maintenance aspects
3   Design and construction – monitor maintainability aspects
4   Installation and commissioning – evaluate product support activity by vendors and enforce contract provisions. Develop planned maintenance system, plant records, and technical information system. Arrange training programmes
5   Post-commissioning – finalize technical information system, review planning system, update as necessary.

FURTHER READING

Report by the Working Party on Maintenance Engineering, HMSO, London
The Terotechnology Handbook, HMSO, London
White, E.N., *Maintenance Planning, Control and Documentation*, 2nd edition, Gower, Aldershot, 1979
Planning a Preventive Maintenance Programme, White, E.N., Winnersh, Wokingham, RG11 5HX

Part Seven

WAREHOUSING AND DISTRIBUTION

37 The total cost approach to distribution

J C Gentles

The more management focuses the company's efforts on cutting distribution costs, the less successful it is likely to be in reducing the real cost of distribution. This apparent paradox is no abstract play on phrases. It explains why so many companies have diligently pruned distribution costs – in the warehouse, in stocks, in order processing and shipping – only to find that these hard-earned savings have somehow been watered down or washed out altogether by increases in other costs scattered throughout the company.

These 'other cost' increments seem to have nothing to do with distribution. They appear unpredicted and inexplicable at different times and anywhere and everywhere in the business – in purchasing, in production, in administrative systems. But when traced back to their root cause, these gremlin-like costs are not as haphazard as they may seem. They are in fact all interrelated, and they do have one thing in common. They all result from the way the company distributes its products.

Some years ago the concept of a total cost of distribution (TCD) approach to evaluating distribution alternatives was introduced. The main thesis was:

1 Classical distribution costs (transport and warehousing) do not reflect the true costs of distribution. A total view of costs from supply to delivery is more realistic
2 A total cost approach is needed to ensure that the other costs are considered and presented to management as part of a fully developed business proposal.

It is this aggregation of distribution-related costs – rather than the more commonly labelled distribution costs – that make up the *real* cost of distribution. It is these costs – rather than those usually attacked in distribution cost-cutting programmes – that represent the important and increasing drain of distribution on earnings.

The important difference between distribution costs and the real impact of distribution on the total costs and total profits of the business has now been measured and dealt with by a number of hard-headed companies. Their managements have defined this cost complex and brought it under management control by applying the total cost approach.

Since its appearance, the value of this approach has become apparent to many practitioners in the field of distribution, materials and operations management. It has grown in stature with general business management as pressures on costs and efficiency have grown in step with the increasingly difficult business environment and greater competition, especially from Japan. The feasibility of the approach has also increased with the explosion of new computer tools that have allowed managers greater access to more sophisticated techniques and large volumes of data.

Some very tangible results have been achieved:

1 A major food manufacturer, after applying effectively an assortment of belt-tightening techniques, found that TCD enabled him to make additional profits of $3 800 000, enough to add 1.7 per cent to his margin of sales

2 A major merchandiser, already enjoying the benefits of advanced distribution techniques, found that TCD was able to cut from its corporate costs an additional 2.8 per cent of the sales value of its products – while at the same time significantly improving service to customers

3 A large manufacturer of school supplies applied TCD techniques to his return of factories and warehouses and was able to cut his annual distribution costs by over $5 000 000 – a 20 per cent reduction

These success stories demonstrate why even companies which have tightened and tidied their distribution operations can still add substantially to their earnings by a frontal attack on the basic framework of their distribution decisions and practices. They have proved, too, that this broad and basic approach brings continuing returns. Once TCD has defined the most profitable pattern of distribution for the present operations of the business, management has a yardstick for measuring the impact on total profits of any proposed change.

The effectiveness of TCD is illustrated by the two following examples – each a different situation. The first traces the step-by-step process involved in the analysis of the factors that enter into a TCD analysis. The second shows how this information is exploited to provide management with the most profitable answers to some familiar distribution problems.

TCD APPLIED TO A CHAIN OF RETAIL OUTLETS

Consider first the problem which faced the management of a large company whose business comprised a widely dispersed chain of retail shops, plus a few factories which produced some of the goods sold in the shops. The company distributed its products from one centrally located warehouse. The question arose 'Would there be any profit advantage in changing to a system of local warehouses, distributed across the country?'

When the company looked at the combined cost of warehousing and transport that would result from introducing local warehouses it found that the lowest cost system was one with five warehouses. But this would increase its distribution costs by $12 900 000. Thus, on the basis of conventional analysis, the central warehouse method seemed best.

However, when the question of how alternative distribution networks would affect other costs in the company was investigated, the answers were quite different. In the first place, the most efficient warehouse system turned out to be a network of six, rather than one or five, field warehouses. And this six-warehouse system would cut total costs dramatically.

When all distribution cost related factors were considered for the six-warehouse system, increases in physical distribution costs amounted to $13 900 000 but there were substantial reductions in other costs amounting to $20 600 000. This total cost look at distribution demonstrated that the profits of the company could be increased by $6 700 000 a year.

What produced this increase which, incidentally, turned out to represent 22.4 per cent return on the investment required to design and install this field warehouse system? The answer is defined by tracing through the company the 'other cost' implication of this distribution change.

It was necessary first to decide which interrelationships were economically significant. These will differ from industry to industry, and even from company to company. To illustrate this point, and to demonstrate how these interrelationships worked out in this instance, Figure 37.1 presents graphically the impact of a number of cost factors on the profits of the company.

The calculations are quite complex, and these graphs serve only to represent schematically the kind of impact that the addition of field warehouses would have on each cost factor. To do this, each point on this series of curves shows how an optimally designed system including from one to thirty field warehouses would add or subtract from corporate profits.

Graphs (a) and (b) show quite clearly how a consideration of warehousing and transportation costs alone would lead to the answer this management was given when the conventional distribution cost analysis was made. It is the sum of these two graphs which leads to the conclusion that a five-warehouse system was the best alternative, although this would actually increase the costs of these two functions.

A further study of the company's operation showed that for each warehouse added there would be a different rate of inventory turnover, and therefore a change in inventory carrying costs. This is illustrated in graph (c). Including these charges in distribution evaluation is, of course, standard practice in many companies. But even the addition of this consideration would not have led management to the correct decision. A five-warehouse system would still appear to be the best alternative, even though economically unsound.

There are, however, other aspects of inventory which, in this case as in many others, prove to be more significant. These are shown in graphs (d), (e) and (f) of Figure 37.1 and they are:

1   Changes in the cost of obsolescence

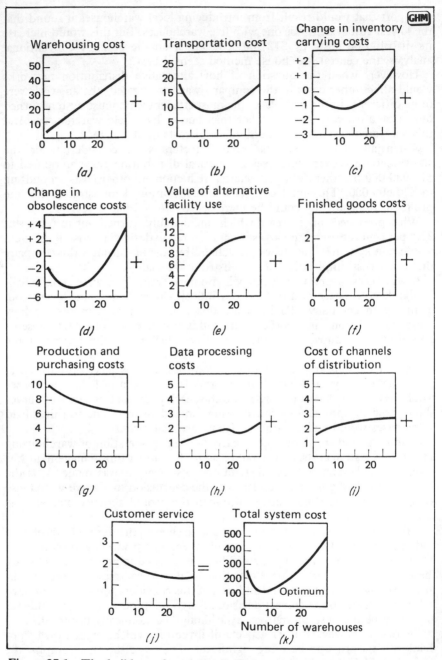

Figure 37.1   The build-up of total distribution costs
Each factor is considered in relation to the number of warehouses possible and a curve of the cost implications plotted. By adding all of these results together, a composite curve is obtained (k), which shows the total costs of distribution in relation to the possible warehouse arrangements

2 The value of alternative use of facilities
3 Changes in the cost at which the company was able to buy finished goods.

When these three cost factors were taken into account, it became clear that the original calculation had been invalid. A total cost curve that included these three factors would shift the decision to a six-warehouse system and begin to show the possibility of substantial profits from such a change.

The interaction between distribution, production and purchasing is traced in the relationships described in graph (g). The number and location of the field warehouses would directly affect the loading of the company's factories, which had a definable impact on the cost of raw materials and components and on production costs per unit.

The company's data-processing costs would, of course, also be affected by decentralizing its warehousing with the resulting need for the ability to exchange information between the field and headquarters. In this case, although there was substantial additional paper work, the cost was not great because it could all be put on the company's existing computer system. The projected results are shown in graph (h).

Finally, and most important, the impact of any proposed change in distribution has to be traced to its point of impact in the market place, for ultimately that is the measure of the effectiveness of the distribution system. Here the two critical elements are the channels through which a company elects to distribute its products, and the level of customer service it decides to maintain.

In this case, because the company distributed mostly through its own retail outlets, the channels seemed not to be an important consideration. There was, nevertheless, an important reason for following out the significance of distribution channels. As this company looked ahead, it could see the possibility that at some time in the future in might want to integrate backwards, and become more heavily involved in manufacturing. In that case, the channels of distribution factor might become more important.

In this kind of analytical exercise it is essential to consider all possible directions that company growth can take. Otherwise, a new distribution system, however profitable it may be under present conditions, might freeze the company into a set of cost factors that would rule out an otherwise profitable growth opportunity.

Customer service is the other marketing decision that plays an important role in any total cost approach. In the last analysis, any distribution system is an effort to achieve at the lowest cost the level of service to customers which will afford the company the greatest opportunity for growth in the market-place. The question is: how much does it cost to improve service to customers and how much can be gained in additional sales by that improvement? Graph (j) shows how warehousing would affect sales lost at the present level of customer service.

When all these factors are added up, they produce a single total cost curve that defines the best solution to this management problem. This is shown in graph (*k*) of Figure 37.1, which illustrates the fact that the six-warehouse system is the best alternative and one that would return a handsome profit to the company. The actual figures from this company's experience for the six-warehouse system are shown in Figure 37.2.

The graphs and figures demonstrate better than words the management meaning of the total cost approach. Study of the cost curves one at a time makes it apparent that the most profitable distribution network is somewhat different for each of these cost factors. This is what leads to distorted decisions when companies look at one, two or six of these variables and fail to consider the others. It shows the pitfalls of considering these various factors as single and static, instead of as interrelated and dynamic. Looking again at the first two graphs, it is apparent how the consideration of distribution

			GHM
Item		Gain or loss ($m)	
Warehousing	*(14.4)*		
Transport	.5		
Total distribution costs			*(13.9)*
Stocks			
Carrying costs	1.4		
Obsolescence costs	4.3		
Value of alternative use of facilities	7.8		
		13.5	
Production and purchasing			
Production and raw materials costs	.2		
Reduced cost of purchased finished goods	6.7		
		6.9	
Data processing		(.2)	
Marketing			
Channels of distribution	.2		
Customer service	1.4		
		1.6	
Total profit impact of distribution-related items			21.8
Pretax profit increase			7.9

Figure 37.2 Profit impact of distribution. Gains or losses projected by a TCD study, based on a changeover from an existing one-warehouse system to a six-warehouse system

costs alone – the cost of warehousing plus the cost of transportation – led to the conclusion that there was no change in distribution which could add to the profitability of the business. Only the final graph summing up all the interacting factors involved, demonstrates unmistakably that a shift to the six-warehouse system would be a very profitable move for management.

These graphs show, too, why difficult distribution problems could not be resolved at the operating levels of the company. In this case, a 'no-go' decision would have been valid if a traffic or transport or warehouse executive had to make that decision on the basis of the cost data available. A reduction in warehouse transport and stock costs would lead to increases in other distribution-related costs, so that total costs would be increased and this significant profit opportunity missed. Only by increasing these distribution costs could total expenses be cut and total earnings increased in this company. It is by this kind of trade-off – robbing Peter to pay Paul – that the total cost approach brings a company closer to achieving its maximum potential profit.

The total cost approach does much more than offer a one-shot solution to a perennial problem. Every time management makes a decision of any magnitude, it ought to be in a position to get an answer to the question: 'How will it affect costs throughout the company?' The total cost approach enables a company to make continuing gains by applying a yardstick to any proposed corporate venture.

Every time manufacturing management designs a new plant or develops a new production process, the pattern of distribution costs will be changed throughout the business. Similar far-flung changes will take place whenever marketing management adds a new product or a promising new group of customers. The total cost approach enables boards to define how these changes will interact with distribution to affect the total costs of the company and its total profits. It tells boards what distribution decisions need to be made to avoid the loss of potential profits, or to add to them.

TCD ANALYSIS OF A LARGE MANUFACTURING ORGANIZATION

How this is done can be seen quite readily in a case in which the TCD approach was used by a division of a large American manufacturing company. This division had an annual business of about $70m, with over 3000 customers located in every state in the USA. It manufactured and warehoused at five points across the country, shipping to customers via both rail and road.

Some of the profit questions this management posed have a familiar ring:

1   Without any major investment, can we increase our profits by changing our distribution system?
2   Can total cost be reduced by shifting some of our equipment from one factory to another?
3   Can we further reduce costs and increase profits by changing our marketing approach?

Then there were some longer-range questions to be resolved:

1 Is there any profit advantage in changing the capacity of one or more of our present plants, or perhaps building a new facility at another location?
2 Could we further improve profitability by changing our warehouse capacities or locations?

An analysis of this company's business showed quite readily what factors and interactions determined the total profit of the product delivered to the customer. Every distribution study has to start with a definition of where the customers are and the requirements they impose on their suppliers. In this case, it was vital to differentiate between the customers that had to be served by rail, and those that had to be served by road.

What was done, therefore, was to determine for each sales district what proportion of sales came into the district by rail, and how much was shipped in by road. And for each sales district data on f.o.b. as against delivered pricing were obtained.

The next step was to determine from which of the five plants and warehouses each sales district should be supplied. This involves an in-depth analysis of the production and warehousing costs per unit in each of the plants and warehouses. This analysis had to be carried out for various volume levels.

The total plant cost is built up by analysing the cost for varying production volume, inbound freight, direct labour and plant overhead. All of these cost elements will, of course, differ at each plant, even within the same company. These plant and warehouse cost calculations were made for each of the company's five facilities.

Figure 37.3 shows these total cost curves for all the plants and warehouses. These costs are, of course, different for each facility at each level of volume. Not only does each curve start at a different point – reflecting different overhead costs – but the rate of increase is also different, reflecting different variable cost factors at increasing volumes for each of these installations.

With some further analyses it became possible to determine, for every unit of product and for all individual customers, the profit contribution under all possible combinations of production and distribution. The problem that remained was to put all these possibilities together into a single solution that would maximize the company's total earnings.

To introduce these data into the computer called for the use of a non-linear programming technique. The technical aspects of this are not important for its managerial implications. What is significant is that the technique does exist, that it does work, and that once the program has been written, this kind of distribution problem can be solved in minutes. TCD was able to provide a very precise answer to each of the questions confronting the management of this company. At the time when the exercise was carried out, it involved a comparatively lengthy process using a mainframe computer. With the advent of such techniques on personal computers this approach is more readily available, and offers

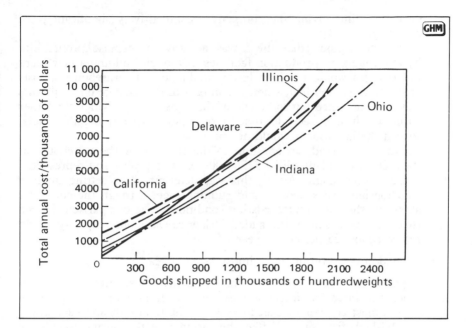

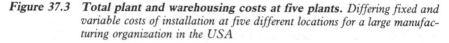

Figure 37.3 **Total plant and warehousing costs at five plants.** *Differing fixed and variable costs of installation at five different locations for a large manufacturing organization in the USA*

greater scope for more detailed analysis. Summarizing the results for this case:

1 By rearranging the company's distribution pattern and making appropriate shifts in production and warehousing loads, it was possible without any change in facilities to increase the company's profits by $984 000 a year.

   The largest ingredient in this change came from reduced materials cost at $400 000, with warehouse savings contributing $366 000. Direct labour savings in the plants added a further $114 000. What is particularly interesting is that transportation, so often overstressed in distribution decisions, turned out to contribute only $108 000 to the total profit improvement package.

2 Additional savings of $360 000 could be effected by shifting equipment from one plant to another. To determine this, it was necessary to develop new production cost curves for alternative arrangements of equipment and run these through the computer, comparing them with the most profitable way of using the equipment as presently located.

3 Additional savings of 894 000 a year resulted if about half of the customers could be persuaded to shift from road to rail delivery. These reduced costs were either added to earnings or passed on to the

customer, thus giving the company a competitively significant price advantage.

4 It was determined that there was no way to increase profitability by any change in production facilities. Although building a new plant in Michigan would result in lower production and warehousing costs amounting to $450 000, when the impact of this change on total costs was seen, it turned out to be one of those instances in which the 'other costs' which have been discussed more than offset any possible gains, so that the investment would not be a wise one.

5 On the other hand, an addition to the capacity of the warehouse at their Delaware plant added $150 000 a year to profits and represented a sound investment. Again, this was determined by setting up new warehousing cost schedules and running them through the computer alongside the costs under existing conditions. The comparison showed that the investment in the added Delaware warehouse capacity would return almost 25 per cent a year.

The total addition to profits was almost $1.5m a year.

The point that needs to be understood is that these profits could not have been generated by decisions based on the insight or the experience of even the most competent executive. Only the total cost approach could have established, for example, that the earnings of the business could be increased by supplying its customers in South Dakota from a plant in Ohio rather than from a much nearer facility in Illinois. Yet when total profits were calculated, this turned out to be an element in the most profitable use of the existing facilities of the company.

Similarly, only a total cost calculation provided the background for estimating the return on investment that could be expected from building a new facility in Michigan. It is this ability to put precise price and profit tags on each pattern of alternatives that makes the total cost approach such an effective management tool.

WHEN THE TOTAL COST APPROACH SHOULD BE USED

1 When the company makes a significant change in its business strategy (for example, going direct versus selling to wholesalers)
2 When the size of the company changes significantly
3 When new businesses or products are added to the distribution system
4 When the company's geographic mix of shipments changes appreciably
5 When one or more of the main elements of cost changes significantly (for example, transportation costs or inventory holding costs)
6 When five to ten years have passed since the last evaluation
7 When any of four symptoms appear

   (a) Inventories that turn slowly
   (b) Poor customer service
   (c) Interwarehouse shipments
   (d) Premium freight charges.

38 Warehouse operation management

Ken Firth

It cannot be said that warehousing has been a source of great inspiration to many who are in senior management positions in the UK. Too often the designing, building, running and controlling of warehousing systems have been left to individuals who have been passed over in their original speciality or those who are approaching retirement and have been given a supposedly less demanding job to do. Such lack of enthusiasm is unfortunate because standards of warehouse efficiency can have far-reaching effects upon customer relationships. A succession of missed delivery dates or failure to deliver a complete order influence a customer's thinking far more than the helpfulness of the salesman who originally obtained the order. Yet warehousing, as one of the least glamorous aspects of business systems, is often starved of resources in both physical and human terms.

Effective warehousing depends, like every other aspect of management, upon a clear understanding of what the system is expected to provide, a carefully outlined plan, and, above all, continuously supervised implementation with great attention to detail. The rewards can be considerable to small and large organizations alike, for although small systems cannot take advantage of economies of scale they often have a considerable edge in their ability to give personal service through effective managerial control.

MODERN WAREHOUSING

The seeds of modern warehousing operations were planted more than a hundred years ago with the arrival of crude but effective pallet handling equipment. Such equipment enabled human beings to move modular loads around manufacturing systems which would otherwise have been difficult to handle. It was not until the advent of a machine which could lift modular loads one above the other as well as undertaking horizontal movement – in the form of the early fork-lift truck – that the revolution in warehousing method took place. This started in the 1930s and accelerated very rapidly during the Second World War when the United States Army recognized that such machinery could revolutionize their approach to logistics. The result was that warehouses ceased to be multi-storey affairs convenient to manhandling, and modern wide-span steel or concrete portal frame building predominated. Since that time there has been unremitting design effort to improve the lifting height capacity of fork-lift trucks and at the same time reduce operating aisle widths. The objective is to take maximum advantage of building cube in storage areas in the knowledge that building costs per cubic metre provided are substantially reduced between the heights of 6 to 15 metres for steel portal frame construction, thereby reducing the total systems cost. The term 'total systems cost' is important because in the context of the firm it is that cost which must be minimized – there are many circumstances where it is justifiable to increase warehousing operating costs *provided that greater savings are made elsewhere*.

The basis of modern warehousing is the principle of load unitization, combined with the remaining principles of materials handling which are:

1   Utilization of cube
2   Minimization of movement
3   Flow effectiveness
4   Safety and security

all at lowest total systems cost.

LOAD UNITIZATION

Although load unitization is commonly associated with pallets and fork-lift trucks, there are many other forms of unit-load, large and small, which have an important place in warehousing and should not be overlooked – tote pans for small components is a typical example.

The underlying concept of load unitization is the combining of like products together on some regularly dimensioned load board or in a container, so that they may be more easily handled by man or machine. Simple though this idea is, it is only too easy to make mistakes either through not recognizing the problem involved or not being sufficiently stringent in applying the standards laid down.

Two main aspects have to be considered: on the one hand, the physical characteristics of the product including its protective packaging; and on the other, the most suitable kind of load board or container for the job in hand. When stacking products upon flat timber pallets it is preferable to have rectilinear packages or cases which are modular to the pallet dimension (to avoid loss of utilization) and at the same time ensure that the packages will 'brick' together in layers (Figure 38.1) thereby ensuring good load stability. A package which is a perfect cube is undesirable because it cannot be bonded to its partners except by the use of strapping, stretch wrapping or other devices. Packages which overhang pallets are to be avoided because they offer scope for damage.

In building up suitable pallet patterns it is usual to construct the largest feasible load because by so doing movement is reduced. The achieving of this objective is conditioned by many constraints, typical of which are the

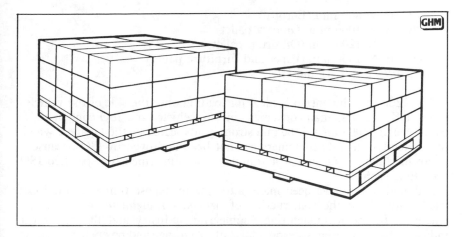

Figure 38.1 **Cartons stacked on pallets.** *Here are two ways of stacking cartons on pallets. The wrong way (left-hand pallet) allows each pile of cartons to sway and topple. The right way prevents this, because the cartons are arranged in an interlocking pattern*

overturning moment of the load, crush loading of packages, the height available within the warehouse, the lifting heights of the fork-lift trucks available, and by the type of vehicle on which the pallet might be transported.

Arriving at the best answer is often a matter of compromise but where overturning or lack of stability is the problem there is a variety of devices, such as layer interleaving, strapping, stretch or shrink wrapping which help to overcome the difficulty. In cases where pallets and loads need to be stacked simply one on top of another, it is essential to perform stacking tests over a period of weeks to be certain that progressive stack collapse will not take place. Such factors as poor carton design or high humidity may well cause stacking problems which cannot immediately be detected.

Once a unit load has been properly formulated and agreed it should be recorded – if necessary the pallet stacking pattern can be printed on the outer package so that anyone not familiar with the correct procedure can ensure uniformity.

In specifying a pallet board or other form of container it is fundamental to obtain a piece of equipment which will provide least cost over its *total life cycle*. The lowest available price is no criterion if the pallet has not been adequately designed and tested to carry its specified load, has poor resistance to damage and is difficult to repair. The attempts to achieve the ideal pallet have caused more contention than any other aspect of materials handling and a great lack of standardization prevails. However, the International Standards Organization (ISO) supported by the British Standards Institution (BSI) and other overseas organizations have slowly approached the problem of standardization of through-transit pallets and dimensional and testing standards for the following sizes exist:

1200 mm × 800 mm (Europal)
1200 mm × 1000 mm (Grocery pallet)
1200 mm × 1200 mm (Oil drum pallet)
1200 mm × 1800 mm (Paper and furniture pallet)
(BS 2629 Parts I, II and III.)

The 1200 mm dimension is ideal for loading onto the side of flat vehicles in the UK, but less than convenient in box vehicles and ISO containers. A pallet size of 1100 mm × 1100 mm strongly advocated by the Japanese which fits perfectly into ISO containers has not been approved by ISO because it is not modular to 600 mm × 400 mm × 400 mm which is a specified ISO unit dimension.

Although there have been many attempts to depose timber as the most used material for the construction of pallets, no adequate substitute has emerged. In the manufacturing engineering industry and the motor car industry there has been widespread use of metal cage and box pallets because of their longevity under the arduous conditions in which they have to work and because of their ability to handle awkward shapes. Many experiments have been made with plastic pallets but their cost, which has escalated since the oil crisis, tends to restrict their use to applications where hygiene is a paramount consideration. The most used pallet in the UK is the 1200 mm × 1000 mm 4-way entry perimeter-based pallet built to BSI specification 2629. A typical life of a wooden pallet in the UK is said to be three to five years, but whether this is entirely due to fair wear and tear is a matter of some doubt. In recent years the company GKN/Chep has introduced a pallet pool exchange system which is worthy of consideration, particularly in the case of companies which have large pallet populations which have to be transported over great distances and where collection of empty pallets and their return is a costly and haphazard operation.

Loaded pallets should not normally be stacked one on top of another to a height greater than six times the minimum base dimension of the pallet and only then when the condition of the pallet and its environment have been carefully checked. For example, uneven floors can create stacking difficulties and lightly loaded pallets stacked outside can be affected by high winds. In adverse conditions the height of stack should be reduced to four times the minimum base dimension or less. There can, of course, be exceptions to such rules, but any change should be agreed with the appropriate safety representatives.

The care given to unit-load design must never be relaxed and what is certain is that as handling and storage sophistication increases, so must the attention to design. There are endless examples of mechanized equipment being damaged or rendered useless through permitting off-dimension or damaged pallets into the system.

Thus the establishment of the unit-load is the first step towards efficient warehouse operation and from this follows good use of the cube, minimization of movement, creating effective flow, all in keeping with high standards of safety and security at lowest total systems cost.

UTILIZATION OF THE WAREHOUSE CUBE

The price of new warehousing can vary quite considerably due to a variety of factors, such as location, degree of refinement of the facilities, negotiating variations and the economic circumstances prevailing. In mid 1986 a figure between £200 and £300 per square metre would not be regarded as unusual for a warehouse building complete with a limited amount of office space and services to an acceptable standard. At such prices it is common-place to discover that the building and building services can account for as much as 40 per cent of the operating cost of the warehouse. Support for the conservation of warehouse space has long been given by UK fork-lift truck manufacturers who have always been at the forefront in the design of narrow aisle height lift trucks. Very narrow aisle equipment which will lift 1.5 tonne loads at heights of 12 metres is readily available for use in gangways only 1.5 metres wide. Whilst reducing gangway widths is an obvious approach to the reduction of space costs, increased lift height is less so. Although increased lift height means more expensive equipment, which is also more expensive to maintain, the disadvantage is offset by the fact that as single-storey warehouses increase in height up to about 15 metres their costs per cubic metre reduce because most of the cost is in the roof and floor. This fact can produce a favourable trade-off of building cost against equipment costs.

The efficient storage of palletized loads demands a careful analysis of the stockholding profile within the warehouse. That is to say stockholding data must be collected for each product stored and the products then ranked in order of quantity of pallets held. A ranking of products in order of through-put quantities should also be prepared. Although the determination of the method of storage is primarily dependent upon the quantities by stocks held, throughput must be taken into account when considering what handling equipment is most suitable. Once the stockholding analysis has been completed it is useful to make use of the simple flow diagram (Figure 38.2) to produce a list of alternatives which require consideration. It is important to remember when using the diagram that whilst all pallet profiles can be randomly stored by individual pallet, they are not all readily block stackable. The objective of using the flow chart is to eliminate looking at unnecessary alternatives.

Pallet block storage

The concept behind palletized block storage is that of stacking pallets one above the other and in rows of suitable depth. The rows of pallet stacks (identical product within each row) are assembled side by side to form a three-dimensional matrix (see Figure 38.3).

The operation of this simple idea can become very complicated in execution due to various constraints which can be placed upon the system and the warehouse manager may find that because of such constraints, his

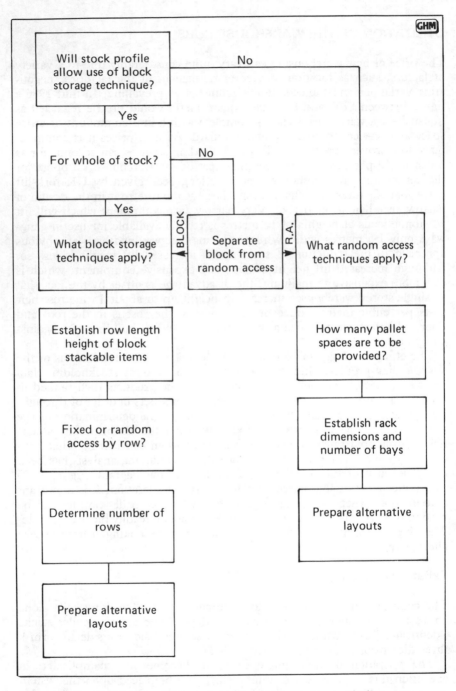

Figure 38.2 Simple flow diagram for palletized bulk storage design

Figure 38.3   Simple block stack

warehouse is badly utilized so that only 60 per cent of the pallet spaces provided can actually be occupied by physical stock.

This may be brought about by one or more of the following ways:

1   Insufficient stock per line item to form significant blocks of storage which leads to 'honeycombing' and loss of cube
2   The use of a fixed location system for products when there is a significant variation between maximum and minimum stocks. This problem may be solved by arranging rows of product randomly within the warehouse at the expense of a control system
3   Incorrect row length. At first glance the longer the row length the better the relationship between stack and gangways. Space utilization is, however, a function of stock quantity and time of occupancy which the following simple calculation illustrates:

Twelve stacks of pallets are received into stock and the stockholding time is estimated at 24 days. The options on row length vary between 1 row of 12 stacks and 12 rows of 1 stack, but each row has the same area of gangway allocated to it.

For example, if we say that a stack occupies 2 m^2 and the gangway allocation per row is 3 m^2 the area required for a single 12 stack row will be 27 m^2. Moreover, the area will be unavailable for re-use until the last pallet is withdrawn after the 24th day has elapsed (unless double handling or poor stock rotation is accepted). The 'cost' incurred amounts to 24 × 27 m^2 = 648 m^2 days. A 2-row approach will mean that half the original space occupied will be free for use after 12 days and the space cost incurred will be only 540 m^2 days – a significant saving. The calculation for all the variants is as follows:

1 row	648 m^2 days
2 rows	540 m^2 days
3 rows	528 m^2 days
4 rows	540 m^2 days
6 rows	588 m^2 days
12 rows	780 m^2 days

In this instance a row length of 4 pallets is the most suitable choice. It is possible to conceive that this approach to row length can be considerably refined to optimize warehouse block storage layouts

4   Limitations upon stacking height. With simple block stacking i.e., pallets simply supported one on top of each other, the problem is usually that of overturning or crush-loading. This may be prevented by the use of 'drive-in' racking which has all the attributes of block storage whilst separating pallets vertically (Figure 38.4)
5   First in, first out rotation of stock can be a problem with simple and drive-in block storage systems – the best situation usually achievable is rotation by row. When stock is fast moving this does not present a significant problem, but where it is, the options of pallet live storage,

Figure 38.4 Drive-in racking

or powered mobile storage offer a solution. Although in both cases the storage equipment cost is high, it usually represents a very small proportion of the total warehouse cost and there are many instances where the higher space utilization provided by more sophisticated systems has resulted in a favourable trade-off against building costs

6 The orientation of block storage in relation to building dimension and the choice of direction of entry of forks into a four-way entry pallet can materially affect the number of pallet spaces available to the system and also the distances travelled by handling equipment. Care has to be taken that the advantage of increased storage does not interfere with flow or impede managerial control.

Palletized random access storage

Virtually every form of palletized random access storage is associated with a racking system and this means, almost by definition, some form of adjustable pallet racking. A random access system, as its name implies, enables individual access to every pallet, the disadvantage being that a record of what is held in each location has to be kept, on a first in, first out basis by product, and this can be prone to error. The other significant advantage of adjustable pallet racking is that it enables the utilization of headroom in a building to levels beyond what is generally acceptable for simple block storage systems (provided the building headroom is available), but when used in conjunction with counterbalance or even reach fork-lift trucks can be wasteful of space due to the relatively poor aisle space to rack occupancy relationships. This disadvantage can be largely offset by the fact that the pallet space utilization factor can be as high as 95 per cent and when this factor is coupled with a very narrow aisle system at heights above 6 metres can result in cube utilizations considerably superior to most block storage systems (see Figure 38.5). The significant exception is powered mobile storage which combines the attributes of both block and random access and can result in total cube utilization factors in excess of 45 per cent.

The simplest way of overcoming the problem of error in placement and removal of stock is to operate a ticket system which indicates the co-ordinates of the pallet position but at the same time incorporates a random check digit which the operator has to record in placement or retrieval. If a mistake occurs this can be rapidly checked by the pallet location control clerk and the fault rectified before too much time has elapsed. The most recent development of stock location validation is the fitting of microprocessors complete with optical character readers, which enables the driver to scan the pallet ticket and pallet location to ensure a match. In the event of a mis-match, a warning signal is activated.

Damage to racking and products caused by fork-lift trucks for whatever reason is a cause of concern. The problem can be alleviated by proper training of fork-lift drivers and what is probably more important by adequate supervision once the training has been completed. It is wise to ensure that racks conform to an approved standard – that of the Storage Equipment

Figure 38.5   Very narrow aisle racking and truck

Manufacturers Association is appropriate to the UK – and equally important that the racks are competently constructed and fixed to the floor. In the event of damage the section of the rack affected should be unloaded and remain so until the faulty component has been replaced. Efforts to straighten thin section members once distorted should be avoided.

High-bay pallet silos

The high-bay pallet silo (Figure 38.6) serviced by automatic storage and retrieval machines (stacker cranes), although by no means a new concept, is arousing increased interest for storage and warehousing throughout the world, nowhere more so than in the USA and Japan at the present time. The reasons for this surge of interest are many but a common one is the economy of not having to move storage off an existing site as more and more companies become locked into urban sprawl with limited expansion potential. In addition, computing and control expertise has developed rapidly over the past ten years, both in the area of data and power transmission, which has greatly increased availability potential of such installations. It must be admitted that the cost justification in straightforward accounting terms can be difficult, but it is becoming increasingly apparent that this kind of equipment can offer tremendous advantage in terms of speed and accuracy of operation, which in turn makes levels of service available previously unachievable with manually operated systems.

MINIMIZING MOVEMENT

Movement, like warehouse space, is a costly resource whether it be attributable to man or machine. Whilst there are many techniques available to reduce movement time, both in a system and an equipment sense, all can be rendered virtually useless if adequate standards are not imposed. A guaranteed way of ensuring continuing poor performance is to overman when setting up a new warehouse – this may be due to the absence of standards or over-anxiety by management in their desire to have a smooth start. Another failing on start-up is to do so without adequate commissioning of equipment or sufficient staff training. Warehouse planning should ensure that a start-up happens slowly and, for preference, at a quiet time of the year. Synthetic time study data for a variety of materials handling tasks is available which can be used until properly measured work standards can be applied.

Order selection tends to be the function of warehousing which is the most intensive user of labour per unit of throughput, although in some applications where load modularization and quality control is extensive goods receiving comes a close second.

An order-picking system (see Figure 38.7) should be organized in such a manner that a fully representative range of stock is presented in the smallest possible area conducive with safe operation, so that orders may be selected accurately at the service level demanded, avoiding unnecessary stockouts and without excessive movement from reserve to forward

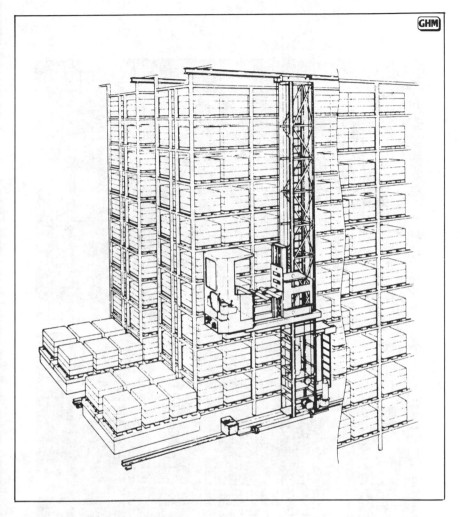

Figure 38.6   High-bay warehouse

location. Because many of these requirements are not complementary to one another, the process is essentially one of compromise making use of the minimization techniques appropriate to the stock and throughput profiles of the picking systems under study. The techniques available are:

Functional separation

This is the consideration of whether to keep order picking and reserve storage in separate parts of the warehouse or physically integrate the two. In simple terms the answer depends on the ratio of stock held in reserve to that

705

Figure 38.7   Second level order-picker

required in order picking. If the difference is large there is scope for holding the reserve in a specialized stockholding area making use of a space efficient storage system, such as high-rack stacking or drive-in storage. Where there is a closer relationship say 3 to 1 or less, it may be more sensible to hold reserve pallets in racking immediately above the order-picking pallets (see Figure 38.8). Where reserve is a very small proportion, it may be feasible to pick from multi-level locations.

Popularity

An analysis of movement within an order-picking store usually demonstrates that 80 per cent of the visits to collect product are made to only 20 per cent of locations. Knowledge relating to these products makes it theoretically possible to arrange them in a layout which minimizes the movement of the order pickers. However, there are many factors which can render the concept infeasible such as congestion, seasonal changes, promotions and cataloguing difficulties, which suggest that caution should be exercised in implementing the idea. Popularity is probably of greater significance when related to a fixed-location palletized bulk loading operation or when the popularity of products can be accurately monitored by computer, provided that in the latter case the stores movement involved does not result in confusion.

Batching orders

In instances where there is a large range of products covering a wide area and the average quantity picked per order is small, it is often feasible to group orders together to be picked upon a single circuit of the order-picking area. Inevitably, some sorting must be carried out either on circuit or at the end of the pick and the justification is that the cost of sorting is less than the cost of the time saved by reduction of movement around the system. The objective should be to maximize an order-picker's carrying capacity for a given picking circuit within the limits of the capability of his handling equipment. This means that if on average single orders satisfy this requirement a batching system is usually unnecessary. There are occasions where a batch pick of a day's work is brought to a forward area and sorted, the advantage being that this serves as an automatic checking device provided that balancing errors in sorting have not occurred.

Zoning

Some large warehousing systems, notably mail order, find it advantageous to divide their systems departmentally according to merchandise or by size and throughput of product. The procedure is to route orders only to the departments concerned with the specific items required on an order and bypass the rest. Order pickers are allocated to each department or zone and only pick in that restricted area, passing the order and goods to the next department featured on the picking list, until the full order has been picked. This not only reduces pedestrian movement but permits specialization.

Figure 38.8   Base location order-picking system

Randomization of order-picking locations

By far the majority of order-picking systems in the UK are based upon fixed-location systems which allow the order picker to learn, relatively quickly and easily, the location of any product. Some wide-ranging systems with constant obsolescence and introduction of lines find it impossible to cope with fixed location because when a bin has been vacated by an obsolete product, it has to be replaced by another. This automatically randomizes the locations, but does keep the picking face within reasonable dimensions. A consequence is that the location is first identified by its co-ordinates and secondly by its contents. Control of such systems has to be comprehensive because a product once lost is hard to find; additionally the administrative complexity is so great that computer control is almost mandatory.

Goods-to-picker techniques

It is not unknown for an order picker to have to walk more than ten miles a day to complete his or her work, which clearly may take up more than 50 per cent of the time available. Provide a system where the goods can be brought to the picker and that time is available to carry out a lot more picking (see Figure 38.9). With a few exceptions, the endeavours to achieve such savings in a case-picking environment have met with little success – the costs, under UK conditions, have been greater than using conventional techniques. On the other hand, the potential for using goods-to-picker techniques on small components applications appears considerable because these are often associated with high range and relatively small volumes and weights per line item. The control complexity required to implement an effective system should not be underestimated.

It is important to remember that whilst one or more of the above techniques may be used to reduce movement in an order-picking system,

Figure 38.9   Horizontal carousel order-picking machine

their applicability can only be determined through a full understanding of the system's requirements.

PAPERWORK REDUCTION

Research into the control of order-picking systems has shown that up to 30 per cent of the time spent by an operative can be in handling paperwork. This can be brought about in a wide variety of ways, for example, looking up stock locations records and stock cards, documentation that is difficult to read, products listed in a sequence which does not follow the picking run, etc. It is interesting to observe that the incidence of such problems is being greatly reduced by the introduction of the small computer into warehousing which operates in real-time on either a stand alone basis or as part of a distributed system. The speed and accuracy of a well-designed warehouse computer system rapidly repays the effort and expense involved and can do much to improve customer and staff relationships. It is little wonder that more and more companies are embarking upon such projects.

RECEIVING AND DISPATCH

A surprising number of relatively well-planned warehousing operations have been let down to some extent by the inadequacy of their load/unload facilities. One possible reason is that the work involved, particularly in the receiving area, is dependent upon external factors which can be difficult to control. Much more attention is being paid to how products are being delivered into the warehousing system, how well they are modularized, whether the quantities delivered relate accurately to the order quantity, whether the delivery is on time, early or late, and how easy is a consignment to identify. Lack of attention to these and many other factors has caused delays, congested loading docks and made unnecessary work, but above all inadequate communication has contributed to the confusion. More and more VDU terminals are being located directly at the receiving point. Their ability to identify rapidly whether a consignment is required, to state what level of quality control should be applied and to show where the product is to be located, contributes greatly to the smooth and accurate flow of product.

The other major factors are what areas should be allocated to the function, how many loading bays are required, whether the loading bays should have raised docks or be at floor level, and whether the loading and unloading areas should share common facilities or be separated. Their determination is by analysis of the products and their load unitization, the quantities throughput per unit of time, the kinds of transport entering and leaving the systems and other criteria such as the value of the product together with safety and environmental requirements. The increasing costs of transportation are forcing some companies to consider more carefully ways of turning around vehicles

Figure 38.10   General view of a modern loading bay

to maximize productivity, nowhere more so than in Japan, where much attention is being paid to the mass-loading of different types of road vehicle.

Figure 38.10 is a general view of a modern loading bay.

CONCLUSION

Much remains to be done to improve standards of warehouse operation and management but evidence exists that over the past ten years the business world has become increasingly aware of the importance of the subject and how its costs need to be controlled. This may be seen by looking at the organizational and managerial changes which have been taking place in specific companies and recognition that formalized training in the skills of distribution are a necessity. Slowly universities and other educational establishments are beginning to introduce courses which will enable future warehouse managers to establish status which equates with that of more fashionable disciplines. Perhaps by the year 2000 a new professional class will be fully established.

FURTHER READING

Burton, J.A., *Effective Warehousing*, 2nd edition, Macdonald & Evans, Plymouth, 1979

Gattorna, J. (ed.), *Handbook of Physical Distribution Management*, 3rd edition, Gower, Aldershot, 1983

39 International trade

R C Horsley, Dennis Lock and Avison Wormald

It is obvious that any company seeking to achieve a high volume of sales will want the biggest possible market. In this context, export markets are ignored at the company's peril. The benefits of high export performance are well known: in addition to contributing to the balance of payments, higher levels of production should reduce product costs and thus improve the company's competitive position nationally and internationally, increasing profitability and creating jobs.

Unfortunately, export markets often seem remote and involve dealing in strange languages, currencies and national customs. Moreover, every new exporter is faced with a formidable barrier of unfamiliar legislation, documents and jargon. This chapter explains some of the terms associated with international trade and outlines the procedures involved.

FREIGHT FORWARDING AGENTS

The use of a good freight forwarding agent will be found invaluable to any company sending goods overseas by any mode of transport. Indeed, the agent can usually advise on the best method of transport to adopt in any individual case. One very important aspect of a forwarding agent's services is found when relatively small consignments are to be despatched. The agent is often able to 'consolidate' such small loads from a number of clients to form one bulk consignment – probably large enough to fill a container or large vehicle and so effect economy of scale.

Although they are termed 'forwarding agents' the role of such organizations is not confined to the loading of goods on to a ship, aircraft, train or road transport vehicle. There is an equally important function to be performed at the receiving port or airport and at international frontier customs posts. The agents operate international networks, either with their own offices overseas or through collaboration with other agencies. Using telex and other rapid forms of communication the progress of all consignments is monitored and necessary action taken to minimize delays at customs offices and to ensure smooth transfer from aircraft to truck, from ship to rail, and so on.

When road transport is used, agents are more likely to be able to make up bulk loads which quality for TIR treatment. This is an arrangement where the total load is sealed within a vehicle or container by customs officials before the start of a journey. A *transport international routier* (hence TIR) carnet is issued. Provided that the seals are not broken by unauthorized persons, the whole load enjoys a smoother passage through overseas customs formalities. Such loads are identified by the familiar TIR plates fitted to the backs of trucks.

(Within the European Economic Community (EEC) there is an arrangement that simplifies trans-border customs formalities which is known as the Community Transit System. Details of this, and of the TIR system, are obtainable from any local office of HM Customs and Excise.)

Unfortunately, any operation connected with the consignment of goods seems to be weighed down with complicated documents. Some of these are outlined in the following section of this chapter. Here again the freight forwarding agent's experience will be found useful – invaluable in the case of companies new to exporting.

DOCUMENTATION

This section describes the main documents involved in international trade.

Bill of lading

A bill of lading is used when goods are transported by ship. It records the contract entered into between the shipper and the exporter and, when sent to the buyer, acts as a document of title enabling him to claim the goods. An example is shown in Figure 39.1.

The principal information given on the form includes:

1 The bill of lading serial number
2 The name of the shipping company
3 The name of the ship
4 Port of loading
5 Port of unloading
6 The final destination
7 A description of the goods
8 The number of separate cases, with their weights, dimensions and markings
9 Name and address of the exporter
10 Name and address of the consignee, or the organization to be notified when the goods arrive (in the latter case the bill is made out to 'order')
11 A statement indicating whether or not freight charges have been prepaid, and where such charges are payable.

The document is usually prepared as an original plus one or more copies, the number of such copies (all called 'originals') being shown on each one. The exporter signs each original. The set customarily comprises two or three such originals, each of them signed by the ship's captain or his agent when

GHM

BILL OF LADING FOR COMBINED TRANSPORT SHIPMENT OR PORT TO PORT SHIPMENT

Shipper

B/L No

Shippers Ref.

F/Agents Ref

LOX LINE

TRANSATLANTIC

Consignee

Carrier

Notify Party/address

Place of Receipt

Vessel and Voy. No.

Place of Delivery

Port of Loading

Port of Discharge

Marks and Nos. Container Nos.	Number and kind of Packages, description of Goods	Gross Weight Kg	Measurement M³
	ABOVE PARTICULARS AS DECLARED BY SHIPPER		

Movement

Freight and Charges

Received by the Carrier from the Shipper in apparent good order and condition (unless otherwise noted herein) the total numbers or quantity of Containers or packages or units indicated ✱ stated by the Shipper to comprise the Goods specified above for Carriage subject to all the terms hereof (INCLUDING THE TERMS ON THE REVERSE HEREOF AND THE TERMS OF THE CARRIER'S APPLICABLE TARIFF) from the Place of Receipt or the Port of Loading whichever applicable to the Port of Discharge or the Place of Delivery whichever applicable. In accepting this Bill of Lading the Merchant expressly accepts and agrees to all its terms conditions and exceptions whether printed stamped or written or otherwise incorporated notwithstanding the non signing of this Bill of Lading by the Merchant

Ocean Freight Payable at	Place and date of issue
Number of Original Bills of Lading	IN WITNESS of the contract herein contained the number of originals stated opposite have been issued, one of which being accomplished, the other(s) to be void.
★Total No. of Containers/Packages	For the Carrier.

Figure 39.1 A bill of lading

GHM

JARDINE
AIR CARGO

A MEMBER OF THE MATHESON GROUP OF COMPANIES
Jardine Air Cargo (UK) Ltd
Service House, Great South West Road
Feltham, Middlesex. TW14 0PL
Telephone 01-890 1355 Telex 934157
Reg. office 3 Lombard Street, London EC3
Reg. no. 445388 England
IATA International Air Cargo Consolidator VAT Reg. no. 244 2321 96

CRN | Invoice No./HAWB
Booked Flight Date | Date
Destination Airport | Master Air Waybill No.
Departure Airport | Import Waybill No. (if transit)

Shipper | Shipper's Reference | Shipper's Account No.
Consignee | Destination A/c No. | A.L.A. c No.
Tel | Telex | Branch | Wt
Attention of | Consignee's Order No. | Final Destination
Invoice to (if different) | Also Notify | Rotation No.
Tel | Telex | Air Consignment Waybill
NOT NEGOTIABLE

Nature and Quantity of Goods, including any Special Packing Instructions	Method of Packing	Marks and Nos	Dimensions or Volume	Rate Class	Chargeable Wt lbs kgs	Rate lbs kgs £	Charge £	No. of Packages	Actual Gross (Weight kgs)

Documents Accompanying Air Waybill | Total | Total-in figs | Total-in figs

Amount of Insurance - in words | Amount of Insurance - in figures

Shipper's COD - in words | Shipper's Declared Customs Value

Shipper Certifies that the particulars on the face hereof are correct and agrees to the conditions on the reverse hereto.
By Broker/Agent

Carrier Certifies above described goods were received for carriage SUBJECT TO THE CONDITIONS ON THE REVERSE OF COPIES 1 & 8 the goods being in apparent good order and condition except as noted hereon.

We hereby certify that the goods described were despatched by AIRCRAFT/SERVICE NO on the to the above mentioned Consignee and that a copy of this Consignment Note was forwarded to the Consignee by the Aircraft carrying the goods.

Note of any Advance Payments | Executed on
Cash Received
Date | Signature of Issuing Carrier or its Agent
Signature

7 Airline VAT

At Originating Branch | 8 Sub Agents Comm | This invoice is VAT rated at Zero

PREPAID CHARGES £	VAT Code	COLLECT CHARGES £	VAT Code
2 Transit Charges		2 Transit Charges	
3 FOB		3 FOB	
4 Misc		4 Misc	
5 Cartage		5 Cartage	
Sub Total Comp. Chge		6 Sub Agents Disb.	
1 Air Freight		7 COD	
8 Airline Charges		8 COD Fee	
Pre VAT Total		1 Air Freight	
0 VAT			
9 Total		9 Total	
PAYABLE BY SHIPPER		PAYABLE BY CONSIGNEE	

All Business is undertaken subject to the Company's Conditions (on the reverse of Copies 1 & 8) which incorporates the 1981 Standard Trading Conditions of the Institute of Freight Forwarders Limited.

Payment is due now, unless credit terms have been agreed, remit to: HEAD OFFICE, Service House, Great South West Road Feltham, Middlesex, TW14 0PL

TATE BUSINESS FORMS LTD

1. ORIGINAL - FOR THE SHIPPER

Figure 39.2 Air waybill *(Jardine Air Cargo (UK) Ltd)*

the goods are loaded. The exporter is given all the originals, and these are known as the 'negotiable' copies, any one of which can prove title to the goods. One original, negotiable copy is sent to the buyer or his agent, by a route faster than the sea voyage, to enable him to clear the goods at the destination port. Other non-negotiable copies are prepared and kept for control and record purposes.

Air waybill

Goods sent by airfreight are consigned under cover of an air waybill (alternatively spelled airwaybill or airway bill). An example is shown in Figure 39.2. Air waybills do not have the same commercial significance as the bills of lading used for shipping, but they are used to control and progress the passage of goods and to identify the consignment through all its stages. In this context, the air waybill number is the vital reference. When a freight forwarding agent is used, he provides his own air waybill forms (known as house air waybills) and it is one of these which is shown in the example.

Commercial invoice

The commercial invoice is an invoice prepared on the exporter's usual invoice form, for despatch to the buyer as a claim for payment. However, additional copies will have to be supplied for use by the customs authorities at the exporting and importing ends of the journey. Requirements vary from one country to another, and some require additional information to be given, such as import licence number, the commission payable to local agents, details of freight and other charges, and so on.

Special requirements

Some countries add their own demands to the weight of paper needed. Such extra forms may include a *certificate of origin*, where the exporter declares the country of origin of the goods, and a *consular invoice*, which is a form of invoice dictated by (but not provided by) the government of the importing country. An example of a form which combines both of these documents is shown in Figure 39.3. The exporter usually has to obtain his own stock of such forms from a printer.

Certificate of insurance

Where the exporter arranges insurance, cover should be obtained for all stages and operations of the journey. The certificate, which must not be dated *after* the date of the bill of lading, air waybill or similar evidence of despatch, is sent to the buyer with the shipping documents.

717

GHM

In accordance with Nigerian Government Notice 1989 of 1970.

FEDERATION of NIGERIA

Combined Certificate of Value and of Origin and Invoice of Goods for
Exportation to Nigeria

C.16

CERTIFICATE OF VALUE

I, ...

of . . . .

*Manufacturers/Suppliers/Exporters of the goods enumerated in this invoice amounting to . . . .

hereby declare that I have the authority to make and sign this certificate on behalf of the aforesaid *Manufacturers/
Suppliers/Exporters and that I have the means of knowing and I do hereby certify as follows: —
(1) That this invoice is in all respects correct and contains a true and full statement of the price actually paid or to
be paid for the said goods, and the actual quantity thereof.
(2) That no different invoice of the goods mentioned in the said invoice has been or will be furnished to anyone.
(3) That no arrangement or understanding affecting the purchase price of the said goods has been or will be made
or entered into between the said exporter and purchaser or by anyone on behalf of either of them either by way of
discount, rebate, compensation or in any manner whatever other than as fully shown on this invoice.

CERTIFICATE OF ORIGIN

(1) That all the goods mentioned in this invoice have been wholly produced or manufactured in . . . .

. . . .

(2) That all the goods mentioned in this invoice have been either wholly or partially produced or manufactured in

. . . .

(3) That as regards those goods only partially produced or manufactured;
(a) the final process or processes of manufacture have been performed in . . . .

(b) the expenditure in material produced and/or labour performed in . . . . calculated
subject to qualifications hereunder, in the case of all such goods is not less than 25 per cent of the factory or works
costs of all such goods in their finished state. *See note below.

(4) That in the calculation of such proportion of material produced and/or labour performed none of the following
items has been included or considered: —

Manufacturer's profit, or remuneration of any trader, agent, broker or other person dealing in the goods in their
finished condition; royalties; cost of outside packages, or any cost of packing the goods thereinto; any cost of conveying, insuring, or shipping the goods subsequent to their manufacture.

Dated at . . . . this . . . . day of . . . . 19 . . . .

(Signature) . . . . (Signature of Witness) . . . .

Note: (1) The person making the declaration should be the principal or a manager, chief clerk, secretary, or responsible
employee.

(2) The place or country of origin of imports is that in which the goods were produced or manufactured and, in
the case of partly manufactured goods, the place or country in which any final operation, has altered to any
appreciable extent the character, composition and value of goods imported into that country.

(3) In the case of goods which have at some stage entered into the commerce of, or undergone a process of
manufacture in a foreign country, only that labour and material which are expected in or added to the goods
after their return to the exporting territory, shall be regarded as the produce or manufacture of the territory
in calculating the proportion of labour and material in the factory or works cost of the finished article.

(4) *Delete the inapplicable.

Enumerate the following charges and state whether each amount has been included in or excluded from the above selling price to purchaser :—	Amount in currency of exporting country	State if included in above selling price to purchaser
(1) Cartage to rail and/or docks . . .		
(2) Inland freight (rail or canal) and other charges to the dock area, including inland insurance . . .		
(3) Labour in packing the goods into outside packages . . .		
(4) Value of outside packages . . .		
(5) If the goods are subject to any charge by way of royalties . . .		
(6) OCEAN FREIGHT . . .		
(7) OCEAN INSURANCE . . .		
(8) Commission, establishment and other charges of a like nature . . .		
(9) Other costs, dues, charges and expenses incidental to the delivery of the articles		

State full particulars of Royalties below:—

Form No. 731 Published and Sold by FORMECON SERVICES LTD., Gateway, Crewe, CW1 1YN, England. Tel: 0270-587811 Telex: 36560 Eurofs G.

*Figure 39.3 Combined certificate of value, certificate of origin and consular
invoice (in the format specified by the Nigerian Government)*

GHM

INVOICE No.............................   .... 19..........
                                                         (Place and Date).

State   INVOICE of   consigned
here
general
nature or   by   of
class of
goods   to   of

             to be shipped per

             Order Number............................ ....
                                                       Country from which consigned.

Country of Origin.	Marks and numbers on packages.	Quantity and description of goods.	Selling price to purchaser.	
			@	Amount

Figure 39.3 (concluded)

TERMS OF TRADE USED IN INTERNATIONAL BUSINESS

(with acknowledgement to the International Chamber of Commerce)

Ex works

'Ex works' means that the seller's only responsibility is to make the goods available at his premises (i.e. works or factory). In particular he is not responsible for loading the goods in the vehicle provided by the buyer unless otherwise agreed. The buyer bears the full cost and risk involved in bringing the goods from there to the desired destination. This term therefore represents the minimum obligation for the seller.

Free carrier (named point)

This term has been designed to meet the requirements of modern transport, particularly such 'multimodal' transport as container or 'roll on – roll off' traffic by trailers and ferries. It is based on the same main principle as FOB except that the seller fulfills his obligations when he delivers the goods into the custody of the carrier at the named point. If no precise *point* can be mentioned at the time of the contract of sale, the parties should refer to the *place* or *range* where the carrier should take the goods into his charge. The risk of loss of or damage to the goods is transferred from seller to buyer at that time and not at the ship's rail. 'Carrier' means any person by whom or in whose name a contract of carriage by road, rail, air, sea or a combination of modes has been made. When the seller has to furnish a bill of lading, waybill or carrier's receipt, he duly fulfils this obligation by presenting such a document issued by a person so defined.

FOR/FOT

FOR and FOT mean 'free on rail' and 'free on truck'. These terms are synonymous since the word 'truck' relates to the railway wagons. They should obviously only be used when the goods are to be carried by rail.

FOB

FOB means 'free on board'. The goods are placed on board a ship by the seller at a port of shipment named in the sales contract. The risk of loss of or damage to the goods is transferred from the seller to the buyer when the goods pass the ship's rail.

FOB airport

FOB airport is based on the same main principle as the ordinary FOB term. The seller fulfils his obligations by delivering the goods to the air carrier at the airport of departure. The risk of loss of or damage to the goods is transferred from the seller to the buyer when the goods have been so delivered.

FAS

FAS means 'free alongside ship'. Under this arrangement the seller's obligations are fulfilled when the goods have been placed alongside the ship on the quay or in lighters. This means that the buyer has to bear all costs and risks of loss of or damage to the goods from that moment. It should be noted that, unlike FOB, an FAS transaction requires the buyer to clear the goods for export.

C & F

C & F means 'cost and freight'. The seller must pay the costs and freight necessary to bring the goods to the named destination, but the risk of loss of or damage to the goods, as well as of any cost increases, is transferred from the seller to the buyer when the goods pass the ship's rail in the port of shipment.

CIF

CIF means 'cost, insurance and freight'. This arrangement is the same as C & F but with the addition that the seller has to procure marine insurance against the risk of loss of or damage to the goods during the carriage. The seller contracts with the insurer and pays the insurance premium.

Freight/carriage paid to

Like C & F 'freight or carriage paid to. . .' means that the seller pays the freight for the carriage of the goods to the named destination. However, the risk of loss of or damage to the goods, as well as of any cost increases, is transferred from the seller to the buyer when the goods have been delivered into the custody of the first carrier and not at the ship's rail. It can be used for all modes of transport including multimodal operations and container or roll on – roll off traffic by trailers and ferries. When the seller has to furnish a bill of lading, waybill or carrier's receipt, he duly fulfils this obligation by presenting such a document issued by the person with whom he has contracted for carriage to the named destination.

Freight/carriage and Insurance paid to

This term means the same as 'freight or carriage paid to. . .' but with the addition that the seller has to procure transport insurance against the risk of loss of or damage to the goods during the carriage. The seller contracts with the insurer and pays the insurance premium.

Ex ship

'Ex ship' means that the seller shall make the goods available to the buyer on board the ship at the destination named in the sales contract. The seller has to bear the full cost and risk involved in bringing the goods there.

Ex quay

'Ex quay' means that the seller makes the goods available to the buyer on the quay (wharf) at the destination named in the sales contract. The seller has to bear the full cost and risk involved in bringing the goods there. There are two ex quay contracts in use, namely 'ex quay (duty paid)', and 'ex quay (duties on buyer's account)' (in which the liability to clear the goods for import are to be met by the buyer instead of by the seller). Parties are recommended always to use the full descriptions of these terms, namely 'ex quay (duty paid)' or 'ex quay (duties on buyer's account)' otherwise there may be uncertainty as to who is to be responsible for the liability to clear the goods for import.

Delivered at frontier

'Delivered at frontier' means that the seller's obligations are fulfilled when the goods have arrived at the frontier – but before the 'customs border' of the country named in the sales contract. The term is primarily intended to be used when goods are to be carried by rail or road but it may be used irrespective of the mode of transport.

Delivered duty paid

While the term 'ex works' signifies the seller's minimum obligation, the term 'delivered duty paid' when followed by words naming the buyer's premises denotes the other extreme – the seller's maximum obligation. The term 'delivered duty paid' may be used irrespective of the mode of transport. If the parties wish that the seller should clear the goods for import but that some of the costs payable upon the import of the goods should be excluded – such as value added tax (VAT) and/or other similar taxes – this should be made clear by adding words to this effect (for example, 'exclusive of VAT and/or taxes').

DUTY

Duty is the money payable by a consignee to the appropriate authorities before he can take receipt of goods imported or released from bond. Types of duty as far as the UK is concerned are:

1. Customs duty
2. Excise duty.

Customs duty

Customs duty is money payable by a consignee or his agent to the customs and excise when goods are imported from abroad. It includes all levies and charges due in respect of the Common Agricultural Policy of the European Economic Community (EEC) which are collected on behalf of the EEC and paid to Brussels. The amount of duty payable is shown in the customs tariff.

Customs duty ad valorem

Ad valorem duty is expressed in the customs tariff as a percentage of the CIF value of the goods (invoice value, plus freight, plus insurance and plus other dutiable charges).

Customs duty specific

In this instance the amount of duty payable is expressed in the tariff as a sum levied against the quantity of goods (for example, 1.645 European units of account per hectalitre).

Payment of customs duty

Duty can be paid immediately by one of the following methods:

1 cash
2 guaranteed cheque
3 banker's draft

Payment may be deferred.

Deferred payment of customs duty

Importers or their agents are allowed to defer payment of certain customs duty and other charges for a 30-day period subject to the lodgement of adequate security (usually a guarantee from the consignee's bank that the money will be available when called for by direct debit). Excise duty and sums payable in respect of underpayment on previous imports cannot be deferred.

Duty free goods

No customs duty is payable on the following types of goods:

1 Those shown in the customs tariff as 'free'
2 Those imported into the UK from the EEC and supported by the correct EEC documentation. (Note: To obtain release of these goods

723

duty may have to be paid on deposit if the documentation is incorrect or incomplete).

The expression 'duty free' is used by customs to imply that customs duty has, in fact, been paid. In regulations affecting customs warehouses the expression is used constantly and care must be taken to avoid the misconception that duty was not liable at any stage of the import.

Excise duty

This is a UK tax on certain imported goods and the money collected remains with the Exchequer. The money is payable by a consignee or his agent to customs and excise when goods which attract the duty are required to be released from customs control. The amount of duty payable on such goods is shown in the tariff and the types of goods which attract such duty are:

spirits
wines
beers
tobacco
hydrocarbon oils
cigarette lighters.

Excise duty payment

Excise duty cannot be deferred and must be paid before release of the goods by customs. Payment can be in cash, by guaranteed cheque or by bankers draft (as described for customs duty above), or by deposit in advance to enable customs to maintain a gross payment account.

Excise duty – gross payment accounts

Gross payment accounts are maintained for each of the differing classes of goods (separate accounts for spirits, wines, and beers and so on). The consignee or his agent pays to customs and excise a sum of money to cover anticipated needs over a trading period, adding to it as it is used so that there is always sufficient money in the accounts to cover duties payable on goods to be withdrawn from the store.

Goods subject to customs and excise duty

Goods subject to excise duty will, if imported from outside the EEC, also attract customs duty. The customs duty may be paid at the port of entry, in which case the goods are stored in bond as customs duty paid (described by customs and excise as 'duty free'). If, however, the customs duty has not been paid then the goods are stored as customs duty unpaid. Customs duty liable on goods in store may be paid in advance of or concurrently with excise duty before release of the goods. This customs duty may be 'deferred' but the excise duty cannot be so treated. Customs duty may, however, be paid through a gross payment account if such is maintained.

BONDS

A bond is a cover, negotiated by a consignee or his agent with his bank or insurance company, to ensure that all sums due in respect of duty or penalties imposed will be paid by the bonder in the event of the consignee or his agent failing to meet customs demands or to comply with the regulations.

Removal bond

A bond required to cover the movement, from one place to another, of goods on which duty, customs and/or excise duty is liable and has not been paid. Such bonds can be individual for single movements or standing.

Transhipment bond

A bond required to cover the transfer of goods from an arrival port (sea or air) when such goods are subject to customs and/or excise duty. Such bonds are usually standing.

General bond

A bond which embraces both removal and transhipment, and acts as security for the payment of duty when goods subject to customs duty are moved, removed or held pending their use in manufacture.

(Penalty) bond

This is a bond in a sum laid down by customs and excise in respect of duty (customs and/or excise) payable in respect of goods stored under control, pending payment of such duty. This is the type of bond which covers the operation of a warehouse in which goods subject to excise duty are stored.

BONDED WAREHOUSES

Bonded warehouses are premises approved by the Commissioners of Customs and Excise for storage of goods without payment of duty. An authorized bonded warehouse can only be used for the storage of those goods for which it has been approved.

Types of bonded warehouse

There are four types of bonded warehouse:

1 *Customs warehouse* – for the deposit, without payment of duty, of imported goods which are liable to customs duty but which are not liable to excise duty
2 *Excise warehouse* – for the deposit, without payment of excise duty, of goods which are liable to excise duty. In this case the customs duty, if applicable, will have been paid
3 *Customs and excise warehouse* – for the deposit, without payment of customs or excise duty, of goods which are liable to both customs and excise duty
4 *Tobacco warehouse* – for the deposit, without payment of customs or excise duty, of tobacco and tobacco products liable to customs and excise duty.

Categories of bonded warehouse

There are two categories of bonded warehouse:

1 *Crown locked* – controlled by the presence of a customs officer. The building is secured with Crown locks and the warehouse keeper's own locks, so that the warehouse keeper only has access to the goods under supervision of the customs officer
2 *Open warehouse* – in which the premises are not normally Crown locked and a customs officer is not constantly present. The warehouse keeper has unrestricted access to the goods during the hours of opening.

Classes of open warehouse

Open warehouses are described as class A or class B according to the following rules:

Class A warehouses

These warehouses are approved for beer, wines and spirits. In this class of open warehouse the goods must be kept within strictly defined and secure limits. Storage must be arranged so that consignments are easily identifiable, and to separate those goods liable only to excise duty from those which are liable to excise and customs duty. Such a warehouse will be the subject of a bond, the limits being set by HM Customs and Excise.

Class B warehouses

These warehouses are approved for goods other than beer, wines and spirits. The goods may be stored anywhere within the warehouse, subject to their being easily identifiable by a visiting customs officer. A bond is not normally required but the company is expected to maintain a duty deferment in a sum which is at least equal to the amount of duty payable on the goods stored. Class B open warehouses subdivide into two further kinds:

1 *General warehouse* – where the space is to be available to the general public on demand
2 *Franchise warehouse* – for the storage of a manufacturer's own goods pending operation for re-export.

FOREIGN EXCHANGE

The simplest international transaction can lead to problems in pricing and payment. The price to a foreign buyer can be in the seller's currency, in the buyer's or in a third 'international' currency such as the US dollar. For the seller, his own currency has the advantage that he knows exactly how much he is going to receive, although he (or his government) may prefer another currency if his own is depreciating rapidly, in value.*

The buyer, on the other hand, will have to purchase the necessary foreign currency, and in most cases the rate of exchange between his own currency and the foreign currency will not be fixed. So at least between the time of quotation and the acceptance there may be a change, favourable or unfavourable. He therefore may well prefer a quotation in his own currency or a third, such as the US dollar, which may be more familiar to him than the seller's.

The fact that the foreign exchange transaction offers both sides the opportunity for gain as well as loss is generally immaterial, since the businessman, either buyer or seller, will generally prefer not to have to bother about the speculative element. That is for the professional risk taker in currencies.

In the first place, the buyer can merely purchase the necessary foreign exchange to pay for the goods when he decides to accept the offer made. In this way he knows exactly how much the goods cost him. The foreign exchange can be deposited in a bank and will earn interest. The rate of interest, however, even on a time deposit, will frequently be below that obtainable by some alternative use of the funds. But in this way virtually all the risk has been covered, although if the exchange rate moves in favour of his own currency there will obviously have been a *'manque a gagner'* or a lost opportunity, since he would not be able to buy the currency more cheaply.

It will not always be convenient to immobilize funds in this way, a long time ahead perhaps of the payment which has to be made, or the rate of interest which can be earned may not be considered sufficient. In this case there exists the alternative of the forward exchange market. This may be of advantage to the seller also, in the contrary case where he has quoted in the buyer's currency, or in a third currency; he may wish to know at the time of concluding the transaction how much he will receive in his own currency.

The forward exchange market, to which access may be obtained through any major commercial bank, will provide a quotation for a contract to buy or sell a wide range of currencies for delivery up to normally six

---

* The text of this chapter from here on is taken directly or adapted from Avison Wormwald's chapter in *Handbook of Financial Planning and Control*, Gower, 1981

months ahead. Contracts for longer periods are possible but can be very expensive.

According to the view the international money market takes of the two currencies involved, the price of the currency purchased may be higher or lower than the present price. Equally, when the contract matures and the currency is delivered it may be found that the contract price may be higher or lower than the then prevailing price. The rates for the principal currencies against the pound sterling are quoted daily in the London *Financial Times* for one month and three months.

If the forward exchange contract is made through the buyer's normal bank it may involve no down-payment at all, and therefore the funds are available for different uses. In other cases it may involve the payment of 5-10 per cent of the value, according to the credit status of the buyer and the risk involved in the particular currency. The buyer of the 'forward exchange' now knows exactly how much he will eventually have to pay, if he is the buyer of the goods, or receive if he is the seller. He will not have tied up his funds, but he will have preferred the judgement of the market to his own as regards the future relationship between the two currencies concerned.

These two arrangements can be combined in some cases (and dependent on exchange control regulations that may be in force) to produce a *foreign currency swap*. In this case the foreign currency is purchased in the 'spot' market and simultaneously a forward contract is arranged to sell the same amount of the currency at a future specified date. This is to cover the case when, for example, funds have to be advanced but will later be repaid in the same currency. There are also credit 'swaps' available in some countries: a bank in the foreign country makes a loan to a local borrower, for example a subsidiary of a foreign multinational, accepting the foreign exchange risk but of course charging interest on this loan. The foreign company then grants a loan to the bank outside the country, and normally this loan will be larger than the first so that the bank is compensated for the exchange risk and expenses.

All the foregoing arrangements are 'hedging' or safety devices to limit the risks implied in handling transactions involving foreign currencies. (In the strictly technical sense these measures are used to eliminate or reduce 'uncertainty', which is distinct from 'risk' in that it is possible to assign probability values to the latter.) It should be noted that normally it will be considered that the domestic currency is 'safer' than the foreign currency, since in effect the main part of the business of the buyer or seller is in any case inextricably involved in its own currency, good or bad. To take a 'bear' view of one's own currency and to hold funds in foreign currencies is normally considered to be speculative and, of course, may even be illegal.

PAYMENT AND CREDIT IN INTERNATIONAL TRADE

The question of payment arises in the simplest international transaction and it is therefore natural that there should be a wide range of methods for dealing with it and with the related problem of credit. These arrangements also cover the important aspect of 'bridging' finance: that is to say financing the exporter's outlay over the (frequently long) period between the shipment of goods and receipt of payment.

The letter of credit

The normal risks of commercial transactions are greatly increased in international trading, frequently because there is less knowledge on the part of one or both parties to a transaction about the other. Commercial practices differ greatly from country to country and there may be difficulties, imaginary as well as real, in obtaining recourse in the courts against one of the parties. The exchange risks already discussed also affect the arrangements in most cases.

The letter of credit has an important place in the list of arrangements designed to reduce risk. It consists essentially of an undertaking given by a bank, on behalf of its client, to a third party to the effect that it will honour its drafts on it provided that they comply in every respect with the requirements specified in the letter itself.

Since it constitutes an obligation to pay, the bank will require that it be backed by the necessary funds or that the bank should have control, partial or complete, over the goods involved in the transaction. Normally the credit will be irrevocable; if it is 'revocable' (in very rare instances) then the conditions under which it can be revoked will obviously have to be very precisely spelled out, otherwise the credit is valueless as a guarantee.

Letters of credit have value to both buyer and seller and the initiative to use them may come from either party to a transaction. To the seller it guarantees that the funds for payment are available; if it provides that payment may be made in his own currency it eliminates the exchange risk. If the credit is 'confirmed' through a branch or correspondent bank in the seller's country the guarantee obviously extends to payment as distinct from the availability of funds and then becomes virtually total. To the buyer also the letter of credit may have value since it immediately establishes, normally at very little cost, that his creditworthiness is unimpeachable, while it removes any risk there might have been in advance payment, if such were required by the seller.

The form of letters of credit, the legal situation, the costs and extent of discounting facilities differ from country to country so that both sides should obtain detailed information from their banks on these points. An example of an irrevocable letter of credit is shown in Figure 39.4.

The choice of payment method

Briefly the choices are between an irrevocable credit opened by the buyer in a bank in the name of the supplier and other methods mentioned above. The irrevocable letter of credit gives total security of payment, as far as both buyer and seller at least are concerned, but the seller may not obtain the funds until the goods are delivered. It is also mainly used where the seller has some doubt at least about the creditworthiness of the buyer.

Broadly speaking the choice of other methods will be between bank loans,

GHM

EXCEL BANK LTD

From:-

Excel Bank Ltd.
Registered in England
(No. 00000)

Registered Office
1074, Lombard Street,
London EC2P 2BX

Overseas Branch
P.O. Box 181760
70 St. Mary's Avenue
London EC3P 3BN
Telephone 01 000 0000 Extn:3259
Telex 000000
Telegrams Excelbank London

To:-

Camside Engineering (Cambridge) Ltd.
Chesterton,
Cambridge.

Advice of:-

Popular Bank of Africa
Mtwara
Tanzania

*Irrevocable credit which bears the confirmation
of Excel Bank Ltd.*

Dear Sirs,

We inform you that the above-named bank have opened with us their irrevocable credit in your favour on account of Haji Bwanamkubwa and Partners, of 24 Port Compound, Mtwara, Tanzania, to the extent of £8,000.00 (say Eight Thousand Pounds) valid at this office until 12 noon on 23rd September 19...., on or before which your drafts on us at sight may be paid if accompanied by the undermentioned documents evidencing current shipment from Liverpool to Mtwara, Tanzania of the goods described below. The buyer's order number and reference is U.K. 1754. Part shipments prohibited. All documents to be in English. We confirm that no import licence is required for these goods on entering Tanzania.

Set of 3 clean shipped Bills of Lading issued in favour of Popular Bank of Africa, Mtwara, Tanzania, marked "FREIGHT PAID" showing the amount of freight paid.

A clean Report of Findings must be obtained from General Superintendents, Liverpool, and must accompany the other documents; also a packing list in 3 copies.

Copy of your advice note sent to Popular Bank of Africa advising details of shipment for insurance purposes, enabling them to insure in good time.

Commercial Invoice in 9 copies, showing the F.O.B. value and freight charges shown separately, giving in all a C & F value.

Covering 8 Water Purifying units Type SD1756 at agreed price of £640 per unit
2 aerators Type TD15 at agreed price of £540 each

We are informed that insurance will be effected by the buyers with State Insure,(Tanzania) Ltd, Mtwara, Tanzania.

Shipment must be effected in Palmate Line Vessels only. All drafts drawn under this credit to bear the clause "Drawn under Doc. Credit No 17,777,777."

We are requested to advise you of the terms of the credit, which is irrevocable on the part of our principals and also bears our confirmation. Subject to Uniform Customs and Practice for Documentary Credits (1974 Revision) International Chamber of Commerce Publication No. 290.

Figure 39.4 **An irrevocable letter of credit** (*Formecon Services Ltd*)

or overdraft facilities (especially in the UK), and commercial paper which can be discounted or sold outright in the bill market. The value of commercial paper depends essentially on the credit standing of the parties concerned, and on whether it has been 'accepted' (see below) by a recognized financial institution, in the UK, a major commercial bank or an 'accepting house' or merchant banker. When the paper is graded first-class it is the cheapest available source of funds, normally being at least 0.25 per cent cheaper than bank loans, and in times of tight money this spread can be up to 2.0 per cent. This method also has the advantage that it does not affect the general debt structure of the business, since it is self-liquidating. It should be clear that it can be used independently of shipping documents; in other words the sale can be on 'open account' if the relations between buyer and seller make this preferable, while the financing arrangements are made in parallel but independently of particular shipments.

Documentary credits, in the form of bills of exchange payable for example at 30, 60 or 90 days are generally preferred since they can be discounted in the bill market through the seller's bank and enable him to obtain his money much earlier. In most countries banks themselves will advance loans on bills of exchange, where the credit of the supplier is sufficiently good. A frequently used form of bank credit is the time draft which is drawn on the bank at the same time as the bill of exchange. Whichever method is used depends on the credit standing of buyer and seller, which in turn will affect the cost of the transaction, and the extent to which the seller at least can finance the transaction himself.

The residual risk in these transactions is covered partially at least as far as the bank is concerned by insurance of the goods, sometimes material proof that the goods exist in the form of warehouse receipts, frequently stipulations as to the nature of the goods, e.g. that they should be readily saleable in the event of default, and finally credit insurance.

Credit insurance

This originated some sixty years ago and has increased steadily in volume and scope. It can confidently be said that the bulk of trade with the communist countries would not have been possible without it because of the lack of experience of most firms in the West in dealing with these countries, the very stringent requirements laid upon them by the buyers and the long credit terms frequently required.

The manner of operation of the British Export Credits Guarantee Department (ECGD) is typical of the many institutions, governmental and private, which now provide these services in all the principal trading countries of the west. There are 'tailor-made' policies for large capital goods, and similar transactions. The ECGD guarantees can be used as security against bank loans and thus greatly facilitate the financing of longer-term projects. Normally of course a proportion of the risk, sometimes quite small, must be assumed by the seller.

These facilities, although increasingly used, are likely to be rather expensive so that other alternatives may be considered. Either the seller or the buyer, for example, can raise money through an issue of debt either in the national or the international money market, the terms being geared to the length of the repayment period, long-term rates tending to be higher than short-term.

HELPFUL ORGANIZATIONS

British Overseas Trade Board
1 Victoria Street
London SW1H 0ET

Department of Trade
Export Services and Promotions
  Division
Lime Grove
Eastcote
Ruislip
Middlesex
HA4 8SG

Export Credits Guarantee Department
Aldermanbury House
Aldermanbury
London EC2P 2EL

H M Customs and Excise
King's Beam House
Mark Lane
London EC3R 7HE

Technical Help to Exporters
British Standards Institution
Linford Wood
Milton Keynes
MK14 6LE

FURTHER READING

Croner's Reference Book for Exporters, Croner Publications, New Malden, Surrey, UK (by subscription: updated monthly)
Croner's Reference Book for Importers, Croner Publications, New Malden, Surrey, UK
Croner's World Directory of Freight Conferences, Croner Publications, New Malden, Surrey, UK (by subscription: updated monthly)
Export Education Packages, Formecon Services Ltd, Crewe, CW1 1YN, UK
Katz, B., *Managing Export Marketing*, Gower, Aldershot, 1987

40 Managing transport services

Frank H Woodward

The transport function is called upon to provide a service to every single function within industry. It is hard to name a function which at some time will not require goods, services or personnel to be moved. Because of this broad responsibility to give a service, those engaged in managing transport come into direct contact with all other departments within a company and will incur costs on behalf of those departments. With this licence to accept costs comes the added responsibility of ensuring that value is received for costs incurred, and of checking costs and performance of all activities within the function constantly against alternative services available.

ORGANIZATION STRUCTURE

The person responsible at board level for the control of transport operations can vary from the sales director to the company secretary, from the production director to the chief executive. With increased activity in the distribution of goods, and escalation of costs in all areas of transport operations, arguments over the rightful place of the transport function in a company organization continue. Despite the strength of many proposals, it has become increasingly obvious that there is no answer which would be suitable or acceptable as a general rule for all types of industry.

A company whose activity is centred around the packaging, warehousing and distribution of goods to retail outlets would find that 'transport', a word used in the broadest sense, is responsible for anything up to 40 per cent of annual turnover and would justify direct representation on the board of directors to ensure that a full account of this expenditure is presented at the highest level in the organization. A company whose transport requirement is only a few cars would not need such total executive responsibility. Unless a company 'sells' transport as a means of adding directly to the profit of the company, in other words, a company engaged in road haulage, then transport is a service function in exactly the same way as the catering activity of a company. The value of this service to the profitability of the company will determine its correct place in the organization structure.

Line or staff. Line management is that which is responsible for achieving the main objectives of the business. Staff functions are those which assist line management to achieve those objectives. Transport is primarily a line function, especially when applied to the movement of a company product. To manufacture goods and to leave them at the end of the production line is not 'achieving the objectives of the business'. They must be placed before a customer, and to achieve this implies movement or transportation of the product.

The management organization of a road haulage operation would be of line responsibility, in that the main objective of the business is to achieve profit by selling transport services. In the manufacturing industry, it all depends on who gives the instructions about the movements. If the manufacturing or sales function states where, when and how the goods are to be moved, then the transport function has no line responsibility and merely provides the service requested. On the other hand, if the transport function takes over the final stage of customer satisfaction, and is able to decide the method of movement after having been given instructions on where and when, then it is in a position of line responsibility, accountable for its own decisions. Figure 40.1 shows the distinction between line and staff functions in an industrial transport services activity.

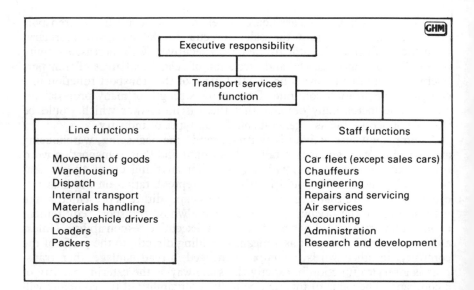

Figure 40.1   Line and staff functions within the transport services activity

Developing the organization structure

Figures 40.2 to 40.4 show different types of organization structure suitable for the transport services function of a manufacturing company. The transport services requirement is of a general nature and is not confined to a warehousing or retailing operation. It is intended that the types of organization illustrated will assist readers in developing their own organization structure after taking into consideration their own special needs.

A typical organization for the transport services function of a single factory location of a small company with only a few cars and light vans and one heavy truck used on local deliveries is shown in Figure 40.2. Dispatches are by local carrier and rail. All vehicle maintenance is carried out at local garages. A dispatch section is established which is responsible for packaging and loading goods on to vehicles.

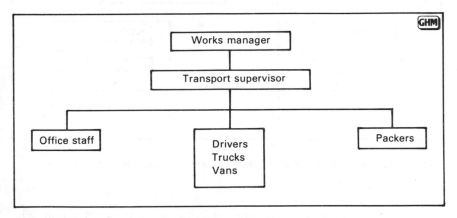

Figure 40.2   A simple organization for a small company

Organization for the transport services function of a medium-sized company with two factory locations is shown in Figure 40.3. There are twenty cars for management and sales staff use, a number of light vans for customer after-sales service, four trucks for goods delivery to customers and a personnel carrier for personnel movement between factories. Distribution is by company transport and local carrier as well as by rail services. A company garage is available to service and repair the majority of company-owned vehicles.

Figure 40.4 shows the organization for the transport services function of a large group of companies with many factory locations spread across the UK. A mixed vehicle fleet of over 2000 has to be controlled and administered, consisting of executive and management cars, a large sales fleet of cars and light vans, and a truck fleet exceeding 200 vehicles. A full distribution service from all factory locations to customers is carried out using company vehicles. Local carriers are used to meet peak demands. Extensive use is made of rail

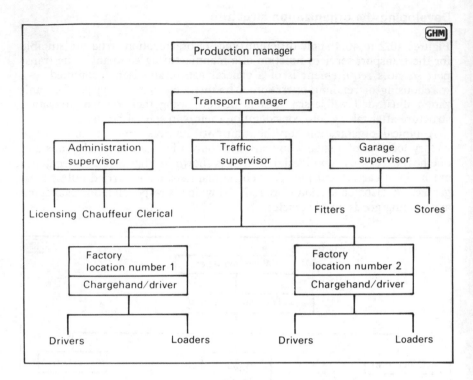

Figure 40.3   Transport services organization for a medium-sized company

facilities. Company garages are established in each transport location. The whole of the transport function is based on a regional organization with line responsibility for the movement of company products. A corporate air service is the responsibility of the transport services function.

TRANSPORT MANAGEMENT

One of the conditions for the granting of an operators' licence is that the 'person' named in the application to manage that transport operation is 'professionally competent'. This means that managers in the road haulage industry have to pass an examination in order to obtain this standard, and a certificate will be issued stating that the person named therein is 'professionally competent'. Although this requirement for the granting of an operators' licence only applies to 'hire and reward' operations, the Certificate of Professional Competence is a qualification available to 'own account' transport management where the transport services are not offered for hire and reward. In recruiting or promoting managers to any transport operation, this 'certificate' should be the minimum standard qualification required.

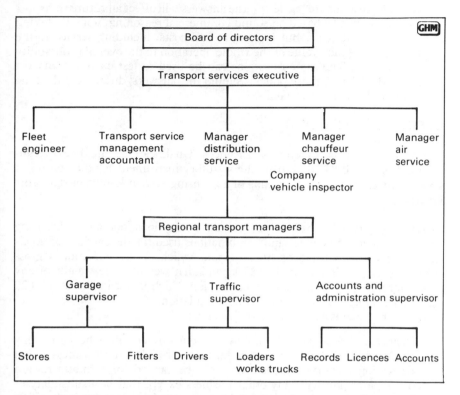

Figure 40.4 Transport services organization for a large group of companies

Before starting to develop any vehicle plan, a number of questions need to be asked:

1 Does the distribution of the product, or movement of personnel need vehicles? Liquids and gases can be distributed by pipe-line, personnel can communicate by telephone, closed circuit television, electronic mail etc.
2 If vehicles are needed, must they be road vehicles? Will railways, waterways or aircraft give a more efficient and economic service?
3 If road vehicles are needed, is the service of a haulier or contract distribution more efficient than the company operating its own vehicle fleet?
4 If road vehicles are to be operated by the company, should they be leased, on contract hire, or owned?
5 If it is finally decided to have company-owned vehicles, how should they be financed, how many are required, what types are needed, and where are they to be based?

These vital questions are 'ageless' – the answers will affect all future transport planning and must be based on sound commercial reasoning, not only taking into account basic costs, but looking at real costs, including service to the customer and the total value of the whole operation to the overall profitability of the company. The same questions can be used to test current transport policies and to change those policies should the 'answers' differ from the time those initial decisions were taken.

OPERATORS' LICENSING

The Goods Vehicles (Operators' Licences, Qualifications and Fees) Regulations 1984 (SI 1984 No.176) is the statutory instrument for the control of goods vehicle operations by means of a licensing system known as operators licensing.

Scope of Regulations. Subject to certain exemptions operators' licensing applies to all goods vehicles and combinations used for the carriage of goods in connection with trade or business and which exceed 3.5 tonnes gross plated weight or, if unplated 1525 kg unladen weight. The weight of any trailer forming part of a vehicle combination which is not in excess of 1020 kg unladen weight is discounted in the calculation.

There are three types of operators' licence:

1 *Restricted licence*. Issued for 'own account' operators who carry only goods as part of their trade or business provided the business is not professional haulage. Goods must not be carried for hire and reward or in connexion with any other business except that of a subsidiary or parent company. A restricted 'O' licence permits operations both within the UK and abroad. The applicants for a restricted licence must satisfy the licensing authority that they are 'fit and proper persons' and 'have appropriate financial standing'. There is no requirement for the applicant to be, or to employ a person who is 'professionally competent'. The holder of a restricted licence using a goods vehicle for hire and reward is liable on conviction to a fine of up to £500.

2 *Standard national licence*. Issued for professional haulage operators who carry goods for 'hire and reward' and to 'own account' operators who may from time to time carry goods for hire and reward. Hire and reward operators are limited to the UK but 'own account' operators issued with a standard licence may operate abroad subject to a restriction of carrying their own goods. Applicants for a standard national licence must satisfy the licensing authority that they are of good repute and have the appropriate financial standing *and* must be, or must employ someone who is, *professionally competent in national transport operations*.

3 *Standard international licence*. Issued to professional hauliers and to own account operators and permits the carriage of goods for hire and reward both within the UK and abroad. Applicants must be of good repute and have appropriate financial standing *and* must be, or must employ

someone who is, *professionally competent in both national and international operations.*

Operating centres. An application for an 'O' licence has to be made to the traffic area in which the vehicle operating centre is located. An operating centre is defined as *the place where the vehicle is normally kept.* This in effect is construed to mean *where the vehicle is parked when not in use.*

Applications for an 'O' licence. Applicants for an 'O' licence must advertise their intention to apply in a local newspaper in order that people living near to the operating centre can make representations against the granting of a licence. Full details of how to apply for a licence and the conditions to be met are contained in Department of Transport publication *A Guide to Goods Vehicle Operators Licensing* (GV74).

The Certificate of Professional Competence (CPC)

A person will be considered professionally competent if holding:

1 A certificate issued by the licensing authority prior to December 1979, conferring on the holder so-called 'grandfather rights' after proving qualification by experience. This certificate will be accepted to support an application for both types of standard licence.
2 Membership of one of the professional transport institutes confers the professional competence qualification according to grade of membership:

 (*a*) for national and international standard licences:
 – Fellow or Member of Chartered Institute of Transport
 – Member or Associate Member of the Institute of Transport Administration
 – Member or Associate Member of The Institute of Road Transport Engineers
 – Fellow or Associate of the Institute of the Furniture Warehousing and Removing Industry
 (*b*) for national operations only:
 – Licentiate of Chartered Institute of Transport
 – Associate (by examination) of the Institute of Road Transport Engineers
 – Graduate or Associate of the Institute of Transport Administration
 – Holder of the General Certificate in Removals Management issued by the Institute of Furniture Warehousing and Removing Industry.
 (*Note:* The above membership must be in the road haulage sectors.)

3 *Examination.* A certificate of competence issued by the Royal Society of Arts after taking the examination for proof of professional competence. Examination 'pass' certificates act as proof of qualification. The RSA examination is held at centres throughout the UK, usually four times each year. The examination is in two parts:

(*a*) national transport operations

(*b*) international transport operations.

VEHICLE MANAGEMENT AND VEHICLE STANDARDS

The object of setting vehicle operating standards is to obtain the most efficient utilization of a fleet of vehicles. This is the key to a minimum cost operation. Standing costs now account for more than half the total operating costs of a vehicle and it follows that the higher the utilization, the cheaper the cost per mile. Figure 40.5 shows the standing costs and running costs of various types of vehicle.

There are four main areas of vehicle operation where an attack on utilization can be made, and which can provide a basis for comparison of planned performance against actual performance.

Vehicle preparation

This includes checking of the vehicle before a day's work, driver administration and documentation. Work study techniques can be applied to this area of work, and standard times are easy to establish.

	Rigid truck	Articulated trucks			Chauffeur car
	12.50 tonne GVW	24.19 tonne GCW	32.52 tonne GCW	38.00 tonne GCW	2.8cc (diesel)
Standing costs per year	£	£	£	£	£
Licences	430	1 200	2 500	3 150	100
Insurance	900	1 578	2 135	2 504	450
Depreciation	3 630	5 132	7 950	9 560	5 400
Driver costs (50 hrs)	6 447	7 544	8 025	8 426	9 200
Total	11 407	15 454	20 600	23 640	15 150
Running costs based on 36 000 miles per year					
Fuel	4 975	6 825	9 752	10 501	3 762
Lubricants	90	122	133	133	46
Tyres	1 210	1 850	2 401	3 744	240
Maintenance	5 443	6 034	7 168	7 704	670
Total	11 718	14 831	19 454	22 082	4 718

Figure 40.5 Standing costs and running costs of various types of vehicle (costs as at April 1986)

Vehicle loading and unloading

One way of achieving a higher productivity is to keep loading and unloading time to a minimum. The use of demountable 'swop bodies', containers and trailers are all ways of preloading vehicles while the motive unit is delivering another load. The size of pallet, side loading, double-deck loading, lower deck height, are all areas where a work study investigation may be applied with advantage. The use of vehicle mounted handling aids such as tail lifts, cranes, and special tracking, will speed up the unloading of a vehicle at customers' premises. Standard forms of label and consignment note, colour coding identification of depots, factories, warehouses or customer delivery areas, are all ways of speeding up the loading procedure and assisting the driver to make an efficient delivery.

Vehicle running time

The running time of a vehicle between two points is governed by the speed limit of the road over which that vehicle has to travel. Figure 40.6 shows the present speed limits in the UK and acceptable vehicle speeds used in transport operations as a basis for calculating time taken over road routes. The working day of a delivery vehicle can be divided into three sections:

1 Proceeding to actual delivery area
2 Delivering the goods in the delivery area
3 Returning to base

The speed-limit factor will only effect the first and last sections as the main controlling factor in the delivery area is the number of delivery points and the number of units to be delivered at each point.

Delivering the goods

This is an area of uncertainty when trying to calculate standard times of performance and the approach to the problem will differ with each company and product. Calculations can be based on:

1 Number of delivery drops
2 A basic time allowance for each delivery point
3 Standard times for handling each parcel delivered
4 An average speed for the vehicle when delivering in towns

The setting of vehicle and operating standards in a transport operation is called 'load assessment' and there are many ways of applying this technique. The object in every case is to establish a standard against which the performance of a driver can be measured.

Type of road	Type of vehicle	Maximum legal road speed	Acceptable GHM average speed for route calculations
Restricted to 30 mph (built-up areas)	All types of vehicle	30 mph	22 mph
Dual carriageways (other than motorways or roads restricted to a lower limit)	Car-derived van or dual-purpose vehicle	70 mph	55 mph
	Rigid goods vehicle not in excess of 7.5 tonnes gvw	60 mph	45 mph
	Articulated vehicle or rigid goods vehicle in excess of 7.5 tonnes gvw	50 mph	38 mph
	Rigid vehicle and trailer in excess of 7.5 tonnes laden weight	50 mph	38 mph
Motorways	Rigid goods vehicle not exceeding 7.5 tonnes gvw and not drawing a trailer	70 mph	55 mph
	Rigid goods vehicle exceeding 7.5 tonnes, articulated vehicles and rigid goods vehicles drawing a trailer	60 mph	48 mph
Other roads (when derestricted)	Rigid goods vehicles, articulated vehicles not exceeding 7.5 tonnes gvw and rigid vehicles drawing a trailer where the aggregate maximum laden weight of the vehicle and trailer does not exceed 7.5 tonnes	50 mph	35 mph
	Goods vehicles including articulated vehicles in excess of 7.5 tonnes gvw and rigid vehicles drawing trailers with an aggregate laden weight in excess of 7.5 tonnes	40 mph	30 mph

Figure 40.6   UK speed limits for goods registered vehicles (April 1986)

DRIVERS' HOURS AND RECORDS OF WORK

Drivers' hours

New regulations governing drivers' hours and rest periods came into force on 29 September 1986. EEC Directive 3820/85 sets out the drivers' hours rules for most goods vehicles with a gross plated weight in excess of 3.5 tonnes. The new rules are now the same for drivers engaged on national and international journeys and all the old duty restrictions contained in the Transport Act 1968 have been abolished for drivers of vehicles falling within scope of EEC Directive 3820/85.

From 29 September 1986 two sets of drivers' hours rules apply in the UK:

1 *National and international operations.* For *national and international* journeys the rule applies to drivers of goods vehicles exceeding 3.5 tonnes gross plated weight including the weight of any trailer drawn, not exempted under UK legislation and to passenger vehicles with a maximum of 17 seats including the driver and operated wholly within the UK.
2 *Domestic operations.* This rule applies to drivers of goods vehicles which are exempt from EEC rules including those vehicles below 3.5 tonnes gross vehicle weight.

National and international operations

The following is a summary of drivers' hours rules for national and international journeys:

Daily driving – 9 hours maximum, extended to 10 hours maximum twice a week.

Driving in any two consecutive weeks – 90 hours maximum.

Consecutive days of driving – 6 days maximum.

Definition of 'fixed week' – The period between 00.00 hours Monday and 24.00 hours Sunday.

Continuous driving – Limited to 4.5 hours accumulated driving either in one block or a number of shorter periods of driving not separated by a legal break.

Daily rest – 11 hours minimum, with a reduction to 9 hours on 3 days per week subject to an equivalent period of rest being taken as compensation before the end of the following week.

Weekly rest – 45 hours minimum, with reductions to 36 hours at base or 24 hours away from base, subject to each reduction being compensated by an equivalent rest taken *en bloc* before the end of the *third week* following the week when the reduced rest was taken.

Breaks from driving – 45 minutes minimum after an accumulated driving period of 4.5 hours or, three 15-minute breaks spaced out over and at the end of that period.

It is to be noted that under the new regulations there are no limitations on the duty hours which a driver can work.

Note: EEC Regulations allow member states to exempt certain other vehicles and operations at their discretion and to make special exemptions in particular cases, but generally the restrictions on *maximum driving periods* are applied without exception. Information on exemptions and variations are available from the Road Haulage Association or The Freight Transport Association.

Domestic operations

Daily driving – 10 hours maximum.

Daily duty – 11 hours maximum.

The above rules are the only limitations placed on the driving and working hours of drivers of goods vehicles exempt from the EEC rules. It is to be noted that there are no requirements to take a legal break during a driving or duty day, or daily/weekly rest minimum.

Drivers' records of work

The use of a tachograph to record the work and driving hours of goods vehicle drivers applies to all goods vehicles in excess of 3.5 tonnes plated gross weight which are not exempt from the EEC drivers' hours rules. Tachographs and compliance with EEC drivers' hours rules also apply to passenger vehicles constructed to carry more than 17 persons including the driver. The relevant EEC Directive is 3821/85 which was brought into effect in the UK on 29 September 1986 and amended the previous rules which had been in operation since 1 January 1982. The revised rules do not apply to crew members other than the driver who is defined as *any person who drives the vehicle even for a short period or is carried in the vehicle in order to be available for driving if necessary.*

Where a tachograph is fitted to a vehicle it must conform to the detailed specification as laid down in the EEC Directive. It must be able to record:

1 distance travelled by the vehicle
2 speed of the vehicle
3 driving time
4 other periods of work of the driver
5 breaks from work and daily rest periods
6 opening of the case containing the tachograph chart.

The tachograph chart must also have a facility by which the driver(s) can continue recording driving and duty time in the event of the instrument becoming unserviceable during a journey. Once a vehicle has been fitted with a tachograph, the instrument must be calibrated and sealed at an approved centre.

The tachograph record

An employer must:

1 issue each driver with sufficient charts for the journey
2 organize each driver's work so that the relevant provisions of the regulations can be complied with
3 make periodical checks to ensure that the provisions of drivers' hours and tachograph regulations have been complied with and, if infringements are found, to take the appropriate steps to prevent repetition.
4 ensure that drivers return charts within 21 days of use
5 retain tachograph charts for a minimum of one year after use and produce or hand over any charts on request by an authorized inspecting officer.

The driver must:

1 use a tachograph chart on every day on which he is driving, starting from the moment he takes over the vehicle. The same chart should continue to be used until the end of that daily driving period
2 enter on the chart:
   (*a*) surname and first name
   (*b*) date and place where the record chart begins and ends
   (*c*) the registration number(s) of the vehicle(s) driven
   (*d*) the odometer readings:
   – at the start of the first journey
   – at the end of the last journey
   – at each change of vehicle, plus the time at which a change of vehicle takes place
3 produce charts for inspection if requested by enforcement officers of the Department of Transport
4 retain with him charts for the current week *and* the chart for the last day on which he drove a vehicle in the previous week.
5 return charts to his employer within 21 days of completion.

A specimen tachograph chart is shown in Figure 40.7.

Written records

Drivers of vehicles which are exempt from EEC drivers' hours regulations are required to maintain written records for vehicles over 3.5 tonnes gross plated vehicle weight, or if not plated, with an unladen weight in excess of 1525 kg. The record is required to be in a prescribed form and there is a duty

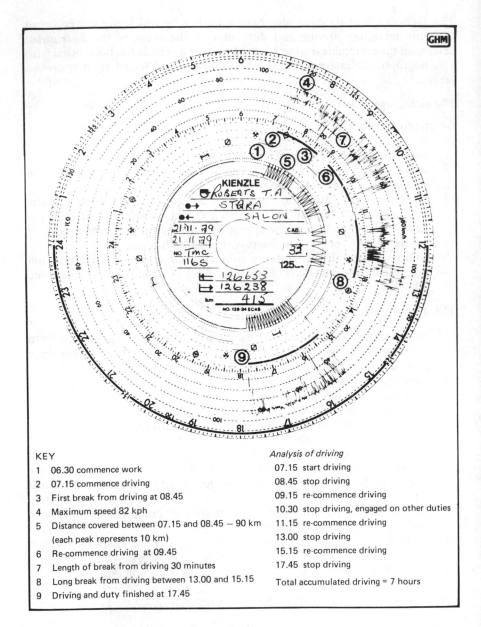

KEY

1	06.30 commence work
2	07.15 commence driving
3	First break from driving at 08.45
4	Maximum speed 82 kph
5	Distance covered between 07.15 and 08.45 — 90 km (each peak represents 10 km)
6	Re-commence driving at 09.45
7	Length of break from driving 30 minutes
8	Long break from driving between 13.00 and 15.15
9	Driving and duty finished at 17.45

Analysis of driving

07.15 start driving
08.45 stop driving
09.15 re-commence driving
10.30 stop driving, engaged on other duties
11.15 re-commence driving
13.00 stop driving
15.15 re-commence driving
17.45 stop driving

Total accumulated driving = 7 hours

Figure 40.7 Example of a tachograph chart
This is an actual record of a European journey

on the employer to check and sign each record. There is no requirement to keep written records for those vehicles which do not exceed 3.5 tonnes gross plated weight or have an unladen weight not in excess of 1525 kg.

VEHICLE SELECTION AND DESIGN

The efficiency of any distribution operation depends upon the selection of the right truck 'for the job to be done'. For the 'own account' user, it is the essential element in achieving an effective customer delivery service; for the haulier, it provides the means to maximize profits. Selecting the right truck to meet a given set of criteria can only be achieved after full discussion with all functions within the total distribution chain: a full understanding of the size, weight and types of load to be carried is necessary in addition to a knowledge of the routes over which the truck is to operate. As the product structure of a company changes, vehicles designed specifically to carry that product may become obsolete. Long-term planning is essential and a degree of flexibility needs to be built into the design features of any industrial fleet.

Setting the body specification

The body of a goods vehicle is that part of the vehicle on or in which the load is carried. This part of the specification must be set first, then a chassis specification to accommodate the 'body'. This specification covers:

1   internal and external dimensions, and floor height
2   size, type and location of doors, shutters and tailboards
3   materials to be used, including provision for insulation and temperature control equipment
4   internal fittings and load security fitments
5   load handling equipment, vehicle mounted or carried
6   requirements for carrying hazardous loads
7   painting and company livery requirements

Truck design and legislation

The Motor Vehicles (Construction & Use) Regulations 1978, as amended, will determine the maximum dimensions and permitted gross weight of the chassis on which a truck body is to be mounted. A brief outline of the weights and dimension legislation is as follows:

1   *Length*

rigid vehicles	11.0 metres
articulated vehicles	15.5 metres
draw-bar combinations	18.0 metres
semi-trailers manufactured from 1 May 1983	12.2 metres*

(*Note:* ⋆ this is the internal load space measurement, but the total length of the tractor and semi-trailer must not exceed 15.5 metres.)

2 *Width*

All vehicles	2.5 metres

(*Note:* under certain conditions a refrigerated vehicle is permitted to have a maximum width of 2.55 metres.)

3 *Height.* None specified except for articulated vehicles where the semi-trailer has a plated gross weight in excess of 26 000 kg and the total laden weight of the tractor and semi-trailer when driven on the road exceeds 32 520 kg. In such cases the vehicle is subject to a height limit of 4.2 metres.

4 *Maximum permitted gross weights*

2-axle rigid vehicle	16 260 kg
3-axle rigid vehicle	24 390 kg
4-axle rigid vehicle	30 490 kg
Rigid vehicle and tow bar trailer (must be fitted with power assisted brakes)	32 520 kg
Articulated vehicles:	
Tractor and semi-trailer with total of 3 axles	24 390 kg
Tractor and semi-trailer with total of 4 axles	32 520 kg
Tractor and semi-trailer with total of 5 or more axles	38 000 kg

The above maximum weights depend upon meeting a number of conditions in respect of 'axle spread' and 'overall length'. These need to be carefully checked before setting a design specification for a truck.

Environmental legislation

With the increase in permitted vehicle operating weights up to 38 tonnes (38 000 kg), legislation has been introduced to meet higher safety and environmental standards. These include:

1 Sideguards
2 Antispray protection
3 Rear under-run protection
4 Noise levels
5 Minimum ground clearance.

The choice of vehicles for the carriage of goods varies from a small van to a '38-tonne' gross articulated vehicle. The design of vehicles within this range is just as varied. The use of unit load movements is an important element in achieving a high utilization of both vehicle and driver. Containers, demountable bodies, semi-trailers and draw bar combinations are used in all types of distribution operations. The ultimate test of vehicle design is the efficiency of the vehicle to do the job it was intended for. In setting design specifications it is also necessary to ensure compliance with Health and Safety at Work Regulations.

ACQUIRING VEHICLES – THE FUNDING OPTIONS

The market-place is full of schemes 'blended' to tempt industrial management to acquire assets, including vehicles, by different methods of funding. Many 'names' are used to market these options, but within all the different methods there are only two ways by which to fund a vehicle.

1 purchase
2 rental

The Finance Acts give a clear definition of determining each basic option:

If a company acquires plant (etc) under a contract whereby that contract provides that it may or will *eventually have title of such plant, then the equipment will be regarded as belonging to that company and will be a* purchase;
if the contract does not lead to or offer an 'option' to eventual title, then the contract will be rental.

Purchasing

A number of different options fall under the purchase heading:

1 Reduce current cash balances
2 Establish or increase a bank overdraft
3 Arrange a bank loan to be repaid over a predetermined period
4 Hire purchase: hire purchase is normally associated with a credit facility for a private purchaser. It has advantages for the smaller business and is usually referred to as a *conditional sale agreement*
5 Lease with the 'option to purchase': A lease which gives the lessee (the hirer) the option to purchase the vehicle at the end of the lease period and to acquire title by payment of a stated sum.

Finance leases

A finance lease is a term generally used to mean the same as 'hire'. It excludes any option or agreement on the part of the lessee to acquire legal title. The repayment will be in the form of *equal rentals over a predetermined period*. The finance company will purchase the vehicle in its own title and the asset capitalized in the financial accounts. The lessee is responsible for all the costs of operating the vehicle, including road fund licence, insurance and maintenance. At the end of the lease period, the vehicle is sold and the lessee is usually credited with up to 95 per cent of the proceeds as a refund of rentals. In the case of trucks, a clause in the agreement may provide the lessee with the choice of continuing the lease for a secondary period at a nominal rental usually one half per cent of the total rental payments per annum.

Contract hire

The growth in the use of the contract hire option by companies has continued to increase since 1980 – it can be best described as *paying a rental for the use of a vehicle over a stated period of time and/or miles*. A contract hire agreement will provide:

1 supply of a vehicle ready for the road
2 road fund licence during period of contract
3 all repair and maintenance costs of the vehicle
4 tyres/batteries/exhaust systems etc.
5 replacement vehicle in the event of the contract vehicle being under repair
6 roadside recovery and repair services.

Many contract hire companies now offer insurance as part of the agreement; the objective is to provide the user of the vehicle with no liability for costs other than the monthly rental. Most contract hire agreements have a mileage limitation. If the mileage is exceeded an extra cost is charged based upon a 'pence per mile' calculation. Contract hire agreements for trucks, especially for periods in excess of 3 years, usually have the maintenance element of the rental linked to an index or a clause providing for this to be reviewed each year.

Advantages of vehicle contract hire

1 fixed costs and cash flow over the period
2 simple and easy to forecast budgets
3 reduced administration
4 maximum availability of the vehicle
5 reduced downtime
6 no risks on residual value or maintenance costs.

Value added tax

Each funding option is affected in a different way as regards the treatment of VAT.

Purchase

Vehicles are subject to VAT based on the invoice price of the vehicle. This means that if higher discounts are obtained which reduce the invoice price, the VAT amount is less. VAT on goods vehicles is an input and recoverable through the VAT account on quarterly settlement dates set by the HM Customs & Excise. VAT on cars, including dual purpose vehicles (estate cars) is not recoverable, so a reduction in the invoice price by negotiating discounts also reduces VAT and is a *real saving*.

Hire purchase

VAT is payable on the invoice price of the vehicle the same as if the vehicle had been purchased outright. No VAT is payable on the repayments of capital or on the interest element of the repayments.

Lease with option to purchase

No VAT is payable on the lease rentals when vehicles are acquired by any conditional sale agreement.

Finance lease

VAT is payable on all rentals and this requires additional funding. For those companies registered for VAT, the charge is recoverable as an input through the quarterly VAT account.

Contract hire

VAT is payable on all contract hire rentals.

Note: VAT costs on finance lease and contract hire rentals is an additional cost to those organizations not registered for VAT – e.g. some local government departments, and when using these two funding options to acquire cars, VAT is being paid twice – on the invoice cost of the vehicle which is built into the rental, and then on the rentals paid.

Balance sheet disclosure

One advantage of selecting a lease option when funding assets was that the funding 'was off balance sheet', which improved the gearing ratios of a company. From 1987 SSAP21 (Statement of Standard Accounting Practices) requires certain leases to be shown within the balance sheet of a company. The test is *whether the lease transfers substantially all the risks and rewards of an asset to the lessee*. Vehicle finance leases fall within this definition and under SSAP21 are required to be recorded on the balance sheet as an asset. Where vehicles are acquired under a contract hire agreement, the lessor takes all the risks under the contract. Such leases are called *operating leases* and are not required to be treated as an asset in company balance sheets.

Effect of taxation on purchase, leasing and contract hire

An argument used in favour of leasing and contract hire is that the payments (rentals) are wholly allowable for tax purposes. This is true, but the fact is that tax is neutral. No matter by which method a vehicle is acquired, the payments, either revenue or capital, qualify for tax relief, the only difference is in the *pace* at which relief is given.

Capital allowances

Capital allowances are the names by which an asset acquired by purchase is depreciated by an annual writing down allowance which is used to reduce the tax liability of a company. Vehicles come under the category of 'Plant & Machinery', and from 1 April 1986 there is no difference in the way goods vehicles or cars are treated under the rules of capital allowances.

Annual writing down allowance

1 Goods vehicles are eligible for an annual writing down allowance of 25 per cent on a *reducing balance* from the date of acquisition. This is defined as the date the obligation to pay arises
2 Cars and dual purpose vehicles are eligible for an annual writing down allowance of 25 per cent on a *reducing balance* from the date of acquisition, but restricted to a maximum of £2000 per annum. Example:

Invoice cost of car	£11000
Year 1 writing down allowance	2000 (restricted)
balance forward	9000
Year 2 writing down allowance	2000 (restricted)
balance forward	7000
Year 3 writing down allowance	1750 (25%)
balance forward	5250

The balance of capital expenditure carried forward after applying the first year annual writing down allowance is transferred to a pool of qualifying expenditure for writing down allowances.

De-pooling of short life assets

The 1985 Finance Act introduced a method of de-pooling for assets expected to be sold within 5 years of acquisition. The objective is to give companies the benefit of applying the total depreciation of the asset at the time it is sold. The rules of de-pooling are that:

1 it only applies to assets previously eligible for 100 per cent 1st year allowances. This includes goods vehicles but excludes motor cars and dual purpose vehicles
2 it only affects assets acquired on or after 1 April 1986
3 election to de-pool must be taken within a period of 2 years from the date of acquisition
4 if the asset is not sold within 5 years, any balance of capital is to be transferred to the asset pool of qualifying expenditure.

Tax allowances and hire purchase

The Finance Acts provide that if a person incurs capital expenditure (including vehicles) under a contract whereby he becomes the owner (e.g.

hire purchase or lease with option to purchase), then capital allowances may be taken on the total cost of the asset purchased at the date of entering into the contract.

Tax allowances on contract hire and leasing rentals

Because the ownership of the asset does not pass to the user under a contract hire or leasing agreement, no capital allowances are allowed to the user of the asset. The rentals under contract hire and leasing agreements are treated as revenue expenditure and the total rentals paid in any one financial year are allowed against taxable profits for that year. For cars costing more than £8000 retail, the tax relief on rentals is restricted using the following formula:

$$\frac{\text{retail price of car} - £8000}{2 \times \text{retail price}} = \text{percentage of rental disallowed}$$

Examples of the amount of tax relief lost on vehicles with a retail price in excess of £8000 are:

Retail price £	Rentals disallowed %
10 000	10.0
12 000	16.7
15 000	23.4
20 000	30.0
30 000	36.7
50 000	42.0

Timing of acquisition and taxation benefits

Normally, tax benefits from allowances are received at the end of a company financial year following the year of entitlement.

Capital allowances

Capital allowances claimed on assets purchased at any time during a tax year are allowable in full.

RECOMMEND
If the company has taxable profits acquire vehicles (purchase, hire purchase, or lease with the option to purchase) before the end of a financial year.
If no taxable profits are forecast, delay acquisition until the period immediately following the end of a financial year.

Revenue expenditure (lease rentals, contract hire rentals)

Only the amount of rentals paid are eligible for relief against taxable profits. The timing of the commencement of such agreements has little effect on the receipt of taxable benefits.

Capital budget planning

The timing of vehicle acquisitions and disposals is an area where real savings in total operating costs can be achieved. The disposal prices of vehicles are governed by the trade values in *Glass's Guide* and similar publications. Purchasing a vehicle in the last quarter of a calendar year is seriously reflected in the price obtained when the vehicle is sold. The *Guide* uses the 'year' as a bench mark for assessing the residual value and this value drops when the vehicle becomes 'a year older'. Examples:

> *Vauxhall Cavalier 1600 GL (5 dr)*
> registered   December 1984
> trade value   May 1986   £4325
> registered   January 1985
> trade value   May 1986   £5000
> *difference of £675*
>
> *Truck: Ford Cargo 0708*
> registered   December 1982
> trade value   May 1986   £3250
> registered   January 1983
> trade value   May 1986   £4200
> *difference of £950*

Vehicle fleet management (VFM)

Fleet management is not an alternative funding option but simply the administration of the selected option by an outside agent for a fee. It is usually associated with the company car fleet. The objective is to reduce costs and administration. A vehicle fleet management package will include:

1   operational management of the vehicles:
    (*a*) acquisition
    (*b*) maintenance
    (*c*) fuel credit cards
    (*d*) licensing
    (*e*) disposal
2   financial analysis of costs:
    (*a*) fuel
    (*b*) maintenance
    (*c*) depreciation
3   advice and consultancy:
    (*a*) vehicle make and models
    (*b*) replacement policies
    (*c*) funding options

What does VFM cost?

1   all purchases by the fleet management company on behalf of the user company are charged at cost *plus*

2 a set fee per vehicle per annum usually based on a percentage of the invoice cost of the vehicle.

MAINTENANCE POLICIES

Before an Operators' licence can be issued an applicant must satisfy the licensing authority that vehicles will be kept fit and serviceable at all times when used on the public roads. The licensing authority may also request a copy of any maintenance contract or letter of agreement if the servicing and repair of vehicles is carried out elsewhere than in a company garage workshop, and in all cases may request examples of the forms used for vehicle safety inspections. It is also a requirement for the issue of an 'O' licence that proper arrangements are available for drivers to report safety faults in vehicles as soon as possible. The Department of Transport publication *A Guide to Goods Vehicle Operators Licensing* (GV74 4/84) sets the following guidelines around which vehicle operators should formulate a vehicle maintenance policy:

1 Two separate vehicle checks and inspections should be carried out:
   (a) daily running checks
   (b) vehicle safety inspections and routine maintenance at set intervals on items which affect vehicle safety, followed by repair of any faults
2 The daily check is normally carried out by the driver and consists of checks on basic items including brakes, tyre pressures, lights, windscreen wipers and washers, and trailer couplings
3 Vehicle safety inspections and routine maintenance should be carried out at set intervals of time or mileage. The items should include wheels, tyres, brakes, steering, suspension, lighting and all safety components
4 Staff carrying out inspections must be able to recognize faults found and be aware of the acceptable standard of performance and wear of parts
5 Records must be kept of all safety inspections to show the history of each vehicle. The records must be kept for at least 15 months. Where an outside garage carries out the safety inspections, maintenance records must still be kept
6 Adequate facilities must be available for carrying out the inspection, especially equipment for measuring braking efficiency and setting lights
7 Drivers must report vehicle faults to whomever is responsible for having them put right. The reports must be in writing
8 Users are responsible for the condition of hired vehicles and trailers. The user is defined as the employer of the driver
9 Where maintenance work is contracted out to a garage or other vehicle repairer, a written agreement must be entered into setting out the conditions and periods of safety inspections.

Planned maintenance and inspection

A number of ready-made planned maintenance and inspection schemes are available to operators, all of which have been designed to ensure compliance with the legal requirements. Basically, each contains the following documents enabling a complete history of a vehicle's maintenance and inspection to be recorded and preserved:

1 Driver's defect report
2 Vehicle inspection check sheet
3 Servicing sheet for predetermined intervals of time or mileage
4 Stores requisition form
5 Work order sheet or job card
6 Servicing, planning and record chart
7 Vehicle history folder.

No matter what method of planned maintenance and inspection a company adopts, whether it be in company premises by company employees, or by contracting out the entire task of maintenance, inspection and documentation, the onus of responsibility for the roadworthiness of the vehicle is always with the vehicle operator. He is still responsible in law even though an outside contractor providing the service and maintenance facilities has been neglectful.

The use of computers

There are many computer programs available designed to meet the requirements of all sizes of fleet. For an outlay of under £3000, small 128K personal computers with printer and a fleet management program are available which can handle all the records and maintenance control information for a fleet of up to 100 vehicles. It must be stressed that 'a computer' does not replace the need for written records. The Department of Transport inspectors will require to see the original documents – invoices, service and repair sheets.

FINANCIAL CONTROL OF THE TRANSPORT FUNCTION

The only way to ensure a cost-effective operation is to establish a system of budgetary control and accounting responsibility which ensures that any overspending is immediately highlighted at the point where the cost was incurred. The best way to impose effective financial control on the transport services function is to make it an independent cost centre within the company.

The whole range of transport services is now on offer to companies who do not wish to invest in a fleet of vehicles. From the acquisition of company cars through to the distribution and storage of the company product the range is available on contract terms. By setting up the company transport services function as an independent cost centre, a correct evaluation of both cost and service can be carried out using 'in house' services or using the services of outside contractors.

A rate schedule for the carriage of goods within the company and to customers should be produced in exactly the same way as one would expect to see from a haulier. Similar rate schedules can also be prepared for the use of other services such as chauffeur-driven cars, allocated company cars, and even for the repair and maintenance of vehicles in company garages. These rate schedules should be fixed for the period of a company financial year and published to all departments to be used as a basis for determining the transport and distribution costs borne by the product. By adopting such a system, the transport function receives regular revenue for its services against which it incurs costs.

To be cost-effective two requirements must be met:

1 Actual expenditure should be within the budgeted expenditure
2 Recoveries should equate with actual expenditure.

This last point should be stressed – excess recoveries only add an unnecessary price burden on the product, and an under-recovery will indicate a loss due to an insufficient charge being made for the services provided.

To establish financial disciplines, it is necessary to keep adequate costing information for each vehicle and also to have a system of budgetary control in order that over the whole of a financial period regular checks can be made on areas of excessive expenditure and corrective action taken by management if necessary.

COSTING THE OPERATION

There are two main components of vehicle costs:

1 *Standing costs*. These generally include:
    (a) Depreciation cost of the vehicle, together with a charge equivalent to the interest which the capital invested in the vehicle can earn
    (b) Licences, including road fund and operators' licences
    (c) Insurance, for both vehicle and goods in transit
    (d) Wages of the driver.
2 *Running costs*. These are the result of operating the vehicle on the road and include:
    (a) Fuel and oil
    (b) Repair and maintenance
    (c) Tyres
    (d) Driver's expenses
    (e) Driver's overtime.

The most informative costs of own-account transport operation are the running costs of a vehicle.

Monthly cost record

The vehicle monthly costings record (Figure 40.8) ignores all costs other than those directly associated with day-to-day operation. These are:

1 *Fuel.* Issues from company bulk installations are shown separately from the fuel picked up from garages by means of agency cards or cash. This helps to control the amount of fuel picked up from outside sources and to maximize the higher discounts available by having bulk stocks.
2 *Lubricants.* Only issues during normal running are recorded. Oil changes will be recorded on maintenance job cards
3 *Tyres.* Expenditure on new tyres is recorded from invoices received. Sale or old casings will be entered as credits
4 *Repairs.* A distinction is made between repairs and maintenance carried out in company garages and repairs by outside agents
5 *Miles run.* This is recorded from driver tachograph charts and gives a simple but clear picture of vehicle utilization.

This vehicle costing record also shows registration number or fleet number, make, vehicle group and operating base. Dividing a fleet into groups of similar vehicles, e.g. vehicles under 3.5 tonnes GVW, vehicles 3.5 tonnes GVW to 7.5 tonnes GVW, etc. allows the costings to be arranged in groups and this will highlight any variance within a group so that action can be taken to investigate the reasons for the variance.

Vehicle operating cost sheet

A layout for a vehicle cost sheet is shown in Figure 40.9. All costs recorded refer to the direct operation of the vehicle. Overheads, rent, rates and wages are excluded as these would tend to reduce the value of the costings as a means of comparing the costs of operating different types of vehicle. The following vehicle data are shown:

1 Registration or fleet number
2 Make, group, type, gross vehicle weight, unladen weight (3/3/B indicates the HGV driving licence class, the size of the vehicle in that class and 'B' denotes a box van)
3 The invoice cost of the vehicle, reduced by the value of a set of tyres and the expected life of the vehicle in miles
4 Details of tyre size and cost of complete set. The estimated tyre life is used as a basis for costing
5 Standing costs will include interest on capital invested, licences and insurance costs
6 Depreciation is calculated in terms of cost per mile, based on the actual cost and the estimated life of the vehicle in miles ($^{18473}/_{300000} = £0.0616$)
7 Tyre costs per mile ($^{1260}/_{40000} = £0.0315$).

The details of running costs are taken from the monthly vehicle costing record and over the life of the vehicle a permanent record is built up. The following points are to be noted:

1 *Fuel.* Calculating mpg is suspect unless the tanks on the vehicle are full at the start and end of a monthly accounting period
2 *Oil.* Calculating mpg or miles per pint serves no useful purpose. Excessive oil use can be seen quite easily from total usage each month

	Vehicle costing record			Speedometer reading	GHM
Registration number **C888 XYZ**			Finish	**29155**	
Make **FORD CARGO 0813**			Start	**22108**	
Depot **WATFORD**			Miles	**7047**	
Vehicle group **3/3/8**					
Month **MARCH 87**					

Day	Fuel issues (Gallons)		Lubricant (pints)	Tyres (£)	Repairs and service (£)		Miles
	Bulk	Agency			Workshop	Agency	
1	16						22121
2	32		4		39·60		22471
3		10					
4	14						23372
5	18					44·00	23768
6	26		2				24191
7							24597
8							
24							
25							
26	8			247·50	97·20		
27	24						26923
28		6	2				
29	22				8·40		28058
30	10		4				28509
31	16						28732
Total agency	28						
Total bulk	293						
Totals	321		16	247·50	145·20	44·00	

Figure 40.8 **Layout of a simple monthly vehicle costing record** *(Costs shown here are to demonstrate the layout only and are not intended to be representative of current cost levels)*

VEHICLE OPERATING COST SHEET

VEHICLE DATA

Reg. No.	C 888 x Y Z
Make	FORD CARGO OF 13
Cost group	3/3/B
Date purchased	Oct. '85

Invoice cost (less tyres)	£18,473.
Estimated life	300,000 ML.
Gross vehicle weight	74·90 Kgs
Unladen weight	3979 Kgs

STANDING COSTS

Interest	£1,662.
Licences	£570
Insurances	£580
Total per annum	£2,812
per month	£234·33

TYRES

Size	85 R 17·5
No. per set	6
Cost per set	£1,260.
Estimated life	140,000 MLS

ESTIMATED COST PER MILE

Tyres	£0·0315
Depreciation	£0·0616
LAST DATE COSTS UPDATE	January 1986

Month	Mileage	Fuel Gallons	Fuel Cost (1)	m.p.g.	Oil Pints	Oil Cost (2)	Tyres Est. cost (3)	Tyres Actual	Servicing/repairs Work shop	Servicing/repairs Agents	Servicing/repairs Total (4)	Depreciation (5)	Total running costs (1–5)	Running costs per mile £	Standing	Operational	Operational costs per mile £
1985																	
Oct	4284	211	321	20·3	7	2·10	135	–	84·80	3·20	88·00	264	810·10	0·19	234·33	1044·33	0·24
Nov	4291	214	325	20·0	8	2·40	135	–	16·80	55·20	72·00	264	798·40	0·19	234·33	1032·73	0·24
Dec	4838	236	354	20·5	6	1·80	152	–	93·94	2·50	96·44	298	902·44	0·19	234·33	1136·77	0·23
1986																	
Jan	6083	297	445	20·5	14	4·10	192	–	182·60	4·20	186·80	375	1202·90	0·20	234·33	1437·23	0·24
Feb	2612	124	181	21·1	7	2·00	82	–	42·90	22·70	65·60	161	491·60	0·19	234·33	725·93	0·28
Mar	7047	321	469	22·0	16	4·75	222	247·58	145·20	44·00	185·20	434	1314·95	0·19	234·33	1549·28	0·22

Figure 40.9 Example of a vehicle cost operating record sheet

3   *Tyres.* Calculations are based on the tyre wear. Actual purchases are shown and if the estimated mileages are correct, then actual expenditure on tyres should balance the estimated costs over the agreed mileage

4   *Depreciation.* Obtained by multiplying monthly mileage by estimated cost per mile

5   *Running costs.* Total cost of fuel, oil, estimated tyre wear, repairs and depreciation, divided by miles run. This figure can be compared with the performance figures of other vehicles in the fleet within the same vehicle group, with its own performance figures over previous months and with cost tables published by the transport journals.

6   *Standing costs.* These are now added to the total running costs to give the total monthly operating costs. The total operating cost per mile is of little use as this entirely depends upon the mileage recorded for the period. It will be seen from the example that total operating cost per mile varied from 22p per mile to over 28p per mile whereas the per mile figure of running costs was reasonably constant.

MOVEMENT OF PERSONNEL

The transport services function should be responsible for personnel movement in order to minimize the problems involved and to increase the overall efficiency of the company by reducing the fatigue associated with people moving.

Sales and service function

The responsibility for the mobility of the sales force of a company comes within the function of transport services in that the provision of small vans, cars, and estate cars and the maintenance and servicing of such a fleet is the direct responsibility of the transport department of a company. The transport services function will need to advise on the choice of vehicle allocated to personnel of the sales and service force, and will need to know the difference of law and taxation in the use of this type of vehicle.

Law on small goods vehicles

A small goods vehicle is defined in s60(4) of the Transport Act 1968 as:

> One which does not form part of a vehicle combination and has a gross plated weight not exceeding 3.5 tonnes including the weight of any trailer drawn, or if not having a plated weight, has an unladen weight not exceeding 1525 kg including the weight of any trailer drawn.

The law for the small goods vehicle and its driver can be summarized as follows:

Operators' licences: exempt.

Vehicle testing: an annual test for roadworthiness when three years old or more.

Speed limits:

1   Dual carriageways other than motorways and not drawing a trailer
60 mph
2   Dual carriageways other than motorways when drawing a trailer
50 mph
3   Other roads   50 mph
(The above subject to the road not being restricted to a lower speed limit.)
4   Motorways:
Not drawing a trailer   70 mph
When drawing a trailer   50 mph

Trailers: subject to the weight of the vehicle not being less than the weight of the trailer being towed, the speed limit on derestricted roads and motorways is 50 mph. A 50 mph disc must be displayed on the rear of the trailer, and the kerb weight of the vehicle and the maximum permitted unladen weight of the trailer must be shown on each.

Driving licences: Ordinary driving licences Group 'A' or Group 'B' if restricted to automatic transmission vehicles.

Drivers' hours: goods vehicles with a gross plated weight not in excess of 3.5 tonnes including dual purpose vehicles (estate cars), are required to conform with the British Domestic Hours rules which have been revised and simplified effective from 29th September 1986. The rules are.

1   Maximum daily driving   10 hrs
2   Maximum daily duty   11 hrs

There are no regulations governing the hours of continuous driving, break periods, weekly duty or weekly rest periods.

Drivers' records: completely exempt (written records and tachographs).

Servicing and maintenance of sales and service vehicles

Although this class of vehicle is exempt from the requirements of operator licensing, it is important to understand that any convictions against a company or a vehicle user for contravention of the Construction and Use Regulations 1978, or for instances of using, or causing to be used, vehicles which are found to be unroadworthy, may be taken into consideration when application is made for the renewal of, or the initial granting of an 'O' licence. A system of reporting defects by the driver of the vehicle is recommended and a suitable form is illustrated in Figure 40.10. Drivers should also be asked to send in weekly reports showing any work done on the vehicle by outside garages.

The company car

Mobility of personnel costs money. Just as the cost-effectiveness of a goods distribution service is judged on its contribution to the total profitability of a company by giving an efficient customer service, the value of a fleet of company cars should also be assessed on its contribution to the efficient mobility of management and executives, as well as the part it plays in recruiting the right calibre of person to fulfil the needs of the company. There are many different approaches to determining a policy for the supply and allocation of cars to company employees. Each company will decide its own policy based on its own needs. For a medium-sized fleet, there are several ways of obtaining cars:

1 Outright purchase or hire purchase negotiating the best terms
2 Leasing, generally without maintenance but sometimes with the cost of the vehicle licence included
3 Contract hire, with maintenance cost, licences and a replacement vehicle included in the monthly rentals.

Each of the above methods has advantages and disadvantages and, as stated in the section dealing with the purchase of trucks, it all depends on the financial position of a company, and how it views its cash flow. There

---

GHM

DRIVER'S REPORT OF VEHICLE DEFECTS

Date _____

This form to be used only to report defects and must be handed to the Transport Office IMMEDIATELY on your return. No verbal reports please

Depot _____

Registration number _____ Make _____

NATURE OF DEFECT. Faults must be reported at once, even if only of a minor nature

Speedometer reading _____ If anything is wrong, don't be afraid to say so

Driver's signature _____

Date rectified _____ By _____

Figure 40.10   Form for reporting vehicle defects

is no doubt that provided the cash-flow situation of a company will permit, outright purchase at the highest discount, followed by a direct disposal policy to trade outlets, is the most cost-effective way of obtaining cars.

A company car issued to an individual is considered as a benefit in kind and as such the car user is liable to be taxed on the assessed benefit. The annual Finance Bill states the taxable benefit on types of car and these are sub-divided into groups either by engine capacity or retail cost. Fuel supplied to car users for private use is also liable to tax and full details are included in the Finance Act published after each year's budget presented by the Chancellor.

Replacement policies

Any replacement policy will again depend upon the cash-flow situation of a company, and any policy should be flexible in order to take advantage of changes in secondhand market values, or impending price increases of new cars. It is possible to negotiate guaranteed buy-back prices for cars when they are purchased, but this type of arrangement tends to become less flexible and arguments will arise over delays and damage when vehicles are returned to the dealers. A well tested policy which has an in-built flexibility is as follows:

1 Outright purchase of all cars after negotiating for highest fleet discounts
2 Replacement policy:
  (a) Cars 1600cc and under, replace after 2 years
  (b) Other cars replace after 60 000 miles or 3 years whichever comes first
3 Disposal policy. Sell to the trade (not to the dealer who supplied the original vehicle) or through car auctions where special fleet terms are available

With the above policy, the transport services function will be carrying out a responsible task and obtaining every possible cost benefit for the company. The policy is flexible in that no firm contracts are entered into and the purchase and disposal dates can be delayed or brought forward for reasons of cash flow, to avoid heavy repair bills or to take advantage of minimizing the impact of taxation balancing charges which may become due at the end of a company financial year.

Chauffeur services

One of the neglected areas in a transport function is that of the provision of an efficient and well-managed chauffeur operation. Even the smallest company will have a driver, whose duties will include meeting visitors at airports and stations, and driving customers between company locations. Larger companies have chauffeurs allocated to directors and executives, whose duties may include tasks other than driving a company car. A chauffeur should be trained to keep himself and his car in immaculate condition, so as to portray an image of an efficient organization. Very often a chauffeur is the first contact a visitor will have with a company, and the initial impression can be of vital importance.

Company air services

The company aircraft, owned and operated by a company for use by company personnel, is now firmly established in the UK. The need for a company air service and its justification on financial grounds are very difficult to assess, and indeed any cost exercise based solely on financial justification must fail. The task of the transport services function is to operate a service based on the highest standards of safety and also to minimize the additional costs which accompany the operating of a company aircraft. Safety, comfort, punctuality and reliability are the most important features of an efficient company air service. Safety means operating to a high standard and strict compliance with the current Air Navigation Orders. Comfort of passengers means a reasonably comfortable cabin layout, quiet, facilities for reading and writing, temperature control, and above all, commonsense thinking of the crew to find a comfortable flying altitude for that particular journey. Punctuality and reliability are the two features which will test the efficiency of the service. Crews must ensure that the aircraft is always waiting for the passengers. Timings are important: not only must the passengers know the take-off time; they must also know at what time they will be at their destination.

There are several ways to acquire the use of an aircraft:

1 Charter from a company which specializes in this type of operation. They will supply the aircraft, crew, and carry out all maintenance, route-planning and management
2 Lease – an aircraft lease can be written in two forms of agreement:

   (a) A finance lease for the aircraft only, including all the instrumentation required to meet the standards of the C.A.A. This will be written over a period of years at the end of which, the aircraft can be made the subject of a secondary lease at a much lower rental.
   (b) An operational lease which will provide an aircraft to the required level of specification, fully maintained to C.A.A. standards and with the provision of the crew.

The administration in both cases would be under the control of the company using the aircraft.
3 Purchase the aircraft and contract out all maintenance and management and also the provision of crews to an operating company.
4 Purchase the aircraft and employ your own crews as well as providing the necessary management and maintenance controls.

Operating the aircraft

Owning your aircraft does not give you the right to operate outside the public category, and if the crew is supplied by a charter company and not employed directly by your company (that is, on the company payroll), then the operation will be subject to all the restrictions placed by the Department of Trade and Industry on a public category operation. By employing your own crew to fly the aircraft, it is possible to operate in the private category using aircraft with an 'all up weight' not in excess of 1500 lb. All aircraft above this weight are required to meet the full standards of operation as laid down for operating within the public category. It is always advisable to operate at the highest standards of safety irrespective of the type of aircraft used.

Selecting the aircraft and costing the operation

A wide variety of aircraft is available which are suitable for company operation. They range from the single engine helicopter which flies 'point to point' at speeds of up to 150mph to the twin fan-jet aircraft capable of speeds approaching 600mph. The costs of operating helicopters and fixed-wing aircraft range from:

Helicopters	Single engine (turbine)	£325–400	per hour
	Twin engine (turbine)	£700–850	per hour
Fixed-wing	Twin engine (piston)	£175–200	per hour
	Twin engine (turbine) pressurized	£425–525	per hour
	Twin engine (jet)	£1000–1400	per hour

FURTHER READING

Commercial Vehicle Buyer's Guide, Kogan Page, London

Duckworth, James (ed.), *Kitchens Road Transport Law* 25th edition, Butterworth, London, 1985

Cooke, P.N.C., *Financial Analysis of Motor Transport Operations* Gower, Aldershot, 1974

Cooke, P.N.C. *The Company Car*, Gower, Aldershot, 1975

Cooke, P.N.C. and Woodward, Frank H., *Controlling Company Car Costs*, Gower, Aldershot, 1985

Cooke, P.N.C. (ed.) *Car Fleet Administration and Finance 1985*, Professional Publishing Limited, London, 1985

Gattorna, J. (ed.), *Handbook of Physical Distribution Management*, 3rd edition, Gower, Aldershot, 1983, page *704*

Lowe, D., *Transport Managers' Handbook 1986*, Kogan Page, London, (published annually)

Lowe, D. *A Study Manual of Professional Competence in Road Transport Management*, Kogan Page, London, 1978

Thompson, B.A., *Croner's Road Transport Operation*, Croner Publications, New Malden (by subscription, and updated monthly)

Thompson, B.A., *Professional Driver's Guide*, Croner Publications, New Malden, 1985 (revised every two years)

Toyne, C.C., *Motor Vehicle Technical Regulations*, 2nd edition, Liffon Engineering Services, London

Tables of Operating Costs (annually), *Commercial Motor*, IPC Business Publications, London

Woodward, Frank H., *Managing the Transport Services Function* 2nd edition, Gower, Aldershot, 1977

Part Eight
ADMINISTRATION

41 Company law

F W Rose

A company registered under the Companies Act 1985 has a legal existence and personality quite separate and distinct from that of persons holding shares in the company. Many legal formalities must be complied with before such a company comes into existence. When formed the company has rights and liabilities in law which depends upon a careful analysis of the relevant statutory rules.

It may be necessary when an individual makes an agreement with a company to determine its precise power to contract, its financial position and future prospects. If the company is experiencing difficulties in trading profitably, the rights of the shareholders to control the company may be of vital importance.

This chapter explains some of the more important legal provisions. Use of technical language which would be unfamiliar to non-lawyers has been avoided. Legislation dealing with company law issues has been consolidated in the Companies Act 1985, replacing material in five previous Acts stretching back to 1948. Other relevant material is embodied in the Business Names Act 1985 and in the Company Securities (Insider Dealing) Act 1985.

FORMATION OF A PUBLIC LIMITED COMPANY

A private company is often formed to carry on a family business. Frequently there are only a handful of shareholders, usually members of the same family. A private company may trade successfully for several years, but further expansion will require additional capital which cannot be supplied by existing shareholders. A public company may be formed to take over and carry on the business; members of the private company will exchange their shares for shares in the new public company. The additional capital for such items as land, new buildings and machinery will be provided by issuing shares which the general public may purchase if they wish. About 2 per cent of all UK companies are public companies.

Registration

The company must be registered. This is effected by filing the following documents with the Registrar of Companies:

1 The memorandum of association
2 The articles of association
3 A statement of nominal capital
4 A list of persons to act as directors and secretary, together with their signatures as evidence of their consent to act as such.

These formalities are usually dealt with by a solicitor, accountant or a company formation firm specializing in this type of work. This person or body also files a declaration that the company has complied with all formalities necessary for registration. The Registrar then issues a Certificate of Incorporation which is conclusive evidence that the company has been properly incorporated.

In law the company now has an existence separate and distinct from that of the individual members who hold shares in the company. The company:

1 Can own property, and members have no rights in that property: their interest is in the shares they hold
2 Can make contracts with other individuals, companies or members
3 Will continue to exist irrespective of the death of an individual member, whose shareholding is then taken over by the person who succeeds to his property.
4 Must act through the medium of human agents who will control its affairs, such as directors.

A public company is subject to stringent rules designed to protect persons investing money in the company, for example, by prohibiting loans to directors from company funds.

The memorandum of association

This is the charter of the company embodying its constitution and powers. It must state:

1 The name of the company, indicating that it is a public limited company with 'Public limited company' as the last words of the name
2 The location of the registered office of the company
3 The objects to be carried out by the company
4 A declaration that the liability of members is limited
5 The share capital and its division into shares.

The objects clause
This states the company's main business objective. It is followed by a

large number of ancillary clauses giving the company power to effect other objects incidental to the main purpose. Examples would include power to buy land, borrow money and purchase shares in other companies. In practice, the objects clause will be widely drawn to include almost every conceivable business objective, coupled with a declaration that they should be construed as main objectives and not subsidiary powers.

The original purpose of the objects clause was to delimit the company's powers so that capital subscribed by investors could be used only for the company's main and, presumably commercially sound, objective; not in some other subsidiary and risky enterprise in which the investor would not have chosen to place his capital.

The concept of limited liability

An investor who purchases shares must pay to the company the purchase price agreed upon. Usually shares must be fully paid for at the time when they are allotted to a shareholder by the company. If they are only partly paid for, then the shareholder is contingently liable to pay the sum still outstanding, even if the company is in liquidation. Once the shares have been fully paid for, the shareholder's liability is complete. He cannot be required to make further contributions, even if the company fails and is unable to settle debts owed to creditors who have supplied goods and services to the company.

Limited liability is one of the most important attractions of shareholding in a public company. After fully paying for his shares the investor has fixed the amount of money that he is prepared to place at risk. However disastrous the company's financial collapse, he cannot be called upon to pay more.

Articles of association

These govern the internal management of the company, regulating the rights of the members among themselves on such matters as:

1 Appointment and power of directors
2 Issue, transfer and forfeiture of shares
3 Rules regulating meetings of a company
4 Payment of dividends
5 Preparation of accounts and auditing
6 Alterations to the capital structure of the company
7 Rights of different classes of shareholders.

It is usual for a company to register its own special set of articles which make specific provisions on matters of internal management, particularly suited to the needs of that individual business.

The prospectus

The usual object of forming a public company is to raise money from the investing public to finance the company's policies of expansion. A company may apply for a stock exchange quotation so that shares can be easily bought and sold through the medium of stockbrokers and jobbers. The company will issue a prospectus which sets out:

1 The objects it will pursue
2 Reports by experts on property owned, its financial position and trading prospects for the future
3 The names of directors; if the board of directors includes well-known experts it may be an inducement to buy the shares
4 The details of the company's capital structure.

These details will enable the investor to determine whether he wishes to purchase shares.

CAPITAL AND SHARES

The authorized (or nominal) capital is the amount of money that the company is authorized by the memorandum of association to raise from the public, for example, £5 000 000. In practice the company may not require this amount immediately, but it can issue shares up to the limit specified at any time when it wishes to do so.

The issued capital is that part of the nominal capital which has been actually issued to the public for cash or other consideration, such as land or buildings, in return for an allotment of shares, for example, an issued capital of £2 500 000 out of the nominal capital of £5 000 000. If a subscriber is required to pay only half the amount due on his share allotment, then the capital actually received by the company (that is the paid-up capital) will be only £1 250 000 in the above example. The amount not yet paid up on the shares issued is referred to as uncalled capital and it may be declared by the company to be incapable of being required from a shareholder except in a winding-up of its affairs.

Certificate of entitlement to commence business

A public company may not commence business after incorporation or borrow money unless it has received a certificate to this effect. This will not be granted until the issued capital is at least equal to the authorized minimum permitted (at present £50 000). In addition at least one-quarter of the nominal value of each share, plus any premium payable as part of the purchase price, must have been paid up.

Serious loss of capital

As a result of adverse trading or other factors, a company may have lost much of the capital that it has raised to finance its operation. Where the net assets of a public company are half or less of the company's called-up capital, then the directors on becoming so aware must convene an extraordinary general meeting of members within the next twenty-eight days. The meeting itself must be held within fifty-six days of becoming aware of the position. There are no legal provisions requiring any specific type of action that the company must take to deal with the problem. The meeting will give shareholders the chance to consider the company's financial position before insolvency supervenes to stop further trading activities.

Payment for shares

The person allotted shares in a company may pay for them in money or 'money's worth', that is granting some form of benefit instead of cash. Payment in a form other than cash may result in the company not receiving the full value of the shares given in return; thus the law has been strengthened to prevent such abuses. A public company cannot accept an undertaking by an allottee of shares to do work or perform services for the company as consideration for an issue of shares. If there is a failure to observe this requirement, the allottee still remains liable to pay the required sum in cash.

A public company is permitted to allot shares in return for an 'undertaking' to transfer a non-cash asset, such as land, within five years from the date of allotment. The non-cash asset must be valued by an independent person qualified to act as a company auditor to ensure that the company is receiving proper value in return for its shares. These provisions are inapplicable where one company takes over or merges with another company and shares in the company being taken over are exchanged for shares in the company that has made the takeover.

Increasing capital and pre-emption rights

When a company has issued all of its capital and received payment in full from shareholders, it may require further cash to finance an expansion of its operations. The company will usually be authorized by its articles to alter the capital clause in its memorandum and, if the members in general meeting so decide, an ordinary resolution may be passed to increase the share capital. Shares can then be issued to raise the additional capital. Suppose that prior to the issue of the new shares for cash, an existing shareholder, Jones, holds 60 per cent of the company's total shareholding. In effect he controls the company as a majority shareholder. The issue of new shares to other persons could take this away by reducing his percentage of the total number of shares now in issue. The Companies Act provides that a company must not allot shares for cash unless an existing shareholder has been given the opportunity to buy the new shares in proportion to his existing holding. Thus, Jones could, if he so wished, buy 60 per cent of the new shares on offer and retain the same percentage interest in the company's capital. The company's articles, or members by special resolution in general meeting, may give power to directors to exclude or modify pre-emption rights from all share allotments for a maximum period of five years. This power can be revoked at any time by ordinary resolution of members or extended for a further period up to five years maximum.

Power over unissued shares

A takeover bid occurs when one company (Company A,) offers to buy or has already acquired a majority of the voting shares in another company (Company B). The directors of Company B may wish to resist the takeover as undesirable, or because they fear that they will be removed from office once the takeover has been achieved. In the past if Company B had not yet issued all of its authorized capital, the directors could have used a power, often granted to them by the articles, to issue new shares representing hitherto unissued capital to themselves and their supporters. This manoeuvre may have given the directors and supporters control of a majority of the voting shares and so thwart the takeover to which the other shareholders were agreeable.

Now directors may not exercise any power of the company to allot shares, or other securities such as debentures which can be converted into shares at the holder's option, unless authorized to do so by an ordinary resolution of members in general meeting or by the articles. The power so granted may be a general authority to allot, or limited to a specified amount. When such authority is granted it must state the maximum amount of securities that may be allotted, the date of expiry of the authority and its duration, which must not exceed five years. The authority may be renewed for a further period (maximum again five years) by members in general meeting. Nonetheless members now control the directors' actions in this area, since any authority given may be varied or revoked at any time by ordinary resolution in general meeting.

MEMBERSHIP

A shareholder is a member of the company entitled to the following rights:

1 To attend meetings and vote on issues affecting company policy, including the appointment and removal of directors. He may requisition a meeting if he wishes to discuss any matter of concern provided that he alone, or in conjunction with his supporters has at least 10 per cent of the issued share capital carrying a right to vote, or some lesser proportion as prescribed by the articles
2 To receive an annual report and accounts giving details of the company's affairs

3   To share in the profits made in the form of a dividend declared by the directors
4   To share in the assets of the company if its affairs are wound up, provided any property remains when the rights of other creditors with prior claims have been met
5   To transfer his shares when he wishes by selling or giving them to another person
6   To present a petition to wind up the company or ask for an order controlling its affairs.

Different classes of shares

A company usually issues different classes of shares, each having its attractions for the investor.

Preference shareholders are entitled to the following payments in priority to ordinary shareholders:

1   A yearly dividend out of profits, at a fixed though moderate percentage of the capital invested, for example, 7 per cent. Unless the articles of association state otherwise, arrears of dividend not paid in a previous year when there were no profits are carried forward and must be paid in future years when sufficient profits are available
2   Repayments of the capital contributed to the company when it is wound up, if, as is usual, the articles so provide.

Ordinary shareholders are entitled to:

1   The remainder of profits available for distribution, which will secure a high rate of dividend if the company is successful. However, if a loss results in any trading year a dividend may not be paid at all
2   Return of capital contributed to the company when it is wound up, if sufficient assets remain to satisfy these claims.

The market value of shares will rise if the company trades successfully and the ordinary shareholder, in particular, may make a capital profit on selling his shares.

Ordinary shareholders bear the risk of substantial loss if the company fails; consequently, they have a right to vote at meetings and control the company's affairs to the exclusion of preference shareholders who are usually entitled to vote only if:

1   Their dividend is six months in arrear
2   Their rights as a class are affected by some issue under discussion at the meeting
3   On a resolution to wind up the company.

MAINTENANCE OF COMPANY CAPITAL

A company raises capital to finance its business operations by issuing shares in return for cash or property. The amount so raised may increase or decrease, depending on the relative success or failure of the company's trading activities. Suppliers of goods extending credit to the company, whether on a secured or unsecured basis, do so in the knowledge that even if the company is sustaining trading losses, there should be sufficient capital to meet their claims for payment. The capital so available must not be reduced and placed beyond the reach of creditors by returning it to the members (as where the company buys back a member's shares and so refunds his capital contribution).

There are a limited number of exceptions to this rule. Preference shares may be issued on terms that permit redemption by the company, and this principle has now been extended to ordinary shares. Capital may be raised for a limited time to finance a specific programme and then returned to members, thus eliminating the need to continue paying dividends on these shares. Such shares offer temporary membership of a company, with repayment of the nominal value of these shares (in some cases plus a premium) when the period of membership expires. Membership will end after a fixed period of time or, at the company's option, in accordance with the agreed terms regarding redemption. On repaying members their share capital or redemption, the company must replace the capital by issuing other shares to raise the money so lost. Alternatively, the company may transfer a sum from its distributable profits (which would otherwise have been paid over to members as a dividend) to a capital redemption reserve, which is then treated in exactly the same way as capital. The provisions permit listed companies to purchase issued redeemable shares at less than the redemption figure (if the company has resources available to finance a purchase at an earlier date than that agreed) from a willing seller.

A company may redeem its own ordinary shares through a purchase from a willing seller, even though the shares were not issued by the company on the understanding that they were to be redeemed. Such a purchase must first be approved by members in a general meeting. The purchase may be made through the medium of the Stock Exchange or direct from a member who wishes to sell.

Acquisition and transfer of shares

When shares are first issued by a company an investor may make an offer to purchase them by submitting an application form. Allotment of shares by the company creates a binding contract with the investor. Shares may be issued at a premium; for example, 50p may have to be paid for a share with a nominal or face value of only 25p. This means that existing shares already issued have a market value of 50p, thus the real worth of a share is determined by reference to the market value, not the face or par value.

A share certificate will be issued by the company stating the name of the shareholder and the extent of his shareholding. The register of members, kept by the company, will record the shareholder's name and address and the number of shares held.

The shares of public companies are quoted on the Stock Exchange and the shareholder can determine the present value of his shares by referring to the Stock Exchange list which is published in leading newspapers. One of the main advantages of shareholding is the ability to sell quickly and realize the value of the shares.

Register of substantial shareholdings

A public company's register of members may not disclose the real identity of shareholders. Often the legal title to shares is held by one person as a nominee of another, and the company cannot by law enter the beneficial owner in its register. The register may not reveal that a group of members are acting 'in concert' as business associates who, between them, control a significant proportion of the voting rights at a general meeting (thus being able to exert some influence on company policy). Such 'concert parties', secretly holding over 30 per cent of the voting rights, would not have to make a mandatory bid to purchase all other voting shares, whose holders would effectively be in a minority position (being unable to communicate easily with one another to establish a coherent view on how the company should be managed). Sometimes such a power base can be used to launch a takeover bid without prior warning. There are now very detailed provisions for such disclosures to be made.

Debentures

A company needing finance for a programme of expansion may be reluctant to raise the additional capital required by issuing more shares. The money will only be needed until the new equipment purchased earns sufficient profits to repay the capital borrowed, the company may not wish to raise capital on a permanent basis for such relatively short-term needs, since regular dividends must be paid. The company borrows money from the lender and in return issues a debenture, redeemable at a fixed or determinable time or at the company's option. The debenture holder is entitled to:

1 A fixed rate of interest which must be paid even if it is paid out of capital, not profits
2 Repayment of the principal sum when due
3 A charge on the company's property. This means that if the company fails to repay the loan and interest when due, the debenture holders may satisfy their claims by disposing of the company's assets. These claims have priority over, and must be satisfied before, claims by all types of shareholders.

MEETINGS

The company is obliged to hold various types of meetings from time to time to transact business. An annual general meeting must be held every year to deal with:

1. Declaration of dividends
2. Consideration of the accounts and balance sheet and the report of directors and auditors
3. Appointment of directors
4. Appointment and fixing of the remuneration of auditors.

Members must be given twenty-one days' notice of the meeting.

An extraordinary general meeting may be called by directors if important business needs to be transacted which cannot await the next annual general meeting. Holders of one-tenth of the paid-up share capital with voting rights may requisition such a meeting, even against the directors' wishes. Members must be given fourteen days' notice of the meeting.

DIRECTORS

Every public company must have at least two directors and a secretary. A proportion of the directors, usually about one-third, retire at each annual general meeting, and the members may re-elect them or appoint others in their place. A director may be removed by an ordinary resolution passed by members, but the director may make representations on the issue showing why he should not be removed.

The directors must manage the company's affairs by taking decisions at board meetings, otherwise they may be personally liable for their actions.

A director may be required by the articles to hold a certain number of shares in the company which are called his qualification shares, otherwise he must vacate his office. This gives him a personal interest in furthering the fortunes of the company to the best of his ability.

The articles may provide for the payment of a fixed fee to a director, but his remuneration is often stated in a service contract which he makes with the company. His remuneration must be disclosed in the annual accounts. A director is not entitled to compensation for loss of office or on retirement, unless approved by the shareholders.

The powers of the company, as determined by the memorandum and articles, are usually delegated to the directors in so far as they are not exercised by the company in general meeting. Members in general meeting cannot interfere with the manner in which the directors exercise their powers, unless they alter the articles accordingly. If directors exceed their powers the members may ratify their actions, provided the act is within the powers of the company.

Publicity concerning directors

The company must make available the following information about a director:

1 A register of directors and secretaries must be kept at the registered office and open for public inspection, specifying a director's name, address, nationality, business occupation and other directorships held, except directorships in wholly-owned subsidiaries

2 A register of directors' interest in the company's shares and debentures must be kept at the registered office or place where the register of members is kept. It must be open for public inspection. Such holdings by a spouse and minor children must be disclosed

3 Details of a director's service contract must be kept at the registered office, or place where the register of members is kept or at the company's principal place of business. It must be open for inspection by members

4 The names of directors must appear on business letters, trade catalogues, circulars and show cards.

Shadow directors and connected persons

The various statutory provisions that impose numerous legal obligations and duties on directors, also cover any person occupying the position of director whatever name is used to describe his office. 'Shadow' directors are also treated as if they were directors for some purposes. This concept covers persons giving directions to directors, who then are accustomed to follow them irrespective of any legal or other obligation to do so. Thus directors may manage a company in accordance with the policy dictated by the controlling shareholder. That shareholder becomes a 'shadow' director. A person giving professional advice, such as an accountant, does not thereby become a 'shadow' director. Persons 'connected' with a director may also have the same restrictions placed upon their activities as the director himself. A 'connected person' includes:

1 Director's current spouse and his children up to the age of eighteen

2 Trustees of a trust which has as one of its beneficiaries the director, his children, his current spouse or an 'associated' company

3 Partner of the director or a partner of the director's spouse, his children or his trustee

4 A company with which the director is 'associated' where the director and his connected persons hold one-fifth of the nominal value of the 'associated' company's equity share capital, or where the director, his connected persons and any company he controls hold one-fifth of the voting rights at a general meeting.

Disclosure of interest in contracts

A director may have a personal interest in a contract made by the company with some other body, such as a partnership in which the director is himself a partner, or another company in which he holds shares. The company is entitled to the unbiased advice of a director, unfettered by conflict between personal interest and duties owed to the company. Every director having an interest, direct or indirect, in the contract which the company is about to enter, must disclose that fact to the board of directors when the matter is discussed. Such disclosure permits the director to make a personal profit from the contract which the company enters into, but failure to disclose enables the company to rescind the agreement so made. These principles also apply to 'shadow' directors.

Where directors have wide powers of management the risk arises that a director may sell his own property to the company at an inflated price with the connivance of fellow directors, or purchase the company's property at an undervaluation. An 'arrangement', which covers transactions not strictly enforceable at law as a contract of sale, cannot permit a director or his connected person to acquire a non-cash asset from the company or its holding company above the 'requisite value' of over £50 000, or one-tenth of the value of the company assets if over £1000, whichever sum is smaller. Further, a director or his connected person cannot sell a non-cash asset over the 'requisite value' to the company or its holding company. Arrangements exceeding the requisite value are permitted, however, if approved by members in general meeting. The holding company must consent as well as the subsidiary company directly involved. Here the shareholders have the opportunity to assess the advisability of the arrangement and will give their consent only if the company's interests have been safeguarded.

Service contract for a director

A director may be dismissed by a majority vote in favour of his removal passed by members in general meeting. To protect himself financially the director may have an express, written contract of service with the company for a fixed period of time (for example, ten years). If removed from office before expiration of the period he may claim damages for salary, less tax, that he would have earned during the unexpired portion of his service contract. The sum involved may be considerable, thus dismissal can be an expensive luxury for the company. Shareholders are given the opportunity of voting at general meetings on whether directors are to be given such long-term service contracts.

A service contract for less than five years' duration, or for over five years' duration but terminable by giving reasonable notice (which means in practice about six months' notice) may be approved by the board or the managing director, depending on the person or body to whom the requisite power has been delegated. The consent of the members in general meeting is required for a service contract over five years' duration if not terminable by notice, or only terminable in specified circumstances. In the absence of such consent the contract itself is valid, but the term on duration is void, and the contract may be terminated by giving reasonable notice.

These provisions are designed to prevent abuses whereby directors negotiate such contracts on terms set by themselves immediately prior to an anticipated takeover bid or removal on a vote by members, so that on loss of office they recoup substantial sums as damages for breach of contract.

Loans to directors

There are strict limitations on companies making loans to directors. Their position as managers may permit abuses at the company's, and consequently the shareholders' expense, as by making loans on terms that are commercially unsound.

A company is prohibited from making a loan exceeding £2500 to its own or a holding company's director, or providing a guarantee, indemnity or security in connexion with a loan by some other person to such a director. However, a company may provide funds for a director to meet, or avoid incurring expenditure he has or will incur for company purposes, or to enable him to perform properly his duties as a company officer. Members in general meeting must give their prior approval with knowledge of the purpose and amount of the loan, or retroactive approval before or at the next annual general meeting. In the absence of such approval the loan becomes repayable, and the resultant liability must be discharged within six months of that meeting. Not more than £10 000 must be outstanding by way of loan at any one time to a particular director or his connected person from a 'relevant' company.

PROVISION FOR EMPLOYEES

A company may make provision for its own employees, or former employees, or those of a subsidiary company, when that company or one of its subsidiaries ceases business or transfers its business to a new owner. This provision permits a redundancy payment to an employee losing his job above the maximum sum authorized under the Employment Protection (Consolidation) Act 1968. The proposed payment must be sanctioned by members in general meeting approving an ordinary resolution. The articles or memorandum may state that a resolution by the directors suffices, or give a greater element of control to members by requiring a special or extraordinary resolution in general meeting.

DIVIDENDS

Dividends are trading profits divided among members in proportion to the number of shares held. The directors are responsible for fixing the rate of dividend, with the sanction of the general meeting. Shareholders cannot demand a dividend if the directors refuse to declare one, even though the annual profits seem to warrant some payment. Profits do not have to be distributed as dividends, as the directors may think it wiser to use them to offset past losses, or to transfer them to reserve to meet future liabilities. Once a dividend has been declared, however, a shareholder may sue to recover the sum he is entitled to receive if payment is not made.

INSIDER DEALING

An insider dealer is someone connected with a company such as a director, company secretary, auditor, employee or other person in a business or professional relationship with the company, who has acquired in confidence specific information; that is, unpublished price-sensitive information, materially affecting the value of that company's shares and debentures or the securities of a company in the same group. The insider dealer then buys or sells such securities on the Stock Exchange without disclosing this information, which is not generally known to those persons who deal in, or would like to deal in, the securities affected. Persons who receive unpublished sensitive information are prevented from dealing in securities to which the information relates.

An individual who has price-sensitive information and/or is prohibited from dealing in a company's securities must not counsel or procure another person to so act, knowing or reasonably believing that such dealing would occur.

Contravention of these rules is a criminal offence under the Company Securities (Insider Dealing) Act 1985. There does not appear to be a civil remedy in this situation. In principle, if someone (such as a director) buys or sells shares in his company because he knows inside confidential information affecting their value, then the profit so made (or the loss so avoided) should in theory go to the company, since he is making an improper profit out of his official position. In such a situation it seems difficult to provide recompense to the shareholder buying from or selling to the director concerned, since the shareholder acted on his own initiative and was not induced to do so by that director. Nor is there a recognized duty to reveal the relevant information to the shareholder involved on an individual basis.

Theoretically, following a conviction for insider dealing, the court could order compensation to anyone suffering from the crime under the Powers of Criminal Courts Act 1973, though there could be problems in determining the precise amount recoverable. The register of a director's interest in shares of his company, together with the interest of his spouse and minor children, may help to establish insider dealing by illuminating his sales and purchases.

FURTHER READING

Northey and Leigh, *Introduction to Company Law*, 3rd edition, Butterworth, London, 1983. Good coverage in a style that is easy to follow

Mayson and French, *A Practical Approach to Company Law*, 2nd edition, Financial Training, 1985. Well researched and informative book with a wealth of detail

Smith, K., and Keenan, D.J., *Company Law*, 4th edition, Pitman, London, 1983. Some excellent background material and a useful summary of case law.

42 Contracts between companies

F W Rose

There are several essential elements that must be present before an agreement becomes a contract binding in law. Although the examples given concentrate on the sale of goods, the legal requirements are the same for all types of contract, whether the subject matter is a contract for the sale of goods or supply of a service by one company to another, or by a company to a private individual (or vice versa), or a contract of employment between employer and employee.

OFFER AND ACCEPTANCE

An offer is a definite indication by one party that he is willing to contract with another party on specified terms. A binding legal contract will come into existence if the terms are accepted without qualification and this fact is brought to the attention of the party making the offer. The conclusion of a contract is often preceded by lengthy discussions between the parties, but from these negotiations it must be possible to extract a firm offer followed by a firm acceptance.

Company *B* may ask further questions to induce better terms from Company *A*, but without intending to reject the original offer which will be accepted without qualification if better terms cannot be secured, for example, whether a total purchase price of £20 000 can be paid in instalments.

Any variation between the terms of the offer and the acceptance prevents the formation of a contract. For example, if Company *A* offers to sell Company *B* one hundred office desks at £500 each, the offer is not accepted if Company *B* agrees to buy at £400 each. Company *B* has rejected the original offer and made a counter-offer which is capable of acceptance by Company *A*. If Company *A* rejects the counter-offer, Company *B* cannot accept the original offer, unless Company *A* agrees. By this time Company *A* may have sold the goods to Company *C*. Company *B* cannot sue Company *A* for £10 000 damages for breach of contract if desks of the same type have to be purchased elsewhere for £600 each.

Keeping the offer open for a stipulated time

If a company offers to sell goods on stated terms, the company to whom the offer is made may be allowed a period of time to reach its decision. If an acceptance is communicated before the time allowed has elapsed, then a binding contract comes into existence. Although the company making the offer may feel morally bound to allow the company to whom the offer is made the stipulated period of time for reflection, the offer may be revoked at any time before notification of acceptance, even if the stipulated period for consideration has not ended. This right may be exercised where changed circumstances render conclusion of the contract undesirable, for example, where the market price of the goods has risen.

To safeguard its position the company to whom the offer is made may take an 'option' on the goods. This is a separate, binding contract whereby a period of time is given to reach a final decision on purchase. If during the period of the option the offer is revoked, the company making an offer commits a breach of contract for which damages are recoverable. Since the option itself is a contract, it must satisfy all the essential requirements of a contract. This usually means that the company making the offer must be paid for granting the option.

Lapse and revocation of an offer

An offer lapses if it is not accepted within the stipulated time. Where a given period of time for acceptance is not prescribed in the offer, there must be acceptance within the time that is 'reasonable' in the circumstances of the case.

An offer may be revoked any time before acceptance, but revocation is effective only when actually communicated to the party to whom the offer was made. It is important to choose a reliable means of communication, so that the company to whom the offer is made cannot claim that it has not heard of the revocation. If the post is used, a revocation is effective only when it is actually received. If the communication is lost in the post the revocation is ineffective. Notification of the revocation may be made through some reliable source, such as the company's sales manager.

If telex is used as a method of communication, then the contract is concluded at the time when the acceptance is actually keyed out. If the message is received in some other country, then the contract will be governed by the laws applicable in that foreign country, not by English law.

Need for a special method of acceptance

The company making the offer may request an acceptance in a particular form, such as telephone, telemessage or telex, a likely possibility where a speedy answer is required. Acceptance by another method, for instance a letter, would then be invalid. If the method of acceptance were quicker than the one prescribed by the offeror, such as a telex instead of a letter, this would probably be a valid acceptance.

Where a speedy reply is not required, but a particular method of acceptance is stipulated, use of the alternative method will not invalidate the acceptance if the circumstances suggest that there was a choice. For example, pending execution of a standard written agreement containing contractual terms, an informal letter of acceptance may suffice, especially if the party making the offer expressly or by conduct waives the condition as to the special mode of acceptance.

Sometimes when a particular method of acceptance is stipulated any alternative form of acceptance will be invalid. A company selling its goods may have drafted a written contract embodying all relevant terms to cover issues (such as problems relating to delivery) which may give rise to difficulties between the contracting parties. The seller will insist on the buyer signing the written agreement to signify assent to these standard terms. Refusal to do so will result in the seller failing to contract, or to negotiation of different terms which are mutually acceptable.

Standard contracts of this type often embody an exemption clause, a term used to describe a contractual clause which is inserted into a written contract attempting to limit or remove the legal liability of the contracting party who has insisted on its inclusion. Experience may have shown that a seller will be exposed to extensive liability in certain situations where goods supplied prove to be defective: consequently the right of action by the party suffering loss is removed at the outset, by mutual consent. The problem here is that such clauses are often imposed by the dominant party to the contract against a weaker party, who is left with little choice but to accept the exemption clause or abandon the idea of contracting. Usually most, if not all, suppliers of a particular type of goods impose similar exemption clauses.

Tenders

A company may invite a tender from businessmen for the supply of specified goods or services. Every tender submitted is an offer and the company can accept any tender to bring a binding contract into existence.

Where tenders are invited for the supply of goods as services as and when demanded, the company submitting the successful tender is making a standing offer. There is a separate acceptance by the company requiring the goods or services each time an order is placed with the party who has submitted the tender. A fresh contract is made each time an order is placed.

Where this type of agreement includes an estimate of the quantity required, there is no obligation to order goods of any particular quantity or indeed any goods at all. On the other hand, if the buyer undertakes to purchase all his requirements in relation to specified goods from the person whose tender is accepted, there is a breach of contract if the goods are bought elsewhere.

The standing offer may be revoked at any time by the party making it, except in relation to any goods or services that have been ordered. To prevent this happening there is usually a binding undertaking between the parties to keep the standing offer open for a stipulated period. This usually means that a sum of money must be paid to the party making the standing offer.

CONSIDERATION

The majority of contracts made are simple contracts and the presence of valuable consideration is essential to their validity. This means that each party to the contract must confer a benefit on the other party in return for the benefit received. If Company A sells goods to Company B for £1000, Company A loses the goods but receives the purchase price of £1000. Company B has to pay the £1000 but receives the benefit of the goods in return.

Consideration is a more complex doctrine than this simple illustration may suggest. It can take the form of an exchange of promises, with Company A promising to sell and deliver goods by 1 January and Company B agreeing to accept and pay £1000 for them. If Company A refuses to deliver the goods on 1 January, then Company B may sue for breach of contract or, alternatively, if Company B refuses to accept delivery, Company A may sue for breach of contract.

Consideration must be valuable. If must have an economic character and be worth something. The court will not determine how much the goods sold are worth and then determine whether the price paid is adequate. It is for business men, not courts, to make commercially sound agreements. No attempt is made to balance the respective promises or acts of the parties to determine whether the bargain is fair, provided each party has received some benefit.

FORM OF A CONTRACT

In most cases a contract does not have to be concluded in writing, but writing is useful since the precise terms agreed upon are then easily ascertainable. The following contracts must be in a written form however:

1 Bills of exchange, promissory notes and cheques
2 Contracts of marine insurance
3 Hire-purchase contracts
4 Contracts for the transfer of shares in a public company.

Although writing is not essential at the time when the contract is made, there are two cases where writing is needed for purposes of evidence. These are:

1 Contracts of guarantee whereby A promises B that he will settle C's debts to B if C cannot meet his own commitments
2 Contracts to sell or lease land.

If the writing does not exist the contract cannot be enforced in a court of law. The written document may be quite informal: a letter will suffice, provided it includes:

1 The names of the parties, or a sufficient description of them
2 A description of the subject matter
3 All material terms
4 Consideration, except in a contract of guarantee
5 The signature of the person being sued or his agent.

A few contracts must be embodied in a deed, that is a written agreement, that is signed by the parties, sealed and delivered. Such contracts are:

1 A conveyance of land or interest in land, including a lease for a term exceeding three years
2 Gifts; a promise to give embodied in a deed is binding and enforceable, although consideration is not provided in return by the recipient.

Intention to create legal relations

If an agreement is supported by consideration it is assumed that the parties intended it to be legally enforceable one against the other, especially if it relates to a commercial matter. The parties are free, however, to state expressly that their agreement is not intended to be legally binding. Then it is an obligation binding in honour only and not subject to the jurisdiction of the courts. For example, collective agreements between unions and management may fall into this category if there is an express declaration to that effect.

Such an approach to commercial contract is exceptional, but there is often an arbitration agreement, which has been framed in order to prevent either party taking court proceedings under the contract until the dispute has been referred to arbitration and an award made. Arbitration may be preferred because it is cheaper, less formal, and adjudicated upon by an expert with special knowledge of the problems involved. Under the Arbitration Act 1950 if, contrary to his agreement to submit to arbitration, a party starts court proceedings, then the court (upon application by the other party) may order a stay of the court action to allow arbitration to proceed; or the court may refuse to order a stay of action (as where the only issue is a point of law) thereby breaking the arbitration agreement.

CAPACITY TO MAKE A CONTRACT

A company does not have the contractual power to negotiate an agreement which falls outside the scope of its objects clause. Subject to the qualifications discussed below, any such agreement is void and ineffective (*ultra vires*), even though the other contracting party was unaware of this fact. The company's main business objectives are stated in the objects clause of the memorandum of association. It is followed by ancillary clauses granting power to effect other objectives incidental to the main purpose such as buying land and borrowing money. In practice the objects clause will be widely drawn to include a wide range of business objectives, with a declaration that they should be construed as main objectives. This reduces the risk of any contract negotiated by the company being held void.

The powers of the company, as set out in the memorandum and articles, are usually delegated to the directors, if not exercised by the company itself in general meeting. Members in general meeting cannot interfere with the manner in which the directors exercise their powers, unless they alter the articles accordingly.

A contract is enforceable against a company if the subject matter is fairly incidental to its main objects, though not specifically authorized by the memorandum. For example, a trading company may lease premises for the purpose of carrying out its business.

The European Communities Act 1972 (Section 9) has vitally affected the law on contractual capacity of a company. Any agreement concluded by company directors, acting collectively as a board, or by a single director or other officer, for example, a company secretary acting by delegation from or with the authority of the board, will be deemed to be within the company's capacity though in fact it is *ultra vires*. The contract is enforceable by the other contracting party (or outsider) against the company, but is unenforceable by the company itself. The outsider must have acted in good faith and be unaware that the contract was *ultra vires*. He is not bound to make enquires to determine whether the company has contractual capacity to make that particular contract. The directors are liable to the company for any losses suffered as a result of negotiating the *ultra vires* contract.

Any transaction agreed upon by the directors collectively as a board, which exceeds their powers, but is within the company's powers, will be deemed to be valid. It is enforceable against the company and may be enforced by the company if ratified by the appropriate authority, usually the company in general meeting. The outsider must have acted in good faith and be unaware that the agreement was *ultra vires*. He is not bound to make enquiries to determine whether the company has contractual capacity to make that particular contract, but if he knows that it exceeds the directors' powers he cannot enforce it.

An individual director may exceed his authority when negotiating a contract. If the contract is within the company's contractual powers it is enforceable by the company and against it, if the director's actions are ratified by sharehold ers,or alternatively an inspection of the memorandum and articles by the outsider would not have revealed that the director was acting outside the scope of his powers. His restricted authority to contract may be a matter of internal management of which the outsider is unaware.

MISTAKES IN THE CONTRACT

A contract may have been concluded under a misapprehension as to a material fact. Where both parties mistakenly believe the subject matter of the contract to be in existence when this is not so, then the contract is void.

For example, a seller may conclude a contract to sell goods which are stored in his warehouse to a willing buyer. Unknown to both parties, at the time of contracting the goods have actually been destroyed by a warehouse fire. The buyer is not obliged to pay the contract price, because the parties have contracted about a non-existent subject matter.

A mistake by both parties concerning the quality of the subject matter does not avoid the contract, where they have agreed on the same terms on the same subject matter, if for example, A and B mistakenly believe that land about to be sold has valuable mineral deposits. The buyer cannot claim his money back and return the land. In this situation the court may be willing on occasions to set the contract aside, thus relieving the party who suffers most because of the mistake. This would only apply on terms which are fair as between both parties, for example, allowing the seller to claim any expenses incurred.

A binding contract does not exist if the parties have negotiated completely at cross-purposes and made a mistake as to the identity of the subject matter. For example, one party intends to sell a cargo leaving New York in March on board a ship named 'Eastern Star', while the buyer intends to purchase the cargo on board a similarly named vessel leaving New York in January. The ambiguity of the circumstances make it impossible for the court to determine with reasonable certainty which cargo is subject matter of the contract. Conversely, an enforceable contract will exist on the terms as understood by one of the parties, if the mistake is basically the fault of one party only. For example, if a purchaser buys land mistakenly believing that it is more extensive in area than the plot being sold, he cannot avoid the contract simply because he failed to check the specifications of the sale which were readily available to him.

A contract is void if one party is mistaken as to a fundamental fact concerning the subject matter and the other party knows of the mistake and takes advantage of it. If Company A offers to sell goods to Company B for £1250 when Company B's previous offer to buy at £2000 had already been refused, it is obvious that Company A really intended the price to be £2250. Company B cannot accept the offer of £1250 and enforce the agreement against Company A. On the other hand, if one party's mistake is not appreciated by the other party who accepts in ignorance of that mistake, then a binding contract exists. If Company A offers to sell goods at £350, when, because of an arithmetical error, £400 was intended, an acceptance of the offer by Company B is binding, provided the circumstances do not suggest than an obvious mistake has been made in the price charged.

Mistaken signature

A party may be induced to sign a written document embodying an agreement which is fundamentally different in nature from an obligation he intended to assume and the party inducing him to sign may be aware of the mistake. The mistaken party can escape liability in pursuance of the agreement only in the most exceptional cases, such as blindness or illiteracy. Company representatives signing contractual documents should carefully scrutinize the contents of the agreement and ensure that the agreement being signed is the agreement that they intend to sign and that all the individual terms are acceptable and have not been altered contrary to any verbal understanding that preceded the execution of a formal written document.

MISREPRESENTATION

A company may be induced to contract because of misrepresentation by the other party. A misrepresentation is defined as a false statement of a fact that is material to the agreement, made by one party to the other during negotiations leading to the agreement, which was intended to operate and did operate as an inducement to enter the contract.

A false representation is fraudulent if it is made with knowledge of the falsity, or without belief in its truth, or recklessly not caring whether it is true or false. Honest belief in the truth of a statement negates deceit, even though the representation is stupid, careless or negligent. A belief is not honest, however, if the representor deliberately shuts his eyes to the true facts or purposely abstains from investigating them. The aggrieved party may either avoid the contract with or without suing for damages for deceit, or affirm the contract and also seek damages.

Although fraud is difficult to establish, it is present in contractual situations where a seller has grossly misrepresented the profits and turnover attributable to a business that is being sold, often accompanied by the production of false accounts and returns.

A contract cannot be avoided (rescinded) where the aggrieved party elects to waive his rights by affirming the contract, for example, if he takes benefits provided by the contract with full knowledge of the misrepresentation, as by using goods purchased.

A contract further induced by fraudulent misrepresentation must be avoided within six years of either discovery of the fraud, or the time when it could have been discovered by using reasonable diligence.

If the parties cannot be restored to their original positions by taking back the purchase price and goods respectively, then the contract cannot be rescinded. A buyer may have radically altered the property he purchased before discovering the misrepresentation or electing to rescind the contract; for example, there may have been substantial extractions from a mine that has been purchased. Damages may be recovered, however, to compensate the party misled where the property is now worth much less than he anticipated because of the misrepresentation.

It is too late to rescind where property has already been sold again to a third party who now has rights to the property in question.

Although a representation may be made with an honest belief in its truth, thereby negating fraud and an intention to deceive, nonetheless the representor may display a lack of care in either making the statement at all, or alternatively in failing to correct it before conclusion of the contract, when the true facts have been discovered or by using reasonable diligence should have discovered that the representative's actions were negligent.

A person possessing special skills and competence who has made a negligent mis-statement may be liable in tort at common law for the financial loss suffered as a result by the person acting in reliance upon it, if he owed the recipient of that information a duty of care to use his special knowledge when making the statement. For example, a firm of accountants might over-value stock while preparing audited accounts for their client. They would be liable for a breach of duty of care to anyone foreseeably relying on those accounts as representing the true position and, in consequence, contracting to buy the business from the client.

A party induced to a contract as the result of a negligent misrepresentation may sue the representor for damages as of right in respect of losses suffered. The measure of damages is the same as for fraudulent misrepresentation. The party misled by negligent misrepresentation may also seek rescission of the contract. The representor has an effective defence to any claim against him for damages, if he can prove that he had reasonable grounds for believing that the statement was true at the time when it was made and continued to hold this belief up until the time when the contract was concluded.

A false representation will be wholly innocent if reasonable care has been taken to check its accuracy before making it. The person misled may claim rescission of the contract instead. The court may award damages, if this is fairer to the party responsible and an adequate remedy for the party misled; where, for example, the falsity is of relatively minor significance in relation to the transaction as a whole. Damages cannot be claimed in the first instance as of right.

When the remedy of rescission is granted, the injured party may, in some instances, also claim an indemnity for losses suffered as a result of the contractual obligations undertaken, in order to be restored effectively to the position originally occupied before contracting. The injured party cannot be placed in the same position in which he would have been if the contract had been properly performed, since the effect would be the same as the granting of an award of damages. For example, if a lessee is induced by innocent misrepresentation to take a lease of premises, an indemnity will cover losses incurred by virtue of the lease terms (such as rent, rates and repairs) but will not recover for injury to health because the premises proved to be insanitary.

Terms of a contract

The parties themselves may state expressly the detailed terms that are to govern the manner in which the contract will operate, such as delivery dates and time of payment. In addition to these express terms, others may be implied by custom or trade usage. For example, in a contract of employment the express terms may regulate many of the more important rights and duties of the employer and employee on such matters as salary, hours of work, holiday and duties to be discharged. However, an employee is also under an implied duty to obey lawful instructions, while the employer must indemnify his employee against any losses incurred while discharging his contractual duties.

In any type of contract the court may imply a term in order to fill in a gap left by the parties in the terms expressly agreed upon, which fail to regulate their respective rights and liabilities. The judge effects the presumed intention of the parties in order to give the contract business efficacy, by adding the kind of term that the parties themselves would have drafted if they had considered the matter.

Where the owner of a wharf contracts to permit its use by another to unload a cargo, there is an implied belief that the wharf is safe for use by that particular vessel. If the vessel is damaged because it rests on a layer of hard rock just below a muddy river bed, then the wharf owner is liable, even though responsibility for the river bed is vested in another person.

In many contracts a number of terms are automatically implied by statute, irrespective of the intentions of the parties themselves. Exclusion of the operation of these implied terms is permissible only in specified circumstances. A number of very important terms are implied by the Sale of Goods Act 1979.

The seller of goods is bound by an implied condition that he has the right to sell the goods and can therefore transfer title to the buyer as a result of the contract sale, or will have the right to so transfer title at the time when the property is to pass, where there is a mere agreement to sell at some time in the future. A consumer sale is a sale of goods by a seller acting in the course of a business where the goods are of the type ordinarily bought for private use and consumption and are sold to a person not buying them in the course of a business. Other sales are non-consumer sales, as where the seller disposes of goods to a company which buys raw material in the course of business.

In a contract for the sale of goods by description there is an implied condition that the goods shall correspond with that description; this usually covers cases where the buyer has not seen the goods and relies on the seller's description. For example, if goods are described as 'new' it is a breach of this implied term to supply secondhand goods.

Where goods are sold in the course of business there is an implied condition that they are of merchantable quality except where the defect is specifically drawn to the buyer's attention before the contract is made, or the buyer examined the goods before contracting and the defect ought to have been revealed upon examination. Merchantable is defined as fit for the purpose(s) for which goods of that kind are commonly bought as it is reasonable to expect, having regard to any description applied to them, the price (if relevant) and all other relevant circumstances. For example, a new vehicle is not merchantable if, after purchase, it has a history of continuous breakdowns due to a number of different mechanical faults.

Where goods are sold in the course of business and the buyer, expressly or by implication, makes known to the seller the particular purpose for which the goods are being bought, there is an implied condition that the goods supplied are reasonably fit for that purpose, whether or not this is the purpose for which such goods are commonly supplied. If a buyer asks the seller to recommend a vehicle that is suitable for use by a commercial salesman covering long distances, the car sold should have those qualities of reliability and comfort that the buyer is expressly seeking in his purchase.

A specially drafted clause in the contract of sale may exclude the operation of the protections given in relation to description, merchantability or fitness. Such an exclusion clause if embodied in a consumer sale is void. In non-consumer sales exclusion or restriction of these implied terms is permitted if reasonable. Such reasonable exclusion or restriction may be imposed by express agreement, inconsistent express terms, trade usage or a course of dealings. In ascertaining reasonableness the following issues may be considered, if relevant, to the situation in question:

1 Relative bargaining strength of each party to the other, taking into account alternative means of meeting a customer's requirements
2 Whether the customer received an inducement to accept the exemption or restricting clause in relation to liability; whether when accepting it he had the chance to make a similar contract with others not imposing such a clause
3 Whether the customer knew or ought reasonably to have known of the existence and extent of the exemption or restricting clause and whether trade customs or previous dealings between the parties show that such clauses are usual
4 Where an exemption or restricting clause only operates if the customer fails to follow a prescribed procedure. For example, failing to report to the seller defects in goods purchased within a reasonable time limit, as specified. Here it is important to ascertain whether it was reasonable when contracting to expect that compliance with the procedure would be practicable
5 Whether the goods were manufactured, processed and adapted to the customer's special order.

Remedy for breach of an implied term

If goods supplied are not in accordance with the contractual description, if the seller is without title, or if the goods are not 'merchantable' or 'reasonably fit' then the seller is in breach of a contractual condition. The buyer may rescind the contract by returning the goods. He may reclaim the purchase price and additional damages, if appropriate, in respect of losses that are not too remote. Alternatively, if he wishes the buyer may claim damages only; that is monetary compensation for the difference in value between the goods delivered and the value they were supposed to have. Here the buyer retains the goods purchased. The condition is treated as a warranty, for breach of which only damages may be recovered. The buyer cannot return the goods, but may claim damages only, where 'property' in the goods has already passed to the buyer. This means that the buyer has 'accepted' the goods purchased and used them for some time before making a serious complaint. A buyer does not 'accept' goods delivered to him unless he has had a reasonable opportunity to examine them.

Unfair Contract Terms Act 1977

Liability may arise in the course of a business or from the occupation of premises used for business purposes ('business liability') for a person's death or personal injury while on the premises. If death or injury is attributable to negligence, such as failing to ensure that business premises are safe to use, then liability cannot be excluded or restricted by an exemption clause in a contract or a notice.

An occupier of premises will not be liable if a lawful visitor is injured by using a defective lift, provided that the occupier has engaged an independent contractor, who is reasonably believed to be competent, to inspect, service and repair the lift regularly. Such an occupier is not negligent. It will be otherwise if he permits an obviously dangerous situation to arise on his premises without taking adequate preventive measures, as for example where accumulations of ice and snow make it difficult to walk safely between buildings in the employment complex.

Business liability for loss or damage (other than death or personal injury) resulting from negligence, such as damage to clothing or personal belongings, can be excluded or restricted by the person responsible by a contractual clause or notice, provided it satisfies the reasonableness tests discussed above. A defaulting party may rely on a contract term or notice restricting liability to a specified sum, by proving that it is reasonable to do so by reference to his resources to meet liability and whether he could insure against it. For example, liability may be limited to a specified sum for loss or damage to goods left in a cloakroom where payment of a small fee cannot cover loss of expensive items of clothing. A non-contractual notice may exclude or restrict liability if fair and reasonable in the circumstances, with the burden of proof resting on the party relying on the notice. For example, a notice in a pub car-park may exclude liability for loss or damage to any car parked there or its contents. The injured party's awareness of the existence of a restricting or exemption clause is not, in itself, voluntary acceptance of any risk of loss or damage imposed by the clause, but if the injured party is unaware of the clause it cannot be operative.

DAMAGES FOR BREACH OF CONTRACT

If one party has broken the terms of a valid contract, the innocent party is entitled to recover damages for any loss suffered. He must be restored to the position he would have been in if the particular damage suffered had not occurred, in so far as money can be sufficient compensation.

Recovery may be confined to those losses that arise naturally in the usual course of events from the breach, and are thus assumed to be within the contemplation of the defaulting party. In a contract for the sale of goods, where there is a market for the goods, the measure of damages recoverable by the buyer is the difference between the contract price and the market price of goods at the time when the seller ought to have delivered them. The buyer can purchase goods similar to the contract goods in the market. On the other hand, if the buyer has refused to accept delivery, the seller recovers the sum by which the market price falls short of the contract price at the time when the goods ought to have been accepted. The seller can dispose of the contract goods in the market.

If there is no available market but the buyer has agreed to resell the goods, the resale price may be taken as representing their value. The buyer's damages will be the difference between the sale and resale prices, though the seller is unaware of the sub-sale. A loss of profit is recoverable for breach of a trading contract made between experienced parties if they can be taken to understand the ordinary practices and exigencies of one another's business.

If the seller is a dealer selling goods at a standard market price, this will be the same as the contract price, for example, the contract price and the market price of machinery may be £5000. For refusal to accept delivery the seller may recover from the buyer the profit that he would have made if the sale had been completed. Even if the item is readily sold to a new buyer, the seller has made the profit on one sale only instead of upon two sales in cases where he has plenty of stock for disposal. Conversely, if a particular items can be sold as quickly as it comes into the seller's stock, the buyer's default is a matter of indifference to the seller. In such cases only nominal damages are recoverable; for example, where a certain type of machinery is in short supply because of strikes.

Owing to special circumstances known at the time of contracting to the party ultimately committing a breach, a loss may be suffered outside the usual course of events. The defaulting party may pay damages in respect of the exceptional loss. For example, a vendor of land may know that the purchaser intends to develop the property and make a large profit. If the seller refuses to complete the sale he is accountable for this loss of profit.

The amount of damages awarded may be reduced to reflect a claimant's liability to reduce the losses suffered, if this is possible, as by selling or buying goods elsewhere.

Distinction between liquidated and unliquidated damages

Damages are unliquidated where one party to a contract sues the other to recover whatever sum the court holds to be the proper measure of damages in the circumstances. A contract may provide that, in the event of a breach, the innocent party may recover from the defaulting party a sum stated in the contract itself: this sum is called liquidated damages. This type of arrangement has the advantage of saving the time, trouble and expense of litigation should a breach of contract occur. Only the agreed sum is recoverable, even if the actual loss suffered greatly exceeds the sum fixed by the contract. If damages are to be assessed by the contract itself, it is essential to estimate with precision the monetary effect of any possible breach.

Distinction between liquidated damages and a penalty

A sum agreed as payable in the event of a breach of the contract may be liquidated damages or a penalty. The distinction is of vital importance. If the sum is liquidated damages it can be recovered from the party in default. It is regarded as a genuine pre-estimate of the damage suffered by the innocent party.

If the sum fixed by the contract is deemed to be a penalty, then essentially it is a threat held against the party likely to violate the contractual obligations. The intention of a penalty is to attempt to compel performance of the contract by severely punishing the party who refuses to implement it. The defaulting party is made liable to pay an extravagant sum, exceeding the greatest loss that could possibly result from the breach. A penalty is irrecoverable and the injured party is limited to recovering the actual loss he has suffered. If a company wishes to guard against breach of contract, a penalty clause is not the method to use.

An example will illustrate the practical operation of these rules. Company A may agree to install machinery on the premises of Company B. A term of contract may provide that if the work is not completed by 1 January, then for every extra working day taken to complete the installation Company A must pay Company B £1000. If a delay of twenty working days results in lost production and lost profits of £20 000, this sum is recoverable from Company A as liquidated damages if the sum is a genuine pre-estimate of the loss likely to be incurred. In the same circumstances, if the actual loss is £30 000, only £20 000 is recoverable. Here Company B is confined in its claim to the genuine, though incorrect, pre-estimate of the likely loss.

On the other hand, if Company B's maximum loss of profit for one day's lost production could not possibly exceed £200, the clause in the contract stipulating £1000 will be recoverable is a penalty. The court will disregard the clause and only the actual loss suffered will be recovered by Company B.

Specific performance

Damages may be an inadequate remedy and the court may order the defaulting party to perform specifically the obligation undertaken in the contract. This is a discretionary remedy usually given the breach of a contract to sell or lease land, or sell chattels with unique qualities. In these cases it may be difficult for the disappointed purchaser to acquire similar property elsewhere.

FURTHER READING

Kay, R. and Sewell, T., *A Practical Approach to Contract and Consumer Law*, Financial Trading, 1984. An effective summary which is interesting and easy to read

Treitel, G.H., *An outline of the Law of Contract*, 3rd edition, Butterworth, London, 1984. A clear, concise summary of all the important basic principles

43 Insurance of company operations

Commercial Union Assurance

The modern business has many opportunities to succeed. However, more than ever before it essential for the businessman to protect his company. Competition, health and safety legislation, the complexity of products, environmental considerations, a whole host of natural disasters from fire to flood, and man-made catastrophes from burglary to fraud can spell disaster for any size company. Insurance is one form of protection against many of the accidental or natural disasters.

For over 300 years there have been risk takers who, for a fee called a premium, are willing to assume financial responsibility for losses incurred following a variety of events. The premiums of the 'many' pay for the claims of the 'unfortunate few' who have to claim. However, some business risks are not insurable – if they are pure business risks which depend on the successful businessman making good commercial decisions. Risk management involves appraisal of risks that might affect the performance of the company. Once the risks have been identified, a business plan needs to be designed to cope with them.

A number of risks are unavoidable. They have to be catered for in business plans (obsolescence, over-optimistic sales forecasts, etc.). The remedy for countering such risks lies in competent research, development and marketing. Other corporate problems can be answered by taking advice from accountants, bankers and solicitors.

But what about the unpredictable risks? This is where the insurance company or broker play their part in a company's prosperity. Insurance provides a financial indemnity from accidental and unpredictable risks. The aim of properly arranged insurance is to put the insured company back into the position that it enjoyed before the unpredicted incident (fire, flood, storm damage, burglary etc.). What follows explores some of the factors involved in business insurances.

Over 300 insurance companies and Lloyds make up the insurance market today. Some of these companies only handle life or pensions business. Those who handle both life and non-life business are known as composite insurers. They are predominantly the large companies, the nationally known names.

All non-life and composite companies are limited liability companies, but Lloyds are different again. Insurance is placed only by Lloyds insurance brokers, with syndicates of individual underwriters who act for the syndicates' members. The members have to satisfy Lloyds of their financial standing and integrity, and are liable without limit to the full extent of their individual wealth. Most Lloyds syndicates specialize in specific classes of risk (marine, aviation, motor, property etc.).

INSURANCE LANGUAGE

Before looking at the insurance cover itself it might be useful to look at some common expressions used in the insurance industry. While many insurers in the present day attempt to produce insurance contracts which are in a 'Plain English' format, there are still some fundamental principles on which most insurance contracts are based. In addition, some words have developed a common usage within the insurance industry. The following glossary is included to provide a basic understanding of some of those principles and terms.

Adjuster	A specialist appointed by the insurer to investigate the circumstances and negotiate settlement of a loss. Usually an independent specialist whose fee is paid for by the insurer.
Assessor	A person who acts on behalf of the insured at the insured's expense to negotiate claims with the insurer and, where necessary, the insurer's *adjuster* (see above). An assessor can also negotiate on behalf of third party claimants.
Average (non-marine)	A principle of insurance (mainly insurance of property) where the insurer will only pay for the same proportion of a loss as the sum insured bears to the actual value of the property at the time of the loss. For example, if an item covered by the policy is 'subject to average' but is only insured for half its value at the time it is damaged, the insurer will only pay half of any claim for repair.
	For this reason, insurers recommend policyholders to select a sum insured not less than the full value.
Betterment	See *Indemnity*.
Broker, insurance	A professional insurance adviser who, following discussions of the cover required with his client, will negotiate and place the business with insurers. The broker must meet the standards required by the Insurance Brokers (Registration) Act, 1977, which includes a statutory 'Code of Conduct', and they may be a member of B.I.B.A. (British Insurance Brokers Association).
	Note: The description 'insurance broker' may only be used by individuals who have required (if a company, enrolled)

under the Act. Sometimes the term 'broker' is used colloquially. When the new financial services legislation comes into force, it is likely some brokers who specialize in Life Business only will 'de-register', and be under the control only of the regulatory organization set up under that legislation.

Code of Conduct/Codes of Practice

Brokers are required to 'follow a statutory Code of Conduct under the Insurance Brokers (Registration) Act.' Other insurance intermediaries are required to follow a Code of Practice agreed between insurers and the Department of Trade and Industry. There are two Codes – one for general (non-life) business, one for life business – and each code is in two parts which distinguish between those who sell and those who merely introduce (*introducers*).

Days of grace

When a non-life policy falls due for renewal, the insurer concerned is usually willing to hold cover under the terms for renewal pending payment of the premium, providing the policyholder intends to renew.

Under motor policies, there are no 'days of grace'. However, as it is necessary for a certificate of motor insurance to be delivered to a policyholder for it to be effective, insurers usually provide 15 days' temporary cover beyond the renewal date to enable the insurer to date the new certificate from renewal date, and deliver it within the period of temporary cover.

Should a life assured die in the days of grace specified under a life policy before the renewal premium is paid, the position must be ascertained from the policy or the insurer.

Debris removal

Under a policy covering buildings and/or machinery against damage, the cost of removing debris can be included providing the costs have been allowed for when deciding on the sums to be insured. If the costs are insured as a separate item under a policy covering commercial property, they are not subject to *average*. Similarly, debris removal of stock can also be insured as a separate item under a policy covering commercial property.

Disclosure

The rule of Law whereby a prospective policyholder must tell ('disclose') the insurer any facts known to the prospective policyholder which are likely to affect acceptance by the underwriter or his assessment of the risks proposed. If the prospective policyholder fails to do this, the policy may not provide the cover required, or the policy may be invalidated altogether.

Excess

If expressed in money terms (which is usual), it is the uninsured amount for which the insured is responsible in the event of a claim. See also *Franchise*.

803

Ex gratia	Voluntary payment made by an insurer, without admission of liability under the policy, as a gesture of good will.
Fees, professional (architects etc.)	Under a policy covering buildings, and/or machinery against damage, it is possible to insure fees incurred in the rebuilding/repairing of damage in a variety of ways. These are normally calculated as a percentage of the value of buildings or machinery, and are limited to the scales of professional bodies. If insured separately under a policy covering commercial property, such fees are not subject to *average*.
Fidelity guarantee	This insurance protects employers against 'direct pecuniary loss' which they suffer by all acts of fraud or dishonesty committed by any of their employees. The term 'direct pecuniary loss' refers to the loss of monies, stock and other items of value belonging to the employer, which can be proved and the employee(s) responsible identified, though insurers do not insist on prosecution. Unaccountable deficiencies or losses are not covered.
Franchise	If expressed in money terms, there is no payment by the insurer if the total claim is below that figure; above that amount, the agreed claim is payable in full. Some policies, e.g. certain personal accident or engineering contracts, may have time franchises. These operate similarly; thus, only if the time franchise is exceeded is the claim payable and the agreed amount will then be paid in full.
Indemnity	Principle of common law by which the policyholder after a loss shall be put in the same financial position as he was immediately before the happening of the event insured against. In practice this often means that, in the event of a claim, payment is based first on what it would cost to replace new a lost or damaged item, but then deducted an amount to take account for. Such a deduction is sometimes called 'betterment'. *Note:* This principle naturally does not apply to life assurance, permanent health or pensions contracts. Nor does it apply to personal accident and sickness cover, although medical expenses insurance does provide indemnity for costs incurred.
Insurable interest	A policyholder has an insurable interest if the insured event would involve him in financial loss or diminution of any right recognized by law or any legal liability, or for the consequences of his own bodily injury or illness. As regards life and personal accident policies, a person is

deemed to have an unlimited insurable interest in his or her own life, or in the life of his or her spouse. Insurable interest may also exist between employer and employee, debtor and creditor and other cases.

Insurance agent

An insurance agent is primarily the agent of the policyholder not least when passing information to the insurer with a view to obtaining insurance cover. He can also be the agent of the insurer, in particular when collecting premiums due to the insurer.

An insurance agent can be in business either full time – such as an 'insurance broker' or an 'insurance consultant', probably acting for a number of insurers – or he may only act for one insurer, such as a company that specialises in the sale of industrial life business (where premiums are collected weekly/monthly from the policyholders' premises).

Insurance consultant

A professional insurance adviser whose business is similar to that of an *insurance broker* (q.v.), but who has not registered/enrolled under the Insurance Brokers (Registration) Act. While unlikely therefore to meet the standards required under the Act, they are required to follow a 'Code of Practice' agreed between insurers and the Department of Trade and Industry.

Introducer

An insurance intermediary who merely introduces a prospective policyholder to an insurer, but who takes no part in the subsequent selling process.

Local Authorities Clause

In the event of damage, current building regulations may well be applied to the structure, thereby involving additional expense when it is rebuilt. If the insurance is on a 'reinstatement' basis, this clause can be added extending the policy to meet the additional expenses on rebuilding for the damaged portion, though the sum insured must have been increased to allow for such expenses.

Proposal form

The form completed by a proposer. A completed Life Proposal forms the basis of the contract between the guarantee and the insurer.

Reinstatement

(a) Where property is destroyed, it means the rebuilding of the property if a building, or, in the case of other property, its replacement by similar property, in either case in a condition equal to (but not better or more extensive than) its condition when new.

(b) Where property is damaged, it means repair of the property to a condition substantially the same as (but not better or more extensive than) its condition when new.

The sum insured needs to represent what it would cost to fully rebuild/replace, at the time the property is actually rebuilt/replaced, and any under-insurance will result in a proportionate reduction of the amount paid in accordance with the average principle – see *Average (non-marine)*'.

Renewal notice

Form sent to insured advising the approaching renewal date and inviting renewal on payment of a stated premium.

The insurer is not bound to issue a notice, but it is the normal practice.

The renewal invitation is provided on the basis of information already given the insurer. Other than for individual life, pension or permanent health insurance, if that information is affected by any change of circumstances or additional fact known to the policyholder, the insurer (or his authorized agent) should be told. It could be that, as a result of the additional information, the insurer will wish to revise the terms on which renewal is being invited.

Subrogation

The substitution of one person or thing for another so that the same rights and remedies which attached to the original person/thing attach to the substituted one.

Surveyor

Person who inspects property to advise the underwriter about the risk. He may also require or recommend improvements to the risk to lessen the likelihood of fire, burglary, or other incidents occurring, or to minimize the effects of them.

Time-on-risk charge

Premium charged for a period (often limited to a number of days) during which an insurer is holding a risk covered, for example, by means of a cover note.

Underwriting

The process whereby a risk is assessed for insurance purposes, on the basis of information supplied to the underwriter often by means of a proposal form. The underwriter will decide whether the risk is acceptable to the insurer, the terms on which it may be acceptable, and the premium to be charged, before issue of the policy.

Utmost good faith

Legal duty imposed on both parties to an insurance contract to disclose all facts material to the contract (see also *Disclosure*).

Warranty

A policy condition or requirement which, if not complied with, may have the effect of invalidating the policy. It may relate to woodworking in a motor garage or to the absence of certain property (e.g. no oil stored in the hardware shop or only certain types of oil kept).

Having looked at some of the basic principles it is now necessary to consider the practicalities of arranging insurance for a company. These can be described under four basic headings, which are:

1 Property protection
2 Loss of income
3 Legal liabilities
4 Personnel.

PROPERTY PROTECTION

Essentially we should regard the insurance arrangement as a complete form of protection where, if a loss occurs, within certain criteria, then the insurer will resolve the problem by way of financial compensation. Such an insurance will include wide cover for stock, machinery, fixtures and fittings and furniture, employees' belongings, and other items for which you may be responsible. Obviously the structure, if owned, would come within this category or alternatively a tenant could arrange for the insurance to cover that portion of the structure and interior decorations for which he is responsible. Specific requirements within a lease would obviously have to be complied with.

Fire insurance

There was a tendency in the past to be particularly selective in terms of which contingencies a company might wish to insure against. It has now become almost standard practice for insurers to offer a package which includes the basic traditional calamities such as fire, lightning, explosion, and the like. There are available on the market many special features and extensions which are worthy of consideration. For example, many insurers now refer to 'all risks' cover which could be more accurately described as accidental damage cover. In addition, many companies now offer 'new for old' although this would require the sums insured to be on a full reinstatement value basis.

Additional standard extensions include property which has been temporarily removed, architects', surveyors' and other specialists' fees, removal of debris costs, special provision for local authority legislation, and even damage to the underground service pipes and cables which the business might rely on.

Theft

Theft and loss of money are now two of the prime security considerations in many businesses and cover for such eventualities will almost inevitably now carry a proviso from the insurer that a certain degree of minimum security is observed. Certain manufactured goods, and even raw materials, have become prime targets to the criminal world and insurers now require their policyholders to endeavour to improve the quality of the safes, locks and alarm protections at their premises rather than solely rely on charging a higher premium for a risk as it stands.

Cash

Money cover can carry a variety of limitations and requirements and particular attention should be paid to the observance of such conditions in the day-to-day business of the company. For example certain safes will have insurance limits as to the amount of cash which can be kept in them overnight and there may well be conditions relating to the amount of cash which can be taken in transit on any one trip. Where large volume cash transits are involved security companies have become more and more prevalent. On a lower degree the insurer may require more than one employee to be present during a delivery of cash (to the bank or to a point of wages payment for example).

Loss of money as a result of theft should not be confused with what insurers describe as fidelity guarantee insurance which would be dealt with separately.

Glass insurance

Apart from the traditional concept of insuring against breakage of glass in doors, windows etc. extensions once more apply which can include breakage of sanitary wear, damage to neon signs, damage to burglar alarm foil lettering, painting etc. Again insurers look to their policyholders to take some positive steps to reduce risk in certain areas, and the use of grills, roller shutters, or perhaps large excesses could apply in areas where the insurers' experience has been particularly poor.

LOSS OF INCOME

This feature of the insurance portfolio protects the business when it is interrupted as a result of loss or damage insured under the sections which have been described above. It covers loss of gross profit due to a reduction in business income. It also covers increased cost of working incurred to reduce the loss of profit so long as these do not exceed the loss of profit which would otherwise have been paid.

Once more, a variety of extensions are available to protect the business against financial loss and these can include damage to property in the vicinity which prevents access to company premises, or damage at the premises of any supplier. This extension would normally carry a limit in respect of any one supplier.

This particular style of insurance has its own special definitions, the principal one being 'indemnity period'. This is intended to relate to the maximum period of time during which the business might suffer loss as a result of the interruption. Traditionally, the indemnity period has run for a period of 12 months following the incident although longer periods are now commonplace. Such insurance normally requires the service of a professional accountant should a claim arise and therefore it is normal practice for the insurer to include the professional accountant's charges as part of the sum paid in the event of a claim. Very careful consideration should be given to the calculation of the 'sum insured' in this context. Future company projections should be meticulously examined when deciding on a sum insured. It is not appropriate to rely on the previous year's gross profit figures as a basis for fixing sums insured. For example if a two-year indemnity period were to be selected and the loss were to take place at the end of a particular insurance year, then at the expiry of the indemnity period it is quite possible that the sum insured originally fixed could almost be three years out of date.

To compensate for future projections the insurer will accept audited declarations in retrospect and adjust premiums to reflect the actual risk as compared with the projected one, paying appropriate rebates back to the policyholder. As insurers have had to recognize steep curves in inflation trends, they developed more sophisticated means by which to adjust this cover. Consultation with a professional intermediary or insurance advisor is highly recommended in this context.

LEGAL LIABILITIES

If any one thing could bankrupt a company at one stroke it would more than likely be a heavy court award and therefore no matter how far a company may consider that they can set aside the need for insurance this particular segment which the insurance market offers is essential. The cover relates to legal liabilities to pay compensation in the following circumstances:

To employees. For bodily injury, illness or disease arising out of and in the course of their employment in the business for an unlimited amount. Any person working for you for the purpose of gaining work experience is automatically included. This cover is a statutory requirement under the Employers' Liability (Compulsory Insurance) Act 1969.

To members of the public For bodily injury, illness or disease or loss of or damage to material property, which arises in connexion with a business, including liability arising from the sale of goods, for an amount of (say) up to £500 000 for any one occurrence. Increases on cover are available on the payment of an additional premium. In addition, all litigation costs and expenses are paid when incurred with the insurers agreement. As with almost all sections of the insurance market there are certain extensions and special features available. Some of these include:

Defective premises Cover for liability incurred under Section 3 of the Defective Premises Act 1972.

Damage to rented premises Cover for damage to premises rented or hired by you (other than if liability is assumed by you under an agreement which would not have attached in the absence of such agreement). You may be asked to pay the first £100 or thereabouts of each loss unless the damage was caused by fire or explosion.

Health and Safety at Work Act   Cover for your legal costs arising out of any prosecution under Part 1 of the Health and Safety at Work Act, 1974, but excluding any fines or penalties imposed an any costs incurred as a result of a deliberate act omission.

Contingent liability   Cover for liability incurred by the employer as a result of the use by any employee of his own vehicle on company business. As a result of the tendency in the USA to make very large court awards, the UK insurance market is now particularly sensitive to this area. For obvious reasons therefore if your company is involved in the supply of materials or products to that part of the world then it is highly recommended that your insurer should be informed. It is commonplace for insurers to exclude public liability claims which arise from motor vehicles licensed for road use, professional negligence, or for property which is held in your custody or control and should cover be required in these areas then special arrangements should be made.

PERSONNEL

Personal accident insurance

This is the least expensive of the covers and normally takes one or two forms:

1   *Occupational accident cover.* This type of cover applies to all accidents at work including those not directly the fault of the employer. It is one of the cheapest forms of protection and can be extended to include accidents on the way to and from work.
2   *24-hour accident cover.* This cover applies 24 hours a day, every day of the year at home and at leisure anywhere in the world. Clearly, as the cover is extended, the costs increase and will vary depending upon the occupation of the staff involved. These covers can be arranged either for specific members of staff by name, specific groups of staff or for all employees.

Personal accident policies usually include capital sums and weekly benefits. They can be arranged either by a fixed benefit or a figure related to the employee's earnings. Capital sums are paid following accidental death or serious injury and can be used as compensation to the injured employee or made payable to the firm to offset the very high costs often involved in replacing a key individual (see key man assurance). Weekly sums, usually for short term absence by reason of accidents, are normally payable for 104 weeks only.

Personal accident and sickness insurance

The personal accident only cover can be supplemented by cover in respect of sickness as well. This extension of the basic personal accident policy would normally provide a weekly benefit in the event of illness on the same lines as for personal accident only. There is usually a two-year limit (104 weeks) on the weekly benefit payable.

Rates of premium are often based on a percentage of the wage roll and the rates vary according to occupation. In general, the employer would collect premiums and pay them in bulk to the insurance company. From the insurance company's point of view the group schemes covering most or all employees would be at a cheaper rate as there is a wide spread of risk among administrative as well as manual staff.

Personal accident insurance, including or excluding sickness, is renewable every year. This means that if there is a run of bad accidents or illness, the insurer may wish to revise the terms of the cover. For key employees permanent health insurance can be the answer.

Permanent health insurance

This has two advantages over personal accident and sickness insurance. First, it provides regular monthly income for as long as the employee is ill, there is no limitation of say, 104 weeks benefit. Payments can continue, if necessary, right up to retirement age. Because the possible amount payable by an insurer is far greater, premiums are more expensive. To keep premiums at a reasonable level, it is usual for the first 13 or 16 weeks of disability, known as the waiting period, to be excluded from the cover. Often an employer will pay full salary for the first six months of illness and there would be a duplication of payment if this was included in the permanent health cover.

The second great advantage that permanent health has over personal accident insurance is that once effected, the insurer cannot subsequently withdraw cover or change the terms of that cover however disabled the member of staff becomes through recurrent health problems. Furthermore, if the employee becomes totally disabled and takes an early retirement pension through illness, or has to take some lower paid professional occupation, a reduction benefit will still be paid under the permanent health policy.

Key man assurance

There are certain members of staff who are particularly valuable to the company and whose loss, either permanently or temporarily, can affect the financial stability of the company. Statistically, it is more likely that a 45-year old businessman will die before he is 65 than that his business premises will suffer a serious fire in the same period. But while the businessman would not dream of failing to insure premises and contents against fire, very few take steps to combat the equally serious loss following death or illness of one of their key people.

Key man assurance can be made to measure, arranged so that it covers exactly what is needed and nothing more. It is specific to the individual and his or her contribution to the company. In addition, because no employer knows precisely what the future holds, benefits can be changed to suit changing circumstances.

Here are the basic kinds of key man assurance:

To protect profits against a key person's death   The cheapest way to offset the effect on profits of a key person's death is by means of term assurance or convertible term assurance. In either case, the policy is often arranged to pay a lump sum in equal instalments spread over, say, ten years to minimize corporation tax. There is an option for a lump sum to be payable. The sum to be assured will depend on the value of the employee.

With term assurance, cover ceases after a set number of years. With convertible term assurance there is the option of coverting at any time into a permanent whole life or endowment policy, or a further term or convertible term policy, without the employee having to undergo a further medical examination.

For a small additional premium, many assurers will include a guaranteed insurability option which allows the sum assured to be increased without further medical evidence at certain intervals and within certain limits.

The premiums involved for life assurance are remarkably small, £100 000 cover on a 10-year term assurance, assuming a non-smoker would typically cost approximately £300 per annum and from this corporation tax would often be deductible.

Key man – permanent health insurance   The long absence of key people through illness or injury can be as disruptive as their death. A regular income for the company whilst the key employee cannot work is best provided by permanent health cover. Statistically, there is a one in six chance of a 45-year old key employee suffering long term disablement through illness or accident during the next 20 years.

Normally a key employee policy is for a period of 10 years, but a slightly higher premium can usually secure an option to extend for a further 10 years without further medical evidence. Monthly benefits are usually limited to two years including the 'waiting period' of 13 or 26 weeks. Usually the loss of a key person is not a problem in the very short term and, similarly, the firm might reasonably be expected to replace or retain by the end of two years.

The key man permanent health policy is designed to tide the company over the short-term financial difficulties arising from the serious incapacity of a key employee. If the key person is incapacitated more than once, benefits start again on the same terms as on the first occasion provided a different illness or injury is responsible. If there are separate periods of incapacity due to the same illness or injury, these are aggregated and benefits are paid for only two years in total, less the original waiting period. The waiting period is not repeated for related illnesses.

If while in receipt of payments under the policy, the employee takes early retirement and a pension, or takes up some lower paid occupation, a reduced benefit is payable during the remainder of the benefit paying period.

Again, premiums are relatively inexpensive. As an example an employer would pay an annual premium of approximately £88 to provide a benefit of £10 000 per annum payable for 104 weeks less a waiting period of 26 weeks assuming the employee was in an administrative or clerical occupation.

Medical expenses

Substantial group discounts are available for groups of employees from firms specializing in medical expenses insurance schemes, such as BUPA and Private Patient's Plan. A common practice is for the employer to arrange such schemes on behalf of their employees, as an employee benefit, with premiums paid by the employee by deduction from salary.

The advantage to the employer is that they obtain the benefit of private medical insurance at comparatively low cost because of the group discounts, whilst the employer has the advantage of faster medical attention available to his employees who can then resume work much quicker.

The employee usually has the choice as to which plan he wishes to opt for, but it is usually recommended that as hospital accommodation charges form a large part of the claim it is better to assume hospital treatment at the rates shown for the London area rather than take up cover on the basis of the provincial hospital charges.

Death in service benefits

Benefits payable following death from any cause are usually part of a company pension scheme. Nonetheless, provided it is arranged by the employer, cover can be paid for by deduction from salary or else subsidized in all or part by the employer. There are two basic forms of 'death in service' schemes:

Capital sums In this type of arrangement, a lump sum is payable which is either a sum directly related to salary, e.g. once, twice, three times, or a maximum of four times the employee's salary at death, or alternatively a sum which bears no direct relationship to the salary.

Widow's 'death in service' benefits This scheme can be in addition to the lump sum benefits and provides an income to the widow or dependants of the deceased employee from the date of death until he or she would have reached retirement age.

Under both these schemes there are certain limitations laid down by the Inland Revenue. In respect of lump sum benefits the maximum is usually four times current salary. In respect of widow's death in service benefits the maximum is normally 44 per cent of current salary.

The previous sections have attempted to cover the fundamental principles of insurance in relation to business practice. There are however very many specialist forms of insurance which are designed to cater for the insurance of fraud or dishonesty of employees, breakdown of computers, explosion of central heating boilers, breakdown of refrigeration plant, death of livestock; in fact the considerations are almost endless.

Insurance is now a highly competitive market no longer inhibited by tariffs or market agreements. As a result the need for specialist advice is paramount, particularly if your business has any degree of specialism in itself. The events which a company insures itself against were traditionally described as perils. Perhaps the greatest peril of all would be to ignore the existence of insurance altogether.

44 The administration of commercial property

Philip Westwood

The company secretary or office manager may be required, as part of his duties, to administer the property within which the company carries out its business, or to advise the directors in matters related to the company's buildings or land.

In normal circumstances, a company secretary will take over the company property from his predecessor, and many of the decisions discussed in this chapter will have been made for him. But like all other aspects of the company's activities, the continuing suitability of its premises should be regularly reviewed. This chapter is intended to aid that process, and assist in the correct decisions being taken as the company expands or contracts to meet changing circumstances.

All proprietary interests in land are at law 'real' property, as distinct from other property including chattels, animals, stocks and shares etc., which are 'personal' property. Thus 'real estate' includes freeholds and easements, which are rights by virtue of land ownership over the land of others (for example, a right of way).

The nature of a company's real estate will depend on its activities. It may consist of retail outlets, administrative offices, warehouses, garages for the repair and maintenance of the company's transport, factories, research and development facilities, leisure and training facilities, and company houses for the accommodation of its staff. If a great deal of property is involved, then the company would be best advised to employ its own staff with professional expertise in the selection and maintenance of buildings. A small company may feel unable to afford such help, and will look to the office manager or company secretary to fulfil these duties, whilst taking professional advice when required.

FACTORS AFFECTING THE SELECTION OF A BUILDING

The process of choosing a building to suit the needs of a company will involve the review of a number of factors, including the location of the building, choice of site, type of building proposed, and the extent of refurbishment, repair, or new building work needed. The choice of freehold or leasehold purchase is dictated by the availability of suitable buildings and will generally have little effect on the decisions taken.

Location

A modern business should be located so that it can achieve the most efficient use of its resources. Traditionally, businesses are located near their markets, their raw materials, or the labour and power necessary for the conversion of that material into goods for sale. In the nineteenth century, the development of the railways allowed the increased separation of these elements and introduced the additional need for proximity to railway depots and marshalling yards. Many heavy industries had their own railway sidings. The decline of the railways coupled with improvements in the road network and suitable vehicles has resulted in a substantial transfer of distribution of raw materials and goods to the roads. Docks and airports are vital for businesses which enter the export market. As trade becomes more international, the availability of alternative means of fast distribution remains an important consideration in the location of a company's premises.

The location of industry and commerce is therefore dependent upon easy access to raw materials, easy delivery of products to markets, docks or airports, and the availability of a suitable labour force.

Commercial undertakings generally begin in locations which favour the small scale of the enterprise. As the company grows the commercial environment may alter to such an extent that the factors which worked in its favour in its early development are either neutralized or begin to work against its interests. It should be borne in mind that relocation could be a solution to the problems of inefficiency resulting from labour problems, unavailability of space for expansion, or the need to reorganize production lines without interrupting output.

Selecting a site

A company wishing to establish itself on a new site, either by conversion of an existing building or by building afresh, will find its choice of site limited by planning legislation, which controls the location of commercial and industrial development. This control, as well as preventing certain types of development in particular areas, also encourages the establishment of special commercial and industrial zones or estates. Sites within such zones are available for light industrial use, allowing the letting of existing purpose-made factory or office units, or the erection of buildings to the company's own design. The government, in partnership with local authorities, also attempts to direct the location of new business to areas of high unemployment. Tax and rate allowances are available in favour of some regions, particularly the North-East and South Wales. In these areas, specially designated 'enterprise zones' have been established where special provisions apply (for example, no general rate payable for the first year of trading in the area). If the business is large or politically important enough, local authorities will generally be prepared to consider proposals for new development and negotiate special terms, consisting of low interest loans, rate reductions etc., in order to attract the business to its area. Similar opportunities apply abroad, particularly within the EEC. A company considering relocation would be well advised to explore all these options before settling on a suitable site.

New towns have been established over the past 50 years or so, to take the overspill population from the large cities. These towns were designed as self-contained economic units, with their own industrial and commercial centres. The sites for these new towns were generally chosen to take advantage of good communications and other facilities, and offer many amenities to attract business and labour.

The long-term benefits to companies of relocation include continuing rate and insurance bills lower than in the centre of the large cities, and a more contented workforce, not hidebound by traditional working practices.

Building location checklist

The following checklist includes factors to be considered when choosing a location for premises.

1 *Communications*
   (*a*) Standard of trunk roads available
   (*b*) Proximity of railhead
   (*c*) Access to international airport
   (*d*) Access to seaport
   (*e*) Average distance from suppliers and consumers (as small as possible)
2 *Services*
   (*a*) Electric power available without restriction
   (*b*) Mains gas supplies available
   (*c*) Adequate water supplies
3 *Climate and topography*
   (*a*) Temperate climate throughout the year
   (*b*) Area/site well drained and free from flood danger
   (*c*) Site sheltered from high winds and extreme weather
   (*d*) Surrounding area pleasant; good outlook from site
4 *Government and local authority*
   (*a*) Area scheduled as development area, (or enterprise zone,) and eligible for investment grants
   (*b*) Planning restrictions in the area minimal
   (*c*) Friendly and cooperative local authority
5 *Labour and labour relations*
   (*a*) Local branches of trade unions moderate and cooperative
   (*b*) Key staff willing to move into area
   (*c*) Good supply of skilled or suitable workpeople already living in the area

817

6 *Amenities*
   (*a*) Housing prices low, good supply of houses of all types (private and local authority)
   (*b*) Good schools available, with possibilities in the area for higher education
   (*c*) Good local transport facilities for commuters
   (*d*) Good local health services and hospitals
   (*e*) Adequate recreational facilities in the area
   (*f*) Theatres, cinemas and other entertainments
   (*g*) Police and fire services efficient
   (*h*) Churches of all denominations accessible
7 *Specific site factors*
   (*a*) Means for disposal of waste/effluent
   (*b*) Access on good local roads
   (*c*) Etc. as required by the particular industry

Choosing a building

The choice of building will depend on a number of factors which must be considered carefully together.

The activities and processes which are to be undertaken within the building must be analysed so that their requirements can be satisfied in its design. A report of the requirements of manufacturing processes, the storage of raw materials and finished products and the methods of packing and distribution should be requested from the managers responsible. Office accommodation also requires specialist consideration, and office services are discussed more fully in Chapter 47. All must be considered and a brief prepared to enable the appropriate building to be sought.

Unless the requirements of the firm are extremely specialized, it is likely that a choice will be made from among a number of buildings with varying degrees of suitability. The first consideration is whether the firm wishes to rent or purchase the property, and if the latter, whether an existing building is being sought or specially built premises are required. There are a number of factors affecting the first decision. The time factor is very important, since a new building may take one or two years to complete (depending on its complexity) after all necessary consents are to hand. The design stage may add a further six to twelve months to the process. If the company can afford to purchase the freehold the building will represent a valuable asset and surety against the rent reviews inevitable in leases.

It is almost inevitable that any building taken over either by lease or purchase will require capital expenditure in adapting it to the needs of the company. This may range from a complete refurbishment, with the installation of air conditioning, improved insulation, and modern welfare facilities, to minor redecoration work and carpeting. If the use of the building is to be changed, then work may be needed to meet the requirements of special legislation or a licensing authority, and planning permission obtained.

PROFESSIONAL ADVICE

At this stage it is appropriate to consider the appointment of a professional who will be able to advise on the selection, conversion or construction of suitable premises. It is advisable to make this appointment at an early stage to avoid problems which may arise from the purchase of a building which is ill fitted to the company's requirements for technical reasons. There are many considerations which require professional expertise in their assessment; for example, the suitability of the structure to carry the loads required, the capacity of the existing drains to cope with the increased use envisaged, and the requirements of the fire authorities.

The choice of suitable qualified professional help has never been wider. In the past the architect has dominated this area, and may well be the only professional who springs to mind when considering building work. Of recent years the emergence of the surveyor, particularly of the building surveyor, as an expert in conversion and refurbishment work, has allowed the client greater choice and a range of skills which go beyond that offered by the architect.

Building surveyors, with their quantity surveying colleagues, are able to offer a full range of services which include structural surveys, cost feasibility studies, advice on the appointment of contractors and the design and supervision of the conversion work. Building surveyors are usually graduates who qualify under the examinations of The Royal Institution of Chartered Surveyors. They use the title Fellow (FRICS) or Associate (ARICS). Architects must be registered with the Architect's Registration Council of the United Kingdom (ARCUK) and are usually Fellows (FRIBA) or Associates (ARIBA) of the Royal Institute of British Architects. Both the RICS and the RIBA publish registers of practitioners which are available in most public libraries.

The correct choice of someone who is going to be closely linked with large expenditure on a company's behalf is of vital importance. It would be prudent to interview prospective candidates. References from recent clients should be sought, and work in progress or recently completed should be inspected.

The architect/surveyor may be appointed to carry out the complete task (from advising at the inception of the scheme to the final hand-over of the completed work) or appointed to deal with specific stages of the work, perhaps for the feasibility study only, or up to the selection of the contractor to carry out the work. The scale of fees would be varied accordingly.

The architect/surveyor will require a brief of the company's requirements, with particular emphasis on any special areas of concern. For example, special provision will have to be made for areas of high fire risk, heavy loads such as safes or heavy equipment, and ventilation and air conditioning. Account must be taken of any constraints upon the layout of offices and workshops arising from working practices, manufacturing production lines, open plan or individual offices etc., vehicular access and parking for staff and deliveries, catering facilities and special service requirements for high voltage electrical substations or generators (for computers or major machinery).

Selecting a contractor

One of the architect/surveyor's duties will be to advise on the selection of a contractor to carry out the building work. Since it is particularly difficult to control building costs associated with conversion work, it is essential that the selection process produces a contractor and price for the works which can be relied upon. The traditional method of choosing a contractor is by a process of competitive tendering, whereby a number of contractors are selected to bid for the work. Generally, the contractor offering the cheapest price is awarded the contract. The architect/surveyor will normally conduct a process of selection of contractors capable of undertaking work of the type and value required prior to the tender itself. The preparation of a list of suitable contractors circumvents any difficulties which may arise if an unknown contractor submits the lowest price in an open tender. The additional confidence in a contractor chosen by the selective tender process, and the time saved in the selection may well be worth the possibility of a higher contract price.

A number of other systems of selection and contracting are available which may be used where suitable. These will now be discussed briefly in turn.

Management fee contracts, whereby the contractor undertakes to manage the contract for a fee established in advance. This allows the appointment to be made at an early stage in the design process and the introduction of an important new member to the professional team. The intention is that the contractor cannot be said to gain from increases in the value of the work, a useful factor if large-scale refurbishment is contemplated.

Package deal and turnkey systems are those where the whole of the design and construction work is undertaken for a total cost, the client being handed the key to the completed building on completion (hence 'turnkey'). Contracts of this type are offered by companies with an interest in providing a standardized form of construction, and are often used for standard factory or warehouse units on industrial estates. They are therefore more suitable for new building work rather than for refurbishment, but they may be used for extensions to existing buildings, or for new building work within an existing site.

Design and build contracts are similar to package deal contracts, but with a greater emphasis on the client's special design requirements.

Separate contracts or the alternative methods of management system (AMM) involves the use of the architect/surveyor as usual, but the various aspects of the work are let to individual contractors, as appropriate, avoiding the appointment of a single main contractor. The architect/surveyor manages the contract. This approach involves the client in the selection of a number of contractors, each carrying out their own part of the works. Refurbishment work could be carried out using this system.

Project management contracts place the responsibility for all the various aspects of the work, design, supervision and performance on one organization. No single profession has emerged as the legitimate leader in this type of contract. Architects, surveyors and main contractors are all conducting contracts of this type at present. Essentially, the functions of each are being carried out by a team consisting of architects, surveyors and contracting staff, but all under the one contract. It generally depends on the professional background of the team leader as to which profession claims to be the project manager. Advantages of the system include the removal of the litigious barriers between the members of the team, who can all be seen to be working together for the good of the project.

The British Property Federation System is a client-based alternative system. It is biased towards the interests of the client, which may mean that better contractors will avoid it. The system contains many previously untried processes, and may not prove as advantageous to the client as it at first appears.

It is as well to remember that the cheapest initial price may not prove to be the cheapest final contract figure. Costs arising from delays, claims or the bankruptcy of contractors caused by the enforcement of onerous contract conditions may not be assessable or recoverable. It is worthwhile spending some little time ensuring that the right designer, supervisor, and contractor are chosen, and that the building requirements are fully worked out and understood before work is started on site.

BUILDING LEGISLATION

There are approximately 200 Acts of Parliament and nearly 300 regulations affecting building operations.

Of course, not all the legislation applies to any particular building. Many types of buildings or uses to which a building may be put have their own specific regulations, but some of the general legislation, such as the building regulations, applies in most cases, and should always be considered.

Many of the regulations apply only to particular classes of building, or to buildings used for special purposes, such as the Asbestos Regulations, which only apply to premises where asbestos processes are carried out.

There are 26 Acts and regulations for buildings in general, and if the building is of some architectural or historical significance, a further 8 Acts or regulations apply. The number of items applicable to commercial buildings depends on the proposed use of the building. Offices and shops for general purposes have 18 Acts and regulations (in addition to the 26 mentioned above). If it is a food shop or market, a further 8 must be added, and if it sells medicines, another 9. Industrial buildings have 12 general Acts or regulations, a further 22 if it is a general factory, 9 more for the manufacture of medicines. Residential buildings also have various Acts and regulations depending on use. Private domestic housing does not have many, but there are 28 Acts or regulations to do with housing, improvement grants and home insulation grants, some of which are applicable to private as well as public housing.

In addition there are the fire precautions Acts, town and country planning legislation, and health and safety legislation.

Legislation affecting particular commercial and industrial applications would normally be well known to a company working in that field. It is therefore proposed to discuss only the main items of legislation of general concern to building owners.

Planning control

The use to which a building may be put is controlled by planning legislation exercised by the local authority under the Town and Country Planning Act 1971. The Use Classes Order 1972 categorizes a number of uses for land. Although land, and the buildings on the land, may continue to be used for purposes within the same use class, any change in use class constitutes development, and requires planning permission. For example, a greengrocers may become a newsagents, but not a fast food restaurant, and a factory producing clothing may switch to the assembly of electronic components, or other light industrial use, provided no noxious emissions result from the process.

Planning permission can be sought in two stages. Initial application can be made for outline planning approval. A prospective user can explore the likelihood of permission to use land for his purpose without the need to fully develop the scheme, even before he has obtained any legal interest in the site. Care needs to be taken here, since the value of the land may increase considerably if planning consent is given. For this reason, consent is generally given to a particular individual or company, and may lapse if that company sells its interest to another party. Before development can take place, detailed proposals must be put forward and full planning consent obtained.

As well as the nature of the use of the development, the local authority will be concerned with the appearance and height of the building, means of access, car parking provision and, increasingly, the employment opportunities offered by the development.

If it is felt that planning approval may be required, then the advice of the planning authority should be sought. Planning permission cannot be awarded retrospectively. The local authority are required to order the removal of any building for which planning permission was not obtained, and to restore the land to its former use.

Building control

In addition to the need to satisfy the planning authorities, any development which involves the construction of new work or alterations or extensions to existing buildings may have to satisfy the requirements of the building regulations. Building control is also exercised by the local authority, and it is common practice to submit plans for building regulation approval at the same time as an application is made for planning approval. The practice of submitting plans for scrutiny and approval prior to the commencement of building work has been criticized in the past as causing unnecessary delay, particularly in circumstances where the work required is straightforward and simple, like the installation of a washbasin or the erection of a small shed. Since November 1985, alternative procedures have been available whereby the local authority is notified that the work will be carried out, and inspection takes place on site, without the prior approval of plans. The building owner loses certain protection afforded under the older system, but gains time in circumstances where the risk of failure to comply with the regulations is less likely. A third method, using inspectors approved under the Approved Inspectors Regulations instead of the local authority inspectors has also been introduced, but at present the only approved inspectors are the National House Builders Registration Council, who deal with private housing developments.

The building regulations lay down standards of design and construction essentially in the interests of public health and safety, and to conserve power and the water supply. Sections of the regulations deal with structural strength, means of escape in case of fire, drainage and sanitation, ventilation, thermal insulation and water supply.

Despite the alternative inspection systems available, the building owner is held responsible for compliance with the building regulations. Failure to do so can lead to a fine, and an order to put right or remove offending work.

Fire precautions

Fire precautions are considered to be an important part of the safety of premises, and are dealt with in two ways. New building work is dealt with primarily under the building regulations, but existing buildings are dealt with under the Fire Precautions Act and related legislation.

The Fire Precautions Act 1971 deals with the adequate provision of means of escape in case of fire. It includes the provision of fire fighting equipment, alarm systems, etc. It is primarily concerned with the protection of life, but the measures necessary to meet the requirements will provide some protection to property in the event of fire. In addition, there is a requirement to instruct staff on necessary action in case of fire, and records must be kept of fire drills, alarm tests, maintenence checks and incidents involving fire. Registers are provided for the purpose. The provision of special equipment, sprinkler systems and the like, may be used in order to prolong the time available for escape and to protect property where there is special risk. Sprinklers and smoke detection devices may be required in special circumstances, for example, basements and storage areas for inflammable materials.

In order to invoke its powers, the minister must place before Parliament a designating order, which brings the types of buildings specified by the order under the Act. The Act was intended eventually to cover all buildings which fall into one of the following categories of use:

1 Recreation, entertainment or instruction or for any club, society or association
2 Teaching, training or research
3 Institutions providing treatment or care
4 Any purpose involving the provision of sleeping accommodation
5 Any use involving access to the building by members of the public, whether on payment or otherwise
6 (Since the enactment of the Health and Safety at Work etc. Act 1974) the use of the premises as a place of work.

At present there have been only two such designating orders. The first dealt with hotels and boarding houses, the second with premises previously covered by the Factories Acts and the Offices Shops and Railway Premises Act. In both cases there is a minimum size related to the number of people on the premises below which certification is not required.

A number of other categories of building are presently covered by other regulations with respect to fire control. For example, nursing homes and residential care homes are among the categories which may come under the Act with the introduction of a future designation order. At present the fire officer's requirements in this area are covered by the Residential Homes Act 1984 and the Residential Care Homes Regulations 1984. In this case the registration by the area health authority under the Act includes the requirement to satisfy the fire officer in the same areas of concern covered by the Fire Precautions Act.

Under the Fire Precautions Act, the owner of premises which come into a category designated by a designating order must make application to the fire authority for a fire certificate. The fire authority is required to inspect the premises and advise on standards. If necessary, he may provide written notice of the steps required to achieve a certificate, and stipulate a time to carry out the work. After the time specified, a final inspection takes place. On being satisfied that the appropriate precautions have been taken a fire certificate is issued. If the work is not carried out to the satisfaction of the fire officer, then the business must cease trading. If the owner feels that the schedule of requirements, or any decision of the fire officer, is unreasonable an appeal must be made within twenty-one days.

The provision of fire protection systems may be prudent in situations not at present covered by the Fire Precautions Act. Suitable detection and fire control systems can prevent serious damage from fire by early detection and local control, and may allow normal business to recommence more quickly after an incident involving fire. Constant vigilance and inspection are necessary to maintain standards and ensure that the measures taken are not undermined by careless action. In a recent fire at a large oil company's head office in London, a fire which broke out in a basement storeroom caused £100 000 damage despite almost instant detection and the attendance of the fire service after less then two minutes. The subsequent disruption caused by repair work added a further £200 000 to the bill. Fire doors had been wedged open, and communication ducting and the air conditioning conducted the smoke as far as the tenth floor.

Insurance companies will look favourably on a company with a sound fire prevention policy. Whilst it is unlikely that there will be a reduction in premiums, the additional premiums required to cover high risk areas or materials may be avoided.

FUTURE ALTERATIONS AND EXTENSIONS

When reviewing the suitability of a company's property due allowance for future expansion should be made. If considering the purchase of existing property the possibility of taking over adjacent property in the future, or of buying a building with a greater floor area than present requirements demand should be explored. The extra space may be let on a short lease until required. If a new building is contemplated, the architect or surveyor responsible for the design should be informed of future plans so that he may make allowance within his design. The additional cost of building stronger foundations and structural members to take an extra storey in the future will be minimal compared to the cost involved later. The choice of location of the building may be influenced if site investigations show that the extra loads take the design beyond the bearing capacity of the ground, or likely planning restrictions inhibit the anticipated development. The incorporation of larger capacity service mains may also be considered.

A company is entitled to extend its property within normal planning constraints up to 10 per cent of the original development without the need for further planning approval. If an extension of less than the full 10 per cent is made, then further expansion up to the total of 10 per cent of the original development is possible. It should be noted that the limits stated relate to the building, not the occupier, and care should be taken to establish if the development allowance has been used up by earlier owners. If expansion beyond the gross 10 per cent is contemplated, a new planning approval must be sought.

If the property is leasehold the lessor's consent will be required, and at this stage it should be considered whether notice should be served under the Landlord and Tenant Act 1927, to protect the tenant's position at the end of the lease.

DISPOSAL

In addition to the initial design alteration or extension of any building it is well to have in mind the possibility of eventual disposal. The more specialized a building in design the more difficult it is to sell, as it cannot easily be adapted for use other than that for which it was originally designed. An extreme example of this would be a steelworks, although such buildings as multi-storey Thames-side warehouses have been converted into flats. In office buildings partitioning arrangements will almost certainly be unsuitable to a subsequent occupier, and open office floors should therefore be subdivided by demountable partitions that are easily removed or adapted.

MAINTENANCE AND REPAIR

An important aspect of the management of property is that of maintenance and repair. Buildings consist of materials of varying durability, with 'lives' ranging from a few years to centuries. Some, such as timber joinery, can be protected by impregnation at the manufacturing stage or the application of surface treatments (paints, stains, or varnishes) throughout their life. Others, such as heating appliances, wear out after a number of years' use, and need overhaul or replacement well before the rest of the building deteriorates.

Failure to carry out repair and maintenance at the appropriate time can lead to a considerably more expensive replacement becoming necessary later, or even danger to the building occupants if, for example, a faulty gas appliance continues to be used.

Whilst not all equipment and materials need to last the whole life of the building, such materials used in parts of the building which are difficult to reach without severe disruption should be designed to do so. Indeed, the replacement of a boiler may provide an opportunity for a review of the heating and ventilating requirements of the property, resulting in the introduction of more efficient systems.

There can be very few buildings over twenty-five years old which still boast the original heating system, or even retain the same internal layout as envisaged in their original design.

When evaluating the suitability of an existing building, or approving the design of a specially commissioned building the importance of ease of maintenance should not be under-estimated. There are a number of hidden costs associated with maintenance which may be overlooked when comparing alternative materials. In addition to the cost of carrying out the work itself, there is the cost of disruption to the normal routine whilst the work is carried out. The cost to the company of misplaced documents or files because they were moved to allow the painters in, or of a vehicle access blocked by scaffolding may be extremely high. Also, the additional security risk of unauthorized access via scaffolding cannot be overlooked. Some of these maintenance costs cannot be avoided entirely, but choices taken during the design or refurbishment of premises at the time of purchase can reduce their effect or frequency.

In some cases, the initial cost of incorporating materials or design requiring low maintenance into a building will be greater than would otherwise be required. Consideration will then have to be given to the loss of earnings or interest on the extra capital against the expected savings in the future. Maintenance is an area which is particularly vulnerable to the company's financial circumstances. It is all too easy to delay maintenance if costs need to be saved. For this reason the temptation of agreeing to a cheap specification and relying on future maintenance being carried out on a regular basis should be avoided. The idea of spending money today in anticipation of problems which may not arise for twenty or thirty years is a difficult one, particularly if a board of directors or shareholders has to be persuaded. It can be argued that companies are more concerned with current expenditure than future expense, but the value of designed maintenance is becoming better appreciated, and may be reflected in the value of the property if it comes to the market before the maintenance is required. A compromise between designing a cheap specification with high maintenance costs or an expensive specification with little or no maintenance must be reached, and the architect or surveyor should be able to advise here. In the discussions the terms 'costs in use' or 'life cycle costing' may be used. These terms describe procedures where on paper, future expenditure is discounted to present values for comparison purposes.

Maintenance programmes should be prepared by the prudent building owner. In order to identify the maintenance requirements of the building a survey should be carried out and a programme of maintenance appropriate to the materials and design incorporated within its construction should be followed. This programme can form the basis of a maintenance budget which should be approved at the highest level, particularly in view of the vulnerability described above.

Care must be taken to establish the varying needs for maintenance in different parts of the building. Little used or carefully used rooms and corridors will require less frequent redecoration and consequently savings can be made in the maintenance budget if they are identified. Reception areas and other prestigious parts of the building will require redecoration more frequently than is strictly necessary for the protection of the fabric, in order to maintain or promote the corporate image of the company. Parts of the building where the fabric is exposed to corrosive processes or where hygiene requirements must be considered, for example in food preparation areas, will also require redecoration more frequently than normal.

Provided the building is brought up to a good standard of repair when purchased, then expenditure on maintenance will not be great in the first few years of occupation. Depending on the decisions taken on the incorporation of low maintenance materials, maintenance will generally involve the repainting of external painted surfaces every three to five years and redecoration internally as required. Longer-term maintenance such as the replacement of boilers or electrical rewiring can be planned in advance and included within an annual maintenance budget.

Labour for maintenance may be provided by a contractor selected by the procedures described earlier in this chapter, usually employed to carry out specific tasks either in accordance with the previously agreed maintenance programme, or to cope with emergencies. Minor repairs and the replacement of consumable equipment like fluorescent light tubes is usually carried out by staff directly employed by the company. In some areas of high office concentrations, it is now possible to obtain all such services from specialist maintenance contractors who will undertake a 24-hour comprehensive service.

LEASEHOLD PROPERTY

A high proportion of commercial property is leasehold, and in most cases the lease contains a review clause which allows the rent to be reviewed at fixed intervals during its term. At each review date the current market rent is assessed and substituted for the rent previously payable. The dates or interval between reviews should be expressly stated in the lease, together with the procedure which must be followed. Recent court decisions have been concerned with the rights of the parties if the procedure is not followed, for example, if the landlord does not give notice of the review at the time stipulated or implied by the lease. The view is that the landlord will forfeit the right to a review until the next review date if time is of the essence of the agreement. Time will only be of the essence if it is expressly so provided in the terms of the lease, or if there is some indication in the lease or in the surrounding circumstances that time is to be of the essence. Generally, surveyors or valuers acting for each party meet and negotiate the new rent. Provision is usually made within the lease for the appointment of a third independent surveyor to settle the matter by arbitration if agreement is not reached.

Full repair covenants

Leases for commercial property may contain a full repair covenant, which will require a tenant to leave the property newly decorated and in a condition of good repair at the end of the tenancy. Even if in disrepair at the commencement of a lease having a full repairing covenant, a tenant must put the premises into good repair and so hand them back at the end of the term.

The law of dilapidations is complex and a subject for experts; but the principle should be borne in mind that the measure of dilapidations when they have to be valued is the amount of injury to the landlord's reversionary interest. If it is the landlord's intention to demolish the building for redevelopment, he will fail in a claim against the tenant if the building is in disrepair, as he has suffered no loss.

A tenant of business premises may be entitled to a new lease on the expiration of an existing lease should he desire to continue in occupation under the terms of the Landlord and Tenant Act 1954. The rent of the premises is subject to review under the new terms, and the landlord can regain possession, thus avoiding granting of a new lease, if he proves intention to redevelop the premises or requirement for his own occupation. Provision is made in the Landlord and Tenant Act 1927 for compensation for tenants making improvements, or establishing goodwill in business premises at the end of the term of the lease. Alternatively a new lease may be granted.

VALUATION

The valuation of freehold or leasehold property should be carried out by an expert valuer familiar with the value of similar properties in the same market. The value depends on the purpose of the valuation. Valuation for insurance purposes will be the full cost of rebuilding on the existing land, and consequently should not include the value of the land. The cost of rebuilding should include the cost of site clearance, professional fees and legal expenses. Insurance should also be taken out to cover the cost of disruption to production or temporary accommodation required whilst the work is carried out. The value of a property for the purpose of sale or the setting of rents will depend on its location, and the demand for property of its type and condition in the area. Perhaps surprisingly, it has no direct relationship to the cost of building, particularly where the advantages of the location may be overwhelming, and there is a scarcity of building land in the area. It is prudent to undertake a revaluation of a company's real estate at intervals, as it represents an asset which is often undervalued in the accounts with a consequential effect on the company's value in the market place.

RATING

The responsibility for valuing property for rating purposes rests with valuation officers of the Inland Revenue, who establish a gross value for the property or hereditament concerned. The rating authority levies a rate in the £ or 'rateable value' for each property, based on the valuation officer's assessment. Valuation lists for England and Wales contain all rateable hereditaments for each rating area together with their assessments.

Rates are levied on the occupier of a property, although the owner may be liable for rates on unoccupied premises.

The basis of the valuation is an estimate of the rent at which the particular property might be let according to the statutory definition defined within the General Rate Act 1967. The current valuation lists came into force on 1 April 1973, and any subsequent alterations to those assessments, or properties being assessed for the first time, should not exceed the value that would have been ascribed to the particular hereditament had it existed in the year prior to 1 April 1973. This is called the 'tone of the list' and it is important to ensure that should reassessment occur, for example as the result of building alterations, the addition in assessment is not excessive and the 'tone' has been properly applied.

Under the General Rate Act 1967 it was intended that a revaluation of the list would occur every five years. This provision was abolished by the Local Government, Planning and Land Act 1980. The further removed 1 April 1973 becomes the more difficult it is to assess new buildings satisfactorily. Plans are at present in progress to revalue all commercial property with effect some time in 1990, the date still to be announced. A ratepayer has the right to seek a reduction in assessment at any time by making a proposal, although the operative date of any reduction in assessment can only be, at the earliest, from the beginning of the rate year in which the proposal was served, i.e. 1 April. The majority of appeals are determined by agreement negotiated between the ratepayers' professional advisers and the valuation officer. If agreement cannot be reached, the matter will be heard by a local valuation court. From their decision there is a right of appeal to the Lands Tribunal and on a point of law to the Court of Appeal and thence to the House of Lords.

Grounds frequently exist or arise where an appeal is justified, particularly if the valuation officer is not aware of special difficulties associated with the premises in question. For example the premises may be outmoded for their present use or irregular in shape. They may have difficult access, poor natural light, low headroom etc. The effect of building works either within the hereditament or adjacent to it can give rise to a temporary reduction in assessment. In view of the foregoing, and the high rate burden carried by the business community, it is sensible for a company to review its rating assessment at periodic intervals and appeal if grounds exist.

ADJOINING OWNERS

The owner and occupier of a property has a responsibility to his neighbours and the community at large in respect of his use of the site. Nuisance and negligence at legal torts which may arise between adjoining owners as the result of the use of property. Nuisance can arise in the generation of smoke, fumes, noise etc., by a neighbour causing grievance to a property owner. If a substance is dangerous, such as toxic chemicals, or is stored in a dangerous manner on a neighbour's land, for example a reservoir of water, he will be liable should it escape and cause damage. There is also a legal responsibility embodied in legislation such as the Health and Safety at Work Act 1974 and in planning legislation referred to elsewhere. Failure to comply can result in prosecution under the legislation.

The boundary to a property is usually defined on the site by a boundary wall or fence. Disputes can often develop concerning boundaries, particularly about their ownership, maintenance and repair. The title to the property may define the ownership of the enclosure, but in the absence of such evidence, the convention is that the fence stands on the property of the owner, for example the posts are on the owner's side, and the face of the fence usually represents the boundary. Boundary walls may be built on the owner's land, or they may be party walls. Walls separating buildings are usually party walls, the law relating to which is well defined, requiring notice to be served by the party initiating works on the neighbours, and if the works are not agreed surveyors have to be appointed by both parties, to negotiate agreement. A third surveyor may be required to arbitrate if agreement cannot be reached.

There may be rights of way across an owner's land in favour of an adjoining property. Such easements may be limited to a particular purpose or use, and generally are limited to a predetermined path or route. It should be borne in mind that if an access be taken and used openly and as of right by a neighbour across an owner's land a *prima facie* right will be established in twenty years, which could become a burden and frustrate development. Rights of light can be acquired by the windows of a neighbour's building enjoying light and air across an owner's property for a period of twenty years. Such rights cannot be obstructed, and can restrict an owner's future development of his property.

Disputes between owners of business premises are rare. When a neighbour is in residential occupation however, every consideration should be shown by the occupier of business premises as it will be seen that a business use could be very intrusive to the quiet enjoyment of residential property.

FURTHER READING

The BWC Partnership, *Business Property Handbook*, Gower, Aldershot, 1982

Woodfall's Law of Landlord and Tenant, Sweet and Maxwell, London, 1978, with updating service

Cross, C.A., *Principles of Local Government Law*, 6th edition, Sweet and Maxwell, London, 1981

Town and Country Planning (Use Classes) Order 1972, HMSO, London

Fire Precautions Act 1972, HMSO, London

Housing and Building Control Act 1984, HMSO, London

The Building Act 1984, HMSO, London

Guides to Fire Precautions Act 1971, HMSO, London

The Fire Precautions Act in Practice, Architectural Press, London, 1977

Taylor N., *Property Managers' Guide to Fire Legislation in Commercial and Industrial Premises*, F.P.R. Distribution, 37 Dumbarton Road, Glasgow

Fire Precautions Register, F.P.R. Distribution, 37 Dumbarton Road, Glasgow

Underdown, G., *Practical Fire Precautions*, 2nd edition, Gower, Aldershot, 1979

Franks, J., *Building Procurement Systems*, The Chartered Institute of Building, London, 1984

Warning! Not using a Chartered Surveyor can put you at risk, Royal Institution of Chartered Surveyors, London, 1986

Mole, J.M., *Landlord and Tenant* 2nd edition, M & E Handbooks, 1984

45 Security

John Wilson

Managers have unpalatable facts to consider in connexion with security matters, and the potential threat to profitability is difficult to predict. A progressive increase in crime shows no sign of abating; indeed it is claimed that in the USA (a good sounding-board for future developments in the UK) white collar crime will soon be the dominant source of losses. Although prepared to give advice through their crime prevention officers, the overstretched police force are not always able to follow up small thefts and the official view is that industry must put its own house in order and that responsibility for safeguarding property falls on the owner. Managers have to decide what action they can take to avoid becoming the targets of internal and external predators.

Courts and prisons suffer from the same overload. Trials can be delayed for many months, the eventual punishment often seeming inadequate as a deterrent and inconsistent with the victim's loss. The media have brought to notice successful criminal ploys (for example, in television plays) which have been copied by criminals. Inevitably the emphasis upon computer-linked frauds and their potential will produce an unwanted reaction in a field where it is often difficult to establish that any misbehaviour has taken place. There is some evidence that this process has already begun.

Fire is often regarded as part of a security responsibility remit. While this chapter will not deal with fire in any detail it should be borne in mind that many more firms are permanently put out of business by fire than by theft. Arson in the UK has recently reached an all-time peak and whether the cause is malice or intended concealment of evidence of theft is an academic question to the firm which has suffered loss of all its records or productive capacity. Since arson is rarely attributable to employees, the exclusion of intruders is an obvious security objective.

All in all, the immediate prospect is one of increasing problems, with no foreseeable solution. The impact on the business world will have to be mitigated by internal action rather than with external assistance.

ASSESSING THE RISK

It is easy to give 'security' priority at board level once a major loss has been suffered. It is far more difficult before the event, when a dispensation of immunity appears to have been granted and the only impetus to discussion is foreboding, or a knowledge of something catastrophic which has happened to another business.

There are no divine dispensations and ultimate responsibility for security of a firm's property and that of its employees cannot be disclaimed by senior management. The nature of the business may be such that the potential losses are minimal or acceptable, but without giving positive thought to what targets exist it is impossible to evaluate economically feasible defensive precautions. Such action does not necessarily involve additional manpower. Many sources of opportunity of temptation can be removed by changing procedures and documentation or by introducing checks into systems, without impeding the normal functioning of the firm.

The Police crime prevention officers relish being invited to advise before incidents happen and their training is sufficiently broadly based to enable them to comment on most aspects of activity. However, their responsibility is a public one which limits the time that can be devoted to a particular client and this may not be adequate for all problems of a medium or large firm. Even so, guidelines will be given which can be used by management as a basis for more detailed action.

The larger commercial security firms will provide consultants but it must be appreciated that use of their companies' equipment or manpower will colour their advice. Independent security advisers or consultants have no qualifying standards whereby their efficiency can be measured, other than by personal recommendation from a reliable source. They may be self-appointed in their role, lacking essential experience and expertise. Before time and money are committed to a survey from any external source an acceptable level of competence must be established.

However the assessment is carried out, departmental heads must be fully involved. Each should be the person most conversant with the risk within his own area of operations, and with the subsequent application and monitoring of agreed security measures by methods that will not detract from the efficiency of his department. But a manager is primarily concerned with his own main purpose; security may be viewed as an inconvenient and irrelevant distraction with unpopular disciplinary connotations. There is a reluctance to admit that weaknesses exist, and this can also lead to concealment of losses which might be regarded as a poor reflection on the competence of the person in charge. It may become necessary to tell individuals forcefully that, whether they like it or not, security is part and parcel of a manager's job content, to be given serious consideration, and to be discussed where appropriate with colleagues and subordinates.

AREAS OF RISK

Obviously the areas at most risk vary according to the nature of a firm's products, location, workforce, and to the susceptibility of its operations from damage through theft or pilferage, major disaster (fire, explosion, flooding), criminal damage (arson, sabotage), loss of information and disruption through problems with industrial relations. Departments deserving special scrutiny are listed in Figure 45.1.

Department	Risk exposures	GHM
1 Research and development	Information leakage to competitors regarding successful and blind-alley projects and future objectives	
2 Sales and marketing	Leakage of planning, pricing and advertising campaigns, customer lists and discounts, confidentiality of tenders	
3 Computing	Fraud, accidental or deliberate damage, industrial espionage	
4 Cashier and wages	Physical attack, frauds or thefts by employees, interference with pre-signed cheques, etc.	
5 Transport and warehousing	Collusion to defraud between employees and customers or suppliers, weights and measures frauds and credit card mal-practices by drivers, genuine and faked hijacking	
6 Purchasing and materials disposal	Corruption by suppliers or customers	
7 Stores and goods inward	Undetected staff pilferage, collusion with suppliers	
8 Production	Espionage directed at process secrets, sabotage, thefts, bonus and other employee frauds	
9 Selling areas and retail shops	Corruption of employees, employee purchase frauds and thefts, customer trespass into unauthorized areas, shoplifting	
10 Personnel and industrial relations	Confidentiality of records and negotiation data, salary structure data	
11 Company secretary's and directors' offices	Policy and planning decisions, data affecting share performance, mergers and takeovers, etc.	

Figure 45.1 Departments deserving special scrutiny

An evaluation of contributory weaknesses was included in a detailed survey of losses within the metal-using industries. The results are worth inclusion here, since they have wider application. Even item 4 in the following list, which is peculiar to those metal-using industries, is likely to have equivalent counterparts elsewhere:

1   Management failure to fully investigate discrepancies; to instigate enquiries at a sufficiently early stage; or to accept that theft is a possible causation before all other alternatives have been exhausted; neglecting to incorporate adequate checks in systems and procedures to spotlight errors and shortages

2   Failure to note and take appropriate precautionary measures, when incidents involving substantial loss have occurred in like industries, and in circumstances which could be duplicated internally

3   Inadequate internal liaison on matters which may give rise to risk of loss through dishonesty or other criminal action (i.e., new procedures, new products or processes, new building or structural alterations); failure to communicate information on losses that have become known

4   Failure by management on many occasions to appreciate the potential contribution to profitability from reclaimable metal waste correctly handled, and disposed of to best advantage; allowing accumulation to a point that sheer quantity provides opportunity and temptation, or conceals loss

5   Adhering to a belief that managerial status in itself is an endorsement of integrity in the holder – failure to accept that problems may derive from a manager rather than from other possible alternatives

6   Allocating localized security responsibility to a disinterested manager; recruiting manpower for security purposes and failing to train, instruct and utilize adequately

7   Inadequate care in driver recruitment and other posts where integrity is of importance; not taking up references when recruitment is that of supervisory staff status and above

8   Accepting transit losses as primarily insurance matters and indulging in prolonged correspondence before making positive enquiries. Failure to check that contract carriers have adequate insurance cover

9   Absence of adequate inclusion of security-based requirements in conditions of contract applied to contractors working on sites to ensure adequate supervision of their employees and transport.

DOCUMENTARY LOSS

The modern company, be it large or small, has to maintain a huge and ever increasing number of books, documents, records, and other sundry items, either because of statutory requirements, or in the interests of efficient administration. Some of these have to be retained permanently, for example minute books, registers of members, directors, certificates of incorporation and of business-name registrations, and the common seal; many will have to be kept for the full term of their viability – such as title deeds and leases, or for their term plus 12 years as in the case of correspondence and papers relating to property transactions, particular types of contract, and so on. In certain other matters, 6 years' cover has to be maintained, and into this category would fall sales and purchase ledgers with their associated records, wages and salaries registers etc.

Although the foregoing have little intrinsic value to make them attractive to a common thief, loss or damage could have serious consequences and absorb much time, money and effort in their replacement – assuming replacement was actually possible.

There is distinct virtue in having a periodic survey made or commissioned to ensure the right items are being retained for the right periods of time under the right conditions of security. Attitudes vary from having a total lack of security classification, to endorsing everything as 'secret', and of building up files of dust-covered documents which will never be consulted and never need to be. A survey list could readily be made summarizing, say:

1　The individual document, book or other item
2　Its proper retention period
3　Its security classification ('secret', 'confidential', 'unclassified' – or 'high', 'medium', or 'low') – this will largely determine the necessary degree of fire or other protection that should be given
4　Its custodian
5　Its present housing, for example safe (fireproof, fire-resistant, or thief-resistant), steel filing cabinet, steel or wooden cupboard, drawer, or open shelf etc
6　Feasibility of reducing and storing on micro film or microfiche (this would be of use in evaluating space-saving or increased security proposals)

A list of this nature would enable any necessary or desirable changes in practice or housing to be highlighted and also pinpoint where a change of custodian should be implemented.

Books, records and documents may be vandalized by thieves but are rarely their actual targets, other than during acrimonious industrial dispute, or when their contents are of industrial espionage interest. Fire is a greater threat and this is a factor which has to be borne in mind, coupled with the possibility of water damage in consequence of extinguishing an outbreak. This may also apply in older premises with a risk of storm damage or other causes of flooding – winter breakage of water pipes – so there could be merit in siting repositories in some cases above basement or ground floor level.

Specially constructed safes and fireproof cabinets are very expensive items and specialist advice should be taken when making purchases. The company's insurers will have such information readily to hand and should be consulted. In the areas of low fire risk, obsolete or obsolescent safes primarily designed to be burglar proof may be suitable for the purpose since they carry ballast linings of a fire-resistant nature, but this should always be checked with a safe specialist, since some cash safes are not proof against a serious fire, and older safes that were designed to be fire-resistant can deteriorate.

Duplication is a reasonable precaution for essential matter so that the originals can be lodged elsewhere, perhaps in a safe deposit, and copies retained for daily use. There is an unexpected source of risk associated with housing papers inside small old safes, especially if these are sited on the ground floor. Many thieves prefer to take safes from premises prior to what might be a noisy operation in opening them and experience has shown that anything up to a ton dead weight is liable to be removed. This can be cir-cumvented by sinking rag bolts into a concrete base to match corresponding holes in the base of the safe which is then bolted down onto them. This is a subject where the advice of a police crime prevention officer, or an insurance assessor, would provide guidance.

Nevertheless, the most likely source of interference with the documents lies in the threat of theft of information from them.

THEFT OF INFORMATION AND INDUSTRIAL ESPIONAGE

Provided a document is actually stolen the law of theft can be applied; if, however, information is simply copied, photographed or memorized and then used to the detriment of the owner, the law is vague in the extreme. Where an employee is obtaining the material for a competitor on repayment, if may be possible to prove corruption, which is criminally actionable, but the very few prosecutions under the Prevention of Corruption Act 1906 have been virtually restricted to public bodies and for purposes other than business espionage. Civil actions for redress are even less promising and more likely to benefit the lawyers involved than any other participants. It should be noted that cases have failed on grounds that a firm took no steps to ensure privacy of what it subsequently claimed to be important, nor did it emphasize to employees that the operations were regarded as being in any way secret.

The Data Protection Act 1984 has changed the situation, however, and has brought the term 'reasonable security' into law. (See Chapter 48 for a summary of the main provisions of this Act.)

A company may not regard itself as a worthwhile target for any form of information theft and in many cases this may be almost true. Regrettably and increasingly the threat is becoming less fanciful, at least 50 companies manufacture electronic 'bugging' equipment and a similar number produce devices for detecting their use – including one leading UK manufacturer. In addition, 'Marketing Information Research' appears among the services offered by some organizations whose previous claimed capabilities have lain mainly in the private detective sphere. It is said that at least twenty such firms have been identified as having an active interest internationally in trade spying. A US survey showed that nearly 50 per cent of the private investigation agencies contacted admitted that they would do electronic eavesdropping themselves or would recommend others that did to clients. Finally, both the French government and the Institute of Directors in the UK have produced documents dealing with counter-espionage.

A simple test for any firm in doubt about its vulnerability is to ask itself two simple questions:

1 What, if anything, do we not want our competitors or others to know about our business?
2 What information would harm our industrial relations if it became generally known?

The initial answers might indicate sufficient risk to justify a board level decision to ask more searching questions, and to conduct a complete survey to pinpoint areas where precautions are necessary. The board would also establish the amount of effort and expense that is justified.

Potential target areas

These could include departments working on:

1. Plans for production and sale of new products
2. Plans for new advertising campaigns
3. Customer lists coupled with rebate and discount particulars
4. Marketing projections
5. Evaluations of possible acquisitions or mergers
6. Sources and costings of raw materials and components
7. Policy decisions on future activities, redeployments, closures, etc.
8. Contractual or trading agreements, and customer contacts
9. Specifications and tenders
10. Research and development projects.

Of less interest to competitors but more immediately embarrassing are those matters which can cause industrial unrest. Obtaining information about these may be more a case of human curiosity than anything savouring of industrial espionage – but nevertheless can be crucially embarrassing if made general knowledge. They would include:

1. Rationalization and redundancy plans
2. Personal files and confidential reports
3. Wage-negotiation preparatory material
4. Confidential instructions on industrial relations negotiations
5. Salary structures and job-weighting factors.

Document classification

This is a basic requirement, and a simple system, used and understood by everyone, is required; if left to individuals, all sorts of terminology will be used, and the tendency will be to classify everything, no matter how innocuous. Fixing the degree of restriction is the responsibility of the originator, and the recipients should conform to his wishes, unless they have permission to treat the material otherwise.

'Confidential' implies the sender's wish that the contents should not be general knowledge, but allows a discretion to divulge the information to those who need to act upon it or must know of it for their work. 'Secret' is much more emphatic and means not be divulged (without the express permission of the sender) to anyone other than those upon the circulation list, which should be attached or marked upon the document.

Naturally an outer envelope which is marked 'secret' will attract attention and it is suggested that it should simply be marked 'personal' – which would convey nothing to a handler. Personal secretaries will open all mail, unless their masters decree otherwise, so that if an originator feels that the contents are such that they should be restricted purely to the named person, a second envelope may be put inside the external one and endorsed 'secret – to be opened only by. . .'

For projects vital to the profitability of the firm, an authorized circulation list should be agreed, which can be expanded as the project develops. If necessary a code word can be given to a project and it should then always be referred to in this way, either in correspondence, or in telephone conversation. The specific number of document copies needed should be printed and marked sequentially with each person on the authorized circulation list allocated an identification number. Highest priority matter is best transmitted by hand and against signature by the recipient.

Production of documents and minutes

Highly sensitive papers should be typed only by trusted personnel who are informed of the importance of secrecy and, ideally, all copying should be done by the same people. This is not a job for temporary employees from an agency who conceivably might work for a competitor, or may realize the value of what is being handled and try to capitalize accordingly. A danger lies in recipients wanting further copies for their own use for unauthorized dissemination to their subordinates or others; 'not to be copied', or some other endorsement should be overstamped on the originals and retribution follow any reproduction carried out without permission.

Many firms are working on the development of paper that will be impossible to photocopy. At the time of writing, only Rank Xerox have a system (which relies on the use of special paper and a security device fitted to the photocopier) which will actually prevent a photocopy being made.

Plastic typewriter ribbons of 'once only' use should be burnt and spare copies, carbons, shorthand notes, or other sources of information should be put into a shredder. Fortunately, most firms use only longstanding and trusted employees for the sorting and movement of mail internally, but documents of prime importance should be passed to the office of the recipient so far as possible by hand. A risk that does arise lies in the fact that mail delivered to a department is likely to be dropped in an office tray at a designated reception point where a variety of people will have access to it: if they can recognize the importance of the particular envelope, it is then at their disposal.

Safekeeping of documents

All precautions can be invalidated by a careless executive who leaves his desk littered at night with confidential papers; or the secretary who is given them to file, then leaves them in an office tray until it is convenient to do so; or locks them away, then leaves the key to the cabinet in an unlocked drawer, the top of a typewriter, or the pull-out accessory tray in her desk.

Standard locks on the doors of offices likely to hold restricted information can be replaced by a master-keyed suite of locks of high security rating with restricted key-holding. Human nature being what it is, where such a system is instigated, inevitably it will be found the special lock becomes something of a status symbol which practically every manager or executive will find substantial reasons for having on the grounds of the importance of the material he handles.

Filing cabinets are rarely resistant to any forcible attack and have a major disadvantage in that the keys are usually fairly available for purchase from the number which is printed on the face of the lock. Despite the somewhat disfiguring effort, it is suggested these numbers be obliterated by drilling. An alternative is to fit a pair of brackets and a removable steel bar which can be padlocked across all drawer fronts.

Any discussions affecting documentary secrecy should include checks to ensure that important papers are not persistently left out on desks; a 'clean desk' end-of-work policy should be advocated, and practised, by all staff.

Destruction of papers

The importance of a document does not of necessity lapse when the project to which it refers is terminated. This is particularly true of industrial relations-linked matters. After being handled with every care and precaution during their lives they are then handed over for destruction to what may be the lowest paid and least skilled class of worker who is employed. It is asking too much to expect that such an individual will not be interested in any document which is stamped with 'secret', or some similar intriguing title. For immediate destruction small cheap shredders are available for departments or larger ones can be centrally sited; and in some industries the cost may be offset by the use of the shredded paper produced for packing purposes. The computer department is of special importance, although the printout material may be meaningless to most people. Disintegrators are available to destroy printouts and tapes; these should be installed, either in the department, or in a suitable room closely adjacent.

Failing destruction on the premises, there are specialist firms who will, for a fee, collect and destroy confidential material. When choosing such a firm, it is best to select one which allows the entire procedure to be witnessed, from collection to destruction.

Potential forms of attack

Typical means of unethically obtaining information are:

1   Exploiting the carelessness, boastfulness, or negligence of employees

2　Corrupting employees, or forming an emotional attachment and inducing confidences

3　Inserting an agent into the workforce

4　Deliberately recruiting an employee from a position where he holds the requisite information

5　Holding a detailed interview of a knowledgeable employee for an advertised, financially wonderful, but non-existent job

6　Electronically 'bugging' telephones and offices, or using other specialized forms of surveillance

7　Entering premises to locate information either:

(*a*) as a visitor or

(*b*) as an intruder by force.

Far and away the simplest method of operating is to walk in and see, if the target firm's procedures are so lax as to make this possible. A skilled observer, apart from possibly acquiring or having sight of the paperwork, might recognize the processes and materials in use, the general level of activity, and innumerable other factors which will supply the information wanted.

If there are areas where there must be the strictest control on personnel entering, a constantly manned reception desk could be installed, or electronic control of access may be more economic. This could be a coded lock, magnetic card-operated lock, or combination of card and code, or even a card and code linked to a minicomputer which monitors and provides a permanent record of who goes there. A further variation has a pocket transmitter which causes an electronically controlled bolt to be automatically withdrawn when the carrier approaches. Photo-identity cards can be affixed to lapels for easy recognition, and colour variations in these can clearly indicate areas to which the wearer is entitled to have access. Control of entry to a computer room has a non-security merit – it prevents distraction and interference with the work of highly paid operators.

A word of caution is necessary in connexion with systems which, even with busy, constantly used doors, require a card and/or a code to open them. They will always, sooner or later, be abused: usually the door will simply be jammed open. Another risk is that properly authorized staff will exercise their good manners by holding the doors open for others, without however first checking their identity. To remove the temptation for jamming open constantly used doors, a 'hands free' (for example, radio activated) system is required.

The subject of access control is very much a specialized one, given the power and scope of centralized control systems. Access control can now use signature verification, fingerprint or even retinal scanning. Systems can, for example:

1　Be linked with closed circuit television (CCTV) and/or with an intruder alarm

2　Control various environmental factors, such as lighting or heating

3   Provide a bewildering array of computerized options, from flexi-time working through to time zoning (for example, allowing access to cleaners only between set times such as 6p.m. to 8p.m.).

The best advice is to consult a specialist!

Entry by subterfuge

This is one of the ploys of professional investigators engaged to obtain information. Latitude in asking questions and moving about premises is often given to persons carrying out safety surveys or appreciation of equipment, or posing as prospective customers etc. Impersonation of telephone engineers, gas and electricity supply employees, laundrymen, window cleaners, etc., have all been used. Preventive action is largely a matter of common sense and developing a suspicious mind. Most public utility employees will have identification cards to produce if challenged. A system of handling visitors efficiently should be devised and they should not be allowed to roam the premises unattended. Others worth bearing in mind are cleaners and temporary staff – the wastepaper basket remains one of the most prolific sources from which information can be gleaned. It may be possible to make special arrangements for the cleaning work in sensitive areas to be carried out during working hours when there is supervision on the premises. Every care should be taken to avoid the use of temporary staff on projects of importance; if this cannot reasonably be done, the supplying agency could be asked of details of the person's service with them and the firms to which he/she has previously been allocated, so that there is at least an informed option to accept or refuse. If used, there is no objection to impressing on the incumbent the confidentiality of the position.

Electronic surveillance devices

The use of 'bugs' is not widespread in the UK; the extent to which they have been used is a matter for some speculation, but the publicity which has been given to them may lead to temptation to try them. They are easily concealed and can be fitted into table-lighters, wall decorations, stuck under tables etc. A standard telephone bug is a transistorized oscillator which is powered by the telephone line current, using the line itself as an aerial. Variations can allow the microphone to be active even when the hand set is not in use. Offices can be checked visually, but this must be done thoroughly and patiently with a knowledge of what to look for, and where. Electronic detection equipment can be bought, but the best varieties are very expensive, and the limited number of larger private detective agencies who provide a checking service have charges which are very substantial. Where leaks are suspected there is merit in holding vital meetings at off-site venues arranged at short notice.

Precautions – checklist

1 Define key posts and areas, applying stringent selection and vetting to applicants for the former, and restricting entry to the latter
2 Establish classification, handling, copying and safe-keeping instruction procedure for documents, etc.
3 Provide means of destroying the secret material and anything connected with its production, (shredders for example)
4 Restrict copying
5 Ensure wall charts, graphs, or other visual aids are not left where they can be freely seen
6 Instigate occasional out-of-hours checks upon offices for important papers carelessly left out
7 Indoctrinate staff
8 Instigate a policy for treatment of any person with access to secret information, who is to leave the company employment for any reason.

Inadvertent disclosure

The unworldly scientist, who 'discloses all' in a learned paper for some technical journal or at some sophisticated symposium, is difficult to cater for; the best that can be hoped is that he will conform to the restrictions that may and should be contained in his contract of employment. However, ideas, inventions, and information in general may be released without thinking in the normal course of business.

It is possible to protect ideas and inventions by means of one or more patents, design registrations, registered trademarks and copyright, but it is also often the case that such protection is unobtainable or impracticable on the grounds of cost, or the idea lacking the right degree of novelty or inventiveness. At times it may be best to keep a good idea firmly under one's hat and in such instances the advice of a good patent agent is desirable and may prove invaluable.

Customers, students, prospective buyers and others may by tradition be shown around the factories and workshops with frank answers being given to their questions. Care must be taken, at the risk on occasions of causing genuine or simulated offence, to be judicious in what is shown and to decline to answer queries which would reveal too much of the firm's business. In one instance, a private detective posing as a potential (and bogus) customer's 'quality assurance expert' acquired secret process detail in all good faith. The same care may be needed in dealing with market research questionnaires, intended student thesis projects and enquiries from the media. The basic question in such circumstances is 'Will my disclosure in any way be detrimental to my company?' Sadly, the answer may well follow the US pattern, where large firms (including many with household names, once famous for providing conducted tours of their plants) are now halting the practice of allowing touring parties access, and are referring all enquiries for information to a press department which is briefed to protect vital secrets.

SECURITY POLICIES AND DISCIPLINE

A high proportion of disciplinary matters arise from incidents with security connotations and the process of enforcing security is as productive as any for industrial discord. It is therefore advisable to have clearly defined policies and procedures in those areas where ambiguity or opportunity could create controversy or a temptation to dishonesty. Such policies and procedures could include:

1   Action to be taken in respect of a criminal offence, where the firm is the complainant, committed:
    (a) By employees – suspension, dismissal, prosecution
    (b) By contractors – prosecution, expulsion from site, other alternatives etc.
    (c) By outsiders – prosecution, or other alternatives
2   The matters to be referred to the police and at whose discretion
3   Dealing with lost and found property
4   Working of notice by person who has been dismissed, or has resigned from a position of special risk
5   Permission of sales of products to employees and the procedures to be used
6   Work permitted for company staff utilizing company's labour on repayment
7   Use of firm's facilities for private purchase, i.e., discounts
8   Policies in respect of giving references
9   Communication sources for media in the event of newsworthy items, i.e., accidents, industrial action and losses, etc.
10 Policy towards losses by employees on premises – disclaimers, and permission for facilities for cash holding, i.e., collections in company safes
11 A policy to cope with drug abusers.

These are really only sample matters and policy statements could include the use of insurance to offset risks (including the fidelity bonding of employees), bomb threats, major incidents and cash handling procedures, in addition to those already mentioned in connexion with the security of documents.

THEFT

It is important to establish a firm policy line on the treatment of employee theft. Since this is likely to be associated with dismissal, no grounds should be allowed whereby an appeal could arise from a legal nicety. The types of serious misconduct which would merit dismissal should, of course, be listed by a firm amongst its rules. That of theft is generally accepted by industrial tribunals as a perfectly valid reason (*Trust House Forte* v. *Murphy, 1977*).

The following ruling is recommended in the light of changes in legislation and from case decisions:

'If any act of theft, or attempted theft, or other form of dishonesty, or criminal damage, is admitted, or on reasonable grounds found to have been committed by an employee in connexion with company property, or the property of another employee, then the employee responsible will be dismissed and, where company property is involved, the company will exercise its discretion in whether the matter is to be reported to the police'.

Discretion

A ruling of this nature does not cover all criminally actionable offences that may be committed, either on the firm's premises, or elsewhere and contrary to its interests. The inflicting of injuries, and sexual offences, are of rare occurrence, as are those involving customers, the consequences of which would be prejudicial to the company interests. Too wide definition would prove unwieldly and the nature of the other criminal actions which can be envisaged is sufficiently serious that dismissal for their commission would be an acceptable reason to a tribunal.

The definition as it stands leaves an ultimate discretion whether or not to prosecute and allows the taking into account of mitigating circumstances which could have bearing on the decision. The prime objective is to achieve consistency on the aspect of dismissal, rather than on that of prosecution.

Right of search

Even where a company includes a 'search clause' in its conditions of employment, there is no legal right of personal search without the consent of the individual being searched. Nevertheless, Employment Appeal Tribunal decisions have indicated that where such a condition is included, refusal can constitute reasonable grounds for dismissal; conversely, where it is not included, dismissal for refusal was found unfair, despite the fact that there were grounds for suspicion of theft. Whilst there are no publicized decisions to the effect, it would seem probable that any search productive of stolen property would be considered justified – dismissal of course being for the theft, not the refusal.

Dismissal without prosecution

This is an expedient to be applied with care in the current industrial climate. No avenue should be provided for a claim of unfair dismissal, but a successful prosecution is not a prerequisite for action by the employer. This has been made clear by several judgments, one of which – *British Home Stores Limited* v. *Burchell* (20 July 1978), an Employment Appeal Tribunal decision on dismissal for suspected involvement of theft where there was no prosecution – is worth quoting in full.

> 'In a case where an employee is dismissed because the employer suspects or believes that he or she has committed an act of misconduct, in determining whether that dismissal is unfair an Industrial Tribunal has to decide whether the employer who discharged the employee on the ground of the misconduct in question entertained a reasonable suspicion amounting to a belief in the guilt of the employee of that misconduct at that time. This involves three elements. First, there must be established by the employer the fact of that belief; that the employer did believe it. Second, it must be shown that the employer had in his mind reasonable grounds upon which to sustain that belief. And, third, the employer at the stage at which he formed that belief on those grounds must have carried out as much investigation into the matter as was reasonable in all the circumstances of the case. An employer who discharges the onus of demonstrating these three matters must not be examined further. It is not necessary that the Industrial Tribunal itself would have shared the same view in those circumstances.'

Burchell has become a definitive industrial appeal case in that *W. Weddel Ltd.* v. *Tepper*, Court of Appeal, 1980 declared its three-stage test should be used to determine whether an employee dismissed for *any* alleged misconduct had been fairly dismissed – not simply in cases of dishonesty.

Where there is an admission of theft, and the employer does not wish court proceedings, it is highly advisable that the admission is in a form that cannot be retracted for the purposes of an appeal against dismissal. It is suggested that a signed admission be obtained or one made under circumstances which would preclude any such retraction. This could be in the presence of witnesses or of the offender's own representative.

Dismissal in the face of a denial of guilt could lead to appeals causing cost and inconvenience beyond any normal police court proceedings and a tribunal is less restricted in the evidence that it will accept than criminal courts (*Dockerty* v. *Reddy* 28 September 1976); it is therefore recommended that instances where guilt is firmly denied should be referred to the police.

There are a number of points arising from other tribunal decisions which are worthy of note in this connexion:

1　An opportunity must be given for an explanation of facts by the suspect before the dismissal decision is made
2　There is no necessity of a successful prosecution to justify dismissal
3　As shown above, it is adequate that those formulating the decision to dismiss have reasonable grounds for their belief in the facts before them when making their decision

4 The decision must be based on the facts that are known at the time of the decision, not those that may arise subsequently
5 There must be as much investigation as is reasonable before the dismissal is made.

Suspension with or without pay

Suspension without pay, where such a power is not included in the contract of employment, is held to be tantamount to dismissal and therefore is subject to the normal appeal procedure.

Suspension with pay is reasonable in cases of strong suspicion pending the accumulation of all the available evidence bearing on a decision. However, if this suspension is extended to the termination of court proceedings it can be extremely expensive since the accused, by various ploys, can defer the hearing of his case interminably. In one instance five employees were suspended on average earnings for two years and six months. The evidence was such that they had to plead guilty, but the cost of their wages far exceeded the value of the theft.

No dismissal

There are cogent reasons why every instance of proven or admitted dishonesty by an employee against his firm should result in immediate dismissal. A company ruling of the type previously mentioned is invalidated if any exceptions at all to it are allowed – precedents are highly important to industrial courts and management could find great difficulty in explaining a variation in policy which it had naively hoped would escape notice.

Other reasons of importance exist:

1 Leniency could cause others to copy in the belief no retribution would follow
2 A repetition of the offence by the same person would invoke caustic comment from board level on the individual who has taken the lenient view (some would say the easy way out!)
3 Retention is unfair to the offender's colleagues and the atmosphere in a department would be impossible if a fellow worker's property had been involved
4 The offender will inevitably be the focus of attention should any further offences occur, even if he is not responsible, and his continued presence be an embarrassment not least to himself.

Police notification

The reporting of a theft is not mandatory nor is, as the Criminal Law Act 1967 clearly defines, the prosecution of an individual known to have stolen from a complainant, who is also legally allowed in making a decision to press charges or not, to take into account whether the loss or injury caused by the offence is to be made good or reasonable compensation paid – a matter which could of course be made quite clear to an offender. If the police are called in, they are unlikely to be familiar with procedures, persons and places all of which might have to be explained. Their presence automatically attracts attention and workers may have to be taken from their jobs to be spoken to. The consequential loss may be out of all proportion to the effect of the offence which is being investigated. However, once they have been notified, it is highly advisable that the question of prosecuting should be left entirely in their hands – even if this causes embarrassment or inconvenience. Otherwise future cooperation might be jeopardized – and they have the power to disregard representations for the withdrawal of charges.

No prosecution

There are circumstances which can militate against a prosecution which at first sight might be justified by the nature of the offence. Amongst the considerations are:

1 Will the firm receive adverse publicity by:
   (a) A lax system putting temptation in the way of the employee?
   (b) Having put a lowly paid man in a position where he is handling property of a value out of all proportion to his salary?
   (c) Permitting the ventilation of a grievance in open court which would reflect adversely on the firm?
   (d) Compulsorily disclosing matters in court which the firm would desire should not be known?
2 Will the prosecution spotlight a weakness in the security system which could be exploited by others and which may be difficult or impractical to remove?
3 Is the end product of prosecution worth the effort and inconvenience; or considering the age, length of service, and good repute of an employee, would dismissal be a greater penalty than any the court might impose?

It must be remembered that malpractices, actual or alleged, by an employer have greater news value than routine theft by an employee.

The Police and Criminal Evidence Act (1984)

The Police and Criminal Evidence Act (1984) is now with us, and security people throughout the country have been thrown into confusion by it. Letters in magazines such as *Police Review, Security Times* and others have all asked to what extent the new law will affect the position of security personnel and store detectives.

The main area of contention arises from the sections 66 (Codes of Practice which replace the former Judges' Rules) and 67 (parts 9, 10 and 11). Section 67(9) of the Act states:

> Persons other than police officers who are charged with the duty of investigating offences or charging offenders shall in the discharge of that duty have regard to any relevant provision of such a code.

The code mentioned (in Section 66) covers stop and search, premises search, seizure of property, detention and treatment of persons and the identification of offenders.

The arguments revolve around whether a security officer can be said to be a person 'charged with the duty. . .' And if he is such a person, to what extent must he then abide by the Codes of Practice? For example, if a store detective detains a suspected thief, must he administer a caution? And how will that affect the suspect's rights if and when the police are called in? What about statements? Detention facilities? The list goes on and on. . .

The answer is for once fairly simple: *nowhere* in the Act is the security officer mentioned in any capacity. And the Act does not materially affect any security officer in as far as existing legislation is concerned; his/her powers remain the same. The Home Office, in a letter to the International Professional Security Association (IPSA), states:

> This Act does not alter in any way the position of security personnel and store detectives under law. They have no special power of arrest, search, entry or seizure. If they make an arrest, it is a citizen's arrest which involves no power of detention for questioning, and they must bring the person arrested before a Justice of the Peace or a police officer as soon as reasonably possible. Security personnel are not charged with a duty of investigating offences within the meaning of Section 67 (9) of the Act. However, the Codes of Practice represent good practice in the investigation of offences, and it is clearly advisable that people who may take it upon themselves, whether by virtue of a contract of employment or otherwise, to investigate a crime or a category of crime, should have regard to the standards set in the codes so far as in common sense they are applicable to the work they do and the limited powers they have.

The Act does, however, give both security personnel (and, of course, all of us as members of the general public) slightly wider powers. Section 24(4) and (5) outline the circumstances where any person may effect a citizen's arrest, and sub-sections (1) to (3) define arrestable offences.

Basic advice to all security officers working in a firm is to use common sense when interpreting the Act and its Codes of Practice; involve police at a fairly early stage when such a course of action is necessary; be fair-minded, and act fairly, and remember to keep your temper regardless of provocation. And make a note of everything said as soon as is possible.

Intruders

The considerations which apply to employees do not, however, apply to offences by non-employees. If these are involved in any offence of any consequence the police should be informed – particularly where identifiable property has been stolen and police assistance is the only means of recovery. Outsiders should be given no indication that they can steal from a firm with impunity: a consistent policy of prosecuting all should be followed as a deterrent to others.

Thefts from employees

Despite the fact that an offence may take place upon company premises the right to decide whether it should be referred to the police is vested in the loser and he is entitled to object if the company tries to interfere with this right. It follows that he also has the right to prosecute or not to prosecute should an offender be detected. However, this in no way affects the rule of dismissal for theft from company or employee. The employee himself may have pressure put upon him by friends of the offender not to prosecute and he may so agree, but this does not invalidate the issue of dismissal.

Prosecution

The Law of England does not (at the time of writing) preclude any person or body from instituting or carrying out criminal proceedings in which the police will assist, but, unless there are very good reasons, there is little point in acting as a private prosecutor. Once notified, the police will ensure that all necessary statements are taken, the case is prepared and witnesses warned of the time, date and place of hearing; the police solicitor will present the evidence and there can be no suggestion of bias in the conduct of the whole affair. In other words a minimum of inconvenience and cost is incurred by the firm.

DRUG ABUSE

A policy for dealing with drug abusers is now vital in the UK, as it is almost certain that medium to large firms will harbour some drug abusers. In the USA firms require job applicants to undergo urine/blood sampling for drug testing as a routine – even the White House has a policy. In the UK, the government's hard line legislation can be summarized under the following four points:

1 Power for the courts to seize the assets of 'drug barons'
2 Reform of banking laws, allowing closer examination of drug traffickers' financial records
3 A new offence, similar to that of handling stolen goods, for the handling of assets acquired from trading in hard drugs

4   A reversal of the burden of proof, so that drug barons will lose homes, cash and luxury assets unless they can prove that these were not purchased out of drug income. This is, perhaps, the most important section of the law.

A written statement of the firm's policy on drugs (*all* drugs, including alcohol and drugs legally obtained) is the first step. The statement must set out graphically the firm's position on drugs, and the penalties awaiting staff found abusing drugs. It should, too, offer help to employees with problems – and contact with local social and advisory services should be established and maintained.

A typical statement should include:

1   Health considerations, pointing out not only the consequences of loss to the firm through absenteeism resulting from drug-induced illness, but also the potentially disastrous outcome of drug abuse to the abuser
2   Safety considerations, particularly where machinery is being operated, where vehicles need to be driven, or in any situation where one worker relies for his safety on the competence of another
3   Quality control, deterioration in the quality of production affecting not only the individual products being sold by the firm but also, eventually, the jobs of all concerned
4   Security, not only in the short term, but in the long term too. The US experience has already included horrific levels of so-called petty crime by opportunists with a heavy drug habit to fund
5   Morale of the entire staff (which of course can depend on many factors other than drug abuse, such as general attitudes to work, dress, time-keeping, etc.).

The statement should also set out what the firm expects of its staff, how they are expected to act while at work, and what specific actions cannot be tolerated. Factors in this statement should include:

1   The firm's reputation, how it is regarded by the public, and how this in turn affects the firm's expectations of its employees. The higher the profile in the marketplace, or the more trust placed by public and/or customers in the firm, the higher must the standards be set
2   The relationship between drug abuse and fitness for work: how the firm views acceptable and unacceptable standards
3   What help the firm is offering drug users. This could take the form of a confidential advisory service, operating through a suggestion box type of method, with the anonymous inquirers being advised by means of a statement on, say, a company notice board
4   Asking employees to help in the drug prevention programme, and to tell senior staff about abusers and, particularly, about pushers. Anonymity can be preserved, again, by a suggestion box type of technique, or a 24-hour telephone answering machine can be

employed (such as that which the Metropolitan Police have used with success).

A clear line must be taken to distinguish between 'legal' and 'illegal' drugs, so that there is no loophole in policy.

Legal drugs, such as alcohol or any drug prescribed by a doctor (and the latter can include heroin substitutes where the user is a registered addict), should be looked at in the light of whether or not they affect job performance. If they do, then the easiest way out is to treat abusers as being 'ill', which means sick leave. But this should only be temporary: continued abuse of any 'legal' drug should subject the abuser to normal sanctions and penalties. Where alcohol is abused actually on the firm's premises, a very stern line needs to be taken.

Illegal drugs will include all those whose sale is restricted or prohibited, or whose use or possession is restricted or prohibited. The firm's policy should take the form of outright bans, i.e.

1 Any employee arriving for work under the influence of any drug so that his/her work is adversely affected
2 Any employee found using a prohibited drug while at work
3 Any employee found buying, transferring or possessing illegal drugs
4 Any employee found selling, or offering to sell illegal drugs. In this case (and possibly others) the firm should reserve the right to bring in the police.

The most obvious penalty is immediate suspension pending an investigation. A team approach to the consideration of the individual problem is worth considering – security, personnel, safety, training and medical people should all be involved, as well as a representative(s) from the employee('s) trade union.

Enforcement of the penalties, however, is absolutely essential. Once set in motion, an anti-drug policy has to be maintained, and all drug users should be treated equally. This means careful attention to such definitions as 'adverse job performance.' For instance, such a definition might include improper use of company equipment, incompetence, physical or mental incapacity, plain carelessness, negligence, lateness on the job, unauthorized absences from both the firm and the designated place of work, unwarranted abuse (verbal or physical) of other staff, especially senior staff, and so on.

Problems will include the possible abuse of cocaine by executives and especially by high-powered sales people, who feel that this drug can enhance their performance. The problem is particularly acute where such senior staff spend most of their time away from the office. The approach here probably comes best from an executive of the same, or higher, rank and it should be made clear to the abuser that the company policy applies to *all* employees.

Finally the questions of employees' rights and legal liability should be thoroughly researched by the company lawyer before the statement is formulated. Make sure, too, it reaches *all* employees, possibly through the company letter/newsletter if you have one. Despite the government's proposed new laws, the profits from drug peddling remain so vast – and Britain remains such a soft target, along with most of Europe – that the plague will continue. Recommended reading is *Drug Abuse in the Workplace* by Henry J. Balevic, which gives an excellent outline of what currently faces American employers and how they are dealing with it.

RESPONSIBILITY FOR SECURITY

Every commercial and industrial concern should have a member of senior management who has designated responsibility for the security of its property and the safety of its employees and their belongings while they are engaged at work. The status of that person will depend on the size and importance of the concern and can range from a member of the board of directors downwards in the operating structure. For instance, at a factory engaged on government classified contracts it is likely a director will be responsible. In other circumstances, the senior man on the site, though he must have ultimate responsibility to the board or shareholders, is likely to delegate routine supervision to a subordinate manager.

The amount of attention a person given the responsibility for security should devote to that job will depend on a number of factors which will also determine the degree of expertise in security practices and techniques which he should acquire. These factors will include, apart from the size of the organization, the known losses and unexplained deficiencies, the value of materials at risk, insurance requirements, the location and type of premises, and the calibre of employees. It could well be that security is included among other responsibilities. If so, and the incumbent has neither training nor aptitude for it, the attention he will give may be far less than he gives to his other duties.

Security is not the most popular job if incorrectly handled. If the factors creating the need for a security function are cogent, the time has then arrived to consider the appointment of a qualified individual whose overriding responsibility will be that of security, bearing in mind there are other administrative spheres in which his presence can be utilized.

Such an individual can be titled security manager, security officer, or chief security officer if he is responsible for personnel engaged on security duties. The status to be given must reflect the importance the management attaches to his position, his responsibilities and the staff he controls. He normally would be a member of the management structure which would assist him in dealing with all levels of employees. He would wear civilian clothes or protective clothing in the same manner as other managers.

COMPANY SECURITY STAFF

Where circumstances justify the employment of security officers it is essential that they should be of good calibre, and properly trained and utilized. It is a total waste of money to follow the outdated practice of internal recruitment from redundant or ageing employees – worse, this gives an impression that security surveillance exists whereas the resultant inefficiency causes the reverse to be true.

Authority

An effective security force must be capable of earning the respect and cooperation of the whole workforce. To do this the policies adopted in security matters must be fair, clearly spelt out and applicable to all. Impartiality, good humour and a friendly attitude are all essential attributes. Smartness in dress and deportment are consistent with an image of efficiency and authority.

Duties

The duties required must be committed to writing in the form of 'Standing Orders', which in effect may be a much expanded and detailed version of their job description. The two combined, amongst other things, must specify what they are expected to do, their line of reporting and the degree of discretion allowed.

Fire-fighting and first aid are customary inclusions among responsibilities, but every firm will have others where continual presence of responsible men on premises can be utilized. The contribution that security staff can make in accident prevention is very relevant but it would be unrealistic to give special training unless there were exceptional circumstances of recurrent risk. Nevertheless, there are a number of things which may be temporarily overlooked by personnel intent on production where common sense observation by a patrolling officer may be used to advantage.

Instructions should be given to deal with these matters tactfully to avoid apparent intrusion into the disciplinary authority of line management, bearing in mind also that a procedure that appears unsafe to the uninitiated may be one which has been considered and found acceptable.

If unsafe practices are seen, security staff should draw them to the notice of the supervisor and not approach the worker himself, unless the matter is one of immediate physical risk or serious contravention of works rules.

Staff selection

For the actual operational implementation of day-to-day security, and advising or recommending where needed, an 'in-company' appointed security manager has advantages of familiarity with persons, places, products etc., but he has to be trained to a knowledge of essential law and security expertise. Perhaps most important, he has to think in terms of security priorities as having an importance he did not perhaps previously accord them, and develop a suspicious and enquiring mind that he did not previously need for his job. This type of appointment is best for a small firm with limited problems, or for a unit within a large organization with centralized security control and expertise which can be called upon for assistance and advice; training is however essential.

If the risk dictates that professional experience is called for, the main sources of supply are ex HM Forces SIB (Special Investigation Branches), ex police, existing senior security personnel in industry or the commercial security service supplying firms. Alternatively, an outside consultant can be retained for services as required – which is unlikely to be financially advantageous – and care has to be taken in checking ability to carry out contractual obligations in the light of existing commitments.

At one time ex-senior police officers were appointed to in-house security positions in the belief that they would, by virtue of their old connexions, have access to criminal records files. Now computerized, these files are closely monitored, and serving officers who have obliged outsiders – including ex-colleagues – on being asked to 'check on so-and-so' have suffered suspension and dismissal as a result. It is not, therefore, possible to rely on 'inside knowledge' of former police officers employed on company security staff: clearly it is not viable that they should be asked to endanger the careers of serving officers.

Selection from 'second career incumbents' can produce know-how but a judgement must be made as to whether the job is being taken with real interest or as a means of supplementing a pension with minimum personal effort and inconvenience.

It must be expected that someone being inducted from a disciplined service into commerce and industry will have problems of adjustment and it is advisable that colleagues, with whom the prospective incumbent will have closest contact, should have an opportunity to meet and assess short-listed candidates for compatibility before the appointment is made.

It must be remembered that candidates for security posts are not exempt from the Rehabilitation of Offenders Act, which means that potential security officers may have criminal records which they need not (by law) disclose.

Training

Security heads are apt to be drawn from the older age bracket, especially when they are 'second career' selections. One possible danger is that they become agoraphobic in attitude with their interest limited to the physical perimeter of their responsibility. If this happens, their knowledge of law and practice becomes outdated, they do not learn from the misfortunes of others, and they miss the advantages of discussion with contemporaries. Arrangements should be made for at least 'brush-up' attendance at security courses and seminars, and they should be encouraged to develop liaisons within their own industry and locally for mutual advantage.

At security guard level it is frequently forgotten that these employees need training as much as, if not more than others – their potential to hurt the firm by unwise action through ignorance is greater than that of others of considerably higher status. Apart from instruction that is available on site, it is advisable that they should have basic instruction amongst others similarly employed – if a suitable course is available. Commercially organized one- or two-day seminars are occasionally held for senior security officers and management but few, if any, at the lower level. However, the International Professional Security Association holds basic, intermediate and advanced courses throughout the country; these are essentially practical in nature, the lecturers are primarily drawn from members with specialized expertise who hold senior positions with industrial firms. Details of what is available at any given time can be obtained from the Secretary of the Association.

HIRING THE SERVICES OF A SECURITY COMPANY

Commercial firms provide a variety of services:

1 The transporting of cash to and from banks and if so required, at most branches, the making up and paying out of wage packets
2 Transporting computer tapes, data, etc.
3 Security attention to premises, with or without guard dogs
   (a) Continuously over twenty-four hours, seven days a week
   (b) For specified shorter periods
   (c) For visits at regular intervals
4 To act as key-holders of premises to reduce the inconvenience of having to attend them at all hours in consequence of some incident which requires attention
5 To protect especially valuable property on display at, for example, exhibitions and provide guards at sporting functions etc
6 To survey premises and to recommend security measures
7 To provide a store detective service in retail premises and make check purchases
8 In some instances a facility to carry out internal investigations; in others to give a debt collection service.

In addition to these, there are of course the alarm, lock, safe, television, etc. specialist firms.

Transporting cash

When a contract is arranged for this service, it must specify the place at which the delivery is to be made. It is not sufficient to give just the address:

the precise location of the transfer must be given, for example, the cashier's office on the second floor. Regrettably attacks during cash deliveries occur frequently, so the precise liability on the carriers at the time of the theft is important. The nationally known cash-in-transit companies have adequate cover spread over several insurers, but positive written confirmation of that cover should be available and the wording of contracts carefully studied. Those with current national coverage are Securicor, Group 4 and Security Express, but other internationally known – and equally reputable ones – also operate in the larger cities.

A wage packeting service is available in many areas, for which the charges made vary little from one company to another. However, the level of these charges has risen to the point where internal make-up could be more cost effective.

Very firm arrangements must be made with the carriers, and with the bank authorities, to agree procedures for cheque submission, cash collection and delivery, with adequate means of identification of both signatures and persons, to preclude any possibility of fraudulent attack.

If an unknown person purporting to be from the security company attends premises to collect cash or anything valuable, his identity documents must be inspected and his employers telephoned to confirm his instructions – his documents might have been stolen or forged.

Cash-in-transit – own personnel

If it is intended that wages or, for that matter, any large sums of money, should be carried in circumstances where they are exposed to attack, the insurers *must* be consulted. They are not enthusiastic about sums in excess of £2000 being carried without extra precautions by way of guards and vehicles which probably will outcost the expense of a professional carrier. This of course is a reasonable ploy by the insurer since it transfers the period of greatest risk to someone else's insurance.

If, however, the amounts are relatively small, or a decision is taken to accept the risk, the advice of the police crime prevention department should be sought, and their recommendations strictly followed as to how the job should best be done having regard to the special risks of the area. Special waistcoats, alarmed bags and others that deface the contents, or throw out clouds of smoke, are commercially available.

Cash-in-transit: security advice and checklist

This is too detailed to be dealt with here and reference should be made to Wilson and Oliver (1983).

SECURITY OF CASH IN OFFICES

Money in any form is just about the most attractive target for theft; it is normally non-identifiable, does not need the intervention of a receiver, and there is no delay in benefiting. Insurance against loss can be obtained either in transit or on premises; the cost is progressively rising, and premiums will be heavily loaded if claims are made – the first £100 or more will probably be excluded in any case.

The weight of claims has caused insurance companies to insist on rigorous security measures, including installation of burglar alarms, without which they will not offer cover. Even so, failure to observe elementary precautions may cause the refusal of a claim, such as has happened with an unguarded till in retail premises and failures to set alarms or to lock doors on delivery vehicles.

Cash on premises should be the minimum for needs; if it accrues to a greater than desirable amount, transfer arrangements to the bank should be made. Key holding for cash boxes and safes must be kept to an absolute minimum and locks must be changed immediately in the event of a key-loss. A spot check should be made on cashiers' petty cash holding – often amounts in excess of insurance cover are kept for purely personal convenience. Excess cash (which might include unpaid wages packets) is safer on deposit at the bank, where it can also accrue interest.

Companies are apt to regard safes as continuing to fulfil their purpose long after they have become antiquated. If an insurance company insists on an examination prior to renewal of policies, many will be condemned as unfit for the storage of cash, and cover will not be extended to them. The surveyors have a classification which includes all types of safes in manufacture and equates them with the maximum amount of money the insurers are prepared to accept that they should hold. Before buying new safes, it is therefore essential to obtain confirmation that they will meet the insurers' requirements.

Petty cash and floats must not be left in locked drawers overnight but should be returned to safes and withdrawn again the following morning. Special care should be taken of cheque books, and the absolute minimum of presigned cheques be retained at any time. If possible, these should be restricted to the control of a single person. The value of presigned Giro cheques for payments to pensioners may be overlooked and a close check should be kept on these. All spoilt presigned cheques must be retained for audit purposes; the signature block and cheque machine key should have separate holders and be kept in safe places.

Cash in private possession

Employees must be told clearly that the company will not accept responsibility for any personal money kept on the premises, unless it is handed over to the cashier or other nominated person for safe keeping. This should apply also to holiday club collections, sports and social clubs funds and the like. Any discovery that this rule is not being followed should result in a verbal reprimand and, if a theft does occur, the opportunity should be taken to stress the need for everyone to comply.

Paying-out stations

Increasingly, attacks are being made on offices where money is in the process of being paid out. Shotguns and pickaxe handles are frequently used – and there should be no heroics in the face of a gun. Consideration should be given to providing personal attack alarms (button or foot operated) in cashiers' offices and at pay points. Thieves are under strain and may be 'trigger-happy', so there should be no audible alarm at the scene but an indication at a safe point from which police assistance can be sought.

Where new positions are being constructed to act as pay points, thought must be given, and if necessary professional advice obtained, as to protection from violence, including the threat of firearms, for those paying out. The point must also be so devised as to prevent casual theft of wage packets through the pay window. Complete armoured glass window and shelf units are available from specialist suppliers. It is also good practice to exhibit at each paying out point a notice that clearly indicates that the recipient is responsible for his own wage packet after collection. Where control of the pay packets and pay points changes during a wage issue, proper checking and handing over should take place between the clerks concerned. The paying out system itself should be such that the possibility of an employee being able to draw another's pay packet fraudulently is minimized. This can be done by issuing payslips twenty-four hours before the pay-out. False allegations of an unauthorized packet collection are not infrequent – all such claims should be thoroughly investigated before a repayment is authorized. Where packets of a type that allow checking of contents are used, no claims of shortage should be entertained if the packet has been opened.

The Wages Act 1986 completely repealed the Truck Act, which gave manual workers the right to be paid in cash. However, where employees already have an existing *contractual* right to be paid in cash, the repeal of the 1831 Act does not affect that right. The NFU (National Farmworkers' Union) were known to be concerned that payment by cheque in small rural communities would lead to the size of the pay cheques becoming common knowledge throughout the village. One compromise to avoid the risks of cash payment could involve installation of automatic telling machines (ATMs) but these carry risks of their own, especially involving fraud. Any company considering the installation of ATMs should first seek specialist advice.

BUILDINGS

Old property, though satisfactory in every respect of location, floor space and amenities, may be totally unsuitable for high-risk commodities. If this is suddenly realized after acquisition, considerable unbudgeted expenditure may be needed to rectify the condition and this will reflect on the foresight of those who conducted the negotiations.

New construction does not offer the same difficulties, provided that – from the draft-plan stage – civil engineers, architects, planners and builders have in mind what is at risk and the steps that can be taken to minimize it, without jeopardizing the essential functions of the building. If no company specialist is employed, the police crime prevention officers will be delighted to give their views and advice – they regard this stage as the best time to utilize their services. Simple adjustments to plans can easily cut out avenues for walk-in theft, or such invitations to a thief as obscured windows or doors which may be forced at leisure. Indeed, some police forces are appointing 'architectural liaison officers', whose speciality is to advise on plans before building starts.

A few basic essentials: endeavour to keep all parking facilities outside the premises proper; provide maximum lighting on perimeters; restrict the number of entrances to the building or site to the absolute minimum (it is much harder to do so when employees have become accustomed to using them); ensure that persons using any entrance can be seen, either by a receptionist, or by occupants of adjoining offices; restrict keys to an absolute minimum and prohibit the making of duplicates. Leaving some interior lights on all night can deter prospective intruders, especially if they can be turned on and off at intervals by an automatic switch. Do not overlook the possibilities afforded by the use of closed circuit television (CCTV), which can be used (for example) to survey several entrances from one central point, and can be coupled with the electrical or electronic remote control of locks.

Alarm systems

The electronic alarm industry has grown to major proportions and many firms have nationwide coverage. Their equipment can be extremely sophisticated; its cost therefore should be in relation to the risk. Whole areas or selected danger points can be covered; warning can be by immediate bells, '999' connection to the police, or by direct line to the police (where this is still permitted) or to a central station operated by the alarm company. Delayed bells can be fitted so that the message can be transmitted to the police but loss restricted if for some reason their arrival is delayed. Reliance on bells alone is a dubious proposition – little attention is paid by the public. Facilities offered include ordinary door contacts, rays, pressure pads, tautened wiring, radar and sonic detectors; new conceptions are continually being developed. When costing such an installation, it is advisable to consult and seek estimates from at least three unconnected companies. Knowing that others are in competition, none will recommend an unnecessarily expensive system which might exclude their quotation. The police crime prevention officer may be willing to indicate those that have the local servicing facilities that are essential to eliminate waste of time. He cannot be expected to recommend any particular one.

A certain number of false alarms must be anticipated in the early teething stages of an installation but should clear within two or three weeks. The police will look with a jaundiced eye if false alarms continue thereafter since they implement a prearranged plan to cover the premises on each occasion as a priority to other duties; they also require key-holders to be nominated who are conversant with the contents of the building, have means of transport and preferably are available by telephone.

There are three UK organizations which aim to safeguard customers and abide by BS4737, the British Standard on alarm installation. These are:

1 The National Supervisory Council for Intruder Alarms (NSCIA), which is the largest and most powerful (set up in 1972)
2 The British Association of Security Installers, set up in 1985, based in the south-east of England (London and the Home Counties) and consisting of small firms (but with insurance company recognition)
3 The Inspectors Approved Alarm Installers, based in the north of England, with a grading system for small to large firms, and again installing to the requirements of BS4737.

In any case, when considering the use of any alarm installation firm, the insurers should always be consulted. Contracts should be carefully scrutinized before acceptance, liability restriction clauses and the precise supplier obligations under 'maintenance' merit special attention. An alarm log, showing dates and nature of work done on the system, and recording false calls with their causes should be kept.

Locks and keys

A lock is just as good as its price, and a key as good as the precautions taken to restrict the holders and the opportunity to copy it. For security purposes, a five-lever lock is the minimum insurance requirement and again the insurers' advice can be obtained in cases of doubt: for privacy the 'Yale-type' lock will suffice. The locking of internal doors can frequently result in excessive damage by intruders and it is a waste of time and money putting a first-class lock on a poor door. The same is applicable to padlocks – the best are close shackled and of hardened steel, and must be used with hasps of equal calibre. Both padlocks and ordinary door locks of all kinds can be 'master-suited', which implies that the keying is such that, for example, an executive will be able to open all doors within his jurisdiction with the one key he holds, his departmental managers will have access to the offices in their departments only, and individuals will only be able to enter their own offices. The same sort of arrangement can be implemented in research departments which contain areas of different security importance.

Duplicated locks on doors are not desirable, even with cheap locks, but the main danger is that of desk locks where it is not unusual to find a single key will open almost all drawers in an office. If the desk contains matters demanding privacy, the lock itself should be unique in its environment. To obtain a desk or filing cabinet which will resist forcing, even with limited violence, is well-nigh impossible – fire-resistant cabinets are the nearest available type and even the smaller substantial ones may reach £300 in price, old safes are preferable. Keys must always be kept in personal possession.

Use of dogs

Trained dogs can be a valuable aid for patrolling or guarding premises, particularly on dispersed sites. They afford protection and given confidence to those using them and their very presence is a formidable disincentive to potential intruders.

Liability for injury caused by them is governed by the Animals Act 1971, which lays down that a keeper is not liable for damage if (a) it is wholly due to the fault of the sufferer, (b) the sufferer has voluntarily accepted the risk (an employee is not regarded as a 'volunteer'), or (c) it is caused to a trespasser by an animal kept on premises and it is proved that either it was not kept there for protective purposes or if so used, it was not unreasonable to do so.

Section 1 of the Guard Dogs Act came into force on 1 February 1976. This lays down that a guard dog shall not be used on any premises unless:

1 There is a warning notice of its presence at each entrance
2 It is in the charge of a capable handler at all times, except 'while it is so secured so that it is not at liberty to go freely about the premises'.

It seems unlikely that any other sections of the Act will now be brought into force and in any case they do not relate to the dog 'which is only used as a guard dog at premises belonging to its owner'. A Divisional Court case Hobson v. Gledhill (1977) did indicate that a handler was not always required when a dog was so tethered that a safe space was always available for the intruder to escape into, but also said that each case would be judged on its merits. There have been very few prosecutions indeed.

Closed-circuit television

Closed-circuit TV is increasingly being found of value particularly in retail concerns for observation of purchasers and employees. It is possible to create permanent records for later scrutiny by means of video-tape recording. The simple combination of fixed camera and monitor can be enhanced by special low light or infra-red lenses, pan and tilt facilities for the camera mount, all-weather protection, screen washing and wiping, heating units etc., all of which grossly increase the basic price, but make the installation much more multi-purpose adaptable.

A further use, which could result in substantial manpower economies, is that of remote control of doors and gates by coupling TV observation with microphones for 'speak-through' and electronic control of the entry lock thereby allowing an under-utilized receptionist to be more gainfully employed.

As yet, 'moving' pictures cannot be sent via ordinary telephone wires. But a picture can be built up line-by-line. This technique, called slow-scan television, is especially valuable for monitoring remote sites at low cost. There is no restriction on distance: for the price of a telephone call a security officer in the UK could monitor a remote site in Australia and (using the same telephone) alert the Australian police.

It is advisable to point out reasons for installing a system to employees before doing so. To avoid opposition, it may be necessary to agree not to take any action if purely disciplinary matters are seen. Dummy cameras may be used to apparently extend a system and can be interchangeable with the genuine if necessary.

FIRE

The creation of an immediate avenue of notification to the company secretary of happenings that might result in claims or proceedings is important. A fire assessor wants to know of damage as soon as possible after it has occurred so that he can survey it to ascertain extent and causation. Any delay in checking the details of an accident can result in essentials being missed and possible failure to inform the Factory Inspectorate of one of notifiable gravity. A standardized and comprehensive system of reporting should be instituted, especially in connexion with accidents.

Fire prevention officers

Full use should be made of the services of the local fire prevention officer. Under the Fire Services Act 1947, the fire authority must maintain efficient arrangements for giving, on request, advice to firms in its area on fire prevention, means of escape, and the restriction of the spread of fires. Consultation with the fire prevention officer should always take place when building alterations or new buildings are contemplated, to avoid unnecessary work and later recriminations. Advice will also be given on the provision and siting of extinguishers and other means of putting out fires. Fire drills should be carried out at regular intervals – it is too late to do so after a tragedy. Very explicit instructions should be given so that all staff know exactly what to do in emergency, and appropriate notices should be displayed. The appointment of fire wardens to be given proper training to combat fire is well worth while, and again the fire prevention officer will be glad to cooperate.

Fire: security checklists

Detailed guidance is given in Oliver and Wilson (1983).

PRECAUTIONS AGAINST TERRORIST ACTION

Regrettably, it has now become necessary for all firms to consider precautions against apparently indiscriminate and senseless acts of violence designed to achieve political ends. These are not entirely confined to the IRA or to the anti-Israeli organizations; others are being tempted to emulate. Terrorism – coupled perhaps with kidnapping – may increase before final containment. There is also ample evidence that criminal elements are involved in some aspects for financial gain.

The threats and actual risks can take several forms, ranging from malicious telephone calls to explosive and incendiary devices, and letter bombs. The first steps that need to be taken are those of formulating and agreeing policies to deal with particular contingencies, giving due weight to the views of those who will be asked to carry out specific duties such as searching for suspect objects.

Bomb-threat calls

These may be direct call, anonymous letter, or via a third party, i.e., the police or newspaper office; the IRA have used a code to the police to confirm the presence of a bomb but this is by no means an accurate yardstick of veracity. If sufficiently prevalent, and treated as needing automatic evacuation, these calls can disrupt a firm's activity almost as effectively as a device itself can. The decision is not easy and any individual, whatever his convictions about the validity of a message, will have at the back of his mind the consequences of ignoring a genuine call; this decision therefore must rest with the senior person available, who should be influenced by pre-considered guidelines.

Bomb-threat policy

Fundamentally, there are three basic possible alternatives:

1 To evacuate and search before re-entry
2 To search without evacuation
3 To ignore the message.

Amongst points to be considered are:

1 Nature of the call – apparent age of the caller, speech, attitude, general approach, etc.
2 Recent history of such threats, genuine or otherwise, locally and nationally
3 Prevailing conditions of industrial tension, strikes and political unrest in the neighbourhood and at the recipient's premises particularly
4 Any trading relationships between the company and countries whose opponents have used bombs
5 The implications and dangers of an evacuation.

In all instances, police and fire authorities should be informed immediately, whether an evacuation is to be ordered or not. As a neighbourly gesture, adjoining firms should be told what is happening.

It must be anticipated that the police will be reluctant to take the initiative in advising on evacuation or otherwise – unless they have positive information.

Telephone operators

As first recipients of a message, it is most important that operators have clear instructions on what to do so that there is a minimum of alarm and subsequent confusion about the content of the message. In addition to the instructions suggested below, a stereotyped form of the type shown in Figure 45.2 could be provided to the operators, and its mere availability could relieve natural tension.

Guidelines to telephonists

1 Let the caller finish his message without interruption
2 Get the message exactly – bearing in mind the points shown
3 If it is possible to tie the supervisor or another operator into the conversation, do so

---

GHM

Signal your supervisor and conform to prearranged drill for nuisance calls: tick through applicable word below, insert where necessary.

TIME . . . . DATE . . . .

Origin	STD		Coin box		Internal	
Caller	Male		Female		Adult	Juvenile

Voice	Speech	Language	Accent	Manner	Background
Loud	Fast	Obscene	Local	Calm	Noises
Soft	Slow	Coarse	Regional	Rational	Factory
Rough	Distinct	Normal	Foreign	Irrational	Road traffic
Educated	Blurred	Educated		Coherent	Music
High pitch	Stutter			Incoherent	Office
Deep				Deliberate	Party
Disguised				Hysterical	atmosphere
				Aggrieved	Quiet
				Humorous	Voices
				Drunken	Other

Text of conversation

Figure 45.2 Bomb threat checklist for switchboard operator
(note that most bomb threats prove to be hoaxes)

4   Ensure that senior management or a pre-designated person are told exactly the contents of the call as soon as possible
5   If the caller is apparently prepared to carry on a conversation, encourage him to do so and try to get answers to the following:
    (*a*) Where has the bomb been put?
    (*b*) What time will it go off?
    (*c*) Why has it been done?
    (*d*) When and how was it done?

In general, if the caller is prepared to continue, try to get him to talk about possible grievances as they affect the firm, and anything which bears upon the truthfulness of the message and the identity of the caller.

It is essential that senior management should be told as soon as possible so that there is no delay in implementing policies and procedures.

Evacuation

Communications should be such that the general warning to evacuate is given simultaneously in all parts affected; otherwise there will be confusion, with people coming and going, difficulty in checking that everyone is out, and garbled messages being passed. If time permits the warning to be given verbally through a managerial chain, it should be on the lines 'At 2 p.m. instruct your staff to begin evacuation, ensure that it is complete not later than 2.15 p.m.'

Based on experience in the USA, a clear radius of 100 yards should be allowed from the threatened area, 200 yards if a car bomb is suspected. Assembly points for evacuation will not of necessity coincide with those used for fire drills. Car parks are definitely not acceptable, for obvious reasons, and there are advantages in housing evacuated staff in substantial buildings if of suitable size and outside the prescribed distance. There must be facilities for checking employees to ensure complete evacuation, the passing of messages and for expediting the return to work. A handheld loud hailer will be found invaluable to those in charge.

In case of evacuation

1   Persons who are instructed to get out must, if time permits, collect and take their personal parcels, bags and other belongings to avoid complications during searching (particularly important in cloakroom areas and office blocks generally)
2   If the time-limit given by the warning permits, there should be a quick search by supervisory staff and/or designated employees before the premises are vacated. A system should be devised to ensure that everyone is out. (Special provisions may be needed for disabled employees).
3   After the time-limit of the threat has elapsed, a reasonable margin should be allowed before a search by security/supervisory personnel,

and employees are allowed to re-enter. (Searching of course is a voluntary matter but, in general, supervisors will cooperate.)

No evacuation

A search should be made by security/supervisory personnel of likely 'planting' areas, i.e. entrances to buildings, cloakrooms and toilets, and the perimeter of buildings – with special attention to parked cars. Police and fire brigade should nevertheless be informed.

Search

1 Responsibility for search of premises lies with the occupiers. The police cannot be expected to accept this task by themselves, since they will be unfamiliar with buildings and likely contents, but they will almost certainly offer their assistance
2 Bearing in mind the multiplicity of forms that a bomb may take, it is the unusual object – not the normal in the particular environment – which is suspect. Again the occupants are best qualified to identify
3 Any search made must be methodical with areas designated to individuals to ensure that the whole is covered, and with a co-ordinator to make certain that this is done
4 Unaccountable or suspect objects should not be interfered with. If such are found the police should be advised and they will then instigate any necessary action.

Recognition of explosive/incendiary devices

These can be encountered in almost any form. In retail premises, small incendiary packets put in pockets of clothing left in cloakrooms or among inflammable textiles may be one of the reasons why the arson rate has escalated over the past few years. From the terrorist point of view, they have the virtue of completely eliminating any sign of their existence.

Explosive types have been planted in parcels, suitcases, dustbins, post-boxes, biscuit tins, or where large bulk has been used, lodged in hijacked cars. On casual inspection, they may not be recognizable for what they are and it is not unusual for the obvious device to have been booby-trapped as a means of attacking anti-bomb personnel. A relatively new type is clearly identifiable and potentially very lethal to those nearby – a conventional bomb is placed with polystyrene padding between two cans of petrol and then lowered into premises where inflammable matter is contained, via a hole cut in the roof.

It follows that anything of a foreign nature – rough parcels, plastic shopping bags left in odd corners or near entrances, dustbins out of place, etc. should be regarded as suspect. In effect, there is no easy way for a layman

867

without special equipment to identify or otherwise a potential bomb, and at the risk of repetition, it is the unusual thing that just should not be where it is which should immediately arouse suspicion.

In the near vicinity of a suspect bomb, the military advise that personal or other types of radio intercommunication be switched off as a precaution against activating a sophisticated device.

General precautions

A general tightening of precautions in or around plant and offices can reduce the opportunity for incidents and at the same time have the added benefit of minimizing other sources of loss. For example:

1   If not already in existence, inaugurate a registration system for immediate identification of cars and motor cycles used by employees (helps quick location of owner when lights left on, tyres flat etc.)
2   Control entrance of visitors, suppliers and contractors to the site. Visitor and vehicular passes can be used to provide a record, and to check that the person or vehicle leaves (improves privacy of firm's operation)
3   Do not allow visitors to enter on any pretext without prior confirmation that they are expected/welcome (excludes unwanted, time-wasting callers and stops a common form of impersonation to get into premises to steal). Arrange collection from reception point in cases of doubt. Always check identity of purported public officials – gas, electricity repairmen etc. – who will be in possession of the necessary cards
4   Review physical protection of buildings, i.e. adequacy of fencing, external lighting, doors, ground-floor windows, fire escapes, alarms, etc. (leads to strengthening of physical defences against intruders)
5   Ensure that the standard of housekeeping around buildings is such that unfamiliar objects will at once become noticeable
6   Restrict parking outside particularly important facilities such as computer installations, gas terminals and power substations
7   Establish a central control point which will not be evacuated unless there is a substantiated positive danger to it. This should have means of communication with outside authorities should the firm's switchboard be obliged to close down, and it should be easily accessible to incoming police and fire services
8   In the event of a bomb warning, small rough parcels and plastic-type shopping bags left in odd corners or near entrances should be at once suspect; likewise unfamiliar cars parked haphazardly, especially those with Irish registration plates.

Letter bombs

There is of course no warning given in respect of these; reasons can usually be thought of as to why a particular target has been selected but the senders are irrational, and immunity for lack of causation should not be assumed. It has been suggested in one instance of injury that the employers may be liable in that no guidance, appropriate to present circumstances, had been given to the person opening the mail.

Letters or parcel bombs mainly take the form of substantial envelopes not less than five millimetres thick or of parcels containing paperbacked books delivered through normal postal channels. The weight in letter form is unlikely to exceed 120 grammes.

General features

1 Letter bombs are made to withstand the handling that any normal letter or parcel would sustain during delivery; they are to all intents and purposes safe until steps are taken to open them, and can be handled normally until then
2 So far as is known, no letter/parcel bomb has been received which has borne a franking mark on the envelope or wrapping, but a franked stuck-on address label has been used on letter bombs originating on the Continent
3 Spraying with an aerosol of the Boots pain-killing type as used for sporting purposes or Holts 'Cold Start' (the first is the better) may make a manila envelope or wrapping sufficiently transparent for contents to be identified enough to alleviate suspicion if not to establish dangerous nature
4 Conventional components include detonators, connecting wire and minute batteries; no device yet used has been known to have been activated when tested with a low-power metal detector or X-ray (a wide variety of hand-held metal detectors are commercially available). The military advise that if X-ray equipment is used, it should be operated by remote control
5 The police have already dealt with innumerable suspect but innocuous letters/parcels and may be able to give immediate clearance if provided with pertinent details, i.e. town of origin, size and shape, franking or other distinctive stamping.

Points which may make unfamiliar material received suspect

1 The postmark, if foreign and unfamiliar
2 The writing, which may have an 'un-English' appearance, lack literacy, or be crudely printed
3 Name and address of sender (if shown), if address differs from area of postmark
4 'Personal'/'Only to be opened by' or 'Private' letters addressed to senior management under the job title, e.g. Managing Director
5 Weight, if excessive for size and apparent contents. Thickness: $^3/_{16}$ inch or more
6 Weight distribution, if uneven may indicate batteries inside

7 Grease marks showing on the exterior of the wrapping and emanating from inside may indicate 'sweating' explosive

8 Smell – some explosives smell of marzipan or almonds

9 Abnormal fastening – sealing excessive for the type of package. If such an outer contains a similar inner wrapping, this may be a form of booby trap

10 Damaged envelopes which give sight of wire, batteries or fluid-filled plastic sachets should be left strictly alone; those that rattle or feel springy should be treated with caution; and naturally, any ticking noise should be treated as a 'red' alert. Pinholes in the outer wrapping may indicate where devices for the safety of the bomb-maker have been removed. Where conventional paperback books have been used, the resultant parcel bomb may be discernibly softer in the centre than at the edges.

If suspicions cannot be alleviated

1 Do not try to open the letter/parcel or tamper with it

2 Do not put it in water or put anything on top of it

3 Isolate it where it can do no harm with minimum handling, i.e., enclose it in a nest of sandbags but ensure that it is in a position for easy visual inspection

4 Open any windows or doors in the vicinity. Keep people away from it

5 Inform the police and seek their guidance: give them full details of the letter/parcel, its markings and peculiarities which have led to suspicion.

KIDNAPPING

In Great Britain, kidnapping has not materialized other than in infrequent instances. In the Americas, it is sufficiently widespread for the term 'executive kidnapping' to be applied to a practice which is being used for both financial gain and political advantage. Some American security firms do tender advice on the precautions that should be taken, and insurance can be obtained against it from Lloyd's. If the company secretary is called upon to arrange an itinerary for a senior director in an area where instances have occurred, there is nothing to be lost by enquiring to the appropriate government department for guidelines to be followed. This advice is now available but the essential ingredients are: maintain low profile and minimum publicity, accept that there is a risk however unattractive a target you consider yourself, and use common sense precautions in your behaviour and movements accordingly. The countries of current highest risk are the Argentine and Italy, but publicity of success elsewhere could easily create new trouble points.

INDUSTRIAL ACTION

We are not concerned here with peaceful industrial action or protests arising from disputes. Unfortunately, such action is not always peaceful and, for whatever reason, those with grievances sometimes commit acts of sabotage or violence.

Picketing during strike action

Picketing in furtherance of an industrial dispute is lawful but certain acts if carried out during it are offences. There is no right to encroach on private land and police assistance can be called for the purpose of effecting removal; the police can order the limiting of numbers if they consider these are unreasonable and likely to cause a breach of the peace; violence to persons or property and the hiding of tools are offences, and the picketing of a place where a person lives is prohibited.

Works closures

Regrettably, works closures have become commonplace during recent years. They bring with them security problems which are often unexpectedly serious. The risks start when the news of closure is announced, and can persist long after the intended closure date. By no means all workforces react badly, but there have been many incidents where ill will has led to theft, vandalism and fraud – to the extent that a group of senior security officers have produced guidelines for action during such periods to limit damage to disposable assets.

These guidelines, which are too detailed for inclusion here, are obtainable from The Secretary, International Professional Security Association, 292a Torquay Road, Paignton, Devon, TQ3 2ET UK.

A HOLIDAY SECURITY CHECKLIST

This checklist has particular relevance at Christmas shut-down, when the short days give villains longer 'working hours' of darkness, police and security guards are at a premium because of the holiday and there are generally fewer people about, especially in industrial estates, to deter intruders. The executive responsible for security should have made all necessary arrangements, especially if it is felt extra guards/patrols would be beneficial (check early as most contract companies will be under heavy pressure). But after the last office party, and as the site/building is closed down, we suggest you check the following, just in case:

1   *The power* – make sure all unnecessary plugs are disconnected; check that heating and lighting controls are set properly (particularly pilot lights/burners), and check/observe all frost and flood precautions

2   *Access Control* – whatever system is used, be it standard locks with keys or the most sophisticated access control system, make sure that all cards/keys etc. are properly accounted for

3   *Company vehicles* – if they are to be left on the site they should be immobilized even if they are fitted with an alarm system. If should, too, be company policy to have lockable petrol caps to frustrate those whose idea of Christmas cheer is to pour sugar or water into fuel tanks.

4   *Petty cash* and any other easily convertible/portable forms of ready money (e.g. postage stamps) should be securely locked away or banked. Make sure, too, that any pre-paid meters (e.g. staff telephones) are emptied before Christmas. And where possible, leave safe doors open

5   *Storage tanks* particularly fuel of any kind (especially butane and other specialist gases) should be thoroughly secured. Fuel is expensive, and a favourite target

6   *Small and valuable items* such as computers, calculators and any other items easily 'fenced' should be locked away securely. Or in some cases, ask staff to take them home

7   *Security lighting* has always been an undervalued tool. And today, for less than £20, an electronic randomly programmed time switch is available to deter thieves. Some form of 'surprise' lighting is also a good idea (and a useful aid to staff who have to turn up early while it's still dark). For about £50+ simple 40/60W light units activated by a built-in body-heat sensor are available for strategic entry/exit points (useful for external stores/sheds particularly). The better models of these will also drive up to 1000W of auxiliaries – flood/spot lights etc.

8   *Windows and doors* should be checked by the security staff of course, but it does no harm to have a last look yourself. And if you have any worries (a lock which has been 'playing up', or a window with a broken or vulnerable catch for example) sort them out now

9   *External stores* must be properly secured, especially if they hold valuable tools, fuel containers or the like. Large stores, especially garages, can be further protected by parking a company vehicle across the door. The vehicle must, of course, be immobilized – and a visible form (such as the dreaded clamp used by London's police and which is now commercially available) will signal the situation immediately to would-be intruders

10 *Climbing aids* – the most obvious are ladders, which must be securely locked away out of sight. But such items as pallets and any other handy aid must not be overlooked

11 *The alarm system.* Make sure there are no problem areas where sensors continually false alarm (which is how the Buckingham Palace break-in happened) and which guards ignore. Make sure there are no by-passes on the system

12 *And finally* – be sure the police know how long you will be shut down for; how they can get in touch with the keyholder(s) throughout that

period, and anything else you can think of vital to your specific security (particularly if specified in your insurance agreement).

FURTHER READING

Balevic, Henry J., *Drug Abuse in the Workplace*, Personnel Services Inc., 2303, W. Meadowview Road, Greensboro, NC-27407, USA

Bologna, Jack, *Corporate Fraud*, Butterworth, London, 1985

Bottom, Norman R. and Kostanosk, John, *Security and Loss Control*, Macmillan, London, 1983

Hughes, D. and Bowler, P., *The Security Survey*, Gower, Aldershot, 1982

Oliver, E. and Wilson J. *Practical Security in Commerce and Industry*, 4th edition, Gower, Aldershot, 1983

Post, R., and Kingsbury, A., *Security Administration*, 2nd edition, Springfield, Ill., 1973

Purpura, Philip P., *Security and Loss Prevention*, Butterworth, London, 1984

Saunders, Michael, *Protecting your Business Secrets*, Gower, Aldershot, 1985

Walsh and Healey, *Protection of Assets Manual*, Merritt Co., Columbus, Ohio.

Walsh and Healey, *Industrial Security Management: A cost effective approach*, Merritt Co., Columbus, Ohio

Wright, K.G., *Cost Effective Security*, McGraw-Hill, Maidenhead, 1973

46 Energy management

R Dick-Larkam

The industrial revolution, largely brought about by the invention of the steam engine and the exploitation of coal, was the beginning of an exponential rise in energy consumption. The energy crisis of 1973, about 150 years after man started using fossil fuels, produced a realization that at the present rates of consumption these would not last for ever. Coal might last for several centuries, but oil and gas, the preferred fuels of the twentieth century, will probably be used up in a few decades.

Apart from the need to conserve energy for future generations and to give time for the development of more permanent sources (such as nuclear, solar, wind, wave, etc.) shortages will progressively produce much higher costs. Energy costs have already increased dramatically, so that they are no longer the insignificant costs for industry that they once were. It is thus essential that every effort is made to use energy as economically as possible. Hence the need for energy management.

It has been estimated that over half the energy used by man is wasted. There are, of course, practical difficulties, but there are very many areas where savings can easily be made and these can reduce the consumption by anything up to 20 per cent in a very short time. Once the commitment to an energy-saving programme has been made, there are four stages to go through. These are:

1 Analyse the present methods of working which use energy; with very little change or expense it is often possible to achieve the same results using less energy. An 'energy audit' is an essential part of this analysis
2 Encourage everyone in the organization to become energy-conscious, so that good energy housekeeping is established. Even turning off unwanted lights, closing windows and doors, and similar simple actions, can produce significant savings
3 Following on from the energy audit, and using ideas derived from the good housekeeping campaign, make short-term expenditure to achieve the more obvious and cost-effective energy savings
4 Make long-term plans. These may involve the commitment to invest considerable capital sums against the longer-term conservation of energy.

AUDITING AND MONITORING THE USE OF ENERGY

As with any other form of management, the first requirement is to know the present position. An audit must be conducted to find out exactly what energy is being used, where it is used and from which fuel it is derived. Energy should be accounted for in the same way as money, so that management can identify and tackle the uneconomic areas. It is surprising how many firms have no idea how the energy that they pay for is really used. No two energy users employ their energy in precisely the same way, and it is not possible to suggest an approach to auditing which is more than a general guide.

Measurement in money terms is usually comparatively easy but cost inflation can be misleading when monitoring progress from one audit to the next. Using energy units presents a problem because the terms used vary from fuel to fuel, so that to find total usage or to compare one fuel with another for doing similar jobs, it is necessary to reduce them all to some common unit. Basic units in the Imperial system are British Thermal Units (Btu) and therms; in the SI metric system, megajoules (MJ). For many managers, however, these terms will have little meaning and for this reason it seems more logical to use the basic unit of one tonne of coal equivalent. This is almost the same as the old Imperial long ton (1 tonne=0.984 ton) and is an amount that can be visualized by most people. Conversion merely entails multiplying by the factors as shown in Figure 46.1. It must be remembered that these conversions are not exact, as the calorific value of fossil fuels varies from sample to sample, but they are sufficiently close for all practical purposes.

Initially the audit need not be very sophisticated and the aim should be to obtain the results quickly. As time goes on it can be improved in the light of experience as it will undoubtedly reveal many inadequacies in metering and measurement. The first thing to be done is to find out exactly how much

		Equivalents		GHM
Fuel	Unit	Therms	Megajoules	Tonne of Coal
Gas	1 therm	1	105	0.0040
Electricity	1 kWh	0.034	3.6	0.000137
Heating oil	1 gallon	1.77	187	0.0074
Derv	1 gallon	1.62	171	0.0065
Petrol	1 gallon	1.48	156	0.0058
Kerosene	1 tonne	470	49 600	1.70
Propane	1 kg	0.47	49.6	0.0017
Coal	1 tonne	261	27 500	1.0

Figure 46.1 Approximate energy equivalents

energy is being bought and used. This should be available in the form of invoices from the various suppliers and can be put together in common units of both energy and money. This information will be very useful in forecasting; in the past the cost of energy has tended to be neglected as it has not been very significant, but that is no longer the case.

One of the principal purposes of an audit is to try to cut consumption and costs. The audit must therefore be taken further so that each individual use can be given much closer scrutiny. The next step is to try to see how all the energy is used or wasted. Electricity, for example, is used for lighting, for driving motors and perhaps for process heating in the factory. Separate meters, installed for different areas, can be read and the different uses divided. But factories often do not have many separate meters and in these cases the amount used for lighting can be fairly closely estimated by the wattage of the lamps and the average length of time in use. By subtraction the power used for other purposes is estimated and by repeating the process the total can be broken down.

This procedure will show precisely what energy is used, how it is used and where it is used. If a few areas emerge where the use of energy is extremely high, it is obviously here that the biggest savings can be made. Each energy use must be investigated to ascertain whether there is excessive waste and if so, how it can be corrected or if there is a less wasteful way of doing the job. In most cases elimination or even reduction of losses will produce a substantial saving in the total use of energy.

By carrying out regular audits it is possible to compare, both in total and for individual areas (or fuels) how consumption of energy is rising or falling. Of course the amount of energy used will depend not only on how carefully it is used, but also on the level of activity and the weather. The first of these factors can be overcome by relating the energy consumption to the volume of production or (in the case of service industries) to turnover, due allowance being made for inflation.

To allow for weather, which has a special bearing and a considerable effect on space heating, the degree day concept is used. The degree day is defined as the daily difference in degrees of temperature between a base temperature and the 24-hour mean outside temperature when it falls below that base temperature. The base temperature taken is 15.5°C (60°F) and if, for example, the mean temperature on a particular day was 8°C, that day would count as 7.5 degree days. If on another day the mean temperature was anything over 15.5°C this would count as zero degree days. By monthly totals of degree days, which are issued by the Department of Energy each month for different regions of the UK, it is possible to compare that month with other months and with the same month in previous years.

An example of how degree-day information can be related to fuel consumption for space heating is shown in Figure 46.2 which compares oil usage in a factory over a two-year period. Between the two years, work has been carried out in an endeavour to make the boiler and the heating system more efficient. November, December and January of year 2 were noticeably warmer than in year 1 and it might have been assumed that the 5500 gallons of fuel were

| Month | Degree days °C | | Fuel consumption | | Gallons/degree day | |
	Year 1	Year 2	Year 1 Gallons	Year 2 Gallons	Year 1	Year 2
October	172	237	2 842	3 301	16.5	13.9
November	286	237	4 686	3 365	16.4	14.2
December	319	218	5 318	3 065	16.7	14.1
January	280	254	4 586	3 527	16.4	13.9
February	274	290	4 544	4 079	16.6	14.1
March	296	313	4 904	4 456	16.6	14.2
April	207	212	3 469	3 056	16.8	14.4
Totals	1 834	1 761	30 349	24 849	16.6	14.1

Figure 46.2   Oil usage for factory space-heating analysed using degree days

saved because of this. February, March and April, though colder, were not very much colder and by the time May came round, when figures were compared, the fact that October was a lot colder would have been forgotten. By comparing the amount of fuel necessary to heat the factory per degree day it will be seen that this has improved by about 2.5 gallons (the efficiency had been increased by about 15 per cent) and that only about 4 per cent of the oil was saved by better weather conditions.

GOOD HOUSEKEEPING

In any organization the person using the facilities either wastes energy or conserves it and for this reason everyone must be involved and committed to saving energy if the campaign is to succeed. National campaigns have done much in recent years to make people in the UK aware of the need to save, but human memories are very short and it is easy to revert to old ways. Publicity is a powerful weapon but, to be effective, posters must be replaced frequently or they become part of the decorations and have no effect. Adhesive labels exhorting people to 'Turn it off' on light switches, radiators or hot-water taps are effective for a time, but again lose their impact as people become used to them.

Other ways of arousing interest and involvement are competitions and suggestion schemes. Competitions between departments on saving the most energy week by week or month by month have proved very effective and often public acknowledgement is enough reward. Results of such competitions, suggestions and other exhortations to save energy can well be made in a bulletin issued at regular intervals, copies of which should be freely available to all concerned.

Small working parties meeting for a short time regularly to discuss and suggest how energy can be saved are very useful. They should consist of people who are actually using the energy and to sustain them the membership should be changed from time to time. Yet another way of involving people is to appoint wardens of small areas of the factory or offices, whose job is to make sure that lights are switched off when not required, that radiators are turned down when the temperature is too high, that windows and ventilators are not opened unnecessarily, that outside doors are kept shut and that the many other ways of wasting energy are not practised.

SHORT-TERM EXPENDITURE

The third phase of an energy-saving campaign is often a development of good housekeeping, as many of the ideas put forward during this phase will require moderate capital expenditure. Spending a small amount of capital can often pay large dividends and it must be remembered that when the payback period has passed the savings will then become a direct contribution to profit. The most obvious savings in this area are those which can be made in buildings and services, but large savings can also very often be made in machines and equipment used in the production process.

LONG-TERM PLANS

These, of course, must be unique to any organization; in the past, due to the low cost of energy, many processes were very energy intensive because they entailed much lower capital costs initially. Now, however, with higher energy costs they are not the most economic. Forms of lighting, heating and building construction may have been the cheapest at the time they were installed or built, but it would be more economic now to pay a higher initial cost in order to save energy afterwards. All plans for the future should be studied from the point of view of energy consumption during their life and this will often influence the original choice.

THE CONSERVATION PLAN

When putting a plan into operation it is essential that someone should be responsible; in a large company it is usual to appoint an energy manager, but with smaller concerns this may not be possible and in such circumstances a manager should be nominated to take on the task in addition to his other duties. The following are the steps that should be taken:

1 Measure what is being used and where it is being used
2 Obtain the cooperation and involvement of everyone concerned
3 Make everyone practise 'good housekeeping'
4 Monitor and publicize the results
5 Make short-term capital expenditure
6 Monitor and publicize the results

7 Prepare long-term plans, for introduction when possible.

ENERGY-SAVING METHODS

There are innumerable ways in which energy can be saved. Most of them are obvious when pointed out, but because in the past the supply of energy has been so readily available, and cheap, they are often missed. A number of practical ways in which energy can be saved, without curtailing any activities and without lowering standards, are set out below.

Lighting

Buildings cut out a considerable part of daylight, despite windows, and they therefore need artificial lighting. Also, of course, we often have to work at night. It is said that lighting consumes such a negligible quantity of energy that it is not worth worrying about, but in commerce and industry this is not so. Office blocks and factories can have lighting loads of several hundred kilowatts, and a saving of only 10 or 20 per cent of this is worth while.

The best use of daylight which does enter a building is not always made. Windows and roof lights are often not very clean and the layout of workplaces often leaves a lot to be desired. For some jobs a lot of light is required while others do not need so much; the former should be situated near the windows or under the roof lights, while the latter can be away from the natural source. When artificial light is being used one of the first things that should be done, when looking for energy savings, is to measure the level of illumination at all workplaces. These measurements can be compared with the Illuminating Engineering Society's code for interior lighting which gives recommendations for various jobs and, while it is not suggested that the lighting levels should be less than they recommend, it is wasteful to exceed them. Look also at corridors, storerooms and other places where people do not usually work. These too can often be overlit.

If an office or a factory is arranged properly, for part of the day many people who are close to windows will not require artificial light. There are, however, other areas which do need lights. Yet very often the switching is such that lights near windows and lights in the dark areas are on the same circuit and this usually means that all the lights are on. At comparatively little expense this can be altered and will greatly reduce the load during daylight hours. It is not unusual to see yard lights on during daylight hours; a light-cell switch will overcome this and can also be useful for controlling lights in corridors, stairways and toilets where switching lights on and off is really no one's responsibility.

The maintenance of lights is very important to retain the lighting level and use the minimum of engyer. With age all lamps give less light, and light will also be lost due to dust build-up. Figure 46.3 shows the loss in light from a fluorescent fitting in an average factory, assuming 3000 hours use per year, and it will be seen that without maintenance for two years the light given out is more than halved.

Light sources vary very much in their efficiency as is shown in Figure 46.4; the variations with each source depend on the type and size of the lamp, generally the larger lamp being the more efficient. It will be seen that tungsten lamps (still used extensively) are very inefficient, using nearly four times the energy for the same amount of light as that used by fluorescent tubes and nearly seven times the high-pressure sodium consumption. Installation and lamp cost is, of course, the cheapest for tungsten lighting, but the overall cost over a period of time, taking the cost of electricity and the shorter lamp life into account, is very much higher. To anyone using tungsten lighting the capital cost of changing to a more economical form will be repaid very quickly.

When planning new buildings or extensions it is well worth while to investigate the total cost of the more efficient lighting systems; that is not only the initial cost of installation but the cost over the period of years that the building will be in use and to compare these with the cost of lower efficiency lighting. It is also important to ensure that the building is not overlit for 'aesthetic reasons'.

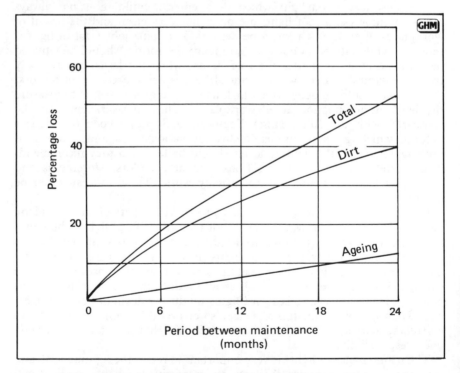

Figure 46.3 Deterioration of fluorescent light source with age and accumulated dirt

	GHM
Light source	Lumens per watt
Tungsten lamp	10–22
Mercury lamp	41–59
Fluorescent tube	42–75
Mercury halide lamp	60–80
High-pressure sodium lamp	68–120
Low-pressure sodium lamp	130–175

Figure 46.4 Comparative efficiencies of various light sources

Ventilation

It is necessary to ventilate any building in which people work not only because the oxygen gets used up but more especially because the concentration of carbon dioxide and humidity rise. Two changes of air per hour is all that is generally needed, but, due to air leaks round windows and doors and the passage of people to and fro, four or more are the general rule in office blocks and factory buildings. Each time the air is changed the fresh air must be heated from outside temperature to that in the building.

On the windward side of buildings leaks can often be felt as draughts. It must be remembered that where cold air can get in warm air can get out, particularly on the leeward side of the building. The elimination of draught is one of the easiest and cheapest ways of saving energy. The use of foam, rubber or metal draught excluder will usually stop the leak and still allow doors to be opened and the windows in summer. In factory buildings the eaves, roof ridges and walls must also be looked at and in these cases draughtproofing can save as much as between 20 and 25 per cent of the energy used in heating the building.

Windows offer very poor thermal material insulation and even when draught proofed it may still seem that cold air and draughts are coming from them. This is because the air near the windows is cooled and, being heavier than warm air, starts a downward circulation. Double glazing is the best way to prevent this, but is, of course, rather expensive. Tight-fitting screens covered with polythene sheet are a cheaper alternative and very often just as effective although not so attractive aesthetically.

Many modern buildings have an air-conditioning system installed. These systems can, if not carefully maintained, consume large quantities of extra fuel when they go out of adjustment. It has been found that savings can be made without affecting anyone working in the building by turning them off about one hour before work stops.

Where air-conditioning is installed a great deal of extra energy can be used in summer by the building heating up due to solar gain; sun shining on windows produces a glasshouse effect. There are basically two ways of overcoming this problem – by suitable tinted or reflective glazing or by the use of blinds. Film is available that can be applied to ordinary glass which achieves a similar effect to tinted or reflective glass and at the same time improves the thermal efficiency of the glass. There are many types of blind, but outside blinds are far superior to those fitted inside the building as when these heat up in the sun's rays they cannot radiate this heat within the room.

Space heating

The Factory and Office Acts in the UK lay down that the temperature in any building in which people are working must attain 16°C (60.8°F) during the first hour of work, but regulations to promote energy conservation make a maximum 20°C (68°F). Thus the temperature of workplaces is confined within four degrees of Celsius and generally a temperature of 18°C is acceptable to most people not doing manual work, although for those with more strenuous occupations lower temperatures are more pleasant. It has been estimated that a 1°C increase in the temperature of a building requires an expenditure of 6 per cent more fuel, so even a small reduction in temperature will make a significant difference to the amount of energy used. Controlling the temperature is not always easy with the crude thermostatic control on most systems. Increasing the number of thermostats (or, ideally, fitting each radiator with one of its own) is one way of doing this, but careful adjustment can achieve much on any system. It is advisable to provide thermostats which cannot be reset by unauthorized persons.

Areas and offices not being used, even if only temporarily, should have their radiators or heaters turned off and should be isolated by keeping the doors closed. Doors leading to the outside, when left open, can reduce the temperature very quickly and thus require extra fuel to reheat the area. The simple remedy is to fit a spring, but this is not always convenient and it may be necessary in offices to fit either automatic or double doors. In the factory rubber doors or strip curtains can be used. Air curtains can be provided for doors which have to be open for a large percentage of the time. Hot-air curtains are expensive to run and waste a lot of energy. Cold-air curtains are effective where lorries and trucks, rather than people, pass through the door, but the most effective and economical on energy is the air curtain that takes its air from the roof space of the building (where it is hotter) and blows this across the entrance inside the building. A further way of wasting energy is to open windows in winter. Where the ventilation is adequate (about two changes per hour) radiators should be turned down instead.

Most offices and factories have some means of reducing the heating during nights and weekends when the buildings are not in use but the most economical ways are not always employed. Reliance is often placed on staff coming in early to start the boilers but little or no account is taken of the ambient temperature. There are many ways of controlling the heating cycle, some very sophisticated, but a great deal can be done using time-clocks and thermostats and very great savings can be made by installing some kind of control.

As with all plant and machinery, heating systems require maintenance. Very often they do not get the attention that they need, resulting in energy losses through inefficiency.

Undoubtedly one of the largest areas of energy waste in the UK is poor heat insulation of buildings. By observing a building it is possible to judge whether extra insulation might be economically feasible. If, for instance, snow on the roof melts quickly, the roof dries very quickly after rains, walls are of corrugated asbestos or iron, or are thin, being built of single bricks or blocks, or the building cools quickly when the heat is turned off, then the insulation is not good enough.

Every building must be considered on its merits. The internal temperature required, the external climate, the form of heating and other factors must be taken into account to arrive at an economic thickness of insulation which should be applied to the shell of the building. With many factory buildings it is possible to reduce the energy used in heating by between 60 and 70 per cent and the capital involved in carrying out insulation would be repaid in three to four years by savings on fuel.

The economies of insulation and draught-proofing can be shown most easily by means of an example. A factory building measured 30 m long, 15 m wide and 6 m in height. Walls and roof were clad with corrugated asbestos cement sheeting, except for the glazed areas which accounted for 15 per cent of the total roof and wall area. The floor was concrete. The internal temperature was maintained at 20°C with steam unit heaters when the outside temperature was 6°C. The steam heaters consumed 192 kW under these conditions. Modifications were carried out to the building in four stages; the first consisted of fitting vertical trunking to the unit heaters to pull the heat down from the roof area, insulating all steam pipes, sealing all air leaks with plastic sealer and fitting self-closing rubber doors. This reduced the heat requirement to 149 kW, a saving of 22 per cent.

Second, the roof was insulated with insulating board, leaving an air gap between insulation and roof. The heat requirement was further reduced to 98 kW, saving another 27 per cent. The third modification was to fill the air gap between the insulation board and the roof with fibre glass and insulate the walls in the same way. This reduced the heat requirement to 60 KW (a further saving of 20 per cent) or a saving of 69 per cent in all.

The final modification was to double glaze all the windows, but this only reduced the heat requirement by 5 kW, saving less than 3 per cent. Double glazing is not usually effective as an energy saver, but it does reduce cold draughts and receipt of outside noise.

Boilers

Boiler plant is needed in most factories, office blocks and other buildings to supply space heating in winter. In factories, however, the major use is usually for the supply of hot water or steam for process work. When boilers are installed the principal factor that determines the choice is usually the initial cost. The cheapest boiler is rarely the cheapest to run. As fuel and maintenance costs for one year usually equal the initial cost of the boiler it is wise to spend more initially on an efficient boiler and save expense over its years of service.

The efficiency of any boiler falls as the load is reduced from its maximum, so that if the load is high it is often more economic to install two boilers, each of half capacity. Then, when the load decreases, one boiler can be cut out, keeping the other at its most efficient working capacity. This also gives greater safety if a boiler breaks down or has to be taken out of service for maintenance. When it is not possible to install more than one boiler attention should be paid to the boiler's part-load efficiency; some are far better than others.

With coal- and oil-fired boilers always ensure that the fuel being used is the kind for which the boiler was designed. Using the wrong fuel can seriously affect the efficiency of the boiler. Correct combustion is also important; if the fuel is not being completely burnt energy is lost up the chimney. To obtain maximum energy from fossil fuel the proportions of air and fuel must be correct. This can be checked by monitoring the carbon dioxide levels in the chimney, either with instruments provided or by portable instruments. Any fall in carbon dioxide level or a rise in flue gas temperature indicates that the firing equipment needs adjustment or cleaning, or that an air leak has developed.

A boiler system should never be run at a temperature higher than that for which it was designed as this will waste considerable amounts of heat by radiation both from the boiler and the transmission lines.

In a closed system, such as used solely for space heating, the water is continuously recirculated and the amount of make-up water is small. But for boilers producing steam or hot water for process work, water must be continuously fed into the boiler to make up the losses, even if the steam is condensed and returned. It is essential that this make-up water is treated to prevent scaling up of the boiler or the efficiency will go down quickly. Energy can also be conserved by heating the make-up water using waste heat from some other process or from the waste heat that is going up the chimney. Obviously the hotter the feed water to the boiler the less heating is required from the fuel.

Equally, savings can be made by pre-heating the air required for combustion. Cold air has a cooling effect on the flame and if heat, which would otherwise be wasted, is used to bring this air nearer to flame temperature efficiency will be increased. There are several patented devices on the market which may be used for this purpose; one uses radiant heat which would otherwise be lost in the hearth. Alternatively, there may be some process in the factory emitting very hot contaminated air through a chimney that could be used as a source of heat via heat exchangers.

In common with all equipment, boilers need maintenance, particularly because of the combustion process. A layer of soot on the heating surfaces or scale on the water side can cut down the rate of heat transfer quite dramatically. Burners and firing equipment need periodical cleaning and adjustment.

In recent years the design of boilers has improved enormously and efficiencies of about 80 per cent are not uncommon. Very many boilers in use were made and installed many years ago and it is unlikely that these will have an efficiency of more than 50 per cent, even if they have been well maintained. Replacement of old boilers can very often give a return of capital cost by fuel savings in the first year.

Distribution of heat

It is generally inconvenient and inefficient to use the energy contained in a fossil fuel by burning it at the point at which it is required; thus the energy is converted at a central point to a form that can be transmitted and used where it is wanted. Unfortunately there can be severe loss in transmission. Electricity is an example of this. There are considerable losses in the grid, but even so it is more efficient to generate at large stations and have transmission losses than to generate in several small stations.

The same applies to the transmission lines that link a boiler-house with the points at which the energy is required, but much can be done to reduce losses. It is not uncommon to see a wisp of steam rising from a flange or a drop of water from a valve; leaks like these, because they are continuous, can be a large drain. A leak equivalent to a 3mm (⅛") hole will lose 400 tonnes of steam a year at a pressure of 11.5 bars (165psig). In a large system it would not be unusual to find a number of such leaks, amounting to a sizeable loss.

Lagging of hot-water and steam pipes is, of course, vital if losses are to be avoided, but the question arises as to the optimum thickness of insulation. Many tables are published showing the heat lost from bare pipes, and from pipes with different thicknesses of insulation, of different temperatures. If these tables are used to calculate the cost of the heat loss, this can be plotted against insulation cost with increasing thickness. By combining the two curves, as in Figure 46.5 the total cost can be found and thus the economic thickness of insulation. It will be seen that if fuel costs increase faster than insulation costs, the economic thickness gets progressively greater. Flanges and valves are often left uninsulated and can account for considerable loss; it is estimated that a flange is equal to one metre of bare pipe and a valve to about three metres.

In many factories transmission pipes are carried underground in ducts from building to building. These ducts invariably collect water and although the lagging is waterproofed initially, this covering loses its properties with time and the lagging becomes wet. Wet lagging is a little better than no lagging at all. It is useful to observe the top surface of ducts during wet weather.

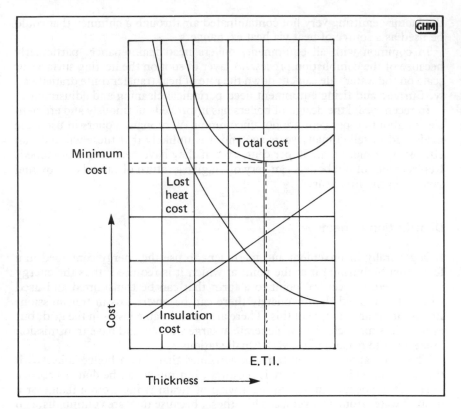

Figure 46.5 Optimum insulation thickness

Quick drying is an indication of heat loss and of the need to investigate lagging.

Compressed air

It is estimated that about 10 per cent of all electrical power used in industry is employed in compressing air and as much as 30 to 40 per cent of the air compressed is wasted in losses. In almost any factory these leaks can be heard during a break when the factory is otherwise quiet but the compressor still running.

Small leaks account for quite big losses. Figure 46.6 shows the amount of air lost by leaks equivalent to 3-mm and 6-mm holes in the pipeline at various air pressures. Maintenance of the air lines is therefore of paramount importance. Leaks are not the only cause of energy waste. Excessive pressure drop, caused by inadequate pipe sizing, choked filters and wrongly sized couplings and hoses, gives high velocities and wastes energy by friction in the pipe. This can be as significant as leaks.

Compressor performance can contribute a great deal to energy usage and it

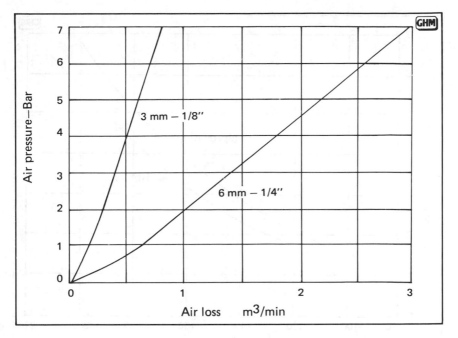

Figure 46.6   Air loss due to leaks

is essential that they are continuously maintained and checked. The loading of the compressor is also important as it is most efficient on full load. For this reason, if there are high peak demands it is often more economical to increase the size of the receiver (which acts as a reservoir for the compressed air) than to increase the size of the compressor.

The choice of pressure in a pipeline system affects both the initial cost and the energy consumption per unit of compressed air. Figure 46.7 shows the power required to generate 30 m^3/min (1060 ft^3/min) of free air at different pressures and it will be seen that the same quantity of air at 7 bar (100 psig) requires 15 per cent more power than at 5 bar (70 psig). It is, therefore, essential for greatest economy that the line pressure is no higher than necessary.

In compressing air a lot of the energy used is converted to heat energy, which is removed either by air or water cooling. The energy contained in both can be used; the air by ducting for space heating and the water either via a heat exchanger or direct for washing, boiler feed or even space heating.

Ovens and furnaces

At some stage almost all manufactured articles go through a process of heating. The equipment used can broadly be termed an oven or furnace and may vary from a heated tunnel through which the products are moved on a

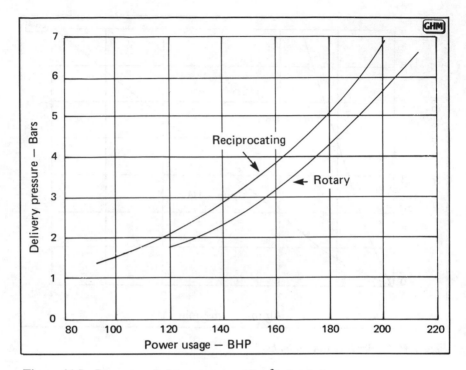

Figure 46.7 **Power needed to compress 30 m³/min of air**

conveyor belt to an insulated box lined with refractory material and heated by almost any fuel.

Few small furnaces are now fired by solid fuel, but oil, natural gas and liquid petroleum gas are often used. The thermal efficiencies of these small furnaces can be as low as 10 per cent and they rarely exceed 50 per cent, due to the losses in combustion and waste gases which are discharged at high temperature. Electric furnaces can be much more thermally efficient as there are none of these losses, but owing to the high cost of electricity as a fuel they are not always cost-effective.

The type of refractory material used in a furnace can influence the amount of fuel used. Where furnaces are used continuously the thermal capacity of the insulation is unimportant, but where they are used intermittently it is very important as high heat storage means a great loss in residual heat. Hot face refractory or ceramic fibre insulation can reduce these heat losses by up to 90 per cent over those suffered with ordinary fire brick.

To obtain optimum efficiency care should be taken to ensure that a suitable burner is used, consistent with the design of the furnace. The firing should also be regulated to give the correct fuel to air ratios as with a boiler. It is usually advantageous to run a furnace at a pressure slightly above atmospheric as this ensures no leakage of cold air through doors and other openings.

Considerable fuel savings can be made by paying detailed attention to furnace loading. An empty furnace can use 75 per cent of the fuel used when it is fully loaded. It is, therefore, necessary to plan the throughput so that it is constantly fully loaded. This may mean that the furnace is running for only part of the day and this will obviously make a saving. Attention should also be paid to furnace doors to ensure they fit tightly and that the load is ready to insert with minimum of door-open time.

Where furnaces and ovens are in use there is usually plenty of opportunity to recover waste heat as they invariably have large quantities available in the exhaust gases. This can be put to use in other parts of the factory or can usefully be used to preheat the combustion air of the furnace itself.

Choosing a fuel

When a source of energy is required there is often some difficulty in deciding which type of fuel to use. With lighting and power sources for machines there is really no difficulty as electricity is almost decided for us; but for firing a boiler, or for heating an oven (for example) there is a variety of fuels that can be chosen.

The choice of fuel is most often made on economic grounds. At any one time the cost of a particular fuel may show an advantage over others, but prices change quickly and not always uniformly. There are, however, other economic considerations. Natural gas and electricity do not have to be stored. Coal, oil and liquid petroleum gas all present problems in this respect, although the last three offer far greater protection against shut-down through loss of supply. All these factors must be taken into account when choosing the fuel.

Electricity

This is one of the most expensive fuels but it offers so many advantages and cost-saving features in use that, overall, it is often less expensive than other fuels. There is no storage requirement and transmission to various parts of the factory is relatively cheap with little or no maintenance on the cables. Breakdowns are rare and usually quickly corrected, so that standby equipment is not normally required.

The choice of the right tariff does not in any way conserve energy, but it can affect the price paid for the same quantity of electricity. It is often extremely rewarding to examine the various tariffs available and choose the right one. Off-peak use can usually reduce the price considerably. Electricity accounts should be studied and the total price per unit calculated. This can then be compared with what the charges would be on other tariffs.

Most factories, whatever the tariff, work on a maximum demand and great savings can be made if this figure is not exceeded or, better still, reduced. The maximum demand is usually only made for short periods over the day, and by studying the load and planning the work accordingly it can often be reduced. For example, if larger receivers are installed on the compressed-air system, the compressor could be shut down for a short time over peak loads. There are many sophisticated devices for giving warning and even shutting off load to avoid overrunning the maximum demand, but much can be done with a simple warning system.

Apart from electricity to perform work, some electrical equipment requires additional current for magnetizing purposes and this lags behind the work current and is not registered on normal meters measuring kilowatts. The total current supplied can be registered on a kilovolt-ampere meter. The ratio of the current effectively used as read on a kilowatt meter and the total current supplied as read on a kilovolt-ampere meter is known as the power factor. In most factories without correction this is usually 0.6 to 0.85, but if there is a lot of arc-welding plant it can be as low as 0.35. Electricity boards penalize for low-power factor and it is usually well worth while to fit capacitors to correct it.

Natural gas

This has a calorific value about double that of the old town gas made from coal or oil. Gas is a very clean fuel with no harmful ingredients such as sulphur, and if correctly burnt will give no solid emissions, ash or sludge. Gas is a piped supply, delivered at a pressure which usually eliminates the need for any pumping or compressing before it is used on site. No storage of fuel is necessary.

Due to limited supplies of natural gas and occasional large peak demands, gas boards sell gas to industrial users on 'interruptible' tariffs. On such a tariff the user can have his supply cut off for considerable periods and to guard against interruption of production users have to store an alternative fuel, such as propane. This entails capital expenditure for the installation of pressure tanks, cash tied up in fuel stock, and space occupied by storage. These factors must be taken into account when deciding on the fuel to use.

Fuel oils

Although not so consistent as gas, these have undergone a process of refining where quality control is exercised. Basically there are two types of fuel oil: distillate fuels which have a low viscosity and require no heating in storage or at the burner, and heavy oils which (because of their high viscosity at low temperatures) require heating in order to flow along the pipelines. By volume the heavier oils have a higher calorific value and are cheaper, so that the cost per therm can be about two-thirds the cost of gas oil. But the cost of heating tanks, desludging etc. more than balances this saving except in large installations.

Storage for fuel oils initially costs far more than for any other fuel. They take up a lot of space and fire precautions are stringent. On the other hand, delivery to the point of use is easy and requires no labour. Although with heavy oil there is the cost of heating, it is clean in burning and there is no ash, but the sulphur content can cause trouble through corrosion.

Solid fuels

Coke, manufactured fuels, lignite or even wood are used as solid fuels, but in the industrial context coal is the solid fuel used most widely. It is the easiest fuel to store from the point of view of capital cost of storage equipment, but it occupies quite a large area. Handling of coal is both dirty and labour intensive and solid fuels have the additional disadvantage of producing ash when burnt, which entails removal and disposal.

Coal is usually the cheapest fuel in terms of energy content, but the handling costs often make it uneconomic in comparison with other fuels. On the other hand, coal is the one fuel which is likely to be available for some hundreds of years to come.

Liquefied petroleum gases

Butane and propane are used in industry for heating and other purposes. These are clean fuels with very little sulphur content. Storage requires pressure vessels sited away from other buildings. Strict fire precautions must be taken, particularly during refuelling. Sometimes it is necessary to install evaporators in order to achieve the high take-off rates where consumption is high, and this adds to the cost because heat has to be supplied to these evaporators.

SOME COMPUTER APPLICATIONS

Computers are used for handling management information, so that energy achievement can be recorded and compared on a month by month basis, and they can also be used actively to manage energy consumption. Increasing use of computers in design of plant and buildings allows energy factors to be more readily calculated, with more efficient plant and buildings resulting.

Computers can be extremely useful in process industries, for example in the industrial gas-producing industry, which relies entirely on electricity for energy, and with its plants spread all over the country. Computers can be used to measure the quantities of industrial gas in stock, and thus predict the production quantities needed from time to time against forecast usage. Having carried out these calculations the computer can go on to choose the plant or plants which are able to produce this gas most economically, including the timing of production needed. In this way production costs are optimized and over- or under-production is kept under control. Although it could be said that the overall amount of electrical energy used to produce the gas is not necessarily reduced, the computer is able to schedule production so that as much energy as possible is transferred to times when its cost is at lowest off peak rates, when the Electricity Generating Board is keen to attract the additional load.

Another increasing use of computers is in the total management of building systems, with a central computer used to monitor and control all aspects of safety and security (intruder and fire alarms) and the actual operation of heating, lighting, ventilation and air conditioning plant. Such computing systems may be centralized to the extent that one computer 'manages' more than one building, typical applications being premises owned by local authorities for health and welfare services. It is not even necessary for the computer to be housed in any of the buildings being monitored and controlled. The control centre can be installed in an energy manager's office, with monitoring and control circuits connected by land lines or by other communication means.

These are just some examples of the increasing use of computers to monitor and control energy usage, with the objectives of optimizing consumption and reducing costs.

FURTHER READING

Dick-Larkam, R., *Cutting Energy Costs*, Gower, Aldershot, 1977. An expansion of this chapter

Dryden, I.G.C..(ed.), *The Efficient Use of Energy*, IPC Science & Tech. Press. A comprehensive work of reference on energy utilization

Fuel Economy Handbook, National Industrial Fuel Efficiency Service, Graham Trotman Dudley Publications. A practical handbook on good practice to save energy

Illuminating Engineering Society Guide, Illuminating Engineering Soc. Defines lighting standards

Payne, G.A., *The Energy Manager's Handbook*, IPC Science & Tech. Press. A useful handbook on energy management

Windett, A.S., *Reducing the Cost of Electricity Supply for the Industrial and Commercial User*, 3rd edition, Gower, Aldershot, 1982

A variety of publications is issued by the Department of Energy, the Department of the Environment and the Electricity Council.

47 Office services

R S Henderson

No firm can hope to operate effectively, and therefore profitably, unless it is properly supported by all the necessary services and facilities that go to make up a modern office. These range from the maintenance and cleaning of the building to the provision of stationery; from well-established security and emergency procedures to the handling and distribution of the post. The task of administering all these services is almost always a thankless one. If all goes smoothly the service is taken for granted; when it falls down, everyone looks for a scapegoat, who is invariably the unfortunate office manager.

The office manager – always underestimated, at least as far as the importance of his job is concerned – finds himself managing by complaint. He is responsible for a large number of diverse and individual systems which he probably has inherited from a predecessor, and which tend to operate much as they always have done. He hesitates to examine their workings too closely for fear of causing disruption, and indeed is probably too busy to do so thoroughly and methodically until he gets a complaint from above. He is then forced to react quickly and as a result may make ill-considered changes with potentially disastrous results and certainly unfavourable reactions from the operating staff.

ORGANIZATION OF OFFICE SERVICES

In setting up an office services department, senior management should consider:

1 The person they charge with looking after the running of the building and its supporting services and facilities will probably have one of the largest budgets and workforces in their organization. The department may not be a profit centre, but it has tremendous significance in terms of total operating cost

2 The quality of the service provided by this department impinges on all aspects of the business, including the profit centres. If that service is efficient, reliable and flexible it will be a positive aid towards profitability

3 To maintain a high level of service the office manager must be able to predict future demands to be made upon his department. He will only

be able to do so if he is kept informed and preferably forewarned of all policy changes and decisions which affect his areas of responsibility.

These three points lead to the clear conclusion that the role of office administrator should not be regarded as an inferior occupation. It should have a clearly defined place in the organizational structure with direct links to top management. Only in this way can channels of communication be maintained to ensure that the planning of office administration is based on full and accurate information.

The scope of office services

Figure 47.1 shows the potential range and scope of the services and facilities needed by a medium-sized company occupying its own office block. For smaller firms some of these items would be reduced in scope but the range of services and facilities applies to all. Even a company with only twenty or so office staff will undoubtedly need an element from each of the main headings. At this level it will probably be the company secretary or his equivalent who will be responsible, but the same principles will apply to their organization and management as for a much larger firm.

Organization structure

In Figure 47.1 the range of services has been grouped under ten headings. For administration and organization purposes they could be brought together as indicated in Figure 47.2. There are obviously many variations on this theme, and much will depend on the size of the company and the complexity of the administrative services needed. However, the aim should always be to avoid having every query finishing up on the office manager's desk. He should be a manager rather than a supervisor.

He should be able to plan for the future, to budget, to introduce new methods and systems, to improve existing ones; he should study trends in the development of new equipment with the aim of phasing it in as the opportunity arises; he should train and develop his staff, particularly the younger ones, to take on new responsibilities as the need occurs; and above all he should manage the administration of the office so that it runs smoothly, effectively and economically.

OFFICE LAYOUTS

This whole chapter is devoted to the provision of efficient services to the office operation and how these contribute to the smooth running of the company. An essential element of these office services and one that is often overlooked or neglected is the responsibility for the layout of the offices. All too often layouts of partitioning, and even of desks, are inherited from a previous occupier, with cost dictating a minimum of alterations, and the

GHM

Reprographics	Telecommunications	Security and Safety
Printing	Telephone exchange	Security guards
Photocopying	Internal systems	Fire precautions
Stationery issues	Paging system	Emergency procedures
Microfilming	Public address	Industrial and com-
	Telex, telecopier	mercial espionage
	terminals	measures (e.g.,
		shredding equipment
		and counter-
		surveillance measures)
		Statutory requirements

Reception	Post	Central services
Main reception	Postal service	Typing
Commissionaires	Messengers	Secretarial
Booking of meeting	Document	Filing
rooms	movement	Word processing
Travel arrangements		Library

Staff welfare	Transport	Purchasing
Canteen	Company cars/vans	Stationery
Refreshments	Chauffeurs, drivers	Equipment
Social/recreation	Transport records	Furniture
First aid/medical	Car park allocations	Leasing arrangements
Rest room		Contract arrangements
Shop		

Building maintenance

Building:	Cleaning, upkeep, repairs, redecoration, rubbish and wate disposal, external upkeep (e.g., grounds and car park).
Plant and equipment:	Maintenance contracts for heating/ventilation/ air conditioning, lifts, window cleaning gear, day-to-day maintenance of plant, plumbing services, electric power and lighting, clocks etc.
Office equipment:	Typewriters, calculators, printing equipment, furniture, filing systems, etc.
Office layouts:	Planning layout revisions, alterations to lighting, partitioning, telephone and power points, furniture moves, etc.

Figure 47.1   The scope of office services

895

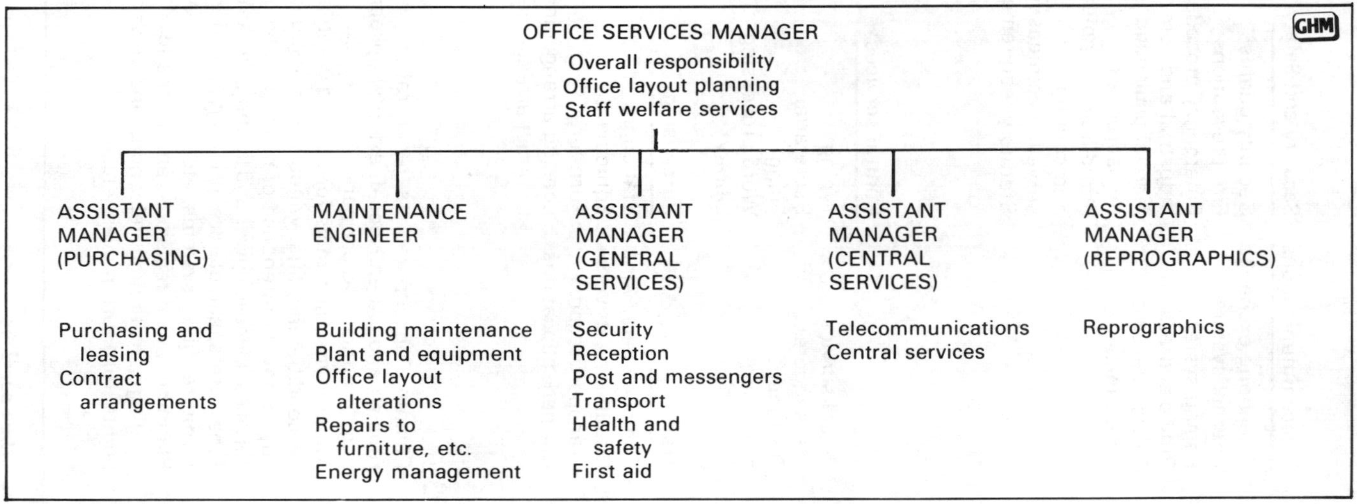

OFFICE SERVICES MANAGER
Overall responsibility
Office layout planning
Staff welfare services

ASSISTANT MANAGER (PURCHASING)	MAINTENANCE ENGINEER	ASSISTANT MANAGER (GENERAL SERVICES)	ASSISTANT MANAGER (CENTRAL SERVICES)	ASSISTANT MANAGER (REPROGRAPHICS)
Purchasing and leasing Contract arrangements	Building maintenance Plant and equipment Office layout alterations Repairs to furniture, etc. Energy management	Security Reception Post and messengers Transport Health and safety First aid	Telecommunications Central services	Reprographics

Figure 47.2 An office services departmental organization
This is just one of a large number of possible organizations which might be found in an office services department. Obviously the organization must depend on the size of a company and the activities which it performs; the arrangement shown here might be found in a medium to large engineering company

896

new users having to adapt their work routines to suit. Even when the layouts suit requirements in all respects on initial occupation, very few organizations remain static for long. Very soon, growth and/or changes in operations and structure inevitably call for modifications. If these are not responded to there begins an, at first unremarked, deterioration in the working arrangements.

Piecemeal changes in shared or open offices, even of an apparently minor nature, can have a domino effect leading to overcrowding in some areas and wasted space in others. It is a fairly straightforward matter to establish a routine whereby the office manager is consulted and controls all layout changes. It is perhaps more difficult to make sure that he has the authority to make his proposals work. In any event, a major reorganization or relocation exercise may overstretch his resources, and it would be unwise to treat this as part of the normal office services role. If an outside specialist is called in on these occasions, it should be to work with rather than instead of the office manager. The professional planning consultancy will need his advice and guidance and his detailed knowledge of the building at all stages if their schemes are to be effective and worth while.

The subject of office planning is worthy of a book in its own right, so it is impossible to give comprehensive advice here. However, the few guidelines reproduced below may be helpful to the hard-pressed office manager.

Office planning guidelines

1. Do not underestimate the importance of planning office layouts to meet individual functional needs
2. These needs change from time to time as new working methods are developed to meet changing market forces
3. Do not assume knowledge of how people perform their day-to-day tasks and how they relate to each other in a department or organization
4. The first step is always to study requirements by formally interviewing both the management concerned and as many of their staff as practicable
5. Base the layout plans on your analysis of needs. For example, private rooms, only for those with a high proportion of their time spent on confidential matters; more space in the open office for those who need some measure of privacy and freedom from distraction
6. Better to arrange informal groups of desks reflecting, perhaps, a team approach, than to adopt a schoolroom regime
7. Avoid rows of private offices along one side of the office floor with the open area on the other. This promotes the idea of 'them and us'. Try to site offices where they are needed and to create pools of related open space between them
8. Walkways and escape routes in open offices need not be straight, but should always be clearly demarked by items of furniture such as low screens and filing cabinets
9. Open planning does not necessarily save any space, but it is more adaptable to change. If properly done, it can result in pleasant working conditions for everyone.

REPROGRAPHICS

Reprographics is the business of reproducing the written word or picture. It is a vast and growing subject in itself. There is hardly an office without at least a simple photocopying machine of some kind, and sophisticated in-house printing facilities are commonplace. The reprographics function also includes the printing of plans and technical drawings and, especially in more recent years, microphotography (alternatively called microfilming or micrographics). Any but the very smallest reprographics department uses materials and bought-out services at an expensive rate, takes up a lot of office space, and needs equipping with costly machinery. Effective supervision of the department is essential in order to keep operating costs down.

Photocopying

It is necessary to be aware of the abuse to which the simple photocopier can be subjected, from the illicit production of private copies to the bigger problem of wastage by taking more copies than are really needed. In the same way as the original Mr. Colman is said to have made his fortune from the mustard left on the side of the plate, so must the paper and copier manufacturers be doing from the high volume of unnecessary copies.

The most effective way to control copy quantity – and quality – is to place every photocopier within a central reprographics department, staffed by one or more trained operators, and with copies only given against duly authorized requisitions. Under such supervision, the machines will prove more reliable, and print quality can be maintained at a good level.

In a large organization, a centralized photocopying facility may not be convenient to all staff, where the ability to obtain a few copies quickly saves the time of senior people and helps to promote efficiency. The wastage inherent in allowing staff free access to unsupervised copiers can be more than offset by the time saved. One solution to cut down wastage at local copier stations is to lock the machines, and provide suitable staff with keys. Another, less cumbersome approach is to provide machines for local use capable of giving the cheapest possible copies consistent with readable quality and reliable performance. Copies for internal use do not have to be up to exhibition standard. Where high quality or large numbers are justified, then the central facility must be used.

Photocopier technology continues to develop rapidly. The basic principles come in several quite different categories, each with its own multiple variations. Plain paper copiers using xerography (an electrostatic process) produce cheap prints at the cost of high technology and, therefore, expensive machinery. Copiers using coated paper may be electrostatic, photographic or with an infrared or ultraviolet source of light. In addition to wide variations in the cost per print, each method produces different degrees of response to the colours in the original document; some copiers will not copy faint blue images and others are relatively insensitive to red.

Many factors need to be considered when choosing a copier for the first time. Will it take the size of paper needed (usually the choice is between B4, A4 or A3)? Some machines can reduce the image if required, for example printing out an A4 copy from an A3 original. A flat bed copier is useful when books have to be copied (observe the copyright law!).

Apart from the number of copies which the machine can make in a minute (i.e., the copying speed), a telling factor is the time needed to make the first copy. Some copiers take ten minutes or more to warm up, with the result that they are left switched on all day to consume and waste electrical power and to emit heat and noise into the office. Some form of automatic or semi-automatic document-feeding device is often justifiable as a time saver, and it may also be desirable to include a sorter than can collate multiple sets of copies into convenient stacks ready for binding or stapling. One or two copiers even do the stapling.

As with the purchase of all office equipment, it is prudent to seek out other users of similar equipment and find out whether they would recommend it. The supplier will usually be willing to give introductions to such referees, although he is unlikely to be very open about sites where major problems have occurred.

The total cost approach is essential when choosing copiers. The starting point is to determine the number of copies to be made each month at each copying station. This is bound to be a variable figure, depending on seasonal factors and the level of activity in the business generally. In addition to an estimated average usage per month (for annual budgeting) it is also necessary to estimate the maximum and minimum numbers. Knowledge of the maximum number of copies will eliminate some copiers at the outset because they would simply be too slow or too unreliable to cope with the workload predicted. Manufacturers often specify the maximum capability of their machines, although they sometimes tend to be optimistic.

The reason for estimating the minimum number of copies needed over slack periods is purely one of economics. It is important not to commit expenditure to a machine which is too big for its job, since to do so must result in the cost per copy at low levels being inflated through the high burden of machine rentals or depreciation costs.

In the total cost approach it is useful to draw a graph for every machine under consideration relating the monthly copy volume (x axis) to the total cost of those copies (y axis). This total cost should certainly include machine rentals (or depreciation), all materials such as paper, toner and consumable spares plus maintenance costs. It may also be possible to estimate operator costs, although this is not essential and may be too difficult. Where alternative tariffs are quoted for the same machine, one graph should be drawn for each option. The curves will indicate clearly penalties payable where copy volumes are low and fixed costs high, in addition to the more straightforward cost per copy at higher rates of usage. This is a practical application of marginal costing. Photocopier salesmen are persistent people, unwilling to take 'No' for an answer; they are however easily impressed and intimidated when faced with a carefully produced set of graphs that provide a good basis for negotiating discounts and reduced terms in the face of their business rivals.

Printing and duplicating

Although some large plain paper photocopiers are able to produce fairly cheap long duplicating runs, spirit duplicators or stencil machines can be considered where low cost is the only consideration, to the exclusion of high quality prints. If it is essential to maintain decent print quality, then offset litho printing commends itself.

In the offset process, an image is prepared on a printing plate by direct typing or by photography. The image is transferred to an intermediate surface in the machine (and reversed) and thence to the paper (reversed back again). Thus it is not necessary to work with a reverse print master. Copy quality is excellent, long runs are possible, and the process is cheap. A skilled operator is essential for best results.

Once an in-house printing facility has been set up it is inclined to grow. Machines for sorting, collating, punching, folding, stapling and binding may have to be acquired. Still more expense occurs when artwork and typesetting capabilities are taken on. As these facilities and their attendant staff proliferate, so may the volume of printing itself increase to take advantage of the 'cheap' service available. It becomes easy to modify forms and produce infinite variations on letterheads and other printed documents. The result can be a very expensive and unjustified operation, generating high volumes of unnecessary forms and scrap paper.

No firm should embark on an in-house printing installation without a very careful study of its requirements. When evaluating the cost performance of a proposed internal unit, it is easy to underestimate the cost of the space which the department will occupy – not only the rent and rates but also service charges, heating, lighting and a share of the upkeep costs of the building. Although a small department may be essential to some companies, it may be better to use a local printer, and ask him to stock stationery and forms for availability against call-off orders.

Plan printing

Printing of engineering drawings and plans is almost always carried out using the diazo process. Masters are drawn on translucent or transparent material, and in the printing process a coated material is exposed to ultraviolet light, passed through with the original in close contact with the print, and the positive image is developed by ammonia. Such machines consume a considerable amount of electrical power – often in excess of 10 kW – and the heat and ammonia fumes produced have to be ducted off into a flue. The process is ideal for producing large-sized prints on paper, or on any other film or sensitized medium.

MICROFILMING

Any office manager responsible for providing office space is aware that document filing is usually very space consuming, and staff continually request more and more filing equipment. Indeed, it could be said that any company will eventually choke to death on its own paper files if the growth of such files is allowed to continue unchecked. Clever filing equipment, some of it mechanized, is available to minimize the space needed; this is achieved by transporting the documents within the system in such a way that waste space (e.g., roof voids) can be used. Other measures include the provision of storage space off site, in a warehouse or similar building, where files can be boxed and held available for occasional reference at (say) a day's notice.

A more drastic and usually sensible way to reduce filing bulk is to question the need to keep documents at all. Certainly, when a member of staff asks for an additional filing cabinet, he or she should be asked first to clear out unnecessary paper from the other cabinets and drawers in the office. Nevertheless, a considerable amount of information has to be stored within easy reach in most companies, and a cost-effective and convenient approach to the problem is to hold the documents on microfilm, which dramatically reduces the space needed for storage. Properly managed, access time to any required document can also be reduced, simply because the files are concentrated in a small area, and no walking is needed to retrieve items. Accurate and sensible indexing is the essential requirement for microfilm retrieval.

Microforms

There are several variations on the microfilming theme, each suitable for a particular office application.

16-mm film is used widely for the storage of complete files. The original documents can be any size up to foolscap. Longer documents can sometimes be filmed so that the image lies along the major axis of the film. By mounting the film in a cassette, and using viewing equipment with a suitable indexing device, rapid retrieval of the document required is possible. Approximately 1500 A4 original documents can be held on a 100 ft (30m) roll of film. The roll film method is only really suitable for files which will not be updated because the replacement of a document would entail cutting and splicing the film.

16-mm jacket fiche is a system based on the use of 16-mm roll film, but which allows editing, additions and revisions. Documents are filmed on to the roll, which is then processed and cut up into individual documents or groups of documents according to the file index. For example, one subject could be the name of an individual in a personnel records system. Using a special jig, the strips of film are inserted into transparent plastic sheets, which allow a grid of frames to be assembled. The sheets contain a series of horizontal channels to accommodate the film. Outdated information can be removed from the jacket fiche using tweezers. Additional or revised information is filmed and inserted in the appropriate place in the jacket.

Retrieval is achieved with a special fiche viewer, using an index system that first identifies the particular jacket fiche, and then locates the frame on the sheet by a grid reference system.

Microfiche is similar in some respects to jacket fiche, but the degree of reduction is greater. Many more documents can be held on one fiche, which is a single piece of photographic film of a size suitable for filing in a card index tray. Every frame is photographed onto the fiche sequentially to form a pattern of images in regular columns and rows. As with jacket fiche, any single frame can be identified by a grid system of co-ordinates but, since microfiche is a direct photographic image on film, it can only be updated by changing a whole fiche. Microfiche is applicable to whole books (since books do not get updated in general, and a whole book can be contained on only a very few microfiche sheets). The method is also used for catalogues and spare parts lists, the whole set of fiche being replaced when a new issue is required.

35-mm film allows larger documents, such as engineering drawings, to be microfilmed without the loss of definition which would result from any attempt to use 16mm. Drawings up to A0 size can be filmed successfully on 35 mm. *70-mm film* is used in limited applications where even greater definition is needed.

35-mm aperture cards are similar in appearance to data processing punched cards, but a rectangular aperture in the card carries a single 35-mm image frame. Usually, drawings are filmed on to a 35-mm roll, which is then cut up into individual frames for mounting into jackets cemented on the face of the aperture cards. Aperture cards can also be obtained in magazines, with the film already in place on each card. Exposure takes place in a special camera, which also develops and processes the image automatically. The advantage of aperture cards over unmounted roll film is in the ease of handling and retrieval made possible. In fact, provided care is taken not to damage the film, aperture cards can be punched and printed with the relevant drawing number and title, and mechanical sorting and automatic feeding to a printer becomes possible.

Quality control and techniques

With all microforms, quality control is essential at every step in the process. The exposure must be right, the original document must be well and evenly illuminated (sometimes from underneath using a glass table), the degree of reduction should be accurate in order to maintain the correct scale on reproduction, and of course the image must be in focus over the entire area. Developing, fixing and washing also require careful control to ensure that the film will keep without deterioration – especially important for archive micro-filming. Good conditions can be obtained using automatic equipment which is electronically controlled. Otherwise, a reliable bureau should be employed. An incidental, but extremely important, extension of quality control and supervision is the care given to the original documents during the process to prevent damage or loss. Obviously such originals must be protected until the microfilm has been processed and the image quality checked.

Storage and copying

Ordinary photographic film, using a silver halide emulsion, is referred to as 'silver' microfilm for short, and this is the material with the longest storage life for archival purposes – say up to fifty years or more. The diazo process can be used to make cheap contact copies from roll film or from aperture cards or fiche. Such cheap copies are usually of very high quality, with adequate storage properties for normal use. For widespread publication of books, catalogues and the like in microfilm, diazo copies are ideal. In engineering offices, 'satellite' reference files of drawing aperture cards can be arranged in a number of locations to give local access to drawing information while the silver masters are locked away for security.

Viewing and printing

A wide range of commercial viewers, viewer-printers and printers is available. There are also projectors. Many of these viewers are fitted with a retrieval device, allowing a particular frame to be found easily on a roll film cassette or fiche. Printing methods include xerography on to plain paper, an electrolytic process, and heat-developed image using photographically sensitized paper.

Computer output on microfilm (COM) is a system in which the need for a paper document is discarded. Instead, the data output from the computer is photographed directly on microfilm from a viewing screen. More modern techniques use lasers, and video discs will replace some microfilm techniques altogether, with information stored in digital form from which an image can be printed out or projected on a viewing screen. At this point the discussion leaves the realm of office services and becomes more a question of data processing.

TELEPHONES

Telephones are often said to be the life blood of a company, although they certainly can be the death of sustained concentration for the individual! Nevertheless, a well-run telephone service is important, particularly in the way calls are handled by the operator. The first impression a potential customer receives is often from that anonymous voice. If it is helpful and obliging, and above all seems interested in being so, the impression is going to be a favourable one. It will become part of the company's image and reflect its standing in its market.

There is, of course, much more to this than making sure the operators have good telephone manners. For example, the internal telephone directory must be kept meticulously up to date, or the image will very quickly be tarnished.

They should also be involved enough in the company's business to be able to direct a vague enquiry about a new product, for example, to the person dealing with it. This applies just as much to the full-time operators of large PABX systems as to the maid-of-all-work who is combined receptionist, switchboard girl and part-time invoice clerk/typist.

Another aspect of telecommunications which the office manager has to be aware of is the need to establish and foster good relations with the local British Telecom engineers and sales staff. They can be remarkably helpful over an unexpected need to move telephone extensions or to cope with some other crisis. Certainly their advice and assistance can be invaluable in planning a move of any size, a new layout, or the introduction of new equipment.

The subject of telecommunications is, of course, a complex and rapidly developing one. It is neither appropriate nor necessary to deal here with all the possible ramifications which might come under the office manager's wing. There is a wide range of equipment available to meet most needs, including electronic mail, radio-paging and mobile telephones. With the end of British Telecom's monopoly this choice has become even wider. Similarly, as electronic systems become cheaper and more commonplace, so will the twin technologies of data processing and telecommunications become more interdependent. Such developments are discussed in Chapter 49.

SECURITY AND SAFETY

Not so long ago security measures were aimed at preventing pilfering and, occasionally, thought was given to safeguarding confidential information. Now vandalism and even bombings can necessitate converting buildings into fortresses and, once again, it is the office manager who is responsible for seeing that the drawbridge is raised. It is a manifestation of rapidly changing society that buildings planned and designed only a few years ago for ease of access for goods and staff and the general public are now considered vulnerable and therefore ill-conceived.

As usual, technology leaps to the rescue and sophisticated services abound to cope with each new problem as it arises; protective film for windows, closed circuit TV systems to monitor the thieves' progress; anti-bugging devices to confound the electronic eavesdroppers – all these and many more are readily available to cope with specific security problems. The drawback is, however, that apart from the cost, they nearly all impose constraints and discipline on the law-abiding users of the building. It is important, therefore, to strike a balance between security risk and acceptable constraints. The office manager should assess the risks and make his recommendations so that management can decide the appropriate level of security precautions necessary.

No avoidable risks should be countenanced, however, when it comes to fire precautions. These really fall under two headings – minimizing the risk of fire breaking out and spreading, and the provision of safe means of escape from the building in the event of fire. In both instances close liaison with the local fire officer and strict compliance with his recommendations, however irksome, are essential. In renovating older premises these may well include having to shorten escape distances by the provision of protected corridors, or even the construction of an additonal fire escape.

Whilst under the provisions of the Health and Safety at Work Act the employer has a legal obligation to ensure as far as is reasonably practical the health, safety and welfare of all his employees, the office manager must relate the spirit of the law to the services for which he is responsible. For example, there are a number of very real hazards which can be created by the mis-use or irregular maintenance of electrical services. Frayed or trailing cables, the use of multi-socket adaptors, damage to electric cabling caused by inadequate protection at outlets and changes to electrical heating systems without consideration of current loading are all common examples of dangerous practices. Similarly, with the increasing use of furniture systems it is essential that components are put together strictly in accordance with the manufacturer's instructions to avoid, for example, accidental tipping of screens carrying storage units.

BUILDING MAINTENANCE

Chapter 44 deals with the administration of commercial property, but some aspects of building maintenance are worth touching on here in so far as they fall within the ambit of the office services manager.

There are, of course, the routine daily processes of cleaning and disposing of rubbish and waste and there is the contract maintenance of a wide range of items from typewriters to lifts. These, though, can be dealt with satisfactorily, once they have been set up, with only routine supervision and an occasional detailed check on performance. What is all too often overlooked, however, are the opportunities for preventive maintenance and planned replacement procedures.

For example, most office building leases have clauses requiring tenants to redecorate externally and, sometimes, internally on a regular basis. Apart from financial planning, or budgeting for what could be a major item of expenditure, it makes sense to plan ahead for the disruption that internal redecoration can cause. With forethought it can be done progressively, taking advantage of the inevitable changes of layout as they occur and which take place regularly in any dynamic organization. This is far better than expensive out-of-hours working with attendant security problems, or having to shuffle people around to create working space for decorators.

Also on the preventive maintenance side, it pays to include an annual wet clean of all painted surfaces in the cleaning contracts. Here again, this can be done progressively and should show a considerable saving on the redecoration bill. The same principle applies to toilet installations, floor coverings, kitchen equipment and so on, where the work can be carried out by specialist contractors.

CENTRALIZED SERVICES

Even a relatively small organization will consider at some time or another the centralization of typing and secretarial services. With the advent of the word processor there is now even wider scope for providing an efficient and comprehensive service. Here is yet another area which demands a proper study of the users' needs before investing in new technology. There is a wealth of information available through specialist magazines and so-called seminars, but most of it is devoted to describing what the equipment will do. Very little is said about how to analyse the need for word processing and how to match that need with an economic system. However, there are plenty of companies with direct experience of using word-processing systems, from stand-alone machines to complex intercommunicating systems. Most of them are quite happy to pass on the benefit of this experience, not only concerning the equipment, but also their staff reactions to it, and this represents a valuable source of information.

As with all change, the new ideas and methods have to be introduced in a planned way; the operators themselves should be made to feel involved in the process and some care should be taken over their physical working environment. The goal should be to make them feel that they are being brought together and provided with expensive computerized equipment, not with the aim of creating a typing factory, but to give them the opportunity of contributing to the business, whilst sharing the workload fairly between them and helping each other out as the need arises. It should be emphasized that there is no need for this centralized service to be restricted only to typing. With the right staff and the right telephone arrangements the group can provide a very efficient central secretarial service, handling messages, appointments, travel arrangements and so on for the whole company. The executive then should not feel deprived at the loss of his personal secretary; in fact he will get an even better service. The typists have their job horizons broadened and their working day is therefore more varied and interesting.

Other contenders for centralization are reprographics, stationery and filing as well, of course, as the more common services such as post and messengers, tea and coffee services, etc. In all instances centralization should be approached with some care and a great deal of planning. It is no good setting up a photocopying service with fast, expensive equipment only to find people wanting to retain their individual machines because they need instant copies and cannot get them. Similarly, an elaborate stationery store which is only open for half an hour every fortnight will soon lead to the creation of individual mini-stores throughout the office.

A final note of warning concerns the continuing need to keep an eye on the future. In this rapidly changing world, all equipment is obsolescent virtually on the day it is installed, but awareness of this fact can help avoid costly errors.

FURTHER READING

Books

Beattie, D. (ed.) *Company Administration Handbook*, Gower, Aldershot, 6th
   edition, 1988
Denyer, J.C., *Office Administration*, 3rd edition, Macdonald & Evans,
   Plymouth, 1978

Journals

British Journal of Administrative Management
Business Equipment Digest
Business Systems and Equipment
Management Services
Office Equipment Index
Office Equipment News
What to Buy for Business

48 Managing the electronic office

Ted Bennett

Until recent times, each aspect of office equipment development could be seen as a separate, clear-cut path of progress. Thus the typewriter was the forerunner of the word processor, early mechanical calculators gave way to powerful electronic computers, plugboard telephone exchanges were the start of a communications industry which now produces fully electronic exchanges, and the handling of stored information has progressed from large paper filing systems, through microfilm techniques to data stored in digital form on video-disc. Although their origins were completely separate, each avenue of development has ended with one common feature. In every case, the handling of information is entrusted to electronic circuits using microchip circuitry, with the information coded in digital form. With this convergence has come the possibility of communication between office machines – and between remote offices – which were until recently regarded as separate entities.

This chapter summarizes the more important recent technological developments, and discusses their role in the electronically integrated 'office of the future'.

WORD PROCESSING

The preparation of documents by word processor is, in essence, an extension of the traditional secretarial tasks of typing/retyping documents of all kinds to produce a finished product. The basic method of performing those operations is by using text composing/editing/amending software resident in a digital computer with an associated keyboard, printer and display screen. The document is entered via the keyboard, as in a normal typing operation, with the text appearing on the screen as it is typed. The format of each document may be predefined, leaving the operator to type as fast as he/she feels comfortable, without having to worry about tabulations or other format rules. If any errors in spelling, punctuation, etc., are seen on the screen, they can be corrected easily. The document may be amended, edited and even rearranged by moving sections of text from one part of the document to another. The final version is printed only when it is perfect.

Word processing equipment ranges from the personal microcomputer with a television screen and simple matrix printer, through a single screen/keyboard word processor with single-element printer, to a multi-station word processing installation using a comparatively large central computer, high volumes of disk storage and several printers. It is also possible to provide word processing facilities using a large mainframe computer offering time-sharing services and specialized software to support text manipulation; in this case it is not likely that letter quality printing will be widely available unless special arrangements are made. From being a simple replacement for the electric typewriter, word processors have developed so that they now offer, amongst others, the following facilities:

List processing, to produce, for instance, mailing lists
Sorting of information
Statistical/mathematical software packages
Text communication with other word processors or equipment
Spelling software, in various languages
The possibility of mixing graphics with text.

Use of all the available options associated with up-to-date word processing equipment, far from deskilling the secretary's job, has produced a new job classification of word processing operator – exponents of which trade can demand, in general, higher salaries than traditional typists.

Printing facilities can be chosen to suit the exact requirements. For drafts and other documents where high print quality is not essential, a high-speed matrix printer can be used to give a legible, but inelegant typeface. For letter quality printing the options are multipass matrix printers, single element devices (golfball or daisywheel), or inkjet or laser technology printing. These last two types use more expensive technology, and they are more likely to find use as a shared unit serving several work-stations until costs reduce.

The development of word processing has been rapid, and will continue. The software offered by the various suppliers will become more sophisticated including graphics and more advanced communications facilities as well as varied application programs. As the cost of microcomputer technology decreases, word processors will perform many or all of the functions of existing small business systems.

COMMUNICATIONS

Telephones

The most obvious basis for developing inter-office communications is the public telephone network. This is because the telephone system is already in place, serves all locations and handles large volumes of traffic. It is not necessarily the best communications medium for every office, but it should not be discarded out of hand. Of the two basic systems, analogue and digital, analogue transmission is only suitable for voice and alarm signal traffic. Thus all further discussion here refers to digital equipment.

Modern private automatic branch exchanges (PABX), controlled by a digital computer, offer a wide range of communication aids both within and between office buildings. It is possible, for example, to 'camp on' a call to an engaged number: this means that the caller can arrange for both handsets to ring when the line becomes free. Calls can be redirected automatically to follow a person around a building, simply by setting up redirection instructions from the base extension. Simultaneous connexion of several extensions to give 'conference' facilities is another useful feature. The exchange can be programmed to dial external numbers which are frequently called by a shortened number – the so-called 'short code' facility. Because the exchange is controlled by software, changing extension numbers becomes a job which can be done by the subscriber. When office removals take place, there is no longer any need to worry about the appearance or non-appearance of engineers: a simple re-programming job allows all staff to retain their existing extension numbers.

For cost-conscious managers, call logging equipment can be attached to the PABX, providing a record of numbers dialled from each extension and the call durations – a good way of detecting abuse of the system. The level of service from every extension can be predetermined, so that at the lowest level no access to the outside service is possible at all, at the intermediate level local public exchange calls can be made, and at the highest level of service complete access to the STD (subscriber trunk dialling) and IDD (international direct dialling) is allowed.

Further applications of digital automatic telephone exchanges will be examined later in this chapter.

Telex and facsimile

Another area of improvement is in the transmission of telex and facsimile documents. Telex is, of course, a very well-established method of sending information but it is also relatively cumbersome and fraught with difficulty when time zone changes are involved. Telex switch equipment, using VDU consoles to prepare the message, electronic media to store the text, and digital computer techniques to control the transmission of the text, relieve many of the problems associated with the traditional telex methods. The introduction of teletex transmission standards and systems will also ease the successful transmission of messages across the world. Facsimile transmission of documents has its place in the office world, especially where a combination of speed and the need for an 'original' document is necessary. The development and widespread implementation of facilities to store the document images electronically and transmit them at the appropriate time will, as with the telex, improve the acceptability and use of facsimile devices, as will increases in transmission speed.

Text transmission between word processors

Combining the use of word processors and modern telephone techniques opens up another area of aid to the harassed office worker. This is the transmission of documents produced on one word processor, via the telephone system, to another word processor which could in theory be across the world although it is more likely to be a matter of metres away. This is the famed 'electronic mail' system, although the term is misleading, implying as it does that every person has access to a word processing screen. This technique has great utility where it is feasible. This does mean that it is *only* possible to communicate with a compatible device; casual interchange of text will not be possible until all manufacturers comply with a single standard or set of standards for text interchange (or until the advent of a truly omni-function adaptor for word processor communications).

All-purpose communication system

The developing market in digital technology based telephone exchanges offers a potential for using these exchanges as message-switching devices for controlling a classical 'star' network for computer-type applications, allowing access to any 'extension' on the network, whether it be a telephone or a more sophisticated device. Such exchanges offer all the usual services associated with advanced telephone equipment as well as, for example, an electronic mail or 'message store and forward' service; they may also be used to provide links into the telex/teletex system.

When the exchange is used as a message-switching device, the particular mode of communication used is not material, the circuit being left open until one of the parties 'hangs up'. Other forms of local network rely on various methods of providing broadcast facilities for the propagation of messages. These may be electrical, radio link, or optical-fibre cables. Most current local area networks use transmission of addressed packets of data as their basic method. All rely on the recipient(s) recognizing data which is addressed to them and processing it accordingly. There are several variants of such systems in use, all essentially incapable of communicating with each other directly.

With the evolution of international standards for information exchange it should become possible to communicate with any site anywhere either because the different suppliers will adopt the standard, or because there will be a series of adaptors available to interface with the standard protocols. Whichever option is chosen by a supplier, it is always wise to determine this method of complying with the standards, as there would be great loss of flexibility if there were no such compliance.

Choice of supplier will also be determined by technical factors such as line capacity which will be discussed later in the section relating to how to implement office automation projects.

The Integrated Service Data Network (ISDN)

The ISDN is now being developed in several countries, and will eventually replace the existing public telephone networks. Network users will be able to use the facility to transmit voice, data, facsimile etc., over a single communications medium.

DOCUMENT STORAGE AND DATA RETRIEVAL

The basic storage medium for word processing equipment is the 'floppy disk', a device allowing up to 2 million or so characters per exchangeable disk. This is a not inconsiderable volume of storage when the sole requirement is the preparation and storage for reprinting of documents, some of which may be quite lengthy. The separate ('stand alone') word processor is not suitable for information retrieval, as this function is not normally part of the design considerations for this type of equipment.

The main requirements for storage and sensible retrieval of information are a screen/keyboard to access and display the information and a large volume of disk or other storage media together with powerful information retrieval software. The specific equipment requirements for text storage and retrieval will depend upon the environment and use to which the system is to be put and this will be discussed in detail in the section relating to project execution. Below we shall discuss in general terms what might be used for the purpose.

The major element is fixed disk storage, either in the form of the small, high density 'Winchester' disk or the large, high-volume disks as are normally attached to mainframe/mini computers. The maximum storage volume available with these devices will depend, in real terms, upon the number of disk controllers with which the processor used can cope without any gross degradation of service. It will thus be obvious that the larger and faster the processor used, in general, the higher the volume of disk storage which may be made available.

The software required to make effective use of the disk storage will increase in sophistication with the increase in storage volume. Access to text will, in the simplest cases, be via document name or reference. As the software becomes more complex, access will be via keywords with or without Boolean operations – this means that keywords may be specified in combination. The most sophisticated software offers 'full text' retrieval, or access on any field in any document stored, this may also include Boolean algebra facilities. At this most useful, and most complex software level, the processor used is either a large minicomputer or a dedicated computer which is often referred to as a 'database machine'. This latter device is used solely to maintain the disk files and to provide rapid access to the database.

Storage of text need not be restricted to disks. In some cases, especially for archive purposes, it is perfectly reasonable to store documents on magnetic tapes; access is slower but this need not be a problem. Other techniques for archiving may include storage on microfilm or videotape with microprocessor-controlled access via electronic cameras to give display on normal video screens.

For comparatively low-volume storage requirements, sophisticated electronic devices such as 'bubble memory' and holographic storage may be used. These give very rapid access to data, but are expensive in comparison to disks and are not really suitable, as yet, for large volume text storage and manipulation uses.

The main requirements of any document storage and retrieval system, of whatever level of complexity and sophistication are:

1 Physical reliability, especially for floppy disks, some of which are mechanically suspect
2 Consistent and reliable software operation; this need not be a function of the size of the supplier, but does tend to relate to the number of units sold
3 Predictable response; it should be possible to know, within reason, how long it will take to retrieve a document when using a specific retrieval method
4 Coherent support for maintenance and recovery from failure. Some suppliers provide systems built from parts produced by several different manufacturers and provide their own software. This can lead to problems
5 'Suitable' software products. If it is predicted that a fairly sophisticated method of retrieval is to be used at some time, it must be possible to achieve this without major re-equipping to do it.

In general terms, the future requirement, up to say three to five years as a minimum, for storage and retrieval should be the guideline for selection of the hardware and software for the system. It may be that in the early stages of system use the system is over-sophisticated; this is preferable to major disruption when it becomes obvious that the initial system is inadequate.

A LOOK AHEAD

There are a number of developments of which a great deal is heard but of which little, so far, has been seen.

Voice response systems

Computer systems which recognize and respond to the spoken word, either with vocalized output or a more normal computer response, have been in existence for some time. As yet, the main applications of this technique have been for 'command' systems in process control and aircraft control. Here the system responds to spoken commands to initiate specific actions. The general purpose computer system which will pause and respond to normally spoken sentences in a natural language is still some way off. As and when such systems come, fully developed, to the market, a new era in office systems will begin, offering the elimination of current conventional input techniques for the small price of clear diction.

Video-disc storage

Video-disc storage devices are available now, in a prerecorded form, for reading via video screens in the same manner as the already accepted video cassettes. For office system use, a reliable and cheap method of recording the information on the discs is required. When this device is made available to the general user, the storage of massive amounts of information in small, cheap, replicable plastic discs will be possible. At the time of writing systems costing approximately £80 000 are available for storing both electronically prepared text and data from paper media. The availability of video discs will not alter the requirement for transient data storage devices such as magnetic discs, because the video discs are not normally re-usable. Any information added to such a disc is permanent and, although it can be rendered unreadable, it cannot be erased and re-used in the same way as magnetic media.

Voice storage systems

With the advent of digital technology telephone systems has come the possibility of using digital computer techniques to store bit pattern representations of telephone messages for processing, or for onward transmission to another telephone handset. This is true message store and forward technique, giving great flexibility to a digital telephone system and allowing better communications within the office. The reproduction of such a stored message might be rather depersonalized, indeed it may not even be possible to recognize the sender of the message, but the message will be received.

Fibre optics technology

This technology is being developed rapidly and gives greatly enhanced transmission speeds to data transmission networks. This will be especially useful for local area networks in the office environment. The interface devices for fibre optics are more complex than for electronic technology, involving frequency division multiplexing techniques which are much more costly to develop and implement than the time division multiplexing techniques which are in common use.

IMPLEMENTING THE CHANGES

The introduction of any office automation, from a single word processor to a fully integrated system, can be a source of problems within an organization. These problems will include:

1   Provision of space for the equipment, together with a suitable environment
2   Recruiting, training and establishing salary scales for staff to operate the equipment
3   Organizing equipment systems, sometimes leading to quite radical changes in the office
4   Planning for the expansion of services as the equipment gains acceptance.

These and other problems will now be discussed in the context of carrying out a project to install office automation equipment of a non-specific type. The methods presented are applicable to any kind of office automation project, and to any type of equipment. Before actually starting, however, project planning is essential. Each stage of the project has to be identified and defined in terms of work to be done and the output expected in the shape of reports, plans, statistics and so forth. If possible, an estimate of the effort required for each stage should be attempted, in order to plan realistically. The separate stages will now be described.

Definition of project objectives

Objectives might include:

1   *Improvement of secretarial services:* faster document preparation, better quality of product, more efficient use of secretaries' time, increased throughput with the same staff
2   *Improved communications:* better voice, telex, facsimile and data processing communication facilities
3   *Replacement of paper files:* less storage space, easier and faster information retrieval, better security and easier transmission of documents
4   *Operational improvements:* more flexibility, more ability to cope with change, lower unit costs and wider availability of facilities.

Setting the project scope

The areas of the organization to be studied must be determined, based upon the stated project objectives. Both the different types and levels of staff, as well as the physical areas within the organization, must be specified and this must be communicated to those involved. If the reaction to the news is unfavourable, then attempts must be made to win over opinion, as the type of project under discussion is virtually impossible to implement successfully without active cooperation.

It is obvious that some project objectives, such as improvement of telephone facilities, will affect all areas of the organization, whereas others may concern only specific parts. Studying a part of the organization as an experiment, or proving ground for technology, is worth consideration as a way of gaining both experience and approval from the staff involved.

Studying the organization

Whichever elements of the organization are studied, the following are the actions from which a selection must be made depending upon the objectives of the project proper.

1 Produce a register of all the equipment currently installed; this must include:
   (a) Word processors/typewriters
   (b) Copying machines/printing facilities
   (c) Facsimile and telex machines
   (d) Computers – mainframe/mini/micro
   (e) Telephones
   (f) Microfilm equipment
   (g) Viewdata sets/services.
   Both numbers and locations should be specified.
2 Survey secretarial staff to determine:
   (a) Total workload, broken down by type of work – typing, filing, photo-copying, dictation etc.
   (b) The different kinds of documents typed: letters, proformas, telexes, reports, statistical typing, originals, retyping
   (c) The need for facilities not currently available
   This survey should include both secretaries and typing pool staff
3 Carry out a mail census, of 'normal' mail, telex, facsimile and any other forms of document transfer. The volumes moving between groups within the organization, as well as between the organization and its environment must be measured over a representative period, excluding holiday times and any other odd periods. The disposition of the mail should be noted, whether it is filed, read and destroyed, read and redistributed, passed on, etc.
4 If it is possible, a census of telephone usage should be taken. This will indicate the numbers of calls, successful and otherwise, both within and without the organization and any facilities such as call-blocking and re-directing which might be required
5 Audit the computer services available, to determine the information retrieval facilities offered and their likely expansion throughout the organization. Note that in many organizations information retrieval system use is fragmented. As part of the information retrieval audit, any library and paper-based information services should also be studied
6 Survey the staff involved in the study to determine how the installation of office automation equipment might improve their performance. It should be made clear that the object is not to automate the functions which the staff carry out; it is rather to remove bottlenecks in the performance of the mundane and release time for more productive effort.

Collating the information

When the survey is complete, a picture of the current information system of the organization and of its needs for the future may be drawn up. At this stage no commitment to specific equipment should be made, despite any particular items already in place. Following the digesting of the information, the next stage may be embarked upon.

Developing the strategy

A strategy for the provision of the required facilities may now be developed. The strategy will indicate the systems which must be developed, the equipment and software which must be used to support the systems, the development timetable for the installation of the systems and the staff training required for effective operation. The systems to be developed will be of several types and might include:

1   Advanced telephone systems based upon digital technology private exchanges
2   Shared facility word processing systems, either of a proprietary nature or constructed from a variety of suppliers' equipment linked with a local communications network. Cabling is often the most disruptive activity associated with office automation: it must be carefully planned
3   Powerful reprographics facilities based on laser technology printers; these may be linked to computer systems or word processing systems
4   'Electronic mail', based either in word processing networks or digital telephone exchange equipment
5   Connecting a variety of word processing, computing, information retrieval and telex terminals, large volume magnetic storage and printing facilities.

The costs of all the elements of the strategy must be estimated, together with the effort involved in all stages of the strategy implementation.

Strategy implementation

The strategic plan will include a series of stages and will indicate which elements of the strategy should be implemented at each stage. Care should be taken that each stage is completed and accepted before the next stage is begun, so that the implementation proceeds in an orderly and controlled fashion.

Post-implementation view

When the implementation of the project is completed and all the systems are operating, a review should be undertaken. Each of the systems implemented (for instance, a shared facility word processing system), should be audited

917

and measured against the stated objectives of that system laid out at the beginning of the project. Depending upon the results of the comparison, it may be thought necessary to re-evaluate the original objectives, or to amend the implemented system to meet the original objectives.

THREE CASE STUDIES

To illustrate the practical achievement of office automation benefits in a reasonably straightforward manner, three different examples are given below.

Productivity improvement from word processing

A survey established the case for word processing in several offices within a commercial company. A common equipment range which suited the general requirement was selected. However, the system was installed first in one representative department. The work done in this department was analysed and figures for time taken for each type were obtained prior to the change-over.

After the new system was operating routinely, measurements of increase in productivity for each type of work were made.

The categories of work and productivity gains are given in Figure 48.1. Also shown are relative proportions of different types of work. Evaluation of work mixes in other departments were then made and these results applied to them. It was clear that some departments did not merit word processing as originally thought, whilst in others the productivity increase to be expected was greater. It all depended on the relative work mix.

The company gained benefits where they were genuinely available and

Time saved (a)	Type of work	Proportion of total office work (b)	Weighted time saving (a) × (b)
25%	Reports	25%	6%
20%	Letters and memos	30%	6%
70%	Standardized letters	35%	25%
80%	Tabulations	10%	8%
	Totals	100%	45%

Figure 48.1   Productivity improvements from word processing

avoided marginal cases. Throughout, compatible equipment was used which facilitated both staff training and the achievement of later links to mainframe computing.

Combined data processing/word processing/microform techniques

This second example illustrates the evolution of a successful real time sales ledger processing system into wider office automation techniques.

The ledger handles tens of thousands of customers and many million invoices annually. For audit reasons, copies of customer accounts need to be dumped regularly and stored for years. Also, signed copies of the invoices as proof of delivery need to be stored for many months. All this storage was in paper form, requiring a heavy print load, much storage space and significant staff time in retrieving documents.

The account records are now stored on microfiche produced from a magnetic tape at a computer bureau. The invoices are photographed internally on to microfilm. Fast access to any given record is achieved by using indexes maintained on the normal real time system and by auto searching of the microfilm. A common reader is used for both microform media.

Figure 48.2 illustrates this system and shows also a word processor connected on-line to the computer for production of high-quality automatically addressed debtor letters.

This company achieved great benefit from space and staff time saving by introducing this system in a single department and it affected the work of no other department. The only disadvantage could occur in the area of equipment compatibility. If different departments installed other makes of word processor and microform equipment, problems of the transferability of skill could arise.

Combined text and voice communications

The company concerned consisted of a head office with a number of large branches and had the following problems:

1 Difficulty of tracking staff within locations for telephone contact
2 High telephone line costs and frustrated calls through trunk line congestion
3 Considerable 'electronic mail' within UK and worldwide at all locations using telex with resulting:
    high cost of equipment and staff cost in establishing connexion
    inconvenient input
    lack of consistent recording of messages
4 Need for timely status reports from branches to head office: for example for senior management meetings at 9.00 on Monday mornings a mixture of voice messages, dictation and telexes gave an unsatisfactory system

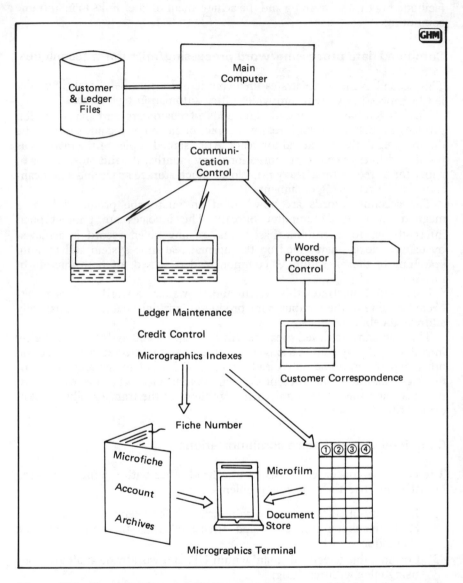

Figure 48.2   Example of an evolutionary approach to a combined word processing, data processing and microfilm system

requiring considerable activity in finalizing and collating reports prior to the meetings.

A study of voice systems identified the need for linked electronic PABX systems to facilitate staff tracking and provide other benefits. Traffic analysis identified considerable savings (£200 000 a year) from use of tie lines between locations.

At the same time it was realized that simple text input terminals with limited text editing facilities could be installed in all locations. They were linked to a message switching computer which had a central telex link. Telex messages in convenient format could be input or received at any location.

This equipment was no more expensive than the telex devices it replaced. However, in addition a company-wide electronic mail system was possible. Messages were electronically pigeon-holed at the central message switch and retrieved as well. This provided the basis for a much more timely and convenient status reporting system.

Transmission costs for the electronic mail system were very cheap. Pairs of multiplexers enabled the text transmission to piggy back on the same lines as the voice network. The two systems used separate frequency channels within the line and were physically separate at each end.

The benefits to this company were major cost savings associated with a more integrated communications capability. Since they did not have to justify the electronic mail system other than on the grounds of replacing telex and an inadequate status reporting system, they could confidently install the new terminals in each location.

Growth in other uses of the electronic mail facility has threatened the capacity message switch, but this is a simple component which they foresee will be easy to enhance. The system is summarized in Figure 48.3.

THE DATA PROTECTION ACT (1984)

The scope of the act

The Data Protection Act, although it strenuously avoids the use of the word computer, refers to data which are or have been, processed on a computer. The Act is also restricted to personal data, which refer to an identifiable, living, human being.

The requirements of the Act are, broadly:

1 That all personal data and the uses of it shall be registered
2 That personal data shall not be used, disclosed, or sent abroad except as defined in the registration document
3 That every computer bureau handling personal data must be registered
4 That the person about whom the data are held (referred to as the data subject) is entitled to know (on request) what those data are
5 That a data user shall abide by the principles of the Act.

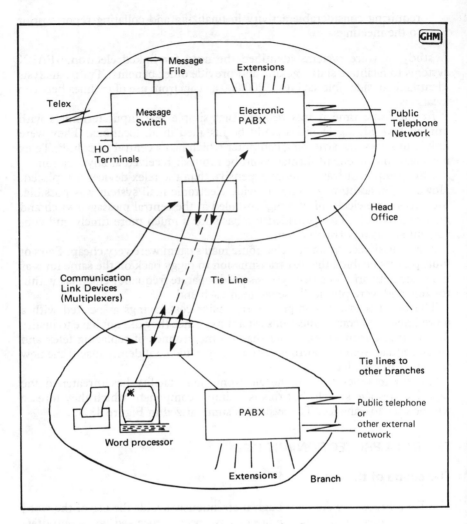

Figure 48.3   Combined text and voice communications

The principles of the Act

There are eight principles, based on articles of the Council of Europe Convention, and similar to the ten principles set out in the Younger Report. The principles are:

1   That the information to be contained in personal data shall be obtained fairly and lawfully, and shall be so processed

2   That personal data shall be held for only specified and lawful purposes

3   That personal data held for any specified purpose or purposes shall not be disclosed in any matter which is incompatible with that purpose or those purposes

4   That personal data held for any purpose shall be adequate, relevant and not excessive in relation to those purposes

5   That personal data shall be accurate and up to date

6   That personal data shall not be kept for longer than is necessary for the stated purpose

7   That an individual shall have the right:

(a) At reasonable intervals, and without due delay or expense

(i) to be informed by any data user whether he holds data of which that individual is the subject, and:

(ii) to have access to any such data held by a data user, and

(b) Where appropriate, to have such data corrected or erased

8   That appropriate security measures shall be taken against unauthorized access to, or alteration, disclosure or destruction of, personal data, and against accidental loss or destruction of personal data.

These principles should be followed by all data users, these being persons who control the contents and use of data. Computer bureaux are expected to abide only by the final principle, the others being the responsibility of the users of the data processed at the bureaux.

The operation of the Act

The data user shall apply to the Registrar for details of his data to be entered in the Data Protection Register. He will receive from the Registrar notice of acceptance or refusal, and may also receive:

1   An enforcement notice, telling him to change his practices to comply with the Act

2   A transfer prohibition, preventing data being sent abroad

3   A deregistration notice, removing his details from the Register and so preventing any further legal processing.

The data subject will apply to the data user for copies of records concerning himself, and may also request any errors to be corrected. He may inspect the Data Protection Register and, for a fee, obtain a copy of part of it. He may also make complaint to the Registrar if he cannot obtain satisfaction.

The Registrar deals both with the data users and data subjects and keeps the Register up to date. The Registrar must promote the observance of the eight principles, and give advice on data protection matters. He may investigate complaints, encourage the adoption of codes of practice and issue appropriate guidelines.

The data user must register his data and also comply with the principles.

Some definitions related to the Act

Data are defined as 'Information recorded in a form in which it can be processed by equipment operating automatically in response to instructions given for that purpose'. In today's world, this is a parliamentary draughtsman's way of saying 'data held on a computer'.

Data are personal if they consist of 'Information which relates to a living individual who can be identified from the information'. The information need not include the name of the individual; anything which uniquely identifies the person will suffice, (e.g. 'the Prime Minister in 1963'). The identifying information need not be held on the computer; it might just be in the possession of the data user.

Personal data include 'any expression of an opinion about the individual, but not any indication of the intentions of the user in respect of the individual'. The interpretation of this phrase is unresolved; nobody is really certain what it means except that intentions passed on to the data user from a third party are not excluded.

A data user is one who controls the contents and the use of data. The data must be part of a collection of data which are, or are to be , processed. Processing is defined as amending, augmenting, deleting or rearranging the information or extracting the information and, in the case of personal data, means performing any of these operations by reference to the data subject. This seems to exclude any chance reference to any individual within any otherwise non-personal file.

Exemptions

Exemption may be gained for a variety of reasons, apart from those of national security, government use and medical/caring services ethics, and data which are by law available to the public.

Exemptions for the normal business user are only concerned with:

1 Exemption from the Act as a whole:
   (a) payroll, pensions and accounts data
   (b) names and addresses etc. held solely for distribution purposes.
2 Exemption from subject access:
   (a) statistical and research data
   (b) data held under the Consumer Credit Act
   (c) all back-up data.
3 Exemption from the non-disclosure principles:
   (a) disclosed to the data subject or his agent
   (b) disclosed to persons working for the data user
   (c) disclosed in response to urgent need to prevent injury or damage to health.

In many of these cases, the definition is not explicit, and will have to be tested in the courts before all becomes clear. In conjunction with this, if exemption is to be claimed, it is essential that the user is certain that any future use of the data will not cause loss of the exemption. The most straightforward advice is that, if there is any doubt at all, the data user should register the data.

Registration under the Act

Each entry in the Register must include the following:

1 The name and address of the data user, and the registered company number if the user is a limited company
2 A description of the data and the purposes for which it is used
3 A description of the sources of the data
4 A description of the data recipients
5 A statement of any other countries to which data may be sent
6 The address to which data subjects must apply for access to their records. It is not a good idea to name a responsible person, as the Register would require amendment every time the name changed.

A decision must be made regarding single or multiple registrations. Multiple entries are simpler to make and maintain, and restrict the volume of data to which access is available via a single enquiry. As each such registration uses up about two man-days, multiple registrations may be expensive.

If there is any doubt regarding the particulars of registration, or usage of the data, then the opinion of the Registrar should be sought. It is better to find out that usage is prohibited *before* an application is developed, rather than be forced to scrap it afterwards.

The rights of data subjects

A data subject has the right to be told if a data user holds personal data about him. If the data user does hold such data, then the subject has the right to see the record. If there are errors in the record, the subject may also demand that it is corrected or erased. These rights may be enforced by the Registrar, or by the courts.

A request for a copy of the data should be accompanied by sufficient information to identify the enquirer and to locate the required record. A fee may be demanded by the data user, and each request for data will cover only one entry in the Register. If records from more than one entry are requested, multiple requests (and multiple fees) are required.

It is stipulated that a response should normally be made within forty days, except for examination results which may be delayed for up to five months or until the results are published (presumably, whichever is the longer).

It is not necessary to provide computer-produced output; hand-written or typed information will suffice. The data must however be comprehensible, so that anything which is coded or encrypted must be translated or accompanied by a translation table. Note that computer installations in Wales should be prepared to provide information in English or Welsh, but not both, to an enquirer.

Disclosure of data

Disclosure, in the sense of misuse of data, has two meanings under the Act:

1 The deliberate passing of data to a third party not declared in the registration. This also includes passing exempt data in a way which invalidates the exemption
2 Unauthorized disclosure, where data are passed through carelessness etc., without the consent of the user. This contravenes the eighth principle, and such disclosure could bring a claim for compensation.

The Act obviously requires that any form of data misuse be avoided by all means.

FURTHER READING AND REFERENCES

Harvey, David, *The Electronic Office in the Smaller Business*, Gower, Aldershot, 1986
Jarrett, Dennis, *The Electronic Office: a management guide to the office of the future*, Gower, Aldershot, 2nd edition, 1984
Price, S.G., *Introducing the Electronic Office*, National Computing Centre, Manchester, 1979
Saphier, Michael, *Planning the New Office*, McGraw-Hill, New York, 1978

For information on the Data Protection Act 1984:

Office of the Data Protection Registrar, Springfield House, Water Lane, Wilmslow, Cheshire, SK9 5AX. tel 0625-535777.

Part Nine
HUMAN RESOURCE MANAGEMENT

49 Manpower planning

E S M Chadwick

The need for companies to take a searching look at their future manpower requirements has become more and more evident, and manpower planning is more important for management than it has ever been. There are three main arguments in favour of manpower planning at the level of the firm. Firstly, there is considerable evidence to indicate that for some time to come there will be a shortage of quality manpower, particularly technological and scientific manpower, the demand for which is steadily increasing. Secondly, changes in manpower requirements in skill terms are likely to be much more rapid in the future than they have been in the past. No longer is a man able to learn a skill in his youth which will carry him through the whole of his working life; it is probable that the young, and the not so young man will have to change his skill once, or even twice, in the course of his working life. Thirdly, the ever increasing costs of manpower. Demands for higher standards of living and increased leisure are tending to push these up at an even faster rate.

Assuming that the *average* stay in a company of a newly recruited graduate engineer is twelve years, and that such a recruit makes normal, but not exceptional, advancements; then the cost in salary alone over the twelve-year period is likely to be (at current values) of the order of £180 000. If, however, one adds on the other costs of staff pensions, National Insurance payments, various fringe benefits, accommodation and office services, etc., then the total cost is of the order of £275 000.

No one contemplating the purchase of a piece of plant or equipment, with a similar life-span, costing that amount would do so without the most careful study of its suitability for the purpose for which it was intended, its capacity, the means by which that capacity could be utilized to the full, its place in the scheme of production, and the expected return on the investment. Few companies apply the same level of criteria or consideration to manpower. The reason for this difference in approach lies in the traditional attitude to manpower as a cost rather than as an investment. Yet while machinery depreciates and eventually becomes obsolete, properly developed manpower can continue to grow in usefulness and capacity.

The view that there is likely to be a shortage of quality staff over the longer term, or that one presently exists, is not universally shared. Some take the view that there is considerable under-use of talents and abilities, and that there is a large, as yet untapped, potential for the exercise of higher skills if only adequate training and education can be made available. This, in itself, is a very large subject. The objective of manpower planning is, and must be, to improve manpower utilization and to ensure that there is available manpower of the right number and the right quality to meet the present and future needs of the organization. It must, therefore, produce, *inter alia*, a realistic recruitment policy and plan and must be very much concerned with costs and productivity.

ROLE AND CONTENT OF MANPOWER PLANNING

Manpower planning has to reconcile two apparently different sets of views: those concerned with the accepted managerial yardsticks of costs, trends, projections, and so on, and those involved in the more traditional staff management approach of 'concern for individuals'. There are people, particularly in the older age groups who have long been concerned with personnel management, who see planning as a de-humanizing process. In fact, the contrary is the case. These two viewpoints are not in opposition but complement each other. The really skilful manager is the man who is equipped to consider the immediate implication of an individual case in a long-term company and national context. Decisions and advice given after consideration of both short- and long-term factors are likely to be of more value both to the individual involved and to the management.

Manpower planning, in its broadest sense, covers all those activities traditionally associated with the management of personnel – records, recruitment, selection, training and development, appraisal, career planning, management succession, and so on. But it is important, both for analytical purposes and ultimately for executive purposes, to disentangle these activities and to think of them as a number of sequential phases. It has been found convenient to think of three main phases. These are illustrated in Figure 49.1. They are:

Phase 1: The development of manpower objectives. This is concerned with the development of forecasts of the manpower necessary to fulfil the company's *corporate* objectives; with looking at the totality of situations rather than at individuals. In this phase, analysis, forecasting and the setting of targets is carried out in terms of total numbers, skill groups, organizational groups, total costs, etc. It is concerned with detailed analysis in order to identify and foresee problem areas, to assess future demands and to establish how those demands may be met. It is directed towards the development of manpower *strategy* as an integral part of company strategy.

Phase 2: The management of manpower. In this phase, the question is one of managing manpower resources to meet objectives and the development, in more specific and individual terms, of recruitment plans, training and development plans, succession plans, appraisal systems, etc.

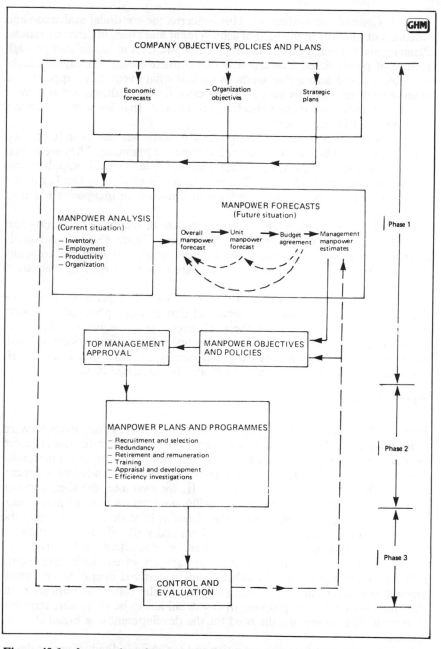

Figure 49.1 A procedure for manpower planning

Here, the three phases of manpower planning are shown in their logical sequence, together with the information feed-back loop which must result from the final phase of control and evaluation

Phase 3: Control and evaluation. This concerns the continual evaluation and amendment of plans in the light of achievement and changing circumstances. Planning starts from a given factual position and tries to look ahead through a range of possibilities. Evaluation in this context means thoroughly checking forecasts and forecasting methods against what eventually happens, and making such revisions as may prove necessary. Any planning activity must have a system for this regular checking built into it. In other words, planning must be a continuing process.

The components of the second phase are fairly familiar in industry and are often taken to be synonymous with manpower planning. They are a part, but not the whole. Phase 1, on the other hand, while obviously supplying the general context in which phase 2 must operate, is much less familiar and it is in this area that recent developments in thinking on manpower planning have occurred.

It is the ultimate aim of any complete system of manpower planning that all three phases should be fully integrated (see Figure 49.1). It is equally clear that manpower planning must be fully integrated with the company plan. Indeed, without a company plan, there can be no realistic manpower planning.

This chapter deals primarily with phase 1. Various aspects of phase 2 are dealt with in other chapters. It is essential that this first phase of manpower planning is well understood if the vital second phase is not to take on an atmosphere of uncertainty and become an operation entirely concerned with short-term tactics, without any particular strategy in mind. The equally vital, and again less familiar, third phase will also be discussed here.

TIME SCALE

How far ahead should one attempt to plan? Obviously, as one looks forward in time, forecasts become increasingly tentative. As a generalization, one can say that the plan period should be that which, having regard to the particular circumstances of the time and the activity, will give the lead-time necessary to deal with most manpower situations. If, for example, the time between the decision to re-equip and the installation and operation of the new equipment is two years, then one must look ahead at least that time to assess the manpower implications in terms of numbers and skills. If there is significant recruitment through apprenticeships whereby productive work is five years removed from recruitment, then for that category of employee one should look five years ahead. On the other hand, occasional operating or organizational situations can render some aspects of the future so unpredictable that, for the time being, planning in any detail has to be very short-term but even with such situations, the need for the development of a broad strategy remains.

It is also true that for some activities and for some individual career development plans, five years can be a comparatively short period. Consequently, in some individual cases, a five-year planning period, although only possible to cover part of the plan concerning an individual, is a *practical* period for looking ahead in terms of the actual action contributing to the long-term aim.

LIMITATIONS OF MANPOWER PLANNING

It is important to bear in mind what can reasonably be expected of planning. The aim is the reduction of uncertainty, but the possibility of doing this varies inversely with time. It must be appreciated that the forecasts covering the later years of the planning period are increasingly tentative. It may be more appropriate to think of the five-year period as comprising a two-year plan (a plan implying action), followed by a three-year forecast (indicating the broad path to be followed).

Manpower does not lend itself to precise measurement and docketing; it often behaves in a quite unpredictable way. The trading and technical situation is also fluid and targets and plans have often to be radically adjusted at short notice. Consequently, the manpower planning activity shares, in a particularly acute way, the essential characteristic of all planning in an uncertain world – it is a never-ending adjustment of expectations and aims to meet changing goals within a very uncertain environment. Its language and results will, of necessity, be probabilistic in nature and will *not* be inflexible commitments to some postulated single course of events.

Above all, it is not a new and revolutionary approach to problems that have only recently been identified; much of it has long been common practice in many companies. What manpower planning, as here described, sets out to do is to bring these practices together into a systematic approach that directs attention to the future and to identification of potential but avoidable manpower problems.

This chapter sets out to describe a number of possible analytical approaches which have been found to be useful. But there is no single universally applicable *system* of manpower planning, though the concepts have been found to have general applicability. It is for each company to consider the various methods which seem appropriate to its own situation. The checklist given in Figure 49.2 may be helpful in identifying particular needs.

ANALYSIS AND FORECASTING

It is axiomatic that no forecast is any better than the data upon which it is based and the judgement of the forecaster. It follows that the first essential of any planning and forecasting is data and analysis of the data in order to reveal trends, changes that have taken place in company activities and objectives and their influence upon manpower requirements. Only then can one consider future changes in company objectives and their manpower implications.

Manpower data traditionally tends to be organized with the primary aim of supplying information on individuals. For planning purposes it is vital that such information should be organized in a manner which permits

	Room for improvement	Adequate	**GHM** Good – no weaknesses
1 Top management and organizational support for manpower plans and programmes			
2 An adequate information system on manpower			
3 Anticipation of future manpower requirements			
4 Integration of manpower programmes with overall company objectives			
5 Anticipation of organizational changes and preparing for their manpower implications			
6 Recruitment of necessary number of well-qualified staff at each level			
7 Effective placement of newly engaged graduate/professional staff to make them productive			
8 Filling key middle and top management posts with well-qualified staff			
9 Management of age structure to minimize wastage problems and avoid promotion blockages			
10 Reducing wastage at all levels			
11 Providing significant jobs for managers throughout their career			

Figure 49.2   Manpower planning checklist

				GHM
12	Evaluating the current performance of all staff			
13	Evaluating the potential of all staff for promotion and of managers for higher responsibilities			
14	Providing sound promotion and career opportunities for all staff with potential			
15	Motivating managers to develop their subordinates			
16	Development of managers for higher-level responsibilities			
17	Keeping the remuneration system up-to-date and effective as a motivator			
18	Investigation into the causes and solutions of serious manpower problems			
19	Measuring productivity improvements			
20	Maintenance of a system that enables the cost of manpower and its contribution to the company effort to be evaluated			
21	Maintenance of a comprehensive and systematic programme of training to enable staff to adapt to new procedures and techniques and to equip them for higher responsibilities			
22	Maintenance of a sound and flexible organization structure			
23	Integration of the manpower management programme			

Figure 49.2 (concluded)

information to be easily available on groups, and in such a way that it can be sorted and arranged to illustrate not only the present position in any group or combination of groups, but also the changes that have taken place over time and to measure the trends that have become apparent. Various systems are available for this purpose from simple needle-sorting punch card systems up to computers. The decision as to which to use will depend on cost, facilities already available, the size of company, and so on.

The present position and the analysis of trends

In manpower planning there are three basic elements to be considered: the present stock of manpower; wastage; and future requirements for manpower. By a proper analysis of present manpower and wastage rates, for example, conclusions can be reached as to how much of the labour force will still be there in five or ten years time. Figure 49.3 shows such an analysis and projection by age groups. Analysis should also be done by category, department, sex, etc.

The starting point of any plan (and any control system) must be careful analysis of the position as it exists at the beginning of the planning period. Information will be needed in a series of permutations according to the needs of the company. The following are the basic 'building blocks' that will probably be needed in most circumstances:

1 Present total manpower
2 Manpower resources by appropriate planning groups, for example, sex, grade, function/department, profession/skill, qualification, age group, and length of service
3 Total manpower costs
4 Total costs by appropriate component elements, for example, salaries, wages, pension contributions, welfare, canteen, etc.
5 Costs by functions/departments
6 Costs indices and ratios (see control and evaluation below)
7 Total numbers related to sales, production, or such other criteria as may be appropriate, in physical and financial terms
8 Attrition and retention rates by appropriate groups, that is, overall, by function/department, profession, sex, age group, etc.
9 Recruitment patterns by age, education, etc., for each function/department
10 Resources of promotable staff.

The manpower pattern revealed by this analysis will be operating in a specific context and the manpower plan will have to keep this context in mind. Obviously a large number of subtle pressures will be at work and these pressures will vary from company to company. Many of them will not normally be of immediate day-to-day concern to management but they underline how important it is to keep informed. Among the questions to be borne in mind will be: the general position of the company in relation to

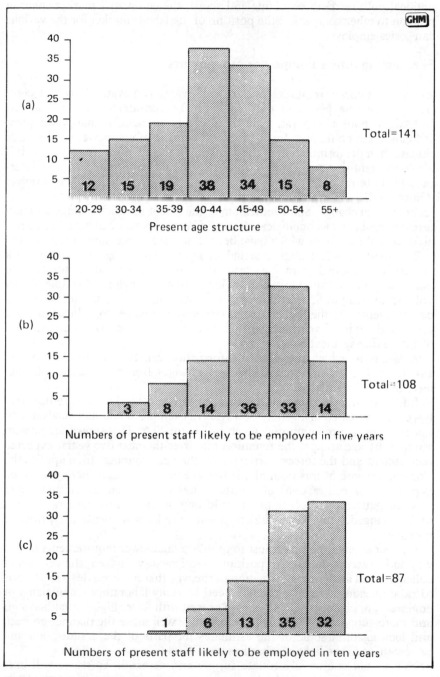

Figure 49.3   Age analysis

national policies, both economic and social; the company's market share in relation to other companies; the position of the labour market for the various categories employed.

Forecasting future manpower movements

Future manpower requirements are self-evidently governed by the company's corporate plan and they can only be considered in that context. Indeed, without a corporate plan there can be no realistic manpower plan. It follows that no forecast for the forward demand of manpower can be more precise than the formulation of the company's overall objectives. Clearly, it is also important that a company's objectives should be so stated as to be interpretable in terms of manpower involvement. The factors affecting manpower demand fall into two main groups: trading and production patterns, and technological change. Some indication of the extent to which volume and patterns of trade, and technological change affect manpower will have been gathered from the analyses which have been described in previous paragraphs.

The method of calculating actual manpower needs against stated work targets, as indicated from the corporate plan, will depend on the type of manpower in question. On the shop floor it may be a matter of simple output volume to manpower relationships, with due allowances for technological developments. At the higher levels, ratios of manpower to volume of work are less likely to be valid, and it then becomes necessary to define the form of future management roles.

A means by which this sort of information can be gathered is given in Figure 49.4. It is emphasized that any changes from the present position have to be substantiated.

Information, estimates and forecasts so gathered need to be carefully analysed and evaluated in a variety of ways. An example of one such analysis and a method of its presentation is given in Figure 49.5. This shows the present strength by age groups, the retention rate over the next five years, expected recruitment and the forecast strength by the age groupings then applicable. For the purpose of this example, it has been assumed that there will be no expansion (or contraction) of numbers and that present recruitment and wastage patterns will continue. Should any of these three factors change, or be changed, only the arithmetic would need amendment; the principle remains.

It is not enough, however, just to build up manpower requirements in this way and to accept the present position as satisfactory. Indeed, the very act of collecting and analysing information in the way that has been described tends to raise questions. Does one really need so many laboratory technicians, or engineers, or chemists? Could one do as well with fewer highly qualified staff and more support staff? Such questions may well make the planner go back and look again at some of the estimates for parts of the organization and review them in the light of what has been found.

Nor should one merely equate supply and demand. To do so will only perpetuate the misuse or under-use of manpower, where it exists. It is,

Categories of staff	Actual number at time of estimate	Expected number at year end 1986	Increases and decreases in requirements and year end balances				
			Estimated		Forecast		
			1987 − + =	1988 − + =	1989 − + =	1990 − + =	1991 − + =
Totals							

Estimates of staff numbers 1986-91 GHM

Functional sector ....

Department ....

Brief statement of reasons for increases and/or decreases:

Signed _____ Date_____
Departmental Manager

Signed _____ Date_____
General Manager

Figure 49.4   Manpower forecast sheet

GHM

Manpower age brackets	20-24	25-29	30-34	35-39	40-44	45-49	50-54	55-59	TOTAL
A Present strength	12	31	28	55	33	29	19	23	230
B Expected intake for 5 years	21	30	9						60
C Average retention rate (percentage)	92	94	95.5	97.5	99	99	97.5	87.5	–
D Expected retention of present employees after five years	8	23	23	50	31	27	14	–	176
E Corrected age brackets for retained employees	0	8	23	23	50	31	27	14	176
F Expected retention of intake after 5 years	11	24	16	3					54
G Forecast strength in 5 years	11	32	39	26	50	31	27	14	230
H Net change after 5 years	–1	+1	+11	–29	+17	+2	+8	–9	0

Figure 49.5   *Derivation of the quantitative five-year forecast for a function*

Grade group	Existing jobs at year-end 1987	Vacancies arising due to					Possibilities to fill vacancies			Surplus of promotable staff
		Retirement	Promotion	Wastage	New jobs by year-end 1988	Total	Promotion	Recruitment	Total	
Male										
A										
B										
C										
D										
Total										
Female										
C										
D										
Total										

Figure 49.6 Recruitment targets 1987, 1988

941

therefore, essential that the manpower planning activity goes hand-in-hand with productivity studies and other studies of manpower utilization. One needs also to give particular consideration to the composition of the overall manpower profile, the proportions of various levels of skills in each of the main employment categories.

Out of these studies and analyses can be built up realistic recruitment targets (Figure 49.6). This shows the expected vacancies arising over the next two years by grade level from retirement, wastage and additional jobs, and how it is expected they can be filled, that is by promotion or recruitment. In the case of recruitment, a further analysis by age group, as shown in Figure 49.5, is necessary.

What has been said up to now has been concerned with the medium-term demand for manpower. The longer-term picture must also be kept in mind, even though this may have no immediate influence. The factors here include the local and national environment, the size and shape of the firm in fifteen to twenty years time, its share of the market, what the market will be, demographic projections and the rate of technological change.

Equally, one must look at the supply position. It is no good setting requirements that cannot be met. A study of the availability of the different types of manpower will be needed. The ability of the industry and the firm itself to attract recruits must also be considered. This is true of both the short and longer term.

The question of supply is not nearly so difficult as it might at first seem. All the manpower that can enter into planning studies over the time-scale is already in existence; it is simply a matter of finding out where it is and what will be done with it in terms of education. The numbers and subjects of study in the top classes of education are known and since, of all things, the education system is slowest to change, reasonable forecasts can be made. Obviously, the size of the total working population has some bearing on this. Forward projections of the working population are prepared and published by the Department of Employment.

But as important as, if not more important than, the mere numbers is the matter of quality, and the ability of the education system and industrial training in its many forms to provide the skills which will be required as a result of changing technology. The problem of manpower obsolescence at all levels is real and urgent. A high proportion, possibly as much as 50 per cent, of a company's present manpower may still be in its employment fifteen years from now (see Figure 49.3). Will they have the knowledge and skills which will then be required of them? Manpower planning has thrown up the need for some form of occupational/skill classification which can be used to indicate the changing pattern of skill requirements and the changing manpower profile.

Projections

What has been discussed up to this point is the assessment of manpower needs to meet task objectives, the supply of manpower and environmental influences and constraints. Another aspect of manpower planning is the use of mathematically based prediction techniques to detect trends, to assist in policy decisions to indicate the futurity in present courses of action, to assess the probable future consequences of alternative possibilities. They have been found to be particularly useful in examining wastage – a whole subject in its own right – and the development of balanced recruitment policies directed towards a stable age structure.

These projections are not an alternative to managerial manpower fore-casting such as has been discussed but are supplementary to it. They are generally only applicable in larger companies but the approach, if not the mathematics, can be used universally.

For the purposes of projections, the basic need is for a bank of historical data over a minimum of five years. From such a store of information, it is possible to extract such essential factors as turnover rates in whatever category is required, related to age and/or length of service, movements within or between categories, the probability of promotion between grades as related to age, length of service, and qualifications. By this means one is able to gain insights into, and an understanding of, situations and the relationships which brought them about, to isolate problem areas, present or future, and the action needed for their solution. By establishing this picture of how the system has worked, it also becomes possible to consider projections of the future to assist in policy decisions by indicating the probable future con-sequences in alternative courses of action. There is, of course, no method of establishing a staff position which, in five years time, will *inevitably* be achieved; decisions can, however, be made which will, in all probability, approximate to that position. The aim is to examine a variety of trends and see whether the projected position achieved by these trends is satisfactory or not. The *executive decision* lies in deciding what position is desirable, what trend produces this position, and what action, if any, is necessary in order to produce that trend.

This method of approach, which is the one that appears most to engender distrust or, perhaps, fear of manpower planning as it has developed, has the object of attempting to see a problem as it really is, not what people think it is. In order to take a decision, one must have solved a problem, and to do that one must see the problem as it really is.

It is a matter of making logical deductions in relation to a situation in which some, at least, of the elements have been measured. Logical analysis of this type of situation cannot be taken very far before running into math-ematics. The choice is therefore either to use mathematics or to stop the logic short at that point. Everything depends on how much analysis is needed to solve the problem. If logic stops short, the chances are that the problem has not been solved and the decision is, therefore, likely to be wrong, and the consequences that flow from it are not those that were being aimed at.

The choice is not between something simple and good but something difficult and not to be trusted, but between something which gives the right (or best available) answer and something based on intuition and guesswork, the consequences of which cannot be foreseen.

CONTROL AND EVALUATION

Two broad and complementary approaches to the control and evaluation of the manpower plan are necessary, one in terms of numerical trends and the other in terms of costs and costs criteria.

Assuming that the planning period is five years, then the plan prepared in 1986 would go through to the end of 1991. In the autumn of 1987, the plan should have been reviewed and up-dated where necessary and extended to include 1992. The first step is, as has been stated, the review and up-dating of the corporate plan. This normally takes the form of a package of expectations and objectives, all of which are considered mutually consistent and feasible. The strategy for achieving these objectives determines the form of organization to be used and the amount and form of resources required, including manpower.

In this review, management will want to question the degree to which the various specific goals of the manpower plan were achieved. This can be shown by the use of a number of numerical controls and gauges, such as changes in numbers by total/department/function, changes in wastage (turnover) rates and the reasons for wastage, changing age structures and their implications, all related to the original targets set.

Another approach which has been found useful in giving a comparative picture of the contribution being made by personnel to the operation of the company is the development of cost ratios.

The concept of productivity is very complex in practice and raises considerable theoretical questions of definition and data. Nevertheless, a number of simple indices can be used to illustrate the changing contribution and costs of manpower. It should be emphasized, however, that these give no more than a 'broad-brush' view and should be treated with caution, particularly in making any sort of comparison between one function and another and, more particularly, between different companies. Reliance on a single index could itself be misleading but, taken together, they can give an indication of trends and the movement of manpower costs related to company activities as a whole (see Figure 49.7).

CONCLUSION

In a world of rapidly changing technology with an ever-growing demand for more and different skills, the need to plan manpower is as great as the need to plan any other resource. The prosperity and growth of any company rests, in the end, on the quality of its manpower and the extent to which their talents are utilized to the full.

Manpower planning is concerned with safeguarding the future, with preventing the loss of opportunities through lack of appropriate human abilities and the wastefulness of 'over-braining' the organization. It emphasizes the need for rationalization in keeping with modern needs and technological capabilities and the development of organization structures to match.

It is not some separate, rather esoteric, activity carried on by a few people

Year	Present	1987	1988	1989	1990	1991
Sales index-units	100					
Production index	100					
Sales proceeds index	100					
Manpower costs index	100					
Staff costs per sales or production units	100					
Total staff costs/ Total operation cost	100					

Figure 49.7   Index approach for assessing trends in contributions made by manpower

in back rooms in large companies. It is, or should be, part of the normal conduct of business which can, and has been successfully and advantageously practised in a wide range of companies in size, background and activity.

At the beginning it can appear to be a large and somewhat daunting task; it certainly needs perseverance and determination to achieve results. It is something which is best learned by doing. It is better to start simply, linking planning with an existing system, such as annual budgeting, and building from there.

FURTHER READING

Bramham, J., *Practical Manpower Planning,* 2nd edition, IPM, London, 1978

Chadwick, E.S.M., *Integrating Manpower Planning with External Manpower Planning and Programmes,* OECD, Paris, 1970

Pettman, B.O., and Tavernier, G., *Manpower Planning Workbook,* 2nd edition, Gower, Aldershot, 1984

Smith, A.R., (ed.), *Corporate Manpower Planning,* Gower, Aldershot, 1980

50 Recruitment and selection

P T Humphrey

No matter what has been written or said about recruitment and selection, everyone believes that he is an expert in this field. It is probably the one area of personnel management where 'the professional' is inevitably challenged by 'the layman', whatever the circumstances. Nevertheless, it is one of those situations where often a manager or supervisor has to face up to the problem of becoming totally involved in the recruitment and selection process without quite knowing how to tackle what is in reality a complicated task, in spite of the apparent simplicity of the ultimate decision to be taken – 'to hire or not to hire'.

However, before going into detail a few basic points must be established and emphasized. Almost everyone in any organization has at some stage the responsibility for requesting materials or finance in order to carry out their work effectively. These requests which can lead to heated discussions between superior and subordinate, or between peers, are essentially concerned with inanimate objects – 'vegetable, mineral or abstract'. But the request for a replacement as someone is leaving the organization, or for more staff to carry out the work, will inevitably lead to consideration of the 'animal' category. The true relevance of this is the ability, apart from the right of this 'animal' category to hold and undoubtedly voice opinion and comment, constructive or destructive, about the way in which the recruitment and selection process is handled. This 'answering back' facility is acknowledged by all professional recruiters, who ignore it at their peril. It is probably the one point which many managers do not appreciate, for when they are dealing with the accustomed human problems within their own job functions they are dealing with known people, in a specific and generally accepted framework. But job applicants are not subject to, nor do they hold, the corporate values (real or imaginary) that form part of the everyday working lives of those already employed.

The second point, which follows on naturally from the first, is that the principle of 'do unto others as you would be done by' underpins the total recruitment and selection procedure. The job applicant, whatever the level, expects to receive the normal human courtesies not only in the face to face situation but also at all other points of contact during the decision making process. In spite of the obvious economic nature of employment, a great deal of attention must be placed on the underlying social processes.

Thirdly, it is important not only to acknowledge but also to understand that the situation is not one sided as far as the decision taking process is concerned. The conclusion of a recruitment task does not occur with the decision 'we'll offer you the job'; this is merely a unilateral decision. The conclusion in reality only comes when the applicant says 'thanks, I accept your offer'.

In any organization there is at the same time both a buyer's market and a seller's market as far as jobs are concerned. It is important to distinguish between them, for while the same basic administrative approach is both necessary and applicable, the tactics to be adopted can differ widely. This is equally true of shop floor and boardroom situations. Bearing these points in mind the objective now is to provide managers at all levels no matter whether they are experienced or inexperienced, with positive guidelines to tackle the job effectively, and to gain, by the end of the day, a sense of personal satisfaction from a task well done. The recruitment process has its part to play in the public relations policy of the organization. The projection of the corporate image is reinforced through the job advertisement and even more in the handling of candidate response by the recruiters who themselves have a unique opportunity for reinforcing as well as maintaining the image. Many recruitment 'failures' can be attributed to the lack of consistency between the organization's perceptions of itself and those it projects through the media and its current staff.

BASIC PLANNING AND PROCEDURE

Everyone will realize and readily acknowledge that all organizations including one's own family must have financial resources in order to function at all, and to utilize these financial resources correctly some systematic methods must be devised and implemented to account for income and expenditure. But not everyone is prepared to acknowledge that the same principle has to be adopted in relation to recruiting and terminating staff, in spite of the fact that no organization can function without staff! The total cost of recruiting an employee of average skill can be assessed at approximately three to four times the weekly wage, and very much more for senior grades. So any organization that does not set up an effective system for handling recruitment is likely to put at risk sums of money in the immediate short term which under normal circumstances would be referred to board level for approval.

Statistical information on the numbers already employed in the organization categorized by status, department, works or site, and sub-divided in relation to occupational skills required, levels of work involved or merely by job titles, must be available in order to provide a reference point from which the whole procedure begins.

The subsequent steps are as follows:

Stage 1   Run up

1   Preparation, authorization and issue of a requisition for replacements or additional staff
2   Gathering information about the job
3   Checking against obvious internal sources
4   Advertising the vacancy – internally and externally
5   Processing of applications

Stage 2   Face to face – the employment interview

6   Setting up the interview
7   Conducting the interview
8   Administering appropriate tests
9   Making the appointment

Stage 3   Follow-through

10   Introducing the new employee to the organization
11   Following up the progress of the new employee
12   Reviewing and evaluating the recruitment and selection process.

On examination, even the most *ad hoc* example of recruitment reveals that the above procedure has been followed and that often the tactics/approach/mechanics vary in relation to the nature of the job to be filled. In many instances it is the level of the vacancy which is the determining factor. Therefore, where applicable, attention will be drawn to the different requirements in recruiting staff at the following levels:

1   Managerial, including supervisory
2   Clerical and technical
3   Operational.

STAGE ONE: THE RUN-UP

Requisitions

The need for a sound method of producing the right statistical information, such as number employed, labour turnover and absenteeism, has already been stressed. However, even in cases where this information exists, many organizations are quite indifferent to the way in which requests for replacement or additional staff are made. In many respects the underlying attitudes which permitted this have been altered by economic circumstances. Closer scrutiny of labour costs is taking place and the requisition for staff at all levels has almost the same cachet now as the capital requisition.

Information on a staff requisition form should include:

1   Name and location of originating department
2   Job title

3 Main job function
4 Salary or grade
5 Reason for requisition
   (*a*) Replacement
   (*b*) New appointment
   (*c*) Additional appointment
6 Required by: (date)
7 Signatures . . . . Department Head: Authorized date

While it is appreciated that it does take a certain (minimal) amount of managerial time to complete such a requisition, nevertheless its value to the person responsible for recruitment is incalculable. The main advantage is that it leaves no room for doubt. No one has to rely on the recollection of what was said about the job during a lunch-time conversation which ranged from detailed shop talk through gossip to personal letting hair down. Far too much valuable managerial time can be wasted in reference back by telephone or by personal visit to verify the position. Certainly the time of the recruiter can be spent to better effect in the next step of the process.

Job information

A great deal of confusion exists over the different terms used in this area. The term 'job description' means different things to different people, and indeed the context in which the term is used can alter its apparent meaning. Nevertheless an attempt has been made by the Department of Employment in its publication *Glossary of Training Terms* to standardize usage of such terms:

> A *job description* is a broad statement of the purpose, scope, duties and responsibilities of a particular job.
> A *job specification* is a detailed statement of the physical and mental activities in a job.

However, jobs must be viewed as part of a dynamic organization, with the result (as so many management writers have said) that the job description presents at best only a point-in-time interpretation. Consequently many managers who inevitably feel 'pushed' in the everyday situation will question the necessity of having a job description at all. But there are simple operational reasons which can help in the argument to overcome such resistance. These are:

1 The job description acts as a basic means of communication between the manager and the recruiter as far as the position to be filled is concerned
2 It is an invaluable mechanism for discussing and finalizing the tactical approach to the selection process
3 It can yield vital information for the candidates who have come to have a high level of expectation in terms of job information. This certainly

has a useful 'plus effect' in promoting confidence about the organization amongst the candidates

4   It ensures that there is an accepted factual basis from which information can be selected for advertising purposes

5   Finally it provides the reference point against which all decisions taken and judgements made can be evaluated.

Time sensibly spent on this important preparatory work can yield significant dividends in preventing over-interviewing and indeed in ensuring that advertising and other expense is used to maximum effect.

The job description

What information, therefore, needs to be included in the job description? The following items are essential no matter what level of appointment is being considered:

1   Job title: this must be self explanatory wherever possible and certainly where either unusual technical terms or terms specific to the organization are used, adequate explanation must be given

2   Name of department: as in (1)

3   Accountability: the job title of the person to whom the job holder is responsible

4   Main job function: a brief but lucid statement of the purpose of the job

5   Responsibilities for people and/or equipment. No need to detail every nut and bolt, but include categories and numbers of people to be supervised together with major items of equipment.

Additional items are required when considering managerial, supervisory, or technical positions. These include:

6   Limits of authority – particularly in relation to spending money

7   Levels of contact – this is of special importance in a multi-divisional organization and with working relationships outside the organization.

Useful questions to keep in mind during this process of gathering information and writing the job description include:

1   Is the informant's statement accurate?

2   What degree of bias is contained in the statement?

3   Who can provide a second opinion?

4   Does the written description contain all the relevant facts?

5   Is it accurate?

6   Can the layman understand it? (In other words is it too simple or too complicated?)

The job specification

The job description now has to be extended and interpreted specifically in relation to the physical and mental activities of the job, and the consequent demands to be made on the job holder.

While it might appear that there is considerable difference in requirements at the various levels of appointment, nevertheless, five basic categories of the job specification can be defined as follows:

1 Qualifications, knowledge appropriate to the job
2 Specific skills, abilities and aptitudes required
3 Experience required
4 Personal attributes
5 Physical attributes.

These categories can be qualified as appropriate for each selection by a scale of relevance – vital/desirable/of no consequence.

Qualifications. This category is the bane of every recruiter's life, for more heat can be generated over this than almost any other topic to do with recruitment. The standpoint to take must be 'is it relevant?' Is a PhD really vital to do the job of sales manager in an electronics firm? It might be. On the other hand, it is certainly not a vital qualification for the sales manager with a confectionery firm. A sense of reality must be maintained, for it is just as easy to be swayed by degrees and professional qualifications as it is by medals and decorations. Indeed the relevance of City and Guilds qualifications to the craftsman and technician, is probably more deserving of the recruiter's attention than has been the case in the past.

Instead of qualifications it is often more advisable to list areas of knowledge which are required, e.g. plastic injection moulding for a production manager, standard costing for a senior cost clerk, export procedures for a shipping clerk.

Specific skills, abilities and aptitudes. This category is not be regarded as a rag-bag for glossy management 'in' phrases, which result merely in directing attention away from the main purpose. Rather the intention is to define accurately (and quantify if at all possible) those factors which are regarded as necessary to achieving success in the job. For instance the skills required in negotiating with trade union officials, or the different skills required in the negotiation of commercial contracts with suppliers, must be stated in the appropriate specifications. Abilities to be considered can include the ability to sell 'an idea' or a product, or even the ability to see 'the wood for the trees'. Aptitudes that readily spring to mind are verbal, numerical and mechanical, where great strides have been made in assessing and quantifying them among the population at large. All this must be geared to reality, and fanciful ideas of what might be required should be discounted. Simplicity really is the keynote in this section.

Experience required. This is most important, and every attempt should be made to build up an accurate picture of the previous experience required. Accuracy in this respect can often lead to better advertisements, easier preselection and more searching interviews. What kind of detail then is necessary? Early 'formative years' experience – apprenticeships, studentships, exposure to more than one commercial or industrial situation, or maybe service in the Armed Forces or Merchant Navy.

First post of responsibility – chargehand, section leader – technical responsibility, e.g. in chemistry laboratory, secretary to a departmental manager, territory salesman. Subsequent responsibility requirements can then be added depending on the nature and level of the post being specified.

Indeed a relationship must be established between the foregoing and the environments in which the experience was gained. For instance with the post of foundry manager, experience of working with specified materials or in making a certain size of castings is very relevant. So also is information concerning the general standing of the companies or organizations in which the experience was gained.

The other most important aspect of the experience required is in relation to the major tasks of the job. This is just as important at operational as well as the other levels where, for example, garage fitters in general are not experienced in maintaining high-speed packing lines at peak performance. Another example can be taken from a supervisory situation which calls for experience in handling a large department of 600 employees. However, unless it is specified whether the employees are all males or all females, there is considerable scope for some fascinating misconceptions!

Personal attributes. More attention is being paid now to this category. The impact of the new individual on an existing work group and vice versa can be vital, particularly where incentives are based on group performance. Some attempt must be made to analyse the 'chemistry' of the situation – acceptability is probably the key word in this context.

However, on occasions it may well be absolutely necessary to specify what might appear to be unwelcome attributes. Abrasiveness is one such attribute which nevertheless can be vital in stimulating complacent teams at all levels. Preparedness to accept a challenge, to work under trying circumstances, or to subordinate one's own convictions in certain situations are other examples.

Physical attributes. A great deal of emphasis has been placed, through legislation on the employment of the disabled. This is more obvious in relation to physical disabilities, but it is often found that only lip service is being paid to the mental health aspects of the working situation. The question of stress and the individual's capacity to absorb stress is very important, especially at certain decision making levels; also where working hours (such as 12-hour shifts in noisy, dusty conditions, or train or aeroplane crews having to 'stop over') can have a serious effect on an individual's necessary domestic or social relationships.

These attributes must be specified accordingly and whenever possible professional advice must be obtained. The amateur doctor or psychologist can do untold harm, and such an occurrence must be avoided.

Having gone through all these steps in describing the job and obtaining the specification, a firm basis has been established. The recruiter can now proceed with great confidence to find 'Mr or Ms Right' for the post in question.

Internal sources

Many companies still have the tendency to overlook the bank of talent contained in their existing work forces despite publicity aimed at management succession plans, or schemes for 'growing your own'. It is therefore very important to look inwards to try to identify potential internal candidates from all parts of the enterprise. In doing this the political pressures of the organization will come into full play, and therefore it is essential to maintain a very independent stance throughout the exercise. This independence is sustained by the very nature of the factual information contained in the job description and the subsequent specification. Nevertheless if potential internal candidates are found, it is vital that they are subjected to the full selection process. This must not be regarded as an act of 'bloody mindedness' or 'bureaucracy', for its very purpose is to safeguard, for the organization, the integrity of the process itself as well as of all those who play a part in it, especially the candidates.

Advertising

The job advertising market is now a multi-million pound business, and inevitably it produces fads and fashions from time to time. Special job advertising agencies have been set up, and selection consultants, office staff bureaux and appointment registers have followed the trend by extending the range of services available. A great deal of material has been published on the subject and indeed many professional recruiters, depending on their own personal inclinations, are either disappointed or delighted if their daily postbag does not include at least one printed circular on job advertising.

The main purpose in advertising a job is to attract sufficient candidates of the right calibre, thereby securing a reasonable field from which to choose the most appropriate person for that job. How does one tackle this attraction process?

1 Define the audience (i.e. the type of people to be reached)
2 Decide on the means and establish the cost of making the contact
3 Write the message
4 Monitor the results.

The audience

The level and nature of the position to be filled will largely define the audience both in terms of volume and geographical spread. At the operational level there is on most occasions a local audience which can be tapped, but from time to time instances occur when special skills are sought, which are not available from the local audience. When this happens, some preliminary investigation is called for, in order to establish the location of the required audience as well as the potential available. This also applies in the clerical and technical level, though there is a tendency for technical people to restrict their own availability by becoming too clearly identified with particular processes, even within the one organization. However, this does not seem to be the case with computer staff, whose skills and knowledge have almost universal application and whose mobility transcends national boundaries.

It is at managerial level that the audience becomes national in character. It is also pertinent to define the audience at this level in broad functional terms – e.g. accountants, engineers, buyers. In addition, consideration must be given to defining current salary levels from which potential candidates can be drawn.

The means

A great deal of detailed information from many sources is available to the recruiter on such matters as circulation of papers or publications of professional bodies, types of people who can be reached and the costs involved.

Decisions therefore have to be made on the worth of national coverage against local coverage, the amount of space needed and whether any apparent extraneous points, i.e. company image, or wider public relations exercise, need to be taken into account. While it seems natural to turn to press advertising, consideration must also be given to other methods. These can include:

1 Television or cinema advertisements
2 Posters in places where the appropriate audience is likely to congregate – newsagents, public halls, schools and colleges
3 Leaflet distributions, especially on housing estates
4 Word of mouth – with the inevitable discount for mis-statements
5 Notice boards outside the place of work
6 Notice boards inside the place of work
7 Job Centres
8 'Recruitment circus' i.e. using a caravan as a travelling recruitment centre, e.g., for the armed forces
9 Use of a pre-recorded message on tape or video which can be distributed.

Most of the above means are more appropriate when considerable numbers of people are required at the same time, especially when a new site is being manned or expansion is taking place. The 'milk round' for graduate recruitment has become firmly established as part of Britain's recruitment scene. Most organizations involved use a number of the above methods in a variety of combinations, depending on their own requirements. Eventually and inevitably cost must play its part in the final decision.

The message

Above all simplicity is the keynote, together with the need to use technical terms on a restricted but meaningful basis. There is certainly an art in constructing the message, for a basic emotional appeal to the audience is necessary. However, not only must one present this appeal, but also sufficient hard information. These two together must make the appropriate candidates reach for their writing pads, cause them to telephone, or make them sufficiently curious to make a personal visit. However, the message must be tailored to suit the means chosen. Consideration must also be given to technical detail, especially size of print, headlining, number of words that can be used, for the message includes everything within the defined physical boundaries of the medium, whether it be words, white or black space, line drawings, or company symbols. Indeed from time to time it is necessary to consider whether or not it is important to write in English or another language. But advice on many of these details is readily available from advertising agencies and public relations consultants. Most organizations have working relationships with services of this kind, either on a local or national basis. A great deal of help can be obtained from such sources, particularly on technical matters.

The results

It is extremely useful to keep a record of the response to advertisements whatever the means used. This enables the user to evaluate in financial terms the relevance of certain media in reaching the required audience. The main statistic is 'cost per reply' which can be refined in relation to numbers interviewed, candidates shortlisted and appointed from that particular source. A relatively simple form can be designed and maintained at negligible cost by a clerk or a secretary. The type of information required includes:

1 Appointment title
2 Media used
3 Size of advertisement
4 Cost
5 Number of replies
6 Cost per reply
7 Numbers interviewed
8 Numbers shortlisted
9 Numbers appointed.

It is quite surprising how useful this information can be, not only in relation to developing realistic advertising budgets but also in settling arguments and destroying preconceived ideas.

Equally at this stage use can be made of the advertising agency in obtaining comparative data on a confidential basis from other agency clients, in order to place one's own data in a wider and perhaps more meaningful context.

Processing of applications

The greatest sin in recruitment is not so much to lose an application (which is bad enough) but to ignore it, to leave it unacknowledged. Most applicants are prepared for the occasional 'mislaying' of letters, but noone will tolerate being ignored. This again is in the realm of extending natural courtesies to the people who have been sufficiently interested to respond to the message.

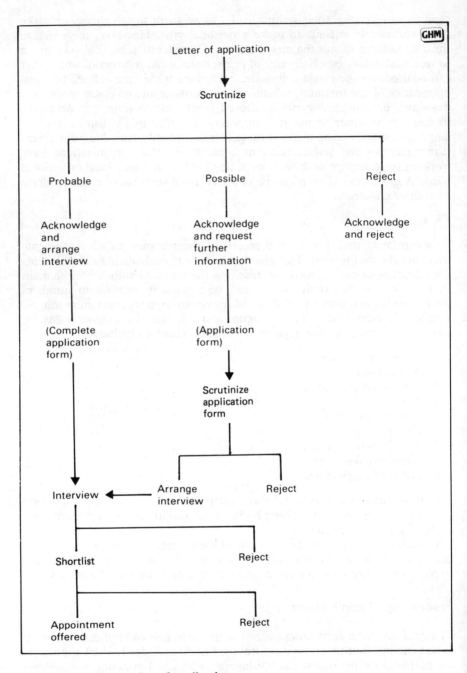

Figure 50.1 Processing of applications

Keeping track of applications over the selection period which can extend on occasions to several months demands a good administrative system, preferably one which dovetails with the sorting process. A suggested outline appears in Figure 50.1.

Most organizations revise their application forms from time to time, but it is important to remember that the form itself can be so designed to promote effective administration by allocating space for action signals at appropriate points.

With the advent of word processing there is an even stronger argument for having individually addressed standard letters. The amount of time that can be saved is considerable, apart from the important question of maintaining cordial relations with the candidates. Admittedly a certain amount of time is taken up initially in constructing standard letters, but it then avoids the necessity for dictating individual replies. This is doubly relevant when 50 to 60 replies are received and demand equal attention. The major standard letters should cover:

1 Acknowledgements of receipt of application
2 Invitation to interview
3 Request for further information
4 Rejection

A well thought out and well tried system will not only keep candidates and recruiter happy, but will also avoid the unwelcome letter to the chairman from an aggrieved candidate, which will inevitably lead to an embarrassing post mortem!

STAGE TWO: FACE TO FACE: THE EMPLOYMENT INTERVIEW

Up to now all work on which the recruiter has been engaged has been directed inwardly on the job to be filled and outwardly only in terms of the audience to be contacted. However, the next stage – 'face to face' – is the one where many managers feel quite exposed. Confrontation is a large part of any manager's job, but it tends to be in a specific commercial or operational context where individuals are aware of the institutional constraints which surround the meeting. The employment situation cannot be classified in the same way, and therefore a framework must be constructed and a number of ground rules established.

However, before discussing the framework in more detail some explanation is necessary in order to highlight the special nature of the employment interview as compared with other aspects of confrontation. First of all, for any situation to be described as an interview it must meet the following criteria:

1 It is a tool of the communication process
2 It is a vehicle for the transmission of information from one person to another

3 It focuses upon specific subject matter that is relevant to its situation, occasion and purpose
4 It requires the participation of at least two people who interact freely with each other
5 It is initiated to achieve one or several objectives
6 It takes place in a particular physical and social setting
7 It occurs as part of a procedural sequence of events.

Having established the intrinsic nature of the interview, a further simple classification test can take place. It is for:

1 Information exchange: simple acquisition or dispersion, taking down details of a person's career history, obtaining information on attitudes – sampling for market research purposes or opinion surveys
2 Problem solving: aimed at resolving conflict; changing attitudes, altering behaviour patterns; career guidance
3 Decision making: objective demands agreement on a course of action, order giving, if necessary terminating employment, engagement interview.

It will be found that most confrontation situations can easily be classified into one category or other, but such is the subtlety of the employment interview that its various stages, not necessarily in sequence, can encompass all categories. This is of tremendous importance, for quite often it is vital for the interviewer to identify these various categories during the actual interview in order to remain in control.

It is also of value to understand the various levels or planes on which the interview takes place:

1 The primary level deals mainly with facts
2 The secondary level deals with both facts and judgements
3 The tertiary (or depth) level deals with motivation and attitudes.

This basic background will help to establish a framework for the interviewer, and from this position he will then be able to develop his own pattern and style to suit the interview which he will have to handle.

Setting up the interview

There are three equally important aspects to be taken into account when considering this task. They are the administrative back-up, the physical setting and the social setting.

Administrative back-up

Sufficient attention is not paid to the detailed arrangements that are a necessary preliminary to the actual interview. On the pure documentation side all relevant papers for each interviewee must be to hand – original letters or copies of all correspondence, application forms, the job description and specification, plus all other documents, such as company reports, product/service brochures, conditions of contract booklets, which contain information which the candidate might want or which the interviewer wishes to pass on to the candidate. While it is quite possible to go to extremes in providing such information, too often the reverse happens to the detriment of all concerned.

It is also vital to ensure that all people to be involved in the interview process are given adequate warning and briefing. This must include internal staff such as receptionists, security officers, secretaries or personnel clerks who have the very considerable responsibility for greeting those who may ultimately become employees of the same organization.

The question of domestic arrangements should not be neglected either. Awkward situations can arise through lack of foresight or experience, in dealing with travel arrangements, overnight accommodation where necessary, and prompt reimbursement of travelling expenses.

All these considerations are not just chores, but contribute to the interview by setting the tone to the meeting. This is just as important to the craftsman or operative applicant as it is to potential general managers.

The physical setting

Privacy is a prime requirement, rather than the scale or type of furnishings, for nothing can be more disturbing or distracting to both the interviewer and interviewee than being knowingly overheard. While in a certain sense the interview has a social context, it is nevertheless a business meeting. Therefore the furnishing of the room has to be functional, especially if it is a room that has been specifically designated as an interview room. Should the interview take place in an office it may well be necessary to reflect upon such things as tidiness, positioning of chairs and desks, barring the internal telephone and turning off loudspeakers. Privacy includes the avoidance of interruptions as well!

Social setting

The tone of the interview is as important to the interviewer as it is to the interviewee. While conditions of physical discomfort can assist in setting the appropriate tone, nevertheless every effort must be made to establish rapport with the candidate. This can be summed up in the one word 'consideration'. If this ingredient is missing, then the chances are that the objective of the meeting will not be achieved unless a deliberate stress situation has been brought about for a specific purpose. It is a good tactic to try to establish cordial relationships with candidates by setting the necessary tone during the exchange of letters. It is also important to ensure that necessary courtesies are extended to candidates during any waiting period which may have to elapse before they are seen. Feelings of being isolated or ignored can so easily be aroused in candidates through inattention or lack of foresight as to what can happen during the waiting period. Once a candidate has been placed in this position, it does take a tremendous amount of effort and time to overcome these effects. Never cause interviewees to lose their dignity. Whatever their own personal motivations they have, after all, volunteered to attend the employment interview.

Conducting the interview

While of necessity the discussion so far has been about the employment interview, it is nevertheless most important to define the context of the particular interview in question. For example, four different contexts can be defined:

1 Preliminary interview which may well only be concerned with meeting a person in order to exchange information and form initial judgements
2 Background information – where the purposes could be merely to record all relevant detail about a person in preparation for another occasion. One such example is assisting a candidate to complete an application form
3 Discussion, where the main objective is to elaborate on information already available and to talk around potential or real problems
4 Group situation – where a candidate is facing a number of interviewers at the same time. This can easily develop into an uncontrolled state, where the only person to benefit will be the candidate – for he always acts on his own behalf, and therefore will be the only consistent factor in the proceedings.

These then are some of the different contexts in which an interviewer can find himself. When the context has been defined the interviewer has to decide on which level he wants to operate, and also he has to determine the style which he is going to adopt. The levels have been discussed earlier, but in terms of style there are fundamentally three choices: directed, non-directed and probing.

Directed

This involves direct questions which require definite answers. There are always circumstances which demand the adoption of this style, but there are also occasions when this is the style necessary for the total interview. It is especially appropriate with school leavers, with applicants who have complicated job histories and when there is a suggestion that 'facts' may be in dispute.

Non-directed

This means asking open questions which allow the respondent to choose an answer. This is the best way of searching out a person's real views on a particular matter, or to allow the person to project into a situation and develop a point of view. When using this approach it is useful to develop the technique of promoting. While each interviewer will develop his own pattern, the subtle prompt – 'and so, then what happened' – places a real burden on the respondent to continue with the story, or to reveal something which was not intended. An alternative method is for the interviewer to keep silent, so allowing the pressure to build up on the interviewee, who usually cannot resist the need to fill the vacuum by continuing to talk.

Probing

This style of interview covers and recovers the same ground by different questions. In many situations the interviewer needs to check on work done, or claimed to have been done, or to check on apparent or real inconsistencies in the job history or even on attitudes displayed which may not be in character.

Although these three styles are not mutually exclusive, nevertheless it is important that the interviewer should make a positive decision to adopt a certain style. But in addition the interviewer should develop an awareness and sensitivity which will assist him to change styles during the course of the interview without losing control.

However, practice makes perfect, and indeed a great deal of experience is required before the interviewer can intentionally change style, and purposely lose control and still achieve his objective. The newly fledged recruiter must guard against losing control even accidentally until he has become fully proficient.

A few words about control are necessary. In the majority of cases the interviewer starts off in control of the situation and if he is to achieve his ends, he must remain in control. However there are many occasions when the interviewee will try to assert himself and assume control. These attempts can be thwarted relatively simply by a rapid change of subject, or asking an innocuous question like the date of his wedding anniversary, or even why he is married or not married. The main element here is the buying of time to re-group one's thoughts and to recommence the questioning along the required lines.

Every interview has its own sequence but there are five distinct aspects of the employment interview which must now be discussed:

1 Opening
2 Giving and receiving of information
3 Recording
4 Guiding
5 Closing.

Opening

In any sales training programme a great deal of attention is paid to developing a salesman's skill both in opening and closing a sales 'interview'. The same degree of attention must also be paid to the employment interview – opening and closing.

In opening the interviewer must attempt to put the interviewee at his ease, and also at the same time to win his confidence. Normal courtesies form a base from which to operate, and it is important to get the interviewee to speak about something in order merely to loosen his vocal chords – the squeaky hesitant voice or dominant aggressive tone must be eliminated at the outset before it forms an important part of the interchange between the parties. A useful opening 'gambit' is to outline the time limits for the interview, or to clear any domestic problems over travelling, or best of all to try to establish a common link with the interviewee which assists in forming a bond between the two people. This latter gambit must be free from any social or racial

GHM

Date:	Time:	Ref. Number:
Name:	Age:	Job:

Education, training and qualifications	*Impact*
	Appearance
Relevant experience	
	Personal

Figure 50.2 Interview notes

overtones. In addition the interviewer must be able to conceal any prejudice, particularly in relation to ethnic origin, forms of dress, regional speech, sex or physical appearance. Conversely he must not appear to be attracted by affinities – old school ties, the shapely form of a potential secretary, or someone who plays a certain sport. Apparent objectivity is the keynote to establish at the outset.

Giving and receiving of information

The why, what, where, whom and how – this is the kernel of the interview. It is at this point that the quality of the preparatory work is tested. If this preparation has been reasonably thorough, then the interviewer will be able to answer most questions; however it is an invariable rule of the professional recruiter not to stretch the truth too much, and to admit openly that an answer cannot be provided if that is the case. An honest approach to difficult or unanswerable questions or problems will be accepted by the interviewee on most occasions.

While one must always give the candidate every opportunity to ask pertinent questions about the nature of the job and its context in the organization, and to have them fully answered, the interviewer must make sure that he has enough time to check all relevant details of the candidate's background and work history.

Recording

Often a great deal of information about the candidate will have been recorded already – either in correspondence or on an application form. However, interviewers can never hope to remember the answers to all the questions put to the candidate; therefore it is necessary to have some policy and method for making notes during the interview. Most candidates will expect this, but it must be done in the least obstrusive way possible. A common document for all interviews is useful, particularly one which allows the interviewer to complete a preliminary assessment after the candidate has left. One such example is shown in Figure 50.2. Quite often it is suggested that a person cannot really do more than one thing at a time, but the proficient interviewer should be capable of asking questions, listening closely to the answers and taking notes at the same time. However there are times when something is missed, and then the interviewer must be strong enough to ask the candidate to repeat his answer.

Guiding

This is part of the control process; nevertheless it is important to keep the discussion within bounds both of subject and time. It is really surprising how often candidates are allowed to ramble on on unimportant points, and this then leads to pressure on time, with an inevitable dropping of standards. It must be stressed that the interviewer is in the driving seat and therefore can and must guide the candidate and the discussion along the appropriate lines. The hallmark of a first-class interviewer is his capacity to listen; not to intrude while the candidate is speaking; and not to 'hog' the conversation with questions, rhetorically answered, and personal anecdotes.

Closing

This is possibly one of the most difficult parts of the interview to handle effectively. The interviewer must be absolutely sure of what he has to do to end the interview. A lot obviously depends on the actual place of the interview in the selection procedure, but it is very easy to mishandle the situation and promote unnecessary uncertainty and suffering in the candidate. Above all a positive approach must be taken and the candidate made aware of the position; e.g. he will be receiving a letter to let him know the outcome within 10 days; or his name will be placed on the short list; or you are sorry but you will not be able to take his application any further; or will he be good enough to wait in reception while you contact the next interviewer.

The 'silent' interview

Before going on to what might logically be described as the next step – namely the assessment – a short pause is required to think upon what may be described as the 'silent' interview. During the actual interview, while the participants have been talking, a great deal of non-verbal interaction has taken place, and this occurs on two planes – the psychological and the physical. Some of the relevant points have already been touched upon, but it is necessary to draw the attention of all interviewers to the non-verbal aspects.

First the psychological aspect: each of the participants will bring in to the interview certain expectations – to sell himself well, to gain a good understanding of the candidate, to show them just what a good chap he is, to demonstrate yet again that the candidate cannot put one across him.

There will also be individual prejudices and biases which will colour the situation. Irrational fears often promote feelings of inadequacy in candidates, while on the other hand interviewers are susceptible to 'halo' effects and stereotypes.

Next the physical aspect: apart from the actual interview surroundings which, depending on the colour scheme can convey a sense of lightness (pastel shades) or of depression (brown and battleship grey), the degree of comfort or austerity contributes in some measure to the quality of the interview. Physical proximity and position – chairs too near for comfort, especially with a fidgety person – can soon lead to unease without a single word being spoken. Gestures and postures provide a visual means of communication either emphasizing or qualifying a verbal statement. Eye movements can also be important in establishing and maintaining contact, although most people tend to comment adversely on the person who is 'shifty-eyed'. This is very similar to the 'limp handshake' phenomenon. Voice expression conveys its own message which need not be connected with the words used. Especial care needs to be taken with the person who hesitates or stammers.

Awareness of these factors is most important for the person new to

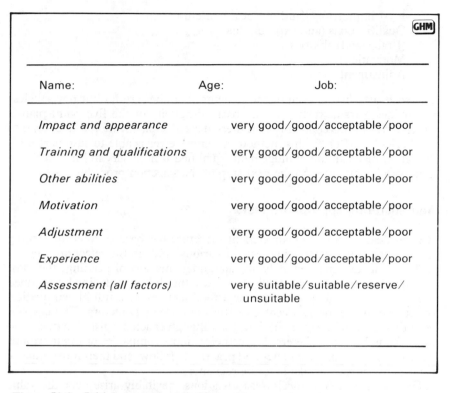

Figure 50.3   Initial assessment and interview summary
This list should be attached to the interview notes

employment interviewing, for by being aware one can be on one's guard, and with experience gradually learn to cope with and interpret such phenomena.

Assessment

At the conclusion of each interview it is necessary to stop and think and ideally to make an initial assessment of the candidate. This can be done quite quickly and effectively by using the outlines of the seven-point plan in Figure 50.3. The value of this initial assessment cannot be over-stressed, especially when there is a considerable time interval or delay between interviewing candidates and the final decision.

The five-point plan developed by J. Munro Fraser from the initial seven-point plan devised by the National Institute of Industrial Psychology and A. Rodger draws the interviewer's attention to five separate points that need to be observed, discussed, and finally assessed. These points are:

First impressions (and physical make-up)
Qualifications (and expectations)
(Brains and) abilities
Motivation
Adjustment

The scale attached to each of these factors is rather crude, but nevertheless it provides a framework, and the basic simplicity of the five point plan is so attractive in this context that in these days of sophistication it does tend to be overlooked. But by this method the interviewer is able to summarize his thoughts, make an initial judgement (qualified if necessary in his notes) and then turn his attention to the next step of the selection procedure.

Administering appropriate tests

A great deal of space in management literature has been devoted to arguing the case for and against using tests of various kinds in the selection process. Although it does not generally appear under this sort of heading, the most common test applied is the medical one, whether it be a screening by a trained nurse before engaging operators for a food factory, or a full blown medical conducted at the medical centre of the Institute of Directors. The case for even this test can be argued both ways, although enacted legislation does tend to set some basic parameters. Nevertheless most companies or organizations have a reasonable defined policy and practice to follow, and therefore guidance is probably already available to the recruiter.

However, in non-medical areas questions inevitably arise over the value of using tests in the selection process. In many instances a case can be made for using appropriate tests, especially where there is already sufficient information available to establish the validity of the tests in that particular context. But a word of warning is necessary, for certain safeguards have been introduced by the National Foundation for Education Research in England and Wales, in conjunction with the British Psychological Society into the administration of many tests in the UK. Where there are any possible problems over the use of tests in selection or management development, reference to the above bodies, to a qualified person, to the test constructors or to a commercial organization such as the Independent Assessment and Research Centre is a must.

What can tests test? Skills like manual dexterity, intelligence, aptitudes, abilities, interests, colour blindness and various aspects of the personality are some of the areas where additional and important information can be gained about candidates in order to make a full and final assessment about their suitability for the job in question.

Managerial level

This is an area where the impact of an individual personality can make a great deal of difference – both positive and negative. In terms of tests, therefore, thought must be given to the main personality characteristics which can contribute to successful performance, and to those which could be contra indicators, i.e. would detract from successful performance. Abilities, interests and aptitudes are important especially in making decisions about people who are starting out on a managerial career for the first time, and especially at this time when many people are likely to find themselves switching career paths once, twice, or even three times in their working life. Therefore in constructing a test package for a particular selection procedure leading to a managerial post, professional advice must be sought, and due weight given to professional opinions in the final assessment.

Clerical and technical

Here keyboard skills are obviously crucial, but in many routine clerical jobs tasks such as checking information against source documents are important. Tests of accuracy are available, and indeed, with the growth of mechanized accounting systems, quite a number of tests of proven validity have been constructed and developed. Sometimes it is important to administer even simple arithmetic and verbal comprehension tests which can be constructed to suit local needs, provided of course that the recruiter knows what he is trying to achieve.

Operational

Tests for would-be apprentices, dilutee craftsmen, plant operators and assemblers are available to those qualified to use them correctly and interpret the results properly. The test of their acceptability is one which can only be resolved in each individual case. But since a great deal of time is required in training those selected to do the job properly, the use of tests must often be justified on financial grounds.

While most tests give detailed instructions on procedure, test administration is nevertheless important, and the recruiter should make certain that he achieves as near to optimum conditions as possible for all test sessions. The correct physical conditions and the right psychological tone are essential to good test performance by the candidates, and if these conditions are not available then the test session can become a futile exercise in apparent sophistication. A guarantee as to the confidentiality of the result is highly important to candidates, and the approach to be encouraged is that of the medical profession in dealing with personal information of this nature.

Making the appointment

The moment of decision has arrived! Again it must be stressed that the decision to offer the position to one of the candidates is one-sided, and until the offer has been accepted, the recruitment task has not been completed.

At this stage the 'evidence' on all the candidates should be available for review and final assessment. In all probability, at least two people will be concerned in the final decision, and in most cases they should meet together to discuss the matter as fully as necessary. Sometimes one candidate stands out among all others, and consequently the decision comes easily. But on many occasions a 'debate' occurs with an informal cataloguing of the pros and cons, and inevitably some sort of compromise has to be made in relation to the 'ideal' job description and candidate specification prepared at the beginning of the recruitment and selection process. Indeed in filling some positions the selection decision is made, not by comparing candidate against candidate, but by assessing the candidate in relation to the specification.

The important point here is to approach the decision making session in a systematic way, so that the reasons for the choice of one candidate and the rejection of the others become quite clear. No one should be afraid of stating and if necessary restating that a liking for a candidate has tipped the scales in his favour. As Robert Townsend says in *Up the Organization*, 'The important thing about hiring is the chemistry of the vibrations between boss and candidate; good, bad, or not there at all'. Any manager who denies this truism has already reached his level of incompetence.

Having made the decision, this must be conveyed in written form to the successful candidate. The formal offer of employment should always be qualified with the phrase 'subject to obtaining satisfactory references', unless of course references have already been obtained. No self respecting potential employee will accept and act upon a mere verbal offer, and until an acceptance letter has been received the process has not been completed. It is also useful at this stage to clear with the appointee any remaining matter relating to the conditions under which he will be employed.

STAGE THREE: THE FOLLOW-THROUGH

Introducing the new employee to the organization

Any new employee will require a period of familiarization before he can begin to perform his job properly. In many cases it is possible to set up a formal introductory course through which new employees learn about the policies and practices of the organization. Sometimes it is possible to put a number of employees through the same course, while for others the introduction will have to be tailor-made. The main aim of induction, whether conducted on a formal basis or informally by the new employee's boss, is to integrate the newcomer as soon as possible. This is not an altruistic concept, but is based on sound economics, for the sooner a person is settled the sooner performance reaches standard.

Perhaps the best basis from which to start the induction process is the question: what does the newcomer want or need to know? A programme of induction must cover such matters as conditions of employment, departmental information, general health and safety. Remember also that new employees will find it difficult to assimilate a mass of information at one sitting, and a suitable time scale should therefore be devised.

For induction programmes at technical, supervisory or managerial level, a useful guide is to be found in the pamphlet *Induction – Acclimatizing People to Work* by W.R.Marks, published by the Institute of Personnel Management. However, the important principle to bear in mind is that the programme must be constructed around the requirements of the job to be done, and the time scale must also be realistic, for most newcomers just want to settle down and prove their worth.

Following up the progress of the new employee

This is of specific importance where a probationary period of employment (not more than 12 weeks) has to be served successfully before confirmation of the appointment takes place. In these cases a formal procedure has to be adopted in order to maintain adequate records and background information for the decision which has to be taken. If the review takes place on a weekly or monthly basis then the employee should be given some idea of what progress he or she is making. This need not be on a formal basis, for given good supervisors, the effect of an 'informal chat' can result in either a mending of the ways or a spurring to even better performance.

In general terms though, contact needs to be maintained with new employees until it becomes quite apparent that they have settled down and become part of the team. This contact between the recruiter, the new employee and his boss can be of considerable benefit in developing an awareness, in the recruiter, especially of the sorts of people who successfully survive the hesitation of the first week or month and become settled members of the company or organization. In looking at labour turnover figures it is not surprising to note that in many instances most of the leavers quit within the first three months of being employed. There is therefore a real economic meaning and purpose to follow up after induction.

Reviewing and evaluating the recruitment and selection process

In basic terms most organizations check their recruitment and selection methods on the exception principle – the new recruit who doesn't fit in becomes the stick with which the recruiter is beaten about the head, no matter how many 'successes' can be listed! However, it is possible to examine the actual methods by which the final decision is reached in a more objective way. Such questions must be asked: Are we advertising the vacancy properly? Are we attracting the right sort of candidates? Are we treating the candidates in the right way? Have we got the right system for obtaining the preliminary information about the job? Generally are the candidate specifications lucid enough? Are we getting the right sort of information about candidates from the tests we use? How long do new employees of various categories stay with us? Is this a result of over- or under-recruitment?

The answers to some of these questions will give an indication of what is going on in the selection process, and provide a reasonably sound base for further improvements.

969

In respect of the competence of the recruiter himself, it is to the advantage of the organization to ensure that its 'gate-keepers' can discriminate (in the nicest possible sense) between those who should or should not be admitted. Apart from professional competence as an employment interviewer and a test administrator, the recruiter must be able to maintain the confidence of his peers and colleagues within the company, as well as enjoy the confidence of the candidates who come in front of him. Integrity is a vital word in this context both from a professional and personal point of view as far as the recruiter is concerned. Indeed all managers eventually build up a 'track record' on their effectiveness in taking on the right people for the tasks in hand.

Finally it must be stated that most companies and organizations are now beginning to realize that the recruitment of the necessary human resources requires the same attention, effort, and concentration as purchasing essential raw materials, plant and supplies. In the last analysis it is people who, collectively or individually, make or break the company as a viable concern. The cost effectiveness of the recruitment and selection process must be of prime concern for top management, especially as the annual company report now contains the average numbers of people employed over the year and the amount of wages and salaries paid to them. In the last analysis, value for money is the unspoken question in the selection decision.

THE IPM RECRUITMENT CODE

The Institute of Personnel Management first launched its recruitment code in 1978, after much debate and heart-searching amongst interested parties, recruiters and applicants alike. Its declared aims include the promotion of 'high standards of professional recruitment practice by encouraging recruiters and applicants to adhere to common guidelines', and the provision of 'guidance on those matters that most commonly cause difficulty to recruiters and applicants'.

Among topics covered by the code are such matters as dealing with unsolicited applications, failure of applicants to honour interview appointments, payment of interview expenses, the taking up of references, and discrimination against applicants on the grounds of sex, race, disability, or past convictions for criminal offences.

The code sets out the obligations of recruiters and applicants, and the following extracts are taken from the fourth edition.*

Recruiters' obligations

1 Job advertisements should state clearly the form of reply desired, in particular, whether this should be a formal application form or by curriculum vitae. Preferences should also be stated if hand-written replies are required.

* Extract from the IPM Recruitment Code used with permission of the Institute of Personnel Management, IPM House, Camp Road, Wimbledon, London SW19 4UW.

2 An acknowledgement or reply should be made promptly to each applicant by the employing organization or its agent. If it is likely to take some time before acknowledgements are made, this should be made clear in the advertisement.

3 Applicants should be informed of the progress of selection procedures, what these will be (e.g. group selection, aptitude tests etc.), the steps and time involved and the policy regarding expenses.

4 Detailed personal information (for example religion, medical history, place of birth, family background, etc.) should not be called for unless it is relevant to the selection process.

5 Before applying for references, potential employers must secure the permission of the applicant.

6 Applications must be treated as confidential.

Applicants' obligations

1 Advertisements should be answered in the way requested (for example telephone for application form, provide brief details, send curriculum vitae, etc).

2 Appointments and other arrangements must be kept, or the recruiter be informed promptly if the candidate discovers an agreed meeting cannot take place.

3 The recruiter should be informed as soon as a candidate decides not to proceed with the application.

4 Only accurate information should be given in applications and in reply to recruiter's questions.

5 Information given by a prospective employer must be treated as confidential, if so requested.

FURTHER READING

Higham, M., *The ABC of Interviewing*, IPM, London, 1979
Plumbley, P., *Recruitment and Selection*, 2nd edition, IPM, London, 1976
Sidney, E., (ed.) *Managing Recruitment*, Gower, Aldershot, 1988

51 Salary management

Keith G Cameron

Managing the reward of employees can be complex and difficult. Putting to one side the statutory requirements for tax and social security deductions, the control of discretionary elements requires careful judgement. The simplest and most comprehensive approach is to view the subject as reward – a combination of wages, salaries and other benefits. The topic of benefits is sufficiently wide-ranging to deserve a chapter of its own (see Chapter 53).

The distinction between salaries and wages is becoming blurred. The Wages Act 1986 removed some of the obstacles to paying manual workers via the bank transfer system, a procedure previously restricted through the Truck Acts. In terms of pay management, the executive and the company need to manage carefully the relationship between wage and salary systems as the factors which kept them separate disappear.

The astute manager should have a pay policy which incorporates the intentions applicable to salaries, to wages, and to the relationship between them. However, it is still appropriate to approach the subject of pay management under the two headings of salaries and wages, since the overwhelming practice is to operate two different systems. Chapter 52, therefore, is assigned to wage management.

NEED FOR A SALARY POLICY

Companies employing up to fifty staff normally have an informal salary policy – and rightly so. However, when total staff exceed this number, anomalies begin to appear in the system and some form of framework is necessary. This is particularly so when rapid expansion is taking place.

Although there must be a co-ordinator, the responsibility for salary management is that of line management. What is needed therefore is a salary policy laying down administrative parameters within which discretion may be exercised and providing salary ranges based on simple job evaluation.

Involvement of line managers at this point is essential in order that they recognize the need for regularizing salary management and make a positive contribution towards drawing up a salary policy.

EXAMPLE OF A SALARY POLICY STATEMENT

Introduction

The aim of this document is to set down the company's policy with regard to salary. It is the responsibility of all who apply it to explain it fully to their subordinates.

Aims

The aims of the company's policy are:

1 To recognize the value of all jobs relative to each other within the company and in comparison with similar jobs outside
2 To recognize the value of the individual to the company and to relate this to the salary range applicable to his or her job.

The foregoing is subject to government legislation, as appropriate.

Salary structure

The salary structure will be based on job evaluation. Each job will have a declared minimum and maximum salary range and it is the company's policy to pay at least the minimum for each job

Job evaluation

It is the policy of the company to ensure that staff are fully involved in job evaluation, including representation on the job evaluation committee.

Job evaluation is a continuing process and once salary grades have been established, the committee will meet regularly to deal with re-evaluating existing jobs as well as evaluating new jobs.

Initial salary

In determining an individual's salary on appointment, no differentiation is made on the grounds of sex. In addition, the following features are taken into account:

1 The value to the company of the relevant experience he or she brings
2 The individual's value in the outside market
3 The individual's value compared with existing staff who hold similar jobs.

Performance appraisal

An integral part of salary management is the regular appraisal of staff. This is the basis on which management counsels individuals in order that everyone has maximum opportunity to develop his or her own potential. In order that individuals utilize their abilities to the full, short- and longer-term objectives will be mutually agreed with management.

Salary reviews

It is the policy of the company to review quarterly the salaries of all staff under the age of eighteen years. At age eighteen years and over, all staff salaries will be reviewed annually. Performance increases, if any, will be paid effective from 1 April.

Promotion

When an individual is promoted to higher-grade work, his or her salary will be increased by 10 per cent or she will be paid the minimum for the new grade, whichever is the greater. If the individual fails to measure up to the needs of the new job, he or she will be made aware of his or her shortcomings and given an opportunity to improve and, failing this, to move to a more suitable job. If this results in moving to work of a lower grade there will be no salary decrease. Instead there will be a salary standstill until the rate for the new position equals that of the old.

Progression within salary range

Everyone will know the salary range for his or her job. Those who do their job particularly well will reach the maximum for their salary range within four years.

Long-serving staff who are already on their salary ceiling will be subject to a salary review every third year to a maximum of six years.

Grievance procedure

Anyone who feels that his or her salary indicates that an injustice has been done has the right to appeal first to his or her manager and then to the managing director whose decision will be final. The individual has a right to bring along a colleague to help support his or her appeal.

Communication

As important as the preparation of a salary policy is the need to communicate it to everyone concerned; indeed there is no reason why every staff member should not have a copy of the actual policy statement.

By far the best way of passing on information is for each departmental manager to call a briefing meeting with all his or her staff to explain what the policy covers and, more important, how it will affect each individual. Care should be taken that each employee's questions are answered sympathetically and honestly. Employees should also be fully aware of the company's intentions regarding possible salary anomalies.

JOB DESCRIPTIONS

In every company there are formal and informal arrangements about who reports to whom and how work is done. It is important, therefore, to establish and seek agreement on an organization or accountability chart. Job titles can be very misleading and some renaming may be necessary. This in turn involves the writing of *job descriptions*.

A job description is a basic statement covering such features as:

Job title
Department
To whom responsible
Date
Tasks/areas of responsibility
Job titles of subordinates
Training and/or experience required for job

The completed description must be agreed by both the job holder and his or her supervisor. (Where disagreements arise, the grievance procedure should be operated.)

A specimen job description follows.

Specimen job description

Position: Secretary to Chief Mechanical Engineer
Department: Project Engineering

Date:

Overall Aim: To provide a complete secretarial service to Chief Mechanical Engineer by organizing the routine aspects of his work

Daily tasks:

1 On receipt of mail, sort into order of priority, attach previous correspondence, if any, and type routine letters for signature

2 Take dictation from Chief Mechanical Engineer and deal also with urgent correspondence dictated by senior mechanical engineers

3 Against a tight timetable, type detailed statistical tables connected with department's project work

4 Deal with department's travel arrangements and prepare all travel itineraries

5 Maintain simple time records concerning progress of experimental projects. Ensure that progress charts are kept up to date

6 Act as an assistant to Chief Mechanical Engineer by dealing with the more routine aspects of his work

7 Act as a 'shield' by dealing with callers personally and on the telephone

Weekly tasks:

1 Prepare for accountant short summary of personal expenses incurred by department during previous week, and allocate to individual projects

Monthly tasks:

1 Collect brief reports prepared by senior engineers on their respective projects and type draft of progress report for the Project Engineering Director

Six-monthly tasks:

1 Transfer old files to basement and make out new files for next six months

Annual tasks:

1 Type statement of account showing income over expenditure on previous year's projects

Minimum age:	Twenty-one years
Educational qualifications:	Five 'O' levels (including English language) and secretarial college training
Experience:	Three years' practical office experience including one year in a similar firm
Induction:	Three months
Other information:	The Chief Mechanical Engineer is frequently off site and the job holder is expected to deal with all routine problems arising during such absences

JOB EVALUATION

Many companies avoid installing job evaluation because they feel it is either too costly or too sophisticated. This need not be the case. Two methods should be considered as practicable:

1 Ranking
2 Job classification

Ranking involves the study of each job description and placing it in order of importance. Note that it is the *job* which is being graded and *not* the person doing it. Here is a likely plan of attack.

1 Constitute a committee of, say, three people who have a good knowledge of all the jobs being covered
2 Select about 15-20 jobs as being a good representative sample of all the jobs being covered. These are the benchmark or key jobs and form the basis of job evaluation

	GHM
Job title _____	
Department _____	
Responsible to _____	
Agreed by _____	Date _____
1 What is the overall objective of the job?	
2 Draw up a family tree showing the job in perspective	
3 Give a concise description of the main areas of responsibility in the job. Take it area by area and stress the important features	
Daily tasks	
Weekly tasks	
Monthly tasks	
Quarterly tasks	

Figure 51.1 Job questionnaire

GHM

| Half-yearly task |
| Annual tasks |
| 4 Give the titles of the jobs which you *directly* supervise |
| 5 Contacts – With what levels of people in other departments and/or outside the company do you have contact in order to carry out the job effectively? Is contact by telephone or in person? Comment on the reason for contact

Internal |
| *External* |
| 6 Comment on the qualifications and/or previous experience necessary to do the job effectively |
| 7 Other information |

Figure 51.1   (concluded)

3 Write job descriptions of the benchmarks
4 Separately rank those jobs in order of importance and seek agreement with other committee members
5 Design a job questionnaire (see Figure 51.1)
6 Brief all employees on how they should complete the questionnaires (see Specimen briefing notes below)
7 Ensure that all questionnaires are agreed by the respective supervisors
8 The committee finally slot in jobs according to benchmarks to reach an overall rank order

Specimen briefing notes

Introduction. Job evaluation is a method of looking objectively at jobs and ranking them in order of importance. By comparing them one with another, each job will be placed in a salary grade relative to its worth. However, it must be stressed that it is the *job* which is being considered and *not* the individual.

A job evaluation committee has been formed under the chairmanship of Andrew Brown, the company secretary. The other members of the committee are Alan Garnett and Jill Pepperell.

The scheme. After a great deal of investigation, the committee has decided to use a classification or grading scheme, a copy of which is described later in this chapter.

Completing the questionnaire

1   *Overall objective.* One sentence will normally suffice here. It should be concise and give the reason for the job's existence in order that the committee has 'something to hang its cap on' before looking at the job in depth. For example:

> Process all orders ensuring that departmental computer data codes are included and that the VAT figure is correct

2   *Family tree.* A clearer picture of your job is given if you draw up a family tree of your department showing your job in relation to all other jobs

3   *Job description.* It is always difficult to write one's own job description: consider therefore that you are transferring to another department in the company and that you must prepare a note for your successor covering the main elements of the job. Describe the job as it is now and not how it should be. Do not be afraid to go into detail.

Write down the area headings first, such as correspondence, planning, queries, staff; and describe the responsibility involved under each heading. For example:

> Correspondence – on receipt of mail, decide what can be delegated to subordinates and retain non-routine letters. Where necessary give instructions regarding the handling of particular letters.

4   *Supervisory responsibility.* Supervisory responsibility can only be assessed fairly by examining carefully the job descriptions of those jobs under his or her jurisdiction. By looking at the situation as a whole, the supervisory aspect should be accorded its proper degree of responsibility.

5   *Contacts.* The strength of the company lies in the service given to customers. This does not diminish the value of internal contacts. What is important is the level at which contact is normally made and the reason for contact in the first place.

6 *Qualifications and/or experience*. Comment should be made here regarding the minimum qualifications and/or experience which must be brought to the job *before* it can be done effectively. It may be possible to state an actual qualification or the job may simply call for 'an aptitude for figures'. Experience required must be quite specific. For example: six months' practical experience in credit control.

7 *Other information*. No questionnaire can possibly cover all aspects of a job and since it is important that every member of staff has the opportunity to comment on all areas of the job which are important, space is provided for this. For example:

> Large proportion of work is concerned with meeting tight time schedules.

These comments should cover features which are an integral part of the job and not temporary difficulties.

Completion date for questionnaires. All questionnaires must be completed and returned to Jill Pepperell by Monday 29 January.

Completion date for job evaluation exercise. With the cooperation of everyone, the committee expects to complete the evaluation exercise by 15 March.

Right of appeal. Any member of staff who feels his or her job has not been fairly evaluated has the right to appeal to the committee through his or her head of department. The individual can then expect to be invited, along with his or her head of department to discuss the job in detail with the members of the committee.

Paired comparisons

An extension of ranking – *paired or forced comparisons* – should be considered. Each job is compared with every other job and a decision is made about which job is the more important. An example of a paired comparison is given in Figure 51.2. A word of warning. Fifty different jobs is the maximum number which can be ranked manually. Once this has been done, a matrix is drawn up showing the jobs in rank order (Figure 51.3).

Grading/classification

Grading/classification is a means whereby jobs are separated into natural/ homogeneous groups on a whole-job basis. This is achieved by:

1 Writing 15-20 benchmark job descriptions
2 Ranking them

GHM

	Accounts clerk	Invoice typist	Receptionist/ telephonist	Wages clerk	Messenger	Costing clerk	Director's secretary	Shorthand typist	Stock clerk	Sales Clerk
Accounts clerk	X	1	0	0	2	0	0	0	1	0
Invoice typist	1	X	0	0	2	0	0	0	1	0
Receptionist/ telephonist	2	2	X	1	2	1	0	1	2	1
Wages clerk	2	2	1	X	2	1	0	1	2	1
Messenger	0	0	0	0	X	0	0	0	0	0
Costing clerk	2	2	1	1	2	X	0	1	2	1
Director's secretary	2	2	2	2	2	2	X	2	2	2
Shorthand typist	2	2	1	1	2	1	0	X	2	1
Stock clerk	1	1	0	0	2	0	0	0	X	0
Sales clerk	2	2	1	1	2	1	0	1	1	X

Figure 51.2 **Ranking chart**
Reading from the left, compare each job in turn with every other job shown along the top. If the job is more important, insert 2; if equally important, insert 1; if less important, insert 0. For example in this chart an accounts clerk is considered less important than a receptionist, more important than a messenger and the same as an invoice typist

3 Marking natural 'break points' between those groups of jobs which have the same relative work
4 Defining in short paragraph form the common features of those jobs in each group
5 Writing job descriptions for the remaining jobs and matching them against the appropriate grade/classification definition

GHM

Director's secretary	2	2	2	2	2	2	2	2	2
Receptionist/telephonist		2	2	2	2	1	1	1	1
Wages clerk		2	2	2	2	1	1	1	1
Costing clerk		2	2	2	2	1	1	1	1
Shorthand typist		2	2	2	2	1	1	1	1
Sales clerk		2	2	2	2	1	1	1	1
Invoice typist							2	1	1
Stock clerk							2	1	1
Accounts clerk							2	1	1
Messenger									0

Figure 51.3   Job evaluation matrix
Derived from the ranking chart shown in Figure 51.2

Example of a grading or classification scheme

Grade 1   Tasks are simple and conform to clearly laid down procedures. No training or experience required. Continually supervised. All written work and calculations are checked. Up to a few weeks' training required.

Grade 2   Tasks are subject to laid-down procedures but can involve a limited measure of initiative. Work subject to spot checks. Up to six months' training or experience required.

Grade 3   Tasks are carried out and decisions made in accordance with standard procedures, subject to infrequent superivision. Routine contact, externally and internally, up to own level to obtain and provide information. Probably minimum of two years' experience.

Grade 4   After specific direction, plans and arranges work within main work programme with little or no supervision. Only non-routine problems referred to superior. May have supervisory responsibility. Can have contact at higher level than own, externally and internally, to obtain and give information which may be of confidential nature. Specialized knowledge may be required. Probably four to five years' experience.

Grade 5   After general direction, plans and arranges work with little or no supervision. Tasks can involve work of a non-routine nature requiring an original approach as to planning and method. Would normally have contact at a higher level than own, externally and internally, to obtain and give information which may be of a confidential nature. Can be required to make decisions as to daily action and direct work of subordinates. More than five years' experience required.

Analytical job evaluation

The methods of job evaluation described so far are relatively simple and are known as non-analytical schemes because they look at jobs as whole entities and compare them without analysis and comparison of the elements within jobs. For example, in the approaches previously described, information about a job will be garnered under a selection of headings (contacts, experience needed etc.) but comparison of jobs by comparative analysis of the individual components is not a feature.

If job evaluation is being used to provide not only order and control for management but also a perception of fairness for the employees, the non-analytical systems of ranking and grading/classification may be thought to be too arbitrary. In this case, a simple form of analytical job evaluation, culminating in a points score for each job, can be designed and introduced in the following way.

Example of analytical job evaluation scheme

1 Constitute a committee with good knowledge of the jobs to be evaluated and representative of the various functions/areas of the organization
2 Select a set of factors to be measured for each job which cover the important elements in the set of positions to be evaluated. Although these will vary from company to company, a typical list of factors can normally be selected from the following:
   (*a*) training
   (*b*) knowledge
   (*c*) skill
   (*d*) experience
   (*e*) contacts
   (*f*) accountability
   (*g*) complexity
   (*h*) working conditions
3 Using the same principle described under the Paired Comparisons scheme, prepare a questionnaire for each committee member to complete which compares each selected factor with the others chosen for the scheme as shown in Figure 51.4.
4 Define the importance of the factors by each committee member deciding which factor is more important when forced into comparison with the other factors, counting the frequency with which the factors appear as choices and allocating a range of points per factor in line with the factor's number of 'wins' in relation to the total number of choices. In the example in Figure 51.4, accountability 'wins' three times out of ten. If this was replicated by the other four committee members, then

Knowledge v Skill		K
Accountability v Contacts		A
Experience v Knowledge		E
Knowledge v Accountability		A
Contacts v Skill		S
Experience v Accountability		A
Knowledge v Contacts		K
Accountability v Skill		S
Skill v Experience		S
Experience v Contacts		C

Figure 51.4   *Questionnaire of paired comparisons used in analytical job evaluation*

    Accountability would score fifteen out of a possible maximum of fifty points

5   Derive the points range per factor. Continuing with the same example, a multiplication factor of 20 could be used for convenience. This would make the theoretical maximum score for a job 1000 points (50 times 20) and produce a maximum score of 300 for accountability, 100 for contacts (1 win × 5 committee members × multiplication factor 20)

6   Evaluate each job in committee, each member awarding points per factor on the derived points scales, then averaging or, preferably, arriving at a consensus score per element. The total of the agreed points per factor is the score for the job and the total points bands can be defined to produce grades, or the points can stand in their own right and be used to determine pay.

This analytical job evaluation method can be used for manual jobs as well as managerial, professional and administrative. The facility to choose and weight factors according to the circumstances of the organization provides the maximum scope and flexibility.

SALARY BANDS/GRADES

Five grades ought to suffice up to and including supervisory level. To have more will mean that differentials between grades will be reduced and staff will see little financial advantage in taking on more responsibility. Alternatively, the salaries co-ordinator will be faced with an excessive number of appeals for upgrading each time there is a slight increase in responsibility.

In general, jobs will tend to fall into broad groups but there are bound to be some jobs which will cause much soul-searching. The establishing of grades completed, the jobs on either side of the break point must be scrutinized carefully to ensure they are in the right group. In the event of appeals being raised, it is likely that they will spring from this grey area.

Salary ranges

Now comes the problem of allocating actual cash to each band or grade. A number of structures is possible, but a structure like that in Figure 51.5 is recommended for its flexibility.

Grade	1	£5 000 ——— £6 600		GHM
	2	£5 800 ——— £7 800		
	3	£6 800 ——— £9 100		
	4	£8 000 ——— £11 000		
	5	£10 000 ———£15 000		

Figure 51.5   Salary structure
Overlapping salary structure

As will be seen, the salary ceiling is roughly a 30-50 per cent addition on the base figure and the base for the next grade starts at approximately the midpoint of the previous grade. This means that on promotion an employee may move easily from one grade to another. It also recognizes that an employee on his or her ceiling on a grade 3 job is worth more than one about to start on grade 4 with less experience of the company's business.

SALARY SURVEYS

Although salary comparison is a continuing exercise, a particular effort must be made to obtain factual information when designing a new salary structure. This can be done in four ways:

1 By consulting national or local salary surveys
2 By telephoning your opposite number in other companies in the area and exchanging information
3 By sending to selected companies a job description from each grade and asking for a comparison. (It is wise to telephone personally to enquire if the company is willing to take part.) This must be followed up by sending to the participants details of the survey but excluding actual company names
4 By inviting four or five opposite numbers in your area to form a Salary Comparison Club with the first meeting on your premises. An agreed agenda should be drawn up stating the jobs to be discussed in order that salary information is forthcoming. Even at this point, the salary ranges cannot be thought conclusive until a thorough internal costing is completed.

USE OF GRAPHS

The use of graphs is invaluable when creating a new salary structure. Only when the situation is presented visually do anomalies stand out. Using a bar graph to study the number of people in each grade, for instance, a crude distribution curve will be obtained, i.e. the bulk of the jobs will likely be in the middle grades.

As an *aid* to determining what jobs should finally be in which grade it is helpful to do a scattergram (see Figure 51.6). Here is how it is done:

1 On a graph plot each job holder by basic salary and grade. This will give you the scatter on your current salary structure
2 Draw a (curved) line through the centre of the scatter so that there are roughly the same number of points above as below the line. This will give you the mid-point of each new salary range. (The technical description for the line is 'line of best fit')
3 The pure approach is to fix 15-25 per cent above and below the line the minimum and maximum salary figure for each new salary range
4 The jobs falling above and below the minimum and maximum are, of course, anomalous in the new structure.

DECIDING HOW MUCH TO PAY

You now have (a) an external salary survey; and (b) a formal salary structure which reflects accurately the *current* company position. It is likely these two aspects require reconciliation.

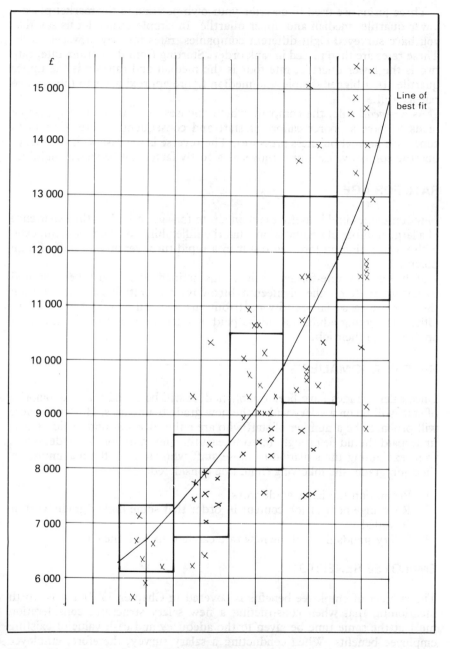

Figure 51.6   Comparison of old and new salary structures

Three terms are used to describe your own position in the market-place – lower quartile, median and upper quartile. In simple terms, let us say that you have surveyed eight different companies' rates for, say, a wages clerk. These rates are then placed in rank order. Starting from the bottom rate, rate two is the lower quartile, rate four is the median and rate six is the upper quartile. In a bigger sample, the median figure approximates to the average rate as well.

As a *general* rule, the company which chooses to be in the lower quartile tends to have a poorer calibre of staff and consequently more of them to cope with normal business pressures. The reverse is the case with the higher quartile company. Labour turnover is a costly factor not be viewed lightly.

RATE FOR AGE

Few companies find it useful to retain a rate-for-age scale. It is the experience of a large number of organizations that the inflexibility of such a system, even with merit rating on top, can result in a rapid turnover among staff of high potential.

If however a rate-for-age scale is maintained, care must be exercised to ensure that, on the eighteenth birthday, recognition is made of both the increase in social security contributions and rail travel (if applicable). Otherwise young adults should be paid at least the minimum of the grade applicable to their job.

SALARY ANOMALIES

Once salary grades have been established, it will be found that the majority of staff will be on a salary within the new grade boundaries. However, there will probably be a number of staff who are either over- or underpaid. Those underpaid should be brought up to at least the minimum for the grade. Apart from explaining the situation to those staff who are over the maximum for their job grade, the following should be considered:

1 Promotion to higher-grade work
2 Rearrangement of job content in order that some higher-grade work is included
3 Salary standstill until the new rate catches up with the old

EMPLOYEE BENEFITS

The subject of employee benefits is covered in Chapter 53, but it is worth mentioning that when constructing a new salary structure, consideration must at the same time be given to the adequacy and cash value of existing employee benefits. When conducting a salary survey, therefore, employee benefits must also be taken into account.

Staff accept fringe benefits as a fact of life but different social groups within the company and indeed within the area will view different benefits with varying degrees of interest. Young people are more attracted to a company by the promise of a realistic salary than by the offer of a generous sick pay or pension scheme. Assisted house purchase, membership of a hospital scheme and profit sharing is likely to appeal to management.

In designing the salary structure, therefore, it is important to consider how much influence employee benefits need have on the salary ranges.

DEPARTMENTAL BUDGETS

Every department should have a budget and within this, there should be an agreed figure for salaries. This should be decided one year in advance and should take into consideration staff retirements (with recruitment on a lower salary level), promotions and increases in staff complement. It should also take into account a figure to be set aside for salary increases. This can either be an arbitrarily agreed lump sum or, more usually, something like 3-4 per cent, excluding cost-of-living increases.

SALARY REVIEWS

Most organizations conduct reviews of salaries in a systematic and regular manner but there are many differences in the way they go about the process.

Frequency and scope

The most common practice is an annual review of salaries. The anniversary date of the review will vary from company to company and may be related to the end of the organization's financial year or to a convention (or formal agreement) within the particular industry. Two-year pay programmes are, however, growing in popularity for salaried staff as well as for manual workers. The two-year programme enables the employer to plan and control costs better and is more acceptable during times of low inflation. Six-monthly salary reviews for organizations do exist, although their incidence is greater during times of high inflationary pressure.

The 'rolling review' system is also used by organizations and entails individuals having their salaries reviewed on the anniversary of their starting date with the organization or appointment to the present job. While gearing increments to a full year's review, and so being very specific, the administration and budgeting is intricate if more than a handful of people are involved.

The salary review may not apply to two groups of people: those who are on a different programme (e.g. young staff who may be given rises every six months) and those who do not justify a pay increase. Some systems, however, do not recognize the latter category.

989

Salary review methods

Putting to one side the 'fixed increment' system (e.g. the Civil Service) and formally negotiated salary reviews, the conventional methods are the general increase, general increase plus merit increase, and merit increase only. The general increase is a fixed amount or percentage for the group or for each category within the group. The other two approaches require a method for varying the amount to be paid to different people and this entails assessment of individual performance.

Performance appraisal

Performance appraisal is a valuable technique in its own right. A formal method of relating performance to expected standards and goals enables managers to examine rationally and agree upon corrective action, areas where training may be required and scope for development and promotion. Additionally, the majority of companies wish to reward individual performance and so link the results of appraisal to salary increases. The 'general plus merit' approach entails payment of an increase to all those eligible based on some generally applicable indicator like cost-of-living movement or, more frequently now, changes in the pay market which will have been quantified by the salary survey methods described earlier.

Some companies gear salary increases entirely to individual performance and this can be achieved by gearing fixed percentage increases to the particular appraisal or merit ratings. For example, the performance appraisal system may have five categories, with A defined as 'Fails to meet the requirements of the job', B being 'Fails to meet some requirements of the job' through to E which states 'Achieves considerably more than is required by the job'. Against such an A to E scale the company could award the following percentage increases to the base pay of individuals: A–0, B–2, C–5, D–8, E–11. Control of the amount available for the salary review is vested in the regulation of the numbers in each performance category. Using the example above, the cost of the review should be 6–7 per cent as the bulk of employees would be in C with a significant minority in D. There should be relatively few individuals in A or B as most cases of poor performance should have been dealt with by management action during the year. Similarly, E should house relatively few people if the targeting standards for individuals are properly set. The suggestion that there could be significant numbers in D is based on the assumption that the company is meeting its fiscal targets and this constitutes an improvement on the previous year. Although such an approach relates reward specifically to performance, it can have an adverse compounding effect if the base salary to which the percentage increase is applied is low. In these circumstances, an increase of 8 per cent to an £8000 salary for good performance yields £640 while 5 per cent for standard performance on £12 000 means £600. Both individuals could be in the same grade with a midpoint of range of £10 000. A matrix can be developed to account for the individual's position in the salary range as well as the merit rating but, without being so elaborate, companies can take account of this factor

Name	Job title	Date appointed to job	Date of last increase	Amount	Present salary	Grade	Salary range	Performance rating	Increase proposed	New salary

GHM

Figure 51.7 Form suitable for administration of merit based salary review

by being flexible with the standard percentage for each rating, and shading this up or down slightly.

For the administration of a merit-based salary review, a form similar to that shown in Figure 51.7 should be used.

AUDITING THE PAY SYSTEM

Although the mechanisms already outlined provide rules and, in many cases, checks to ensure that salary (and wage) systems operate correctly, there is a need for an auditing method. The purpose of the audit should not only be to validate the accuracy of the pay process but also to provide information about the appropriateness of the systems in use. So although the salary review process incorporates a check on the pay levels in the market-place by salary surveys and other comparisons, a sensible auditing system will complement this activity. For example, a check on the occupancy levels of various grades compared to the distribution of jobs within grades from the previous year may indicate 'grade drift' if there has been an upward migration without a change in the company structure to justify such a change.

Establishing the audit process

The critical elements of any audit are the power of the process – senior management endorsement – and the positive recommendations for change and improvement which stem from the data. The steps in the process are as follows:

1 Appoint a senior manager to have control of the audit process. The manager should be conversant with the process of pay and have sufficient authority to secure all the necessary information. The manager should not, however, have daily responsibility for pay; otherwise the critical and distanced stance is unlikely to be achieved
2 Inform all the individuals and groups who may be involved in the process. This should include union or staff representatives as well as all administrators
3 Define and agree the rules. In addition to the 'accounting' rules there needs to be agreement on the approach. What is going to be audited on a given date and what is going to be reviewed over the last twelve months?
4 Locate the information required. In addition to the obvious places, information should be gathered from other sources such as management control reports
5 Collect and plot data on rates and earnings levels
6 Collect and plot information on pay related matters (e.g. labour turnover, exit interview results)
7 Monitor structural aspects of reward (e.g. membership of grades)
8 Pay special attention to bonus schemes and other methods of variable reward with a particular view to changing aspects of scheme design

9   Identify interfaces with other systems and monitor the effectiveness of the system and methods in use
10 Summarize the findings in a formal report and ensure that the findings are presented and that there is endorsement or rejection of the findings.

The audit should be a powerful tool in keeping the salary and wage system dynamic – which is an essential element in its successful operation. The process of salary and wage management is not completed with the introduction of various systems and techniques: monitoring and adjustment to reflect changes in the company is an integral part of the process.

FURTHER READING

Bowey, Angela M. (ed.), *Handbook of Salary and Wage Systems*, 2nd edition, Gower, Aldershot, 1982
Lupton, T., and Bowey, Angela M., *Wages and Salaries*, 2nd edition, Gower, Aldershot, 1983

52 Wage management
Keith G Cameron

DESIGNING A COMPANY WAGE POLICY

The wage structure must be linked to what the company is trying to achieve. It is not unusual to find a company with a wage structure in direct conflict with the company's overall objectives. For example, a company may plan to produce a high-quality product while at the same time it may have a direct incentive geared to quantity. These questions must be asked:

Apart from profit, what are we in business for?
Where are we going during the next two to three years; in the next five to ten years?
How do we plan to get there?
What influence will these plans have on our wage structure?
How can the wage structure aid the company in meeting its objectives?

From this a business plan is built up, in simple terms, expressing the company's short- and long-term objectives and how these will affect specific areas. It may be, for example, that in two years' time a massive capital investment is planned. In terms of human resources this will probably affect the way work is organized, manning arrangements and job demands. Care must be taken, therefore, to ensure that the new wage structure will form a satisfactory springboard to cater for future developments. Consideration must also be given to the spin-off which will affect the whole company.

Management style

It is necessary to identify the company's management style. Is it predominantly autocratic, paternalistic, participative or *laissez-faire*? Incompatibilities arise if a wage structure is implemented in isolation of this consideration. An autocratic management style for instance is in conflict with a Scanlon/Rucker plan. Since the pay structure expresses to employees how the company values them, a real attempt must be made to draw up a declared wage policy. A framework for a policy statement is given later in this chapter.

CHANGING A WAGE STRUCTURE

The desire to change a wage structure usually springs from an existing structure which management no longer controls. Common features are that the present structure suffers from wage drift, that it has numerous rates which are inequitable in terms of individual contribution and there has been a gradual build-up of 'special' allowances.

Most companies, when faced with the need to change their wage structure, begin by looking for alternative incentives. In reality this is prejudging the issue. The first step should be an investigation to ascertain the pressure points which exist in the present structure. Only by discovering the 'lumps and the bumps' in the present system will the way ahead seem clear. A discussion with the senior wages clerk will be an enlightening experience since that individual, more than anyone else, is fully aware of the inadequacies and inequities of the existing system.

Wage analysis

This should be based on a thorough examination of the gross pay earned department by department, for say, a 'typical' week at two points in the year. All special allowances should be examined and the totals expressed as a percentage of labour cost. Consideration should be given to the effectiveness of the incentive element.

Overtime

The number of hours overtime should be broken down and scrutinized to see what indicators exist. Excessive overtime working usually means an unrealistic basic hourly rate. What, for example, would be the result if overtime working were curbed? If overtime earnings were consolidated in the basic rate on the understanding that productivity was maintained, would the need for overtime working cease? And would this be socially acceptable in your locality?

Work study

One of the main reasons why a company decides to change its wage structure is because work study values have worked loose and wage drift has become a dominant feature. For example, is the pace of working closely related to that shown on the time sheets? Too often top management assumes that because performances are high on paper, all is well. If the company's present work study team cannot cope with the situation, the use of consultants should be considered. An alternative is to employ experienced work study personnel on a short-term contract.

Labour turnover

Annual figures should be produced and broken down by department. These figures are normally associated with the social aspects of employment but it is not by any means unknown for a definite correlation to be established between them and the method of payment. For example, it is possible that a very low labour turnover linked to a very high rate of absenteeism indicates that earnings may be unusually high for the area but working conditions are intolerable, leading to low morale: the employees cannot afford to leave. In other words, it is just as problematic to grossly overpay people as to underpay.

Age and sex

On a departmental basis, figures should be produced for both men and women grouping them by age, for example 16-18, 19-25, 26-40, 41-50, 51-60, 61-65, 65+. Men and women in particular age groups have different attitudes to work and how their pay packet should be made up. Additionally, they will have fairly specific ideas about what they are prepared to do to earn £x per week. It is doubtful, for example, whether a middle-aged male work force would be enthusiastic about the introduction for the first time of direct incentives.

Attitude survey

Ideally an attitude survey should be made to ascertain what needs have to be satisfied through a wage structure. What are the employees' attitudes towards the current pay structure and what are their deeper expectations? The pay structure to a large extent determines and reinforces attitudes. Two of the areas a survey ought to highlight are the reasons why employees work for a particular company and what motivates them. Every company has a reputation as an employer and if it has achieved, for example, a 'quick buck' image, it will attract a particular type of employee. Thought must therefore be given to the kind of image the company wants to have and how it plans to achieve it.

What motivates people in your geographical area? What kind of incentives are socially acceptable, for instance? The whole of the Midlands is almost incurably on direct incentives and a firm that works otherwise is viewed with suspicion. In a free bargaining situation, a company introduced a new incentive scheme which theoretically should have increased take-home pay – and the impact was nil! An investigation highlighted the fact that the social custom was for young people to lay their unopened pay packet on the kitchen table each pay day and to receive in turn a fixed amount of pocket money. A little unusual in the 1980s, perhaps, but knowledge of this factor would have saved the company much time and trouble.

The survey should be done by an outside specialist in order to gain the confidence of the work force.

Influence of production method

Insufficient consideration is normally given to the link between the technological aspects of production and how people are paid. It is obvious that this is important and yet many operatives in a machine-controlled situation are on direct incentives intended to make them work faster! Similarly, it is not unusual for a company specializing in one-offs to have a direct incentive scheme which entails on-the-spot bargaining between, say, a rate fixer and a shop steward for every unit produced: the result is a hardening industrial relation climate.

These questions should be asked:

1 Are runs short, long, one-offs?
2 How important is quality, quantity, accuracy, consistency?
3 Is the operation operator- or machine-controlled? And what happens in *practice*?
4 What are the capital investment plans for the next 3-5 years? Will these developments influence pay structure?
5 What are the market pressures? Are there seasonal fluctuations?
6 Can buffer stocks be kept or is the product perishable?
7 How much is lost through scrap? (If the material is reconstituted, cost this.)

JOB EVALUATION

Job evaluation is an essential exercise if a company is to be truly in control of its wage structure. Certainly it is the only answer to leapfrogging pay claims and escalating special allowances.

Job evaluation can be as difficult or as expensive as a company likes to make it. Ranking is quite satisfactory; the basis of job evaluation is ranking anyway and all other methods are, in simple terms, administrative systems which are an aid to maintaining the original rank order of the benchmarks. Points rating is the most commonly used system, however.

Nowadays it is normal for a joint management/union committee to introduce job evaluation though this depends to a large extent on the industrial relations climate. It is important, however, for the committee to be trained before embarking on an exercise.

At the other end of the industrial relations scale, however, is the multi-union situation, or long-established union militancy, or a combination of both. In such a situation, the unions should be consulted regarding their role but they will probably prefer to let management make all the decisions while they reserve the right to object on behalf of their respective members. In any case, such unions are probably accustomed to an autocratic management style and a large dose of participation is just as difficult for the unions to countenance as for line management. Obviously, union participation simplifies the situation but involvement does not guaranteee instant success: there will still be appeals. What is important is that job evaluation is regarded as quite separate from negotiating actual rates.

The Industrial Society's book entitled *Job Evaluation* is useful.

COSTING

The basis of a carefully considered wage structure is sound costing. The company accountant, therefore, has an important role to play. Here are the major areas to be scrutinized for key indicators:

1 Budgeted labour cost for the coming year
2 Trend of total labour cost over the last five years
3 General breakdown of cost of the various wage components which contribute to the total labour cost for, say, the last two years
4 Earnings distribution for each department for two typical weeks
5 The unit cost of producing each selling line and the proportion of labour cost attributed
6 Cost of employee benefits. Frequently overlooked, these benefits are nonetheless part of the total labour cost
7 Cost of labour turnover. As a rule of thumb, a routine factory worker who leaves after, say, three months, has probably cost the company approximately £1000. This figure includes recruitment costs, interviewing time (allowance must be made for the average number of interviews to fill each job), initial training and a scale linked to the likely contribution an individual will make as his skill and know-how increases. A new employee does not begin to function as a member of a team until one or two weeks have elapsed.
8 Cost of absenteeism. (Absenteeism is being used in a wider context than simply illness). It is a useful pulse to take: if, say, absenteeism is running at a steady 20 per cent, possible causes are overmanning, overpaying or simply low morale. The cost of morale is not a balance sheet item but it is nonetheless an important hidden cost which must not be ignored.

FINANCING THE WAGE STRUCTURE

It is inflationary to set out to design and implement a new wage structure without first agreeing with the unions concerned that the increase in the wage bill must be found from within the company's resources. The actual cost of changing a wage structure is about 5 per cent of the wage bill, excluding cost-of-living for example. At first glance this figure will appear to be high: in effect a redistribution of cash and control is taking place with a short-term gain for the operatives involved and a medium-term gain for management. In a stable economy, no matter how sophisticated a company's techniques and know-how, it is possible to find savings to cover this cost. Of prime importance at the beginning of the exercise is agreement by management and unions on how the savings are to be achieved and shared.

Running concurrently with the initial investigation should be the operation of productivity groups or quality circles bent on finding savings. These groups under the leadership of their supervisor should comprise *operatives* meeting on a sectional or departmental basis during working hours or at the end of a shift (on overtime). Their remit should be a broad one where they may discuss every aspect of the organization and planning of the work in their immediate working area.

While the structure of the groups will depend on the size of the section or department, the numbers meeting at any one time should not exceed eight to ten. A simple record of decisions made should be kept by each group for the sake of continuity and an effort made to communicate this within the group. Training will be necessary to help the groups to assess each problem, devise probable solutions and make recommendations. Many companies underestimate the wealth of untapped potential which exists at shopfloor level. However, companies who have attempted a similar exercise have discovered that operatives are quite capable of using simple problem solving and costing techniques, for example. Provided the groups understand in essence the services provided by, say, the company's work study or production engineering specialists, the groups will ask for expert advice if the need arises.

DESIGNING THE WAGE STRUCTURE

Having established the realities of the existing structure, the next step is to design one which will meet the company's needs. The trend is for a company to have a two-tier wage structure: a basic hourly/job rate tier accounting for 80-85 per cent of the wage bill and an incentive tier (if any) accounting for 15-20 per cent.

Number of grades

The trend is to have four to six grades covering all factory personnel. The more straightforward the production process, the less reason for numerous grades. Without prejudicing the situation in the early stages of the investigation, there should be at least £7.50 per week differential between each grade. To have less will act as a disincentive to internal promotion. In effect this means reducing the number of grades to a point where the differential is a significant demonstration that work in a higher grade really is more important to the company. If the pay steps are too small, management will be faced with numerous requests for regrading jobs every time a fraction of responsibility or a grain of dirt is added to the job.

The decision regarding the break point for each grade is largely arbitrary. It will probably be a negotiating point. On the whole, jobs tend to fall into homogeneous groups but no matter where the break points are made, 'grey area' jobs on either side of the line will give rise to much tooth-sucking. It is from this area that job evaluation appeals usually spring.

As an aid to deciding where the break points might be, it is useful to produce some scattergrams showing how, for example, the results of job evaluation compare in relation to job holders' basic rates as well as gross pay (see Figure 52.1). The next step is to determine the 'line of best fit': in simple terms a line is drawn through the centre of the points already plotted It is then possible to determine roughly what the pay steps might be. In practical terms this is a quite considerable exercise and it may be that a 30 per cent sample, say, of all jobs might suffice.

Yet another statistical aid is the use of bar graphs. In most companies the bulk of the jobs will be in the middle two grades with roughly the same number in the bottom and top grades.

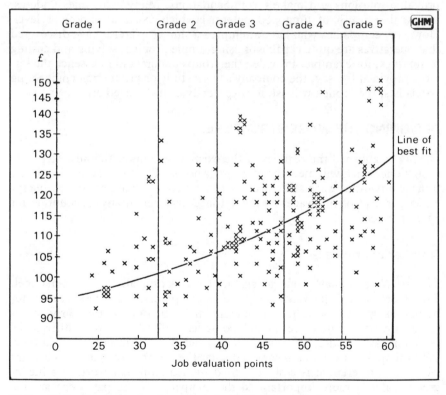

Figure 52.1 Scattergram of earnings (excluding overtime)
Related to job evaluation points as well as to possible break even points between grades and new pay steps

Deciding the basic rate

Traditionally, manual workers have been in a position where the ratio of basic rate to incentive was 2:1. However, this ratio now tends to be nearer 4:1 largely because companies moving towards single (staff) status are rightly challenging the concept that a manual worker's earnings should fluctuate with the company's production throughput.

The case for greater security of earnings should therefore be considered as a matter of course. If nothing else, a proportion of 2:1 is a prime cause of wage drift. Theoretically, a wage survey should be conducted with other firms but since the make-up of gross pay is so variable from company to company, it is difficult to establish any meaningful form of parity. A company must examine its own costing system in terms of budgeted labour cost and the relationship this bears to unit cost. In other words, management must decide how much of the budgeted labour cost should be attributed to basic rate and how much to incentive, if any. Since this is negotiable, management should also know in advance the influence on unit costs of different break points or alternative basic rates.

One company employing about 1000 people avoided this problem by taking the budgeted labour cost for the coming year and giving to the unions concerned three different 'mixes' of total wage cost. This was broken down into 3, 5 and 7 grades complete with incentive calculated at 80, 90 and 100 BSI. (80 BSI is a good average rate of working). The unions were told that they could produce another option still coming to the same total if they so desired. The company in question, while unused to this level of participation, had a history of good industrial relations. Obviously some unions will question the budgeted labour cost but this does not detract from the principle proposed.

Dealing with anomalies

Once the job evaluation exercise is completed and new basic rates determined, a scattergram will pinpoint those jobs which are likely to be over or underpaid in relation to the new rates. Provided the old structure was not completely out of control, the bulk of the jobs will be just about right with roughly the same number over as underpaid. The options open to management are:

For overpaid employees

1 Retrain the individuals concerned in order that they can take on work of a more responsible or skilful nature and therefore justify the new level of payment
2 Make the difference between the old rate and the new a personal allowance which would be eroded each time a new basic rate was agreed. In time the new rate would catch up with the old
3 As for 2, but the old rate – sometimes called a Red Circle Rate – is retained for ever and ever. This is not advised. In time this becomes a thorn in the side of other employees

4   Buy out anomalies by paying a lump sum comprising the difference multiplied by a negotiated figure. This is a strong negotiating area. What must be considered is the percentage of employees involved and whether or not the majority of differences will be swallowed up within twelve to eighteen months anyway

For underpaid employees. There are no options here: the individual's pay must be brought into line.

INCENTIVE ELEMENT

The word 'incentive' is synonymous with the word 'effort' in the minds of many. But this is not so. An incentive is some form of financial encouragement recognizing a particular contribution made by the work force. It is, in effect, a sum of money additional to the basic rate which a company pays to ensure that its most important production aspects are being optimized. For example, a capital-intensive company might have an incentive linked to machine utilization; a company making diamond-tipped tools might put particular emphasis on a low scrap value while still maintaining quality. Nonetheless many companies insist that effort is the only factor to recognize despite the fact that automation is very much with us.

Thought must be given to the *cost* of maintaining any one incentive: how many work study personnel, bonus clerks, tally clerks and inspectors are required to maintain standards? Can it be done in a more simple, effective way? Need there be an incentive? Will people only work on a carrot and stick basis? Will you, the reader, only work on this basis or are you different? What contribution does first-line supervision make to motivating people? Will the system encourage or stifle the growth of tomorrow's supervisors?

The basic decisions to be made about the incentive element are whether or not it is going to be individual, group, department or company based or a combination of these. The other important feature is whether the incentive is to be based on a straight-line formula (the more units produced the more earned *ad infinitum*) or on a curve where rather less is earned proportionately the more units produced, sometimes with a cut-off point to limit production and thereby restrict bonus. Yet another approach is to have a cut-off point beyond which any bonus earned is placed in a common pool. This in turn is used to help finance basic rates when these are renegotiated.

Direct incentives

Definition. A method of payment whereby a bonus is paid in direct relation to effort.

Advantages

1   Appropriate where a high level of physical effort is necessary and it is difficult to supervise workers effectively
2   Can generate substantial motivation as payment occurs shortly after achievement
3   Flexibility in allocating added reward for added effort
4   Introduction can mean a reduction in labour
5   Can be useful in the short term to increase the pace of working as an interim step to moving on to a more sophisticated system

Disadvantages

1   Management is not in control of production
2   Tendency to ignore avoidance of waste
3   Supervisors in time may earn less than their subordinates, skilled less than semi-skilled
4   People learn how to achieve earnings without undue effort, for example by qualifying for special allowances, avoiding promotion to non-lucrative jobs, embarking on slow-downs during 'testing' of new rates
5   Can ruin industrial relations
6   Mobility of labour becomes virtually impossible
7   Supervisors become good progress chasers but rarely good managers

Measured daywork

Definition. Measured daywork is a stablized direct incentive system where the incentive element is consolidated in the basic rate, thereby achieving a high, non-fluctuating weekly wage or salary.

It is based on sound training, sophisticated work measurement techniques and sound management. It is still payment by results except that the underlying philosophy is one of trust – that an individual will work at an agreed pace provided work is available for him or her. The most common types are:

High day rate, which is suitable in an assembly-line situation. Each new employee is fully trained before starting work on the factory floor. He or she will be expected to produce work of a specified standard and to maintain a fixed working pace of, say, 90 BSI. The aim is to achieve a controlled work flow: those individuals who have a naturally high pace of working would normally be transferred to indirect work. Those who have a naturally slow pace are subject to warnings and then either transferred to indirect work or dismissed, following reasonable warning.

Advantages

1   Simplified pay structure usually based on job evaluation
2   Considerable operating flexibility

3 Trust and responsibility given proper emphasis
4 Management is in control of production and uses work study standards as a condition of employment as well as for management information

Disadvantages

1 Not always possible to elicit acceptable levels of performance without the 'pull' of a direct incentive
2 Sophisticated control techniques, such as daily computer data, are necessary
3 High calibre of supervision is essential
4 Disputes can be tougher than in direct incentive plants as employees can slow down without impairing earnings

Philips premium pay plan is suitable where individuals can control the pace of work. The same principles as those for high day rate apply except, perhaps, the problem of disputes since PPP is based on individual effort.

The pay structure is a simple one, usually based on job evaluation, but unlike high day rate, it is graded in steps according to the pace of working (see Figure 52.2). Each individual contracts through his supervisor to work for a period of three months at a particular pace. If this pace is not maintained and the fault is not that of management, a warning is given. If the pace of working does not meet the agreed standard during the following three months, he or she is either retrained or moved back to a lower pay band. If he or she is unable to maintain an acceptable pace, he or she is liable to dismissal.

GHM

SALARY AND WAGE ADMINISTRATION

GRADE	80 BSI £	90 BSI £	100 BSI £
I	113.00	122.00	131.00
II	104.00	112.00	120.00
III	95.50	102.50	109.50
IV	87.50	93.50	99.50
V	80.00	85.00	90.00

Figure 52.2 Example of a wage structure of the Philips Premium Pay Plan type

Group/departmental incentives

Definition. A method of payment whereby a bonus is paid either equally or proportionately to individuals within a group/department as a result of, say, *output achieved* over an agreed standard.

Advantages

1 It encourages team spirit
2 It breaks down demarcation lines
3 The group disciplines its 'slackers'
4 Job satisfaction is achieved through seeing the complete operation within the group area

Disadvantages

1 Management is not in control of production
2 The bonus ceases in time to be an incentive and management might as well consolidate the rate
3 Individual effort is not rewarded

Plantwide incentives

There are three main types:

Factory throughput. Linked to, say, tons leaving the factory, the bonus is distributed either equally or proportionately according to skill. Basic concept is that workers become more closely associated with the company's aims.

Advantages

1 Improved atmosphere
2 Demarcation less pronounced
3 Employees are aware of the production targets the company plans to achieve

Disadvantages

1 Individual effort is not recognized
2 Employees find it difficult to associate themselves directly with the bonus
3 To safeguard against bad weeks/months, companies sometimes maintain a bank, so that the bonus becomes an employee benefit
4 If a bad week/month is experienced it's always the fault of 'other' departments

Scanlon plan. An alternative name is share of production plan. The nub of the system is the formation of a joint management-union productivity committee which has *executive authority*. The bonus is based on productivity improvements and is usually calculated monthly.

Rucker plan. An alternative name is cost reduction plan. The basic theory is that there is a constant relationship between wages and production or added value. A joint management-union productivity committee is formed but it has *advisory authority* only. Savings made by reducing costs are shared either equally or proportionately and are usually distributed on a monthly basis.

In a nutshell, Scanlon is strong on industrial relations and weak on mathematics and Rucker vice versa. In practice, the best of both methods is adopted. The share-out is usually about a third of total savings. The basic concept for both is that manual workers have very much more to offer to a company than simply effort.

Advantages of Scanlon/Rucker plans

1   Can encourage better use of resources and raw materials and thereby produce substantial savings
2   Focuses attention on cooperation and teamwork to reduce costs
3   Trust and responsibility given proper emphasis
4   People accept change more readily
5   Normally covers direct and indirect workers and can include staff directly linked with production
6   Work group has a stake in how well management performs – and has freedom to criticize poor decisions: it therefore keeps management on its toes

Disadvantages of Scanlon/Rucker plans

1   Cannot in themselves create a willingness to cooperate or a management capable of exploiting cost reduction
2   Some groups have more control over results than others and some contribute more than they receive
3   Parochialism can result: good communication is essential
4   Success largely hinges on sophisticated cost control techniques over a long period – and deciding on the 'right' calculation for distribution of savings

Profit-sharing

Definition. On the basis of company profits, employees either receive an annual cash bonus or actual company shares. Basic concept is participation.

Advantages

1   Thrives in non-union firms
2   From management's point of view, extra rewards are allocated only when they can be afforded
3   Improved teamwork and cooperation. However, to optimize this, management must communicate the economic facts of life
4   The system is self-adjusting although the method by which profits are calculated or the form in which the money is distributed may come under attack

Disadvantages

1   Workers have little control over final profit achieved
2   An industrious worker does not necessarily achieve extra payment

3 Tendency to withhold part of the profit to be shared against less fortunate times, thus making it a handout or employee benefit
4 Many schemes do not pay sufficient money to make an impact on motivation

Merit-rating

Definition. A method of payment based on management decisions about an individual's personal *qualities and aptitudes*. Basic concept is that management reserves the sole right to pay people individually.

Advantages

1 Supervisors regularly consider each subordinate's contribution
2 Method of payment is flexible
3 Employees feel they are being treated as individuals

Disadvantages

1 Because it is usually a subjective assessment, it is difficult to discuss problem areas without an element of emotionalism – always supposing they are discussed at all
2 Economic pressures often result in the system being bent with everyone ending up at the top end
3 Supervisors find it easier to pay everyone the same so that it effectively becomes an employee benefit

ADDED VALUE

It is a well-established fact that in a *stable economy* there is an almost constant relationship between labour costs and added value. It follows, therefore, that this provides a useful formula on which to calculate savings: these in turn can be used to fund annual wage increases on a plantwide basis.

For example, assume that unions and management agree (as a result of information provided by the company's auditors) that over the last five years labour cost has been 34 per cent of added value.

	£
Sales	100 000
Less raw materials, utilities and depreciation	55 000
Added value	45 000
Labour cost	15 300
Labour cost: Added value	34%

It is agreed that any savings made in labour cost beyond this reference point of 34 per cent will be shared equally between management and unions.

Assume that sales increase 20 per cent and that with no additional increases in basic cost the cost of providing raw materials is a further £11 000, and that labour costs increase by 10 per cent. The situation would appear thus:

	£
Sales	120 000
Less raw materials, utilities and depreciation	66 000
Added value	54 000
Labour cost	16 830
34% × £54 000	18 360
Saving in labour cost	1 530
Proportion contributed to plantwide increases	765

A total of 4.5 per cent on the total wage bill

It will be obvious that companies will be required to open their books if the operation of the added-value concept is to maintain credibility. Set against this is the fact that the more information which can be produced prior to negotiation, the less conflict there will be between management and unions. Approximately half of all disputes leading to stoppages are caused by friction over wage rates. A removal in part, even, of some of the reasons behind these stoppages would give both management and unions more time to contribute to other important areas.

PRODUCTIVITY AGREEMENTS

A productivity agreement is a statement jointly agreed by management and unions on how work and people may be more effectively organized to mutual benefit. Two types of agreement are:

1 An agreement using the 'buying out' principle on the basis of quid pro quo. In effect, this type of agreement covers immediate wage increases in exchange for relaxation of rigid demarcation lines; elimination of tea breaks; forfeiture of mates; reduction in manning levels
2 An agreement which lays down a framework for allowing savings to be accumulated over six to twelve months. These savings are normally shared equally between management and shopfloor employees

In a nutshell, the difference between the two is 'jam today or jam tomorrow'. In selecting the right approach, a company must consider what will best match its industrial relations climate *and* its overall company objectives. It may be that its lack of operating flexibility demands a 'buying out' agreement in the short term but its longer-term objectives require phased steps towards a position where greater participation will fund wage increases as well as strengthen the company's future. But it must be *planned*.

In times of high unemployment, productivity agreements of the buying-out type are not popular with unions. In any case, it is narrow to assume that increased productivity can *only* be achieved through a reduced labour force: there are numerous options which are equally valid. For example, what would be the effect of better machine utilization, improved work flow, reduction in scrap value, introduction of shift work? It is rather a question of selecting the right tools in order to make the best use of human resources.

Whatever form the agreement takes, it is, in effect, a *statement of intent* signed by both parties: what must not be overlooked is that it is not a once-and-for-all effort but a document calling for positive action throughout its term with regular progress reviews properly communicated. All too often companies negotiate excellent productivity agreements but fail to follow them through.

SINGLE STATUS

Employee or fringe benefits provide an element of security, a security which up until the last few years was the preserve of staff and management only. With the trend towards removing the differences in conditions between blue- and white-collar workers, unions are becoming increasingly aware of the value to their members of negotiating, for example, increased pensions. If the incentive element influences employee attitudes, how much more that of employee benefits? Sometimes overlooked, the Equal Pay Act requires equality in particular employee benefits as well as pay. If single status is the ultimate aim, a phasing operation must be planned in order that costs may be absorbed. The point being made is that employee benefits are part of the total labour cost and must be taken into account when looking at overall pay and conditions.

COMMUNICATION

An important area not stressed sufficiently is the need to communicate effectively. *The need to know* what is happening must be satisfied. Managers are often as starved of information as operatives! Will your present system cope? It is not the shop stewards' job to communicate management's intentions. Can your supervisors brief their subordinates face to face? What can you do to help them? Above all, every individual affected by the new pay structure must *understand* how it works. Could a simple booklet be produced? These are the main points concerning communication but since it is vital to the success of the whole project, readers are strongly advised to read the Industrial Society's booklet on 'Communication' in the *Notes for Managers* series.

SUPERVISORY STRUCTURE

Because many companies are attempting to move away from direct incentives, it is wise to comment on the need to investigate the existing supervisory structure and to consider the calibre, in effect, of first-line managers. Whatever management decides in terms of a new structure, first-line supervisors will be required to manage more effectively. Apart from training needs, the span of control must be examined. If a supervisor is to manage effectively, the most he can control and motivate is fifteen to twenty operatives. The successful implementation of a new wage structure hinges on how carefully this aspect is handled.

EXAMPLE OF A WAGE POLICY STATEMENT

It is the intention of management that this document be issued to every employee whom it concerns. It is the responsibility of first-line management to explain it fully to their subordinates. Should anyone feel that any aspect of this policy is not operating in practice, he should as a first step discuss this with his supervisor.

Aims

The aims of the policy are:

1   To recognize the value of all jobs in relation to each other within the company
2   To take account of wage rates paid by companies of similar size, product and philosophy
3   To ensure stable earnings
4   To enable individuals to reach their full earning potential as far as is reasonably practicable
5   To ensure employees share in the company's prosperity as a result of increasing efficiency.

Job evaluation

The basis of a sound wage structure is job evaluation. It is in the interest of both unions and management that this is carried out on a joint basis.

Job evaluation is a continuing process and therefore must be maintained if it is to retain its usefulness. To ensure that the scheme is still relevant, it will be reviewed jointly by unions and management at the end of its third operating year.

Wage structure

In designing the wage structure, the company aims to make the best use of its employees in order to achieve the company's short- and longer-term business objectives. By achieving these objectives the company hopes to remain a leader in its field, thereby ensuring greater job security for all concerned.

Rate for the job

No one will be paid less than the recognized rate for the job. Equal pay is in force on the basis of 'equal pay for work of equal value'. While the company recognizes the right of the unions' joint negotiating panel to negotiate on behalf of its members, management believes that first and foremost rates should be linked to the company's prosperity.

The company does not aim to pay the top rates in the area but rather to place the emphasis on good working conditions, security of employment and an atmosphere in which individuals may reach their full potential. Nonetheless the company aims to be in the top 15 per cent as far as total earnings are concerned. (Total earnings includes employee benefits.)

Number of grades

The number of grades will be as few as possible in order that differentials are of a sufficiently high level for real differences in responsibility and/or skill to be recognized.

Incentives

The company does not accept that its employees will work only on a carrot and stick basis; neither does it believe that its employees will give of their best if earnings fluctuate from week to week. This policy is reflected in the company's wage structure which is based on measured daywork.

Every employee should, wherever reasonably practicable, have the opportunity to reach maximum earnings for his grade. Provided work is available, employees are expected to work at a mutually agreed pace. Where work is not immediately available, employees will not lose financially but will be expected to move to alternative work in order to maintain production.

Where individual targets are not maintained, and management is not responsible, an employee must expect to be counselled, disciplined if necessary and, as a last resort, dismissed.

Work measurement

The basis of the wage structure is work measurement. The company aims to use the most advanced methods available. However, it does not intend to wrap these methods in a jargon not easily understood. All production managers (including first-line supervisors) and shop stewards will attend jointly sponsored appreciation courses in order that any disagreement over standards is discussed in full knowledge of how the system works.

Indirect workers

Indirect workers such as maintenance, cleaning and catering employees play an important support role in the overall production process. It is not possible to apply work measurement techniques to indirect jobs at an economic cost. An enhanced day rate will therefore be payable to employees in this category.

Minimum earnings

No employee will receive less than £80.00 for a 40-hour week. This ensures that lower-paid employees are paid a 'living wage', but employees in other grades must not expect that established differentials will necessarily be maintained.

Overtime

The wage structure is designed to ensure that excessive overtime is both unnecessary and unattractive. Overtime is a requirement which will only arise in very exceptional circumstances. Since it is management's responsibility to plan work effectively and determine manning requirements, 72 hours' notice will be given of the need for overtime working, except in very exceptional circumstances.

Promotion

The company operates a policy of internal promotion, wherever possible. When a promotion takes place, the individual will immediately take the 'rate for the job'. However, if the individual is on maximum earnings for his old grade, he will retain the old rate for three months until he has established himself in the new grade.

In exceptional cases where the individual fails to maintain a satisfactory level of performance, he will be transferred to lower-grade work. He will, however, retain the higher rate until the annual negotiation of wage rates when his personal rate will be eroded.

A similar policy operates for staff promotions.

Single status

It is company policy to remove progressively all differences in employee benefits for blue and white collar employees. To this end, the cost of such benefits will be included in overall labour costs. The ultimate aim is to move towards a 'package' concept negotiated annually.

Share of prosperity

The company believes that employees have a right to share in the company's prosperity. It also believes that increases in its labour bill should not be passed automatically to its customers. A special formula has therefore been agreed between management and unions whereby all savings made as a result of shopfloor participation will be divided on a $^{50}/_{50}$ basis and used to finance increased wage costs.

Negotiating information

The company believes that only by providing its recognized unions with sound, factual information can a positive industrial relations climate be fostered. Agreed information will be issued quarterly to the joint negotiating panel.

CHECKLIST: CHANGING A WAGE STRUCTURE

The following checklist is intended to provide a starting point for discussion before installing a new wage structure. The list is by no means exhaustive but answering such questions should enable managers to decide the direction in which they plan to go in the short and longer term.

Company objectives

1 Apart from profit, what are you in business for?
2 Where are you going during the next two to three years; in the next five to ten years?
3 How do you plan to get there?
4 What influence will these plans have on your wage structure?
5 How can the wage structure aid the company in meeting its objectives?

Product

1 Are runs short, long, one-offs?
2 How important is quality, quantity, accuracy, consistency?

3 Is the process operator- or machine-controlled?
4 What are the capital investment plans for the next three to five years? Will these developments influence the pay policy?
5 What are the market pressures? Are there seasonal fluctuations?
6 Can buffer stocks be kept or is the product perishable?
7 How much is lost through scrap? (If the material is reconstituted, cost this.)

Work measurement

1 Are measurements loose, tight or a mixture of both?
2 Is pay related to effort? Is this what you want anyway?
3 To what extent are you subject to wage drift, that is, increasing labour costs with little or no increase in productivity?
4 Do your supervisors and shop stewards understand the principles of work measurement?
5 Have you enough industrial engineers to ensure that three separate studies are made before each standard is decided?
6 Are your existing studies sufficiently accurate to allow you to consider the introduction of synthetic ratings?
7 How about method study?
8 Will it be necessary to employ contract work-study personnel? Or experienced industrial engineers on a short-term contract?

Wage analysis

1 How many wage rates exist?
2 Where do national agreements fit in?
3 Is there a 20 per cent differential between supervisors' pay and the average gross pay (less overtime) of those they supervise?
4 What is the budgeted labour cost for the coming year? Does it include the cost of employee benefits?
5 What is the trend of *total* labour cost for the last five years?
6 How many elements make up gross pay? How many of these do you wish to consolidate? Or buy out?
7 What is the earnings distribution for each department for two, separate, typical weeks?
8 What trends are indicated from a breakdown of overtime worked?
9 What is the cost of producing each selling line and the proportion of labour cost attributed?
10 What is the cost of labour turnover?
11 What is the cost of absenteeism?

Job evaluation

1 What is the simplest possible method you could use which would satisfy the company's and the job holders' needs?

2 Should there be a joint job evaluation committee?
3 Should it be a full or part-time exercise?
4 To what extent can you involve the job holders?
5 Who should write the job description? The job holder, a job analyst or a member of the job evaluation committee?
6 How much information are you prepared to give to job holders about the scheme? Do you mean, for example, to tell each job holder the number of points allocated to his job? Could you give everyone concerned a copy of the scheme?
7 Will your existing appeals procedure match the needs of a job evaluation exercise?
8 Could you time and cost in advance the implementation of job evaluation?

Financing the wage structure

1 Can you finance from within the increased cost of the new wage structures?
2 Could you negotiate initially the share-out between company and employees of any savings made?
3 How can you communicate effectively the aims of the exercise?
4 What training will have to be undertaken?
5 How can you involve your supervisors in order that they make a major contribution to the exercise?

Social aspects

1 What is the age and sex distribution by job and department?
2 What motivates your employees? What are their aspirations? Would an attitude survey be useful?
3 What kind of image does your company have? Is it what you want?
4 What kind of incentives are people used to in your geographical locality? Would your proposals cut across the expectations of your employees? What can you do to engineer the change?
5 How do you rate your industrial relations? How can this exercise improve them?
6 What is the company's predominant management style? Will the new wage structure alter this in any way? How can you involve middle and senior management in such a way that they become party to the proposals?
7 What plans have you regarding such things as security of employment and earnings; single status?
8 How important is a stable work force to the company? Is it company policy to promote from the shop floor? Will the new pay structure influence or detract from this?

Designing the wage structure

1 From scattergrams of the existing situation, what anomalies exist? How many of these can you hope to get rid of first time around?
2 Using the scattergrams, how many grades ought you to have in the short term? What are you aiming for in the long term?
3 How can you involve your company accountant in order that the exercise is properly costed?
4 Is an alternative incentive planned? Do you need incentives anyway? If you do, will they be individual, group or company based? Or a combination of these?
5 What effect will the incentive element have on your products, the way you plan work, the way you manage people, employee attitudes?
6 Could you work out three possibilities for, say, a 3, 5 or 7 grade structure complete with differentials and incentive element, if any, each coming to the total budgeted labour cost?
7 How competitive would these rates be locally?
8 What is your policy on equal pay?
9 What will your unions be expecting at the negotiating table?
10 What kind of productivity agreement do you need? To what extent can you make it a charter for the future?
11 How far can you go in giving information to your unions in order that negotiation may be constructive?
12 How will you handle pay anomalies?

Implementing a wage structure

1 How can you improve your methods of communication in order that everyone *understands* what is happening?
2 Do senior managers understand how the new pay structure might affect them? Marketing and sales, for example?
3 What training can you give to your supervisors in order that their status and respect is strengthened and not weakened by the demands of the new pay structure?
4 Is your supervisory structure adequate in relation to the needs of the new pay structure? Can you give your supervisors more scope for decision-making without reference to the next level? Is their span of control about right in view of the demands which will be put on them?
5 What training should you give to shop stewards in order that they are aware of the implications of the new structure?

FURTHER READING

ACAS, *Advisory Booklet No. 1 – Job Evaluation*, Advisory Conciliation and Arbitration Service, London, 1979

Bowey, Angela M. (ed.), *Handbook of Salary and Wage Systems*, 2nd edition, Gower, Aldershot, 1982

Lupton, T., and Bowey, Angela M., *Wages and Salaries*, 2nd edition, Gower, Aldershot, 1983

53 Employee benefits

John Muir

Company reports invariably allude to the contribution made by the employees. This acknowledgement of the role of employees in the success of the firm itself reflects the fact that without their efforts little could be achieved. Increasingly, however, it is being recognized that the employment of a workforce is a costly business. The pressure of rising costs and greater competition is driving employers to seek ways of using that workforce more effectively. Some ways in which this can be done, like work measurement, skill flexibility and so on, are outside the scope of this chapter; but the factors which lead to a stronger sense of participation through financial means, and to a feeling that the firm's reward system is structured to meet the needs of the employee, are matters which can be examined under the heading of employee benefits.

BENEFITS IN RELATION TO OTHER EMPLOYMENT COSTS

The costs incurred in employing staff are not just the obvious items like overtime payments, allowances and direct wages. The state makes a major intervention in terms of the employer's contribution to pensions and social security benefits of all kinds and, for all but the smallest firms, the whole cost of redundancy payments falls to the employer. It has been estimated that in 1986 UK employers were paying some 35 per cent over and above basic wages to cover obligations like social security contributions, payment for public holidays, sick pay and holiday pay. That figure will rise if costs relating to maternity pay and statutory sick pay fall to the employer (being mooted at the time of writing). In comparison with a number of other countries in Western Europe there is still some way to go. A recent study showed that in Sweden such extra costs amounted to nearly 70 per cent of basic wages. In Holland they were almost 80 per cent.

Whether because the employer has to contribute by law, whether he does so on a range of additional items to keep up with his competitors or whether he does so because he feels that certain benefits are important for his workforce, the net result is a big increase over his direct labour costs. So a starting point for any employer is to determine the total amount he wishes to spend, or can afford to spend, and then to consider how this sum might be split as between direct pay and benefits. Very rarely does a company provide a single benefit; they normally come as a package which operates alongside, and very closely with, the salary structure. The best benefits package is one that combines the optimum benefits to employees with the optimum benefits to the employer. In other words, while it might at first sight seem that benefits are provided primarily for the benefit of the employee they should as a matter of equal importance provide a benefit to the employer in the form of higher motivation, more efficient working, increased cooperation and a better working atmosphere.

When establishing a complete set of benefits it is important to realize that it will be effective only so long as the salary structure is satisfactory. That structure must have integrity and be able to reward employees according to the responsibilities they carry. It does not necessarily have to be rigid in its application but any variations from established principles must have a proper basis and be capable of being explained against objective criteria. Perhaps the structure should also accommodate the notion of meritorious performance by being incremental. Whatever the detail of the scheme it should be fair in operation. The best benefits package may make a partly defective salary structure just about acceptable, but it will not turn a bad salary structure into an acceptable one. On the other hand a poorly designed benefits package can make what might otherwise be a good salary structure into a singularly unattractive feature.

What are employee benefits? Some indication has already been given in referring to pensions, social security insurance, redundancy payments and holidays. Indeed the list is a long one – house purchase, life insurance, meals and so on – and the opportunity will now be taken to examine a number of items in detail. It is important to recognize that some benefits may be more applicable to one group than another. A current feature in employment is the gradual removal of the distinction between blue collar and white collar workers. The development of personnel policies, including the benefits package, has for instance largely seen the disappearance of the holiday differentials between one and the other – indeed some would argue that the pendulum has swung the other way! Furthermore, the very considerable degree of unionization has meant (a) that the benefits package has figured in union demands and (b) that many middle managers and some senior managers are themselves in bargaining units with their conditions of employment subject to the outcome of negotiations. The employer is thus increasingly being required to consider the whole cost (salary and benefits) in his dealings with unions. To argue that for this reason there is less flexibility in dealing with benefits would be to misunderstand the nature of collective bargaining. It may be that the respective emphasis which unions and employer put on benefits will differ according to the industry, and economic indicators, but it should not stop the employer from making his offer partly in cash and partly in benefits if that is what he thinks is good for his workforce. Flexibility still has a major part to play in the managerial area where the senior executive and the company can negotiate what comes in cash and what in benefits.

The total cost concept of a benefits and salary package

The cost of an employee is made up of three components: salary, benefits and overheads. The last is difficult to quantify but the other two add up to so many pounds per year. Companies are increasingly taking the view that they should offer the senior executive a total compensation package, i.e., a ceiling is set to an employee's total compensation. For the sake of argument, assume that for a senior manager the total compensation is £25 000 pa. Within this total, certain minima and maxima are set. For example:

Salary	55-100 per cent of the ceiling
Car	£5000-£8500
House purchase	up to £8000
Insurance, medical and otherwise	up to £1500
Children's education	up to £3000

Thus an employee with a ceiling of £25 000 with two children at school might choose £2000 for their education, £5000 for his car, £4000 for his house purchase and £14 000 for his salary; whereas his older colleague, whose children have left school, who wants to buy a new house and who dislikes driving could choose £8000 for his house purchase, £1500 for insurance and £15 500 salary.

The obvious advantage of this system is that each employee can choose the benefits which are of most use to him. Furthermore, an employee who has no need of a particular benefit will not feel hard done by if his colleague avails himself of it because he knows that he can take other benefits or a larger salary.

The disadvantages are first that too much flexibility can create administrative difficulties and, second, an executive who chooses unwisely may feel aggrieved later in his working career. These drawbacks can be reduced to manageable proportions by limiting choice within components; for example, a particular insurance may not be reduced during its period of existence or the car may not be changed more frequently than once every three years.

CATEGORIES OF BENEFITS

In devising its remuneration policy a company will regard certain benefits as most important – like a pension or a car – and then other benefits as less so. While this approach is sound, care should be exercised in taking away or trimming back these 'other' benefits, or indeed in not adding to existing benefits on the grounds that they are trivial, lest this conflict with employees' perceptions. It is surprisingly easy to make a wrong move in this area. All benefits clearly have a monetary value which is important to the recipients, but the true value of some of them bears less relation to this than it does to the intrinsic nature of the benefit. Employees' attitudes and wishes should be taken into account – a feature which will be examined later.

Benefits can usefully be divided into three groups: status, security and work benefits.

Status	*Security*	*Work*
Cars	Pension	Office accommodation
Meals	Housing	Sabbaticals
Holidays	Share schemes	Management training
Telephone	Medical and insurance	Subscriptions
Gifts	Scholarships for children	
Entertainment facilities		Discount, company purchase
Foreign travel	Creche	Sports and social clubs
	Notice period and redundancy	
		Retirement counselling

STATUS BENEFITS

Cars

The provision of company cars needs to be undertaken within a well defined policy. Without a policy, or if a policy exists but is regularly disregarded, then the potential benefit to the company is severely reduced since recipients spend their time and energy pressing for something better and complaining in the process. Car provision can make for the extremes of satisfaction and effectiveness. Apart from office accommodation, no other benefit so easily identifies an executive's seniority in the firm. Therefore it is important for it to achieve its maximum effect.

The actual policy can have many components. Some firms stipulate that cars must be of domestic origin; others restrict the choice to EEC manufacture while a smaller number give unlimited choice of make. The cost of car will depend upon the position of the employee in the firm but here the importance of clearly defined and understood rules becomes clear. If the firm has a graded structure then the different levels of executive can be readily identified. At any particular level the employee concerned will know his entitlement. Again the policy does not have to be completely inflexible. Perhaps a group of employees undertakes representational duties where a more expensive car would be consistent with the image the company wishes to maintain. There must always be a sound reason for departing from general rules.

The type of car supplied can be determined by engine capacity, or by price, or by letting the price of one selected car determine the upper limit for that group. Some firms allow executives to add their own money, within defined limits, to car purchase but care should be exercised to avoid creating the impression that the car policy as such has been ignored.

The administration of a car scheme will inevitably entail the use of staff resources. The vehicles will have to be bought and individual requirements taken into account. It is desirable to have a policy which is as unrestrictive as possible. An entitlement to a car, however expensive, whose make is unacceptable to the individual concerned diminishes very substantially the perceived value of the benefit. The criteria in operating a car policy should be flexibility and choice within the company's administrative capability.

Meals

The provision of meals to executives is another highly sensitive area. Dining facilities do not just represent a cost saving to the individual concerned, though this can be significant. Provision of a dining room permits the company to entertain customers and clients in agreeable surroundings and it develops a corporate sense amongst executives. While it need not be a prime purpose the fact remains that informal discussions over drinks and a meal can make a material contribution to keeping executives abreast with developments and problems elsewhere in the organization. The operation of dining facilities should be kept simple. Restricting the range of drinks for less senior staff, for example, can be very divisive indeed.

The provision of subsidized canteens for employees can be a very useful benefit both in cash terms and in convenience. In setting up a canteen or deciding to continue an arrangement a company should consider the true cost of the benefit being provided. A meal which costs the company a certain amount will not necessarily be recognized as worth that much to the employee; if left to his own devices he would almost invariably settle for something simpler.

Holidays

Differentials in holiday entitlement as between one group of staff and another have tended to disappear over the past few years. Furthermore, discussion about the length of the working week has, in some industries, been in the context of the length of the working year. In other words holiday absence and the working week have been coupled together. Both are cost items and while the calculations will vary according to the industry or job, every extra day's holiday can be expressed in money terms. While the trend is towards a common entitlement, many senior executives will still enjoy a substantial holiday allowance but claim that, due to work pressures, they are unable to take the full entitlement. If there are indeed such pressures companies should examine the reasons. It is a well-established fact that holidays, far from being a benefit in the sense of being an extra, are essential to the good health of employees in general and senior staff in particular. Companies should explore the possibility of encouraging its executives to take holidays, say, at the end of a business trip on which their wives have accompanied them, or to take a sabbatical.

Another feature of holiday absence relates to domestic and personal circumstances. Maternity leave, subject to a two-year service qualification with the employer, is an employee's right but many employers now offer more than the statutory entitlement as an employee benefit. Furthermore, a substantial number of employers give paternity leave – usually about three days – so that the husband is on hand to cope at least with the first wave of changes which come with a new arrival in the family. Bereavement leave is also an established benefit and is designed to permit the immediate relative to make the necessary funeral arrangements.

Telephone

In the great majority of firms there will be key staff when it comes to out-of-hours incidents. If the refrigeration in a cold store breaks down the senior executive will need to know, even though the maintenance engineer will be the person to take action. If there is a walkout on the evening shift, the personnel director will need to know. So these, and people like them, must be contactable by telephone. There is good case for the company paying the whole of the rental. Other senior staff may or may not be crucial in this sense but the ability to contact them by phone may be sufficient reason and justification for paying part of the rental. Companies will have to weigh the strength of the case against the cost involved but there is little doubt that support with telephone costs is a useful benefit.

Gifts

Until fairly recently most companies could boast about the number of long-service employees. Nowadays really long service (say twenty years or more) is far less common. Nevertheless, a substantial number of companies continue to operate a long-service gift policy as a means of identifying the individual with the company and rewarding loyalty. Generally speaking the arrangements find favour with the recipients. It is, however, fair to say that many employees prefer cash, either as a lump sum or an increment to salary.

Entertainment facilities

Entertaining may be an extension of the working arrangements commented upon in the discussion on dining facilities, or it can be, for certain executives, a fundamental part of their job involving home and leisure time. In fact it is not leisure, in that the executive is entertaining the firm's clients in the interests of business. The pressure on many businessmen today has meant that entertainment for entertainment's sake is rapidly declining but that, as a means of finding extra working hours, it is extremely useful.

If entertaining at home is not possible then access to appropriate club facilities can fill the gap; and many companies in recognizing this pay the club subscription. It could be argued that this is truly a business expense but on the other hand many executives see the arrangement as a benefit in that the facilities offered by the club can be used by the whole family.

Foreign travel

Like entertaining, travel is probably considered an attractive benefit initially but loses its glamour when it becomes a regular feature of the job. Indeed if this aspect of the work assumes too large a proportion it can become burdensome. However, the absence of business travel can again be counter-productive to an executive who has been used to going abroad. To executives not heavily involved in foreign travel, the occasional trip to overseas customers or overseas offices is a genuine attraction and can be used productively. There is a real gain to be made in establishing personal contact and in undertaking a representational role. It is well worth while a company considering whether wives can accompany their husbands on the occasional trip; this will not only lead to greater identification of an executive's family with his work but will also provide some compensation for the commitment he may be called upon to make to his work.

SECURITY BENEFITS

Pension

Pension schemes in the private sector are now commonplace but it would be a mistake to think that everyone is covered. Most managerial and executive staff would be, but large numbers of blue collar workers would not be in an occupational scheme. While on the one hand, therefore, many employees would regard a pension scheme as a normal feature of employment, it remains a real benefit. After all, a normal funding basis would be that for every 1 per cent of salary contributed by the employee, the employer would pay double – and indeed more if, as has generally been the case, pension schemes have run into an actuarial deficit due to inflation. A normal pension scheme has four main features:

1　A retirement pension payable at a predetermined age
2　A facility to commute a part of the pension to a lump sum free of tax
3　A death benefit
4　A widow's and dependants' pension in the event of the death of the employee in service or in retirement.

The rate at which pension accrues is often $^1/_{60}$th of salary for every year of service leading to a maximum of $^{40}/_{60}$ths but the salary determination has itself been subject to widespread improvement in the past few years. Good schemes looked at the salary of the last three years of service and took an average; nowadays the best schemes take the most advantageous definition of final salary. Part of the pressure to take the final year has been a direct reflection of inflation but the net result has been that inflation by itself plus now final year salary for calculation purposes has vastly increased the cost of funding pension schemes. Much of the burden has fallen on employers.

Apart from the basic benefit element in a good pension scheme, attention has increasingly been paid to flexibility within the scheme itself. Thus better transfer value arrangements, added years for short service, payment of accrued pensions (or pensions calculated on what would have been total service) in circumstances of ill health or involuntary retirement, additional voluntary contributions, are all features which are commonly found. Voluntary retirement can be a way of making room for new managers and creating promotion opportunities.

Pension arrangements should be seen both as a significant benefit and as a management tool (certainly a vital one in the 1980s).

Housing

Banks and financial institutions have provided house purchase facilities to their employees for a long time. Many other companies have housing support schemes. They may not lend the money direct to the employees, but will offer a degree of mortgage support. The real benefit is in any case substantial. It enables the employee to buy his own property and perhaps more importantly to buy at a higher standard of housing than his salary would otherwise support. Furthermore, as house prices continue to rise and as companies expect their executives to be more mobile, it is becoming a matter of prime importance to consider the scale and extent of house purchase facilities and mortgage support. Another question is whether the facility should be open to all employees or if not then to what level. In addition to the question of cost there is a danger that employees will be 'locked in' to the company by their dependence on the loan or the support. Provided care is taken to avoid these dangers, house purchase or housing support schemes can provide a very genuine attraction in recruiting and retaining appropriate staff. Such schemes are considered very important by the employees themselves.

Employee share schemes

There are now three Inland Revenue 'approved' employee share schemes: the Profit Sharing Scheme enacted under the Finance Act 1978, the Savings-Related Share Option Scheme enacted under the Finance Act 1980, and the Selective or Executive Share Option Scheme enacted under the Finance Act 1984. In each of these schemes, the approved status granted by the Inland

Revenue enables the participating employees to enjoy income tax relief on the gains made on their shares acquired under each of the schemes.

A company's profit sharing scheme is established by a trust deed and rules under which independent trustees are appointed to administer the scheme on the employees' behalf. The profit declared by the company for the scheme is used to subscribe for newly issued or to purchase existing shares in the company, which are then held by the trustees for the employees for a minimum of two years. If the shares are released to the employees between two and five years from this date of appropriation, then income tax is levied. Reliefs are available in compassionate circumstances. After five years, the shares are passed to the employees free of all tax. The legislation provides that employees must be treated on similar terms and all full-time employees with five or more years' service must be included in the scheme. The statutory maximum value of shares which can be distributed is £1250 per annum or 10 per cent of the salary if greater, with an overall limit of £5000 per annum. The shares must be in the company in which the participant is employed, although employees in a subsidiary company can participate in a parent company scheme where the parent company is a quoted company. The Association of British Insurers, whose Investment Protection Committee acts as a watchdog for institutional investors, has laid down guidelines for such schemes and has limited the amount of profit that a company ought to set aside for such a scheme at 5 per cent of profit before tax. In February 1986, the Inland Revenue had approved over 500 such schemes.

A savings-related share option scheme provides for options to be granted to employees to purchase shares which are financed from an employee's own Sharesave Contract with a building society or the Department of National Savings. The scheme consists of two contracts; the first being the grant of the share option by the company to acquire shares, exercisable in five or seven years from the date of grant, but at the share price then prevailing although a discount of up to 10 per cent of the share price may be allowed. The second contract is a savings contract in which the employee contracts to save a set amount of money each month to acquire those shares in five or seven years' time.

This time period must be specified at the outset. The amount of the contracted savings, together with the terminal bonus determines the number of shares over which options will be granted to the employee. At present, the terminal bonus consists of the equivalent of 14 months' savings for a five-year contract, and 28 months' savings for a seven-year contract. The decision to exercise the option is not made until this maturity date, at which time the participant can either exercise the option in whole or in part, or withdraw his savings and bonus from the Sharesave account. The legislation provides for limits on the savings contract between a minimum of £10 per month and a maximum of £100 per month, as well as concessionary provisions for involuntary termination of the employment. In February 1986, the Inland Revenue had approved over 500 such schemes.

Under the selective or executive share option scheme options to acquire shares are granted selectively by the company to employees without any contractual savings provisions. Employees working 20 hours (25 in the case of directors) a week are eligible to participate. The limits on the value of share options must not exceed the greater of £100 000 or four times the participant's emoluments. An option is exercisable between three and ten years from the date of grant and can be exercised in whole or in part, subject to a three-year gap between partial exercises. In February 1986, the Inland Revenue had approved over 1300 schemes.

In all employee share schemes, the employees and the company benefit from the common objective to achieve an increase in the prosperity (and the share price) of the company. The employees can monitor the value of their stake in the company and benefit from the increased participation by their direct interest in its success and profitability.

Insurances

The provision of additional insurance cover for employees can be a significant benefit. The insurance cover can be provided as part of the company's pension plan or it can be additional to it. Insurance cover can be restricted to the time when the employee is working on company business or it can be operable on all occasions. If it were easy to draw a sharp line between time spent on business activity and own time the former would be an obvious choice. If, however, the employee has tasks which make it uncertain whether time is official or private who can say what insurance cover operates? If an executive is meeting a potential client out of normal hours but as part of his job, the question is: 'Is it worth risking a dispute whether insurance cover operates or not when, for a small extra cost, overall cover can be secured?' Total cover is one area where the company can get a cost-effective deal because insurance is relatively cheap to provide on a group basis.

In cases where the employee has died in service the benefits both tangible and intangible for his widow can be very large. Similarly at small extra cost provision can be made to cover permanent incapacity to work, even from month one of employment, on the simple basis that very few people indeed suffer such a misfortune. But for the individual concerned and his family the benefit accruing is very highly regarded.

In the field of medical care insurance arrangements organized by the company at no cost to employees or reduced cost are well established. This is a field hitherto almost exclusive to manager and executives, but fairly recently a major craft union negotiated such arrangements with the employer covering staff generally. Not only does this form of insurance normally provide more comfortable care in the sense that privacy is invariably a feature, but it also ensures that for treatment of a non-urgent kind specific dates can often be arranged to suit the convenience of both the employee patient and the company. Furthermore, private treatment can usually allow an executive to carry out important parts of his work from his hospital bed. This should be seen both in the context of the firm getting service out of employee and of the employee feeling that he is continuing to make a valuable contribution to the company. In this situation such insurance may be seen to be prudent from the company's point of view and (subject, naturally, to the employee's true state of health), therapeutic in so far as recovery is concerned.

While occupational sick leave is common it should nevertheless be seen as a true benefit. There is no legal requirement to provide it; all the employer is legally required to do is to say whether such a scheme is in operation or not. For many blue collar workers a sick pay scheme is still an absent feature but its implementation can act as an added security benefit. Payment during sickness can be effected via insurance cover if the company does not want to bear the risk itself. Clearly the smaller the firm the greater the cost of having an employee away for a long period and insurance cover would appear to offer the better solution.

On-site medical facilities are likely to be of less importance to the average senior executive or manager – although it is as well to bear in mind the incidence of heart attack. However, where he is responsible for a plant or factory which is not close to medical facilities on-site provision can be useful.

Scholarships for children

Few companies are prepared to take the lead in providing facilities for the payment of school fees for the children of employees though some companies have set up machinery whereby an independent panel consider applications from employees and recommend awards accordingly. There is certainly a recognition on the part of senior management in companies that this is one area where executives are likely to be faced with increasing costs. One way in which the executive can be materially assisted to meet such cost is for the company to arrange for personal financial-planning consultants to advise its executives on a group basis, with the company paying the consultants' fees. Such a service, which is already fairly well established, has the advantage of giving individual freedom of choice; and it certainly indicates the company's interest in the welfare of the employee and his children.

Crèches

The increasing demand for able managers and the greater freedom being demanded by women means that a higher proportion of senior posts will be held by women in the future. The dual role of wife/mother and executive is already established but further encouragement will need to be backed up by the provision of child care facilities. Many companies have a formal equal opportunities policy. This feature, coupled with statutory provisions on rights to the job after maternity leave, has already led companies to consider the scope and extent of such support. Facilities in this area can be regarded as a benefit to both employee and employer. On the employee's side there is confidence in that care is being provided while on the employer's side there is continuing access to the employee's skills and experience. That skill and experience was probably a heavy cost to the company in terms of recruitment and training. Providing child care facilities is clearly more sensible than starting all over again with a new employee.

Notice period and redundancy pay

It may seem a contradiction to be discussing security benefits in the context of the employee leaving the firm. Nevertheless, for a variety of reasons many employees, including many executives, will find that their jobs come to an end. It may be due to merger and rationalization, to a changing market which reduces the need for certain expertise, or to the need to insert fresh thinking into senior posts by promoting other able people. The benefit in employment terms comes with the appreciation that if the job finishes there will be reasonable compensation.

Minimum notice periods are fixed by legislation. For service with the employer of twelve years or more, twelve weeks' notice must be given to the employee. In cases of redundancy or job loss, pay in lieu of notice is often given. Notice pay can therefore be a substantial sum and many employers in recognizing the seniority of the employee have given via the employment contract notice periods of six and twelve months.

Since 1965 redundancy pay has been a statutory requirement. The maximum statutory entitlement is bounded by a limit of twenty years' service and an upper pay limit of £155 per week. Weighting is given for age but it means that no more than thirty weeks' worth times £155 is available. Shorter service below age forty gives a simple one week's pay for each year times pay or £155 whichever is the lesser sum. Very many employers, both private and public sector, have greatly enhanced scales of payment so that on leaving a job the employee goes with a substantial sum of money. The current tax-free limit is £25 000 so that job loss – if notice pay and severance pay are right – need not represent disaster.

WORK BENEFITS

Office accommodation

Along with the provision of the company car, the most visible sign of executive seniority is the type of office occupied. Properly planned and furnished office accommodation can reflect the general standing of the company and the importance of executive job holders and at the same time be achieved at modest cost.

Sabbaticals

Allowing senior executives a sabbatical (a specific period of leave, for example, six months or a year's leave with pay) after they have served a number of years (typically fifteen or twenty) has been an established practice for some time in the USA. It is rare for UK companies to provide such a facility. However, as pressure on executives tends to increase, this facility is likely to become more widespread. There are two clear advantages: from the executive's point of view it enables him to 're-charge' and come back fresh to his position; and from the company's point of view, provided it has some control over the study or work undertaken during the sabbatical, it prevents senior managers from becoming too stereotyped and blinkered in their approach to the job.

Management training

This benefit comes more in the shape of skills and knowledge acquired by the employee rather than in cash terms, except that the acquisition of a formal qualification can mean an addition to salary. There has been a move away from the practice of sending executives away on general management courses unrelated to their work or potential. This reflects growing awareness of the cost and a better understanding of training needs. With more careful selection of the individual and the course or with the use of in house training (either with own resources or engaging a consultant) management training can be continued effectively within the budget.

The need for executives and senior managers fluent in another language is rapidly increasing. The company, in providing language training either direct or by way of financial support, improves the general quality and contribution of its staff. From the employee's point of view it greatly improves his own marketability. This, of course, is not an objective of the benefit but the point should not be ignored. Many companies who specify the need for someone to be fluent in a given language before making an appointment are unnecessarily limiting the scope of their choice. In many cases, it would make more sense to recruit somebody suitable for the post and provide the necessary language tuition afterwards.

Some companies also offer support to employees in relation to courses of study undertaken at their own volition. It would, however, be exceptional to find unqualified support irrespective of the subject. A company would normally wish to be satisfied that the course was in some way related to work.

Subscriptions

Membership of a professional body or an organization reflecting business interests is often of concern to the employee. Such membership keeps him in touch with current trends and legal requirements and helps him to keep abreast of developments through contact with fellow members. Those leads are of considerable use to the company as well, in so far as the executive is better informed and therefore a more valuable member of staff. While subscriptions to such bodies are tax allowable many companies recognize the importance of the membership and pay the subscription in full.

Discount and company purchase plans

Many companies take advantage of their purchasing power or of their importance in the trade to provide facilities by which employees can buy goods and services at favourable prices. The company's own products can also be sold to staff at a discount. It is difficult to assess the extent to which such facilities contribute to retention and a long-term identity with the company but the value of the benefit should not be underrated.

Sports and social clubs

Like dining facilities and canteens, sports and social facilities are also a long established benefit. They are one of the best ways by which identification with a company can be achieved by an employee and his family and such facilities are normally well accepted. Bearing in mind that from the employee's point of view a main friendship area is his place of work, the development of that circle on a family basis can be of very considerable benefit.

In the provision of facilities two problems arise. First, when setting up a club some companies make the mistake of trying to over-economize and produce facilities which are unattractive in comparison with similar facilities elsewhere. Second, in the large conurbations these facilities can be out of reach of a large percentage of the workforce. In such circumstances, it is possibly better to concentrate on providing first-class social facilities close to the place of work.

The need to keep in touch with pensioners is more readily recognized by companies than in the past. This can be regarded as a benefit in the sense that employees and pensioners themselves see the company taking positive steps to maintain contact and take a continuing interest in old employees. If there are sports and social facilities these can readily provide a focus for pensioner interests.

Retirement counselling

Clearly associated with work, but towards the end of a career, comes retirement counselling. The break between work and retirement is enormous. Not only is there the loss of work on a regular basis but also a significant financial change. More and more companies are recognizing a responsibility to make employees aware of the need to adjust to the new circumstances, to find useful alternative employment (normally of a voluntary nature) and above all to plan for the next ten years and more on a sound financial basis. Pre-retirement courses can make a substantial contribution to a successful transition from work to leisure; and the provision of such courses is welcomed by employees and clearly seen as a benefit.

CONCLUSION

This chapter has examined a wide range of benefits but the question may be asked 'Why provide benefits at all?' The answer is simple. Benefits are often a much more efficient way in tax terms of providing part of a total remuneration package and their provision often directly reflects the company's real appreciation of employees' needs and the value of fostering an identity of interest between the company and its staff. Clearly, few companies can afford to provide all the benefits described (even so the list is not exhaustive) and therefore there is the question how the benefit programme should be constructed.

The two basic steps which a company should take are, first, to define precisely what it hopes to achieve by introducing the benefits or reshaping its present programme; and, second, to ascertain what level of effectiveness flows from any current programme. In defining what it wants to achieve, a company has to decide whether it wants its benefits to be linked to the performance of the company or whether it wants to give them as reward to employees so as to create, for instance, an enhanced sense of security. If a company decides that it wishes to build up a total compensation package related to the company's performance, it should be prepared to investigate and have designed either or both shares schemes and profit-sharing schemes. If, on the other hand, the emphasis is to be on non-performance-related benefits, items like pension, house purchase and retirement counselling will be of primary importance.

A company should recognize that its own assessment of what employees want in terms of benefits is not necessarily a reliable guide. For instance, generous pensions may be a desirable aim in the benefit field and socially desirable but it does not follow that all sectors of the workforce will see it in the same way.

In order to obtain the maximum effect from a benefits programme the company should be aware of the perceived effectiveness of its present arrangements. To obtain this information an audit may be carried out of the benefits currently provided and how these are received by the staff. For a company to undertake this programme by itself is not on the face of it particularly difficult but in practice problems arise which tend to invalidate the answers. The form of questionnaire may be unsuitable, employees may think that there is a desired answer, particularly if the enquiry is conducted in house with no chance of confidentiality. The use of outside consultants could make this a more feasible operation not only in the form of the exercise but in terms of confidentiality. The results would not identify individuals in any way and employee preferences would be expressed as percentages out of the total number of employees involved.

A typical programme would involve deciding which benefits should be included in the survey and also any attitudinal points of special interest which should be covered in interviews with a cross-section of recipients and potential recipients. The recipients would then be interviewed to see if they understood precisely what benefits they were receiving and how much these were worth to them and how much they cost the company. Furthermore, they could also be asked what further benefits they would like to receive or would prefer to receive in place of benefits already in existence. This aspect touches very clearly on the notion of personal choice in electing to take some benefits in place of others or of at least scaling the size of benefits to fit in with the changing needs of the employee.

The results of this survey could be cross-referenced with the cost of a company's benefits programme and a realistic view of the cost-effectiveness of the programme worked out. The company would then be in a position to decide precisely how the programme should be amended or added to or indeed how such a programme should be undertaken. It is important that, once the new programme is introduced, great care be taken to see that its effectiveness is duly checked and essential that the full impact of the new programme is communicated to the recipients and potential recipients. A regular update or audit is necessary to see if the hoped-for effect is achieved and whether failure to achieve it is due to the programme itself or to a failure to communicate it properly to employees.

It is both surprising and worrying that so many companies pay scant attention to the need to communicate. Even companies which by any standard have good benefit features in this total remuneration package, often do not take the trouble to inform staff about them. They assume that the details are understood but regrettably there is no clear understanding and in the meantime the company is getting little or no credit for its policy. Sometimes a company will content itself with an explanatory booklet or memorandum but often couched in semi-technical jargon incomprehensible to recipients. It would make better sense and certainly improve the effectiveness of the company's programme if companies took the time and trouble to make sure that their personnel department, for example, had a specialist who was responsible for communicating the programme.

A company embarking on a benefits programme or reshaping its existing policy should be prepared to take the following steps:

1 Clearly define the aims of the programme
2 Ascertain what the programme gives and what benefits are received
3 Ascertain what employees would like to receive
4 Work out what can be afforded in relation to a benefits programme
5 Draw up a new benefits programme, bearing in mind the very wide range of benefits which could be given
6 Make sure the programme is communicated fully and effectively to all recipients
7 Check regularly to see that the benefits programme is achieving its aims and objectives
8 Be prepared to change the programme if it is not achieving its aims
9 Consider the possibility of giving flexible benefits to employees so that their personal election fits in with their changing needs
10 Be prepared to employ specialist personnel both internally and externally to ensure that a benefits programme is properly constructed.

FURTHER READING

Beacham, R., *Pay Systems: Principles and Techniques*, Heinemann, London, 1979

Beattie, D. (ed.) *Company Administration Handbook,* 6th edition, Gower, Aldershot, 1988

Di Palma, V., *Your Fringe Benefits,* David & Charles, Newton Abbot, 1977

Greenhill, Richard, T., *Employee Remuneration and Profit Sharing*, Woodhead Faulkner, Cambridge, 1980

Keneghan, F., and Redfearn, A., *Determining Company Pay Policy*, Institute of Personnel Management, London, 1979

Toulson, N., *Managing Pension Schemes*, Gower, Aldershot, 1986

Wood, D., and Turton, D., *White Collar Productivity Schemes*, Oyez Publishing Ltd., London, 1979

54 Working conditions

Patricia George

Good working conditions minimize, if not prevent, accidents at work. They also make an important contribution to the health and wellbeing of staff, enabling the attainment of improved work standards.

STRESS AT THE WORKPLACE

Stress at work can be costly for the employer. The symptoms of stress are many, ranging from headaches, higher absence levels and deteriorating relationships to more serious physical disorders. Recent research in France and Denmark has, for example, pointed to premature births, infertility and menstrual disruption in female staff subjected to noise and other stress. The effects of stress are dealt with at greater length in Dr Melhuish's chapter at the end of this book.

Stress can be caused in many ways, examples of which are:

1 Poor workplace layout, so that staff cannot find the tools and materials needed, and with the danger of knocking into obstructions
2 Bad lighting and glare, especially in work such as draughting and the use of VDUs
3 Inappropriate allocation of work or job design, so that routine and boring tasks are not relieved by sharing them out and interspersing them with the more interesting jobs
4 Shift working systems
5 Insufficient rest pauses (for example when sitting at a typewriter or VDU)
6 Poor environmental control, with inadequate ventilation or draughts, smells, noise, and temperature or humidity problems
7 Inadequate instruction or training for the duties expected.

In recent years the moral responsibility of management to provide reasonable working conditions for their employees has, more and more, been taken over by legislation. No one would deny that the objectives of such legislation are well founded, but so much has been produced that a summary will help to ensure that readers obey the letter, as well as the intent, of the law.

HEALTH AND SAFETY AT WORK ACT 1974

One of the main purposes of this Act is to provide a comprehensive and integrated system of law to deal with the health, safety and welfare of people at work. Based on the concept of a general duty of care, the Act has been drawn up in such a way that it can be changed, expanded and adapted to cope with risks and problems in industry for many years ahead. It has been described as the most significant statutory advance in this field since Shaftesbury's Factory Act of 1833. The Act applies to all people working in any capacity: employers, employees (except domestic servants in private employment), manufacturers, contractors, the self-employed and to certain members of the public.

The basic obligations of all employers and all employees, which the Act deliberately couches in very general terms, are given below.

Basic obligations of employers

The employer must ensure, so far as is reasonably practicable, the health, safety and welfare at work of all his employees. To assess what is reasonably practicable, the employer must balance the risk against the cost of measures to prevent or minimize the risk. If the risk is clearly established as dangerous it is likely that even the most expensive measures would be deemed to be reasonable. This duty includes the provision of (and maintenance of, as appropriate):

1 A safe, healthy working environment with adequate facilities and arrangements for welfare at work
2 A safe, healthy place of work with safe means of access and egress
3 Safe, healthy plant and systems of work
4 Means, etc., to use, handle, store or transport articles and substances without risk to health or safety
5 Information, instruction, training and supervision necessary to ensure the health and safety of employees
6 A written statement of the employer's current general policy for the health and safety of employees, and the organization and arrangements for carrying out that policy.

Employers must, in specified circumstances, allow their employees to appoint their own safety representatives, consult with them and, if so requested, set up safety committees.

Directors will be required to give information in their annual reports to shareholders on what their companies are doing in this field. The Companies Act 1967 was amended accordingly by s79 of the Health and Safety at Work Act on 1 April 1975.

Additionally employers have a duty to ensure the safety of persons other than employees who enter their premises and to ensure that their activities do not endanger anybody outside their employment.

Basic obligations of employees

Every employee has a duty to take reasonable care for the health and safety of himself and of others who may be affected. He must cooperate with his employer to enable the duties and requirements of the Act to be carried out.

Many processes or activities are now, or will be, governed by regulations or approved codes of practice. In general contravention of the appropriate regulation will be an offence. A person will not however be open to criminal proceedings for failing to observe a particular code of practice but in the event of criminal proceedings any relevant code of practice is admissible in evidence.

Administration and enforcement: the Health and Safety Commission, Executive and Inspectorate

In general, the Commission is responsible to the Secretary of State for Employment for making whatever arrangements are appropriate for the general purposes of the new legislation. It has an information, education and advisory role and the power to carry out investigations and inquiries within the health and safety field.

The Health and Safety Executive, responsible to the Commission, is its operational arm and has been set up to carry out the Commission's functions under the Commission's direction. In its turn, the Executive is empowered to appoint inspectors to carry out its enforcement and advisory functions. Inspectors of factories, mines and quarries, nuclear installations, alkali and clean air and explosives have been transferred to the Executive for this purpose.

Inspectors can enter an employer's premises at any reasonable time to carry out their functions (at *any* time in a situation which is dangerous in an inspector's opinion).

Improvement and Prohibition Notices. An inspector will be able to issue Improvement and Prohibition Notices.

Improvement Notice. Requires the employer to remedy a contravention of the Act or a regulation under it within a specified period.

Prohibition Notice. Requires the employer to stop (immediately if necessary) any activity which carries risk of serious personal injury.

There is a right of appeal to an industrial tribunal against these Notices. Improvement Notices will he held in abeyance pending the appeal but Prohibition Notices will remain in force unless the employer satisfies the tribunal to the contrary, by application prior to the hearing.

Employment Medical Advisory Service

In addition to having an advisory role, the Act:

1   Authorizes a medical adviser to carry out a medical examination of any

employee whose health is believed to be in danger because of the work, provided the employee consents

2 Requires an employer to inform the local careers office when recruiting a person aged less than eighteen to work in a factory, specifying the nature of the work

Disclosure of information

The Commission can serve a notice on any person to reveal information affecting health and safety.

An inspector can in appropriate circumstances inform the employees at a workplace of matters affecting their safety, health and welfare.

The Safety Representatives and Safety Committees Regulations 1977 require employers to make certain information available to safety representatives.

Enforcement of the Act

The Executive is required to make adequate arrangements for enforcement except where regulations made by the Secretary of State place the duty on local authorities or other bodies.

Responsibility for fire prevention and fire precautions. S78 amends the Fire Precautions Act 1971 so that the fire authorities and the Home Office can deal with general fire precautions (means of escape in case of fire, fire-alarm systems, fire-fighting equipment and so on) under the Act. The Commission and Executive remain responsible for control over risks of fire associated with particular processes or the use of particular substances, and for all fire precautions in certain scheduled premises (which will include major hazard factories).

Offences. S33 lists the offences and the type of penalty which may be imposed for each: fines and/or imprisonment.

Action by management. Management should:

1 Prepare and issue a written safety policy statement
2 Set up an accident prevention programme
3 Provide training in safety policy and practice
4 Designate line and functional responsibilities for health, welfare and safety.

The main provisions of the Act came into force on 1 April 1975 and largely replace most of the existing law on safety and health in industry. Among the major Acts which will eventually be replaced or mainly replaced are the Factories Act 1961, and the Offices, Shops and Railway Premises Act 1963. For the time being, many of their provisions remain in force.

THE FACTORIES ACT

Many provisions of the Factories Act 1961 remain in force for the time being. The Act applies to all factories as defined in s175 of the Act, as well as to certain other premises, such as building sites, which are not factories in the normal sense of the word. For the purpose of the Act, a factory is defined as a place to which the employer has right of access or of control and where two or more persons are employed in manual labour, by way of trade or for the purpose of gain in any of the following operations:

1 Making any article or part of an article
2 Altering, repairing, ornamenting, finishing, cleaning, washing, breaking-up or demolishing any article
3 Adapting an article for sale
4 The slaughtering of cattle, sheep, swine, goats, horses, asses or mules
5 The confinement of such animals while awaiting slaughter at other premises provided those premises are not maintained primarily for agricultural purposes and do not form part of the premises used for holding of a market in respect of such animals.

Furthermore, whether or not they fall within this general definition, s175(2) specifically applies the Act to the following groups of premises, provided that persons are employed in the following manual operations:

1 Packing articles, washing or filling bottles or containers incidental to the purposes of the factory
2 Sorting articles prior to work in a factory
3 Printing or bookbinding carried out as a trade or incidental to a business
4 Making up or packing of yarn or cloth
5 Laundering carried on as an ancillary to a business or public institution. (Ordinary commercial laundries are factories within the general definition quoted above.)
6 Constructing, reconstructing or repairing vehicles, locomotives, or other plant used for transport purposes, when ancillary to a transport, industrial or commercial undertaking (other than running repairs to locomotives)
7 Production of films. (It would be wise to assume that the production of recordings on videotape might be treated as coming within this definition, though the point could lead to much legal argument).
8 Making or preparing articles for the building, fishing and engineering industries, the theatre and for films
9 Making or repairing metal or wood incidental to business for trading, etc., using mechanical power
10 Construction, repair or breaking up of ships in dry docks
11 Gas holders of over 140 cubic metres.

Certain sections of the Act also apply to electrical stations and substations, warehouses, docks, wharves, ships and sites where building and civil engineering are carried on.

Premises that come under the definition of a factory but are used by public authorities or charitable institutions may still be subject to the Act even though they are not actually operated 'by way of trade or for the purpose of gain'. The same applies to factory premises occupied by the Crown or a local council.

A place sited within the factory precincts is not a part of that factory if it is used solely for a purpose different from the processes carried on in the factory; for example the office buildings in the factory may not be part of the factory.

The principal matters legislated for under the Factories Act are:

1 Drainage, cleanliness, overcrowding, temperature, ventilation, lighting, sanitary conveniences, washing facilities, drinking water, seating and accommodation for clothing.

Drainage

All floors liable to become wet must be drained.

Cleanliness

Dirt and refuse must be removed daily from floors and benches in workrooms and from staircases and passages. Workroom floors must be washed or otherwise cleaned at least once per week. All inside walls, partitions and ceilings must be periodically washed, painted, whitewashed or otherwise treated as prescribed by the Factories (Cleanliness of Walls and Ceilings) Regulations 1960, amended by S.I. 1974 No. 427. Factories must be kept free of effluvia from drains, sanitary conveniences, etc.

Overcrowding

Workrooms must not be so overcrowded as to be dangerous to health. The employer must allow at least 11 cubic metres of space for every person employed excluding any air space more than 4.2 metres from the floor.

Temperature

The temperature must be reasonable. If a substantial proportion of the work in a particular room is done sitting and does not involve serious physical effort, the temperature must be at least 16°C after the first hour and at least one thermometer must be provided in every such workroom. However, Statutory Instrument 1980, No. 1013 restricts heating to a maximum temperature of 19°C, unless certain industrial processes require more heat.

Ventilation

Fresh air must be circulated to provide adequate ventilation, and measures taken to protect employees from inhalation of dust, fumes or impurities which may be injurious or offensive.

Lighting

Lighting, artificial or natural, must be sufficient and suitable.

Sanitary conveniences

The Statutory Rules and Orders 1938 No. 611 as amended by S.I. 1974 No. 426 setting out the minimum requirements for factories can be obtained from the Stationery Office. The conveniences must be maintained, kept clean and effectively lit. The general scale is one convenience for every twenty-five men or twenty-five women but when employing more than a hundred this scale may be varied by the substitution of urinals for water or chemical closets.

Washing facilities

Must include a supply of clean, running hot and cold or warm water, soap and clean towels or other suitable means of cleaning or drying and be suitable and adequate for the number employed.

Drinking water

The employer must provide an adequate supply of drinking water, with an upward jet convenient for drinking or with suitable drinking vessels and facilities for rinsing them.

Seating

The employer must provide suitable seating where an employee (male or female) has reasonable opportunities for sitting without detriment to his/her work.

Accommodation for clothing

Adequate and suitable accommodation must be made for clothing not worn during working hours, with arrangements where practicable for drying such clothing. The risk of theft is an element which must be taken into account in deciding whether accommodation is suitable.

2　*Safety.* Safe conditions of workplaces, including floors, stairs, passages and gangways, and the means of access to places where people have to work. The requirements for handrail and fencing are stipulated for means of access, for workplaces, and for openings in floors.

Precautions against dangerous fumes, dust and other health and safety hazards, protection of eyes, restrictions on lifting heavy weights.

Fencing on dangerous machinery and parts of machinery which are in motion or use, restriction on cleaning machinery by persons under eighteen and women, training and supervision of young persons required to operate certain machines.

Safe construction and safe operation of cranes, hoists and other plant with special hazards.

3　Restrictions on the employment of women and young persons, including limitations on normal hours, overtime and holiday work.
4　Statutory registers kept and statutory reports made, regarding (for example) accidents and industrial diseases, inspection of factories, lists of homeworkers in certain trades and other administrative matters.

In addition to the requirements of the Factories Act itself, many specific processes are subject to special regulations made by statutory instruments under the Act. These include detailed requirements for certain types of machinery, (e.g., woodworking machinery) and for certain types of industrial employment, for example, building operations and works of engineering construction.

OFFICES, SHOPS AND RAILWAYS PREMISES ACT

Many provisions of the Offices, Shops and Railways Premises Act 1963 are still in force for the time being. The Act extended to these premises some of the requirements that formerly applied only to factories. $S1$ details what premises are covered, and these can be summarized briefly as follows:

Office premises: A building which is used solely or principally for office purposes, from filing or telephone operating to the preparation of material for publication. Premises used in connection with office premises, such as storerooms or canteens, are also subject to the Act even if they are not physically part of the office premises.

Shop premises: In addition to a shop of the ordinary kind, the term is defined to include any building or part of a building

> 'of which the sole purpose or principal use is the carrying out of retail trade, for example the sale to the public of food or drink for immediate consumption, retail sales by auction and the lending of books or periodicals for the purpose of gain
> occupied by a wholesale dealer or merchant who keeps goods there for sale
> which members of the public visit to deliver goods for repair, etc. or to carry out repairs, etc. for themselves
> used to sell solid fuel'.

The Act does not apply to:

> Offices in which the total number of man hours worked does not exceed twenty-one a week
> Moveable office structures in which people work for less than six months
> Permanent buildings in which persons work for less than six weeks
> Premises where only the husband, wife and/or immediate family work.

The Offices, Shops and Railways Premises Act is mainly concerned with the following:

1 Physical working conditions: cleanliness, ventilation, lighting, drinking water, seating, accommodation for clothing.

Overcrowding: the employer must allow at least 40 square feet of floor space for each person normally employed in a room, or where the ceiling is lower than 10 feet, 400 cubic feet per person. Furniture, fittings, machinery and other such items should be ignored when measuring the size of the room.

Temperature: unless the room is used by the public and it is impracticable to do so, a reasonable temperature must be maintained. Where a substantial proportion of the work does not involve severe physical effort the temperature must not be less than 16°C (60.8°F) after the first hour but not more than 19°C (66.2°F). The employer must provide a thermometer on each floor in a conspicuous place for the use of the employees.

Sanitary conveniences and washing facilities: the Sanitary Conveniences Regulations 1964, SI966 and the Washing Facilities Regulations 1964, SI965 lay down the minimum requirements

2 Constructing, maintaining and keeping reasonably free from obstruction floors, stairs, passages and gangways
3 Restrictions on lifting heavy loads
4 Fencing dangerous machinery, restricting the cleaning of certain machines by persons under eighteen and training and supervising persons using certain prescribed machines which are registered as particularly dangerous
5 Registration of offices and shops with the local council, obtaining a fire certificate from the fire authority, and other administrative matters
6 Eating facilities for those working in shops
7 Safe construction and safe operation of hoists and lifts

THE SHOPS ACTS

The Shops Acts are designed to ensure that shop assistants do not have to work excessive hours and that they are allowed adequate periods of rest and leisure.

REGULATIONS

As noted earlier, many regulations have been made for special processes and industries. They are too numerous to quote here, and most apply only to a few specialized processes, but mention should be made of the regulations for safety representatives and safety committees, building operations, and canteens.

Health and Safety (First Aid) Regulations 1981

These regulations require an employer to make adequate first aid provisions for staff and to inform them of these arrangements. Help and guidance concerning arrangements including first aid boxes, kits and other equipment, first-aiders and appointed persons are provided in the Approved Code of Practice and Guidance Notes prepared by the Health and Safety Executive.

The Safety Representatives and Safety Committees Regulations 1977

These regulations provide for the appointment of safety representatives, describe their functions and given them the right to certain time off to carry out their tasks and for training. The representatives are also empowered to carry out inspections and have access to certain documents and information. The setting up of safety committees is also prescribed if at least two safety representatives make such a request in writing.

Safety Signs Regulations 1980 (SI 1980 No. 1471)

All safety signs must comply with these regulations.

The Reporting of Injuries, Diseases and Dangerous Occurrences Regulations 1985 (SI 1985 No. 2023)

Employers must under these regulations report major injuries, accidents/conditions, diseases and dangerous occurrences to the relevant enforcing authority and keep various records for at least three years.

Noise

It is likely that regulations will be published in the near future on exposure to noise.

Building operations

Regulations apply not only to the erection of new buildings but to the repair and maintenance of existing buildings, including redecorating, repointing and external cleaning of buildings. They thus affect firms, who without being engaged in the construction industry, employ their own teams of maintenance workers. The main requirements for such operations are contained in four sets of regulations:

> The Construction (Working Places) Regulations 1966
> The Construction (Lifting Operations) Regulations 1961
> The Construction (General Provisions) Regulations 1961
> The Construction (Health and Welfare) Regulations 1966
>   and Amendment 1974

Building Regulations

Part III of the Act, which will be the responsibility of the Secretaries of State for the Environment and for Scotland, extends the power to make building regulations governing the structure of buildings.

Canteens

Staff and works canteens are included under Food Hygiene (General) Regulations 1970, made under the Food Act 1984. These regulations include provisions for cleanliness (and personal cleanliness) and other precautions against the contamination of food. A canteen within the curtilage of a factory and used by employees working on the manufacturing process is also subject to the Factories Act. A staff canteen used by office workers, whether part of the office premises or not, is subject to the Offices, Shops and Railways Premises Act.

A guide to these regulations can be obtained free of charge from the local health education units or environmental health officers.

CODES OF PRACTICE

Regulations will, where appropriate, be supplemented by Codes of Practice. These will not be statutory requirements but nevertheless may be used in criminal proceedings as evidence that statutory requirements have been contravened.

Codes of Practice have been issued on the appointment and time off for training of safety representatives, on the establishment of safety committees and on first aid.

EMPLOYERS' LIABILITY (COMPULSORY INSURANCE)

The Employers' Liability (Compulsory Insurance) Act 1969 prescribes that all employers must insure against liability for personal injury and disease sustained by their employees and arising out of, or in the course of, their employment. The Social Security Act 1975 does not exempt the employer from taking out this insurance.

FIRE PRECAUTIONS ACT 1971

There must be means of escape in case of fire, adequate in regard to the circumstances and number of people employed, and suitable fire-fighting equipment and systems must be available. Inspectors from fire authorities have the power to enter and inspect premises. Application must be made to the local authority for a certificate that these requirements have been met.

CHECKLIST OF NOTICES TO BE POSTED

In the following list of statutory notices which have to be displayed, where relevant, the numerical references are to the sections of the Factories Act (FA) and the Offices, Shops and Railways Premises Act (OSRPA) in which the requirement appears. An asterisk against an item indicates that the notice displayed has to be in a prescribed form, copies of which can be obtained from the Stationery Office.

1   A statement showing the health and safety policy. The organization and arrangements that are in force for carrying out that policy must be brought to the notice of all employees
2   *Prescribed abstract of the Factories Act (FA 138). The employer is required to show on this the addresses of the employment medical adviser and the district inspector
3   *Prescribed abstract (or a copy) of any statutory regulations made under the Factories Act and applicable to the premises (FA 139)
4   *Prescribed abstract of the Offices, Shops and Railways Premises Act, unless every employee affected has been given a copy of the prescribed booklet containing the same information (OSRPA 50)
5   *Notice in each factory workroom showing the maximum numbers of persons permitted to work in that room unless the factory inspector exercises his power to exempt a factory from this requirement (FA 2)
6   A notice giving the locations of first aid equipment and facilities, together with the names and locations of staff with first aid responsibilities
7   *Notice of any exemption for or granted under the Offices, Shops and Railways Premises Act (OSRPA 46)
8   Notice showing the hours of work, times of meal breaks, etc. for women and persons under eighteen (FA 88, 90, 94 and 115)
9   *Cautionary placards required to be displayed under regulations for certain special processes, for example, chromium-plating and power-press regulations
10   Placards showing the recommended treatment for electric shock, if electricity is used at voltages above 125v ac or 250v dc
11   Notice in sanitary conveniences used by persons handling food, requesting them to wash their hands (this is a requirement of the Food Hygiene Regulations 1960)
12   Notice showing the piecework rates payable for certain prescribed operations (FA 135 and orders made under the Act) unless every employee is given a written note of these rates
13   Fire regulations and drill instructions may be required to meet the terms of the fire certificate
14   Certificate of insurance against liability to injury or disease incurred whilst at work

15 In addition to notices, thermometers must be provided. There must be one in every workroom in a factory in which a substantial proportion of time is spent sitting and where the work does not involve serious physical effort, and there must be one on every floor in an office.

It is an offence for any person to deface or pull down a notice displayed under the Acts.

CHECKLIST OF NOTICES TO BE SENT TO FACTORY INSPECTOR OR OTHER AUTHORITY

The following notices must be sent to the district inspector of factories, unless otherwise stated. The numerical references are to the relevant sections of the Factories Act (FA) and the Offices, Shops and Railways Premises Act (OSRPA). An asterisk against an item shows that the notice must be sent on a prescribed form obtainable from the Stationery Office.

1 *Notice that premises are to be used as a factory (FA 137)
2 *Notice to local council that premises are to be used as offices or shops (if the offices are to be on factory premises, the notice must be sent to the factory inspector instead; if at a mine or quarry it must be sent to the inspector of mines and quarries) (OSRPA 49)
3 *Application to the fire authority for a fire certificate for a factory, office or shop. Small factories, offices and shops are exempt
4 Notice to fire authority when material structural alterations are made to premises, or number of employees materially increased, after fire certificate has been granted (FA 41 and OSRPA 30)
5 Notice to the local careers officer of the Youth Employment Service when recruiting a person under eighteen (a requirement under the Health and Safety Act Part II) to work in a factory
6 Notice of any fatal accident or major accident injury to any person, whether or not an employee, and of dangerous occurrences, accidents causing more than three days' incapacity for work, certain work-related diseases, and certain gas incidents. The notice should be given to the relevant enforcing authority, as set out in the Reporting of Injuries etc. Regulations. Accidents and dangerous occurrences should be reported to the Health and Safety Executive (or other authority of it) by the quickest possible means (usually by telephone) and confirmed by a written report within seven days.
     Free leaflets advising when and how to make such reports are available from local area offices of the Health and Safety Executive
7 *Notice to factory inspector and also to employment medical adviser of any cases of industrial disease. These diseases are prescribed in s 82 of the Factories Act and in various orders made under it
8 *Notice of intention to employ women or young persons on overtime (FA90)

9 *Notice of intention to employ women or young persons at different times from those stated on routine notice posted in factory (FA 88)

10 *Notice of intention to take advantage of permitted exemptions to the legal hours for women and young persons allowed in certain industries (FA 99 to 112)

11 *Notice of intention to employ persons in an underground room, i.e. one with at least half of its height below ground level (FA 69)

12 *Biannual return to local council (in February and August) of any out-workers working on certain processes (FA 133 to 134)

13 *Intention to begin building operations or works of engineering construction expected to last for six weeks or more (FA 127).

The special regulations for certain processes also contain the requirement that the use of such processes shall be notified to the factory inspector.

CHECKLIST OF REGISTERS TO BE KEPT

Most of the following records and registers must be kept on the prescribed forms, published by the Stationery Office.

1 General factory register. This provides a record of young persons employed, periodical painting or limewashing of the factory, accidents and dangerous occurrences, cases of industrial disease, persons trained in first aid, testing of fire warning systems, and any exemption granted by the factory inspector concerning the hours worked by women and young persons (FA 140)

2 Certificates, etc. attached to general registers. Reports and certificates of various examinations and test of plant required by the Factories Act and regulations made under it are, in most cases, required to be entered in or attached to the general register. The fire certificate issued by the fire authority must also be attached to the general register

3 Records must be kept of accidents, dangerous occurrences, reportable diseases and gas incidents

4 Health registers. The regulations for certain special factory processes require the medical examination of workers engaged in them; the results of these examinations must be recorded in the prescribed health register for the process

5 Register of overtime. This must be used to record overtime worked by women and by persons under eighteen (FA 90)

6 Record of hours worked by van boys, etc. This must be used to record the hours worked by young persons employed outside the factory on business connected with the factory, for example as van boys or messengers (FA 116)

7 Registers of homeworkers in certain trades.

ADVICE AND FURTHER INFORMATION

There are public enquiry points, open between 10.00am and 3.00pm at the following offices of the Health and Safety Executive:

Baynards House
1 Chepstow Place
London W2 4TC
Tel 01-229 3456

Magdalen House
Trinity Road
Stanley Precinct
Bootle
Liverpool L20 3QZ
Tel 051-951 4000

Broad Lane
Sheffield S3 7HQ
Tel 0742 752539

Advice on health and safety can also be obtained from local offices of the Health and Safety Executive, which are represented by HM Inspectorate. A list of their addresses is given below:

Health and Safety Inspectorate addresses

Area	Address	Local authorities within each area
1 South West	Inter City House Mitchell Lane Bristol BS1 6AN Tel 0272 290681	Avon, Cornwall, Devon, Gloucestershire, Somerset, Isles of Scilly
2 South	Priestly House Priestly Road Basingstoke RG24 9NW Tel 0256 473181	Berkshire, Dorset, Hampshire, Isle of Wight, Wiltshire
3 South East	3 East Grinstead House London Road East Grinstead West Sussex RH19 1RR Tel 0342 26922	Kent, Surrey, East Sussex, West Sussex

4	London NW	Chancel House Neasden Lane London NW10 2UD Tel 01-459 8844	Barnet, Brent, Camden, City of London, Enfield, Hammersmith, Harrow, Hillingdon, Hounslow, Kensington & Chelsea, City of Westminster
5	London NE	Maritime House 1 Linton Road Barking Essex IG11 8HF Tel 01-594 5522	Barking, Hackney, Haringey, Havering, Islington, Newham, Redbridge, Tower Hamlets, Waltham Forest
6	London S	1 Long Lane, London SE1 4PG	Bexley, Bromley, Croydon, Greenwich, Kingston-upon-Thames, Lambeth, Lewisham, Merton, Richmond-upon-Thames, Southwark, Sutton, Wandsworth
7	East Anglia	39/43 Baddow Road, Chelmsford, Essex CM2 0HL Tel 0245 84661	Boroughs in Essex except the London Boroughs in Essex covered by Area 5; Norfolk, Suffolk
8	Northern Home Counties	14 Cardiff Road, Luton LU1 1PP Tel 0582 34121	Bedfordshire, Buckinghamshire, Cambridgeshire, Herfordshire
9	East Midlands	5th Floor, Belgrave House, 1 Greyfriars, Northampton NN1 2LQ Tel 0604 21233	Leicestershire, Northamptonshire, Oxfordshire, Warwickshire
10	West Midlands	McLaren Building, 2 Masshouse Circus Queensway, Birmingham B4 7NP Tel 021 236 5080	West Midlands
11	Wales	14th Floor, Brunel House, 2 Fitzalan Road, Cardiff CF2 1SH Tel 0222 497777	Clywd, Dyfed, Gwent, Gwynedd, Mid Glamorgan, Powys, South Glamorgan, West Glamorgan

12	Marches	The Marches House, The Midway, Newcastle-under-Lyme Staffs ST5 1DT Tel 0782 610181	Hereford and Worcester, Salop, Staffordshire
13	North Midlands	Burbeck House, Trinity Square, Nottingham NG1 4AU Tel 0602 470712	Derbyshire, Lincolnshire, Nottinghamshire
14	South Yorkshire	Sovereign House, 40 Silver Street, Sheffield S1 2ES Tel 0742 739081	Humberside, South Yorkshire
15	West & North Yorkshire	8 St Pauls Street, Leeds LS1 2LE Tel 0532 446191	North Yorkshire, West Yorkshire
16	Greater Manchester	Quay House, Quay Street, Manchester M3 3JB Tel 061-831 7111	Greater Manchester
17	Merseyside	The Triad, Stanley Road, Bootle L20 3PG Tel 051-922 7211	Cheshire, Merseyside
18	North West	Victoria House, Ormskirk Road, Preston PR1 1HH Tel 0772 59321	Cumbria, Lancashire
19	North East	Arden House, Regent Centre, Regent Farm Road, Gosforth, Newcastle-upon-Tyne NE3 3JN Tel 091-284 8448	Cleveland, Durham, Northumberland, Tyne & Wear
20	Scotland East	Belford House, 59 Belford Road, Edinburgh EH4 3UE Tel 031-225 1313	Borders, Central, Fife, Grampian, Highland, Lothian, Tayside and the island areas of Orkney & Shetland
21	Scotland West	314 Vincent Street, Glasgow G3 8XG Tel 041-204 2646	Dumfries and Galloway, Strathclyde, and the Western Isles

Many employers' organizations, trade associations and trade unions can also provide guidance, as do the British Safety Council and the Royal Society for the Prevention of Accidents. Detailed information about the responsibilities of employers in regard to working conditions will be found in the following standard works.

FURTHER READING

Birnbaum, R., *Health Hazards of Visual Display Units with Particular Reference to Office Environments*, TUC Centenary Institute of Occupational Health, London

Chandler, P.A., *Croner's Health and Safety at Work*, Croner Publications, New Malden, Looseleaf. Updated guide to the law

European Foundation for the improvement of living and working conditions, *Physical and Psychological Stress at Work: Summary Report*, Shankill, Co. Dublin, 1984. (Seminar held in Dublin 3-4 September, 1981)

Fife, I. and Machin, E.A., *Redgrave's Health and Safety in Factories*, Butterworth, London, 1976 and Supplement 1979 and 1981

Fife, I. and Machin, E.A., *Health and Safety at Work excluding factories and mines*, Butterworth, London 1980

Goodman, M.J., (ed.), *Encyclopaedia of Health and Safety at Work*, Sweet and Maxwell, London. Looseleaf. Updated.

Grandjean, E., *Fitting the Task to the Man: an Ergonomic Approach*, Taylor and Francis, London, 1980

Melhuish, A., *Work and Health*, Penguin, Harmondsworth, 1982

Orlans, V. and Shipley, P., *A Survey of Stress Management and Prevention Facilities in a Sample of UK Organisations*, Birkbeck College Stress Research and Control Centre, London, 1983

The Stationery Office publishes the texts of all Acts and regulations, the prescribed forms, codes of practice, guidance notes and various advisory booklets. Details are given in the publications catalogue available from the Health and Safety Executive. Many employers' organizations, trade associations and trade unions also publish booklets and guidance notes.

55 Industrial training

Derek Torrington

A recent report by the Manpower Services Commission included the following statements:

> Britain's future international competitiveness and economic performance will be significantly influenced by the speed with which substantial improvements can be made in the scale and effectiveness of training by British Companies

and

> Few employers think training sufficiently central to their business for it to be a main component of their corporate strategy; the great majority did not see it as an issue of major importance – a few openly stated as much.

Those responsible for training in companies often regard their work as vulnerable. If times are hard, then training programmes are among the first to suffer cutback. It was partly to change this situation that we had the 1964 Industrial Training Act to boost the provision of training in companies. That intervention was only temporarily successful and the more rigorous circumstances of recent years have shifted governmental priorities in the UK towards provision for the unemployed, and companies are less constrained by the requirements of industrial training boards.

Company training budgets remain vulnerable because training is often regarded as an optional extra: 'without proper training we may not be here in five years, but without more productivity and cash in the bank we won't be here next week'. Sadly some training programmes are indeed expendable because they are not geared to real organizational needs and are of dubious effectiveness. The purpose of this chapter is to make a case for training and then to review some methods of putting it into practice.

THE NEED FOR TRAINING IN COMPANIES

The advantages of training range from more effective use of resources to considerations of the overall purpose of the enterprise.

Resources

The people in an organization are its main resource. If they are not appropriately trained for the work they have to perform they will not do it as efficiently as they could and operations will not be as profitable as they might be. Some degree of investment in training can make the human resources at the disposal of the management more productive and more profitable.

Fragmentation of work

Specialization is growing so that the work to be done within the undertaking is constantly being broken up into smaller parcels. New departments are set up to specialize in a particular aspect of the company's affairs, and each employs people to work in a specialized rather than in a general field. In the management ranks this produces the functional specialist who can do one or two things well, replacing the gifted amateur who could do many things with reasonable competence. This means that each employee needs training to undertake his duties, and this need is likely to become greater.

New skills and knowledge

One consequence of specialization is obsolescence in skills and knowledge. Many people in the financial and administrative field, for example, have forced themselves through the traumatic experience of accepting electronic data processing in the last decade. This acceptance has made it necessary for them to take some training so that they understand the monsters that are spewing forth information at such an alarming rate. The arrival of the computer has rendered obsolete some of the established administrative skills. This effect of technological development is apparent in every part of commercial and industrial activity. Few if any people will still be practising at forty the skills they learned at twenty. The new skills have to be taught.

It is short-sighted, expensive and impractical merely to hire new people who happen to have picked up the new skills elsewhere. The challenge of retraining the adult has to be faced, both by the employer and by the individual concerned. With managerial staff especially, there is the even more demanding need constantly to develop new understanding of the environment in which the organization is functioning. Changes in law, economic circumstances and in the community outside the organization have great influence on affairs within the organization, and knowledge of the environment is essential to managers.

On the job training

Some people counter this sort of argument by saying that training should take place outside the field of employment, and that the substantial proportion of the gross national product channelled into further education should take care of industrial training needs by training people in colleges and government training centres in the whole span of skills and areas of knowledge that are developing. Those who make this point would usually be surprised by the extent of what is done in this way, but still the training that is done off the job cannot be completed off the job. Just as a person learning to drive has to sit in the driving seat and drive along the street during his training, so the apprentice engineer, the trainee typist, laboratory technician, supervisor, personnel officer, sales manager and other industrial trainees all have to get their academic training in practical perspective, which is best done in the working situation. Also much necessary training is in routines which are peculiar to one company so that although a supervisor may learn much of great value on a supervisor's course at the local college it will be equally important for him to learn his own company's disciplinary procedures, and this can obviously come only from an agent of the employer.

Employee expectation

There is a standard of expectation which prospective employees have about what the company provides for its recruits. They will expect canteen facilities and locker rooms. Many will expect pension provision and sick pay. If these basic expectations are not met, they will not come and work for the company unless they have no choice, or unless they are likely to earn much more money than they would elsewhere.

Employees who have no choice of employer may not be influenced by the training that is provided – or not provided – but those who can afford to be selective are much influenced by the training opportunities that a particular opening offers. Here is a comment from a 25-year-old expert in information technology:

> When I came out of university all the employers were trying to outbid each other on the money and the perks, but that's not what you want. The non-contributory pension scheme means nothing to you until you're on your way out, and who needs free medical insurance? I went for a job that was worth doing, and where there was proper training, so that I could do it well. Some of my friends who were attracted by the money are in their third and fourth jobs now, but getting nowhere: they're just ripping off one company after another without making any sort of future for themselves.

More and more employees are expecting to receive systematic training for the job when they join a new company rather than having to 'sit next to Nellie'. A well-run training scheme will be an aid to recruitment. Complete lack of training will be a disincentive to prospective recruits.

Social purpose

All administrators and managers have a view of the purpose of their enterprise that goes beyond mere survival and profitability. One of management's many objectives is that the company should be a place worth working in, and that the people working there can to some extent achieve personal fulfilment. Assuming that a company has a personnel policy which recognizes its employees as people rather than simply resources, then the requirements for industrial training are the requirements of the people employed as well as the requirements of the employer.

ADMINISTERING THE TRAINING FUNCTION

The passing of the Industrial Training Act led to many companies taking the concept of specialization too far, and training departments were set up where the managers reported directly to the managing director or to the general manager quite independently of the personnel department. The reason for this was usually the calibre of the incumbent personnel manager, or the alarm of the managing director at the prospect of being 'fined' by his industrial training board for not meeting their requirements. In the mid 1960s many personnel managers were limited in their thinking to aspects of employee welfare such as canteen, lavatories and record-keeping rather than taking the broader view of personnel which is common today. As a result this type of personnel manager was not considered the appropriate person to be responsible for training with its new levy sanction, and most of the bright, keen training officers who started emerging were not prepared to report to that type of company executive.

This produced a split in the personnel function. Fortunately this practice is now less common except in the largest organizations with substantial training requirements, but it is important to appreciate that personnel work is an amalgam of many activities including training, employment, payment, trade union recognition, discipline, grievances, the design of jobs and consultative arrangements. Each of these interlocks with the others and they have to be co-ordinated and administered under an overall personnel policy. One cannot be isolated from the rest without risks. Effective training depends on effective selection, improved industrial relations often require new training programmes and training innovations frequently influence the industrial relations environment. In considering how the training function is administered, it is therefore of primary importance to see it as part of personnel work.

The personnel function should not usually report to a line manager. If the responsibility for any aspect of personnel comes under, say, the production manager, then managers in marketing, R and D and other areas will regard it as a specifically production function – as may the production manager. It must be seen to be available to, and necessary for, all company functions. Furthermore, the responsibility of the training specialist does not interfere with the line authority of the manager. The training officer provides a specialist service to all line managers in the organization. His particular usefulness lies in his understanding of the requirement of the training board for the relevant industry, his expertise in the skills and the knowledge needed to administer a training programme, his awareness of how people learn, his knowledge of courses and potential visiting lectures. He has a general responsibility for the quality of training provided in the organization, but the individual line manager remains responsible for the performance and competence of his own staff. The line manager needs to appreciate what the training function can do for him in developing that competence: he cannot wash his hands of the responsibility and 'leave it to personnel'. They can only provide him with some services that he has to understand and use.

Integration with other functions

Responsibility for specialist training services needs to be integrated with the whole of the personnel function, which must in turn be integrated with the management of the enterprise. Personnel and training are actively concerned with ensuring that the organization meets its business objectives, not some parasitical unnecessary growth imposed by an outside agency.

Objectives

Corporate objectives need to be reappraised to consider the place of training within the total personnel activity. What are its objectives? How do these fit in with the existing business objectives? What targets have to be achieved? This procedure sounds obvious, but it is perhaps the aspect of training which is most often ignored, with the consequent vulnerability of the training arrangements.

Identification of training needs

The person responsible for training has first to establish what the training needs of the organization are. He will consider two aspects of this. First he will investigate the operational efficiency of the organization. Later he will look at the training needs of individual people, and the need of the organization for people to be trained. In considering operational efficiency, he will seek to identify those jobs within the organization that appear to be holding back to the achievement of proper levels of performance and where training may help to lift this level to one that is acceptable. He will take note of the various indicators which personnel people use to 'take the temperature' of working groups.

Absenteeism, labour turnover, punctuality, sickness, changes in output level, complaints and labour troubles can all be indicators of the state of morale in a department, and low morale may be caused by inadequate training. There may be data available from work study officers who feel that the work standards in a particular department are not satisfactory. Conversations with managers and supervisors will suggest other areas requiring attention.

The training officer's own experience and training will suggest others, as will the officers of the industrial training boards.

The training officer will therefore collect a mass of information about the training needs that exist within the company, and can then begin to draw up proposals about what training should be done and in what order, the priority usually being determined by the likely pay-off. He may suggest, for example, that the training of typists could be altered to enable newly recruited school-leavers to reach an acceptable level of proficiency in half the time now con-sidered as necessary, at a saving of £x a year, followed by specially designed programmes of operator training in selected departments to reduce the level of labour turnover and to boost output. He might suggest middle managers attending courses at a business school, or supervisors having a series of dis-cussions on the implications of recent legislation. Whatever the particular proposals, he will draw these up and require them to be endorsed by his man-agement colleagues or superiors, so that he has a mandate to start work.

Implementation of the training programme

When the training officer has received his mandate he will also be empowered to spend some money to implement his programme. This will be based on his prediction of how much he can produce in the way of operating economies. The expenditure will come broadly under two headings. First there will be expenditure on hardware and fees, which are outgoings that would not be incurred if the training were not done. Hardware can range from boxes of chalk to overhead projectors, teaching machines and fully equipped, sound-proof lecture theatres. Fees will be either the fees payable for employees to attend courses, or payable to outside experts to come and take part in internal courses. The training officer, like any other executive submitting a budget for approval, is likely to ask for more than he needs under this heading, as he expects those who have to sanction his budget to cut it. It may be sensible for a newly established training function to start off with a minimum of equipment and to invest more heavily when experience has been gained. The reason for this is that most training programmes change fundamentally after a spell of running in and the benefits of experience. Heavy initial investment can result in an accumulation of expensive equipment that is unused, and a dearth of equipment that is needed but not available because the budget has been overspent.

The second category of expenditure is salaries and wages of trainees, where the administrator perhaps needs to scrutinize proposals clo.sely Employees away from work on training courses are still being paid. In the case of most managers and supervisors this adds nothing to the cost of their duties being carried out. Someone else will deputize for them in their absence, they will catch up with their work when they return, and that is that. In some other cases, however, there may be expenditure of either increasing the establish-ment for a department so that people absent for training can be covered, or arrangements for colleagues to work expensive overtime to make up the shortfall. The training is necessary, but this type of consideration needs to be thought of before the training begins so that the cost implications are fully appreciated.

As well as hardware, the training officer will need some space to run his schemes in. Some training will be done on the job or in a training section of the normal job environment, such as the apprentice bench in an engineering shop. Some training will be carried out away from the premises altogether, as when a young manager goes to the nearby polytechnic to take a management course. But there will be a need for some of the training programme to take place away from the job but on company premises. Typists are often trained in a small school within the company, and a number of short courses may be run to give managers or others an appreciation of a subject or to give training in certain skills that are needed.

Evaluation of training effectiveness

Finally in setting up a training function, there is a need for some means of evaluating the training, and this is one of the most nebulous and unsatisfactory aspects of the training job. The starting point is to compare the results achieved with the original objectives and, where possible, to measure the degree of improvement. This can be done in such areas as labour and material utilization, or the reduction in the number of despatch errors being made in a warehouse. It can only be guessed in the more difficult areas such as the quality of supervision by a foreman before and after a training course. This often depends on a subjective assessment that may be influenced by the reactions of the trainee.

Another possible means of evaluation is to measure the benefits that are set as objectives at the beginning of the programme. It might be a drop in labour turnover and other measures of improved efficiency and employee morale. There may be fewer accidents or reduced levels of overtime. It is also important to attempt some evaluation of the intangibles, such as atmosphere in industrial relations, customer satisfaction, self-confidence among managers and so on. To some extent this can be done by the use of an outside adviser who can come along for a day to examine the situation relating to training within the organization and then report upon it, rather like an auditor.

It is useful from a training point of view to carry out some form of performance appraisal regularly among employees. If this is done systematically over several years, the validity of training arrangements will be confirmed – or otherwise.

TRAINING FOR DIFFERENT CATEGORIES OF EMPLOYEE

Operators

The largest single grouping in the employed population is the operator on the shop floor who has no craft skills – the general worker. His job may require such a small amount of skill and knowledge that he needs no training other than a short period of 'being shown how' by his supervisor. There are, however, very few jobs which genuinely fall into this category. Most would be done better by more satisfied employees if they were preceded by a period of training, which covered induction to the organization and the place of the job in the manufacturing process, as well as the mechanics of how it should be done.

As operator jobs in manufacturing are usually specific to each employer, the training needs to be set up and run within the company, as there is no outside body either with the understanding of the job or any alternative source of supply of trainees. The training officer will need to study the operations and to use a process of skills analysis to devise a programme of training to be carried out by an instructor instructing trainees. Seldom is the training load large enough to justify a full-time instructor, and it is usual for an experienced operator in each department to be trained in instruction so that he does all the instruction needed by new recruits. Another method is for the foreman to be trained so that he inducts and trains all those in his department. This may be the best method as long as the training job is not going to take up too much of his time.

Skills analysis can be learned at one of the many introductory courses for training officers run within the further education system. Alternatively there are short crash courses available. Instructors can be trained by one of the Training within Industry (TWI) courses provided by the Training Services Division of the Manpower Services Commission.

Clerical

Very little training is provided in clerical duties in most organizations, although the provision of training is spreading and companies find that it pays big dividends in cost savings and employee satisfaction. The practice of clerical training is similar to that for operator training, although there are certain more general occupational skills involved, so that the further education system is more helpful.

Widely available is a course in office skills which is taken by young people on leaving school. They attend technical college for one day a week and learn simple office skills and routines to fit in with the working experience they are beginning to acquire.

There are also many courses in shorthand and typing, although the demand for shorthand is declining and the word processor is rapidly replacing the typewriter as a professional tool. Technical colleges still have some difficulty in equipping their classes with word processing facilities for student practice, but equipment suppliers provide on-the-job training when they install new machines. Many secretaries are still left to struggle with the instruction manual for a new piece of office machinery when it is delivered, and instruction manuals often seem to be designed to confuse rather than instruct.

The important development marked by the word processor is that this is an introduction to computing skills. Many secretaries are now manipulating numbers and elaborate programs with the same facility that they acquired initially by mastering the discipline of a word processing package.

Craft

One of the first areas to repay attention is the training of craft apprentices, as this is a long and expensive business. Some of the training boards gave the largest amount of their attention to this area in the first few years of their operation.

Apprentices are recruited at the age of sixteen on leaving school, and serve an apprenticeship of several years before being accepted as craftsmen at the end of their training, usually at the age of twenty-one or twenty-two. Most apprentices are young men, although young women do follow apprenticeships as well, but these are heavily concentrated in hairdressing. Many companies follow the customary practice of binding apprentices by indentures, under which the apprentice is obliged to stay with the employer until finishing his 'time' and the employer agrees to provide his training.

A major part of the apprentice's time is spent in further education at a local college, learning the theoretical background of his craft and some manual skills. While with the employer, he needs to practise the skills he is learning and to develop them by applying his knowledge and ability to a growing range of work. Traditionally this has been done by watching, helping and copying a craftsman at work. Gradually this method is being replaced by systematic and full-time training under an instructor in charge of a group of apprentices.

If an organization is not big enough to warrant the services of a full-time instructor, it is often possible to join a group training scheme, in which a number of small and medium-sized companies pool resources to employ a training officer who organizes the training of the apprentices in all the companies. In return, the individual company pays a relatively modest fee to the group scheme. Also, the individual apprentice has a better training as he probably moves from one firm to another in the group.

There are usually national agreements between employers and trade unions regarding the employment and training of apprentices.

Technician

A category in which the number of employees is growing is that of technician, who is one step up from a craftsman and is likely to be concerned more with design than with manufacture. In the field of engineering, the fitter is the craftsman and the draughtsman is the technician, although there are many others classified as craftsmen and technicians respectively in that industry. To some extent the training needs are common, as the basic technology is the same, but the technician's training needs go further. He is likely to have better educational qualifications at the outset and his further education will go to a higher theoretical level. His practical training will tend to lie in conventional white collar rather than manual operations. It is usually carried out in close conjunction with a qualified man.

Technologist

It is difficult to distinguish between technicians and technologists and in many industries such a distinction cannot be drawn at all. A rough and ready identification would be by the word 'professional'. In engineering, for example, the technologist is the professional engineer who has achieved membership of one of the constituent bodies of the Council of Engineering Institutions. This requires a high level of academic qualification together with the appropriate working experience.

In this category will be the ex-technician who has taken the HNC/HND route through day release or evening courses, as well as the technical graduate who starts his working life in his early twenties. These are the people on whom the technical competence and progress of the organization will depend. The HNC/D method of qualification has been replaced by the scheme of the Technical Education Council (TEC). Courses for technical graduates now have the interesting development of a small number of courses in selected universities that combine engineering and management studies, usually over four years of study.

The man who comes up through the ranks will need facilities to pursue his academic studies, either by day release or by sandwich course. His practical expertise will be acquired almost incidentally as long as he has reasonable opportunities for varied working experience, rather than being classified as a trainee who cannot be given a proper job because he has not finished his education.

The technical graduate who joins industry in his early twenties with academic qualifications of a high order but no practical experience usually needs some form of graduate apprenticeship while he spends a number of months acquiring the practical experience that is needed to go with his theoretical grounding.

Management

Training managers is a very different matter from training other categories of workers in industry. This is largely because a smaller proportion of the manager's job content can be isolated and taught. To be effective a manager needs to learn management techniques, such as various methods for the quantification of data so that decisions may be soundly based. He also needs knowledge in such areas as the behavioural sciences so that he can understand how employees may react in certain situations, and so that he may plan sensibly for the future. Beyond this, however, there is still a large area of training or development needed for the individual management trainee, so that he acquires the stature and confidence needed for the job of leadership, gains judgement and determination and develops good timing and a sensitive awareness in handling people.

Largely because of the difficulty and lack of definition in the task of management training, most large organizations separate this particular aspect of training and give the responsibility to management development officers within the training function. The body of knowledge and some of the skills can come from the educational system. In addition to the business schools, which cater for a small fraction of the total amount of management training, there are a number of polytechnics and universities with management departments running courses with recognition from some professional body. The most widely recognized management qualification available in the field of further education is the Diploma in Management Studies, run under the auspices of the Department of Education and Science. It is operated at a limited number of centres and provides a broadly based management education for the well-qualified entrant with limited practical experience. There are also courses run under the aegis of, for instance, the Institute of Personnel Management and the Institution of Industrial Managers which provide a broad management education with particular emphasis on the specialism that the professional body represents.

In conjunction with further education, the trainee manager will need controlled working experience and career development so that he can apply his developing skills and knowledge. He may also need careful coaching to help him develop qualities such as judgement and timing. All managers need constantly to bring themselves up to date with new techniques or with new knowledge. Thus, professional bodies like the British Institute of Management and many firms of professional consultants conduct admirable short courses, running for a few days or a few weeks, to update the experienced manager. Typical of these have been the endless variety of courses and conferences to brief managers on unfair dismissal legislation, safety and health, or negotiating skills. The next chapter deals with management development in more detail.

Supervisory

Training of first-line supervisors is generally unsatisfactory in the UK, and the foreman has more than once been referred to as the forgotten man of British industry. Much of the problem lies in the uncertainty about the nature of the job. In the early years of this century the foreman was a man of considerable power and authority in a factory, with extensive discretion in decision-making, and was often a general manager in all but name. Since then we have seen the professionalization of management and the development of shop steward authority. The professionalization of management has spawned countless middle managers who have taken bits of the foreman's job away from him, like the production engineer and the training officer. The development of shop steward authority has largely done away with the foreman's role as representative of shop floor feeling, and he is constantly bypassed as shop stewards negotiate with middle and senior managers at meetings he is not invited to attend.

As the position of first-line supervisor is so difficult to define, training for it presents obvious problems. The most useful approach is probably the in-company course which aims to inform foremen of the changes taking place around them and give them an understanding of company procedures together with an introduction to such vague but necessary subjects as leadership and human relations. An attempt to establish a course for foremen within the further education system has not received widespread support.

Administrative

The term 'administrative' covers an amorphous group of people who are lumped together because their work is neither clerical nor managerial. They are such people as cost accountants, computer programmers and systems analysts, salesmen and O and M staff.

For the cost accountant, training will usually be on the job as a cost clerk while he makes his way through the further education courses for cost and management accountants, perhaps after starting with an Ordinary National Diploma in Business Studies while he is making up his mind about the area in which he wishes to specialize.

The training of computer personnel operates at various levels. Most courses in management include some elements of computing, even if only at the appreciation level, and there are a number of degree courses in computation. Computer operators and data input personnel are still mainly trained by computer manufacturers or specialized private agencies.

Shop stewards

The final category is shop steward. It is the joint responsibility of management and trade unions to train shop stewards. The best courses for stewards are provided by the trade unions, and an introductory course for newly elected shop stewards is run at many educational centres under the auspices of the TUC. It is difficult for many employers to provide satisfactory courses of their own, as stewards are likely to be suspicious of them, but this field of training will no doubt develop.

TRAINING METHODS

Teaching someone to *do* something requires a different approach from teaching someone to *understand* something. This broad distinction between training in skill and training in knowledge has been refined by research in the training field to produce a division of all types of learning into five basic types.

Some learning involves theoretical subject matter, knowing how, why and when certain things happen. This is *comprehension*: examples are the laws of thermodynamics, the currency structure of the EEC, or the arguments justifying the recognition of trade unions. *Reflex* learning is involved when skilled movements or perceptual capacities have to be acquired, involving practice as well as knowing what to do. Speed is usually important and the trainee needs constant repetition to develop the appropriate synchronization and co-ordination. Typing is one of the many jobs that requires reflex learning. *Attitude* development is concerned with enabling people to alter their attitudes and social skills. *Memory* training is concerned with learning how to cope with varied situations and *procedural* learning is very similar except that the drill to be followed does not have to be memorized, but located and understood. This categorization produces the mnemonic CRAMP.

Learning for comprehension requires the whole subject to be treated as an entity and the lecture or training manual are appropriate methods. Attitude change is typically handled by group discussion, but reflex learning is best handled by part methods, which break the task down into sections, each of which can be studied and practised separately before putting together a complete performance. Memory and procedural learning may take place either by whole or part methods, although memorization is usually done by parts.

FURTHER READING

Bass, B.M., and Vaughan, J.A., *Training in Industry*, Tavistock, London 1968

Industrial Training Research Unit, *Choose an Effective Style: A Self-instructional Approach to the Teaching of Skills*, ITRU Publications, Cambridge, 1976

Kenney, J.P.J. and Reid, M., *Training Interventions*, Institute of Personnel Management, London, 1985

MSC/NEDO, *A Challenge to Complacency: Changing Attitudes to Training*, Manpower Services Commission, Sheffield, 1985

Stammers, R.B., and Patrick, J., *The Psychology of Training*, Methuen, London, 1975

Winfield, I., *Learning to Teach Practical Skills*, Kogan Page, London, 1979

56 Management development

Michael Day

This chapter takes the conventional view that the success of an organization depends on the quality of its management. Since the quality of management is all important, the long-term future of an organization depends on a continuous supply of competent, experienced and well-trained managers, alert to the changing environment.

A competent manager is the result of many differing factors. He is certainly not the product of a recognized training system like a skilled craftsman, a doctor or a pilot. Some of the factors which make for quality may be controllable, yet the effectiveness of any total system for producing managers has never been adequately measured in terms of efficiency; there have only been attempts to measure the parts (e.g., human relations training), and those with varying degrees of success. It is not possible therefore to discuss methods in terms of their cost-effectiveness; indeed it is this lack of knowledge that has led management development to be an area particularly prone to fads and fashion. Yet though many of the packages which are offered are found wanting, the subject is still felt to be important because quite clearly organizations differ in their success and the only discernible reason can be the difference in quality of their management.

For this reason this chapter takes the widest view of the way an organization may act in order to meet its manpower needs for managers. To do this it must concern itself with three areas:

1 The attributes of the individual himself
2 The effect of the opportunities and the environment as they affect the individual
3 The form of administrative assistance that may be given.

ATTRIBUTES OF THE INDIVIDUAL

In theory, senior managers have to pass through the most stringent system of selection in that to arrive at their position they must have passed a series of stages where they could have been accepted or rejected. In practice most selection systems, if they are not dependent on the decision of a single individual, rely heavily on an appraisal system.

As will be mentioned, there have been some attempts to identify the essential characteristics of a good manager, but there is no general agreement on what these may be. Such attempts have been initiated, primarily, in large companies which have a greater problem in selecting people for wider 'exposure'.

On the whole, research indicates that leadership is specific to situations and perceived leaders share specific attributes with their groups but at a higher level. It follows that a manager should possess sufficient knowledge of skills to a level acceptable to the group he controls. The first point for training is that first-line managers must have sufficient technical knowledge. This will be even more important in a situation of changing technology; the danger of skill obsolescence is becoming greater and is an increasingly common reason for retiring managers prematurely.

The second point is that the skills of management are discontinuous; thus the attributes of a good lieutenant are different from those of a good general. This implies that training must be both different in content and continuous to meet the needs of an advancing career.

The third point is that organizations are formed of successive layers which interact. A good organization is the product of mixing attributes, knowledge, skills, etc., into a complementary whole. For instance, research has indicated that a dominant creative person works best as leader of a less creative submissive group; put such a man in a group of people similar to himself and little is produced but argument. Alternate layers of good communicators and administrators and good conceptualizers are very desirable. Hence building a *team* is an important objective of management development.

There are also general personal characteristics that are likely to be important:

1 *Intelligence*. This is not only necessary because management requires the ability to deal with abstract matters, but also because learning must take place quickly and effectively in order to deal with the changing environment
2 *A willingness to grow*. Pym's research concluded 'people who aspire to growth in their work are likely to be numbered among the more effective in mentally demanding jobs and in situations where changes increase the uncertainty of work roles'
3 *Accuracy of self-perception*. Effective people are conscious of their strengths and weaknesses and learn to play their strong points
4 *Versatility*. Administrators operate very largely by labelling; however, longitudinal studies of careers show that it is increasingly common for individuals to make major switches in profession. Indeed it is commonly predicted that most of us must be prepared to have two or more careers in our lifetime. Versatility is therefore a characteristic that must be identified; most selection puts greatest emphasis on choosing an individual for a particular job, though viewed longitudinally the individual will occupy it for a short time in his career.

Success in management therefore largely rests on factors outside the scope of training, but fortunately the growing individual is likely to have the best view of what his needs are. We should attempt to operate a system of self-appraisal and self-education.

In any case most ambitious young men are well aware that an increasing number of their contemporaries (compared with the present generation of managers) have had some form of management education. This may be a pity because the desire may merely be to attend such a course, and concern for the content, effectiveness and relevance becomes secondary.

THE OPPORTUNITIES AND THE ENVIRONMENT

A man is the product of his history; but though one can trace the effects backwards, forecasting outcomes is very dubious. Specialists usually have more limited career patterns than generalists. This is not because they lack ability but because the decision-maker will rule them out for 'lack of experience'. The pattern for specialists is therefore largely determined very early in their careers. Paradoxically many organizations can point to individuals who were thrust into positions of responsibility and are very successful – the 'Truman phenomenon'.

The rate of progression of an individual within an organization depends on three factors (apart from his own abilities). These are:

1 Age structure of the organization (or the manpower pool to which he belongs)
2 Rate of expansion or contraction of the organization
3 Degree of change of organization, structure, functions, etc.

For example it is obvious that a thirty-year-old who has already had a varied experience in an expanding organization with elderly management has very bright prospects.

In a small organization the problem of getting the right experience is not difficult; the rate of progression allows ample time to master new situations and yet gain a reasonable understanding of other functions. However, this escalator approach is not always possible. It is a simple arithmetical exercise to compute the time a high-flying individual might stay in each level of an organization. Thus a man spending forty years in a company which has eight layers must spend five years in each; in practice, speed through layers is usually quicker at the start of a career and gradually slows. This computation also implies that the company will be run by old men; this is commonly not a desired objective, hence the speed of movement for a future head of a large organization must be very fast indeed. But the danger is that this makes for a narrow career, i.e., the individual has been moving up so fast he has little time for lateral movement.

The escalator also has its dangers. It can carry an individual up because of the age structure rather than because of his outstanding abilities until he appears the only possible choice for the top job. The result can be unfortunate for the organization and eventually calamitous for the individual.

Given the right environment, individuals will grow by learning. For this to happen, feedback must be effective and positive. An organization with a good system of counselling where the individual can discuss job performance and objectives, together with his personal wishes to expand his knowledge, skills and experience, will ensure an adequate supply of potential material for promotion.

Many social scientists believe that managerial systems based on trust give the employee a better opportunity to achieve growth at work (McGregor's theory Y). Such a climate may be produced as a result of a programme of organization development or the drive of a key individual. It can occur because an organization is in a state of fairly rapid change when decisions are made by those possessing the key knowledge rather than a high position in the hierarchy. Jobs and responsibilities are not highly defined and opportunities are there for those with initiative. This accords with the common observation that radically new situations, e.g., in war time, cause new talents to emerge.

Lastly there is the fortunate accident of working under a first-class manager; many would say that this is the best form of management education. Some organizations try to institutionalize this by having a system of coaching but as Gellerman points out 'most people in management are rewarded for making themselves successful not for making other managers successful'.

It can be seen that becoming a successful manager is a very chancy thing. The first-class man will usually come through; the rest need some help. If the human resources of the organization are to be used and a 'cadre' of professionally efficient individuals is to be built up, then some assistance in the form of a management development system is desirable.

FORMAL ASSISTANCE IN MANAGEMENT DEVELOPMENT

Many organizations have tried systems of management development, many of which have failed or waned. What is required is not gimmickry but a system in which the management have faith in the overall conception, and the operation of which is built into the normal working of the organization. As Wilson says, it must become institutional in character, that is, it must operate with an agreed and acceptable set of procedures and it must have the ability to handle the inevitable conflicts which will arise (since individual managers incur short-term loss of efficiency for the organization's long-term gain).

On the assumption that the personnel function is given the organizing responsibility, it has a delicate role to play. If the total system is seen as a piece of personnel gimmickry wished on the organization, it will fail. The chief executive is responsible for the long-term viability of the managerial team; he cannot delegate this but only the staff work and the organization of the activities. The personnel function can assist managers to develop their subordinates; they must never seek to impose their solutions.

The overall scheme for a management development is shown in Figure 56.1. A number of elements of the scheme, manpower planning and appraisal, are discussed more fully elsewhere in this book.

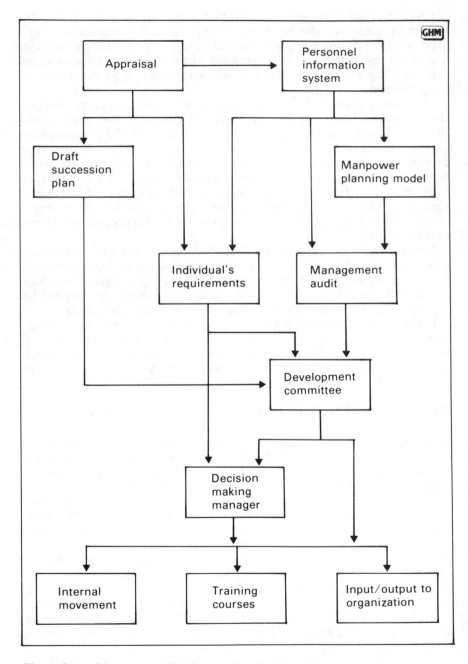

Figure 56.1 Management development system

There are three parts to the programme:

1 Information collection and analysis
2 Decision making
3 Action.

The scheme is elaborate but can be simplified for small organizations.

INFORMATION INPUTS

Personnel information system

This is a necessary adjunct to a manpower planning model. Apart from its obvious use as a single comprehensive source of information, it acts as a useful discipline to prevent overlooking minor parts of the organization and particular individuals. A management development system must scan the total manpower resources and not rely on the chance knowledge of the decision-makers.

Manpower planning

This subject was discussed in Chapter 49 but the particular aspect relevant here is the ability of a plan to predict the requirement for managerial manpower some years ahead and also the pattern of the probability of promotion for different groups e.g., departments, professional/skill groups. Some authorities see the desirable planning horizon as fifteen years; others believe that only five years is practical.

Appraisal

Again this is discussed elsewhere (Chapter 51), but to reiterate, appraisal provides essential management information for decisions about people and particularly for management development. It will be seen from the diagram that appraisal information underpins many parts of the management development system. Particularly important are:

1 The assessment of potential for promotion
2 The readiness for a move
3 Specific recommendations on training, movement, etc.
4 The reported views of the individual

Draft succession plans

Succession plans must be layered, that is they encompass distant levels within the hierarchy, e.g., branch, department management, top management. A typical chart is shown in Figure 56.2 and is self-explanatory. Such a document is completed by the senior manager in the 'layer', usually with the assistance of a specialist in manpower development or a personnel officer. It should be discussed by a management development committee to ensure that all possible candidates are considered.

Job	Holder	Age	Year successor required	Possible successor
Manager, Northern Sales Div.	Evans, W. S.	55	1988 (R)	Brown, J. (44) MacPherson, A. (42)
Manager, Newcastle Branch	Brown, J.	42	1987	(E) Jameson, P. (53)

R: Retiring; E: Emergency only

Figure 56.2   A succession plan

The main objectives are to stimulate management into thinking about their succession problems and to identify areas where special action is called for, e.g., an adequate successor for Brown in Figure 56.2.

Management audit

The object is to collate and analyse the available information in order to arrive at an appraisal of where the organization finds itself now and may find itself in the foreseeable future with respect to its management manpower. The audit might contain a number of elements:

1   An age distribution of manpower now
2   The same distribution in five years
3   The expected promotion prospects
4   Distribution of potential (see Figure 56.3)

Grade	Number	Immediately promotable	Foreseen potential grade					
			1	2	3	4	5	6
1	100	24	52	20	15	8	4	1
2	54	16	—	32	11	8	3	0
3	32	15	—	—	12	16	3	1
4	12	3	—	—	—	8	4	0
5	3	1	—	—	—	—	2	1
6	1	0	—	—	—	—	—	1

Figure 56.3   Distribution of potential

Organization levels	Numbers	Core[1]	Expected numbers[2]	Require- ment	Numbers ready now for promotion
A	10	5	10	5	—
B	30	25	32	12[3]	7
C	100	75	110	47[4]	16

1 Numbers remaining at the end of 5 years
2 Allows for change in size of organisation
3 Allows for five promotions to level A
4 Allows for 12 promotions to level B

Figure 56.4   Relationship between requirements and resources over five years

5   Relationship between requirement and resources over five years (see Figure 56.4).

Individual information

Personal histories and particulars will be required but these can be included on a special card which can be used as a visual aid when discussions are taking place. The individual cards can be displayed in a format corresponding to the organization structure. The card may contain:

Photograph of individual
Age
Grade
Performance rating
Potential rating
Present job title
Job history
Qualifications

This device is certainly useful in larger organizations where not all individuals will be directly known to the decision-makers.

Decision-making

The locus and form of decision-making will vary with the style of the organization. It may be the head of the function or organization alone; he may be advised by a senior group; or a committee representing different functions may be formed. No best way exists; however failure will follow if those dealing with management development have no power. To repeat, decisions about people are an important part of management responsibility, therefore the decision-making structure must be coincident with the power structure of the organization.

It is desirable to minimize the time consumption of managers by having relatively infrequent meetings and by good staff work. One meeting a year is usually adequate.

It is clear that any manager or committee should only survey a limited number of individuals. A layered system will be required; the number of layers will depend on the organization, but there should be basically three, all interlocking:

1 Top management
2 Department, function or geographical location
3 The working unit.

The objectives of the decision makers will be:

1 To review the manpower position. Without reviewing the overall position it is possible for organizations to run into problems of shortfall, over abundance or maldistribution of talent. Few organizations are in equilibrium
2 To ensure that sufficient numbers are available to fill foreseen management requirements. In practice more people must be available than can be promoted because at the moment of decision a number of candidates will not be available for many different reasons, e.g., recent transfer, personal circumstances, etc.
3 To ensure efficiency and equity in movement. Individuals are often penalized because they belong to a less well-favoured part of the organization. Alternatively there is unnecessary professional exclusivity for certain jobs (e.g., accountants)
4 To encourage the utilization of talent. Many individuals benefit from movement even if no promotion is involved; it encourages self-renewal or the use of talents for which there is little opening in the present position. Gellerman believes that such moves should always stretch a man by giving more responsibility than he is judged to be ready for; failure in practice is rare and growth is accelerated
5 To resolve conflict about the use of individuals. There will always be a limited number of outstanding individuals, and their current managers will always be tempted to try and keep them. Given the scarcity, this is unlikely to be the best strategy for the organization as a whole, so some supra-body is required to resolve competing claims.

ACTION

Although recruitment and dismissal must be part of the scheme, in a well-run organization these should be rare events; resorting to either points to the failure of the management development programme.

Movement

Action tends to two extremes, either 'opportunistic' or 'predetermined'. Opportunistic movement operates where the decisions are made in the light of the previous analysis and recommendation but the act is dependent on an opening occurring. Predetermined movement initiates a succession of inter-related moves. The opportunistic system is perhaps less efficient but has the advantage that it allows greater choice to the individual as the system can still operate if he refuses a move. Predetermined moves depend on the individual being willing, say, to move location; in return he can be reasonably certain of where his next job will be.

Movements (promotion) can take the following forms:

1   Transfer – in practice exchanges of individuals are administratively easier than a chain of movements if only because of the problem of handover
2   Projects – these are valuable because they can provide an opportunity to try an individual in a new role, e.g., putting him in a managerial position without an almost irreversible commitment to keep him in his new status. It is a useful mechanism for spreading experience of a new technique throughout the managerial group by making each man serve as a project leader for a limited spell
3   'Secondments' – opportunities for these are rare but may include the civil service, education establishments and companies with close commercial relationships
4   Action learning – Revans (its progenitor) describes this as 'Learning to learn-by-doing with and from others who are also learning to learn-by-doing'. In its most usual form it involves undertaking an assignment in another company (or part of the same company) which in turn nominates an individual to form part of the learning group. The whole process is carefully guided with the group of participants meeting weekly to talk through experience and problems, with the aid of a specialist adviser.

Continuous movement is part of the way of life in some companies, but it has a cost penalty attached to it. In theory there must be a 'learning curve' for each person entering each job. This implies that for a period of time there will be a continuous but reducing deficit of efficiency.

Against this the organization has increased the asset value of its man-power. Indeed, the R.G.Barry Corporation in the USA (among others) has shown changes in the value of its human resources in its annual reports. The desirability of this can readily be seen for organizations such as architects' groups, advertising agencies and accounting practices whose strength lies primarily in the quality of the people they employ; however this form of accounting presents great technical difficulties and no agreed conventions exist.

It does indicate the need for the decision-maker to balance the cost of movement and training against the increase in asset value of the manpower.

Training

Two fundamental assumptions are made; first, training must be continuous, and second, training content must vary with the stages in the individual's career. It follows, therefore, that management training cannot be a 'one-shot' injection.

Training must be continuous because the individual changes over time, because the work environment alters, and because new knowledge and techniques are being created at an increasing rate.

Four stages in an individual's career can be identified and with each there are corresponding training needs.

Professional phase

Few start as managers; initially the individual often works as a professional – a chemist, accountant or personnel officer. This phase exploits any academic qualification. Training is predominantly a 'topping-up' process in order to keep him up to date and prevent skill obsolescence.

Gradually he is likely to acquire greater managerial responsibilities. The corresponding management training need is to introduce him to topics so that the self-educational process can start. These might include:

1 Company knowledge – this has the object of breaking down parochialism and facilitating interaction. Much of this training happens informally by virtue of mixing course members from different parts of the company
2 Information handling and analysis – introduction to accounting and numerical analysis techniques
3 Manpower planning, assessment, training, industrial relations. Broad management theory.

It is stressed that the treatment will be introductory; teaching in depth has no direct value unless the individual has the opportunity to practice new found skills. The exception may be social skills, e.g., lecturing, presentation of cases, interviewing and running meetings, though these are best deal with as separate 'modules' when a need is clear.

Initial management appointment

It is common for a manager to be confronted with a requirement to undertake a number of specific administrative actions related to local procedures on taking up his appointment. These might include:

1 Budgeting method
2 Completion of assessment forms
3 Grievance procedure
4 Procedure for replacing staff
5 Authorizing expenditure
6 Handling communication with subordinates.

In the first months this can be bewildering and needlessly embarrassing; costly errors can result from ignorance. So on appointment either a course or a series of individual discussions should be arranged to accelerate the learning process and the building of confidence. The actual content must be determined by a thorough analysis.

Mature management

This is one of the most difficult phases for which to cater because of the very varied experience of management matters possessed by each individual. It is a common experience that managers sent on a general management course complain that 'it was very interesting but it only partly touched on topics that are important in my job'. Such courses are not very efficient in time usage and may be positively harmful if they reinforce a latent feeling that all such training is 'useless'.

The answer would seem to be either a carefully chosen series of modules, or courses with a high degree of flexibility to meet personal needs.

The principle of selection for modules should be that the manager is certain to practise the new-found skill on return to his desk. The principle of the method is that the skill must be advanced to a level on the course where he can go through the process without outside assistance on his return; this implies a fair level of practical work on the course.

Informational topics have their place but mainly to change attitudes or to reinforce the process started in the professional phase.

Modules can be linked in time so that they run consecutively provided that a homogeneous group can be brought together, e.g., a group of marketing managers. This enables technical topics to be taken in depth.

An important module for many managers will be industrial relations. Traditional approaches have been to trace the history of trade unions or to place the emphasis on the legal aspects; such approaches are useful as an introduction but are rarely useful practically. Knowledge of local agreements and procedures is vital, and many companies use simulated disputes where course members role play the parts. Trainees can experiment with different responses, and feedback can be provided by discussion or preferably by playing back a video tape of the process. One of the advantages of role playing is that it encourages flexibility together with the realization that no single mode of response is effective in meeting all types of situations. The process of role reversal, i.e., playing the part of the union official, fosters a deeper understanding of the powers and limitations of the full-time officer.

An approach, of which one is likely to see more, is some variety of flexible training. The theory is that all parts of the course should be tailor-made to meet the needs of every individual. For instance, if the topic is discounted cash flow, one group may be very familiar with the topic and so would be more interested in the advanced aspects, the largest group may have only a nodding acquaintance and so need their skills brought up to the working level, and one group may know nothing. The first step is to discover the groups; this can be done by self-evaluation or self-testing, though this is only a guide since the individual may choose which group he joins. The difficulty is the administration and the availability of highly flexible tutors. An alternative would be the use of self-teaching aids or guided reading. Surprisingly few managers' courses are based on reading; books appear to be for self-educators, not course-goers. There is certainly no lack of suitable material.

Higher management

The potential member of top management, if caught young enough, presents no great training problem, most large companies send such people to prestigious courses which draw their membership from all over the world. The business schools are favourites. Such a course has many advantages:

1 It will enable the 'young lion' to test himself against international standards
2 It will expose him to some of the best minds whose jobs it is to think about business
3 It will break down parochialism and cause him to think afresh about his own organization.

Such courses are usually expensive and long, so organizations send only the cream. This carries the danger that unless the man is mature, with a long history of achievement, the organization may feel it is necessary to arrange a glittering career for a man whose lustre, in fact, fades as he progresses. The comment 'we had to promote him, he'd been to . . .' is not unknown. In such instances the organization is caught in a dilemma since young men increasingly expect to be sent on such courses, and will leave if they are not.

For the more mature manager, training is more difficult. He is unlikely to take kindly to being lectured at; nor is he very happy with the new techniques. Probably the best solution is to let these men educate each other, with stimulation from outside. This is likely to be fruitful because each will possess a depth of experience, but unless the skill of communication is present to a high degree the best format would appear to be some form of team project.

Board members rarely attend courses (unless they are that way inclined). Pressure of work is certainly one factor, but if as a pundit once said 'the mark of a great manager is the power of infinite self-delusion' then the motivation is also likely to be lacking. Perhaps this is the biggest gap in management education.

Internal v. external courses

The choice between an internal course run by the organization and an external course, particularly those run by academic institutions, must be decided by its relevance and an assessment of cost/benefit. For the small organization the choice does not exist because of the difficulty of mustering enough people and resources to make an internal course worth while.

Internal courses ought to be more relevant but this will depend on the skill of the training specialist. There is a good case for making practising managers or specialists give the lectures; the discipline is always beneficial. Naturally some training in lecturing is desirable beforehand. The course gains the added benefit of seeing, in action, managers of functions with which the individual does not come into contact.

There should be a freshness of ideas if the academic institution also undertakes research, and there may be an opportunity to hear the leaders in particular fields. Such courses have the use of opening up new areas and introducing ideas which do not exist in the parent organization.

Again compromise is possible and desirable. Academic lectures can be inserted into the internal programmes; increasingly, organizations and academic institutions are collaborating to form tailor-made courses to meet special needs. There is evidence of considerable mutual gain.

A special word must be said about business schools, in particular the immediate postgraduate courses. The quality of the courses is usually high but there is a clear problem on timing. From the discussion on phasing earlier in this chapter it will be seen that such courses do not fit the desirable sequence since they occur *before* the professional phase. There is evidence from Livingston writing on the 'myth of the well-educated manager' that such courses are not producing managers but new sorts of professionals, (e.g., planners, consultants, etc.), for it is in these fields that their academic knowledge and analytic skills can most quickly be applied. Though high salaries can be commanded initially it appears that the high rate is not sustained comparatively; hence the low correlation that has been found between academic success and business achievement.

Organization development and management training

A problem that has been hinted at in the discussion above is that it is relatively straightforward to teach informational subjects, certain social skills and to foster an analytic approach, yet the sum of these does not turn a professional into a manager nor do they produce those subtle changes of behaviour that lead to greater efficiency. Coupled with this has been a growing body of evidence concerning the effectiveness of various management styles. Early attempts to capitalize on this were not successful because the behaviour learned on the course was not reinforced in the work situation. It is unrealistic to expect an individual to change his way of managing when his superior does not. This was particularly true when the subjects were foremen. Foremen were singled out because they formed the essential link between management and the managed; yet in many ways they were dupes. As many foremen observed 'you shouldn't be telling me but teaching my boss'. The conclusion is clear; changes in management style can only be effective if applied to a group as a whole. The ideas can be introduced into courses, but the real change can only be brought about by a process of 'organization development' as it is now called. Usually the object of the changes is to transform an organization's climate from the rigid and mechanistic to something more flexible or organic.

The techniques used are T-groups (or sensitivity training), Blake and Mouton's management grid or Reddin's '30' training. A number of successful applications has been reported, but they are not exempt from the usual requirements for successful innovation within an organization. They must start with a wholehearted commitment from the top, and they must have competent practitioners or 'change agents'. However, the logistical problem of encompassing a whole organization (to say nothing of the internal politics) has caused this to be a declining area of training.

The training situation, the trainee and the stages of training

Training courses rightly take place outside the immediate environment of work (if only to prevent interruptions). The training situation, therefore, takes place on a 'cultural island' – a special place, a particular pattern of time allocation and an institutionalized form with its own norms of behaviour.

The trainee, on the other hand, may enter with some doubts. At worst he may come from an organization where only those that can be spared are sent on courses. The average course-goer is unlikely to have been told why he was selected, what is expected of him (except to 'have a good time') or what will happen when he returns. He may believe he was sent to have deficiencies remedied, rather than to be developed. Finally, training courses have been known to be used to get individuals out of the way while changes are made.

Because of all this, the role of the course tutor or training officer is crucial. He will set the style of behaviour of the newly formed group; he can motivate, reassure and guide. First-class administration will not make a poor course good but the lack of it can make an inherently sound course into a failure. Very largely he controls the expectancy and context of the training; this is the first of the stages.

The second stage is concerned with exposure, trial and reinforcement. The training aim must be clarified and the appropriate technique selected to achieve the objective. The various methods are now familiar but it is wise to scan the possibilities before finally deciding. The range includes:

> Lecture (including the use of visual aids)
> Video recording and playback
> Film
> Discussion group
> Case study
> Project
> Self-teaching aids (either by book or even using a computer)
> Role playing
> Business games
> Social learning situations

But, as much educational research shows, the crucial factor is the instructor; his skill with the chosen medium, his acceptability, his knowledge and his ability to kindle the interest of his audience are all important. A cursory knowledge of the technique and a poor style are disastrous.

The next phase is the transfer of skills and knowledge to the work situation. If the situation is right this will happen automatically, but this is rare. *It is this stage where the greatest loss of value occurs.* It is uncommon for the returning individual to be debriefed adequately not only to get his evaluation but to understand what he has learnt and how it might be applied. Ideally, the man's superior should be seeking opportunities for practice and either acting as the 'apprentice-master' or arranging for someone else to play this role (this is one of the values of the change agent in the organization development situation). In reality, life is usually too short for proper follow-up so the waste of new-found skills is immense. This is probably one of the main causes for doubt concerning the value of management training. The course notes stand on the bookshelf like a trophy from the hunt; like the stuffed antelope head, they gather dust and occasionally stimulate a memory of a past event.

Evaluation

Selection of topics for training is usually based on desirability rather than a knowledge of whether it is technically possible to achieve that objective. Yet it might be argued that it is better to teach something the result of which can be guaranteed, than a topic, however important, which has a low probability of successful outcome.

Changes in method and content will be more dependent on fashion than information, unless attempts are made to evaluate effectiveness, though the difficulties of doing such an assessment adequately are considerable.

Warr, Bird and Rackham have pointed out that there are three levels of outcome from training.

1 Immediate: new knowledge, skills and attitudes which are present immediately after training
2 Intermediate: new knowledge, skills and attitudes present in the work situation
3 Ultimate: changes in organizational effectiveness.

Immediate outcomes are the most commonly attempted in management training by means of discussion or questionnaire at the end of the course. For external courses, such a method is incorporated in the National Training Index in which a number of companies participate. The danger is that unless such an evaluation is done vigorously, one gets an 'Index of Euphoria' commonly associated with the end of courses. It is better therefore to evaluate each section of the course for:

1 Relevance
2 Content

3 Presentation
4 Enjoyment.

The evaluation is usually in the form of ratings.

Intermediate outcomes are usually based on measurement (or ratings) of the individual at periods after his return to work.

Ultimate outcomes should be based on economic criteria or, less satisfactorily, on a questionnaire comprised of 'before' and 'after'.

Foreman and supervisor training

In principle the training (as opposed to development) of foremen does not differ from management training. In practice it is complicated by the curious role position of foremen. If he were clearly part of management then there would be no problem, but in practice this is not so. In career terms foremen tend to lie near the top of the ladder starting with the skilled or semi-skilled worker; with the increasing number of graduates and professional workers he is less and less seen as being on the way to higher management. Thus he has been variously described as 'the man in the middle' and the 'victim of double-talk'. Because much foremen training has ignored the organizational context, it has often a curiously unreal air to it. This does not mean that no training should be given, but that the dangers must be foreseen. Certainly courses will not cure any gross ineffectiveness of foremanship within an organization; the roots of this problem are much deeper.

The phases of training for foremen correspond to the initial appointment at the mature stages of management. The same principles apply though the style and content will be different. Style is particularly important because of the length of time that usually has elapsed since they last attended a full-time educational institution; adaptation to the course environment will need special care. The emphasis should be on practicability, e.g., the discussion and role playing of case studies presented by film or film strip. Industrial relations is an essential topic since the foreman is involved with this at the grass-roots level. As the Industrial Relations Code of Practice states in section 8, 'The supervisor is in a key position to influence industrial relations. Management should ensure that he . . . is fully briefed in advance about management's policies as they affect his work group'. Communication is, therefore, another important area and includes not only content but an increase in the skills necessary for its accomplishment.

FURTHER READING

Blake, R, and Mouton, S., *The New Managerial Grid*, Gulf Publishing Co., Houston, 1978

Boydell, T., and Pedler, M. (eds), *Management Self-Development*, Gower, Aldershot, 1981

Easterby-Smith, M., *Evaluation of Management Education, Training and Development*, Gower, Aldershot, 1986

Gellerman, S.W., *Management by Motivation*, American Management Association, Inc., New York, 1968

Jones, J.E., and Woodcock, M., *Manual of Management Development*, Gower, Aldershot, 1985

Livingstone, J.S., 'Myth of the well-educated manager', *Harvard Business Review*, Jan–Feb 1971

Mumford, A. (ed.), *Handbook of Management Development*, 2nd edition, Gower, Aldershot, 1986

Revans, R.W., *Action Learning*, Blond & Briggs, London, 1980

57 Employee relations

J L Cookson

This chapter deals with regulating the working relationship between employer and the employees collectively. It is an unrealistic and oversimplified view of management that sees managers making decisions and issuing instructions for others to obey. The conception – shaping and implementation of executive action in organizing – is a complex process that depends heavily on employee consent. This consent is ceded to managers by employees individually, as they decide to accept rather than decline an offer of employment, as they work with enthusiasm rather than apathy and direct their activities towards the objectives of organizational success that managers determine.

Consent is also, however, ceded to managers by the employees collectively who give, implicitly or explicitly, a mandate to managers to make decisions and issue orders. There are many ways in which managerial action can be frustrated by collective employee resistance which would be beyond the scope of employees individually. There are not only the extremes of industrial action, but cooperative or uncooperative working within the guidelines of union agreements, the degree of enthusiasm with which changes are accepted and implemented, the care with which safety routines are followed, flexibility of manning arrangements, and many more.

Whatever the level of national unemployment and economic gloom, and no matter how tightly collective agreements are worded, managers depend on the collective consent of employees to *allow* and *support* them in their duties. That consent can perhaps be required or even forced in some situations for a short time, but sustained and productive consent has to be won: it is won by managers who earn it through paying close attention to the working relationship.

The most recent empirically based research findings (published in 1985 and 1986) attest to the continuing importance of employee relations. Despite recession and technological change, workplace trade union organization has proved durable, and workplace employee relations stable. There is no evidence of decline in the importance which senior management attaches to employee relations and, to personnel practitioners, it remains pre-eminent (the activity upon which they spend most time and to which they assign most importance).

TRADE UNION RECOGNITION

When a trade union has recruited a number of members in an organization it will seek recognition from the employer in order to represent those members. What is recognition? It involves first of all that the employer singles out that trade union from others, so that the step of recognizing by an employer means that, while he will have to take seriously the representations of one union, he will not usually have to deal with others as well for the same group of employees. There are exceptions to this, especially when the number of union members is low, but it is a normal component of recognition. The second aspect is that the employer has to allow the recognition to affect his behaviour by taking seriously what the union representatives say to him. This does not necessarily mean agreeing to their claims, but it does mean taking time to talk with them to seek accommodations. It is an important, irrevocable step away from all decisions lying unilaterally with management. There are three points to consider about recognition:

1 The timing of recognition – when to recognize
2 Identifying the people, or groups of people, whom the union should represent
3 Deciding which topics should fall within the scope of recognition – or what to recognize.

Reasons for recognition

Why should an employer recognize a union at all? Is there any advantage or is it simply an unfortunate yielding to pressure? The answer to that question depends on the wishes of the employees. If they collectively want trade union representation it is unlikely that they will cooperate with the employer who refuses it. They will want recognition partly because of their general experience and beliefs about working life and partly because of their particular experience with the individual employer where a recognition claim is brought. Manual employees tend to regard trade union representation as normal and necessary, managerial employees tend to regard it as abnormal and unnecessary, and administrative and clerical employees lie between these two extremes.

A more positive reason for recognition is the benefits which can flow to the employer from having representatives with whom to discuss plans and problems. It offers at least a useful method of communication and can be a way of contriving improved working relationships, hastening necessary change and developing trust in the motives and competence of the management.

When to recognize a union

The time at which to recognize a union is a fine judgement for managers to make. If it is too soon there will not be enough support among employees, who may feel that what should be *their* decision is being made for them. A union with only 5 per cent of the employees in membership has a small and potentially clique-like constituency, recognition of which might antagonize the majority. At the other extreme, the refusal to recognize a union which has 95 per cent of the employees in membership would be antagonizing the majority of the labour force in a different way, possibly with more serious results.

In the days when unions could seek recognition by legal means if an employer refused, the Advisory Conciliation and Arbitration Service (ACAS) often recommended recognition when the proportion of union members was below 40 per cent. The factors influencing the decision of when to recognize are the degree and efficiency of union organization, the number of representatives, the size of constituency and the degree of opposition. Nonetheless the key indicator is obviously the number of union members. It may be useful to ballot the employees to determine their wishes, although the greatest stimulus for a management to recognize union *A* is often the fear that union *B* may start recruiting members. Only recognition by management can check that move towards multi-unionism.

Identifying the groups of people to be represented by a recognized union

Another judgement to be made is to define the group of employees to be represented by the union. If the group is too large its members do not have enough interests in common for representation to be feasible. If it is too small there may be other employees, outside the group, who claim the same treatments as the union members because the terms and conditions of employment are similar. The employer either concedes the same benefits and antagonizes the union members who regard the others as 'riding on their backs' or refuses and antagonizes the non-union members. The normal test is to consider what different groups of employees have in common.

Some of the more common boundaries are between manual and white collar workers, where members of the two groups are seldom represented by the same union or involved in the same procedures and agreements. Another boundary is manual skill, where union membership or *grade* of membership is often jealously guarded on behalf of those who have completed a craft apprenticeship or other preparation that is acknowledged to justify special representation. In some situations the Amalgamated Union of Engineering Workers may represent employees who are skilled as well as those who are semi-skilled and unskilled, but the grade of membership would be different and arrangements with the employer would recognize that difference. The same union, through its Technical and Supervisory Section, may well represent white collar employees in the same company, but that would be through a different section of the union, with different officials and different agreements.

More difficult boundaries are those connected with status in the organizational hierarchy. Should the supervisor and those he supervises be represented by the same body? In manufacturing industry it seems that he will usually be represented separately, to cope with the problem of the union member seeking representation against the management action of his supervisor, who is a member of the same union and entitled to the assistance of the same union official. In local government it is quite common for the Chief Officers in an authority and the most humble clerical personnel all to be members of the National and Local Government Officers Association.

What to recognize

A union can seek recognition on anything that might be covered in a contract of employment, but the employer may agree to recognition for only a limited range of topics. The basis is to recognize a union to represent the grievances of members. That excludes any consultation on payment, terms and conditions, working practices and the other potential ingredients of a recognition agreement. It may be that an employer will proceed progressively with recognition, so that the range of topics grows with familiarity in the negotiating relationship. It should be noted that the potential benefits for management from a recognition arrangement come only when recognition is on a wide basis. Also, if the employees are up in arms on an issue, it may be pedantic to refuse discussion because it is not covered by the recognition agreement.

The legal position on recognition

The fragmented structure of collective bargaining in the UK is partly attributed to the traditional abstentionist policy of the state, departed from only in statutes prescribing the structures of nationalized corporations. During the 1970s, however, both major political parties were agreed upon the necessity for statutory machinery to resolve recognition disputes. The purposes embodied in the recognition provisions for the Industrial Relations Act 1971 were largely frustrated by the policy of non-cooperation on the part of the labour movement.

The Employment Protection Act 1975, sections 11-16, represented an attempt by the state to steer a course between legalism and voluntarism in this area. These sections permitted a recognition issue to be referred by an independent union to ACAS for examination, inquiry and report. If an employer failed to comply with a recommendation by ACAS for recognition and conciliation failed to resolve the dispute, the union could present a claim for specified terms and conditions to the Central Arbitration Committee (CAC) for unilateral arbitration. Any terms and conditions awarded by the CAC would thereafter take effect as part of the contracts of the employees.

During their currency, these provisions were subjected to several criticisms:

1 The statutory processes culminating in unilateral arbitration could only be invoked by the union side
2 Inquiry procedures were protracted
3 ACAS's functions were capable of being seriously impaired by the absence of any requirement that employees should cooperate in enquiries, and by judicial review of ACAS's exercise of its powers
4 The ultimate sanction fell short of requiring an employer to recognize a union.

The response of the Conservative Government elected in 1979 to these criticisms (in the Employment Act 1980) was to repeal sections 11-16, returning to voluntarism in union recognition.

Despite the dismantling of statutory recognition machinery, recognition disputes continue to be referred to ACAS, and to represent a significant element (approximately 14 per cent) of ACAS's collective conciliation activity.

The closed shop

In some ways the logical development of union recognition is the 'closed shop' which is an agreement whereby *all* employees in a particular category should be members of the recognized union, as a condition of employment.

Perhaps nowhere is 'the dilemma between the function of the law to protect the individual and its function to help adjust power relations in Society' (Kahn-Freund) more clearly demonstrated than in the debates which have raged since 1970 over the issue of the closed shop in British industrial relations and the extent to which the state should extend or restrict its operation. At the level of public policy, the issue is whether, given the ostensible commitment of the political parties to the system of collective bargaining, it is appropriate to provide individuals with a statutory right of disassociation and if so, in what circumstances.

The provisions of the Industrial Relations Act 1971, heavily influenced by doctrines of individual rights which paid little heed to the realities of collective labour relations, aimed to outlaw the closed shop notwithstanding a pledge of support for the principle of collective bargaining. In the event, established closed shop arrangements remained largely unaffected by the 1971 statutory measures, and it came as no surprise that the incoming Labour Government of 1974 should remove the right of disassociation from the statute book, thereby re-legalizing the closed shop though providing limited statutory protection for religious objectors. Undoubtedly, statutory support for union membership agreements during the period 1974-1980 reinforced the willingness of employers (based upon administrative convenience) to conclude such agreements to the extent that, currently, approximately one-fifth of British employees and two-fifths of trade union members are covered by some form of closed shop arrangement.

The Employment Act 1980 is calculated, if not to render closed shops unlawful, at least to limit their objectives and restrict their future development. The 1980 Act significantly narrows the circumstances in which employees may be dismissed fairly for not being a union member. It is now unfair to dismiss an employee:

1 Where the employee genuinely objects on grounds of conscience or other deeply held personal conviction to being a member of any trade union whatsoever or of a particular union. Interestingly, the courts have held that a deeply held personal conviction does not require that the objection be based on conscience but may cover dissatisfaction with the performance or conduct of the union (see Home Delivery Services Ltd v Sackcloth, E.A.T. 1984 and Thorpe v General Motors Corporation, Bedford Tribunal 1984)

2 Where the employee was a member of the class of employees covered by the closed shop agreement before it took effect and has not subsequently been a member of a union which is party to such agreement

3 Where the closed shop was introduced on or after 15 August 1980 and has not been approved by a secret ballot of affected employees showing that at least 80 per cent of those entitled to vote supported the agreement.

Employers may also require a union or other person to be joined as a party in unfair dismissal proceedings where the employer claims that the dismissal was the result of pressure exerted by such union or person calling or threatening industrial action because of the complainant's non-membership of the union. The 'joined' party may be ordered to contribute towards the compensation awarded if the complaint of unfair dismissal is upheld.

A further significant feature of the Employment Act 1980 is the restoration of statutory recourse to law for individuals who, in relation to employment subject to a union membership agreement, are unreasonably excluded or expelled from membership of a specified union.

Further statutory reform of the closed shop laws is embodied in the Employment Act, 1982. Given the practical importance of the closed shop in British industrial relations and the doubts, based upon the experience of 1971-74, concerning the extent to which long-standing practices can be eradicated by law, the Conservative Government's intention is not to outlaw closed shops altogether but to impose further restrictions upon their operation. The Act makes the following provisions:

1 Increased compensation for unfair dismissal for refusal to join a union. The 1982 Act introduced a minimum basic award of £2000 for unfair closed shop dismissals. Additionally, the dismissed employee will be entitled to receive the conventional compensatory award. Most significantly, an employer who dismisses an employee unfairly in a closed shop situation, and who refuses to implement a tribunal reinstatement order, is liable to pay the employee a further special award of three years' pay or £15 000, whichever is the greater. The Government's rationale for these increased levels of compensation is that they provide more adequate compensation for an individual who loses his livelihood unfairly. They appear also calculated to cause employers to think more

carefully and to exercise greater reserve, both before entering into a new closed shop agreement and before dismissing objectors

2 A dismissed employee may 'join', as a party to tribunal proceedings, the union that has contributed to the dismissal by exerting pressure on the employer. An award may be against, and be recoverable directly from, that union

3 Periodic ballots at five-yearly intervals to ascertain current support for continuance of existing closed shops. It is unfair to dismiss an employee refusing to join a union not receiving the support of 80 per cent of those covered or 85 per cent of those voting

4 Compensation may be payable by the Secretary of State to victims of closed shop agreements who were dismissed under legislation passed by the last Labour government and who would have been protected as existing non-union members or conscientious objectors if the EA 1980 closed shop provisions had been in force

5 It is unfair to dismiss an employee for not being a union member in a closed shop which took effect before 15 August 1980, unless in the five years preceding dismissal it had been supported in a ballot by 80 per cent of the employees covered or 85 per cent of those voting

6 Control of the exertion of pressure on a contractor, by the person engaging his services, to employ only union labour, since this requirement can involve conscription into unions of disinterested employees. The Act stipulates that:

(a) any clause in a contract will be void if it requires the employment only of persons who are members of a union, or persons who are not members

(b) it is unlawful to discriminate, in inviting tenders, or making contracts, to require that those employed to perform that contract should be trade union members, or alternatively should not be members

(c) immunity is removed for industrial action which interferes with performance of a contract primarily on the grounds that those employed to do so are, or are not, union members.

The impact to date of the new closed shop laws has been mixed. In the private sector, existing union memberships have rarely been subject to balloting, and remain largely unimpaired. In the public sector also there has been little balloting activity but three major employers (British Rail, British Gas and The Post Office) have announced their abandonment of long-standing union membership agreements.

ARRANGEMENTS WITH TRADE UNIONS

Within the framework of a recognition agreement, which may or may not have closed shop features, there are a number of arrangements which may help to put management/union relationships on a satisfactory footing.

Collective procedures

Procedures provide a structure within which the parties can engage each other in discussion, problem solving and negotiation at the same time as exercising some degree of control over each other. Some actions are laid down to be followed and others to be avoided, so that it is commonplace for a procedure to state that an employee with a grievance about his employment must seek redress *first* from his immediate superior. It is also typical for a procedure to state that industrial action will only be resorted to when procedural steps are exhausted and that changes in payment or other major terms and conditions of employment will not be made without prior consultation.

The essence of a procedure is to predetermine how matters shall be handled, so that everyone knows what the next step is if they cannot solve a problem or reach agreement. There is a similarity to legal procedure, with its clear path from court to higher court, but it is an area of industrial relations activity that remains free from law. It is quite possible for employer and union to make legally binding agreement, but it remains most unusual.

The most common procedures cover discipline and grievance. The law relating to the contract of employment assumes that there will be a grievance procedure and the law on unfair dismissal assumes that there will be a procedure for discipline, so these are becoming almost universal, although the degree of sophistication is seldom great. The next most common are procedures for negotiation and consultation, which only exist when employer and union have reached the stage of recognition that embraces more than terms and conditions of employment. There is also a frequent link with a procedure operated by an employers' association on a regional or national basis. Procedures are likely to bring clarity, fairness and consistency to employee relations, but they have limited effectiveness in altering the custom and practice of the workplace and they can make change difficult.

Rights of employee representatives

An inevitable consequence of recognizing trade unions is the need for union representatives to have some facilities.

Conventional industrial relations wisdom holds that the conduct of collective labour relations is improved by ensuring that employee representatives are informed and enjoy those facilities which they require to perform their functions. Thus, it has been an aim of public policy in recent years to strengthen the quality of workplace representation, primarily as a means of contributing to the creation of more orderly employee relations.

Under section 27 of the Employment Protection Consolidation Act 1978 officials (including shop stewards) of independent, recognized unions have a right to take time off from work with pay to a reasonable extent and subject to reasonable conditions, in order to carry out their duties concerned with industrial relations between the employer (or associated employer) and the employees or for the purpose of undergoing training relevant to those duties.

Such training must be approved either by the TUC or the official's own union. For safety representatives, an analogous right is provided by the Safety Representatives and Safety Committee's Regulations. Under the stimulus of the statutory provisions, basic courses for workplace representatives have trebled, and health and safety courses have increased by four times.

Disputes concerning whether these rights have been denied are ultimately determined by industrial tribunals, which may seek guidance from the recommendations of the ACAS Code of Practice 3, *Time Off for Trade Union Duties and Activities* (1978). This jurisdiction forced tribunals to the heart of workplace industrial relations in so far as disputes concerning time off require close consideration of both the structures of collective bargaining and of the functions which it is appropriate for shop stewards to perform.

The Code of Practice (para 13) gives examples of union officials' duties, though the list is not intended to be exhaustive:

1 Collective bargaining with the appropriate level of management
2 Informing constituents about negotiations or consultations with management
3 Meetings with other key officials or with full-time union officers on matters which are concerned with industrial relations
4 Interviews with and on behalf of constituents on grievance and discipline matters
5 Appearing on behalf of constituents before an official body such as an industrial tribunal
6 Explanations to new employees, whom he or she will represent, of the role of the union in the workplace industrial relations structure.

The code offers no guidance, however, upon whether, in the case of multi-site organizations, time off with pay should be afforded to allow stewards from one site to consult with those from another. This has been the central issue in much of the case law to date. Tribunals have usually applied a restrictive interpretation of the statutory provisions, though more recently, the Employment Appeal Tribunal (Good *v*. GEC Elliott Process Automation Ltd) rejected the contention that an official's duties can only be those which fall within the area of recognition. And in Beal *v*. Beecham Group Ltd (1982) the Court of Appeal held that attendance at a union representatives-only meeting, called to discuss matters of an industrial relations nature *and* to plan a co-ordinated union strategy, constituted a duty concerned with industrial relations.

The courts have also demonstrated a willingness to place a liberal construction of 'relevant' training for workplace representatives. In Young *v*. Carr Fasteners Ltd (E.A.T. 1979) it was held that training may be 'relevant' under the statutory provisions if it relates to a subject which may, in the future, form part of the representative's duties.

Perhaps the most important recommendation in the Code of Practice (para. 10) is that employers and trade unions should reach agreement on arrangements for handling the time-off facility in ways most appropriate to their particular situations.

Disclosure of information

During the 1970s, public policy supported the view that disclosure of information by employers to employees and their representatives is conducive to sound industrial relations and improves the processes of bargaining. Subsequent experience, however, reveals a marked lack of consensus, both within British employers and trade unions, concerning what information should be disclosed and why or how its disclosure would assist bargaining and influence its outcome.

The Employment Protection Act 1975 substantially re-enacts the disclosure provision of the Industrial Relations Act (never activated) by imposing a duty upon an employer to disclose (on request) to representatives of an independent, recognized union information relating to his undertaking or that of an associated employer without which the representatives would be materially impeded in their conduct of bargaining and which it would be good practice to disclose.

ACAS was required to produce a Code of Practice for the guidance of the parties. The Code on Disclosure, published in 1977, represents a disappointing gloss on the statutory provisions. Noting that the relevance of information is determined by the particular structure within which collective bargaining takes place, ACAS rejects the possibility of formulating a list of items which is universally relevant and disclosable. Instead, it provides examples of items of information which could be relevant in particular situations. These cover pay and benefits; conditions of service; manpower; performance; and finance. The central recommendation of the Code is that the parties should reach voluntary agreements on what information is to be disclosed, when and in what form. The scope of the statutory duty to disclose is restricted by the provision of certain safeguards for the employer, who is not required to disclose information communicated in confidence or which relates to an individual unless consent is given and, most importantly, which would cause substantial injury to the employer's undertaking.

Upon complaints of failure to disclose, the Central Arbitration Committee is empowered to declare what information an employer should disclose and by what date. As formerly with recognition claims, the ultimate sanction for failure to comply with such declaration is for terms and conditions to be determined by unilateral arbitration.

The Employment Protection Act provisions on disclosure are less stringent than the obligation of US employers to 'bargain in good faith' under which certain information is presumptively relevant and disclosable. Nor do they make provisions for disclosure to individual employees.

Perhaps the most striking feature of the statutory disclosure machinery since its establishment has been its low utilization by trade unions. This suggests either that they feel no need to invoke the machinery to obtain the information desired (because they can get it in various other ways) or that they continue to be suspicious of company-provided information (especially that disclosed to support an 'ability-to-pay' bargaining position). Thus the impact of the disclosure measures appears to have been minimal, although the existence of the statutory measures and the recommendations in the Code of Practice *may* have had a beneficial influence on the attitudes of some more reticent employers.

Picketing

UK picketing laws have been the subject of public controversy. Given the variety of criticisms directed from so many different quarters, it is hard to understand how the Donovan Commission concluded that the law on picketing was satisfactory. Statutory changes were introduced in 1971 and 1974; litigation arising out of picketing received prominent coverage by the media; and the subject was a prime target of further legislative change via the Employment Act 1980. The main aims of the Act's picketing sections are to curb secondary picketing such as by miners at power stations, mass picketing as at Grunwick; and the phenomenon of the 'flying picket' used in the building industry dispute of 1972. Additionally, the Act increases the scope of legal remedies available to employers who suffer as a result of unlawful picketing.

Section 15 of the Trade Union and Labour Relations Act 1974 (as amended by section 16 of the Employment Act 1980) renders it

> lawful for one or more persons in contemplation or furtherance of a trade dispute to stand at or near *his own place of work* or if he is an official of a trade union, at or near the place of work of a member of that union who he is accompanying. . . for the purpose only of peacefully . . . persuading any person to work or abstain from working.

Special provisions apply to mobile workers and to employees who have been dismissed during a strike. Generally speaking, therefore, it is unlawful for workers to picket, albeit peacefully, at premises other than those at which they work. Picketing which is accompanied by violent, intimidating or obstructive behaviour also exceeds the lawful limits of section 15. In respect of such unlawful picketing, employers may seek legal redress via an application for an injunction. It should also be noted that lawful picketing is confined to attendance 'at or near' a worker's place of work, not inside, which constitutes trespass.

The Code of Practice (1980) makes reference to picketing with excessive numbers and suggests that, as a general rule, the purposes of peaceful communication and persuasion can reasonably be achieved by six pickets or fewer at an entrance to a workplace. Since the Code must be considered by a court during legal proceedings, this suggestion may crucially affect the outcome of an employer's injunction application. Evidence that more than six pickets were present may be construed as indicating unlawful purpose.

Hitherto, the legal remedies (injunction and/or action for damages) available to employers in respect of industrial action have been statutorily restricted via civil immunities conferred upon the organizers of such action. An extremely important feature of the Employment Act 1980 is that for the first time, such immunities (under TULR Act 1974, section 13), are linked to the legality of picketing. Where picketing exceeds the limits set by section 15, the immunity from civil liability no longer applies so far as the organizers of the action are concerned, though trade union funds remain protected. In this way, the opportunity for employers, customers and suppliers to exercise legal remedies is significantly increased.

In applying for an injunction to remove an unlawful picket, the employer must name the organizers (usually a full-time union official or shop steward) and submit evidence by affidavit that the picket was unlawful and that damage has been sustained. If granted, the injunction will ordinarily apply to both the named organizers and to others acting on their instructions or on their behalf. Employers may experience difficulty in identifying the organizer(s) of an unlawful picket. Identification, however, remains the responsibility of the employer, not that of the police, and a suggestion that the police be required to assist employers in this context appears unlikely to be implemented legislatively.

STATE AGENCIES

Several state agencies are charged with a duty to advise employers on aspects of industrial relations practice. On specific matters there is the Equal Opportunities Commission and the Commission for Racial Equality or the Race Relations Advisory Service of the Department of Employment. The main agencies are ACAS and CAC.

Advisory, Conciliation and Arbitration Service (ACAS)

ACAS is a body run by a council that has both employer and union members, and there are offices in most large UK cities. An employer can obtain from them advice on the full range of employment practice, from how to draw up a contract of employment to the administration of job evaluation. This advice is also available to unions and members of the public.

Conciliation is provided in an attempt to solve problems between employers and employees, or ex-employees by informal discussion with one or both parties. The most widespread call on this service has been in many cases of dismissed employees seeking compensation, but it is also available to assist with collective issues, such as pay claims or other disputes.

When agreement between employer and union cannot be reached by the parties themselves, or after conciliation, ACAS can offer the services of a single arbitrator or a panel. In these situations, the arbitrator decides the matter for the parties after hearing evidence from both sides.

Central Arbitration Committee (CAC)

The statutory framework governing the processes of conciliation and arbitration was established by the Conciliation Act 1896 and extended by the Industrial Courts Act 1919. These statutes were largely repealed by the Employment Protection Act 1975. Following the creation of ACAS and to give final effect to the aim of establishing an independent (and therefore, more acceptable), conciliation and arbitration agency, the Central Arbitration Committee replaced the Industrial Arbitration Board as a permanent, arbitral body maintained at state expense but expressly protected from ministerial direction.

Its composition is tri-partite with legal chairmen plus representatives of employers and employees, all appointed by the Secretary of State after consultation with ACAS. It may sit publicly or privately and, since its creation, it has proved to be a more regional body than its predecessor; approximately 80 per cent of its hearings have been outside London. The Committee has developed its own procedural rules having the overriding aim of achieving informality and flexibility – an aim further encouraged by the fact that there exists no direct right of appeal against its awards. In line with tradition, the Committee's awards are usually not legally enforceable. Its principal statutory functions include:

1 Adjudicating on claims under the Fair Wages Resolution 1946
2 Amending discriminatory agreements and pay structures under the Equal Pay Act 1970
3 Determining complaints from independent unions of employers' failure to disclose information under the Employment Protection Act 1975.

The Committee's philosophy is innovative and clearly expressed in its First Annual Report 1976:

> The Committee is not a court . . . its proceedings and hearings are structured so as to achieve . . . informality. The aim is to encourage the approach by way of problem-solving rather than by emphasising the aspects of conflict and verdict. Above all, there is a commitment to the principles of sound industrial relations and workable solutions.

Thus, the Committee attempts to locate both problems and solutions in an industrial relations context. The 'general considerations' section preceding the 'award' is used by the Committee to try to assist the parties in resolving industrial relations difficulties from which the issue in the terms of reference has arisen.

FURTHER READING

Advisory, Conciliation and Arbitration Service, *Industrial Relations Handbook*, HMSO, London, 1980

Brown, W. (ed.), *The Changing Contours of British Industrial Relations*, Blackwell, Oxford, 1981

Farnham, D., and Pimlott, J., *Understanding Industrial Relations*, Cassell, London, 1979

Muir, J., *Industrial Relations Procedures and Agreements*, Gower, Aldershot, 1981

Suter, E., *Employment Law Manual*, Gower, Aldershot, updated regularly

58 Redundancy

Peter Mumford

The Redundancy Payments Act, which set out to assist employees who were dismissed because of redundancy, came into force in 1965. Since then, many hundreds of thousands of people have been affected by redundancy.

STATISTICS

No reliable or comprehensive figures for the actual numbers involved seem to be available. The Department of Employment, who are the responsible ministry having incorporated the 1965 Act into the Protection of Employment (Consolidation) Act of 1978, maintain several sets of figures:

1 Records of notifications of impending redundancies – these do not include cases where less than 10 workers are to be dismissed. Nor will all the anticipated redundancies actually take place
2 Records maintained by local employment offices following up statutory notifications with the employers concerned. They are more reliable than the original notifications, but still do not include cases where less than 10 are dismissed at one time
3 Finally, the department maintains records of the number of claims for payment. There is a very marked difference, however, between these figures and the others because those under twenty, or with less than two years' service, do not qualify.

This situation is often compounded by 'last in, first out' policies which ensure that those with less than two years' service are first to go again. There are, therefore, in the total figures many who have suffered multiple redundancies.

Some figures

January 1981	Statutory notifications	120 349
January 1981	Confirmed redundancies (Employment Office figures)	41 300

January 1981	Redundancy payments	52 348
1984	Confirmed redundancies	237 343 (all industries)
1985	Confirmed redundancies	227 328 (all industries)
January 1986	Confirmed redundancies (provisional)	14 282 (all industries)
February 1986	Confirmed redundancies (provisional)	11 770 (all industries)

(*Sources:* F. Noble, 'Redundancy Statistics', *Employment Gazette*, June 1981, March 1986 and April 1986)

Whether officially or unofficially recorded according to the Act, first time or 'Oh God, not again', the total presents a massive pattern of industrial change and disturbance. Even more so does it represent enforced change on the lives of the people directly affected and also their families and associates. Redundancy is a common feature of current society and, for those in industries subject to constant change, an ever present threat.

Redundancy need not, however, always be a threat. For many individuals, as well as organizations, it can be an opportunity – an opportunity to get out of a strait-jacket which is no longer appropriate to changed circumstances and a chance of a release of potential for new activities and achievement of new objectives.

The degree to which this more satisfactory situation can be achieved will undoubtedly depend to a very great extent on external economic, environmental or political circumstances, such as changes in oil prices, government policies on nationalization etc. However, these effects can be anticipated or, at worst, reacted to swiftly and with maximum consideration for those likely to be affected if the organization has an effective policy for dealing with redundancy. The requirements of the Redundancy Payments Scheme will ensure a high degree of fairness and make financial and other provision for those affected, but it cannot anticipate or plan in advance to take positive advantage of a developing situation.

To do this, the organization needs its own strategic planning and forecasting system with built-in manpower planning and, again, as part of this, a comprehensive redundancy policy. This will have two broad objectives: first, the continued health and success of the organization and, second, the safeguarding of the interests of individuals affected by possible redundancy.

We have, therefore, to examine two aspects of redundancy: the statutory requirements and benefits of the Employment Protection Act and the organization's own plans for forecasting and controlling its manpower requirements.

LEGISLATION

The Redundancy Payments Act 1965, which was later embodied in the Employment Protection Act 1978, covers the following aspects of redundancy.

Scope

The Act covers nearly all classes of employees between 18 – 60 for a woman or 65 for a man who have been continuously employed by the same employer for a minimum of two years (full-time employees). For people working between 8 and 16 hours per week, the qualifying period is five years. A few categories of employed people cannot claim redundancy payments: these include civil servants, registered dock workers, merchant seamen, share fishermen and the self-employed.

Note: To be entitled to payment, an employee must be formally dismissed because of redundancy. Entitlement will be lost if an employee leaves voluntarily because of anticipated or threatened redundancy.

Definition

The Act defines redundancy as dismissal due solely or mainly to:

1 The fact that his employer has ceased, or intends to cease, to carry on the business for the purposes of which the employee was employed by him, or has ceased, or intends to cease, to carry on that business in the place where the employee was so employed, or
2 The fact that the requirements of that business for employees to carry out work of a particular kind, in a particular place, have ceased or diminished, or are expected to cease or diminish

It should be noted that whilst it is the employee who is dismissed, it is the lack or change of work which is the criterion. Employees cannot be made redundant for reasons of poor work, discipline or ill health. If there is a reduction in overtime working or re-arrangement of working hours and workers are dismissed for refusing to accept the new arrangements; they are not considered redundant so long as the same number of that grade of worker is employed.

Lay-offs and short-time working

Employees may claim redundancy, however, if:

1 They have been kept on short-time working or laid off (less than half a week's pay per week for four or more consecutive weeks)
2 They have been kept on short-time working or laid off for six weeks or more in a period of 13 weeks of which not more than 3 were consecutive.

The employee must give written notice of an intention to claim within four weeks of the last day of the lay-off or short-time working.

The employer may make a counter-claim in writing within seven days that there is a reasonable expectation of full-time working resuming within four weeks and continuing for 13 weeks. Lay-off or short-time working caused by a strike or lock-out does not count for this purpose.

Proof of redundancy

Employers have to prove that dismissal is not due to redundancy if an employee makes a claim.

Selection

Where a choice has to be made from a number of employees, this must be based on custom and practice in the organization or the industry, an agreed procedure or, last in first out, where this is customary.

Notice of redundancy

Each employee to be dismissed is entitled to notice on the following scale according to length of service:

Continuous service	Notice or pay in lieu
4 weeks	1 week
2 years	2 weeks
3 years	3 weeks

at the rate of 1 week per year up to a maximum

12 years or over	12 weeks

Employees may leave during this period without forfeiting payment or compensation, providing they obtain their employer's consent.

Consultation

To give adequate time for consultation, the employer must give the following warning of impending redundancy to the Secretary of State for Employment on form HR1 and also to the recognized Trade Unions according to the following scale:

If 100 or more are to be dismissed within a period of 90 days or less	90 days of the first dismissal
Between 10 and 99 employees within a period of 30 days	30 days

For 10 or fewer employees

Consultation must begin as soon as possible

The following information must be given to Trade Unions involved, whether or not the employees actually belong to the Union:

1 The reasons why the employees have become redundant
2 The numbers and descriptions of employees whom it is proposed to dismiss as redundant
3 The total number of employees of any such description employed by the employer at the establishment in question
4 The proposed method of selecting the employees who may be dismissed
5 The proposed method of carrying out the dismissals, including the period over which the dismissals are to take effect.

In the course of consultation the employer shall consider any representations made by the Trade Union representatives and reply to them and state the reason, if any of their representations are rejected.

Compensation

Compensation is payable at the following rates to those dismissed:

Age of employee	Scale for each complete year of employment
18–21	½ week
22–40	1 week
41–59 (women)	1½ weeks
41–64 (men)	1½ weeks

For the purpose of this calculation, only full years of employment count. Working back from the date of dismissal, any part of a year's employment which falls into a high age scale is calculated at the lower rate.

Earnings above £155 per week do not count for compensation. Compensation under the Redundancy Payments scheme are free of tax up to the maximum of £4650. Occupational pension payments made at the time of, or shortly after redundancy may be offset against redundancy payments.

Rebates to employers

The enormous drains on the redundancy fund have meant that from 1 October 1986 only employers with less than ten employees may claim rebates from the redundancy fund. Thirty-five per cent of the payments made may be claimed. Claims must be made within six months of the payment, and the following information is required as well as a receipt for payment from the employee:

1   The employee's name and sex
2   The employee's national insurance number
3   The employee's income tax reference number
4   The employee's date of birth
5   The date on which the employee commenced his period of continuous employment
6   The date on which notice was given to the employee
7   The date on which the employment terminated
8   The reason for the termination of employment
9   The amount of a week's pay calculated in accordance with form
10 An indication of how the payment has been calculated.

Insolvency

Claims for redundancy payment against employers who are insolvent should be made by the employee to the employer's representative, who may apply to the redundancy fund for payment. Payments should include other outstanding items of pay, such as maternity and medical suspension pay covered under the Bankruptcy Act of 1914, as well as:

1   Arrears of pay up to a rate of £155 a week for a period not exceeding eight weeks. Pay includes salaries, wages, statutory sick pay, commissions, guarantee payments, medical suspension payments, payment for time off to look for new work or to make training arrangements and remuneration under a protective award
2   Holiday pay up to a rate of £155 a week up to a limit of six weeks according to entitlement in the last year
3   Any payment outstanding in respect of a basic award (by an industrial tribunal) of compensation for unfair dismissal
4   Pay in lieu of notice up to the statutory minimum entitlement under the Employment Protection (Consolidation) Act 1978
5   Reimbursement of apprentice's or articled clerk's fees.

Appeals

Employees who feel they have been unfairly treated by selection for redundancy, or for entitlement to compensation, may claim to an employment appeal tribunal in the normal way. Claims may also be made for insufficient notice and failure to consult.

An employee may make claims for payment for redundancy and compensation for unfair dismissal at the same time.

Procedures for making claims are set out in the following leaflets:

FORM IT1   for employees seeking decisions on their entitlement to compensation and the amount due.

FORM IT17   for employers seeking a decision on their entitlement to rebate against redundancy payments.

FORM IT18   in all other cases.

Alternative employment

Employees may be offered alternative employment to avoid redundancy. The alternative offered must be reasonable i.e., the work itself; pay and conditions should not be substantially different from the original work; nor should travel or access be significantly more difficult.

An employee is entitled to a trial period of four weeks, plus an agreed training period, if this is relevant. During the trial period, either the employer or employee may give notice to terminate the new contract, and the employee will then be considered as having been made redundant under the original terms. The employer is entitled to claim that the refusal was unreasonable.

Compensation and awards

A tribunal may make:

1 An order for reinstatement in the original job
2 A protective award covering an individual or a group of employees who shall be paid for a period up to 90 days if 100 or more employees are affected, 30 days if 10 or more employees are affected, or 28 days' pay in any other case.
3 Compensation under the redundancy payments scheme.

Claims must be made by individuals or trade unions on their behalf on form HR1.

COMPANY POLICY

Most organizations will consider these statutory requirements as a minimum and will need a far more comprehensive approach to redundancy as a part of their manpower policy and planning. To some extent, indeed, a redundancy situation may be seen as a failure of manpower planning.

In practice, however, changes may arise over which organizations have no possible control and inadequate warning may occur, which make redundancy essential for the survival of the organization. In these cases, protection of the organization becomes of prime importance and redundancy policies must have adequate arrangements for reducing numbers and/or costs rapidly in those categories and activities affected.

In other circumstances, the organization may stand to benefit from changing the structure of its workforce, e.g. adoption of new technology. Under these conditions it is reasonable that those adversely affected should be treated more generously.

CORPORATE PLANNING

Organizations which have adequate corporate planning will be geared towards future development, taking advantage of new situations and circumstances.

They will protect their investment in the future, whether it be in equipment, premises or, most important, in people, by having effective monitoring of the success of their plans, changes in the total environment in which they operate and interpretation of the impact of these changes.

A company redundancy policy needs to be concerned with:

1 Objectives
2 Social and corporate considerations
3 Methods of avoiding or reducing the impact of redundancy
4 Selection methods
5 Consultation
6 Compensation
7 Re-engagement
8 Assistance to those dismissed

Both the legal requirements of the Employment Protection Act and the human aspect must be taken into account when drawing up the policy.

Objectives

It is essential to clarify these to give guidance to the decisions which will have to be made when framing the policy and, even more important, implementing it if a redundancy situation should occur.

Objectives need to be formulated, therefore, in the areas of:

1 Protecting the economy and development of the organization
2 Safeguarding the interests of the employees
3 Avoiding adverse effects on the local community.

The priority given to these objectives may have to vary according to whether the redundancy is forced on the organization because of outside circumstances, or it plans it to achieve greater profitability, new products or business.

Social and corporate consideration

If the efficiency of the labour force were the only consideration, it would probably be desirable to use a redundancy as an opportunity of getting rid of the unwanted, the trouble makers, the least able, the least adaptable and the least hard working.

It is at least arguable that if management had allowed any significant number of these categories to continue in employment until the need for redundancy occurred, the task of recovery would be particularly difficult for them. At the same time, using redundancy as an excuse in these cases is neither legal nor desirable. Management must also consider the social implications of their actions, both upon individuals and the community in general.

So far as individuals are concerned, the chief considerations must be the comparative degree of hardship they will suffer, which will be affected immediately by their commitments and family responsibilities and, in the longer term, their age, fitness and the employment situation locally which will affect their ability to find alternative employment.

In a community where there is a shortage of various categories of labour, the release of suitable staff by one organization would obviously be welcomed.

Where there is already unemployment and redundancy, as in so many communities, where one organization is a main or sole employer, then redundancies will have far-reaching consequences on the community.

Where the redundancy is foreseeable, as part of changes which will benefit the organization, consideration should be given to the possibility of timing, either by speeding up or delaying the dismissals to suit the circumstances in the community.

The prospect of substantial redundancies should be notified to the Chairman of the Regional Economic Council, any government department having special responsibilities for the industry, and local authorities. Particularly in development areas, the Department of Trade and Industry should be advised also, in addition to the statutory notification to the Department of Employment.

These notifications should take place as early as possible, so that the authorities concerned have the maximum time in which to assist in finding suitable alternative employment.

The enormous efforts made by organizations such as British Steel and British Coal, who have had to handle massive redundancies over long periods, are classic examples of attempts to meet community interests.

Methods of avoiding or reducing the impact of redundancy

In a period of economic recession for the organization, it is still possible to avoid or reduce the impact of redundancy if sufficient advance warning is available.

Methods which can be used include:

1 Identifying and attempting to sell surplus capacity even at marginal cost in order to retain skilled staff
2 Bringing subcontracted work into the organization's own workshops
3 Stopping overtime so as to share out the work available
4 Restricting recruitment and filling vacancies by internal transfer and retraining wherever this is possible
5 Dismissing employees who have been allowed to work on past normal retirement age
6 Dismissing part-time workers – assuming there are full-time employees available with the required skills
7 Short-time working – for a limited period

8   Stocking up if the downturn is likely to be short-lived. In a period of rising costs, holding stock may be cheaper than paying compensation to long service staff

9   Transfers. The numbers to be dismissed can often be reduced, or a valuable person retained in the organization, by transferring staff from one department to another or even to another company in a group.

10 Voluntary retirement is a useful method of reducing the impact of redundancy which has the added attraction of relieving the employer of the need to make the choice between individuals.

The last has been used extensively by large organizations to reduce a surplus of senior staff who would otherwise clog the avenues of promotion for younger people who must be developed for the future.

By making a direct financial appeal to the individual, it has been possible to break through the total resistance to any job losses which some Trade Unions have tried to enforce.

It depends for its success on generous cash payments and subsidy of pension funds to ensure that the income available will be adequate.

There is no reason why the voluntary principle cannot be extended to earlier age groups. Many staff will welcome the lump sum and the opportunity of an early start in looking for other work.

Selection methods

The most controversial aspect of any redundancy is the method for selecting those who are to be dismissed.

The simple solution is last-in first-out (LIFO), based purely on length of service. This is favoured by many unions, is easy to operate, understandable and allows people to know fairly accurately where they stand. The Redundancy Payments Scheme itself favours this method by making it more expensive to dismiss long-service employees.

If all employees were of equal worth and if all sections of the organization were equally affected, then this policy could satisfy most needs. In most redundancies, and particularly in those caused by technological or product changes, it is unlikely that all departments or all grades of staff will need to be reduced by the same amount, and even in those departments whose overall numbers have to be reduced, there will be certain key jobs for which skilled workers are in short supply and whom it would be quite wrong to dismiss.

Additionally, there will be problems created by hardship cases, the registered disabled, those under training for skills required in the future and, perhaps most important of all, the future age structure of the company.

The effect of a number of even small-scale redundancies can be to bias significantly the age structure upwards, which may in turn create difficulties in, say, five years' time.

From the broader social point of view, there is also a danger of creating a category of worker who will always be first out and who, through no fault of his own, will never be able to build up any service to qualify for redundancy payments.

Where LIFO is used, it is essential that jobs are categorized within departments so that selection can be made within a group of skills, rather than across the whole department which may include skills which are still required. Arrangements must also be made to ensure that key personnel, whose absence could affect the output of other sections, are not dismissed purely because of seniority.

An ideal selection method would strike the balance between the requirements of the organization and the social needs of individuals. Factors to be taken into account would be:

Organization needs

Types and variety of staff and skills, as shown by the corporate and manpower plans; the worth of each individual in terms of their potential contribution to those plans; the cost of their replacement, and development.

Individual needs

Commitments and needs; age; service; likely difficulty in obtaining new work or retraining.

Such an approach would firstly enable each individual to know where he stood and, more important, enable him to improve his relative security rating by greater effectiveness and higher skill.

For the organization, it would enable it to recognize people more easily as the valuable asset which they are and treat them accordingly.

Whatever selection methods are used, it is essential that they are known and agreed beforehand with the representatives of the people likely to be affected.

Consultation

Although management must make the decision about the need for redundancy and the scale of it, the more employees are consulted about the way in which they are to be treated, the better.

Employees need to be advised about current and future business prospects and changes likely to affect them. This information can, of course, be interpreted in a number of ways and, indeed, exploited. It is therefore essential that such information is carefully presented and that staff are able to interpret it in a positive way. This, in turn, will depend on a build-up of trust and confidence between senior management and staff.

Once the decision has been taken on the need to reduce staff, full consultation on timing, methods, selection and so on, must take place.

The existence of a detailed and agreed procedure will greatly reduce the need for ad hoc negotiation and bargaining.

In federated firms, the vehicle for consultation will be the convenor, shop stewards' committee, or their equivalents, as appropriate.

For the large numbers of firms with no union representation, staff committees or meetings of representatives from appropriately sized departments or sections should be instituted. Such representations will have far wider uses then consultation on redundancy, and they should be set up so that they are recognized and working well in normal, as well as emergency circumstances.

Consultation involves notification that redundancy is likely. The Act requires that minimum periods of notice be given, so that the consultation process may begin.

In cases where the changes can be foreseen in advance, it would seem reasonable to give longer notice of intention than is legally required. Should, however, such announcements precipitate a rush of key workers to secure first place in the queue for scarce jobs in other organizations, so putting the continuance of the existing methods in jeopardy, then little will have been accomplished.

Staff can, of course, be encouraged to work out their notice by a system of premium payments, and may lose their entitlement to redundancy payments under the Act if they do not obtain their employer's permission to leave before the expiry of their notice. Even so, severe unemployment locally can make it more attractive for individuals to secure the long-term advantage of another job than a once-only cash payment.

The best policy is to restrict formal notice to the requirements of the Act, but to give notice of intention as part of the consultation procedures as early as possible. This will maintain good faith with employees and prevent the spread of rumour and loss of confidence.

Compensation

Many employers consider that the statutory level of payments represents a minimum and supplement them by scales of their own, usually related to length of service. A simple way of doing this is to add a fixed percentage to the statutory payment.

It is much easier to justify more generous treatment where the redundancy is due to circumstances from which the company will benefit and there is, therefore, merit in making additional payments in these circumstances only. Certainly in the extremes of redundancy where the organization is insolvent, only the Redundancy Scheme scale can be applicable.

An alternative method of supplementing payments is to make weekly and monthly payments – again on a scale according to service – until the employee has either used his entitlement or obtains alternative employment. To avoid reducing entitlement to unemployment benefit, these payments must be limited to one third of normal earnings.

Occupational pension payments which commence within a short time of redundancy can normally be offset against these payments.

The transferability of pension rights already earned, but not yet due for payment, must be protected in the normal way.

Re-engagement

Should circumstances change more rapidly than anticipated, it may be possible to re-engage those dismissed, the fairest way being to re-engage in reverse order to dismissal.

Before re-engagement takes place, the question of service must be clarified. If payments under the Redundancy Payments Scheme have been made, then clearly service under the re-engagement can count only from this date and similarly, if payments against pension rights have been made, then pensionable service must restart from the date of re-engagement.

Providing no payments have been made, it is usual to count service for pension purposes as continuous if the period between dismissal and re-engagement does not exceed one year. Thereafter, it is preferable to regard any re-engagement as a completely new period of service for all purposes.

Assistance to those dismissed

The increasing recognition of social, as well as commercial, objectives by organizations of all types has encouraged greater attention to assisting employees who have been made redundant. Assistance includes:

1 *More generous compensation.* Severance payments greatly exceeding the statutory requirements are now common and may include enhancement of pensions, as well as ensuring the legal portability of pension rights already earned
2 *Counselling.* Although the incidence of redundancy has been so high in recent years, it is still a traumatic experience for most people, especially those in mid-career or too young even for early retirement. Skilful counselling to determine needs and aspirations can be of immense benefit in opening up the range of options available in many cases, creating the opportunity for entirely new careers or occupations. In addition, counselling will help to rebuild the essential confidence and morale. Many specialist organizations now exist to carry out counselling and job search programmes on an individual or organizational basis
3 *Assistance with job hunting.* With high unemployment in many areas, job hunting is a skilled and demanding activity. In addition to requirements for time to seek new employment, assistance through contacts, use of services, identification of skills, guidance in writing CVs, interviewing skills and use of typing services, are all of extreme value. A number of self-help groups have been set up with a high degree of success
4 *Assistance with setting up in business.* For many, compensation or the availability of marketable skills point to self-employment. In some cases where the organization still requires part of the service, a part-time consultancy agreement, leaving the individual free to build up business elsewhere, works well. Grants are available under the Enterprise Scheme of the Manpower Services Commission

5   *Retraining.* To enable individuals to acquire skills which are more in demand, or to update their existing skills, training schemes are run by the organization, or by colleges, or by specialist agencies. These are invaluable. For skills in high demand, there may be grants available from the Manpower Services Commission.

Many of these activities are costly and time-consuming for the organization, but their value in rebuilding morale and faith in the organization by remaining staff and the community in general, will usually more than justify this.

EMPLOYMENT SERVICES AND AGENCIES

The Manpower Services Commission is responsible for providing a wide range of services to industry and individuals including:

Advice on manpower planning and forecasting methods
Assistance and advice in documentation for redundancy
Guidance on alternative employment available for dismissed employees
Temporary employment subsidies
Guidance on assistance and service available to help those dismissed
Advice on retraining facilities
Advice on appeals and industrial tribunals.

Where large numbers of staff are to be dismissed, an employment office can be set up on the organization's premises.

Initial contact with the services should be made to the local Department of Employment office. The larger offices have specialist departments for dealing with all aspects of redundancy.

The following leaflets are available:

RPL1 Offsetting pensions against redundancy payments
RPL2 Ready reckoner for payments
RPL4 Service calendar
RPL5 Calculation of a week's pay for employees on shift and rota work
RPL6 Summary of information for employees

FURTHER READING

Carew, T., *Get Up and Go Job Search,* Percy Coutts & Co., London
Employment Protection (Consolidation) Act 1978, chapter 44, HMSO, 1979
Golzen, S. and Plumbley, P., *Changing Your Job,* Kogan Page, London, 1981
Golzen, S., *Working for Yourself,* Kogan Page, London, 1981
Guidelines for the Redundant Manager, 2nd edition, British Institute of Management, London, 1981
Kemp, F. et al, *Focus on Redundancy,* Kogan Page, London, 1980
Croners Reference Book for Employers, New Malden, looseleaf with updating service

Part Ten
THE SKILLS OF MANAGEMENT

59 Management self-development

Michael Williams

It is widely believed that management development = management training = 'send him on a course'. This view assumes that management development is 'done' by someone to someone else – applied, in other words, like an external treatment.

Management development planned in this spirit rarely involves the person who requires development in either the diagnosis of the problem or the formulation of the prescription and follow-up. Thus he tends to find himself playing a largely passive role in important activities concerned (as the case may be) with:

– his growth as a person
– his development for future promotion or transfer
– improving his current performance or increasing his contribution as a manager
– helping him make the transition from specialist to managerial role
– developing his skills in specific areas.

Traditional forms of management training, moreover, are more likely to be 'off the peg' than tailor-made, and may not always be the most suitable for the individual in question.

Perhaps most serious of all is the constant failure to recognize that ultimately the company, a boss, or the management development manager is not responsible for the development of the organization's managers. The managers themselves are. The boss's responsibility is to encourage, support and 'facilitate' the process of his subordinates' self-development and therefore is principally one of helping them to help themselves to develop and become more effective.

At its most fundamental, management development means self-development – that is, a conscious response on the part of the individual to deal with what *he* recognizes as his development needs. Real development takes place when the individual sees, for himself, the need to modify his behaviour, change his attitudes, develop new skills, improve his performance, or prepare himself for a different role. The rationale that 'only the learner will learn' is recognized in some organizations and by a growing number of management development specialists, tutors and trainers.

Because many of the barriers to self-development that exist in companies and within boss – subordinate relationships are self-imposed and psychological, the process needs stimulation, guidance and sensitive managing. The next level up in the management hierarchy often serves as the best excuse for not getting things done and provides a frequent let-out for the individual who chooses to deny his responsibility for his own development:

> 'I'm employed by the company: it's up to my boss to decide what my development needs are. I don't know which way my career is going to go'.

Such self-imposed constraints are not strategies for success. They need to be recognized by managers as recipes for mediocrity. The evidence that such self-protective behaviour is prevalent at managerial and supervisory levels usually takes the form of:

– scepticism and a general 'don't want to know' attitude
– unwillingness to take ownership of problems
– reluctance to exercise initiative and authority
– opting out and buck-passing
– failure to take necessary risks leading to a record of lost opportunities
– forfeiture of influence as a 'power source' within the organization.

The true basis of self-development – namely that the individual takes responsibility for his own learning – may be quite alien to some managers. Traditionally much education (schools, further education and training) has put the emphasis on teaching rather than on learning. That approach tends to create inappropriately high levels of student passivity towards developing new attitudes and behaviours (It's up to *them* to teach *me*').

To some people the idea of taking responsibility for their own learning is even seen as threatening, because it involves a personal shift from a largely uncommitted or passively receptive state to one which demands the individual's commitment and action.

Others may be so disillusioned with their particular lot or with the company in general that they are demotivated and demoralized to the extent that they cease to care about self-development altogether. To people in such negative states of mind the process is likely to be seen at best as 'pie in the sky'.

More probably it will be viewed with suspicion as a management confidence trick, personnel department propaganda or (by the real cynics) as a 'do-it-yourself hangman's kit'.

Some managers may take a tougher, more calculative view and expect to see direct links between any effort on their part in self-development and the company's reward system.

Finally there will always be managers (usually senior executives) who assume inviolability. They claim, with or without coyness, that they have already 'arrived' and that 'this sort of thing is all right for other people'.

SELF DEVELOPMENT IN THEORY AND PRACTICE

There are two aspects of the human personality which are relevant to the understanding of self-development. These are:

1 The 'self image' (the 'me as I see myself') by which each individual identifies himself, his personal values, beliefs, knowledge, wants, needs and fears as well as his physical presence
2 The 'ego ideal' (which amounts to the individual's 'me as I would really like to be'). In essence this consists of the attainable 'plus me' which exists in every individual in addition to the hopes, dreams and wishes which may make up the idealized or fantasy self.

Personal growth (which by definition is largely determined by self-development) is the linking route from the self-image to the ego ideal. This is illustrated in Figure 59.1.

Practical self-development in management, necessarily, is concerned with attainable realities – what have been termed the 'plus me', rather than simply with the individual's fantasy world. The 'plus me' represents the difference between what the individual currently does, how effectively he operates, what contributions he makes in his present role and what that person is realistically capable of doing and being, within *self-selected periods of time*. The concept of the 'plus me', therefore, is related to a series of progressively emerging horizons – rather than to some ultimate limit which he or others have put on his potential. The horizons become more readily discernible as the individual consciously links his current behaviour and performance to what he feels are, for him, *requisite* standards, levels or modes of behaviour and which he judges are within his identifiable capacity. In practical terms the 'plus me' can be related to and reinforced by what Hodgson and Myers refer to as the 'plus job'. This is an attainable, realistic and viable role in which there are opportunities for increased satisfaction for the individual, coupled with increased contribution to the organization in which he operates.

Identifying the 'plus me' and the 'plus job' involves the individual manager working through a series of key questions, preferably with his boss and (where available) a management development specialist. From the responses are built up pictures of how the individual wants to grow as a person and how his job, or role, might be realistically developed to cater for and capitalize on that person's growth. The next stage is to evolve appropriate action plans, principally within the scope of the manager's work environment. Exercises are given later in this chapter which illustrate the processes and show how more diagnostic information can be obtained in order for the prescriptive action plans to be evolved for individual managers and for managerial teams. The crucial following activities are monitoring, review and follow-through, without which there would only be action plans – not action.

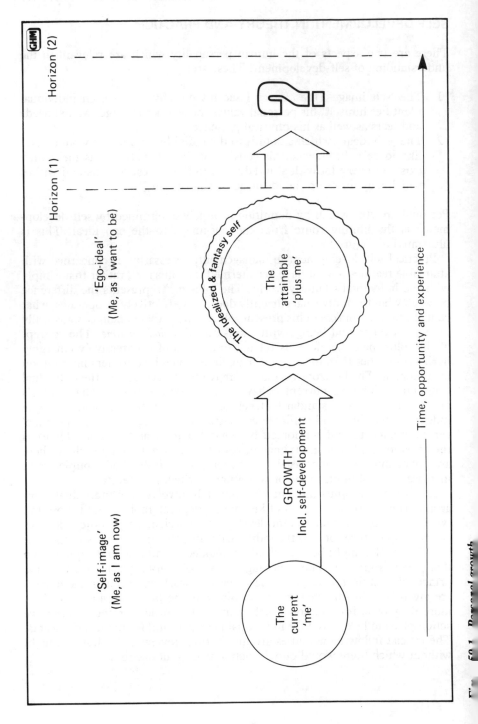

Fig. 50.1 Personal growth

SELF DEVELOPMENT: DISCLOSURE AND FEEDBACK

The self-diagnosis described above represents a systematic analysis of a manager's performance, especially his behaviour in role and, therefore, his *management style*. The evidence of his immediate boss, his boss's superior, his peers and his subordinates represents crucial feedback to help him identify his real training and development needs for himself.

Informal performance reviews by his boss, periodic discussions with colleagues whose opinions and judgement he values, together with the data available to him from formal appraisal interviews all help him to place himself in relation to the demands of his job. Similarly, discussions with effective and experienced management development or training managers should provide valuable feedback and insights into how others see him and his contribution.

The process of feedback, however, is often best enhanced by *disclosure,* that is by disclosing expectations, needs or concerns which invite response and discussion. By specifically asking for information about personal effectiveness, management style, role as a colleague or boss, or contributions as a subordinate, a manager can build up a picture of both confirmatory and contradictory evidence about his perceived competence in his job. For example, he can turn what is so often the rather sterile ritual of the annual appraisal into a fruitful discussion by taking the initiative himself and encouraging his boss to ask the right questions. By using a simple self-appraisal instrument which more or less parallels the questions and areas of analysis of the company appraisal form he can prepare himself (and his reviewer) for a worthwhile and relevant diagnosis of his real performance improvement or development needs. One of the hallmarks of the really effective manager or specialist is his capacity to 'manage upwards'.

Influencing superiors is not the same as falling into the trap of self-weakening by *delegating* authority and responsibility upwards. Rather, it means letting a boss know exactly what you need from him, in order to do your own job more effectively. Equally, it means finding out from him where he needs you to change your behaviour in some way. The process is about helping a superior to act as a necessary and appropriately supportive source of organizational authority in order to open doors or give sanction to requisite innovation. Some managers may well feel vulnerable when the significance of their epaulets is drawn to their attention by a subordinate who is saying, in effect – 'Come on, you're the boss, so act like one and give me the authority to go and do what we need to get done'.

Generally most far-reaching changes require management at, at least three levels within the organization, as Figure 59.2 illustrates. First, there is the level at which the innovation or change is to be implemented. Immediately above that is the superior who may have to go out on a limb in order to give the necessary 'go-ahead' – hence the sense of vulnerability at this level. Then, above him is the 'umbrella' often necessary to provide senior managerial or organizational cover for the venture, even though all the evidence suggests that the change will result in necessary performance improvement.

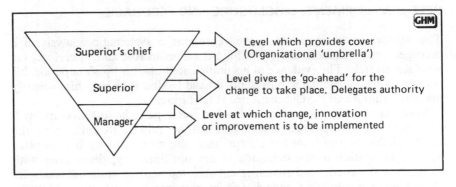

Figure 59.2 Hierarchical support needed for change to be implemented.
This diagram shows the levels of support required to implement and sustain far-reaching change and improvement

Much of the art of the process lies in the extent to which both joint and mutually exclusive areas of accountability are identified and spelled out. In this way, mutual perceptions and expectations about obstacles to effective results and about opportunities that should or should not be exploited can be clarified. Such disclosure and feedback need to be 'core' features of any boss – subordinate relationship in management, as a matter of course not just during periods of innovation and change. As an essential part of the personal (and hopefully mutual) stocktaking which is what the annual performance appraisal should be, then at least the following questions need to be raised and worked through from the subordinate's point of view:

1 'These are what I see as my current priorities'
2 'This is what I believe(d) you (my boss) expect(ed) from me' or 'This is what I believe is/was expected of me in my job'
3 'These are the results I believe I have achieved'
4 'This is what I feel I have done well'
5 'This is where I see I need to improve'
6 'This is where/how I need you (my boss) to act on my behalf (or to give me support) in order for me to do my job more effectively'
7 'These are areas where I see our relationship as

– Good
– Less than satisfactory

8 'What do you need me to do differently in order for you to

– act more effectively as my boss?'
– do your own job more effectively?'

9 'I see these as my main training development needs'
10 'What training or development do you feel I need?'

THE 'FLY-ON-THE-WALL'

A process which provides detailed minute-by-minute data about a manager's role and performance over several short periods of time is that of direct observation, accompanied by feedback and discussion. The purpose of the observation is to identify, record and review what a manager actually *does* in the course of several working days. Observation takes the form of a 'fly-on-the-wall' technique, which involves the observer sitting in with the manager so that the latter's every work activity can be recorded under appropriate headings and subsequently fed back to him for review and analysis. As a tool for learning, self-development and performance improvement it is invaluable, given an observer who is a credible, competent and sensitive individual in whom the manager being observed has confidence. The observer therefore may be a management development or training manager, external consultant, colleague, superior, or in some cases a subordinate.

The process can be structured to suit the situation, status and role of the manager being observed and the relationship between the observer and the observed. A case study later in this chapter illustrates a structured observation over a period of several hours. The subject in this case was a typical middle manager at work. His activities have been recorded in detail, in this format, in order to provide him with accurate data about:

1 How he spends his time in a variety of management situations, covering a range of managerial activities. In particular, where he needs to create periods of uninterrupted time for himself
2 Where he could or should delegate and make greater use of other people – especially his secretary
3 In which situations and with which people he needs to control his 'boundaries' more effectively by developing more assertive approaches
4 How he could acquire vital information from other functions in a more timely way, with less effort
5 Where he needs to develop a more effective 'eyes and ears', or 'field intelligence' service through other people to reduce the amount of time he personally spends seeking information.

The amount of time required and frequency of observation for a 'fly-on-the-wall' exercise will vary, dependent upon:

1 The purpose and intended outcomes of the observations
2 The role and nature of the activities of the manager under observation
3 Whether or not remedial work is to begin after the first session or once all observation is at an end and diagnostic feeback has been completed.

Generally the process takes place in four or five phases, which are described below.

Phase 1: Initial discussion and decision to mount the exercise

This includes:

1 Agreement of the 'contract' between the observer and his client about mutual expectations and intended outcomes (Note: the client may well not be the person to be observed; it could be his immediate superior, or other more senior executive)
2 Ice-breaking and establishment of relationship between observer and observed
3 Agreement on whether to hold observation sessions on set dates, or turn up on a random basis
4 Confirmation of what are and are not legitimate activities for observation.

Phase 2: Observation

This phase may consist of any number of sessions but, typically, four or five half-days over a period of two weeks represents the minimum necessary. During those sessions the observer is virtually 'glued' to the manager so that he may record the latter's activities and *reactions* in adequate detail. Normally the observer will use a log with appropriate headings under which he can detail what he sees happening (or not happening, since part of the observer's role during later stages will be to talk through significant omissions in the observed manager's behaviour). A typical log is illustrated in the case study later in this chapter (see Figure 59.3). Codes used are also explained in the case study. Others may be added as necessary. This is largely a matter of matching the tool to the task and evolving a relevant shorthand vocabulary which is convenient and quick to use.

Phase 3: The feedback stage

At this stage copies of the log are given to the manager. This may be done either at the end of each observation session, when his memory is fresh, or as a complete 'package' at the end of the exercise.

To stimulate review and analysis and to help the manager draw out the necessary learning points the observer usually works through a series of relevant questions, typified by the following:

1 How far do the observations match your understanding of what happened?
2 Are there any surprises in the data contained in the log?
3 Does time actually spent on some activities fit your recollections of the time you believed you spent?
4 What can you learn about the way you analyse situations, make decisions and take action?
5 When are you most effective? Which situations do you handle well?
6 When are you least effective? Which situations could you handle better?

7   What could and should you be delegating?
8   How well do you plan against contingencies and cope with events that you could not plan for?
9   How effective are you in obtaining the information you need to do your job?
10 How well do you warn others of impending difficulties, or actions likely to affect them?
11 What exactly do you need to do differently in order to be more effective at your job?
12 From all the above data what skills do you need to improve in order to be more effective and how best can you develop them?

Phase 4: The action plan stage

Both the data presented and the manager's response to that feedback provide the basis for his personal development action plans. Where appropriate the action plans may well be discussed with the manager's superior and a specialist from the personnel department or an external consultant. The plans need to be implemented and followed through to ensure that the requisite changes in operation, management style and personal development *are* taking place.

Phase 5

As a variation on a theme, a team workshop consisting of all the managers who have been through a 'fly-on-the-wall' exercise may be run to confirm development needs and action plans to meet the needs. Each manager (who is well known to the others) presents the essence of his feedback and the lessons drawn from it, together with his action plans for treatment. These are added to, modified and ratified by his colleagues or team mates on the basis of their knowledge of him. They are then implemented by the team on a mutually supportive basis which ensures a high level of monitoring, review and follow-through.

SELF-DEVELOPMENT: CASE STUDY IN ACTIVITY ANALYSIS

John Walton is a transport manager. In this exercise the procedure is described by which over three hours of his working day were recorded on an activity log in order to obtain an impression of his typical work pattern. The activity key looks fairly complicated, but it becomes relatively simple when considered under the four right-hand columns, as described below.

Format of the activity log

A proforma is used to record the activities, with the layout shown in Figure 59.3. A shorthand key is used to speed up the entry process and condense

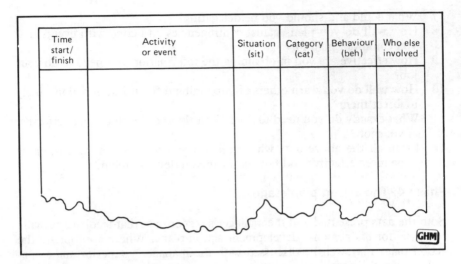

Time start/ finish	Activity or event	Situation (sit)	Category (cat)	Behaviour (beh)	Who else involved

Figure 59.3 Format for activity log

data into the limited space available on the form. In this example, the shorthand codes used were as follows:

Under 'sit' (the situation in which the individual was observed)

AW	working alone
TI	taking an incoming telephone call
TO	making an outgoing telephone call
D	discussion with one other person
MI	meeting – informal
MF	meeting – formal
O	outside own office

The above can be used in combination, and might have been supplemented by:

WSP	with superior
WSB	with subordinate
WSBS	with more than one subordinate
AD	dictating to secretary
AT	working alone – thinking

Under 'cat' (the category of managerial activity observed) the codes used were:

PA	establishing causes of problems
SA	clarifying situations or problems
GD	giving data/information
BV	briefing verbally
XCA	checking data for relevance and accuracy
SDI	seeking data/information

E	evaluating or reviewing progress
O	organizing
OGI	organizing and giving instructions
RH	requesting and requiring help

Other possibilities which might have been used under this heading are:

DA	making decisions (choosing between alternatives)
P	planning
PP	protecting the plan (contingency planning)
CO	controlling
S	social chat
A	arbitrating

The following codes were applied under the 'beh' column, where the behaviour of the observed individual was recorded

PA	positive/assertive
LA	listening attentively
Q	questioning
D	disagreeing
X	confused
U	constructive
C	composed (when under stress)

To these codes might have been added:

UN	uncertain/indecisive
CR	critical
DI	dominant
DG	domineering
E	emotional
DF	defensive
SWO	switched off
DY	switched on (dynamo)
GA	playing psychological games
AG	aggression
H	humour
NU	nurturing/building

Codes under 'who else'

are simply the initials of others involved in the observed situation

Activity log for Mr John Walton

The activity log compiled for John Walton is shown complete in Figure 59.4. The impression gained is that the period of observation involved activities and work patterns which were typical of John Walton's normal work load and working style. Assuming this to be so, then what emerges as a representative picture is the following:

Manager observed: John Walton
Position   :   Transport manager
Date(s) observed   :   3 August 19XX
Times observed   :   11.09am-12.30pm and 1.45pm-3.45pm

Time on/off	Subject/activity/event	sit	cat	beh	who else?
11.09		AW	PA	PA	
11.10	Arthur collects notes on transport routes	D	SA	LS	ART
11.11	Graphic statistics – analysing what, where and when	D	SA	Q	BRI
11.12	Checking\details/facts/figures with supervisor	D	SA	Q	
			PA	PA	BRI
11.13	J. goes out to collect outwork book, disagrees on section III; agrees on sections I and II	D	SA	D	BRI
			GDI	PA	BRI
			BV	Q	BRI
	J. seeking reliable accurate information (given contradictory 'facts')		BV	X	BRI
				Q	
11.18			SA	U	
11.19	Telephone call to Transport Haulage Company	TO	SDI	PA	
	– seeking information on lorries and drivers		SDI	Q	
11.26	– ? work completion notes to clerk	D	E	PA	CLE
11.27	Recommences work with BRI	D	BV	PA	BRI
11.28	Query work in progress	AW	O	PA	NEV
11.28	Telephone call	TI	SDI	PA	
11.28	Second telephone rings (J. also takes this one over from secretary)	TI	SA	PA	
11.29	First call finished and first 'phone rings again	TI	SDI	PA	Visitor
11.31	Organizing people to do things, including	D	SA	PA/Q	Secret
11.35	gathering information	D	OGI	PA	MIK
		D	OGI	PA	DON
11.38	Given more wrong data (goes out to TER next door)	MO	SA	X	TER
	Checks paperwork with loader (loader unhelpful)	MO	SDI	PA	LOA
11.39	Wrong feedback – visitor gets data/information mixed up	D	SA	XQ	DON
		D	SDI	Q	
11.40	Talks to driver	D	GI	PA	Driver
		D	SA	PA	
11.40	Clarifying delivery situation on goods	D	SA	PA/Q	MIK
11.42	Discussion with driver – gives more information	D	GI	PA	Driver
11.46	Reaffirms delivery date on goods	D	SA	PA	MIK
11.47	MIK returns regarding possible shortages	D	E	Q/PA	MIK
11.47	Checks numbers of 'look in'	MO	GI	Q	TER
11.52	Checks/queries tonight's deliveries	D	GI	LS	PAC
11.55	Gives routes/delivery runs and quantities	D	SA	PA	BRI
12.00	Request for transport	TO	RH	PA	
			XCA	Q	
12.05	Availability of drivers' mates for twilight shift	TO	SI	Q	RON
			DA	PA	
12.07	Call for information (no-one there)	TO	RH	Q	
12.09	Request to J. for transport and driver	TI	GDI	PA	ANON
	J. goes out to talk to driver	MO	SDI	Q	Driver
12.13	Request for situation report	TI	GDI	PA	RAY
			DA	PA	

Figure 59.4   *Activity log compiled for John Walton, Transport Manager*
            Entries would, in practice, be hand-written

Time on/off	Subject/activity/event	sit	cat	beh	who else?
12.14	Checks up on transport availability	TO	SDI	Q	VIC
		D	SA	PA	TER
	Do we have a car? Do we have a driver?		SA	Q	
12.19	Spare driver?	D	SA	Q	MIK
12.19		TO	SA	Q	CLI
12.20	Situation report	D	E	PA	MIK
12.21	No driver	TO	GDI	PA	
12.22	Briefing caller	TI	BV	PA	RAY
			GDI	PA	WIL
12.23	Situation report	D	BV	PA	MIK
		TI	DA	PA	PAU
		D	SA	PA	WIL
		TO	GDI	PA	CLE
12.25					
12.28					
LUNCH					
1.49	Planning procedures	D	GDI	PA	CLE
1.51	Making up loads for tomorrow	AW	DA	PA	CLE
2.06	Phone call	TI		PA	?
2.11	Clarifying schedule	D	PA	PA	MIK
2.12	Taking message	TI	A	PA	DIC
2.14	Phone (wrong number)	TI	A	PA	?
2.15	Call TER	TO		PA	out
2.17	TER calls back	TI	XCA	Q	TER
2.22	Goods (southern deliveries)	TI	SDI	Q	PAT
2.24	Meeting	MI	SDI	Q	NOR
			GI	PA	
2.28	Goods (Midlands deliveries)	TO	SA	Q	PAT
2.30	Parcel arrives – goods components				PET
2.31	Makes out rail notes	MIO	DSI	PAQ	
2.32	Clarifying/explaining procedures	TI	E/BV	PA	CLI
	+ action: sorts out detail		O/DA	QPA	JON
2.42	Parking ticket from driver	M	XCA	QPA	Driver
2.42	Clock card	D	GI	PA	PAC
2.44		D	GI	PA	Driver
2.50	Calls for notes	D	SA	X	Driver
2.57	Writing	D	SA	PA	CLE
2.57	Sorts out Midlands/North deliveries	D	E/ GDI	C	ART
3.09	Delivery of two reels of cable	D	SDI	Q	Driver
3.10	Electricians call	TI	BV	QPA	RAY
3.15	Ring for transport	TO	SA	PA	PAU
3.22	Needs information for PAT for goods (southern)	D	DA	PA	Visitor
3.24	Despatch priorities: goods (southern)	D	SA	PA	DER
3.28	Phone call	TI	SA	PA	DON
	Another call holding		SA	Q	ADR
	OBSERVER REJOINS PERSONNEL DEPARTMENT				

Figure 59.4 (concluded)

1   About 5 per cent of his time is free to work along (thinking and planning time)
2   95 per cent of his time is spent face-to-face with someone, or on the telephone
3   50 per cent of his time is spent seeking information and clarifying situations
4   30 per cent of his time is spent giving instructions or briefing
5   The remainder is spent in arranging/organizing transport, solving problems, etc.

Some questions raised by the analysis

Given that the above *is* typical of John's working day then some questions that need to be asked are:

1   How could JW create more thinking and planning time for himself?
2   How much of the time he personally spends chasing up data and information could be reduced by
    – using other information sources (production planning and control)
    – delegating to his subordinates the task of securing much of the information
    – the introduction of an up-to-the-hour information service to JW from production (or production planning and control)?
3   How much more, generally, could and should he use his subordinates and push responsibility for solving problems back down to them?
4   The very nature of a transport manager's role especially when combined with that of chief despatcher, is fraught with fire-fighting problems. Being at the 'end of the line' inevitably means collecting everyone else's rubbish, to some extent.
    BUT, there is much that JW's immediate superior could do to reduce the pressure on John by
    – sitting down with him and analysing the what, how, when and who of JW's work
    – assuming a higher profile and more assertive stance in managing the boundaries between finishing and transport/ despatch.
    Ultimately, of course, many of the decisions to delegate or not delegate rest with John himself.
5   Finally, there is the question of organization. Is the structure of work done and current reporting relationships appropriate or is there a need to rethink and reorganize the whole question of ordering and using transport both at incoming and outgoing stages? This is obviously a far wider issue but inevitably the organization structure is a major determinant of work loads, work patterns and comparative efficiency/inefficiency of managerial time.

ACHIEVEMENT OBJECTIVES AS A MEANS FOR SELF-DEVELOPMENT

Used either as a natural consequence of discussions at the end of a 'fly-on-the-wall' exercise or as an alternative approach, specific achievement objectives can lend structure, direction and impetus to a manager's self-development. Based on a diagnosis of needs, set within the context of a manager's role and agreed with his boss, achievement objectives represent yardsticks of attainment against which the manager can measure his performance and development.

Obviously the practice of setting objectives takes various forms in business. These range from formalized management by objectives (MBO) schemes to informal (but specific) targets set between bosses and their subordinates or within a work group set up to resolve a particular problem. The very process of management is about moving from a current situation (X) to a requisite state of affairs (Y) – usually within a set time limit. Typically managers work to the basic criteria as part of their day-to-day role, namely: quantity (how many and how much); quality (how well done or in what manner); cost (how much in financial terms); deadline (by when started/completed).

At the most senior levels philosophy, policies and strategies are normally based upon certain corporate goals – even though they may be sometimes more implicit than explicit. Normally corporate objectives are then translated appropriately at different levels down the line so that, necessarily, there will be a mandatory aspect to manager's objectives as well as a discretionary one.

In setting and agreeing personal achievement objectives as a means of stimulating self-development and improving managers' effectiveness, the diagram in Figure 59.5 illustrates the basic scope open to bosses and their subordinates. That scope can be refined by a structure which enables managers to select, define and sharpen objectives in a disciplined way that more closely relates the performance of individuals to the goals of others.

First, it is helpful to determine what objectives are and what they are not. Management objectives:

are	*are not*
required results	activities
achievements	effort
accountabilities	duties
what is required	how it must be done
'musts'	'shoulds'

Second, there are different types of management objective. The principal categories are those which reflect the results to be achieved, under the following headings:

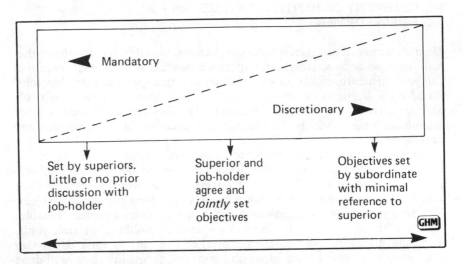

Figure 59.5 **The extent to which objective setting between superiors and sub-ordinates may be mandatory or discretionary**
Some objectives will be mandatory themselves by their very nature (budget targets for instance) but how they are to be achieved may be largely discretionary within the boss-subordinate relationship

1 Targets: to meet a deadline, programme of activities or product launch
2 Improvements: for example, to increase profitability levels, productivity rates or quality standards
3 Resolution of specific problems: examples are the removal of obstacles or constraints in order to correct deviations and restore previous conditions
4 Innovation and change: this would include introducing and implementing something new which represented a departure from previous practice
5 Control: aimed at ensuring or maintaining a given set of conditions
6 Personal or team development: principally aimed at acquiring the behavioural knowledge and levels of skill needed to operate more completely.

Undoubtedly some areas of activity are easier to measure than others in terms of results. It is usually possible to apply at least one specific, quantified objective. This is particularly the case where the type of objective has been determined ('target', 'improvement', 'problem solving', 'innovation', and so on). Even in areas of activity such as research and development or operational research, where the final outcomes might be very difficult to predict realistically, it is still possible to set quantified objectives. This can be done by making the objectives of the form 'submit and present an interim report at the progress review meeting on 13 May and show all findings to date' (for example).

Objectives need to be realistic, attainable, accurate and expressed in clear language if they are to appear credible and relevant as a self-development exercise. They must not be couched in vague terms. For example:

1 'Reduce the use of consumable materials on numbers 1 and 2 lines to budget level by the end of December, and by a further 10 per cent by the end of March' NOT 'Cut down drastically on consumables'

2 'Submit proposals by the end of the month for reducing steel procurement costs by at least 12 per cent. Method: by the use of alternative transport arrangements from the mills' NOT 'Investigate methods for reducing steel procurement costs'

3 'Revise your own and your subordinates' job descriptions by mid-January, clarifying the principal accountabilities for each person. Progressively ensure that only agreed principal accountabilities are retained and that all other work is delegated and reallocated to section heads by 31 January' NOT 'Delegate as much work as possible to subordinates'.

In some organizations people of high potential may be deliberately moved into the 'fast line' in terms of career progression by being appointed to specially designed 'development posts'. Although they usually carry out necessary functions the real purpose of their move is to groom them for a more senior, longer-term position. In most organizations this probably does not happen and only selected tasks and objectives may be available for the job-holder's development. Where this is the case the opportunities for self-development could well lie outside the mainstream of the role in the areas of:

– Short-term tasks and objectives
– Priority objectives
– Innovation and change programmes
– Trouble shooting and problem solving

Figure 59.6 represents the typical structure of many managerial jobs where objectives are divided between mainstream and short-term goals.

SOME VEHICLES FOR SELF-DEVELOPMENT

Once the task and personal objectives have been agreed, there is the question of work opportunities through which to achieve those objectives and ensure the process of development. A crucial factor in the process is the extent to which the manager's boss facilitates his subordinate's self-development by:

– providing the necessary 'trigger' and encouragement
– sustaining and restimulating it
– capitalizing on it to the advantage of both the individual and the organization

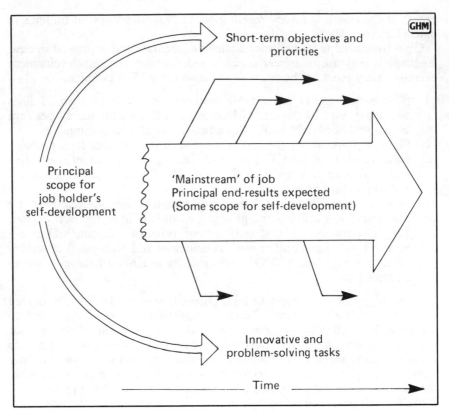

Figure 59.6   Scope for self-development within managerial jobs

— pressing on the appropriate 'nerves' when unnecessary obstacles get in
  the way

Learning is fundamental to self-development and most people in managerial
roles tend to learn as the result of *experience*. However, that experience
needs to be analysed, discussed and worked through in order to draw the
appropriate lessons from it.

Learning by experience, within a management job, is likely to involve the
'learner' in at least:

— *doing* – followed by analysis and review
— experimenting with new or different experiences and activities
— questioning and testing out existing knowledge, custom and practice,
  prejudices, values and beliefs
— experiencing (and reviewing) both success and failure
— examples and models (other managers) against which the learner can
  compare, assess and, if necessary, modify his own management style
— study and reflection, in order to put experience into perspective and
  context.

Well-tried learning vehicles which provide opportunity for experiential learning and self-development including the following:

1 Keeping a work diary which is reviewed daily or, at least weekly, by the learner with his boss and/or a management development specialist

2 Setting up projects which are *relevant* and *realistic* and which have *real pay-off* for the company, the department and/or the individual. Such projects often carry far more weight when there is major representation to be made by the trainee to the chief executive or a senior panel, so that a sense of occasion is attached to the experience and it is seen to be important

3 Cross-functional assignments involving multi-disciplinary teams of subordinates working together (for example marketing, product planning and engineering or production, industrial engineering and finance) where end results rely on cooperative, co-ordinated effort

4 Presentations on key issues – or contributions to key issues – to top management

5 Team development workshops in which members review:
  – 'our key objectives and priorities'
  – 'obstacles to achieving them'
  – 'my personal contribution to the team's goals'
  – 'our strengths and weaknesses as a team and as team members'
  – 'our action plan for the next 12 months'

6 'Bespoke' tutorials for individuals or groups using external professionals who test thinking and action plans by inputs of expertise, rigorous questioning and a wider perception

7 'Action learning', involving cooperation with managers from other companies and organizations, in the identification and resolution of each other's operational problems

8 Participation in junior 'boards', working parties, 'think tanks' or research teams, with or without senior executives involved, but where the outcomes are deemed to be important and relevant

9 Deputizing for the boss:
  – by representing him at meetings, or on committees
  – visiting important external contacts, on his behalf
  – acting in his capacity for days/weeks/months at a time as appropriate

10 Setting up and running an entirely new product, department, function or small subsidiary company

11 Lecturing on personal accountability or a field of expertise to:
  – internal courses and seminars
  – professional courses run by universities, polytechnics or local colleges
  – educational programmes run by national, local or professional bodies

12 Planned reading, regularly reviewed and discussed with the trainee by one or more of the following acting in a mentor role:
  – his immediate superior
  – his superior's chief

– appropriate in-company specialists, managers or supervisors
– external professionals

Planned reading also involves keeping up-to-date by regularly choosing different areas of developing technology, important disciplines or relevant current events and systematically scanning the appropriate professional journals.

These, then, represent some of the learning opportunities that are available to enable a manager's self-development to take place at little or no cost to the company and with minimal interference with the day-to-day job that he is there to do.

The term 'self-development' means exactly what it says. The real drive to make it happen must come from within the individual himself, but his superiors can do much to ensure an encouraging supportive climate in which self-development can thrive and become regenerative.

SOURCES AND RESOURCES

Some organizations and bodies concerned with self-development

Organization	*Contact*
Anglian Regional Management Centre High Street, Stratford, London E15 2JB 01-590 7722	I. Cunningham
Association for Education and Development Polytechnic of Central London, 35 Marylebone Road, London NW1 5LS 01-486 5811	M. Greatorex
Centre for the Study of Management Learning, University of Lancaster, Gillow House, Lancaster LA1 4YX Lancaster 65201	J. Burgoyne R. Boot
Hodgson Myers Assoc. 103 Walton Street, Oxford, OX2 6EB Oxford 52353	A. M. Hodgson
Human Resource Associates 18th Floor St. Alphage House, Fore Street, London EC2Y 5DA	T. Jaap

The Open University   B. Lund
Walton Hill, Milton Keynes,
Milton Keynes 74066

Polytechnic of Central London   J. Bowden
School of Management Studies
35 Marylebone Road,
London NW1 5LS
01-486 5811

Sheffield City Polytechnic   M. Pedler
Pond Street, Sheffield S1 1WB   T. Boydell
Sheffield 738621

Michael Williams & Partners   M. Williams
Fairfield House, Quarry Park Road,
Pedmore, Stourbridge
West Midlands DY8 2RE
Hagley (0562) 883485

FURTHER READING

Austin, B., *Time and the Essence – A Manager's Workbook for Using Time Effectively*, British Institute of Management, London, 1979

Boydell, T. and Pedler M. (eds.), *Management Self-Development*, Gower, Aldershot, 1981

Humble, J.W., *Management by Objectives*, Gower, Aldershot, 1975

Mumford, A., *Making Experience Pay*, McGraw-Hill, Maidenhead, 1980

Pedler, M., Burgoyne, J. and Boydell, T., *A Manager's Guide to Self-Development*, 2nd edition, McGraw-Hill, Maidenhead, 1985

Revans, R.W., *Action Learning*, Blond & Briggs, London, 1981

60 Personal organization

A N Welsh

It has been suggested that the better manager is the better organized manager, who makes the best use of his time and best use of the time of his staff. However, just as there is no such think as a born manager, so the effectiveness of a good manager cannot really be taught. *Effectiveness has to be learned* and the suggestions in this chapter are only some pointers as to how you can look at your work, develop a personal approach, and make the best use of your time.

THE NEED FOR PERSONAL ORGANIZATION

When I had my first managerial job, I naturally found it very exciting and very demanding. I would come in on or before time, and to digress, a good manager should sometimes come in before time and perhaps stay after time. All sorts of things happen outside normal working hours: some people who get their work wrong or do not complete it within the day will stay behind or come back later to finish off, others will use company facilities for private purposes. However, I would come in on or before time and work furiously throughout the day, and by the end I had never completed all that had to be done and my head was full of all that was happening. In particular, I was concerned by matters affecting the well-being of others, and also attacks on my department's activities or my own standards of performance.

When I arrived home my head was buzzing and I would wake up in the middle of the night remembering things I had forgotten to do or thinking of new ideas. I had the choice then of lying awake during the rest of the night remembering whatever it was, or going to sleep again and forgetting the matter. At least I did not decide to hold a meeting about the situation!

CREATING A LIST

I listed all the jobs which I had to do, all the work in my in-tray and the functions which I had to supervise. I kept a diary, and a brought-forward file. The latter in my case was a concertina file with slots for the days 1 – 31 and for the remaining months of the year. I would pop into the brought-forward

1136

file any correspondence, assessments, buying orders and the like which I wanted to review at a future date; these items were brought into the list as they 'came up'. Having made the first rough list, I then sorted it into order of importance and urgency. At the end of each day I used to go through the list and cross off what I had done and also any items which had ceased to be relevant. I would add to the list new jobs or problems which had arisen and then I would note which jobs I planned to do the following day.

In the morning there was my list telling me what I had to do that day. Obviously unexpected matters arose – in an operational situation one can almost budget for the unexpected – but by and large I worked through the list each day.

Communications

One of the standing items on the list, apart from going through the diary and brought forward file, was to see *all my subordinates*. I kept at hand a list of all subordinates and made a point of seeing each one even if only to say 'hello', every day. It could be, of course, that you are often away, or that you have too many staff to see. Perhaps in the first case you should consider whether you are away too much to do your job properly, in the second case either you may have too many people directly under you or should delegate some of the communication process to subordinates. Communications is the name of this game: people require *regular contact* and in particular from their boss, and they will often say things, or you will be able to sense a problem which they would be diffident about bringing to your office.

Incidentally, what does your office look like to a subordinate? Can he come and talk to you, or are you involved most of the time in meetings, discussions or telephone calls? Communications can only exist on face-to-face basis, and they are of prime importance at every level. Many managers with considerable responsibilities in large organizations do not know the names or faces of their top management and directors. An even greater proportion never see, or are seen by, their top management in any operational situation from year to year end. *No amount of personnel work can make people think you care about them if they never see you.*

Personal planning

The first list of work is much more difficult to produce than the subsequent amendments, and to help you produce it there is a checklist of questions in Figure 60.1. These are general and analytical questions to be used in any review of your responsibilities, but they would assist in preparing the first list. When, you may ask, would there ever be time to do this, and is it possible with everyone rampaging around and the telephone constantly ringing?

Well, do you intend to spend the rest of your life in a managerial pigsty, and are you seriously going to say you are too busy to do your job? Half

GHM

1 What are the objectives of my department or function?
2 Am I satisfied that I feel these can be achieved – that I have a plan(s) for this?
3 In what ways can my department or area be improved?
4 Is the work in my area altering in nature, quantity or quality?
5 Can the work be done in a better way?
6 Have I the right equipment and facilities?
7 Have I the right number of staff?
8 Am I happy that all my subordinates are correctly placed and loaded?
9 Are my staff doing what I want them to do?
10 Do any of my staff need further training or experience? Have I a training plan?
11 What are staffing trends?
12 Are my staff happy? Do I spend enough time with them?
13 Have I a trained deputy?
14 Am I satisfied personally? Have I defined my personal objectives?
15 Is my authority defined and adequate?
16 Is my relationship with my senior management satisfactory?
17 Where is my next promotion coming from?
18 Am I doing too much routine or administrative clerical work?
19 Have I enough time for thinking?

Figure 60.1   Checklist for reviewing your function

an hour's planning can save hours – even days – of misdirected effort; the crisis anticipated proves to be no panic, and you should find in the normal situation that if you pursue this type of personal planning for a few months, you will get right 'ahead of the game' and that you can start looking for additional responsibilities.

Decide now on a specific half hour in the coming week to go through the list. Ask someone else to take the telephone calls and say you do not want to be disturbed (unless it is the Chairman!). Some of the questions will require further investigation, but whenever you reach an unsatisfactory answer, answer the question: 'What am I going to do about it?'

THE CONSTRAINT OF TIME

Managing is conducted within a large number of constraints. What is your biggest constraint? Is it capital, working finance, material resources, machinery, property or is it people? People can be a big limiting factor, but you can always train them. Are you limited by the presence of other aspects?

Many factors can constrain you, but *the biggest restriction of all is your own time*. You never have enough of it. There are only twenty-four hours in a day, seven days in a week, 52 weeks in the year and so many years in your career. You cannot produce more time; it keeps slipping away. Yesterday can never come back.

We would say, therefore, that we do not have as much time as we need, but would this be equally true for everybody, or would it apply in particular to you? Time can be replaced. Certain tasks can be performed by machinery and certain office work can be done by computers. Some tasks can be delegated to other people, although this is really a transfer of time. However, *the manager cannot delegate his management work* to a machine and seldom can he share it with anyone else. There is no substitute for time as far as he is concerned. Everything he does takes time. All business, all activity, all work uses time and takes place in time.

However, we do not manage our time naturally – as a whole we take it for granted. Now we could talk for a long time about this problem, and we could say that the unhurried, unheroic manager with a clear desk, and a reliable organized office is the efficient or effective manager, but what do you do about it?

Step 1

First of all, accept that, other things being equal, *the best and happiest manager* is the one who *makes the best use of his time*. If you do not accept this, then this chapter was not written for you. But if you feel that you can make better use of time, and that if you do so you will be a better manager, then please read on.

Step 2

The second step comprises finding out what you are doing now. A simple method of doing this is to list various activities which you perform, and record for a week or a fortnight (or on random days over a longer period) how much time you spend on them. This can be done by using a simple daily diary sheet. At the end of the period the daily diary sheets are analysed into what is called a work distribution chart. This work distribution chart will show quite clearly what you are doing and what proportion of your time is spent on your various activities.

A specimen manager's activity list (with the activities given for example only) is as follows:

1 Visiting customers
2 Visiting suppliers
3 Queries from staff over technical matters
4 Customer complaints
5 Planning and control work
6 Training
7 Supervision

8   Reading mail
9   Chasing overdue accounts
10 Checking stocks and reordering
11 Management meetings
12 Recruiting
13 Staff problems
14 Personal.

Simple forms for the daily dairy sheet and for the work distribution chart are shown in Figures 60.2 and 60.3.

The work of a manager is variable, particularly as regards the subject involved. Completing a work distribution chart will not give a 100 per cent accurate picture of what the manager does or should do, but it will give a representative view of the proportions of his time spent on various activities, e.g., queries; accounts queries may relate to different transactions, but they will still be accounts queries. Once the work distribution chart

Date:				1. Ines- sential	2. Some- body else could do	3. Wasting others' time	GHM
Time	Activity	Inter- ruptions	Phone calls	1. Ines- sential	2. Some- body else could do	3. Wasting others' time	Notes
8.30 8.45 9.00 9.15 9.30 9.45 10.00 ,, ,, ,, ,, 5.30 5.45 6.00 Evening	Enter number against time whenever activity changes	Enter a '1' for each, e.g., 1, 11	As for interruptions. Note incidence and quantity. Analyse if too many.	Record impressions, if any, at the time.	Record impressions, if any, at the time.	Record impressions, if any, at the time.	Note anything unusual or 'special'.

Figure 60.2   Specimen manager's diary sheet

Activity no.	Activity title	Daily times										Total time	% of total	Comments and action
		1	2	3	4	5	1	2	3	4	5			(You can also do this kind of analysis with your staff.)
														These are taken to the nearest quarter hour.
										(No)	(No) (No)			If phone calls and interruptions occur which are separate from the activity being recorded – multiply by 3 minutes; if the totals exceed 15% of the day, then analyse them. Possibly something is wrong.

GHM

Figure 60.3   Manager's work distribution chart

has been completed, one can then move on to the next step.

Step 3

The third step is the analysis of the work distribution chart. A number of questions need to be asked at this stage.

WASTED TIME

1 What would happen if I did not do this kind of activity?
2 Am I spending too long on it?
3 Am I doing it ineffectively – for example, am I getting it properly set up and spending enough time on it? Short periods of supervision are of limited value with persons engaged on complex work
4 Am I failing to do any task which would contribute to the business because of the lack of time?

Supervision

A manager should be able to spend time with his staff – encouraging, training, supervising and just getting to know them and keeping in touch. The time required for this varies with the staff and the complexity of the work, but a rough quick figure is an average of forty minutes per person per day. This includes normal management duties, reports and 'personnel' work. It does not include 'checking' as distinct from normal supervision and training.

Checking

Checking should be considered carefully. Twenty or thirty years ago commercial convention looked for a high degree of literal accuracy, and salary costs were lower in proportion to other expenses than they are now. There is a satisfaction in getting everything 'right', but we should first consider what the customer really needs. Checking is expensive and frustrating: it is no longer a motivating factor (if it ever was) for staff to have all their work checked.

Your work distribution chart will show how much of your time is spent checking, but you should consider whether the cost of checking is justified by the errors discovered and how much these matter. If the errors do matter you may have to continue to check, but you can consider whether random checks, occasional and unexpected, will serve as well where generally quality standards and methods are the main concern.

List of jobs

In the end you will finish with a list of jobs which you want to do and which you have to do, and a subsidiary list of jobs which you feel you should not be doing but perhaps you still have to do for one reason or another. (We are, of course, well aware that you cannot get rid of all inessential tasks, but you can reduce them.) You will *rank the list of jobs in order of their importance* to the business, and estimate what general proportion of your time and energy should be spent on each.

You will have considered where time is being wasted on unnecessary work, and where time could be saved by better personal organization and work methods. You should move to the next heading in your analysis of the work distribution chart.

DELEGATION

Ask yourself which of your activities could be done by somebody else to an adequate standard, or as well as you, or even better. The manager is paid to do his work, but if there are others at lower salaries who can do part of it and have the time, then is it better for the manager to be fully occupied or for the junior staff?

Another factor which comes out of this analysis is that the more senior people become, the larger becomes the proportion of their time spent on moving about and travelling, and you should think about this.

There will be certain customers who are very important, and who are accustomed to dealing with you personally; it may well be that you can introduce them to someone else who can deal with the routine parts of the account but, of course, you will remember to watch what is happening to the account from time to time subsequent to this arrangement. This would apply also to 'important jobs' and to important senior managers!

The present managing directors of several companies in the UK were in very humble positions only a few years ago; in fact, consider where you yourself were five years ago, and now you are performing much more important work. Quite possibly within your area you have the managers or senior managers of the future, and you should keep a look out for them and give them a 'chance' as soon as you can. Not only will this be good for them, but it will also free you. Think about how to develop the business and to perform your other managerial tasks.

One thing which is very irksome to staff is to see people senior to them performing activities at greater salaries which they could perfectly well do themselves. In one major British company staff are asked the question 'What does your supervisor do that you could do yourself?' Could you ask this question of your staff, and would they know how to answer it? It is worth considering that they may have views on this subject themselves.

SUBORDINATES' TIME

A manager becomes a manager by promotion or appointment. He learns to be a manager by observing other managers, who themselves have been taught by observation, and by being shown, and from what is called the 'hard way'. There are certain training courses, but they are normally very short, and as a result most managers devise their style and system of management from

1143

their own experience. Often this is very good, but once personal inclinations creep in, funny things start to happen.

You should ask yourself the following question: 'Is there anything I do which wastes subordinates' time without contributing to their effectiveness?' You can begin to answer this question from your analysis of the work distribution chart, and you may even be able to ask it of the subordinates themselves.

Waiting around

For instance, how much time do your staff spend waiting for answers from you, items to be checked or approved, action to be taken, or for you to be available? Consider whether in your area you ever have two or more people involved in work which should be done by one person only. Normally it is more satisfying and efficient for a job which can be done by one person to be done by one person and not split between two or three. Staff learn from observing you (or colleagues), but sometimes you may be playing to an audience unnecessarily (and distracting the others).

Remember when you were a member of staff or a worker. Did your manager or foreman ever waste any of your time while you waited for him when he was late, when he had to check your work, while he had to get around to this or that but was (or allowed himself to be) interrupted by a variety of other matters? Did this frustrate you as well as waste your time? Staff are paid less than managers, but with overheads the difference is not as great as it once was. Are you working too hard; are you paying the proverbial dog then doing the barking yourself?

Crises

One thing which wastes time, particularly of subordinates, is a crisis. In many organizations crises occur regularly, and there are so many things which are unforeseen that one could almost describe crises as routine. However, a recurrent crisis is a symptom of slovenliness. Certain crises such as making up the returns, the budget figures, sales figures, payroll, the peak season, are all known in advance. If the manager uses sensible planning and scheduling techniques he may well be able to provide for these, in which case they will become routine occurrences and not crises.

Panic action is expensive. People rushing off to make special deliveries, special visits to the post office, special trips out to acquire stationery, other things that are needed, people dropping things in the middle of picking up others and so on, all lead to ineffective use of time and also mistakes.

IMPROVEMENTS

The question here is, how can you use your time more effectively? The first thing to consider is your attention span. Are you a person who works best by sitting down quietly and for extended periods looking at a particular problem, or do you keep things running around in your mind? What are your best methods of working, and with whom and when?

Discretionary time

You need to have a certain amount of 'discretionary time', i.e., time at your free disposal, time available for important matters, perhaps the things you are paid for, and this must be kept in usable chunks. Not many managers feel they have much discretionary time, even after cutting out wasted time, but they can generally set aside an hour or so each week. The question arises as to how much discretionary time is desirable. This is rather like maintenance on a car; you do not buy a car in order to service it, but if you do not carry out a certain amount of maintenance on the car it will not perform satisfactorily.

Your function

The same applies to your function. You need from time to time to review the total operation of your area and to go through the checklist given previously; you need to make sure you see the staff regularly and review their situation. On a daily basis you may want to keep a list of the tasks which you have to do, and the problems with deadlines and priorities, and perhaps revise these either last thing at night or first thing in the morning. Also you may well want to use a brought-forward file or diary system so that you are automatically reminded of things that need to be done in the future. How long this should take is like the service on the car, except that it is you rather than the garage that must make the diagnosis and the decisions.

Suggestions

Simple suggestions for using your time more effectively are to concentrate on one thing at a time; deal with first things first, and one at a time. Allow enough time for what you are doing – nothing ever goes completely right and one thing you can always expect is the unexpected. Do not hurry, do not try and do several things at once. Do not assume that everything that was important yesterday is important today. Ask yourself the question 'If we had not already started on this activity would we start it now?' It is just as difficult and just as risky to do something small as something which is big, so allocate your time to the most important parts of the business.

When you have analysed your work distribution chart comparing the proportions of time spent on the various activities with their importance in terms of obtaining income, business and profit or other advantage for the company, you will most certainly find that you are spending a lot of your time on small irritating matters. Consider whether some of these can be allowed to slide without damage to the business, and whether things would be improved by concentrating on the main managerial requirements of the organization.

FURTHER READING

Drucker, Peter F., *The Effective Executive*, Heinemann, London, 1967

Lakein, A., *How to Get Control of your Time and your Life*, Gower, Aldershot, 1985

Welsh, A.N., *The Skills of Management*, Gower, Aldershot, 1980

61 Negotiating
Bill Scott

This chapter is in three parts. The first describes a style of negotiating designed to produce the greatest area of agreement in the joint interest of both parties. This is a pattern of negotiating in which the parties work together, creatively, *towards agreement*. The second pattern is one in which each party is concerned more with its own advantage than with the joint advantage. Goodwill and agreement are still important, but the overriding consideration is that which is *to independent advantage*. Third, when goodwill is not important, negotiations can sometimes deteriorate into a pattern of *fighting*.

NEGOTIATING TOWARDS AGREEMENT

When the parties are concerned to work together creatively towards agreement the key activities are exploration of one another's position, and creative recognition of what is in their joint interests.

Those phases of exploration and creativity, however, hinge on having first created a suitable climate and on having some procedure which helps the parties to work together. There is no cause for heavy use of negotiating tactics but there is a need for effective preparation.

The sequence in this section will therefore be:

Creating the climate
Opening procedure
Sequence in negotiations
Exploration
Creativity
Subsequent phases
Preparation

Creating the climate

Negotiators usually operate best when the climate is brisk and businesslike. When negotiating towards agreement, they need a climate which is also cordial and cooperative.

The pace of a negotiation, be it brisk or lethargic, is set very early. Within seconds of the parties coming together, during the rituals of meeting and greeting, a pace is established which is durable. It should be a brisk pace – briskness established by the pace at which the parties are moving about and by the speed at which they are communicating.

The cordial character is established in an ice-breaking phase. As the parties first meet and interact with one another, they need to adjust and to build their regard before getting into possibly controversial areas. The ice-breaking, therefore, needs to be a period in which they focus on neutral topics – the football, the weather, the journey and so on.

The ice-breaking is an essential preliminary, so important that it deserves possibly 5 per cent of the prospective negotiating time: a couple of minutes even at the outset of short negotiations; a preliminary dinner and evening out before protracted negotiations.

The brisk and cordial character is thus very soon established. The development of the businesslike and cooperative characteristics comes as the parties sit down and move towards business. Timing and the form of first remarks at the negotiation table should provide the 'business-like': timing, by an immediate statement so that there is no long gap as members get seated; and the form of the opening remarks focusing on business, towards agreement.

The cooperative character can be set too at this early stage. This depends on effectiveness in handling the opening procedure.

Opening procedure

There is nothing more likely to produce a cooperative atmosphere than the immediate question, on sitting down: 'Well, gentlemen, can we first agree on procedure?'

Note that the word 'agree' is used at the outset. Note that the question is one which will almost certainly produce the answer 'Yes'. Note that the two parties both establish the 'agree' mood from the outset.

There are four procedural items which should be explored and agreed in this opening stage: the four Ps.

1 Pace
2 Purpose
3 Plan
4 Personalities.

The *pace* is the speed at which the parties need to move together. There needs to be harmony on this pace if parties are to work together effectively. There will not be such harmony if one believes that there is a whole afternoon available whereas the other has another engagement in half an hour.

The *purpose* is the reason why the parties are meeting. If one party thinks that the meeting is purely exploratory, while the other believes the purpose is to achieve a final settlement, then the parties are going to be working at cross-purposes.

Even when the purpose has been established in preliminary communication, it is still important at the outset to refresh the consciousness of that purpose, and to take the chance to emphasize that both parties *agree* on that purpose.

The *plan* should be in the form of a short agenda – some four main stages through which the meeting should move.

These first three Ps – Pace, Purpose and Plan – should be agreed at the outset of every negotiation.

The fourth P in the opening procedural stage is Personalities: the introduction of members who do not know one another, their backgrounds, what they can contribute to the meeting. Skilfully used, this opening procedure has great advantages:

1 The meeting can proceed with both parties recognizing joint objectives and a joint means of moving forward
2 The plan gives a framework for control of the remainder of the meeting
3 The mood of agreement can be quickly stated and established
4 The groundwork is set for a smooth and cooperative entry into the later stages of the negotiation.

There is a consistent sequence in these later stages of any negotiation. The sequence is:

1 Exploration
2 Creativity
3 Shaping the deal
4 Bidding
5 Bargaining
6 Settling
7 Ratifying.

These phases are – or should be – found in any negotiation, even though they may sometimes become mixed and muddled. The importance of each phase varies a great deal, however.

In negotiating towards agreement, the key phases are those of exploration and creativity.

Exploration

When two parties come together, each has its own distinctive view of the aims and possibilities for the negotiation. If the parties want to work together to bake the biggest possible cake, it is imperative that each should

(*a*) recognize what both see in the same way,
(*b*) recognize and respect what others see in a different way, and
(*c*) be clear about the way in which their own interests are distinctive.

From such recognition can spring the creative spark of what is then most in their joint interests.

To achieve that recognition each party should independently make a broad statement of its own position, and give opportunity for the others to seek clarification. Then get a comparable 'broad picture' of the other party's position, and clarify that.

Each opening statement needs to cover:

- Our understanding. The broad area within which we believe the negotiation will take place.
- Our interests. What we would like to achieve through the negotiation.
- Our priorities. What are the most important aspects for us.
- Our contribution. The way in which we can help to our joint advantage.
- Our attitudes. The consequence of our previous dealing with the other party; their reputation as it has come to us; any special hopes or fears which we may have for collaboration.

Characteristic of the opening statement are the following points:

1 The opening statements of each party should be independent. Each should state its own position, and not attempt at this stage to state the joint interests of the two parties
2 They should not attempt to put assumptions about the position or interests of the other party. (The giving of this assumption serves only to irritate, to confuse and to introduce disharmony).
3 The statements should be general, not detailed, not yet quantitative
4 The statements should be brief. Each should give the other party an opportunity to come into the discussion quickly, both so that the parties can quickly interact and so that others do not get a sense of being overwhelmed by either the duration or the complexity of an opening statement. Keep it short.

As one party makes its opening statement, the other party needs to listen, clarify and summarize.

Listen

Do not waste energy by thinking up counter-arguments.

Clarify

If in any doubt, question to get clear what he is trying to say. But note: question for clarification. Do not question for justification – that forces the other negotiator on to the defensive and runs counter to the creative climate being sought.

Summarize

Feed back the key points of what you understand him to be saying, so that he can check.

Having got clear the view of one party then comes the time for the other party to offer its own opening statement, and for first party's corresponding response – listen, clarify, summarize.

For really creative negotiations, there is a need for these opening exchanges to be carried through frankly in an environment of mutual trust and respect. For these reasons great attention has been paid to creating a positive climate and to underlining agreement and preparing minds in the opening process.

Skilled negotiators are skilled at giving and getting information. They are also conscious that some other parties will seek to exploit them. They therefore look out for danger signals which would suggest a need to change strategy.

If in the ice-breaking, the other party insists on probing about business matters ('How's trade? cash-flow? quality?') beware. Probably he is simply an unskilled negotiator, but possibly he is aggressive, seeking information that he can later use aggressively. If he is highly assertive in the phase of proposing and agreeing procedure – then again we must beware. An amber light is flashing.

If he is excessively anxious that we should be the first to make an opening statement, or in challenging that opening statement: then a further amber light is shown – indeed, this is virtually a red light.

Given a succession of amber lights, or just one red light, then the skilled negotiator will be prepared to change his strategy. He should seek a recess, even though it is still an early stage of the negotiation, reconsider the other party's behaviour and decide whether he needs to change to either of the strategies in later sections of this chapter.

But skilled negotiators practising this characteristic style of negotiating towards agreement can normally produce a positive response.

There is thus a great need for negotiators to develop the skills of creating a cooperative climate, of agreeing procedure, and of openness in the exploratory phase.

Creativity

Agreement-oriented negotiators now have a unique opportunity to achieve something to joint advantage, something bigger than either party could get when negotiating to independent advantage. This is the moment to be seeking together to bake the biggest possible cake.

To achieve that creativity they need first to be imaginative. Later they must impose the forces of reality, but the most productive of ideas may not be seen unless the parties are prepared to range as far as the borderline between reality and fantasy. Be imaginative.

Scandinavian negotiators have a special phrase to launch into this phase. Having summarized the respective positions of the parties as discussed in their opening statements, they say 'All right then – what are the creative possibilities?'

In looking for those creative possibilities there are a few guidelines:

1   The pattern of generating the ideas must be broad in its sweep, and interdependent
2   It must be broad because immediately the parties focus on one suggestion (either criticizing or exploring in depth), their minds cannot revert to broad and imaginative thinking
3   It must be interdependent, not only to sustain the cooperation between them, but also because each fresh suggestion can kindle a new spark in the imagination of the other. The parties have great potential to be creative together.

This process of recognizing creative possibilities should generate a number of different ideas. There then comes the need to form a bridge between the world in which the parties have been thinking imaginatively, and the world of reality in which their performance must be measured by business criteria. They must decide which of their imaginative ideas offer realistic possibilities. They must then assess and agree on the action needed to turn possibility to mutual advantage.

Subsequent stages

The critical periods of negotiations towards agreement are the exploratory and creative phases. From them springs the recognition of mutual interest. There is, of course, need for the later realities to be foreseen, for agreement on the commercial conditions, and for the establishment of realistic plans to implement decisions. Given however the creative atmosphere, then views and possibilities for these commercial and planning discussions can be developed in a similarly open atmosphere.

The approach – 'Let us now explore together' – can be sustained through these later stages without the need to get into the tough bidding and bargaining encountered (and to be further discussed) in the context of other strategies.

However, before starting any negotiation, each party must arrive at the negotiating table well prepared.

Preparation

For any form of negotiation, the negotiator must have done his homework beforehand. He must know the facts, the figures, the arguments.

He needs also to have prepared in two other respects. First, preparing for the procedure. He should think through the Pace, Purpose and Plan which he will suggest for the meeting. And having thought them through, it is advisable to jot down the headlines of pace, purpose and plan on a postcard, to serve as a reminder during the meeting.

Second, he needs to have prepared his opening statement: his under-standing of the matter for discussion, his interests, priorities, contribution, attitudes; and again, to jot the headlines on a postcard.

It is important, when negotiating towards agreement, not to over-prepare. The negotiator who has built a detailed framework of prices, deliveries and so on in his preparations is so mentally committed to those preparations that he obscures the possibilities for being creative in any wider sense.

To summarize, when their strategy is negotiating towards agreement, the parties must first create a climate which is brisk, businesslike, cordial and cooperative. They must them establish and agree on a procedure helping them to work together effectively. From the opening procedural discussion they move into important exploratory and creative phases, and thereafter should be able to sustain the high cooperation already established. This must be founded on effective preparation by each party before the event.

NEGOTIATING TO INDEPENDENT ADVANTAGE

Different skills are needed when the negotiator is concerned with gaining special advantage for his party. In some ways these skills mirror those needed when negotiating towards agreement; in other ways, new and different skills are needed.

In particular, bidding and bargaining become the crux of the negotiation. Early moves set the framework; and a different form of preparation is needed. The sequence of this section will therefore be:

1 Opening moves
2 Bidding
3 Bargaining
4 Preparation.

Opening moves

The negotiator working to independent advantage must approach the negotiation with a difference of attitude. No longer is his concern to work creatively together with the other party. Rather it is to establish the best deal in the interests of his own side.

Assuming however that the deal will need the other party's cooperation to be implemented, or that there will in due course be a need to negotiate some other deal with the same party, it is important that goodwill should be sustained. Aggressive tactics and power struggles should be avoided.

The negotiator's attitude should not be that he will work towards the other party's disadvantage. His attitude must be to find the best way to divide the cake to give satisfaction to both parties. If he likes icing more than fruit, and the other party likes fruit more than icing – there is no problem. Both sides can 'win'. The skilled negotiator thus works towards influencing the other party to value the fruit more than the icing.

The opening moves will again establish the climate for the meeting. Because of the concern for sustaining goodwill it is again important that the climate should be brisk, businesslike, cordial and cooperative; and it is again important that procedure should be agreed at the outset.

Exploration now takes a different form. It becomes necessary to identify the shape of the deal quickly, rather than to look creatively for some new shape. In this process, both parties become more concerned with 'what our party wants'.

The response to the other party needs to be one of probing, to find out which issues or which ingredients are important to the others. Are they, for example, more concerned about price than delivery, quality, terms of settlement?

It is important in these exploratory stages to keep the dialogue on a broad front. If the move to discussion of a particular item (such as price) is taken too soon or too deeply, it is likely to lead to a premature conflict and also to erode some of the most effective possibilities for later bargaining.

Bidding

In negotiating to independent advantage, the guideline to bidding is to start with that which is the highest defensible. (For buyers, the corresponding phrase is of course 'lowest defensible offer.')

The opening bid needs to be 'the highest' because

1 The opening bid sets a limit beyond which the party cannot aspire. Having once made it, no higher bid can reasonably be put at a later stage
2 The first bid influences others in their valuation of our offer
3 A high bid gives scope for manoeuvre during the later bargaining phases. It gives something in reserve with which to trade
4 The opening bid has a real influence on the final settlement level. The higher the level of aspiration, the greater the prospective achievement.

The opening bid needs to be high. At the same time it must be defensible. Putting forward a bid which cannot be defended does positive damage to the negotiating process. It is found to be offensive by the other party; and if it cannot be defended when challenged in subsequent bargaining; there is soon a loss of face, a loss of credibility, a forced retreat.

The content of the bid of course usually needs to cover a range of issues. The components of the opening bid in a commercial negotiation will not simply be price, but a combination of price, delivery, payment terms, quality specification and a dozen other items.

The 'highest defensible bid' is not an absolute figure; it is a figure which is relevant to the particular circumstances. It is specifically a figure which relates to the way in which others are operating. If they are pressing to their independent advantage, then we must open with a high bid; but if faced with a lot of competition, the bid must be tailored to the level at which it will at least enable us to be invited to continue the negotiations. If we have established cordial relationships with others, possibly over a long period of time, then we shall know the style in which they will operate and the degree of cooperation we can expect – we know the level at which it is prudent for us to make our bid.

On each individual item the opening bid needs to be the highest defensible. We are certain, when negotiating to independent advantage, to be pushed by others to compromise on one or two issues. We cannot be sure which until the bargaining process is under way; we must aspire high on all issues and keep room to manoeuvre.

The manner in which the bid is stated is important. It should be put firmly – without reservations, without hesitations – so that it may carry the conviction of a conscientious negotiating party.

It should be put clearly so that the other party recognizes precisely what is being asked. The creation of a visual aid, i.e., taking a sheet of paper and writing figures on it within the sight of the other party, whilst one is stating the bid, is powerful reinforcement.

It should be put without apology or comment. There is no need to apologize for anything that can be defended. There is no need to comment since the other party can be expected to raise questions on matters which concern it. And voluntary comment (before others ask for it) simply makes them aware of concern about issues which they might never have considered.

Those then are three guidelines to the way in which a bid should be presented: firmly, clearly, without comment.

In responding to bids by the other party there is a need to distinguish between clarification and justification.

The competent negotiator first ensures that he knows what the other party is bidding. Precisely. He asks any questions which are needed to ensure that he gets the picture clear. He makes sure, in the process, that the other party recognizes that these are questions for clarification and not demands to justify. And once satisfied, he summarizes his understanding of the other party's bid, as a check on the effectiveness of communication between them.

First party should at this stage deflect questions which demand that he justifies his position. He has put a bid, and he has a perfect right to know what other is prepared to offer in return.

Bargaining

The first two steps in the bargaining process should be:

1 Get it clear
2 Assess the situation.

It is vital to establish a clear picture of other party's requirements at the outset. We should have got a clear picture of *what* he is bidding already. Now we need to know *why*.

The need is increasingly to build an understanding of what will give him satisfaction and of how to trade to advantage whilst giving him that satisfaction.

We must discover what for him are essentials and what else is desirable but not essential, and what aspects of his bid are really of fringe interest only – where he could readily give.

To achieve this clarity, the guidelines are:

1   Check every item of his bid. Enquire why. Ask how important the item is and how much flexibility he could introduce
2   Never speculate on his opinions or on his motives. A speculation only irritates. Moreover it is often misconceived – it is out of our frame of reference, not his, and confuses the negotiations between the pair of us. Never put words into his mouth
3   Note his answers without comment. Reserve our position. Avoid deep diving or premature diving into any issue. Keep it on a broad front.

Assuming significant difference between the parties there are now three options for the negotiator:

1   He can accept
2   He can reject
3   He can carry on negotiating.

If he decides to carry on negotiating then he must be prepared for the next round. His options at this stage are:

1   To make a new offer
2   To seek a new offer from the other party
3   To change the shape of the deal (vary the quantity or the quality or the use of third parties), or
4   Embark on give-and-take bargaining.

The steps for preparing for that give-and-take are:

1   Issue identification – list the issues in the package
2   Prepare the bargaining position:

   (*a*) an essential conditions list – those issues on which it is impossible to concede anything

(b) a concessions list – those issues on which concession is conceivable. For each such issue, a progression stepped from the minimum which could be offered (against counter-concessions from the other party) in the next round of bargaining, to that ultimate limit which might be forced in successive rounds.

During the bargaining stages, each successive negotiation meeting should be opened with a new round of climate formation and with agreement on procedure. Each round should be concluded with the establishment of some means of resolving outstanding difficulties.

In between, the negotiations should be conducted laterally rather than vertically. That is to say, the aim should be to reach agreement in principle on a broad front, then to tackle more detailed negotiations, still on a broad front. A sequence of several successive moves across the broad front; not a succession of narrow penetrations.

When the time comes for compromise, neither party will readily 'lose face'. Neither party will readily concede on one issue without having some corresponding concession on another. It is thus important to solve difficulties on a broad front or, at the least, two at a time; not simply one at a time.

For example, when the parties have been exploring a difference between them in price and when they are reaching the stage of preparedness to make concessions, it is helpful to both parties if one of them interjects a comment such as 'Well, just before we finish that discussion on price, could we at the same time tie in this question about (e.g., the shipping risk) and who is to be responsible for that?'

And so sustaining goodwill and sustaining efforts to keep a cooperative climate even through tough bargaining – the negotiation should move towards settlement to independent advantage.

Preparation

As ever, preparation is of critical importance, and the general pattern of preparation should repeat that previously described – with one important difference. This is the need to be more specific during preparation processes. Whereas in creative negotiations it is important to keep one's preparations general and to preserve flexibility, in more divisive negotiations the negotiator needs to be protected from exploitation. He needs to have considered his bids at an early stage. There is this constant dichotomy between the need for flexibility and the need for precise preparations. The one is the enemy of the other. The choice should reflect the strategic situation which will be referred to at the end of this chapter.

To summarize: bidding and bargaining are the key phrases in negotiating to independent advantage. It is a type of negotiation needing distinctive attitudes and skills. Bidding and bargaining become more important than exploration. Climate formation and procedural development remain important. So does preparation though it takes a slightly different form.

FIGHTING

Warfare is not a commendable form of negotiation. Nevertheless, negotiators do become involved in confrontations in which the aim has to be 'win' – or, at any rate, to ensure that they do not 'lose' at the hands of an aggressive party.

This section will review:

> the use of fighting methods
> the pattern of a fighting negotiation
> fighting tactics
> counter-measures

The use of fighting methods

The fighter's aim is to win and to make the other party the loser.

This is a dangerous attitude to negotiations. It puts goodwill at risk; it obscures the possibility of creative cooperation; it naturally provokes the other party to fight back, causing delay and putting at risk the fighter's chances of success. Even when the fighter batters an 'opponent' into submission, he is not likely to find the deal implemented energetically.

The means which the fighter uses are powerful. Both by his personal behaviour and by the negotiating tactics which he uses, he seeks to reinforce the power of his position. His methods include:

- a constant search for gain at every opportunity
- at each successive stage in the process of negotiating, he wants fresh advantage
- any withdrawals must be deliberate, tactical withdrawals, designed only to promote greater advance
- power-methods; high in terms of the pace, size and forcefulness of demands, low in readiness to listen or to yield
- task-centred. Concern for his special advantage. Not concerned with other party's pride or dignity nor with their feelings. Forcing them to 'accept or else'.

The pattern of a fighting negotiation

The central concern of the fighting negotiator is to win. This winning takes place in the fighting phase of the negotiation – a special version of the bargaining phase, at which he is expert and best able to use his personal characteristics. Quickly he leads the negotiation to the point at which his form of bargaining becomes the dominant activity.

This leaves little time or interest for the early stages of negotiating, little time to get on the same wavelength as other party, or to agree on a plan; little time to explore mutual interests. Even issue identification is hastened and the negotiation quickly becomes focused on his first chosen issue.

The pattern of the negotiation is then 'vertical', deep diving on the first selected issue. He aspires high and pushes until he 'wins' on that and each successive issue.

Fighting tactics

He knows a lot of tactics and manoeuvres, and regularly uses a number. He has his own repertoire, and admires (and tries to emulate) tactics which have been used 'against' him by other negotiators. Here are some of them:

1 *Probing from the start*
   The fighter enters the negotiating room, shakes hands and wishes us 'Good morning' and immediately starts probing – about our business situation, about the product or service in which he is interested, even about one's personal situation.
   The advantages he seeks are in getting information, in building a picture about other party and especially in recognizing weaknesses and vulnerabilities. Additionally, he establishes a power position – a pattern of aggressive leadership

2 *Get/give*
   He is concerned to get something before he will give anything – to get a small concession before he will give a small concession, and a big concession before he will give a big concession; to get information before he will give information; to get the other party's bid before he will give his own bid; to get the power of being the first to make an opening statement.
   Get/give tactics used by skilled negotiators can have positive commercial advantages in the short term. They may well gain ground during the early stages of a negotiation; but in the long run, they lead to delay and deadlock (neither party being willing always to give before it gets)

3 *Showing emotion* (anger, for example)
   Loud and emotional statements, possibly banging the table: the form of eye-contact, posture, gesture and voice, all displaying emotions

4 *Good guy/bad guy*
   This is the tactic for use by a team of two negotiators. One takes the role of the 'bad guy', being aggressive, making excessive demands, dominating, un-cooperative. He holds the stage for a long time whilst his colleague remains quiet. When he has softened up the 'opposition' with his tactics, the 'good guy' takes over the lead role, constructively offering solutions, quietly trying to reach a mutual understanding.
   The tactic parallels the archetypal method by which prisoners of war are cross-examined; the prisoner first ruthlessly interrogated by a tough investigator, then offered the sympathy of a different personality to whom – with luck – he would open up.

5 *Poker-faced*
   Giving away nothing by expression, tone, posture or gesture, an important part of the fighting negotiator's armoury

6 *Managing the minutes*
Taking responsibility at the end of each session for production of the record, slanting interpretations of what has been agreed, always to his advantage. Readiness to include the odd item 'which ought to have been agreed' even if there was insufficient time to include it in the discussion – provided, of course, that the odd item is favourable

7 *Getting upstairs*
When unable to come to an agreement with the other negotiator, taking steps to contact his boss, or boss's boss's boss!

8 *PR*
Many fights are conducted by negotiators acting on behalf of other group-ings. For example, the union negotiator representing the workforce; the government negotiator representing his country. It is here important for the group which is represented to be kept informed and influenced so that they continue to give their backing to the negotiator. His ability at public relations is thus an important part of the fighter's armoury

9 *Forcing moves*
There are, of course, yet other moves which some negotiators use: bribery, sex, blackmail, bugging. Most negotiators would see such devices as rankly unethical; but people negotiating very important deals are at risk and need to be on their guard.

Counter-measures

Counters to those who fight are in two forms: long-term and short-term measures.

In the long term, where there is expectation of repeated rounds of negotiations (for example, in labour negotiations) there is a need for the development of attitudes, skills and relationships.

This development takes place best when the parties can come together at a place remote from their normal battlefield, and at a time during the off-season for fighting. Especially fruitful is the practice, which has been well developed in Scandinavia, of holding joint working seminars for two or three days. The product of such seminars is not only the development of relationships but the planning of subsequent joint activities.

That is a long-term approach. In the short term, measures to counter the fighter fall into three categories:

1 Head him off
2 Control the battlefield
3 Cope with his tactics.

The most satisfying way of coping with him is of course to head off the fight before it develops. If this is to be achieved it must be done in the critical opening seconds and minutes:

- deflect his opening questions
- preserve a neutral ice-breaking period
- do not be drawn by his probing questions
- do not let him assert leadership
- do not let him dominate the early moments – what is being talked about, when to stand and when to sit, the seating arrangements

We are able to control the skirmishing if we can somehow control the battlefield. In negotiating terms, this 'control of the battlefield' is control of the procedures of negotiating. Guidelines are:

1 Seek for form and plan for the proceedings
2 Seek for opening discussion of purpose, plan and pace
3 Keep bringing him back to the agreed plan
4 Keep things fluid. Use the 'broad front' approach
5 Seek compromise. He will be impervious either to searches for creative resolution of differences, or to sensitive attempts to influence him. His metier is that of compromise. If his position is that he is asking £120 and ours is that it is only worth £100, then settlement is likely to be at the compromise amount of £110. Bargain slowly until you get him down to at most £110.

Above all, keep control of the process – keep control of what is being negotiated and in which sequence – keep to the plan. It will irritate him. He much prefers to be able to run free, but do not worry. A caged fighter cannot do as much damage as one on the loose. To cope with some of the fighter's tactics: When he is using the 'get/give' tactic, we must not give too easily, for if we give before we get, he will regard this as a sign of weakness. He will want to get yet more and will change the tactic into 'get/get/give' and soon will be aspiring even higher to 'get/get/get'.

We must not give in. We must trade scrap of information for scrap of information, scrap of readiness for scrap of readiness, scrap of concession for scrap of concession.

The only counter to displays of anger is to suspend negotiations, either temporarily or permanently. The human brain is such that emotions (such as anger) are handled in one part of it, rational thinking in another part. Once the brain becomes focused on emotive thinking, then the rational part is cut off. The angry party cannot receive rational messages and it is no use the other party trying to instil them. So the counter is to suspend operations.

It does not matter if first party's anger is simply a display rather than real anger. Second party has no way of being sure about the matter. First party has behaved in ways which are not acceptable and second party should immediately suspend.

The 'good guy/bad guy' tactic is difficult to recognize and difficult to counter. But, of course, if it has been recognized in one round of negotiating then the negotiator will be alert for it during later rounds and must hope either to be able to ignore the bad guy or to separate the two 'opponents'.

The counter to 'getting upstairs' is to state strong objection to the tactic and then to arrange for our own boss to come in and make it clear that theirs was a losing tactic.

Formality is, inevitably, a device used to try to bring order to such negotiations. However, the fighting negotiator becomes expert in framing and fighting for a rule-book which is to his advantage. He is expert not only in drafting and amending rules but in interpreting and manipulating them. The effective negotiator from the other side therefore is forced to build his own corresponding expertise.

Preparation is, as ever, of critical importance for effectiveness in negotiating. When faced with a fight it is imperative to be well prepared procedurally and to have precise objectives, targets and prepared concession lists. There is special need to prepare options ('scenarios' in the current jargon), alternative approaches which could enable both parties to move forward whilst minimizing loss of face.

The counter to his competence at public relations is to develop equal competence and to ensure that the relevant public is suitably influenced.

In meeting with a fighting 'opponent' then, the negotiator is operating in a world of power. He needs skill to control the battlefield and to prevent his being exploited.

But that is a short-term approach. The longer-term interest demands that he should work for some joint development of attitudes, skills and relationships with the other party.

SUMMARY

This chapter has been concerned with three distinct forms of negotiation. First, with negotiations in which two parties seek to move forward co-operatively to create the best possible deal in their joint interests. Second, with patterns of negotiation in which both parties aim to preserve goodwill whilst at the same time trying to maximize their independent advantage. Third and finally, with fights in which continuing goodwill is not treated as being important.

The choice amongst these approaches to negotiating will depend on a number of strategic issues:

1 The extent to which the parties will need to come together again from time to time
2 The respective strength of the parties in the market place
3 The character and quality of their negotiators
4 The time-scale and the importance of the prospective deal.

These strategic issues are considered at greater length in the last two books given in the further reading list which follows.

FURTHER READING

Karrass, C.L., *Give and Take*, World Publishing Co., 1974. A good treatment of the tactics used by American negotiators.

Marsh, P.D.V., *Contract Negotiation Handbook*, Gower, Aldershot, 2nd edition, 1984. Excellent treatment of negotiating strategy of general interest. Preceded by a mathematical/economic analysis of bidding – also excellent, but demanding a reader with mathematical talents.

Scott, Bill, *The Skills of Negotiating*, Gower, Aldershot, 1981. A highly readable expansion of his ideas by the author of this chapter of the handbook.

62 Effective communication

Gordon Bell

As a director, a manager or an aspiring manager you will be interested in facts. A survey of over 5000 men and women such as yourself revealed the following data:

1 On average, they had each received about fifteen years of formal education
2 Approximately a third of them gained degrees, diplomas or other paper qualifications
3 Only one in twenty-three felt that their subsequent achievements in life matched their abilities, qualifications or early ambitions
4 Fewer than one in twenty had taken the trouble to equip themselves with skills such as effective speaking, clear writing, handling meetings.

From the chairman of the largest industrial group to supervisors and staff, everybody uses words. Every business man and woman writes letters, reports, memoranda, orders. Reasonable people will agree that words are a vital tool in industry. The higher we go up the ladder of management the more important words become.

Many business meetings produce nothing but frustration and expense. The average executive spends a third of his working life talking at interviews, conferences and committees (to say nothing of the time and hassle involved in arranging them and getting there). How much of this talk is productive? How many business men are either confident or competent when making a presentation or delivering a speech?

The nub of effective management is communications. Time and effort that you invest in developing your own skills as a communicator must produce dividends. In this chapter we shall discuss three aspects of communications:

1 Speaking
2 Report writing
3 Meetings.

SPEAKING

Speaking is for other people. This fact about effective speaking is so obvious and so simple that many overlook it. An audience always evaluates a speaker subjectively. What did they get from the talk? The answer to this question measures the speaker.

A manager needs to command attention at conferences and other meetings: he must be able to make oral presentations to his board and to professional organizations; to brief his staff, to persuade, to convince. Particularly if he is a specialist, he must be able to clarify specialized concepts so that others, not necessarily qualified, can share his thoughts. Even the most brilliant man is useless until his ideas can be shared by others who can use them.

A successful speaker is a man who gives his audience a success.* Many managers, both male and female, suffer from the delusion that speaking in public is the same as a theatrical performance, or something suitable only for extroverts. This delusion often serves as a defence. The plain truth is that they fear exposure of their limitations as speakers. This state of affairs is deplorable. If a man has something worth saying, he should not only say it but also learn how to say it with full effect. 'Why should the devil have all the best tunes?' asked General Booth. It is also pertinent to ask, 'Why should the image-makers and the tricksters have a monopoly of effective speech?'

Let us examine the fear, sometimes amounting to terror, that afflicts otherwise intelligent men when they are asked to speak. What causes this fear? The unpopular but accurate answer is vanity – too great a concern with 'How am I going to do?' and not enough concern with 'How are they – the audience – going to do?' This truth is a hard one to face yet it applies at both ends of the scale. Vanity causes the glib, arrogant, loud-mouthed, no-nerves-at-all-I-can-talk-at-the-drop-of-a-hat chap to subject his audience to a flood of waffle: it also causes the timid to worry about themselves at the expense of their hearers. If you face this fact now you can save yourself a lot of trouble.

A successful speaker is a man who gives his audience a success. The speaker's success stems from the audience reaction. If his audience reacts in the desired manner, the speaker has been effective. There is no other criterion.

Newton's third law of motion says, roughly, 'To every action there is an equal and opposite reaction'. A given stimulus creates the same response if conditions remain constant. Herein lies one of the most important points that a speaker must consider. An audience is never a constant factor. There is no such thing as a production-line human being. Everyone is unique. People in an audience vary in social levels, technical knowledge, prejudices, age, sex. Even the same people gathered together at different times or under different conditions can change as an audience.

*A note for women readers: I apologize for using words like 'man', 'his', 'him' throughout. Of course women are included in the thinking behind this chapter.

Effective speaking is a human relationship, not something that one person does alone and in isolation. A speaker wishing to get the desired reaction must obviously begin with a study of his audience. Unfortunately, many speakers begin with themselves and end in disaster.

So, the first point that a would-be speaker must think about is his attitude to his audience. His thinking must be positive and outward – not so much 'What subject am I going to talk about?' as 'How can I create a powerful relationship with my audience using the subject as both the generator and the cement which binds that relationship?'

Can you imagine anyone erecting Tower Bridge or building a locomotive who would begin by laying the first brick or polishing the whistle? A rational man starts with a purpose and a plan. So does a professional speaker – and you, whether you realize it or not, are a professional speaker, a professional report-and letter-writer and a professional meeting man. If you analyse your job as a manager you will find that you do little else but talk and write and discuss. Given equal knowledge of his business, a man who knows how to speak, how to write and when to listen always has the advantage over one who does not.

Preparing an effective talk

Many speakers complain that they have no time to prepare properly. If you know your subject you can prepare a talk in one hour. The method we shall discuss now is the one-hour method. There are three stages, roughly twenty minutes each. (When you have ample time, say, three weeks or six, simply extend each stage accordingly.)

Stage 1: Gathering subject matter

Arm yourself with plenty of large sheets of paper and write down at great speed *every* idea on your subject that enters your mind. Make no attempt to think these ideas through. Get them down in rapid notes, symbols or any other shorthand form that will enable you to recognize them when you arrive at Stage 2 - the plotting stage. Work at speed. Your aim during Stage 1 is quantity; to amass hundreds of facts about your subject, various opinions, prejudices, misunderstandings, possible visual aids, thoughts about the audience, the occasion – anything which in any way may bear on your proposed talk. Note direct facts, oblique, tangential and even remotely relevant facts. Set down page after page of rough notes.

During Stage 1 it is most important that you concentrate and work non-stop at great speed. If time allows, do this several times until you have at least ten times more material than your final talk demands. Fix nothing, solidify nothing. Bear in mind that what might be old stuff, obvious to you, might well be new or in need of explanation to your hearers. So get it all down. Note everything. A thought unnoted often disappears for ever.

Give yourself all the options. Review the whole subject. This review jogs your memory, gives you flexibility, acts as a solid background for your talk and can prove particularly helpful if you are required to answer questions.

Instead of having to excavate facts from the deep recesses of your mind, you have them near the surface, fresh and ready for use.

Quantity. Now you have raw stuff to work on, stacks of it.

Stage 2: Purpose and people

Establish your precise purpose. What reaction do you wish to induce in your hearers? What job has the talk to perform? Write down your purpose; rewrite it several times until you express, exactly, in a few cogent words, the effect you wish to achieve. Know what you are doing, explicitly. Be thorough about this. Do nothing else until you have got your objective clear.

Now that you have ample subject matter and a vividly clear purpose, you must ponder on the real material for your talk – the people who will listen to you. Examine every link they have or might have with your subject because they will be completely uninterested until what you say has something to do with them. Obvious, isn't it? What is their technical level, their social, financial level; what are their needs in connection with you and your subject? Study the people until you can see their view of your subject. You can only put your view across in relation to theirs. If you do not know anything about your audience, you would be well advised to find out at once. A discussion with the organizers, even a telephone call, can prove useful. Get to know your audience and integrate them into your presentation *now*; it will be too late when you are on your feet talking.

So, purpose and people. These two essential elements for an effective talk rarely receive enough thought or attention.

Stop here, please.

You must go no farther until you have checked that you have the driving force of a clear purpose working for you. You must go no farther until you have developed a real interest in your audience and their needs. These two factors should already be allies helping you to establish a partnership with your audience.

Purpose.   People.   Theme.   Main points.

After your talk, what message will your hearers carry away with them? What big points supported your thesis? No audience will remember everything that you said. Decide at this stage in your preparation what basic theme you wish them to remember. As with your purpose, write down your theme and work on it until it becomes simple, straightforward and crystal clear. Next, separate the one, two or three really important points from the lesser points. Which are the really big points that you want them to have working in their minds? If you do not establish them clearly now, they will not stand out prominently enough in your delivered talk. Your job as a speaker is to clarify the subject for your audience. You cannot do this unless you first clarify it for yourself.

Now build your talk on the foundation of your purpose, your people, your theme and your main points.

A few reminders. A successful speaker knows his subject and is enthusiastic about it.

He makes certain that he is well prepared.

He has considered his audience and believes that the subject is important to them.

Bad speakers are usually people who think about themselves too much.

Pertinent questions to be answered at the end of Stage 2:

1 What exactly is my subject?
2 Why am I speaking about it to this audience and what do I know about them?
3 What are the most important things I must tell them?
4 Have I picked out the main points which must be highlighted?
5 Have I arranged these points so that this particular audience will fully understand them and be involved in them?
6 Have I made sure that there is a glowing, dominant theme?
7 What will the audience gain from this talk?

Stage 3: Delivering the goods

The audience must at once be made confident that the speaker knows what he is doing. They must find his first thoughts intensely interesting. This, of course, rules out the usual dreary opening, for instance, where the speaker talks about himself and his worries as a speaker.

The three-sentence technique can secure a telling impact on opening:

Sentence 1. You make any vivid, unexpected, off-beat, truly interesting remark you like (always of course bearing in mind your audience).

Sentence 2. You link, skilfully, sentence 1 to your subject and make clear exactly what your subject is.

Sentence 3: You *involve* the audience in both your opening remarks and your subject.

It is essential that you economize and discipline yourself to use only three sentences for this effect. There must be no woolly edges around these three sentences, no 'hums' and 'hahs', no interpolated oddments, no clutter. You are seeking a clean, crisp, immediate communication, a direct response. Experiment until you have got a really good beginning. Excite, Link, Involve. Do not be satisfied with the first openings you think of: try at least six ways before you decide.

Avoid the word 'I' for at least one minute. Substitute 'you', 'your', or group words describing the audience, such as engineers, Scotsmen, managers. Be as specific as you can. Talk about them and their links with the subject. Get the focus firmly on to them and away from yourself.

As soon as your impact has been achieved and the audience knows what your broad subject is, define your limits so that they will not waste their attention on parts of the subject outside the scope of your talk. Tell them where you intend to take them within your subject, sometimes even which aspects you intend to leave out. From the start concentrate their mental energy on the relevant aspects. Give them clear signposts, briefly.

Now, you have a dynamic purpose in your mind; you and your audience know where you are going. They have been intrigued by your opening remarks and are ready for the statement of your basic theme, ready for the development of your first main point supporting that theme – and they are eager to find out how and where they fit in and what you have to say.

The elements are prepared for you – the catalyst – to do your work.

There are no dull subjects. Everything under the sun teems with interest. From even such beginnings as a dirty ashtray or the Industrial Training Act a lively mind could create a fascinating talk. How are you going to tell your story, how give your facts their full value as facts plus that life which also gives them interest? The key to power in story-telling is to bind everything you say to people and things – the concrete rather than the abstract. You might well be talking about some entirely abstract technical concept. Human beings and physical, tangible things judiciously woven into your presentation will vitalize even the unlikeliest subject for a potent talk. Also, wherever you can, link your examples directly to your listeners. An earthquake killing thousands in China could leave your audience unmoved: but a gas explosion in Clay Street, Manchester will engender great interest – especially to those of your audience who live in Clay Street, Manchester.

Facts are sacred and must not be tampered with. Concrete examples emphasize facts and make facts stick in the mind. The closer the examples are to the experience and the environment of the audience the more surely your points will find their target.

Contrary to a common opinion, facts do not always speak for themselves. They need good men to speak for them. No fact of life need be colourless or less interesting than fiction. You must adroitly develop the story of each fact, giving it a good beginning, a lively motif, substance, excitement, strong, close-to-home examples and a language suitable for your hearers.

Words worry people. They say 'I have plenty of ideas but I haven't the vocabulary to express them'. This assertion is based on a fallacy. Words (or some other set of symbols such as mathematical formulae) are essential to clear thought. If you are fumbling for words, you have not clarified the thought.

Technical language and jargon incur much scorn and contempt; but they have their uses as a shorthand for the initiated. On the other hand, to use such esoteric stuff to show how clever you are or because you lack consideration for your hearers is unpardonable. Use your audience's language or explain your own. Otherwise you will waste your breath and, what is worse, waste their time.

Speaking style

A hypnotist wishing to put someone to sleep employs a subdued, monotonous voice and single soporific thought repeated and repeated and repeated until the patient gives up and slumbers. To arouse the patient he makes some sharp noise and brings his own voice to life by using a complete change of tone. The patient wakes up.

Human voices possess an immense range of volume, tone, pace, attack. Why be monotonous? Why be dull? Why mutter or bawl like a bull? Why not work out beforehand how you can give variety and the appropriate vocal clues to each part of your talk? Think in terms of main headlines and paragraphs and make sure that each new idea comes to the audience with a change in vocal approach. Particularly when introducing a fresh point, give your voice a lift. Watch sentence length; see to it that a few crisp short ones intervene between a series of protracted sentences. Watch the ends of sentences: a rising pitch holds more interest than a dying fall.

It is an odd fact of speaking technique that absolute silence for a few seconds – under control – can be the most effective part of a speech. Try to find, perhaps, two such moments when you can hold your audience to your thoughts during your calculated pauses.

The human voice is only one of the channels through which ideas can flow. Sound, sight, touch, smell, taste all provide means of conveying to other people. A good speaker gives his audience a chance to use as many of their senses as the occasion permits. With a little ingenuity you can give their ears a rest and switch channels. One obvious way of doing this is to show them the point, to demonstrate it. The term 'visual aids' does not mean only blackboard – chalk-and-talk stuff – or flipcharts or films or overhead projectors; solid physical, three-dimensional objects have much more effect. If it is practicable show them the actual thing you are talking about. Let them handle it, smell it, taste it. Use your zest, imagination and enthusiasm to create a worthwhile experience for your audience. You can develop a reputation as a first-class speaker if you work at it and stop worrying about yourself. They will say you simply have a flair for this sort of thing, a gift. You must not mind that. A judicious use of the five senses will help you. However prosaic your subject, give it vigour, colour – life.

Please arm yourself with a pencil and a sheet of paper because we are going to create a graph. I would appreciate your comments in it and your physical cooperation. To begin with, here are the axes (Figure 62.1). Please read the notes, draw the axes exactly. Then proceed to Figure 62.2.

Commentary

The shading at the foot of Figure 62.2 represents the grey sludge area at the beginning of so many talks, during what the poor speaker calls 'warming up'. The monologue here tells how unaccustomed the speaker is and what a trying ordeal he is experiencing in facing such a difficult, awesome set of people. In general, the self-centred blockhead isolates himself and destroys the goodwill of the audience by focusing in the wrong direction. No wonder he is nervous. No wonder the audience already begin to doubt whether they should have come.

Eliminate the sludge area altogether. Instead, get some vigour, elevation and impact into your beginning. Hoist the value-and-interest line clean through the sludge up to X, which marks your impact at opening.

Signposts help your hearers to concentrate on the special aspects of the

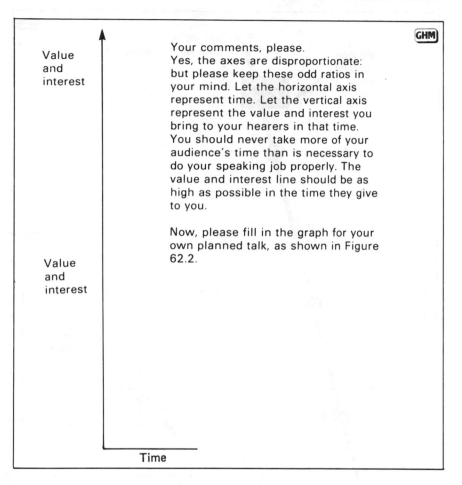

Figure 62.1 Axes for graph of value and interest against time
Use the proportions shown here to prepare the graph described in the text

subject that you intend to cover. Define your limits, briefly.

Now drive towards your first main point (*a*). You have it clear. You have already worked out how to make your facts come to life, how to link your vivid example both to the facts and to your audience. Follow your line, the theme, and support that theme with facts. Develop your message.

Summaries are a matter for your judgement. At least you must make certain that each main point holds fast in the minds of your audience before you tackle the next point.

Signposting internal to the talk, again, is a matter for you to decide. Will summaries and signposting help the audience? If so, use them.

When you reach the climax of your talk, when you ram home your message

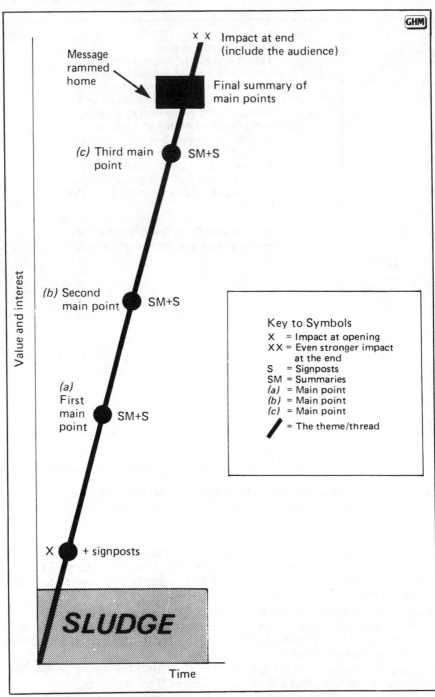

Figure 62.2   Graph of value and interest against time

you must remind your audience of the main facts which support your theme. Summarize crisply: remind them how the matter of your talk affects them and do have a powerful line at the end. (Make a really sharp, hard, strong point and sit down on it!)

Speaking for special occasions: case presentation

Please engrave this sentence into your mind: Nothing induces agreement faster than self-interest – the other fellow's self-interest.

Many business men have to recommend changes that will cost money. In most companies there is a procedure for this. The proposer has first to prepare a document setting out his proposal in detail. This goes through normal channels and may sometimes be agreed to or rejected as it stands. More frequently the proposer will be asked to appear before some board or committee to explain his proposal and to answer questions about it.

The written part of a proposal is a persuasive report and should be written with that in mind. The oral presentation is part speech, part meeting and part interview.

In preparing such a presentation, the proposer should ask himself these questions:

1 Do you know exactly what you want?
2 Do you really believe in your case?
3 Have you got all the facts that support your case and have you checked them?
4 What are the strongest arguments for your case?
5 What are the benefits for your listeners?
6 Why must the present situation be changed?
7 What is their problem?
8 Who else is affected? (Unions, other divisions, etc.)
9 What are the arguments against your plan?
10 What are the alternatives to your plan?
11 Do your benefits clearly outweigh these arguments and alternatives?
12 To whom are you presenting your plan? Have you done any lobbying? Do you need to?
13 Do you know who your probable allies and opponents are?
14 Have you discussed the finances with the experts?
15 Have you prepared hand-outs of any complicated figures?
16 It was a good idea when you first thought of it. Is it still – from their point of view?
17 Have you prepared a really effective presentation? (Time plus the value and interest ratio are particularly important in case presentation.)
18 How will you sum up and end?
19 Are you ready for questions?
20 Have you emphasized the benefits they (your listeners) will gain? Remember: nothing induces agreement faster than self-interest – the other fellow's self-interest.

The board is probably only interested in this question: 'Have they a problem and does your proposal solve it for them?' Ask yourself: 'Will your proposal satisfy their need, their greed, their self-esteem – or all three?'

Social speaking

Social speaking has one simple purpose: to give pleasure. What will make your audience purr? What will cause them to cry 'Hear! Hear!'? What will make them laugh? What will make them proud that they belong to this club, this company, this band of people brought together with a common cause? What sentiment will bring a lump into their throats? What will make them say afterwards 'Oh, I did enjoy that'?

Deliver the answers to these questions and they will be glad that you spoke, especially as you delivered with obvious affection for them, and warm appreciation of their values and you did so without going on and on and on. Work out a good line to end your speech and do not separate it by too long a time from your first-class opening line. Give them pleasure and enjoy the pleasure of their company.

One-to-one talking

An encounter across a desk can often make or break a manager. Failure follows almost inevitably if you present your ideas at the wrong time or if you insist on pushing a proposal from your own point of view.

By all means be relaxed but before you go in to win your point, or before the other fellow calls on you, do your homework. Get your purpose clear, have your facts ready. Know his problems in relation to your suggestion and start the disucssion of the basis of his problems. Until you have established his problems and have shown that you understand them and are in sympathy with them, you must not try to sell him anything. You want him to react, to say 'Yes'. He will not react in your favour if you spend your time putting yourself across. Try it the other way round. Put him and his problems in the forefront. If what you have to sell solves his problems, he'll agree.

Some thoughts

Make contact with people. Use your eyes. Look at them. Include them in what you say. This is simply good manners. Take the trouble to prepare properly to ensure that you give them value in exchange for the time they are giving you. Develop a respect, even an affection for your audience. Remember that, however expert you may be, every man and woman there is superior to you in some way and could teach you something.

Speaking is probably the oldest form of human communication. It is certainly the most natural to modern man but, unless other minds can process and use what is said, speaking is just a useless shifting of wind.

There are few things more exhilarating than an audience reacting with interest, excitement and the sheer pleasure of enjoying a first-class speaker. Deserve such a reaction and your world will be that much better for having you around.

REPORT WRITING

John Logie Baird's discovery of the principles of television was useless; Einstein helped nobody with his thinking on relativity nor did Fleming with penicillin until they made their facts and theories known to other people. Knowledge locked away in the recesses of a single mind has little value until other minds receive the key and gain access to it. Many specialists believe that their work stops when they have uncovered the facts. A question was asked of them. They worked on it, investigated it thoroughly and found the answer. And that, they say, is the end of their job. But is it?

Why do industrial concerns employ scientists, accountants and other specialists? The answer to that question is simple. Industrial concerns employ specialists in order to get from them information, and expert guidance towards profitable action. Yet although specialists study and sweat for 5, 10, 15, 20 years, a lifetime, to equip themselves as experts they rarely study the techniques of passing their hard-gained information to other people. And their readers do the sweating.

A report is a working document that helps the other man to do his job. A record may well form the basis for a report but it is not a report. Samuel Pepys' diary recorded his times, brilliantly, but scholars had to delve to extract the meat. Nobody expects to have to delve into a modern business report; readers expect you to present the meat ready for digestion. A long report is not necessarily better than a short one, if only because fewer people will bother to read it. On the other hand, if you are writing for qualified people who want to know not only the conclusions and recommendations but also the detailed results and the methods used to obtain them, your report must contain such facts in full.

A report is not a detective story. Agatha Christie could take a set of facts and cloak them so skilfully that few readers can get the crucial point until the final page. The facts are all there if only one has the nous to spot them. There should be no mystery about a report. The facts should be clear and the development logical so that the conclusions and recommendations follow them naturally.

There are five main considerations in thinking about reports:

1 Circulation and distribution
2 Physical layout
3 Numerical information
4 Visual aids
5 Language.

Circulation and distribution

All communications are a struggle for other people's interest and attention. The furniture in any busy man's office always includes a yawning wastepaper basket. If you have put this busy man on your circulation list for reasons of self-advertisement or because his name happened to be on a routine list, unedited for years, beware!

Before you begin to shape your report, please take the trouble to sort out the people whom it will help in their jobs. Nobody else should have it.

Many a report suffers from a false start. The managers who asked for it did not bother to discuss with the writer either the purpose of the report or the intended readership. Or the writer just said 'Yes' and ploughed on blindly into a document which did not meet the real requirements. Such a report will fail or at least have to be rewritten. Both the senior man and the writer contributed to the failure and caused the extra labour, the frustration, perhaps the anger ensuing from a job badly done.

So, before you write a syllable, establish who is going to use your report and what they have a right to expect from you. What is the purpose of the report from their point of view?

In many companies, the circulation is tacked on to the completed report as an afterthought. This deplorable custom should be opposed vigorously. Additions to the circulation list should be exceptional; better still, they should have been considered and meshed into the writer's reckoning from the start.

All this does not mean, however, that the facts should be coloured or slanted to affect the truth; no specialist worth his salt would wish to gain a point by distortion or trickery. His credibility would quickly disappear if he did, and rightly so.

Above all, your reader must find your report useful and the facts presented in such a way that he can absorb them easily and accurately. You cannot use suitable language, suitable layout or even select the material properly unless you know whom you are talking to and what he wants from the report. Consider your reader from the beginning. You cannot expect to do this unless you fix the circulation list at the outset. A report looks so forlorn in the wastepaper basket or even put aside – to be read 'later'. Do not plague people with reports they do not require for their own work. People have enough to do. All they want from you is help. Your useful reports will receive a welcome at the right time, at the right place and from the right man.

Physical layout

Your company has probably issued instructions on how its reports should be laid out. Such instructions were not written to while away an idle hour and it is the duty of every report writer to study them. The research department requires for its reports a different approach from the sales or public relations departments. Monsieur Ritz, the hotelier, made a fortune by following the precept 'the customer is always right'. The layout of a report depends almost entirely on how the readers like it. There are no rules, just a few principles. Your reader must be able to find his way about the report. If he is accustomed to a summary on the first page, that is where you put it. If he prefers all the graphs, tables, charts and detailed figures in appendices, put them there.

Reports should look as if they expect a welcome and want to be read. The ninety-third copy from a worn-out duplicator lacks inspiration and deserves neglect. The general appearance of a report must be appropriate to the contents and its purpose.

First appearance

The cover should immediately indicate the type of report that is inside: glossy for the chairman's annual report and other such public relations stuff; perhaps blue for research, green for personnel, or whatever the company's standard practice demands. The title and security classification must, obviously, be prominent before a page is turned.

The busy man's page

The first page must include the date of the report, the title, the author's name and that of the issuing authority and a reference/file number. Some readers also like a short circulation list on the title page – it is often useful to know who else has the report – and a very brief synopsis. This busy man's page should tell the busy man the object of the report and the reason why the work was done. It should give him a well-pruned summary of the investigation, the *main* results, the *main* conclusions and the *main* recommendations for action. He should get the guts of the report in fewer than 200 words, if possible on one page.

Any report longer than six pages should have a table of contents, clearly indicating where readers can find the special bits of the report that are all they intend to read. (Do not flatter yourself that everyone will read the whole of your tome.) Even avid readers will want to know where things are. A table of contents, reflecting a logical layout with clear, expressive headings, immediately creates an impression of order, thought and consideration.

So, you have already given your reader:

A cover that immediately tells him the style, title and security classification of the report.
A title page that tells who wrote it, when it was written, who authorized it and, sometimes, who else has the information.
A synopsis – the main elements of the report in a nutshell.
A table of contents that tells him where he can find all the details he wants.

Many of your readers, especially top management and laymen, will go no further into a report. They have all they need – a general appreciation of your work and enough information for discussion or appropriate action at their level. It is advisable to avoid technical language at this stage.

Your fellow specialists will now wish to dig into the report. They will expect an introduction which informs, or reminds, them of the circumstances which prompted your work. They will want to know how you set about your investigation, what methods, what tests, what equipment you used. They will expect a complete validation of your results and figures and to know what standards of accuracy you worked to. They will expect you to separate facts from opinions. The headlines for the main body of the work could read:

1   Introduction
2   Experimental details
3   Results
4   Discussion
5   Full summary
6   Recommendations
7   Appendices

This format cannot fit all circumstances and must be adjusted to suit the needs of your readers and the purpose of the report.

Please acknowledge the work of other people who have helped you, if only in a bibliography.

Information by numbers

Numbers form the backbone of most reports. Measurements of time, frequencies, distances, etc., are fundamental in presenting facts. Few readers need all the numbers; all readers need the significant numbers and wish them to be displayed significantly. Do not bury them or wall them up behind the background data. When you are planning your report, establish the vital numbers early on so that you can give them due prominence when writing.

Your reader will want to know your tolerances and to what degree of accuracy your figures are presented. Do not bother him with five decimal places if the approximate whole number will suffice for him. The main body of the report will flow more easily if the script is uncluttered by a mass of figures. Many thoughtful writers quote only those figures that make the point and then guide those people who may be interested in greater detail to an appendix which contains more complicated items such as mathematical formulae.

With numbers, significance is all – or nearly all.

Visual aids

If you were a sales director, how would you prefer to have the sales figures from May to October presented – as in (a), (b), (c) or (d) of Figure 62.3?

Sometimes readers would rather see the point than have it related to them. Please consider this.

GHM

(a)
The sales for May were 20 of type 1, 32 of type 2, 38 of type 3; for June, 28 of type 1, 30 of type 2, 36 of type 3; for July, 40 of type 1, 30 of type 2, 28 of type 3; for August, 26 of type 1, 18 of type 2, 28 of type 3; for September, 26 of type 1, 18 of type 2, 30 of type 3; and for October, 44 of type 1, 20 of type 2 and 28 of type 3

(b)

Sales figures for May to October

	Type 1	Type 2	Type 3
May	20	32	38
June	28	30	36
July	40	30	28
August	26	18	28
September	26	18	30
October	44	20	28

Figure 62.3 *Four ways of displaying a set of numerical results*
This shows how careful thought can result in a more effective display (see also pages 1180 and 1181)

Language in reports

'Tests showed that the handle gets too hot'

or:

'The results of a period of *ad hoc* experimentation supplemented by both statistical analysis and consideration of empirical factors thought to be universally viable in the context of the areas in which utilization could be expected to approach a maximum indicated that the thermal conductivity of that portion of the equipment designed for prehensile digital contact was such as to present a surface whose temperatures would markedly exceed the generally accepted threshold of sensory discomfort.'?

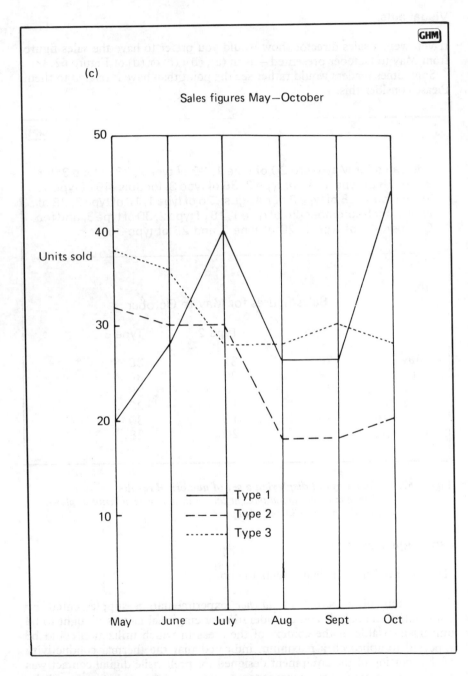

Figure 62.3 *(continued)*

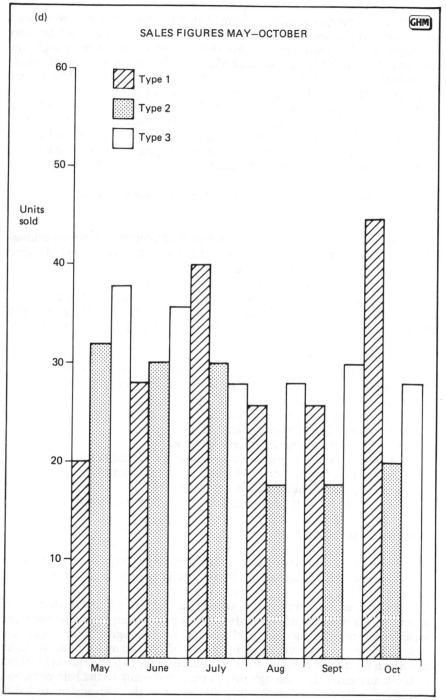

Figure 62.3   (concluded)

Why do so many technicians, trained in logic and precision, write such twaddle? Is it because they are suspicious of the arts, afraid that what they do might lose 'mystique' or it is that they cannot bother to bring logic and precision into their use of language? Many a brilliant young man, on reaching middle age, wonders what went wrong with his career. Let him re-read some of his reports. The answers could be found in them.

We have no space here to discuss grammar and the techniques of clear English, but you should learn a few basic points of control in your writing. You can then leave the rest to your genuine wish to help people to understand you. For instance, most readers will want to recognize, without much effort, two things about each of your sentences:

(*a*) The grammatical subject – whom or what you are talking of
(*b*) What happens – the action.

Let us look at (*a*) first. Concrete words such as 'polecat', 'sewing-machine', 'policeman' give your reader an exact image of what is in your mind. Abstract words and phrases leave room for doubt.

So prefer concrete words as subjects of your sentences.

Now (*b*). Your reader will readily understand the what-happens part of your sentence if you convey the action as simply as you can with power verbs, preferably active. Let us clarify this. Please examine these four sentences:

1   Oil lubricates bearings.
     The subject of the sentence, 'oil', is concrete, tangible, clear.
     The subject does the deed of the verb so the sentence is active.
2   Bearings are lubricated by oil.
     The subject, 'bearings', is concrete.
     The subject does not do the deed of the verb:
     it gets done to, so the sentence is passive.
3   The lubrication of bearings is carried out by the use of oil.
     The subject, 'lubrication of bearings', is an abstract phrase.
     The subject does not do the deed of the verb:
     it gets done to, so the sentence is both abstract and passive.

Structure 3 often leads to:

4   In so far as the process of lubrication with respect to bearings is concerned, this is carried out by the use of an application of oil.

Exaggerated as it is, sentence 4 shows the beginnings of the decay that attacks so many specialists from about the age of twenty-eight. In any large organization roughly one-third of the people over the age of twenty-eight are dead. They have accumulated sufficient cliché phrases and routine attitudes to lean on until their pensions turn up. There seems to be no reason for them to think any more. It is enough just to react according to the rule book and the jargon – 'We are in receipt of your favour of the 19th instant to hand,

and it must be pointed out that in view of the fact that . . .' 'The conceptual philosophy of commonality and standardization at this point in time could be said to have, perhaps, groundings in feasibility which, with the basic assumption that . . .' '. . . the viability of these parameters, shiftwise. . .'. All non-think stuff, torture for the reader and highly dangerous for the writer.

Danger? What danger? We live in a sea of words. What is wrong with drifting along in the fashionable waters, swallowing the stuff and regurgitating it into the faces of our fellows? Why not? It's easier than thinking.

What happens to a muscle that gets no exercise? It becomes flabby. What happens to a machine that lies idle for years? It becomes rusty and useless. What happens to a brain that does nothing but gather verbal cobwebs? Adult thinking is impossible without a language or some other set of symbols that label the elements we develop into thoughts. If words, for instance, are the bricks and mortar with which we build the wall of thought does it not follow that the sort of words we habitually use is the sort of thinker we are? Near-enough words, that'll-do words, other people's tired old clichés provide neither keep-fit exercise nor nourishment for an active mind. A factory girl whose eight-hour day consists of fitting component A into component B and endlessly repeating the dreary process to feed some production line would go mad if she thought about it very much. So she works mechanically and dreams of her boyfriend or being a duchess. But this will not do for expensively trained managers.

Technical language has the advantage of being clearly defined. Used properly, it assists constructive thought and communication among those who understand it. Abused, or flaunted because you want to imply that you are superior to people outside 'the club', it can cause trouble – for you as much as for your victims. The English language provides one of the most precise, subtle, flexible and vigorous aids to clear thought and effective reports. No manager can claim to be more than half-baked if he does not learn how to control it.

Report writing checklist

Before drafting a report ask yourself:

1 Have I insisted on a thorough briefing from whoever requested the report and discussed with him in detail: (a) that there is a need for the report, (b) the exact purpose of the report, (c) who is going to read the report, (d) the exact scope of the report?
2 Have I collected all the information I may need?
3 Have I selected from this the information the readers need?

When drafting a report, ask yourself:

1   Does the layout comply with any company standard and does it make things easy for the reader?
2   Is there a 'busy man's page' and does it contain the right information for him?
3   Does the report look good and can it be reproduced using the equipment available?
4   Is everybody who 'needs to know' on the circulation list?
5   Have I arranged for library copies and spare copies?
6   Is the circulation too wide?
7   Does the report need a security classification?
8   Have I used sufficient active verbs and concrete nouns?
9   Have I used short sentences and simple construction?
10 Are any technical or scientific words likely to be unknown to the readers?
11 Have I avoided padding and waffle-words?
12 Will the reader easily understand what I have written?
13 Have I avoided slant and bias?
14 Have I clearly stated conclusions and recommendations?
15 Have I used sufficient visual aids?
16 Are the visual aids in the right place, clearly labelled and cross-referenced?
17 Have I shown scales, dimensions and magnifications on my visual aids?
18 Are the tables and charts displayed in the best way?
19 Have I shown the units? Are units consistent and do they comply with British or other accepted standards?
20 Will the visual aids still be clear and easy to follow when reproduced by the available process?
21 Should I invite someone else to read the draft and discuss it with me?

A report is a working document that helps the other man to do his job. A manager who learns to write effective reports adds value to himself and his work.

MEETINGS

Believe it or not, some companies use up more cash at meetings than they spend on the raw materials with which they make their products. Much of this cash goes straight down the drain. Before you dismiss this thought as whimsical, consider the cost of meetings – air and rail fares, cars, hotel bills, salaries and expenses, conference and boardroom rents, rates, cleaning, postage of reports and other documents, typing and more money for many more items. Any large organization spends millions of pounds each year so that people can discuss, decide and, one hopes, energize some profitable action. The waste is colossal.

Money is important – only a fool would deny that – but much more important is human life. Ineffective meetings not only waste money but they also devalue people's time and shrink the people concerned with them. Human relationships can be soured by bad meetings. A wise man takes the trouble to find out how meetings work and how to make them work for him and his associates.

A definition of business meetings might be 'two or more people getting together for a specific business purpose'.

The meeting itself forms only one link in a chain of events. If the other links lack strength the meeting can become merely the place where the chain breaks. Ninety per cent of an effective meeting happens before the meeting starts. Forging the before-the-meeting link requires thought, horse-sense and skill. If you intend to call a meeting, be completely clear about its intended purpose. What specific business should the meeting achieve? Is it to decide on action, to brief people, to inform, to persuade? What in specific terms – no vague abstractions – is the business purpose of the meeting? You must then face what might be a deflating question: is a meeting necessary at all? Must you deprive people of their time and put the company to expense? Can the business be done – the decision made, for instance – in some other way – a few telephone calls or half a dozen letters? Why are you proposing to call the meeting?

So you decide that your meeting is a necessity; the business cannot be accomplished without a combination of other minds, interest and experience. Which people can provide you with such a combination? Nobody else should be invited. You want to get some business done. Avoid the hangers-on and the strange creatures who go to meetings just to get out of their own offices for a while. If your business is to get a decision and action, beware of the second-string man who cannot give a firm yes or no. He has to report back to his boss. Then there will have to be another meeting for his boss or even his boss's boss. Invite and accept only the people who can do the job properly. Do not forget, as so often happens, to invite the man who will have to take any action you decide upon. If your meeting decides to change the production line you cannot expect joyous cooperation from the production manager who was elsewhere when you decided how to run his department.

When and where the meeting takes place depends on the urgency of the business and the convenience of the people concerned. Be considerate about this. Merely the fact that you operate from Plymouth does not necessarily mean that your Glasgow and Ipswich colleagues will agree that your office is the perfect location. Must you start your meeting at 0900, which means an overnight trip for everyone except you? Timing, the date and the hour, can show you to be a thoughtful organizer.

If your colleagues have to examine reports, plans, figures or must equip themselves in other ways in preparation for the meeting, give them a fair chance to do so. Also make it clear to them precisely what the business of the meeting will be and that you expect them to come prepared. A meeting which has to be recalled because the relevant facts are missing reflects no credit on the convenor or the members. More meetings fail because the preparation has been neglected or skimped than for any other reason. No one should go to a meeting ill-prepared. Even if the meeting happens to be a quick get-together, and at short notice, a few minutes' thought beforehand will increase your value as a meeting-man. At least one man, you, will be able to talk sense.

The businesslike chairman will see to it that he or his secretary arranges a suitable conference room. He will indicate when the meeting is likely to finish; he will arrange breaks for the creature comforts of the conferers, and for telephone messages to be collected, outside the conference room – no interruptions will be allowed except for desperately urgent calls. He will plan an approximate timetable for the agenda so that timeworthy items get their due. Documents and, if required, suitable equipment for presentations must be available. Name cards help people to know who's who; make them bold and do have them spelled correctly. There are of course a hundred and one other details, any of which might be important. A meeting succeeds in direct ratio to its intelligent preparation.

The formal rules for running meetings become more important when the gathering is a large one. For most business meetings, formal rules matter little. It is the spirit in which people attend the meetings that produces a good or bad meeting.

No real progress can be made without agreement. The object of meetings is to produce agreement. Even if, after disagreement, action results because of fear or force of personality, the action will only be half-hearted and possibly poorly performed. The chairman of a meeting must always be striving for agreement, not surrender.

Preparation for the meeting

The chairman

The chairman must decide whether the meeting is really necessary (especially important with routine meetings which often occur even when there is nothing to be discussed or decided). He/she must also:

Decide on the purpose of the meeting

Decide on the subject or subjects

Decide on the place and time

Decide who is going to attend the meeting. Only those with something to contribute or who need to know exactly what was said and by whom should be present. Other people can get any necessary information from the minutes. The chairman should ensure that those attending are of sufficient standing, that they really represent their departments, and have the authority to commit them to action.

Decide on the agenda and roughly how much time to allow for each item. It is imperative that items are stated in concrete terms. Abstractions will inevitably result in rambling discussion that leads nowhere. One or two simple items first will get the meeting off to a good start. Even if the meeting is summoned hurriedly by telephone, members should be told what they are going to discuss. This is the agenda.

Study the subjects. The chairman must be sufficiently familiar with the subjects being discussed to be able to keep the discussion on the right lines.

Study the people attending. He must know the personal alignments that will help or hinder the meeting; who will not talk even though he has valuable contributions to make, and who will talk even though he has not.

The secretary

The secretary is responsible for all the mechanics of the meeting; he/she must obtain for the chairman any points for the agenda and names of those attending; suitable accommodation; arrange for paper, etc., arrange for refreshments to be available when the chairman wants them, and arrange to disconnect the telephone.

He/she must circulate the agenda in good time and must prepare all the papers the chairman may require.

Members

The members must:

Study the subjects to be discussed and, if necessary, departmental opinions and agreements.
Study the chairman and his idiosyncrasies.
Study the other members.
Work out how they are going to sell their ideas. (Refer back to Speaking for special occasions – case presentation.)

Conduct of the meeting

The chairman

The meeting must start on time, even if there are absentees. If the chairman is absent the next most suitable person should start for him. If the speaker on the first point is absent, switch the agenda.

Start briskly, laying down the purpose, the time available, and any other conditions that will help to control the meeting. A chairman cannot demand respect: he can only earn it – usually by giving it to others.

The chairman must watch the time. If he sees that he is getting behind time and wants to extend the meeting he must warn the members early, so that they can make any necessary arrangements to get a move on.

The chairman must keep feeding back to the members the state of the discussion, to ensure that everyone understands the situation. This is particularly important at the end of each item. This will also enable the secretary to set down an immediate, accurate record of the decisions reached, who is to take action and by what date, without any risk of error.

The chairman must try to be impartial and only produce his own opinions late in the discussion, if at all. Otherwise he will inhibit proper discussion.

The chairman may have to keep reminding members of the subject and aim in order to keep them to the point.

The chairman must ensure that everyone has the opportunity to express his opinion, at the same time preventing any individual from taking up an excessive amount of time. A member with very strong views that he is determined to express should be given his head, unopposed, the chairman, at least, giving all his attention to what is being said. The chairman should try to extract the relevant points from what may be a confused discourse and ensure that they are properly considered by the meeting.

The chairman must summarize, clarify and emphasize the action arising from the meeting, name specifically who is to be responsible for taking action and record who should do what in precise terms.

The meeting should finish at the stated times unless the members have agreed to go on late.

The chairman and the secretary should leave the room immediately after the meeting is over; otherwise another meeting might ensue.

The members

A member must disagree without being disagreeable. A member must be clear in his mind what points he wants to get across and do it with the aim of convincing the other members that he is right. At the same time, he should have a sufficiently open mind to be able to change his opinion if someone else produces better arguments or ideas.

Avoid distracting personalities.

The secretary

During the meeting the secretary must take copious notes unless he/she can be sure that the chairman will provide minutes as the meeting goes along. It is therefore impracticable for a member to act as secretary and do both jobs adequately.

Chairmanship – reminders

Before

Ensure that there is a clear, worthwhile purpose.
Check who will be attending.
Check on the points to be discussed.
Ensure that the secretary has organized everything.

During

Introduce the meeting and purpose.
Define the limits of the subject and time available.
Control the members. Ensure that all have a fair say and none dominate.
Keep the meeting to the point. Be quick to spot when people are wandering.
Feed back. Ensure that everyone is keeping up with discussions and understands the points that are coming out of the discussions.
Summing-up. Make sure that everyone knows the conclusions reached and especially who is to take action. Be impartial. Earn respect.

After the meeting

As quickly as possible after the meeting the secretary should write up the minutes, either for rapid circulation or to go on the files. The minutes should be kept as short as is practicable.

The essential parts of the minutes are the decisions, agreed action and who is to take it and when. These must stand out.

At an appropriate time after the meeting someone, probably the secretary, should check that members are getting on with action they undertook or were instructed to take.

The chairman must have at the front of his mind all the time, and occasionally remind members, that the object of the meeting is to benefit the whole organization and not any section or individual. He should strive to ensure that profitable action will result from the meeting.

Anybody can talk, anybody can write, anybody can hold a meeting, but only he who can also obtain the desired responses ranks as a good communicator. A computer memory and its processing unit contain great quantities of facts; but the computer is simply a speedy automaton, subject to its program. The human memory and its processing unit contain facts, experiences, feelings, prejudices, social attitudes, business needs, expediency, cussedness, warmth, love, hatred and the breath of God.

Programming a computer to obtain a useful print-out – the response – demands skill and knowledge. How much more demanding is the need for a manager to acquire the knowledge and the skills for better human relationships. At least you can make a start by speaking more effectively, writing reports that help and by making your meetings successful.

FURTHER READING

Bell, Gordon, *The Secrets of Successful Speaking and Business Presentations*, Heinemann, London, 1987

Eyre, E.C., *Effective Communication Made Simple*, W.H. Allen, London, 1979

Jay, Antony, *Effective Presentation: the Communication of Ideas by Words and Visual Aids*, Management Publications Ltd, London, 1970

Scott, Bill, *The Skills of Communicating*, Gower, Aldershot, 1986

Wells, Gordon, *How to Communicate*, McGraw-Hill, Maidenhead, 1978

Williams, Beryl, *Communicating Effectively: A Manager's Guide to Getting Through to People*, Thorsons, Wellingborough, 1977

63 Executive health

Dr Andrew Melhuish

There are two things to aim at in life; first to get what you want and after that to enjoy it. Only the wisest of mankind achieve the second.

Logan Pearson Smith

The objective of this chapter is to encourage executives to look at their lifestyles: to discover if there are ways in which they can enjoy life more and remain well longer.

THE BENEFITS AND HAZARDS OF EXECUTIVE LIFE

First let us look at executives in general. Is there scope for improvement? The answer, coming from modern research, is a firm yes. Executives enjoy good health compared with the population in general but are equally prone to heart disease. They certainly could improve their health and happiness. Second, and most important, can you yourself improve? Consider your present lifestyle. Do you whole-heartedly enjoy work; or are there times when it is too demanding, too time-consuming – or boring? Do you have time to enjoy the expensive home and holidays you earn by your hard responsible work? Do you have enough time with your wife and children? Even more important, would they agree? If you have the balance right, well done! I fear you are in a minority. Unfortunately most executives can manage with expertise their complex jobs, but fail to manage effectively the apparently more simple balance of work and home life and the maintenance of their own bodies.

The reasons for this are many. There will always be a high demand on the successful executive's time at work, creating pressures on his time at home. His success is usually due to his commitment, independence and drive at work; and these qualities can lead him to neglect or under-rate his own health and happiness. Many managers would die rather than admit they are exhausted, unable to cope, unfit. Some do! Executives are usually well trained to do their job; it is rare for them to be trained to manage their own lives.

In order to manage his body and his life successfully the executive needs to know the particular challenges he faces from his executive lifestyle. Then with sufficient motivation, he can use this knowledge to devise strategies to modify his lifestyle and improve his health. Before proceeding further, it may well be helpful for the reader to list his own satisfactions at work and the pressures which go with them. Each executive has his own unique lifestyle with its own rewards and problems. Awareness of these will help him to review the balance of his life.

Some benefits of executive life

1 *Job satisfaction*. Most executives are involved in challenging and, usually, interesting jobs.
2 *High financial rewards*. These benefit the manager and his family.
3 *Autonomy*. Most executives exercise some degree of control over their working hours, work content and working conditions.

Risk factors to be weighed against benefits

The demands of the job

Much is known about the problems faced by executives at work. Cary Cooper's book *Coping with Stress* summarizes these well. My own experience is that most executives can produce high quality work; their main problem is that they do not have enough time to achieve this high quality. The more senior they become, the greater the responsibility they have, the more they must come to terms with deadlines and priorities. There is very real conflict between high standards and expediency.

Interpersonal relationships also create much pressure; dealing with people is so much more difficult than dealing with things, and the more senior the executive becomes the less the support he can expect from his colleagues at work. It is lonely at or near the top. The relationship which has a great effect on most executives however is with his 'boss', but colleagues and staff can be equally demanding.

Work load can also be a problem. To complete his work satisfactorily the manager may spend long hours at work, returning home late. Worse, however, is the automatic assumption in most firms that the executive's work does not stop when he leaves the office. The bulging briefcase is the obvious sign of the pressure he faces: work to be completed during the evening, during the weekend and even during his holidays, that is, if he feels able to take his full allocation of holiday entitlement.

Finally, concerns about his career structure together with the politics and infighting associated with high position and authority can create great pressures.

Sedentary nature of the job

Most executives work behind a desk and move around very little during the working day. The more senior they become, the less they move; staff and colleagues come to them, they park close to the office and they may not even have to walk to lunch. Executives tend to be concentrated in big cities so, if they choose to set up home outside the city limits, they must travel to and from the office by car or train. This is sedentary, unhealthy and takes valuable time. When the executive reaches home his ability to take exercise as relaxation or enjoyment will be reduced by his long hours at work and the extra work he may take home. Executives spend many hours flying. Air travel is a particularly striking example of remaining sedentary for long periods. Few British companies provide good exercise facilities at the office or encourage organized activity breaks during the day – unlike their Japanese, Russian or North American counterparts. It is difficult for most British executives to get enough physical exercise.

Entertainment as part of the job

The entertainment of customers is a necessary part of many executives' jobs. Important customers expect to be well entertained, and it is difficult to entertain well without drinking or smoking too much. Entertainment at lunchtime will affect work performance later in the day while entertainment in the evening can lead to neglect of home life. Expectations about entertaining are changing: successful firms, such as IBM, ban alcohol during the working day, and most German executives bargain over a frugal healthy lunch. But the mushrooming hospitality tents at Ascot, Wimbledon and Henley show how many British executives enjoy the fruits of their labours.

Insecurity of executive employment

Unemployment in Britain has increased over the last ten years and executives are in no way immune from it. Estimates of redundancy in executives vary, but all figures are unacceptably high for, if an executive should lose his job, he and his family are at high risk and they have high expectations from life. High mortgages are encouraged by the British tax system and private schooling is expensive. Loss of his job can be a total disaster for the executive – both to his morale and to his ability to support his family in the way to which they are accustomed.

Relocation as a way of life

In many companies executives move regularly; it is a necessary part of a successful career structure. Relocation is a great pressure on the executive and, increasingly, on his family. More than 60 per cent of wives in Britain now work regularly. For them, finding new employment in a new locality may be difficult. Children need stability to benefit from their education. Job uncertainty can only make relocation even more frequent and stressful, for the executive must prove himself in a new company in addition to moving location. As discussed later, change is a major cause of executive stress. There is no greater change for an executive than relocation.

THE HEALTH OF EXECUTIVES IN GENERAL

This long list of pressures and short list of benefits might suggest that many executives are unhappy or unwell. This is quite untrue. In the league tables rating job satisfaction and health the British executive does remarkably well. In terms of mortality – when we die – and morbidity – how well we live – executives compare favourably with the general population. The most recent health census showed that, as members of social class 1, they are about 40 per cent less likely to die between 35 and 65 than the lowest social class, class 5. Sickness absenteeism shows an even more dramatic difference in favour of social class 1. The death rate in the group of managers being researched by Professor Cary Cooper and myself is at present about 10 per cent of that predicted for the population in general.

The two most important factors contributing to this good health are:

1 *Job satisfaction*
   In a *Which* survey of job satisfaction in 1977, executives were high in the league of those satisfied with their jobs. The report on this survey noted that high job satisfaction correlated well with a high level of control over how the job was done.
2 *Habits*
   In general, executives share with other members of social class 1 much better habits than the other social classes. The most dramatic change in habits over the last ten years has been in cigarette smoking, with social class 1 reducing from about 60 per cent smokers to as few as 20 per cent today. Over the same period, social class 5 actually increased from 60 per cent to 65 per cent. Eating habits and exercise also strongly favour social class 1. It is only in terms of alcohol problems that social class 1 fares badly, the risk of alcoholism being highest in this class.

Current health patterns

Although the executive is less at risk than most other workers, his health will still be influenced by the prevailing pattern of illness in Britain. This has changed dramatically during this century as Western civilization has evolved. Eighty years ago, more than 90 per cent of men dying between 35 and 65 did so due to infection or malnutrition. Today the most important causes of death in this age group are the two 'modern killers': coronary heart disease and lung cancer.

The emergence of these 'modern killers' reflects the variety of the spirits released from the Pandora's box of modern Western civilization. Good living conditions and advances in medical care have wiped out malnutrition and greatly reduced infection. At the same time the abundance of pleasures – smoking, eating and drinking – and the freedom to indulge them, often to excess, have led to the dramatic rise in heart disease and lung cancer. Too many cigarettes contribute to lung cancer; excess food, cigarettes and alcohol are important risk factors for heart disease.

Once established, coronary heart disease and cancer are dangerous and destructive. But much can be done to prevent them, The occurrence of coronary heart disease in young people can be dramatically reduced by simple changes in diet and cigarette smoking. Lung cancer would be a fairly uncommon illness if no-one smoked. Finland has long been known to have the highest rates of heart disease in Europe. In the late 1970s The Karelia programme offered to a selected group of Finns regular health screening along with practical advice on diet and stopping smoking. It nearly halved the occurrence of heart attacks in this group. In America, the increased awareness of the importance of weight reduction, diet and cigarette smoking has resulted in a significant fall in heart disease in the last ten years.

Executives share equally with the general population the increased risk of coronary heart disease. Sensible modification of their lifestyle will reduce this risk. Indeed, they stand to benefit even more than other workers for there is convincing evidence to implicate their particular lifestyle as contributing to coronary heart disease.

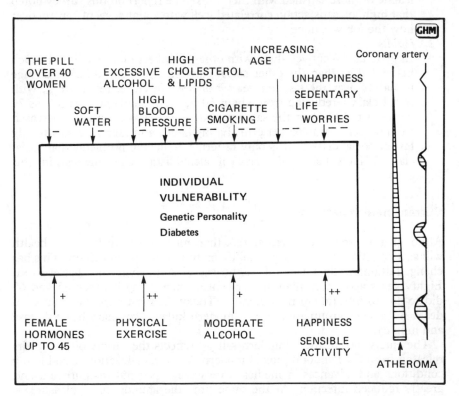

Figure 63.1 Summary of factors known to influence the onset of coronary heart disease

Figure 63.1 summarizes the factors known to influence the onset of coronary heart disease. Coronary heart disease is the result of clogging up of the arteries supplying the heart itself – the coronary arteries – by atheroma. Blood flow to parts of the heart can be reduced (causing angina) or fully blocked (a heart attack or coronary thrombosis).

Atheroma is a fatty deposit containing cholesterol and other fatty materials. The formation of atheroma is clearly associated with cigarette smoking, so the executive who uses cigarettes to help him to cope with his working pressures is at risk in this way. Raised blood pressure is also an important factor in increasing the risk of heart disease. Success in executive life is often related to the ability of the manager to control and to hide his emotions. He learns to carry on calmly; but at what cost to his system? It is probably no coincidence that the Italians, who enjoy expressing their emotions, are relatively free from heart disease. But probably the greatest risk to the executive lies in the combination of his hard-working responsible job and the lack of exercise that goes with it. To understand this better we need to look briefly at the natural response to stress or challenge. This will show that it can now be inappropriate, and so a danger, to the modern executive's lifestyle.

The stress response

Inert matter and living organisms respond to increased challenge or stress by improved performance. But the pattern of this response is different. Figure

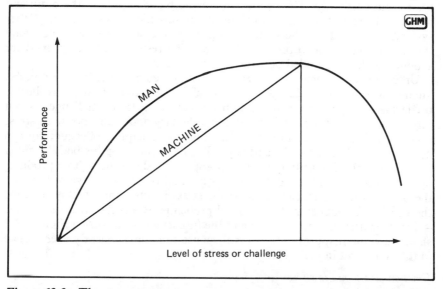

Figure 63.2 **The stress response**
> *For a machine or an inert material, the response to increasing stress is gradually improved performance, up to a point where breakdown suddenly occurs. The human response to stress is more rapid initially, with the eventual collapse less easy to predict owing to the complexity of mind and body*

63.2 shows how the physical response of inert matter is entirely predictable, performance increasing steadily to a maximum beyond which the system is destroyed. Physiological response, from living organisms, be they animal or man, is quite different. At low to moderate levels of pressure the response is dramatic, with small increases in pressure resulting in much improved performance. Then, as the levels of pressure become higher, the response falls steadily away. Finally, the organism will fall apart, like the machine. The time of such collapse is not predictable, however, because the organism is complex, with a mind and body of its own.

The practical applications for man are obvious. Very little challenge or stress (boredom) produces poor performance. Too much stress (overload, burn-out) destroys. In between, there is the area where stress enhances performance, improves life. Stress cannot be avoided; it must be kept at a manageable level. Executives, through their natures and their jobs, will be at risk from too much stress. So it is important to know how excessive stress can harm – and what clues can be detected to warn that it is becoming excessive. The answer lies in the physical and emotional response to stress.

Physical response to stress

Faced by challenge, animals and man respond in the same well known, scientifically proven, way – the 'fight or flight response'. Figure 63.3 shows how the organism is helped to survive. The message comes from the brain and is mediated through the adrenal glands which produce adrenalin and the steroid hormones. The result is increased blood supply to the brain and muscles. The heart and lungs work harder to provide this extra blood. Other systems lose blood. At the same time, glucose and small fat molecules flood into the bloodstream to provide the fuel. The result is a body primed for action, the choke is pulled out, the booster let in.

Unfortunately, a new type of animal has evolved over the last forty years, 'homo executus'. He faces just as many challenges and pressures as did his predecessors – perhaps more; but his response to these challenges is not physical; it is emotional. His habitat is sedentary and his response to stress is controlled. He cannot hit his difficult boss or unhelpful colleague; nor can he run away. He must smile and cope. But he cannot stop his body priming itself for the physical activity it feels appropriate and it is the unused products of that priming – the raised blood pressure and pulse, the surge of fats into the bloodstream which can harm. If the stress is acute and quickly resolved the benefits far outweigh the potential problems. But if the stress is chronic – if work is frustrating, unhappy and the future uncertain – then Figure 63.3 shows how the inappropriate stress response can damage nearly every organ in the body, and in particular the heart.

Emotional response to stress

The natural emotional response of the body to stress or challenge is a powerful adrenalin-induced stimulation. Concentration is high, reflexes are quick. The mood is serious. Sleep or relaxation are impossible. Faced by a crisis this stimulation is beneficial; a difficult job can be completed more quickly

	Normal (relaxed)	Under pressure	Acute pressure	Chronic pressure (stress)
Brain	Blood supply normal	Blood supply up	Thinks more clearly	Headaches and migraines, tremors and nervous tics
Mood	Happy	Serious	Increased concentration	Anxiety, loss of sense of humour
Saliva	Normal	Reduced	Reduced	Dry mouth, lump in throat
Muscles	Blood supply normal	Blood supply up	Improved performance	Muscular tension and pain
Heart	Normal rate and Blood Pressure	Increased rate and Blood P	Improved performance	Hypertension and chest pain
Lungs	Normal respiration	Increased respiration rate	Improved performance	Coughs and asthma
Stomach	Normal blood supply and acid secretion	Reduced blood supply Increased acid secretion	Reduced blood supply reduces digestion	Ulcers due to heartburn and indigestion
Bowels	Normal blood supply and bowel activity	Reduced blood supply Increased bowel activity	Reduced blood supply reduces digestion	Abdominal pain and diarrhoea
Bladder	Normal	Frequent urination	Frequent urination due to increased nervous stimulation	Frequent urination, prostatic symptoms
Sexual organs	(M) Normal (F) Normal periods, etc.	(M) Impotence (decreased blood supply) (F) Irregular periods	Decreased blood supply	(M) Impotence (F) Menstrual disorders
Skin	Healthy	Decreased blood supply, dry skin	Decreased blood supply	Dryness and rashes
Biochemistry	Normal: oxygen consumed, glucose and fats liberated	Oxygen consumption is up. Glucose and fat consumption is up	More energy immediately available	Rapid tiredness

Figure 63.3 Effects of stress on bodily functions

and efficiently. The loss of relaxation and sleep does not matter. As with the physical response, problems will only arise if the stress response continues for too long. Unfortunately, for many executives it does; adrenalin-induced stimulation seems to become an addiction in just the same way as can alcohol or heroin. As so many addicts cannot stop gambling, so the executive cannot stop working under intense pressure. If he finishes the job in hand he will find another to maintain the pressure.

Many executives can cope with this lifestyle and do so happily. But there are several disadvantages to it. One is that the ability to work long hours and the inability to relax at the end of that work easily create pressures at home. A second is that such dependence on work for satisfaction leaves the executive desperately at risk when he cannot work. Twenty years ago this problem was postponed until retirement. In 1968 superannuation figures from a large British firm showed that 65 per cent of their senior executives, who retired at 65, died during the next year. Early retirement has taken away this particular risk: usually the executive can decide when to retire and most of those taking early retirement remain reasonably well. Early retirement seems the silver lining to the cloud of redundancy, evidence that there is worthwhile life after work. Unwanted redundancy has replaced retirement as the medical hazard.

In general, the executive fares well in terms of mental health compared with other workers. But mental illness, particularly anxiety and depression, is common; and executives are not exempt. Some executives, such as those involved in research, may be vulnerable by virtue of their brilliance. There is a real association between genius and mental instability. Others may be put at risk by the increasing pressure of competition at work or the dual career family at home. Few women now see their role in life as the passive supporter of a successful husband. So the support of a solid stable home base for a successful career is fast becoming an illusion. Our research at Henley has already identified lack of social support as an indication of risk for mental illness and breakdown.

HELPING OURSELVES TO BETTER HEALTH

Happiness and good health are the two objectives that executives should be seeking to achieve. Happiness for ourselves and for our families is the most important. Health is part of this happiness – but only a part.

Figure 63.4 shows diagramatically the complex factors which determine our health and happiness. Each of us floats in a sea of life. Whether we float or sink in the sea depends on our response to the many factors affecting us. How we respond is governed physically by our bodies and emotionally by our minds or personalities. Each of us is unique, with different bodies and different personalities, the products of nature and nurture, heredity and environment. Therefore our responses cannot be predicted. There can be no precise rule as to what makes us buoyant, giving good health and happiness, in just the same way as there is no precise rule as to what makes a good executive. But there are many guidelines, which will help most executives to live well, just as there are management procedures which will help most executives to manage well.

The factors affecting us divide easily into two areas: what we do to our bodies and what our environment – work and home – does to us. What we do to our bodies, body maintenance, is mainly determined by our habits. These are difficult to change, as Mark Twain said. But they are, at least, within our control. Our environment is not. There will be good times, when we are doing well at work and our families and friends are happy and supportive. There will also be bad times when work is uncertain and when illness or unhappiness affects our support systems. It is during these bad times that we need to be most buoyant, when we need a healthy body to help us to cope. Figure 63.4 also summarizes the medical concept of being under stress. Stress or pressure is part of every executive's life. On the whole he enjoys the challenge it provides and he is rewarded well because he copes well with stress. He becomes under stress when he fails to cope well, when he is sinking in his own sea. Many circumstances may contribute: excessive pressures at the time, poor support, poor body fitness, vulnerable personality are some examples. The downward trend can be reversed by reducing the pressures or increasing the support – provided that no irreversible physical

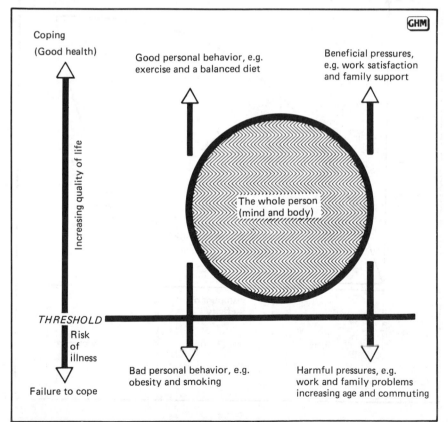

Figure 63.4   Habits, environment and health

or mental damage to the individual has occurred while he is down.

What practical advice can be given to executives to help them to remain buoyant and so able to resist stress? The one word which best describes how to live well is 'moderation'. It was inscribed on the walls of the temple at Delphi to guide the Greeks. George Bernard Shaw wrote 'If you give up everything you like you can live to be a hundred, or at any rate it will seem like it!'

Figure 63.5 shows the body's response to stress in terms of performance and adds a second response – the harmful effects of stress on the body. These are minimal at low levels of stress, but increase greatly when stress levels become high. The gap between benefit and harm determines the net effect that stress has on the body: the gap is greatest at low stress levels.

Let us now apply this concept to the executive's lifestyle, looking first at

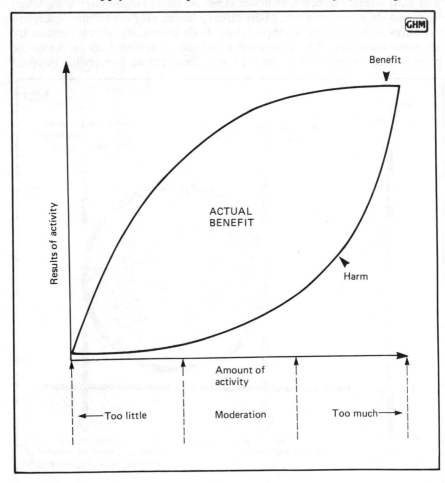

Figure 63.5   The 'Rugby ball'

the way he manages his body and then at the way he manages his work and family environment.

Smoking

Smoking has its benefits. Why else would the majority of British have smoked cigarettes throughout the last war? Emotionally it stimulates but at the same time provides relaxation. Medically it reduces the weight. Unfortunately it became apparent to medical researchers in America and Britain soon after the war that smokers became ill and died earlier than non-smokers. Their studies confirmed the high medical risk of cigarette smoking in terms of coronary heart disease and lung cancer – and subsequent research has confirmed this important association.

Doctors are convinced that the medical risks of cigarette smoking are so high that the accepted advantages of the habit cannot even start to tip the balance towards its support. The medical lobby against smoking grows stronger and at least on this occasion, doctors have practised what they preach as only 15 per cent of the profession in Britain now smoke. The dangers of smoking cigarettes are real, very unpleasant and proven.

These strictures only apply to cigarette smoking in excess. Unfortunately, excess is more than 8 – 10 cigarettes daily, and few smokers can stick at this level. The smoker, smoking 20 cigarettes per day who gives up at 35 should also be safe. Even better, the older smoker, providing no irreversible disease is present, will have removed the extra risk factor within 3 years of stopping smoking.

The dangers of smoking apply less to cigars and very little to pipes. The executive who badly needs to reduce tension should therefore stick to his pipe – empty if possible! The cigar smoked after dinner on occasions provides pleasure and quality of life – with no medical penalty. Filters sadly do not significantly reduce the risk of cigarette smoking; they reduce the risk of lung cancer but not the more important risk of heart disease.

There are many ways to stop smoking. Success needs careful planning so that motivation can be maintained during the period when smoking is stopped, and afterwards when temptation must be avoided. Acupuncture, hypnosis, aversion therapy can all help. Family doctors will be encouraging and can suggest therapeutic support such as nicotine chewing gum.

Alcohol

The cigarette smoker puts himself at risk. He can be considered a social nuisance and passive smoking does provide a small medical risk to others. But he is not an addict in the medical sense of the word. He does not need more and more of the drug to achieve the same results nor does he get the real addict's withdrawal symptoms. Nor does tobacco demean, degrade or destroy. Alcohol does all these; alcohol represents total destruction to the executive who becomes addicted to it, who becomes an alcoholic. Not only is he destroyed; so too are his family and his colleagues – and even those he has never seen, but may hurt with his inadequately controlled car. Despite this, public opinion is more agressive towards tobacco smoking than towards alcohol. The reason probably lies in the social acceptability of alcohol; the fact that most of us drink moderately and enjoy it, doctors more than most. It is difficult to condemn others for what we condone ourselves.

Yet condemn them we must, and help them too. Alcoholism is a significant problem of British executives. Not just the British, of course, for in France and Belgium, behind the Iron Curtain and in the USA, alcoholism is even more common. The number of alcoholics in the population is always under-estimated. At a national level this may reflect the government's need for revenue. A *British Medical Journal* leader in 1986 stated 'The government is far more addicted to alcohol than any individual alcoholic'. At a company level, it is because the alcoholic dissembles and hides; since he can fool himself that he does not have a problem, it is not surprising that he can fool other people.

Here are a few observations about this very important problem:

1   Although difficult to estimate, most informed sources agree that in Britain 6 – 7 per cent of executives (1 in 15) have an alcohol problem
2   Women executives can drink only one half the amount of alcohol drunk by their male colleagues without risk of damaging their brains or livers
3   Figure 63.6 shows the daily consumption of alcohol above which most doctors agree that the person is at high risk from alcoholism.
4   Half this daily consumption – 4 units – taken over 2–3 hours with an average meal will produce a blood level of approximately 80mg of alcohol in every 100ml of blood. This is the upper legal level for driving in Britain. Above this level, heavy fines and long periods of disqualification from driving are common. For many executives: 'there but for fortune. . .'
5   Increased alcohol consumption is a common symptom of stress. It impairs performance by anaesthetizing the brain and by diverting its blood supply. Work suffers, stress increases; another vicious circle is started.
6   The alcoholic can be recognized by his impaired performance, particularly when associated with irritability or absence from the office after lunch
7   If you suspect that colleagues or staff have an alcohol problem, face them with it at once and insist they seek medical help. Unless treated early, the alcoholic's hopes of recovery are small. Treated early, he can resume a totally normal life.

Eating

Another way we reduce stress is to put food into our mouths. Unless this input is balanced by considerable physical activity or unless the individual is blessed with a high metabolic rate and so burns off excess fat, the result will be weight gain or obesity. Executives often entertain, so naturally they are at risk from weight gain.

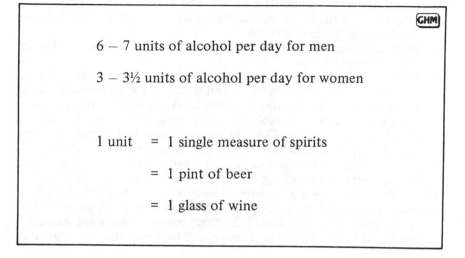

6 – 7 units of alcohol per day for men

3 – 3½ units of alcohol per day for women

1 unit   = 1 single measure of spirits

       = 1 pint of beer

       = 1 glass of wine

Figure 63.6   Maximum safe level of alcohol consumption

Luckily, obesity is not too serious a health risk for young people. It does not increase the risk of cancer and in itself is not a risk factor for heart disease. But it can raise the blood pressure and the blood fats, both of which are risk factors for heart disease. The overweight executive will feel better slimmer and he should have his blood pressure and blood fats checked regularly. Current medical opinion recommends bran, dislikes animal fats and encourages moderation. It does not support drastic diets: just sensible care and good variety of food. Michael Spira's book (see Further Reading) has many good tips on losing weight. Learning to leave food is perhaps the most important. Most British people are programmed to destroy all food put in front of them. However, Figure 63.5 showed that we get most pleasure at the moderate level. So try to leave any food you are not enjoying and encourage the cook to serve small helpings.

Exercise

Unfortunately a lot of exercise is needed to burn off excess food. Luckily exercise has many other advantages. Indeed, as was explained earlier, it is the sedentary lifestyle of the executive which helps to put him at risk from heart disease and sensible moderate exercise is the obvious answer.

The key word is moderate. With excess exercise comes an increasing risk of injury or illness and little medical benefit. Executives must not muddle athletic fitness with medical fitness. Athletic fitness means exhausting training, means marathons. Medical fitness means keeping the body sensibly fit and this can easily be achieved by two or three 10 to 15 minutes sessions of jogging or Canadian Air Force exercises weekly. Here are some suggestions:

1   If you are unfit, start exercise gently. This is the high risk period. Kit yourself out well. Warm up for 5 minutes before exercise; it helps to avoid muscle and joint damage
2   Swimming, jogging, badminton and tennis provide appropriate, healthy exercise for executives
3   Squash and team sports such as rugby are less warmly recommended as they are vigorous and competitive and so can encourage the competitive executive to excess. Squash, however, is often a very appropriate exercise for executives – enjoyable and not too time-consuming. As a rule of thumb executives under 40 are fit to play squash if they play regularly once weekly. Above 40 they need to play twice weekly to keep fit.
4   Exercise need not be vigorous or with a ball. Climbing stairs and brisk walking during the working day or at airports carry great benefits.
5   Ideally exercise should be taken during or at the end of the working day – to burn off the unused fuel generated during the stressful day. But expediency is important. It is often easier to make time for exercise early in the morning and such exercise is far better than no exercise at all.

Sleep

The benefits which can be obtained from sleep also follow the slope of the benefit curve in Figure 63.5. Maximum benefit comes in the first 3–4 hours. After 7–8 hours there is little benefit. We all have an optimum period of sleep and usually know it. It varies from 6 to 8 hours. One hour in the afternoon can balance 2–3 hours lost in the night. Thus a late night can be made more enjoyable by an hour's rest the afternoon before, and its bad effects reversed by an hour's sleep the next afternoon.

Under stress, the executive may buy time for extra work by missing sleep. He may get away with it for some time but chronic lack of sleep will affect performance and may cause sudden collapse.

Sex

Until the last two years it would have taken a brave doctor to quantify what is moderate in sex. The advent of AIDS and the increase in venereal disease, both usually the result of excessive indiscriminate sex, have changed this. Between couples frequency of sex is a question of mutual agreement. Certainly there is no medical risk attached to sex. Quite the reverse – it provides happy healthy exercise and enhances relationships. The only recent medical input relates to faithfulness. Two studies, one in Japan and the other in France revealed identical results; heart attacks during sex were very rare – but twice as common in 'away matches'. You can live a double life, but only for half as long!

A real problem for executives is the effect of their busy lives on their sexual drive. Partners usually interpret lack of performance as lack of interest and care. Another dangerous vicious circle may result.

Relaxation

For most executives life is hectic and every minute full. How to get everything done is their main concern. Relaxation is the natural antidote to all this hustle. Medical evidence supporting relaxation is mounting. It is now accepted that relaxation reduces blood pressure, pulse rate and blood fats – all risk factors for heart disease.

Relaxation can be achieved in two ways. The first is to carry out any activity which distracts the mind from work. A happy home life, religious activity, gardening, sport, hobbies; all of these are good forms of relaxation. The second form of relaxation is through a formal discipline such as yoga, transcendental meditation or autogenics. Sessions can be once daily for up to half-an-hour or for short periods during the day. Hubert Benson writes well about relaxation and has done much to demonstrate its value (see Further Reading).

Regular medical checks

The Americans probably have excessive medical checks – many cannot believe they are well until told so by their doctor. The British certainly have too few. When their relative value is compared it does seem remarkable that so many companies should service their cars and yet fail to 'service' their executives.

Regular medical checks take many forms and are usually recommended more often as the executive grows older. Ideally, a straightforward annual check is recommended. This should include weight and blood pressure recordings, together with a careful discussion of the executive's lifestyle. Every 2–4 years a more thorough medical with blood screening and testing and exercise cardiograms is valuable.

One reason for the lack of medical checks in Britain is that the National Health Service cannot finance this luxury. Most GPs will carry out the simple annual check-up for NHS patients and the full checks can be arranged through the BUPA and PPP centres.

Air travel

Air travel for the executive soon loses its glamour. It is a frustrating and tiring business which can take up far too much of his time and energy. It is also a risk factor to his health – during flights he is even more sedentary than in his office, even more at risk to the temptations of excess alcohol and food. Some simple hints are:

1. Book in early and take a vigorous walk before the flight starts
2. Avoid alcohol completely whilst flying; spirits in particular actually cause dehydration by pushing fluid out from the body
3. Drink as much fluid as possible; ideally so that you need to walk to the toilet once an hour

4 When not drinking fluid, sleep; it is the best way to arrive fresh at your destination
5 Travel first-class when possible; it makes a tremendous difference to your comfort and health at the end of the trip.

THE WORK AND HOME ENVIRONMENTS

However well the executive looks after his body, his health ultimately will be determined by his happiness at work and at home. At work the fit between his personality and his job control the satisfaction that he achieves. His happiness at home will be influenced most by his choice of partner, and by their ability to discuss honestly their feelings about having a family. The more successful the executive is at work the more time he will want, or be asked, to spend there. The happier he is at home the more he will want to be there. In the end his happiness and that of his family will depend on his awareness of these conflicts and his ability to resolve them as well as he can.

Ten years ago I asked a large group of executives – 30–40-year-olds attending courses at Henley Management College – to look back over their managerial life and identify the source of their greatest stress so far. Sixty per cent identified this stress as coming from their family lives; 40 per cent from their work. This conclusion has been confirmed by a much more detailed and ambitious study in America by Holmes and Rahe. They set out to explore the concept that stress could cause illness. They chose to work with managers and they based their study on the idea that stability is safe and healthy. Stress, they argued, came from change.

A large number of American managers was asked to list the main changes that could affect their lives and then to rate their importance in comparison with the greatest change they could meet – death of a spouse. Figure 63.7 shows the resultant ratings. The scores from the changes were added together every 6 to 12 months to quantify the amount of stress. Figure 63.8 shows a typical result; mental and physical illness occurring at times of high change scoring – providing scientific support for the version of 'Sod's Law' which states 'You get ill when you can't afford to'. In fact illness came in the days or weeks after the change. The stress response boosts performance and at the same time discourages illness. It is during the flat time after the stressful period that we can become ill; or when stress goes on and on. The results seemed to confirm Holmes and Rahe's suggestion that change causes illness. There are two important applications of this concept:

The additive nature of stress

Life change units are relative, not absolute. A high life change score does not mean that someone will become ill; just that they are more likely to. However, study of the table does show that several small changes in a short period can produce a much higher score than one big change. While surprising, this conclusion does seem to be borne out by what we see in

Rank	Life event	Mean value
1	Death of spouse	100
2	Divorce	73
3	Marital separation	65
4	Jail term	63
5	Death of a close family member	63
6	Personal injury or illness	53
7	Marriage	50
8	Fired at work	47
9	Marital reconciliation	45
10	Retirement	45
11	Change in health of family member	44
12	Pregnancy	40
13	Sex difficulties	39
14	Gain of a new family member	39
15	Business readjustment	39
16	Change in financial state	38
17	Death of a close friend	37
18	Change to a different line of work	36
19	Change in number of arguments with spouse	35
20	High mortgage	31
21	Foreclosure of mortgage or loan	30
22	Change in responsibilities at work	29
23	Son or daughter leaving home	29
24	Trouble with in-laws	29
25	Outstanding personal achievement	28
26	Spouse begins or stops work	26
27	Children move to new school	26
28	Change in living conditions	25
29	Revision of personal habits	24
30	Trouble with boss	23
31	Change in work hours or conditions	20
32	Change in residence	20
33	Change in schools	20
34	Change in recreation	19
35	Change in church activities	19
36	Change in social activities	18
37	Mortgage or loan less than £10.000	17
38	Change in sleeping habits	16
39	Change in number of family get-togethers	15
40	Change in eating habits	15
41	Vacation	13
42	Christmas	12
43	Minor violations of the law	11

Figure 63.7 **Life events points rating scale**
Adapted from: Holmes and Rahe

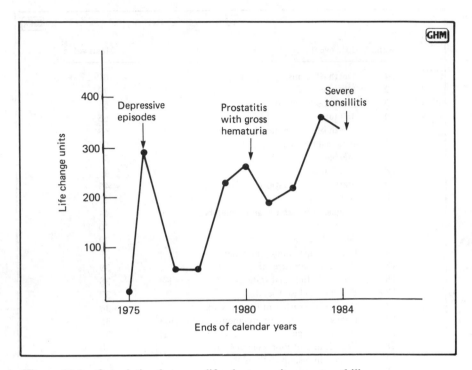

Figure 63.8 Correlation between life change unit scores and illness
This chart shows the results from observing one individual over a number of years.

general practice. Executives usually come through bereavement intact; but the same does not apply to their ability to cope with an event which actually scores a lot higher on the rating scale than bereavement – namely relocation. Relocation is a frequent event in many executives' lives. In one survey, IBM executives moved on an average every 27 months. Relocation scores 137 on the life event rating. The executive must prove himself in a new job, his family must find a new house, his wife must start work again and the children must adapt to a new school. In my own practice, two tragedies have affected executives in the last two years. I believe it to be no coincidence that both occurred four months after the executive had been moved to a new location and was having great difficulty adjusting to the change.

Management must recognize the pressures produced by relocation and moves must be thought through carefully. The executives concerned must be fully involved in the decision and have as much time as possible to plan it. Once they have moved, the manager and his family need all possible support for the next six months. The executive must involve his family fully in the decision to move and be prepared to take their views into account. In the last ten years more and more executives have declined moves for these reasons.

The important sources of stress

When the 43 life events are divided into their areas of origin it is immediately obvious that the majority come from this area of family life. There seems no doubt that in order to gain maximum fulfilment from his life, to be really happy, the executive must achieve the best possible balance between his work life and his home life. Family life provides him with his greatest risk factors; it also provides him with something worthwhile to work for and enormous pleasure. Not only this, it provides him with his most effective counsellor. The most important antidote to stress is to talk about what is happening. In this way the vicious circle by which lack of insight can lead to a totally irrational view of current problems is broken. When asked who provided them with their greatest help in times of stress, 80 per cent of the executives on our survey at Henley answered their wives.

How then can the executive check that he is achieving the right balance between his work and his family? At work, his performance will usually be checked once or twice yearly by his boss at an appraisal and counselling session. In addition, he will see his boss when things are out of control. From these meetings suggestions for future behaviour will be agreed. There is no reason why he should not use the same procedure to monitor his health and happiness. He has two resources:

1 *His doctor.* A regular medical examination by an appropriate doctor should keep the executive aware of the effects of his lifestyle on his habits and his health. The same doctor would then be in the ideal position of knowing the executive well and so being available for consultation at times of medical crisis. It would be helpful, therefore, if companies made available such a service, either within the company or at a nearby medical centre
2 *His wife.* The same routine annual meeting could again apply. The agenda for discussion will be the happiness of all the family. Any changes agreed can be monitored at future meetings. The meeting must not be open to interruption or have a short time limit. Time is necessary for open, honest discussion.

As at work and with the doctor crisis meetings may also be appropriate. The reasons for such a crisis meeting serve as a reminder of the effects of stress on the executive (Figure 63.9).

FEMALE EXECUTIVES

I hope that this late specific mention of female executives will upset neither those who feel they should have had more space for their own particular problems earlier nor those who see themselves as no different from their male counterparts. The use of the male prefix throughout this chapter is

	GHM
COMPLAINTS OF	Poor performance, lateness with work, indecision from partners and colleagues from work, family and social groups
INCREASED	Eating, drinking, smoking, irritability, 'feeling tired', lack of concentration
DECREASED	Time for family, leisure, sense of humour, sleep, insight into problems, exercise, relaxation, preparation for holidays, sexual drive
In general:	
AT WORK	Inability to finish work in reasonable hours; too great a workload to tackle; frequently being late; rushing; exerting extra pressure on staff and long reports at last minute. Altering appointments because overbooked or over-committed. Not taking holiday entitlement
AT HOME AND WORK	Periods of poor health; change in sleep patterns; waking tired; more than one traffic accident; minor accidents at home due to carelessness; needing to take tranquillizers or sleeping tablets

Figure 63.9 Indicators for a crisis audit

partly for stylistic ease, and partly because most executives, particularly the more senior, are male. Considerable effort was needed to track down the small sample of women executives taking part in our Henley research project. Britain is still 20 or 30 years behind Scandinavian equality.

In general, women between 30 and 50 are protected against heart disease by their female hormones. However, recent findings show clearly, and the early results of our research confirm, that female executives, by achieving success in a previously male world, have lost this protection. Their risk of heart disease is the same as their male colleagues and as so many women managers smoke their risk of lung cancer is high. In addition women face the additional risk of breast cancer and female executives are well advised to schedule into their busy timetable an annual well-woman screen.

It is not surprising that the British female executive should have an increased health risk. She has needed to succeed in a chauvinistic world, for it has been suggested that female executives need to be 30 per cent more competent than their male counterparts to earn promotion. Her success at work can destroy her happiness at home. Many husbands cannot cope with a successful wife. Even if they do cope, they may well expect her to look after the home as well as work. Without a man at home life may be no easier; as Renèe Short said, 'What every working woman needs is a wife at home'. Perhaps female executives should be declared an endangered species and for them there is an even greater need for genuine concern for their health.

CONCLUSION

Achievement of good health and happiness must remain the important objective for every executive. Achieving success in both is partly a matter of luck, partly skill. Skills can be acquired; and even luck can be influenced but this requires careful planning. The executive who does control his lifestyle and discipline his habits has so much to gain. He really can help himself to better health and happiness.

USEFUL ORGANIZATIONS

The BUPA Medical Centre Ltd
Webb House
210 Pentonville Road
London W1

Appointments: Tel. 01-837 8641

PPP Medical Centre
99 New Cavendish Street
London W1M 3FQ

Tel. 01-637 8941

FURTHER READING

Benson, Herbert, *The Relaxation Response*, William Morrow and Company, New York, 1976
Carruthers, Malcolm, *F40 – Fitness on Forty Minutes a Week*, Futura, London, 1976
Cooper, Cary and Davidson, Marilyn, *High Pressure, Working Lives of Women Managers*, Fontana, London, 1982
Marshall, Judi, *Women Managers, Travellers in a Male World*, John Wiley & Sons, Chichester, 1984
Melhuish, Andrew, *Work and Health*, Penguin, Harmondsworth, 1982
Royal Canadian Air Force, *Physical Fitness*, Penguin, Harmondsworth, 1971
Selye, Hans, *Stress Without Distress*, J.B. Lippincott Company, New York, 1974

Index